LAST MISSION OVER LOC NINH

The commander promised them a milk run. But as the big Huey approached Loc Ninh, their radio crackled. "Blackhawk Niner Two-Five, this is Bird Dog One. There are a few things you need to know that they didn't tell you. I think I can put down enough firepower to get you down there. But I guarantee you, if you get in, you'll not fly out!"

Loc Ninh Village and the ARVN Camp had already fallen. By the light of the flares, all four men could see that the star-shaped Special Forces perimeter had been breached once already and was under heavy attack. At twenty-five hundred feet, they saw flashes from the ground as enemy troops opened fire.

QUANTITY SALES

Most Dell books are available at special quantity discounts when purchased in bulk by corporations, organizations, and special-interest groups. Custom imprinting or excerpting can also be done to fit special needs. For details write: Dell Publishing, 666 Fifth Avenue, New York, NY 10103. Attn.: Special Sales Department.

INDIVIDUAL SALES

Are there any Dell books you want but cannot find in your local stores? If so, you can order them directly from us. You can get any Dell book in print. Simply include the book's title, author, and ISBN number if you have it, along with a check or money order (no cash can be accepted) for the full retail price plus $2.00 to cover shipping and handling. Mail to: Dell Readers Service, P.O. Box 5057, Des Plaines, IL 60017.

CREW CHIEF

Jesse T. McLeod

A Dell Book

Published by
Dell Publishing
a division of
Bantam Doubleday Dell Publishing Group, Inc.
666 Fifth Avenue
New York, New York 10103

ISBN: 0-440-20555-7

Reprinted by arrangement with Daring Books
Printed in the United States of America
Published simultaneously in Canada
March 1990

10 9 8 7 6 5 4 3 2 1

KRI

DEDICATION

*To Molly and Galen. May this book
in some small way help you to understand
why sometimes I cry, and
you don't know why.*

Acknowledgments

The author is grateful to the following persons for their help: Deborah McLeod, who gave me the courage to start what ended up taking seven years to finish; Dave Keck, who planted the seed for the book in a hayfield and kept encouraging me through the years (Dave also helped with editing and provided me with the sourcebook I needed by Shelby L. Stanton titled *Vietnam Order of Battle*). Paul Streater and Rupert Sparks, Jr., helped me most with R&R. Doctor "Al" Bachman put me in touch with Major Richison and others of the Ohio Army Aviation Reserves such as Mr. Guest and Mr. Lindsay, and others too numerous to mention. Thanks also to Joan McLeod, who did the final editing before it was sent to the publisher, and to all my family and friends who kept encouraging me to keep writing.

My special thanks go to Judy McLeod, without whose patience and many typings I could never have finished. I am also greatly indebted to Dr. Richard Pinkerton of California State University, who was instrumental in helping me to get the book published. Finally, these acknowledgments would be incomplete without crediting Jesus Christ, whose divine protection not only kept me alive in Vietnam, but also enabled me to recall many of the events and conversations that took place so many years ago.

Contents

Introduction

I fell out of bed one night in the midst of a nightmare. My wife asked the obvious question, "Were you dreaming?"

"Yes."

"Would you like to tell me about it?"

"I don't remember what it was about."

That was what came out of my mouth. Oh, how I wanted to pour out my heart, to share my memories, to release what was locked within me, yet, I could not. To talk about Nam, the real Nam, the Nam of pain and suffering and fear was, for me, an impossibility. Sure, I could tell of an occasional funny experience or of the long hours of boredom, but not the stuff nightmares are made of.

Not long after that, I was at a luncheon meeting where one man seated at my table seemed to be doing all the talking. "Why can't these guys from Vietnam just forget about it and get on with their lives? Why do so many of them have marriage problems? After all, a lot of those guys have been back for ten years or better, and it's time to quit crying about it. They're just a bunch of crybabies."

I looked up from the tabletop I'd been staring at and saw the one man in the group (a WW II vet) who knew I was a Vietnam vet. He looked me in the eye and I knew he wanted my approval to speak. I shook my head ever so slightly as if to say, please don't tell him, but he spoke anyway.

He asked the first gentleman, "Have you heard any of their stories? Have you felt their fear or experienced their humiliation at the hands of people like yourself? If you haven't walked in their shoes, then maybe you should keep your big mouth shut."

The thing that bothered me most was, "How were people ever going to understand if no one told them what we went through?" Sure, the vast majority of guys who served in Nam never saw that first minute of combat. There was only a small percentage of us who were exposed to combat almost every day. How do you explain to someone what it was like? The ups, downs, the harassment, the fear, the constant fatigue. These aren't things one tries to explain in a half hour.

After much thought and encouragement by a high school history teacher, I decided to write this book. My goal is to help those who wish to understand us to come a little closer to that end. For me, it has been very painful to remember and write about and I apologize if the content of the stories or language offends anyone. I ask the reader to remember that the average age of the Vietnam vet was only 19, and many pray like David, "Remember not the sins of my youth and my rebellious ways; according to Your love remember me for You are good, O Lord," Psalms 25:7 NIV. Some of the story is my own, some of it belongs to others I've known, but most all of it has a basis in fact.

I will begin during the 1968 Tet Offensive.

My personal experience was that Tet was a time of the most vicious and most intense fighting during my tour. I didn't like living part of it. You may find parts of it you don't like reading. Yet, these are some of the stories locked in our memories, so I ask you, "Is it worth remembering?" To me, it was necessary.

I have talked with fellow Vietnam veterans who were in companies similar to mine. Some of these men have only good memories of Nam and consider it to have been a "good gig." One former pilot told me he'd never been shot at, let alone taken any hits or been shot down. The one thing that is obvious to me as I speak with other vets is that no two men had the same experience. As I thought about it, I realized that each company had its own rules and those rules changed with a new commander. The constant moving of men from spot to spot and the shifting of personnel from company to company caused a stirring that made it impossible for one vet to say whether or not another's stories were true. For example, I had three different "permanent" pilots and countless spot pilots during the time I flew. The co-pilots changed on a daily basis as did (for the most part) the door gunners. I did have several permanent door gunners on my ship, but none lasted more than thirty to forty days. My point in all of this is that there are combat veterans who didn't experience any trauma and some are questioning those who did. Every person alone knows what he went through, and for some it's impossible to explain or discuss those feelings.

Jesse T. McLeod

1

Guard Duty

"Prepare for War! Rouse the warriors! Let all the fighting men draw near and attack."
                                    JOEL 3:9 NIV

Jim MacLaughlin enjoyed his job as a crew chief on a UH-1 Huey about as much as he hated pulling guard duty. He took a great deal of pride in his work. As a result, he was well-liked and respected by most of the officers and enlisted men in his company. He always did his best to be as clean as possible and to present himself as a soldier who was proud of his uniform.

He had been "in country" since May and had been flying since early October. It was January—to be exact, the twenty-ninth of January. The first day of the Vietnamese New Year would start tomorrow. In honor of that event, both sides had declared a thirty-six hour truce which would start at 1800 hours that night.

Pulling guard duty in Jim's company was a fact of life for everyone whose rank wasn't sergeant or higher. On this night, Jim had two more hours before he had to report for guard. Of all the different types of duty he had pulled, guard was second only to KP (Kitchen Police) in terms of undesirability, although guard wasn't so bad if you were lucky enough to be assigned to interior as opposed to bunker duty. Of all the times he had pulled guard duty, only once had it been interior duty. The rest of the time (about every ten days) he'd been stuck on the bunkers. Interior duty was preferred because one never had to leave his own company area and thus could sleep in his own bed when not on duty. The responsibility when on interior duty was simply to walk around the company area looking for anything or anyone who wasn't supposed to be there. This walk occurred sometime during the night and usually lasted only two hours. The officer in charge of guard duty hardly ever checked on the interior guards once they started their duty—primarily because he usually couldn't find them. There wasn't any assigned pattern they had to follow. Each man was responsible for waking the next person and was not supposed to leave his post until the replacement had dressed and relieved him.

Bunker duty was a lot different. The bunkers were musty little one-room hollow mounds made out of sandbags. The outside of the bunkers looked like they wouldn't withstand a good, big, healthy wind, let alone an enemy attack. The sandbags were so deteriorated that many had broken open, spilling their contents. Since the bags had been filled with local soil, the bunkers gave the appearance of large gray warts that had died after hemorrhaging from various ulcers and open sores.

Some of the guys called the local soil "laterite." Jim was sure it was some type of red clay with a high mineral content and just enough small stone to make it hard to shovel. Filling sandbags with it when it was wet required two shovels—one shovel to dig the soil and the other to scrape it off the first. When the bags and their contents dried out, it was like one solid block of concrete. Filling sandbags with it when it was totally dried out required the use of a pick first. But then, one of the first things a soldier learned about sandbags was to never, ever, put sand in them. Sand is simply too easy to shovel and put into bags, plus it doesn't require all the extra work of the locally available soil. It wasn't hard to look at a bunker and tell which part had been built with wet soil and which with dry. When the wet soil in the bags dried, the bags themselves rotted away and a solid block remained.

To enter the bunker, one walked through the open doorway, made an immediate right turn, took three steps, turned left, took three more steps, turned left again, and arrived in one large room. The entranceway had wood pallets for flooring, which had two purposes: first, they kept the guards out of the mud during the rainy season, and secondly, they made it impossible to enter the bunker quietly. Once in the bunker, one had all the comforts of home. The walls were decorated with leaky sandbags, and there was a twenty-five watt bulb in the middle of the six-foot ceiling. Each bunker came equipped with a set of bunk beds and mattresses, with barely enough space between the top and bottom to turn over. The mattresses looked and felt like they were left over from WW II. The floor was dirt and there was the ever present musty smell one would expect from a medieval dungeon. In the wall that faced "no mans land" was a series of three small openings, through which one could shoot or simply look out.

Jim decided he should quit thinking about the bunkers and start getting ready. He still had a lot to do and only two hours before reporting for guard. One good thing about bunker duty was that it meant getting the next day off and as much as Jim enjoyed flying, he was more than ready for a day off. Being a crew chief with the 187th Assault Helicopter Company had provided him with a lot of different experiences. Some of the things he did, he enjoyed; others he found to be disgusting, nauseating parts of the war. He badly wanted and needed a break, even if for only a day. His body felt tired and his mental alertness had begun to slip noticeably from the long, stressful hours. He had been on more single ship night missions in the last two weeks than during the whole time he'd been flying. Single ship night missions were usually death-defying feats of bravery with a high casualty rate and, consequently, were hated by most guys.

Jim had several misgivings about this cease fire. The first was that if they could stop the fighting for thirty-six hours, why couldn't they stop it forever? His second and primary concern was that everywhere he looked, he saw signs of a massive build-up by the enemy, and almost every day his company saw North Vietnamese Army Regulars (NVA), or at least some signs of their existence. American troops were involved in more sustained fighting—something the Vietcong wouldn't do under any conditions. The NVA alone would stand and fight. Only a month ago, American troops were complaining that the Cong wouldn't fight, they just melted away. Now, almost every day, they were seeing heavy action and were taking some pretty severe losses. The enemy fire directed at Jim's company was a lot more accurate of late, and it seemed that every day at least one chopper took a hit. A month ago that was unheard of.

The M16 in Jim's bunk had been completely broken down and cleaned, a job he performed almost every night. When in a hurry, Jim cleaned only the two spots that would inevitably cause jamming: the firing chamber and the trap door spring. If the firing chamber had sand or dirt in it, the bolt wouldn't seize onto the shell and eject the spent cartridge, a situation that had cost more than one GI his life. As Jim reassembled his M16, he made sure each part was spotless and would thus pass the inspection that was always a part of guard duty. Jim put the reassembled rifle in his wall locker, got out the shoe polish and started on his boots. The easiest way to stay out of trouble on guard duty was to be very sure every part of his uniform was perfect before reporting for duty. Jim finished his boots, stripped, put on a towel and his shower thongs, picked up the soap, and headed for the showers. He had just recently started to wear the thongs to the enlisted men's showers. No one had thought it important until one of the guys from maintenance stepped barefoot on a scorpion. He was taken to the hospital screaming with intense pain.

The water was nice and warm as usual in the early afternoon. Jim looked around and saw that some of the other guys going on guard that night were already present. All the showers in Tay Ninh were of the same construction: large black water tanks mounted on overhead platforms, which allowed water to flow by gravity to the shower head below. This arrangement worked fine unless one was unfortunate enough to be taking a shower when the water ran out. Then, not only was there not enough water to finish, but one also got covered with sand and dirt drawn from the nearest river by the transport truck earlier that day. Having finished his shower and brushed his teeth, Jim headed back to the hooch to dress.

Jim's hooch was like all the rest, a building about 16' by 30' with a cement floor, wood sides half way up and wire mesh up to the metal roof. Inside was one large room with an aisle through the entire length and doors at either end. On both sides of the aisle, spaced every so often, was a foot locker. Behind each foot locker was an army bunk with green mosquito netting held up by four three-foot poles. Beside each bunk, and against the wall, was each man's wall locker.

He could smell the sickeningly sweet aroma of pot almost from the moment he entered the hooch. His company was in the process of drawing up battle lines between the pot users and the non-users. Jim had never been a user but, like most guys, had simply kept his mouth shut and looked the other way. Now, he was falling more and more into the camp of the radical non-users. He'd heard all the arguments from both sides, yet, when he sat back and looked at it, it was only the users who claimed what a great thing it was and how it didn't affect their personalities or performance. Jim didn't agree, for he had witnessed more than one GI who had been a good soldier, proud of himself as reflected in his dress and conduct, until he'd started smoking pot. Once on pot, there seemed to be a gradual change in his conduct and general outlook on life.

In fact, he had seen it enough times that he could draw up a typical transition profile of a user. The almost undetectable change in users started with neglecting little things like haircuts. Progressing into heavier use, it seemed to cause a kind of laziness exhibited by neglect of one's personal appearance and surroundings. Little things, like not sweeping up their area each morning or making their bunks, were usually followed by personal degeneration. Wearing clean clothes became unimportant, hair was left unwashed and often showers were skipped altogether. Eventually, a user became a general slob and his vocabulary dwindled to a handful of words. Their performances on the helicopters were much the same. Jim disliked flying with a pothead, regardless of his job or rank. More often than not, the door gunners didn't clean their guns, and one never knew what a stoned pilot was going to do. Crew chiefs really into pot flew in ships that Jim wouldn't get into for anything. Fortunately, he now had enough time in the company and enough respect that he rarely had to fly in someone else's ship. He knew from observation that some of the potheads didn't change oil filters, pull inspections, grease bearings or do a lot of the things a crew chief was supposed to do. Sloppy maintenance was easy to get away with as long as one took the time to adjust the log book accordingly.

If a crew chief didn't feel like pulling his fifty hours inspection, which took about two hours by himself, and included such things as engine and transmission oil filter inspection and oil changes, he could get away without being caught by turning in his log book as though it had been done. As a result, it was nearly impossible for anyone other than the crew chief, whose ship was parked next door, to know if the inspection had been pulled or not. So Jim knew who around him was and was not pulling inspection. After all, if he spent two nights a week pulling inspections and performing other tasks on his ship, it wasn't too hard to figure out why the guy on his right never did.

It was the crash about a week ago of a chopper in Jim's platoon that had really brought things to a head and started the conflict between the users and non-users. Things had been really slow that day when, suddenly, the next to the last ship in the flight went down. The flight had just dropped off troops and started to climb, when at about one hundred feet, a MAY DAY came over the radio.

"May Day! May Day! This is Chalk Nine going down!"

That was all the pilot had time to get out before the ship crashed. The chopper behind Chalk Nine circled and landed but found no one alive. Since there hadn't been a fire or explosion, the wreckage had been sling-loaded back to Tay Ninh.

Late that night, a group of guys collected at the club to discuss it over a beer. During the conversation, the company clerk said he had been ordered to fill out paperwork as though they had been shot down by enemy fire and were, thus, listed as "killed in action." The crew chief on Chalk Ten reported that it looked to him like Chalk Nine's main rotor had quit turning, but he really wasn't sure. The fellows from maintenance thought that made a lot of sense, since one of them (against orders), sneaked out to the wreckage and pulled the transmission and engine oil filters. He claimed the engine filter looked okay, but the transmission's internal filter had so much metal in it, he could hardly get it out to look at it. As the crew chiefs talked about it, no one could remember seeing the crew chief do any recent maintenance. No one in the group disputed the fact that their dead comrade was a lazy pothead. The next day the wreckage was sling-loaded to Saigon. The cause of the crash was supposed to be determined there, but no one heard any more about it. If it hadn't been for the fact that one of the most well-liked pilots in the company had been killed in that crash, nothing more would have come of it. As it was, that crash was the constant topic of conversation, and a lot of the guys blamed the potheads for his death. Things that were tolerated a few days earlier no longer were, and a lot of the men were making it tougher on the users.

Pot had a smell all its own, and once Jim walked into his hooch he knew it was in use. Slowly he walked down the aisle looking in each bunk for the perpetrator. There wasn't anyone in the hooch, but Kenny's bunk looked like someone had spent the day in it. Jim figured it must have been Kenny, but whoever had been smoking before he walked in must have walked out the other door only seconds before. Since no one was around, he headed back to his own bunk to finish getting ready for guard.

Jim put on a clean uniform and the boots he had just polished. As he dressed, he began to wonder if he would get stuck with perimeter duty tonight or get to pull interior duty, where he could sleep in his own bed. By now he was ready to go. His watch told him he still had fifteen minutes before time to report. This was a good time to add a few lines to a letter. As he sat down on his foot locker, the platoon's main flunky, Bob Kenny, came in the door with his pet monkey.

Sp/4 Kenny, a short, stocky man with round features, had been a door gunner who hadn't taken very good care of his guns. As a result, he rarely flew and was put on details such as driving water trucks, picking up the platoon's gunners after the flight had landed, and supervising the Vietnamese civilians doing manual labor in the company area.

"Hi, Mac, I see you've got guard tonight."

"Yes, in about fifteen minutes. Put on a record, would you please?"

Kenny put the monkey down, got his record player out and put on The Supremes. Kenny's favorite record started right out with "I Hear a Symphony." The monkey had climbed unnoticed into the rafters and started squawking. Jim couldn't help but laugh, thinking that Diana Ross wouldn't appreciate that accompaniment. Suddenly, something hit Jim on the left shoulder. He turned his head to look and by reflex his hand went up to brush it off, when the foul smell and sight of monkey shit on his clean uniform hit him.

Jim's face went red with anger.

"Dammit, Kenny, that sorry-ass monkey just threw shit at me. Man, I've told you before, I'm going to kill that son of a bitch and this is the day."

"Mac, don't use your M16. You'll have to clean it again before guard. Besides, you should be leaving right now."

Jim was so mad he couldn't see straight. He knew Kenny was right. It was time to leave and now he had to change shirts and wash his hands. He hurriedly changed as he told Kenny, "I hate that damned monkey and everybody else in the hooch does too. You'd better get rid of it before it does something to the captain or one of the pilots."

The monkey sat in the far corner of the rafters screaming with delight. "Mac, twenty years from now you'll think about this and laugh. You'll remember it as part of the good times."

"Kenny, there is nothing about this place that is worth remembering. Especially you and that damn monkey!"

Jim fell into formation just as his name was being called by the sergeant of the guard. He was assigned bunker duty, and it wasn't long before the inspection was over. The OD* didn't seem any happier about being on guard than any of the enlisted men. He made sure each man knew what was expected of him and that his weapon was clean. After chow they would be given the code.

Everyone but the officer ate together. So Jim asked around until he found someone from the OD's company. "What's Lieutenant Tetley like?"

"Oh, he's fair enough, doesn't believe in pulling chicken shit on you. Do your job and he won't bother you, screw up and he'll hang ya."

Jim's bunker was at the west end of the flight line. Every-

* OD—Officer of the Day—Officer in charge of guard detail.

thing that took off and landed had to fly over his bunker. He was really kind of glad it worked out that way. All he had to do was listen for the gunships to take off and land and he would have a pretty good idea of how the truce was holding up. If the gunships were constantly going in and out, it wasn't going to be a quiet day tomorrow. He wasn't too concerned, though. He had tomorrow off.

There were four men in the bunker with Jim. They cut a deck of cards one guy had brought to determine who had what shift. When Jim pulled the card that gave him the one o'clock shift, he thought the only way for things to get better would be for him to go to bed at once. He'd had a monkey throw shit on him, got stuck on perimeter duty, and then got stuck with the worst time slot possible, one to three in the morning. Jim found a bunk and lay down.

"Hey, man, wake up. It's your shift."

"I'm not on until one o'clock."

"It is one o'clock, get up so I can go to bed."

Jim got out of bed and asked what had been happening.

"Not a thing."

"Phone hasn't rung, no flares, nothing?"

"You got it."

"How about the choppers, they been flying?"

"Yeah, they've been going in and out all night. The guy with the shift before me said it started about ten or ten-thirty, and it's been going on ever since. Why did you ask about the choppers?"

"It's my company and, if there is that much activity, the truce has to be long since over."

Jim picked up the starlight scope and looked out through the darkness in front of his bunker. The ghostly green light that enabled him to see into the darkness showed him that nothing was moving out front. He looked for the orange strip on the claymores'* backs, found each one and felt a lot better at once.

_____

* Claymore mine—a mine that is flat, thus being a one-directional mine. The front is filled with large steel shot and the back is filled with plastic explosive and used to propel the shot outward in a sixty-degree arc. Strictly antipersonnel and used in defensive positions by American troops. It was

He knew the orange strip was put on a claymore's back so the defender could tell where the mines were after dark. Jim had heard more than one grunt* tell about watching an orange strip slowly turn, or look out and see their claymores still there but no orange strip. The VC** had turned them around so that when the GI blew the claymore, he blew it at himself.

Jim placed his M16 where he could grab it to fire in a hurry, then pulled the blackout curtain before turning on the light to check the M60.*** It checked out okay. So Jim again killed the light and opened the blackout curtain, then turned on the starlight scope and looked around. Nothing, absolutely nothing, was moving, and the orange strips were all still where they should be. Suddenly, he could hear, then see, two gunships coming in. Looking at his watch he saw it was only ten after one. What in the world was he going to do to stay awake 'til three? He played with the starlight scope for awhile, mentally broke down and reassembled the M60, and it was still only one-twenty.

Boredom rapidly set in and he found his head bobbing as he started to fall asleep. He got up and did some jumping-jacks and would continue until three if he had to. It certainly was a lot better than going to jail for six months if he got caught sleeping on his shift. He spent some more time playing with the starlight scope and still it was only one-thirty. An hour and a half to go yet. How in the world was he going to make it 'til three?

The whop, whop, whop of the helicopters taking off helped wake him. He watched the flight take off and counted each ship 'til all ten passed over. There was only one reason the whole flight would be leaving at one-thirty in the morning; some troops somewhere were getting the hell kicked out of them.

---

connected by a wire to a hand-held generator that had to be squeezed to fire the claymore mine.

* Grunt—American infantryman (slang).

** VC—Vietcong.

*** M60—Machine gun used for medium to heavy fire support. Fired a 7.62MM round. Also used as door gun on Hueys (helicopters). Fired six hundred rounds per minute.

There was no question about it, the truce had to be over almost before it started. He counted three more choppers taking off and could tell by their sound that they were gunships. Almost immediately, two more ships took off. Jim wondered if the flight was taking both a heavy and a light fire team* with them or if the guns were being sent someplace else.

Boredom. It was without question the worst thing about guard duty. It was one of the few times he really wished he smoked, just so he would have something to do to stay awake.

Suddenly, Jim heard the wood pallets squeak telling him someone was coming in the bunker entrance. He picked up his M16 and pointed it at the entrance, pulled the blackout curtain, put his hand on the light cord, and said, "Halt."

The intruder stopped and his frame was now visible to Jim. He pulled the light cord and could faintly see an American uniform. He wished the lightbulb was more than twenty-five watts. He decided to give the password. After all, the GI was probably getting nervous looking at the business end of his M16.

"Black"—the response came back—"Velvet."

It was right and he sure was glad. "Enter and identify yourself."

In walked a PFC** followed by Lieutenant Tetley. Jim snickered to himself that the gutless lieutenant made his driver walk in first.

"I'm Lieutenant Tetley, the OD. Everything okay?"

"Just fine, Sir."

"Good. We'll stop by later. Let's go, Private."

"Lieutenant, is the truce over?"

"Just about. How did you know?"

"I'm with the helicopter company and the only time we fly night missions is in an emergency. I just watched the whole flight leave. How bad is it?"

"It begins to look like almost everybody but us has been hit. Keep your eyes open."

* Heavy fire team—Three or more gunships. Light fire team—Two gunships.
** PFC —Private first class, third lowest ranking soldier in Army.

The two men turned and left. Jim looked at his watch. It was one-forty, another hour and twenty minutes to go. At least he was wide awake. Jim shut off the light, opened the blackout curtain and looked out. Nothing but black. He turned on the starlight scope and looked around, checked the claymores and started praying that Tay Ninh didn't get hit.

The time really dragged on until just after two o'clock when the artillery opened up. Jim walked out the back door long enough to see the shells hitting across camp with three flares scattered above the far perimeter. Jim hurried back to his starlight scope and stayed there. He knew Tay Ninh had been hit. Probably just a probe at first, with the real threat coming later. As the artillery continued to fire, he knew he wouldn't have any trouble staying awake the last hour.

It was two-fifteen when the phone that connects each bunker to the command post rang. "Bunker number forty-three. Specialist MacLaughlin speaking, Sir."

"This is Lieutenant Tetley. Manchu Company's* bunker line is under severe pressure. I want two men awake until further notice. Understand?"

"Yes, Sir."

The phone went dead and Jim had to decide who to wake up, the man before him or the one after him. For no particular reason, he woke the man after him and told him what was going on. There was still some artillery firing when Jim saw the slicks** come in. He counted nine ships and looked at his watch, two-fifty. Wherever they went, it wasn't far in order to get there and back in only one hour and twenty minutes. The one missing ship didn't overly concern him since it was common to have one sent off by itself. At 0300 hours Jim decided he might as well stay up for another half hour since two people had to be awake. Besides, he found it a lot easier to stay awake with the second man up. The only trouble was this guy smoked

* Manchu Company—4th Batallion, 9th Infantry, part of the 25th Infantry Division.
** Slicks—Slickship—Huey helicopters UH-1 used for troop transport and resupply missions.

and it wasn't long before Jim decided to step outside for some fresh air.

He had been outside only a short time when a jeep stopped on the road parallel to his bunker. The man beside the driver hurriedly jumped out and moved quickly toward Jim. Jim decided to challenge him just in case it was the OD again.

"Halt!" The man stopped moving and Jim spoke again, "Black."

"Velvet. I'm the sergeant of the guard. I'm hunting for Specialist MacLaughlin."

"That's me. What's up?"

"We got a call from your CO*. He wants you back ten minutes ago."

"Why?"

"I don't know. Just get your gear and let's go."

Jim and the Sergeant went back in the bunker, told Private Khalid what was happening, picked up his gear and left.

Once back in his company area Jim found Gillett, a tall New Yorker with thinning hair, and asked what had happened that the CO had pulled him off guard.

"Mac, all hell has broken loose out there. We've been pulling Manchu out of forward encampments since about one-thirty, and in the process we've run out of crew chiefs. If anybody else gets hurt, I'm going to have to fly myself. Get your flight gear and let's go. Nine two five [pronounced Niner Two Five] is waiting on you."

"Well, so much for days off."

When Jim got to his ship, Blackhawk** 925, he found the rest of the crew there waiting. Mr.*** Walker, a tall well-built warrant officer, was the ship's pilot. Mr. Glass, the co-pilot or peter pilot as everyone called them, was already in the right-hand seat. Jim thought to himself that was typical of a peter pilot. Climb in and sit down.

* CO—Commanding officer, company commander, also called "Six" as in Blackhawk "Six."
** Blackhawk—Call sign and name of the 187th Assault Helicopter Company.
*** Mr.—Proper way to address a warrant officer.

A short plump Sp/4, Mike Polaski, had already started untying the main rotor blades. Polaski was an excellent door gunner. He didn't mind helping a crew chief out and always took good care of his guns. If you flew with Polaski, you knew the two M60 door guns weren't going to jam.

Jim put his gear in the ship and checked the log book. Mr. Walker started to crank the engine and Jim could hear the familiar whine of the turbine as it began to turn. He put the log book back, put on his chicken plate* and flight helmet, then turned on his intercom.

"Mr. Walker, you on line?"

"Yeah, Mac, welcome back. We ready to go?"

"The log checks out okay. How thoroughly did you preflight** this thing?"

"Polaski and I went over it just like you taught me. So if we didn't do it right it's your fault."

Jim laughed and the two men looked each other in the eye. Their faces showed the respect they felt for each other. Mr. Walker gave the thumbs-up sign and Jim responded the same way saying, "Okay, let's fly."

Mr. Glass saw Polaski connect his intercom and said, "Climb in, Polaski. It's time to go play war."

* Chicken plate—Bullet proof vest worn by flight crews.
** Preflight—Visual inspection of aircraft before flight.

2

It Begins

"Beat your plowshares into swords and your pruning hooks into spears: let the weak say, 'I am strong.'" JOEL 3:10 KJV

As the chopper grabbed the sky Jim looked at his watch, 4:15 a.m. It was going to be a long day. Mr. Walker came over the radio. "Blackhawk Lead, this is Blackhawk 925. Do you copy? Over."

"This is Blackhawk Lead. What's your status, 925?"

"We picked up MacLaughlin, refueled, and are south bound out of Tay Ninh. Where do you want us to join you? Over."

"Pick us up at Cu Chi, 925. Lead, out."

Polaski's familiar nasal twang came over the intercom. "What time did you start guard last night, Mac?"

"One o'clock, and I want to tell you I thought I'd never stay awake. What'd you do last night?"

"Oh, the usual. Played a little golf, went swimming, watched TV, and read the evening paper. What the hell do you think I did? I got drunk and went to bed until a little after one when Gillett got us up. That's what!"

Jim laughed to himself. He liked flying with Polaski. He had a real sense of humor. He remembered the time Polaski had turned on his radio to broadcast outside the ship and shouted across the company frequency, "I'll take a banana cream pie a la mode to go, please."

The Blackhawks had already made several extractions before Jim's ship joined up. So once in the flight they became known

19

as Chalk Nine. They continued to pull troops out of forward positions to beef up base camps and almost every extraction turned into a hot LZ*. Fortunately, all the hits taken were in noncritical areas. Jim could tell from the radio traffic this was a major offensive. Saigon and Ben Hoa both were having house to house fighting with the American Embassy and the Cholon district being major confrontation points.

The Blackhawks were now on their way to make the last extraction from this outpost. These were always the worst because there weren't any ground troops left for protection and, in this case, they started receiving fire before they'd even gotten on short final approach. The flight was in a staggered right formation to give it more concentrated fire from their door guns. In only seconds they were in and out and the last of the grunts were safely on board. The only trouble was that they weren't out of reach of enemy fire yet. Jim and the other three crew members heard it—it almost always sounded the same: the sharp *thunk* of metal hitting metal. Polaski not only heard it, he felt it. His first thought was that he had been stung by a bee. But when he looked down at his left leg, his pants were turning red. He began to feel the warm flow of blood down the side of his leg as he looked down and saw his blood already becoming a part of the dirt that covered the chopper floor. He thought of the phrase, "from dust to dust . . ." In that same moment a controlled but tearful Polaski keyed his mike. "Mr. Walker, I'm hit! Mac, HELP ME! I got it in the leg!"

"Sit tight, Polaski. I'll be right there." Jim looked for a way to get to his door gunner, but the grunts were in his way. There was a lieutenant seated with his back to Jim. He grabbed the surprised lieutenant by the collar and pulled his body backward and shouted in his ear. "My door gunner's shot, get him up here!" The lieutenant shouted orders, and in only seconds, Polaski was on the ship's floor with a PFC putting direct pressure on the open wound while another applied bandages to his leg. From the moment Polaski had made his plea for help, Walker had been busy.

* Hot LZ—Receiving fire from landing zone.

"Lead, this is Chalk Nine. We're breaking formation for Cu Chi medical; Polaski's been hit, Chalk Nine out."

The only sound in reply was the click click of Lead's mike being double keyed in response.

"Mr. Glass, dial Cu Chi Tower. Get clearance for the medical pad, then dial the medical unit and tell them we're in bound with one WIA.*" As he was talking, he broke the ship from formation and increased the ship's airspeed until it was redlined on the airspeed indicator. Jim heard Mr. Glass call Cu Chi Tower and get clearance for the medical pad. While Mr. Glass was changing radio frequencies, Jim came over the intercom.

"Mr. Walker, as many hits as we took, you better keep an eye on your gauges."

"Oh shit, Mac, we're losing hydraulic pressure!"

"Mr. Walker, if that gauge is correct, you're going to start feeling it in the stick shortly. We'll have to land on the runway instead of the medical pad."

"Well, the gauge is correct. I'm starting to pick up some vibration. Mr. Glass, you work the pitch and RPM.** I'll take the stick. Mac, get up here and read instruments."

Jim worked his way through the ship and grunts and over Polaski, who smiled at him as he carefully stepped over his prone body. By the time Jim had positioned himself behind the radio console between the two pilots, the ship was shaking violently from the loss of hydraulic assist on the controls. It was all the two pilots could do to maintain control. Each was required to use both hands on their respective sticks.

"Mac, dial 41.8 Cu Chi Tower on the UHF radio and tell them what happened and ask for a new landing spot."

"Roger." Jim dialed 41.8 and changed his controls to broadcast outside the ship. "Cu Chi Tower, this is Blackhawk 925. Over."

"This is Cu Chi Tower, 925. Over."

"Roger, Cu Chi Tower. We've lost hydraulic assist and have one WIA on board. We will not be able to land at the medical unit as previously requested. Will you give us an alternate land-

---

* WIA—Wounded in Action.
** RPM—Revolutions per minute.

ing spot and advise medical unit to have transportation for wounded meet us."

"Roger, 925, I'll advise medical. You can land direct at far end of helicopter maintenance area. Please advise your ETA.* Over."

Walker came over the intercom. "Two minutes, Mac."

"Roger, Cu Chi. Our ETA is zero two minutes. Over."

"925, be advised winds are steady at zero two knots from the west. Make direct approach and we now have you on visual. Also be advised extreme pressure on east perimeter from Charlie. Cu Chi out."

"Did you get that, Sir?"

"Yea. Thanks, Mac. How's Polaski?"

With a quick glance backward Jim responded, "He'll make it —if we do."

The two pilots worked together to bring 925 into Cu Chi. Jim read off airspeed, altitude, engine RPM, and main rotor RPM all the way down. The three men worked together like the team they should be; each did his job and trusted the others without question to do theirs correctly.

Once safely on the ground the grunts helped load Polaski into the ambulance. Jim opened the pilots' doors, slid back the bulletproof plating for pilot protection and spoke. "Mr. Walker, I should be able to fix this thing if there's not too much wrong. Suppose you could get that lieutenant to give us one of his men to take Polaski's place?"

"No. But I can ask." Mr. Walker walked over to where the lieutenant was standing. "Could I speak to you, Lieutenant?"

"Sure. By the way, you did a great job of landing this crate. What's wrong with it, anyway?"

"We lost hydraulics, which makes it a lot like driving a car with the power steering out. Plus, as you noticed, the rotor blades turning causes a terrible vibration."

"I noticed. I thought we were going to bounce out of the ship. What can I do for you, Sir?"

"I need a door gunner. Could you give me one of your men who knows how to use and work on an M60?"

* ETA—Estimated time of arrival.

"You're not going to fly that thing like that are you?"

"Oh, no, Sir. My crew chief thinks he can fix it without too much trouble."

The lieutenant walked over to where his troops were standing around smoking. "Hey, any of you guys want to fly as a door gunner?"

PFC Green's hand went up in a flash. "I will, Sir."

"Okay, Green. Get your gear and report to that warrant officer."

"Yes, Sir." Green was all smiles. He figured being a door gunner was the easiest job in Vietnam. "Sir, PFC Green. The lieutenant told me to report to you."

Mr. Walker returned Green's salute and told him where to put his gear. Jim was busy inspecting the ship and, as he walked around the left side, Mr. Walker spoke. "Mac, this is PFC Green. He's our gunner 'til we get back to Tay Ninh. Private Green, meet Jim MacLaughlin. He's the crew chief on this ship. If you have any questions ask him. He's one of the best."

"Sir, I'm going to have to crawl under this ship and get up in the hellhole*. I can't find any broken lines out here. Why don't you tell Green what his job is and what's expected of him." With that, Jim lay down on his back and started to crawl under the chopper's belly and up into the hellhole. "Mr. Glass?"

"Yeah, Mac. What do you need?"

"Get my tool box out of the storage compartment and give me a 3/4 inch open end and a crescent wrench, please."

Mr. Glass found the two wrenches and crawled under the ship. He placed them in Jim's visible hand reaching out from the hellhole. "Find the problem, Mac?"

"Yes, Sir. Evidently a bullet just grazed this line, causing a slow leak. You should see this place. It's a mess, and I'm covered with oil." Jim took off the ruptured line, handed it to Mr. Glass and crawled out. "Okay, Mr. Glass, here's what I want you to do. Take this line over to the parts tent. Here's my book.

---

* Hellhole—Hole in the bottom of a Huey where the cargo hook sticks out. It is directly under the transmission, very oily and barely large enough for one man to fit in from the waist up.

I'll open it to the page where this line is shown. Sir, take the book also and you shouldn't have any trouble getting the correct part. Bring me back the new line and enough hydraulic oil to completely refill this thing—please. In the meantime, I'll finish checking out the ship. Okay?"

"Hey, I'm a warrant officer. I don't run errands for enlisted men."

"Look, Mr. Glass, I'd send the new door gunner but he doesn't even know what type of helicopter we're flying. I can't send him after parts. Mr. Walker and I can finish inspecting this thing. You wouldn't know what to look for. Besides, as a warrant officer, you shouldn't have any trouble getting the parts I need, just act like you know exactly what you're doing and nobody will question you. Work it right and you might even get a jeep ride back."

Mr. Glass looked at Walker who was now standing beside Jim. Mr. Walker smiled and waved bye-bye. Mr. Glass slowly shook his head and picked up the part and book and started to leave.

"Hey, Mr. Glass, don't forget the oil and bring me some rags to wipe off with also, please. Mr. Walker, get a Phillips screwdriver and open up that inspection panel in the floor where the bullet hole is, please. I'm going to climb on top and check the rotor head and blades."

The new door gunner stepped forward and said, "Specialist, what do you want me to do?"

"You can start by calling me Mac, just like everyone else. I'll tell you what, why don't you check out those M60's? All of Polaski's stuff is under his seat on the left side. Green, just one thing to remember while you're going over those guns: if we ever get this thing flying again where we're going, I guarantee you, you'll want 'em to work."

Each man went to work. It didn't take Jim long to determine that everything was okay on top. As he started down the chopper's side, Mr. Walker spoke. "Mac, I got all except two of those screws out, but they just won't come."

"Okay. You put some constant pressure on 'em and let me tap the top of your screwdriver at the same time with a hammer. Sometimes that will break them loose." In this manner the last two screws were removed and then the inspection plate. Jim had really expected to find a control rod with a bullet hole in it. To his amazement, not one thing had been hit except the aircraft's skin. The inspection panel was replaced and the three men sat down. Mr. Walker kept glancing at his watch. Finally, Mac said, "What's the matter, Mr. Walker, you got a hot date this afternoon?"

Walker laughed as he responded, "Why?"

"You can't keep your eyes off your watch."

"Oh, just thinking. Six* is going to be wondering where we are."

"See if you can raise him on the radio. Besides, it'll take me, oh, about a half hour yet after Mr. Glass gets back."

"Yeah, I think I will." Mr. Walker put on his helmet and turned on the radio.

"Mac, I got a question."

"What's that, Green?"

"How do you get away with talking to officers like you do? I mean, you give them orders just like some PFC and they do it. You don't say 'Sir' all the time or anything. They would court martial your butt in a second in the infantry."

Jim laughed and looked to see that Mr. Walker still had his helmet on. "I'll tell you, Green, it's all a matter of timing. Do it at the wrong time and you're in trouble. It's that simple. For example, I'm the guy who knows how to make this thing fly again. If they want it to fly, and if I need help, then they do what I say. Of course a lot of it's in the tone of voice I use. I never use a tone that says I'm the boss. It's always a tone that says you're the boss but I need some help from you. As for saying 'Sir' all the time, well, it just gets in the way. Most all the pilots are pretty good about it. Again, as long as the tone of voice implies 'Sir' they don't really care. Just say it once in a while to show them that you're willing and you'll be okay. Remember, too, that we spend an awful lot of time together. Like Mr. Walker and I. We've been together for ten to twelve hours a day every day for the last couple of months. We're a lot alike and we have a lot of respect for each other. In fact, we've

* Six—Designates a commander—company, division or otherwise.

become very good friends. You just have to be very careful with an officer you don't know. Also, I say please."

Mr. Walker finished his radio conversation and the three men sat down to eat their C-rations and shoot the bull.

After what seemed like hours, Mr. Glass arrived. He had the part and the oil, but no rags. "Mr. Glass, thanks for getting this stuff."

"No problem, Mac. By the way, Mr. Walker, I stopped by Operations. They had word that Charlie had broken through one of the walls."

"Which wall?"

"I don't know. Everyone started getting excited so I left." As the three men looked at each other, it dawned on them what they had been hearing.

Mr. Walker was the first to speak. "Mac, hurry up and get that line on. That small arms fire we've been hearing has to be what this is all about."

Jim crawled under the ship and up into the hellhole. The three remaining men moved to the side of the ship where the firing was coming from and could see rapidly approaching American troops. Mr. Walker shouted at a staff sergeant to find out what was going on. He could hardly believe it when told the place was being overrun and to fall back to the maintenance area drainage ditch.

Instantly, Walker started shouting instructions. "Mac, get out from under the ship! Green, Mr. Glass, get the guns and ammo off the ship!"

They now found themselves on the edge of a major fire fight and in the thick of the retreat. Jim picked up his M16 and all the M60 ammo he could carry. Mr. Walker had already taken one M60 off its mount and wrapped as much M60 ammo around him as he could carry. Mr. Glass had the other M60 and some ammo and Green had his M16 and the rest of the M60 ammo. As the four men retreated, the two pilots took turns firing cover with their M60's. They had been joined by several other GI's but now were being pursued by an even larger number of NVA. They were only about fifty feet from the drainage ditch when it happened; the spine-shivering scream of Mr. Glass as he fell to the ground. Jim shoved his weapon and ammo in someone else's hands. An unknown GI picked up Mr. Glass's M60 as Jim bent down. The adrenaline in Jim's body was flowing in abundance, so it was with relative ease that he threw Mr. Glass over his shoulder in a fireman's carry. In this manner, he ran as well as he could the rest of the way to the ditch, with the warm trickle of Mr. Glass's blood running down his back. As the American troops jumped in the ditch, they cleared a field of fire for those already there. The ensuing discharge of lead caused the pursuit to drop off. Jim laid Mr. Glass down in the bottom of the ditch. He didn't have to check for life. He knew Glass was dead. Mr. Walker and Green came over and gave Jim his M16. it was then that Jerry Green saw the blood-soaked dead American. Green looked up and, before he knew what was happening, he had thrown up all over himself and Mr. Glass. Mac took him by the arm and turned him away.

"Don't be embarrassed, Green, it happens to a lot of us the first time. We just don't have time for it now. Get that M16 off your shoulder and start firing."

Jim said a quick prayer and looked up, his own eyes moist and one cheek wet. The enemy pursuit stopped soon afterward. The same staff sergeant came by and gave everyone orders. He put Mr. Walker and Jim on one M60 and, about twenty-five feet away, Green and another GI on the other M60. The sergeant got everyone placed and shouted, "Get ready, because the next time they come, it will be a mass suicide charge."

"Mr. Walker, you fire, I'll feed the gun."

"Okay. Oh, shit! Mac, I just peed my pants."

"Hey, don't worry about it. No one will notice. Mr. Walker, we're going to make it."

"Yeah, but if I don't, who wants to be sent home with pee in his pants?"

Both men could now hear the familiar whap, whap, whap of approaching Hueys. Turning to look, they saw two gunships approach just as they banked to make their run on the gathering enemy troops. Jim recognized the boomerangs painted on the noses of the choppers. The Blackhawks had worked with this company before. The first gun run finished, both ships made a sharp bank and came right back in. Both were mini gunships and Jim knew the 6000 rounds per minute that the miniguns fired had to be taking a fierce toll on Charlie. All the American troops in the ditch were cheering. Mr. Walker shouted, "That a boy! Go get 'em." Then, "Mac, they're leaving. Oh, shit. They must be out of fuel or ammo."

Someone shouted, "Here they come!"

Jim looked back down in time to see enemy troops charging at them. Their screams sent shivers down his spine. Bullets were hitting all around them but no one seemed to notice. Every man in the ditch was firing at the human wave charging his way. Both Jim and Mr. Walker were too busy to feel fear, with each totally in control of himself now. All of their thoughts and energies were directed to the task before them. The fire coming from the ditch was taking a terrific toll, but it was the two M60's from Jim's chopper that were holding the line and making the real difference.

(Several years later, Jim visited the battlefields of Gettysburg. As he stood at the high water mark of Pickett's Charge, looking out over the open space those southern boys traversed, his chest swelled with emotion and his eyes broke with the tears of a day gone by. His knees buckled, he sat down and wept as his mind raced back to that ditch and the stand he'd made half a world away. One of the guys he was with at Gettysburg sat down beside him and asked if he was okay. Jim nodded his head yes. He was unable to speak. He shrugged his shoulders, blew his nose and said, "Sometimes it just happens like that.")

The human wave charging their way had been reduced to just a handful of NVA by the time it reached Jim's ditch. Jim ducked a fixed bayonet and a screaming NVA who lunged by his head. As if by instinct, he'd known the action was too close for an M16. His hand reached into his pocket and, in a flash, he held the Army issue switchblade. In that same moment the enemy soldier turned and Jim buried the blade in his chest. Jim prided himself on keeping the heavy blade very sharp—as a result it slid smoothly between the ribs with surprisingly little effort. In the same movement he pulled it out and stabbed again, this time in the guts. He heard Walker scream and turned in time to see an NVA about to thrust his bayonet into Walker. Jim's knife found its mark in the NVA's back as

Walker sidestepped the pained man's thrust. Jim grabbed the man's hair, yanked his head back and, with his blood drenched knife, slit the NVA's throat. Out rushed a mixture of air and blood that bubbled down his chest. Walker looked at Jim. "Thanks." Jim simply nodded his head. it was over quicker, by far, than it had begun.

American reinforcements were jumping over the ditch in hot pursuit of the few remaining NVA troops. Neither man spoke. Jim wiped his knife and his hands as clean as possible. He picked up his M16, grabbed the M60, and climbed out of the ditch without speaking. Medics busied themselves with the wounded as reinforcements continued to arrive. There was nothing left to be done at the ditch so Jim simply turned and walked away. Green, with his guns, found Mr. Walker and the two men turned and followed Jim. They were all still hyped up from the events just past and, about one hundred feet from the ditch, Walker put his arm around Jim's shoulder and gave it a squeeze.

"Mac, you want to fly right seat back to Tay Ninh?"

"Sure. You know I just had a thought. Why didn't they blow our ship?"

"It probably didn't occur to them or they didn't have time."

The three men put their weapons and ammo down. Mr. Walker and Jim walked around the chopper—their eyes scanning every inch of the ship.

"Mr. Walker, they took the time to pull the soundproofing down and to take the first aid kit out but not to blow it. Why?"

"You think it's booby trapped?"

"Yeah. There has to be something under that soundproofing they took down."

"Hey, Mac."

Jim looked up to see Green pointing at the front end of the skid. There, wedged under the curved part of the skid, was a fragmentation grenade. Jim reached down and removed it, being careful not to allow the handle to spring loose.

"Okay, you two. See if you can find the pin laying around someplace." After searching and coming up empty handed, Jim decided to take it to a clearing and give it a toss.

"Hey, here it is. You know what they've done? They've pulled the pin and given it a toss!"

Jim carefully worked the pin back in the hole and bent the end over slightly. He gave the grenade a toss to Green and looked at Walker. "I'll still bet there's something under that soundproofing. Probably another frag."

"Probably. But what if there isn't. What if it's something else? At least with a frag, if the pin pops, you have a couple of seconds to pick it up and give it a toss. If it's something else, you're not going to know what it's going to do or how to handle it."

"Sir, they're not going to be carrying anything special. It's all going to be dual purpose stuff."

"True. Can't you gently feel for something solid under it?"

"Why do you automatically assume me? Green, how long you been in country?"

"Not quite a month. Why?"

"I just thought maybe you might have worked with booby traps before."

"Nope."

"Okay. I'll do it. If nothing else, I can always run like hell." Slowly, and very gently, Jim felt the soundproofing blanket for something solid. Every instinct he had told him something was there. He just hoped it was a frag and only one. As he felt the blanket he prayed. "Lord Jesus, help me please, please help me." There it was! He'd hit something solid. With great care he tried to determine what it was. The all too familiar pling told him all he needed to know. With a frag you had only seconds. With one hand, Jim tore off the blanket and, in one fluid movement, he grabbed the frag and threw it. Jim said another prayer, this time in thanks, that it had blown harmlessly on its way to the nearby clearing.

Jim walked over to where Green and Mr. Walker stood. He sat down on a thirty gallon drum and took a long deep breath. Mr. Walker spoke first. "This is turning into one hell of a day! Mac, you know I've never really believed that story you tell—that you have a guardian angel. I just want you to know. I believe!"

Jim looked him in the eye and, at that moment, the realization of all he had recently been through caused him to lose his composure. Fatigue, stress and emotional strain swept through his body. He bent over and lost muscle control, the convulsions and weeping almost knocked him off the barrel. It was Mr. Walker who stopped Jim's fall and cradled his head to his chest. The two men shut out all time as they wept together and embraced, drained of emotion.

It was a full ten minutes before Jim felt he was in control of himself again. He got some C-rations and sat down for a snack. The pound cake, cheese and crackers tasted good. He ate and then checked the ship for more grenades. He found none. Green had left to get some of his personal gear while Walker put the soundproofing back up. He also mounted the door guns and put the ammo back in the left seat box, since there wouldn't be anyone flying behind the right door anyway. Jim crawled back under the chopper and up into the hellhole.

"Mr. Walker, I just had a thought. Get my flashlight and look in the fuel tank for a frag, will you? If there's one in there, it'll have a rubberband around it instead of a pin in the handle."

"Sure, Mac. What do I do if I see one?"

"Well, say so and I'll get the hell out from under here, for one thing!"

"I don't see anything, there isn't anything in there. Did you hear me, Mac?"

"Yeah, thank you."

By the time Jim had finished putting the line on and filled the hydraulic reservoir, Green was back. Mr. Walker was the first to see him coming, carrying a foot locker over his shoulder and a duffel bag in one hand.

"Green, what are you doing?"

"I packed all my stuff and moved out."

"You what? You can't do that! We just borrowed you for one day. I'm not sure we can keep you that long now that I don't have a peter pilot."

Green's face showed every bit of disappointment he felt. Laying his stuff down he looked at Walker. "Sir, I thought I was to be a permanent part of your crew."

"Look, Green, you need orders to change companies. We lost

a gunner and, to keep from flying back to Tay Ninh just for a gunner, your lieutenant let us borrow you. Now, I've got to go get a co-pilot."

Jim felt really sorry for Green. It was obvious he really wanted to fly.

"Mr. Walker, Gillett told me this morning that the only people he had left to fly were Kenny and himself. So unless you want Kenny as a gunner, we'd better find a way to keep Green."

Mr. Walker looked at Jim with dismay. Jim slowly nodded yes. Walker shrugged his shoulders and said, "Okay, Green, put it in the ship, I'll see what I can do. Mac, we ready to go?"

"Yes, Sir."

"Okay. Let's go get a peter pilot."

Jim untied the main rotor blades and helped Green put on his chicken plate and helmet. He showed him how to work the lip mike and how to turn his radio on and off. Mr. Walker had climbed in and started to crank the engine before Jim had Green strapped into his monkey harness*. Walker had the ship running by the time Jim climbed in the peter pilot's seat and, after putting his helmet on, heard Green say, "Can everybody hear me?"

Walker looked at Jim and laughed. Green came over the intercom, "Gee, Mac, this is neat."

Walker casually reached down and switched his and Jim's radio to private. "Mac, he's like a kid with a new toy."

"Give the guy a break. Remember how excited you were the first time you climbed in one of these things! Besides, it wasn't him who peed his pants back in that ditch." They both laughed.

Walker spoke. "Man, I'd never been so scared in all my life. I couldn't control myself anymore than a bitch in heat."

"Oh, but you did, not your bladder obviously. But you con-

---

* Monkey harness—Restrainer straps that went around the waist and over the shoulders and interlocked in the front with a quick release buckle. A long tail (thus the name) comes from the back of the harness and hooks onto a ring or secure part of the ship. This tail allowed movement while still being strapped in.

trolled your mind enough to make the rest of your body do what it had to do. You sure made that M60 sing."

"Mac, while we're on the subject, I may never get another chance. Thanks for saving my life. If it wasn't for you and that switchblade, I'd be dead."

They looked at each other and Jim nodded his head. "You're welcome. Although it's not me you should be thanking. But I do appreciate it. You should be thanking Jesus. Without Him we both would be dead, I don't even remember getting the knife out of my pocket." As the two men looked at each other, they knew a special bond had been formed.

Walker turned the radios back to the previous setting and made contact with the tower for clearance to taxi to the runway and leave.

Once airborne and headed for Tay Ninh, Walker contacted "Six" in C and C*. Walker spoke briefly about what had happened and stated they could rejoin the flight after picking up a co-pilot. "Six" said that he would advise Operations so there would be a co-pilot ready.

---

* C and C—Command craft that is filled with communications gear. Used to direct and coordinate operations from the air.

3

You Do What
You Have to Do

*"The trouble he causes recoils on himself;
his violence comes down on his own head."*
                                        PSALMS 7:16 NIV

No one spoke as they landed at Tay Ninh and taxied as close as possible to Operations. Somewhat miffed at not having a co-pilot waiting on them, Mr. Walker headed for Operations. Jim helped carry Green's foot locker and duffel bag into the hooch, where Gillett was in the process of cleaning out Polaski's gear. Introductions were made and Gillett told Green that he might as well have Polaski's spot. They were giving Gillett a quick account of what had happened when an Sp/4 came in.

"I'm from Operations. I'm looking for a PFC Green."

"That's me."

"We're going to try to get some orders cut, but we need some information."

"Let me put this stuff away and I'll be right over."

"I'd appreciate it if you make it as quick as possible. Furthermore, don't get too settled in, because I'd be very surprised if we can keep you."

"Okay, I'll be right there."

The Sp/4 left as Green stuffed his duffel bag in the wall locker. Once this was finished, Jim and Green headed for Operations. As they walked across the company area, they heard someone shout, "MacLaughlin."

Jim turned to see Mr. Halsey headed their way. "Oh, great,

here comes trouble! Green, just keep on walking and tell Mr. Walker that Mr. Halsey has me."

"Mac, you . . ."

"Get out of here before he gets you, too!" Jim turned and waited for Mr. Halsey.

"MacLaughlin, where's your hat?"

Jim looked the tall, thin, sunken chested, acne-scarred warrant officer in the eyes and knew it was harassment time. "In the helicopter, Sir."

"Specialist, you know perfectly well you're supposed to have on a cap. STAND AT ATTENTION when I speak to you, Specialist!" Halsey's voice expressed the hatred he felt. His face was twisted as he made a real effort to look mean. Jim came to attention but couldn't help smiling as he watched Halsey's face. "You find something amusing, MacLaughlin?" Jim just stood there without answering. "Answer me, Specialist!"

"What makes you think I find anything amusing, Sir?"

"Don't get smart with me, Specialist! By the way, don't you salute officers anymore, Specialist?"

"Yes, Sir." Jim brought his right hand up in salute.

"That's better. Now, what is it that you find so funny?"

"I'm not laughing, Sir. I find nothing funny."

"MacLaughlin, you've got oil and dirt and who knows what else all over you! You look like hell, you know that, soldier? Your personal appearance is disgusting. How long has it been since you changed fatigues? Your boots need shining, plus you need a haircut."

Jim thought, *So do you, you SOB, right below the chin.* "I put on clean clothes this morning, Sir."

By this time, eight or ten people had gathered at a safe distance. Some were maintenance people, some were platoon sergeants like Gillett, and some were the walking wounded. Halsey walked around Jim checking his uniform. Jim stood at attention wondering, "What's next?"

"Specialist, your back pocket is unbuttoned."

Jim couldn't help but smile. After what he had just been through he really didn't care if it was unbuttoned.

"MacLaughlin, just what is it that you continuously find so funny?"

"Nothing, Sir."

"Soldier, when you stand at attention, you don't smile. So, I'm going to take that smile off your face. Get down and give me fifty."

Jim's smile disappeared alright. In its place was a look of pure hatred. Halsey thought for a moment that he finally had him. All he had to do now was push MacLaughlin just a little more, and he would do something that he could be sent to jail for.

"Don't you find that funny, MacLaughlin?" Jim just stood there and looked Halsey in the eyes. "I'm giving you a direct order, Specialist. Get down and give me fifty."

Jim sat down and started to count, "One, two . . ."

"What the hell do you think you're doing?"

"I'm doing what you told me, Sir, giving you fifty. You didn't say fifty what, so I'm counting to fifty for you."

"You insubordinate, smart-mouthed, little bastard. I'm going to bust your ass to an E-fucking-nothing!"

"On what grounds, Sir? I've done everything you told me to do!"

Halsey knew he was right. MacLaughlin had beat him again. Maybe. In a perfectly calm voice Halsey made one last try. "Okay, MacLaughlin, I want you to do seventy-five pushups and count out loud as you go. If I hear one word otherwise, I'll court martial your ass."

Jim sat there on the ground and looked up at Halsey. Each man showed the hatred he felt for the other. Jim thought about what he had just gone through a short time ago. He tried to stare Halsey down as he wondered why creeps like him lived, while the nice guys like Glass got it. However, Halsey could hold his own and said, "Now, MacLaughlin, not ten minutes from now."

Jim took a deep breath, looked around and saw Gillett standing by the hooch door with a look of disgust on his face. Jim rolled over very slowly and even more slowly started the pushups. "One . . . Two . . ."

Suddenly, Jim heard Walker's voice shouting from across the

company area, "MacLaughlin, what are you doing? The XO*
has been waiting on you."

"Sir, Mr. Halsey thought I should do seventy-five pushups
first." Walker had walked up to where Halsey was standing and
shook his head. "Mr. Halsey, would it be okay if my crew chief
went on a mission with me—or should I tell the XO what
you're doing is too important to interrupt?" Jim laughed to
himself. Man, you could cut the sarcasm with a knife.

Halsey spoke as he walked away. "He's all yours."

Jim stood up, brushed himself off and said, "Thanks. What
took you so long?" They laughed together as Walker gave Jim's
shoulder a squeeze with his hand.

"Mac, you're just lucky I got here at all. Green waited until I
got finished talking with the XO before he told me Halsey had
you."

"Mr. Walker, we both know there's no such thing as luck.
Jesus Christ, yes; luck, no. By the way, what was the XO's
problem?"

"He needs a ship to go pick up some ARVN's [Army of the
Republic of Vietnam] at Chon Thanh and take them to An
Loc."

"We're not going back to the flight?"

"Nope."

"Who do we get as a peter pilot?"

"Ratcliffe."

Mr. Ratcliffe was a short chunky man with a roly poly face.
He wasn't one of the best pilots by a long shot, but he was still
new in the country and fresh out of flight school. When they
got to the ship, Green couldn't wait to ask, "Hey, Mac, what
was that officer's problem?"

"Oh, he's a hard nose, Green. He believes in harassment for
the fun of it. Just forget it."

They untied the ship and hovered to the fuel dump. From
there, they went to the ammo bunker and re-armed.

Once airborne, Green couldn't contain his curiosity any
longer. "Mac, tell me about you and Mr. Halsey."

"Not now, maybe later tonight."

* XO—Executive Officer, second in command to Company Commander.

Ratcliffe spoke up, "Hey, don't worry about me. I don't like the guy anymore than most of the EM* do. Besides, I'd like to hear your side of the story. Halsey claims you screwed him."

"Yeah, and he didn't even get a kiss." There was a pause as Jim wondered if he should. "Okay, everybody, it's story time. First you have to understand Halsey. He's the kind of person who never had any responsibility, authority, or respect before in his life. Once he did get a little authority, he couldn't handle it. One look at him and you know he never was involved in any kind of sports; in fact, I wonder how he ever got in the Army, let alone made officer. Once he became an officer, he simply didn't get respect, so he figured he could order people to give it to him, and of course, that just doesn't work. Then, to show how mean he is, he started harassing the EM.

"I didn't have any more trouble with him than anyone else did. Oh, the usual, shine your boots, button your buttons, and get a haircut—until I had to fly with him one day about two months ago. We had a single ship mission that we had to leave on before daylight. It was just getting light when Halsey decided to do some low level flying through the Hobo Woods, of all places! That was right after they'd gone through the Hobo with plows and knocked down trees and everything. Well, of course, I objected to putting it on the deck and said so. Halsey told me not to get smart with him, that he was an officer and would make the decisions on the ship, that I was a stupid enlisted man and my job was to sit behind my M60 with my big mouth shut. Now, understand, I didn't object to flying on the deck. I objected to it because we didn't have enough light, and because we had no idea what was still sticking up, or had been put back up. Basically, I think Halsey is a hot dog without the skill of a hot dog. So, he takes it down. He starts flying so low that I'm looking up at some of the bushes. I figured surely he'd get us all killed, especially when I looked at the airspeed indicator and saw it sitting on 110 knots. We were just about out of it when WAPP! Well, to make a long story short, Halsey had hit a twig that was still standing and busted out the Plexiglas bubble covering his foot pedals. In the process, he got his leg cut up.

* EM—Enlisted men.

The jerk tried flying without the foot glass but the wind kept blowing dirt up in his face, so he had to go back to Tay Ninh to get a new bubble. When we landed, he gave everyone strict orders that we were to say we took a hit when we landed at Duc Hoa.

"The maintenance officer took one look at the bubble and knew a bullet hadn't done it. Neither Polaski nor I felt like lying for the guy so when the maintenance officer asked how it happened, I told the truth. This made the major as mad as a wet hen. He left Polaski and me, swearing he would make Halsey pay for that bubble. The best part was that Halsey had gone to change his pants and clean up his leg. While he was in the shower washing it off, the flight surgeon came in and, of course, asked how it had happened. Halsey told him that we had taken a hit in his foot window, that it had shattered the Plexiglas and a piece had cut him. Well, the flight surgeon insisted on treating him and filling out the papers for a purple heart. So Halsey didn't have any choice but to go along, or to tell the truth. By the time he got back to the ship, it was ready to fly and the flight surgeon and maintenance officer were converging on the CO's office at the same time. Man, I have to laugh just thinking about it. There must have been so much smoke in that office it's a wonder the place didn't burn down. To make things even better, neither Polaski nor I told Halsey what we had done to him. He flew the rest of the day so darned happy with himself you would have thought he was the cat that ate the canary.

"When we landed that night there was a jeep waiting for him. Before he got out of the chopper, he asked if we were all going to report it like he told us to. Polaski and I both said, 'Right'; that's all, just one word, 'right.' He took it just like we wanted him to. Plus, the peter pilot was so busy kissing his ass that if Halsey had turned real quick, he would have broken the dude's nose. The jeep driver took him straight to the CO. I'm not sure what happened there other than he got an Article 15 and fined two hundred dollars, plus he had to pay for the window and labor to replace it—no purple heart and reduced to peter pilot status for thirty days. Which is, of course, the ultimate insult, and he figures it's all my fault. Now, any little chance he has to get even, he takes.

"I think the guy figures I'm stupid enough to do something during one of his little harassment sessions that he could use to get me court martialed. Then, he could have the last laugh by sending me to jail."

"Mac, I don't understand why the CO lets him get away with it. It's pretty obvious what he's doing!"

"I don't know, Mr. Ratcliffe, unless the CO figures he treats all the EM that way. Which he does, I just get it more severely. What do you think, Mr. Walker?"

"I think we're about ready to land at Chon Thanh and I need the radios. We'll finish talking about it on the way to An Loc."

It wasn't long until the ship was on the ground at Chon Thanh. Sitting there waiting for them was a South Vietnamese major and three NVA prisoners. Each of the NVA's were bound; their hands were tied in front with a stick wedged against their backs and between their elbows. Their feet were tied together with a rope running from the stick to the bindings on their feet. Each prisoner had to be partially lifted up and put in the chopper. The major sat facing the three NVA's who were kneeling on the chopper floor with their backs to the pilots. Jim found it a little unusual that the major would spend so much time and effort obviously placing each of the three in the chopper and on the floor, exactly in the location he wanted them.

As the chopper took off, Jim looked at the four passengers. The ARVN major was no bigger than his three prisoners, the biggest of which couldn't have been over five feet tall. In fact, they looked almost identical—short and skinny. The helicopter was high enough that Jim allowed his M60 to drop into the rest position, that way he could watch what was going on. The major was ranting and raving at the three NVA on the floor. It didn't take a student of psychology to see they were three distinct personalities. The one seated on the far end was a hard nose, whose mere presence kept the other two from telling the major what he wanted to know. On the other end was your basic follower, who probably didn't know anything anyway. It was the man in the middle who was getting most of the major's attention. Jim figured he probably was an officer, but not as high ranking as the Hard Nose. He, more than likely, knew what the major wanted to know but was afraid of Hard Nose.

The major was screaming at the three in Vietnamese. Jim wished he could understand what was being said. The poor guy in the middle looked like he was scared stiff but wasn't going to talk with Hard Nose sitting there. That's when it happened. The major simply grabbed one end of Hard Nose's stick and gave it a flip. Hard Nose disappeared out the cargo door. Jim was stunned.

"Green, did you see that?"

"Yeah, and I think he's getting ready to do it again to the dude on the other end."

The major was really putting the pressure on the two remaining NVA and, in fact, was threatening to do the same to each of them if they didn't talk. It was Walker who came over the radio next. "Mac, what are you two talking about back there?"

"That ARVN major just threw one of his gooks* out the door, and I think Green's right, he's about to do it to this other dude."

"Well, don't let him. We're not barbarians!"

Jim really didn't know what to do, so he shouted, "Hey, Major!"

At the same time the major grabbed one end of the stick and with little effort, rolled the resisting NVA out the door. He then turned to Jim. "No problem, GI. No problem, all done."

He turned back to the one remaining NVA, smiled and asked a question. The prisoner was terrified and his pants showed the dark spot of a man who had just lost control. It didn't affect his tongue, though, as he began to talk so fast the major had to slow him down. There was no more hesitation in answering questions when the major asked.

The rest of the way to An Loc, Jim thought about what had happened. He even shut off all his radios except the inter-ship conversation. It was almost as if he were being mentally ripped in half, one half said so what, especially after what he had been through. Besides, what was the difference? The enemy was the enemy and if he died being thrown out of a helicopter, it wasn't any different than if he got shot. Further, the third dude did sing like a canary, which was, of course, the whole purpose.

* Gook—Slang for any Southeast Asian person.

But his other half told him that what had been done just wasn't right. Jim looked down at his clothes with dried blood all over them and thought of the morning at Cu Chi. Yet, the look of total terror on the two men's faces as they went out the door caused a shiver to go up his spine. How could he condone what had been done. Still, he couldn't bring himself to feel truly sorry for the dead NVA. The fatigue, pressure, stress and general conditions were beginning to get to him. He found himself praying to God that he would get shot—a nice clean wound that wouldn't do any permanent damage but would send him home, and he meant it.

When the chopper landed at An Loc it was met by a jeep. Out stepped an American full bird colonel who wore a Big Red One shoulder patch. He returned the major's salute and it became quickly evident the two men knew each other. Jim had to snicker at the Mutt and Jeff contrast between the two men: the colonel's six and a half foot, two hundred fifty pound frame really made the major look like a midget. Walker shut the chopper down and Green let Walker out of his door before the blades had completely quit turning.

"Colonel, my name is Mr. Walker, I'm the pilot. I would like to have charges brought against this man for throwing two NVA prisoners out of my helicopter at 2000 feet."

"Mr. Walker, I don't really give a damn what he did just as long as he got results."

"Colonel, I . . ."

"Mister! I don't have time to worry about two dead NVA. Listen, the truce started at 1800 hours last night and was called off by 0900 this morning. We've been getting the hell kicked out of us since 2300 last night. Just in case you aren't aware of it yet, Mr. Walker, we are in the middle of the biggest battle of the war. They've thrown everything they've got at us, and we're going to be very lucky to hold our base camps. It wouldn't surprise me in the least if we get kicked completely out of the country, lock, stock and barrel. To help prevent that, I need to know some very important information about the enemy troops in this area and I need it now. I don't have time for niceties, and I don't have time for stupid court martials. Do I make myself clear?"

"Yes, Sir." Mr. Walker saluted, turned and met Jim's eyes with his own. Jim saw "I tried," just as Walker saw the response "I know, and it's okay."

The flight back south to join the rest of the company was quiet. Jim turned Saigon back on and listened to whatever music was playing. Green daydreamed, Ratcliffe and Walker were busy driving and getting artillery and air strike clearances.

It was almost midnight when the flight finally landed for the night. Jim introduced Green to Kenny and asked him to show Green where to clean and store the guns. He pulled his daily inspection as quickly as he could, filled out the log book, so he could turn in the daily log sheet and headed for the hooch. He had just walked in the door when Gillett yelled at him, "Mac, you had anything to eat lately? The CO has the mess sergeant fixing supper for the flight."

"Man, that sounds good! Come on and eat with me, Gillett, I want to talk to you."

The two men went through the line filling their plates with mashed potatoes, gravy, corn and roast beef. The coffee tasted like burnt acid, but there wasn't any ice for water and, without ice, the water always reminded Jim of recycled piss. The food didn't have much taste but was hot and therefore good. Jim had long ago decided the mess hall food was good if it was hot and bad if it was cold.

A short time later, Green and the rest of the gunners came in. Gillett asked, "What in the world have you guys been doing, spit shining those guns?"

One of the gunners answered, "No, Gillett, the CO ordered the guns left on the ships tonight, so we had to get them out of armament and get Kenny to take us back out. Hey, Gillett, what's going on anyway? We never left the guns on before."

"All I know, fellows, is Charlie has evidently decided to play for real."

After the flight crews finished their meals, most of the men headed for one of two places, the club or the showers. On the way out of the mess hall, Green asked Jim where both were located. "Let's get a shower first while there's still some water." The showers weren't quite full of guys when they arrived. The shouts as the ice water hit bare skin bounced off the shower walls and into the night.

"Hey, Mac, is it always this cold?"

"Only late at night. Just be glad there's still water. When it runs out, the last bit of water is full of sand and grit, and you never know when it's going to hit you." They had just left when the obscenities started.

"That, Green, is what it sounds like when the water has just run out."

Back in the hooch Green spotted Jim's shirt. "Hey, Mac, you going to keep that shirt?"

"Of course I'm going to keep it. It'll wash out and you'll never be able to tell it from any other."

"No, no, I mean why don't you keep it like it is and send it home? You could have it framed and wouldn't even have to stretch the truth to impress all the girls."

Kenny spoke up. "Mac, I'll tell you what I'll do, I'll buy that shirt for ten bucks."

"What for?"

"I know a guy in supply who really goes in big for that kind of stuff. You should see some of the letters he sends home. He's a real Saigon warrior*. He would probably rip your name tag off and sew his on, then send it home with some cock and bull story, I mean really, the thing looks like you've been through hell with it." Kenny held the shirt up to get a good look at it. "I'll tell you what, since the thing is almost totally covered with blood and oil, I'll give twenty bucks top for it."

Jim looked Kenny straight in the eye. "Go to hell, Kenny. I wouldn't sell it to you for a hundred bucks!" With that, he grabbed the shirt from Kenny's hands and stuffed it into his dirty clothes bag.

It was almost one-thirty a.m. when Jim got into bed and pulled his mosquito netting down. Sleep came the instant his head hit the pillow.

Jim's eyes felt it first—then his brain seemed to explode with

* Saigon warrior—Person who has not seen combat and tells fictionalized combat stories.

the blinding light in his face. "Mac, wake up, I need a crew for a single ship night mission. You want it?"

"Yeah, I'll go, but get that flashlight out of my face, please. What time is it?"

"Almost two-thirty. I'll get Green up and drive the two of you to the flight line."

"Two-thirty! Gillett, I've only been in bed an hour."

"I know, Mac. You want me to get someone else?"

"No, I'm awake. I'll go."

Jim could really feel the fatigue; his chest felt heavy and it was almost more than he could manage just to crawl out of bed. Gillett helped put their gear in the truck and it wasn't long before they were at the aircraft. Jim was untying the main rotor when the two pilots arrived. They looked like they came out of the same mold: tall, dark and skinny. John O'Neal was from Wyoming and Dave Gabrys was from Colorado.

"Mr. O'Neal, Mr. Gabrys, how did you two get stuck flying tonight?"

As O'Neal placed his gear in the chopper, he turned to answer Jim. "We both had yesterday off, so they figured we would be in the best shape for tonight. Besides, Walker has enough hours that if he flies tonight he'll be over the hour limit. Is this crate ready to fly, Mac?"

"Yes, Sir, I always preflight before I quit for the night."

"Okay, I'll take your word for it, especially since it's so dark." In no time at all the ship was airborne and headed east of Tay Ninh.

"Mr. O'Neal, where we going?"

"Mac, we're headed for Xom Bau Dau. Manchu company had a couple of snipers on Nu Ong* who sniped on more than they could chew. They're supposed to be headed north on Highway 14 in an effort to stay alive."

"How in the world are we going to spot them at this time of night?"

"They have a radio and an M14 with a starlight scope on it, so they should be able to contact us. For that matter, they should see us a long time before we see them."

---

* Nu Ong—An area containing three mountains in a very flat area.

"How long they been on the run?"

"I'm not real sure. Evidently, they got in trouble about 0100 and have been trying to get picked up ever since. Let's cut the chatter now so we can raise 'em on the radio."

Mr. Gabrys had already tuned into their frequency and was listening for their transmission. The wait seemed forever as the single Huey glided silently east over Highway 13 toward the point where 14 and 13 met. O'Neal looked over to Gabrys who was studying a map and asked, "How much further 'til we meet up with Highway 14?"

"About four miles, yet."

It was then that they all heard it, very faint, almost a whisper: "This is Frog calling Lizard. Do you read me? Over."

O'Neal spoke at once. "Roger, Frog. This is Blackhawk 925. We're inbound to your location. By the way Frog, Lizard sends his regards. Can you give me your exact location? Over."

Again, in a voice that betrayed his exhaustion, they heard a whisper. "Negative, Lizard, on the location. Charlie is on this frequency. Can you lock on this frequency if I leave my mike on and find me? Over."

"We can come close. I understand you should be able to see us. Is that correct? Over."

"Affirmative. Over."

"What highway are you now on, Frog? Over."

"Negative, Blackhawk, be prepared to decode. Wait one! Okay, look, Charlie is getting hot again. I've gotta leave this location. I'll leave the mike on, DO NOT, I repeat DO NOT contact me. I see you. I'll call you. Out!"

O'Neal spoke. "He's crazy as hell if he thinks I'm going through that decoding garbage. If he wants a ride he can just tell us where the hell he's at."

"Dave, can you use that radio direction locater? He must be on 13 headed west."

"Yeah, you're probably right! I haven't used a beacon locater since school though." After about two minutes Gabrys spoke. "Okay, I've got him dead ahead. It's a pretty strong signal so we must be close."

"Blackhawk 925, this is Frog, land on the flashlight signal, out!"

"Mr. O'Neal, that wasn't the same man, was it?"

"No, but, Dave, they said there were two of them."

"Blackhawk (huff, huff), this is Frog (huff, huff). Disregard that transmission (huff, huff). It was Charlie (huff, huff). We have (huff, huff) you on visual (huff). Charlie is about two hundred meters back (huff, huff). You just flew past us (huff). Do you have us (huff)?"

"What direction are we turning, Frog? Over."

"To your (huff, huff) left. Come get me, PLEASE!" (Huff, huff.)

"John, we did fly over the signal and it is now behind us. He also got the left turn right, but then he had a 50-50 chance."

"Okay, let's go get him. You two in the backseats awake?"

"Yes, Sir."

"Yes, Sir."

"And, Green, don't fire your M60 until we are on the way out. If Charlie is only two hundred meters back, he's close enough to hear us but not see us. However, the flash of that gun will give them a spot to aim at."

O'Neal came over the radio. "Okay, Frog, we're on our way down. Give us a talk down."

"Roger, you are directly to my north (huff). Now (huff), you're flying by me (huff). You're over the highway and fifty meters (huff) in front (huff). Set it down. I'll come to you. Out."

"Sir, what if it's Charlie?"

"Then cut loose with that M60."

"Green, don't worry about it. If it's Charlie, you'll be dead before you know otherwise."

"Mac, you really know how to encourage a guy."

"I love you too, Green."

"Cut out the chatter back there. Damn, it's dark. I wish I could turn on some lights. I don't even have our navigation lights on. Can anybody see how close the ground is?"

"No, Sir."

"Can anybody see anything?"

There was total silence as every eye searched for some clue to the ship's proximity to earth, tree or, hopefully, highway. Finally, Jim spoke as Mr. O'Neal slowly eased it downward. "Sir,

Frog said we were directly over the highway. All you can do is ease on down."

At that point they felt the skids touch down. Instantly, two men jumped on board and Jim could see one raising his arm upward. Jim almost screamed as the adrenaline pumped through his body. "They're on. Let's go!" With that, O'Neal put everything he had into it and the ship jumped upward and away. Jim could see plainly the flashes of enemy fire and hear the all too distinct thunk, thunk as his chopper took hit after hit. It was all he could do to keep from blindly spraying the area, but he knew every fifth round he fired was a tracer. The trail it left would be like saying, here I am, everybody, shoot. In only seconds, they were out of the area and on their way back to Tay Ninh.

"Mr. O'Neal, we took some hits, so keep a close eye on your gauges."

"Got you covered, Mac."

Their two passengers had begun to regain their breath and had taken seats on the bench. One was seated close to Jim. He placed his hand on Jim's shoulder and pulled the crew chief towards him. Looking at the grunt, Jim realized he wanted to say something. Placing his face only inches from the grunt's, he keyed his mike so everyone could hear. The voice was full of emotion and all knew he had to be crying. "Thank you. Thank you for coming to get us. We've been running almost all night trying to stay ahead of them. Every time we thought we had lost them they would turn our direction and we had to start moving again. You guys looked like a chariot from heaven sent to pluck us from death."

Jim shouted back at the man so he could hear, "Who did you shoot? Ho Chi Minh?"

"We got their CO."

With that the conversation ended and both men leaned back to rest. The next voice Jim heard was O'Neal's. "No wonder they spent so much effort pursuing those two. Look, Mac, these gauges read just fine and we're about five minutes out of Tay Ninh. Where do you want me to put it down?"

"Just take it right on in to maintenance and park it. I know it took several hits that will have to be patched."

It was 0433 when Jim took off his boots and shirt and lay down on his bunk. Sleep, as always, came instantly for him, but it didn't last long.

"Mac, wake up, it's five fifteen, What time did you get back last night?"

"Gillett, it was four-thirty this morning. That's forty-five minutes sleep I got last night and the night before I was on guard duty. That's only five or six hours sleep in the last forty-eight hours."

"Mac, if I had someone else to fly in your place, I'd set you down, but I just don't. In fact, I've got to send Green to Cu Chi for a flight physical today. Come on, I'll eat breakfast with you and you can tell me about last night."

"Man, that was something else. We picked up these two guys, one was a radio man, the other a sniper. You should have seen this guy's rifle, Gillett. He had an M14 with a starlight scope on it and a silencer on the end that must have stuck out a foot. I don't know how much that thing weighed, but he had to think it was a ton after running up Highway 13 from Nu Ong and then down 14, 'til we picked them up. Come on. Let's go eat and I'll tell you all about it."

Breakfast was the same as always: eggs done to your choice, toast—sometimes donuts, and the ever present coffee. Whenever the cooks were fixing omelets Jim always had one. His favorite was ham and cheese, but any omelet had flavor, and that was more than he could say for eggs sunny side up or over easy, which usually ended up being over hard. Unlike a lot of guys, he always took his malaria tablet. But then he didn't get the diarrhea like some of the other guys, so he really didn't mind.

The two men were about finished with their meals when Gillett poked Jim with his elbow. Pointing to a guy at the end of the table putting Tabasco sauce on his eggs he said, "Mac, what septic tank do you suppose that guy lived in that taught him to put Tabasco sauce on his eggs?"

"Mexico!" Both men broke into laughter. They looked at each other and laughed that much harder. Before long, they had the whole mess hall looking their direction.

Jim placed his steel pot* with the ice cold shaving water on his bunk between himself and his mirror. He was well lathered and had started to shave when he saw it. There in the rafters was Kenny's monkey directly over Bob Athia's bunk. It didn't dawn on Jim what was happening until he turned around and started laughing at the spectacle above. Bob Athia was a well-built man of about 5'7" and one hundred fifty pounds. An Oklahoma boy with brown hair and eyes, he already had a big dislike for Kenny's monkey.

"Hey, Bob, Kenny's monkey's about to come all over you."

Athia looked up to see the masturbating monkey directly over his bunk. Grabbing a combat boot, he threw it at the monkey and shouted, "I'll kill you, you son of a bitch."

The boot missed but caused the monkey to move just as he ejaculated, spreading semen on Bob's bunk, the floor and Dick Hunter's wall locker. Dick Hunter stood six feet, weighed about one hundred ninety pounds, and like most of the other men in the hooch, he didn't have any love for the monkey. So with the mess on his wall locker that now confronted him, he picked up his M16 and with the actions of a man who meant business, he jammed in a full magazine and pulled back the bolt.

Kenny, who had been watching with Gillett and Jim, jumped on Hunter before he could take aim. Athia's temper was on full boil. He jumped on Kenny and a full scale fight was under way. Gillett started forward to break things up when Jim grabbed his arm and said, "Let 'em fight. It'll do Kenny good. Maybe he'll even decide to get rid of that damn monkey."

Gillett ignored him and moved forward shouting, "Alright, you guys, I'm giving you a direct order: break it up. I mean it. Stop it." The three separated as Gillett shouted, "attent-hut," and came to attention facing Gillett, who started his lecture. "Kenny, Mac thought I should have let them beat the hell out of you and believe me I would have if I was sure that Athia and Hunter would be flyable. You just might have gotten lucky and really hurt one of them, so I had to stop it. However, Kenny,

* Steel pot—Steel part of an infantryman's combat helmet.

YOU WILL get rid of that monkey and YOU WILL clean up the mess he just made! Do you understand me?"

Kenny nodded his head, "Yes".

"Hunter, you know perfectly good and well it's an automatic Article 15 for unauthorized discharging of a weapon in the company area. So you should be glad Kenny stopped you. Okay, let's get finished up in here, you're supposed to be on your ships shortly."

The truck ride to the flight line was filled with conversation and bet-taking on when, if at all, Kenny would get rid of his monkey. One thing about a group of GI's, they were willing to take bets on anything. Once at the ship, Jim started his pre-flight inspection. It wasn't long before the gunners were dropped off. They usually went to the armament bunker for ammo and smoke grenades before going to their ships. Jim's ship had been fixed and moved out of maintenance and into its revetment. The first thing he checked was the log book to see what maintenance had been done. As he had suspected there was no major damage to the ship, only superficial wounds which required some simple skin patching.

Jim was almost finished with his preflight when Gary Broadnex, his gunner for the day, showed up. Gary was a short, five-foot-five, stubby fellow with a roly poly disposition. Yet his one hundred sixty-five pounds of mostly muscle made him very physical, "Hi, Mac, I heard that new guy has to go get a flight physical today. My ship's in maintenance, so for today, I fly with you."

"I'll tell you, I'm glad to see you. I was afraid I'd get stuck with Kenny or one of our pothead friends."

"How are you betting on Kenny's monkey?"

"Oh, it'll still be there tonight."

It wasn't long before Mr. Walker and Mr. Valadores walked up. Mr. Valadores looked every bit the Spaniard his name indicated. A full faced man of medium height and build, Valadores hoped to be a comedian once out of the service. Everyone enjoyed flying with him because of his great sense of humor.

In another twenty minutes, the flight of ten ships and two gunships was airborne. Their mission for the day was to put troops in position to start a sweep in the direction of fire support base BURK. BURK would then act as a blocking force, along with troops from the First Infantry Division.

BURK was located alongside a dirt highway surrounded by trees, except where the engineers had cleared them to allow for a good field of fire. No one liked flying in or around trees. They were hard to get over on takeoff and made it hard to find a safe place to land in case of power failure or other emergency.

It was a long, boring flight from Tay Ninh to the drop sight, although no one was in a real hurry to get there. Jim pulled the sun visor down on his helmet and pulled his seat belt tight to take a nap. The boredom and exhaustion was putting him to sleep. He awoke when he heard Valadores say, "Is that our LZ?"

Walker's response was only to shake his head in the affirmative. Jim looked out the door and saw they were on long final approach to the hour glass.

It was called the hour glass because, from the air, that's what it looked like. In reality, it was a grass clearing surrounded by trees. Everytime the Blackhawks had landed there they had been shot at and this time wasn't any different. It started with small arms fire as they came in on short final. The bottom right side of the hour glass suddenly looked like a fire works display. Jim could only guess at what it looked like from the ground as all twenty M60's opened up, each firing a tracer every fifth round. Unfortunately, the worst was to come as the ships touched down. Out of the hour glass's neck came fire that Jim couldn't see but Broadnex announced, "We're getting shot at by a bunch of 50's. There are four, no eight of them. That thing must be a dual quad fifty*. As the flight started to lift off, Jim could see fire coming from his side of the bottleneck. It was Valadores who asked the question first. "My Lord, those look like basketballs coming at us! Mac, what is that thing down there?"

"It's got to be an anti-aircraft gun." Jim continued to fire his M60 at the ack-ack gun, hoping to silence it long enough to get past. His voice was full of agitation and emotion as he related to the others what he saw as he looked backward. "Oh, shit,

* Dual quad 50—50 caliber machinegun with eight barrels firing together.

Chalk Seven just took a direct hit from that ack-ack. It just literally blew up."

Jim hadn't finished speaking when the intership radio cracked, "Lead, this is Chalk 10. Chalk 7 just took a direct hit from anti-aircraft fire. He went down out of control and is on the ground in flames now. There appear to be no survivors. Trail, out."

The mike clicked twice. The big question on everyone's mind now was, who was in Chalk Seven? It was a First Platoon ship, so no one on 925 knew who was in it. Of course, it just wasn't right to go on the radio and ask.

"Trail, this is Lead. How many ships did we leave behind? Over."

"Lead, this is Trail. Two by my count. Over."

"Six, this is Lead. Do you copy? Over."

"Roger, Lead. We're over the LZ in C and C. Take the flight back to BURK and pick up troops there and insert them ASAP*. I'll get Saigon and see if we can't get some fixed wing help up here. Six out."

The flight had already turned to head for the dirt road alongside BURK. In no time, troops were on board and headed back to the hour glass. This time, though, there was more prepping of the LZ for their landing. The first time in, the gunships had made a couple of runs but drawn no fire, which meant, of course, the NVA troops on the ground were well disciplined. So this time the LZ was also prepped with artillery fire from BURK's 105MM guns.

All the friendly troops were supposed to be on the left, so only those guns on the right side of the ships opened fire as they approached the LZ On command, the right side guns opened fire with each person expecting at any second to see the basketball sized tracers start blowing them out of the sky. The ships were on the ground and the troops out and nothing—not even small arms fire. The flight took off and was gone without receiving that first sign of enemy fire.

"Mr. Walker, you know I'm enormously glad we didn't get shot at again, but I don't understand why."

* ASAP —As soon as possible.

"The only thing I can figure, Mac, is that when they started getting artillery fire on them they packed up and left."

"But, Sir, with those two guns working together they could have blown every one of us out of the sky, then taken the troops on the ground at their leisure."

"Wouldn't you guess that was their plan to begin with, but the guys they had operating the fifty and ack-ack were such poor shots they didn't get the job done. I mean, after all, the 50 only got one ship and the anti-aircraft one, and either one of them alone should have gotten all ten of us. But at the worst, both together should have knocked down seven or eight of us. When that didn't happen, they figured correctly that we would be right back with more troops, and it did only take us about thirty minutes turn around time. You can bet they didn't want to lose those two guns, so they figured since plan A didn't work, use plan B. Pack up and leave."

"Yeah, you're probably right which means two things: one, someone in Saigon told them where, when and with what we were coming, and two, they also knew where the trap was laid and were not about to get caught in it."

"You got it, Mac. We'll put a little red apple on your tree tonight and send you to the head of the class."

"You're so kind."

Valadores broke in. "Hey, you guys, I've had my UHF* on. Six has been talking to Tay Ninh. They're going to let us get fuel this time but that's it. No more fuel except for gunships until they can get the bridges the NVA blew fixed to get a convoy through. And, of course, they'll probably have to have the Air Force fly in fuel first."

Jim reached up and flipped his UHF and VHF** switch on just in time to hear Six calling Lead, "I read you loud and clear, Six. Come on in."

"Roger, Lead. You can only get the flight topped off once at Tay Ninh. I've tried Quan Loi and Dau Tieng and they're both

* UHF—Ultra high frequency radio—used for long range communication (mostly Air Force).
** VHF—Very high frequency radio—used for medium range communication.

out of fuel except for gunships. The next closest place is Cu Chi. They said they have a reasonable supply, but with everyplace else running low, Cu Chi won't last long either. I'll keep you advised. Six, out."

It wasn't long until the flight landed at the fuel pumps, refueled and picked up troops.

Jim always thought that, in many ways, the ferrying of troops was one of the worst parts of the war. It was the boredom, hour after hour of the same patch of sky to look at, the same jungle or rice paddy, the same trees and water from eighteen hundred feet was very monotonous. Boredom, long, long hours of boredom combined with the ever present fatigue, made it extremely hard to stay awake.

It took about thirty minutes to get to the LZ with American troops on both sides of the hour glass. There wasn't any firing of the ship's M60's. It was a routine landing and take off. Now they had to make the forty-five minute flight to Cu Chi, then up to Tay Ninh to pick up troops and back to the LZ. Jim figured it would be an easy two hours before they got back to the LZ again.

He could hear Lead asking Six what kind of resistance the grunts had met. The response didn't surprise Jim. No contact with the enemy. Of course, the American troops hadn't moved until the second lift had been put in. By that time, the NVA had broken down their big guns and split. By the time our troops got there, they could see by the crushed grass the spot where both guns had been. No other sign of their existence was present: no shells, nothing. The walk to BURK would be just as uneventful. No question about it—the NVA had planned on a very big slaughter. Lack of skill by the guys working the fifty and ack-ack had caused a very quick change in plans. Jim realized their plan was good—very, very good. If the NVA had as few as one hundred fifty troops in the area, it would have been easy pickings because there couldn't have been more than fifty or sixty U.S. troops on the ground, depending on how many of the flight crews survived in fighting condition.

The tension seemed to release as Jim leaned back, allowing the fatigue to consume him. Before falling asleep he said, "Thank you, God."

Jim awoke to hear Broadnex and Walker talking. Cu Chi was in sight and before long, the flight had refueled and then relocated on a side road. Jim was glad he hadn't gotten caught sleeping and, also, that there'd been a change in plans, even though he didn't know what or why. The flight was now in Cu Chi sitting on a side road shutting off the engines, which meant they were going to be there for a while.

Almost as quickly as the engines were shut down, the crews broke out the C-rations. The pilots took their C's and walked up to lead ship to discuss the day and get instructions from Six. Jim had tied down the main rotor blade and started to open his C-ration box, when a chaplain stuck his head in the ship and said, "I've got a jeep over there in the clearing," as he pointed in its direction. "I'll be holding services in three minutes and I'd like to have you men join me." With that, he turned and walked down the line of choppers and made the same invitation to each man he saw.

Jim turned to Broadnex and said, "Come on, let's go."

"Mac, that's sissy stuff. I'm not going over there."

Without responding, Jim gulped his C-ration and walked over to the jeep taking a seat on the ground along with some grunts who had come over and the handful of Blackhawks. There were about a dozen men present. The chaplain started, "In the name of the Father, Son and Holy Ghost. Amen. Men, I've only been in country a few weeks, but in that short time, I've learned these impromptu services are often more meaningful to you than the regular Sunday services I hold. I've also learned those choppers won't wait for me to finish, so I better get the most important part done first. Is there anyone here who hasn't been baptized and would like to do so now?" The chaplain looked quickly around and seeing no response moved on. "Is there anyone here who already knows the Lord Jesus Christ and believes in Him?" This time the response was unanimous as each man raised his hand. "In that case, is there anyone here who would like to receive Holy Communion?"

The response was slower but, again, several hands went up, including Jim's. It would be his first communion since he left the States and he knew he had many sins of which to repent.

His first thought was of R&R* and all he had done there. The chaplain's voice continued. "Very well, men, all I have is a canteen of water and some C-ration crackers. Under the circumstances, though, I don't think the Lord will mind their use." He then placed the canteen and crackers on the jeep's hood and said, "Let us pray. 'Our Father, who art in heaven. Hallowed be Thy Name. Thy kingdom come, Thy will be done on earth as it is in heaven. Give us this day our daily bread; and forgive us our trespasses as we forgive those who trespass against us and lead us not into temptation, but deliver us from evil. For Thine is the kingdom and the power and the glory. Amen.' Men, our Lord Jesus Christ on the night He was betrayed took bread and when He had given thanks, He broke it and gave it to His disciples saying, 'Take, eat, this is My Body which is given for you, this do in remembrance of Me.' After the same manner also, He took the cup, when He had supped and when He had given thanks, He gave it to them saying, 'Drink ye all of it, this cup is the New Testament in My Blood which is shed for you and for many for the remission of sins. This do, as often as you drink it, in remembrance of Me.' The Peace of the Lord be with you always. Amen. The table of the Lord is ready.

"Men, those of you who believe in the Lord Jesus Christ as your personal Savior and who truly repent of all your sins, rise and receive the Lord's table."

Jim and most of the men rose and moved forward. The words just spoken rang in his ears, emotion filled his chest and a tear fell from his eye down the side of his face as the chaplain handed him a small piece of stale cracker and said, "Take, eat, this is the Body of Christ given for you." Each man was served and the chaplain picked up the water canteen, passing it to each man as he said, "Take, drink the Blood of Christ shed for your sins."

After all the men had been served, he had them take their seats on the grass again and spoke once more. "The Body of our Lord Jesus Christ and His precious Blood strengthen and preserve you in true faith unto everlasting life. Amen." After a

* R&R—Rest and recreation.

short pause, he addressed the group as though giving a sermon. Jim's eyes were full of moisture and the emotion he felt at that moment would haunt him always. He wanted to weep openly but forced back the tears, not wanting to seem unmanly. He had just received the most meaningful communion of his life. It was the chaplain's voice that brought him back from his own deep thoughts. "Men, like me, some of you have only been in country a short time, others are probably about to rotate home." As the chaplain spoke he could look over the men in front of him and see the helicopters parked behind them. The pilots in the first chopper were climbing out and quickly moving back towards their ships. Knowing he now had only seconds before the flyboys in his group would have to leave, his message became shorter, "I can never know your trials because, like millions of others, I'll never walk in your shoes." He could see the main rotors being untied. "There will be times when you think Christ has forsaken you. However, take a lesson from the old Jews. They sinned and the Lord punished them but he never forsook them. He always loved them and was always with them just as he will always be with you. That doesn't mean you won't be killed. St. Paul and Peter were killed because they loved Jesus. He will always be with you, even in death, and for that reason, LIVE without fear!"

The all too familiar whine of the chopper engines starting to turn reached their ears. The flyboys all stood at once and started to leave but were stopped and turned around by the chaplain's words. "Men, give me only one second more." He raised his right hand and said, "The Lord bless you and keep you. The Lord make His face to shine upon you. The Lord lift His countenance upon you and give you His peace. Amen."

With his still raised hand he waved them on. To a man, they turned and ran to their respective ships. Watching them go he was reminded of a phrase he had heard before, but couldn't quite bring to mind, something about the flower of American youth.

Broadnex had already untied the rotor and Walker had started to turn the engine. Jim quickly put his chicken plate on and then his helmet. Having plugged his helmet in he spoke. "What's happening?"

Walker responded, "To make a long story short, there was only one way out of our trap at BURK. Naturally, that's the way the NVA are going. Since we now have to go to Saigon to get fuel, we're simply going to let them go and pull our own troops out. It seems the turn around time will be too great to chance putting in a blocking force."

The flight back to BURK and the Hour Glass was uneventful, giving Jim time to think about the chaplain's words. They picked up the same troops they had dropped off earlier along with the flight crew that had been shot down. The charred remains of the other ship still lay in a broken, ugly heap. The second ship had been chinooked out earlier. What little was left of the four men who had been burned in the chopper hit by anti-aircraft fire lay on the ground beside their ship.

"Mr. Walker, did you see those bodies as we took off?"

"Yeah, Mac, I did. Not a nice way to die."

"Sir, where are we dropping these troops?"

"Since the pressure is off at BURK, they're going all the way to Saigon. We're supposed to put them in a polo field the French built. In fact, it's alongside a building used as a French academy. Evidently the Cholon district of Saigon is catching hell. We heard on the radio that the MP's have finally secured the U.S. Embassy."

The flight down to Saigon seemed to take forever. Jim was overwhelmed as they approached the old French polo field. He had no idea that any such place existed in Vietnam. Old world money and lots of it was very evident. A brick fence surrounded the polo field and a brick two-story building that might have been a barracks or school at one time stood just outside the field. Half round red tile roofing lay broken on the ground beside the building. Grass was growing in the cracks around the old flag pole in what had once been an area where ceremonies were held. The grass on the field had been recently mowed like someone expected to play one day this week. Only the trash on the field told of the departed army that had used its grounds as a camping area.

The flight landed on the edge of the polo field not far from the old barracks. There were still signs of the recent heavy combat that had taken place in and around the field but the flight didn't draw any fire. From the polo field they went to the fuel dump to put on fuel.

"Flight, this is Lead. A jeep will approach one of our ships; whoever the lucky one is that they pull up beside, you're to get four rubber bags and take them back up to BURK with you."

As Jim put fuel in his chopper, he listened to the radio and hoped that jeep driver didn't pick his ship. Broadnex's voice told him he hadn't hoped hard enough. "Oh, shit, why us? Eight choppers sitting here and that bastard has to pick us."

Valadores said, "Broadnex, this is just your lucky day. Stop bitching and go get the bags."

When Jim climbed back on board, there in the cargo area were four neatly folded black rubber bags. He hated those bags and if he never saw a black rubber bag again, it would be too soon.

The flight back to the Hour Glass seemed to take forever. It was the routine of the long flights and the boredom that once again made it really tough for Jim to stay awake.

Once at the LZ, Walker hovered their ship over to where the bodies lay. Two grunts ran over to give assistance as Broadnex and Jim stepped out of the chopper, each carrying two bags. It was the close-up sight of the bodies that first made Jim look away. He tried not to look but the sickly sweet smell violated his nostrils and tightened his throat almost to the choking point, forcing him to look at the badly charred body before him. The sight and smell was almost more than he could stand. He put his handkerchief to his mouth and tried to block out the smell as the other hand unzipped the bag. The flies were all over the bodies, like bees on honey. Already swollen considerably, the bodies looked and smelled worse than words could describe. Jim bent over and with Broadnex's help, tried to roll the first body on top of the opened bag. It was as if on cue they both turned and vomited. Gagging and choking and vomiting, they finished the gruesome task and zipped up the bag. The second body was just as bad as the first; both started dry heaving when Broadnex pulled off a large chunk of cooked flesh and meat in his hand. Unable to pick up the charred remains, they tried to push the body into position. Finally, the job was done and with the grunt's help, they were loaded onto the ship. All four men tried to wash the bitter taste out of their mouths with ice water from Jim's cooler, to no real avail. They swished it around, gargled and spit. Only the air rushing over their bodies as the ship flew along prevented them from smelling the odor that had attached itself to their clothing.

Jim settled back in his seat for the long flight back to Saigon. It was already starting to get dark, and the total exhaustion that overcame him was more than he cared to resist.

"Mac, you awake? Mac, wake up!"

"I'm awake, Mr. Walker. I'm awake!"

"You were, like shit, MacLaughlin! Now, stay awake, damn it! There are too many other choppers around, plus jets. I don't have to tell you that a phantom's nose wouldn't look at all good sticking out of our cargo door."

"Mr. Walker, do you know how much sleep I've had the last few days? Not more than three hours. I'm beat. Besides, these sixty minute lifts are boring as hell back here. Not to mention the fact I just had the dry heaves."

"MacLaughlin, there are millions of people in the world you could never convince that flying in a helicopter and getting shot at is boring. Get another drink of water and you'll feel better."

"Sir, I could care less what people think and I'm not thirsty."

"Okay, Mac, let's change the subject. I'm supposed to have R&R next month. You just went. Tell me about it."

Jim figured why not, it'd take his mind off everything, "Okay, it was January 17 through 21. I went to Manila but you could care less. You just figure that if I'm talking, I won't go to sleep."

"That's not true, I really want to hear about it, and if it helps keep you awake, so much the better. Start with picking up your orders."

"Okay, I don't mind telling you about it because I had a great time. In fact, if I can work it out, I'm going back. I picked up my orders from the company clerk that morning. I was all on my own as far as getting there and back, so I hopped a ride on the courier flight down to Cu Chi. At Cu Chi I had to do some processing out of country and get my shots updated. I spent most of the time standing in line. You know the Army, hurry up and wait. Since it was night by the time I got done, I stayed with the 116th Flight Platoon. The Hornets had an empty bunk."

R&R

*"I noticed among the young men, a youth
who lacked judgment."* PROVERBS 7:7
                                                    NIV

Yes, Jim thought to himself, it had been quite an experience,
but he didn't want to tell Walker the whole story. His mind
drifted back to that first day of R&R. He remembered checking
in and taking his sheets to the hooch he'd been assigned for the
night. He found an empty bed, decided that it looked as flea
infested as any of the others available, and unrolled the mattress to lay the sheets down. Someone touched him on the arm
and said, "Aren't you Jim MacLaughlin?"

Jim turned and, seeing a slightly familiar face, shook his
head and said, "Yes."

The other GI laughed and said, "I'm John Seiko."

Jim was stunned. He hadn't seen John since high school,
where they had been classmates almost two years ago. John
had grown at least four inches and had lost all his baby fat. In
school, John had been at least one hundred pounds overweight.

"Jim, you didn't recognize me!"

"John, I hate to admit it, but I didn't. Man, you have
changed!"

"I know! Joining the Army was the best thing that ever happened to me. Look, Jim, you coming or going on R&R?"

"I'm going, how about you?"

"I just got back from Hong Kong and have the day to kill;
then tomorrow, I check out of here and head back to the Big

63

Red One over at Di An. Look, let's check in your M16 and ammo and go get a drink."

"John, that sounds great, but I have to check in at reception in about fifteen minutes."

Together, they made Jim's bunk and walked over to check in his ammo and M16. From there they headed to the reception center, where Jim was given a list of do's and don'ts and a departure time for the next day. From there they hopped a ride on a jeep to Saigon. The staff sergeant driving turned out to be a nice guy who took them to a bar and told them to have a good time.

The place was packed with people, and it didn't take long until they decided to leave. Once on the street Jim remembered why he hated Saigon. The place was a pigsty and the people were barbarians. The two GIs hadn't gone fifty feet down the road when a little boy about six years old, with bare feet, ragged shorts and no shirt approached.

"Hey, GI, you want number one woman?"

"No, kid, we're not interested. Now beat it!"

"Come on, GI, you want layed? Buy my Mama San, she virgin, number one lay, GI. Number one, you like, you like!"

John decided to have a little fun with this kid, so he said, "Hey kid, your mother good-looking?"

"Number one, GI, number one, you like."

"You sure she's a virgin, kid?"

"Sure, GI, she virgin, you like, number one, number one!"

"Beat it, kid! We're not interested in your mother. Go on, get out of here!"

John laughed and laughed. "I'll tell you, Jim, this is some country where little kids try to sell you their mother and sisters."

"Yeah, and look at those kids—the streets and the buildings."

"Hey, GI, you no want Mama San? But sister, she pretty."

"She a virgin too, kid?"

"Sure, GI, she virgin, number one, you like very much."

"Hey kid, how many kids your Mama San have?"

"Eight, you want sister?"

"No! No! No! Now beat it kid, go on, git!"

Jim pulled on John's arm and pointed down the alley. There, beside a bunch of old crates and boxes, squatted a Vietnamese man with his pants down having a bowel movement and the whole area smelled like it wasn't the first time it had been used as a toilet. Jim wasn't really surprised, though, as there was garbage and trash all over the place and the streets were covered with dirt and sand. From the same alley, an old woman came out of a restaurant with a pail of slop and gave it a sling into the gutter. The street was lined on both sides with bars, restaurants and open-air shops. The shops were filled with varied and sundry goods. Some had meat hanging that was covered with flies, some were filled with black market goods. Everything from guns, ammo and other weapons of war to booze and C-rations was available. As the two men walked by the bars, they were accosted by men and sometimes women. Each tried to sell the age old folly of soldiers in any army: drink and girls—girls on stage, all nude girl reviews, all nude go-go dancers, strip shows, topless waitresses, girls for sale by the ejaculation or by the hour, day or week—girls were definitely available.

As they walked, they were stopped by a very attractive girl in the doorway of a bar, who was pleasant and spoke fairly good English. As she talked, she put her arm around John's waist and began to rub his crotch. As she worked on John, Jim couldn't help but be stunned by her beauty. She was a small woman, of about sixteen, he would guess. Her hair and makeup were perfect and her oriental dress, slit to her hips, showed enough of her petite figure in a provocative sort of way to cause both men to give consideration to the offer she proposed. She had John sold and knew it from her hand, so skillfully manipulating his engorged shaft. In a sexually playful gesture, John began tickling her under the arms and on the tummy. It was this that caused both men to lose interest instantly in her and move on. "My God, Jim, did you see those teeth when she started to laugh?"

"Unfortunately, yes. I have never seen such a disgusting mess in my life. Those teeth were half rotted away with just stubs sticking up and what was left had a sickly black and green color. I thought I was going to gag."

"Jim, you thought you were going to gag, how about me? I could just see myself screwing that broad and me laying a few French kisses on her. I think I'm going to be sick. Come on, this looks like a half way decent place. I'll buy you a beer."

It was a typical small bar, not much space, with only three tables and bar stools running the length of one wall. The table they took was made of wood, but didn't look like it would hold the two beers they ordered. The bamboo walls showed various sized holes and cracks. The floor was dirt and was probably raked out once a week, whether it needed it or not. They ordered only American beer in cans and insisted that they remain unopened before being placed on their table. Time slipped by quickly as the two old friends discussed their high school and Army days.

Very late that night when they left, the kids were still selling their female relatives and the men on every street corner were still selling watches and cigarettes. Both GI's were in a silly, drunken condition and when Jim asked to see a watch hawker's selection, they literally fell over each other laughing. The watch hawker had pulled up both sleeves. Watches covered both arms from his wrists to his elbows. Then he pulled up both pant legs exposing more watches on each leg from the ankles to the knees. From there they caught a taxi back to the base and left the Saigon shanties behind.

(In three years, Jim MacLaughlin would attend his high school class reunion, where the emcee would tell that John Seiko had been killed in action in South Vietnam at some place called Hobo Woods. Jim immediately recognized the date as being only days after they had been together in Saigon. Jim's chest would fill with painful emotion, his head would drop into his hands and on down to the table. Tears would fill his eyes until, finally, overcome with emotion, he would weep openly.)

Wake up time for Jim was 0500 hours. He watched for Seiko, but didn't see him. So he decided to try to look him up again when he got back from R&R. When Jim reported in at the reception center, he was told to turn in his bedding and be ready for departure at 1000 hours. He already had his bedding, so he could go straight to the supply hooch, and from there to the mess hall for the predictable Army chow which he knew was as big a mess one place as another. Jim arrived back at the orientation center at 0945 hours with khaki uniform on, suitcase in hand and ready to go. At 1035 hours, an Army sergeant began the briefing by saying they were going to hurry, as they were running late. The sergeant checked everyone's orders and, when finished, told the group they would be met in Manila and given a briefing. From there the sergeant led the group to the finance center where their M.P.C. (Military Pay Currency) was exchanged for real American greenbacks. As each person walked through the finance center door, the sergeant directed him to a waiting bus.

Jim found himself somewhat amused at how tough some tours of duty were in Vietnam. Here there were numerous soldiers doing nothing more each day than driving a bus and directing other people around, but he knew this was nothing new. He had often been told that it took eight or more support people for each combat soldier. Still, he couldn't help but wonder if these Saigon Warriors wouldn't be the ones to tell the biggest war stories back home.

The bus arrived at Tan Son Nhut airport at 1200 hours. The group was led by the same sergeant from the customs area. Going through customs wasn't any real problem. It was a simple matter of opening one's suitcase for inspection and then passing through the turnstile.

Once more they followed that fine old Army tradition, "Hurry up and wait." At 1245 hours, the group finally was ready to board an Air Force DC-6 for Manila. Standing in line, it occurred to Jim there weren't any officers or women in the group of about thirty enlisted men. He decided they probably sent officers in separate groups, but he wondered how women went on R&R.

When Jim got on the plane he was horrified. There weren't any seats! Halfway panicstricken, he looked around to see what the others were doing. They, for the most part, were looking around to see what everyone else was doing. One Sp/5 had started unfolding the plane's fold-down benches from the walls. Jim's only thought was, "You have got to be kidding me!" as he sat down and looked for the seatbelt that wasn't there.

The Sp/5 seated next to him said, "They could have at least told us it was a no frills flight."

Jim laughed and commented, "With the no-expenses-barred treatment we have received so far, I'm afraid to see what the stewardesses look like."

He didn't have to be concerned. There weren't any. Somewhat to his surprise, the plane managed to get off the ground. It landed at Clark Air Force Base, Manila, at 1805 hours. As they disembarked, they were led into another customs center and from there to the briefing room.

The staff sergeant entering the room looked like a hundred other young men. He was about twenty-one, tall, thin, with a fair complexion. Despite his squeaky voice, he tried his best to sound like a nail-biting drill sergeant. "Good evening, men. My name is Staff Sergeant Pedro. I'll be giving you a lot of information, so listen up. First, each of you must pick one hotel from the list on the blackboard. Write the name of said hotel in the space marked hotel on the white sheet of paper you were given as you entered this room. If you don't know anything about any of the hotels, just pick a name that sounds good and write it down. We are not allowed to give out any more information about the hotels."

Jim looked at the list and wrote down Shoreline Hotel. He wished he knew more about it than just the name. Sergeant Pedro explained what they could and couldn't buy (mostly what couldn't be bought and taken through customs), and where they could not go in Manila, since part of the city had known Communist sympathizers. They were not to wear their uniforms at all, from the time they arrived at the hotel until the morning they dressed to return. If they became ill or needed any other services, such as legal or medical, they were to call the base operator or present themselves to the MP at the gate. Sergeant Pedro also stressed the importance of not being arrested by the local officials.

Finally, he had the group finish filling out the required paperwork. "In conclusion, gentlemen, I welcome you to Manila and assure you that there is no reason each of you shouldn't have a very nice visit. To help you enjoy yourselves we have compiled a list of bars that we strongly recommend. You can visit them tonight. At these bars you can buy drinks and female companionship without fear of MP disapproval. The girls are checked out on a regular basis by a doctor. We also recommend that you pay in advance for your room for the duration of your stay. That way, if anything happens to your money, you have a place to stay and you can eat here on post. If there are no questions, pick up your suitcases and file outside. You are to get on the bus marked with the name of the hotel you chose. Have a good time, men. Move out."

The bus ride to the hotel took about thirty minutes. In no time at all, Jim had checked in and arrived at his room on the tenth floor. He was pleased with the room. It was clean, with one large bed, a bath and shower, dresser, desk and chair. In general, this is what he would expect in a nice but older hotel in the states. Jim quickly showered and changed. He wanted to eat and then find a bar. He walked out the hotel door and saw several taxis. One of the drivers approached and asked, "You need a taxi, Sir?"

"Yes, I do."

"Get in, Sir, get in. My name is Joe. Where you want to go?"

"I'm here on R&R. I'd like to get something to eat and drink."

"I know the exact place, sir. And let me add, I would consider it a privilege to be your personal guide and driver while you're here."

Joe started the '58 Ford he used for a taxi and drove off into the night, and Jim started on an adventure that would affect his relationship with women and his future wife more than he could possibly realize.

"Joe, I'm not sure I understand your offer. How much do you want for this service?"

"Nothing, Sir, except the usual taxi fee. You see, it works out good for both of us. You have me for a guide around the city, and I'll take real good care of you—even give you some advice and answer all your questions. You'll want to go various places and I know the best. Besides, you won't have to worry about a taxi. I'll always be there as your personal driver, not taking any other fares while you're here. It's a good deal for me, also; I can count on your using my taxi, so I'll have a fare each day. You simply tell me what time to be at the hotel in the morning and I'll be there waiting."

"Joe, how do you charge? By the mile, day, or hour?"

"By the mile, Sir. Look, business is bad right now and I know how much the average GI travels on R&R. So, I know I'll make more money working for you than by trying to hack it, and you get a good deal in return."

"Okay, Joe, you've got a deal under one condition. Stop calling me Sir. My name is Jim MacLaughlin. Call me Jim or Mac, or MacLaughlin, but don't call me Sir. Okay?"

"Okay, okay, Jim. You've made a wise decision. Here we are, Howard's Bar and Restaurant. I'm sure you can find everything you want in there. When you're ready to leave, I'll be here waiting. You're going to like it here."

Jim got out of the taxi, a little unsure of himself. He had never done anything like this before, but he sure wasn't going to miss his chance now. He just hoped he didn't lose his nerve. Upon entering, he noticed several young girls standing around. As much as he hated it, he knew he blushed when they smiled at him. The maître d' met him and asked if he would like to go to the bar or the restaurant. Jim chose the restaurant and dined on the best steak, mashed potatoes and peas he'd had since the States.

After dinner, he paid his bill and proceeded to the bar. He was shown to a table where he ordered a whiskey sour. A short, heavy set Filipino man approached the table and sat down. "Hi, my name is Manuel Romulo. You're here on R&R?"

"Yes, I am. My name is Jim. Have a seat, make yourself at home."

"Thank you. Are you interested in a girl, Jim?"

"Sure, you the boss?"

"Yes, I am. Do you have a girl picked out?"

"No, and I have to admit I've never done this before."

"Jim, my good friend, that's no problem."

Manuel slapped his hands and shouted to no one in particular in a language that Jim didn't understand. In a routine that was obviously standard procedure, all the girls who weren't sitting with a man moved to a bench along one wall and sat down. There must have been fifteen girls on that bench. They were different in many ways. They ranged in age, from what Jim guessed to be about fifteen, to what must have been forty-five or forty-six. Some were just plain ugly, some homely, some plain, some attractive, and some were very, very pretty. There were fat girls, skinny girls, and everything in between. All but a few were dressed in western clothing. Manuel gave Jim several minutes to look the girls over and make a selection. Finally, Jim smiled and looked over at Manuel, who had been in the business long enough to know that this is where he should take the lead.

"Jim, would you like to go up and take a closer look?"

"No, I don't think so."

"Is there one that you would like to have come over? Would you like to talk to her?"

"How about the one with the deck of cards in her hands?"

"An excellent choice, Jim. She is one of my very best girls."

Manuel motioned to the girls and directed the one Jim had picked to his table. The rest of the girls dispersed and Jim watched the slender, young beauty walk to his table. She had a graceful walk and held herself in a manner as if to show that she had grown up in an above average home. She had a light complexion and dark hair and eyes. Her skirt ended well above her knees, revealing two beautiful legs. As she sat down she smiled at Jim. He realized instantly she hadn't shown any teeth. Manuel spoke first.

"Jim, this is Rose. Rose, I'd like you to meet Jim."

Rose looked Jim in the eye and said, "Hi, you're very nice looking."

"Thank you, and may I say, you're the most beautiful Rose I've ever seen." Jim paused for a moment and said, "I know this sounds strange, but could I see your teeth?"

Rose flashed him a very toothy smile and a very puzzled look.

Manuel spoke, "Is everything okay?"

"Yes, just fine, thank you."

"Would you like to use the bed in the back room before you decide?"

Jim shook his head and said, "No, that won't be necessary."

Manuel and Rose exchanged several words in the local dialect. This irritated Jim, but he didn't think it wise to demand they speak English. It was obvious that Manuel was giving Rose instructions, since he was doing most of the talking. She simply responded with one or two words or a nod. Finally, she left and Manuel turned to Jim and said, "Now then, we can talk business. Do you want her for all four nights that you're here, or do you wish to change girls each night? Let me add, there is less cost if you keep her for the duration of your stay."

"I'll keep her for all four nights. How much?"

"Twenty dollars a night, that is eighty dollars for the four."

Jim was shocked and it showed on his face. Manuel saw it and responded at once. "I told you she is one of my very best girls, and she costs accordingly."

"Okay, no problem. When do you want paid?"

"You can do it right now. Would you also like some herbs to smoke?"

"Herbs? You mean pot?"

Manuel held out his hand to take the money Jim was counting and said, "Yes."

Jim's response was a curt "No!"

"That's perfectly fine. Now if you have any problems with her of any kind, please let me know. If you wish for any reason to change girls at any time, feel free to do so. There won't be any additional cost."

The two men shook hands. Manuel turned and motioned to Rose, who, at some time during the discussion, had taken a seat on the bench. She picked up a small handbag and approached them. Jim, watching her movements in the very short dress, was filled with great anticipation.

"Let me carry your bag, Rose."

She handed him the bag and took his extended arm.

Outside, Jim looked around for Joe and he spotted him getting out of his taxi parked just across the street. Joe hurriedly crossed the street, took the bag from Jim, and led the couple to his taxi.

Once inside, the couple made small talk. Jim learned that English is taught in the schools along with the local dialect. That explained why everyone he met spoke English, and why many of the signs were in English, also.

At the hotel they got on the elevator just behind an older Filipino couple who appeared to be in their fifties. As the elevator started its rise, the older couple looked Jim and Rose over closely. The man spoke very curtly to Rose in the local dialect. Her response was one or two short words with her head down looking at the floor. Finally, the elevator stopped at Jim's floor. He took Rose's hand and started out the door. The man shouted at them as they left. Rose turned and responded very sharply. As the elevator doors closed between the two antagonists, the man spit on the floor at Rose's feet. Jim took her arm and led her down the hall.

"I take it he doesn't care much for you, or me—and neither of our professions."

"Oh, he likes yours all right. He still thinks General MacArthur is God's second son. It's me he doesn't approve of."

Jim unlocked the door, put the bag on a chair, closed the curtains and embraced Rose. Their kiss was long and passionate. Jim's hand moved to the top of her dress and pulled on the zipper. Rose wiggled and the dress dropped to the floor leaving her in only her very lacey bra and small bikini panties.

She was very pleased with herself for having spotted him when he first entered Howard's. She had smiled and shuffled her cards as he shyly glanced her way, and watched as he blushed and moved on past. She liked these American boys who blushed. They always turned out to be very kind and gentle. The fact that this one was also very nice-looking made it just that much better. It had been a simple thing to make herself scarce until he moved to the bar. Then, to make sure he noticed her again, she had moved by his table shuffling the cards, before Manuel had sat down with him. Once Manuel ordered the girls to the bench for his scrutiny, she'd made sure she got the seat directly in front of him. Thus, the first girl he saw would be her. And she knew that the shuffling of the cards would subconsciously attract his attention. All she had to do then was to give him her most inviting smile. If his choice was close, the cards would tip the balance in her favor, and this would also make his description of her to Manuel that much easier.

Sometime later Jim opened his eyes and watched her dry him

with a towel before lying down beside him. "You know, Rose, you're beautiful and Manuel was right, you're very good."

"Thank you. I like you, Jim, and I'll try to make you very happy while you're here. We'll make love more than you ever made it in your life."

Jim laughed and said, "That wouldn't be hard to do. I'm a virgin, or rather, I was. Wow, is that an embarrassing thing to admit."

"It doesn't matter. In fact, I'll make you a promise: before you leave Manila, I'll be so implanted in your mind that you'll think of me on your wedding night."

"That, Rose, is some promise. Come on, let's take a bath."

Rose moved off the bed and wrapped a large towel around her. Jim had already started the bath and climbed in when Rose entered. She picked up a wash cloth and a bar of soap. Then she got down on her knees.

"Come on, Rose, get in, it really feels good."

"Later, Jim. First, let me bathe you."

She started scrubbing his back and shoulders and watched his muscles roll under his bronzed skin as she rubbed. She sensed that he possessed a great deal more strength than his stature indicated. He lay back in the tub completely relaxed and allowed her to start on his feet. The pleasure he felt at that moment was indescribable. "Rose, this feels wonderful. How did you ever learn to bathe a man?"

"My mother died when I was thirteen and I assumed her duties, one of which was bathing my father."

Jim looked up at her. "You said her duties. Does that include sleeping with him?"

"Of course not. I assumed only her jobs and responsibilities. Of six children, I was the youngest and only daughter."

"What did you do, run away?"

"Oh, no. My father was fairly rich and I had a good life until he was killed in a car crash when I was almost sixteen. Then I came to Manila to live with my oldest brother and his family. Once here, I started dating American boys from the base, which my brother didn't like. We got into a real big fight one day, and he kicked me out. I'd already met Manuel a few months earlier through one of the guys I was dating, and he'd extended me an offer to work for him. So, there I was with no money, job, or place to stay and only in Manila about six months. There wasn't a whole lot I could do. Besides, the money's good and I do enjoy my work."

The excitement that had started to stir in Jim disappeared after hearing Rose's story. He simply lay there totally relaxed and touched by her story, while her soft hands finished scrubbing his body. She rinsed him off and helped him rise from the tub and step out. "Jim, I'll take a quick bath and be right out. Okay?"

"Take your time, Rose."

Jim closed the bathroom door behind him as he heard her step into the bath. He put on a shirt and sat down at the desk to look through the pamphlets provided by the hotel. Suddenly, he began to feel very tired and it occurred to him that it must be pretty late. He had left his watch on the bedside table, so he rose and started in its direction, intending to check the time and go straight to bed. He dropped the shirt to the floor and picked up the watch. He was shocked: it said 2:35 a.m.

Jim awoke, and for a moment was disoriented. He moved just slightly and felt Rose's body beside him. With that touch, he realized where he was, and why. It was pitch dark so Jim figured it couldn't be time to get up yet. He reached for his watch; the luminous dial said 5:05. He lay there trying to go back to sleep but couldn't. About ten minutes later he decided it was useless, got up and went to the bathroom.

Jim really didn't know why he was taking a shower, but it sure felt good. He washed and then just stood there letting the water beat down on his fatigued body. The pounding water massaged and relaxed him until, finally, it took an enormous effort to shut it off. He dried slowly and contemplated shaving but the watch said only 5:45, and he really didn't feel like doing anything but going back to bed.

Awakened by Rose pulling the sheet from his body, he opened his eyes enough to see that it was daylight. Thinking it couldn't be more than 6:00 or 6:30, he glanced at his watch and was surprised at the 10:45 reading. He felt Rose enter the bed and glanced down at her naked body. She bent over and kissed him. Immediately, a shiver went up his spine. He watched with both surprise and pleasure as Rose kissed her way up his leg.

Jim again stepped out of the shower. It was already past 12:30. He had shaved while Rose showered, and it was a good thing. He'd told Joe to be out front at 12:00. Opening the bathroom door he could see Rose seated at the dresser fixing her hair. As he dressed, he found himself thinking what a beauty she was, even the morning after.

"Ready to go get something to eat, Rose?"

"Anytime you are."

Jim rested his hand on her shoulder and directed her through the door. Then he allowed his hand to slide gently down her back to her bottom, where he gave her a little pat. What he was really doing was checking for a bra and panties. The bikinis were there, but no bra. With the pat, Rose turned her head toward him and each gave a knowing smile.

Jim was glad no one else was in the elevator, especially after last night's encounter. It also gave him a chance to look Rose's dress over a little more closely. It was about three inches above her knees and very clingy. It was a red silk-like fabric with a large yellow floral print. It had a mandarin collar and buttoned to her waist. Rose had left the top two buttons undone, and it looked very appealing.

"Well, do you like what you see?"

"I was just admiring your dress. It's very pretty, almost as pretty as what's in it." Rose couldn't help herself as she reached up and gave him a kiss on the cheek. She was beginning to like this American GI. His boyish innocence and charm, the combination of honesty, shyness, and sexual vitality all began to tear at the invisible wall that usually protected her emotions in these situations.

As they reached the sidewalk, Joe pulled up with his taxi. Rose wasn't surprised when Jim held the door for her and allowed her to enter first.

"Where to, Jim?" Joe asked.

"I don't know! Rose, you pick a place. As long as it's a place with good food, I don't care what kind."

"Joe, take us to the Jade Palace, please."

"Okay, Rose. Well, Jim, did you sleep well last night?"

Jim broke into laughter: long, hard, and deep laughter. When he finally got control of himself he looked at Joe through the center rear view mirror and said, "Somehow, I just don't believe that's what you really wanted to ask."

There was a long silence during which Joe decided he had been put nicely in his place. Jim wasn't going to volunteer any information. So, how was he to report to Manuel?

"Jim, it'll take about an hour and a half at the Jade Palace. Is there something you would like to do after lunch?"

"Yeah, Joe, I'd like to shop for some clothes, maybe a suit."

"Okay, no problem. I know just the place. I'll even give you some free advice: when you find what you like, let Rose deal for a price. Here we are, at the Jade Palace. Have a nice lunch!"

Before he could get out, Rose gently pulled on Jim's arm and said, "I'll need $5.00 for the head waiter."

Jim wondered why, but gave her the five spot and got out. He opened the door to the Jade Palace and followed her in. Rose greeted the head waiter politely, trying not to show her familiarity with him or the place, yet it was obvious she'd been here frequently. Jim smiled to himself as the two haggled in the local dialect. Rose opened her hand, showed the five, and ended the argument.

The head waiter led the two through the main dining room which had a Polynesian decor. After winding their way through the tables they entered a hallway. On each side were four doors, all closed. The head waiter opened the third door on the left and Jim followed Rose in.

After seating them, the head waiter gave each a menu, asked if there was anything they desired and left. Jim looked around. It wasn't much more than an enclosed private booth. The only light was from a single candle placed in the center of the table. The walls were painted with a continuous mural which included the door. The painting was of fishermen, boats, islands and birds. It was really quite good. The tablecloth was scarlet with a velvet texture.

"This is quite a place, Rose."

"Do you like it?"

"So far, although I've never been in a private dining room for two before."

"You'll like it. The food and service are excellent and the privacy allows us to do most anything we wish. The walls are all soundproofed so there won't be any distractions from the people on either side of us. You know, these booths are used by some very important people both in and out of government."

"I'm surprised you could get one for only $5.00."

"Oh, you couldn't during their busy hours—it would cost $20 or $25 during lunch or dinner. As late as it is now, though, he more than likely had a couple of them empty."

"How do you call the waiter?"

"You see that handle on the door? You pull it up and it drops a little green flag. Each door has one at a different height so the waiter can see them all at once. What would you like to eat?"

Jim looked at the menu. "You're obviously familiar with this place, what would you recommend?"

"Well, you said you like all kinds of seafood. Why don't you try the filet of flounder stuffed with crab meat? It's sautéed in butter and is delicious. You get rolls, butter and a tossed salad, with the dressing of your choice, plus tea or coffee."

"I'll take the coffee and French dressing on my salad."

Rose laughed and shook her head slightly. "They have an excellent house dressing. Why don't you try it?"

"No, thanks. I really like French. If they don't have that, then I'll try the house special. What are you going to have?"

"Tea, house special on the salad and I believe I'll take the monkfish."

"Monkfish? I've never heard of monkfish."

"It's a type of saltwater fish. I'll give you some and you can see how you like it."

"Would there be a problem, Rose, if you ordered for the both of us?"

"No, I can do that if you like. In fact, it probably would be easiest that way. Are you ready?"

Jim nodded his head yes and Rose flipped the handle up. In about thirty seconds there was a knock and the handle dropped down. Rose spoke and the door opened. The waiter entered, smiled and took their orders. He didn't speak the first word of English. He placed a pitcher of ice water and two glasses on the table and left closing the door behind him.

"Why won't he speak English?"

"The owner won't let anyone speak English during work. I don't know why."

"Do we have to drop our flag again in order to get our food?"

"No, he should be back shortly with the salads, then he'll be back in about ten minutes with our meals. Once he leaves the meals, you'll have to drop the flag to get him back."

The waiter knocked on their door and waited for Rose to speak. He placed their salads, smiled at them and left. In a few minutes the same procedure was repeated for the main course. Along with the meal the waiter brought pots of coffee and tea.

Jim's meal was excellent. He hadn't eaten crabmeat before, but found it very tasty. Rose's monkfish was absolutely delicious, and he decided to remember monkfish when he got back to the States. During the meal the conversation centered around the usual small talk of weather and food. As both finished eating, Rose slid off her shoes and rested her feet on the bench beside Jim. Jim had refilled both cups. "I hope you didn't mind my waking you this morning."

"No, it was past time to get up, and I had told Joe to pick us up about 12:00. Besides, I loved the way you woke me. You can wake me every morning the same way." Jim placed his hand on Rose's leg and started caressing her calves.

"I'm glad you enjoyed it."

She placed her foot between Jim's legs and with her toes began to massage him.

"Rose, you keep that up and we'll have to go back to the hotel instead of shopping."

"Why would you want to wait 'til then?"

The surprised look on Jim's face asked, "Here? You've got to be kidding?"

Rose smiled seductively and put her feet back on the floor. The next thing Jim knew she was under the table. The emotions that swept over him at that moment were shock, surprise, disbelief, and fear. However, they were soon displaced by great excitement and anticipation. He felt her hands working his zipper.

When they left the restaurant, Joe was seated on a bench just outside. In the taxi, Joe spoke first. "Well, how did you like the Jade Palace?"

"Hey, okay, I really liked that place. The food was excellent, the service just right, I'd certainly recommend it—I can't wait to see where she takes me tonight."

"You still want to do a little shopping?"

"Yes, I do." Jim watched the city slip by as Joe drove. He was amazed at the four lane super highway on which they traveled; for some reason, he hadn't expected Manila to be a city of expressways. Joe stopped the taxi on a small side street. Now this was what Jim thought Manila would look like: the shops were so close together they shared sidewalks. It was obviously an older part of the city, for the store fronts showed the effects of time and age.

They walked a short way down the street and entered a men's clothing store that had large plate glass windows with protective iron bars. Once inside, Jim was really surprised at how small it was. Each wall was stacked to the ceiling with bolts of fabric separated into types of cloth and again into colors, plaids, checks, and stripes. Jim was amazed. He had never seen so many different selections in one place before. The center of the room was only about five feet wide and had two tables, each about three feet wide and five feet long. The room couldn't have been more than thirty feet long, with fourteen or fifteen foot ceilings. As Jim looked around a tall, well-built Filipino man of about forty-five approached.

"May I help you, Sir?"

"Yes, you may. I'm interested in having a suit made."

"Well, we can certainly help you in that department. What type of fabric were you interested in?"

"I don't know. I hadn't thought that far."

"Why don't you let me show you some fabrics and we can go from there?"

Jim spent considerable time looking at the fabric. Finally, he decided on a light blue cashmere and asked the shop owner, "How much?"

"Well, Sir, that depends. Do you want a vest? How many pairs of pants? And what type buttons, single or double breasted?"

"Single breasted, vest and one pair of pants."

"Ninety dollars should cover it."

At that point, Rose and the shop owner got into a heated discussion. Jim figured Rose was trying to get him a lower price and that the shop owner wasn't giving much. Finally Rose took Jim by the arm. "Come on, we're leaving. There are other clothing stores."

As they started out the door, the shop owner said, "Okay. I'll go forty-five, but no more."

Rose nodded approvingly, and Jim said, "Deal."

At that point, the owner pulled out a tape and started measuring Jim. As he did so, they discussed fabrics and before Jim left, he'd bought a second suit of a wool blend, with two pair of pants.

When they left, Jim asked Rose if they could just walk and browse for a while. Rose took his arm and they started down the street. By the time Joe found them, Jim had bought an onyx bull for his father, a jade Buddha for his mother, and various charms and trinkets for his sisters. Once back in the taxi, Joe asked, "Where to?" Jim glanced at his watch. "I'm hungry. Rose, pick a restaurant!"

When Jim got out of the taxi he looked at the sign, "The Bay Restaurant." They were seated outside a boardwalk-type area. The brightly lit harbor loomed in front of them. Jim ordered lobster, baked potato, peas and salad. Rose ordered oysters on the half shell with rice and clam chowder. As they ate, Rose explained that this was Manila Bay and Harbor. She gave him the history of the harbor and even told him from where some of the ships had come. Jim was surprised. There was even a rich man's yacht about a half mile out in the harbor, all lit up just like in the movies.

Jim's meal was excellent though Rose had tried unsuccessfully to get him to try an oyster. Every time he looked at one, all he could think of was trying to swallow snot!

The room at the Shoreline Hotel looked mighty good to Rose, who was tired and had done more walking than she cared to think about. After all, they'd walked about four hours and then, after dinner they'd walked around the harbor. Now all she wanted to do was to go to sleep. However, she was out of luck for Jim felt good and wasn't at all sleepy.

Sometime later Rose awoke and realized Jim wasn't in bed. Looking around the room she could see him sitting in a chair gazing out the window. "Something wrong, Jim?"

"No, I just couldn't sleep. You know, Rose, this is quite a view."

She got up, put on one of Jim's shirts and knelt beside him. By moving her hand along Jim's thigh, she could tell that he, too, had on only a shirt. She had learned a long time ago there was one surefire way to make a man tired. This time sleep came quickly and restfully for both.

Rose woke before Jim and decided she would shower and attend to her toiletries before he awoke. The next thing Jim knew he was dreaming, or so he thought. Opening his eyes, he saw Rose once again waking him with her mouth. He felt good, refreshed and he certainly enjoyed waking up this way.

By 12:30 they were in a little oriental restaurant. Jim's plate of sweet and sour pork was very good. He was glad he hadn't taken more than one of Rose's stuffed mushrooms, though. Unlike the small, crisp, firm mushrooms back in the States, these were a soft mushy variety that Jim did not care for.

After eating, they went back to the tailor's where he made some final alterations. Jim was very pleased with both suits and looked forward to picking them up the next day. From there Jim wanted to visit the American cemetery. Joe asked if he had a relative buried there.

"No, Joe. I just want to see it. Okay?"

Neither Joe nor Rose was happy about the trip to the cemetery as their silence showed. Once there, Rose asked if she could wait in the taxi.

"Have you ever been here before?" Jim asked.

"No."

"Well, maybe the walk would do you both good. After all, if not for these men and thousands like them, you would be speaking Japanese now. In fact, you, Joe, would be driving Jap men around, while Rose would still be Rose. Come on, Rose, the walk will do you good."

They walked through the entrance and followed a path into the midst of many crosses. The military precision was perfect; no matter which way they looked the crosses formed a perfectly straight row. Jim was reminded of a poem he was supposed to have memorized in school. It was something about Flanders fields and row on row, the poppies grow. The quiet beauty was magnificent and he could feel a special presence, something he would never be able to describe.

"Come on, Jim. Let's go."

"No, Rose, I need to stay awhile. You know, I can feel their presence. It's strange, I know, but I can feel them. You don't understand, do you?"

She looked him in the eye and shook her head.

"You see, they're my brothers. We're comrades, these men and I bonded together by our country and its love of freedom. It's hard to explain. Most people don't understand what we, these men and I, have in common is mostly boredom. One could describe our jobs as long hours of boredom interrupted by short moments of total terror. At any moment we know that we could join our brothers in a place like this; yet none of us really accepts the fact that we could be killed. It's always the other guy who gets it. Only in very special moments would you find any of us willing to admit that each of us could die." After several minutes of silence Jim looked down at Rose. "Go on back to the taxi, Rose." She gladly left. To her, the place was beautiful but morbid, a place where only old people visited.

Jim walked alone among the rolling hills, the crosses in perfect formation, the trees and bushes placed in equally perfect locations. He came to an oval with a tower at one end. The tower had an altar and was obviously there as a place of worship. The oval was broken into different sections by walls, with the names of the men buried there carved in the stone. It was very impressive, but most impressive of all were the rooms on the end. Using different colors of stone, various battles were mapped out on each wall. Jim spent a lot of time reading and looking at the maps. It was beginning to get dark when he finally returned to the waiting taxi.

"Joe, tomorrow I want to go to Corregidor."

Joe shook his head slowly. "You don't have time, Jim. You have to pick up your suits tomorrow afternoon and Corregidor is an all day trip. You can't pick up the suits the following day because you have to be at the R&R center by seven in the morning."

"You sure we can't get back in time to get the suits tomorrow night?"

"No way, Jim. I'm sorry."

"Okay, let's go get something to eat." Jim was bitterly disappointed and even considered taking a chance on the suits but decided Joe should know best. After all, he lived here.

Once again, Rose took them to a seafood restaurant, where she ordered shrimp and Jim ordered red snapper. After their orders had been taken, Rose started the conversation. "I'm really glad I had the opportunity to spend these last few days with you. It's been very enjoyable and, in this short time, I've grown to like you very much."

"That's nice of you to say, Rose. I've really enjoyed Manila and the days we've spent together. But most of all, I've liked the nights and you."

"Jim, I love you. I don't want you to leave me. Take me back with you, please."

Jim was shocked. He hadn't expected this and didn't know what to say. He liked Rose, but he didn't want to marry her; however, he certainly didn't want to hurt her feelings.

"Rose, I can't do that! I leave day after tomorrow."

"We could go to the U.S. Embassy tomorrow and make application for marriage. Then, when you get back to the States, you could send for me. I'd make you very happy. I'm an excellent cook. I'd make love to you whenever and however you wanted. All the American men I've known say that American women won't make love except when they're in the mood. According to the Americans I know, that isn't very often. I'll do it every night and even during the day if you want. I'll even wake you in the morning just like I've been doing. I could fix your breakfast while you shave. Jim, you'd love it. I'd make you so happy."

"Rose, no one can make someone else happy. Each person

must be able to do that for himself. Besides, I don't love you, and when I marry, I'll love the girl. End of subject, okay?"

"Okay. I'm sorry. I just thought, well, I . . ."

"Rose, forget it. I like you, I really do. You're a nice person, great in bed and you have many other fine qualities. You'll make some lucky man an excellent wife. You're very pretty and before this war is over, you should be able to find an American husband, if that's what you really want. But, not me. Okay?"

Rose felt like a fool and was sure Jim figured all she wanted was a ticket to the States. The fact that he was partially right was the main reason there was very little conversation for the rest of the evening.

Later that evening, they had sex in different positions until Rose told him they had just "pointed the compass." He didn't tell her that he had never heard of pointing the compass. All he wanted to do at that point was go to sleep.

Jim awoke first and was relieved, though he didn't know why. By the time he was finished shaving and showering, Rose was also awake. They ate in the hotel dining room and Jim was surprised that their ham, eggs, coffee and orange juice cost almost as much as their lunch had the day before. After breakfast, they visited Old Fort Santigo, where Jim was impressed by the twelve foot thick walls. From there, they went to pick up Jim's suits. He tried each one on before paying and found both fit perfectly. As he looked at himself in the mirror he glanced at Rose standing behind him. The smile on her face told him he looked good, so he couldn't resist asking, "Well, how do I look?"

"Stunning, absolutely stunning. You'll have all the girls back home chasing you."

It was almost 2:00 when Jim asked the shop owner if he would keep the suits while they got some lunch. Not too far up the street they found a sidewalk cafe. Rose ordered a rice ball and shrimp for the two of them. When it came, the shrimp, rice and indistinguishable vegetable was all rolled into a softball sized wad. Jim's first thought was, "That looks awful." But he decided he should try it. Much to his surprise, it was very good and had a sweetness that he hadn't expected. After lunch, they went back and picked up his suits and from there Joe took them back to the hotel.

Jim had already decided he was going to have Rose one more time and then take her back to Manuel. Once in the room Jim hung up his suits. Rose started packing his bags, since she had packed hers while he had been in the shower that morning.

Rose was bent over at the end of the bed folding clothes when he took hold of the zipper on the back of her dress.

They were in Joe's taxi on the way back to Howard's when Jim decided that this was the best time and place to say good-bye. "Rose, I want to thank you for a wonderful time. I really enjoyed myself, largely because of you. I wish you the very best and honestly hope you'll someday find the husband you need."

"I'd be happy to take you. I love you and I could make you happy. I'm a great cook and I really enjoy it when we make love."

Jim felt like a rat. He liked Rose, he really did. And she was always ready and willing to make love, which greatly pleased him. "Rose, I'm not going to, so please just quit."

At Howard's they ordered dinner. As they were finishing, Manuel approached. "Good evening, I trust you have enjoyed Manila and Rose's company."

"Manila has been very nice, thank you. As for Rose, well, she has been an experience beyond words. She has been truly wonderful . . . a delight to be with and a very nice person."

"I'm pleased you liked her. I'm also curious. Why did you bring her back one night early?"

"Simply because I have to get up at four-thirty tomorrow morning and I would like to get a good night's sleep."

"You're sure that you don't desire her services tonight?"

"I'm sure."

"Very well. Rose, we have a new R&R group in tonight. Time to go back on line."

Rose and Jim's eyes met for the last time. "Good-bye Rose, and thank you."

"Good-bye Jim. I really enjoyed being with you. Remember me."

"Oh, I will. Of that you can be certain. Good-bye."

Manuel held out his hand to Rose. She took it, stood, and walked into a hidden corner of Jim's mind, where she would be remembered by him forever.

Four-thirty came before Jim was ready. In one hour, he was back in the R&R center going through customs. His suits were already packed in a shipping package. That way, once he got back to Vietnam where postage was free, he could send them home. At 0745 the DC-6 left Manila and arrived four hours later in Saigon.

At the airport, he sent his packages home and went to the R&R center. Jim picked up his M16 and, as he started out the gate, a jeep stopped.

"Hey, GI, need a lift?"

Jim looked at the MP* driving and figured, "Why not."

"Sure, if you're going the direction of Hotel Three**."

"Sure, that's my area. Hop in."

Once at Hotel Three, he headed for the dispatcher's office and asked about a possible ride to Tay Ninh. If not, were any of the Blackhawk ships in Saigon air space.

"Sorry, Specialist. No on both accounts."

"How about Cu Chi? Anything headed that way?"

"No."

Jim was beginning to wonder what to do next when a major general walked up. "Specialist, you with the Blackhawks?"

"Yes, Sir. I'm a crew chief. I just got back from R&R this morning and thought maybe I could catch a ride back to Tay Ninh from here."

"Well, Specialist, you're in luck. I'm going to Nui Ba Den***. I'll give you a ride."

"Thank you very much, Sir." Jim picked up his gear and followed the general out the door and said a silent prayer of thanks for once again making things work out so well.

It was 1430 hours when he walked into the hooch. After getting clean bedding, he spent the rest of the day in the club

* MP—Military police.
** Hotel 3—Main heliport in Saigon.
*** Nui Ba Den—Mountain just outside Tay Ninh. On top was a Special Forces camp protecting a long-range radio complex.

drinking beer and writing letters. He wrote one long one to his parents telling them all about the things he had seen. Then he allowed R&R to retreat into his subconscious mind, where it would affect him in many ways for years to come.

5

You Did It, Then You Talked About It—But Only Once

"Do you not know that your body is a temple of the Holy Spirit?" I CORINTHIANS 6:19

NIV

Once at Saigon, no one seemed to know they were coming; so again, the flight had to sit and wait. Finally, the bodies were loaded onto a quarter ton pickup.

The flight back to Tay Ninh took even longer than usual, with artillery fire coming from most every fire base. Finding a route home around it was tough. The cloud cover made it even darker than usual that night, but the flash of the big guns reflecting off the clouds was unmistakable as they flew along.

Jim shut off all his radios and turned his intercom switch to private. This allowed him to hear himself talk without anyone else listening, unless someone else on the ship had also turned his intercom switch to private. Then there would be a hot mike situation between their respective head pieces. Jim was mumbling to himself about nothing, interspersed with a short song every now and then when he heard, "Hey, Mac, is this a private party or can anyone join in?"

"Come on in, Broadnex. You getting lonely, too?"

"Yeah, I guess. It's funny how people get to the point where they simply need to talk to themselves and hear themselves respond."

"Especially after a day like today."

"Yeah, isn't that the truth. I'll tell ya, Mac, I still have that burnt flesh taste in my mouth."

"Me too, I keep wishing I could brush my teeth. I hope I never have to do that again."

"Yeah, look, could we, uh, change the subject?"

"Sure, Broadnex, that suits me just fine. What do you want to talk about?"

There was a long pause before Broadnex said very softly, "Look, Mac, I'm sorry about calling you a sissy for going to that chaplain's service earlier today. I know that's your way of coping mentally, and getting by, and I shouldn't make fun. Besides, there might be something to it."

"There is something to it, Broadnex, and thank you for the apology."

Once the flight was on the ground, Jim pulled the necessary inspections and headed for the showers. Much to his disgust, there wasn't any water, so he put on clean clothes and headed for the enlisted men's club. He got a beer and joined Green, who was already seated at one of the big tables.

"Hi, Mac, I heard about your day."

Jim gave him a surprised look. "How?"

"Broadnex was here. In fact, he just left."

"Well, Green, you can be glad you had to take a physical today. Which reminds me, did you pass?"

"Sure, the only time I had a problem was when this doctor put on a rubber glove and said, 'bend over.' I'll swear, Mac, that man had a twelve-inch finger. You wouldn't believe the hand this dude had on him. He wouldn't have any trouble palming a basketball. I'll bet he got picked for the job just because of the size of his hand. Of course, he just had to make a big production of putting this glove on and then sticking it over his finger. I'm telling you, that finger grew an inch right before my eyes. I almost asked if I could have something to bite down on when he told me to bend over. I don't know what he was feeling for, but I thought for a moment he was going to push it out my belly button."

As Green told his story, several other guys joined them at their table. Soon they all found themselves laughing so hard it hurt.

Two of the guys now joining the group were Hunter and

Athia. Green decided to have some more fun. "Hey, Hunter, I see your favorite monkey is still around."

"That son of a bitch Kenny, I knew he wouldn't get rid of that damn monkey. Green, how did he get out of it?"

"I don't know, other than he was telling Gillett when I got back that he couldn't catch it."

"Well, did he at least clean up my wall locker?"

"Oh, you mean you don't want to keep that little present that came this morning?"

Hunter's glare made everyone at the table laugh that much harder. Another round of beer was ordered and a general round robin started.

"Well, what are we going to do about that monkey?"

"I vote, kill him."

"Look, Hunter, I don't think anyone here would object to that. The question is how? We'd never get away with shooting him. Hey, Barkeep, bring us another round."

"We could put poison in its food."

"Okay, Genius, where you going to get poison?"

"I've got it! We could lace his food with enough pot to kill him."

"How about, if every time one of us walks in the door, we throw a couple of combat boots at him. Maybe he'll get the idea and leave."

"No, it would be our luck the bastard would think it was a game. I can just see it now, we throw a boot at him and he throws a fist full of shit at us."

"Look, Mac, you're Gillett's friend. Why don't you talk to him about it? Maybe you can get him to do something."

"Athia, don't you think I have? I've been trying to get him to make Kenny get rid of it for I don't know how long. However, if you're buying another round I'll have another talk with him."

"You got it. Barkeep, another round please."

While the barkeep was collecting Athia's money, Jeff Stihl came in and joined them. Jeff was probably the best looking crew chief in the company; 5'10, 185 pounds, blond hair and blue eyes with just enough of the man coming through the boy to make him a very striking person.

Dick Hunter turned the conversation in another direction by asking, "Jeff, weren't you in the chopper that was shot down today?"

"Yeah, talk about a day not worth remembering, this is it."

"Didn't you enjoy being a grunt for a day?"

"Not in the least."

"Well, come on, Jeff, tell us all about it! By the way, did you see that anti-aircraft gun?"

"Hey, look, if I'm telling the story, somebody else is buying the beer."

"Barkeep, set 'em up again!"

"To be honest, we were already on the ground when that gun opened up. The fifty was on the other side so I didn't see it, but, man, did I hear it! We were unloading when he first got us. He must have hit us a dozen times. Then, almost at the same moment, the flight lifted and must have diverted his attention from us. I'll tell you, I can still hear that ship's skin rupturing, thump, thump, thump. He had to have hit the engine. I could hear it die, and Mr. Marshall said, 'We lost the engine. Let's get the hell out of here.' I got the door open for Mr. Barr who was flying peter pilot. Just as he stepped out, Chalk Seven got it direct. Man, I was so scared I didn't know what to do first, crawl in a hole or check to see if I had shit in my pants. Of all the days to get stuck flying with a couple of potheads, you'd know this was it. I had Conrad for a gunner and he and Barr were so stoned, Marshall and I had to practically drag them to safety.

"I really had to laugh at Barr, he had left his camera in the ship and was going back after it. Marshall wouldn't let him, since the flight was gone and that fifty was taking target practice on my ship. I expected it to blow any minute, but it never did, and Barr was sitting there arguing with Marshall to let him go get his stupid camera. Anyway, I'm getting ahead of my story. Did any of you guys see Chalk Seven get it?"

Several of the men including Jim said they had. "Talk about an explosion, those guys never knew what hit them. One big boom followed by a fire ball and a bunch of burning pieces all over the place."

"Well, Jeff, what did you do all day?"

"Sat around mostly. When we first got in the woods we helped set up defensive positions with our M60's. The captain in charge of the grunts was positive Charlie was going to come get us. When you guys put in the second lift and didn't draw any ground fire, the captain didn't know if he should shit or play with himself. I don't know how long it was before he sent a scout team out, but it was quite a while. When they didn't make contact, he moved everybody out. There was absolutely nothing to show anyone had been there but us, no shells, nothing.

"I went back and checked out my ship. That poor baby looked like swiss cheese; you guys should have seen that thing. Every window in it was shot out. I counted thirteen holes in the tail boom and was ready to start on the cargo area when some lieutenant came up and told me Conrad and I had to lay the guys from Chalk Seven out. Man, talk about a sick job, that was it."

Jim said, "Hey, I know all about it. Broadnex and I had to put them in bags."

Jeff pointed his finger at Jim as he said, "I'll tell you, Mac, you couldn't have had it as bad as us, other than they had already started to swell when you got them. At least when you bagged them, 'rig' had already started to set in. When Conrad and I tried moving them, they weren't stiff yet, which made it twice as tough. Plus the smell, I don't think I'll ever forget that smell. I got so sick I ended up with the dry heaves. That damn Conrad was so high on pot he was making sick jokes. I'll tell you, I've had it with those potheads. I don't know what I'm going to do, but I'm going to do something."

Gillett had entered and approached the table unnoticed. Laying a hand on Stihl's shoulder he asked, "You're going to do something about what?"

"Gillett, I didn't see you. Grab a chair and sit down! Want a beer? I'll buy."

"Sure, I never turn down an offer like that."

"Barkeep, set 'em up again, please."

"Come on, Stihl, you didn't answer my question!"

"Oh, I was just talking about Conrad and the rest of the potheads in this company. I'm getting awfully tired of flying with these guys, Gillett. Sooner or later, one of them is going to get someone killed besides himself."

"Well, there isn't anything I can do about it unless I see one of them with a joint in his mouth."

"Come on, Gillett, if they're stoned they're stoned and you know it as well as anybody else."

"That's right, but I can't prove anything. Even if I could, the Brass isn't going to do anymore to them than they are to you guys. Look at you, every one of you is drunk on your butts. Not one of you is fit to fly. If we had to scramble in ten minutes you'd all be a health hazard. Yet, you'll get in those choppers and go and do your job. The Brass figures there isn't any difference between you guys who are drunk, and a stoned pothead, just as long as you or they get the job done."

Hunter spoke up. "Look, Gillett, why do we have to fly with them at all? Why can't you put the potheads on one ship and us on another?"

"The biggest reason is, I don't assign the officers. What are you going to do when a stoned pilot walks up to your ship and says, 'Hi, I'm your AC* for the day?"

"Okay, Gillett, I've got a question, and I'm not being funny. I want an honest, serious answer!"

"With a prep like that I can hardly wait. What's your question, Athia?"

"What could they do to us if we all stuck together and refused to fly with any pothead?"

"Other than throw your asses in jail, not much, I suppose."

"Come on, Gillett, if all of us at this table stuck to it, do you really think they would press it, especially since pot is illegal?"

"No, I suppose not. It would be very touchy though, and you guys would have to watch your mouths. Man, I'll tell you, the more I think about this, the less I want to do with it. I'm going to bed. You guys just forget I was in this conversation." Gillett drank the rest of his beer in one gulp and stood to leave. Jim finished his beer at the same time and also stood.

"Come on, Gillett, I'll stagger back to the hooch with you." Jim looked back towards the table, "If you guys decide to

* AC—Aircraft commander.

blackball the potheads, I'm with you all the way. I think if we stick together, we can beat 'em."

The two men walked out together and headed for the urinals, which were two fifty-five gallon drums cut in half with each half buried to an inch of the top, then filled with rock and covered with a fine mesh screen. The whole thing had a roof over it with wood walls on both ends and on the side facing the prevailing winds, leaving the back side open. After all, one would not want to pee into the wind. The two friends stood and relieved themselves as they talked.

"Gillett, I see everybody's favorite monkey is still with us!"

"Yeah, that damn Kenny, I don't know what I'm going to have to do to get rid of that thing."

"Put Kenny in the air one day and give it to the gook house maids."

"That's fine except for two things. One, since this Tet thing broke out, there are no more Vietnamese on post. Two, do you want to fly with him tomorrow?"

"Hell, no!"

"That's right, and nobody else does either. By the way, I wish you would have kept your big mouth shut back in the club. You gave them just enough encouragement, I'll bet they try it. If you hadn't piped up with 'count me in,' it would have died right there, but not now."

"How come they're not letting in the hooch maids?"

"Somebody up there figures they'll give aid to the enemy. So until this offensive dies down, no more hooch maids, KP* workers or detail people."

The two men finished their business and started to walk to their hooch. They both heard it at the same moment. The sharp, shrill whistle of the Soviet-made 122MM** rockets. Their reaction was instantaneous and without hesitation. They dived for the ground and covered their ears as the grumbling and grating sound started, telling them it was going to be close, real close. The explosions shook the ground they lay on severely enough that Jim could feel his body bouncing. He looked

---

* KP—Kitchen police.
** MM—Millimeter.

up in time to see one hit about ten feet from the officer's shower. The concussion and shrapnel were enough to blow the shower walls down. Another rocket hit, almost at the same time, just outside one of the officers' hooches. The screams of pain and calls for a medic left no doubt that one of the pilots had been hit, probably while still in bed. One of the enlisted men's hooches took a direct hit and blew up like the proverbial match box.

Jim was scared, this was the heaviest bombardment in which he had ever been; plus, lying out where he could see everything didn't help any. It seemed like hundreds of those 122MM rockets were dropping on his company area. The sound was deafening. He closed his eyes and tried to get closer to the ground. Suddenly, it stopped. Jim's eyes felt like they were going to burst out of his head and his ears ached from the ringing.

"You okay, Mac?"

"Yeah, other than I've got a terrible headache. I'm just thankful I was leaving the pisser instead of heading for it. You okay?"

"Yeah. I was just thinking, you don't suppose we were lucky enough that Kenny's monkey was in that hooch that got it?"

"That's about as much wishful thinking as hoping it's not going to start again any second. You want to try to make it to the bunker?"

"No, Mac, didn't you notice? Almost all of 'em hit in the hooch area. They probably have a spotter in that church steeple at the end of the runway again. They had one up there earlier today, until a gunship put a rocket in its bell tower. We're probably safest right where we are."

Just as he finished speaking the shrill whistles started again. "Mac, in case we don't make it, I want you to know your name is on the list coming down tomorrow for promotion to E-5."

The company's buildings were once again the main targets. "Gillett, why the devil didn't you tell me that at the pisser? I could have been happy about it then!"

"I thought about it, but figured you might get so excited you'd pee down your leg!"

The two looked at each other and started laughing. Rockets

exploded all around and they lay there laughing so hard at each other, their stomachs hurt.

After twenty minutes, the rockets stopped and almost immediately someone went running through the area shouting, "Gun crews, man your ships."

"Gillett, they'll just about get to those ships, and it'll start again."

"Yeah, but if they can get off the ground, they'll get it stopped."

"They'll have to go to Cambodia to do that and you know it."

"Ten bucks says they go, plus they'll probably make a run on that steeple again on the way out."

"I hope they blow the bastard down. Well, at least we stopped laughing. I'll bet we look like the drunken fools we are."

The gun crews were running across the area headed for their ships when it started again.

Jim and Gillett were still lying in the same spot watching when the whistles started sending shivers up their spines.

"Here they come, Gillett, this'll be the big one!"

"It can't be bigger than that first group."

It was. Rockets started dropping all around, not only in the living area, but also along the flight line. Jim watched one of the gun crew members running to the flight line, run right into the path of a rocket. One moment he was there, the next he wasn't. The noise was deafening as the rockets screamed and grated, followed by an explosion. Jim watched as three guys from maintenance tried to run from the club to a bunker. He couldn't believe they were up and moving. He kept thinking, why didn't they get down. Finally, they made it to the three foot deep drainage ditch in front of the hooches. Jim sighed with relief as he saw each man jump in. Then wincing with pain, he saw a rocket jump in behind them, throwing their body parts back out. Gillett poked Jim in the ribs and pointed with his head to what had just happened. His gesture was his way of asking if Jim had seen it happen. Jim looked him in the eyes and shook his head yes. Jim's ears began to hurt even worse and the ringing in his head was getting louder and more painful, so he pressed his hands even tighter against his ears in an effort to block out the spine shattering noise, and to help keep his head from exploding. He began to think that nothing could live through this pounding when, suddenly, off to the northwest corner of the post, it started to look like the Fourth of July: fire balls, flares and rockets were going off. He knew that it could only be one thing. What a magnificently beautiful display of grandeur, unlike anything he had ever seen. But the fact that he knew only the ammo dump going up could make such a display, caused a certain amount of anxiety to pass over him. After almost thirty minutes, the rockets stopped, just as though someone had shut off a water faucet. One moment rockets were exploding all around, the next, it was perfectly quiet.

"Mac, you okay?"

"Yes, you?"

"Yeah, other than I've got a splitting headache and my ears hurt."

"Gillett, some of those things didn't hit more than ten feet from us. At least that should be the last of it for tonight."

"I hope. Come one, let's go help clean those guys out of the drainage ditch."

"Okay, let me go take a leak first, though."

Gillett headed for the ditch and Jim for the urinal. Once at the urinal, Jim relieved himself again and then walked around behind the club. Staying in the shadows, he made his way to the back door of the hooch. He'd had all the bagging of bodies he could take for one day. Opening his wall locker, he found his box of post cards and thought, "why not." Using a flashlight to see, he addressed a card and wrote "free" where the stamp would go. "Dear family, Not much seems to be happening here, though I understand there's some trouble down at Saigon. I'm fine, enjoying flying, although it does get boring a lot of the time looking at nothing but rice paddies. Gillett and I just got back from having a beer at the club. Nothing new happened today. Spent day flying troops in and out of LZ. Didn't draw any fire. Hope all is well with you, also. Love, Jimmy." He stripped, threw his clothes into the wall locker and was asleep within seconds of pulling the mosquito netting down over his bunk.

Deep within his subconscious, Jim heard an explosion, but it took the second one to bring him fully awake. Now, he was aware they were being hit again, and with that awareness, he simply rolled over and out of his bunk onto the concrete floor. As he hit the floor he heard Gillett call from the floor beside his bunk, "Mac . . ."

"I'm right behind you, Gillett, let's go!"

The two men low crawled out the door, around the corner and into the bunker. Like everyone else, they were dressed only in olive drab boxer shorts.

"Mac, you got your watch on?"

"Yeah, it's quarter 'til five. The bastards could have waited another fifteen minutes 'til it was time to get up."

By this time the shelling had stopped and the bunker slowly started to empty out. "Gillett, did all these guys spend the night in there?"

"Yeah, did you know we got hit again about three o'clock?"

"No! Really?"

"That's what I thought. You went to bed after going to the pisser last night, didn't you?"

"Sure, I was tired, I came in and went to sleep."

"Well the rest of the company worked 'til about two thirty cleaning up Charlie's mess. We lost the three guys in the ditch, plus Lolofft, and I don't know how many officers were killed in the bunker. Evidently a rocket hit right in their doorway; it killed a half dozen or more, and seriously wounded several others. There was also the pilot that got it right to begin with. He was still in bed. We saw that one hit, it got the officers' shower at the same time. We had to clean up the hooch to the south of us that took a direct hit. Anyway, we were just about done when it started again and everybody got in the bunker. They only hit us for two or three minutes, but everybody had decided to spend what was left of the night in the bunker. Everybody but you, that is. I couldn't find you. Finally, I looked in your bunk and sure enough there you were sleeping like a log. I figured I couldn't leave you there all alone in case we got hit again. You might sleep through it forever. I figured, what the hell, I couldn't have better company to go out with, so I stripped down and went to bed."

"Gillett, you're a real friend. Here, mail this for me please, while I go take a shower."

Gillett looked at the postcard and laughed. "Mac, you jerk! Your parents will hear on the six o'clock news that Tay Ninh got the hell kicked out of it last night. Especially since the NVA overran part of Manchu's bunker line."

"No shit, how far in did they get?"

"Clear into their company area. You mean you slept through that also? You couldn't have been in bed. That happened shortly after we split up last night. They even sent officers through all the hooches moving everyone out."

"Well, I didn't see anybody or, at least, nobody saw me. Back to the postcard, Gillett, who are my folks going to believe? Somebody they never met on TV or that postcard? Besides, they won't get it for four or five days."

Gillett just shook his head as Jim headed for the showers. "Mac, wait a minute, there isn't any water."

"I know, I'm going over to the hospital."

"Don't get caught."

Much to his surprise, there was still water but it was very cold. He got in and out as quickly as possible and was glad none of the good doctors saw him.

There wasn't anyone at the mess hall, which allowed Jim to move right into the serving line. As he picked up a malaria tablet a voice behind him spoke, "Those things will give you the shits."

Jim laughed as he turned. "Green, if you've got the squirts you don't have to fly. Besides, after you've taken them as long as I have, they don't bother you."

"I better take two or three in that case. I didn't get any sleep at all in that bunker last night. We were packed in so tight you couldn't lie down or stretch your feet out. Where did you spend the night?"

"In more than one place. Hey, what did you guys decide about the potheads after Gillett and I left?"

"They decided to refuse to fly with 'em. As for me, I'll do whatever you do. By the way, did you hear two of 'em got killed last night?"

"No, who?"

"Holiday and Gomes, I'd just met them yesterday after I got back."

"How did they get it?"

"We had to clean up the hooch that took a direct hit and also the guys in the ditch. But Holiday and Gomes climbed up on the roof of the next hooch down the line. They were sitting up there watching the ammo dump go up. You know that place had fireworks all night. Mac, you should have heard those two. Gillett was trying to get them to come down and they were going on about this being the best Fourth of July fireworks display they'd ever seen. Anyway, they wouldn't come down. We started getting hit with rockets again so everybody else went to the bunkers. I don't know who found them this morning, but they were on the ground dead. The fireworks must have gotten too close."

"Come on, Green, eat! We have to get going."

Just for
the Fun of It

"Your eyes saw my unformed body. All the days ordained for me were written in your book before one of them came to be."

PSALMS 139:16 NIV

Jim picked up the day's C-rations and his gear. On the way out to the chopper he couldn't help but feel good for being alive. He'd gotten a fair amount of sleep last night, so maybe things would go better today. He stowed his gear and had just finished pulling the preflight inspection when Green showed up with his guns, mounted them and helped Jim clean up the ship. They were finishing when Jim spotted Halsey approaching. "Oh happy day, Green, here comes Mr. Halsey, commonly called the Admiral. Let's hope he walks on by to another ship."

"Looks like he's drawn a bead on this one, Mac."

"Well shit, let's look like we're busy. Go fiddle with your M60, I'll climb on top and mess with the rotor head."

Both men went about their busy work in hopes Mr. Halsey would see their activity and not take time to harass them.

Jim's heart sank as it became obvious Halsey would be their co-pilot. Mr. Halsey put his helmet in the peter pilot's seat, and turning back around, his eyes lit upon an object lying on the ground next to the revetments wall. "MacLaughlin, what the hell is that laying there?"

Jim knew without turning around to what he was referring. "What's what, Sir?"

Mr. Halsey reached down and picked it up. Jim halfway expected him to put it to his mouth and blow it up like a balloon. As Halsey held it in front of his face giving it close examination, Jim had a terrible time not laughing as he answered, "I believe it's called a rubber, Sir."

"What do you find so funny, MacLaughlin?"

"Nothing, Sir."

"This is your revetment isn't it, Specialist?"

"Yes, Sir, but I didn't put that there."

"If you didn't, who did?"

"Sir, I can only guess that some officer has brought one of the nurses who sells it out here to my ship and screwed her. When he finished, he ripped that rubber off and gave it a chuck against the revetment."

Halsey's face took on an even greater expression of disgust. "Why didn't you throw it in the trash, MacLaughlin?"

"Because, Sir, I just didn't like the idea of picking up someone else's old used rubber."

"Look, MacLaughlin, this is your revetment, it's your job to keep it picked up. Here, put this thing in the trash!"

"Sir, it's right behind you. Would you please put it in the trash for me?"

Halsey looked Jim in the eye and threw it on the ground. As Jim saw his response he thought, "You bastard, you probably put it there to begin with." In fact, he wouldn't have been surprised if Halsey had picked his ship to use just so he could hassle him with it.

"I'm giving you an order, Specialist. Pick it up and throw it away!"

"Yes, Sir." Jim slowly climbed off the helicopter roof, picked up the rubber and threw it in the trash. "You happy now, Sir?"

"You're a real smart mouth aren't you, Specialist? Green, front and center. I want the both of you at attention." Halsey walked slowly around the two men standing side by side. "You two are a disgrace to the uniform you wear. Neither of you has a hat on. Where's your head gear?"

Jim responded, "In the helicopter, Sir. I was under the impression we were about to put on helmets and fly."

Halsey looked Jim in the eye. "Specialist, did you shave this morning?"

"Yes, Sir."

"You must not have used a blade in the razor. I've half a mind to send you back to shave again." Jim thought he had one thing right, *he only had half a mind.* "Your left breast pocket is unbuttoned, you need to button your blouse, and you have a pants pocket unbuttoned. Where do you think you are, MacLaughlin, back on the block? That's a uniform you're wearing. There is a correct way for it to be worn, but you don't seem to understand that, do you?" Jim made no response as anything he said at this point would be wrong. "How long has it been since you had a haircut? . . . Answer me, Specialist."

"I don't know, Sir."

"MacLaughlin, get a haircut tonight. I don't care if you have to shave it off, it's too long. Get it cut."

"Yes, Sir."

Halsey then turned to Green. "Private, you obviously haven't changed uniforms in the last week."

"Sir, I put it on clean this morning."

"You couldn't have put it on clean unless its been wadded up in a duffel bag for a month, which is about how long it's been since your boots have seen any polish. I'm afraid to stand close to you for fear your boots will rape mine for their Kiwi. Here come the pilots now or so help me, I would send both of you back to the hooches to straighten up your acts. Button your buttons and you're dismissed."

As Jim buttoned up he saw Mr. Walker put his gear in his seat. "Good morning, Mac, how are you this morning?"

Jim saluted and said, "Morning, Sir. I was fine a few minutes ago. Mr. Halsey, could I ask you a question?"

"Sure, what is it?"

"Are you flying peter pilot on my ship today?"

"Yes, I am." Halsey had a great big smile that told Jim he was looking forward to the day. Jim didn't say a thing. He just picked up his helmet, rifle and water jug and started to walk away. He could hear Halsey shouting at him as he continued to walk down the flight line. "Specialist, where do you think you're going?" Jim just acted like he didn't hear him. "Specialist, come back here. That's an order!" Jim made no response, he didn't even turn his head. "Specialist, I'm giving you a direct order! You come back here or, damn you, I'll court martial you!" Jim just kept on walking down the flight line.

The thing to do now was find Gillett. He walked over to Athia's ship and asked if he had seen Gillett. "Yeah, Mac, I just saw him over at Captain Wolf's ship." Jim turned and headed for the captain's helicopter. As he approached he could see Gillett and Captain Wolf talking. Gillett turned to him with a look of surprise.

"Mac, what are you doing here?"

Jim saluted Captain Wolf as he spoke. "Captain Wolf, Gillett, I've got a problem. Mr. Halsey is flying peter pilot on my ship and the first thing he did was start on me. So I walked off because I'm not flying with him. You can put me back in maintenance. I don't care. I'm not getting in the same helicopter that Mr. Halsey is in."

Gillett turned to Captain Wolf. "Sir, could we switch crew chiefs with you for the day?"

"Sure, although I've got a better idea, let's switch co-pilots. It'll give me a chance to find out what Mr. Halsey's problem is." Captain Wolf walked around to the left side of the chopper where Mr. Gabrys was lacing his boot. "Hey, Dave, I want you to go with Mac and fly right seat on 925 today. Tell Mr. Halsey he's flying with me today. Okay?"

"Yes, Sir." Dave Gabrys picked up his helmet and without showing any signs of displeasure for being switched, looked at Jim. "Where you parked, Mac?"

"I'm on my way if you want to walk with me."

The two men turned and started back down the line. Once out of Captain Wolf's hearing Jim started the conversation, "I'm sorry about causing you any inconvenience, Sir."

"Oh, that's okay. For a West Point man Captain Wolf isn't bad. There's just something about flying with the boss that makes a person uneasy."

"It's been my experience, Sir, that the guys from West Point are usually pretty nice and easier to get along with than a lot of the 'ninety day wonders' walking around."

"I guess if a person puts up with four years of harassment at the Point they have a better understanding of what the troops go through. What's your problem with Mr. Halsey, Mac?"

"We have what's called a personality conflict. It's not just me, Halsey has problems with all the enlisted men. The only difference is, since I refuse to fly with him, he feels it's his duty to break me."

"Why won't you fly with him?"

"Because my life and the lives of everybody in that ship depend on our ability to get along with and respect each other's opinion. Halsey and I don't respect each other and that's a prime ingredient for making four dead men." They walked the rest of the way in silence. Once at 925 Mr. Gabrys spoke to Mr. Halsey, who gave Jim a hate look and started collecting his gear. Jim wondered what Mr. Gabrys had told him. It was obvious he wasn't supposed to hear, or Mr. Gabrys wouldn't have taken Halsey aside and spoken softly into his ear. Mr. Walker and Green both welcomed Jim back and inquired as to how he had managed to get Mr. Halsey switched.

After Mr. Walker walked over to where Gabrys and Halsey were standing, Green looked at Jim and shook his head. "Mac, back in the infantry they didn't put up with guys like Halsey."

"Other than shooting him in the back, what would they do?"

"Oh, you could frag him, or almost as good, a fake fragging."

"What's a fake fragging?"

"That's where you fix a fragmentation grenade so it's a dud, then throw it at him."

"Throw what at whom?"

Both men turned in surprise to see Mr. Walker standing there, but it was Jim who responded without hesitation and thus convincingly. "Throw an open can of cold beans and wienies in Halsey's face."

Walker laughed and said, "That's a good way to get busted for sure." As Mr. Walker climbed in his seat he shouted back, "Untie it, Mac. Lead's starting to crank."

The familiar whine of turbine engines starting to turn reached Jim's ears at the same time he released the rotor blade from its tie down strap.

The day started off much the same as many others with the flight flying resupply to various outposts. As with the previous day, there wasn't any fuel anywhere except in Saigon, so it wasn't long before the flight headed south for Saigon and fuel. Artillery strikes were such that it was necessary to go around to the west and come up the Saigon River. As they approached Saigon, flying at about twenty five hundred feet, Green came over the intercom, "Why do I suddenly smell something rotten?"

It was Mr. Walker's laughing voice that answered, "Why, Green, that's the Paris of the Orient you smell, usually called Saigon. We just flew into its upper air currents."

"Sir, why does it stink so bad?"

"Because, Green, they're burning their shit. That's how all the military posts get rid of their shit from the day before. You obviously haven't been on many details yet. When you take a crap in the latrine it falls into half a fifty-five gallon drum. The next morning some private drags it out, pours a couple gallons of fuel on it and lights it. With several hundred of them burning at once around Saigon it makes a pretty bad smell up here. In fact, on a clear day when there isn't any wind you can see the smoke rising up from Saigon at fifteen hundred feet over Cu Chi. It's strange though how it does just suddenly hit you."

The flight had started its descent as they crossed the Saigon River. Mr. Walker spotted an island floating down stream that gave him a thought. "Hey, Green, what do you suppose that island floating down the river is made of?"

"I suppose moss and sticks and various debris that float in any river."

"Wrong, it's shit. What happens is the good people of Saigon crap in the streets and alleys. Next time you're in Saigon notice the gutters in all the streets. Those people do their thing in the gutter, or else in a pan and then throw it in the gutter, then a rain comes along and washes it all away. Just like magic they have nice clean streets again. The only trouble is it all gets washed out to the Saigon River, where it collects along the banks until a bunch breaks off and floats out to that big septic tank called the South China Sea. The best part is, Mac and I have been flying along the river before Tet broke and could see people water skiing around that stuff. I checked it out after the first time I saw it. Come to find out, there used to be a French resort on the river here in Saigon which the Americans have turned into an officers club where all the male and female officers in Saigon can go to socialize and, as it turns out, to water ski and swim."

"Sir, do they know what they're swimming in?"

"I would certainly think so."

It only took a short time to refuel and the flight was back in the air, flying more resupply. As with most of these missions the boredom of landing, taking off with supplies, flying for a half hour, dropping off the supplies and then back again began to wear on most everyone. Jim looked at Mr. Walker who was driving, from there his eyes shifted to Mr. Gabrys. He was sitting there smoking a cigarette with his right arm stuck out his window.

"Hey, Green, what are you doing?"

"Oh, just thinking, Mac. Why?"

"What are you thinking about?"

"To be honest, last night. Tell me something, will you? How long does it take till you quit thinking about getting killed? I mean, I lived through last night, but will I live through today and tonight, and if I do will I live through tomorrow, or is tomorrow the day I get it?"

Mr. Walker spoke first. "All I can say is get used to it, Green, because it's part of life over here." Mr. Walker looked back at Jim who shook his head slowly.

"I don't agree. It is true there are times when we're all sure we're going to die. There are times when we look back and think that by all rights we should have been killed. It's also true we have to deal with death most everyday, though not our own, others will have to deal with that. Green, I look at it this way, there is a book in heaven with my name in it and along side my name are many items including the time and date of my birth, also the exact time and date of my death. That is set by God. When my time is up, my time is up and there is nothing I can do short of suicide to change it. To spend time and energy worrying about it is a waste, since there isn't any difference where we're at when out time is up, it's up. Back in the States or here, we're still going to die and there isn't anything we can do to prolong it. It's up, it's up, you're dead, your family weeps, but life goes on."

The long period of silence that followed left each man to his own thoughts. Jim's were broken by something moving across the floor. He turned in time to see Mr. Gabrys' cigarette flutter across the floor and out the cargo door. Jim looked up to see Mr. Walker who looked at him and winked. Walker's hand reached down and switched his radio to private. Jim knew instantly that was his cue to do likewise. Reaching up, he switched his intercom over to private. "I'm on, Sir."

"Mac, let's give Mr. Gabrys a hard time about that cigarette."

"Okay."

Both men switched back their radios and Mr. Walker started. "Hey! I smell something burning!"

Jim picked it right up. "Yeah, me too! I just thought it was my imagination, we're on fire!"

"No, none of my instruments show it. It's getting stronger though."

"Mr. Gabrys, I think it's coming from you. Are you on fire?"

Mr. Gabrys spoke up. "I sure the hell hope not."

Mr. Walker decided to turn the screw a little tighter. "Dave, what happened to that cigarette you were smoking?"

"It was right here in the ashtray a moment ago."

Jim said, "Mr. Gabrys, your seat must be on fire, I can see smoke coming from it. I'll bet that cigarette is down there."

Mr. Gabrys hurriedly unbuckled his seat belt and frantically tried to climb out of his seat. He looked at Jim and Mr. Walker who were both about to burst with laughter. Mr. Walker was laughing so hard he could hardly drive. It was a good thing Jim was strapped in, or he would have laughed himself right out the door. Mr. Gabrys still wasn't sure if his seat was on fire or not, but seeing no smoke or flames, he decided to sit back down.

"Well, I hope you two had a real good laugh at my expense. Just out of curiosity, where did the cigarette go?"

Mr. Walker had gotten control of himself enough to say, "On the floor and out Mac's cargo door. You should have seen yourself, Dave. There you were at two thousand feet flying along with your ass stuck up in the window. It's a good thing you didn't fart just then, or you would've scared yourself right over the radio console and out the cargo door."

Gabrys said, "Well, at least we're not talking about getting killed anymore."

7

Another Single Ship Night Mission

*"A thousand shall fall at thy side, and
ten thousand at thy right hand, but
it shall not come near thee."* PSALMS 91:7
KJV

Lunch was to be in a remote staging area just outside Saigon.
All the pilots were to report to Lead ship, so each took a box of
C-rations with him. Jim was glad he wasn't the crew chief on
Lead's ship. He didn't like the idea of playing garbage man for
all the pilots. Jim looked for Green but he wasn't to be found,
so he picked up a C-ration box that read "ham and eggs" and
headed for Hunter's ship.

Jerry Green had known for the last hour what he was going
to do if time and chance permitted. On the next to the last lift
he had talked a grunt into giving him a fragmentation grenade.
Once on the ground for lunch, Green grabbed the frag and took
off. He needed a place far enough from the flight that they
wouldn't notice the bang from the percussion cap. It didn't take
long to find a secluded spot where the engineers had piled up
some dirt. Jerry climbed half way down a slope and sat down.
He pulled out the grenade and, leaving the pin in place, very
carefully unscrewed the top, thus separating the percussion cap
from the explosive body of the grenade. He then sat the body
down beside him and holding the percussion half so that the
spring wouldn't pop, he pulled the pin. Jerry placed the pin
beside the grenade and, watching for the spring, he gave the top
a flip about twenty feet in front of him. The ensuing *pop* at-
tracted no attention and in a moment, Jerry had collected the

111

top and the spring. He replaced the spring, folded the handle back over it and reinserted the pin. That done, he then screwed the body back into the exploded percussion cap and wiped off the powder burns. Jerry held it out in front of him and gave it a good inspection. He was pleased but a bit nervous. He hoped no one had seen what he had just done and that the grenade would pass visual inspection. Placing it in his pocket, he calmly walked back to the flight and his ship. Nobody was in his helicopter so he picked up the last carton of C-rations. Beans and wienies was the label on the box, and the idea of the cold, grease coated beans didn't really excite him, so he ate everything except the beans and wienies, cleaned up his mess and stretched out on the chopper floor for a nap.

Sleep came quickly and easily for him. The next thing he heard was Jim's voice. He came to as Jim shook his foot and said, "Wake up, Green, time to earn your pay."

Green slowly lifted his head and said, "I'm awake, Mac, we leaving?"

"Yeah, the pilots are on their way back to the ships. Hey, Green, where did you disappear to after we landed?"

"Oh, man, you wouldn't believe how bad I had to pee. I began to think my back teeth were going to float out."

Jim laughed so hard he had to hold his stomach. After all, he'd had the feeling in the past himself.

Mr. Walker approached and said, "Untie it."

Once in the helicopter and ready to take off, Mr. Walker spoke up, "Well, we've got a new mission. The Brass thinks Charlie is retreating from the Saigon area back towards Cambodia, so we're to put in a blocking force in the Hobo Woods and the Michelin rubber plantations just south of Saigon."

Jim had been listening to Saigon radio and had just heard the news broadcast before they had landed.

"Mr. Walker, from what I've heard on the radio, the Cholon District* of Saigon must still be getting hit pretty good."

"Yeah, I know, Mac, there's still house to house fighting in parts of Saigon. However, the people who should know think it

* Cholon District—Chinese area of Saigon.

will be only rear guard personnel left by tomorrow with most of the NVA trying to slip back over the border."

The first two lifts were taken into the Hobo Woods. On the first insertion, they had received some small arms fire, but nothing that anyone considered out of the ordinary. Their last three lifts for the day were to go into the Michelin rubber plantation. They were completed without incident and the flight was released for the day. They flew north along Highway One up to Go Dau Ha where they would pick up Highway 22 to Tay Ninh. Jim started to think out loud. "Mr. Walker, considering where we put troops in this afternoon, would it be correct to assume that tomorrow we're going to be working in the Iron Triangle area?"

"They were talking about tomorrow during lunch today, and there are three possibilities; all are for putting in blocking forces outside Saigon. Someplace in the Iron Triangle is one, the sugarcane fields around Dong Hoa, or someplace in the Plain of Reeds between the Song Vam Co Dong River and the Parrot's Beak."

"Sir, the Parrot's Beak is in Cambodia. Were they talking about crossing the border?"

"No, unfortunately, there isn't much chance of that happening. The sad thing is we could end this war if we could cross."

It was well after dark when the flight landed for the night. Jim pulled his post flight and headed for the club. Green pulled his guns off the ship and took them in with the rest of the platoon gunners and started to clean them. He had just finished when Mr. Euclid walked up.

Mr. Euclid was a tall, lean, black man who looked like the former high school basketball, football and track star he had been. He was also one of the better liked peter pilots, because of his easy going attitude. Several of the crew chiefs who didn't have permanent pilots were hopeful that Mr. Euclid would be assigned to their ship once he made pilot.

"You Green?"

"Yes, Sir."

"I've been looking for you. Your ship's got a night mission to fly. Come on, I'll help you carry your guns back out."

"Okay, Sir, they're both ready to go, you going with us?"

"Yeah, I've got the privilege of riding right seat. Gillett is looking for Mac and I don't know who's flying AC or left seat. It won't be Mr. Walker, though. He left for the other side of the post to see somebody he knew."

Each man picked up an M60 and walked towards the waiting helicopter.

Meanwhile Gillett had found Jim in the club along with several of the other crew chiefs. Gillett had just come from Operations and figured this would be as good a time as any to pass the bad news. "Good evening, men."

Hunter turned and said, "I hope this is a social visit, Gillett."

"Yes and no, do you want the good or the bad first?"

"The good."

"Okay, I'll have a beer. Now for the bad."

"Wait a minute, where's the good news?"

"My drinking a beer with you guys is it."

"Oh, great, I just can't wait for the bad news."

"In that case, I'll get on with it. First, Mac, you have a night mission to fly. Before you go, though, I have to tell everybody: as you all remember last week, we had to take all the cargo doors off the helicopters. Well, this week the Colonel has decided that you should put them all back on."

The vulgarity that followed wasn't totally unexpected by Gillett. Athia spoke up. "Hey, Gillett, you can't be serious."

"Unfortunately, I am. The old man wants all the doors put back on."

"Well, you can give him a message for us. Tell him to go screw himself, he's doing more to destroy morale than Charlie has done since I've been here. What the hell does he do, lay awake nights thinking up things for us to do?"

"Okay, okay knock it off. It's not going to do any good to get all upset about it, just do it. End of discussion, okay? Mac, I don't know anything about your mission except Operations wanted a ship, so you had better get going."

Jim got up and headed out the door. As he walked across the company area Hunter joined him. "Hey, Mac, you going to put your cargo doors back on?"

"Hel-l-l-l, no!"

"How you going to get out of it?"

"I'm going to go to supply and order the neoprime rollers that hold the doors on. Since supply hasn't had any call for those in the past, they're not going to have them in stock. And, since they're not critical to the ship's safety or flying ability, they're not going to be put on rush order, so it should be three to four weeks before they come in. Once they're in I'll go back to supply and order the door tracks. If I'm asked, I can just say, 'Gee whiz, I didn't realize I needed both 'til I got the rollers and saw how worn the track was.' It should take another three to four weeks to get the track into supply. Since it's going to take sheet metal work to put on the track, they'll wait 'til my ship comes in for a PE* to put it on. Since I've been having a PE about every six to seven days lately, it could end up being seven to ten weeks before my ship's got its doors back on. In that time span a lot could happen. I mean, I could have two or three helicopters by then. Or the old man could forget all about cargo doors and be hot on something else for us to do. For that matter, he could decide to take 'em all back off again in two months time. Just one thing, Hunter. If you do that, make sure you've got it written up in your log book that you have the parts on order. You could write something like, 'Cargo doors removed due to excessive wear of gromlets, parts on order.' Make sure you put the order number in there also. Okay?"

"Sounds good to me. Have a good time out there tonight, Mac."

"Right, see you later, Hunter."

The two men entered the hooch and went to their respective areas. Jim picked up his helmet and M16, then headed for the flight line. Hunter sat down on his foot locker and started to write a letter.

With pad and pen in hand, he paused to think before starting and happened to look up. There, watching him very intently, was the monkey. "You son of a bitch, I'd like to cut your sorry ass throat." It was almost as though the monkey understood his every word. Instantly, he spread his lips, showed his teeth and gave off a loud screech. He took his fist and started pound-

---

* PE—Periodic inspection of ship which is done every one hundred hours. Takes five men about eight hours to do if they find no major problems.

ing against the rafters while shaking his head in every imaginable direction. Chattering wildly, the monkey's whole body went through contortions and gyrations. Hunter decided it would be easier and safer to write his letter in the club. Collecting his writing paper, he put the pen in his pocket and started down the aisle of the hooch. As he went by Kenny's bunk, he very smoothly, and in the blink of an eye, reached down and picked up one of Kenny's combat boots and in the same motion, he raised and threw the boot in the monkey's direction. He missed, but the mere gesture was enough to cause the monkey to go wild. Hunter ran out the door, letting it slam shut behind him.

When Jim got to his ship, there sitting in the cargo area was Green and Mr. Euclid carrying on a conversation like old buddies. "Good evening, Sir."

"Hi, Mac."

"Where's Mr. Walker?"

"On the other side of the post, visiting some old friends."

"In that case, who's driving?"

"I don't know yet. Captain Wolf was trying to find someone who wasn't too close on their hour limit."

Jim turned on the inside lights and started to write in his log book when Mr. Hill walked up and said, "Ya all ready to go?"

Mr. Hill was one of your basic good ole southern boys from Georgia who had lost most of his accent, but not the drawl. He was well liked by both the enlisted men and the officers. His general attitude was "You don't cause me trouble, and I'll not cause you any," and he'd built a good rapport and working relationship with the enlisted men. His five foot eleven height was built around a small-boned, petite frame that gave the first impression of belonging to a feminine-type person.

Jim looked up and closed the green, plastic-covered log book as he spoke. "Mr. Hill, you driving tonight?"

"Yep."

"Aren't you supposed to rotate home tomorrow morning?"

"Yeah, well I just couldn't stand the idea of leaving without one more time in the sky."

"Mr. Hill, that's the dumbest thing I ever heard."

"Well, there isn't much I can do about it."

"You could refuse, you don't have to fly. My God, man, you're supposed to go home tomorrow; not get killed on some stupid ass single ship night mission."

"Look, Mac, I can't refuse and you know it. Captain Wolf came up and said he needed me to fly one last mission. One simply doesn't tell Captain Wolf, no; although I did kind of try by telling him I didn't have any flight gear—no helmet or gloves, nothing. He just told me to borrow some. So, I've got my roommate's."

"Mr. Hill, if you don't get killed tonight it'll be a miracle, you know that, don't you?"

"Look, I don't have any more choice than you do, so stop telling me I'm going to get it! Okay?"

The expression on Jim's face told all of them he truly thought Mr. Hill's flying was stupid. He had one more thought. "Sir, tell you what I'll do. Give me your left hand and I'll break your index finger for you. Just tell Wolf you fell down in the dark on the way out here and did it. That way, you'll still go home tomorrow without having to fly tonight."

"Mac, just shut up and untie this thing! Will you?"

"You're really going to fly it?"

"Yep. Look, Wolf said it's a simple resupply mission. All we have to do is go to Dau Tieng, pick up a load of beehives* and take them up to Loc Ninh, that's it. We should be back in a couple hours." A look of surprise came over Jim's face. Goose pimples rose on his arms and a shiver went up his spine.

Almost shouting he said, "Beehives! Mr. Hill, there's only one reason Loc Ninh needs a night resupply of beehives and that's because they're catching hell. Captain Wolf doesn't care about you. All you are to him is a warm body in the pilot's seat."

"Mac, that's enough! Captain Wolf is just like the rest of us. He has a job to do and he did it. Now go untie the rotor blades and let's go!"

Jim shook his head in a slow no motion as though to say one

---

* Beehives—Small needle like darts tightly packed in an artillery canister. Fired from an artillery piece as an antipersonnel weapon at close range. Approximately 20,000 needles per shell.

last time "This is dumb," and stood up to go untie the rotors. The two pilots climbed into their seats and Green strapped on his chicken plate.

Dau Tieng was only a few minutes flight time away. The area between Tay Ninh and Dau Tieng was densely wooded forest with heavy underbrush. It looked during the day like a big, puffy, green canopy. At night, it was just one huge black expanse. Jim had often thought in the past it would be a most unpleasant place to go down, especially since the highway between Tay Ninh and Dau Tieng had become known as Ambush Alley. Like many of the military posts in Vietnam, Dau Tieng was named after the village next to it. The military complex was located directly on top of the mountain, with only a few two seat observation choppers stationed at Dau Tieng. Its main purpose was as a forward staging area for the 25th Infantry Division.

One of the interesting things about Dau Tieng for Jim was a little house that looked like it was only big enough for one room. It had white, freshly painted walls and a bright red tile roof with a big white swastika painted on the red tile. Each time Jim saw that house, he wondered why a Nazi swastika would be painted on it. It was almost a month after he had started flying that he found out that it was also a Buddhist insignia.

Mr. Hill dialed 36.8 for Dau Tieng control. "Dau Tieng control, this is Blackhawk Niner Two-Five, we're inbound to your location. ETA, zero five minutes. Over."

"Roger, Blackhawk Niner Two-Five, you're clear to land. Winds are calm and there is no artillery fire at this time, over."

"Roger, Control, we're supposed to pick up a load of beehives, could you advise us as to their location, over."

"Roger Niner Two-Five, try the truck parked on the east side of the runway, over."

"Roger Control, Niner Two-Five, out."

Mr. Hill keyed his mike. "Well, Mac, if that truck really has our beehives on it, this part of the trip will have been easy enough."

"Yes, Sir, but then this isn't Loc Ninh and we both know Charlie is in love with Loc Ninh. To change the subject, I was just thinking things are looking up, I mean we could be going to Saigon for fuel if the Air Force hadn't brought up those fuel wheels today."

"Wonderful outfit, the Air Force. Did you hear, Mac, that the first day of Tet, Charlie had a gun set up at the end of Tan Son Nhut's main runway, so the Air Force had their F-4's taking off and dropping their payloads almost as soon as they were off the ground."

"No, I hadn't heard, but for that matter, I haven't heard much of anything in the way of news. Man, that would have been something to see."

The deuce and a half waiting at the end of the runway was loaded with beehives, and three GI's, who hurriedly loaded Jim's ship. Once loaded, the artillery sergeant supervising gave Jim a thumbs up sign, and Jim waved good-bye as he said into his mike, "Mr. Hill, I just got a thumbs-up, let's go see what's happening at Loc Ninh."

"Roger, Mac, have they got those boxes balanced and secure?"

"Yes, Sir."

"Okay, Dau Tieng control, this is Blackhawk Niner Two-Five at the northeast end of the runway, requesting clearance for takeoff and artillery, over."

"Roger Niner Two-Five, you're clear to take off and we now have artillery firing from the east end of post at a maximum altitude of two thousand feet going into Tango November. Out."

Mr. Hill said, "That's Tay Ninh. I wonder which bunker line is under attack tonight? Well, we can always look on the bright side. We could be back at Tay Ninh sitting in those damn bunkers, huh, Mac?"

"Mr. Hill, that's why I fly all these night missions. It's better than getting my ass blown off in a ditch. Besides, I get the message, Sir, and I'll tell you what, nothing would make me happier than to say at the end of this flight, 'I was wrong and you didn't get it.' I really, honestly, hope I get to say that."

"Believe me, I hope you can, too. Okay, we've got clearance to leave. We can fly east around those guns and then head north. Mr. Euclid, I'll drive, you keep us clear of artillery."

Niner Two-Five was airborne and headed north before anyone spoke again. Mr. Hill, like all the short timers, couldn't help rubbing it in. "Well, you guys, in about forty-eight hours I'll be on that big freedom bird heading home. You poor saps still have all that time left. Mac, how long you got yet?"

"Oh, about three months, too long to start a 'short timers' calendar. It's Green and Mr. Euclid that you should work on, neither one's been in country three months yet."

"Nine months, man, if I had nine months left over here I'd walk in to the club tonight and get so drunk I wouldn't wake up the whole time.

"I'll tell you what I'll do, just for you guys, in memory of this flight tonight. It takes about twenty minutes to get home from the airport, so just for you guys, I'll let my wife suck me off all the way home and, I promise, I'll not once think of any of you. Man, just think, in about seventy hours I'll be fucking my wife in my own bed. Oh, wow, I can feel her legs up over my back now."

Mr. Euclid broke in. "I hate to interrupt when you're just getting started, but I've checked Quan Loi artillery. They must have every gun in reach of Loc Ninh firing on it, they also have a Puff* operating in the area. I've got him on UHF and he'll give us a lead in. However, the only way I see we can get in and out is to come up along the Fish Hook** and swing in almost directly from the west. Loc Ninh sits at about two hundred feet altitude, so we'll have to maintain at least three thousand feet. The artillery is all going in on the south and east side of the air strip. With the Special Forces camp on the west side of the air strip, we shouldn't get within two hundred meters of any artillery. Now, did you get all that, Mr. Hill?"

"Yeah, three thousand feet, come in from the west and if I cross the airstrip we get blown to hell by our own artillery."

Mr. Hill moved the control stick so the aircraft would head toward the west and the Fish Hook. Unseen from the ground, it

* Puff—Air Force C-47 aircraft with three mini guns on one side, each firing 6,000 rounds per minute. On each pass the C-47 fired 18,000 rounds per minute with every fifth round a tracer.

** Fish Hook—Nickname for an eastern section of the Cambodian border.

glided like a giant bumble bee, carrying its cargo of death northwestward into the night sky and the destiny that awaited its four masses of pollen, called humans.

Jim's voice broke the silence. "You know, this will be the first milk run I've ever been on where we had Puff give us an escort in. Besides, anybody got a coat I can use? Three thousand feet is going to be very cold."

"That's a fact, that's why I'm not taking her up there 'til I have to."

Green spoke next. "I hate to be showing my ignorance, but what's Puff?"

Mr. Hill answered, "Green, it's an Air Force C-47 with three mini guns stuck out one side, each firing six thousand rounds per minute. There's no real way to describe what it looks like, other than it does look like a dragon spitting fire. It's quite a sight! Three thousand feet, here we are, Mr. Euclid, what's that thermometer read?"

"Five degrees centigrade, which would be about forty to forty-two in normal temperature."

Mr. Hill turned the ship sharply eastward and made a straight line for Loc Ninh. Jim sat there shivering, he was freezing. Between the temperature and the wind, it seemed like time was clicking by all too slowly. He was on his way and would just as soon get there, get it over with and get out. If Puff was there, plus all that artillery, he knew it wasn't going to be a pleasant visit. As they approached, they could see the flares light the night above and around Loc Ninh. Jim listened as Mr. Hill talked to the driver of Puff and to the radio operator on the ground in Loc Ninh.

"Loc Ninh control, this is Blackhawk Niner Two-Five, we're about ten minutes out. What is your status at this time? Over."

"Niner Two-Five, this is Loc Ninh. We've had a few uninvited guests try to drop in, nothing we can't handle with the help of your cargo. We will get a C-130* drop first light. See you in zero nine minutes, winds are steady at five knots out of the south. Your approach should be from the west straight in

---

* C-130—Air Force cargo plane.

and down, land with your nose on the flashlight and turn off all lights. Over."

"We're on our way, Niner Two-Five. Out. Mr. Euclid, where's Puff?"

"I don't know. I just talked to him and he'll give us an escort in. He said he has us on visual and promised not to shoot us down. Also, he had me dial up an air traffic controller in a Bird Dog*. I'm on hold now."

"Well, at least we've got a friendly Puff."

"Blackhawk Niner Two-Five, this is Bird Dog One over Loc Ninh. I monitored your call to Loc Ninh and there are some things you need to know that they didn't tell you. To start with, the place is under extremely heavy attack; Loc Ninh Village and the ARVN** Camp have already fallen, and the American Special Forces camp has had its perimeter breeched once already. I have two F-4's, one light Huey fire team and Puff up here, plus artillery. To make a long story short, I think I can get you in! I'm not sure, and I won't promise, but I think I can put down enough fire power to get you down there. I will, however, almost guarantee you, if you get in, you'll not fly out! Charlie has several mortars firing on 'em, and there is a dual quad fifty set up and well sand-bagged in what used to be the Frenchman's swimming pool right beside the main house. I have two F-4's dropping napalm and five hundred pounders on it, do you understand what I'm trying to say to you? Over."

"Roger, I understand. Wait one." Mr. Hill then spoke to the crew of his ship. "Well, crew, I assume you all heard, so what do you think?"

Several seconds passed before anyone spoke. Finally Jim said, "Sir, we came here for a reason, if we don't take 'em their beehives will they be able to hold? I guess I vote to do what we came up here for. Let's take 'em their beehives and, what the hell, if we can't fly out, I always wanted to be a Green Beret— but I'm not the one going home tomorrow!"

Green and Mr. Euclid quickly agreed, leaving the decision to Mr. Hill who said, "Well, what the hell, it might be fun."

* Bird Dog—Fixed wing, single engine aircraft used for observation.
** A.R.V.N.—Army of the Republic of Viet Nam.

Mr. Euclid said, "What about your wife?"

"Hey, she's done without this long, she can wait a couple more days if we don't make it out."

Keying his switch to broadcast outside the ship, Mr. Hill said, "Bird Dog One, if you can get us in we'll take out chances on getting out. Over."

"Roger, Blackhawk, follow same approach as given by Loc Ninh control. I have you on visual at about thirty five hundred feet and circling just west of Loc Ninh. Is that correct? Over."

"That's affirm. Over."

"Roger, most aircraft are in position, shut off your navigation lights at this time. Thank you. Begin descent on my command." There was a short pause.

Both Green and Jim checked their monkey harnesses and pulled their M60's up into firing position. Mr. Hill spoke. "You two ready?"

"Yes, Sir. Yes, Sir."

"Blackhawk, this is Bird Dog One. Go! And good luck!"

"Okay, here we go. Mac, there's nothing friendly out there on your side. Green, you've got the village down the hill plus the ARVN camp. Don't be afraid to hit either one. We're at twenty five hundred feet and I don't hear either gun firing back there."

Both men knew that was their cue to open fire. Each pulled his trigger, bringing a small smile to Mr. Hill's face. Loc Ninh was now only a short distance away and Mr. Hill could see the star shaped perimeter by the light from the flares. Niner Two-Five was now on short final approach. All four men could see the flashes from the ground as the enemy troops opened fire on them. Jim had just decided that it would take a miracle to get them in and out when it happened—out of the black sky came a steady stream of red fire streaking towards the ground. Green came over the intercom with the almost typical response to the first time observer of Puff.

"What the HELL is that?"

Mr. Hill laughed and said, "That, Green, is Puff the Magic Dragon."

"I don't think Peter, Paul, and Mary would approve," said Green as he watched the tracers race to their destination below.

He really couldn't believe anything could live through that on-slaught, if unfortunate enough to be caught in its path. He watched as the last stream of burning hail balls streaked to-wards the earth just like a giant hand had shut off the flow of fire and was now pushing the last breath from the dragon's mouth downward with open palm. He realized his own gun was still firing into the darkness and that Mr. Euclid was call-ing out altitude and airspeed for Mr. Hill. Both Green and Jim stopped firing at about the same moment as the chopper settled gently down into a blanket of dust. Instantly two men dressed in combat gear and camouflage paint appeared on each side of the helicopter and started unloading the crates of beehives. Their movements were strained, and showed a forced hurried-ness as they jerked the crates, weighing approximately one hun-dred sixty pounds each, out the door. Jim heard the pop but didn't make the connection until he heard the second pop at the same time he saw the explosion, followed by another and an-other as the mortars were slowly walked their direction. All four Special Forces soldiers were now lying prone on the ground, starting to low crawl to protective cover.

"Mr. Hill, this place is getting mortared and we're empty, let's get out of here."

Mr. Hill turned up the RPM and started to talk to Bird Dog One. Mortar shells were falling all around them as Bird Dog One came over the radio. "Roger, Blackhawk, please wait as the gunships aren't yet in position."

Jim could feel the chopper leap up and forward as Mr. Hill shouted, "Fuck you, Bird Dog!"

"Puff, this is Blackhawk Niner Two-Five, we're on our way out, give 'em hell!"

"This is Puff, Niner Two-Five, hell's on its way," and indeed it was as the dragon's breath spewed forth lead and fire. Mr. Hill had Niner Two-Five red lined as he tried to make good their escape. Tracers flashed over their ship as it sped away giving them the necessary protective lead curtain. Jim, looking back, could see the explosion at the swimming pool and two gunships starting their run with rockets and mini guns blazing.

"Puff, Bird Dog One, everyone, this is Niner Two-Five, we're homeward bound, thanks for the help out."

"Niner Two-Five, this is Bird Dog One, we were all glad to be of help. Too bad you can't stick around for the show."

Mr. Hill was ready to get back and had nosed it over to the one hundred twenty knot red line; with any luck he could get back before midnight.

"Loc Ninh, this is Blackhawk Niner Two-Five, we're out safe and homeward bound, sorry we couldn't stay for the party, but your uninvited guests weren't being very nice. Niner Two-Five, out."

"Niner Two-Five, this is Loc Ninh. You're always welcome here at sunny, scenic Loc Ninh. Come back again and thanks for the supplies, without them, we wouldn't make it. Loc Ninh out."

"Thanks for the invitation but I go home tomorrow morning, I'm SHORRT." Mr. Hill laughed as he yelled short, short, short into the mike. "Well, Mac, we made it much to your chagrin."

"My chagrin? Bullshit! I'm just as happy we made it as you are. Besides, where did you get that ten dollar word in this land of the fifty cent vocabulary?"

"Hey, I'm almost a civilian again, I've got to start acting like one.

"You know, gentlemen, there are a lot of reasons I'm glad to be leaving this place, not the least of which is our new XO. Any of you guys met that man yet?"

All three said, "No." "No." "No."

"Mr. Hill, I didn't even know we had a new XO; what happened to the old one?"

"He got promoted and given a command someplace down in the Delta. I'll tell ya, Mac, you EM are just going to love this guy." The sarcasm in Mr. Hill's voice was obvious as he continued, "I met the man this afternoon in the officer's club, he's a Major. I can't remember the name but the guy thinks he's John Wayne. I'll give him this much, he is a big dude, about six foot six and I'd guess two hundred fifty pounds, blond hair with a flat top and he eats nails for breakfast."

"Mr. Hill, could I ask a question before I forget it?"

"Sure, Green, shoot."

"At Loc Ninh they said something about a Frenchman. What Frenchman?"

"Didn't you take history in school, Green? This place belonged to the French. A handful stayed on after the French Army got kicked out, primarily to run the various plantations. There's one that lives in a mansion at the far end of the runway. He's got a swimming pool located between the house and the Special Forces camp, or at least, he used to. Next time you're up there during the day look for it. There's a pretty good sized little village on down the hillside with his mansion about halfway up the hill. Anyway, the Frenchman who lives there runs the rubber plantation that's all around Loc Ninh. He, of course, pays the Vietcong protection money. Whenever they're going to have an offensive against the Special Forces camp, he gets the word. Then he moves all his valuables into the basement, drains his pool, packs his bags and climbs in his little yellow airplane for a few days vacation."

"Sir, how does he know when to come back and where does he go?"

"Oh, they probably tell him how long the offensive will last and he probably goes down to Saigon or Vung Tau. You see his plane around every now and then. He could even go over to Bangkok. I've heard that the Special Forces guys know if he's leaving on business, or if he's getting out before an attack, by whether he drains the pool first or not, but that's not important.

"There is one thing, Green, you should remember about tonight. In fifteen or twenty years when you tell this story, no one will understand or comprehend what it was like seeing all those tracers going by you. In fact, most people won't even believe we went in there with a helicopter. There are a lot of pilots who wouldn't have gone close to Loc Ninh tonight, let alone landed there. For that matter, in this company you'll go a lot of places people won't believe you've gone. Isn't that right, Mac?"

"Yes, Sir, we'll fly into a hornet's nest if someone needs help. Just out of curiosity, Mr. Hill, tell me more about our new XO."

"Oh, he's got more good ideas than a cat has lives." The sarcasm in Mr. Hill's voice was obvious as he continued, "I think the one all you guys will like the most is, he wants all the cargo doors put back on the ships."

"That's where that idea came from!"

"Oh, you've already heard about that one?"

"Yeah, Gillett told us about it tonight before sending me to the flight line."

"You going to do it, Mac?"

"Why, Mr. Hill, you know I'd never disobey an officer's order."

"Yeah, just like I'm not going home tomorrow. You'll do whatever you damn well please. The thing I want to know is how you are going to get away with it. 'Cause I know you're not going to put those doors back on."

"Well, you're right. I'm not happy about it, they are a big pain in the neck. I have to shut the right door every time I put fuel in, then open it again and snap pin it open, plus I'll have to unhook the ammo belt and then hook it back up again every time the doors are opened or shut. Of course, every time I want into the engine or storage compartments, I'll have to shut the door. It wouldn't be so bad if it wasn't for the fact the machine-guns are on the outside and the ammo is inside."

"So, how'll you get out of it?"

"Hard to say, Sir, something may come up. What else does he have up his sleeve for us?"

"Oh, cute little things like painting the rocks, raking the sand, police call* before the flight takes off, washing and waxing the helicopters and their blades. He's got this idea that waxed rotor blades give a chopper ten percent more lift. He was saying in the club today that Colonel Appleton and he decided to split the duties. Appleton would have the flights, and he would have the company area. It will be his mission to clean the place up and make it look like the first class unit it should be, which means a lot of painting, raking and shoveling."

It wasn't quite midnight when Mr. Hill sat Niner Two-Five down in its parking revetment. Everyone was in a hurry to get back. Mr. Euclid immediately climbed out and walked off,

---

* Police Call—Picking up everything that isn't supposed to be in the area, such as cigarette butts.

while Jim was tying the main rotor blades down. Green came around to the tail of the ship and asked, "Mac, do I have to take those guns in tonight?"

"You're supposed to, but why don't you hide them in the corner of the revetment?"

Jim walked forward to the pilot's door. He wanted to talk to Mr. Hill before he left and was glad to see he was still there writing in the log book.

"Well, Sir, I was wrong. We made it, you made it, and I'm glad you did. You've been a good officer and a good pilot. I always enjoyed flying with you."

"Thank you, Mac, that's very nice of you to say. For the most part, I've enjoyed the year I've spent here, but then I've been really lucky. You know I wasn't shot down that first time, although I have to admit, I really figured we'd never get out of Loc Ninh tonight. Speaking of Loc Ninh, did we take any hits tonight?"

"Not that I know of, but then I haven't really checked it out yet. You know, Mr. Hill, it's kind of strange how we can fly through Hell like we did tonight, not take any hits and yet be in a flight of ten and come out looking like a peg board."

"Yeah, that's one of the benefits of being a member of an all combat assault team. We go places and do things other general purpose units wouldn't touch."

The two men shook hands and said good-bye. Mr. Hill headed back to the company area and officers' club while Jim started his post flight inspection. Green had already hid his guns and headed back.

So You Want
to Play Games

*"Whatever a man soweth, that shall
he also reap."* GALATIANS 6:7, KJV

On the way to the company area, Green fingered the grenade in
his fatigue pocket. He knew what he was going to do, he just
didn't know quite how to go about it. He knew if he got caught,
he'd go to jail. So he just didn't dare make any mistakes. Suddenly he had to pee something terrible. Squeezing all the way to
the urinal, he still almost wet his pants while trying to get it
out. Control, that was the key, he had to get control of himself
and his nerves. If he couldn't, he might just as well forget the
whole thing.

Taking a deep breath, Green moved into the shadows and
started working his way into the officers' area. As he walked, he
tried to look as casual as possible, like he belonged there. Staying in the shadows, he passed the officers' club and latrine. The
area in front of the officers' quarters was well lighted. Green
stood and looked at the L-shaped building that made up their
two-man quarters. There wasn't any way to get closer without
exposing himself to the light and possible discovery. He stood
and watched for several minutes before deciding the only thing
to do was walk down the row of doors and read the names on
the outside. Hopefully, he wouldn't be seen by anyone. There
hadn't been but a couple officers in sight the whole time he'd
been standing there. He looked around very carefully for other
people and, seeing none, started toward the row of doors. As he

walked he was struck by the similarity between this building and some of the fleabag motels he'd seen in the States. He was now close enough to spit on the first door and he still couldn't see any names. There was enough light for him to see a few doors down the row and they were all the same, no name, just numbers. Turning quickly, he moved rapidly away and back into the shadows. He was visibly shaken and now very uncertain just what to do next. It had never occurred to him that the doors wouldn't have the officer's names on them. Now he had a real problem: how could he go about finding Halsey's quarters without anybody knowing he wanted to know? One thing was sure—after he made his move, everyone would hear about what had happened. If he asked questions, someone would surely remember.

Somewhat dejected, Green sat down. Not really knowing why, he just sat there looking at the empty space in front of him. Finally, he decided he might just as well go to bed. As he started to get up, the officers' club door flew open and a group of officers staggered out. Searching each face, hoping to locate the one belonging to Halsey, he again felt the disappointment of failure.

As he watched each man enter his hooch he also saw two female nurses leave the club together. They went straight to the latrine, almost as though they had been there before. Green was really surprised when they walked right in. After all, it was an officers' latrine, for men. As he thought about it, it did make sense. There wasn't a female latrine outside the hospital area, and that was a quarter mile away. It did strike him somewhat strange though as he pictured those nurses sitting down on the pot beside some pilot. The more he thought about it, the more he became convinced it was probably so dark in there that they would have a hard time finding the pots, let alone seeing who was next to them.

Again the club door opened and two men walked out. Green's heart jumped—one of them was unmistakably Halsey. Suddenly Green felt chilled and he again struggled to control his nerves. After all, it was a dud. He wasn't going to kill him— just scare the hell out of him.

As Halsey walked by he thought about just throwing it and

then running. No, that simply would not do. There were far too many people around; the guy with Halsey and the two nurses still in the latrine, who surely would be coming out any second now. Green watched and waited as the two men headed to their respective doors. Halsey's was the second from the inside corner. That meant he would have to walk by a lot of officers' doors in the light before getting to Halsey. Then he would have to get out. He'd run to the shadows and then make his way back to the hooch as quickly as possible without being seen.

He looked back toward the latrine, not understanding why the nurses hadn't yet emerged. To his surprise there they stood just outside the door, partly hidden in the shadows of the latrine wall. He would have missed them, if not for one of them moving. Now why were they standing there? It was almost as though they too were watching for something or someone and not wishing to be seen. Maybe they had spotted him. That was it, they had seen him! It just didn't make sense. He had been very careful not to move anything except his head and that only slowly. He watched two of the pilots emerge from the club and move quickly to the latrine. Not spending but a few minutes inside, they left by the door where the two nurses stood. Now he knew what the nurses were doing. The four people exchanged words, looked around for others and holding hands as couples often do, moved quickly, almost at a run, towards the officers' quarters. Green almost broke out laughing as both couples entered the door beside Halsey. He knew that was one door that wouldn't open, no matter what. Almost at the same moment Halsey's light went off.

Green knew this was it. Carefully, he looked for any signs of someone else in the area or about to enter the area. He was moving quickly now like a man with a purpose. Stopping in front of Halsey's door he looked around to see if anyone was about. Seeing no one, he gave two quick firm raps on the door, ripped the pin from the grenade, opened the door and threw the frag inside. In the same movement he turned and ran back to the shadows as though the devil himself was behind him. He'd only taken three or four steps when he heard Halsey's voice yell, "Grenade."

He was in the shadows now and his whole body was shaking

so badly he could hardly run. Once back in the protective darkness, he slowed to a brisk walk. Still his nerves kept his body shaking so badly his knees would hardly function. He fell twice before finally reaching his hooch's back door. The back door was his choice of entrance so he wouldn't have to pass by Gillett's bunk. Finding his bunk in the darkness wasn't easy, but he didn't want to fall over anything and wake someone up. The army cot he slept on felt good, like a child's security blanket. Yet his heart continued to pound violently. So fierce was it beating, he thought it might burst. Even breathing deeply to try to regain control of himself was almost an impossible effort. Yet, he knew he must get into bed as quickly as possible before bed check. The combat boots had to come off. He struggled with the strings, with fingers shaking uncontrollably. Finally, the boots came off and the shirt pulled over his head without unbuttoning. The pants weren't too much trouble and he found himself in bed. Still shaking, he wondered if he would ever get control, would he really get away with it? Man, he wished he hadn't done this. It was the dumbest thing he had ever done. His heart was still pounding as though trying to escape his chest cavity. So fierce was the pounding and shaking that his whole bed was moving. Finally, after some time he began to settle down and fatigue was once again setting in. Ever so slowly, like a slowly melting snow, he began to relax. The shaking and pounding had stopped and his eyelids settled gently over his eyes.

The squeak of the main entrance door being opened shot through Green like a spear. He lay there trying to pretend he was asleep, certain they had come for him. Yet nothing happened. He lay there straining to hear what was going on. For some reason someone had awakened Gillett, who was now getting out of bed.

Mr. Halsey hadn't been in bed but a short time and sleep was rapidly shutting down his bodily functions. The knock on his door irritated him more than anything else. After all, he was comfortably in bed. As he threw off his sheet and flipped up the mosquito netting he mumbled under his breath. "This better be good." He was never sent on any of the night missions so that wasn't it. Who would be knocking on the door? His roommate

would just walk on in. Besides, he was probably still in Bangkok on R&R and wouldn't be back for a while. The grapevine
claimed that Bien Hoa had been closed since Tet started. As a
result, all R&R activity had stopped, with the guys still out of
country being held over.

Mr. Halsey had just stood up when his door opened. With
the light in the background, he could just make out something
small and round being thrown in. He could tell it was something relatively heavy the way it traveled through the air. It
was the spring throwing open the handle that told him what. In
that same flickering of a heartbeat he yelled, "Grenade" and
dived into his bunk. As he hit the bed, the mosquito netting
over it became tangled in his arms and body, breaking off three
of the four poles holding it up and ripping a big long tear in the
netting where it was attached to the fourth pole. Realizing his
bed wasn't the safest place he could be, he allowed his momentum to roll him over onto the floor. Trying his best to hug the
floor, he covered his ears with his hands and awaited the pain
he knew would come. His only hope now was to live through it
because he was going to be hurt, yet there was no ear shattering
explosion. Why not? Was it possible he had misjudged what
had come in his door and bounced like a steel ball onto the
concrete floor? He searched the floor with his eyes trying in
vain to find the mysterious object. If it was a frag, it should
have blown long before now. He began to wonder if he should
stand up or try to low crawl to the door and the light switch.
Finally, he started to move, slowly at first, almost as though his
very movement might set off the awaited explosion. As he
moved closer to the door, he moved faster and faster until he
resembled a bug on a hot surface. Once at the door, he stood up
and turned on the lights. There it was in the far corner, just as
big and black and ugly as a fragmentation grenade could be. He
stood there staring at it for several minutes trying to figure it all
out.

Why had it not blown? The spring was off and the handle lay
several feet away. It was obviously a dud, but had someone
made it so; or was someone disappointed he wasn't dead? But
who? MacLaughlin, of course. He really couldn't picture Mac-
Laughlin doing this—it just didn't fit his personality—but he

was the only logical one. It had to be MacLaughlin. That son of a bitch, he'd send his smart ass to jail for the next twenty years.

The thing he had to do now was make sure he did everything the right way. The first thing he did was bang on the door next to his. Mr. Halsey's heart was still pounding pretty hard as he shouted, "Hey, you guys, wake up! There's a live frag next to your wall in my room." The response from behind the closed door was strained.

"Get lost, Halsey, we're busy."

"I'm not kidding you, guys. Somebody threw a frag in my door and it's laying against your wall."

With that he could hear a woman's squeal and a great flurry of activity. The door flew open with a bang and a disgusted Mr. Lucas stood there, a bulge protruding from the pants he was hurriedly trying to buckle. Halsey knew the activities had already started. That knowledge, plus the sight of Lucas standing there with nothing on but his pants almost made him laugh. Lucas was a tall man, over six foot, but thin as a rail. His most distinguishing characteristic was his prematurely bald head. He kept the rest of his head and face shaved, which gave a very strange appearance.

"Halsey, you know something? You're an asshole."

"Hey, man, I'm just trying to help you out. I'm going to go report that grenade to Captain Wolf, and you know how he feels about hookers."

Mr. Lucas looked down at Halsey standing there in nothing but his green boxer shorts. There wasn't any question in his mind that Halsey would pull this kind of trick, just out of meanness. Yet there was something about the pathetic little bastard that told him his story might just be for real.

"Halsey, don't jive me. Nobody in this outfit would do something like that."

"Hey, I'm not going to stand here and argue with you. I was just trying to be a nice guy."

"Halsey, I'll tell you what. There damn well better be a grenade in there, or I'll kill you myself."

Lucas turned and slammed the door behind him. Once inside he looked at both girls, who had finished dressing. "Come on, girls, he was just kidding. If there was a frag in there it would have blown long ago."

"I don't care! Either way we're getting out of here. We didn't ask for this, and we're not staying."

Lucas found himself wishing the grenade had blown Halsey's ass off.

Once the door had been closed in his face, Halsey turned and started towards Captain Wolf's quarters. He had only taken a few steps when Captain Wolf and Major Hobbs came out of the latrine. Major Hobbs was indeed a big man, as Mr. Hill had said. He had a dark complexion with blond hair, cut in a half-inch flat top. Worst of all, he tried his best to give everyone the impression he ate nails for breakfast.

It was Captain Wolf with a big smile on his face who spoke first. "Halsey, what are you doing out here in your shorts?"

"Looking for you, Captain! Someone just tried to frag me!"

At that moment, Mr. Lucas' door came open and out ran the two nurses. Almost running into Wolf and Hobbs, the two nurses came to an abrupt stop. Wolf said, "At attention, Ladies."

"You happen to be speaking to a Captain, Mister, and I expect to be treated like one."

"Then you should try acting like one. Furthermore, I'm also a captain; the difference is, you're on my turf!" Captain Wolf's voice continued to build in force and volume.

"Lucas, Euclid, get your butts out here!"

Both officers came through the door fully dressed acting like two little boys who had just been caught with their fingers in the pie. Captain Wolf's voice was now back to normal, but still very forceful. "I've told you guys before, no women in the rooms. As long as you're in my platoon, you'll follow my orders, or wish you had."

Mr. Lucas spoke up. "Captain, it's not what you think. I just invited the girls in for a minute to look at some pictures I'd gotten back."

"Lucas, unless you want to be put on every asshole flight or shit detail for the rest of your stay, don't treat me like I'm stupid." Turning to face Euclid he asked, "How much did they charge you?"

Euclid shrugged his shoulders and looked at the ground, then said, "One hundred dollars each." Wolf's eyes bulged and his mouth dropped as his head slowly turned to the two nurses. In a soft but forceful voice he asked, "One hundred dollars each! What were you going to do, gold plate it for 'em?"

Neither nurse said a thing as one looked at the ground and the other looked hatefully at Halsey, who was standing a few feet behind and to the side of Hobbs.

"Okay you two, because of this fragging, I don't have time to mess with you now. Just get out of here and don't ever come back. Not here, not to the club, not anywhere in this company area, or I'll personally see to it you stand court martial for prostitution. You're a disgrace to your country and your uniform. As officers, your conduct is inexcusable, and insulting. There are countless fine women who serve as military nurses, but you two are scum. Now get out of my sight and stay out."

Major Hobbs had moved close enough to Wolf so that he could speak in his ear without any of the others hearing and without its being obvious he was speaking. "I hope you never have to spend time in one of their hospital beds."

Captain Wolf slowly nodded his head in agreement and said, "Right."

Wolf now turned to Lucas and Euclid still standing there watching as their dreams walked rapidly away. "As for you two, it is going to be a very expensive night. You can sign the papers in the morning in the orderly room. Shall we say another two hundred dollars each? That'll make it a three hundred dollar night for you two love birds."

Neither man said a word but both looked straight at Halsey, who had now moved behind the massive body of Major Hobbs. Halsey's attempt to hide was unsuccessful, and seeing their stares, he simply shrugged his shoulders and curled his mouth as though to say, 'I'm sorry, fellows.'

Captain Wolf now turned to Mr. Halsey and said, "Now, tell me about this fragging."

Mr. Halsey related the story as best he remembered it. At the end Major Hobbs said, "Let's go see it."

The light was still on as Halsey opened his door, allowing Wolf and Hobbs to walk in. Major Hobbs spotted the ominous looking grenade and said, "Well, Captain, I used to be in the infantry. This sort of thing is one of the reasons I transferred to aviation. You fly boys aren't supposed to have this type of problem."

"To my knowledge, Major, it's a first, at least in this company. What do you think, Major?"

"I think it's an intentional dud. In fact, I'm willing to bet on it." He walked over and carefully picked up the frag. Gripping the top with one massive hand, he gingerly turned the bottom off. Once the two parts were separated and the major could see the exploded percussion cap, his face lit up with a big smile. Turning to face the two men still standing in the doorway, he flipped the spent percussion cap over to Captain Wolf, who caught it and quickly examined it. Standing fully erect now, Major Hobbs turned to Halsey. "Didn't I hear your name is Halsey?"

"Yes, Sir, that's right."

"I've got a question for you, Mr. Halsey. When this thing bounced across your floor what did you do?" Adding very sarcastically, "Jump in your bed?"

"Sir, it was dark in there. The lights were off and when I realized what had just come through my door, I just dived for the floor and hit the bed in the process."

"I can see that. Did you pull your covers over your head also?"

"Major, this isn't a joking matter. Someone tried to kill me, and . . ."

"Wrong! Mr. Halsey, somebody tried to scare the hell out of you, not kill you. At least not this time. That cap has been previously exploded, intentionally. Someone's gone to a lot of trouble to separate the body, blow the cap, pick up all the parts, and then put it back together. You didn't see who did this?"

"No, Sir, but I've got a real good idea!"

"Who?"

"A Spec Four named MacLaughlin."

"Any particular reason why him?"

"Yes, Sir, we've had problems in the past, and this morning was just a typical example of his arrogance and insubordination."

Mr. Halsey started to relate a very shaded account of Jim's refusal to fly with him that morning.

Captain Wolf just couldn't imagine MacLaughlin doing something like this. Yet somebody had, so until he knew more, he wasn't about to say anything one way or the other. He did notice that Halsey's account of this morning's activities wasn't quite correct. Yet again, he felt it best to listen and remember.

Once Halsey had finished, Major Hobbs suggested they go talk to Colonel Appleton after Halsey put on some clothes. As they headed out the door, Mr. Euclid reached over and tapped Captain Wolf on the arm. The major and Halsey were already on their way as Euclid said to Captain Wolf, "Captain, Mac was on a night mission with Mr. Hill and I tonight 'til after midnight or later. I don't believe for a second he did this. For one thing, whoever did it has been sitting out there someplace for a long time, watching for Halsey. Mac just hasn't been in the company area that long."

"Okay, go on back to bed. By the way, I'll draw up the papers for you and Lucas to sign before I go to bed. See you in the morning."

Colonel Appleton walked through the orderly room into his office, followed closely by Major Hobbs, Captain Wolf, Mr. Halsey and shortly thereafter, by Mr. Walker. Colonel Appleton positioned himself as comfortably as possible in his office chair. He'd had a long day and was sound asleep when Captain Wolf pounded on his door. Why in Heaven's name did it have to be his company? In the infantry, one could maybe expect it, but not an aviation company. Not an outstanding company like his. There had never been any trouble before this. Oh, sure, the usual amount of Article 15's. All for small time things like insubordination, mostly talking back to one of the officers; but nothing of this magnitude where a man's life was threatened.

The biggest question he had to answer besides who, was how should he handle it. He sure didn't want the publicity and problems that went with this kind of thing. If at all possible, Appleton wanted to keep it right here within the company.

Halsey was positive MacLaughlin did it. Maybe he'd get unbelievably lucky and MacLaughlin would confess and he could be on his way to the LBJ* before morning. Well, he'd better get this thing started so he could get back to bed. Leaning back in his swivel chair, Colonel Appleton shouted at the CQ**. "Hey, Sergeant, come in here!"

The CQ quickly jumped up from his chair and headed into the old man's office. He didn't know what was going on, but at this time of the morning it had to be something big for all that Brass to be up walking around.

"Sergeant, I want to get Sergeant Gillett up and have him find Specialist MacLaughlin. Don't tell them anything except I want to see MacLaughlin in my office at once."

"Yes, Sir!"

"One more thing, Sergeant. Don't send your runner. I want you to go personally. I also want you to pay close attention to MacLaughlin's reactions."

"Yes, Sir!" He saluted the colonel, turned and headed out the door. Once in the outer office, he checked the duty roster. Finding Gillett's name on it, he glanced across the board to find his hooch number and was on his way.

"Now then, Mr. Walker, do you know why we're all gathered here in the middle of the night?"

"Yes, Sir. Mr. Halsey told me when he got me up."

"Okay, you probably know MacLaughlin better than any other officer. You are his AC, aren't you?"

"Yes, Sir, I am."

"What kind of soldier is he? What kind of person is he?"

"He's a nice guy and well liked. He's smart and disciplined. In fact, I'd say he does nothing on impulse. As a soldier, he's one of the best crew chiefs in the company. He does his job and doesn't bitch, no matter how bad things get. He knows that Huey inside and out, and how to fix anything on it. I believe Captain Wolf will verify that he flies most every single ship night mission we have. They used to ask for volunteers and he always went, so they just quit asking. Now they just go get MacLaughlin. As to whether I think he would do something

---

* LBJ—Long Binh jail.

** CQ—Charge of quarters, always an E-5 or above; usually there was a lesser ranking EM used as a runner.

like this, no, Sir! There's no way he'd frag someone, not even Mr. Halsey! His personal conduct and appearance is always what you would expect. One other thing, Sir, as a pilot, he makes my job a whole lot easier. I know I can depend on him no matter what. I personally don't believe for a second that he did this. It's against everything he stands for. I've never once heard him advocate anything even close to this.

"As you know, Sir, Mr. Halsey and MacLaughlin haven't gotten along since Mac turned him in for falsifying those records. I wonder if that hasn't clouded Mr. Halsey's judgment in this matter?"

"Mr. Walker, you obviously like the man a great deal."

"Yes, Sir, we're very close. We've gone through a lot together. He has never shown me any disrespect. He has, however, given me a lot of reasons to greatly respect him."

"All right, Mr. Walker, you can go back to bed now. Thank you very much for coming in and giving me some background information."

Mr. Walker was stunned at being so quickly dismissed—but having no choice, he came to attention, saluted, turned and left. Once outside, he thought about waiting for MacLaughlin, but decided against it. If the CO found out he'd talked to Mac before going in, he would find himself in almost as much trouble as Mac.

The CQ had no trouble locating Gillett's bunk. It was right where all platoon sergeants bunks were supposed to be—the first bunk on the right after entering through the main entrance. His flashlight shone in Gillett's face and with a gentle shaking, Gillett came to enough to say only, "What?"

"Sergeant Gillett?"

"Yeah, what do you want?"

The CQ had moved his light from Gillett's face to help ease his reintroduction into the waking world, "Sergeant, I'm the CQ. Colonel Appleton wants to see Specialist MacLaughlin ASAP."

"What's he want with Mac?"

"You'll have to ask the colonel that, Sergeant."

"What time is it?"

"Almost two."

Gillett stretched and slowly sat up on the edge of his bunk. He couldn't imagine why the CO wanted to see Mac at this time of night. Oh, well, at least Mac wasn't hard to wake up. He'd had a real education about waking people up since he'd become platoon sergeant; some guys you didn't dare touch or they'd get upset and start swinging, always under the pretense of being startled out of sleep. With others, he had to exchange verbal blows each morning. Not Mac, though; he always woke easily and without a hassle. All he had to do was shake his foot or shoulder gently and say, 'Mac, wake up,' and he would, without a fight of any kind.

Gillett turned on a flashlight and walked over to Mac's bunk. Reaching down to Jim's foot he gave it a gentle shake and said, "Mac, it's me, Gillett. Wake up!"

The CQ had positioned his light so it shone directly in Jim's face causing him to squint and turn his head to one side.

"Gillett, get that light out of my eyes!"

"It's not me, it's the CQ."

"I don't care who it is, just get it out of my face, will you?"

The CQ lowered his light slightly, enough to allow Jim to remove the hand which had been shielding his eyes. "Gillett, where're you sending me now, Loc Ninh again?"

"No, Mac, the CO wants to see you."

"The CO! What time is it?"

"Two, or there about."

The CQ had put the direct beam of his light full force in Jim's eyes once again. As Jim sat up he said, "I don't know who you are, but I'm not going to tell you again to get that light out of my face. I'm about ready to stick it down your throat."

"Look, Specialist, I was told to get you up and watch your reaction and that's what I'm doing."

Jim was now seated on the side of his bunk, so it was a simple and seemingly natural move to gradually reach for a boot. Gillett spotted the movement and realized the potential problems it could cause if Jim put his boot up alongside the CQ's head. At the same time Gillett spoke, he reached out and moved the light. "Forget it, Mac, it's not worth it. Look, Sergeant, go on back and tell the CO we'll be there just as soon as we finish dressing."

"Okay, Gillett, but if you two aren't there in five minutes, I'll be back for you."

The CQ turned and left. Once out the door, Mac asked Gillett, "What's the CO want with me at this time of night?"

"I don't know anymore than you do, Mac."

"One thing is for sure, he didn't get me out of bed to give me a promotion!"

"Right! Did you get in trouble going up to Loc Ninh tonight?"

"No. I gave Mr. Hill kind of a hard time about flying a night mission when he's going home tomorrow. That's it though, hardly something major."

"Well, one thing is for sure, the CO isn't going to get himself out of bed for something that isn't serious. Did you and Halsey have more trouble?"

"Just this morning and you know about that. Gillett, maybe it's not something bad."

"I'm not so sure. That CQ said he was told to watch for your reaction when you were told the CO wanted you. Now, I ask you, why would he be told to do that if it was something good?"

"Gillett, I can't figure it. You about ready?"

"Yeah, just as soon as I finish tying this boot."

Jim stood and walked to the door, where he waited for his friend. Gillett finished, picked up his light and walked out the door with Jim. The two men walked in silence with the aid of Gillett's flashlight to the orderly room. As they approached, yet still out of hearing range, Gillett took Jim's arm and shut off his light. "Look, Mac, I don't know what this is all about so let me give you some advice before we get there. First, it might be something good, it might be something bad, and it might be neither, so until you know exactly what's going down, don't do or say anything you don't have to. Give 'Yes, Sir' and 'No, Sir' answers, don't volunteer anything. Remember your military procedures for saluting and your physical stance. Stay at attention until he tells you otherwise. If by some remote chance, and I can't think why there would be, but if there is anybody else there, you talk only to and respond only to the CO. Unless, of course, the question obviously has the CO's blessings. You got any questions?"

"No, I guess I'm ready. Let's go find out what the old man wants."

Gillett turned his flashlight on and the two men resumed their walk. Jim kept searching his brain for any kind of clue—his continuing struggle with Halsey was what he kept coming back to. This morning's refusal to fly with him must have been the last straw. Still, that didn't make sense. The CO would just have waited until morning . . .

After leaving Gillett and MacLaughlin, the CQ walked directly back to the orderly room. As he walked in the door, Colonel Appleton, Major Hobbs, Captain Wolf and Mr. Halsey were all coming out of the old man's office. Colonel Appleton spoke before the CQ had a chance to do anything but shut the door.

"Well, Sergeant, did you find him?"

"Yes, Sir. He was in bed asleep."

"Tell me everything you did just as it happened."

The CQ told his every action in great detail including the fact that Gillett was going to accompany MacLaughlin. This pleased the CO. After all, it is a platoon sergeant's responsibility to assist his men in this type of situation. He smiled to himself as he thought about what a fine example Gillett was making. He'd have to remember Gillett.

After the CQ had finished, the CO thanked him and turned to Captain Wolf. "Captain, let's go over these duty rosters and see where we stand on personnel."

The two men looked at the roster of names in each platoon trying to get some idea of how to shuffle people around. "Colonel, as I see it, we have one extra gunner in second platoon and one extra crew chief in the first platoon. If we lose Mac, we'll have to leave a ship on the ground anytime one of the crew chiefs gets sick or can't fly for some reason."

"That only leaves us with two options. One, take a man out of maintenance to fill a crew chief's spot or start making the two flight platoon sergeants fly."

"Colonel, the flight platoon sergeants have too much to do as it is. Those guys have to work on the next day's flight schedule after everyone else is in bed. They have to coordinate ships in and out of maintenance with the personnel available. They often don't get to bed until 0200 or later, then get up at 0445 to get their people up and going. Those men have to be able to rack out during the day. We put them on a chopper and they'd sleep most of the time."

"Captain, maintenance is almost as bad. They used to have five work crews of five men each; three day crews and two night crews. They're down to one five-man night crew and two day crews of five men each. I've already eliminated all supervisory personnel in maintenance, every crew leader works just like one of the crew. I even told the the sergeants they had to start helping out. They're to find a crew they like working with and stick with it until they have to go inspect someone's work. It's to stay that way until we get some replacements. Oh, well, we can make a decision after we talk to MacLaughlin."

Everyone but the CQ followed the Colonel back into his office. As they walked by the last hooch, Jim could see the bright lights of maintenance; several sets of those lights were set up and burning brightly. Jim knew it was going to be another long night for the guys in maintenance. He could remember spending many a time working under those lights all night long. Maybe it was the loner in him, but he actually preferred working at night. There was never any Brass around to hassle you, just a sergeant, and they always left you alone, as long as you did your job. He could still remember, as though it were yesterday, being told he was going on the night crew. He hadn't liked the idea but the sergeant hadn't given him any choice. Besides, he told Mac, they only put their best people on night because they were expected to work without much supervision. Man, that had been an understatement. The only time he'd seen any supervision was when he'd picked up his job assignment along with the rest of the crew, or when the crew he was on needed a tech sergeant to okay something they were doing and then sign it off. Tech would leave and the crew would be on their own again. Jim very quickly saw the advantage of working on the night crew. Almost as quickly, he'd really learned to like working nights. It really did have a lot of advantages; no hassling, the work pace was flexible and you had the next day off. Not to mention the night crew missed most formations due to the working hours. Oh, well, that was in the past.

Gillett and Jim walked up the steps and entered the orderly room. There sat the CQ, who stood up as soon as he saw the two men walk in. "Wait here and I'll tell the CO you're here."

The CQ turned and knocked on the CO's door. The CO's voice was heard. "Come in."

The CQ opened the door, stepped in and said, "Sir, Sergeant Gillett and Specialist MacLaughlin are here."

"Send them in, Sergeant."

Jim wasn't nervous or apprehensive. He couldn't think of any reason why the CO wanted him so he was as relaxed as any enlisted man could be, going to see the CO. The fact that he was still partially asleep helped. Gillett poked him and said, "Remember what I said."

Jim nodded his head and thought about the CO's office. He'd been in it once before when he'd been a CQ runner one night. The old man's desk sat off to the right so that one had to enter the door, take two steps forward, make a right turn and face the CO behind his desk. Jim figured the CO probably put his desk there just to intimidate those entering the room.

Gillett entered first and made a straight path to the CO's desk. Jim noticed that he had made a very unmilitary diagonal path to get there. If he wants military, I'll give him military, Jim thought.

Gillett reported, "Sir, Sergeant Gillett reports."

"At ease, Sergeant."

Jim figured Gillett being told to stand at ease was a good sign. He entered and took a quick glance to his left and there, to his surprise, stood Halsey. The sight of Halsey struck Jim like a hundred needles pricking his spine. Halsey meant trouble and he knew it. Gillett was right, he would have to be very, very careful. Jim took two steps forward, executed a perfect right turn, took two more steps and found himself squarely in front of the CO's desk. Standing perfectly at attention with his eyes straight ahead he brought his right arm up to a snappy salute. "Sir, Specialist MacLaughlin reporting as ordered!"

Jim could see standing off to the left and behind the old man was Captain Wolf; seated to the right and slightly behind the CO was a major whom Jim had never seen. It was impossible to read the name tag without turning his head or eyes, so he didn't. Something was very wrong, this almost looked like a court martial hearing. Jim was now scared. If Wolf and Halsey were both here, he was definitely in trouble. The unknown major bothered him almost as much as or even more than the others, yet the location of each man indicated their importance, and the major held no more important position than did Captain Wolf. The CO brought his arm up to return the salute and the moment he started back down, Jim whipped his hand down in a lost effort to beat the CO's.

Each man was impressed with the other's salute. Most officers gave a lackadaisical type of salute and Jim had expected to beat the colonel's arm down. Colonel Appleton, on the other hand, often measured an enlisted man's military sharpness by his salute and MacLaughlin had certainly passed with high marks.

The colonel sat there looking up at Jim's face as though trying to read his mind. Jim was aware of the significance of his being left standing at attention. No one spoke and Jim knew no one would until the CO did. All the CO was doing was staring at him; if his intent was to make him nervous, he was being very effective. Finally, after what seemed like a lot longer than it really was, Colonel Appleton spoke. "Specialist, how long have you been in country?"

Jim wondered why in the world he wanted to know that. It had to be a lead in; after all, Halsey and Wolf weren't here to find out what they could read on his personnel records. "Going on nine months, Sir."

"Of that time how much has been spent with the Blackhawks?"

"About four months, Sir."

"Specialist, I've looked over your record. It's very impressive. You're obviously a good crew chief. Tell me, do you have any problems?"

"Problems, Sir? Well, Sir, between the long hours, the night missions and the CQ waking me up, I don't get enough sleep."

"That's not what I mean, Specialist, and you know it. Do you want to talk about it?"

"Sir, I don't know what you mean."

Colonel Appleton just sat there giving Jim a very stern look. Very slowly he leaned back in his chair allowing the swivel rocker to tip backwards. Placing both hands behind his head he allowed himself to show a small smile. In a soft friendly voice he said, "At ease, Specialist."

Jim moved very smartly into the more comfortable "at ease" position.

"Did you fly a night mission tonight, Specialist?"

"Yes, Sir."

"What time did you get back?"

"About 1230, Sir. I'm not real sure."

Colonel Appleton leaned forward, opened a desk drawer, pulled out an object, sat it abruptly on his desk and said, "Ever see this before, Specialist?"

The surprised expression on both Gillett's and Jim's faces registered with all the officers in the room. Even Halsey, who had slowly worked his way around the room to where he could see everyone's face, hadn't expected that reaction. Jim shrugged his shoulders. "It's a fragmentation grenade, Sir. Everybody in the army has seen one of those."

"Specialist, the question was, 'Have you ever seen this particular one before?' "

"I have no way of knowing that, Sir. I would say right off the top, no, Sir, I haven't, because I simply don't handle that many frags."

"Disassemble it for me, Specialist!"

Jim looked down at the colonel as though he were crazy, then looked over at Captain Wolf, who was taking in his every reaction. Looking back at the colonel, he spoke. "Colonel, that thing is not a toy. It has one purpose and that's to hurt people. So if it's all the same to you, Sir, I'd rather not play with a live grenade."

"I didn't give you a choice, Specialist. I said take it apart, now!"

"Yes, Sir." Jim picked up the grenade, looked it over and looked back down at the CO. "Sir, having never done this before, I'm not sure one can take a frag apart without blowing oneself into very small pieces."

The expression on the CO's face told him he should start disassembling the frag. Firmly gripping the base with his left hand, he turned the cap off with his right hand. Clearly showing the apprehension he felt, Jim removed the cap and saw the spent percussion clip. The look of surprise on his face was obvious to everyone in the room. Holding the cap in his hand so that it was visible to the others, Jim searched each man's face for some kind of answer. "Colonel, I know you didn't get me out of bed to play a practical joke. Sir, I would appreciate it if you told me what is going on."

"I had hoped you could tell me, Specialist."

The questioning look on Jim's face had convinced the CO by now that Jim wasn't their man, or else he should get an Oscar for his performance. "Sir, I am obviously missing something. I don't know what you want from me."

"Specialist, someone took this grenade earlier tonight and threw it into Mr. Halsey's quarters."

Jim's eyes enlarged, his jaw dropped open and his general look of surprise and shock was clear. "Colonel, you obviously think I did it. I'll be the first to admit Mr. Halsey isn't one of my favorite people, but I didn't do it. In the first place, I wasn't in the company area until sometime around 0100, when I got back from a night mission. You can ask Mr. Hill or Mr. Euclid. They were the pilots."

Halsey spoke up. "You had plenty of time after you landed!"

"Sir, I did a post-flight inspection, took a shower and went to bed."

"I'll bet."

Jim turned to Halsey. "Sir, you can check my log book and ship on the post flight, and smell my arm pit to verify the shower!"

A quick glance at Gillett who was shaking his head "no" and saying "not now" with his lips, moved Jim's glance to Captain Wolf, who gave him the same glance and facial expression. He then turned back to Colonel Appleton and the unknown major. It was only the major whose body was moving as though laughing, and who had covered his bowed face with one hand. The major quickly regained his composure and looked up, showing only a small smile.

Gillett spoke up. "Sir, may I speak?"

"Go ahead, Sergeant,"

"Sir, Specialist MacLaughlin was on a night mission tonight. I don't know what time he got back, but I came in the hooch to go to bed at 0115. I know the time because I had to set my alarm. Mac's bunk is right across the aisle from mine and I checked on him just to see if he was back. He was in bed, sound asleep. When the CQ came in, he was still asleep, and the CQ stood there and watched me wake him up. Could I ask the colonel what time this fragging occurred?"

"About 0100, which makes it pretty unlikely that you were the guilty party, Specialist."

Jim's mind was saying, "Thank you, Gillett!"

"Do either of you have any idea who might have done this?"

Gillett slowly shook his head and said, "No, Sir. I can't think of anybody who would do something like this."

The colonel looked at Jim. "How about you, Mac. Any ideas?"

Jim was struck by the sudden difference in attitude . . . suddenly he was good old Mac. "No, Sir, none of the enlisted men I know would do anything like this." Jim saw a small chance to get Halsey off his back and decided to take it, no matter how far out it sounded. "Colonel, I would like to suggest one possibility for your consideration."

"All right, who is it?"

"Well, Sir, it's common knowledge that Mr. Halsey hassles me every chance he gets ever since I turned him in for falsifying those reports. Sir, the man hates my guts, and has been trying everything he can think of to put me in a situation where he could get me into trouble. Sir, I can't help but wonder if Mr. Halsey didn't fake this whole thing. That would explain why it was a dud instead of a live grenade. Mr. Halsey didn't want his room all messed up."

The rage on Halsey's face was apparent to Colonel Appleton, who spoke before Halsey could. "Specialist, nobody in this room including yourself believes that's a real possibility." The colonel paused and looked around the room. "Okay, we don't seem to be getting anyplace tonight. Captain Wolf, you and Major Hobbs sit tight, everyone else is dismissed."

Gillett and Jim came to attention, saluted and left, followed out the door by Halsey. No one spoke as the two enlisted men picked up their caps and walked out into the night. Once out into the darkness, Jim grabbed Gillett's arm, as the two men turned and watched Halsey walk down the orderly room steps. Halsey paused at the foot of the steps, looked around, pulled out a cigarette and lit it. After taking a long drag, he turned and walked toward the officers' quarters.

Jim felt a great sense of relief. The darkness gave him a sense of confidence and security; he felt a freedom to do things that he would never do in daylight. As Halsey walked away, Jim flipped him the bird. Gillett laughed softly and said, "If I had a grenade right now I might just use it myself. Mac, you didn't really do it, did you?"

"Hell, no, I didn't. By the way, Gillett, thanks for speaking up for me in there. I appreciate it."

"Well, I just hope the CO doesn't check out our stories too closely because, if he does, he'll poke some holes in mine."

"Why do you say that?"

"Mac, I lied through my teeth in there. I didn't lay eyes on you or your bunk from the time I sent you on that mission until I woke you up with the CQ. I just didn't think you did it and I wasn't going to let Halsey hang your ass for it. For that matter, I wouldn't have let him have you even if I thought you had done it. It's just a shame Charlie doesn't shoot that son of a bitch for us."

"Yeah, the only trouble is, that's the kind who makes it all the way through without a scratch. Thanks, Gillett."

"Forget it, Mac, but I would like to know if not you, then who?"

"I don't really know, but if I were to guess, I could think of six or eight guys who wouldn't mind seeing him dead."

"Gillett, how about Green? He's from the infantry, and that's primarily an infantry problem. Plus, he was saying something about fragging this morning."

"I doubt it, but let's go ask him. He just hasn't been in the company long enough."

They walked into the hooch and Gillett tu~~rned the~~ light as Jim made his way down the aisle to ~~Green's bunk.~~ Gillett approached from the other side of the ~~bunk with the~~ flashlight on. Both men raised the mosquito net~~ting on their~~ respective sides and Gillett handed Jim the light. ~~"You take~~ this."

Jim took the light and directed it in such a way as to see Green's face without shining it directly into his eyes. Gillett shook Green's shoulder and as Green started to open his eyes, Gillett spoke. "You certainly have had a busy night haven't you, Green?"

"Hey, man, I don't know what you're talking about. I didn't do anything." Green's heart was pounding so hard that both Gillett and Jim could feel it. Green was obviously very nervous about something and both men knew it.

Gillett put his face down close to Green's and said, "You threw that frag, Green, and we both know it. Listen to me, you son of a bitch, make damn sure you stick to that story about not knowing anything and for sure don't do anything for the next month to draw attention to yourself! Above all, don't be throwing anymore, you got that? Or I'll turn you in myself, even if it is Halsey. Understand me, asshole?"

"Yes, Sergeant." Green looked at both Jim and Gillett and asked, "Does anyone else know?"

"Not yet."

"Sarge, how did you know it was me?"

"We didn't."

Jim walked back to his bunk and went quickly to sleep. It was Halsey who had the most trouble getting to sleep. He'd locked his door behind him yet was startled by every creak and sound. MacLaughlin obviously hadn't done it, yet the little creep had really turned the screws on him there in front of the old man. It was just a good thing the CO didn't believe him; he very easily could have. The thing that bothered him most was, if it wasn't MacLaughlin, then who? Certainly, he'd have to start being a little more careful, and he'd watch all the EM for even the slightest indication of guilt.

In the CO's office, Wolf and Hobbs moved two chairs in front

CO's desk. As always it was the CO who started. "Well, gentlemen, what do you think?"

Both men's facial expressions said, "You go first." Finally Hobbs spoke. "Since I just got here today, maybe I could give a more balanced opinion. I was more positively impressed with MacLaughlin than I was with Halsey. I don't think MacLaughlin did it, he was just too surprised. I have to admit, I didn't think I'd keep from laughing when he asked Halsey if he wanted to smell his armpit!"

Appleton and Wolf both started to laugh as they remembered the scene and Halsey's face. "If Halsey really does hate MacLaughlin as much as he claimed, perhaps we should take more seriously the possibility that Halsey faked it."

Wolf jumped in. "I don't think Halsey has the guts to try something like this. I do agree, though, I don't think Mac's our man, so how do we find the guilty party?"

"Without a major interrogation of all the enlisted men, the only thing we can do is to wait for the guilty party to start telling people he did it. Once the secret is out, it'll get back to the officers, then we can make our move. So, unless one of you two have something more to add, I suggest we all go back to bed."

Everyone was in agreement; flying tomorrow would be a real effort for everyone after tonight's activities.

Colonel Appleton was the only one besides Halsey who had any trouble getting back to sleep. As he lay there in his bed, he kept thinking, Of all the units in country, why his? Halsey was an ass, he knew that, nobody much cared for the man, but he hadn't realized the men hated him so much. Of course it was a dud, so whoever did it meant it only as a warning. Still, it couldn't be tolerated regardless of who, or how bad, the officer was. He wondered how often this kind of incident occurred. It was common knowledge that the infantry had a problem with fraggings—but not aviation companies. He wondered if there were any accurate statistics available. Furthermore, if he didn't have anyone to court martial, he certainly wasn't going to report it. He only had a short time left in country and unless something went wrong, he had a real good chance of being promoted to full bird before his tour was up. The last thing

Appleton needed was a bunch of TV people running around doing a story. The army sure had changed in the years he'd been in it. Who would have thought ten years ago that there would be daily TV coverage of a war? Worst yet, that a company commander would be somewhat inhibited by it in the handling of his troops? The fear that some TV reporter would want to take pictures and do a story changed a lot of things. He would just bet there would be more than one perfectly good officer's career ruined by the TV coverage of this stupid war.

It was 0500 when Gillett woke Jim and the rest of his platoon much too early as far as Jim was concerned—yet there was nothing to do about it but yawn and get up. One of the benefits of flying was not having to stand morning formation, which meant an extra fifteen or twenty minutes of sleep, making the morning a lot slower and easier. Gillett came back through just as Jim finished tying his boots.

"Mac, you ready to go eat?"

"Yeah, let's go."

Once outside the door and headed for the mess hall, Gillett spoke. "I switched your gunners today. I got to thinking about it and decided it would be best if Green flew with someone else for a while."

"That's fine with me, if you don't think it will draw attention to Green."

"Quite frankly, Mac, I really don't care if it does. In fact, I'm halfway tempted to turn him in myself. The only reason I don't is I figure he did it to get Halsey off your back." Both men displayed their meal cards, which allowed them to eat without paying, and picked up their trays. Jim put the malaria tablet on his tray alongside the usual utensils.

"Hey, Cookie, the war must be swinging back our way. That actually looks like food!, I halfway expected to get nothing but dry cereal for breakfast again."

"Gillett, we have a vast wealth of food this morning. The Air Force got a C130 full of food in here last night. Up until then, you were getting cold dry cereal for breakfast this morning."

Jim looked over the selection. There were the ever-present individual packages of cereal, eggs cooked to one's specifications, toast and creamed chipped beef on a bun at the far end.

Gillett took a couple of overeasy eggs and some toast. Jim put four toasted buns on his plate and poured a plateful of creamed beef over them, then followed Gillett to a table where no one else was seated.

"I'll swear, Mac, you'd eat shit on a shingle every day if it was available."

"Hey, man, I like it!"

"Mac, it's gross! It looks like it should be coming out the other end of somebody sick, not something being eaten."

"I don't care how it looks, it tastes good, it's filling and I like it. Besides, I don't cut on your hard boiled eggs that the cook called overeasy."

Both men laughed as they started to eat. Before anything else was said, Kenny walked to their table, put his tray down and asked, "Mind if I join you guys?"

Jim looked at Gillett, who had an "if you have to" look on his face.

"Hey, Mac, I hear you tried to frag Halsey last night."

Jim's shock was apparent. "Kenny, how did you hear that?"

"The guy who was CQ runner was telling me as we stood and pissed on Vietnam together this morning."

"I didn't do it, Kenny. I think Halsey faked it and I hope that isn't an accurate account of what he told you."

"Well, that wasn't exactly what he said; it was more like the Old Man pulled you in last night because he thought you did it."

"Well, it looks to me like Halsey set the whole thing up, so if you tell anybody else about it keep it accurate, will you! Say, Kenny, while I'm talking to you, I'd like to know where you got the water you put in the shower yesterday."

"We had to get it straight out of the river, Mac. Why?"

"Because it had half the river bottom in it. I didn't know whether I was washing the dirt off or just recycling it. It was terrible—dirt, sand, and the way it smelled, a good percentage of it had to be shit."

Kenny said, "I'm surprised there was still water in the tanks."

"Yeah, I was, too. Man, I still remember the first time I took a late night shower and the water ran out; all that grit and grime came pouring out just as I was rinsing my hair. I had to go get a steel pot full of water out of the drinking water trailer and pour it over my head to get the sand out." The three men laughed together as each remembered a similar experience. It was Gillett who finished eating first. He turned to Kenny and said, "Kenny, didn't I tell you to get rid of that monkey?"

"Gillett, I can't catch him!"

"Bullshit!"

"No bullshit, Gillett; you know how wild it is!"

"I'll tell you what, Kenny: if you cage it up, you can keep it, but otherwise it goes."

Kenny's face lit up like a child's on Christmas morning. "Hey man, that's great! Thanks, Gillett, I really appreciate it. I'll get him caged up today. Man, I promise."

"Well, you better, because I'll give it to the gooks as soon as they get back on post. If that monkey isn't caged, it'll be their dinner. You understand me, Kenny?"

"Sure, Sarge, I'll get a cage today, or maybe I'll just make one—but somehow I'll get it caged up, I promise."

Gillett looked over at Jim and saw the disapproving look on his face, but before Jim could say anything, Gillett asked if he had finished eating. If so, he would walk out with him. Kenny stayed at the table and continued eating his breakfast as Jim and Gillett picked up their trays and left. Once outside, Jim turned and said, "Gillett, why did you let Kenny keep the monkey?"

"Oh, a couple of reasons. First, he is the only one who can catch it. Second, once it's caged it won't be throwing shit on anyone and, finally, if it's caged and Kenny goes on a convoy to Saigon it's hard to say what could happen to his poor monkey while he's gone."

"How soon are the highways supposed to be open for traffic again?"

"The last I heard, in a day or so. All they have to do is put up a couple more pontoon bridges where the VC knocked out the old ones and I guess we're back in business."

"Let me guess. You've already volunteered Kenny to go on the first convoy out, right?"

"Right!"

"Gillett, he'll just love to hear that."

"Now, you don't have to be so sarcastic, Mac. Besides, Kenny has gone on several convoys in the past. I think he kind of enjoys it. He gets to spend the night in Saigon, where he can get good and drunk, plus have some broad to lay him."

"Gillett, you're all heart." Both men broke into laughter.

Once back in their hooch, Jim opened his wall locker (which was similar to everyone else's with clean uniforms hanging in no particular order), to get his toothbrush, paste and shaving gear. One of the few nice things about a true combat area was that enlisted men seldom had to stand inspection of their personal area. As a result, most all wall and foot lockers were very unmilitarily organized, if organized at all. Jim had all his underwear in his foot locker, where it was out of the way. Like most men in his company, he long ago had quit wearing underwear. It only retained more heat and held the sweat against his body, causing crotch itch. Also, it wasn't at all uncommon to get back underwear from the cleaners which looked like it had been cleaned in the Saigon River. Whenever one can tell that olive drab underwear isn't clean, it really isn't clean. Jim kept his socks and spare footwear on the floor of his wall locker, he hung up his dress uniforms and clean fatigues and, on the top shelf, he kept his toiletries and hats. On the inside of the door he had taped only two pictures. One was his family, the other his home. He didn't like to hang up nude pictures, as it only made him want what wasn't available.

Jim headed straight for his ship as the crews were all beginning to gather, including a few of the officers flying peter pilot, so he stowed his gear and pulled out the log book. Once satisfied that all the paperwork was in order, he got out his flashlight and started pulling his preflight. The last thing he checked was the rotor head and he couldn't believe there were no holes. It was almost as though a blanket had been thrown over them which nothing could penetrate. As was often the case, he simply stood there on top of the helicopter looking out over the area. From the direction of the company area, Jim could see the trucks bringing the officers out towards the flight line; their preflight briefing was obviously over. With the pilots on their way, Jim climbed down off the chopper's roof as Kenny drove up in the platoon's quarter ton jeep and dropped off the door gunners and their guns. Green and Sp-4 Wright climbed out, but it was Wright who carried his guns over to Jim's ship, where he could set them down, along with his gear, on the chopper's cargo floor. Green picked up his guns from the revetments corner and left.

Sp-4 Wright wasn't that much different from the rest of the guys in Jim's company, standing 5'10" and thin as a skeleton, with brown hair and eyes, and a nose as big as Jimmy Durante's. His nickname, as a result, was The Beak. With a happy-go-lucky personality and almost always in good spirits, it was hard not to like him.

Once the pilots arrived, the rotor blades were untied and the aircraft started. They didn't go far, however; only to the runway where troops were loaded, then into the air, where they formed a trail-right formation and began circling Tay Ninh while one other company landed and put on troops. Once everyone was loaded, Blackhawk Lead turned and headed north to Loc Ninh. It was Mr. Walker who broke the silence. "Mac, you awake back there?"

"Yes, Sir, bright eyed and bushy tailed."

"Yeah, I'll bet! How much sleep did you get last night?"

"Oh, I don't know, about an hour or two."

"You know where we're headed?"

"No, Sir! Where?"

"Loc Ninh! Does that send shivers up your back?"

"Yes, Sir, it does! I take it you heard about last night?"

"Yeah, Mr. Hill was telling everyone about it at breakfast. Sounded like you guys had quite a ride."

The sarcasm was obvious as Jim replied, "Hey, man, that's what we're paid extra for! Why do we have to go back this morning?"

"We're going to be the lead company on a three company insertion into Loc Ninh. We're supposed to land just seconds after daybreak and the two companies behind us will follow us in and, hopefully, out on ten second intervals. Which means we're not going to have time to do anything. If we can't find a place to land, we'll have to hover and let the troops jump."

"Mr. Walker, I've never heard of landing on a ten second interval before."

"Well, don't feel bad, the only time I've heard of it was in flight school, and they told us then not to sneeze or someone would land on top of us. The whole idea is to put in as many troops as possible, with as much cover fire as possible, in as short a time as possible.

"Looks like the lights of our third company forming up on our right. If you guys aren't strapped in, you'd better get ready, because I put us only three minutes out of Loc Ninh."

Jim checked his seatbelt and pulled the visor down on his helmet. He was beginning to see daylight, and could just make out trees below.

"Flight, this is Lead. We're on final approach to the runway with touchdown in ninety seconds, please advise door gunners not to hit the Special Forces camp, everything else is a free fire zone. Also, be advised the Air Force hasn't received any fire from the swimming pool for about an hour now, but we'll still brake right on takeoff as planned to stay away from it. Here we go."

It was now just past daybreak and everyone could see the bodies and parts of bodies all over the ground below. All door guns were now firing and Jim concentrated his fire on the distant tree line which had been shredded by bombs, artillery and small-arms fire. He could make out the bodies of dead NVA nailed to the rubber trees by the darts from the beehives. There were so many bodies on the runway that landing was impossible, so the troops quickly jumped out and started to throw bodies aside to allow the flight on its way in to land. As the Blackhawks turned right and away from Loc Ninh, Jim could see the Special Forces camp with bodies of dead NVA stacked two and three deep on the wire surrounding Loc Ninh.

"Blackhawk Lead, this is Loc Ninh Control. Do you copy? Over."

"Roger, Loc Ninh, we copy. Over."

"Roger, Blackhawk. Sir, my commanding officer wishes me to convey the following message to the men from your company who brought in the beehives last night. We would like to extend our thanks and appreciation to the men of that aircraft, for without their courage we wouldn't have received the bee-hives, and without the beehives we could never have held. Thank you, from all of us, Loc Ninh, out."

Mr. Walker came over the radio. "Mac, did you hear that?"

"Yes, Sir!"

"Hey, you're a real hero!"

"Yeah, and they'll probably give Mr. Hill a DFC for it."

"Yeah, I know it's unfair. You and Green will probably get V-devices on an air medal for it."

"Yeah, that and ten cents and I can buy a cup of coffee. We going to work up here all day, Sir?"

"No, we're supposed to go back to Tay Ninh, refuel, and go someplace else."

The trip back was quiet except for when Lead came over the radio to say that the troops hadn't made any contact other than rear ground action, and that they'd gotten to the swimming pool and found it empty. Not so much as a spent shell had been left by the NVA.

Once at Tay Ninh, Jim quickly removed his helmet and started to pump on fuel and was surprised when he heard the engine start to wind down and die.

"Hey, Mac, come on, we're supposed to have a formation at the CO's ship."

Jim walked around the nose of the ship. "Wright, did you say formation?"

"Yeah, our new XO wants a formation. Mac, have you met this guy yet?"

"Yeah, I think I had the pleasure last night. Wright, as long as I've been here, I haven't stood formation on the flight line. I don't even know where to fall in."

"Well, I've got a feeling you'll find out."

"Why does he want a formation?"

"All I know is Lead came over the radio and said to have all crews meet at the CO's ship for a formation."

"Okay, let's go."

There was quite a crowd gathering at the CO's ship when Jim and Wright arrived. Officers and enlisted men were mingling with each other grumbling about having to stand formation. Even Mr. Hill in his Class A uniform* was there, holding his records and departure orders. As Jim snapped to attention and saluted, Colonel Appleton and Major Hobbs walked around the revetment unnoticed by Jim or Mr. Hill. It was the big smile on Jim's face that caused Mr. Hill to return the salute and extend his hand. Jim shook the officer's hand and said, "Sir, I just want you to know I'm glad we made it last night and I was wrong, plus, I can't think of anyone other than Mr. Walker I'd rather have had driving than you."

"Mac, you're a hell of a soldier and one of several enlisted men I can honestly say I really like and respect. Just between you and me, I can't think of any crew chief I'd rather have had in the back than you."

"Thank you very much, Sir. That's very kind of you to say."

"I mean it, Mac, I truly hope you make it back alive and all in one piece."

"I will, Sir."

"Not if you keep flying all those night missions you won't. Besides, that's what every GI who ever stepped foot in country said."

The two men shook hands again as Jim said, "It looks like they're starting to fall into formation, so I'd better go. Good luck, Sir!"

"Good luck, Mac. Stay alive!" As Jim turned to walk away, he saw Major Hobbs and Colonel Appleton standing within hearing distance. He looked both of them in the eye, saluted, and continued on his way to where Gillett was trying to assemble a formation.

Major Hobbs looked at Colonel Appleton as Jim walked toward his platoon. "Colonel, when I get my own ship, I want that man as my crew chief."

"MacLaughlin?"

"Yep."

"Why, for heavens' sake do you want him? He's constantly on the edge of trouble."

"Wolf says he's one of the best crew chiefs in the company. I've got a suspicion that Halsey is most of the problem, and if

* Class A uniform—the light, short-sleeved khaki dress uniform.

you'd transfer him, you'd probably find that out. To answer your question, I guess there are several reasons. First, he impressed me last night. He's obviously smart and is not afraid of danger or he wouldn't be flying single ship night missions. Also, he's got a sense of humor. I woke up this morning laughing at him asking Halsey if he wanted to smell his armpit. The man's got brass, but still knows his place and how to conduct himself in a military manner. The conversation we just overheard with that warrant officer tells me that. So far, I like everything I've seen from him. He's the kind of GI I want to surround myself with. I would have to earn his respect, but once I've earned it, he'd follow me to Hell and back without a moment's hesitation or complaint."

"I can tell you right now it's not going to be easy for you to get him. Walker won't want to give him up and he won't want to quit Walker."

"Oh, that's no problem, just send Mr. Walker on R&R. Put MacLaughlin on my ship as crew chief—temporarily, of course."

"Of course!"

"By the time Walker gets back, MacLaughlin will have seen all the advantages of being the XO's chief. He'll ask to stay with me."

"If he's all you think he is, when Mr. Walker gets back, he'll go back to him just out of friendship."

"In that case, Colonel, I'll transfer Walker to guns and if MacLaughlin decides to go to the guns, I'll transfer Walker to another company."

"Of course you know if MacLaughlin finds out you're behind Walker being shipped out, you'll never get his respect."

"True, very true."

"One final thought: Major, you don't think there is any chance of being fragged, do you?"

"None. He didn't do that job last night anymore than I did."

Major Hobbs and Colonel Appleton moved out in front of the formation as the company first sergeant called the formation to "ten hut." The flight company slowly came to attention, after which the first sergeant continued, "Men, your company commander wishes to address you."

The first sergeant stepped aside as the CO stepped forward. "Men, I've called you together this morning to introduce you to your new XO. He is a former infantry platoon leader. While serving his first tour of duty in Vietnam, Third Corps Area, he received several citations for valor including the Silver Star. Men, I'm very pleased to introduce the man who will probably be taking my place in a few months, Major Hobbs."

As the colonel stepped back, Major Hobbs stepped forward. He spoke with a strong, deep and husky voice. "Men, I want to tell you how happy I am to be here as part of such an outstanding company."

Jim could hear faintly an unknown voice behind him say, "If he's so happy to be here, he can take my place."

"The record you men have compiled as an all-combat assault company is truly outstanding. You pilots have never refused to go anyplace you're sent. There isn't an outfit in the area that doesn't know that if the Blackhawks are on their way they'll get there. No matter how much or what kind of enemy fire tries to stop you, you get through.

"However, you men are a lot like a tooth that is beginning to show some decay. You need some minor work so you can continue to function in the high tradition you have come to accept as a standard. Colonel Appleton and I have discussed it, and it is the colonel's desire that I make every effort to make this company look as good as it really is.

"Men, together we're going to clean out the bacteria that is causing our tooth to begin to decay; let's start with this sloppy formation." The major paused, then shouted, "Dress right dress!"*

Jim again heard the unknown voice behind him say, "Dress right dress? I haven't done this since basic training. What is with this guy?"

After completion of the dress right dress, the major spoke. "Men, that's much better. Now, we're going to paint the choppers, the hooches and anything else that needs it. We're going to clean up the company area and these revetments where our

* Dress right dress—Means of obtaining proper spacing in a group formation.

hueys are parked; we're going to restack every sandbag pile in the company area and do it in such a way that it will look like you have used a plum line. We're going to fill in all these rocket and mortar holes, so that this place doesn't look like a teenager with an extreme case of acne. We're going to put those choppers back in mint condition. Those without doors will have their doors put back on, all bullet holes will be patched and painted OD.

"I started to count yesterday how many choppers we have with more than one greenish yellow bullet patch on it, and finally decided that most all of them do. Those choppers without the soundproofing or part of it will have it reinstalled. I have already talked to the supply sergeant and he has assured me there isn't any problem getting us paste wax and rags to wash and wax the helicopters and their blades. Some of you may not know that waxing blades and ships will give ten percent more lift.

"I've noticed that several of you men need haircuts. It's always been my opinion that one can tell a great deal about a soldier by his personal appearance. Therefore, I want you men to look as sharp as you are. I've found a man in maintenance who has assured me that he gives excellent haircuts. So I've instructed him to set up a barber shop each day for an hour after the flight has landed. That way, there will be no problem keeping both officers' and enlisted men's hair properly clipped. There isn't too much we can do about the condition our uniforms are in when returned from the laundry. However, each man will be expected to have enough uniforms, so he can put on a clean one each morning.

"Well, men, that gives you a basic understanding of how I will be changing a few things, plus some of the things I'll be expecting from you." The major stood there for a moment looking as though he was as proud as he could possibly be, then turned to the first sergeant and said, "Dismiss the men, First Sergeant."

The first sergeant stepped forward, came to attention and since the troops were still at attention he simply shouted, "Officers, platoon, dismissed! Enlisted men, fall in for police call of the flight line."

Almost in unison a number of voices moaned with, "Police call! You can't be serious." Someone else said, "I've never done a police call of the flight line as long as I've been here." Still another voice was heard. "This guy has to go, fellows!"

Jim and Athia were beside each other as the troops spread out at the end of the flight line, so it was only natural that Hunter found his way over to their location. Just as Gillett started the slow movement of walking vacuum cleaners through the flight line, Hunter started the conversation. "Well, how do you two like our new XO?"

"I can't speak for Mac, but I think he sucks the green wienie."

Jim laughed and said, "He sucks it? My man, the green wienie has just taken up permanent residence at the Blackhawks!" Very sarcastically Jim continued, "I really loved how he kept saying 'we' knowing full well how 'we' are going to do things. He's going to give the orders and all of us underworked EM are going to do it!"

Hunter jumped in. "The part I liked was how he started out telling us how great we are and ended up telling us we stink."

"Yeah," said Athia. "The only trouble is the man isn't any flash in the pan. This guy just got here and obviously plans on taking Appleton's place when he rotates home."

"You know," added Hunter, "he and Halsey should get along just ducky."

Jim added, "Oh, isn't that just a wonderful thought. Halsey was bad enough but at least he didn't have any real power or authority. All he could do was chickenshit stuff compared to this joker. You know, fellows, I think I'll put in for emergency R&R. By the time I get back, he'll have most of this worked out of his system."

"You can't, Mac. They're not letting any flight crewmen or maintenance personnel go on R&R until we get some new people in. I'll tell you what, I don't know about you and Hunter, but I can't see myself out there washing and waxing those stupid helicopters. I mean, give us a break, we fly every day, usually until late at night, and this guy wants us to wash and wax those ships. I mean, I can just see all of us out there between midnight and 0200 washing and waxing our little hearts out.

Oh, well, now we know why Gillett told us to put our cargo doors back on last night. What a pain in the ass! Every time we put fuel in, we'll first have to unhook the ammo belt and shut the door.''

"Hey, Athia, not just when you put on fuel but whenever you want in the engine compartment, or the storage area, anytime you get tools, rags, C-rations, or anything out of the storage compartment, you'll have to go through that same procedure.''

"Yeah, Mac, you're right. I'll tell you what I think I'll do. The first LZ we land in after I put those stupid doors back on, my chopper's going to loose its right cargo door. I'll just put it back on so that all I have to do is unhook the safety pin, slide the door forward a little and give it a good, big kick! Bingo, Chuck just got a new roof for his shack, courtesy of Major Hobbs.''

Jim and Hunter looked at each other and wondered if that wasn't a better plan than the one both of them had already put into play.

The now jagged row of men reached the end of the flight line and started to mill around. Gillett, seeing that the police call had reached its destination, ordered the troops to fall out to their respective helicopters.

"Well, Mac, how many tons did you pick up?''

"Wright, I picked up the same thing the little boy shot at, nothing.''

"Mac, you suppose that guy's so damn dumb he doesn't know the choppers blow everything away that isn't tied down or weighs at least fifty pounds?''

"It sure looks like it. It also looks like whatever little esprit de corps there is left in this outfit will be lost if he keeps this kind of chickenshit stuff up.''

Every man on police call had developed an instant dislike for Major Hobbs. Somehow the idea of policing the flight line didn't make much sense, especially when they all knew sometime today they would be caught up in what was now being called The Tet Offensive. Jim and Wright walked around the rear corner of the L-shaped revetment and up along the open side. There, in the cargo door, sat Mr. Walker just looking out at nothing in particular. "Mac, you okay? You look terrible."

"Mr. Walker, I feel like I'm on the verge of total exhaustion! I've had very little sleep the last few nights, I've gone through hell the last couple of days, and last night I thought sure I'd get killed at Loc Ninh. Then, I have to get up in the middle of the night because some asshole was out playing games with Halsey."

Wright interrupted, "Mac, didn't you really throw that frag?"

With total exasperation Jim looked at Wright. "Hell, no, I didn't." Turning back towards Mr. Walker he continued, "Then I have to go for this silly-ass walk this morning. I'll tell you what, to me, that was the height of insults, to make us go police the flight line. He has to know that anything on the flight line gets blown away by our props during take off. It's almost like he feels he has to show us that he has the power and authority to make us do anything he wants. It was just his way of saying, 'Fellows, get used to the changes I'm going to make, whether you like them or not, they're here to stay and there isn't a damn thing you can do about it!' He might just as well have said in that speech of his during formation, 'Bend over, fellows, cause here it comes and there isn't anything you can do about it!'"

"Come on, Mac, it's not all that bad. In a couple of weeks he'll have it worked out of his system."

Walker and Jim looked each other in the eye, neither man smiled. After a few seconds, Jim turned to see Mr. Mace walk up with his helmet in hand. Mr. Mace, a small man, stood only 5'2", with small bones, small fingers and feet. His frail one hundred ten pounds made something of a comic appearance. "Hi, Mac. Hey, I hear you scared the hell out of Halsey last night."

"Mr. Mace, I didn't do that, and if I had a Bible on me, I'd swear to it. Furthermore, if you ask me, I think Halsey did it himself."

With disbelief, Mr. Walker said, "Come on, Mac, Halsey may be an asshole but he isn't stupid; besides, he made Euclid and Lucas mad as hell at him last night."

Jim looked questioningly at Mr. Walker. "How did he do that?"

"You really haven't heard, have you?"

"No!"

"Well, I'm not sure I've got this story straight. But as close as I can figure it, Halsey caused each to get an Article 15 for two hundred dollars."

"How?"

"Well, Lucas and Euclid had a couple of the nurses in their room fucking their eyes out when Halsey started yelling, 'Grenade.' " All four men started laughing as Mr. Walker continued his story. "The nurses decided they wouldn't spend the night after all. Of course, you always have to pay before you play, so they just packed up and left with their one hundred dollars each. Only trouble was, Captain Wolf walked up as they walked out the door. Now, Captain Wolf has this thing about whores. He must have read those four the riot act. Anyway, he kicked the nurses out of the company area and hit Lucas and Euclid each with a two hundred dollar Article 15."

The laughter from the four flight crewmen made them all feel better. Jim and Mace were seated on the chopper floor laughing so hard they were holding on to each other. Wright had climbed up in his seat and was laughing also as Walker continued, "Needless to say both Lucas and Euclid are a tad bit upset with Halsey right now. Not only did they not get laid, but what started out costing them one hundred dollars each ended up being three hundred dollars each and no ass to brag about!"

Jim stopped laughing. "Mr. Walker, isn't one hundred dollars a little steep?"

"I'd say so personally, but they seem to have a steady business."

Mr. Mace spoke up. "Yeah, you talk about setting on a gold mine, there's more than one broad who'll come out of Nam a millionaire. You know, Walker, that blond one's a good-looking whore."

"You're telling me. She's almost worth a hundred dollars, but the other one she buddies around with isn't much."

"For a couple of guys who've never used their services, you two sure know a lot about 'em."

Mr. Walker and Mr. Mace looked at each other and started to snicker. Mr. Mace responded, "Well . . . , Mac, you have to understand, our officers' club is THE PLACE to hang out. The fact that we're so close to the hospital, and we have more officers than any other company on post, makes ours the ideal place to drum up business. As a result, that's where a lot of the nurses hang out, which makes it impossible for Mr. Walker and me not to know what's going on."

"Sir, how many nurses are whores?"

"Oh, really not many, most of them are nice girls. But like any large group of people, they run the whole gamut. Some won't put out for anybody or anything, others will if you work at it hard and long enough. Then there's the three or four pros who sell it and the price starts at one hundred dollars and goes down the longer it's been since payday."

Jim spoke. "Well, Sir, I guess that's one of the nice things about being an officer instead of an enlisted man, you get the opportunity to waste your money on some sorry broad's ass."

Mr. Mace just looked at Jim, not sure if he was being sarcastic. It was Walker who spoke next. "Mac, go untie it. I see Lead starting to crank."

"Yes, Sir." Jim untied the main rotor blade from its secured position as the other three climbed into their respective seats. Jim put the tie down rope in the ship's storage compartment, put on his chicken plate and helmet, plugged in his headset and climbed into his seat behind the ever present M60. Mr. Walker started to crank the engine over as soon as Jim untied the blades and gave him the thumbs-up sign. By the time Jim was in his seat, the aircraft was running and both Mac and Wright had checked in with Mr. Walker, just as Jim was ready to do. "I'm in, Sir, and ready to go."

"Okay, Mac." Pushing his mike switch down to broadcast outside the ship, Mr. Walker spoke again. "Lead, this is Chalk Five. We're up."

"Roger, Chalk Five."

To Hunt
and to Be Hunted

*"Because he loves me," says the Lord, "I will
rescue him; I will protect him, for he
acknowledges my name."* PSALMS 91:14 NIV

Jim listened as each ship's AC checked in with Lead and received the same response. In less than a minute all ten AC's
had checked in and Lead came back over the radio, "Flight,
this is Lead. Everyone's up, so I'm not pulling pitch and on my
way." One after another, the Hueys moved down the flight line
until all ten were airborne. Once in the air each AC maneu-
vered his ship into its flight spot, and it wasn't long until the
Blackhawks were headed south in a V formation.

"Lead, this is Trail, we're all up and in formation."

"Roger, Trail." It was an unwritten rule that until this message was given there was to be no unnecessary conversation.

"Mr. Walker, where are we working today?"

"We're going down to Saigon to pick up troops, then put
them in the Michelin rubber plantation just outside of Ben
Sue."

"Oh, great, another day of fun and games inside the heart of
The Iron Triangle."

"Does that bother you, Mac?"

"Naw, if we got to be here, I figure we might as well be
where the action is. I don't understand, though, why we have
to go to Saigon to get troops and then all the way back to Ben
Sue."

"Intelligence says the offensive is over in Saigon and the

169

NVA and their VC buddies are pulling out, so we're taking the troops who have been defending Saigon out and putting them in as a blocking force."

Jim figured the flight down to Saigon would take about forty-five minutes to an hour, depending on artillery. He pulled his seatbelt up good and tight, pulled the dark visor down on his helmet so Walker couldn't see his eyes, and then leaned back to get some sleep. It took only a matter of minutes for him to drop off; this kind of flight was always boring and Jim had learned, shortly after starting to fly, the value of a quick nap. One of the gifts he knowingly possessed was his ability to fall asleep quickly anywhere and through most anything.

Mr. Walker, aware of all the night missions Jim flew, let him sleep. Unlike the gunner and peter pilot, who could not easily look at Jim, Walker had only to glance over his right shoulder. It wasn't uncommon for Walker to glance back at Jim during long flights and see him cinched up tight with his dark visor down. It was a dead giveaway because the only time Jim pulled his visor down was on their way into an LZ, or when he didn't want anyone to see him sleeping. However, it was a simple matter for Walker to wake Jim without anyone else on the ship knowing he had been asleep or that Walker had known it. It seemed Jim's ears were tuned to Walker's voice so he could simply start talking, but slightly louder than usual.

The flight to Saigon was uneventful with no radio chatter, until Lead told the flight to change into a trail formation as they would be landing shortly at the fuel dump.

It was the sound of Mr. Walker's voice that woke Jim up.

"Mr. Mace! Would you like to drive for the rest of the way into Saigon?"

"Sure, but you don't have to yell. I've got it."

"Sorry, Mace, I was thinking about something else." Walker glanced back over his right shoulder and saw MacLaughlin had raised his visor. The next time Walker looked back, Jim had removed his seatbelt and put on his monkey harness.

Mr. Walker had flown in and out of this area of Saigon several times. He was struck by all the destruction that had taken place since Tet. Engineers were busy with the earth-moving equipment making new perimeter fortifications. They were on short final approach now, and Walker could see troops waiting off to the side. It looked to him like there were enough troops there for four or five lifts. At that rate, this would be an all day affair.

Once on the ground Jim unhooked his monkey harness tail and stepped out. First, he threw the tail over his shoulder then opened the fuel cap, letting it dangle on its chain. Next he dragged the fuel hose to his ship and started pumping fuel. Meanwhile, the pilots kept their ships running at idle speed while fuel was being added and the grunts started to load. Jim looked up and saw a staff sergeant seated there watching him. Each man looked the other in the eye and knew the other had been there and come back.

"Hi, Sarge."

"Hi, how are you?"

"A little tired but other than that, okay."

"You guys been flying a lot lately?"

"All day and half the night."

"Yeah, we've been busy, too. Until yesterday, then suddenly . . . nothing, just like Charlie packed up and left. You know where we're going?"

"Not exactly! You?"

"Yeah, we're on our way up to Ben Sue. We're to set up a blocking force in the Michelin plantation to keep what's left of an NVA battalion licking its wounds up there from escaping."

"You don't look too happy about going."

"Hey, man, I'm not. I just hope we don't find a thing when we get there."

"You will. We haven't flown in there yet and not caught hell."

When the fuel tank was full, Jim replaced the hose and cap. He gave Walker, who was looking back at him, a thumbs-up sign as he climbed in. Walker reported to Lead that they were up, and after all the flight had checked in, Lead called Six in the C and C ship. In only seconds the engines began to pick up RPM, and they were on their way.

No one said much during the flight to Ben Sue. It sometimes amazed Jim that he could sit for long periods of time with a totally blank mind.

"Flight, this is Lead. Our destination has been switched to Highway 14 just south of Rach Bap. The LZ has been prepped with artillery and we'll have gunship escort all the way in. Let's form a staggered right formation at this time. We'll be landing on the road and in the brush off to the right. Make sure your door gunners understand there are NO friendlies on the ground or in the area at this time. Six advised that when we lift off from the LZ, we'll have to fly straight ahead for a ways due to the height of the rubber trees. Once up, we'll be banking hard left and over the Mekong River. If anyone goes down, try to get it across the river first. There are mostly rice paddies over there where we can make a pickup. Over here you're in trouble. Lead, out."

They were now on short final approach. Jim saw the gunships fly by firing their rockets and mini guns. This was the signal for all the doorguns to open fire, and they did. All twenty machine guns were spitting lead into the rapidly approaching LZ. Trees lined both sides of the dirt, one-lane road, yet there was plenty of room for the flight to land. Jim's chopper hadn't quite touched down when the grunts started jumping out. Small arms fire was coming from the trees to their right as their flight lifted and started to fly out.

Jim heard their engine make a funny sound but continued to fire his M60 as they departed. In only seconds, he could tell by the engine noise they had taken a round through the engine intake. It probably had been sucked on through the engine, taking some of the turbine blades out the other end with it.

"Lead, this is Chalk Five, we're rapidly losing engine power. May Day, May Day, we're going down in the trees, no power!"

"Chalk Five, this is Lead, I read you. Trail, do you see Chalk Five? Over?"

"Roger, Lead, they're down in some trees. There's no way we can put a ship in to pick them up where they are."

"Lead, this is Chalk Five. We're down, nobody's hurt and I didn't hit anything larger than some large twigs with my rotor blades."

Once on the ground, Jim and Wright went quickly to work, taking off their M60's and opening the pilots' doors. Mace climbed out at once and started collecting ammo for the M60's.

"Chalk Five, this is Blackhawk Six. I have you spotted. Do you read me? Over."

"Roger, Six. Over."

"Chalk Five, you're in trouble. The ground troops have encountered heavy resistance from the area between you and them. Your best chance for a pickup is to continue north along the river bank for about a half mile. There are some rice paddies up there where we can put in a chopper."

"Six, be advised we have a scrambler* on board."

"Why the hell!? Never mind! Look, under no condition is that unit to be left. Understood? Over."

"Understood, Six. It's on board because of all the night missions my crew chief flies. Walker out."

Walker looked around and saw Jim grab his M16 and pistol belt.

"Mac, get the scrambler unit out, we have to take it with us."

"What the hell for?"

"Don't give me any mouth, MacLaughlin, just get the damn thing out. Six doesn't want it left under any circumstances."

"Yes, Sir! Mr. Mace, get me my tool box out of the storage compartment, please, while I start unhooking the quick disconnects."

Jim turned and headed for the ship's nose. Mace, who was already standing beside the storage compartment door, turned and pushed the two snap buttons that unhooked the latches. He reached in, grabbed Jim's tool box and turned to leave as Wright walked around the tail section carrying his M60, and his M16 slung over his shoulder.

Jim never saw it, but knew instantly to hit the ground when he heard the AK47 open fire. Walker, who had climbed out his door, dropped beside Jim. Both men looked back at Wright when they heard his M60 open up. Jim's eyes went from the still standing and firing Wright to Mr. Mace, who was lying face down on the ground.

"Mac! I got the three VC but Mr. Mace is hit!"

* Scrambler—Radio unit that garbles all radio transmissions on that wave length. Makes it impossible to understand unless the receiver also has a scrambler.

Jim started to move in a crouched position towards Wright. He could see the three dead VC not more than fifty feet away. Looking down at Mace, he recognized the grotesque signs of a sucking chest wound.

"Wright, cover us! Mr. Walker, pick Mace up and get him out of here! I'll get some ammo and be right with you."

Walker picked Mace up in a fireman's carry and headed in the opposite direction from the dead VC. Wright grabbed as much M60 ammo as he could quickly loop over his shoulder and followed Walker into the brush and trees. Jim strapped on his pistol belt, reached up and grabbed one of the two first aid kits above the cargo door, and, picking up the pilot's map laying in Mace's seat, he jumped out the door and started to run. Then he remembered the fragmentation grenades he had hidden in his storage compartment. He turned and ran back to the ship. The storage compartment door was still open. He reached in, removing the rags covering the frags and pulled out all four, taking only seconds. He put the frags in his jungle fatigue pockets and picked up two smoke grenades, one violet and one yellow, from under his seat. Once again, he started to leave as he heard Wright's M60 open up. This time he dropped to one knee, laid down his M16, pulled out a fragmentation grenade, jerked the pin and threw it at his chopper. Grabbing the M16, he ran like hell. Then, tripping over a branch, he fell just a few feet from Mr. Walker.

The first explosion went off as he was falling, followed almost immediately by the secondary explosion of his Huey. Jim picked himself up and looked back at the fireball that was once his ship. Stepping over a fallen tree, he joined Walker and Mace. Wright had set up his M60 on that same tree log and was watching the VC moving on the far side of his field of fire. The burning Huey started erupting with smaller secondary explosions, as the ammo left on board became hot enough to blow.

Jim knelt beside Mac and unzipped the small, green first aid kit. Walker had his left hand over the entrance hole in Mace's chest and his right hand over the exit hole. Blood was flowing out both holes and had covered Walker's hands and back from carrying Mace. The bubbling and gurgling that came from Mace's mouth told Jim that he was having extreme trouble breathing, as he knew he would. Jim's switch blade cut Mace's shirt open and, as best he could, Jim wiped the entrance hole dry of blood. Walker dried his hands on Mace's clothes and held the plastic envelope from the bandage in place as Jim tried to tape it down. The continual flow of blood made it difficult at best. The wheezing from the exit wound in Mace's back was expelling blood and body fluids with each choking breath he tried to take. Walker rolled Mace over onto his chest, exposing the full extent of Mace's wound. Unlike the small thumb sized entrance hole, the jagged exit hole was not quite the size of a hard ball. Jim cut what was left of Mace's shirt off and tried to wipe a dry area where tape could be applied. There was flesh, meat and even a piece of bone sticking out of Mace's body. Jim picked the bone chips out so they wouldn't rupture the plastic that Mr. Walker then placed over the hole. Once the plastic was in place, the almost impossible breathing of Mace became much more normal, as air now could enter the lungs only through the mouth. Jim dried the back area with Mace's clothes and taped the plastic down as Walker applied the cloth bandage. It was at this point the first word was spoken by either man.

"Mac, Six said we should go to the river and walk north to some rice paddies for a pickup."

"Sir, that's the direction the VC came from."

"Yeah, I know. They're also between us and the ground troops we put in."

"Oh, great! Does that radio you're wearing around your neck work?"

"I don't know yet."

Walker started to open the radio up as Jim reached in his pocket. He pulled out a violet smoke grenade and handed it to Walker along with one of his three remaining frags, and the map. Walker put each in a different pocket as Wright's M60 started to bark once again.

"Mac, I thought you weren't supposed to carry any frags in the ship."

"We're not, but I'm glad I didn't get around to taking them out yet!"

"Me too!"

Wright had quit firing and joined them.

"Mac, where's the other M60?"

"I left it on the ship! I figured we couldn't carry two M60's, Mr. Mace and ammo."

"You're right, come on. We have to get out of here, they're trying to flank us."

Jim picked up his M16 and put Mace in a fireman's carry. Walker took Wright's M16 and several belts of ammo, and followed Jim. Wright, with the M60, brought up the rear walking in a circle as he followed Walker. Jim could hear Walker speak into his radio as they moved deeper into the heart of the Iron Triangle.

"Six, this is Walker, come in, Six! Six, this is Walker, over! Six, please come in! SIX! Anybody! Please, does anybody hear me, over."

Silence. Their hearts sank as they realized their sole means of communication didn't work. It was Walker who verbalized what they all thought. "This damn thing doesn't work."

"Mr. Walker, just keep trying. It only has a fifteen kilometer range. The flight's probably getting more troops and C&C ship could have gone back for fuel."

"You're right, Mac. At least let's hope that's what happened."

"Mr. Walker, is Mr. Mace going to make it?"

"Wright, if we can get him to a doctor in time he should be okay."

"He has blood coming out of his mouth and looks like a ghost."

"He's probably in shock. We just can't stop now and treat him for it."

Walker raised the radio to his lips to try once again. "Walker to Blackhawk Six. Over!"

The radio cracked and to everyone's relief, Colonel Appleton's voice was heard. "Mr. Walker, this is Blackhawk Six. Your situation down there has changed."

Wright spoke. "He's telling us!" Walker motioned Wright to be quiet.

"I've been in touch with the gunships, they spotted VC along the river bank and have sunk one sampan. There's a road that you should intersect about six kilometers ahead if you follow a heading of seventy-five degrees. We can make pickup there. Over."

"Six, be advised Mr. Mace took a chest wound. Over."

"Where's Mr. Mace now? Over."

"We're carrying him. Over."

"There's no way we can get him out until you reach that road. Did you bring the scrambler with you? Over."

"Negative, Six. We didn't have time. It was on the ship when my crew chief blew the chopper. Over."

There was a short silence before Six's voice broke through the radio again. "What did you bring out? Over."

"I got my map and pistol, Mace's pistol, one M60, two M16's and ammo. Over."

"Walker, we'll try to maintain one gunship in the area with orders to monitor this frequency and give whatever support possible. If you need ammo, we can try to drop it through the trees, otherwise, you're on your own till you get to that road. The flight's on short final with its second lift into the LZ. We'll put the next lift in on the road you're headed for. They'll sweep your direction, so you should be able to link up. One more thing, are you being pursued? Over."

"Affirmative. Over."

"By how large a force and how close? Over."

"Unknown to both questions, Sir. Over."

"Good luck, Walker, Six out."

The group had already stopped moving and Jim, as gently as possible, laid the unconscious Mr. Mace down. Jim's face was scratched from the tree branches. Sweat was dripping into his eyes, and the salty wetness burned as it came in contact with his scratches. Mace didn't weigh much, for which Jim was thankful, yet he had quickly tired under the burden Mace presented. Walker and Wright sat down facing Jim, who spoke first.

"Mr. Walker, do you really think they're following us?"

"Wouldn't you be, if in their position?"

"Yeah."

"Look, we can't stay here very long—how much ammo have we got?"

Wright responded first. "I've got six magazines full for my M16 and, I suppose, between you and me we have about three hundred rounds for the M60."

"Sir, I've got eight magazines in my pistol belt plus these three I always carry taped together. And I've got two more frags."

"Okay, that's pretty good, three frags, two smokes and seventeen magazines for the M16's. At twenty rounds each we should be okay."

"Sir, you only put nineteen rounds in each or it'll jam."

"Okay, Mac, that's not important right now. Look, let's get going. I'll carry Mace for a while. One of you take Mace's pistol."

"You can have it, Wright, I don't want it!"

"Okay, I'll take it." Wright took the shoulder harness containing the snubnose 38 off Mace and looked up at Mr. Walker.

"Sir, I think he's dead."

Walker kneeled down and felt for the carotid artery. Finding no pulse, he turned Mace's face so he could look at his still open eyes. "You're right."

Jim looked at his watch for the first time since being shot down, ten after ten. Walker took one of Mace's dogtags, positioned the chipped part between two opposing teeth and pushed his mouth shut, wedging the dogtags in place. Wright spoke as Mr. Walker started to pick up the lifeless body.

"Mr. Walker, wait a minute will you? I've got to take this chicken plate off."

Walker waited while Wright flipped it over his head, then he pulled up his shirt, exposing his black and blue and obviously sore ribs. Most of Wright's left side was bruised and starting to swell. Walker and Jim were amazed.

"Man, am I sore, but I sure am thankful for that chicken plate." Jim pulled the fiber glass plate from its cloth wrapping. There in the left center of the plate was an AK round.

"Wright, when did you get hit?"

"I got it the same time Mr. Mace did; fortunately, I hadn't gotten around to taking my chicken plate off yet." Jim found himself wishing he still had his on. "It knocked me back against the tail boom and I started firing the M60 I had."

Suddenly, Walker grabbed Wright's arm and put his index finger to his lips. Now they all heard it—Vietnamese! Walker quickly picked up Mace and motioned Wright to lead. Jim grabbed the M60 and pointed for the other two to head up a gentle slope. The two took off in a run as fast as they could move. Jim took a frag from his pocket, pulled the pin and carefully placed it under the chicken plate. Then he picked up the M60 and moved quickly up the slope. Once on the top, he moved behind a big tree off to his right and lay there prone. For the first time, he realized they weren't in the rubber plantation anymore; in fact, as he looked at the trees and bushes, it didn't seem much different from the woods he had hunted rabbit and squirrel in ever since he could remember.

Jim's mind drifted back to his childhood and a cold winter day with a newfallen snow, and his dad saying, "Hey, Jim, how about you and me going rabbit hunting today?" Off they'd march into the crisp, sparkly clean Ohio winter. Everything was good then, and natural and safe, with his dad carrying a 12 gauge pump action shotgun and him carrying a stick.

He remembered clearly the Christmas his parents gave him the BB gun. That afternoon his dad and he made a search of the fence rows for some poor unsuspecting rabbit who would be skinned, gutted and carried home with the greatest pride. Many a rabbit had been fired at with that BB gun, and occasionally, one would even be hit and sent jumping in a different direction before his dad, who rarely missed, would drop the floppy-eared creature with the first shot. His dad had been taught to shoot by his father, who had been taught in turn by his father, who had lived in the days of Wyatt Earp and Doc Holliday.

In a few years, Jim progressed to a 22 rifle and squirrel hunting. Then, there was the magic year that he'd saved every penny to buy a shotgun of his own. Finally, with rabbit season approaching, his dad took him one fall day to the local gun shop. The salesman showed him several different guns he could afford before finally bringing out a used, double-barreled 20 gauge Winchester. Its blue steel shone with the luster of a cold, deadly breeze, and the intricate carvings were impressive. The stock was made of a polished dark wood with a rubber butt. The salesman said, "Go ahead, pick it up and bring it up to your shoulder to see how it fits. Good, good, looks just like it was made for you, son. How's she feel?"

"Just fine, Sir."

"Well, young man, that is a mighty fine weapon. She's been used a little but she's been well taken care of. You can tell by the fact there aren't any chips in the stock, and if you'll open her up, you can see the inside of the barrel is as clean as the day she was made. Plus, for a young man like yourself, a 20 gauge is the perfect size; it's big enough to kill anything you'd want to hunt, yet it isn't as heavy or overpowering as the 12 or 10 gauge shotgun. You'd need several more pounds before you could fire one of those without being knocked down by the kick. I'll tell you what let's do, let's go out back and fire both barrels and see how you like it."

Jim was so proud and pleased, he could hardly wait for hunting season to begin. His dad bought three boxes of shells for practice, and a tin can of any size or shape would soon find itself being thrown in the air and shot full of holes. By the time hunting season arrived, he was the scourge of the woods. If a rabbit jumped, he dropped it, but the climax came the last season before he entered the Army. His dad and he had been sitting under a hickory nut tree watching two squirrels go about their business of collecting nuts for the long winter ahead. His dad wanted to take the one on the right and Jim the one on the left but Jim said, "No, wait. I want to try for both at once." And so it was. Jim thought he'd always remember with pride the day he'd killed two squirrels with one shot of his own gun; a piece of wood and steel that made him feel big and strong and powerful and invincible.

Now he lay behind a tree with an M60 machinegun, which fired a 7.62MM round at 600 rounds per minute for more than 300 meters, and he felt like the terrified rabbit he was. He was so scared he wanted to cry but forced himself not to. He felt more and more like the rabbit—it had certainly gone full circle for him. It was then that he decided, if he lived through this, he's never go hunting again.

As the enemy troops became visible he couldn't believe it; they had on uniforms just like him, complete with boots and helmets and carrying AK47's. These weren't VC—these were

North Vietnamese Regulars. He had an overwhelming desire to pee as he counted one, two, three, four, five, six, seven. Seven NVA, man did he have to pee bad! They'd stopped right next to his frag and now two more showed themselves. One had a back pack with an antenna sticking up so the other one had to be the group's leader, with a radio man. Jim had to pee so bad he started squeezing his legs together. He couldn't understand why they hadn't picked up the chicken plate yet. He was going to pee his pants if he didn't get it out in time. So he rolled over onto his left side and opened his fly. The nervous pressure shot a good stream out and for the first time since he'd been shot down, Jim realized he was scared to death.

The shouts from the gooks, followed by an explosion, told him they had found his booby trap. Damn, he wished he'd seen it. He was only about one hundred fifty to one hundred seventy-five meters away with a real good line of vision. Oh, well, he hadn't, now he had to get himself put away and zipped up. That done, he rolled back over where he could see the NVA. There must have been at least one hit since he could hear shouts of pain. Carefully, he place his M60 where he could watch and then fire without moving again. He was so nervous he didn't dare put his fingers on the trigger. Now he wished for the standard handle and butt instead of the two handled aviation system. Man, he had to pee again, but he knew it had to be nerves, he'd just gotten done peeing! Watching closely, he could see one gook start to give orders and others start to fan out. Now there was a group of three in one spot, one of which was their officer. Jim figured they were working on the wounded gook and this was going to be his best shot. Just as he was taking aim, one of the NVA who had fanned out stepped behind a tree between Jim and his target. The gook behind the tree had to go. He was just too close and Jim knew he'd never be able to escape with him there, so he waited and watched as the gook peeked around the tree. Jim drew a bead just beyond the tree and waited. At least they hadn't seen him yet. Over and over in his mind he said, "Oh, God, help me! Please help me!" when the gook started to move quickly to the next tree.

The blast from Jim's M60 caught the NVA full in the midsection, throwing him backwards and rolling him over. In only a flicker of a second, he shifted his aim to the group with the officer. Everyone in that group had started to dive for cover already as Jim opened up on them. He was sure from watching his tracers he'd hit at least one more. He continued to fire into the same area hoping to hit another one. Suddenly the dirt all around him started to explode and tree bark began falling on him. His first thought was, 'What?', then he realized his every fifth round being a tracer, had drawn a direct line to where he was—he was being fired at. Instantly, he rolled over behind a tree and then started to low crawl away. Once far enough away, he got up and ran in a crouched position to a big tree. From there, the elephant grass and bushes would give him enough cover to run standing up. He looked around behind the tree to where he had just been and off to the left he saw a movement. He aimed the M60 and waited for only a second until the gook started moving to the next tree—then he opened fire once more. Again he watched his tracers fly to their target and then suddenly stop as the body they had hit lifted into the air and flew backwards. Jim turned and ran through the woods in the direction Walker had gone.

It wasn't hard to find their trail. Jim's adrenaline was really flowing, so it didn't take long for him to catch up to where he could see them moving ahead of him. He figured he was about three hundred meters behind and just hoped they didn't shoot him.

It was certainly strange going through these woods. There were all different types of sizes of trees, there were places with no undergrowth at all, and other places where there were briars, vines and thick, coarse grass that cut his skin. He had to jump over an ancient rotting tree and tripped in the process. Jim lay there for a moment, his legs ached and his breathing strained. Slowly, he picked himself up and then the ammo belt that had fallen off his shoulder. He tried to wipe the dirt from his face and found blood on his hand. His shirt was totally soaked with sweat, and his panting and gasping for breath made him feel all the more like a scared rabbit fleeing for its life. Breathing was still difficult, especially since he was now crying silently, causing his chest to heave. Cradling the M60, he started moving through the underbrush once again.

He caught up with the others a short time later seated along the bank of a small creek. Walker was looking at his map and Wright was keeping watch. Walker looked up when Wright spoke. "Mac! Man, am I glad to see you! What happened back there?"

Jim told him briefly and then asked whose turn it was to carry Mace. Wright spoke in a soft, dejected tone, "Mine."

"Mr. Walker, which way?"

"I don't know, Mac. This creek isn't on the map."

"In that case, let's go up stream, we know the NVA are downstream behind us. If we walk in this creek, we'll quit leaving a trail a blind man could follow. How are the ribs, Wright?"

"Sore, Mac, really sore, but I'm alive!"

They all cupped their hands and drank from the creek, then Wright picked up Mace and moved into the middle of the creek, followed by Walker and Jim.

"Mr. Walker, I'll trade you this M60 for those two M16's." Walker laughed and handed Jim his M16 with the three magazines he'd taped together and took the M60.

"You look like you could use a break. I'll carry the M60 and Wright's 16 slung over my back—it's no problem."

"Thank you, Sir. Do you have any idea which way we're headed?"

"No, not really. It has to be in the general direction of the road though."

After a while they came to a place on the bank where they could climb out on some rocks without leaving a trail. Each man was glad to finally leave the creek and the mosquitoes, which were eating them up. Walker led them up the bank, followed by Wright carrying Mace and Jim bringing up the rear. They walked around a small clearing not large enough to land a chopper in, and sat down under some trees on the other side. Speaking almost in a whisper Jim said, "Well, if they're following us, that little trip should lose them. At least it does in the cowboy movies. I'm glad that creek wasn't any more than a foot or so deep."

"Mac, did you get any C-rations out of the ship? I'm hungry."

"No, but now that you mention it, so am I."

Jim looked at his watch, ten after one. They'd been on the ground for over three hours. Each man sat there totally exhausted and saturated with sweat. They all knew they should start moving again but nobody wanted to.

"Mr. Walker, rig's got Mr. Mace already."

"You're kidding me! He's stiff already? He hasn't been dead more than an hour."

"He's beginning to smell and the flies are already all over him."

"Well, for God's sake, Wright, don't unhook his belt!"

Jim grabbed Walker's leg and motioned for him to be quiet. He'd seen something move off in the woods and, motioning only with his hand, pointed in the direction of the movement. Now they all saw an NVA moving slowly through the trees. Walker motioned to Wright to pick up the M60, his M16 and move out slowly. Jim grabbed Walker and whispered, "Take Mace. I'll try to hold them one more time."

Walker nodded, picked up Mace and moved into the woods after Wright. Both men tried to keep the trees between them and the NVA. Once out of sight, Walker told Wright to drop back and give Mac some cover.

Jim moved slowly into a prone position beside a large tree with several smaller ones behind him and waited. Fortunately, the NVA hadn't seen them move, and by now Walker and Wright were out of sight. Jim watched as the single NVA moved closer along the bank to where they had come out of the creek. When the NVA got to the clearing, he suddenly crouched down and yelled for what Jim knew had to be his comrades in the creek. This guy had to be a flank man. The NVA officer had learned his lesson. Jim was sure he was now using a point man and flankers on each side, and this guy had found their path. "Well, you smart son of a bitch, you just had to see it, didn't you. Now I'm going to give you a sucking chest wound, you bastard!" The NVA flanker had just finished yelling for his comrades when Jim flipped his selector switch to semiautomatic. Taking careful aim, Jim squeezed the trigger, firing a single round into the body of the crouched man, knocking him over on his side. Jim flipped the switch to full automatic and waited for the NVA troops to come through the tree line from the creek. Nothing. Why didn't they come to help their buddy? Had he hit the panic button and fired too soon? Maybe he should spray the tree line with lead and then run like hell? No, that would just be a waste of ammo and give away his position. He had to get out of there—something was definitely wrong. Those NVA should have moved out of the creek by now. Jim started to low crawl backwards when he heard an M60 open up being him. "Hallelujah! They've found the road and American troops." No more had this thought cleared his head than he heard Wright yelling, "Mac, they're flanking you. You hear me?"

Jim's heart sank as he yelled, "Yes!"

"Mac, I'll fire five second bursts. You move when I open up!"

Wright's M60 opened fire and Jim started running toward him, trying to move so he'd come out behind Wright. As he ran from tree to tree he counted one thousand one, one thousand two, one thousand three, one thousand four and he stopped behind a big old tree. It was a full two seconds before Wright stopped firing, but Jim just stayed behind his tree and panted. Boy, what a sucker he'd been. That gook officer was a smart son of a bitch. He'd just have to be a whole lot more careful from now on. Thank God Wright hadn't left him. He heard the M60 open up again and instantly started running, and once again counted as he ran.

When Walker heard the M60 open up and Wright start yelling, he dropped Mace and started to move back. Then he had another thought. Appleton had said he'd keep a gunship overhead. Turning on his radio and extending its antenna he spoke, "May Day. May Day. This is Blackhawk on the ground, does anybody up there copy? Over!"

"Hey, Walker, I've been trying to reach you. This is your friendly gunship Triple Nickel on station. What can I do for you? Over."

"You can give me some fire support, ASAP. We just moved out of a creek and are approximately one hundred fifty meters west, I think. Over."

"Walker, give me a count. I don't know where in the hell you are. I don't see any creek. Over."

"Roger, one . . . two . . . three . . ." As Mr. Walker

counted, he continued to move towards Wright's M60 sound. Once in position, he stopped counting and asked, "Do you have me yet?"

"Affirmative. Where do you want what—and be exact. Over."

Walker took the violet smoke grenade out of his pocket, pulled the pin and tossed it as far as he could. "Smoke's out and I want one rocket ninety-five meters northeast. Over."

"I see violet smoke. Over."

"You got it."

The Blackhawk gunship rolled in and placed one of its 2.75 inch rockets between the trees as requested.

"Triple Nickel, you're twenty meters too far west and fifteen too far north. Fire for effect this time, smoke is between us and your rocket. Over."

"Roger." The gunship had already turned to start its second run when Walker gave the corrections. On this run, they started firing early and continued a little past where they usually would quit, since they knew where the Americans were.

"One more time, Triple Nickel. Same place, please."

"Roger, roger."

Walker watched with satisfaction as once again the rockets started exploding on target. Giving him even more satisfaction was the sight of Mac and Wright running towards him as the rockets hit. Walker put down cover fire with his M16 just on general purpose.

Once Jim made his second run, he knew that was all the further he'd ever get. Even with Wright's M60 fire, Jim knew he was being fired at for the last couple of steps. When he got to the trees, he tried to make himself as thin as possible and hoped they couldn't cut his tree down with AK fire. This was it, he knew beyond a doubt, this was where he would die. The next time he tried to move he'd be the one cut in half. He was surprised at how much he was in control of himself. Yet he wondered how his parents would take the news, and why he'd been brought to this place to die all alone. He'd just made up his mind to make them come and get him so he could take as many with him as possible when he heard the chopper overhead. He didn't know what was going on but, hearing the explosion, he assumed they'd put a rocket in. He didn't know how or why, but was so thankful it had shown up. Once more, he checked his selector switch to make sure it was on full automatic and hoped that gunship would make another run. If it did, he was going to make another break for it and hope Charlie kept his head down. He could hear the chopper coming and got ready to move. Jim was quite pleased with himself; he was totally in control and perfectly relaxed. As soon as the rockets started to hit, Jim began to run. By the time the rockets quit, he was about ten meters behind Wright on Walker's side.

"Wright, you okay?"

"So far!"

"If that gun makes another run, let's try to get to Walker."

"I'll be right behind you, Mac."

Once more the gunship could be heard coming in on its last run. Wright opened fire from behind his log just as the rockets started to hit. Jim and Wright instantly started running in the direction of Walker's firing M16. What a beautiful sound that thing made as it burped, and in the process led Jim and Wright by its sound to where Walker was hidden. There wasn't any activity from the area where the NVA had been. Once the three were together again, Walker pointed in the direction of Mace, and without saying a word they moved out.

Jim handed Wright his M16 and bent over to pick up Mace. Instead, Jim turned to Walker, who was about to speak into his radio. "Mr. Walker, thanks!" Walker only nodded.

"Sir, Mr. Mace smells terrible."

"I know. Pick him up and let's get out of here. Walker to Triple. Nickel, over."

"Go, Walker."

"Thanks for the help. Now, could you tell me where the hell we are?"

"Not anywhere near where you're supposed to be, that's for sure. But that's good. The flight put in troops on the road you were supposed to be headed for, and after being on the ground about fifteen minutes, found some heavy resistance. There's a major war going on down there. We've put in most of the 25th infantry that's available, part of the Big Red One, and parts of the 199 Light Infantry. To put it bluntly, you're in the middle of a big box that's being squeezed from three directions. How you got turned around, I don't know but you were supposed to be headed northeast and you've been going southeast. You're only about eight kilometers southeast from where you went down."

Wright looked at Jim and asked in a whisper, "How far is eight kilometers?"

"I don't know, about five miles, I'd guess."

"How far have we walked today?"

Jim shrugged his shoulders and said, "Feels like twenty miles."

Both men turned their attention back to what was being said on the radio as they walked.

"There's a thinly wooded area about half a kilometer ahead of you. Once you pass through there, I'll be able to see if you're still being pursued and give you directions to the pickup sight, which is about five kilometers further. Over."

"Triple Nickel, we're exhausted down here. Could you drop some water and C-rations to us? Over."

"I'll see what I can do. There's one more thing you should know. The pickup sight is so small it'll be straight down and straight up, so get there before dark! Over."

Jim looked at his watch, quarter after five. That meant they had about two hours to travel five kilometers. Under normal conditions they would be able to do it easily.

He'd had it, and Wright's ribs were so sore, he was holding his arm strangely and Walker's feet kept tripping over every little stick. Mace felt like he weighed twenty pounds more than when this day began and man did he stink, the flies were all over him.

"Mr. Walker, I can't carry him anymore, I've had it."

"Okay, I'll carry him for a while."

Jim put Mace down and Walker bent over and picked him up. "My Lord, he stinks. That's enough to make a person sick. What would you two think of leaving him?"

"I think it's a great idea."

"Me too."

"So why haven't we done it yet?"

Walker's radio came on just then, causing all three to turn

their attention to it as they walked. "Walker, this is Triple Nickel, do you copy? Over."

"Roger. Over."

"You're starting into the thin part now. Veer a little to your left. There, that's good, try to maintain as straight a line as possible. I'll be turning you over to 714 at this time. See you back at Tay Ninh, Triple Nickel, over."

"Thanks for the help, Triple Nickel. Walker out."

"Walker, this is 714, we have a canteen of fresh water for each of you and three chocolate candy bars from the C-rations. Six said to tell you he'd have the mess sergeant fix supper for you once you're out. I'll make the canteen and candy drop on the edge of the thickest jungle. That way you can move into a more protected area more quickly. I'll maintain a watch over this area to make life unpleasantly short for anyone still on your tail. Do you copy? Over."

"Affirmative."

Once they started into the thinner jungle, the grass and brush seemed to increase in size and thickness. Jim wondered if the giant ant hills, some as high as six feet with eight to ten foot bases, had anything to do with the thinness of the jungle in this area. Certainly they were doing their best to stay clear of all the ant hills, big or small.

Each man found a great deal of comfort in the whopp-whopp-whopp of the Huey blades as it flew across the tree tops. It was like having a big brother who would beat up on anybody picking on them. The NVA had to know they had communication with the chopper, how else could that rocket attack have been put down with such accuracy. The single rocket on the first pass was a dead giveaway of communication with the ground people, who would have given corrective information if necessary. The area they were now passing through was only about two hundred meters wide. Once they were within fifty meters of the thicker jungle, Walker got back on his radio. "714, this is Walker, we're ready for your drop. Over."

"Roger, we're on our way."

Because of the trees, the chopper had to stay about sixty to seventy meters up. It moved slowly, almost in a hover until directly above them. Then, as the chopper slid slowly on by, a package dropped from each side. Walker had already put Mace down and all three ran for the canteens and candy. The canteens had been put in a pillow case and stuffed with wadded up paper. The candy was in an old C-rations box that burst open upon hitting the ground. The stuffed pillow case landed on an ant hill and rolled part way down the side.

Without stopping to think, Wright climbed up and returned with the bag. Walker picked up the candy bars, and all three men returned to the thicker jungle. Jim's switch blade quickly opened the pillow case and the three men drank like the water-starved animals they were. After drinking their fill, Walker handed each a candy bar and that, too, was quickly eaten. More water helped wash down the extremely rich candy that they each had finished off. Jim hooked the canteen on his pistol belt and offered to put one more on it. Walker and Wright put the remainder of their water into one canteen and Jim added it to his now full pistol belt.

As they sat on a log to eat and drink, they could see and smell Mace's body. Each had his own thoughts about Mace, and were torn between leaving him and carrying him on further. It was Wright who finally spoke. "Mr. Walker, I've been thinking about Mr. Mace. We don't have that much further to go. I can't help but think if it was me, I'd want you to carry me out. After all, I'd like to go home, even if it is in a rubber bag."

Walker simply nodded his head in agreement and looked at Jim. "Me, too, I'm just tired of carrying him and it's so damn hot and humid, plus the mosquitoes and flies." They all looked at each other and at Mace's body. It was Jim who spoke next. "Wright, how much ammo is there for that M60?"

Wright looked at the ammo belt in the machinegun and the one on the ground. "Oh, I'd say about forty to fifty rounds."

"Okay, let's leave the M60, we could strip it and put the barrel in one of those ant hills and the firing pin in your pocket, then give the rest a toss. It would mean that much less to carry. I used all three magazines in my Y clip, but I've still got eight full magazines left."

Walker shook his head in disagreement and said, "You can't leave a weapon."

Jim said, "I don't care what you say unless you want to carry it. Look, each of us have only been able to carry Mace for ten to fifteen minutes.''

"Mac, we can't leave a weapon."

"It's the M60 or Mace!"

Wright immediately went to work. First he handed Jim the barrel and then gave Walker the ammo. As Wright continued to strip the M60 down, Walker broke the ammo belt apart into single rounds. Jim took the barrel and headed back to the ant hills. The gunship 714 was still circling overhead when Jim started out for the ant hills. The first one he came to over four feet tall would do. With the nose of the barrel he made a shallow slit in the side of the hill, placed the barrel in it and covered it up as the small red ants emerged. By the time he got back, Walker and Wright were throwing bullets in every direction and the M60 was gone.

"Whose turn to carry Mace?"

Walker looked at Wright, who looked at the bloated body a few feet away and said, "Mine."

Walker, with one M16, took the point and Jim, with the other M16, brought up the rear. Once on the move again, Jim looked at his watch and knew they'd never make it by dark. He didn't know what time sunset was, but it had to be within the next hour. With the sun down, it would get dark fast in this jungle, and the idea of walking in the dark didn't appeal to him.

As they walked, Mace was passed from one to the other with each turn lasting a shorter time, as they became more fatigued; stumbling and falling more frequently.

Once the sun set, darkness came quickly, and they each kept thinking about Triple Nickel's telling them they had to make it to the pickup before dark. Walker had been on the radio most of the time he wasn't carrying Mace, each time hoping to be told they were almost there. Finally, it was just too dark to continue trying to move any further and Walker sat down against a fallen tree stump. He was joined shortly by Jim and Wright.

"Take a break you two, and I'll get hold of 714."

Walker pulled out his radio and extended its antenna. "714, this is Walker. Over." There wasn't any doubt that 714 was up there, they'd heard the whopp-whopp-whopp of its blades all afternoon. "Walker, this is Triple Nickel, we're back on station over your location. What can we do for you? Over."

"It's too dark to walk down here, we're falling over every little stick. How much further to go? Over."

"Well, Walker, that's a problem. I think you're only about one hundred to one hundred fifty meters out yet. We knew you would be close, so Six got a flareship rigged and on its way, along with a heavy fire team. Major Hobbs called a company formation and told everyone your station. He said he was going in to get you out, that it would be a night extraction with only about two feet clearance for the rotors and they would probably get fired at. Then he asked for volunteers to go with him, and I'll be damned if the whole company didn't volunteer. I never realized how popular you guys are. Anyway, the major then asked who the best pilot in the company was and since I was already assigned to gun duty, he picked Lucas to fly AC with him! He's got Gillett and Athia in the back with him. Hold on a minute." They waited in silence for only seconds, then, "I'm done entertaining you guys. My co-pilot says the major is on final approach and the flareship is in position. You guys ready to make one last run for it? Over."

"Anything to get us out of here. Over."

"Okay, flares will be out shortly, start moving ASAP and let me know the moment you hit the clearing. Walker, you'll have to talk Lucas down. Understood? Over."

"Affirmative."

They waited and watched skyward for the first flare to light. The noise from the choppers had increased considerably, telling them there were more than two helicopters up there. Suddenly, as though God himself had struck a match, the first flare lit, then a second and a third, a fourth and finally a fifth. Jim picked up the terribly rancid remains of Mace for what he hoped would be the last time. Then, just as they had done all day, Jim fell between Walker and Wright.

The light wasn't great but for coming through the trees, it wasn't bad either, and the final few meters were traveled without much trouble. They could hear the gunships making their runs ahead of them and knew the LZ would be hit with rockets along the area on three sides. Only the side they were approaching from would be untouched. The jungle would be hit in case the VC were there waiting on them, and the LZ would be hit to explode any booby traps. It was common knowledge that many of these small jungle openings were booby trapped just to discourage helicopters from landing, dropping off, or picking up reconnaissance teams.

Walker stopped before Jim realized they had reached the clearing. He almost bumped into Walker and had to step around him. He looked out into the pickup spot. It was long and narrow, with elephant grass higher than their heads. Yes, it was definitely going to be tight. Walker was already on the radio telling the people upstairs they had finally made it. Then the gunships made a run behind them and more flares popped above.

"Walker, this is Lucas, I'm on my way in. I'll be coming straight down so talk to me 'cause I can't pick up my rotor blades. Over."

"I got you, Lucas, you're looking good, bring it on down." Wright stood there beside Jim, who was still holding Mace. Their faces were pointed upward as they watched the red and green lights slowly descending. Suddenly, a blinding light struck all of them in the face as Lucas turned on both his landing lights and search lights. Still, they watched as the chariot that would take them home settled on down. "Lucas, take it left a foot, that's good, back a couple inches, set it down."

The rotor blast flattened the grass and almost flattened Jim before Wright caught him and helped him toward the now waiting chopper. Jim very rudely dumped Mace on the floor and climbed in, followed by Walker and Wright. They weren't yet seated when Lucas, who hadn't slowed the engine down, put pitch in the rotor blades and started to lift her straight up. Jim was seated on the left end of the bench with Walker in the middle and Wright beside him.

Once the ship was on its way back home, Jim felt a pat on the shoulder. It was Gillett who was flying gunner welcoming him back. With that pat, Jim relaxed for the first time since being shot down. The relaxation of the tension and stress slowly gave way to the well of emotion he'd suppressed all day. He could feel it building low in his chest and steadily swell to consume his whole chest cavity. Tears began to leak from each side of his eyes and, unwilling to suppress it any longer, he lowered his head to his knees and wept. Like a chain reaction, Walker, then Wright broke down and cried.

Once the ship was safely at altitude and on its way home, Major Hobbs looked around at the three men he had just plucked from the jungle. He wasn't surprised to see all three in a state of uncontrollable weeping. He'd known the feeling himself once. Major Hobbs, unseen, turned back around and didn't look back again.

10

Games, Games and More Games

"And then he will reward each person according to what he has done." MATTHEW 16:27 NIV

Mr. Lucas slowly guided his helicopter into its revetment and gently sat it down. Remaining seated, the three passengers waited for the ship to completely shut down. Fatigue had taken its toll and it wasn't until the hospital people had removed Mr. Mace that they slowly climbed out.

Athia tied down the rotor blades, Gillett pulled the guns and the two pilots finished the log book and then climbed out. Major Hobbs stood on one side of the chopper and watched as Mr. Mace was removed. He, along with everyone else, just stood there quietly while Mace's body was placed in a black rubber bag and removed to the waiting truck. Major Hobbs, the ranking officer, was the one who broke the silence.

"Well, gentlemen, you can't stand there all night. The CO has the mess sergeant fixing you supper, which should be ready by now. There's a company formation at 2200 hours in the EM Club and I'm sure at least one of you is on the promotion list that'll be announced then."

For the first time that night, Jim looked at his watch and was really surprised to see it was only a quarter after nine.

Kenny arrived with the platoon truck and everyone climbed in for the ride back. Wright and Jim locked up their M16's, washed their hands and faces and put on a clean shirt before heading for the mess hall. On the way, they were greeted by several of the guys who wanted to congratulate them and just say, "Welcome back!"

Once at the mess hall, they were instructed to go over to the officers' side to eat. The mess sergeant had fixed them a good meal: roast beef, brown gravy, mashed potatoes, peas, fresh rolls and coffee. The servings were ample and both men were eager to dig in. Jim, unsure where to sit, waited for Wright to finish filling his plate so they could walk to a table together. It was Major Hobbs who pointed at the empty chairs at his table and said, "Hey, you two, sit down over here!"

The officers' side of the mess hall was the same as the enlisted men's with two long tables placed end to end, and sixteen chairs total at each table. All the chairs were placed on the table tops upside down for the KP's to sweep and mop the floor, except the ones at the major's table. Jim looked at Wright as though to say, "Are we really supposed to eat with those officers?" Wright shrugged his shoulders and proceeded to their table, taking the open chair on Mr. Walker's left, which forced Jim to sit on his right. They were now seated facing Colonel Appleton and Major Hobbs, who made the expected small talk trying to put the enlisted men at ease. After telling about their day, and having nearly finished their meals, both Jim and Wright felt more comfortable. It was at that point Colonel Appleton asked, "Mac, why did you blow your ship?"

Jim looked directly into the colonel's eyes. He couldn't believe he was being asked that question. Surely the answer was obvious. "Well, Sir, I didn't think I had any other choice. Mr. Walker told me you had given him an order not to leave the scrambler behind. I was in the process of removing it when Mr. Mace got hit. Once he went down, we had one less man to share the load, plus Mr. Mace to carry.

"I just didn't think the three of us could carry two M60's, two M16's, a scrambler, Mr. Mace and the ammo. It was a split second decision I made because I thought it was better than leaving it for the VC."

"Specialist, did Mr. Walker order you to blow your ship?"

"No, Sir."

"You just took it upon yourself to do it?"

Jim was still staring into the colonel's eyes. "Yes, Sir."

"My problem, Specialist, is that I have to account for each and every one of those choppers. Believe me, you have no idea how much paperwork I've got to do because you fragged that helicopter. And speaking of frags, where did you get them?"

Jim turned to Major Hobbs and started to chuckle. Almost at once, his eyes moved back to the colonel. "Specialist, I don't know what you find so funny, or do you just find everything funny?"

The smile on Jim's face disappeared, and his voice became serious. "Sir, there was nothing about the last twelve hours that I found funny."

The colonel paused for several seconds before he spoke again. "So, where did you get the frags?"

Jim was in trouble and he knew it. If he admitted to having the grenades in his ship, he was guilty of disobeying the CO's order to remove all the frags from the helicopters. If he lied, the CO would know it. The colonel wasn't stupid, he knew where those frags came from. If he refused to answer, the CO would just order him to tell and then he would be right back where he was; lie, tell the truth, or refuse to obey the colonel's order. The two men held each other's eyes, yet without malice. It was more a sizing up for both of them.

"Colonel, what do you want me to do, lie to you? I could tell you the grunts left them in the helicopter before we dropped them off. But you're not stupid and you're not going to believe that. And furthermore, I'm not in the habit of lying and I'm not about to start now."

"Mac, I want to hear you say it."

Jim knew he was back in the colonel's good graces or he would never have addressed him as Mac.

"Sir, I kept four in my storage compartment for just such an emergency."

"Four! Where are the other two?"

Jim reached in his pocket and pulled out two remaining grenades and the one smoke grenade. He placed all three on the table directly in front of the CO. "Right here, Sir."

As the CO slowly shook his head, Jim glanced at Major Hobbs from the corner of his eye. The major was sitting there with a half smile on his face. Jim put the last bite of roast beef in his mouth, as the colonel cleared his throat.

"MacLaughlin, you really enjoy living on the edge, don't you? That's why you fly all those night missions, you just enjoy living on the edge! I mean, you've been on the verge of trouble ever since you joined this company. First, you had problems with the maintenance officer. What was it you told him to his face, 'He didn't know what he was talking about'? You came close to getting it on that one; the only thing that saved your ass was that it turned out you were right. Then there was Mr. Halsey. You couldn't just let it go, no, you had to turn him in for, what was it again, 'falsifying records and flying too low'? He's been on your back ever since, and it's hurt the company as a result. You two have got to stop carrying on your own private little war. I'll tell you right now, Specialist, it stops and it stops now!"

"Sir, I had nothing to do with last night."

In a slightly tense voice the colonel continued, "I know that, but the two of you agitating each other constantly precipitated it. Now you have disobeyed a direct order from your commanding officer to remove all the fragmentation grenades from the helicopters. You blew up a helicopter worth about a half a million dollars without being ordered to do so, plus an M60 against your officer's orders, I might add, plus ammo, plus radios, plus a scrambler! Do you have any idea how hard it is to get a scrambler unit? You know, of course, I could make you pay for that helicopter and everything in it! But you also know you're right on that edge again. Just a little bit one way or the other, I could push you right off! I'll give you this much, you've always got your ass covered! Okay, you get away with it one more time but so help me, don't show up in my office in any kind of trouble ever again! One more thing, if there are any medals passed out for this day's activities, you won't be getting any. That's the trade off. Understood?"

"Yes, Sir."

The colonel looked at his watch and then back at the three men seated across from him. "I see you men are finished with your meals and it is nine fifty-five. We'd better head on over to the EM Club."

Colonel Appleton stood, followed by everyone else. He took his hat from the table behind him and looked back at Jim. "Specialist, you're a good crew chief and if I'm ever shot down, I hope you're with me, but I just can't allow enlisted men to make the decision to blow up a helicopter. Worst of all, you disobeyed my orders about the frags. Now you're going to get away with it because of the way things turned out. But you damn well better pass the word, I'm going to personally check each of those helicopters and any crew chief who has frags on his ship loses a stripe, understood?"

"Yes, Sir! About the cost of that helicopter, Sir?"

For the first time Colonel Appleton smiled. "Oh, you don't have to pay for it, you made the right decision—this time!" Pointing his finger at Jim, Appleton continued, "Mac, climb off that edge before you get knocked off."

As everyone followed the CO out, Major Hobbs took Jim's arm. "Mac, I'd like to speak to you alone." The Major waited until everyone else was out the door before he spoke. "Mac, I'm going to make you an offer you're going to love—I'll send Halsey to another company if you give me the name of the person who fragged him last night."

"Sir, do you think I know who did it?"

"Probably not yet, but you will before too long and when you do, I want him. Do we have a deal?"

"How soon after I rat will Mr. Halsey be gone?"

"I'll have him out of here in a week's time, and don't call it ratting—call it maintaining military discipline."

"Will Mr. Halsey know why he's being shipped out?"

"Do you want him to?"

"Sure!"

"Okay, I'll even let you be there when I tell him if you want, do we have a deal?"

"If you'll get him off my back until I find out who did it, sure, you got a deal."

Hobbs laughed. "You drive a hard bargain. How much more do you want?"

"That's all."

"Well, I can't guarantee that but I'll tell you what I will do. I'll talk to Mr. Halsey and tell him I think it's time for this silliness to stop, and I'll try to impress upon him that I mean it."

"Major, can I ask you a question?"

"Sure."

"Sir, why does the colonel hate my guts?"

With a look of surprised disbelief the major replied, "He doesn't hate you at all, quite the contrary. If he hated you, he'd be busting you to PFC instead of promoting you to an E-5."

Jim looked up with surprise. "I'm really on the promotion list?"

"Yep!"

"In that case, I'd better get over there or I'll be in trouble for missing my promotion."

Major Hobbs laughed and opened the door motioning Jim out. Once outside, Major Hobbs put his left hand on Jim's right shoulder. "Mac, Colonel Appleton told Mr. Walker he could go on R&R as soon as that channel opened back up, which will probably be ten days to two weeks. By that time I should have made AC. Would it be all right with you if I flew AC in your ship while Mr. Walker's gone?"

"It would be fine with me, Sir. In fact, I'm honored that you even asked me instead of just doing it."

"Oh, I realize I'm not the most popular person around here right now, and it's not going to get a lot better."

"Why do you want to fly with me, Sir?"

"Because you're good and I like your personality. You know the difference between an officer and an NCO*, which you'll be shortly, and you'll talk to me without pulling any punches. I like that and respect an enlisted man who can carry it off, in a respectable manner, of course. I like the way you handled yourself with that Halsey thing and the way you handled yourself when shot down. You've got a set of balls all right. Just out of curiosity, how come you don't mind flying with me? I have to be on all the EM's lists by now."

"As a matter of fact, Sir, you are about one step below Mr. Halsey. Nobody likes the idea of painting rocks or putting the cargo doors back on the choppers. I mean, it's a real pain to

* NCO—Noncommissioned officer (E-5 and above).

unhook the ammo belts so I can shut the door and put fuel in the chopper, or get into the engine compartment, or the storage area." Jim could tell from the look on the major's face it was time to stop on that subject.

"You didn't answer me, Mac. How come you don't mind flying with me?"

"Because with your rank you're only going to fly lead or trail. Those are the two spots in the flight that are never sent on single ship missions after the flight is released. As a result, I'll be able to finish my post flight inspection earlier and maybe get a little more sleep." Jim opened the club house door and followed the major in. The place was crammed with all the officers and enlisted men in the company; there was hardly enough room to stand, let alone walk, so Jim simply followed the major towards the stage at the west end.

Colonel Appleton had already started handing out the promotions and was in the process of shaking Gillett's hand, along with two other men. All three had obviously just been promoted to Staff Sergeant. With promotion orders in hand they stepped off the stage leaving only the CO. As they climbed off, the First Sergeant climbed up. From a sheet of paper in his hand, he read the names of all the men being promoted to E-5. Jim, whose name was about halfway down the list, quickly joined the others on stage.

Happy didn't describe how Jim felt. He was elated! He'd finally been promoted to Specialist E-5. Sp/5 meant a lot of things besides the obvious increase in pay. I meant no more KP, no more guard duty, other than the possibility of sergeant of the guard and that was an easy job and only pulled about once a year. It meant no more crummy details like filling sand bags or burning shit. Officers, and for that matter most everyone, treated a Sp/5 with considerable more respect than a Sp/4 and that would be nice. It also meant he'd be able to get away with a lot more as a Sp/5, things he wouldn't even try as a Sp/4. Plus, he'd be an NCO. That did sound good to him—Jim MacLaughlin, a noncommissioned officer. He'd almost forgotten that meant he'd be able to get into the NCO side of the EM Club, where he could buy hard liquor. He was only twenty years old and he'd be drinking whisky when guys who were twenty-one or older couldn't if they weren't E-5's.

Colonel Appleton stepped in front of Jim, who was already standing at attention. The CO held out his hand to shake Jim's, than handed him a copy of his promotion orders and said, "Congratulations, Mac!"

"Thank you, Sir."

The CO and Jim saluted, then Colonel Appleton turned to the next man in line. Once the colonel had completed handing out the E-5 promotions, those men were released and everyone else being promoted had their names read off by the First Sergeant. Everyone from E-2 to Sp/4 was lumped together and quickly handed their promotion orders.

Once the CO was finished, he asked that all the new E-5's meet him in the NCO side of the club—he was buying. There was monumental confusion as people tried to leave and others tried to make their way to the just-opened bar. Others, like Jim, were trying to make their way through the NCO doorway. Once in the NCO side of the club, Jim didn't know quite what to do, so he stood along one wall looking around. It was a fair-sized room with several small tables where people were already seated. There was a great deal of activity as men moved from table to table, and some were just looking for a place to sit. Others just enjoyed talking to several people and moved from table to table. The wall to his left housed the bar itself, behind which was the usual display of bottles and glasses. There was one American GI tending bar who Jim recognized as having come to Tay Ninh with him from Bear Cat. He'd heard that during the day two fairly attractive Vietnamese girls tended bar. The thing that held his attention most was the silk parachute used as a ceiling adornment. Major Hobbs was standing at the bar trying to get everyone's attention and for the first time Jim realized how smokey and noisy it was.

"May I have your attention please . . . thank you . . . thank you. Just in case somebody doesn't know me yet, I'm Major Hobbs, your new XO. I'd like to congratulate all of you who were promoted tonight and be the first to buy all of you a drink. Barkeep, the first round's on me for everyone who just got promoted."

Jim felt a hand on his arm and turned to see Gillett standing there. "Mac, you stink!"

"No kidding! What did you expect? I've had a hell of a day and haven't had a chance to shower and change yet."

"So I understand. I can't wait to hear all about it! Come on, let's go get our free-bee. What are you drinking?"

"I don't know, beer I guess."

"Beer! You have to be kidding. Mac, you're not going to drink beer anymore! I want you to get a Jack Daniel's Black and Coke. In fact, since the major's buying, you should buy a bottle and keep it here behind the bar."

"I'll tell you what, I'll try the Jack Daniel's and Coke, but I get the feeling I've got a friend in Major Hobbs, so I'm not about to pull a stupid trick like sticking the man for the price of a whole bottle."

The two men made their way to the bar and Gillett ordered a bottle of Jack Daniel's and a can of Coke. Jim stuck to a single drink of Jack and Coke and followed Gillett to a table where Mr. Walker, Mr. Euclid, Hunter and Athia were seated. Congratulations were passed all around along with inquiries about their day. Several comments were made about the way Walker and Jim smelled and looked, followed by a general discussion about what it was like to spend the day running from Charlie while carrying a dead man. Their table seemed to be one of the main centers of attention, with several officers stopping by to shake hands with Jim, Walker, and Gillett.

It was Major Hobbs who moved most of the flight crews out by getting everyone's attention and then giving final congratulations to all those newly promoted. He then announced that he had to fly tomorrow along with several others in the room, and it would be a good idea to get some sleep.

Once the flyers had left, there were only about a dozen guys remaining. Walker, Gillett and Jim remained at their table only because they knew the line at the urinal would be immense.

"Well, Gillett, I'll tell you this, you were right about the Jack Daniel's, this stuff is nice."

"Mac, would I steer you wrong? I'll even make you a deal. Since the major was nice enough to buy the bottle, I'll share it with you two if you'll buy the Coke."

"That sounds like a good deal to me."

Since the bar was empty it didn't take him long to get back. "Sorry, Gillett, they're out of Coke so I had to choose between Pepsi and root beer."

Gillett looked at the can in Jim's hand, half afraid he'd be holding root beer. "Well, I'm glad to see you made the right choice. While I'm thinking about it, Mac, I want to give you these since I won't be needing them any longer." Gillett reached up to his collar, unsnapped the Sp/5 insignias and handed them to Jim. Genuinely pleased, Jim pinned the insignia onto his collar in place of his Sp/4.

"Thanks, Gillett, I really appreciate this."

"You're welcome."

Walker poured the last of the Pepsi into his glass and with a puzzled look said, "I'd like to know something, Mac, what's with you and Hobbs?"

"I don't know, I guess the guy just plain likes me. Why?"

"I don't know for sure, but before you got to the mess hall tonight, the major pumped me for everything I knew about you. From the questions and comments he made, he'd obviously looked your 201 file* over very carefully."

"What did he want to know?"

"It's hard to say, but my guess is he wants to know why you do the things you do. If you know the risks and do them anyway, or if you're just too stupid to know better."

"I'm too stupid to know better."

"I'm sure that's what you'd like everyone to think and there are times when you do a real good job of playing that part! That little act has probably kept you out of a lot of trouble, but there's nothing stupid about you. You always know exactly what you're doing and all the possible consequences. Nobody knows that better than the three of us sitting here, right, Gillett?"

Gillett nodded. "I think there are others who know it or he wouldn't have gotten promoted. But you're right about Major

* 201 file—Personnel records giving all known information on an individual.

Hobbs, he's after something. He was asking me a bunch of questions about Mac earlier today."

"Well, he must not dislike me too much or he wouldn't have asked me to fly with him when you go on R&R, Mr. Walker."

"I'm not going on R&R for a couple weeks. Appleton said tonight in the mess hall that I would be the first person to go but that won't be for a while."

Gillett took a swig from the bottle of Jack, handed it to Jim and said, "Maybe he's decided he wants you as his crew chief."

Jim shook his head but Gillett continued, "Just think about it, in about a month Appleton rotates home and Hobbs is the new CO. He'll be flying C and C ship and will need a crew chief." Looking at Mr. Walker, Gillett continued, "Why else would he be so interested in sending you on R&R? In two weeks he should've made AC and you'll be gone so Mac has the choice of flying with every loose pilot in the company or with him. You're gone a week and by the time you get back Mac's learned all the benefits of flying with the CO, and bingo, he's only too happy to stay with Hobbs!"

"You know you're just about right; I know he was really impressed with the way he handled himself last night. Hobbs told me this morning he had to bite his tongue to keep from laughing when Mac asked Halsey to smell his armpit, or something like that!"

Jim and Gillett exchanged glances and broke out laughing remembering the moment. Jim, who, like Gillett, was now drinking straight from the bottle of Jack, took another gulp. "I think you're both crazy! He has to know I'd never quit flying with Mr. Walker."

Walker looked Jim in the eye. "Listen to me! If you get the chance to fly as the CO's chief, you'd better grab it."

"Why? I don't want to spend the rest of my time flying in circles at thirty-five hundred feet!"

"It would be a lot better than getting shot at all the time or flying all those night missions."

"But I like flying night missions."

"Do you have any idea what the casualty rate on those single ship night missions is?"

"Zero for me, I've gone down lots of times but never on a night mission."

"You're lucky, that's all."

"Divine protection."

"Look, it's irrelevant. What's important is you keep flying all of them and you're dead. With Hobbs, you're out of it; you get more time off, you'll fly less hours, you'll get back to base before anyone else and you'll get first class service from maintenance. Further, if you won't do it for yourself, do it for me. If Hobbs asks you to crew for him and you say no, he could send me to the guns or to another company."

"Hey, there are a lot of pilots who would give their left nut to be in the guns, besides we're just guessing anyway. Hobbs could have something entirely different in mind."

"Mac, if you could go to the guns, would you?"

"No, I like flying slicks. Besides, I'm too lazy to fly guns, they're just too much work."

"Ditto! But you're right. He might not ever ask. I've got to pee. See you two in the morning."

Jim took another swig from the bottle and handed it to Gillett who did the same. Once Walker had left, Jim felt it was safe to tell Gillett about Major Hobbs' proposition. "Gillett, just between you and me, I think you're probably right about Hobbs. He offered me quite a deal on the way over here tonight. Basically, if I turn in the guy who's responsible for fragging Halsey, he'll ship Halsey out to another company."

Gillett looked shocked. "You kidding me?"

"No."

"What are you going to do?"

"I don't know for sure."

"Have you told Green?"

"No and I'm not going to. In fact, I haven't told anyone but you and I don't think I will either. If Halsey finds out, he'll go crazy. Gillett, tell me something, will you? Why does he want me? I know I'm good at my job but no better than most of the guys in this company. And I'm always closing in on trouble. So why me?"

"I don't know, Mac. The only person who does is Hobbs. If

he ever does ask, and we might be jumping the gun, before you say yes, ask him—why you?"

They both heard it at the same time—the unmistakable scream of a 122 MM rocket. Both men jumped under the table as someone in the background yelled, "Incoming." It only lasted a couple of minutes, but everyone stayed under their tables for several minutes more. Finally, after the first person stood up, everyone else followed. Jim looked over at Gillett who was still holding his bottle.

"Mac, you want this last swallow?"

Jim shook his head and said, "No, thanks. My stomach really doesn't feel too good. I think I'm going to go take a leak and go to bed."

Gillett smiled a knowing smile. "Wait a minute and I'll go with you!" Jim stood and watched as Gillett downed the last of his Jack Daniel's.

Jim's stomach was feeling progressively worse. The fall he took going down the club's steps didn't help any. Fortunately, it was a short walk from the enlisted men's club to the urinals. He was so drunk he couldn't stand without holding himself up. Yet walking didn't seem to be any real problem, though his head kept going around in circles and things looked a bit fuzzy.

"Mac, can you get to the hooch okay without me?"

"Sure, Gillett. You know, I've never been this drunk in my life and I'm never going to be again. I feel terrible."

"Well, look on the bright side, you don't have to fly tomorrow."

"Does that mean I have to stand formation in the morning?"

Gillett laughed. "No, I'll cover for you, go to bed. I've got to run out the few guys who do have to fly and are still in the club."

Gillett turned and headed up the steps of the EM club and Jim headed on to the hooch. He was only a few steps from the pallet used as a bridge across the drainage ditch when Kenny bumped into him. He almost fell over but somehow managed to maintain his balance. "I didn't see you. Where'd you come from, Kenny?"

"The club." Kenny had positioned himself in such a way that Jim couldn't cross the pallet.

"Hey, Kenny, get out of my way!"

"To hell with you, MacLaughlin, just because you made E-5 tonight doesn't mean you can push people around."

"Kenny, you're drunk."

"So are you. So what are you going to do about it!"

Jim was making every effort to be as alert as possible. Something told him Kenny was working up enough courage to take a swing at him.

"And I'll tell you one more thing, get off Gillett's back about my monkey."

"Kenny, you and your monkey can both go to hell for all I care. Besides, what are you going to do about it if I don't?"

"How about busting you in the face for starters?"

"You're drunk, go to bed!"

Jim knew exactly what Kenny was going to do as he watched him make the exaggerated motion with his right arm. Jim's mind flashed with all the moves he'd been taught as a high school wrestler and later refined without the rules, by the army. Kenny's right arm had swung behind his back and started forward with fist clinched. Jim raised his left arm with open hand and caught Kenny's blow. His right hand came up and caught Kenny's armpit at the same time his left hand slid up Kenny's arm and grabbed his wrist. Then, pivoting on his left foot, he turned, bent over, bumped Kenny with his hip, pulled his arm down and flipped Kenny over his shoulder.

Kenny landed with a jar which hurt him physically as much as it did his pride. It had all taken place in a matter of seconds and Kenny hadn't even landed yet when Jim vomited. Jim straightened up only to jerk forward once more, spewing chunks of his supper and slimy Jack Daniel's all over Kenny's chest and stomach. Jumping up as quickly as possible, Kenny lowered his head and charged like a bull. Jim stepped to his left and stuck out his right foot, tripping Kenny, who then fell in the drainage ditch. Jim vomited one last time and turned to where Kenny lay. "Kenny, I'm sick, could we finish this tomorrow? I promise. You let me go to bed and we can finish this tomorrow if you want. I just really don't feel like fighting you right now."

Kenny picked himself up out of the ditch and looked down

at the vomit all over his front. Somewhat dejectedly he said, "I think you'd better go on to bed before I end up with vomit down my back as well. I'll tell you one thing I've learned, I'm never getting in a fight with a drunk again!"

Jim took off his shirt as he entered the hooch and wiped his face with it. Fortunately, he hadn't gotten any on himself. He sat down on the edge of his bunk, took off his boots and lay down. His head and stomach were still spinning, but feeling much better after having vomited, he was soon asleep.

11

Situation Ethics

*"Do you not know that we will judge angels?
How much more the things of this life!"*
I CORINTHIANS 6:3 NIV

The first thing Jim was aware of was someone shouting in the background. Then he realized how much his head hurt and his lips were swollen and dried out. Next his brain became aware of a mouth full of cotton and, finally, opening his eyes, he had trouble focusing.

"Mac, come on, wake up, get up!"

Jim slowly sat up on the edge of his bed, holding his head with both hands. He looked up and to his right at Gillett standing beside his bunk. "Welcome to the world of the living, Mac!"

"You don't have to shout, Gillett! Besides, you said I didn't have to fly this morning."

"I'm not shouting and you didn't go with the flight. It's ten o'clock."

Jim looked down at his watch, Gillett was right. He felt terrible and something stunk. All he wanted to do was lie back down. As he started to fall backwards, Gillett spoke and reached out, grabbing Jim's shoulder. "Oh, no you don't, get back up and go take a shower. You stink! Now that you're an E-5, you can go in the mess hall anytime you like and I suggest after the shower you go get a cup of coffee. At 11:15 the courier ship is supposed to land here and you're going to be on it along with Walker and Wright." Jim looked up questioningly. "You're supposed to pick up a Huey from Depot at Vung Tau.

You got it?" Jim slowly nodded his head. "Mac, you really tied one on last night. How do you feel?"

"Like shit!"

"Well, you smell like it, too. Go get in the shower. Kenny just filled it up."

Jim watched Gillett walk out the door before starting to strip. For the first time, he saw Mr. Mace's dried blood, now an ugly blackish color, caked on his legs, shoulder and arm. Looking at the blood, he felt only a moment's sadness for Mr. Mace. Realizing how close he'd come to death himself, he decided to be thankful he was alive and not to think about Mr. Mace anymore. Jim put on his flip flops, and had just finished wrapping a towel around himself when Gillett walked in holding a cup of coffee.

"Here, drink this. It'll make you feel better!"

"Gillett, thanks, but I really don't think I could drink anything right now."

Gillett pushed the cup forward and said, "Drink it!"

Jim took the cup and drank it in two gulps. "Gillett, I swear to God and anybody who'll listen, I'm never going to get that drunk again as long as I live."

Gillett laughing said, "Sure, Mac, at least until tonight."

"No, I'm serious. I may get a little tipsy, but never totally wiped out, stoned-ass drunk again." Jim picked up his shower bag and headed for the shower. The water was still cold, so he didn't spend any more time than necessary. Once showered and dressed in clean fatigues, he felt a lot better. He still had almost an hour before meeting the courier ship, so he decided to go declare his losses from yesterday to supply.

Supply was nothing more than a big hooch. The first thing he saw once inside was a long counter top with various types of clothing piled on top. There was conversation coming from the shelving just behind the counter.

"Anybody home?"

"Be with you in a minute."

The conversation stopped and Jim waited for more than his minute. Finally, a large, overweight staff sergeant with his gut hanging over his belt buckle approached. "What can I do for you?"

"My name's MacLaughlin. I was shot down yesterday and I lost some stuff when my Huey caught on fire."

"From what I heard, you blew it up; it didn't catch on fire!"

"Does it make any difference, Sarge?"

"Not as far as I'm concerned. I've got your records right here. What did you lose?"

"How did you know I'd be in? For that matter, how did you know about my ship?"

"Mr. Walker and I just finished pulling inventory on Mr. Mace's gear and boxing his personal belongings for shipment home. In fact, that's what I was doing when you came in, putting his gear back in stock."

Jim looked at his watch and decided he'd better get on with it. "Okay. Well, let's see. I lost my ballistics helmet, field jacket, flight gloves, five magazines for my M16, one baseball cap, canteen and my big water jug—I don't know what you would call it, it held five or eight gallons of water and had a bottom spigot."

"Okay, I know what you mean, but I don't have any more in stock and probably won't get any for a while. What else?"

"All my tools."

"You're out of luck there, also."

"You're kidding, how am I supposed to fix anything?"

"Well, you won't have to worry about that until you get a ship. Then I guess you'll just have to borrow, what else?"

"I guess that's it."

"Be right back." The staff sergeant walked off with paper in hand. Shortly, he returned with an armload of items to replace what Jim had lost. "Here you are, Mac, everything but the water jug and tools, including tool box. Try the helmet on and see if it fits." It did. Shoving the receipt form in front of Jim, the sergeant said, "Sign on the line!"

Jim signed, picked up the gear lying on the countertop and walked out. From the supply room, he went to his hooch and put the gear in his wall locker and headed for the mess hall.

It was now five minutes before eleven and Jim figured he didn't have a chance of getting anything to eat. But then, nothing ventured, nothing gained. Once inside he looked around until he saw a mess sergeant. "Hey, Sarge, I've got an eleven-fifteen flight to Vung Tau. Could I get an early lunch?"

"Oh, I think we can fix something up for you. I just wish you'd given me more time. I'll tell you what, Sarge, about the best I can do for you is heat up some C-rations real quick."

"That would be fine." Jim got a cup of coffee and sat down.

It wasn't long before the mess sergeant hollered, "Hey, Sarge, here's your lunch; potato cakes, peas, with beans and weenies."

Jim picked up a plate, "Thanks a lot, Sarge, I really appreciate it."

"You're welcome, Sarge, have a good flight and you had better hurry."

Jim ate quickly, thanked the mess sergeant again on his way out and returned to his hooch, where he picked up his M16 pistol belt, flight gloves and helmet. On his way to operations, he took a detour through maintenance. There he found a roll of gray tape used to temporarily patch bullet holes in rotor blades. In less than a minute he had taped three M16 magazines together, two down and one up, and slammed the single magazine home in his M16. He thanked the maintenance crew for the tape and moved at a brisk pace to operations.

The courier ship was already on the operations pad when Jim got there. Not seeing Mr. Walker, he went on into the operations bunker just as Mr. Walker and a second lieutenant were starting out. Jim could tell the lieutenant was the courier by the combination lock attaché case he had handcuffed to his left wrist. The lieutenant was about 5'10" with dark hair, eyes and complexion. He was big boned and Jim figured he weighed over one hundred eighty pounds. Like most all couriers, he had an Army 45 on his right hip. Since Jim was outside headed in, he decided he'd better salute. Both Walker and the lieutenant returned his salute, but it was Walker who had the big smile.

"Cut it a little close didn't you, Mac?"

"Sir, I was told to be here by the time the courier was ready to leave and here I am." Jim knew that wasn't quite the truth, but he didn't feel like being hassled about not being there on time. After all, the important thing was not when he got there, only that he was there and ready to leave before the courier.

"I'm surprised you can even function this morning. I understand you really tied one on last night."

"Guilty as charged, Sir."

"How do you feel?"

"Oh, I feel okay after getting cleaned up and having something to eat. I'm a little sore from carrying Mr. Mace. But I'll tell you what, I'm never getting that blown away again. You know, I've been drunk on beer before, but never anything close to last night."

"Mac, that's the difference between beer and whiskey. I kind of figured you wouldn't feel too good after watching you drink straight from the bottle."

The three climbed on board, joining Wright who had been there waiting. The Huey engine picked up speed and soon they were airborne. Jim knew there wouldn't be any conversation because of the flight noise, so he leaned back in his seat and watched the scenic view below.

Heading south, they would follow Highway 22 to Go Dau Ha, where they would pick up Highway One to Saigon; from Saigon they'd probably pick up Highway 15 just outside Bien Hoa, and follow it to Vung Tau.

Jim had flown courier flights several times before their company had been changed to an all combat assault unit. He'd always enjoyed flying courier because they went to every outpost that had a landing pad and some that didn't. After all, how else was the military to get their important papers from one post to another? Jim's hope now was that Tay Ninh would be their last stop before lunch. If it wasn't, it could take a long time to get to Vung Tau; if it was, they'd probably head straight for Saigon to eat lunch. Afterward, the courier ship would head back out and spend most of the afternoon flying more papers.

Jim was right about Tay Ninh being the courier's last stop before lunch. Heading south, the jungle, green and lush around Tay Ninh quickly turned to rice paddies outside Go Dau Ha. There was an occasional farmer working his rice paddy as they flew overhead. Twice he saw farmers working their water buffalo. Jim laughed to himself as he remembered eating water buffalo once in a fancy restaurant in Saigon. He and three other guys had paid perfectly good money for the most terrible steaks they'd ever eaten. To say it was strong and tough would be a major understatement. Catsup helped the flavor, but he couldn't cut it thin enough to help the toughness.

It wasn't long until they landed at Hotel Three and the three Blackhawks headed for the Operations room. Mr. Walker got them a ride on a chinook leaving in ten minutes for Vung Tau. Once outside, they found a shady spot and sat down to wait.

"Wright, have you ever been to Tay Ninh?"

"Nope."

"How about you, Mr. Walker?"

"I've flown in and out of it, but never done any walking around. How about you, Mac?"

"Yeah, I've been there several times. When I was in the 191st, my maintenance crew won an in-country R&R at Vung Tau."

"You're kidding me!"

"No."

"Man, you're just full of surprises! Well come on, tell us all about it."

"Okay. They were having trouble getting aircraft out of maintenance, so the maintenance officer decided to give the crew who completed the most jobs in thirty days a trip to Vung Tau. Oh, yeah, to get credit, the aircraft had to pass inspection the first time. The guy I had for a crew leader was really good; he was on his second tour of duty in country, so he knew what he was doing. He said right to begin with that we were going to win it and we did. Don Sunday was his name.

"Our crew was also the recovery crew. If a ship went down, they sent us to fix it or rig it to be sling-loaded home by a Chinook. You know, I haven't thought about that crew for some time. I was on KP one day when the crew went out. For some reason, they couldn't find me so they got someone else to take my place. Everybody in that helicopter was killed." The others just sat there with blank looks on their faces. "I guess that's one reason I believe in divine protection. Anyway, one of the guys I came to Tay Ninh with said one of the pilots in this company found Don's ship shortly after we came to Tay Ninh."

"Was it a Boomerang ship?"

"Yeah, why?"

"I was the pilot."

Jim, obviously surprised, looked up, "Now who's full of surprises? Are you serious?"

"Yeah! I was just flying alone one day, I don't remember what I was doing or where I was going. You know—one of your basic milk runs back when we were a general purpose company. Anyway, we were just outside of Blackhorse when I thought I saw a helicopter crash down in the trees. So I circled around—you had to fly over it just right to see it—but there it was. I could make out a Boomerang on the nose so I radioed Saigon to see if the Boomerangs had lost a ship. Sure enough, about three months before, their maintenance ship had gone down and they never found it. They happened to be working in the area so they came and got the skeletons, which I understand was all that was left."

"Had they been shot down or what?"

"I really don't know, Mac. I heard that they'd hit with enough impact that the pilots' seats had been ripped out of the floor. The pilots were still strapped in and they found the passengers some distance away. From the way that chopper was busted up, it had to hit those trees well over red line. My guess, and it's just a guess, is they got caught in a monsoon and were blown into those trees. But who knows, their transmission could have frozen for any one of several reasons including a bullet hole letting out the oil." Mr. Walker shrugged his shoulders and continued, "That's all I know, Mac. I'm sorry I don't have more information."

"Did Charlie find them?"

"Mac, I just finished telling you, I don't know! I don't even remember if they found their weapons."

"I wonder why it didn't blow?"

"Who knows, maybe they were about out of fuel. Besides, not every Huey that crashes, burns."

"That's true."

"I'm sorry, Mac."

"Hey, don't be. I know more now than I did before. You know, Mr. Walker, one of the things I don't understand now is, I was on the serving line that night in the mess hall. When our

First Sergeant came through he was really surprised to see me, since he thought I was dead. He had me leave the serving line right then, much to the annoyance of the mess sergeant, and report to the company commander, who was in the process of writing the letter home to my parents. Now, what I don't understand is, how did he know, they were dead?"

"I don't know; what time of day did they go down?"

"Early morning."

"Maybe they'd been lost without contact long enough, I just don't know!"

Wright spoke for the first time. "So tell us about Vung Tau!"

"There's not much to tell. We went down on the maintenance ship early one morning. Don had been there before, so he took us to a motel he knew about, named The Thunderbird. We each got a room and spent the rest of the day on the beach."

In unison Wright and Walker said, "On the beach!"

"Yeah, there's a pretty nice beach area where you can swim and just lie around. Then that evening, we went to a fancy hotel for dinner and had buffalo steaks. After that, we hit the bars and got picked up on base the next day about noon."

Walker smiled and said, "Did you ever spend any time on the base?"

"Sure, I used to go with the maintenance ship two or three times a month to pick up parts."

"Good, then you know right where we're going."

"Sure, I've been there several times, it's not hard to find."

"How about passenger pickup area, do you know where that is?"

"Sure, we used to give guys rides out of Vung Tau all the time as long as it was on our way. Why?"

"We're supposed to have a Lieutenant Carson waiting for a ride back to Tay Ninh."

"We getting a new pilot?"

"I don't think so. We're supposed to deliver him straight to Headquarters at Tay Ninh. So I don't think he's a pilot."

"Mr. Walker, do you know what he looks like?"

"I have no idea. I don't even know if he's black or white."

"Well, it shouldn't be any problem to find him, he's probably waiting at Operations. I can show you where to go sign for the Huey, and then I'll go look for our lieutenant."

The three turned to their left and watched a Chinook land and lower its back door, which doubles as a cargo ramp. Out walked several GI's, including one that still had a flight helmet on. Mr. Walker approached the man, figuring him to be the crew chief, and asked if he was headed to Vung Tau. Receiving a thumbs-up sign, Walker motioned for the other two to join him. In only minutes they were once again airborne and headed south.

The inside of a Chinook is like a very noisy, rectangular box. Much of the superstructure is visible, as are hydraulic lines and electrical lines. There are fold-down seats on either side for passengers to sit on, and several steel tie-down rings in the aluminum floor. Unlike a Huey, passengers can't sit and look out the sides because they are solid, with only a few small windows to look out.

It wasn't long until they landed at Vung Tau. Jim showed Mr. Walker and Wright how to find the maintenance offices, with the understanding that he would join them with Lieutenant Carson at the helicopter. Wright was to stand out in the open so Jim could see him.

It was only a short walk for Jim to the Operations office, and he was glad. The sun was directly overhead and it was getting very hot. He knew Operations was air-conditioned so once in the door, he removed his hat and just stood there cooling off.

Seated on the bench on the far side of the room was a WAC Lieutenant. It only took one glance to see she was a real knockout of about twenty-four or five years of age. She had on a dress uniform, complete with hose which accentuated a pair of gorgeous legs. She'd crossed those legs with her skirt hem resting a good three inches above the knee. Jim couldn't help but think, Man, the things I'd like to do with her. He decided he'd better quit staring before she looked up from her paperback book.

Moving over to the counter, he looked for the first time at the staff sergeant standing there. In a whisper, the staff sergeant said, "Didn't strain your eyes did you?"

Jim chuckled quietly. The sergeant continued, "Makes a man wish he was an officer, doesn't it?"

Jim puckered his lips slowly, blew out some air, closed his eyes and nodded. "What can I do for you, Specialist?"

"I'm looking for a Lieutenant Carson."

The sergeant stood up straight and broke into a big grin. With his eyes he pointed to the WAC Lieutenant. It took Jim a moment to recover and only then did he turn around. The first thing he looked for was her collar insignia, which would tell him her job. It was a gold diamond. She's in finance? There aren't any finance people at Tay Ninh! The broad is a whore! Jim was really disappointed, but her beauty still held him captive.

Jim walked over to the bench and positioned himself only about two feet from the lieutenant. He felt sure she had been aware of him and probably had checked him out just as he had her. For one thing, he didn't remember her turning a page of that book she seemed to be reading. He had to admit, she was truly a beautiful woman, even in military clothing. One thing he'd learned, if a woman was attractive in military clothing, she was gorgeous in civilian clothes. Her short brown hair had every strand in place and her makeup was perfect. Unlike so many WACs he'd met who either didn't wear any makeup or put so much on it looked like Indian war paint, hers was truly perfect.

Jim stood there not saying anything, waiting for her to respond to his presence. Very slowly and deliberately she raised her head showing a slight smile.

Lieutenant Carson had been waiting most of the morning for her ride to Tay Ninh. Her rear end and back had long ago begun to ache from sitting on the wooden bench placed against a wall. She was bored to death with the wait, and the novel she'd brought along didn't hold her interest.

There'd been a parade of men through that door and with each one she'd hoped her chariot was parked outside waiting. Instead, each man ogled. Some even went so far as to stand and leer. One, a captain, had even had the nerve to try to pick her up. She didn't mind though, she knew she was very attractive, and in the military she rated higher. In fact, she usually got a kick out of the men's reactions. She had, after all, worked very hard to perfect her ability to get the reaction from men she wanted.

When Jim had walked in the door, she'd shifted her eyes to the top of the page; that way she could watch him without being obvious. He was young, but then weren't they all. He carried an M16, which meant he was stationed out in the boondocks someplace, and there was the pistol belt with ammo packs on it. Of all the guys who had walked through, not more than a couple had weapons, and none had a pistol belt. This guy was either a basic Saigon warrior or the real thing. Somewhat to her surprise, he'd removed his hat and placed it under his arm. Only a few of the officers had removed their hats while inside. As he was walking across the room to the counter, she took the opportunity to look him over good. Not bad-looking, not great, but not bad. A shame he's only a spec-five, and not the pilot sent to get her.

She moved her eyes back to the book and started to read. Much to her surprise, this spec-five started to walk towards her, stopping only a couple feet from her. This was obviously her ride but she was a lieutenant and not about to appear anxious. He just stood there with his feet slightly apart. He didn't seem intimidated by her looks or rank or he would have spoken her name from the counter, not walked over and stood directly in front of her. Slowly and very purposefully, she raised her head to look directly into his eyes. Dark brown eyes. It's too bad it's only in the movies that you can read things in people's eyes. His soft boyish smile caused the woman in her to respond instead of the lieutenant. *I* think *I'll give him a thrill.*

Softly and very pleasantly, she spoke. "Is there anything I can do for you, Sergeant?"

Jim thought, but didn't say, *There's a lot you could do for me, lady!* But something told him she knew exactly what she was saying. So, in a slightly deepened voice, Jim replied, "Yes, Ma'am! And I believe there is something I can do for you. My name is MacLaughlin, but most everyone calls me Mac. I'm with the 187th Assault Helicopter Company stationed at Tay Ninh. I understand you need a ride!"

She thought, *It is just a shame this one isn't an officer.* It was such a rarity to meet a man who wasn't intimidated by her looks. Well, he wasn't an officer, so she'd just have to take this cocky young spec-five down where he belonged. Without smiling, and in a curt tone, she said, "You're right, Specialist, I'm waiting for a ride. Get my bag and let's go!"

"Yes, Ma'am. Lieutenant, Ma'am. Anything the Lieutenant Ma'am wants, Ma'am."

Lieutenant Carson was instantly sorry she'd pulled such a cheap trick. She could have asked nicely. For that matter, she probably hadn't even needed to ask. He probably would have done it on his own. As it was, his response made her feel small. Then there were his eyes. His soft boyish eyes had in an instant turned hard and mean. She wasn't sure whether it was his tone of voice, his eyes, or the M16 he held that made her feel slightly threatened. There wasn't any doubt he'd been there and back, you could see it in his face, in his eyes. Only an instant had transpired since her command. Since he hadn't yet picked up her bag, she started to stoop to do so when his M16 moved in front of her, blocking her hand's path.

With his left hand, he picked up the bag and said softly, "I'll get it, Lieutenant."

Jim was very pleased with himself. He'd put just the right inflection in his voice when offering her a ride to Tay Ninh. Then she'd barked that command to pick up her bag; it was almost as though she didn't like the idea that he wasn't scared to death of her. What did she expect him to do, stand there with his knees knocking? She was beautiful, that was for sure, but he thought she was also a whore, even if she was a lieutenant. And if she wanted to play hardnose with him, he could play, too; even if it was her game. When she started to reach for her bag he figured two things: first it was her way of saying she realized she'd made a mistake; secondly, she had given him an order and he'd better obey it.

Jim reached down and picked up the small overnight bag, which was surprisingly light. He had to smile to himself. His mother would have packed the kitchen sink in this thing and it would have weighed a hundred pounds. That was the worst thing about going on a vacation, carrying the bags his mother packed. Not this bitch, though; she couldn't have more than a toothbrush and negligee in her bag.

He wasn't sure if he had overstepped his bounds with all the "Lieutenant, Ma'ams" he'd used, so to make amends he had smiled and said, "I'll get it, Lieutenant."

Lieutenant Carson smiled faintly and replied, "Thank you."

Jim only nodded and motioned with his M16 for her to lead. Once out the door, the heat and humidity hit them full force. Lieutenant Carson, not sure where to go, had to wait for Jim. In fact, she would be following him, a small but significant role reversal. Jim watched her fidget as he put her bag down and placed his hat back on his head.

"May I call you Mac?"

"I wish you would."

"Mac, where's your helicopter?"

"Lieutenant, I'm not really sure. Someplace in the maintenance area, I hope."

"What do you mean, you hope?"

"My helicopter blew up yesterday when I was shot down, so my pilot, gunner and I were sent here to pick up a new one."

"No co-pilot?"

"He died of a sucking chest wound and shock and there aren't any other pilots in the company."

Lieutenant Carson looked at Jim and held his eyes for a full heartbeat. There wasn't any question but what he'd said was fact.

She walked directly to his left and allowed him to set their leisurely pace. The maintenance area was a good walking distance away and she, for some reason, was enjoying his company. Since he wasn't an officer, he wouldn't try to get into her pants, and with his self-confidence, it was a good thing he wasn't.

"Lieutenant, what do you know about Tay Ninh?"

"Not a whole lot. It's supposed to be a good-sized base. Why?"

"Do you know we get hit with rocket and mortar fire almost every night? We sleep in bunkers, and the base was partially overrun only a few days ago. Tay Ninh is a dirty, dusty hole where people get killed . . . in their beds! It's not a nice place to visit."

They walked on in silence for a while. "Lieutenant, could I

ask why a finance officer is going to Tay Ninh? There isn't any finance operation there."

Somewhat embarrassed, she replied, "That's really none of your business!"

"No, Ma'am, it's not. I just can't help wondering since there isn't any finance and you're all dressed up like you're going to your college R.O.T.C. graduation dance. Don't misunderstand me, you're my idea of a truly beautiful woman. In fact, I hope I end up married to someone who looks like you. But somehow I just don't think you belong at Tay Ninh, let alone dressed like that."

"Specialist, that's enough!"

"Yes, Ma'am!" They walked a ways further. "Lieutenant, I don't understand something. You could have most any man you want, so why?"

"Specialist, that's enough. I'm giving you a direct order, just shut up until we get to your helicopter! You understand me, Specialist?"

"Yes, Ma'am." Jim started to laugh as he shook his head.

In a slightly irritated voice, Lieutenant Carson said, "And just what do you find so damn funny?"

Jim's thought was, *Ah, so, permission to speak,* but said; "You. First, who, besides the two of us have heard this conversation? Secondly, you're not going to court martial me. If you do, it would greatly embarrass you, but more than that it would greatly embarrass the guy you're meeting."

"You're an insubordinate son of a bitch with a smart mouth. Just how do you know I'm not meeting my husband?"

"Because there isn't any wedding ring and any man who really loved you would never take you to Tay Ninh, not for any reason!" She just looked at him. He was on a roll and decided to make one last push in something that really wasn't any of his business. "So what do you get out of it, Lieutenant, Captain's rank?"

"For a spec-five, you've got a smart mouth and a lot of brass that'll get you in a lot of trouble. Okay, Mr. Smart Mouth, let me ask you a question! Have you been on R&R yet?"

Jim understood her point. "Yes, Ma'am."

Lieutenant Carson was obviously upset. "And you're pointing the finger at me?"

"There's a difference."

"Oh, you bet there is, you're a man and I'm a woman, that's the difference!"

Jim tried to respond calmly. "No, the difference is the seller is considered a cheap, slut-whore. The buyer, he's considered just a good old boy and whether it's right or not, that's the way it is, at least in the military and most of society. That's the difference, Lieutenant."

Nothing more was said the rest of the way. Jim spotted Wright and waved his recognition with the M16 and made a direct path in his direction. Three helicopters were parked in a row just behind Wright. Mr. Walker was seated in the cargo doorway of the middle one.

The first thing Jim noticed about the chopper was the First Cav insignia on the tail boom; the next was the lack of passenger seats or soundproofing.

"Mr. Walker, Specialist Wright, I'd like you to meet Lieutenant Carson. Lieutenant Carson, Mr. Walker, my pilot, and my door gunner, Spec Four Wright."

Jim laughed as both men struggled to regain their composure. Still stunned by her beauty, Mr. Walker said, "Lieutenant, you're going to Tay Ninh?"

"That's right and please save the lecture, I've already had the full course from your crew chief."

Walker smiled. "Mac never was one to mince words. I just want to be sure you know what you're going to. Tay Ninh isn't a nice place to visit. If you're accustomed to Saigon or Vung Tau, you're in for a real shock when you reach Tay Ninh."

"Believe me, Mr. Walker, Mac's told me all about it!"

Jim had picked up the log book and was looking through the various pages. "Mr. Walker, is this ours?"

"Yep."

"Did you see how many hours this thing has on it?"

"Yes, but I wasn't given a choice. Besides, I didn't know what I was getting until I got out here and looked at it. Is it really flyable?"

"According to the log book it is, it just looks like the devil.

It's been test flown and signed off, but I'll still give it a thorough preflight inspection. Major Hobbs will have a hemorrhage when he sees this thing."

"Well, Mac, what do you want to do?"

"I'll tell you this, I don't want to fly in it. The log book says it came in because of structural cracks in the transmission mounts. This thing has so many hours on it, metal fatigue is going to be a real problem. Wright, go over to the maintenance area and find a Specialist Six named Dill. He's the Tech Inspector who signed this crate off. Tell him your pilot would like to speak with him. Lieutenant Carson, you might as well sit down, this is going to take a while. Mr. Walker, here's the log book; as I list them, you write 'em up. Remember, each item gets its own line and don't sign 'em or give anything a status symbol."

Mr. Walker picked up the log book as Lieutenant Carson gave him a dirty look and said, "Wait just a minute, Specialist. This man is a Warrant Officer in the United States Army and is not to . . ."

Mr. Walker interrupted her by placing his hand on her arm. "Lieutenant, could I have a word with you, please?"

"Sure."

"Lieutenant, has Mac done something to irritate you personally?"

"As a matter of fact, yes. He's an insubordinate smartmouth who disobeyed a direct order I gave him on the way over here."

"Just what did he say to you, and what was the order he disobeyed?"

Lieutenant Carson thought better of going through the whole thing so she simply replied, "Just forget it, it's not important anyway! Okay?"

"Whatever you say, Lieutenant. I just don't think you understand. He would never be disrespectful to me. Where he and I have been, you'll never go, and the things we've done to stay alive while there, you'll only read about in books or see in the movies. And furthermore, you should give thanks to God above you'll never be put to the kind of test that man has already passed. Try to understand our relationship. We're in combat every day. We get up in the morning knowing we'll be shot at that day. There are times when we just don't have time for military courtesy. As a result, a crew chief and his pilot develop an understanding about a lot of things. How we talk to each other is just one of many examples. Look, if we're going to fly in that helicopter it better be safe, because I can't pull over to the side of the road and park until it gets fixed. Lieutenant, every time I get in a helicopter, my life depends on that man. If you fly to Tay Ninh with us, yours will, too. From the looks of that chopper, we both better hope Mac knows what he's doing. Sometimes it's necessary for me to help him with his job and I'm happy to do it. Do you get my drift, Lieutenant?"

"Yes." Lieutenant Carson picked up her book and sat down on the crew chief's seat.

Mr. Walker picked up the log book and walked around the tail boom to where Jim was checking the tail rotor. "Find anything serious, Mac?"

"No, Sir—well, at least no one thing. I've found a whole lot of little things though that'll keep a crew chief busy for months. You ready to start listing?"

"Yep."

"Okay, first item: four bullet hole patches, tail boom left side needs spot painted O.D. Same for right side: screws missing from tail boom inspection panel, two snap openers missing on tail rotor drive shaft cover, several rivets loose in tail boom on both right and left sides, all soundproofing missing, passenger seats missing, both cargo doors missing, both cargo door tracks have excessive wear, both first aid kits missing, fire extinguishers missing, left pilot seat not safety wired, magnetic compass missing." Jim climbed into the pilot's seat. "There's play in the foot pedals and I get drag which shouldn't be there."

"What causes that?"

"Oh, there are several things that can cause that and none of them are good." Jim climbed out of the pilot's seat. "Window missing in pilot's door, left side, window broken in right door, snap release broken on door to radio nose compartment." Jim continued to list every little thing he could find wrong with the helicopter. It was up on top that he found the most serious problems. Maintenance had put back on the old dampers that had so much moisture in the hydraulic oil, he couldn't see through the sight gauge. There were push-pull rods with a lot of play in their bearings, and several other things which caused him concern.

Lieutenant Carson had never started to read her book. She'd been more interested in listening to Jim list all the things wrong. The longer the list grew, the more she thought about what Mr. Walker had said. As a result, her respect for him grew. She watched Jim climb off the roof and jump into the cargo area, landing in front of her. Pointing with her head she said, "Mac, I think we're about to get company."

Jim noticed the friendliness was back in her voice and that she called him Mac instead of Specialist. All these things, plus the fact she was giving him advance notice, had to mean she was softening towards him, at least partially. Jim glanced back to see Wright and another man approaching.

"Thank you, Lieutenant. I appreciate it."

Lieutenant Carson smiled and said, "You're welcome, Mac. Is this thing safe to fly?"

"Technically, I suppose so, but personally, I wouldn't fly in it from here to the other side of the post. May I sit down?"

Lieutenant Carson smiled and moved over to give him room. Walker came around the aircraft's nose at the same time Wright and a spec-six approached.

Wright spoke. "Specialist Dill, this is my pilot, Mr. Walker, and my crew chief, Specialist MacLaughlin, and Lieutenant Carson."

Spec-Six Dill was a tall man about six foot six and thin, not weighing more than one hundred fifty pounds. Dill saluted, then placed both hands on his hips and developed an all business expression. "What seems to be the problem, Sir?"

"Are you the tech inspector who signed this aircraft off?"

"Sir, if you looked in the log book you know I did."

Jim looked at Lieutenant Carson seated beside him and in a soft voice said, "And you called me a smart mouth."

She only smiled. Walker's voice was now all business. "Specialist Dill, I'm really not in the mood for any smart ass answers, you got that!"

"Yes, Sir."

"Do you let all the aircraft you work on out of maintenance looking like this?"

"No, Sir."

"Then why this one?"

"Because, Sir, that's the way we got it. All we do is depot level maintenance. In this case that meant replacing the transmission mounts. We don't paint or put missing sound proofing in or replace loose rivets. All that type stuff is done on a company level."

Jim said, "You mean to tell me that those push-pull rods on top shouldn't be replaced?"

"I didn't tell you anything of the kind, all I said is we don't do it."

"Not even if its got excessive play?"

"They don't have excessive play!"

"I think they do! How about the dampers? You can't even see their sight gauges they're so cloudy."

"I don't remember looking at 'em."

"Specialist, would you fly this thing?"

"Sure."

"Just like it is for ten hours a day for ten days?"

"I don't know what that's got to do with anything."

"The point is that there isn't any one thing the aircraft can be grounded for maybe, but all together it's an accident waiting to happen. As a tech inspector you should be ashamed of yourself for letting the thing be test flown, let alone released!"

The two NCO's simply stared at each other until Mr. Walker said, "Specialist, I don't understand how this crate can look so terrible and that chopper right beside us look brand new."

"Sir, the biggest reason is that it is almost brand new. As I remember, it doesn't have two hundred hours on it yet."

Jim asked, "What is it in depot for?"

"It came from the 195th Skychiefs up at Long Binh. It had a sudden stoppage."

Lieutenant Carson asked, "A sudden stoppage, what's that?"

Dill looked at Jim and replied, "You're such a hot shot and think you know my job better than I do, you tell her!"

In a very pleasant voice Jim said, "Specialist, I am a Specialist E-5, which, in case you have forgotten, makes me an NCO just like yourself. Therefore, I would appreciate not being insulted in front of two officers and an enlisted man. Furthermore, not because you want to know how much I know, but because I happen to like Lieutenant Carson, I'll answer her question for you. Lieutenant, a sudden stoppage is when the rotor blades hit a solid object, like a tree, causing them to stop suddenly. The problem, Lieutenant, with a sudden stoppage is there isn't any place in the power train to allow for any slippage. Power is delivered from the engine into a shaft called a short shaft, from there, directly into the transmission, directly into the mast, directly into the rotor head; where it is finally delivered to the rotor blades. Since there isn't any place in the system for slippage when the rotors hit something solid enough to suddenly stop them, it causes a massive internal hemorrhage. Gears break, bearings rupture and bolts pop. As a result, everything that turns has to be removed and replaced: engine, transmission, drive shafts, bearings, everything. And that, Lieutenant, is what a sudden stoppage is all about."

Dill nodded his head and said, "Very good, Specialist, very good indeed."

Jim had an idea. "Specialist Dill, who's supposed to get that ship?"

"The 195th gets it back. When we're done with them, they're test flown and if everything checks out okay, they're parked here till picked up by the receiving company."

Mr. Walker said, "In other words, Specialist, you're not going to fix anything on this helicopter to make it safer to fly?"

"Sir, it's been test flown and signed off as safe to fly."

"I guess that's a matter of opinion, isn't it?"

Dill just stood there and looked at the ground before finally saying, "Sir, if there isn't anything else, I'll be going."

Dill was standing between Mr. Walker and Jim, who was still seated beside Lieutenant Carson. Mr. Walker glanced at Jim, who shrugged his shoulders and shook his head slowly in disgust. Walker looked back at Dill and said, "That will be all, Specialist."

Everyone sat there in silence and watched as Dill walked off. It was Wright who broke the silence. "Well, what are we going to do now?"

Jim and Walker looked at each other and each knew what

the other was thinking. Jim spoke. "Lieutenant, would you rat on us if we committed a little grand larceny?"

Lieutenant Carson laughed and answered, "After listening to you two talk, I'm not interested in riding in this one."

Walker said, "Mac, we'll have to get the log book somehow."

"I can think about that while I preflight the chopper. Keep an eye open for somebody who might see me." In a few minutes Jim returned. "Well, I don't see anything wrong with it and Dill is right, that ship's almost brand new. I've got an idea about the log book. Mr. Walker, tell me what you had to do and how many people were there when you signed for this crate."

"There was only a staff sergeant seated at the front desk. There was another desk behind him but no one was there. I told him who I was and what company I was from and that I was to pick up a Huey. He got the papers I signed from a file cabinet, and the log book was with a stack on his desk."

"How many times did you sign?"

"Just twice."

"What did he do with those papers?"

"I'm not sure. One was in duplicate. In fact, I think I left before he did anything with them."

"What drawer did he get the papers from?"

"Top."

"Okay, Mr. Walker, you can't go back in there because they'll recognize you. So if you and I trade shirts and hats, I'll go in and try to find the papers you signed. I'll leave this log book here and pick up 647's book. I'll have to sign your name to new forms."

"Mac, one wasn't a form, it was like a sign-in sheet that was on a clipboard on the front desk. Besides, you'll never get away with this. That sergeant isn't going to sit there and let you go through his files."

"That's where a beautiful lieutenant dressed to knock your eyeballs out comes in handy."

Lieutenant Carson interrupted. "Just wait one minute! I'm not going to have anything to do with this!"

"Lieutenant, please, all you have to do is go in, ask the desk sergeant to show you where the ladies' room is and have him escort you there."

"No! You're talking about stealing a helicopter, impersonating an officer, forgery and enough other things to send you and anyone involved to jail for thirty years. I don't want any part of it!"

"There isn't any forgery unless Mr. Walker presses charges, which you're not going to do, are you, Mr. Walker?"

"I'll swear it's my signature."

"As for the impersonating an officer, who's going to say, hey, you, you're not an officer! Nobody knows Mr. Walker or me, so no one's going to question me. As for stealing a helicopter, if I sign all the forms, it's not stealing. It'll be a simple case of the sergeant giving the wrong forms to Mr. Walker to sign. As for you, nobody will ever connect you with it. After all, you're just a damsel in distress who asked the nice sergeant to show you to the ladies' room."

"You two are crazy, you know that! What if someone walks in on you?"

"I'll have Wright standing outside to warn me." Jim could see Lieutenant Carson warming to the idea. "Come on, Lieutenant, you see this type of thing done in the movies all the time. Now's your once in a lifetime chance to be part of a military operation, usually called something like 'a midnight requisition.' "

"Yeah, except this is in broad daylight."

"And that's the biggest reason it'll work. Come on, be a sport!"

Lieutenant Carson looked at the three men standing there staring at her. "You're crazy, you really and truly are crazy, all three of you!" Looking at Jim she said, "Especially you." She paused for a moment then continued, "You won't go off and leave me?"

Walker answered, "I give you my word as an officer—you'll leave with us!"

"Your word as an officer! You're talking about stealing a helicopter amongst other things and you're giving me your word as an officer?"

"Please, Lieutenant."

Lieutenant Carson smiled and shook her head. "Well, I do need to use a latrine, but I'm not going to help you guys."

Jim smiled at her and said, "Thanks, Lieutenant."

Lieutenant Carson stood up and brushed her clothing. "I'm giving you guys a direct order, forget about this whole idea." With that she turned and walked towards the office. Jim and Walker traded hats and shirts.

"Mac, I sure hope we get away with this."

"If we don't, you can always fly us out of here in this crate and hope it holds together till we get home."

Jim and Wright were almost to the office door when Lieutenant Carson walked out talking to a staff sergeant. "Wright, you wait outside. If someone comes, rap on that door twice and once more when the coast is clear."

"Mac, don't take too long!"

Jim walked in the door and everything was just as Walker had said. He headed straight for the first desk and started frantically hunting for Walker's forms. Surprisingly, it didn't take him long to locate both. This done, he pulled open the file cabinet's top drawer, pulled out the first blank form he found and ripped out the carbon paper. He threw the blanks in the trash and placed the carbon between the two forms. Moving to the typewriter, he picked up the correction fluid and wiped out the helicopter number. As he blew it dry, he was glad he'd thought of this because once he'd seen the forms, he knew there were far too many things to fill in. Once dry, he placed the forms with carbon in the typewriter and typed in the new numbers. Quickly, he threw the carbon away and placed the forms back where he found them. Last, he switched the log book from the sergeant's desk with the one in his shirt, and changed the number on the clipboard form beside Walker's name. As he walked around the desk, he heard Wright rap on the door twice.

Jim walked outside just as a staff sergeant approached. The sergeant saluted and Jim returned his salute. "Sir, can I help you?" the sergeant asked.

Jim responded just as any officer, "Is your CO around, Sergeant?"

"No, Sir, but I can get him for you in just a second, if you'll step back inside."

"Thank you anyway, Sergeant, I've got a couple of other things to do, I'll just stop back in an hour or two."

"Yes, Sir."

Jim looked over at Wright. "Let's go, Specialist."

Jim and Wright walked away as the staff sergeant entered the maintenance office. "Mac, you didn't forget the log book did you?"

"Nope, it's inside my shirt. Man, you talk about being close, I'm sure glad he didn't get back thirty seconds sooner!" Jim, hardly able to control his excitement, slapped Wright's hand. "We did it, Wright, we really did it."

"Mac, let's don't celebrate yet, we still have to get out of here. I just hope that staff sergeant doesn't notice he's got a log book missing."

"I'll drink to that."

They moved quickly back to Walker, who saw them coming and moved to the new ship. Jim handed Walker the log book and said, "It worked like a charm, let's get out of here!"

"Lieutenant Carson isn't back yet, give me my shirt back and go untie the rotor blades."

"Yes, Sir."

Lieutenant Carson approached as they were changing shirts and quickly climbed into the chopper.

"Well, Mac, I see all went well."

"Yes, Ma'am, thank you, we couldn't have done it without you."

"Somehow I get the impression you'd have found a way."

Walker, who was already strapped into his seat, yelled, "Clear!"

Jim responded, "Clear."

Walker hit the start switch and yelled at Jim, "Mac, you want to drive?"

Without responding, Jim climbed into the co-pilot's seat. He strapped himself in and plugged in his helmet. Walker knew keeping a crew chief happy was easy; give him some stick time and treat him like a person should be treated and you got along just fine. Walker asked ground control for permission to taxi.

Permission was given along with instructions for the path to be followed to the runway. As they taxied out of the maintenance area they went by several choppers parked off to the side. Jim had been looking each ship over carefully and on the next to the last ship he saw what he was looking for.

"Mr. Walker, set it down quick! I'll be right back."

Walker, who didn't know what had happened, instantly dropped the chopper to the pavement. By the time Walker had it on the ground, Jim was unstrapped and climbing out of his seat. "Mac, what's wrong?"

Jim didn't answer as he unplugged his helmet and jumped out the door. He ran to the Huey parked only slightly behind and off to the side. In one leap, he jumped through the ship's open cargo doors, grabbed the large water jug and started to leave when he had another thought. Setting down the water jug, he ran around to the right side of the chopper and opened the storage compartment door. There it was, a tool box. Jim grabbed it and ran without even closing the door. The tool box was so heavy, he knew it had to be well stocked. With the tool box in one hand and the water jug in the other, it was all he could do to walk fast. Wright saw him coming and jumped out to help. As Jim threw the tool box on board 647, he looked back to see two enlisted men running towards them as fast as they could. He jumped on board and motioned to Walker to take off quickly. Jim sat in the cargo door briefly and watched the two men grow smaller and smaller as Walker moved it down the runway. As he turned to climb back into the co-pilot's seat, Jim saw Lieutenant Carson smiling at him and slowly nod. Jim returned her smile and winked quickly at her. He then climbed back into his seat, plugged in his helmet and said, "Hi, I'm back."

"I can see! You're crazy, you know that?"

"Yes, Sir, but I got us a water jug and a tool box, neither of which I could get out of supply back at Tay Ninh."

"Any idea who the two trying to run us down were?"

"My guess is they were Skychiefs and that was their aircraft whose load we just lightened. Come to think of it, this was probably their aircraft also. I'll bet that's why they were parked there, they'd brought a crew down to pick up their ship."

All three men laughed a good, deep, hard laugh. Lieutenant Carson, not having a helmet, just sat there wondering what was so funny. Once they'd stopped laughing, Walker said, "Mac, you've got it."

Jim took hold of the controls. "I've got it. We have enough fuel to make it to Tay Ninh?"

"No, but it doesn't make any difference; we have to stop at Long Binh Replacement and pick up some new pilots. We can get fuel there."

"You didn't tell me about that."

"Mac, I don't tell you everything I know, and in case you've forgotten, I am the officer in this crew!"

After refueling, they made the short hop to Long Binh Replacement Depot. Once on the ground, Mr. Walker told Wright to go over to a group of men seated not too far away and ask if any were headed for the 187th. Shortly, Wright returned followed by six warrant officers carrying their duffel bags.

"Mac, are we going to get off the ground with all that weight?"

"I don't know, Sir. If I had known there'd be six of them, I wouldn't have topped it off with fuel. They probably average one hundred sixty pounds each with another eighty in each duffel bag. That's two hundred forty times six, or fourteen hundred forty pounds, plus the three of us and Lieutenant Carson. Of course, we don't have the guns and ammo, and this thing is supposed to have a brand new engine, but the thermometer says forty-two degrees. That's awfully hot, well over one hundred degrees Fahrenheit. I don't know how much humidity there is, but you can bet a bunch. I guess there's only one way to find out, give it a little try and if you can't get it off the ground all we can do is kick one of them out, which should make it light enough to get airborne."

As Jim talked, he and Walker watched the new pilots load their duffel bags and eyeball Lieutenant Carson as they climbed in. It was obvious she was becoming very uncomfortable with the looks. Lieutenant Carson looked up in time to see Jim and Walker looking back over the radio console. Unsnapping her seatbelt, she climbed over the duffel bags and leaned over to talk to Mr. Walker. Walker pushed his lip mike out towards her and keyed his switch to make it easier to hear what she had to say.

"Mr. Walker, take me back to Vung Tau."

"What?"

"You heard me, take me back to Vung Tau."

"Lieutenant, I can't do that. I'm supposed to take you to Tay Ninh. Besides, I'm not really anxious to take this ship back to Vung Tau right away."

"Come on, Mr. Walker, I've changed my mind. I'm not going to Tay Ninh. I want to go back to Vung Tau."

Walker turned just enough to look Jim in the eyes. He shrugged his shoulders and gave an "Oh, brother" look, then spoke into the mike so she couldn't hear. "Sir, she does outrank you."

"Yeah, I'm painfully aware of that." Walker turned back to Lieutenant Carson. "Lieutenant, I've got orders to take you and these men to Tay Ninh. I can't go back to Vung Tau."

"Mister, I don't care what your orders are. I'm giving you new ones. Take me to Vung Tau!"

"Yes, Ma'am." Walker turned around, looked out the windshield, and spoke to himself. Jim didn't need the intercom to tell what Walker had said. He was getting better at lip reading and the "Well, shit" came across Walker's lips as clearly as if he'd keyed his mike.

Jim wasn't very happy about going back to Vung Tau, either. He'd been looking forward to getting home before the rest of the flight and having a couple hours of daylight. He could take a nice hot shower then hit the club before anyone else got there. That was out now. They'd be lucky to make it home before dark. Walker was already on the radio getting the necessary flight clearances. Once airborne, Walker said, "You wanna drive?"

"Sure."

"Okay, Mac, you got it. Keep it on this heading and just shy of red line. I'm not going to fiddle around taking this bitch home. I just hope some bastard at Tay Ninh doesn't raise hell with me because his piece of ass for the night changed her mind."

Jim held it just shy of the one hundred twenty knot red line all the way down to Vung Tau. As a result, it didn't take long to get there. There's a lot of difference between one hundred twenty knots and the casual eighty knot cruising speed.

Once on the ground, Lieutenant Carson jumped out with her bag and took only a couple of steps before setting it down and returning to the ship. She had gotten out on Jim's side, so it was his door she opened. He pushed his lip mike out for her to speak and keyed it so Wright and Walker could also hear what she had to say. "I just came back to thank you guys for a very interesting and unusual day." Looking at Jim, "I'm glad I met you." Glancing over to Walker, "Both of you." Jim smiled as she stepped down and shut his door. She waved good-bye as she stooped to pick up her bag. Walker watched Jim wave good-bye slowly, and with a strange look on his face, turned the wave into a salute. Lieutenant Carson, whose eyes hadn't moved from Jim's, broke into a big smile and returned the salute.

Walker, who couldn't believe what he was seeing said, "What the hell was that all about?" There was only silence for a response. "Mac, what'd you do, fall in love with that whore?"

Jim laughed and said, "Don't be silly."

The two men sat and watched her backside as she moved briskly across the pavement. "I'll tell ya, Mac, that's one hell of a lot of woman!"

"Yes, Sir."

Only slightly sarcastically Walker asked, "Be okay if we go home now?"

Jim, still not wanting to take his eyes off her, nodded his head and replied, "Yes, Sir."

As Walker pulled pitch to the rotors and headed down the runway Jim asked, "Mr. Walker, can we red line it going home, too?"

"Yep. You got it, and I'll get us as straight a path home as artillery will allow."

12

What's in a Hand?

"For he will command his angels concerning you to guard you in all your ways." PSALMS 91:11 NIV

In the west, orange and red rays streaked skyward from the rapidly setting sun. It was beautiful, even though the black bellowing smoke from the burning fuel dump in Saigon made a sobering contrast. VC sapper* squads had blown and burned a large part of the Saigon fuel storage area the night before. As a result, from fifteen hundred feet above Tay Ninh, one could still see the flames that leaped skyward changing into clouds of deep, rolling black smoke, which rose several thousand feet.

Jim was glad they were on short final approach. It meant they'd be on the ground ahead of the flight and with enough daylight left to pull his daily inspection. With just a little luck, he could even get a warm shower and still have plenty of time for a drink at the club.

Once on the ground, Mr. Walker parked beside the fuel pumps for Wright to top it off. From there he took it to their revetment and started shutdown procedures. Once Wright had opened the pilots' doors, Jim climbed out and saluted each new officer and shook hands. He introduced himself and was giving them directions to the company area when Mr. Walker turned around and shouted, "Hey, Mac! Put your helmet on!"

Jim excused himself and motioned to Wright to tie down the

---

* Sapper—VC and NVA demolition people. Usually willing to blow themselves up along with their target.

rotors. He noticed the new pilots just stood around as though they didn't know what to do. As he put on his helmet, then plugged it in he said, "Yes, Sir."

"Mac, the flight's on long final and Chalk Two has lost tail rotor control!"

Jim jumped into the cargo area and flipped the switch allowing him to hear the flight.

"Chalk Two, this is Lead. I've got clearance from the tower for you to put it down on the runway. Flight, the rest of us will move directly into the revetments. Chalk Two, good luck and remember to keep your airspeed up."

"Roger, Lead, see you in the club."

Jim, looking out the cargo door, could see the single ship headed for the runway as the flight approached short final on the revetments. The brave words of Chalk Two's pilot didn't hide the nervousness in his voice as he called out his airspeed and altitude.

The tail rotor's sole function was to prevent the helicopter from spinning like a top at slow speeds. Once the helicopter reached a speed of about sixty knots, the air flowing by it would hold a Huey straight, so to land a Huey without a tail rotor required landing on a pair of skids at about sixty knots. Jim knew the procedure. Twice he'd come in without tail rotor control. Fortunately, on both occasions, his pilots had the skill to do it right; one little mistake meant a crash and roll. There wasn't any question in his mind it was the most dangerous of all the emergency landing procedures. Perhaps it was even more dangerous because the pilots never practiced it. Whatever the reason, Jim was glad he wasn't on board Chalk Two.

Everyone's eyes were glued to the single ship as it rapidly approached the runway. Mr. Walker broke the silence. "He's too high. He'll never make it. I know what he's done, he's forgotten the runway's at twelve feet above sea level and his altimeter is set at zero. He hasn't made the mental twelve foot subtraction. He's twelve feet too high! He thinks he's at twenty-four feet and he's really at thirty-six!"

Jim ripped off his helmet as Walker switched the radio over so he could talk to Chalk Two. Jim yelled in terror, "Wright, he's going to crash! Come on, let's go!" Pointing his finger at the closest pilot still standing there holding his duffel bag, Jim ordered, "You, get the fire extinguisher out of our ship and follow us!"

As they ran, Jim kept praying the pilot would touch down with both skids at the same time. If he didn't, he'd bounce and flip over.

Jim, and the rest of the group behind him, stopped running about a hundred feet from where the broken machine first bounced. They stood and watched as it slid only a short way before spinning and skipping sideways. Then like a giant wounded monster, it flipped over onto its right side and died, throwing rotor blade pieces and various other parts of its anatomy in all directions. Jim and Wright ran to the wounded chopper and started climbing up its skids. Screams of intense pain could be heard inside as Wright opened the pilot's door to help him out. Jim climbed inside to find the gunner struggling to climb out. Shouting at the gunner over the continuing screams of the injured crew chief, Page, Jim asked, "You okay?"

"I see two of everything."

One of the new pilots had climbed up to help. "Sir, help him down; he's got a concussion."

That done, Jim climbed on down inside. The screams of pain coming from both the crew chief and peter pilot caused Jim to lose precious seconds wondering if he could get both out. As he looked at the peter pilot he could see through the window the others were working from the outside to free him. Jim turned to the crew chief. The small of JP-4 fuel penetrated his nostrils and he knew all caution had to be discarded.

The crew chief's left hand was pinned between the ground and the edge of the ceiling. Two bones protruding from the compound fracture made it a grotesque sight with blood seeming to be everywhere. Jim heard the psst!psst! of the fire extinguisher as he ripped his belt from its loops.

"Page, this is going to hurt!" Page only nodded his head and continued to moan. Quickly, Jim slipped the belt under Page's arm, hooked the webbing into the buckle and pulled it as tight as he could. Page let out a scream that caused Jim to look back at him lying there gritting his teeth. But the bleeding had pretty well stopped. Looking up at Wright standing on the skid looking in, Jim shouted, "Wright, try to rock it so we can get his hand free!"

"You got it!"

Looking back at some officers standing there watching Wright, he shouted, "Hey you guys, give me a hand!"

Jim looked at Page and said, "Pull." It was useless, the hand wouldn't budge. Then it happened—Jim heard someone yell, "Fire!"

Wright, still on the skid, shouted down, "Mac, it's on fire! Get the hell out of there!"

Jim felt his heart jump and the adrenaline rush through his system. Page, almost in tears cried, "Mac, don't leave me!"

Jim's hand moved swiftly in and out of his pocket. In the same flick of a second that the blade flashed from its handle, Wright shouted, "Mac! Get out! It's going to blow!"

As though in that same fraction of a second Page shouted in panic, "Do it, Mac! Do it!" The blade was sharp and Jim struck where the bone protruded. With the first slice, Page let out a scream that came from the very depths of his soul, and collapsed into a state of unconscious shock.

As a farm boy Jim had helped butcher hogs and cattle since childhood. He knew how much force it took to cut raw meat and with the second slice the hand was completely severed. Next, he cut the two shoulder straps on Page's chicken plate, with each requiring only one quick stroke. At the same time but with his left hand, Jim ripped open the velcro strap at the waist allowing the chicken plate to fall free.

Only a few short seconds had passed since Wright's first shout of fire. Now there were several people yelling 'Fire!' but Wright was still standing on the skid waiting to help get Page out. Jim quickly refolded the knife and slipped it back into his pocket. With the adrenaline still flowing in his body, he threw Page over his shoulder in a fireman's carry. Using the pilot's seats as steps, he climbed high enough for Wright to reach the still unconscious Page. With the help of a pilot who had joined Wright, they got Page over the side and into the arms of others. Now there was only Wright left on the skid to help Jim out as the others had all started to run away from the burning aircraft. As Jim threw his leg over the side, Wright jumped and

Jim saw the flames leaping up from the engine compartment. He could feel the heat and hear the crackling of the fire. Jumping as far away as he could, he hit the ground and fell, rolling over once and coming to his feet on a run. Only two steps had been taken before the explosion behind him knocked him once again to the ground. This time Walker was there to help him up and the two moved quickly to a safe distance where the rest of the group greeted them with applause and cheers. Everyone wanted to shake Jim's hand and pat his back. Yet the fire behind him drew their attention like a magnet. Jim also turned and looked back and for the first time, heard the screams and realized they hadn't been able to get the peter pilot out. The burning blob of human flesh caused his heart to sink rapidly, and the screams of pain caused shivers to race up and down his spine. The burning body twisted and jerked and its face contorted with pain making it look as though its eyes would jump from their sockets. Someone off to the side asked, "Major, should I shoot him?"

Major Hobbs said, "Give me your M16. I'll do it." Before the major's hand could reach the offered rifle, a second explosion sent a giant fireball skyward. With that explosion the pilot's pain ended.

Jim turned and walked through the crowd hypnotized by the burning mass in front of it. As he passed through the back of the group, he saw Halsey approach and thought, *I hope I don't have to put up with any of his shit.* Mr. Halsey was unaware of all that had just transpired, other than the obviously burning aircraft.

"Mac, what happened?"

Jim, with tears in his eyes, only looked at the ground, then slowly shook his head and his shoulders. "MacLaughlin, you're a mess, no hat, no belt. Where the hell's your belt, anyway?"

Jim never knew why he did it. In fact, it happened almost before he realized what he'd done. Maybe it was just a gut response which caused his right hand to fly up with all the force left in his body and strike Halsey in the left cheek, sending him sprawling to the ground. Halsey looked up in an expression of shock that changed to a smile. Finally, he sat up and laughed as he said, "Thanks, MacLaughlin, you don't know how happy this makes me."

Jim didn't respond. He simply turned and walked away, sure that by morning he'd be, at the very least, a Spec-Four again. Jim hadn't gone very far when Kenny pulled up in the platoon quarter-ton pickup.

"Mac, you've got blood all over you. You hurt?"

Jim looked at himself for the first time and realized how bad he did look. Blood was on both hands, arms and down his right pant leg. "I'm okay, Kenny. Do me a favor, will you?"

"Name it."

"Give me a ride back to the revetment so I can pick up my stuff, and the new ship's log book."

"Hop in." Kenny turned around and drove off quickly.

Once at the ship, Jim collected his gear and was back in the pickup in less than a minute. As Kenny drove towards the maintenance area he said, "Mac, I saw you hit Halsey. I just want you to know I'll swear he fell down on his own if you want."

Jim smiled and patted Kenny on the shoulder replying, "Thanks Kenny, but you don't want to end up in the brig with me, do you?"

"Hey, if it gets rid of Halsey . . ."

Once back in the company area, Jim showered and put on clean clothes. He was in the mess hall eating when Gillett came in. Their eyes met and Jim knew it wasn't good. "Mac, the CO wants to see you."

"Would it be okay if I finish eating first?"

"Sure, I've got to go find Kenny anyway. He wants to see both of you. Why don't you meet me in the hooch?"

Jim entered the hooch and heard muffled sobs. Walking back through the hooch, he found Green sitting on his bunk crying. "Green, what's wrong?"

Green only shook his head and said, "Nothing."

Jim noticed the letter in Green's hand and sat down beside him. "Come on, Green, you might as well tell me."

"I got a letter from my mom. Mary Ann, she's my girl; we were going to get married when I got home. My mom says she announced her plans to marry some guy she met at college. In two months she'll be Mrs. Somebody Else. Oh, Mac, I loved her so much. My chest, the pain . . . the pain! Why couldn't she wait? I waited for her. I never messed around, not so much as a flirt. I love her so much!" Green lowered his head into his hands and cried.

Jim patted his shoulder and said, "I'm sorry, Green, I know how you feel."

Green, between sobs asked, "You got a girl, Mac?"

"No, she dumped me when I joined the Army. I wrote her letters but she wasn't even kind enough to write back."

"She get married?"

"Not yet. She marries the day before I get home. I get the privilege of thinking about her on her honeymoon my first night home."

"How long did it take you to get over it?"

"I haven't. The pain's still there but I go on. They say time heals all wounds; maybe it will, maybe it won't. Right now, Green, I think when I'm fifty I'll still love her, but maybe by the time I'm fifty I won't even remember she ever was."

"Thanks, Mac, but somehow it doesn't help."

"I know, Green. I know. Try getting drunk and passing out, when you're unconscious or asleep, it doesn't hurt anymore."

Green sat there and cried with Jim holding him. Shortly, the hooch door opened and Gillett hollered, "Mac, you in there?"

"Yeah, I'll be right there."

Green fell flat on his bunk and covered his head with a pillow as Jim stood to leave, but turning back he said, "Green, you might as well have it straight. The hurting doesn't go away, it just gets to the point where you think it's normal. Once you reach that point, you'll forget what it feels like not to hurt. Then you'll think you're back to normal and who knows, maybe you are. At least you don't realize you're still hurting."

Jim joined Gillett and Kenny waiting just outside the door. "Hi, Mac."

"Hi, Kenny. What's the Old Man want you for?"

"Oh, Halsey probably told him I saw something."

Gillett interrupted to say, "You two go ahead and go on over to the orderly room. I've got to take a leak. I'll be right with you."

Kenny and Jim headed in the direction of the orderly room. "Mac, this has to be a rather familiar walk for you."

"Yeah, one I'm getting tired of."

"Mac, tell me what you're going to say so I'll have the same story."

"Look, Kenny, tell him the truth. There isn't any point in lying, there were too many other guys standing around. All you'll do by lying is get yourself in trouble, and it won't help me in the end."

They entered the orderly room and were told to sit down. Kenny leaned toward Jim and whispered, "I'm going to tell him I didn't see a thing. I was watching the fire."

Jim nodded his head. The two sat silently for what seemed like hours. Jim tried to think of all the possibilities and decided his only chance was to plead memory lapse, due to what he'd just been through. Gillett came in shortly after they'd been seated and was called into the CO's office. Finally, he came back out and said, "Kenny, Major Hobbs will see you now."

Kenny entered, had the usual problem walking to the CO's desk, came to attention and saluted. "Sir, Specialist Kenny reports."

Major Hobbs returned the salute but kept Kenny at attention.

"Specialist, tell me what you saw happening on the flight line this evening."

Kenny told the Major everything just as he remembered it, except he left out seeing Jim hit Halsey.

"Specialist, did you leave anything out?"

"No, Sir."

"You didn't happen to see Specialist MacLaughlin hit Mr. Halsey, did you?"

"No, Sir. Did he do that, Sir?"

"Yes, he did!"

"Well, Sir, I was watching the fire and driving at the same time and didn't see anything like that."

"Specialist, have any of the other enlisted men said anything about seeing him hit Mr. Halsey?"

"No, Sir."

"Very well, you're dismissed."

Kenny saluted and left. As he walked by MacLaughlin he whispered, "I told Hobbs I didn't see a thing." With that, Kenny walked outside and found a place in the dark, where he could wait unseen and watch the door.

In the meantime, Major Hobbs turned to the three men standing along the wall. "Captain Wolf, what do you think?"

"Well, Sir, he could be telling the truth, or he could be lying. Either way, as long as he sticks to that story, he's worthless as a witness."

"Mr. Halsey, how about you?"

"Sir, I think the man's lying through his teeth. He was in that quarter ton headed straight for us. He had to see it!"

"Yes, so you said. Sergeant Gillett, your turn."

"Yes, Sir. Well, Sir, I agree with Captain Wolf."

Hobbs smiled and said, "Very diplomatic of you, Sergeant."

Captain Wolf turned to Mr. Halsey and said, "Too bad none of the officers saw it."

"Yes, Sir, it is. But just like you, they were watching the fire."

"There wasn't anyone besides you who could possibly have seen anything?"

"No, I don't think so. I got there after everyone else, and MacLaughlin had started to leave by himself."

Captain Wolf, with the irritation he felt showing, barked, "Mr. Halsey, stand at attention! Damn it, you play this game with the enlisted men all the time and that's part of the reason we're here now. I am a captain, and your superior, and you will address me as such! We're not in the club having a beer and you damn well better remember it!"

"Yes, Sir! I will, Sir. The point is, Captain, I was struck by an NCO and I want him jailed for it!"

Major Hobbs broke in. "Captain, Mr. Halsey, this isn't getting us anywhere! Sergeant, did you tell Specialist MacLaughlin why he's here?"

"No, Sir."

"Okay, Sergeant, bring him in."

"Yes, Sir." Gillett walked out to the orderly room where Jim was waiting. Jim's mind had been at work and he had decided several things. One, he wasn't going to admit to hitting Halsey.

Two, they must not have any officers as witnesses or they wouldn't have messed with Kenny. Third, and the thing that bothered him only slightly, was Kenny had said Hobbs, not Appleton. Why would the Major be running things?

Gillett looked at Jim and said, "Your turn, Mac."

"Gillett, can I talk to you first?"

Gillett glanced over to the CQ seated only a few feet away at the company clerk's desk. "I don't think that would be a good idea. Let's go, Mac."

Jim nodded his head only slightly and knocked on the door.

"Come in."

This time he wasn't surprised to see Halsey standing alone against the far wall with Captain Wolf seated in the chair Major Hobbs had occupied only the night before. Once again, he made a sharp entrance and came to attention directly in front of Major Hobbs. "Sir, Specialist MacLaughlin reports."

Jim raised his right arm in salute and it was a real race to see which man got his arm down first—Hobbs returning the salute, or Jim.

"Specialist, I assume you know why you're here."

"I haven't been told, Sir."

"At ease, Specialist. Mac, we're all very proud of what you did to get Page out. You put your life on the line. Captain Wolf wants to put you in for a Silver Star. Personally, I think you deserve it. The only problem is, Mr. Halsey thinks we should send you to jail. What do you think?"

"Sir, I think the medal would be very nice."

Major Hobbs slowly shook his head.

"Perhaps, Sir, it would be best if we just forgot about the medal and also Mr. Halsey's idea. I'm even willing to transfer to another helicopter company, if that would be acceptable, Sir."

"Did you hit him, Specialist?"

There was a long pause, during which Jim tried to figure what Hobbs had in his hand that he was willing to play verbal poker. "Sir, I'm not in the habit of lying and I'm not going to start now."

"That doesn't answer my question, yes, or no."

Jim looked over at Captain Wolf. "Sir, do I have any trouble with any officer except Mr. Halsey?"

"Mac, you're not answering the Major's question."

Major Hobbs spoke. "Yes, or no, Specialist!"

"Sir, if I say yes, what happens to me?"

"We'll talk about that after you say 'yes.' We're not playing poker, MacLaughlin, because your hand's exposed. Now I want a straight answer out of you."

"Sir, can I tell you what happened?"

"Specialist, I'm trying to be nice. Now, I'm giving you a direct order, yes or no?"

"In that case, no, Sir."

"Okay, now that we've finally got that out, tell me what happened."

"Sir, I've changed my mind. I don't care to explain."

"Just who the hell do you think you're talking to, MacLaughlin? I gave you an order. Now I want an explanation, and I don't want anymore of your smart ass answers. You got that, Specialist?"

"Yes, Sir."

"Well, you'd better, or you'll find yourself a PFC just because of your mouth. Now everyone in this room knows you hit Mr. Halsey, so we might just as well find out why!"

"Sir, I'll not admit to hitting Mr. Halsey and I don't think you'd expect me to. I knew their chopper was going to crash, and in my hurry to give aid to the guys in it, I didn't take the time to get my hat out of the chopper I was in. Mr. Halsey stopped me afterwards and dressed me down for not having a hat on or a belt. I'd used my belt as a tourniquet on Page's arm. He also didn't like my uniform being so dirty. It was Page's blood and the dirt from being knocked down when their ship blew."

Jim could see both Major Hobbs and Captain Wolf look over at Halsey. It was obvious he hadn't told them some or all of it. Major Hobbs spoke. "Mr. Halsey, is there anything about Specialist MacLaughlin's story you disagree with?"

"Only that he could have explained, instead of hitting me, Sir. He didn't even try to explain . . ."

Jim interrupted. "Sir, you could have fallen down and busted your nose and blamed it on me."

Halsey shouted, "MacLaughlin, you've got more brass than a fuckin' monkey. You know that?"

Hobbs interrupted. "Okay, stop it! Both of you, at attention! Mr. Halsey, you're dismissed. Wait in the other room."

"Yes, Sir." Halsey saluted and left.

Jim, still at attention, waited for Major Hobbs to speak. "At ease, Mac. How old are you?"

"I just turned twenty, Sir." There was a long pause before Hobbs spoke.

"He's right, you know. You're brass, for one so young. It's really gotten you in trouble this time. I understand you also stole that helicopter today. Oh, don't look so worried. I know all about it. You switched shirts with Mr. Walker and forged his signature. You've had quite a day, haven't you: stole a Huey, cut a man's arm off, and busted Mr. Halsey in the mouth."

"Sir, I never said I did that and unless there is a witness . . ."

"MacLaughlin, shut up before I chew you up and throw you to the dogs."

Jim stood there silently. "Specialist, I'll tell you what I'll do. You accept an Article 15 and I'll only take one stripe and a couple hundred dollars."

"And if I don't accept it?"

"Mr. Halsey will probably insist on a court martial. Which would mean jail if convicted."

"Can I think about it, Sir?"

"Hell, no, you can't think about it! You know that. Make up your mind. Now!"

"Sir, are there any witnesses?"

"That's not necessary and you know it. All you have to do is look at his swollen black eye."

"Sir, I'll take the court martial."

"That's the stupidest thing you could do and you know it!"

"Yes, Sir, but a lot could change between now and then. I could be killed or wounded by then and, if not, I'll go into it denying everything."

"That's enough, Specialist, I get the message! Now let me

give you one: right now, you're only looking at thirty days down at LBJ. You kill Halsey, or even try, I'll see to it you spend the rest of your life there! You got that?"

Jim allowed himself to let only the slightest smile cross his lips. "Yes, Sir, I've got it."

"Very well, you're dismissed." Jim saluted, turned and left.

On his way through the orderly room Halsey's eyes met his. Jim smiled broadly at Mr. Halsey and walked on by. Neither man spoke. Jim stepped outside and took a deep breath. Kenny walked up. "Mac, how did you come out?"

"I took a court martial."

"Damn that Halsey! It's too bad that frag the other night wasn't live."

"You know, Kenny, I'm beginning to think the same thing."

"Come on, Mac, I'll buy you a beer."

Jim put his arm around Kenny's shoulder. "Kenny, that's the best offer I've had tonight."

Back in the CO's office, Major Hobbs looked at Gillett and said, "Sergeant, you're dismissed. On your way out tell Mr. Halsey to step in."

Gillett came to attention and saluted. "Sir, could I speak openly to you?"

"I wish you would, Sergeant."

"Without repercussions, Sir?"

"What do you want to say, Sergeant?"

"Sir, do you know how this feud between Mac and Mr. Halsey got started?"

"I believe it was the broken window incident, where Mr. Halsey ended up paying for the window and getting an Article 15."

"Yes, Sir. Ever since then Mr. Halsey has made life unpleasant for MacLaughlin. I'm surprised he hasn't punched him out a long time ago."

"Or thrown a frag under his bed?"

"Major, you know as well as I do, Mac didn't do that."

Major Hobbs looked startled. "Gillett, you know who did it, don't you?"

"No, Sir."

"Don't lie to me, Sergeant!" He paused. "Wait a minute—you did it!"

"No, Sir, I didn't and I've got enough witnesses as to where I was to prove it."

"Well, then, you know who did!"

"Yes, Sir, I do! And so does MacLaughlin. In fact, he knew when you offered him your deal. But as much as he hates Mr. Halsey, he refuses to burn someone else for trying to help him."

"How did he find out?"

"He guessed, and after leaving here the other night, he simply tricked the guy into admitting it."

"You really like MacLaughlin, don't you?"

"Yes, Sir, I do. And I don't think he deserves what he's going to get out of this. The whole company would be better off without Mr. Halsey. It wouldn't be better off without Mac."

"Who did the fragging, Sergeant?"

"No, Sir. You said I could speak freely. Sir, you and I both know in the States Mac wouldn't stand a chance. But here, Sir, you're the law. You don't have to send him up regardless of what Mr. Halsey wants. Sir, you won't have any more trouble from Mac, he's only got about two and a half months left in country. He's put up with more than he should have had to already. You can hold this over his head if he gets out of line, which he won't, and I think Captain Wolf will agree. That's all, Sir."

"Very well, Sergeant. You're dismissed, and thank you for your honesty."

Gillett saluted and left.

In the club, Jim, Kenny and Athia were all on their way to a good drunk. Gillett walked in, sat down, and was the first to speak. "Well, Mac, how you are going to get out of this one?"

Jim laughed and said, "Something will come along, you have to have faith."

"Mac, I don't think you truly grasp the severity of this situation."

"You're wrong, Gillett, I grasp it. I just don't know what the hell I'm supposed to do about it."

"Well, for starters, you could have taken the Article 15."

"No, I'll get to the court martial and drag out every little shitty thing Halsey has ever done. I may go to jail, but I'll fix it so he never gets promoted again."

"Mac, don't kid yourself; besides it's not worth it."

Kenny interrupted. "Gillett, I've got a question. Do you think we could scare Halsey out of pressing charges?"

"Not without the officers' help."

"They'd help, there are several of them who don't like Halsey any more than we do."

"I don't know. I'm not sure they'd risk it for an NCO. What kind of scare do you have in mind?"

"Well, you know Mr. Lucas is always running some kind of lottery. Maybe we could get him to run one on when Halsey gets killed."

"That's enough! I don't want to have any more of that kind of talk!"

"Gillett, I wasn't going to suggest we really kill him, just talk like we will."

"It could backfire, too, and make the bastard determined to send Mac up, regardless of what happens to him."

"But, Gillett, if the officers will help, they could convince him to drop the charges."

"I don't know. What do you think, Mac?"

"Sounds like the best idea I've heard so far."

Gillett saw Wright walk in and said, "By the way, Wright will get a Bronze Star for helping get Page out of that chopper."

Jim looked at Gillett and said, "Big deal. He can take that Bronze Star and it'll still cost him a dime for a cup of coffee."

Wright walked up and sat down. "Hi, fellows." Everyone returned Wright's greeting before he said, "Hey, Mac, did you hear the good news?"

"What's that, Wright?"

"I get a Bronze Star for this afternoon!"

"Hey, that's great, Wright! I'm really glad, you deserve it! Congratulations."

"Mac, could I fly as your permanent gunner?"

"Wright, I don't really think you'd want to. For one thing, I probably won't be flying more than a day or two."

"What are you talking about?"

Jim and Gillett exchanged glances. "Wright, you get a Bronze Star; I get a court martial."

Wright couldn't believe it. "What in the world for?"

"Halsey says I hit him."

"When did you do that, and why?"

"Why, Wright? I'm surprised at you, not even asking if I hit him." Jim smiled and added, "You know I'd never hit a superior officer."

Wright sat there looking stunned as Gillett said, "Mac, let's go see what's happening on the other side."

The two got up and walked through the door to the NCO side. Both drank Jack Daniel's Black and RC as they talked, figuring it would be their last chance. The hours slipped by quickly. Finally, Gillett reminded Jim he had to fly tomorrow and it was past midnight.

Jim used the latrine and was almost back to the hooch when, on impulse, he made a right turn and headed for the hospital.

Walking through the big double doors, he entered a brightly lit hallway. Not sure where to go he started to walk forward slowly, when a nurse, carrying a tray, stepped out of a door just in front of him, "May I help you, Specialist?"

"Yes, Ma'am, I'm looking for a Spec-Four Page. He was brought in earlier, with his left hand cut off."

"Oh, yes! I remember him. He's two doors down but you can't go in there now, it's almost twelve-thirty. He's had major surgery and wouldn't be coherent."

"Lieutenant, please. I'm the guy who cut his hand off."

"Oh!" There was a short pause before she said, "In that case, we can check and see if he's awake." The lieutenant led the way to Page's bedside and turned on a bedside light. Very softly she said, "Specialist, if you're awake, you have a visitor."

There was no response, so the lieutenant turned to Jim and said, "I'm sorry, but he's asleep and you'll have to leave."

"Lieutenant, could I just sit here in a chair for a while?"

"No, I'm afraid not."

As they turned to leave, a captain walked in. The lieutenant addressed him. "Doctor, this is the man who cut Specialist Page's hand off."

The captain looked at Jim and said, "Tell me about it."

"There's not much to tell, Sir. He was pinned inside a Huey that was on fire. The only way to get him out was to cut off the hand where the arm bones were sticking out."

"What did you use?"

Jim reached in his pocket and slowly pulled out his knife. He held it out slightly, pushed the button and the blade sprang into a lock position with a clang. "This."

The lieutenant's eyes bulged only slightly larger than the captain's, whose mouth was also hanging open. The captain closed his mouth and swallowed, then said, "Where did you get that thing?"

Jim answered as though it wasn't any big deal. "Supply. It's Army issue. Sir, did you happen to save the belt I used as a tourniquet?" The doctor looked down at Jim's waist and then back up questioningly. "Sir, I had another belt, but I would like to have the buckle back."

The captain turned to the nurse and said, "Lieutenant, see if you can find his belt and buckle, please."

"Yes, Doctor."

Looking back at Jim he said, "You can put that thing away. I'd also like to say, you did a good job. Are you going to get a medal?"

"No, Sir, I'm getting court martialed."

"For cutting his hand off?"

"No, Sir. Could I speak to you in confidence, Captain?"

"You bet! I want to hear this. Just a minute, I'll take off my gown. Come on over here and sit down."

Jim told the doctor the whole story, leaving out nothing. He added the necessary background information on Mr. Halsey and had just finished, when the nurse walked in. "Specialist, here's the buckle. I don't think you'd want the belt."

"Thank you, Lieutenant."

The captain stood and said, "Lieutenant, set a chair up beside Specialist Page's bunk for this man. How soon is his medication due?"

The lieutenant took the chart from Page's bunk, looked it over and answered, "In about ten minutes, Doctor."

She handed the chart to the doctor, who looked it over and hung it back. "He gets a couple of shots so he'll be waking up.

You can talk to him then. Just don't stress him. If he falls asleep, let him sleep."

"Yes, Sir. Thank you, Sir."

"You're welcome, Specialist. What did you say your XO's name was?"

"Major Hobbs, Sir. Captain, are you going to talk to him?"

"Oh, I might remind him he could find himself in my care one day."

"Thank you, Sir." The captain only smiled as he left.

Soon the lieutenant returned pushing a medical cart. She woke Page and gave him his shots, then told him he had a visitor. Jim walked over and sat down in the chair she'd provided. Page saw him coming and smiled. "Mac!"

"Hi, Page. How ya' feel?"

Page spoke slowly and with great effort. "Not very good." And yet Jim could see a faint smile as Page continued, "but better than the alternative."

"Page, I'm glad you're not mad at me. I was afraid you'd hate me for cutting off your hand."

Page started to cry softly as tears crept down his cheeks. "You didn't have any other choice. Mac, that chopper was on fire when you climbed in."

Jim slowly shook his head. "No, Wright and I got there at the same time and there wasn't any fire. I probably wouldn't have climbed inside if it had been on fire."

"Mac, I can remember hearing fire extinguishers."

"Yeah, so do I, but not until I was already inside."

"Mac, did everyone else get out?"

There was a second's hesitation before Jim spoke, "No, Page. Your peter pilot didn't make it."

"Mac, tell me everything, just as you remember it, including what I said."

Jim started at the point where Mr. Walker told him to put his helmet back on and finished with his getting into the quarter-ton with Kenny. Page smiled and slightly laughed. "Mac, I would have loved to have seen that. It's just too bad you didn't use a live grenade on him the other night."

"Page, I swear, I didn't do that."

"True?"

"True!"

"Did Halsey get mad about being punched out?"

"Yeah, you should have seen him lying there on his ass. The only problem is, it looks like I take a court martial for it."

"Mac, I'm sorry."

"What for, you didn't hit him."

"I kind of feel responsible."

"You're not!"

"Mac, I may not get another chance—so I want to say, thanks." With broken voice and tears visible, Page continued, "Thanks for my life."

"You're welcome, I'm just glad I could get you out."

"Mac, I feel kind of stupid asking this, but do you believe in God?"

"Absolutely! Why?"

"I once saw a Huey burn! Did you ever see one go up in flames?"

"Three times now."

"It's quite a sight, isn't it?"

"It sure is."

"Mac, the one I saw was up at An Loc. I don't think it was on fire more than thirty seconds before it was completely consumed and exploded. You had to be inside my chopper for a good three minutes. You'd been in there over two before I passed out. So why didn't it go up a lot faster and blow before it did?"

"Well, Page, in the first place, I don't think I was in there that long. Maybe I was, I don't know. I guess the reason it didn't go up was Jesus wasn't ready for us to die yet."

"Us or you? I mean, the second you're out, it goes up."

For the first time that night it dawned on him. Jim knew in his heart that the hand of God had once again reached out and restrained the Angel of Death until they were safe. What was there in his future he was being spared for? Maybe it wasn't him. Maybe there was someone in his life whose prayers for him had been answered. He didn't know which it was but he knew Jesus is no respecter of persons—He cared as much for Page as He did for him.

"Mac, you didn't answer me."

"Page, we're alive tonight because of the divine protection of Jesus Christ. I know nothing more."

"Were you raised in the church?"

"Yes, I was raised a Lutheran, but it was here in Nam that I really came to know Jesus. Now, I'm really thankful for all the Bible background and training that Lutherans stress, because I know what I believe—I'm not perfect by far, but I know Him."

"Mac, tell me about Jesus and what you believe."

Jim took a deep breath. "I believe in Jesus Christ as my personal Lord and Savior. He died on the cross and rose from the dead to take away my sins. In other words, even though I sin, and I know I do, Jesus is able to wipe my sins away as though I'd never sinned, each time I ask Him to forgive me. Because of that, I'm allowed into heaven when I do die."

Page asked questions and Jim answered as best he could late into the night. Finally, Page fell asleep as Jim continued to tell him about Jesus. Even though he knew Page was asleep Jim said, "Good-bye, Page, and may the peace of Jesus Christ be with you always." Jim looked at his watch, quarter after two. He'd have a hard time staying awake tomorrow. He shut off the light beside Page's bed and returned the chair to where the nurse had gotten it. He saw no one on the way out, and even though he thought about looking for that doctor, he simply left, unseen by anyone.

(There are many ironies about the Vietnam war. Howard Page would return to the States and enter school at Capital University in Columbus, Ohio. After being accepted by the Lutheran Seminary at Capital, Howard started writing letters to everyone and every organization he could think of in an effort to find Jim MacLaughlin. He was the one person Howard really wanted at his graduation and also his ordination service, when he would receive the full rights of a Lutheran pastor. Letter after letter came back getting him no further than when he started. Howard even visited the Pentagon one summer in hopes of finding some of Jim's records with a home address. His search was fruitless, as he never found Jim MacLaughlin. Yet, Jim lived only a short distance north of Columbus; his name, address and telephone number were listed in the Columbus phone book.)

News of MacLaughlin's court martial traveled fast. It was the only topic of discussion at the officers' club by the time Halsey came in. He saw Captain Wolf already seated and headed for a table close by. Changing his mind, he approached Captain Wolf. "Mind if I join you?"

"Yes, as a matter of fact I do, but sit down, anyway, I want to talk to you." As Halsey sat down, Mr. Lucas walked up. "Hey, Captain, you want in the pool?"

"What pool?"

"Well, Sir, I'm calling it the Halsey pool. You see I think Halsey is a walking dead man. They're going to kill him just as sure as the sun rises in the east." Halsey sat there almost in shock. "The pool works like this, Sir. You can place a bet on the day they kill him and how they kill him. Each bet costs you fifty dollars. For example, I've got bets they hit him tomorrow and with a door gun in the first hot LZ we hit. The winner of the pot is the person who gets both right. In case of a tie, I'll split it even. You in, Captain?"

"No thanks, I'll pass this one up. Although if I were going to bet, I'd bet on tonight with a frag—a live one this time."

"You know, Captain, that's where most of the money's at. Second high is he gets it in the showers with a grenade tomorrow."

Halsey interrupted. "Lucas, you'd bet on anything!"

"You bet; my old man was a pit boss in Vegas."

"Just what makes you so sure they'll try to kill me?"

"Haven't you heard? Walker was looking for MacLaughlin in his hooch and overheard some of the men talking about how to do it. Plus the barkeep in the NCO Club was here about ten minutes ago and said your demise was the only topic of conversation over there. See ya, Captain. Try to make it through tonight would you, Halsey?"

Lucas turned and left as Walker sat down. "Captain, Admiral, how's it feel to be a walking dead man?"

"Walker, don't call me that, and I don't believe any of this shit!"

"Oh, you can believe it all right. Personally, if I was in your shoes, I'd drop all those charges and see to it the word gets passed before people start going to bed. Did Lucas tell you he's moving into my room for the night? Just in case a grenade does go off in your room, he doesn't want to be sleeping beside it. You know, Halsey, you don't have one friend in the enlisted men's ranks. Mac could have hit any other officer in the company and the rest of those guys wouldn't raise a finger to help him. But with you, they see it as their chance to get rid of you. Try to remember, every one of those guys hates your guts. You know, I've spent a lot of time with Mac. He believes he has a guardian angel, and I've been flying with him long enough to think he may be right. I've seen too many things that did or didn't happen, which should have gone the other way. I'm telling you, Halsey, the man isn't alone. Somebody's looking after him Who's more powerful than either of us. Somehow, I just can't see him ending up in jail. Just look at what happened earlier today. Halsey, that ship was on fire, but it didn't spread until he stepped out of it—then suddenly BOOM, the whole thing erupted into flames and blows—almost like it was waiting for him to get out."

"You're crazy!"

"Halsey! You ever see a Huey go up?"

"Once."

"And how long did it take?"

"Not very long."

"I rest my case. In fact, do me a real favor and stay away from me from now on, I don't want to be too close when it happens."

Walker stood up and said, "Good-bye, Halsey. See ya, Captain."

Halsey looked at Captain Wolf and said, "Captain, you think they're serious? I mean in the infantry, sure, but not in aviation!"

"Halsey, you're a hell of a slow learner. What do you think that fake fragging was all about the other night? That was somebody's way of telling you to back off. These guys aren't any different than the grunts; they all came from the same United States. If I were you, I'd drop those charges before the men go to bed."

"Can't you have MacLaughlin locked up tonight, Sir?"

"I could, but I'm not going to. Besides, it wouldn't do any

good. If he doesn't get you, somebody else will. Anyway, you have to sign the papers and the major said he wouldn't have them ready till tomorrow."

"Captain, I refuse to be intimidated. Just to be safe, though, could I bunk with you tonight?"

"HELL, NO! I'm like Walker, I don't want you anywhere near me. You change your mind, you go tell Major Hobbs. I don't want you close to me after I leave this club."

Halsey had heard all he wanted to and decided to leave. When he got to the door, Walker was standing behind him. "Well, Admiral, it's a long walk and those lights are perfect for a sniper."

"Walker, you don't scare me!"

"I'm not trying to scare you, man, I'm trying to keep you alive."

"Look, they won't try anything here because of the company area guards."

"Halsey, those guards are enlisted men from our own company. Look, you and I've had our problems, but I don't want you killed, especially by our own men. Come on, let's sit down and talk it over."

Once at a table, Walker ordered two beers. "Okay, let's look at the pros and cons of this situation. First of all, if you drop the charges, you lose a little pride and have a black eye for a while. Hey, get somebody to take your picture and send it home, then you can tell everybody at home you got it in a crash. At least you're alive. I mean, man, is the risk really worth it? Halsey, if I'd been fragged, even with a dud, I'd thank God I was still alive and become the nicest guy in the company."

Halsey sat there and looked Walker in the eye, then took a big drink of beer and said, "Okay, I'm convinced, but the SOB shouldn't get away with it."

"He will, Halsey, because you got greedy. If you had asked for company punishment, you'd have gotten away with it. Plus, you could have laughed at him every day. But, no, you had to play hardball and go for the court martial. One final piece of advice, Halsey, your life depends on those men every single day. They fix the helicopters you fly in. You get shot down, who do you think's going to be out there walking through the jungle with you, with a loaded weapon? There've been more than one officer shot by his own men in this war. You get in a fire fight on the ground and, believe me, you want enlisted men around who like you. Man, you don't want to hide from Chuck and your own men. Come on, I see Hobbs over there, let's go talk to him."

Kenny was seated on his bunk when Mr. Walker came in and sat down beside him. "Well, Kenny, we got Mac off the hook!"

"Great, that's really great! How'd it go?"

"Just like we talked about. Now look, nobody knows about this but Mr. Lucas, you and me, and it damn well better stay that way or we could all find ourselves in a sling. You got that?"

"Yes, Sir."

"One more thing, it worked once, it'll never work again. By the way, where is our golden glove friend?"

"Probably still in the club. He and Gillett were beginning to really tie one on."

Walker hadn't been gone but a minute when Gillett walked in. "Hey, Kenny, they're going to try to get a convoy through tomorrow. It'll be a five day trip, so pack a bag. You'll take the company truck and you're to leave at 0500. You got any questions?"

"No. Where's Mac?"

"He should be along any second. We left the club together. You know, I wonder where he did go? He should have been here before now. Oh, well, he can't get lost. See ya in the morning, Kenny."

Jim carefully felt his way into the hooch. It was pitch black in there and he didn't want to wake anyone by falling over something. He made his way to the wall locker, felt for the lock and without much trouble, unlocked it. The flashlight he kept on the top shelf almost fell as he groped for it. Instead, he was able to lay it quietly on his bunk after turning it on. Jim sat down and started to untie his boots when the door opened and an unseen face called, "Sergeant Gillett?"

"He's in the bunk straight across."

The intruder turned his flashlight in Gillett's direction and approaching his bunk said, "Sergeant Gillett, wake up."

"Uh, what? I'm awake, I'm awake, get that light out of my eyes!"

"Sergeant, we need another crew and the names of the men you sent on the earlier mission."

"I don't know who went. I couldn't find MacLaughlin any place! I went next door to see if he was over there and their platoon sergeant said not to worry about it; he had a guy who's been wanting to fly some of those night missions. So I said fine, I'll just let you fill the crew and he did. Why?"

"We've got a dead crew chief, a wounded co-pilot, and a broken ship we have to go get."

Jim said, "Gillett, I'll go."

"Mac, you just getting back? Where the hell you been?"

"At the hospital with Page. Hey, runner, how'd they get it and where are they?"

"I don't know. All I know is they left here about a quarter till one to pick up a long range recon group. The next thing I know I'm being woke up and told to go find Sergeant Gillett, to get the name of the dead crew chief, and have him fill another crew."

"Okay, Gillett, I'm dressed, get me a gunner. I'll go preflight the ship. By the way, what am I flying?"

"Take the new one you brought in yesterday! Hey, runner, you getting officers?"

"Yes, I woke Captain Wolf before coming here; he had me wake up Major Hobbs. He said the Major had been upset that he hadn't been able to go on the earlier one. The major said he'd get a co-pilot. I've got to go."

The runner walked out the door and Gillett turned to Mac. "Mac, how's Page?"

"Under the circumstances, pretty good. He'll make it."

"Mac, you realize the only reason you're not that dead crew chief is that I couldn't find you?"

"I realize. Maybe that's why you couldn't find me."

"You've got no idea what you're going into out there! You don't know where you're going! All you know is the guy who took your place is dead and so you jump right in there and say, 'I'll go!' You got a death wish?"

"No, it's just that I'm already dressed. I just walked in the door. There's no point in waking someone else. See you later, Gillett." Jim locked his locker and left as Gillett tried to wake somebody on down the hooch.

Jim had just started with a preflight of the ship when two officers walked up. He knew from what the runner had said that one of them would be Major Hobbs. Acting like he hadn't seen them approach in the dark, Jim continued with his inspection until Major Hobbs spoke. "Hey, up on top, this is Major Hobbs. Who am I flying with tonight?"

"MacLaughlin, Sir. Sir, I'm almost done and then I'll be right down. I don't know who the gunner will be."

The two officers climbed into their seats. Jim didn't think anything of it when Hobbs climbed into the peter pilot's seat, since he hadn't been made an AC yet. Wright came around the revetment carrying his M60's, so Jim helped him mount them and, since it was already untied, the pilot started to crank the engine. Jim climbed into the cargo area and for the first time looked at the AC who was busy starting the aircraft. Jim felt a streak of panic leap through his body as he recognized the form of Halsey. Now he knew why Hobbs had been watching him so closely as he'd put on his gear. Jim plugged in his helmet and said, "Mr. Halsey?"

"Welcome aboard, Mac!"

"Go to hell! I'm not flying with you!" Jim unplugged his helmet and started to get out of the chopper.

Hobbs, who had been watching him, moved faster than Jim could believe possible; especially for a big man. By the time Jim had removed his helmet and chicken plate, Hobbs had gotten out and grabbing Jim by the shirt, flung him against the revetment wall. With his massive size pinning Jim against the wall, and the Major's two fists holding him by the shirt a couple of inches off the ground, Hobbs spoke in his most forceful and commanding tone. "Listen to me, you smart mouth little son of a bitch! I've just about had it with you. I'm not real sure how, but you managed to get Halsey to drop the court martial. So you're off the hook, but I'll not allow you to talk to my officers like that! You got that?"

"Yes, Sir!"

"Now, I'm going to tell you something else. You'll fly with whomever I tell you to fly with, when I tell you to fly with him, and as often as I tell you. Now, you get your insubordinate little ass on that chopper before I stick my size twelve boot in it!" Still holding Jim's shirt, the major stepped aside and half threw Jim into the chopper. Both climbed into the cargo bay and Hobbs gave Halsey the thumbs up sign. In seconds they were airborne. Major Hobbs, with some difficulty, worked his way over the radio console and into his seat. Jim had replaced his chicken plate and helmet and, like Major Hobbs, returned to his seat.

"MacLaughlin, you on line?"

"Yes, Major."

"Good, flip it over to private."

"You there?"

"Yes, Sir."

"Good! How do you feel right now, Mac?"

"Oh, slightly humiliated, upset and confused. We both know I shouldn't have spoken to Mr. Halsey the way I did, and you could get in as much trouble for shoving me around."

"But I won't, will I?"

"No, Sir, I won't rat."

"Speaking of ratting; who fragged Mr. Halsey?"

"I don't know, Sir."

"Yes you do, and I know you knew it when I first made you a deal. So why didn't you take it, Mac? Then all this unpleasantness wouldn't have happened."

There wasn't any response, so the major pushed him a little harder. "Don't think too long, Specialist, because I only want two answers. One, the name, and two, why you didn't rat earlier."

"Sir, I don't know what you're talking about."

"The hell you don't."

"Major, what makes you think I do?"

"That's unimportant, just give me the name!"

"I don't know it."

"You're lying!"

"Major, this isn't going to get us anywhere, because you're just going to say, yes, you are, and I'm going to say, no, I'm not. So, if you don't mind, would you tell me what you meant by 'no court martial'?"

This time it was the major's turn to pause. "You mean you haven't heard?"

"No, Sir. I spent the evening at the hospital with Page. I just got back to my hooch when they came looking for a crew for this mission."

"Okay, well, it seems that Mr. Halsey has decided that in the interest of 'esprit de corps,' he'll make the first move towards burying the hatchet by not pressing charges against you."

"That's very generous of Mr. Halsey, Sir."

"Yes, it is and you had better decide to reciprocate."

"Sir, it wasn't me who had the problem to begin with. The mere fact that he's the officer and I'm the NCO should tell you who had been harassing whom."

"Yes, I know, but you're not entirely blameless. Okay, Specialist, I'll tell you what I've already done and you damn well better not tell Halsey. He's not going to find out until tomorrow morning. As of then, Mr. Halsey will be in the other flight platoon. I decided not to enter anything into your records. That means you won't get any medal, but when you get to the States nobody will ever know how much trouble you've been in over here or how close you came to jail."

"Thank you, Sir."

"Mac, have you ever considered extending your tour over here?"

"No, Sir!"

"Well, consider it. You're made for it. The colonel's right, you simply enjoy living on the edge and this is the only place you'll be able to. Besides, you've got fifteen months left in the service when you get back. With that much time you'll get sent back over anyway—so you might as well stay to begin with; at least for another six months. That way you'll go home with less than a year left and not get sent back. You can fly with me as my crew chief, once I'm made CO. I'll see to it that you get the medals you deserve, and you won't have to worry about people like Mr. Halsey."

"I don't know, Sir. How can I live on the edge as you put it, flying in circles at three thousand feet? As for the medals, they don't mean that much to me anyway. I don't doubt for a second you could get them; after all, Colonel Appleton got a Silver Star a couple of months ago for flying courageously at thirty-five hundred feet while the rest of the flight got the hell kicked out of them in the Hobo Woods."

Major Hobbs sat there and slowly shook his head. "Mac, you don't respect anybody or anything, do you?"

"Sir, only if it's earned. So let me ask you a question, Major. Why me? Of all the guys in the outfit, why do you want me?"

"Who knows! Look, we're almost to Dau Tieng. Think about extending, Mac. Better switch back to intership commo."

Jim saw the major reach down and heard the click of his going off private. Reaching up, he turned his switch back to intercom also and sat there quietly listening to Mr. Halsey update the major on their status. Soon they were on the ground not far from the UH-23 chopper's hanger. Two warrant officers and a spec-four approached, then one warrant stuck his head in the major's window. Major Hobbs directed them to get in as he said, "Their ship's at the far end of the runway. Let's go see what's wrong. Fortunately, we're not going to lose a pilot; he's just got some small shrapnel in his right arm."

Everybody but Mr. Halsey jumped out almost as soon as they were on the ground, leaving him to shut down. The lone Huey was only about twenty feet away but, for some reason, nobody approached it until Major Hobbs said, "Okay, let's go find out what's wrong with it."

Jim turned to one of the warrant officers and asked, "Sir, why did you land here? I mean, did you lose power or hydraulics or what?"

Major Hobbs shouted, "Don't answer that! Mac, you're supposed to be good at your job, let's find out how good—you tell us what happened!"

Jim shrugged his shoulders and shook his head. "Okay, Major, whatever makes you happy." Jim returned to his chopper, climbed in and turned on the searchlight, lowered it and shined it in the direction of the other chopper. Now he had plenty of light but, just in case, he held on to his flashlight.

The whole right side of the Huey was pot-marked with shrapnel holes. Jim looked underneath and saw a puddle. He put his finger in it and then smelled it—fuel. He then opened the engine compartment and, after checking it, climbed on top. After about ten minutes, Jim walked up to Major Hobbs, snapped to rigid attention, saluted and said, "Sir, Specialist MacLaughlin reports."

Major Hobbs smiled, returned the salute and replied, "I guess I deserved that. Okay, Mac, as you were. Now what did you find?"

Turning to the wounded officer, Jim said, "Sir, you either took a mortar round or a grenade on your right rear side. Which?"

"I don't know."

"Was your crew chief killed instantly?"

"Yeah, along with two of the long range recon people."

"You must have had your arm out the window?"

"No, just my elbow."

"Okay." Turning back to the major, Jim continued, "Sir, I believe a mortar round hit just off their right side and slightly behind the crew chief's seat. As a result, there's a massive rupturing of the chopper's skin, including the right upper and lower fuel cells. They're supposed to be self sealing and some of the smaller holes have sealed but there are just too many that are too large. Therefore, I suspect they ran out of fuel. Also, the engine shows it's taken a small piece of shrapnel through the intake, breaking and chipping off some of the blades. I also suspect they had a drastic loss of power. There's hydraulic oil all over the place but I can't see a ruptured hose, so I suspect it's a small break somewhere. Without the lines being under pressure I can't tell where the break is." Turning back to the warrant, Jim continued, "If you hadn't lost hydraulic assist yet, you would have very shortly." To Major Hobbs, he said, "The tail boom has several holes in it. Without taking the time to open the inspection panels, I'd say there's probably structural damage; possibly damage to the tail rotor control cables. It's unimportant, anyway, because the ship's unflyable. We'll have to get a Chinook to take it home. The only other thing I found was a hole in one of the main rotor blades which probably gave you a vibration. That's all, Sir."

Turning to the warrant officer, Jim asked, "How correct am I?"

"I'm impressed. We landed here because we were losing fuel so fast we couldn't get any further. Hydraulic pressure was taking a steady drop and we didn't have more than two thirds power, plus a pretty good vibration in the stick."

Jim, with a big smile, looked Major Hobbs in the eye. "Will that be all, Sir?"

"Yes, there's no way it'll fly home, right?"

"No, Sir! You might just as well call for a hook."

"You did a good job, Specialist. Let's go home. We'll have it hooked in the morning."

Mr. Halsey was standing beside Major Hobbs. As everyone started to walk away, Jim touched Mr. Halsey's arm, causing him to turn around. Extending his right hand Jim said, "Mr. Halsey, peace?"

Halsey looked at Major Hobbs and then back at Jim. "Yeah, why not, Mac? Peace." Mr. Halsey extended his hand and, somewhat begrudgingly, shook Jim's.

Everyone but Jim and Major Hobbs had climbed aboard. Jim untied the rotor blades and walked around to hold the major's door for him. "Mac, I bet you play a mean game of poker!"

"Major, I don't particularly like the game."

"Well, you've played one hell of a hand tonight."

Jim, not sure of what he meant, showed a puzzled look as he replied, "Sir?"

"Never mind. You been to bed yet, Mac?"

"No, Sir."

"Flying tomorrow?"

"Yes, Sir."

The major looked at his watch and said, "Well, you're only going to get about an hour's sleep. I put the word out last night, everyone has to stand reveille from now on."

"Sir, I thought this was a combat zone, not basic training. Do you have any idea how important those extra few minutes of sleep are to me?"

"I've got a real good idea, but that's no reason to relax military discipline. Get in. Let's go home!"

Jim motioned for the major to climb in, which he did. Jim pulled the armor plating on the seat forward to the lock position and shut the door. Halsey had already started the engine, so as soon as Jim was in his seat, he gave Halsey the thumbs-up sign.

13

Sure I'm Mean—
But Don't Make
Me Prove It!

"The spirit is willing, but the body is weak." MATTHEW 26:41 NIV

Both men were only a few steps from the hooch door when they heard the now familiar whistle of the Russian built 122MM rockets. Jim, who was closest to the bunker, turned and headed through the doorway. Tripping, he fell over a body as he entered. Wright, who'd been directly behind, fell on top of him. Both were startled at landing in an entanglement of hot, clammy bodies that had already started cursing and making unkind references about their mothers. Finally, a flashlight was turned on, showing a bunker packed so full of men they were sitting on top of each other, with no place to stretch out their legs. It had been hot outside, but the added body heat made it unbearable inside.

By now the rockets were falling so fast, one couldn't be distinguished from another. The continuous whistle and grumbling of the incoming rockets had all blended into an ear shattering sound, made even worse by the explosions as the rockets hit. The very ground on which they laid began to shake and vibrate as the pounding continued. Each man pressed his hands to his ears in a futile attempt to ease the pain. This was undoubtedly the worst bombardment Jim had ever been in. Though it seemed to each man that hours had passed, it had lasted only twenty minutes. Suddenly, as though someone flipped off a switch, it stopped.

270

The first sensation Jim felt was the ringing in his ears. Slowly, almost as though someone was tuning in a radio, his ears began to pick up other sounds and tune out the buzzing and ringing. A couple of guys were crying and another was shouting obscenities at the VC, at the Army, at Lyndon Johnson and anybody else who came to mind. Someone turned on a flashlight and the shivering in Jim's spine began to subside. He could see several guys still holding their ears and shaking. Most everyone was wearing only their underwear as they had obviously gotten out of bed. It wasn't much longer before someone said he couldn't stand the smell of mildew and rot any longer; besides, his legs were aching from someone sitting on them, and he was getting out. It was the signal they'd all been waiting for and the bunker slowly emptied. Jim was close to the doorway, and therefore, one of the first outside. Once out he waited for Gillett, who came crawling out wearing only his green boxer shorts.

"Gillett, how long you guys been in that bunker?"

"Since shortly after you left. This last one was the worst by far. How'd you get along?"

"No problem. In fact, I'm glad I went. I wouldn't have gotten any sleep in that bunker. I'm going to bed. See you later, Gillett."

"What time is it, Mac?"

Jim shone the light on his watch and answered, "About five to five."

Gillett shouted to anyone within hearing distance, "Listen up, you guys! You might just as well get dressed, because everybody who's still walking and has it swinging has to stand formation in five minutes!"

There was much cursing and moaning from everyone in the area, but it was Hunter who hollered from the far side of the hooch, "Hey Gillett, if I bind mine up, do I still have to stand reveille?"

"Yes!"

Gillett left to start the generator and shortly the hooch lights came on. Almost at the same time Kenny started screaming. His wall locker had a six inch hole in it. Jim looked at his own bed. The mosquito netting had been destroyed by a piece of shrapnel, but the bed itself had been untouched. Looking up at the metal roof that now had more holes in it than a block of swiss cheese, Jim saw Kenny's monkey still alive and cowering in the far corner.

By the time the company was called to attention, the confusion over where to stand had yet to be worked out. Major Hobbs could hardly believe it; he had a whole company of people and two thirds of them had never stood formation since joining the company. They didn't know where their platoon was, or where to fall in once they'd found it. Others didn't even try to find their platoon, they just fell in the end of the first line they came to. Very few people were happy about the formation. For one thing, it would only take one rocket to wipe out the entire company. Finally, at 0517, the reports were given and the Major stepped forward to address the troops.

Jim heard Hunter behind him say, "I hope he makes this short. I'm getting hungry."

Jim smiled to himself at the typical lack of respect for officers. Major Hobbs spoke, "Men, I know we've all had a rough night, but I'll not accept this kind of slop for a formation. Tomorrow morning every man in this outfit BETTER know where he belongs and be there! We've lost so much time getting into formation that we can't have a police call of the company area—so what I'm going to do is this: you can just get up fifteen minutes earlier tomorrow morning, and you'll get up fifteen minutes earlier every morning until you get it right. By the time the flight lands tonight, I want all the holes in the company area made by those rockets filled. First Sergeant, I also want a work crew to start filling more sandbags and stacking them around the living quarters. Both clubs will be closed until the hooches are patched and the sandbags are raised to at least six feet from ground level around all the living quarters. You might just as well find out now that I've ordered enough paint to paint all the buildings in the company. There are going to be a lot of improvements in this company in the next few days and I know you men can handle it. Finally, I think it's important that you know we're going to be part of one of the largest operations of the war to date, Yellowstone*. First Sergeant, dismiss the company!"

"Yes, Sir. Company, ten hut! Fall out!"

Gillett and Jim were among the first in the mess hall. Each looked at the other with an "Oh, no" type look, as they listened to the conversation in front of them.

"Hey, Cookie, what's the idea of hamburgers for breakfast?"

"Look, it's just this simple, Charlie blew up our powdered eggs, powered milk and boxes of cereal, along with most of our other supplies. About all we've got left is bread and hamburger. I can't even make creamed beef!"

Gillett had just sat down when Major Hobbs approached from the kitchen area that divided the officers' side from the enlisted men's. "Sergeant Gillett, there are some things I need to go over with you. Why don't you bring your tray and join me on the officers' side?"

"Yes, Sir."

Hobbs turned to leave as Gillett stood up. Gillett looked down at Jim and said in a quiet, yet commanding tone, "What did you do now?"

Jim looked up and speaking through his teeth, answered in a slightly forced manner, "Nothing!"

Jim was standing outside the hooch, his steel pot half full of water, resting on top of the wall of sandbags protecting the hooch front. Being careful not to lose any of the toothpaste he was applying to his toothbrush, he didn't see Gillett walk up and slap him on the back. "Well, Mac, I've got good news and bad news, which do you want first?"

"Give me the good and somebody else the bad."

"Sorry, you only had two choices. But to show you what a nice guy I am I'll give you the good news first, anyway. Halsey has been transferred to the other platoon."

"Is that it?"

"Yes."

"Hobbs told me that last night. What else you got, Gillett?"

* Yellowstone—79 day operation (8 December 1967–24 February 1968) small in size and duration—conducted in Tay Ninh Province (War Zone C) with units of the 25th Infantry Division, 1254 known enemy casualties.

"Well, aren't you just full of little surprises. That's all the good. The rest is bad."

"And I'll just bet there's a lot more of it, isn't there?"

"Yes. Well, to start with, Hobbs will be flying your right seat* today."

"That's okay, he's not bad to fly with. Besides, as long as he's on board, there are only two places we'll be flying, lead or trail. I won't get stuck on some side mission."

"You're flying trail."

Jim finished spitting out the rinse water and gave the remaining water in his steel pot a fling. "I hope that's the worst of the bad news."

"It's not. Hobbs had ordered in enough soap and buckets so that we can start washing the helicopters."

"The man is crazy!"

"Mac, that's not the half of it. He also ordered in enough paint to completely paint all the choppers and enough paste wax, in fifteen pound cans, no less, to paste-wax all those suckers."

"The man is totally insane! What time does he want us to do all this? Let me guess, midnight to two o'clock?"

"I don't know, Mac. I also don't know what we're going to do about it. Any ideas?"

"Not right off the top." The two friends stood there looking disgusted. Jim had a thought. "Hey, Gillett, did he also order in rags or sponges?"

"No, he didn't."

Gillett's face broke into a smile. He knew there weren't any sponges in the company, and supply was so tight with rags they had to be signed in and out. An old rag to wipe your hands with was something jealously guarded.

As Jim walked to the flight line, he took time to look over the company area. The place was a mess. Although, for the pounding they'd taken during the night, they'd gotten off pretty cheap. One other hooch had taken a direct hit and been turned into kindling. Another hooch had lost its front and several had roof damage. There were countless pot holes and one place

* Right Seat—Co-pilot's seat.

where the drainage ditch had been widened. Most every hooch had some holes in its sides and several had roofs that looked like someone had tried to open a can with a screwdriver instead of a can opener. The flight line, for some reason, didn't look like it had received more than a few strays.

It was only a little after six and already the heat and humidity had caused sweat beads to roll down Jim's back, soaking his shirt. The sun was up and serving notice. It would be unpleasant today.

There were places the dust was ankle deep, making it hard to walk. In a few weeks it would start raining and that dust would become ankle deep mud, which would be even harder to walk through.

Jim was glad his helicopter was still there. Once up in the air it would be a whole lot cooler; just one of the little benefits of being a flyboy.

Jim opened the left cargo door and put his water jug inside, directly behind the console. Next, he pulled out the green, plastic-covered log book. His entry from just a few hours before was the last one. There wasn't any reason that something should have been added, but one always checked the log book anyway. He could remember more than once going to the ship he'd been assigned, checking the log book and finding anything from a radio to an engine had been pulled out during the night. He'd finished his preflight and was having some water when Gillett drove up in the quarter-ton. Wright jumped off the back and pulled out two M60's. Gillett waved a greeting as Jim shouted, "Hey, Gillett, where's Kenny?"

"I sent him on a convoy to Saigon. By the way, I've some more good news. They decided to let the gook KP's back on post today."

"You don't suppose one of them would like to have monkey stew tonight, do you?"

Gillett smiled broadly and said, "I'd had that thought myself." Gillett drove off.

Jim helped Wright mount his guns as the pilots approached. Wright spoke. "Man, oh man, Mac. Kenny is sure going to be mad when he gets back and his monkey is gone."

"Yeah, he'll flap around like an old rooster that's just been wet on. Won't it be wonderful?"

Major Hobbs, who had just walked around the ship asked, "Won't what be wonderful?"

Jim and Wright came to attention and saluted both Hobbs and Walker. "Good morning, Sir. Wright and I were just talking about how nice it will be to finally get rid of Kenny's monkey."

Major Hobbs smiled. "You mean one of the men has a pet monkey?"

"Yes, Sir, and it's disgusting. It's like living in a zoo. The damn thing shits on people or shits and then throws it at somebody. It jacked off the other day and dumped its load all over Hunter's wall locker."

The major was laughing so hard he had to sit down.

"Sir, I'm glad you find it so funny. Believe me, you wouldn't if you walked in the door and WHAM! A load of monkey shit hits you between the eyes!"

The major regained his composure long enough to ask, "Mac, did you preflight this thing yet?"

"Yes, Sir."

"Do it again. This time, though, I want you to show me everything you're looking for. I want to learn as much about a Huey as I can while I've got the chance."

"Well, Sir, let me be the first to welcome you to Mac's school of preflights." Jim showed the major everything he did on a preflight, and during that time there was a running conversation between the major and the SP-5. Jim asked about Colonel Appleton, since he hadn't seen him for a while. Major Hobbs was pleased to inform him that the CO had been called to Saigon for a few days but would join them today as C and C, thus explaining Hobbs being in the command position. The major was very friendly during the preflight even though Jim took a jab at him when asked about extending. He explained to the major he didn't have any time off as it was, and the idea of washing and waxing Hueys when he could be sleeping didn't excite him. Jim told him that was stateside-type duty, not combat zone. If he was going to pull stateside duty, he might as well be there. They hadn't finished the preflight when Lead ship started to crank. Hobbs quickly climbed inside, called Lead and informed them his ship had been on a single ship night mission and would need fuel. Jim laughed to himself as he could picture the lieutenant flying Lead ship kissing Hobbs's ass by politely telling him to go refuel. Anybody else would have received a not-so-polite chewing out. It wasn't long until they were parked at the fuel dump.

Jim had just climbed back into his seat when Hobbs came over the intercom. "Men, take a good look, because the first day I'm made CO of this company, that's something you'll never see again."

Jim looked up to see a hog* making its usual struggle to take off. A hog was a classic example of the American adage that a little is nice, but a bunch is a whole lot better. It always amazed Jim that a hog could get off the ground at all. Hog pilots had their own routine: they always refueled first, then hovered to the opposite end of the flight line where the ammo bunker was located. There the gunner, crew chief and, if in a hurry, the co-pilot rearmed the ship with rockets and grenades. Once fully fueled, armed and crewed, a hog was about one thousand pounds over maximum gross for takeoff. Thus, the pilot always landed at the ammo bunker with the ship's nose pointed down the runway, because he couldn't hover to change directions. Whatever direction he was pointed, he had to go. Takeoff wasn't so much of a thing of graceful beauty, as it was an accident full of explosives on its way to a happening. The pilot had to bring the engine and rotors up to full RPM, then tip the ship over onto the curved, forward part of the skids, which made it look like it was standing on its nose. Then, by jerking pitch into the rotors giving it lift, the pilot could literally hop down the runway until he had enough airspeed to make the transition into flight. Even then, he had to stay close enough to the ground to use the prop blast from the rotors to help him into the air. Only after most of the runway had been used did a

* Hog—Huey gunship equipped with an XM3 tube type rocket pod system (24 tubes 2.75 inch rocket) on each side. Plus an M5 nose-mounted 40MM grenade launcher. Both the door gunner and crew chief had an M60 machine gun hung by bungi cords.

hog ship have enough airspeed to raise its nose and gain altitude.

After topping off with fuel, Major Hobbs informed Lead he was ready to go. Instantly, Lead pulled pitch and hovered out of his revetment. Everyone in Jim's ship waited patiently as each ship slowly flew by, then the ninth one went by and it was their turn.

Walker pulled pitch into the rotors and hovered away from the fuel dump. He turned the ship to the right and started out over Tay Ninh Village. The major had just finished calling Lead and telling him the flight was up when it happened—there was a crashing sound and Jim instantly knew they'd been hit. In that same fraction of a second, he saw pieces of Plexiglas fly out the doorway and the aircraft rocked as Walker tried to regain control.

It was a startled Major Hobbs who shouted into the mike, "What the hell?"

Jim could see Hobbs trying to climb out of his seat backwards and then sink back down. Walker said, "You okay, Major?"

"Yes, I guess. Turn it around, Mr. Walker, we'll have to change ships while maintenance replaces this windshield." It was then the major picked up the dead duck in his lap and threw it onto the cargo seat.

Jim came over the intercom, "Major, what happened?"

"That damn duck just flew through my windshield and hit me in the chicken plate. I don't mind telling you, it scared the shit out of me."

"Well, Sir, I've heard of a man shitting a brick before, but this is the first time I've ever seen anyone shit a duck."

Jim could see Walker laughing so hard he could hardly drive. Hobbs, now laughing also, said, "I'm just damn glad I had on a chicken plate or that stupid duck would have broken every rib I've got."

"What kind of a duck was it, Major?"

"Hell, I don't know, but it's a dead one now!"

Walker called Lead and told him what had happened, assuring him they'd be back in the air just as soon as they changed ships. Lead wasn't very happy; so after talking to Lead, Walker called Operations and asked where to land and where another ship could be found. They were told to park it on the maintenance pad to get the window fixed because there weren't any other flyable aircraft. Lead had been listening in and made it clear he couldn't understand anyone flying into a duck. Once on the maintenance pad, three men hurried their direction. One carried a tool box, one had a new window still wrapped in its protective paper and the third was a Spec-Six tech inspector. Jim couldn't help but be impressed. Service like this he'd never had before. Maybe flying with a major wasn't so bad after all. He'd put windows in by himself before and it wasn't that easy, plus it took a long time. Something told him this job would be done in less than twenty minutes.

Jim tied down the rotor blades and walked around to where the maintenance men were attacking the broken windshield like ants after a cube of sugar. Since there wasn't any room left for him to work on the windshield, he decided to get out of the sun. The large maintenance tent was only twenty feet away, so he casually walked over and found an empty spot inside on one of the work benches and sat down. Directly overhead was a large NO SMOKING sign that someone was using as a shirt rack. It might just as well have been used as a dart board, since he was the only man in the tent who didn't have a cigarette hanging out of his mouth. It was slightly cooler inside the tent, but only slightly, with a faint, hot breeze moving through the open ends.

There were two slicks parked beside each other having their PE's pulled, each with cowling off, inspection panels open, and in various stages of being broken down and put back together. Jim leaned back against the stiff canvas wall of the tent and closed his eyes. At the sound of heavy footsteps approaching, he opened one eye and saw Major Hobbs standing there looking at him.

"They said I'd find you in here. If you were sleepy, why didn't you rack out on the chopper's seats?"

"Because, Sir, there was a dead duck on it that belonged to you and it's a lot cooler in here."

Hobbs smiled. "It is at that. Mind if I sit down?"

Jim moved over to make room. "You know, Sir, I came over with a company as a maintenance man; I pulled many a PE

Man, am I glad I'm out of that routine. I may not get any sleep, but it's a lot more fun flying. I mean, Major, how many of these guys can go home and tell about having a duck fly through their window? By the way, Sir, you going to have it stuffed or what?"

"I just took it to Cookie and let him know I wanted it dressed and ready to eat the night I make AC. I'll have a special party for you, Wright and Mr. Walker. You do eat duck don't you, Mac?"

"It couldn't be any worse than the zoo I've eaten with the Special Forces before we were made an all combat assault company. Those guys eat whatever their Montagnard friends cook, which could be anything from dog, monkey, rat or snake, to the water buffalo that died of old age, or hoof and mouth. You know, Major, I'll just bet the cook was tickled pink about having to cook that duck."

Hobbs laughed as he replied, "He didn't say much."

"I can imagine that! Major, do you mind if I ask you a question?"

"Go right ahead."

"Sir, you've got infantry written all over you. What are you doing in aviation?"

"Well, to make a long story short, I took ROTC in college, liked it, and decided to make a life of it. I graduated in '63 and was getting nowhere fast in the States, so I went to jump school and then volunteered for Nam. I was sent to Okinawa in January of '65 and joined the 173rd Airborne Brigade. We came to Nam on May 7th that same year and operated out of Bien Hoa. It was a hell of a good unit. You know we were one of the first units into Vietnam. In fact, I remember General Williamson, he was brigade commander, telling us we were only here temporarily until an airborne brigade from the States relieved us. They're still here, up at An Khe, but we were supposed to be temporary because we were the only Pacific command quick reaction unit around. Anyway, I ended up spending eighteen months over here before rotating home. But I hadn't done too badly; I'd been a platoon leader and hoped to make company XO. In fact, that's what I'd stayed for. The only problem was every other officer who had been commissioned since the Korean War saw Nam as a chance for promotion. So I ended up at Fort Bragg with the 82nd Airborne Division behind a desk, doing nothing but reading the newspapers and being bored to death. After about a year of that, I decided this war wasn't going to end in a year or two, and I might just as well get back in it while the getting was good. Besides, I loved it here. This is where it's at. You and I are alike in that respect. You just haven't admitted it yet. You get back to the States, you'll realize this is reality and there's nothing else like it. It's just one hell of an ego trip. Anyway, after my first tour over here, it was obvious that helicopters were where the action was, so I put in for flight school. I'll tell you what, it didn't take that request long to come through. So I was off to Fort Rucker in Alabama and Huey flight training. From there I joined the 101st Airborne at Fort Campbell and we arrived at Bien Hoa on November 19, 1967. I made major in January. About a month ago, I happened upon an old friend of mine in Saigon who worked in Corps Headquarters. During the course of the conversation, he mentioned this unit needed an executive officer, and here I am."

The tech inspector walked in and told them their ship was ready. Jim couldn't believe it. Only seventeen minutes had passed since he had tied the rotors down. Jim picked up a strange looking device that he'd asked one of the guys in sheet metal to make for him a few days ago, and headed for the ship. He explained to Major Hobbs how it was used to cook C-rations. He was also impressed with the speed of maintenance. Hobbs was really pleased when Jim told him it would have taken an hour or more for him to do it by himself. Then, pointing out all the rivets that went all the way around the windshield to Hobbs, he explained how they were removed and then replaced with new ones. The man seemed genuinely interested in learning everything he could and Jim enjoyed teaching him.

They were airborne again and he had a chance to think about the major's story. Jim had been in the Army long enough to be able to read between the lines and there were sure some big holes in that story. Oh, he was probably telling the truth about not getting anywhere after college. It was a peace time army with several Korean veterans still around, and if you're an infantry officer, you just about have to be airborne in order to make it up the ladder. Plus, old Hobbs had been smart enough to see a chance to get that all important combat experience. And it's not too hard to believe that bit about every officer since Korea volunteering for Nam, also. I'll bet he stepped on somebody's toes or he wouldn't have ended up behind a desk doing nothing in the States. If he went over in January '65 that means he went home in June '66. The buildup was underway by that time, new companies were being formed from scratch, and there's just no way a captain with experience as a platoon leader in combat would get filed away. I wonder what he did. He should have been in a position to climb right up the ladder, quick. Whatever it was, he must have been passed over for promotion at least once back in the States because of it; possibly even once before that in Nam, with the 173rd. That would have been twice, once more and he'd have been riffed out of the service. That's why he put in for flight training. If he'd really loved combat as much as he let on, he'd have put in for Ranger school instead of flight school; although helicopters would get him out of the infantry and give him a chance to start fresh. The Army needed helicopter pilots badly, so he got in quick, but I'll bet he shit his pants when he ended up with the 101st Airborne. That's why he went to Saigon and happened upon a friend. Happened upon, my butt, I'll bet he's gone and hunted him up. Old Hobbs had to get out of that infantry unit. Even if he was driving helicopters for them, he was still in the airborne. That friend of his at Corps had enough rank, or else had the right job, with access to records and information to know we needed an XO. I'll even bet he arranged the man's promotion to major. Hobbs did say he'd been promoted in January. I'll bet his buddy's got the promotion and orders sending Hobbs up here all on the same set of orders. After all, if Corps knew we needed an XO, it knew we would need a CO in about a month. If the buddy in Corps had that ability, then there wasn't any reason to believe he couldn't purge Hobbs' records for him, also. Not a bad deal, really. Hobbs had taken out of his records whatever it was that kept him from being promoted, never to be seen again; he gets orders sending him up here, and the promotion to major. When he goes home at the end of this tour, he'll have one of the most important flags on his 201 file an officer could have, command of a company during combat. One thing was certain, any officer who gets a star in the next twenty years will have to have that flag on his records. No combat leadership command, no star. For that matter, it's going to be just about as important for an enlisted man to have Nam on his records. After all, the officers who are promoted will be vets and they'll surround themselves with enlisted men who are Vietnam Vets also. I wonder what Hobbs had to give his buddy at Corps? That might explain Hobbs' attitude towards Halsey and me. Maybe he's walked in my boots. He just might have had a Halsey back in the 173rd without anybody to protect him.

By the time they had rejoined the flight, one lift had already been made. Mr. Walker pulled into the trail position as Hobbs advised Lead of their presence. Troops were picked up at Dau Tieng and added to those already in position. There had been no contact made to this point, so it was beginning to look like another long, quiet, boring day. From the LZ they flew to Tay Ninh and picked up more troops. These were put in a different location and the flight headed back to Tay Ninh.

By this time, Major Hobbs was getting wise to Mr. Walker's way of waking Jim up before each landing, but Hobbs was so tired he didn't really care. In fact, he wished he could rack out also.

They were almost back to Tay Ninh when Six called Lead and told him their mission had been changed. Nothing was happening with the troops they'd put in, and all hell had broken loose up north a ways; so they'd been released from the 25th Infantry and Operation Yellowstone. They were to pick up troops from the 1st Infantry Division at Lai Khe and put them in at an LZ just northeast of Song Be.

The flight up to Lai Khe took half an hour, during which Jim woke up long enough to say "clear right" just prior to touchdown. Jim noticed Major Hobbs was asleep while he put on fuel and troops. Having been to Lai Khe before, Jim recognized the place, but since he'd been asleep he had no idea why they were there, where they were going or why they were picking up troops from the Big Red One. He turned on all his radios after refueling, except AM Saigon, so it wasn't long before Lead's conversation with Six in C and C told him just about everything he wanted to know. Jim figured the flight all the way up to Song Be would take a little over an hour, so once again he pulled his visor down, turned off the radios, and put on his seat belt. Sleep came quickly as he sat there watching the rice paddies turn to woodlands.

Just outside Song Be, Mr. Walker had to wake not only Jim, but Wright and Major Hobbs. The major was very apologetic about dozing off, even though Mr. Walker told him not to feel bad about it and had made light of his sleep-talking.

Song Be was a small village only a few miles from Cambodia and almost to the Second Corp area. It was heavily wooded and slightly rolling; some would say picturesque best described the area. It was also a U.S. Special Forces Camp. Yet for everyone in the flight of ten Hueys on long final approach, it was just another place to land, be shot at, and for some, to be wounded and die. They all knew it wasn't going to be good. An ARVN unit had gotten things started by sending out a patrol that was ambushed and ran. This upset the ARVN commander, so he sent his entire unit out to engage Charlie. The only problem was his men had backbones made of a substance slightly softer than mush. As a result, once the shooting started, they fell in behind the largest trees they could find and had been screaming for help ever since.

Mr. Walker called the roll to make sure everyone was awake. Major Hobbs was upset that Mr. Walker would be checking on him again, and made it clear Walker wasn't to do it again.

"Major, would you like to drive? This LZ is going to be good and hot!"

"Mr. Walker, I'd be glad to drive. What makes you think it's going to be so hot? The gunships didn't get any ground fire during their prep."

"Yes! Sir, that's one reason I think it'll be hot. We know they're down there. I mean somebody kicked the shit out of that ARVN unit. If they've got enough training and discipline not to fire on our gunship, then they're NVA. Believe me, it'll be hot. Okay, you two in the back, we're on short final, once we cross that road just ahead, open up. ARVN is supposed to be all on this side of the road so, Wright, if it moves down there cut it in half!"

"You got it, Sir."

"Mac, you copy?"

"Yes, Sir."

"Okay, there goes the road."

Both door guns opened up, causing the usual vibration. The grunts on board knew that was their sign. They all shifted in their seats and looked a lot more alert: some tightened their chin straps, some checked their weapons, one even retied his left boot. It was eight seconds from the time the doorguns opened up until Hobbs sat it down and the grunts jumped off. Walker had been right. It was hot. It was very hot. There was a steady flow of muzzle flashes coming from both tree lines. As the grunts jumped out, Jim's M60 was working perfectly. He gave the usual one word signal that the troops were all out, "Go!" and instantly the Huey started to lift. Out of the corner of his eye, Jim saw the grunts start to move forward, when one stood up straight, threw both his arms up and out, with his M16 being released and flying through the air. His face showed the pain his scream expressed. In that same movement his arms came back in, clutching his midsection as his knees buckled and his head jerked forward; collapsing his body in a roll on the ground.

Jim shouted into his mike, "Major, put it back down! Now!"

Like any good pilot, Major Hobbs instantly, and without question, followed his crew chief's command and sat it down only ten yards from where they'd dropped off the grunts. Jim waved to the two grunts who had come to their wounded buddy's aid to put him on board. At the same moment, he started firing his M60 into the trees and talking to his pilots. Less than two seconds had elapsed since he'd told Hobbs to set it down.

"Major, I've got a WIA back there!"

"Well, tell 'em to hurry up! We're sitting ducks here!"

As the two grunts helped put the wounded but still conscious GI on board, Mr. Walker called Lead. "Lead, this is Trail, you've got nine ships up. We're still on the ground putting on a wounded grunt."

"Roger, Trail. Take him to Phuoc Binh, Lead, out."

The wounded GI was a large black man with an unusual pot belly for a grunt. He was losing a lot of blood fast as it flowed freely onto his shirt and pants. There was a small white man under his right arm, and another black under his left arm. They quickly lifted him into the chopper's cargo area, with Wright's aid. As they pushed his legs inside, the short white man slammed face first onto the floor as though pushed by some unseen force. He struggled to stand, only to slide off the edge of the chopper's floor. The black man beside him reached down and pulled him to his feet. Blood was now making the back of the little man's shirt soggy. In one big push, the black man shoved the smaller white man into the Huey and then threw in his M16. Mr. Walker had taken the controls and run the RPM up enough so when Jim said, "Go! Go!", the ship literally jumped into the air and disappeared.

As Jim climbed over the seats to help Wright give first aid, Mr. Walker said, "How many hits did we take, Mac? And how bad are those two?"

"Sir, I heard at least two hits, but I was kind of busy, so I wasn't really listening for them. How many did you hear?"

"I counted at least three. Check it out close when we get to Phuoc Binh!"

"You got it! Sir, you asked about these two." Jim had been working as he talked, and it didn't look good. "The white guy's not too bad, he took a slug in the right shoulder. If you can turn around and look at this black guy you should. I've never seen anything like it before."

With that, both officers turned in their seats to look back. Major Hobbs spoke instantly. "Holy shit! He's going to need major surgery; we better get him to Tay Ninh."

Jim said, "Major, he'll never make it to Tay Ninh. I don't know what's at Phuoc Binh, but even if there's only an aid station with a doctor, he can do more than we can to stabilize him until a medevac can transport him."

"You're right, Mac, it would take us a half hour to get to Tay Ninh, and we're on long final to Phuoc Binh now."

Jim had bandaged the shoulder of the wounded grunt who, still conscious, had positioned himself so the black man's head rested on his lap. Tears slowly rolled down his cheek as he softly stroked his black friend's head. Wright had removed the flak jacket and opened the man's shirt only to have his intestines fall out. The bullet had made a perfect incision just below the belly button. What Jim had thought was a pot belly were, in fact, the man's guts hanging out. It was at times like these Jim marveled at the punishment the human body could endure and still survive. Neither Wright nor Jim knew what to do. Every time they tried to push his guts back in, more came out. There was blood all over the place but no place to put a tourniquet. Likewise, there wasn't any place to apply direct pressure as could be done with a muscle wound. Every time they tried to apply direct pressure to the jagged edges of the tear, more guts and blood came out somewhere else. For some reason, there didn't seem to be any sensation in the area because he never once showed any signs of pain. He was obviously in shock. One look at his badly dilated eyes and dazed expression confirmed it. Yet, he never made a sound.

Finally, they landed. A man with a stethoscope around his neck and only an olive drab T-shirt met them. Jim figured he was the doctor. There were three other bare chested men who were taking orders from T-shirt. Jim could hardly believe his eyes as he watched the black hold his own guts on top of himself as the others placed him on a stretcher.

Both crewmen had removed their flight gloves to work on the wounded grunts, but had wiped their hands on the shirts of the infantrymen as T-shirt and his men arrived. Walker was in the process of shutting it down as Jim and Wright threw dirt and sand on the floor to help dry up the blood. Jim opened Major Hobbs' door and slid his seat's armor plating back. He was somewhat surprised when the Major climbed out and said, "Well, Mac, it's turning into quite a day. First we have a duck fly through our windshield, then we have some poor grunt spill his guts all over the floor."

"Sir, I feel sorry for him."

"Mac, me too. You've got to give him credit, though; he's got balls of steel. There aren't too many men who wouldn't have passed out. Then when they put him on that stretcher he just gathered in his guts and held on." Hobbs laughed as he added,

"Just like he was saying, 'By God, they belong to me and no-body else can have 'em!' "

"Major, you are hard! I mean really, making fun of some poor guy who's had his guts shot out." Jim shook his head and walked around the aircraft's nose as Hobbs followed laughing. There was one bullet hole in the fiber glass lid that housed some of the radios and a battery. Jim pointed the hole out to Hobbs. "There, Major, another two feet in your direction and you'd have had that one in the leg. You might have even gotten a free ride to the States out of it."

"I'll be damned! I'd have put a Band-Aid on it, and maybe taken a couple of days off just to help the guys in the company area get things straightened out, and been right back at it."

"Sir, if you want, I'll find you some old rusty nails for break-fast!"

Hobbs at first was taken back, then a small smile crossed his lips, followed by his larger than necessary laugh. "Mac, you're alright, you know that? I like a man who's not afraid to give it to me straight. Something tells me you'd walk right up to General Westmoreland himself, lay it on the line and not give a shit how many stars he's got. You and I'll get along just fine."

They found the second hole in the tail boom. There wasn't any damage to anything except its skin. They looked and looked for the third one that Walker was sure he'd heard hit, but couldn't find. Jim had even started to climb on top for a second look when Wright hollered, "I found it."

One round had passed through the soundproofing in the ceiling, almost in the middle and above the cargo door opening. It had then exited through the track on which the cargo door hung. Once Jim saw it, he tried to shut the cargo door, but it wouldn't go past the bullet's exit hole. Looking over at Major Hobbs, who was standing there watching, Jim said, "Major, we'll have to take this door off once we get back to Tay Ninh, or we won't be able to get into the engine compartment on the left side. Plus, it'll have to stay off until maintenance can get a new track put on."

The major took another drag from his cigar, frowned, slowly nodded and more slowly said, "Why do I get the impression

I'm going to have to crack some nuts to keep the doors on all the helicopters?"

"Because, Sir, the cargo doors are a pain in the ass. Besides, I didn't put that bullet hole there."

It wasn't long before they'd joined up with the flight on their way out of the same LZ. Another Huey company had joined the Blackhawks on this lift and what should have been a major battle was underway. The NVA found themselves in a box. On one side, American troops, on another, ARVN, and both were to be pushing the NVA towards Cambodia. But between Cambodia and them stood the American Special Forces camp of Song Be, and all their mountain friends who hated the North Vietnamese more than anything or anyone else.

There was one more lift put in a different LZ by each Huey company. These were to dig in and hold in an effort to force the NVA towards Song Be. There was only one small problem, the ARVN troops weren't moving. This had irritated the American commander to the point he'd ordered his troops to hold until they'd received confirmation that ARVN was on the move. Thus, the Blackhawks had been ordered back to An Loc.

The flight was on short final approach when Mr. Walker said, "Hey, Mac! Sounds like we might have a little time, how about cooking our C's?"

"You got it, just don't shut it off too quick."

Once on the ground, Walker kept the Huey running at idle speed. Jim quickly jumped out and closed his cargo door. Then, opening the storage compartment door, he pulled out the four C-ration boxes and the metal holder he'd just picked up earlier that day after having one of the guys in sheet metal make it for him. He took the main meals from each box, placed them in his pockets, opened the engine compartment and climbed onto the platform. Then, using Wright's asbestos glove (used for changing gun barrels), he placed the rack with the C's in it inside the engine's exhaust pipe just after Mr. Walker shut it off. The heat still radiating from the turbine engine quickly heated their lunch. Still using the asbestos glove, he carefully removed each can and placed it on the platform beside his feet. Then he removed the holder and threw it on the ground to cool, but it didn't hit the ground until after bounding off a highly polished combat boot. Jim looked down at a short, slightly plump little man wearing a uniform that looked like it had come from a dry cleaners in the States with extra starch. It was then that Jim saw the star in the center of the baseball cap.

Jim saluted as best he could and at the same time glanced at the tall, straight-backed first lieutenant standing with a clipboard behind the general.

"Good afternoon, General."

Both officers returned his salute as the general said, "Good afternoon, Specialist. What were you doing?"

"Sir, I was cooking our C-rations."

"Very ingenious. Did you make this, Specialist?"

"Yes, Sir, with the help of some of the guys in sheet metal."

"Everyone in your company have one of these?"

"No, Sir, just me. That's the second one I've had. I lost the first one after only using it a couple of times when my ship was shot down and burned. My friend in sheet metal knew it, so he made this one and I just got it this morning."

The general bent to pick it up and burnt his fingers.

"Sir, that's why I use my gunner's glove."

The general looked up disdainfully and said, "Get down from there!" Looking inside the aircraft, the General saw Major Hobbs and Mr. Walker still in their seats talking, with the major smoking a cigar. In no time the general had all four crew members standing at attention in front of him. "At ease, men. Do any of you four know who I am?"

The general searched each man's face. Getting no response he started to speak when Jim said, "Sir, I do."

The general turned to Jim, who was standing there looking like he wished he didn't know. "Very well, Specialist MacLaughlin, is that pronunciation correct?"

"Yes, Sir."

"Very well, Specialist, why don't you enlighten your fellow crew members!"

"Sir, you're Brigadier General Anber, Commanding Officer 1st Aviation Brigade."

"Very good, Specialist, and how is it you know that when your major doesn't?"

"Well, Sir, he hasn't been in country that long."

"Specialist, I didn't ask you to make excuses for your officers."

"No, Sir. I was a member of the 191st Assault Helicopter Company at Bear Cat before being sent up here. We had a formation one day, complete with TV cameras, and you were there passing out medals. After you'd finished decorating people, you climbed up on the platform to speak, when you were handed a note. I remember your asking our operations officer if this was for real and he assured you it was. Then, you somewhat disgustedly spoke into the mike and told us a tactical emergency had been declared and all members of the flight crews were to man their ships. I think almost everybody in that formation let out a scream of joy and half of us threw our hats in the air. It was nothing personal, Sir, we just didn't want to stand out there in the sun and listen to speeches. I guess, Sir, I remember your face from that day."

"You mean you remember my nose." Jim didn't respond, but couldn't help but smile. "It's okay, Specialist, I know they call me Hook-Nose-Six. But with a horn like this, I can't blame anybody but my old man. You know, I remember that day also. It sure was hot. Believe it or not, I felt so sorry for you guys I'd decided to cut my speech from fifteen minutes down to just a couple. After all, I've stood in a few of those formations myself. If I remember right, you guys flew all the way down to Cau Mong that night. Got yourself into quite a fight, too, didn't you?"

"I don't really know, Sir. I was in maintenance."

The general simply smiled and said, "Hmmm. This your ship, Specialist?"

"Yes, Sir."

"Why isn't your name on it as crew chief?"

Jim glanced over at Walker, and the major then replied, "Sir, it was just transferred to us yesterday."

"Do you smoke in your aircraft when it's on the ground, Specialist?"

Jim knew what the general had in mind. "Sir, I don't smoke at all, but if I could add, Sir, Major Hobbs has been very kind to me, Sir. I'm convinced he'll make an excellent pilot and commanding officer. He hasn't been in the company long enough to know one isn't supposed to smoke in the ship on the ground."

Again there was only the "Hmmm" from the general before he said in a very commanding voice, "Lieutenant!"

"Sir!"

"Lieutenant, it appears we have three Article 15's to pass out here. Major, you get the first one for smoking in an aircraft on the ground with its engines shut off. That'll cost you one hundred fifty dollars. One hundred dollars for smoking, fifty because you're the company XO and should set a better example for your troops. Give the lieutenant your full name, rank and serial number!"

If looks could kill, General Anber would have dropped dead on the spot. As the lieutenant took the information from Major Hobbs, General Anber asked, "Mr. Walker, you're the aircraft commander?"

"Yes, Sir."

"Then you alone are responsible for everyone on board your ship regardless of whether they're crew members or passengers. They're your responsibility. As a result, they take orders from you even if they are majors. I understand your problem with rank, but you have no choice but to make it clear that you disapprove of their actions. Did you say anything to the major?"

"No, Sir."

"Because you didn't say anything at all to the major about his cigar, it'll cost you one hundred dollars. Give the lieutenant your full name, rank and serial number."

Turning to Wright, who was next in line, Anber continued, "You seem to be the lucky one today. You get off scot free. Just have a seat in the aircraft and see to it you don't move up the line. By this time everyone in this flight who smokes has lit up and I'm going to get every one of them for one hundred dollars. So just have a seat and enjoy your lunch. I'm sure it's still warm."

Then turning to Jim, the general said, "And as for you, I don't know. At least you had good motives."

Jim took this opening as his only chance. "Sir, have you ever eaten cold beans and wienies or, even worse, cold pork slices with so much grease it looked like lard? Then when you ate it, even after scraping off the greasy lard, it stuck to your teeth and mouth until you were willing to use a GI brush to get it off?"

"Yes, Specialist, I have and so have thousands of others and there'll be thousands more after you're gone. Give the lieutenant your serial number."

"But, General, I wasn't doing it just for myself. If everyone could cook their C's, we'd all be a lot happier. Happy troops make better troops, and Sir, I wouldn't keep it for myself. I can very easily see the Army putting one of these in each chopper."

"You're a real humanitarian, Specialist. Now, before you become a Spec-Four, give the lieutenant your serial number!"

Jim decided it wasn't going to do any good to continue on, especially after being threatened with the loss of a stripe. In a voice that clearly conveyed his displeasure, Jim said, "RA* and I USED to be proud of it!"

The general shouted, "Specialist, one more smart-ass remark out of you and you'll be an E-1**. Aren't you afraid of me at all?"

"No, Sir. I always thought a general was supposed to have the good of his troops at heart. So why should I be afraid of someone who's supposed to be looking after me?"

"Just give the lieutenant your serial number."

"Yes, Sir. RA11701118, Sir!"

The two men's eyes held each other's for a full second before the general turned and walked towards the next ship in line. Hobbs, Walker and Jim stood there with their eyes fixed on the general's back. It was then Jim saw Hunter happily cooking away with what he knew had to be a C-4 ball. It was a very common practice. The C-4 plastic explosive came in sticks, and almost every chopper had part of a stick stuck in a corner of the storage compartment. It reminded Jim of Play-Doh. The stuff would stick to anything. Then, when one had enough time to heat his C's, he just pulled a little loose, rolled it into a ball

---

* RA—Indicates a person who has enlisted, as opposed to a U.S. for draftees.

** E-1—Lowest rank in the army.

about the size of a marble, put it between some stones on the ground and set it on fire. The stuff was truly wonderful. It would burn extremely hot, but never explode. It took a blasting cap to make C-4 explode, which made it totally safe to cook with. The only problem was some officers didn't like the idea. Jim knew it was going to cost Hunter one hundred dollars, which made Jim realize the general hadn't told him the amount of his fine.

It was at this point, Major Hobbs spoke. "There goes a truly sorry son of a bitch."

It was Wright seated inside the aircraft who let out a loud, hard laugh that made the other three turn and give him the evil eye. Wright's laughter stopped instantly and he said, "Major, it just reminded me of how I feel about washing and waxing Hueys!"

Jim said, "You know, major, our wonderful commander didn't even tell me how much he's going to stick me for."

The major turned and looked surprised as he said, "You lucky bastard! I'd swear you could fall in a shit pile and come out smelling like a rose!"

Startled, Jim asked, "How do you figure that?"

"If the man didn't tell you how much that Article 15 was going to cost you, then you're not getting one."

"Why not?"

"Because! It's a matter of pride for someone like him. If he didn't tell you how much, then you won't get one. He didn't take your name either, did he?"

"No, Sir, just my serial number. Sir, do you think he forgot, or did I talk him out of it?"

"Mac, it's hard to say, it could be either, or the fact that you knew who he was."

"Sir, he could always stick a figure in later."

"He could, but I'd bet money he won't."

Major Hobbs was right. In two weeks there was a company formation for all flight crews, during which the CO called off the names of all the men who had an Article 15 waiting in his office courtesy of General Anber. Jim's name was not on the list. He often wondered why not, but never knew for sure. All the officers caught smoking in the Hueys paid one hundred dollars for the education they received that day. The enlisted men's education wasn't quite as expensive, but at fifty dollars each, it still hurt.

It was Mr. Walker who turned to Major Hobbs and asked, "Major, you going to warn the rest of the flight?"

The major watched General Anber move on to the next ship up the line. After watching his lieutenant start to write down more names, Hobbs turned to Wright, who spoke before the major had a chance. "Major, if you really don't mind, the general told me to sit here and be a good little boy and that's just what I'd like to do. Unless of course, you order me to walk past that man. I'm sure he wouldn't hold me responsible for obeying a direct order."

Major Hobbs said, "Yeah, I can't blame you for that. You know I could call Lead on the radio, he probably has someone monitoring company frequency in case Six tries to contact us. But what the hell, misery loves company. Mac, any of the C's still hot?"

Jim gave a "How should I know" look at Hobbs and then picked up the four still warm C-ration cans. He placed each can beside its box, but held on to the beans and frankfurters. In the box was a can of crackers and cheese and a pound cake.

He watched with interest who took what meals, as he tore open the accessory packs. Major Hobbs took spaghetti with beef chunks. Mr. Walker took beans with meatballs in a tomato sauce, leaving Wright with the chopped ham and eggs.

Every time Jim opened an accessory pack he had to laugh at the Army. They just couldn't bring themselves to allow anything to keep its common name and the accessory packet was an excellent example. On the pack was a listing of everything inside: matches, chewing gum, toilet paper, instant coffee, cream substitute, sugar, salt and a stimulater interdental. Whoever heard of a stimulater interdental? Who even knew what a stimulater interdental was? It was only through the process of elimination that he'd found it was a toothpick.

They were just about finished eating when Lead's crew chief walked up and told them all the officers were wanted at Lead ship.

Once the pilots left, Jim stretched out on the ship's passenger seats for a nap, using his chicken plate as a pillow. Wright started to play with some local kids who'd come out from nowhere. There was something about Wright that just seemed to attract them. For the life of him, Jim couldn't understand why. All Wright ever did was torment the poor kids. There were five of them ranging in age from about four to seven, each with the same sad little cutoffs as shorts. Two of the kids had shirts on, one still had two buttons but no sleeves and the other had sleeves but only one button. All five were barefoot and their dark skin was deeply tanned. They must have all gone to the same barber who knew one type of haircut, a butch. The biggest one had only a stump where once had been a right hand. No doubt one of the saddest by-products of war.

The saddest thing about the whole group was their eyes; those poor, sad, deep, dark little eyes. Yet, these same little sad eyes could instantly turn to life and sparkle with all the alertness of a normal, healthy child whenever Wright pulled out some little trinket. It didn't take much, something like a roll of toilet paper or a packet of creamer and Wright would have those kids doing all kinds of tricks. Just like training a puppy, you show him his treat, then have him do a trick and you give him his reward. The better the trick, the greater the reward and the same for those kids. Wright's fame in the company came from once getting a group of kids to make a human pyramid for a can of beans and weenies.

Jim awoke to a terrible racket which caused him to sit up. There were three South Vietnamese CH 34's taxiing down the runway. Wright stopped playing with the kids long enough to tell Jim they'd landed for fuel while he'd been asleep. Both GI's watched what were commonly called flying death traps lumber down the runway. The CH 34's had picked up that nickname because the crew chief's seat was located directly under the transmission, which had the tendency to break loose during a hard landing and fall on him. When the CH 34's had been given to the South Vietnamese, their pilots were so short the foot pedals had to be extended for their shorter legs, and the seats raised so they could see out the window.

By this time almost everyone in the area was watching the South Vietnamese pilots roll their helicopters towards the end of the runway. Jim, like most of the other Blackhawks, began to wonder when they were going to pull pitch and become airborne. Like a magnet, all eyes were drawn to the first of the three CH 34's as it reached the end of the runway and rolled down the hillside without ever leaving the ground. The second chopper followed the first in perfect formation right down the side of the hill, being preceded in death by the explosion of the first chopper. Not wishing to be outdone, it also exploded like the first into a giant fireball. The third pilot in line, having seen the fate of the first two, pulled pitch for all he was worth and managed to get his 34 off the ground at the last second. He was obviously unable to maintain flight as he dipped his nose down and disappeared below the trees. Yet, there was no explosion, and everyone who wasn't running in that direction stood with their mouths open, not really believing what they had just seen. Then, as though resurrected from the dead, the third chopper suddenly reappeared above the trees and headed south.

Wright returned to playing with the kids, a group that had expanded to twelve. Jim moved up into his seat behind the M60 and picked up his camera. These were the type pictures he liked to take. Kids doing their thing, local people in their daily lives, and general aerial photographs of the countryside were what he wanted to record on film. Unlike some guys, he'd never taken that first photo of a dead or wounded GI; it wasn't what he wanted to remember. There were guys who took pictures of every dead or wounded person they came across. It was almost as though they needed to prove to themselves or to others they'd been where the action was.

Jim had just finished taking a photo of Wright holding a C-ration can above his head and the kids trying to get it, when one of them grabbed the obvious leader of the group. It was almost like instant panic set in, the Vietnamese kids' normal fast chatter and smiles turned to shouts at machinegun speed, and their smiles were gone. In seconds the whole bunch had left with the smallest one quickly running back the ten feet he'd already traversed to make one final gesture for Wright to give him the can of C-rations.

Wright handed him the can and turned to Jim. "Hey, Mac,

what the hell scared them off? You'd have thought Ho Chi Minh himself just popped up."

"I don't know, Wright. Something sure scared them off quick. It kind of looked like they were afraid of those other kids coming, but there are only five of them, even if they are a little older. Besides, kids usually work their way up the line of choppers. Those little guys just split. I don't understand."

"Ya know, Mac, I had the impression that little guy who came back was trying to tell me something. He kept saying, 'Number ten, number ten,' but I thought he was talking about me making them beg. Mac, hop out, I'm going to shut this cargo door."

Jim put his camera back in the corner and helped Wright slide the door shut. Jim thought about walking on up the line to Athia's ship, but decided it might not be a good idea to leave the ship since they couldn't shut the left door. So he opened the peter pilot's door, climbed in and sat down to watch the ship and Wright until those kids left. Besides, it was so hot his shirt back was soaked with sweat and he wanted to stay in the shade.

There were five kids in this group. All were older than any of the first group, most were in the eleven to fourteen age bracket. Wright started right in on them, just like every other group, by holding a can of C-rations as though he didn't know what to do with it. Both GI's relaxed as this group of kids responded just like every other. Shortly Wright was doing his routine.

Jim turned on AM Saigon. Turning all the other radios off and the volume up on Hobbs' helmet, he could easily hear the DJ in Saigon giving the time and temperature. No wonder his shirt was all wet down the back, 106 degrees in the shade and like the DJ said, "I know all you GI's out there in the bush are in the shade and if you aren't, you really don't want to know how hot it is in the sunshine."

Jim almost jumped through the windshield as a single 38 caliber pistol shot rang out right next to him. Turning, he saw Major Hobbs standing there with smoking pistol in hand.

All the officers had collected at Lead's ship while the flight waited for instructions. It hadn't been long when the pilot monitoring the radios broke up their chatter. He'd just received word the South Vietnamese were sending up an elite ranger unit to help move their infantry unit forward. It didn't take a genius to know how that would work. The rangers would land behind the ARVN unit and simply tell them to move out or be shot. They'd move.

It was almost an hour later when the ARVN choppers landed to put on fuel. As they touched down all kinds of fun was poked at them by their American counterparts. The general lack of respect by the Americans was even more evident as the ARVN aircraft started to roll down the runway. They laughed and joked about how it wouldn't be surprising if the gooks flew those 34's down the hillside instead of into the air. Yet all stood with their mouths open in a shocked state of disbelief as each CH 34 went down the hill. No one moved, the laughter stopped and the American eyes slowly dropped to the ground.

There was a steady stream from the end of the runway of people running towards the downed choppers. It was Major Hobbs who finally turned to the American pilot monitoring the radio and said, "You better call C & C and tell them what happened to their elite ranger unit."

It was over an hour before they received word from Blackhawk Six. The American officer in charge of the GI's on the ground had decided he wasn't sending American boys in to fight North Vietnamese when South Vietnamese refused. The order came down to pull out the American troops they'd just put in. The South Vietnamese troops were to provide cover for the extraction, and then walk out.

Major Hobbs and Mr. Walker had headed for their ship together, talking as they walked. At the helicopter before theirs, Mr. Walker cut between ships to speak to another pilot. It was then that Major Hobbs first looked ahead at the kids beside his ship. There was Wright teasing a group of kids with a can of C-rations, yet something was wrong. As Major Hobbs slowed his pace, he couldn't understand why one of the smaller kids was standing back towards the storage compartment by himself. Each step for the major was slower than the preceding one. His eyes were glued to the little kid standing alone. He was barefoot, with ragged cutoffs and a short sleeve shirt about two sizes too large. The child's haircut was the standard Vietnamese boys cut, a butch, but it was his left hand that held the major's attention. His left hand was holding something inside his partly unbuttoned shirt. Major Hobbs had stopped walking beside the preceding ship's tail rotor. He didn't yet know what was going on but figured, what the hell, they'd be in the air in a couple of minutes.

It was at the same moment, he saw the kid's right hand reach up and open the fuel cap. Major Hobbs shouted, "Hey kid, what the hell you doing?"

With that, the other kids started to run. Wright turned to look at the major as the kid pulled the pin on the now exposed hand grenade. Only a fraction of a second passed, but Major Hobbs knew he was too far away to stop him physically. In that same fraction of a second, Major Hobbs knew what he had to do and he did it. The snubnose .38 came out of his shoulder holster in a flash, and one round was fired just as the kid raised the grenade to stick it in the fuel tank.

No one said a word as the major ran up to the prone kid. He was dead, a bullet hole in the right side of his head just above and in front of the ear. Major Hobbs picked up the hand grenade and without speaking, held it out to show the large rubberband holding the handle in place. There were several GI's from the next couple of ships up the line who stood there gaping.

It was Wright who finally broke the silence. "My God, Major, he was just a kid!"

"Yes! A kid who would have blown this helicopter and everyone on it, including your young ass, into a thousand pieces! Mr. Walker, get on the radio and see if you can get some MP's out here to pick him up! The rest of you, get back to your ships. Now!"

Jim and Wright remained standing beside each other after the others had started to leave. Major Hobbs picked up the pin and placed it back in the grenade's handle. Looking up at Jim and Wright, he spoke somewhat curtly. "What are you two looking at?"

Without hesitation, Jim said, "You, Sir."

"What's the matter with you, MacLaughlin? He was VC. He

just tried to stick a grenade in your fuel tank." Hobbs could see the look in Jim's eyes.

"All right, MacLaughlin, what would you have done? I was clear up to the next ship. There was no way I could have reached him before he dropped that grenade inside your fuel tank. Let me ask you something, Mac. You going to fly in this thing knowing there's a grenade with only a rubberband around its handle in the fuel tank?"

Jim slowly shook his head. "Okay, so if you're not going to fly in it, are you going to help pull the fuel cell out, knowing that every second that passes, the JP-4 fuel had weakened the rubberband a little bit more?"

"I wouldn't be very happy about it, Sir."

"I didn't think so. Look, I'd already hollered at him. That didn't stop him, nothing short of a bullet was going to."

"Sir, it didn't have to be in the head!"

"How the hell do you know? Were you standing where I was standing? Did you see my line of fire? Look at it this way; he had a great future ahead of him as a Vietcong. There are a lot of GI's he'll never kill! Mac, back to the first question, what would have done?"

Jim paused and slowly said, "The same thing, Sir."

Jim turned and walked towards the fuel cap; stepping over the dead kid. It bothered him, yet he knew deep down inside the major was right. He had done just exactly the right thing, there was no question about it. If he'd hesitated for even a second, it would have been too late. Whoever said, "War is hell" was right, but he should have added, "It also makes you want to puke."

There wasn't any of the usual chitchat as the helicopter lifted and fell in line behind everyone else in a trail right formation. It was Major Hobbs who decided he had to do something to get his crew's minds off recent events.

"Hey, Mac, you back there?"

"No, Sir, I took a flying leap."

Major Hobbs decided to ignore the obvious sarcasm. "I was talking to one of your admirers at Lead, a Mr. Gail. He told me quite a story about the one time you two flew together." There was only silence for a response. "Well, Mac, come on, let's hear it."

"Major, I thought you said Mr. Gail already told you."

"He did, but I wanted to hear it from you. There are two sides to every story and I don't care what you called him, it's water over the dam. I'm not going to do anything about it now. But I will nail your balls to the wall if it happens again. So, tell me the story."

"Major, I really don't remember what you're talking about."

"MacLaughlin, I've got hammer and nails back at Tay Ninh. I could start nailing tonight unless you want to tell me a story now! I mean, everybody loves a good story. Wright, you'd like to hear Mac's story, wouldn't you!"

"No, Sir."

Jim laughed to himself, *Good old Wright, the man does have brass.* Hobbs's anger was clear in the tone of his voice. "All right dammit, I've tried to be nice about it; now tell me the damn story and that's an order!"

"Okay, Major, I'll tell you what happened. Polaski was the gunner, Mr. Gail and another pilot from the other platoon drove, and I was the crew chief. Mr. Gail, by the way, is in the other platoon also. That's why I've only flown with him once. I didn't refuse to fly with him or anything like that. I can't remember the peter pilot's name or, for that matter, why we didn't have pilots from our own platoon. You have to remember, Major, that was back before they made us an all C.A.* company. We'd fly maybe one or two C.A.'s per week and the rest were all single ship missions. We called them ash and trash, or milk runs. Basically, you name it and we hauled it, and very seldom were any of them dangerous. I remember one time, just as an example, I spent the whole day flying sampans from Saigon to some little hamlet way down in the Delta. I knew I got picked for that job because I had one of the few helicopters in the company that still had a cargo hook in the hell hole. Most guys take the hooks out because they are hardly ever used and they make it really tough to crawl up into that hell hole. Anyway, this fishing hamlet had been hit by VC the night before

* C.A.—Combat Assault.

and Chuck had, as a parting gesture, burned all the sampans. So our Uncle bought 'em all new ones, and we hauled them down there.''

Major Hobbs broke in, "Mac, what's that got to do with you and Mr. Gail?"

Jim chuckled to himself. "Nothing, Sir. I just thought if I talked long enough, I could stray far enough off the subject that you'd forget what I was supposed to be talking about."

"And you're still trying it."

"No, Sir, I'm getting to it, it just takes a while." Jim took a deep breath and said, "Anyway, we'd spent the morning hauling around a light colonel and a captain from Psychological Operations. Mostly we'd been down in the Delta. We'd take them to this place or that place, and they'd get out and talk to somebody for a little while, then we'd take them someplace else. I remember at one point, we came across an old outdoor oven that had some old pots sitting around it, some were broken, some weren't. That colonel wanted me to break the rest of the pots. So while Mr. Gail circled the oven, I shot up the unbroken pots and then started on the oven. I'll bet I wasted eight hundred rounds on that stupid oven before the colonel decided it wasn't going to shoot back at us. We'd also spent some time over in the Plain of Reeds area dropping leaflets asking Chuck if he wouldn't like to give up, with instructions on how to go about it."

"Mac, would you get on with it!"

"Okay, okay, I'm getting to it. Anyway, when it came time for lunch we took our passengers back to Bien Hoa. They told us we could have an hour and a half lunch. So Mr. Gail got all excited and started hopping up and down in his seat. He was going to the officers' club in Saigon for lunch. Well, we flew on over to Saigon and the two officers hopped out almost before the main rotor blades had quit turning. So I hollered at Mr. Gail as he hotfooted it off, 'Hey, how about us?' You see, Major, they didn't give us C-rations except when we were flying C.A.'s. Otherwise, we were supposed to eat in somebody's mess hall. Well, Mr. Gail said he didn't care what we did, just so we were back and on the ship by 1345. That way we'd have plenty of time to fly over to Bien Hoa by two o'clock. He even suggested we go to the enlisted men's club and eat. Well, I'd been there before and it takes over a half hour to walk one way. There was no way we could have walked there and back, plus eat and be on the ship by 1345. So I asked if we could go to the PX; it was only about a fifteen minute walk one way and we could get something to eat there. Mr. Gail told us, 'Sure, go ahead,' and to pick him up a can of shaving cream while we were there. So Polaski and I headed for the PX. We ate at the snack bar and still had plenty of time, so we decided to walk around the PX for a while. Man, oh man, is that place something. I'd never been in a place like that before, it's enormous. Plus it had everything under the sun for sale: cameras, and lenses the likes of which I'd never seen, diamonds and all kinds of rings and jewelry with rubies and sapphires. You can buy all kinds of clothes, even have a complete suit hand made. There's even one desk there where you can order a brand new car, any make you like, made to your specifications and delivered to the dealer closest to your home or next duty station. Anyway, we both got some things we needed along with Mr. Gail's shaving cream, and got in line to check out. There were only two people in front of us and I remember looking at my watch and thinking we still had about nine minutes to spare. The next thing I knew, three officers walked up and got in line in front of the two guys in front of us. Now we were five people back. The checkout guy was working on the last officer when up walks two captains, and they pull the same trick. I'm beginning to think I'll spend the rest of my tour over here just trying to get checked out. Of course, by this time the line behind us had gotten long enough, you couldn't see the end. The thing that finally got things moving again was when some Air Force Full Bird walked up and wanted to know why the line was getting longer instead of shorter, just as a group of four army warrants jumped the line. Man, did that Air Force colonel get mad. He'd been waiting in line and so could they. When he got done with 'em, they went to the end of the line. I remember he sat his stuff down on the checkout counter and asked where he could find the officer in charge. He was going to put a stop to this crap.

"By this time it was, of course, way past time for Polaski and I to leave. So we sat the stuff we were going to buy down and left. I'm telling you the truth, Sir; we ran all the way back to the chopper. We still got there five minutes late. But from where we were parked it only takes five minutes by air to get back over to Bien Hoa.

"Mr. Gail saw us coming and by the time we got to the ship, he'd untied it and had it running. The last thing Polaski said before we reached the chopper was, 'Mac, what's this guy's problem? We've still got ten minutes to get to Bien Hoa and that's plenty of time.' I told him I didn't know. But if he's in such a hurry that he's got it running already, we can expect to catch hell for being late. Anyway, when I climbed in, lo and behold, there in the passenger's seat sat another warrant officer whom I'd never laid eyes on before.

"We were in the air before I had my helmet or seatbelt on. In fact, I'd climbed in, sat down, and started to put on my flight gloves when he pulled pitch and took it up. Needless to say, I took my own sweet time putting my helmet on and hooking it up. Less than a second after I'd plugged it in, Mr. Gail said, 'MacLaughlin, you plugged in yet?' I told him I was and the first thing he asked me was, did I get his shaving cream? So I told him what had happened to us at the PX and he never said a word. I asked who our passenger was and Mr. Gail said he was an old friend of his from flight school. That was the last thing said until we got back to Bien Hoa. In the meantime, he'd redlined it all the way up to Cu Chi where he dropped our passenger off, and then redlined it all the way back to Bien Hoa. Needless to say, by the time we got back to Bien Hoa we were almost thirty five minutes late, and there, standing on the heliopad at parade rest was our captain. So Mr. Gail says, 'Oh, shit, that man is pissed! MacLaughlin, if I catch hell for being late, I'll nail your balls to the wall.' Well I don't mind telling you, Major, his telling me that really jerked my chain. I told him, 'Hey, look, we'd a been on time if you hadn't taken that joker all the way up to Cu Chi, so you don't need to go sticking the blame on me. Besides, a man admits to his mistakes and you made one, not Polaski or me.' Needless to say, that jerked Mr. Gail's chain completely out of its socket. The only thing that kept me from catching it right then was that we were on the ground and the captain had Mr. Gail standing at attention, chewing him up one side and down the other. To say he was upset would be a major understatement. The funniest part was when the captain had just finished with him, out walked the colonel, and he started in on him, too. Finally, it was Mr. Gail's turn and you could see the little worm passing the buck to Polaski and me. Once he got back in the chopper, nobody said poop to anyone.

"The first place we landed was just outside the Hobo Woods. The infantry had found a VC tunnel and the colonel wanted to talk to the tunnel rat* when he came out, if he came out. Anyway, once we'd landed, the colonel told us to shut it off, we'd be there awhile. So, while I was back there tying the main rotor blade down, Mr. Gail walked up and said, 'MacLaughlin, come here, I want to talk to you.' We walked another twenty feet away from the chopper where it was just him and me. He started in by giving me this line that one of his goals when he'd entered the Army was to spend his time without handing out any military discipline, but it looked like I'd just made that goal unobtainable. So I asked him why, and he said, Two reasons: one I was late reporting for duty after lunch and two, my smart mouth in front of others. As an enlisted man I had no right to question his decisions and I didn't have the right to make smart ass comments or give him any kind of back talk. Did I understand that? Well, to make a long story short, I told him I understood and he wouldn't have any more problems from me."

Major Hobbs interrupted. "Mac, you just skipped the part I've been sitting here listening to all your rambling for. You've made this story as long as you possibly could. Now, Mr. Gail remembers very well what was said next." There was a long silence before the major continued, "Mac, I'm waiting."

"Major, I'd just as soon forget about it if you really don't mind."

"Let's put it this way, I mind."

Again there was silence before Jim finally said, "Sir, isn't there a law against self incrimination?"

Major Hobbs practically shouted, "MacLaughlin!"

"All right, Major. I asked him if he'd passed the buck about

---

* Tunnel Rat—Small G.I. sent in V.C. tunnels.

our being late to me. He told me that was irrelevant. I knew it was just the two of us and that nobody would be able to prove later what either of us had said. So I told him, 'Like hell it was.' I knew good and well he'd been too big of a coward to take the rap himself for his own mistake, and that if he hadn't taken that joker to Cu Chi, we would have been on time and he knew it. Besides, we were out here having this little chat probably because the colonel had told him to. Further, that I personally thought he was lower than a toothless, yellow-bellied swamp snake with the bite of a sabertooth crotch cricket, that not only had a yellow belly, but had a yellow streak running down the center of his back going from one shoulder to the next. And as far as his goals were concerned, there wasn't going to be any military punishment and we both knew it. In the first place, it wouldn't be too hard to find that Air Force colonel from the PX. In the second place, I wouldn't have been in that line if he hadn't asked me to buy him shaving cream, and finally, even if I'd been on time, we still wouldn't have made it to Cu Chi and back to Bien Hoa on time. Anybody with the brains of a stick knows that, including him when he was offering that warrant officer a ride. Well, he started jumping up and down claiming he'd break me to E-1 for talking to him like that. I just told him. 'Look, I won't give you any more trouble on the ship, but I'll deny ever having had this conversation. So it'll be your word against mine, and without a witness, you haven't got any more chance than an ice cube in hell,' which was about how mad he was when he turned and walked away. That's the last I've heard about it until today. Is that what you wanted to hear, Major?"

"Yep."

"Well, Major, how much difference was there between Mr. Gail's version and mine?"

"They were almost word for word at the important parts."

"So what happens now, Sir?"

"I told you nothing before you started and I meant it then just as I do now, nothing."

The major was pleased with himself. MacLaughlin wouldn't be thinking about that kid for a while.

Lift after lift was made without incident and the Blackhawks had quickly settled into the boring routine of extracting troops from point A and putting them in at point B. The day had been long and everyone was tired. It also had been hot, very hot and humid. As a result, the engines weren't putting out as much power as they should have and the men alternated between sweating on the ground during pickups and being chilled when that sweat hit the cooler air at eighteen hundred feet. Thoughts of a cold beer, a warm shower and bed, even if it was an Army foldup cot, began to creep into everyone's mind. One more extraction and they could head home.

Everyone on board Jim's ship had been laughing about how this had been such a bad day, starting right off with that duck and going straight down hill from there. It was agreed by all, they'd feel a whole lot safer back at Tay Ninh on the ground for the night. After all, there were only two worse things that could have happened to them, to go down in the trees, or for someone to take a hit.

One of the unwritten rules on board a helicopter was never to suggest the possibility that one of the four crew members could be killed—wounded yes, but never never killed.

The flight was on short final when Lead came over the radio, "Flight, this is Lead, this is the last extraction for the day. The ARVN troops will be providing ground cover on this lift and then walking out. There are some things your crew chiefs and gunners should remember. First, if we start receiving fire it will probably be on the way in; unfortunately, you won't be able to return it because of the ARVN troops. However, I want you to keep your eyes on those troops. If you see one of 'em turn and open up on us, blow the bastard away. Just be damn sure it's us he's shooting at. Lead out."

Mr. Walker spoke as soon as Lead quit. "Okay, Wright, just for your information, it's on this kind of lift that we usually find a real hot LZ. ARVN will turn tail and run and Charlie knows it, so he won't hesitate a second about trying to put us on the ground with a few grunts. Just to make you feel better, it's usually Trail who gets it the worst. In other words, if you're sitting there looking at muzzle flashes, don't ask permission to return fire, just blow 'em away as Lead says. Any questions?"

"No, Sir."

They were only a few seconds from touchdown when the left tree line erupted like the Fourth of July, with sustained bursts of light. The American troops were on board even before the chopper touched down, and in less than two seconds they were up.

"Flight, this is Lead, open fire on that left tree line."

Instantly, every one of the Flights' ten door gunners opened fire. Jim, being on the right side of the chopper, could only sit and listen as the door gunners opened fire.

The radio cracked with background noise, as first one, and then a second ship reported taking hits. The first ship continued to fly and reported no apparent substantial damage. It was the second one that got everyone's attention; one of the grunts on board had taken a hit as they passed over the tree line.

Mr. Walker had been busy. He hadn't anymore than finished giving Wright instructions than they were in the LZ. The grunts started to jump on before he was on the ground, which he always hated. It's hard enough to land a Huey without four or five guys jumping on the skids rocking it. The temptation was always to just drop it straight down, but if he caught a foot or leg, it'd be crushed. All he could do was try to hold it steady and work it on down. They were all loading from the same side, which made it only slightly easier. Just as he'd gotten it down, Wright had said, "You're loaded, GO!"

He called Lead and said, "Trail to Lead, we're loaded, Sir."

As though lifted by puppet strings from an unseen hand, the flight lifted as one and moved forward.

Walker had heard the first two reports of ships hit and knew it would be a wonder if his didn't take damage, too. That was the worst thing about flying trail, you were the last in and the last out, and you caught the most lead. At times he could just about feel Charlie's frustration. As each ship escaped, the VC turned their attention to the one chopper they could have their guns on the longest, Trail.

Time always seemed to move so terribly slow for Walker as he raced his ship towards the safety of the sky. It just seemed at times like this he'd twist the throttle grip off, his hand would actually ache from the twisting grip he held on that throttle. He even found himself rocking back and forth in a futile effort to gain airspeed and a quicker escape. It was now their turn to cross the tree line where the others had taken fire. Their airspeed indicator read seventy-two knots, which meant Charlie wouldn't have much of a shot at them. Both door guns were raking the tree line with lead and all on board thought they'd made it by safely.

Wright was still firing and Jim had just quit when Major Hobbs' foot pedal bubble exploded, and Mr. Walker saw Hobbs jump like he'd been hit with an electric prod. It was Major Hobbs' voice that the other three crew members heard screaming in their earphones. "I'M HIT, MY GOD, I'M HIT!"

Jim's head jerked to the left in time to see Major Hobbs slump into a fainted position.

Walker yelled, "Mac!" and was interrupted by Jim's "I'm already on my way," and indeed he was.

The monkey belt had been unhooked and a grunt pushed out of the way. The grunts, unaware of what had happened, watched dumbfounded as Jim climbed into the cargo area and half motioned for the grunts behind Hobbs' seat to move as he shouted, "Move! Move!" Dropping to his knees, Jim grabbed both red handles at the bottom of Hobbs' seat. In one big yank, he broke the small safety wires and pulled the seat retaining handles down. With his right hand, Jim reached up to the handle on top of the seat and gently pulled the back down. The grunts, now aware of what was happening, started to help by removing Hobbs' helmet as Jim released the major's seatbelt. This done, they pulled him back into the cargo area. There was so little blood it took Jim a minute to locate the wound. Once located, his switch blade quickly cut away the left pant leg, exposing a nice neat .30 caliber sized hole. Jim went to work bandaging Major Hobbs' leg and almost cried with envy. The man had the perfect wound. It was small caliber and had entered and exited his calf muscle without doing any major damage. It hadn't hit the bone, and from the small amount of blood it was obvious there wasn't any damage to the major blood sources.

Jim had been aware of the grunts' activities over Hobbs. Now, however, for the first time he looked up. To his great surprise he saw a black PFC giving mouth to mouth and another man pounding on Hobbs' chest. Jim sat there stunned, the implication was obvious. The mean, super tough, 'I can eat nails for breakfast,' Major Hobbs had gone into shock and had heart failure, all from a wound that wouldn't even have gotten him out of the country. He'd have spent a week or ten days in a Saigon hospital, followed by another two or three weeks back in the company area on restricted duty. Instead, he lay on the Huey's aluminum floor whiter than show. The grunt giving mouth to mouth stopped long enough to feel Hobbs' neck for a pulse. He slowly shook his head and stopped his buddy still pushing on the major's chest. "He's gone," was shouted over the roar of the Huey.

Jim's response was rage, not only at the grunts because they were quitting, but even more so at Hobbs for dying. Jim's shouts could be heard by all the grunts as he jumped on Hobbs' chest. "Live, you stupid son of a bitch, live, damn you, live!" Grabbing the major's shirt, he shook and shouted at the same time. "Damn you, don't die on me, you son of a bitch, you're so fucking tough, wake up." The tears were gently rolling down the side of Jim's face when the first grunt pulled Jim back and slowly shook his head.

"He's dead, man, he's dead." Then pulling an olive drab handkerchief from his pocket, he handed it to Jim, who wiped his eyes and blew his nose.

They were almost on the hospital pad before Jim plugged in his helmet, which had come unhooked as he climbed forward to pull Hobbs out of his seat. Neither Wright nor Mr. Walker could believe what Jim told them.

The ride home was in silence and seemed to take forever.

14

Is This Really What We Fight For?

"We played the flute for you, and you did not dance; we sang a dirge and you did not mourn." MATTHEW 11:17 NIV

When Gillett found Jim, he was alone at a corner table writing a letter; there was a bottle of Jack Daniel's Black, a can of Coke and a coffee cup to keep him company. Gillett got a Coke from the bar before walking to Jim's table.

"Hi, Mac!"

"Hi, Gillett, have a seat. Help yourself to the bottle."

Gillett took a big gulp of Coke, poured a healthy amount into the can from Jim's bottle and slowly swished it. "I hear you had quite a day. It should make interesting reading for your folks."

"If I was writing about it, it probably would, but I'm writing about the weather and Hobbs making us police the flight line. I haven't gotten to it yet, but I'll add the duck flying through our windshield and that's about it."

"What do you think you're doing, protecting them?"

"You're damn right! At least my parents know I'm here and flying combat missions; that way if I get it they won't be too surprised, but they don't need to know any more. It wouldn't do any good for them to know more." There was a pause before Jim continued, "You know, Gillett, for the life of me I don't know how those guys who tell their folks they're in Alaska get away with it. I mean what in the world would you write about?"

"I don't know, but there are guys who do it and, of course, with only an APO number for an address, they get away with it."

"Yeah, and if they get their brains blown out, their parents go into as deep a state of shock as Hobbs did. I take it you've heard about Hobbs?"

"Yeah, I talked to Wright a little while ago. He also told me about the kid with the frag. Just between you and me, I'm not all that unhappy about Hobbs. I don't like to see anybody killed, but I'm real glad he's not going to be in the company anymore."

"Gillett, he'd have been all right!"

"I don't think so, Mac. He'd a had us playing all kinds of stupid games."

"Only until he made CO, then they would have stopped."

"Well, Mac, we'll never know whether you're right or not, and personally, I'm glad. Speaking of good news, I've got some that should cheer you up. They let the KP's back on post today. So I asked one of them who had done some things for me before if he wanted a monkey. That guy got a long stick, stuck an orange on it and got the monkey out of the rafters with it. Then when the monkey was on the floor eating its orange, the gook clubbed the hell out of it with his stick. Then he tied the monkey to the same stick. I never saw one stick get so many uses."

Both men laughed as Jim asked, "Where was Kenny during all this?"

"Remember, I put him on a convoy going to Saigon this morning."

Jim looked surprised. "Gillett, he was on the EM's side of the club when I came in a little while ago."

"Well, I know he was in the convoy when it left post this morning. I checked. Which reminds me, how'd you get your daily inspection done so fast?"

"I didn't do it, that's how."

Gillett looked disapprovingly at his friend and said, "You'd refuse to fly with anyone who pulled that kind of trick."

"Yeah, I know."

"Mac, you look beat, why don't you finish that letter and go to bed?"

Jim drained the cup as he watched a tall, over six foot, skinny bean pole Spec-Four rank approach.

"Sergeant Gillett?"

"That's me."

"Sergeant, Operations sent me to tell you they need a crew and a ship for a night mission."

Jim responded instantly. "I'll take it, Gillett."

"Just a minute, Mac. Okay, Specialist, tell 'em I'll get a crew and then report personally to Operations. By the way, did that convoy that left this morning come back?"

"Yeah, it got back about an hour, hour and a half ago. The NVA had knocked out one of the bridges between here and Dau Tieng that the engineers had just replaced yesterday, so they just turned around and came home. Will that be all, Sergeant?"

"Yes, thank you."

The walking bean pole hadn't gone out the door yet when Gillett turned to Jim. "Mac, I can get somebody else. Go to bed."

"Oh, I'm okay. Besides, I'd rather fly than sit around here bored to death getting hit with 122MM rockets."

Gillett looked Jim over good. He didn't have to let him go. He could send someone else and order Mac to bed. His eyes were puffy with dark circles and the left one was a little bloodshot. He needed a shave and his face was still splotchy with mosquito bite welts from walking in the jungle. Yet, the fatigue that had been so very obvious just moments ago had already begun to disappear with the prospect of flying.

"Okay, Mac, go ahead. I'll get Wright."

Jim had just locked his wall locker after putting his writing paper away when he heard Meyers let out a loud, long profanity.

"Hey, Meyers, what's wrong with you?"

"Oh, Mac, that damn mother of mine screwed me over good."

"What?"

"A couple of weeks ago I wrote home and told my Mom to

send me five hundred dollars from the money I've been sending home. I'm supposed to go on R&R next week if they get it opened up again. Anyway, I've been sending all my extra money home and having my Mom put it in a savings account for me. She knew it was my money and she knew what I was saving it for. Tonight I get a letter saying she's very sorry but she's emptied my savings and bought my sister a new car. The little bitch just turned sixteen a month ago. You know, Mac, it's at times like these I can understand why my dad used to beat the hell out of that stupid woman. I've wondered for a long time why he ever married her, but I'll tell you, I KNOW why he divorced her."

Jim looked down at the boyish-looking nineteen-year-old Spec-Four from Texas.

"Hey, Meyers, it'll work out; some of us can go together and loan you enough so you can still go. Plus, you might get another pay day in there first, which would help. Just one more thing, you may know why he beat her, but it still wasn't right. It's never right!"

"I know, Mac, and thanks for the offer of money, I really appreciate it."

When Jim got to his ship, Mr. Walker and Mr. O'Neal were already there. Greetings and small talk were exchanged as Jim untied the rotor blades and prepared for flight.

It was Green who walked up and threw his gear on the ship instead of Wright. He explained that Gillett couldn't find Wright, so he'd volunteered. Once in the air, Mr. Walker explained they were going to Saigon to pick up an entertainment group.

At Hotel Three, the group of entertainers loaded their gear quickly and climbed in.

Three women with bags, rabbit fur coats, spike heels and speakers sat awkwardly through the ride back to Tay Ninh. They looked as much out of place as they had to feel. It was the contrast that struck Jim. Only a few hours ago a dead major and infantrymen covered with sweat and mud had sat in the cargo area now occupied by these three women. The fur on the rabbit coats whipped back and forth and each woman tried unsuccessfully to hold her hair in place.

Steadily the craft flew northwestward, going over artillery fire where it could and around it where it couldn't. The women didn't see or know of the F-4 Phantom that shot by on their left, or the B-52 strike they flew around just south of Cu Chi, nor would they ever know of the small arms fire directed their way on short final approach into Tay Ninh. No return fire was given since no hits had been taken and to keep the women from knowing just how far away from the civilized world they really were.

Once on the ground, the three struggled to walk in their spikes. Besides, those rabbits, which probably felt good in the air, had to be terribly hot by now.

They were met by a jeep and a three-quarter-ton pickup. The girls were quickly loaded into the jeep, but not without exposing more than their legs. Once the jeep had departed, the enlisted men loaded the pickup and made numerous comments about the girls, not all of which were nice. Jim rode back to the company area in the pickup and then headed straight for the hooch.

He quickly stored his gear and went to the club. The partitions between the NCO side and the EM side had been removed to allow for greater viewing area. GI's were busy on the stage setting up mikes and other sound equipment; all the tables had been removed and chairs were stacked along the walls. Jim headed for the bar thinking a beer would taste good, but it had been closed until after the show.

It was another twenty minutes before the CO climbed on the stage and asked for everyone's attention. "Men, we're very lucky tonight that our company clerk was able to bring in this entertainment on such short notice. They were supposed to go down to Tan An tonight, but Tan An is under siege, so they're here instead. I just want you men to know I'm damn proud of you, you're the best assault helicopter company in the world. You deserve the best and, believe me, I know you won't be disappointed."

There was a big applause with cheers as the CO held up both hands to regain control. With a big smile the CO continued, "Besides, I explained that I have the only transportation off this island, so you damn well better not be disappointed. Without any further ado, I give you the Australian Pussy Cat and her Two Kittens."

With that the three girls stepped through the door behind the stage. They were jumping, shaking and singing.

By now the club was so jammed with GI's shouting and cheering, it was not possible to move. They were one solid mass of humanity standing and stomping on each others' toes watching the three women singing and wiggling. Their singing wasn't that great, but they did know how to wiggle and that's all most of the GI's really cared about.

The Pussy Cat was dressed in typical show girl attire. Bright blue spike heels and a very loosely flowing full length dress that was split up the left side to just above her knee. There was a long white feather shawl wrapped around her shoulders to partially hide the low cut front of her dress. As the shawl moved and was finally discarded during one of the songs, it left her exposed down to the nipples. She was dark-complected with dark hair and slightly overweight, with hardly enough makeup to hide the fifty some odd years she'd been around. The two backup girls, one light black and one blond, played guitars and wore matching outfits, bright red with high necklines but backless and a hemline about eight inches above their knees.

They told bad jokes, sang poorly and stripped. By the end of the show, the two kittens wore only their shoes and had swung their breasts around enough to have made a man sore, let alone two women. Yet it truly was the Pussy Cat who was the show's star. She, too, had stripped during the course of the show, leaving her with only a G-string and her shoes. It was, however, the muscle control she had in her chest that stole the show. Able to move one breast independently of the other, or together, she had the group of GI's not believing their eyes and shouting for more by the show's end.

Within a few minutes of the show's completion, all the officers and most of the enlisted men had left the club. Jim moved over to the NCO side and ordered a Coke and his bottle of Jack. Hunter, already seated at a table, waved for Jim to join him. It was only minutes later when Athia, with beer in hand, made it a threesome. There was a lot of joking, laughing and discussion of what they'd just seen.

Twenty minutes later Gillett walked up. "Mac, where the hell you been?"

Jim looked up with a bewildered look. "Right here. Why?"

"Because everybody's sitting on your ship waiting for you. You're supposed to take those girls back to Saigon."

"Gillett, you've been telling me I should quit flying all these night missions, so I think I'll just sit this one out. Besides, nobody told me I was supposed to fly 'em back. And I really wouldn't call them girls."

"You what? Get your ass out there!"

"Hey, Gillett, stay cool, man. I'm telling you, I'm not flying them back. Get somebody else or let 'em walk for all I care."

"What the hell is eating you, Mac? Didn't you like the show?"

"Sure, I enjoyed it at the time, but the more I think about it the less I think of it, and I'm not going to waste my time flying them back to Saigon."

Athia spoke up. "Hey, Gillett, I thought it was a great show, I'll fly 'em back."

Jim looked over at his friend. "Athia, you're a jerk, you know that?"

"Oh, Mac, get off your self righteous kick. You enjoyed what you saw as much as the next guy and, in fact, you were probably breathing heavier than most."

"Athia, you're so damn stupid, you can't even see that's the point! What good did it do any of us? Furthermore, the only reason those broads were here in the first place is they can't sing or dance well enough to get a legit job anyplace else. And the only reason they take off their clothes is they couldn't get anybody to pay them to do anything else. Besides, that Pussy Cat is so damn old, the only place she could get anybody to watch her take off her clothes is where there are a bunch of GI's shut off from the world."

Athia, who had risen to leave, turned back towards Jim. "MacLaughlin, you sure know how to ruin a perfectly good evening, you know that? But what do I care, I get to fly 'em back to Saigon. See you later, Sucker."

The alcohol was working on Jim by now and it heightened his anger. "Athia, you're an asshole. What do you think you're going to do, fly 'em home and have one of 'em suck you off on the way? You know that's never going to happen just like I do. In fact, I'll bet you fifty bucks you don't even get a peck on the cheek. They've got their thirty pieces of silver and to hell with you and me and how we feel, or our emotions."

Athia looked down at his friend and said half out of anger and half from a feeling of comradeship, "Fuck you, Mac."

Several days later, Athia and Jim were in the club having a drink. Athia brought it up by saying Jim had been right and he had known it even before he'd left the club that night. Jim laughed and bought the next round.

After Athia left the club, Gillett sat down with Jim. "Mac, you and I are the old soldiers in this outfit."

Jim interrupted. "Yeah, and I just turned twenty years old. Now, ain't that a gas?"

"You know what I mean. You've only got about two months left before your year's up and you go home. I'm the only one in the platoon who's been here longer than you, and that's only because I extended for six months so I could get out of this crummy Army early. The point is, you know I'm not going to pull rank on you unless you back me into a corner, so don't pull that kind of trick on me in front of somebody again. Most of these guys already know you and I are old and close friends. They also suspect I don't treat you quite the same, even though you and I both know better.

"Look, you've had too much to drink, you're tired, and you've had a stressful, trauma-filled day. Besides, you look like you're physically exhausted. Go to bed!"

"Okay, Gillett, just as soon as I finish my drink."

"You hear about Willard and Mr. Tracy?"

"No, what happened to them?"

"Well, you know we've been flushing some of the older engines the last couple of weeks, and Willard's ship had one that should have been replaced a hundred hours ago, but we can't get any new engines. You remember the proper flush procedures?"

"Sure, I've done it enough. Have somebody turn the engine over without starting it while you throw a quart of solvent in the intake. Let it set for half an hour then run it up and throw about five gallons of water through it."

"Right. Well you know how Mr. Tracy is such a know-it-all and us poor crew chiefs are all stupid as hell?"

"That's the one allright."

"Well, Mac, he really stepped on himself tonight. He was mad because he had to help Willard flush his ship, so when Willard told him how it's supposed to be done, Mr. Tracy told him just throw in the solvent while he was running it. Willard told him he was crazy, that he'd just end up ruining the engine. Well, Mr. Tracy gave Willard a direct order to throw the solvent in while it was running. You care to guess what happened?"

Jim was laughing as he answered. "Willard did it, and that would be about like throwing gasoline into a burning pot belly stove, so I'd say he probably blew it up?"

"You got it. The sucker threw about a fourth of its turbine blades out."

Both men were laughing hard enough that others began to look their direction.

"I'll tell you the best part, Mac. Captain Wolf told me just before the show started that the colonel is making Tracy pay for the engine. He has a nice little sum taken out of his paycheck every month, and he also loses his AC status. Don't you know that'll just kill our Mr. Know-It-All."

"You know, Gillett, we had a pilot like Mr. Tracy in the company I came over with, a Second Lieutenant Point. He was the maintenance officer until he got sent to another company. The man had no more idea of how a Huey works than a nurse does. He didn't even know the difference between an open-end and a box-end wrench. Anyway, he was always trying to tell us guys in maintenance how to do things and he was always wrong. So we'd just say "Yes, Sir," and as soon as he left we'd do it the right way. Well, one night he showed up to test-fly a ship we'd just put a new engine in, but he was drunk as a skunk. The guy in charge of our maintenance crew told him he was too drunk to fly and refused to get into the aircraft with him. As you well know, you don't do that. In fact, if anybody on a crew refused to fly on the test flight, you had to pull it back in and do it all over again. But for some reason, our crew leader was able to convince the lieutenant the only reason we wouldn't fly with him was because he was drunk.

Needless to say, Lieutenant Point was mad as hell. He started it up and began to taxi to the runway. He was doing just fine until he started to turn to take off and turned the tail boom into another ship parked, ready to come into maintenance that night. Talk about an instant change in a man's attitude. The good lieutenant hadn't anymore than crawled out of the aircraft than he was trying to buddy up to us. He kept talking about how he'd lost tail rotor control and how glad he'd been that none of us were on board. The man didn't have a chance. He'd totaled it, but it hadn't burned, so we checked out the tail rotor controls that same night. They were fine. The next morning, the CO called our whole crew in, one at a time, and asked what had happened. Everyone of us told him the lieutenant was drunk and unfit to drive, that was why we hadn't flown with him and why he'd crashed. So, to make a long story short, the CO pulled Point's AC status, put him into the flight platoon as a peter pilot and fined him enough so that he'll get about fifty dollars per month for the rest of his time in service. With that on his record, you know he'll never make captain."

Gillett watched Jim finish his drink and said, "Mac, go to bed."

"Okay, I'm on my way."

15

From the Depths of Terror to Euphoria

"They that sow in tears shall reap in joy." PSALMS 126:5 KJV

The sharp pain that struck Jim between the eyes drove itself deep into his brain. Pulling the covers over his head protected his eyes from the overhead lights that Gillett had turned on, but not from the platoon sergeant's mouth.

"Okay! Everybody up! It's another bright and beautiful day! Let's go. Let's go. Out of your rack!"

As Gillett moved on down the row of bunks still shouting and clapping his hands, Jim pulled the covers off his head. He had one terrible headache. For some reason life didn't seem so wonderful, even if it was a "bright and beautiful day." Not only was his headache getting worse, but the rest of his body's sensor controls were beginning to function and report to his slowly operating brain.

His mouth was full of cotton, his eyes wouldn't focus, his tongue was twice as large as it should be, his nose reported a foul, bitter smell and as he slowly stood, his back and shoulder muscles reported they were all still very sore and stiff from carrying Mr. Mace through the jungle.

Jim stood partly bent over with his head resting against his wall locker. One eye was only slightly open as he worked the combination lock, first one direction and then the other, until, with a metal thunk, it fell open. It was Gillett's hand that rested on Jim's left shoulder and Gillett's voice almost in a whisper, "Mac, you'd feel a lot better after a shower. The only problem is the officers' shower is the only one with water."

"What time is it, Gillett?"

"Four thirty-eight."

"I think I'll go take a shower. I feel terrible."

"Don't get caught or your butt will be sore from getting your ass kicked out."

Jim smiled as he headed out into the all consuming darkness.

The officers' showers were constructed basically the same as the enlisted men's. There weren't any lights and it had a gravity fed water system. It also wasn't quite as busy since there were about fifty less officers than enlisted men. Still, of the two hundred fifty men in the company, one hundred were pilots and officers, so it wasn't like the place was never used.

Jim knew the officers didn't like it one bit when an enlisted man used their showers or anything else that belonged to them. But as long as he didn't say anything, no one would be able to recognize him in the darkness. Still he was a bit uncomfortable as he entered since the water from one of the faucets was running. Jim acted like he belonged there and his attire (flip flops and towel wrapped around him) was the same as any officer coming in for a shower. He headed for the faucet farthest from the naked body being rinsed off. Jim had just turned on the water and stepped under its ice cold flow when he heard the all too familiar voice of Mr. Halsey.

"Good morning."

Jim's first thought was, Oh, shit! His second thought was, What do I do now?

Again Halsey spoke, this time a little louder, "Good morning!"

This time Jim stuck a hand out and waved hello.

"Hey, who is that down there?"

By now Jim had quickly soaped and was rinsing off. In a jolly voice Jim answered, "Good morning, Mr. Halsey!"

"MacLaughlin, what are you doing in here?"

"There isn't any water in our shower, Sir."

"Life can be a bitch can't it, Mac?"

"Yes, Sir, especially over here."

"Okay, you've had your shower, now get your smart ass out of here!"

Jim finished drying and wrapped the towel around his waist. "Mr. Halsey, you know, Sir, the two of us are standing here naked and I just can't see any bars tattooed on your shoulders."

"Are you disobeying me?"

"No, Sir, I'm leaving but I do want to know something." Leaning closer he almost whispered, "How old are you?"

"Twenty, why?"

"I was just thinking that if you have any desire to be twenty-one, grow up and start being an officer instead of a jerk. In case you're thinking about it, I'll deny ever being in this shower, let alone talking to you." With that he walked out.

Dawn was beginning to break over South Vietnam, and it was already hot and humid. Moisture dripped down Jim's back, wetting his clean shirt. With each step, miniature dust clouds puffed up, masking the polish on his boots, and the air already reeked with the stench from the burning of human waste.

As he climbed the two steps going into the mess hall, Jim stomped his feet and brushed off his clothes in a futile effort to separate himself from the world in which he lived.

Gillett and Athia were almost finished eating as he sat down. As always, Jim forced down the malaria pill with the heated black water. It was Athia who spoke first. "Mac, you look exhausted!"

Jim looked up from his plate of over easy eggs, smiled and said, "Athia, you looked in a mirror lately?"

All three men laughed. Gillett finished the last bite of toast and asked, "Mac, did you get caught in the shower?"

"No, nobody there but me."

"Good, I was sure with your luck Halsey would decide to take a shower at the same time!"

Gillett hadn't finished speaking when Kenny walked up and said in a very angry voice, "Gillett, you gave my monkey to the gooks! Didn't you?"

Gillett looked up, unsmiling at the still standing Kenny. "Yes, I did. I . . ."

Kenny curtly interrupted. "I don't give a shit what you

think, you son of a bitch, you had no right! It was my monkey. I fed him, took care of him. He was mine!"

Gillett and Jim glanced into each others eyes when Kenny made the reference to Gillett's mother; neither man could believe what they'd just heard. Gillett, trying to control his anger, fingered the staff sergeant insignia, looked up and said sharply, "Kenny, what's this?"

"So you're an E-6, big deal. You still had no right—"

Gillett, who had risen to his feet, leaned with both hands on the table in Kenny's direction. His voice now slightly raised, clearly showing the anger he felt as he interrupted Spec-Four Kenny. "Shut up, you stupid asshole, and come to attention! Just who the hell do you think you are anyway?" Kenny had halfway straightened up. "I said, come to attention! Now! Lock those heels!" Gillett then lowered his voice to a more normal tone. "I want to tell you something. First of all, I am your platoon sergeant and I don't have to justify a damn thing to you, Specialist. Secondly, you're dead weight around here. You don't fly because nobody will fly with you and, if I felt like it, your stupid big mouth would get you a trip to LBJ. Instead, you just got yourself a week's KP, so be good at it or I'll take a stripe just for the hell of it. Finally, I gave you a direct order to get rid of that monkey and you didn't do it. The Captain told you to get rid of it and you didn't do it. So you got any more smart ass questions?"

"No."

"No, WHAT!?"

"No, Sergeant!"

"Okay, you're dismissed, and do yourself a favor, Kenny, don't let me see your face for the rest of the day starting right now! You got it?"

"Yes, Sergeant." Kenny turned and left.

The season's first monsoon had started sweeping across the company area. Rain beat viciously against the mess hall's tin roof, making it impossible to talk without shouting. As a result, each man sat quietly looking out at the force of nature as it swept by. Someone turned on the lights and Jim realized how dark it had gotten, yet it was more than just dark, it was a deep, opaque blackness that worked its way into every crevice. Wind rocked the mess hall roof, walls and floor and Jim felt his smallness in the hands of God.

Suddenly, as though a mystical hand had turned off a valve, the rain stopped. The wind quit blowing and light once again showed itself on Blackhawk land.

Gillett stood and turned towards the guys behind him. In a louder voice than necessary, he said, "Okay, you guys. It's over. Let's go to work. And for you men who just went through your first monsoon rain, get used to it. The one that just went through was a baby. During the peak season, we'll have two or three a day and they'll all be bigger, meaner and longer than that one. Okay, let's go." Gillett gave two quick claps with his hands and watched as the place cleared out. Gillett turned back to look at the still seated MacLaughlin. "Mac, what are you waiting on?"

Jim looked up and smiled as he said, "The applause."

"I'll swear, Mac, you're hard! You know that?"

Jim gave a look of half-surprise and half-amusement that caused Gillett to chuckle. Jim stood, picked up his tray and with Gillett at his side, headed for the trash barrel.

"You know, Mac, this war will go down in history as the one that destroyed military discipline. I mean really, just look at the way enlisted men talk to their NCO's. In the Second World War, you'd have gotten an Article 15 for a smart ass remark like that. And Kenny, he'd have gone to jail for that little outbreak of his."

"Well, Gillett, look at the way we talk to our officers. I know I'm probably worse about it than a lot of guys. But almost anybody who's been here for a few months says whatever he damn well pleases to any of these warrant officers. For that matter, there aren't many of the hard bars who get a lot of respect."

"That's true, but then we don't have to put up with a lot of the bullshit from the officers that our fathers did."

"Hell, no! Gillett, there isn't an officer in country* today who doesn't have some of his actions controlled by the fear of being fragged."

* In Country—In Vietnam.

"Or having his knees shot off."

"True, but you know, Gillett, a lot of us EM are just as smart or smarter than some of our officers. I mean, we're high school grads and that's all most of them are. You have to wonder how some of 'em got through high school."

"There are some good ones though."

"No question about it. There are some who are very smart and are very good officers, plus being nice guys. The trouble is there are too many like Halsey who cause a loss of respect for all officers, not just the bad ones."

"It's called guilt by association. But you're right. If a man doesn't respect his officers, how can you expect him to show any respect for his NCO?"

When the two men walked out the mess hall door, they stopped at the bottom step and looked at the giant mud puddle that had been ankle deep dust when they went in. There was no way around it, so each man resigned himself to having wasted his time and effort putting Kiwi on his boots.

By the time Jim got to his ship, his boots were covered with the reddish brown mud that had replaced the dust. The first thing he noticed was the left cargo door was shut, which meant maintenance had been out during the night and fixed the track. He stowed his gear and checked the log book. Just as he'd suspected, his old friend J.B. had taken care of him once again.

J.B. and Jim had first met shortly after the 191st had arrived in country. Both were in maintenance and ended up living in the same hooch. Although they weren't in the same work crew, they did occasionally work together when two crews would work on one ship. As a result of working and living together, they had become friends. After all the recovery crew except Jim had been killed, he asked to join the same work crew as J.B. Then they both were infused up to Tay Ninh. At Tay Ninh, everyone dragged their duffel bags off the Chinook and fell into formation. The officers were called out by their new platoon leader first, then a staff sergeant stepped forward and called out his crew chiefs and door gunners. When he had all his people, he left with them and the next staff sergeant stepped forward and started reading off the names of his crew chiefs.

J.B. was the last to be called out as crew chief. There was

only one problem, J.B. wasn't a crew chief and didn't want to become one. His response was a surprised "But, Sergeant, I'm not a crew chief, I'm in maintenance."

"Well, Specialist, you're in the flight platoon now!" There was such a look of surprise and disbelief on J.B.'s face that the sergeant looked down at the orders he held in his left hand. After reading aloud J.B.'s full name, rank and serial number, he looked up and asked, "Is that you?"

"Yes, Sergeant, but I don't fly! You can ask any of these guys I was in maintenance with. I didn't even fly on test flights, which caused me a lot of problems until our maintenance officer realized I wasn't just trying to get away with something."

"Look, Specialist, I don't care what you did in the other company. These orders say you're in my flight platoon and that means you're a crew chief, so fall out with the rest of my group."

J.B. didn't move. "Sergeant, look, I promised my mother when I joined the Army I wouldn't fly anymore than absolutely necessary and I'm not going to break that promise!"

In a very sarcastic tone of voice, the sergeant replied, "Well, mommy's boy, I don't care what you promised your mommy. You're either going to fly or go to jail!"

After a short pause J.B. said, "Sergeant, I don't want to go to jail. But I'm not going to fly."

The two men stood looking each other in the eye when Jim spoke. "Sergeant, if I may, I think I can solve this problem."

"Good, how?"

"I'll fly in J.B.'s place."

The sergeant looked at Jim's name tag and then down at his papers. He found Jim's name and read it aloud, along with his rank and serial number. Then he asked, "Is that you?"

"Yes, Sergeant."

"Okay, you're the same rank with the same M.O.S.*, I can do that. It'll be less paperwork than sending your buddy to jail."

That was how Jim became a crew chief. J.B. never directly said thanks, but his signature or initials signed off a great deal

* M.O.S. —(Job title)—Military Occupational Specialty.

of work on Jim's ships. Plus J.B. got him parts other crew chiefs couldn't get. A good example was the fire extinguisher.

It had been about three months ago when Mr. Halsey had been flying as the peter pilot. He'd decided to give Jim's ship a super close pre-flight inspection. Not finding anything wrong that wasn't already written up in the log book, Halsey opened the peter pilot's door. The fire extinguisher in a Huey is held by a quick release clamp on the floor beside the right-hand pilot's seat. For some reason, about a third of the company's fire extinguishers were missing or empty. So when Halsey saw this one he removed it from the clamp and looking at Jim asked, "Does this thing have anything in it?"

"Yes, Sir."

"You checked it lately?"

"Yes, Sir." Jim turned and leaned inside the cargo area to remove the log book with the intention of showing Halsey the page where he'd recorded the date of inspection and weight of the extinguisher. He turned back just as Halsey pulled the pin. Jim, in a slightly raised voice said, "Hey, what are you doing?"

Halsey spoke and squeezed the handle at the same time. "Checking to see if it really works."

A spray of foam shot onto the ground as Jim shouted, "Don't!" With a look of exasperation, Jim said, "You stupid jerk! Thanks to you, now I don't have a fire extinguisher either!"

Lieutenant Buton had walked around the aircraft's nose just as Halsey pulled the pin. He looked at Jim. "Hold it right there, Mac. That man is an officer you're talking to." Lieutenant Buton was an ROTC man who had the respect of all the enlisted men.

"Well, Lieutenant, it's the truth. I HAD one of the few fire extinguishers in the company! Because I took care of it, even to the point I hid it in the ship at night. Then Mr. Halsey comes along and because he doesn't know what the hell he's doing, I now have to fly without a fire extinguisher and if this aircraft has a fire, it's my butt that burns up because of him!"

Halsey, realizing he'd made a mistake, tried to replace the pin as the extinguisher made a soft, almost silent hiss.

"Oh, come on, Mac. All I've got to do is replace the pin and it'll be okay. I didn't waste that much."

"Mr. Halsey, once you pull the pin you can't put it back without first fully recharging the extinguisher, and once you squeeze the handle it'll just keep on leaking until it's empty. And finally, Sir, so you don't decide to do a stupid trick like that again, you check an extinguisher by its weight. When fully charged its weight is at least as great as specified on the tag. By the way, Sir, you can check the log book to see when it was weighed last."

That exchange had taken place what seemed to Jim a long, long time ago. The pilots were beginning to arrive at their respective helicopters. Mr. Lucas and Mr. Euclid were laughing as they simultaneously threw their gear onto the aircraft's passengers seats.

Jim came to attention and saluted. "Good morning, Mr. Lucas, Mr. Euclid."

Each officer returned Jim's salute as Mr. Lucas said, "Morning, Mac! How are you this morning?"

"I'm fine, Sir. Where's Mr. Walker?"

"He's got a toothache this morning." Still laughing, Mr. Euclid added, "He's the butt of all the jokes this morning. The poor guy was hurting so badly he tried to get the dentist during the night. We tried to tell him, "Army dentists don't make house calls, and the club was closed so he couldn't get any liquid pain killer. Finally, somebody found some aspirin but I don't think it helped a whole lot."

"Well, Sir, at least he has a dentist here on post. Think of all the guys who wake up like that and then have to get a chopper to take 'em to a dentist."

"This thing ready to fly, Mac?"

"Yes, Sir!"

"Okay. Let's you and I preflight it."

It was sometime later the flight picked up troops to start another day of search and destroy missions. There hadn't been any activity out of Charlie as lift after lift was made. On the last lift before lunch, the flight was diverted to a new LZ and still there was no activity.

Once on the ground, the C-rations were quickly distributed

and the officers headed for Lead's ship. Jim ate and took the opportunity to get some badly needed sleep. When Wright awakened him, he was soaked from perspiration.

In later years he'd find it somewhat ironic that he often awoke "in country" saturated from the heat, having never had the first nightmare while there. Back in the States, he'd often awake in the comfort of his own bed saturated from perspiration simply due to his dreams.

"Mac, get up! Here come the pilots on a run."

"What's happened?"

"I don't know. I'll untie it."

Jim sat up and put on his chicken plate just as Mr. Lucas came running around the ship's nose. He was very excited, and with a burst of nervous energy, leaped into the cargo area and from there to his seat. As he moved quickly past Jim, he shouted, "Come on, Mac, move it! One of our gunships is down!"

Jim closed the door behind Mr. Euclid, who had entered through the pilot's door and taken his seat. Jim hadn't yet given the all-clear signal when Mr. Lucas started to crank the engine.

Putting his helmet on Jim asked, "Sir, what happened to the gun?"

"Shut up, Mac. I'm listening to Six now."

Jim climbed into the ship and turned on all his radios so he'd be sure to get Six's transmission, but it was over. It seemed to take forever to get troops onboard. Then they sat on the ground at idle speed for several more minutes before Six told Lead to bring 'em airborne. Once in the air and over the crash sight area, Six couldn't decide where to have the flight land.

The other gunship had made several passes over the downed ship and had seen no signs of life. There was a clearing within a hundred meters that was large enough for a single ship to land in. The gunship's AC had asked permission of Six to land and send his crew chief and gunner to check out the downed ship. Six had refused permission since he was the only gunship on station. Almost everyone in the flight disagreed with that decision but no one spoke. Still time slipped by and the flight continued to circle.

Jim had already once advised Mr. Lucas about the chopper on his right being too close; now they were slowly getting closer and closer. "Mr. Lucas, do you have this ship on the right?" Jim could see Lucas turn his head right, followed by the helicopter moving a few feet to the left. It wasn't more than a couple of minutes when Jim once again felt Mr. Lucas had drifted far enough right to be at an unsafe distance. "Mr. Lucas, could you take it left please, Sir?"

In a slightly irritated voice, Mr. Lucas responded, "I've got it, Mac! Okay?"

Jim didn't respond, but the aircraft didn't move left. He sat and wondered what to do and finally decided it would be better to try once more than to die in a crash, all because of some hotshot pilot who lost his cool. So, in a normal voice, Jim said, "Mr. Lucas, you're still flying too close, please take it left to a safe distance."

Mr. Lucas's voice reflected the nervous state he was in. "MacLaughlin, I've told you before and I'm not going to tell you again! I've got him, I see him and I'm getting sick and tired of your mouth! So just sit there and keep your mouth shut until we land! I don't want to hear about the chopper on my right again. I'm beginning to see why you have so much trouble with some of the pilots. You got it, MacLaughlin?"

Jim didn't hesitate. "Sir, you better get something straight! I'm the crew chief on this aircraft and as such I have several jobs besides the overall maintenance of the aircraft. One of those jobs, Sir, is to advise you when you're flying at an unsafe distance to another aircraft! And that, Sir, is exactly what I've been doing and what I'm going to keep on doing until you move it left far enough to be safe and keep it there! Furthermore, if you can't keep it at a safe distance then you should turn it over to Mr. Euclid, which you ought to do anyway because you've blown your cool and shouldn't be driving until you get your act back together! Finally, for you to give your crew chief an order to sit there with his mouth shut is in direct violation of Army General Aviation orders! Not to mention common sense, and it puts his life, your life and the lives of everyone on board this aircraft in danger. Believe me, Mr. Lucas, I don't like telling you to move left more than once anymore than you like hearing it. But you wouldn't look good with this guy on your right's rotor blade stuck in your windshield!"

There was no response from Mr. Lucas or anyone else, and Jim didn't have to tell him to move it left again. The troops were finally put in about a half mile from the crash sight. The flight then returned to Tay Ninh to sit and wait for the troops to find and secure the crash site.

Once on the ground, Jim sat in his seat for a few seconds looking empty-faced at the clay-colored soil. Here or there a weed or bunch of grass made a valiant effort to survive. And behind the row after row of black, L-shaped revetments stood the dirty brown buildings the Blackhawks called home. Slowly, as though resigning himself to the futility of trying to hide, Jim climbed out of his seat. He stepped up on the skid after opening Mr. Euclid's door and watched the gauges as Mr. Lucas shut it down.

Hearing Lucas's voice, Jim looked the pilot in the eyes as Lucas said, "Mr. Euclid, you can finish shutting her down."

Jim watched Mr. Lucas's eyes lead a path to the radio control switch where the pilot's right hand rested. The hand made only a small movement as it turned the control knob and Mr. Lucas's head and eyes moved in a manner to direct Jim to his own radio control switch. Nodding his head in recognition, Jim climbed up into the cargo area, turned his control switch to private and sat down on the passenger's seat. Expecting a first-class chewing out, Jim looked up and slightly to his left.

Mr. Lucas had turned in his seat to the right so he could face Jim when he spoke. "You there, Mac?"

Jim knew perfectly good and well Mr. Lucas knew he was there. He watched him turn his control switch to private, and he could hear Jim's breathing just as Jim could now hear the pilot's breathing due to the 'hot' or live mike situation between the two men. "Yes, Sir."

There was no expression on either man's face as their eyes locked. "Mac, I want you to know I'm sorry for climbing on your back there."

"Forget it."

"No, it's important for me to say. You were right, I lost my cool and I was using my rank to cover it up. You had every right to tell me to keep it at a safe distance. That's your job and that's all you were trying to do. I know that. I'm sorry I lost my cool and I'm sorry I got on you because of it. Thank you for valuing your life and mine enough to stand up to me."

His facial expression told Jim he was finished. "Forget it, Sir. It's over. It's done and who knows, maybe you'll be a better pilot and officer because of it." First there was a big smile, then Jim could see Mr. Lucas's face fight back the tears. "Mr. Lucas, forget it! It's okay, really. Hey look, anybody who's been in combat every day for several months has lost his cool at some point."

"Somehow I can't picture you ever losing yours."

Jim slowly nodded his head and said, "I did."

"How? Why?"

"When I first came over, I was stationed at Bear Cat. We got hit with a few mortars which I never thought were much more than big cherry bombs. After we were there a few weeks, they quit, and we had things pretty easy. Then I got sent up here. I hadn't been here a week when all hell broke loose one night. The CO said later that we had averaged one 122MM rocket hit in our company area every second. I don't remember how long this went on, but it was something like one or two hours. I was in the bunker beside my hooch and I was scared. I mean, I had never been so terrified in all my life. The grating sound those rockets make just before they hit, which you only hear if you're within thirty meters of ground zero, had me totally terrified. Then these sirens started blowing just as the rockets quit. Our platoon sergeant at the time was in the bunker with us and somebody said, 'Hey, Willie, what's that siren mean?' Just then, the rockets started to fall again but not quite as bad. The sergeant shouted, 'It means the post is being over run!' I had goose pimples all over my body. I could just see some gook throwing a frag into that bunker and all of us being killed. Just as I had that thought, I could see, because of a flashlight someone had on, this guy crawl into the bunker. He looked just like a gook to me. He even had on one of those round pointed hats they wear. He squatted down right by the door just like they squat. Mr. Lucas, the Lord Jesus Christ knows every man's heart, and believe me, He and I both knew if I'd had my M16, I'd have killed him. I even looked around trying to find one I could get hold of, and then move real slow so he wouldn't see me pointing it at him. Believe me, I give thanks to God every day that I'd left mine in the wall locker and I couldn't find another. I kept thinking why doesn't he just drop his frag and run? But then I figured he didn't want to get killed by his own rockets and as soon as they quit again, he'd drop it and move out the door. Finally, I got control of myself enough to poke Gillett, who was sitting beside me, and said, 'Hey, look at that guy by the door!' Gillett picked up the M16 he had on the other side of him and, pointing it at the guy, said, 'Hey you in the gook hat, you better speak English and identify yourself, or you're dead!' The guy raised his head and said, 'Who me?' Gillett said, 'Yeah, you! What's your name?' 'Zettler, and what are you pointing that thing at me for?' I knew at that moment I'd lost my cool totally and would have killed a man because of it. It was by the grace of God I didn't have a gun handy. I promised myself then I'd never ever lose my composure again, no matter how bad things got. And I haven't. I later learned the guy was one of the potheads in the other flight platoon who thought it was cool to wear one of those stupid hats. By the way, Mr. Lucas, you're the only person I've ever told this story. Zettler never knew how close he came to being killed that night because of that stupid hat and my fears.

"That's my story, Sir. Now you have yours."

Mr. Lucas smiled slightly. "Mac, you probably know you're quite the point of controversy in the officer's corner. But I want you to know I now understand why Walker and some of the others think you're the best. And I'd consider it an honor, if anything ever happens to Walker, if you'd ask for me as your AC. I really am a good pilot and officer, and after today, I'll never loose my cool again, no matter what."

Jim's face had a great big smile on it as he responded, "Thank you very much, Sir. That's very kind of you. I hope nothing ever happens to Mr. Walker, but if it does, I'll keep you in mind."

Mr. Lucas reached down and turned his switch back to internal.

The flight sat there for about an hour before one of the ships was sent to pick up the remains that had been secured by the grunts. The always present black rubber body bags had somehow not landed on Jim's ship, for which he was thankful. Several minutes after the chopper had left to pick up its cargo, Jim decided to listen in on the company frequency to hear whatever was said about the crash. It was several minutes more before Chalk Seven's pilot came on the radio. "Lead, this is Chalk Seven, do you copy? Over."

"This is Lead, go!"

"Lead, we have all four remains on board and are headed for Saigon. Be advised also my crew chief swears up and down that the mask was cut off by the rotorhead. I will have to agree the rotorhead is quite a ways from the crash site and both the mask and head have some strange marks on 'em."

Suddenly another voice broke in. "Chalk Seven, this is Six! Discontinue this conversation right now! Do you copy, Mr.?"

"This is Chalk Seven. Yes, I copy."

"Very good, Chalk Seven. Now I want to see you and your entire crew at my ship after we're discharged for the night! Understood?"

"Yes, Sir."

"Lead, this is Six, you're to crank the flight at once and go pick up those troops. We're not going far with them, just a few kilometers, and I'll mark your LZ once they're on board. Let me know when the flight's up! Six out."

"Roger, Six."

Jim could see the pilots moving quickly back to their ships as he stepped out. He untied the main rotor blade, put on his chicken plate and helmet. Mr. Lucas had started to crank the engine as Jim plugged in his helmet.

"Mac, you there?"

"Yes, Sir. What do you need, Mr. Lucas?"

"I don't get any engine oil pressure!"

Jim knew exactly where to look for the gauge. It was the second one down on the left just below fuel pressure. Mr. Lucas was right, the gauge that measured engine oil PSI read zero.

"Sir, shut it down, right now!"

Jim heard the reduced pitch in the engine and at the same time heard Mr. Lucas say, "You got it, what's the problem?"

"Probably just a bad sensing unit or gauge but I'm not flying in it 'til I find out."

"Okay, Mac, check it out. I'll call Lead."

Jim finished and walked around to Mr. Lucas, who was just climbing out of his seat, "Sir, I can't find anything, we'll have to call maintenance and have them do a more complete rundown."

Mr. Lucas put on a big smile and tapped Jim playfully on the chest with his finger. "I'm already ahead of you, Mac. I called Operations and they said there was a ship just out of maintenance that was being test-flown now. We're going to trade. I'll bet this is it now."

The dust being kicked up by the landing Huey caused both men to turn their backs and pull up their collars. Sand and dirt went into their ears, hair and down their backs. It was almost as though the maintenance officer who was driving got a sadistic joy out of dusting them off and held pitch in the rotor blades just a little longer than necessary. Finally, he rolled back the RPM and leveled out the rotor blades' pitch. Mr. Lucas ducked under the rotor blades and opened the pilot's door to talk to the maintenance officer.

Every time Jim saw someone walk under the still-turning rotor blades, he cringed and a rapid shiver went down his spine. He remembered well back at Bear Cat, standing and talking to another fellow as a Huey landed on the maintenance pad. The pilot had shut it down and climbed out. With the main rotor on its last cycle, the tall slender pilot removed his helmet and started to walk. He would have been okay if the helicopter had been running, as it wasn't possible for the blades to tip while at speed.

Once the helicopter had been shut off and the rotor blades slowed down to the last couple rotations, the weight of the blades and the slow speed allowed the pilot's controls to be pulled forward. This, in turn, allowed the rotor blades to dip down low enough to strike the pilot squarely in the head. His head exploded like a ripe, slightly rotten pumpkin, sending pieces of hair, bone, brain, skin, teeth, tongue and eyes flying to the left of the slowly falling torso. Jim still, all too clearly, remembered having to pick up every last bone chip, tooth, glob of brain or flesh and putting it in a bucket. When someone from the hospital arrived with the black rubber bag, they placed the torso inside and poured the bucket's grotesque contents into a pile where there should have been a head. They then zipped the black rubber bag shut and left.

As the maintenance officer signed off the log book clearing the helicopter for flight, everyone else moved guns and ammo to the other ship. Jim was pretty upset with himself for forgetting to take his tools, water jug and some of his personal gear. He still had his camera around his neck as he read the log book's last few entries. As he moved back into his seat, Mr. Lucas asked, "Log book okay, Mac?"

"Yes, Sir. It was in for an electrical short but I'm not sure from the way it was signed off that they're sure they found the problem. So it might be a good idea to keep a closer eye on the gauges than usual."

"Anything you say, Mac."

They had just cleared Tay Ninh Village and were about a thousand feet up when Mr. Euclid said, "Hey! We've got circuit breakers going off like popcorn!"

Then it was Mr. Lucas's voice that broke in with control, but still betraying his concern. "Mac! I've got a light on that says engine fire!"

Jim looked out and back at the engine compartment and knew the light was correct. Almost shouting, Jim commanded, "We're on fire, put it on the ground! QUICK!"

Mr. Lucas didn't hesitate. He jerked the controls into a maneuver he'd never practiced but had heard others talk about.

There was only one way to get a burning Huey on the ground from that altitude fast enough. It required laying the aircraft on its left side so it would fall like a rock, unobstructed by the rotor blades. The hard part was to pull it out before you crashed, but not too early.

Jim, still strapped in his seat, looked out his door and suddenly found himself looking straight up at a clear blue sky. Speaking to himself and his God he thought, *Oh, God, help us, we're going to die.* Able to see nothing but the sky as it went rushing by him almost as though he was falling backwards through a tunnel, Jim grabbed the metal support post on his left and waited for the impact. Suddenly he heard a terrible metallic scream. It was almost as though the helicopter was fighting the giving up of its soul as Mr. Lucas pulled it out of its dive and righted it to land.

It wasn't a perfect landing and as a result, the skids were about half-way flattened out. Nobody cared since they were all alive and on the ground, though still in a burning Huey.

Once Jim felt the sudden jerk of the ship being righted, his mind went to work deciding what to do first. By the time they hit the ground he had his M16 in his right hand and his left on the seatbelt buckle. Only a fraction of a second passed between impact and the time Jim had his seatbelt off. He was out of the now rapidly burning aircraft in less than a second and moved in one leap to Mr. Euclid's door. It was jammed shut from the hard impact. Jim could see Mr. Lucas climbing out the other side as he jerked on the still jammed copilot's door. Realizing it wasn't going to open, he grabbed the safety pin on the bottom and gave a big jerk. It came out, and in the same movement Jim threw it, he grabbed the top pin and pulled it out. Before he could get out of the way, Mr. Euclid kicked the door open and jumped out, landing beside Jim. The two helped pick each other up as they tried to run and stand erect at the same time but found themselves stumbling more than running. Finally at a safe distance, they turned to watch the flames leap from the aircraft.

It was Mr. Euclid who broke the silence. "Somebody in maintenance should have their ass kicked."

Jim didn't know why it struck him so funny but he stood there and laughed and laughed. Mr. Euclid started to laugh also, and the two had to hold their stomachs, they were laughing so hard. By the time Wright and Mr. Lucas arrived, they had just about gotten control of themselves.

Mr. Lucas spoke first with hands on hips and head slightly back. "I don't see what you two stupid fools find so damn funny!"

All that did was make the two laughers start all over and laugh that much harder. It was a good five minutes before they finally got enough control of themselves to quit causing each other to laugh by just looking at each other.

After regaining control, Jim sat for a few minutes more in the effort to catch his breath as he looked at his surroundings for the first time. They'd landed in a clearing that separated the jungle from the rice paddies. Another twenty meters one way and Mr. Lucas would have put it in the trees. Fifty meters the other way would have put them on the rice paddy dike where they all now sat. Looking behind him, he could see several villagers heading their way, walking on top of the dikes, past the almost ripe rice that ever so softly waved in the breeze like an endless golden flag.

Rising, Jim walked over to where Mr. Lucas was seated. Sitting down between Lucas and Wright, Jim said, "Sir, you're right. You're a damn good pilot. You did one hell of a good job!"

Looking over at Jim, Mr. Lucas smiled and responded, "I didn't lose my cool either, did I?"

"No, Sir, you didn't. You did a very good job. This is something you can tell your grandchildren about. After all, there will only be a handful of men who will ever do that maneuver and live to tell about it, and you're one of them. Congratulations!"

"Thank you, Mac. Just out of curiosity, how much time do you think we had to spare?"

"Not more than two or three seconds. It was already uncomfortably hot by the time Mr. Euclid got out."

Mr. Euclid looked their way and said, "By the way, thanks Mac, for sticking around and getting my door open."

"You're welcome."

"And I don't think we had three seconds. When my door wouldn't open the first time, I looked around back thinking I'd go between the seats and out the cargo door, but the floor was already on fire."

Wright spoke for the first time. "Do you suppose anyone besides the villagers know we're here?"

Mr. Euclid responded, "I hope so but I only got out one May Day before we hit the ground."

Mr. Lucas kiddingly interrupted. "What do you mean hit the ground? That was a precision, controlled landing!"

"Yeah, that's why the skids were flat and my door wouldn't

open. But don't misunderstand me, I agree with Mac. You did a wonderful job. I think I'll even put you in for a D.F.C.*"

The villagers who came scurrying across the rice paddy dikes were all old men or young children. As three of the old men shouted in Vietnamese and made gestures at the four Americans, the children looked over the charred remains in the background. Mr. Lucas tried without much success to converse using sign language, but the constant chatter from the farmers just kept on coming.

Standing and watching, Jim was impressed by the difference in the two groups. The Americans were all taller, more muscular, in uniforms with boots and each had a mouth full of normal healthy teeth. The locals all stood between five foot or five foot five, but were wiry looking men with an obvious strength beyond their sizes. They wore thin black shirts with four buttons, and pants that ended just above the ankle made from the same material. Each wore homemade sandals constructed from old rubber tires that were probably better for the feet than the jungle boots the GI's wore. Like most locals, their teeth were a mess. Some teeth were missing but the ones that were there made a person half sick to look at them. They were green and black stubs with only the smallest flakes of gray enamel still visible. Some teeth had half moon shapes missing from the sides, others looked like an upside down T, while others were simply points sticking out through the gums.

All the Americans were happy to first hear the whopp-whopp of approaching Huey blades, and then see the familiar silhouette headed their way. None were as happy as Mr. Lucas, who had thrown up his hands in frustration.

Once back in the company area, they learned that Operations had heard their May Day. Operations then contacted the courier ship that was due into Tay Ninh about that time and asked them to pick up the downed Blackhawks.

By the time the courier ship dropped off its passengers and they reported in at Operations, maintenance had also reported Jim's ship as fixed and flyable. Wright and Mr. Euclid went to supply to pick up two new M60 door guns while Jim and Mr.

* D.F.C.—Distinguished Flying Cross.

Lucas checked on his ship. It had been test-flown from the spot they'd left it back into its revetment, so it took them longer than it should have to find it. The first thing Jim did was check the log book. Mr. Lucas stood watching Jim's face as he read the signed-off form.

"Well, Mac, what did they find?"

"All that was wrong was a bad engine oil pressure gauge. They replaced the gauge, test-flew it and signed it off as okay."

"You mean to tell me the four of us almost burned to death because of a bad gauge?"

"That and some dumb ass in maintenance who let that other crate out before it was fixed."

It was several minutes before Mr. Euclid and Wright walked up, each carrying an M60. Jim, in the meantime, had checked his gear and was pleased to find everything he'd left on board still there. From the revetment, they hovered over to the ammo bunker and put on ammo. Jim also picked up two frags and hid them in the storage compartment.

They were told by Blackhawk Six to rejoin the flight at Duc Hoa, picking up ARVN troops for transport over to the Plain of Reeds. It would take almost an hour to get down to Duc Hoa, so Jim dropped the dark sun visor on his helmet and pulled his seatbelt up tight.

He'd just settled in for a nice nap during the long, boring flight, when Wright's voice came over the intercom. "Hey, can anybody see those fixed-wing jobs flying formation at about 10 o'clock and low?"

Mr. Lucas's was the next voice Mac heard. "Yeah, I've got 'em. Those are C-130's. Wouldn't that be something, flying at treetop level in a V formation with three C-130's?"

Wright asked, "What are they doing?"

"Spraying a defoliant," answered Mr. Lucas. "I can't remember what it's called."

Jim said, "Agent Orange."

"Yeah, that's right. I remember now, they got the name from the orange stripes of the drums the stuff comes in. The whole idea, of course, is to kill all the vegetation so Charlie won't have anyplace to hide. Of course, he'll see us coming better, but we're not supposed to worry about that."

Wright said, "If they put enough of that stuff on to kill all the vegetation, what's it do to people?"

Lucas spoke. "Nothing. The only things it hurts are plants."

Jim interrupted. "Not according to some of the Special Forces guys I've talked to."

Lucas said, "Mac, I've seen the poop sheet on the stuff. It's totally harmless to everything but plants. Besides, you know the Army, or for that matter the government, would never use a chemical that could harm people. All that stuff has been thoroughly tested for years before it's used."

"Yes, Sir, I know. But I also know I was on a single ship night mission about a month ago. We picked up a group of Green Berets and, while the pilots were being briefed on where we were going, I got a conversation started with a staff sergeant in the group. I'll tell you what, he was most unhappy about where they were going. He kept calling it Death Valley. I finally said, 'I don't know where that's at. I'd never heard of the place and I'd been almost everywhere in the Third Corps area.' So he said it was just a little ways outside Tay Ninh, that Death Valley was slang for almost anyplace that had been sprayed with Agent Orange. He couldn't understand why they were being sent in there. They never found any signs of Charlie. He was smart enough to stay out of there. The thing I found most interesting was when he told about finding dead birds and animals. He claimed there was nothing alive in Death Valley, not even insects. I remember him saying it was so quiet in there that at night it was really eerie. He claimed it was so dead, even the ant hills were dead. Not to mention the fact there wasn't any plant life—no trees, no bushes, no grass—nothing, and if he had his way he wouldn't ever go in it again."

Mr. Lucas said, "Mac, I can't believe you're so gullible you fell for that story. That man was pulling your leg. He saw someone he could tell a tale to and be stupid enough to believe it."

"If that's so, Sir, then everyone in his group was in on it because they all agreed with him. There is nothing alive in those sprayed areas and anyone that goes into 'em is stupid."

"Mac, look, I don't care what they said. You know the government wouldn't use something that strong. I mean, if it's going to kill animals, it'll kill us and they don't want us dead."

Jim said very sarcastically, "Whatever you say, Sir."

16

"But I Don't Want To!"

"These men lie in wait for their own blood." **PROVERBS 1:18 NIV**

Duc Hoa was just like every other Vietnamese village with its wood shacks, dirty ragged kids and dirt roads. The ARVN camp was undoubtedly the saddest part of all. Whole families lived in ten foot square cubicles, sectioned off inside one long wooden rectangular building with a plywood divider to separate their living quarters. The tin roof was coming loose in several places and was completely gone from one section. It was hard to imagine as many as three generations living in one cubicle.

The ARVN troops were all lined up and waiting. Their uniforms were almost identical to the Americans with the only real difference being the rank insignia. The NCO's stripes were upside down and the officers wore funny little things that Jim seldom could figure out. There was pride in those uniforms, though, as they were clean and most all had been tailored. It was their faces and mannerisms that struck Jim as being the most out of place. Whenever they picked up Americans for a lift they were always quiet, reserved, sometimes openly afraid of where they were going, yet never lacking the courage to climb on the helicopter, even if they were a bit hesitant. Yet here stood ARVN troops, slapping hands, obviously making jokes with their M16's. It was almost as though they couldn't wait to get into combat like green troops who still thought

345

combat would be a lot of fun; a great adventure, a chance to prove their manhood, a place to find fame and glory, and totally believing in their invincibility. Was it possible they didn't yet realize there would be no music, no stirring drum beat in the background, and no trumpet blowing, only the extreme loneliness of their own thoughts and fears?

Climbing on the choppers, they continued to laugh and make brave gestures with their M16's. Maybe they would be lucky and not have any contact with the enemy and could live another day in their illusion of grandeur.

The air blew cold over their charged bodies as it rushed in through the open cargo door. At two thousand feet it hit their sweat-soaked shirts, causing each man to move a little closer to his buddy.

The Plain of Reeds was appropriately named. It was a large flat lowland marsh type area. Grass and various reeds grew to heights taller than the helicopters that would be landing shortly on another dirt road.

From one dirt road to another they had flow. Unlike the first one, this dirt road had been built up several feet to help maintain a dry base and there were no friendly, happy and excited troops awaiting their arrival.

"Flight, this is Lead. Six advises there is pretty good reason to believe we'll be landing very close to a VC command center. Everybody stay sharp, there are no friendlies down there and all guns can open fire at will." With a sudden increase in tempo and pitch the same voice said, "I'm receiving fire from the right! My God, we're going to land right on top of it!"

Jim could already see the muzzle flashes and like everyone else opened fire. He'd only seen this type of fire a couple of times before. It came up at them directly from the ground itself, which meant only one thing, bunkers. They were right along the road and so well camouflaged one could have walked by and never seen that first one. Jim aimed his fire at the flashes directly across from where he would be landing shortly. Every fifth round the door gunners fired was a tracer, allowing Mr. Euclid to follow Jim's tracer rounds as they went in on the opposing machine guns. Each machine gunner knew what he had to do to live, and like the duelist of old, was putting all his skill into that one objective. Jim could now see the gun barrel as it continued to fire on his aircraft and moved ever so slowly to gain a better shot. For a full second more the two machine guns threw lead at each other with all the fury of the machines of death that each gun was. Then suddenly the still firing machine gun barrel protruding from the ground jerked straight upward and fell silent.

Mr. Euclid, with joy and excitement unrestrained in his voice said, "MacLaughlin, that was beautiful! You must have held your fire on him for a full four seconds! I kept wanting to shout, get him, Mac! Get him! I could see those tracers going right down his hole and wanted to shout, 'You got him, Mac! Get him! You got him just hold it on him!' But man I wasn't saying shit, except to myself! Because I didn't want to do anything to distract you! You were doing a fine job and we're one hell of a lot bigger target than he was and not more than fifteen feet away!"

Jim's gun stopped firing, the ARVN troops had started to jump off. As Mr. Euclid stopped speaking, Mr. Lucas pulled pitch and started to leave. As he finished the last few words of his sentence, Mr. Euclid turned to look at Jim. Much to his surprise, there in the center of the bench seat, with his back pressed tightly against the soundproofing, sat an ARVN soldier. Without ever breaking off his sentence Mr. Euclid said, "Hey, there's still an ARVN soldier on board!"

Mr. Lucas, who had only moved it about forty feet, immediately put it back down and said, "Mac, get him out of there!"

Jim unhooked his radio and seatbelt. Stepping around the seat he could see the fear in the ARVN's face. Jim felt no emotions, he was simply following orders, and not wanting to waste any more time in a hot LZ, he grabbed the fear-struck soldier by one arm and tried to rip his clamped fingers loose from the seat. With the second jerk the ARVN's right hand ripped loose, but not the left. The two allied soldiers shoved and pulled at each other for a full five seconds before Jim looked around in frustration at Mr. Lucas, who was looking back in his direction.

With one quick movement of his hand and facial expression,

Mr. Lucas made his meaning clear. "Get him off, and get him off now!"

Jim's movement was quick and without hesitation. The right fist came crashing in hard against the ARVN's left cheek, sending his head backwards and bouncing off the soundproofing behind. Jim grabbed the stunned soldier by the shirt and, in one motion, threw the crying ARVN soldier off the helicopter. As Mr. Lucas pulled pitch to leave, Jim threw the ARVN's M16 off.

Swinging around the bench seats to get back into his own seat, Jim could see the same ARVN soldier running after them down the road with M16 in hand. Suddenly the ARVN stopped in mid-stride. His head jerked backward as both arms flew outward, releasing the M16 into midair. His body leaped forwards and landed several feet ahead of his original position.

Jim sat down and hooked up his seatbelt. It took him longer than usual to reconnect the helmet's radio wires. "Mr. Lucas, I just killed that man."

"For crying out loud, Mac, you didn't hit him that hard!"

"No, Sir, but he got up and started to run. He took a machine gun burst square in the chest."

"Well, we can't go back and get him. We have to join the flight and take in more troops, so we can bring him out then. Besides, it's hard to believe we didn't take any hits back there as it was."

Mr. Euclid said, "You're telling me. I thought sure that bunker would get us but Mac quieted him and then we sat on the ground for a full fifteen seconds trying to get that stupid ARVN off."

Lucas interrupted. "They probably figured we were shot down, unable to fly. So why waste time and ammo on a dead bird, you can always cut his head off later. Besides, Mac, you did what you had to do. If that stupid gook won't fight for his own country, how can he expect us to?"

Jim lowered his head into both hands and wept. No one but the wind could hear him crying as it rushed by his face and melted his sobs into the roar of the engine and the scream of the transmission. Locked in the subconscious of his mind he would remember the ARVN soldier's eyes only in his dreams.

There were two more lifts made into the same area. On the last lift Jim's ship had an American TV man on board. The batteries and camera had to be a real pain to carry around. It was the antenna sticking up that Jim figured would make him no one's friend. Even the greenest of troops knew an antenna would draw fire like bees to honey. After all an antenna usually meant a radio, which meant an officer, and it was always important to remove an officer no matter what side you were on. After the drop Jim watched as long as he could and wasn't surprised to see the ARVN soldiers move quickly away from the cameraman. He tried to stay with them but nobody wanted him around.

After the last lift the flight was sent to Saigon to pick up as much food as they could transport back to Tay Ninh. From the unloading platform the ships refueled and then parked for the night.

Jim had to pull an intermediate fifty-hour inspection. It was already dark when he got started and, by the time he finished, it was almost ten-thirty. There wasn't any question about what he'd do first—shower. The water was cold but felt better than the grease and oil he was washing off.

Once back in the hooch Jim sat down on his foot locker to put a little Kiwi on his boots. He'd just started the first boot when the screen door flew open and in walked Gillett. The giant steps and hunchback stance indicated Gillett was all business.

Using his voice of command, Gillett barked out, "Schott! You got that letter written yet?"

"Yes, Sergeant, right here."

Rick Schott was your basic, good ole Southern boy, complete with Mississippi accent, wiry frame, about an inch shorter than Jim and an easy going, happy go lucky disposition. However, in an irritated manner, Rick walked up and slapped an envelope into Gillett's outstretched hand.

Gillett said simply, "Thank you."

They turning to Jim, "You just get in?"

"Yeah, I had an intermediate to pull."

"Find anything?"

"The only thing was a little metal on the internal transmission oil filter, but nothing I thought was unusual."

"Good. Come on, Mac, put something on besides your shorts and I'll share my bottle of Jack."

"Thanks anyway, Gillett, but I'm exhausted. I'm going to bed as soon as I brush off this polish."

"Okay, see you in the morning."

Jim finished his boots and walked down the aisle to Schott's bunk. Sitting down on the next bed's foot locker so he could look Rick in the face he asked, "Rick, what was that all about?"

Rick sat up on the side of his Army cot and answered, "Mac, this Army is so screwed up I can't believe it, but my sorry-ass mother is worse."

Jim half laughed as he asked, "What are you talking about?"

"My mother, God bless her, called the Red Cross, asked them to find out why her little boy Rickie hadn't sent her a letter for almost a month. So the Red Cross at home called the Red Cross in Saigon. They called the CO who asked the first sergeant to look into it. The first sergeant told Gillett he'd like to meet the asshole who was responsible for the CO having to spend ten minutes on the phone with the Red Cross in Saigon. I'm telling you, Mac, when the man got done with me, I had to check to see if I had any ass left or if he'd chewed it all off."

"So why haven't you written home?"

"I did! I try to get a letter out every week or ten days. Well, you know there hasn't been any mail leave here since Tet opened up until today. So, of course, there's a letter in there, but since it's gone, the first sergeant can't check to see that I'd put a letter in the mail drop the night Tet started. And I had a letter on board that plane that went down a couple of weeks ago. To say nothing about the fact we've been kind of busy lately. I mean, she must think I have nothing to do but write her letters. Anyway, my letter must be laying out there in the jungle rotting, courtesy of the U.S. Air Force. So you'll never guess what I get to do now, Mac. I get to sit down each and every night and write my dear sweet mother a letter. For two full weeks. It doesn't make any difference how late we land, how bad a day I've had, or if I even have anything to write about. Then I have to put it, unsealed, in Gillett's hand each night, who then has to put it on the First Jerk's desk the next morning, who will not read my letter, but check to make sure I wrote a full page worth, before sealing it and mailing it. So I wrote her a real nice letter telling her what she did, and how much trouble she got me into, and that she'll get her fourteen letters and not another single one for the rest of my nine months over here."

The two men just looked each other in the eye before Jim said, "Rick, don't punish your mother for loving you. When she gets your letter she'll realize she made a mistake and did a stupid thing, but she still loves you and that's why she did it. Besides, if you think about it, it's probably easier for us over here than it is for them at home. They know we're in an all-combat assault company and where we're stationed. They watch the six o'clock news every night and know we're right in the middle of the biggest battle of this war. My man, we're right smack in the middle of this thing and they know it. This is just like the Battle of the Bulge in WWII with better news coverage. As a result, those letters are the only thing that they can touch and hold and say 'Hey, at least I know he was still alive and okay when he wrote this letter, dated whenever.'

"Besides, what happened to you that was so terrible? You got a good chewing by Top, and right now you're a little embarrassed. Big deal! That doesn't give you the right to punish her like that, just because she loves her son, does it?"

Somewhat dejected Rick replied, "No." There was a pause before he continued, "Mac, how'd you get so damn smart so young and only a Spec-Five?"

"Hey, when I get home I'm going to college to get my book learning, because I've already had my education."

ABOUT THE AUTHOR

Jesse McLeod served three years in the U.S. Army and 365 days in Vietnam (May 1967–May 1968). He was a member of the 191st and 187th Assault Helicopter companies. He served as a helicopter mechanic, door gunner, and crew chief in Vietnam and returned to Fort Rucker, Alabama, to be an instructor in order to fulfill his military obligation. Military awards include the Aircraft Crewman Badge and the Air Medal with "V" device and 22 Oak Leaf Cluster. Jesse has spent his life in the Columbus/Westerville, Ohio, area. After returning from Vietnam he attended Ohio State University and received a B.S. in agriculture. His primary occupation over the years has been owner and operator of a dairy farm. He recently entered a seminary in Mount Vernon, Ohio, to become a full-time Protestant pastor. He and his wife, Joan, live in Westerville with their three children.

Special Offer
Buy a Dell Book
For only 50¢.

Now you can have Dell's Home Library Catalog filled with hundreds of titles. Plus, take advantage of our unique and exciting bonus book offer which gives you the opportunity to purchase a Dell book for *only 50¢.* Here's how!

Just order any five books from the catalog at the regular price. Then choose any other single book listed (up to $5.95 value) for just 50¢. Use the coupon below to send for Dell's Home Library Catalog today!

DELL HOME LIBRARY CATALOG
P.O. Box 1045, South Holland, IL. 60473

Ms./Mrs./Mr. _____

Address _____

City/State _____ Zip _____

S0-ABY-338

Irving Wallace's
THE MAN
The most exciting political novel of our time!

"It is a book that speaks the Washington language
we speak; whose characters breathe the official air
we breathe . . . that understands our government—its importance, its pettiness, its complexi-
ties, vagaries, shortcomings, and its greatness . . .
A MASTERPIECE OF THE STORYTELLING
ART."

—*Roll Call*, the newspaper of Capitol Hill

"The reading pleasure is immense. The theme is
powerful . . . *The Man* is cast upon a gigantic
canvas . . . Should be required reading for the
candidates of both parties."

—*Denver Post*

"Huge, turbulent, enthralling. It will grip [readers]
with its taut and hard-driving story, and in so
doing will lift the veil on Washington infighting."

—John Barkham, *Saturday Review Syndicate*

THE MAN

IRVING WALLACE

BANTAM BOOKS
TORONTO · NEW YORK · LONDON · SYDNEY

DEDICATED
TO
Sylvia, David, and Amy
WITH LOVE

*This low-priced Bantam Book
has been completely reset in a type face
designed for easy reading, and was printed
from new plates. It contains the complete
text of the original hard-cover edition.*
NOT ONE WORD HAS BEEN OMITTED.

THE MAN
*A Bantam Book / published by arrangement with
the author*

PRINTING HISTORY
Simon and Schuster edition published in 1964
Bantam edition / March 1974

2nd printing . November 1974	6th printing .. February 1977
3rd printing ..... April 1975	7th printing ...... June 1979
4th printing .. December 1975	8th printing .. February 1980
5th printing .. February 1977	9th printing ... October 1981

ISBN 0-553-20731-8

Published simultaneously in the United States and Canada

*Bantam Books are published by Bantam Books, Inc. Its trade-
mark, consisting of the words "Bantam Books" and the por-
trayal of a rooster, is Registered in U.S. Patent and Trademark
Office and in other countries. Marca Registrada. Bantam
Books, Inc., 666 Fifth Avenue, New York, New York 10103.*

PRINTED IN THE UNITED STATES OF AMERICA

18 17 16 15 14 13 12 11 10

One of the author's prized possessions is an original auto-graphed manuscript, written firmly with pen on cheap ruled paper, signed by a former Negro slave who became a great reformer, lecturer, writer, adviser to President Abraham Lincoln, United States Minister to Haiti, and candidate for Vice-President of the United States on the Equal Rights Party ticket in 1872. The manuscript reads as follows:

In a composite Nation like ours, made up of almost every variety of the human family, there should be, as before the Law, no rich, no poor, no high, no low, no black, no white, but one country, one citizenship, equal rights and a common destiny for all.

A Government that cannot or does not protect the humblest citizen in his right to life, Liberty and the pursuit of happiness, should be reformed or overthrown, without delay.

FREDERICK DOUGLASS

Washington D.C.   Oct. 20, 1883

I

STANDING THERE in the cold office, at this ungodly hour, no longer night, not yet day, she felt apprehensive and nervous. She wondered why, but instantly her memory had traced the source of worry, and she knew its answer was right.

From her earliest childhood on the modern farm outside Milwaukee, Edna Foster remembered, she had been raised—by erect parents of German origin—to believe in the virtues of constancy, steadiness, punctuality. Whenever she had given voice to a girlish dream of irregular adventure, her solemn and mustached father, an omnivorous reader of almanacs and books of useful quotations, would repeat verbatim the words of Someone (rarely named, Edna suspected, because her father hoped that the terse homily would seem his own). *"Gott im Himmel,"* her father would say to the ceiling, addressing his approving Lutheran God, "adventures, romantic adventures she wants." Then, glowering down at Edna, he would recite the wisdom of Someone: "Adventures are an indication of inefficiency. Good explorers don't have them."

Her father, she guessed long after, had the approval of his God because he had so carefully anticipated and thwarted the temptations of the Lutheran devil. Her father's devil seduced the weak and erring not with the banal sins of immorality and unrighteousness, but with the Twentieth Century sins of irregularity and confusion. As a consequence of this paternal foresight, Edna Foster's formative years had been boundaried by tan-

1

gible disciplines: the clock at the bedside, the budget in the bureau drawer, the schedule on the kitchen wall.

These rigid lessons had stood Edna in good stead during her attendance at the business college in Chicago, during her first secretarial jobs in Detroit and New York City, and especially when she had come to work for T.C.—yes, he had been T.C., "The Chief," even as a senator—in the Old Senate Office Building in Washington, D.C. In an uncharacteristically long and almost indecipherable letter, her father had hailed her prestigious government job as the inevitable triumph of her upbringing.

It was only after so much had happened to her employer, after T.C.'s nomination, and the exacting and exciting campaign, and the heady election night, it was after all that, when she followed T.C. into the White House with her shorthand pads and special Kleenex box, that Edna had come to realize that the parental standards she lived by were causing her difficulty. T.C. found her indispensable, she knew, because of her efficiency. What he did not know was that his secretary's efficiency depended upon her opportunity to be methodical. Yet the new job, from the start, seemed to have been equipped by the old Lutheran devil. No inkpot could drive that devil off. The office of the President's personal secretary was possessed of furnishings that mocked regularity: clocks had thirteen hours, calendars had thirty-two-day months, light switches had no "off" markings, or so it sometimes seemed to Edna.

As personal secretary to the President of the United States, Edna Foster possessed great pride in her position —she had recently learned to regard it as a position, not a job—and she had believed George Murdock, and giggled with delight, when he had told her over their second martinis in Duke Zeibert's bar, "Edna, if the President's wife is the nation's First Lady, then you are the nation's First Secretary." It was one of the things that she liked about George Murdock, his way of putting ordinary things so cleverly, which of course came from his newspaper reporter training. But then the job—no, position, position, as George kept reminding her—had its burdens, as she sometimes explained to George, and the worst burden of all, the most disconcerting for one of her background, she could never disclose to him, for then he might think her inflexible and dull, and therefore unattractive.

The worst burden, she could tell herself alone, was *emergency*.

It had been so on the farm in Wisconsin. The tread of the Western Union boy's footsteps as he came up the walk, the tinny faraway voice of the long-distance operator, had always meant emergency, and emergency was the enemy of order, peace, security. This enemy, and only this one, had always broken her father's composure, reduced his authority, and its threat had frightened her then and it frightened her still. And now, of all people on earth, it was Edna who had the one job—position— where emergency was an expected weekly visitor, although for her always an unexpected visitor, leaving her as damp and upset as she might be left by a skipped heartbeat.

Last night late, after midnight, there had come the telephone call from Governor Wayne Talley, the President's closest aide, and the word he had used was *emergency*.

"Hello, Edna, did I wake you up?"

"No—no, I was just reading." Then she had realized the hour. "Is there anything wrong?"

"Nothing special. The usual. Look, Edna, are you well enough to come in tomorrow? How's your cold?"

Automatically, she had coughed. "I suppose I'll live. Yes, of course I'll be in."

"I'd like you to make it early, real early. T.C.'s orders."

"You name it," she had said.

"Around six A.M. I know that's rough, but it's rough all over. The Russians are giving us a bad time. T.C. will be at the table early with Kasatkin. When they break, it should be about noon or so in Frankfurt, and that'll make it seven in the morning here, daylight time. It's going to be an open conference call from Germany. We're piping it into the Cabinet Room, so you get set up for seven or eight people. And you'd better hang around in case he has something personal to dictate. Okay?"

"I'll be there, Governor Talley."

"Sorry to do this to you, Edna, but it's an emergency."

There it was. Emergency. And here was she. Disconcerted.

The chauffeured limousine had been waiting before her Victorian-style apartment on Southeast E Street, just off New Jersey Avenue, when she had emerged at five forty-five. By ten minutes after six, she had crossed the empty Reading Room in the press quarters of the West Wing of the White House, and quickly gone to her cubicle between the Cabinet Room and the President's Oval Office.

After snapping on the overhead lights, and hanging her coat beside the bookcase, she had telephoned downstairs to ask someone in the Navy Mess to bring up some hot, hot coffee and a slice of toast. Now, shivering as she waited, resenting the early hour and the loss of two much-needed hours of sleep, resenting even more the nameless emergency that shattered her pattern of work and peace of mind, she began to sneeze. Hastily she sought the package of Kleenex in her leather purse, yanked one free in time to cough into it, and then wadded it to pat her painfully reddened nose.

Trying to ignore the ache between her protruding shoulder blades, determined to bring herself up to the day's beginning, she moved woodenly toward the small wall mirror next to the beige file cabinet, with its ugly security bar still locked in place down the center. With antagonism she stared into the mirror, blinking miserably at her bird's nest of brown hair, all stringy, at the faint crease in her forehead, at her swollen watery brown eyes and the slight bulges below (bags filled by overtime hours), at the shiny long straight nose, and then at the quivering dry lips.

She went back to her desk for her comb and compact. Seated before the gray electric typewriter, holding the compact's mirror above her, she toiled to achieve a semblance of efficient neatness. She had a plain face, she knew, but at its best, all well and rested, it was at least passable. George Murdock said that it was more, and she wanted to believe him, but when so many people had told you that your face had character, you knew for certain you did not have good looks. Certainly it was a face that could not afford tension or sleeplessness or the common cold.

She wondered whom or what to blame for this morning's wreckage. She could not blame George. Dutifully, it having been a week night and with her constant sniffling, he had brought her home early from their dinner. She could not blame herself for staying up until Talley's call after midnight, trying to read but really thinking of the miracle of her eight months with George and speculating about the months to come. After all, that was important, this thinking and daydreaming about George. It was the first time in her entire thirty years that she had had the chance to indulge herself so, that is, indulge herself seriously, that is, in secret hopes for the future.

For six years T.C. and the job for him had been enough to fill her mind. Now there was not only the President, but another, two in her life of equal importance—how it would please George to know his august standing!—and this was a pleasure worthy of her budgeted thinking time. Nor could she blame her ravaged morning face on T.C. for bringing her in here at six o'clock instead of eight. Banish that thought, she thought; veto it, it's unconstitutional. No, not T.C., he was guiltless, a dedicated, wonderful, great man, so far away, arguing and fighting with those Communist leaders about Berlin and about Africa and about the planets.

Then she realized where to put the blame, and since it was on one still so fresh in his grave, she was sorry and ashamed. She could date her teary, tired, streaky face back to the Vice-President's funeral ten days ago. It had rained, and they had stood there, the high and the mighty and herself, too, soaked to the bones, staring at Richard Porter's wet oak casket, listening to the minister's high-pitched supplication, *Unto Almighty God we commend the soul of our brother departed, and we commit his body to the earth; earth to earth, ashes to ashes, dust to dust.* Yet, she had felt certain, all the mourners had

not been listening attentively, for most seemed turned
inward with self-concern induced by the shock of the
suddenness of the Vice-President's massive coronary,
his first, his last, and the mourners seemed to be mentally
determining to drink less, smoke less, eat less, work less,
and have those medical checkups more often. Even the
President, the President himself, young, middle-aged and
strong as he was, a dray horse for work, a tireless robot
on the golf fairways, had gone to Walter Reed Hospital
two days after the funeral, the day before leaving for
Frankfurt am Main, for a thorough physical examination.

The unreality of the Episcopalian funeral lingered in
Edna's mind. She had felt apart from the ceremony at
the time, as she was this moment. The Vice-President's
death had not upset her deeply, nor, as far as she had
observed, had it emotionally moved any of the official
family either, except by its suddenness and its threat to
all mortality. The reason for this, she decided, was
Porter's relative unimportance. His passing left no gap,
rendered the nation no weaker. He had been a good bluff
man, in an affable salesman sort of way, full of clichés
and politics and gallons of bourbon and Throttlebottom
stances the cartoonists so enjoyed. He had been a professional politician and natural Vice-Presidential candidate brought into the campaign in order to lure the uncertain Far West with him. He had served his purpose,
and in death T.C. was his legacy. Because of Porter,
T.C. was Chief Executive by an overwhelming mandate
from the people instead of by a close plurality. Poor
Richard Porter had played his role, served the Party
and the electorate, and without him life would go on un-
altered. It was the seventeenth time in history the government would be without a Vice-President, and no
longer unusual. It was T.C. who mattered, to Edna and
to the country.

Closing her compact, Edna fully absolved the late
Vice-President of responsibility for her head cold and
wretched face, and now, her face repaired, her mind
clearer, she smelled the steaming coffee on the desk behind her. Somebody from the Navy Mess had noiselessly

come and gone, and because of her self-absorption, she did not know who it had been and whom to thank. She sipped the coffee, recoiled, blew on it to cool it, and finally, breaking the slice of toast, munching it, she was able to drink down the contents of the cup.

At last, feeling better, forgiving the day for its earliness, forgiving everyone for everything, she came to her feet. Her platinum wristwatch, a generous gift from the First Lady, showed the time to be twenty-six minutes after six o'clock. Right now, Edna guessed, T.C. and his staff were leaving the Kaisersaal, the splendid dining room of emperors of the Holy Roman Empire located in the Roemer, Frankfurt's five-gabled city hall. The European press, and recently the American papers, had gleefully taken to calling the meeting between the President of the United States and the Premier of Soviet Russia the Roemer Conference, reminding readers that Frankfurt's city hall had been the site, during the Middle Ages, where international merchants gathered to trade.

Well, Edna thought, T.C. has done his trading for the morning. Now, driving the several blocks to the Alte Mainzer Palace, his headquarters in Frankfurt, he is probably considering what problems of the trading he must discuss this afternoon (over there) or morning (over here) with select Cabinet members and Congressional leaders. Edna had seen photographs of the President's ornate Gothic ground-floor bedroom in the ancient Palace—the Bonn government had suggested the President use the ancient Palace for his living quarters instead of the United States Consulate across the Main River, because it was roomier, more picturesque, and nearer the Roemer—and not seeing this fourteenth-century Palace was what Edna regretted most about missing the trip.

Ordinarily, Edna traveled with the President. She had made four trips with him abroad—a wonderland for a farm girl from Wisconsin—but this was one of the two trips that she had missed, because of the darn head cold. Frankfurt was a city she had never seen, and even though Tim Flannery, the President's press secretary, assured her that she had missed nothing, that postwar Frankfurt was a dull, Swiss-type industrial metropolis featuring nothing more exciting than the I. G. Farben Building and the Hesse State Radio Building, both modern monstrosities, Edna knew differently. She knew that the Allied bombers that had leveled Frankfurt's medieval Old City in 1944 had, by some miracle, left almost intact the two dusty near-crumbling architectural wonders of the fourteenth century, the Frankfurt cathedral and the three-story Alte Mainzer Palace that housed the Presidential party. Edna knew that she traveled the way she tried to work, with efficiency, and she was not ashamed that she collected palaces, castles, and museums, with which to educate her children someday. The possibility of children, for one not even married and nearing spinsterhood, brought Edna back to reality, and once more brought her mind to George Murdock. She was sorry to lose the Alte Mainzer Palace for her collection, but there was compensation in not having to be apart from George the entire week.

She realized with a start that she had been standing at the desk, daydreaming away five more precious minutes, and 3,000 miles away in Frankfurt the President was nearing his telephone in the ancient Palace, and she had not yet made the few preparations necessary for his call to the Cabinet Room. Hastily she searched her desktop for the list of those who would be present for the conference call, found no such list, and then guessed that Wayne Talley would, from long habit, have left it on the President's own desk.

Hurrying now, Edna opened the nearest door on her left, and crossed the rug to the sturdy brown Buchanan desk at the far end of the President's corner office. The green blotter held nothing, and neither did the empty card stand, so much like a menu holder, into which T.C.'s daily engagement schedule was slipped. Concerned, she looked about, and then she saw it, the single sheet of paper that Talley had left for her, a corner of it pinned under the weight of the black telephone, the deceptively ordinary telephone that was the much-publicized hot line.

Taking the sheet, she scanned the list typed upon it:

Talley himself, of course; Secretary of State Arthur Eaton, of course; Senator Selander, Majority Leader in the Senate; Representative Wickland, Majority Leader in the House; Senator Dilman, President pro tempore of the Senate; General Fortney, Chairman of the Joint Chiefs of Staff; Mr. Stover, Assistant Secretary for African Affairs in the State Department; Mr. Leach, the stenotypist. Eight in all. That was it for this morning.

Studying the personnel on the list as she slowly left the President's desk, Edna played her deduction game. One did not have to be Scott of the CIA or Lombardi of the FBI to make an accurate prediction, once one was given a set of clues. Edna made her prediction to herself, enjoying the sport almost as much as she enjoyed the diversion of the crossword puzzles and Double-Crostic games that she hoarded for weekends. The emergency conference call from the President, she told herself, would be devoted almost entirely to Africa and the trouble over the new Republic of Baraza. The presence of the Assistant Secretary for African Affairs indicated this. Then there would be talk about pushing something through a balky Congress, probably the unpopular ratification of the renewal of the United States' membership in the African Unity Pact, as well as further economic aid to newly independent African nations. The presence of two senators and one representative and one general indicated this. The attendance of Talley and Secretary of State Eaton furnished no added clues. They were always present when T.C. spoke, always there, his confidants and alter egos.

Yes, Edna decided unhappily, Africa would be the subject, and that promised a dull and wearisome morning. African talk meant almost nothing to her. What was it, really? A black jumble of crazy names like Basutoland, Nyasaland, Malagasy, Gambia, Dahomey, Chad, Rwanda, and lately, Baraza. Even if you were intelligent, you could not tell one country from another, or one primitive face from another (despite those wild robes they wore, despite those odd Oxford or Harvard accents they assumed when they called upon the President). It was all impossible and, for Edna, Africa remained the

Dark Continent, affecting her day-to-day existence in no way whatsoever. And—repressed heresy—she suspected that those comic-opera countries meant little more to T.C. or Talley or Eaton, either. Soviet Russia, now, that was another matter. Russia could blow us up, and ruin everything, everyone, before some of us had a chance to get married and live and have children.

She had paused before the French doors leading out to the cement walk with its overhang and colonnades. Outside—T.C. called it his "backyard"—the darkness had gone, and the gray dawn was brightening. Even in late August, the Rose Garden was still in full bloom, the roses and Shasta daisies and geraniums dominated by early chrysanthemums. At the far end of the garden Andrew Jackson's hoary magnolia tree, partially obscuring the White House rotunda and Truman's Balcony, was thick with green foliage. For a moment Edna was tempted to step outside, join the White House policeman who had appeared on the walk, deeply inhale the cool fresh air, and fully revive herself for the Frankfurt call. But the platinum watch on her left wrist bound her to duty. Swiftly she left the President's office and returned to her own desk.

Yanking open drawers, digging supplies out of them, she was at last occupied with routine and too busy for daydreaming. In a few minutes, her thin arms heavily weighted under a pyramid of memorandum pads, boxes of pencils, shorthand notebook, and spare ashtrays, she went carefully to the door of the Cabinet Room. Balancing her load against the frame of the door, she grasped the knob, turned it, and pushed the door open with her knee.

She had somehow expected to find Arthur Eaton inside. He was usually first, seated and hunched over the long eight-sided, coffinlike mahogany table, his chalky, finely chiseled, aristocratic profile bent over sheaves of briefing notes. But he was not there. Instead, across the Cabinet Room, two khaki-clad enlisted men, plainly Signal Corps, were finishing the wiring of two gray metal boxes that rested on the dark table. Edna recognized the larger box, with its perforated side, as the receiver that would unscramble and the loudspeaker that would amplify the President's confidential conversation from Frankfurt, while the sensitive smaller audio box was the microphone which would pick up any voice in the room, scramble it in a special transmitter, and send it off to the Gothic study in the Alte Mainzer Palace, where it would be unscrambled and made comprehensible through a similar portable system set up for the listening President.

Apparently the two Signal Corps men were too occupied to be aware of Edna's arrival. She coughed, and called out, "Good morning, gentlemen."

The younger, a technician third class, glanced over his shoulder. "Oh, good morning, ma'm. We'll be outa here in a jiffy."

"Go right ahead. We still have fifteen minutes."

Edna lowered her precarious load to the table, then went to the three pairs of green drapes concealing the French doors and opened them, so that once more Jackson's magnolia tree was in her view and the room behind her filled with the filtered early morning light. After shaking loose the Presidential flag, which now hung well, and taking note of the American flag, which was fine, Edna resumed her familiar routine. She distributed memorandum pads, pencils, ashtrays. She filled the water carafes. She was hardly aware that the Signal Corps men were making tests, and then saying good-bye.

She was not yet through when the corridor door opened. Startled, Edna wheeled, expecting Eaton, but instead saw two of the Secret Service agents of the White House Detail, one the red-faced, beefy Beggs, the other the wiry, blond Sperry.

"Got you busy early this morning, hey?" Beggs called out.

"They sure have," said Edna.

"Just want to thank you for Ogden and Otis, Miss Foster," said Beggs. She knew that her face must have reflected blankness, for he quickly added, "They're my boys." Then he said, "First ones in their school with the new Baraza stamps. We're all grateful."

"I haven't had any more from Africa this week," said

Edna. "Most of the mail is from Frankfurt—from Germany—by diplomatic pouch, so no stamps. Of course, some other things drift in."

"Anything'll do, Miss Foster. Boys can use those for trading. Sure appreciate your thinking of us." Beggs's colleague, Sperry, had touched his arm, and he looked off, then turned back. "Here they come, Miss Foster. Be seeing you."

The moment that the Secret Service agents were gone, Leach came through the open door, nodding his skeletal head, carrying his perpetual harassment and his portable stenotype to the table, two chairs from the center where Eaton would sit.

Edna heard more footsteps on the tile corridor floor and waited. The three of them appeared in the doorway at the same time, and then Talley and Stover hung back, deferring to Eaton. The Secretary of State, tall, slender, magnificent in his pin-striped gray Saville Row suit, fedora in his hand, entered briskly.

"Hello, Miss Foster," he said in his deep, well-modulated voice. "Sorry about the hour, but T.C. appears to need our help."

Eaton's appearance, his evident good breeding, always struck Edna dumb, and as ever, she could do no more than duck her head and murmur her welcome. She watched Eaton as he deposited his hat on a bench and walked to the chair where Stover had already placed his alligator briefcase. She could see Eaton with the same eyes that the President, an old friend, saw him, and what she saw was an Easterner of excellent antecedents, schooled in the Ivy League traditions, a careful, moderate, thoughtful man, mellowed by the best of taste, and still youthful in late middle age. Where Eaton differed from T.C. was in the matter of human relationship. The President was gayer, warmer, more flamboyant, the politician's brass section accompanying the subtle chamber-music strings. The President would always be elected; Arthur Eaton would always be appointed.

She continued to observe Eaton as he removed clipped papers from his briefcase and sat down with them. He was the most attractive man currently in public office, she was positive. The press liked to say that he resembled Warren Harding, but Edna resented this, for Harding was not patrician and his historical image was weak. Edna had once seen a portrait of James K. Polk, and although she had heard that Polk had been slight and inconspicuous, she knew that this was the man in American history that Eaton most resembled. Like Polk, the Secretary of State possessed a smooth, sleek pompadour, graying above the forehead and at the temples. His eyes were full and deep, his nose slightly Grecian in its line, his jaw (like his entire face) bony and long. He was Virginia, Andover, Princeton, and perfect.

And now, Edna could see, he had lifted his head from his papers to listen to an exchange between T.C.'s right-hand adviser, Wayne Talley, and Eaton's own Assistant Secretary for African Affairs, Jed Stover.

The short, heavyset, electric Talley was poking a finger into Stover's shoulder for emphasis. "I don't care about your damn facts and figures, Jed. We've done enough for Baraza, more than enough, and you know that. Do you want us to go to war with those Communist apes over some little jungle country not much bigger than a football field? Do you want to fight over 30,000 square miles in West Africa?"

The taller Jed Stover, squirming at Talley's poking finger, patted his bristly eyebrows and scrub of mustache, and said calmly, "It is 33,000 square miles, and has a population of 2,437,000, Wayne. It has gold, a good deal of gold, and diamonds and iron ore. Besides—"

"There's not enough gold in the entire place to pay for what it might cost us in trouble."

Doggedly Stover continued. "Besides, it is our model, in a sense, our creation, our showcase, Wayne. You cannot give an emerging black nation democracy, and then turn your back on it."

"We have enough showcases over there. We have Liberia and Ghana and a half-dozen more. That African Unity Pact was fine when it was first set up. Paper work, good propaganda. We never intended to renew. Now, just because Baraza is in it, I see no reason to change our minds. You people in African Affairs get too involved in your own little world, and you can't see it as a small part of a bigger world with bigger problems. You're like so many whisker-combing scholars, each with one lifetime specialty, and you get to thinking that the truth about Nancy Hanks is more important than the Presidency, or that the significance of democracy in San Marino is more important than Italy. Don't look so damn hurt, Jed. I'm not disparaging all the spadework you fellows do, and how well you serve, but you're all inclined to suffer from funnel vision. I mean it. The President and I have discussed this many times. And I'm sure Arthur understands this even better than the two of us."

Talley had turned to seek Arthur Eaton's collaboration. Jed Stover, who had been about to reply, was immediately subdued by the reference to his superior. He seemed to bite his tongue and make an effort to hold silent.

Eaton, who had been listening, pursed his lips. He considered the President's aide. At last he spoke. "Jed and his department are doing an excellent job, Wayne."

"I admitted that," interrupted Talley. "I was only saying—"

"I heard what you were saying, Wayne," Eaton went on. "There is much to what you have been saying. You can be sure that T.C. and I are perfectly aware of what is going on and what must be done."

Witnessing the verbal scuffle, Edna Foster saw that this time it was Wayne Talley's turn to be cowed. Eaton had made it clear that he and T.C. would make the final decisions on African intervention. He had, in a refined way, reminded Talley that although he was the President's aide, he was not his first adviser, in no way his Gray Eminence, but only his sounding board and runner. He had put Talley in his place, which was not between the President and the Secretary of State, but somewhere behind them, outside them. But it had been carefully done, so that Talley would not lose face before a lesser State Department appointee.

Edna noted that Governor Talley reacted to the encounter, and subtle rebuff, as he always had in the past. His right eye, the one that was slightly crossed, involuntarily began to twitch. His bulbous nose reddened. He seemed less sure of the checkered suit and blue shirt and gaudy gold-coin tie clasp he was given to wearing. He appeared, Edna thought, like the officious manager of a Midwest haberdashery, who had just been reminded by the wealthy absentee owner that he had once been a humble clerk.

"Of course," Eaton was saying now, with a serious smile, "we are dealing with yesterday's facts, are we not? What I know, what you know, Wayne, and what you know, Jed, is useful, as of this minute, but in five minutes the President will be speaking to us from Frankfurt. After another morning with the Russians, he may have new facts, new ideas, and our recipe for a decision on Africa may be considerably changed. Don't you both agree?"

Edna found that she had to keep herself from smiling at the Secretary of State's adroitness. He had taken Talley and Stover in as his equals at last, and they were mollified. Talley, grunting and bobbing his head, circled the table to sit beside T.C.'s favorite. Stover, exhaling satisfaction, found a place opposite his superior.

Edna, realizing that Arthur Eaton was waving to someone behind her, turned, and to her surprise all the others were already in the Cabinet Room. Quickly she stepped forward to show Senator Selander and Representative Wickland to their chairs. Senator Dilman had not waited for her, but had gone off to take the place farthest from the Secretary of State and the President's aide. It was understood by all, Edna knew, just as she herself understood it, that Dilman did not rank with the others, not even with Selander and Wickland. Although Dilman, as President pro tempore of the Senate, had been wielding the gavel since the Vice-President's death, it was known that he held the position as a political gesture.

"Sorry to be the last!" Edna heard a voice boom out from the door. It was four-star General Pitt Fortney, the rigid, scarred Texan, pulling off his leather gloves. "SAC has been bending my ear from Omaha. It wasn't easy to get away." He handed his trench coat to Edna and strode to the table, pulling out a chair and sitting stiffly in it. He addressed Eaton. "Steiny had me on the phone last night. He thinks Premier Kasatkin means business. Even flew Marshal Borov in from Leningrad. Maybe the President ought to have me over there."

Eaton appeared to look down his nose at Fortney. "I think Secretary of Defense Steinbrenner can represent the Pentagon very well, General. I am sure T.C. feels you are needed here."

Noticing that her platinum wristwatch gave them two minutes to conference time, Edna Foster started around the Cabinet table toward Eaton and the portable loud-speaker.

Passing Representative Wickland, she saw him lean across the table and ask Talley, "What's this about Earl MacPherson flying to Frankfurt from Buenos Aires? He was supposed to be here in Washington today."

"Just a one-day detour," said Talley. "The President felt you boys in the House could spare your Speaker for one more day. T.C. wanted him on hand."

"On African economic aid legislation?"

"Probably. If T.C. tells you what's going on, you boys in the House might not listen. If your own Speaker tells you, then you might listen. MacPherson'll be back on the Hill tomorrow."

Edna had taken a position behind Eaton, and was about to inform him that it was precisely seven o'clock, when the telephone rang out shrilly. Instantly the room was hushed.

Edna bent between Eaton and Talley, punched down the "On" button atop the beige loudspeaker, then she hit the "On" button above the microphone box, turned the volume to "Medium High," and stepped away.

She reached her waiting chair and shorthand pad, be-side Leach, as a far-off erratic voice came indistinctly over the loudspeaker, and then suddenly broke out loudly and clearly.

"—calling from Frankfurt am Main, this is Signal Corps Captain Foss calling from Frankfurt am Main. Do we have the White House in Washington?"

Calmly Secretary of State Eaton addressed the micro-phone box. "This is the White House, Captain. This is the Secretary of State. We are assembled and ready for the conference call."

"All right, sir. The President is waiting to speak to you." A muffled crossing of voices slapped against the loudspeaker, and then a jagged arrow of static, and at once T.C.'s hurried, bouncy, unceremonious voice was upon them in the Cabinet Room.

"Arthur, are you there?"

"Everyone is here, Mr. President. How are you? Is everything going well?"

"Never better, never better. In fact, I just this moment talked MacPherson into betting all even on Dartmouth against Princeton next month. I want you to ask Internal Revenue if my winnings are tax-free, since we made the wager in Germany. Remember to do that, Arthur."

Everyone in the Cabinet Room laughed, hoping the laugh would be unscrambled in Frankfurt, and then settled into silence.

T.C. was coming through the loudspeaker again. "We broke up at the Roemer before noon. We're reconvening at two. Our gang stayed over there to eat, but a few of us slipped out on the press and the rest of them, and came over here to talk it out in privacy. I've been sitting in this beat-up old Palace study—it's cold as hell, Arthur—tell Edna she was smart not to come along—and I've been conferring with Ambassador Zwinn, and Secretary Steinbrenner, and our obliging Speaker of the House. One second, Arthur—" There was a long pause, and then T.C. was on once more. "Just said good-bye to the Ambassador—he's heading back to Bonn—and to Steiny—he's needed over at the Consulate. Okay, we can settle down now. There are a few problems to contend with, at once. I want to talk this over with you, and then I'll put MacPherson on, and he can concentrate on Harvey Wickland. Incidentally, Harv, I want to let MacPherson rest here tonight, and you'll have him back in the Speaker's chair tomorrow."

There was a pause, and then T.C. resumed through the loudspeaker. "Arthur—Wayne—all of you there, the problem is Premier Kasatkin. I'd forgotten what a tough bastard he can be. He seems determined to be difficult in

four-letter words, except in Russian they're forty-letter
words, and my backside is aching after these last hours.
I'm determined to get out of here in a few days, but
I want to get out with the knowledge that I haven't given
up New York, Detroit, Los Angeles, Bombay, and
Baraza City to the Muscovites for the right to stay in
Berlin."

Wayne Talley had leaned across Eaton. "T.C.," he
said into the microphone, "this is Wayne here. Is it that
bad? Does Kasatkin mean it?"

Over the loudspeaker T.C.'s retort was urgent. "Does
he mean it? I'm not sure. That is what we have to judge.
We have to decide how far we can go with blank car-
tridges. That is why I wanted to consult you before trying to digest my lunch. When I go back in there this
afternoon, and sit down across from our Soviet friends,
I want to know what ammunition I have or should have.
In other words, I've got to decide how far I can go in
showing Kasatkin and Marshal Borov that we intend to
stand firm on Baraza, support its independence, even
fight for it, at the same time making it clear that we
want to be reasonable and are concerned with more dangerous trouble spots and greater issues abroad. You understand?"

Listening, Presidential aide Wayne Talley displayed
his pleasure, and shot a triumphant grin at Assistant Secretary Jed Stover.

Arthur Eaton was speaking in the direction of the microphone box. "What are the latest Soviet charges against
us, Mr. President?"

"On Baraza?" said T.C. "A whole bill of particulars
to prove the United States is becoming an aggressor in
Africa, using Baraza merely as a beachhead for our eventual domination of all Africa. They argued that we
manipulated Baraza's independence in return for the
promise that they would be pro-democracy and anti-
Communist. Premier Kasatkin carried the ball the whole
morning. He tried to prove that we did not allow Baraza
to hold a fair and open election three months ago. He
accused us of rigging it, and said we got our puppet, Kwame Amboko, in as President. You know what

the Premier's evidence was? That one of our old exchange programs financed Amboko's coming to the United States fifteen years back, and this program financed his brainwashing at Harvard. Hear that, Arthur? Harvard is still giving us Princeton men trouble." He laughed through a rising wave of static, but it was not a mirthful laugh. He went on quickly. "Premier Kasatkin pointed to Baraza's new anti-Communist legislation, which is being debated in their Parliament. The Premier accused us of being behind it. He raved and ranted that we were bending Amboko's arm to get the Communist Party outlawed and the cultural exchange program with Moscow stopped."

"What evidence did the Premier present to support that charge?" Eaton asked.

"He had no concrete evidence," replied T.C. "I could have stayed home and reread your Embassy reports, or the translations from *Pravda,* and known just as much. Kasatkin argued that the economic aid we were giving Baraza came from our government funds, and not from private enterprise, and that we had threatened to cut it off unless Amboko banned the Communist Party and the cultural exchange with Moscow. He said we were afraid of Communism in Africa, because we knew that was what the blacks wanted and needed. He said, 'Those poor people know Communism gives them bread, while democracy gives them a vote and a Letter to the Editor.' He's a real smart aleck, in a sort of kulak way, and absolutely distrustful of everyone. He said not only was our money leading Amboko by the nose, but that we were also using our renewal of the African Unity Pact as a bribe. It all comes down to this—the Soviets are charging us with using Baraza as a launching pad to wipe native Communism out of Africa, so we can exploit the black population, control Baraza's gold and iron ore. That's the picture, my friends. It may look abstract, but it is realism, and we have to cope with it."

"You are perfectly right, Mr. President," Eaton was saying, "we have heard most of that before. The question is—what do the Russians specifically want of us?

After all, they instigated this Frankfurt conference to iron out differences. What are they suggesting?"

T.C. snorted, and the loudspeaker sent the sound splitting across the Cabinet Room like a handclap. "What are they suggesting? Good God, Arthur, they are demanding. Yes, they are demanding that we do one of two things—you see, they say they are being reasonable, ready for compromise—that we do one of two things, either kill the African Unity Pact—the AUP—kill it in the Senate, withdraw from it—or that we use our influence, show our good intentions in Africa, by getting Baraza to drop legislation against the native Communist Party and the cultural exchange program with Moscow. There it is."

"Why this sudden strenuous objection to AUP?" Eaton asked. "They showed only token disapproval when we first went into it."

"Because, according to Kasatkin, when we first went into it, the Soviets regarded it as a weak paper pact, limited to three countries and promising only small economic assistance. But they consider the new AUP as a threat. They point out it involves five African nations, and guarantees our military intervention to protect those countries from aggression. The Soviets argue we're setting up a Monroe Doctrine in Africa. They won't sit still for another NATO—a fledgling NATO they're labeling AUP—unless we allow their own ideology perfect freedom in Baraza. It must be one or the other, but not both."

Representative Wickland called out toward the microphone box, "Mr. President, what if we support both measures—banning of Communism in Baraza as well as membership in the new AUP? What do you think Kasatkin would do?"

"The works, Harv, the works," said the President. "Premier Kasatkin warned me Soviet troops would occupy West Berlin, and redouble support of their adherents in and around India and Brazil. I think he means it this time. And if he does, we're in for a shooting war, and we'd have to fire the first shot."

"But, Mr. President—" It was Assistant Secretary Jed

Stover's pained and trembling voice. "That's absolute blackmail. We're committed to AUP as well as giving Baraza the absolute right to do as it pleases, and apparently Baraza wants to curb Communism. I don't blame Amboko. He has a new and uncertain democratic coalition. His minority of Communists are militant and dangerous. If we give in on either point, drop out of AUP or force Amboko to leave the Communists alone, the Reds might infiltrate every free nation of Africa, and control the continent in a year."

The loudspeaker was quiet, and those waiting in the Cabinet Room were quiet, too, and at last T.C.'s reply came through the loudspeaker from distant Frankfurt. "Jed—all of you—I'm sure we understand our Soviet friends very well. We know what they want. We have to prevent them from getting it. The question is where do we stop them, and when do we see the whites of their eyes? In Baraza? I don't think so. I'd hate to risk American lives over some godforsaken little tract of land in West Africa. I don't want to have the distinction of having been the last President of the United States, the one who encouraged nuclear annihilation. I'm more worried about Germany, India, Brazil than I am about Africa."

"Mr. President." The voice had come from the far side of the coffinlike table, and it belonged to Senator Dilman, whose fingers were drumming the table nervously. "Mr. President," he repeated, "I'm sure you are—are right—yes—but if we back away from Africa, won't we —wouldn't we not only lose Africa for democracy—but show the Russians we are weak? I'm not disagreeing, only I am wondering—"

"Who was that?" inquired T.C. "I don't recognize the voice."

"That was Senator Dilman, Mr. President," said Arthur Eaton.

"Oh, Dilman," said T.C. "Fine, Dilman. Well, I wouldn't worry too much about losing Africa to anyone. Those people know we're with them. They see our money. They see we're really making an effort to solve the civil rights problem in the United States. As to showing any weakness to the Soviets, I'm not concerned about that either. They've counted our ICBMs, you can bet. They know we have muscles. No, I think we stand to gain more by showing a readiness to bargain, to give a little in order to get a little, than by being bullheaded. The question is how to proceed, how to concede with strength, how to conciliate the Russians, while reassuring the Africans we are behind them, and showing our electorate back home that we have emerged from Frankfurt with a victory, that we have preserved the peace of the world?"

Arthur Eaton edged forward in his chair. "Mr. President, what is your impression of Premier Kasatkin this time around? Do you feel that he is sincere? Do you feel that he will keep hands off in Berlin, Brazil, India, if you make a concession about Africa?"

"Oh, definitely, Arthur. No doubt about it. He's a roughneck, and crafty, peasant crafty, but he is blunt and honest. I think he wants to live and let live, if there is no other choice. Anyway, MacPherson and I have been kicking this around, and we have come up with a possible approach. We want your opinion on the strategy. Listen carefully—"

Listening carefully, Edna Foster, seated five chairs from the loudspeaker box, crossed her legs again, ready to hook her penciled ciphers across her shorthand pad, if required to do so. Beside her, Leach stopped tapping away on the stenotype set between his legs. Since all sound in the room had ceased, Edna glanced up. The intent faces of the President's advisers seemed to form human parentheses around the loudspeaker, as each individual prepared to concentrate on what would come next from the Chief Executive in Frankfurt.

Finally there was T.C.'s familiar voice once more, washed over by the atmospheric static above an ocean that divided him from those who heard him. The President's tone was low-keyed and insistent. "When I go back into that Roemer conference room with those bandits this afternoon, I want to tell them that the Senate is going to ratify the African Unity Pact this week. And that I intend to sign it when I return home. This ratification is necessary—I want to tell them that—because we have made a pledge to our African friends, and we want to keep our word. I want to assure Kasatkin, however, that we will never implement the Pact, act upon it, unless we are certain—absolutely positive—that a foreign power is attempting to interfere, militarily, with the sovereign rights of the Pact members. On the other hand, I want to be able to tell Premier Kasatkin, because we want peace, not only in Germany, India, Brazil, but everywhere, that we are ready to use our great moral influence in Baraza to convince its leader not to permit any discriminatory legislation against Communism to be passed into law. That should do it. I think that can wind it up, and I can come home and tell our people they can sleep safely in their beds for another year.

"However, I need your cooperation, need help from all of you there, and I've got to know what you can do for me, and how far I can go with the Russians today. John, I want you to bang ratification of the Pact through the Senate as fast as possible, no matter how long you have to keep in session. At the same time, Harvey, I want you to get that economic aid measure for those Pact countries out of the House committee and onto the floor. And I want it publicized, this support of our African friends. Then you, Arthur, you can call in Ambassador Wamba, and tell him we've got to get that anti-Communist legislation in Baraza quashed. Tell him to let his opposition natives have their little Communist Party. We'll keep an eye on it. Tell him to let his students go to the U.S.S.R. on a cultural exchange. Let him keep an eye on that. Tell him our joining the new African Unity Pact is evidence enough of our continuing support. If he balks, put on the pressure. I won't stand for any nonsense. I am determined to be the President who kept the peace of the world intact. Now, if you approve, what I want from you there in Washington is your promise that—that—wait, one second, MacPherson is calling out something—"

Abruptly the President's voice was gone, and through the perforated holes of the loudspeaker box came a faint tearing sound, like canvas being ripped, and then a tinny whine, and then the ear-splitting falsetto crackle of static, and then dead silence.

Arthur Eaton had reached forward, placing a hand on the microphone box as if to steady it, and quietly he spoke into the box. "Mr. President—hello, Mr. President, we cannot hear you, we have lost you. Try again, please try again." He remained immobilized, head cocked, listening for a response, but there was no sound. His hand shook the microphone box slightly. "T.C., this is Arthur here. Can you hear me?"

The loudspeaker stood mute. Eaton stared at it a moment, then looked about the room at the others. "I think we have been disconnected. We'll have to get him back."

General Pitt Fortney was already on his feet, hurrying to the ordinary green handset telephone at Edna Foster's elbow. "Let me get hold of the Signal Corps," he was saying. "This happens from time to time with the mechanical unscrambler. I'll have them track the trouble down. We'll be hooked up again in a few minutes."

While General Fortney called the Department of the Army, reporting the communications failure, barking his displeasure, demanding that the line to his Commander in Chief be restored, Edna Foster had the mental picture, a Brueghel in animation, of a thousand little enlisted men with repair tools scurrying up and down the ramps of the Pentagon Building.

General Fortney's stars and his ribbons and his raw Texas accent always frightened her, and she wanted to be as far away from him as possible. Since General Fortney was still on the telephone above her, Edna put down her pad, pushed back her chair and stood up. She found the silver silent butler, and began to move about the Cabinet table, emptying ashtrays into it. Here and there, around the table, the participants in the conference call had shifted positions on their chairs to discuss the President's report of what had happened so far at the Roemer Conference and what must be done about it.

Senator Dilman was removing the cellophane from a fresh Upmann cigar, as he listened to Senator Selander and Representative Wickland discuss the possibility of expediting ratification of the African Unity Pact. Selander expressed confidence that he would have sufficient votes to obtain passage of the Pact through the Senate. Still, to win the necessary votes, he felt that he would have to do some shrewd horse-trading in the cloakrooms and at luncheons in the Hotel Congressional. He hated, he was admitting, to make concessions on the important Minorities Rehabilitation Program being debated by the Labor and Public Welfare Committee, but it might be necessary. As soon as the connection was made again with Frankfurt, he would ask the President how much he could concede to the opposition floor leader in return for his full support of AUP.

Cleaning out the last of the ashtrays, Edna could hear Assistant Secretary Jed Stover and Governor Wayne Talley once more locked in disagreement. Stover was saying that any weakness that the American government displayed in Africa would immediately aggravate Negro protest groups in the United States. Talley would not accept this. He tried to reduce Stover to the role of uninformed outsider. Talley was retorting that both he and the President had already met with the Reverend Paul Spinger, and the clergyman had assured them that the vast and conservative Crispus Society, which he headed and which had outgrown the NAACP in membership and power, would be satisfied with the ratification of the African Unity Pact.

"Wayne, I'm not speaking of the Crispus Society or the NAACP," Jed Stover was saying. "I'm not sure they're the voice of protest any longer. Most Negroes are becoming impatient with their drawn-out legalistic efforts. Most Negroes want what they want here and now, and they are turning to more aggressive organizations like the Turnerites. Didn't you read Jeff Hurley's statement in last night's *Post*? He made it clear in that speech in Detroit that the Turnerites were not going to twiddle their thumbs while the Attorney General's office studied illegal voter registration in the South or while the Crispus Society made appeals to higher courts. Hurley said they were on the verge of undertaking a new policy of unremitting demonstration, and if molested for protest, they would retaliate, demanding an eye for an eye.

How do you think this group will react when they learn that the President is forcing Africans to rescind pending legislation in order to please the Soviets? This group and others like it take pride in Baraza's unique freedom, keep using Baraza as their model of equal rights, keep insisting that is all they want here at home. I think—"

"Oh, knock it off, Jed," Talley said impatiently. "Don't lecture me, and don't waste T.C.'s time with that unsubstantiated nonsense. Nobody's listening to the Turnerites or any crackpots like them. They mean nothing, nothing at all. Reverend Spinger admitted to the President that the Turnerites were a small splinter group who'd left his Crispus Society, that he wasn't bothering to denounce or oppose them because they were inconsequential, and that there were always some elements who had to let off steam. Jed, you've got to stop confusing issues. Baraza is one thing. Our own domestic Negro situation is another thing. If the President can keep Baraza happy, and at the same time contain the Russians, then he has achieved a diplomatic marvel. As to our civil rights problems here, when the Minorities Rehabilitation Program is passed into law, that'll put an end to Negro protest. Relax, Jed, just relax. Let T.C. perform as President. He'll manage for all of us."

"There's too much compromise," Jed Stover said feebly, but he seemed helpless, and said it more to himself than to anyone.

Edna Foster, after dumping the ashes from the silent butler into a wastebasket, had been watching and listening. She noticed that Arthur Eaton, slumped in his leather chair, fingers pressed together, eyes narrowed, had been watching and listening also, watching everyone, listening to everything.

Edna realized that General Fortney had completed his calls to the Pentagon, and was marching toward the center of the room opposite Eaton. "Well, finally got those chowderheads hopping," Fortney announced. "Everything checked out on this end. Nothing wrong on this end. Our communication is A-1. Signal Corps reports the disconnection took place on the other end. Line came down in Frankfurt. They're getting in touch with our Army Communication Center in Wiesbaden, and with our Consulate in Frankfurt. They expect repairs to be made on the double."

"Any idea how long it will take?" asked Eaton.

"Ten minutes, no more than ten minutes," said General Fortney. "So we've got a little recess before the President comes on again. . . . Hey, Miss Foster, how's about having some coffee brought up from the Navy Mess?"

Not ten minutes but nearly twenty minutes had passed, and still the direct communications line from the Alte Mainzer Palace in Frankfurt am Main to the Cabinet Room of the White House in Washington, D.C., had not been repaired.

Only General Pitt Fortney, who had asked Edna to order the coffee, had not had the time to finish more than half of his cup. Impatient with the delay, irritated by the unexplained inefficiency, he had been up and down, at the handset telephone and away from it and back to it, belaboring the Signal Corps for not yet making the President's private line operative. Minutes ago he had bellowed into the telephone at some Pentagon underling, "Dammit, Colonel, if you aren't fixing to get those wires up, I'm going to get SAC to fly me over in a B-70 and do the job myself. Now, get cracking!"

They were no longer gathered around the Cabinet table. General Fortney, like a caged and offended beast, was pacing near the telephone. Jed Stover stood beside the bookcase, beneath the mantel with its model ships, examining the titles of the various volumes. Near him, propped on the arm of a chair, Senator Dilman was lighting the stub of his cigar, and again reading a sheet of paper he held in his hand. Before the open door to Edna's office, Senator Selander and Representative Wickland were engaged in a conversation. Secretary of State Eaton, his back to the others, his hands clasped behind him, stood at the French doors contemplating the Rose Garden in the dull August morning. Governor Talley was making an inquiry of Leach, the stenotypist.

Thus it was that Edna Foster found them, as she returned to the Cabinet Room from her office where she had met with Tim Flannery, the press secretary, to inform him that the conference call, while still interrupted, would soon be resumed. Passing Selander and Wickland, she heard a snatch of their conversation.

Senator Selander was saying, "Don't you worry your head none about old Hoyt Watson. He's the most reliable member of the Senate. Southerner or not, he's still aware of our responsibilities abroad. He'll go with T.C. It's that damn troublemaker in your House I'm worried about. Can't you control Zeke Miller and that lousy newspaper chain of his? He hasn't let up a day on our participation in Africa."

Representative Wickland was at once defensive. "Leave him to me, I can handle him. He likes T.C. He's received plenty of patronage from T.C. If I tell him the President wants African aid, why, Zeke Miller won't obstruct him."

Senator Selander appeared unconvinced. "For someone who likes T.C., he's sure raising hell with T.C.'s Cabinet. Did you see what he let Reb Blaser publish in the *Citizen-American* about Eaton? Dirty politics, I tell you."

Edna Foster, who had hung back to hear the last, saw that both Majority Leaders were turning to inspect Eaton. Embarrassed at eavesdropping, she hurried to her purse lying on the table. Opening it to find a cigarette, she cast a surreptitious glance at Eaton, still at the French doors, still contemplating the Rose Garden. She wondered if he was thinking about Reb Blaser's column in the Washington *Citizen-American*. Leaving dinner the night before last, George had bought the newspaper, peering briefly at the baseball scores and Reb Blaser's story as they walked toward her apartment.

George had showed her the column. It had been devoted to the low moral tone of the Department of State, and then boldly revealed information "from an inside informant" that the Secretary of State and his attractive socialite wife, Kay Varney Eaton, were on the verge of a divorce. The gossip column had pointed out that of the

365 days past, Kay Varney Eaton and her husband had been together, in the capital city, only sixty-eight days. In fact, Reb Blaser had pointed out, she was now in Miami, being seen in night-clubs with Cartnell, the renowned decorator, while her equally renowned husband rattled around alone in their elegant Georgetown mansion. "We can only hope," Reb Blaser had concluded, "that our Secretary of State will be more successful in maintaining peace with the Soviet Union than with his wife of two-and-twenty years."

Edna remembered that she had considered Blaser's column disgraceful, and she had blamed his publisher, Congressman Zeke Miller, for allowing, even encouraging, such attacks. She had been surprised to find George defending both Blaser and Miller. He had, he had said, only admiration for their news sense and for their honesty. Edna had quickly forgiven George, understanding that as a member of the White House press corps, he would naturally defend and admire his own.

Now Edna realized that Arthur Eaton had come away from the window, and caught her staring at him. Flushing, she turned away, only to observe Senator Dilman going out the corridor door, probably to the washroom. She decided to talk to Jed Stover at the bookshelves.

Starting toward the Assistant Secretary for African Affairs, she became aware of a folded paper lying on the green carpet behind Stover. Quickly she went to it, picked it up, and opened it in order to find out to whom it belonged. The embossed letterhead, she saw, bore the name "Trafford University." In the left corner was the smaller lettering, "Office of the Chancellor—Dr. Chauncey L. McKaye." It was addressed to "Dear Senator Dilman." Not meaning to go further, but unable to escape the typed words in the single paragraph that followed, Edna realized that the head of the University, at the suggestion of the dean of men, was writing the Senator about his son, Julian Dilman, a sophomore, whose grades had seriously fallen off and who would have to be placed on probation if this continued. She noticed words like "inattentive" and "disrespectful," and the phrase "more interested in outside activities of late than in his schooling."

She folded the letter, embarrassed to have seen its private contents, but for the first time she thought of Dilman as a human being. Of those in the room, she knew Senator Dilman the least. This was because, since T.C. had been President, Dilman had been less frequently in the White House than the others. Only in the few days between the Vice-President's death and the President's departure for Frankfurt had Dilman appeared several times with the Majority Leader. But now this letter in Edna's hand: it gave him a son, a son who was a problem, and it made him a father, not just another senator but a human being.

Noticing that Dilman had reappeared, and was making his way toward Selander and Wickland, Edna hurried to intercept him.

"Senator, I found this on the floor," she said. "Apparently you dropped it. I'm sorry, I had to open it."

Senator Dilman accepted the letter with the slightest smile. "It's quite all right. Thank you."

Edna turned in time to see Wayne Talley approaching Eaton. "Arthur, it's past two in the afternoon in Frankfurt. T.C.'s probably gone back into the conference. Think there's any point in waiting around like this?"

Eaton shrugged. He addressed not only Talley but everyone. "I think we have no choice but to wait. The President just may feel this is important enough to delay the conference. He may want to speak to us further."

As if the deferment in resuming communications was a personal affront, General Fortney charged at the regular telephone once more. For the hundredth time, it seemed, he was calling the Signal Corps.

About to continue to her chair, and shorthand pad, Edna slowed down, listening hard. She thought that she had heard her own telephone ring in her office. She was listening, trying to make it out above Fortney's voice, when she heard Representative Wickland, the person nearest to her open door, call to her, "Miss Foster, your phone."

She darted past the Congressman into her office,

slipped between the electric typewriter stand and the table holding the television set, and caught up the receiver in mid-ring.

"Hello," she answered, "the President's office."

For a suspended moment she heard nothing more than the wavy, swooshing sound that indicates a long-distance call. Then a voice came on, a strange voice from far away, and it said, "Is this the White House? Who is this?"

"This is the President's personal secretary, Miss Foster. May I ask who is calling?"

"Oh, Miss Foster—Miss Foster—" And suddenly Edna felt goose pimples on her arms and a chill across her back, for the disembodied voice was quavering and frantic. "Miss Foster—this is Zwinn—Ambassador Zwinn in Frankfurt—Miss Foster—" The voice seemed to be choked, and then it shouted out, "There's been a terrible emergency—get me someone—Talley—get me Talley!"

With *emergency*, with *terrible emergency*, Edna found herself shivering, and the receiver in her right hand shaking.

"One second—one second, please—" She blinked at the open door to the Cabinet Room, and screamed out, "Governor Talley! Governor, come here, something terrible has happened!"

Talley burst through the door on the run, puzzled, curious, searching her face. She merely wagged her head, wordlessly, and shoved the receiver into his hands. As he took up the telephone, she backed away from the desk, and could see the room rapidly filling with the others, all looking from her to Talley, wonderingly.

"Who?" Talley was saying into the receiver. "Zwinn? Oh, Ambassador, I didn't know—" His speech halted as abruptly as if his throat had been cut. He listened, and listened, and as he did so, his lips began to move, but dumbness remained, and his face turned grayer and grayer until it was finally ghost-white. At last he spoke. "Are you sure? Are you positive? The President?" And then listening, lifting his head from the mouthpiece to stare at Eaton and the others. "Yes, Ambassador," he was saying again, "yes, I understand—I can't believe it

—yes, yes, I do believe you. I'll tell them. We'll get right back to you."

Talley lowered the receiver onto the cradle, and stood rooted to the spot, a portrait of stunned disbelief.

Eaton came slowly toward him. "What the devil is wrong, Wayne? What has happened?"

Talley tried to speak, tried to form the words, mouthing them, then stuttering them out. "The Pres—President —the President is dead!"

"What?" Eaton grabbed Talley's shoulder, roughly shaking him. "What in the hell are you saying? Who was that? What did he say?"

"Arthur, that was Ambassador Zwinn. Part of that building in Frankfurt collapsed—that goddam ancient Palace—the top caved in on two rooms, and one was T.C.'s study—where he was talking to us—that's what happened, that's what cut off the call, broke down everything—fell on him, all of them—killed him. The President's dead, Arthur, dead."

Eaton was ashen, but controlled. "Are you sure? Is it certain?"

"Dead," whimpered Talley. "Killed instantly. Blocks, slabs of granite, fell down on him, crushed him. They have the body. Two Secret Service agents in the room, too. Dead, all dead. Oh, God—God, what a terrible, terrible thing—"

That moment, the corridor door was flung open, and Tim Flannery rushed in, crying out, "Have you heard? Associated Press just got the bulletin from Frankfurt. The President—" He halted, eyes going from one dazed face to the other, and then he knew that they had heard.

Eaton's face was hidden in his palms, and then suddenly he looked up. "The President dead," he said. "That means the Speaker of the House—Wayne, what about the Speaker? Earl MacPherson was in there—what about him?"

Talley did not seem to comprehend.

Eaton spoke louder. "Dammit, man, is MacPherson alive or dead?"

"Alive," muttered Talley. "He—I don't know—I think he's in pretty good shape—nothing critical—

they've got him over at the hospital, they're working on him. This is the worst tragedy in our history. The worst. What's going to happen to all of us?"

Eaton closed his eyes. "Us?" he repeated. "The roof just fell in on us, too."

And when he opened his eyes, Edna Foster could tell, for the first time, that they were wet. It was hard to tell, because she was weeping, and she did not know if she would ever stop. . . .

Night had come to Washington, a city, like the nation, dumbed down in grief and mourning.

Night had come to the late President's Oval Office, where those who had worked with him and for him, who had known him and loved him, who had depended upon him and needed him, now filled the sofas and armchairs, forlorn and disconsolate, stood in corners, heavyhearted and helpless, waiting for they knew not what.

Edna Foster, eyes swollen, lips still quivering, came into the office with the latest special editions of the evening newspapers, and wobbled through the cheerless room, passing out copies. All who had been in the Cabinet Room ten hours before were present here, but now there were also many others. Edna recognized Attorney General Clay Kemmler, Secretary of the Treasury Vernon Moody, CIA Director Montgomery Scott, Senator Hoyt Watson, Admiral Alfred Rivard, and at least a half-dozen more of equal standing. It seemed that every nook and cranny in the Oval Room was filled, except one, and that one, the vacant place tonight, was the late President's high-backed, black leather armchair behind the Buchanan desk.

Having finished passing out the newspapers, Edna found that she was left with one copy. The group beside the French doors that led to the Rose Garden, the group consisting of Senator Selander, Representative Wickland, General Fortney, and Secretary of State Eaton, were reading the front page of the newspaper that Senator Selander held out for them. Or rather, Edna became aware, all were reading the front page except Eaton, whose attention was disengaged, whose attention was turned inward.

Edna lifted the newspaper in her hand and the mammoth headline, six inches high, assailed her: **T.C. DEAD IN FRANKFURT!** The second headline, almost as heavy, proclaimed: WORLD MOURNS ACCIDENTAL END OF U.S. PRESIDENT. The third headline, considerably smaller, read: HOUSE SPEAKER MACPHERSON, PRESIDENTIAL SUCCESSOR, UNDERGOES SURGERY IN GERMAN HOSPITAL.

She felt the sob grow in her lungs and throat, and suppressed it, and looked at the bottom half of the front page. The lead story, in boldface type, spilling across the width of four columns, began:

FRANKFURT AM MAIN, August 26 (AP)—The shattered body of the President of the United States lay in death tonight in a private room of the ancient Frankfurt cathedral while the entire civilized world grieved over his sudden demise.

The President was killed instantly—his smashed gold wristwatch having been stopped at 1:32 in the afternoon (8:32 A.M. EDT)—when a wing of the Alte Mainzer Palace collapsed and crashed down upon him. With difficulty, teams of West German police and firemen removed the corpse from the half ton of debris, mostly blocks of granite and crumbled brick, that showered down upon America's head of state and three others in the historic old library from which the President was making a long-distance call to his advisers in the White House. Ironically, the President died in the ruins and rubble of one of the two 14th-century buildings of Frankfurt's Old City spared by Allied bombers in World War II.

A German official, who did not wish to be named, stated angrily: "The Palace should have been condemned after the War. Not only was it 600 years old, but its structure had been weakened by the bombings, and never properly rebuilt and reinforced. This is a terrible tragedy, and America's loss of one of its most popular and international-minded Chief Executives in modern times is no less our loss, too."

At the time of the fatal

accident the President had served in office two years, seven months, and six days of his elected four-year term.

Among the first to offer condolences was Premier Nikolai Kasatkin, of the U.S.S.R., who had been meeting with the United States President this past week to work out important international differences. The official spokesman for the Soviet Union told the press: "The Roemer Conference may be considered suspended, not canceled. Some progress had been made. The points being discussed, however, still remain unresolved, and the talks must be resumed if the peace of the world is to be preserved. We anxiously await announcement of the late President's successor to the leadership of the United States. As soon as that is made known, we hope to set a date for resumption of the meetings."

Meanwhile, the eyes of the entire world were today focused on Frankfurt's Hauptwache Hospital, where the President's constitutional successor, Earl MacPherson, veteran Speaker of the House of Representatives, injured in the same accident, is undergoing spinal surgery. Three German surgeons, summoned from Munich, would make no prediction as to Speaker MacPherson's chances, but United States Ambassador to Germany Paul F. Zwinn advised assembled reporters that there was every reason for "optimism."

There was much more to the news story, and many more similar stories on the front page, but Edna Foster had no desire to read further. Casting the newspaper aside, she realized that Wayne Talley and Tim Flannery were whispering in the doorway to her office.

Now Talley was returning, heading for Arthur Eaton. "Stand by, Edna," he said. Then, reaching Eaton, he said, "They have an open line to Frankfurt. No word on MacPherson yet. He's been almost three hours in surgery. Tim spoke to Ambassador Zwinn briefly. The first phase of the operation was successful, but there's still a way to go. But everyone is feeling better. They expect to swear MacPherson in, the minute he comes out of the anesthetic. I think Tim and I better draft a press release.

There are more than a thousand accredited correspondents out there baying for news."

"Go ahead," said Eaton disinterestedly.

Talley hesitated. "I know how—how you still feel, Arthur. I know how close T.C. was to you. I can't get used to it myself. I'm numb. Who would have ever dreamt that such a thing—"

"Go draft that release," said Eaton curtly. Then he added, "Let me know the second you receive any flash on Mac."

"Okay."

Edna saw Talley signal her. "Edna," he said, "Tim and I need you. I know it's tough, but we have to dictate something about MacPherson succeeding T.C. as President."

Sorrowfully, Edna Foster nodded her assent, hating this moment of surrender, of bitter truth, when her employer would be supplanted by another. She followed the Presidential aide into her small office, shut the door behind her, and observed that Tim Flannery had already drawn up two folding chairs. Since he and Talley were sitting, she went around the desk to take her accustomed place in the walnut swivel chair. She located her shorthand pad and several sharp pencils.

Flannery waved toward the pencils. "Don't take anything yet, Edna. Wayne and I want to talk this out first." Flannery had already handed the aide a sheaf of papers, which Talley was studying intently.

"Everything here?" Talley inquired, still reading.

"Everything," said Flannery. "The boys on the Judiciary Committee pitched in, and also the justices gave us material, and for the background we had the Legislative Reference Service at the Library of Congress busy. You'll find the Presidential Succession Acts of 1792, 1886, and 1947 in full, with pertinent sections marked out. Then there's a lot of legal and background data, all severely condensed."

"Isn't it amazing how you go along and never think of anything like this," said Talley. "You'd think I'd know most of this, but I don't. I know eight Presidents died in office, before T.C., but I never knew this, that eight Vice-Presidents died in office, also."

"Nine Vice-Presidents, counting poor Porter ten days ago."

Talley looked up blankly. "Christ, I forgot all about him. Today seems to have blotted everything else out."

Half listening, Edna doodled on her pad. Then, as Talley read on, she began to print the names of the nine Presidents, including T.C., who had died in office. She printed: William Harrison, Zachary Taylor, Abraham Lincoln, James Garfield, Warren Harding, Franklin D. Roosevelt, John F. Kennedy, and then T.C. She counted. Eight. Who was the ninth? Then she remembered, and printed the name of William McKinley between Garfield and Harding. Next, she tried to think of the Vice-Presidents who had died in office. She could think of only Elbridge Gerry, Henry Wilson, Garret Hobart, and Porter, and not another. Finally she gave up. There was no use thinking about it. She felt ill.

She heard Talley's strained voice. "I somehow believed that almost every President who didn't finish his term was assassinated, but it says here that not more than four were shot down."

"Lincoln, Garfield, McKinley and Kennedy," said Flannery, fingers pressing his forehead. "Harrison and Harding died, in part, of pneumonia. Taylor's death was caused by cholera morbus. F.D.R. suffered a cerebral hemorrhage. Incredible, but poor T.C. was the only one ever to be snuffed out by an accident." He shrugged. "I suppose it had to happen to someone sometime." Then he added wretchedly, "Only why did it have to be T.C.?"

Edna had been watching Tim Flannery as he spoke, and there was a sweetness about him, behind his whole façade of forced factuality, that she liked very much. He was a tall Irishman, with unruly rust-colored hair, and a small reddish mustache, and a wide, ingenuous florid face, now puffy and blotched by sorrow. He looked as tweedy as his suits, with their suede elbow patches, and he had been a Midwest newspaperman who had written several highly respected history books on the side. It said much for him that most of the cynical White House press corps, and her own George among them, liked Tim Flannery.

"Chrisamighty, but I'm sure not in the mood for this," Governor Talley was saying. His one crossed eye contemplated the ceiling and then reluctantly came down to the papers in his hands. "Well, guess somebody's got to do it. Might as well get it over with. . . . Let me see, Tim, says here that Speaker Earl MacPherson will fill one year and five months of T.C.'s unexpired term. Is that correct?"

"Give or take a few days, yes," said Flannery, almost inaudibly. He seemed to make an effort to pull himself together. "All the past Vice-Presidents who succeeded Presidents had over three years of unexpired terms to fill, except Fillmore, who served two years and eight months of Taylor's term, and Coolidge, who picked up one year and seven months of Harding's unexpired term, and Lyndon Johnson, who served one year and three months of Kennedy's unexpired term. MacPherson will have a long enough way to go in the—in the Presidency."

"Yes, he will," said Talley with gravity. He touched the papers in his hand. "You say here this is the first time in our history we have ever lost both men elected to serve us for four years."

"Never happened before," said Tim Flannery. "But as Clinton Rossiter wrote in *The American Presidency,* 'This is no guarantee for the future.' How right he was." Flannery pointed to the sheaf of papers. "Did you notice that other quotation from Rossiter?"

"Which one?"

Flannery had bent forward and pointed to a paragraph on the top page. "Right there." He read it aloud. " 'If we are only poorly prepared for a double vacancy, we are not prepared at all for a multiple vacancy; and it is this kind of vacancy, so I am told by colleagues who deal in the laws of probability, that we are most likely to be faced with during the next hundred years and beyond.' "

Talley frowned. "I'm not interested in that. I'm interested in the facts, Tim, nothing else. We're faced with a double vacancy, not a multiple one. Let's check the Presidential Succession Act of 1947, just get it straight, before we dictate the release to Edna." He had begun turning the pages, and at last he found it. "Here it is. Okay, clear and simple. If the Presidency and Vice-Presidency are vacant, 'the Speaker of the House of Representatives shall, upon his resignation as Speaker and as Representative in Congress, act as President.'" His gaze moved down the page. "Yes, clear enough—President, Vice-President, Speaker of the House—and after that the order of succession is President pro tempore of the Senate, Secretary of State, Secretary of the Treasury, Secretary of Defense, Attorney General, and so forth through the Cabinet." He raised his head. "Any Speaker even come half this close to the Presidency before?"

"Not while Speaker, no," said Tim Flannery. "One former Speaker, Polk, was later elected President. But none ever—"

"Okay, there's always got to be a first time," said Talley. He handed the papers back to the press secretary. "So it's the Speaker of the House—grumpy old Earl MacPherson himself—who'd have believed it possible? Okay, that's the law, and no matter how we feel, we might as well start dictating some kind of press announcement."

Flannery snapped his fingers. "I forgot to get a capsule of MacPherson's background. Some of that should be in, too."

"Definitely," said Talley.

Flannery twisted in his chair toward Edna. "Can you be a good girl and fetch Representative Harvey Wickland in here? He can give us what we need for now on MacPherson."

Edna came out of her swivel chair, hastened to the door leading to the President's Oval Office, opened it, and then halted, surprised. Everyone in the crowded room was on his feet, all converging upon Arthur Eaton, who stood in the center of the room, in the middle of the eagle of the United States seal woven into the thick green Presidential rug.

Edna turned to Flannery and Talley. "Something's happening!" she exclaimed. "Everyone's gathering around Secretary Eaton."

Immediately, Talley and Flannery jumped to their feet, pushing past her into the room toward Eaton. Reluctantly Edna followed them to the center of the Oval Office.

Eaton, his voice dry and low, was speaking aloud. "I have just been called outside to take a telephone call from Frankfurt. I have terrible news to report to all of you, terrible news, and it grieves me. Speaker of the House Earl MacPherson died in surgery, on the table, under the knife, ten minutes ago. This has been confirmed. Now the Speaker is also dead."

A great gasp swelled through the room, and off somewhere there was someone hysterically sobbing, and after that there was a sickening silence.

Edna heard Tim Flannery, beside her, whisper, almost to himself, "Multiple vacancy."

The first to be heard speaking aloud was Governor Wayne Talley. "I don't believe it."

The second to be heard aloud was Arthur Eaton. "It is true."

Then it was that General Pitt Fortney called out, "Who in the hell is T.C.'s successor?"

Arthur Eaton held up his head. "According to the Presidential Succession Act of 1947, the next in line is the President pro tempore of the United States Senate."

For strange and suspenseful seconds, the Secretary of State's pronouncement hung in the air, and those who heard it were immobilized, allowing it to sink into their minds, as the curved walls with their niches and shelves of dead mementos seemed to close in on them.

"The President pro tempore of the Senate," the Attorney General intoned, as someone might intone Amen.

And then at once, all at once, collectively, each in the room seemed to realize who this was, who their next President of the United States was, and all at once all of them, collectively, turned their gaze upon the one man who stood somewhat apart from them, near the Buchanan desk.

Everyone, it seemed, was staring at Senator Douglass Dilman. And for Edna it was frightening to see that in each person's eyes, without exception, there was registered a look of horror.

Within thirty minutes the group, grown larger from the arrival of other members of the government, had assembled in the Cabinet Room. They stood now in a semicircle, with an opening in the center for two still photographers and two television cameramen representing the press pool, clustered around the long, dark mahogany table.

Once, while waiting, Eaton had asked Douglass Dilman if he had any close relatives or friends in the city whom he might wish to have witness the ceremony. He had replied, in an undertone, "No, sir, no one."

Once, minutes ago, Eaton had beckoned to Edna and Tim Flannery and demanded a Bible. There was much scurrying about, but no copy of the Bible was to be found, until Edna remembered the one in the lower drawer of her desk. She had gone to get it, and found the cheap, battered Bible, a Gideon Bible she had borrowed from a hotel room in Memphis once, on a trip with T.C., and had forgotten to return, and which she now retained for reference purposes. Guiltily, she had brought in the Gideon Bible and given it to Eaton.

She found herself still standing next to Eaton, who leaned against the high-backed leather chair bearing the tiny brass nameplate "Secretary of State."

She heard Eaton inquire of Senator Dilman, "Do you wish this open on any particular passage?"

She heard Dilman reply, "Psalms 127:1." Slowly, Eaton leafed through the book, and then he said, "Is this it? 'Except the Lord build the house, they labour in vain that build it: except the Lord keep the city, the watchman waketh but in vain.'" He glanced inquiringly at Dilman, and Dilman swallowed, his Adam's apple bobbing, and said, "Yes, sir, that is it."

It was during this moment that Noah F. Johnstone, Chief Justice of the Supreme Court, came through the corridor and across the room, gravely nodding at the familiar faces turned toward him. Even without his robes, Edna thought, even in his bow tie and dark suit, the Chief Justice appeared impressive. He was a giant of a man, with a slight stoop and an uneven gait. His sunken face, wrinkled and wise, betrayed no emotion.

He came around the Cabinet table into the glare of klieg lights, nodding to Talley, and then to Dilman and Eaton, and he took his position beside T.C.'s old chair. "Are we ready?" he inquired of no one in particular, and then he accepted the open Gideon Bible from Eaton, squinted down at it, and said to Dilman, "Take the Holy Book in your left hand and raise your right hand. I will recite the oath of office as it is written in Article II, Section I, of the Constitution of the United States. When I have finished, please repeat the oath."

He proffered the Bible to Dilman, who accepted it and held it with difficulty in his left hand, and raised his trembling right hand. Chief Justice Johnstone lifted his own right hand, and measuring each word, he rendered the oath of office.

When he was done, he waited.

After a painful interlude, Douglass Dilman's thick lips moved, and the words that he repeated came out low and slurred.

"I, Douglass Dilman, do solemnly swear that I will faithfully execute the office of President of the United States, and will, to the best of my ability, preserve, protect, and defend the Constitution of the United States."

He halted, and looked around the room, bewildered, as if seeking a friend in a company of strangers. The harsh kliegs, blended with the light of the overhead neon grill, made the witnesses to the historic tableau seem ghostly. He had lowered his right hand, and suddenly Chief Justice Johnstone reached out and grasped Dilman's right hand in his own and shook it.

"Mr. President," the Chief Justice was saying, "we deeply mourn the passing of our beloved President, but the continuity of our government, the welfare of our country, must stand above any one individual in these perilous times. Our hearts go out to you for your double burden—and may the Lord in Heaven bless you and watch over you as the new Chief Executive of this nation—and—as the first Negro to become President of the United States."

"Mr. President," the Chief Justice was saying, "we
deeply mourn the passing of our beloved President. For
the continuity of our government, the welfare of our
country, must stand above any one individual in these
perilous— Our hearts go out to you for your double
burden— I may be of aid in heaven bless you and
watch over you as the new Chief Justice— of this nation—and—as the first Negro to become President of
the United States.

II

IT WAS the muffled sound of argument that awakened
him.

There was a thin line of ache behind his forehead as
he listened, sorting and separating the muffled sound into
two sounds, the first shrill and feminine, cross and indignant, the second low and male, calm and placating.

His head was deep in the fat pillow, so deep that
when he turned, he could not see the time. The pillow
had been handmade by Aldora, almost double-sized and
stuffed with gray goose down, and presented to him on
their first anniversary, so long ago, when their marriage
still had hope.

The cross fire of altercation beyond his bedroom wall,
increasingly abrasive, continued louder. He lifted himself ever so slightly on his forearm and was able to make
out the time on the electric clock humming upon the end
table beside the bed. It was eight fifty-two, and although
the room was darkened by the drawn shades, he knew
that it was morning.

He realized that he had meant to be awakened earlier, had meant to set the alarm, but had forgotten to do
so before falling asleep. The shutoff lever on his telephone had banished all calls, and in his utter exhaustion
he had slumbered on and on. It was shameful, he thought
behind the headache, and, as always, to do anything
shameful alarmed him. Other men could afford mistakes,
small and large, but he could afford none, not the
smallest one. Several times, during his residence in
Washington, he had awakened with the remnant of the
same dream, that he had been treading water in an

enormous aquarium, and that all its sides were painted with blue eyes staring at him. The shimmering fragment of dream had always left him uneasy.

But now, the private hook of humor that he possessed but had not dared to reveal to anyone but Wanda and his closest friends extricated him from the fish bowl, and he was free to admit to himself that he had performed his first act as the President of the United States. He had overslept.

Suddenly the enormity of what had happened last night, and of what he was, oppressed him with its unreality and automatically forced him to retreat into the cup of the down pillow.

He had, he remembered, been told by someone last night that, after formally resigning from the Senate, he had become the President of the United States at ten thirty-seven in the evening. He had not been returned to his brownstone row house until after one o'clock in the morning. It was almost impossible to recollect what had taken place in the time between. He had signed something, yes, his first official signing; he had affixed his name to the proclamation that poor Speaker MacPherson was supposed to have signed, the same statement that had been hastily prepared for the Speaker and was to have been flown to Frankfurt. This proclamation was the official announcement of T.C.'s funeral and the period of national mourning.

He had listened to Secretary of State Arthur Eaton and Governor Wayne Talley expound on the critical Roemer Conference, and he had not absorbed a word of it. He had sat with them, smoking cigars until his eyes smarted and his throat felt blistered, and he had sat with the sympathetic press secretary, yes, Tim Flannery, the redhead, preparing the carefully worded release to all the news media. Then others had swum about them, senators and representatives whom he had known during work hours for years, and T.C.'s Cabinet members, whom he had hardly known at all, and they had spoken of approaches and strategies and public relations and the Party, and he had been grateful that they had addressed Eaton and Talley and Flannery and not himself.

He had been almost physically ill from the tension of the events of that day and evening, and after midnight there had been a stirring and rising, and he had been released, guided to a Cadillac limousine outside the South Portico. He remembered protesting against the two Secret Service agents who had entered the limousine with him, and protesting, with embarrassment, against both the motorcycle escort of police which had preceded him and the second car of agents which had followed him to his home.

He recalled the scene outside his brownstone, and how he had begged Hugo Gaynor, the Chief of Secret Service, who had followed him into his living room, to go home, and how Gaynor had been adamant about staying. And he remembered how he had surrendered from exhaustion, desiring only to escape to his bedroom and sleep alone, away from the blue eyes around the glass aquarium.

The sound of the argument beyond his bedroom wall was persisting. It had probably been going on steadily in the seconds of his introspection. And now, at last, he was able to place himself accurately in the time of day and the routine of his former life, and he knew what was happening in his living room. It was Crystal and a Secret Service agent who were locked in debate.

Crystal had come to him, through an employment agency, during his fourth term in the House of Representatives, and because he had been alone, and was still alone, she had grown fiercely maternal in her devotion to his comfort. Five days a week she appeared at eight-thirty to prepare his breakfast, make his bed, clean his flat, market for him. She worked until twelve-thirty, then disappeared to tend to her own household, which included her sister's family, and then returned at three-thirty, remaining to cook and serve his dinner, often not leaving until eight o'clock in the evening. She was a poor cook, a burner of toast, and a slipshod domestic, a sweeper under the rug, but she was prompt, loyal, busy, and relatively unobtrusive (that is, until recently, when she had taken to carrying on, always quoting her brother-in-law, a gas station attendant, about the Turnerite

Group, who were out to ruin the one chance that the colored folk would ever have for economic improvement through that rehabilitation subsidy act for Negroes that was being talked about).

At once, the reason for the altercation in the living room was clear to him. Crystal had arrived as usual, and found the Secret Service waiting, which was unusual. The irresistible force had collided with the immovable object.

Douglass Dilman threw aside his electric blanket and swung out of bed. He stood up, straightening his blue pajamas, stuck his feet into the misshapen slippers, picked up his polka-dot cotton robe off the chair and pulled it on. He walked to the bureau mirror and looked at himself. His black kinky hair, as always after sleep, was shoved high into a peak at the back of his head. He took the wide-toothed comb and ran it through his full hair, smoothing down the peak. He poked at the inner corners of his bloodshot eyes, to wipe and clear them. He studied his broad indelicate countenance. He was dark—well, black, but not coal-black—and his features were Negroid. His forehead was high, his nose full and wide, his lips heavy and protruding.

Now in his fifties, he was overweight, not yet fat, but stocky and thick. Tim Flannery, he remembered, had asked for the statistics last night, and he had said that he was five feet ten inches (cheating a half-inch for more stature) and 180 pounds. His appearance, a big-city ward heeler had once told him, worked for him. His lack of height, his tackiness, the antithesis of the fearsome young Negro buck, combined with mild, refined Caucasian speech and mannerisms, made him more acceptable to the white labor voters; his unmistakable Negro features made him authentic and agreeable to the black menial voters. Oftentimes in the past, he had wished that he could be all one or the other, like the members of his family. Pitiful dead Aldora had been light tan, often mistaken for a Spaniard, and he was sure this had contributed to what had happened. Wretched Julian, his son, was as dark as himself, black really, but possessed of features less coarse than his own. Pa-

thetic Mindy, his daughter, was (or had been when he
had last set eyes on her six years ago) white and beautiful, white and lovely, which had pleased her mother, had
worried him, had made Julian resentful, and had made
Mindy herself haughty and impossible.

He thought that he heard Crystal's sharp voice through
the wall. "Wake him up!" she was demanding.

He knotted the belt of his robe, crossed to the door,
went through the narrow hallway, and turned left into
the living room.

The sight that met him was not unexpected. Beneath
the arch that led from the entry hall into the living room
stood the shiny, bulging Crystal, shapeless in her tent of
brown coat, still holding the morning newspapers in one
hand and the inevitable huge straw basket (for leftovers
for her sister's hound) in her right hand. Blocking her
way stood lanky, elderly Hugo Gaynor, Chief of the
Secret Service, and the well-proportioned ex-California
athlete whom Dilman recognized as Lou Agajanian,
Chief of the White House Detail of the Secret Service.

It was Crystal who saw Dilman first.

She waved her fat hand and shrieked, "Senator! They
won't let me in——I gotta get up breakfast."

Gaynor spun around, and Agajanian did the same, and
both were instantly respectful and apologetic. "Mr. President," Gaynor said, "we have no idea who this lady is.
We can't let people without credentials in here simply because they say they work for you. Can you imagine
what——"

Dilman nodded. "She's quite safe, Mr. Gaynor. Crystal
has been my housekeeper for years. I should have advised you last night. . . . Hello, Mr. Agajanian, I think
we've met once or twice. . . . Good morning, Crystal.
It's all right now. You can come in."

Obediently the agents parted, backed off, and the
magic of it made Crystal's eyes widen. Her unsubtle
black face was almost comically transformed from indignation to triumph to pleasure to awe. She waddled toward Dilman, halted, eyes blinking. "I——I almost forgot
to say, Senator——President——Mr. President——but I want

to be the first to wish you well, and also for my sister and brother-in-law and the kids."

"Thank you, Crystal, thank you."

She began to go sideways, still awed, and then she stopped. "We stayed up late and it was all over the television. Everyone was sorry about the others, but we're happy that, if it had to be, then mercy, we're sure-enough happy it is you. I—I almost didn't come here this morning. I was sort of sure you'd be in the White House, with a special fancy staff, and not needing me any more."

Dilman smiled. "I won't be in the White House for a while, and you can be sure, Crystal, I'll want you then as much as I want you now."

She seemed overwhelmed with relief. "Thank you, Sena—Mr.—Mr. President—" Suddenly her round face broke into a toothy smile, enamel and gold, and she said, "I'll have to take lessons how to talk to you. What'll it be this special morning, anything special?"

"The same as always, Crystal. Give me fifteen minutes or so. I've got to shower and dress."

She was off to the dining room and kitchen, straw basket swinging, and Dilman smiled at the two Secret Service executives. "She's here every day," he said, "and weekends her niece comes in."

Gaynor said, "We'll have to trouble you for a full list of your employees and friends."

"You'll have it today."

"Mr. President, there are a number of calls that have come in—"

"Anything important?"

"I don't believe anything urgent. The Secretary of State wants to speak to you when you're up. Oh yes, one personal call—well, he phoned two or three times from New York—a young man who claims to be your son."

"Julian?"

"That's right, Mr. President. Gave the name Julian Dilman. Said he'd call back again at half past nine."

"All right. Better give me time to get myself cleaned up and into some clothes." He started to go, then said

over his shoulder, "You can ask Crystal to make something for you. You must be starved."

"Thank you, Mr. President," the two Secret Service
officers said simultaneously.

The tone of their voices hung inside Douglass Dilman's ears as he walked back to the bedroom. He was attuned to every nuance of every utterance that came from
his white colleagues. The changeable inflection of speech
was their civilized weapon of subtle mockery and superiority without insult, even when you were a congressman. This was their best weapon when they found that
your skin was black and thin. You could not prove disrespect, but you could know its vibrations. He remembered one committee hearing when General Pitt Fortney had appeared as a witness before him and the others.
He had posed a question, and Fortney's reply, in print,
on the record, had been beyond reproach. In writing, it
was a general replying sensibly to a senator. Across the
committee tables, verbalized, it had been a West Point
white general speaking downward to a semiliterate jigaboo. Perhaps he had been oversensitive that time, and
on several other recent occasions. For years he had tried
to curb his excessive sensitivity, as other men tried to
reduce their weight. It took diligent, unremitting work.
It could be done. But then, every once in a while, you
put on sudden sensitivity as you put on extra weight,
and suffered for the added burden.

Throwing aside his robe, entering the bathroom, he
decided that the two Secret Service heads, Gaynor and
Agajanian, had been courteous in their behavior. And
now it seemed reasonable that they should have been.
To their dedicated eyes, a Mr. President was a Mr. President, whether he was Grover Cleveland or Woodrow
Wilson or Dwight D. Eisenhower or T.C. or Douglass
Dilman. All that mattered to them, their jobs, their future, their pride, was that they keep the pounds of flesh
entrusted to them, whatever its pigmentation, alive.

He unbuttoned his pajama top, stripped it off, and
removed the pajama trousers. Opening the shower door,
he adjusted the knobs inside, then started the spray of
water. Finding soap and cloth, he wondered how many

other white men would be as courteous as his bodyguards. The personalities whose speeches he had heard,
whose bright remarks he had heard, whose prejudices
he had known, crossed his mind: the Southern congressmen, the Northern committeemen, the Western rightists,
the Eastern Ivy League snobs. A son of Ham, he thought,
in the White House, in the Oval Office of the West Wing,
in the highest seat extant in this red, white, and blue
(not black) republic. Despite the old prediction of
Robert Kennedy, as Attorney General, that there could
be a Negro in the Presidency in thirty or forty years,
there had been no one of equal stature, then or now, no
matter how wise or liberal, who believed that it could
happen then or in this century. Yet it had happened,
by accident.

Stepping into the shower cell, he knew that he had
been insulated since last night from what was happening
out there, in the capital city, in the cities of the fifty
states. How stunned the American people must be this
hour to learn they would have to look up to an outsider,
a member of the ten-per-cent black minority of *their*
white country.

It was not the first spray of the shower that chilled
him, but the first realization of what had happened and
how wildly it would be resented.

He remembered the short poem: "How odd/ of
God/ to choose/ the Jews."

He paraphrased it: How odd of God to choose me, to
choose one who had already gone high enough, too high
for comfort, and had wanted nothing higher for himself,
one who wished only to be limited to his legislative height,
where reticence and diffidence would still keep him an
unresented exhibit that was a sop to the liberal conscience of the North. Then the Chief Justice's wrenching
words of last night came back to him: "may the Lord in
Heaven bless you and watch over you . . . as the first
Negro . . . President of the United States."

His limbs felt weak, so weak, and his heart thudded
inside its chest cavity. There were a million white men
who were right for the job. There were a thousand black
men who would have bravely and defiantly welcomed

the Godsent opportunity, and called it Godsent. Yet something, something, had gone wrong Up There. The Lord had poked His heavenly finger at the wrong name, and now it was too late. He wanted to rebuke the Maker for His blunder, and then, strangely—out of respect to the memory of his mother and father and aunts in the Midwest earth, out of fear of the hellfire that had been sounded in that old Michigan church in the room behind the broken-down social club, when he was in knee pants—he was humble before that God and the Son of God; and his bitterness and fear, really it was deep-down cringing fear, turned to shame. This was no place for kneeling, but when there was the time and the place, he would beg forgiveness and beg for help.

Yet, Jesus, Jesus, why did it have to be himself, Douglass Dilman, who was not white and who was afraid of being black, and who was without armor or grace?

Then as the shower's liquid needles, warmer now, hit his chest, and the foam ran down his stomach and thighs, and as he absently rubbed himself with the soapy cloth and allowed the stream of water to dissolve the soap, he thought that his position, despite his secret inadequacy, was not entirely bad. His mind went backward to last night, or the early hours of the morning, when the White House limousine had taken him home. What had happened then was, in retrospect, heartening.

When he had become a member of the House of Representatives, he had leased the upstairs front apartment of a red brick, two-story apartment building between Georgia Avenue and Sixteenth Street. The three rooms and kitchenette, modest and clean, had been sufficient to serve his widower existence. The location had been comfortably in the midst of a onetime white neighborhood, now occupied by upper-class Negroes. But the apartment had soon become too small for him. Senator Espinosa, who had grown senile and disabled, had resigned two-thirds of the way through his term. The Governor of Dilman's state, to strengthen his position with his vast Negro voting population—which had trebled with the influx of colored families from the South—and with the liberal union leaders, had appointed Dilman to

Espinosa's vacant office for the two years remaining. Dilman as Senator had found himself, briefly, a *rara avis*. Having left Washington, D.C., to campaign in a preponderantly Negro district for his fifth House term, he had returned to Washington as a Senatorial appointee. One of the few Negroes to achieve so high a seat in government, he had been the subject of lead articles in such magazines as *Life, Look, Time,* and *Newsweek,* and he had made the covers of *Ebony* and *Sepia.* He had vaguely felt a freak and been discomfited, but, encouraged by the Party bosses, he had cooperated with one and all.

It had been during this transitional period, when he had been the object of so much attention, when his mail had swelled, when he had received callers (mostly political, mostly pressure), that he had decided that his rented apartment could no longer serve him. He had found that the parlor and kitchenette were too cramped, and there was need of a study and library at home. He had begun to search for a larger apartment, but the rents demanded had appalled him. Gradually he had concluded that it might be wisest to buy a house. Washington was, after all, his adopted city, and would likely remain his home for years to come. While he was a senator from his state by appointment, and only for a short period, and while he had no idea if he would be a senator again, he was confident that he could regain his old House seat. And even if that were not possible, he could go into private law practice in the capital city where, with a population 55 per cent Negro, a highly reputed Negro attorney would have enough clients to keep him occupied and secure.

Guided by real estate brokers, he had visited three brownstones in his neighborhood, and in each instance had felt that the house was overpriced and too expensive for his meager savings. The fourth brownstone had come to his attention by chance. Seated one morning behind his desk in the Old Senate Office Building, he had learned that the Reverend Paul Spinger was in his reception room, eager to see him. A visit paid by Spinger was not in itself unusual. Spinger, as director of the largest Negro

organization in America, the Crispus Society, had often
come to Dilman to discuss civil rights legislation. That
morning, as far as Dilman could recall, there had been
no immediate business to discuss. He had invited Reverend Spinger in, and the elderly but energetic clergyman-
lobbyist had said that the word was around that Dilman
wanted to buy a house. If true, he happened to know of
a house not yet on the market, whose owner had to sell
in a hurry, and which might be bought at a reasonable
price, in view of its value as an investment. It was a ten-
room, two-story brownstone off Sixteenth Street, on
Van Buren N.W., and it was a bargain at $45,000. It
was, Spinger had said, a solid, aged abode, that one day
could stand remodeling, but was comfortable enough
and well located on the fringe of the wealthier Negro
section, near Walter Reed General Hospital. Spinger
knew about the house in advance, he had said, because
he and his wife Rose and a boarder had rented the upstairs for several years. The landlord had lived downstairs. Half jokingly, Spinger hoped that Senator Dilman
would consider it. If someone else bought the house,
they might require all ten rooms and evict the Spingers.
The Senator, Spinger had reasoned, was a widower, with
his son in boarding school, and would have no need for
more than the downstairs rooms.

Senator Dilman had gone with the clergyman to visit
the brownstone, and he had been enchanted by the quiet
residential street with its maple trees, the small green
front lawn, the walk up to the entry hall, the generous,
comfortable rooms and nineteenth-century fixtures. Immediately he had bargained for it and closed the deal.
That had been five years ago, more than five years ago,
and not one day had Dilman regretted the financial en-
cumbrance. For to this brownstone off Sixteenth Street
Dilman owed not only his first real pleasure in having a
place where he belonged, but also his enduring relationship with Wanda Gibson, and, because of last night, he
owed to this house his first feeling of acceptance as the
new and accidental Chief Executive of the United States.

Last night, he thought. And then his memory held on
last night.

The feeling of acceptance had come at some time after one o'clock in the morning. As his chauffeured limousine turned into Van Buren Street, Dilman, sandwiched between the Secret Service agents, had become aware of a phenomenon. This was a well-off Negro neighborhood, but a hard-working one, and its inhabitants went to sleep early. The thoroughfare was always blanketed in darkness well before midnight. But last night, after midnight, the street was lighted with illumination from every house, and alive as a Mardi Gras. And then, as they had neared his brownstone, Dilman realized that Van Buren Street was thickly lined on both sides with people, neighbors and others of the capital city, who had come to be the first to set eyes upon America's new President.

When the limousine had drawn up before his front lawn, and he had emerged, the size of the crowd in attendance had overwhelmed him, almost one thousand persons, he had guessed. The faces, many recognizable, had been mostly black, but there were whites here and there, although Dilman had been unable to discern if they were reporters, Secret Service agents, or simply sensation seekers of the kind who rushed to accidents. As he had walked between the agents to his front door, the applause had begun, then swelled, and there had been cheers. Dilman had paused, deeply moved, and had exhaustedly waved and waved, and then gone inside his house.

He had fallen asleep so quickly, he now supposed, because after the first fear and trepidation, the paralysis induced by change and sudden elevation, he had been warmed by friendship and approval. But now the harsher light of morning was upon him. The soothing blackness was gone. The uncertain whiteness waited.

He shut off the shower, emerged dripping onto the bath mat, quickly dried himself, then went into the bedroom to dress. This was a momentous day, and perhaps he would be expected to attire himself specially for it. He considered his dressiest Sunday black suit, then decided that it would be awkward in the morning. He settled for the charcoal one he had purchased ready-made at Garfinckel's for his first appearance as temporary presiding officer of the Senate, during the Vice-President's last trip abroad, six months before his death.

As he dressed himself, his mind compulsively revived one more event of last night, one that had taken place a few minutes before he retired. Sitting on his bed, wondering if the Secret Service men in the living room could hear his voice, he had dialed the Spingers upstairs.

The phone had hardly begun to ring, when it was answered. The voice he had recognized as belonging to Rose Spinger.

"Hello, Rose, I hope I didn't wake you. This is Doug."

Her response had been pitched high with excitement. "Oh, Doug, we hoped—heavens, I mustn't be calling you Doug any more, or even Senator or landlord—"

He had smiled to himself tiredly. "Please, Rose, no formality. Nothing has changed between us. I—"

"Thank you, Doug. Oh, my heavens, to think of it! Did you see us outside in front, in that mob, waving to you?"

"I'm not sure. I saw Wanda for a second."

"Of course, you would have. We're all so thrilled. We're sorry for that accident in Europe, but since it was God's will, we're happy you will be there to guide us. We need you, Doug, we all need you, and the Reverend says this is the hand of Providence. . . . Oh, heavens, he's telling me to be quiet and let you speak to Wanda. All right. Except I want to say for the Reverend and myself, from our hearts, that we wish you strength and courage."

"Thank you, Rose, I need that."

"The Reverend went to knock on Wanda's door. She's still up. She'll pick up her phone in a second."

"I'll wait. Thanks, Rose."

In the seconds that he waited, his brain had become alive and projected the early pictures of Wanda Gibson. When he had bought this brownstone five years ago, and while it was still in escrow, he had been invited to dinner by the Spingers to celebrate his acquisition. He had met the Spingers before, many times, but always about the Hill, or at Crispus Society affairs, or at parties given by African Embassies near Sheridan Circle. This was the first time that he had accepted an invitation to their home. Twice, as a representative, he had been asked to their dinners, and twice he had declined with fabricated excuses. As a member of the House, he had not wanted to be in the position of having to answer to white colleagues who might charge that, as a Negro, he was being used by the head of the most important Negro organization. His timidity had been ridiculous, he had known, especially since other Negro congressmen and white liberals had attended those dinners in a natural way, and had enjoyed Rose Spinger's cooking. Thereafter he had told himself that if he was ever invited again, he would accept.

The familiar timidity had assailed him but one more time, just before signing the escrow papers on the brownstone house. He had wondered what those on the Hill would think, once it got out, about a senator owning a house in which he permitted the leader of America's largest minority pressure group to live. Nobody, apparently, had cared. Perhaps, Dilman thought wryly, because nobody, apparently, cared what he did at any time. In the Senate, until his surprising selection in Party caucus to serve as President pro tempore of the body when Vice-President Porter was out of town or ill, few had seemed aware of his existence. He was one of a hundred names on the roll call, rarely absent, but almost always silent and withdrawn. He made no speeches, gave no interviews, introduced no bills, and he went along with the Party and T.C. and everyone. Even though, after filling Espinosa's unfinished term as Senator, he had been endorsed by the Party to run on his own (with strong Negro and labor support, against a weak opponent, destroyed by a graft exposé four days before the voting), and he had been re-elected to the Senate on his own, he had felt an interloper.

He had accepted the Spingers' third invitation to dinner not as a senator but as their landlord, and he had gone unafraid, knowing at last that no one, not even such Southern red-neck mouthpieces as Representative Zeke Miller or Senator Bruce Hankins, cared or gave a damn.

There had been six of them at that intimate dinner at

the Spingers' five years ago, the host and hostess, a colored engineer and his colored teacher wife, himself as the personage and guest of honor, and Wanda Gibson. It had been his initial meeting with Wanda Gibson, and for the first time in the many years since Aldora's death he had realized that affection and desire within him had not atrophied but had only been sublimated.

Even then, five years ago, Wanda had not been a girl, but a mature woman—a lady, he had always thought of her as being, a lady—of thirty-one. She was a graduate of the University of West Virginia, with economics as her major; and she had worked for her favorite professor in Morgantown and Charleston, and followed the professor, known for his liberal books, to Washington, D.C., when he accepted a government advisory job in the latter part of the Lyndon Johnson administration. When T.C. had become President, and Wanda's professor had gone back to his university, she had stayed on in Washington. For the last two years she had held a well-paid position as executive secretary to the director of Vaduz Exporters, in nearby Bethesda, Maryland.

From the first, Dilman had known that Wanda was a remarkable find. Her intelligence and wit, her good nature and humor, her well-bred manner, had made it seem incredible that she had not ever been married. As he came to know her better, Dilman had come to understand her avoidance of marriage. Her parents, who had lived in West Virginia, where her father had been a short-order cook, dishwasher, janitor in an all-night diner serving coal miners, had sacrificed much of their comfort, and the futures of her younger brother and sister, to educate and launch her. When first one parent, and then the other, had been hospitalized, and afterward confined to costly sanitarium care, Wanda had accepted full responsibility to support and look after them, not only as daughter but as debtor. She had a burden, and she could not discard it in favor of marriage, for which she was so perfectly suited. But two years ago her father had died, and less than a year before her mother, and at last Wanda had been free to live her own life as her own person.

She had expected him to propose marriage last spring,
Dilman knew, and he had not, and it had created, for the
first time, an undercurrent of unhappiness between them.
She had known that he wanted her for his wife. He had
known that he needed her. The proposal was up to him,
and yet, while he could profess affection and love, articulate his need for her, he could not bring her from upstairs
to his flat downstairs as wife. He had thought about it a
thousand times since spring, and had known that the failure was entirely his own. Marriage was an affirmative
act, and he had been shackled by countless negative
fears. He had tried, time and time again, to narrow in on
specific fears, small ones, avoiding the major one, until at
last he could see what was left and what in himself
taunted him with contempt.

Wanda Gibson was a mulatto. That was the center of
it. As a mulatto, she was more white in appearance than
black. In most communities she could have passed for
white. Her hair, while brunette and curling, was soft and
long. Her eyes were light brown, her nose delicate and up-
turned, and her lips and mouth small. Her figure was trim,
well hipped but otherwise slender. She considered herself a colored woman, and she lived as a colored woman.
But, for Douglas Dilman, how she regarded herself, and
how she approached her life, were not assurances enough.

The nagging cowardice within him, that avoided
marriage to the one good companion of his life, was his
fear of how she would look beside him and how this
would affect his political career. With Wanda as his mate,
he would appear blacker. With himself as her mate, she
would appear whiter. Whatever the facts and truth, it
would give the impression of an interracial marriage. It
might not cause talk in Washington and in his home
state, but on the other hand it might. It was an unnecessary risk. It would rock the boat in times like this.
Or, at least, it might.

Dilman's solution had been to avoid the issue. The
weekly platonic meetings had continued, the Senator
and his ladylike lady friend, in the Spinger living room,
in the loges of Loew's Palace Theater, and, ever so occasionally, in the Golden Ox or the Lincoln Inn. Re-

cently, Dilman had become aware, each rendezvous had
been less comfortable, less warm and communicative. It
was as if they were both present, each desiring the company of the other, but now that she was free of parental
commitment and he was temporary presiding chairman
of the Senate, there had fallen a thick steel grill between
them. You could see; you could hear; you could not
touch. You were two, not one, and might never be one,
and Wanda Gibson, for all her evenness of temperament
and understanding, had begun to resent this failure in
Douglass Dilman.

Since his invisible antenna of sensitivity had picked
up and recorded her disappointment in him, Dilman had
recently taken to reviewing and brooding over this relationship and his own life. Some weeks ago he had almost arrived at the decision to propose marriage, and to
the devil with the consequences, if any. After all, he had
asked himself in a practical way, how could he any
longer be hurt? But then he had been sidetracked by his
activity, and sham importance, in serving the Senate in
the Vice-President's place. And now, overnight, cruel
Destiny had touched him. He had become the President
of the United States. The personal choice ahead was
clear-cut: should he be James Buchanan or Grover
Cleveland? Buchanan had been the only unmarried
President to serve his country. Cleveland had been the
only Chief Executive to be married in the White House.
When the choice was weighed thus, the scales tipped
toward Buchanan. A showy wedding, like Cleveland's
in the Blue Room, before the world and the press, a
marriage to a mulatto, a mulatto who might almost be
mistaken for white, would merely serve to incense the
enemies of his race. His uncertain position and precarious image, before a broken and divided country,
would be worsened.

This had been his rationale last night, as he waited,
the telephone receiver in his hand, to hear Wanda's
voice. His private decision, he had known, was neither
courageous nor honest. It was merely expedient and political. It solved nothing, but simply traded off a personal
problem to avoid a more fearsome one.

Gazing down at the receiver in his left hand, he had wondered why, under the circumstances, he was trying to speak to her at all, at least at this time. He had no idea what he could say to her, yet somehow, as President of the United States for more than three hours, he had to speak to someone before sleeping and then waking to the terrible fact, and the only one who might care about him, reassure him, was Wanda. As he waited for Wanda, his mind drifted to Mindy. His attitude toward the two of them was one and the same. He avoided taking a wife he needed for the same reason that he did not seek out a daughter he loved. He was black and still afraid.

"Hello, Doug." She was calling down to him through a wire from upstairs, and yet she had never been farther away.

"Wanda, I wanted to—to say good night, before going to sleep."

"Doug, it's overwhelming, the whole thing. What does one say? Do I congratulate you? That sounds wrong."

"You commiserate with me, and with the whole country."

"No, don't—don't talk like that. It's not true. That accident in Frankfurt was horrible. But it happened, Doug, those things happen. Remember how we once talked about what our families were doing the moment that they learned F.D.R. had died? And how they felt? They felt the world had come to an end, that they were dying, too, that there was no hope. Yet nothing happened to them, or to us. Life went on. Maybe differently than it might have been had he lived, but not that differently. Well, Doug, T.C. was a good man, I'm sure, and popular, but he was no F.D.R., and neither was MacPherson. I know you'll do as well as or better than either. No one is born to be the only one to be President. Thousands of men could be President just as well as the one who fought to get the office. If it had to be someone else, I think it could have been no one better than you."

"Wanda, don't—you know me too well for that—you know my weaknesses—"

"Everyone has weaknesses, Doug. Be sensible. Stand

off and look around. Lincoln had weaknesses, and T.C. had too many to count, and probably dozens we couldn't see to count. Of course you have weaknesses, but you're strong enough to handle the job. Don't discount your strengths. I can't forget what you refuse to remember. With the kind of background you had, all that poverty, how did you get through the university and then law school? How did you get elected to the House of Representatives four times, and then get into the Senate, and even become its presiding officer? It took *something*. Doug, it took very much. I know you, maybe as well as anyone knows you, maybe better, and I am positive the whole country—once they get over the shock of the—of T.C.'s death—they'll see you for what you are, and they'll be proud of you."

"Wanda, Wanda—you're doing your best, I know—I appreciate it—but, Wanda, I'm black—tomorrow morning 230 million Americans are going to wake up and find their President, one they didn't elect, is black."

"That's true, Doug. . . . Maybe it'll be a good thing for them, for the country."

"Maybe, but—will they think so?"

"I don't know, I don't know what they'll think and neither do you. I only know what I think. If you go at this as you've gone at everything before, with determination, honesty, learning what you have to learn, acting as you believe best, it will be all right. I'm sure it will work itself out."

"You—you sound less certain now, Wanda."

"Do I? I didn't mean to. I guess I'm just concerned about you."

"What do you mean? Tell me exactly what you mean."

"I mean—please don't take it wrong, Doug—we know each other too well for that—but—I mean it would be bad, hurtful, if you started off, went into the White House, feeling you don't belong, feeling you are less than you should be, feeling that way because—because you are colored. Don't misunderstand me, Doug, but—"

"I understand you very well. I'll try not to be like that. I'll try hard, but—you're right, I guess—I am afraid. . . . I'm also afraid for us. That's on my mind, too. I don't know what the demands or the expectations of the office are, except what I've seen and read. I don't know what it is really like in there. I want to see you, speak to you, more than ever. I—I just don't know—will they let me?"

"Doug, nobody owns you. You don't have to wait for anyone to let you do anything, I mean in your personal life."

"You're right, Wanda."

"It's late, dear. You'd better get some sleep. I—I'll be here. You call me when you can, anytime, I'll be here."

"I'll call you tomorrow."

"Anytime. . . . Now sleep, dearest, and know we are all with you. Good night, Doug."

"Good night, Wanda, good night."

After hanging up, he had tried to analyze their talk. She had offered him encouragement, and her language had been warm, and yet, toward the end especially, he had sensed her remoteness. Still, he had thought, as he reached to turn off the bed lamp and then pushed his fatigued body beneath the blanket, she was for him and with him, no matter how disappointed she might be in him, and that was comforting, that was something; and then he had felt drowsiness, and then he had slept.

He finished knotting his knit tie, pulled on the coat of his charcoal suit, and consulted his wristwatch. He was afraid the journey his mind had taken to the events of last night, to the five years with Wanda, had consumed an hour of time. He was amazed and pleased to see that only six minutes had passed. It occurred to him that he had made a discovery no scientist had made before him. He had found what traveled faster than the speed of light: memory. The trouble was, no matter how fast it traveled, memory never stopped.

Determined to retreat no more from the unknown present into the more pleasant past, he left the bedroom and walked briskly into the living room. Lou Agajanian was seated in a chair, under the arch leading into the entry hall, smoking a cigarette. Immediately, the head of the White House Detail leaped to his feet in a pose of civilian attention.

"Mr. President," he said, "the boss—I mean, Mr. Gaynor, he went off to catch a wink of sleep. Another agent, Mr. Prentiss, came in to spell him. He's in the kitchen, at the rear service door."

"Fine, fine." Dilman indicated the chair. "Please relax, Mr. Agajanian."

The Chief of the White House Secret Service Detail remained standing while Dilman entered the small dining room, which overlooked the street. He noticed that instead of his usual yellow breakfast mat and plain pottery dishes, Crystal had set the table with the formal white tablecloth and decorated dishes from the good set. Obviously, for her, this was an Occasion. Amused, he called off toward the kitchen, "Let's go, Crystal, I'm here!"

As he sat down, Crystal rushed in and placed his orange juice before him. "Eggs an' bacon comin', Mr. President!"

Before picking up the orange juice, he studied the messages on slips of paper lying before the telephone: his son Julian had phoned from Trafford University ("Will call you back"); his Senate secretary, Diane Fuller, had phoned from the Old Senate Office Building ("Has to go out on your business, will call you back"); Secretary of State Eaton had phoned from his house ("To inquire how you are"); press secretary Tim Flannery ("Please set aside time for him early today"); Governor Wayne Talley ("Will call back shortly"). Those were the messages. He guessed that there might have been hundreds more, except that his phone number was unlisted, known only to a select handful of persons.

Drinking down the unsweetened orange juice, grimacing at the liquid's bite, he reached over and brought the pile of newspapers before him. There were five to which he subscribed, two New York City dailies, and three Washington, D.C., newspapers, one of the latter a Negro press publication.

Quickly he examined the headlines streaming across each front page. The sensational New York newspaper read:

NATION GASPS! A NEGRO IS PRESIDENT OF THE USA!

The moderate New York newspaper read:

SENATOR DOUGLASS DILMAN SWORN IN AS PRESIDENT LAST NIGHT: FIRST NEGRO TO ACHIEVE COUNTRY'S HIGHEST OFFICE

The pro-administration Washington newspaper read:

CONGRESS AND VOTERS RALLY TO SUPPORT SENATOR DOUGLASS DILMAN

The pro-segregationist, Zeke Miller Washington newspaper read:

NEGRO SENATOR MADE CHIEF EXECUTIVE BY FLUKE; JUDICIARY COMMITTEE MEETS TO DEBATE CONSTITUTIONALITY; CITIZENS PROTEST "UNFAIR" RULE OF MAJORITY BY MINORITY; REPRESENTATIVE MILLER PREDICTS "DISSENSION, DISUNITY, VIOLENCE"

The Negro Washington newspaper read:

HALLELUJAH! EQUAL RIGHTS AT LAST! COLORED PRESIDENT OF SENATE BECOMES PRESIDENT OF US ALL! WORLD APPLAUDS TRUE DEMOCRACY!

Several things were evident at once. To no one would he be simply a public servant who, by the law of succession, had become President of the United States. To both sides, and the middle, too, he would be the "Negro" who had become President. To the press of his own race he was the colored man, the black Moses, who had come to lead his people out of bondage and save them. To the press of the enemies of his race, as represented by Congressman Zeke Miller's newspaper chain, he was a black and ugly thing pulled out from under a rock to wreak

vengeance on the magnolia-scented South, to destroy the
Grand Republic by enforcing equality between black god-
less brutes and white Christian human beings, to enforce
his nigger ideas on their chaste daughters. To the sensational press he was a zoo object, a freak, for the time a
story and circulation builder, who could be contended
with seriously later. To the press of his Party he was
still a senator, to be rallied around until the Party line
toward him could be straightened out. To the moderate,
conservative, thoughtful press he was—he reached for
the respected and balanced New York daily again and
reread its headline—the first Negro to achieve the country's highest office.

Douglass Dilman considered this headline. It was true,
and it was fair. But how many others, black or white,
would be this reasonable? Slowly his eyes went down the
columns of news datelined Washington, D.C. It was all
solid reportage of his being sworn in, of the tragedy in
Frankfurt that had led to his being sworn in, backed up
by full quotations from Tim Flannery's release explaining
the Presidential Succession Act of 1947. At the bottom
of the lead column was a box containing the suggestion
that the reader turn to the main editorial on page sixteen.

Dilman put down his fork and knife, took up the New
York newspaper, turned to page sixteen, folded it back
and then in half. Immediately he found the main editorial
headed THE NEW MAN IN THE WHITE HOUSE, and
then he settled in his chair to read what followed:

At 10:35 last night (EDT), a new, eligible American male
was sworn in as President of the United States, to succeed a
popular predecessor who died before fulfilling his full four-
year term. In itself, this sudden changing of the guard was
neither historic nor unusual. It has happened eight times before in our history. But last night, for the first time, there was
a difference.

When Presidents Harrison, Taylor, Lincoln, Garfield, Mc-
Kinley, Harding, Franklin D. Roosevelt, and John F. Kennedy died in office, their unexpired terms were filled out by
men who had been their campaign running mates, by men
second in line of succession, by men who had appeared be-

side them before the electorate, and by men of their own race and color. While public and Congressional acceptance of a second choice, a substitute President, was not always simple and smooth—as witness Andrew Johnson's troubles when he succeeded Abraham Lincoln in 1865—at least the transitions were familiar enough to cause no national unrest or uneasiness.

However, the overnight accession of Senator Douglass Dilman, to fill the unexpired term of his popular predecessor, presents numerous problems which are deserving of thoughtful consideration. For the first time in our history, not the President's running mate and campaign colleague, not his second-in-command, not his Vice-President, has taken over his vacant seat, but a relative outsider. For the first time, a senator and not a Vice-President, a legislative officer chosen by his Party colleagues and not the voters, has succeeded to the high office. And, for the first time, let it be stated plainly, a colored man, a member of the Negro race, has been catapulted into top command by an accident of life and a hitherto unused provision of law.

There is no reason why, in our view, a Negro should not be President of the United States. Were the country educated for him, prepared for him, were they to vote for him spontaneously and elect him to the high office, it would be a significant moment in our history and in world history. All men of goodwill and good heart have worked toward that moment, and hoped for that moment to come. Yet, unfortunately, this schizophrenic land of liberty is still groping its way toward equality. It still disfranchises Negroes, it bars them from gainful employment, it keeps them from decent housing, schooling, public accommodations. We still live in an era of growth as a nation—we are making our first toddling steps from uneasy tolerance and decency toward full equality—and so we still dwell in an era of constant falls and bruises.

Thus, a republic which continues to oppress its ten per cent Negro population, which continues to be riven by demonstrations and riots and sectional hatreds, finds itself overnight led by one of the minority it has constantly kept in servility. This is a nation that woke this morning and rubbed its eyes in disbelief when it found that a Negro was at its helm, a Negro was its constitutional pilot and leader. In an anguished and shameful period, when Negroes must still be led into schools protected by armed guards, when Negroes must search for segregated washrooms, when Negroes must sit in the rear of municipal buses, in a period such as this, a Negro has become the highest executive in the land, sitting in the seat of Washington, Lincoln, Wilson, becoming every American's face and voice to the outside world.

The problem presented by a Negro in the Presidency is real, and it is grave. The problem is not President Dilman's problem, but rather, the problem of almost every one of his 230 million fellow Americans. No longer, now, has the United States a half century of grace to grow up to its ideal of equality for every citizen. The United States is faced, today, with the necessity, the imperative necessity, of growing up to its ideal of equality all at once, of accepting a Negro as its leader all at once, of accepting colored men as equal to whites all at once. Failure to attain this maturity, by any state or any member of the democratic community, will be a blow to the country as a whole, will send us reeling backward to the edge of the abyss upon which we teetered toward destruction in the terrible months and days preceding the Civil War. If we go backward, if we fall now, all men here and all mankind everywhere will suffer a death of the soul, as they might suffer a death of the body from a nuclear holocaust.

This is not the morning to recapitulate the wrongs that colored men have suffered in this republic, and to plead their case for civil rights so long overdue. It is enough to remark that while the Constitution specifically bars anyone from this office who is not a natural-born citizen of the United States or not yet thirty-five years of age, it does not bar anyone because the pigmentation of his skin is other than white. A Negro has become President of the United States, and there is no reason on earth why he should not be President.

The Southern racists, and the Northern nonthinkers whose prejudices are rarely acted out, cannot deny that American Negroes, when given the opportunity, have been as capable as their white brothers in practicing wisdom, or attaining wealth, success, fame. One need only glance at the record. The black hue of their skin did not prevent Jan Matzeliger from inventing the billion-dollar shoe-last machine, did not prevent Frederick Douglass from becoming a brilliant lecturer and writer, did not prevent Booker T. Washington from becoming a great educator, did not prevent Matthew Henson from helping Peary discover the North Pole, did not prevent Paul Lawrence Dunbar from composing his deathless lyrics, did not prevent Marian Anderson, Duke Ellington, Lionel Hampton, Jesse Owens, Joe Louis, Mahalia Jackson, W. C. Handy from providing entertainment for the entire world.

Nor can the millions awakening this morning prove that Negroes, in the rare instances in the past when they served us in politics and government, acted with less wisdom, courage, judiciousness than did their white brothers. Ebenezer Bassett was our Minister to Haiti. Jonathan Wright was associate justice of the South Carolina Supreme Court. Jefferson P. Long served in the United States House of Representatives. Blanche K. Bruce served in the United States Senate. In more recent times, Robert C. Weaver administered the United States Housing and Home Finance Agency. E. Frederic Morrow worked as administrative aide to President Eisenhower. Ralph J. Bunche served in the United Nations. Andrew Hatcher worked as associate press secretary to President Kennedy. Carl Rowan served as director of the United States Information Agency under President Lyndon Johnson. Douglass Dilman was President pro tempore of the United States Senate in T.C.'s administration.

Each and every one of these leaders was a Negro citizen of the United States. They had earned the right to guide us, help us, not because their colored forebears helped free us and defend us in the Revolutionary War, in the War of 1812, in the Union Army of Lincoln and Grant, in the First and Second World Wars, in Korea, but because they were part of our whole, part of each of us, with the same stakes and goals. Now one of them, really one of us under the laws devised by the Founding Fathers and since, has become our President. The paramount question is not if Douglass Dilman is equal to the burdensome responsibility, but if we are equal to our responsibility as Americans.

Today we start the first day of President Dilman's term, his time of trial and our own, the one year and five months that stretch ahead, and we begin with trepidation induced by a survey of cold statistics. Out of 230 million American citizens, there are 23 million Negroes, and it is supposed that most will accept our new President. Based on recent voting figures, excluding Negroes and Southern whites, there are perhaps 40 million white citizens of liberal and progressive persuasions, and it is supposed that most of these will cooperate with the new President.

On the other hand, there are 47 million whites in the fourteen states of the Solid South, and it is feared that most of them will reject our new President. Again, based on recent voting figures, there are 30 million extreme rightists in the East, North, and West, and it is likely that most of them will refuse cooperation to our new President.

What is the guess? Sixty-three million of us may be behind Douglass Dilman, 77 million of us may be against him. How are we to account for the remaining 90 million of our citizenry, the follow-the-leaders when told whom to follow, the undecideds in countless polls, the great center mass with real faces and real feelings who can go this way or that? How will they respond to a Negro in the Presidency? Will they listen to racists or rightists, or will they consider the pleadings of moderates and true democrats? Or will they react according to feelings long hidden and repressed about Negroes? How have they felt about the racial ferment in this country these last twenty years? Has something of the aspirations of the new and militant Negro leadership sunk deep into their consciences? Has more, or less, of the propaganda of segregationists infused their minds?

For the middle majority of us all, knowledge of Negroes firsthand is probably limited—limited to the colored cleaning woman, who comes twice a week, limited to the colored baseball player who saves or loses a home game, limited to the garage mechanic, or dime-store clerk, or blues singer seen and heard on a Saturday night. To this white majority, the black man is as unknown as once was the heart of the Dark Continent of Africa. Personally unacquainted with their dark-skinned fellow citizens, knowing of their strife only through the printed page, long avoiding real commitment to this issue because they were busy concentrating on their jobs and raises, shopping and picking the youngsters up at school, these white citizens are suddenly confronted with the imperative demand to make a historic personal decision.

There they are, this strange morning, the vast uncounted, staring with curiosity or bewilderment, with the first throbbings of pride or resentment, at a middle-aged senator with kinky hair and dark skin and African face, who has supplanted a leader they chose, and who is now their voice and image in domestic and international affairs.

We wait now for the commitment. We pray they, in turn, will wait for their own judgments to stand the tests of self-exploration and sound intelligence. And when they come to that moment of decision very soon, whether to accept President Dilman as one of us, one of us, and cooperate with him for the common good, or whether to reject him as an inferior alien disguised as one of us, we pray they will, on the eve of their personal commitments, bear one final consideration in mind.

Judgment of a colored man in the White House cannot and should not be made on whether he will or will not be a wise President, better than Harding, worse than Kennedy or Lyndon Johnson or T.C., but whether or not his judges, all the products of independent America, have attained sufficient maturity, have grown high enough, have become citizens enough, to permit a fellow human being, experienced and expert in his calling, to reflect and serve them.

The immediate future is not in the hands of our first Negro President. It is in *our* hands, for better or for worse.

It seemed an eternity that Douglass Dilman sat at the dining-room table, holding the great metropolitan newspaper which had spelled out, frankly and sensibly, what conditions and judgment waited for him beyond the insular fort of his Negro dwelling and Negro neighborhood.

Presently he dropped the newspaper to the table beside the cold breakfast he had hardly touched. He knew that what he had read should have made him feel heartened, even hopeful. Yet the apprehension and fears of the morning shadowed any possible optimism. He thought: Yes, there are men of reason and good will out there; they exist. But then, he also knew, from years of traumatic observation, years of compromising and cowering to survive and get along, that men such as the one or ones who created that reasonable editorial were too few.

Dilman was not a highly imaginative man, not a soarer, a dreamer, a passionate mover or shaker; this he knew and had always known. He was an intelligent man. He was a formally educated man. He was an experienced man in his chosen field, politics, where knowledge of superficial catch phrases, some forensic talent, an ability to smile, a gift for concession, and a knowledge of facts were enough.

The hard factual core of his mind reframed the eloquent content of the editorial. If all men in America read it and were moved by it, he could enter the White House without fear. But what was this New York metropolitan newspaper anyway, in truth? It was a morning paper, the most appreciated by intellectuals in the land. Its total daily circulation was 800,000. How many of these 800,000 would even read the small type of the editorial page? And how many in the broad nation of 230 million would even know of its existence? It was a pebble trying to fell a Goliath of prejudice—a pebble, not a boulder.

The telephone to his left rang out, startling him from his brooding. Too quickly, out of guilt for the self-indulgence of self-concern, he shot his hand to the receiver, pulled it toward him, fumbling, almost dropping it into the eggs.

"Hello?"

It was a long-distance operator from Trafford, New York. He waited.

"Hello—hello—" He recognized the nervous, high-pitched voice at once as that belonging to Julian, his son. "Dad?"

"Yes, Julian. How are you?"

"Me? Forget about me. My God, Dad, they woke me up in the middle of the night with the news. I couldn't believe it. I'd have called you right away, but I was afraid to wake you up. I tried all morning——"

"Yes, they told me."

"I guess congratulations are in order. May I be one of the first to congratulate you?"

"You certainly may. Thank you, son."

Julian went on excitedly. "Everyone's thrilled about it, Dad. It's the talk of the school. Kids are even cutting classes, whole groups roaming the quad, singing, celebrating."

As he went on to describe the activities at Trafford University, Dilman realized that this was the first time in a year that his son had spoken with enthusiasm of the school. Julian had not wanted to go to the Negro university. He had been forced to enroll by his father, and he had never ceased resisting it or complaining about his classmates. Now elation had replaced complaint.

"I don't know that they have so much to feel festive about," Dilman interrupted. "We lost a fine President."

"Sure we did, Dad, but, my God, can't you see? In one stroke we have more than we ever dreamed of. We've got you there. No more lousy uphill fighting. Now you can do it all with a twist of the wrist. They've got to give in to you. You're the President!" He was almost shouting with manic glee. "The shortcut's been made. We'll get our rights without——"

"Julian," he said sternly. He had to put a stop to this Julian in Wonderland. "Don't go around quoting me, or repeating a word I say. This is strictly family, you understand."

"Sure, sure——"

"Nothing has changed that much, at least not for the better. The road ahead is just as long and steep as a day ago."

"Naw, never, Dad. For once, stop being so conservative. You're too close to the picture. You can't see how big it is. I tell you——"

"You've told me enough," said Dilman curtly. "We'll discuss this another time. I've got a lot to attend to today. And I'm sure you have, too."

"Yes, but not today, Dad. My God, they're treating me here like *I* was the President."

Instantly the letter from Chancellor Chauncey McKaye, of Trafford University, came to Dilman's mind.

"Has Chancellor McKaye come down to congratulate *you?*" Dilman asked with slight sarcasm.

"No, not yet, but—"

"I don't think he will. I think he celebrates honor students. Look, son, we'd better have a talk—"

"I want to. When are you moving into the White House? I want to come down with the gang and see the inside and—"

"I don't know yet. I'll know more about everything in the next few days. I want you here as soon as it is feasible, but without your friends this first time. I have something to discuss with you."

"Okay, sure." Julian sounded deflated. "When can I come to Washington? I'm free next Tuesday."

"Tuesday, then. You come to the West Wing of the White House. I'll leave word to let you in. Now, behave yourself and attend your classes."

"Stop worrying, Dad." He hesitated, and then lowered his voice. "I was thinking about—I wonder how *she* feels this morning."

"Never mind about that," Dilman said sharply. "See you Tuesday, and thanks for your call. I appreciate it."

After he hung up, Dilman thought about his son's oblique reference to Mindy, the unmentionable by name, the untouchable, the expatriate from her family and race, and he wondered about her, too. Would he hear from his daughter now? He knew the barter involved. Would it be worth it to her to abdicate her whiteness for the throne of a Negro President's daughter? He guessed the answer, even as he asked himself the question, and he was grateful when the telephone sounded loudly once more.

This time the caller was his Senate secretary, Diane Fuller, and because he could hardly hear her and because she was almost inarticulate, he knew that she was among whites. He accepted her congratulations and then learned that she was in Edna Foster's office in the White

House. Diane explained that T.C.'s personal secretary had summoned her to pick up Dilman's heavy inflow of top-level cables and telegrams, and bring the most important to his apartment, in case he wanted to see the communications early.

As Diane began to recite the names affixed to the cables of felicitations and good wishes—one from the Premier of the U.S.S.R., one from His Holiness the Pope, one from the British Prime Minister, one from the President of France, one from the Secretary General of the United Nations, one from President Amboko of Baraza —Douglass Dilman interrupted her.

"Diane, you leave all that right on Miss Foster's desk," he said. "Tell her I'll be in shortly. As for you, go back to my Senate office and take calls. I'll be in touch with you later."

When he had finished with the telephone, a troubling thought plucked at his sensitivity. The President's personal secretary, the late President's secretary, had telephoned the Senate Building to get Dilman's own colored secretary to pick up the messages for him. Why this roundabout, time-wasting maneuver? Why had not Edna Foster simply telephoned him herself or brought the messages to him? That would have been the normal way, and the most efficient. Was it that she had never been to a Negro neighborhood before? Or was he overreacting? Was it simply that she had been T.C.'s secretary, and was not only grief-stricken but uncertain about her future role?

Resolving to stop these convolutions of sensitivity, he pushed himself to his feet. He would get his hat, and do what he knew he was avoiding most. He would allow himself to be deposited at 1600 Pennsylvania Avenue.

Before he could leave the dining room, the telephone's ring caught him. He took up the receiver. This time it was a more distant long-distance operator. She announced a call from Fairview Farm, outside Sioux City, Iowa. She repeated the number she had been given to contact. Did she have the correct number? Dilman assured her that this was the correct number.

Suddenly he inquired, "Who is calling here?"

In a schoolteacherish tone, she spelled out the name of the caller. Dilman could not help smiling. It was The Judge himself, and Dilman was delighted. No one, of course, ever called The Judge by any other name than that, and Dilman, who had been a member of the House when The Judge was the outgoing President of the United States, had known him slightly, and had liked the crusty, outspoken, nearsighted old ex-President enormously. The Judge—he had been a minor municipal justice of the peace long before he had become a veteran of the Senate and an American President—had been given so little chance to become elected in his time that he had campaigned without vacillating on issues, with astonishing candor, without selling himself to any man or bloc (since there was no need to, because his candidacy was considered hopeless). When he had won the Presidency in a landslide, putting two polls and three magazines out of business, The Judge had come to the office as his own man. The mandate to speak as he pleased, as well as the fact that he had reached an age when he did not give a damn about ambition and had no hopes for a second term, had made him one of the most individual, independent, and refreshing Chief Executives in modern times. When he liked a man, he liked him if he was black or white, a member of the Party or the opposition, a brain or a heel, and he said so in short expletives, and his enemies fulminated, and the nation adored him. In the three meetings that The Judge had had with Dilman, once while The Judge was President, twice later at Party conferences, he had made it clear that he liked Dilman as a person. No patronizing Rastusboy attitude. He liked Dilman and he said so, and Dilman liked anyone who liked him and was flattered.

"Put him on—put him on—" he found himself telling the Iowa operator.

The receiver emitted a sound like that of cylinders misfiring, and suddenly The Judge's nasal voice could be heard. "Mr. President Dilman, are you there?"

"Yes, Judge, how are——?"

"From one old bastard who's hung in the public stocks to another about to be pilloried in the same place, I want to wish you well. Doug, I want you to go in there, keep your left up high, chin tucked in, and belt them straight from the shoulders. No matter what you hear, no matter what you see, just remember you're the boss, you're not Uncle Tom. You think what you think, speak out what you believe, and when you have to, you give them hell. Remember that, young man. Except for those Confederates who still think old Jeff Davis is President, you got your Party right behind you from this day on. And those that aren't behind you, you tell me and I'll whomp them into line. Just calling for me and the Missus to wish you the best on the first day, because you and I and the Missus know you need it."

He began to cough, and Dilman waited, beaming like an idiot, and when the coughing ceased, Dilman spoke. "Judge, I appreciate this, I do, deeply. I don't know how to thank you."

"I've not done anything for you yet, young man, so don't thank me till I do. But I'll tell you what. Me and the Missus are living out here in the middle of nowhere, like Thoreau at the Pond, and all we got is cows and fresh air and time, and time is what we got the most of. So you listen, young fellow, and you remember, if you ever need me at all, not money but advice or a helping hand—both untaxable and both which we got plenty of out here—you come around to me and we'll have a farm breakfast and talk, and set you straight, or if you want and I can move my bones, I'll come up there to you. Remember that. Promise?"

"I won't forget it, Judge."

"Just one more thing, Douglass, and it's a favor." He paused, and then he said testily, "I don't give a damn if you turn that White House upside down and inside out, but one thing I don't want you to do—don't you dare move my portrait out of the Green Room! Good luck, Mr. President, and God bless you!"

Returning the receiver to its cradle, Dilman chuckled. There were more than decent editorial writers out on the land. There were men like The Judge. The morning appeared brighter.

Again the telephone was ringing. Dilman glanced at

his wristwatch. It was a quarter to ten. He picked up the receiver impatiently.

"Yes?"

"Good morning, Mr. President. This is Wayne Talley. I'm in the White House with Secretary of State Eaton. We have some urgent matters—routine, but they have to be settled—to discuss. Are you intending to come over here this morning, or would you prefer that we visit you?"

"I'm on my way to the White House right now," said Douglass Dilman.

He hung up, and it occurred to him that this might be the last telephone call he would receive on his private unlisted number. He was going to another home with many telephones, connections to every state and to all countries, and his telephone number would be known to everyone in the world.

He started out of the dining room to find his hat, and to leave this Negro house and this Negro community behind him. He would try to live in a new house and a new community that was not meant for a Negro but for a man of all the people, because only such a man could serve as President of the United States—that is, a man who was certain that he was a man, and nothing less.

DURING Governor Wayne Talley's brief conversation with Dilman, Arthur Eaton had sat on one of the two black sofas of the Presidential reception room, the Fish Room it was called after the mammoth sailfish that T.C. had had mounted and hung on one wall, staring up at the square skylight in the ceiling.

Arthur Eaton had hardly heard the conversation, so absorbed was he in his own musings. Persistently his mind had dwelt upon the loss of T.C., his closest public friend—in fact his only friend, since he was a person who had never encouraged personal or intimate relationships with other men. Eaton had been in government, a career diplomat, as far back as he cared to remember. His parents, when they were alive, and when there was money, would have been horrified at anything in government under diplomacy. To run for office, to depend upon others for largess, was unthinkable. As a consequence, Eaton had never considered running for any office, although there had been opportunities. His father, before his death—which occurred almost simultaneously with his loss of wealth—had arranged to put him into diplomacy, and in diplomacy he had been throughout his years.

He could recollect many of his previous posts with ease. There had been the minor beginning as a representative to UNESCO in Paris. There had been the appointment as a delegate to the still growing United Nations in New York. There had been three ambassadorships to three corners of the globe. There had been special troubleshooting assignments, where poise and firmness and keen intellect were wanted, from Eisenhower, Kennedy, and Lyndon Johnson. There had been a period of dismay, almost ennui, when the assignments seemed to be blurring, each one resembling the last, with the same polished tables and same calfskin briefcases and same treaties and same Oriental or Semitic or Asian or European countenances uttering the restrained semantics of upper-echelon diplomatic negotiation. Eaton relished protocol, fine manners, the limited games of wits, and yet he had once become bored by it all. It was a period during which he had felt trapped on a treadmill. Worse, as oppressive, was the fact that he and Kay had lived beyond his means, because this was the way they had been taught to live, and more and more he had become dependent upon her inherited fortune. In his career at that time, not so long ago, he had possessed no hope for change or promotion, and in his personal life he had enjoyed no freedom. It was T.C. who had rescued him, and offered him his greatest hope.

He had enjoyed T.C.'s vigor and boundless extroversion since their college years. While their paths had crossed occasionally, Arthur Eaton had watched T.C.'s political fortunes rise from afar. He had observed his friend engage and defeat foe after foe in elections of more and more importance. He had, with admiration mingled with envy, observed T.C. become a national figure. He was not surprised when the convention had nominated

T.C. as the Party's standard-bearer on the third ballot, but he was surprised when Tim Flannery had telephoned from St. Louis to report that T.C. needed his assistance in the campaign and wanted him to fly out immediately.

At the time, Eaton had been between missions, momentarily free of an assignment, and he had gone to T.C. at once. To Arthur Eaton, in that St. Louis hotel suite, T.C. had been as he had always been, only more so, more confident, more exuberant, more stimulating. T.C. had presented his proposition directly. As the Party's candidate, he was well-enough versed in domestic affairs to handle himself properly. But, T.C. had admitted disarmingly, he'd had little opportunity to be involved in international problems, and on the subject of foreign affairs he was a dolt, and he needed help and advice. He had implored Eaton to take a leave of absence from the Department of State, and join T.C.'s campaign for the Presidency as adviser on foreign affairs and part-time speech writer.

Although the idea of accompanying anyone on a grueling campaign junket, leaving air-conditioned rooms and polished tables for grubby, poorly lit hotel rooms, half-cooked food, smelly, disheveled local politicians, revolted Arthur Eaton, he had accepted without hesitation. There had been two reasons for his immediate acceptance. One was the chance to get away from Washington, from Kay and her tiresome social friends, from work that was suffocating him, and the other (and more exciting) reason was T.C.'s promise. "Arthur, you help me win, and I'll see that you have yourself a Cabinet post, not selling stamps or worrying about squaws, but a big one, the biggest. You help me now, and you can help me run this country and most of the world next year."

It had happened exactly as T.C. had promised that it would. Two hours after T.C.'s opponent had conceded defeat on television, and T.C. had become the President-elect, Arthur Eaton had answered the ringing telephone in Georgetown. The caller had been T.C. himself. No sooner had Eaton congratulated him than T.C. had boomed out, "Arthur, you got any enemies in the Senate?" Eaton could think of none, not real enemies. Then T.C. had said, "Think they'll give consent on your appointment?" And Eaton had asked, "To what?" And then T.C., with a delighted laugh that was almost a shout, had bellowed across the wire, "To Secretary of State, my friend. You are the first in my Cabinet, and welcome to it!"

So he had become Secretary of State Eaton, and with Talley trotting between T.C. and himself, he had assisted the President in running the country. Those had been adventurous and stimulating days, those days of the two years and seven months gone by, and they had been his Fountain of Youth. Not only had each morning, with its challenges, been a joy to wake to, but Eaton had found the independence to shake off the yoke of money that held him captive to his wife. He had been enabled to ignore her disdain, her snobbery, her petty values, her Social Register crowd and her avant-garde artist salon. He had, indeed, been able to plead devotion to something that mattered more, survival of his country. This had been the same shield he had always been able to hold up to fend off Kay's barbed anger. Her technique had not varied from its pattern in the past; it had only intensified. She had continued to hack away at his masculinity. When she found that she could no longer bring him down, as she had always succeeded in doing in the past, she had begun to increase her trips away from Washington. She had permitted herself to be seen with her endless bright young men in public. Eaton had rarely speculated on what she might be doing with her companions in private. But more and more, freed of her, he had begun to derive pleasure from the company of attentive and appreciative young Washington women, the single ones. There had been but two short-lived affairs— for he was always aware of the dangers—but they had been gratifying enough to remind him that he was a person still capable of enjoying love and companionship, and that he was more than his wife had tried to make him.

All of this pride and pleasure he owed to the patronage and friendship of T.C., whom he had revered as a

friend and respected as a leader. Twenty-four hours ago
their future had seemed glowing. There were years of
their joint rule ahead of them—the remainder of this
term, and the almost certain second term. Twenty-four
hours ago Eaton's resurrection as an individual, a very
important person, had been secure. And then, shockingly, with the crumbling of that ancient Palace in
Frankfurt, his high hopes and good prospects had crumbled, too. And so he knew that his mourning was not
only for the loss of his friend, but for the loss of something of himself.

Throughout the endless tragic night in Georgetown,
following the swearing in of Dilman as President, he had
received and listened to or overheard the members of
T.C.'s bereft team and the leaders of the Party. Most
of the chatter had been about how to preserve the unity
of the Party, now that a Negro was its head. There had
been a little talk, he remembered, about preserving the
unity of the nation as well. Too, there had been talk,
mostly in Southern accents, about challenging the constitutionality of the 1947 Act of Succession, and there
had been talk, in harder accents, about reviving some
aspect of the old 1867 Tenure of Office Act, which had
once enabled the Senate to try to restrict a President
from removing officers appointed to his Cabinet. In
short, Eaton remembered, the concern had not been
about Dilman's ability to handle the office, and how he
must best be guided, but rather about how to balk him
or, failing in that, to control him, pluck his powers, so
that the nation would not be tainted black and so that
those present might not lose their jobs to colored men
and to bleeding-heart Negro-lovers.

Through the night, Arthur Eaton had not permitted
himself to be drawn into these discussions. His foresight had suffered from emotional cataracts. He had
thought only of the immediate consequences of the fate-
ful night, of the condition of the country and himself
now, in the present, without T.C. as mentor. When his
living room bar and then his library had emptied, and he
had sought sleep, he had still not fastened on the full
realization that even though another, by default, had

become President, this other must be made to understand that it was still T.C.'s country and T.C.'s government and that any successor was there merely as a custodian of T.C.'s ideas and ideals, which Eaton himself might continue to spell out and present.

Not until now, in the Fish Room of the White House —a room, like the Oval Office, restored by T.C. to the decor of the Kennedy administration—had Eaton, after listening to Talley on the telephone, after reviewing all that he had reviewed in his head, finally settled on the idea of what must be done. He had a role, after all, and perhaps now it was more important than it had been before. He must ignore every one of those harebrained schemes about blocking Dilman from the Oval Office, or obstructing the lamentable Negro. He must devote himself, Eaton decided, to keeping T.C. as alive as he had ever been. Only thus could their United States be saved, and, parenthetically, only thus could Arthur Eaton have a continuing, meaningful life.

He sat straight on the sofa, saw that Wayne Talley was standing at the desk near the door, making notes on a sheet that lay beside the quaint early typewriter once used by Woodrow Wilson.

"What are you up to, Wayne?" he inquired.

"Dilman's on his way in. He's an absolute amateur. I'm not saying he's stupid—hell, he's been around the Hill long enough. But he's ignorant of what really goes on, and of things that have to be done. It kills me when I think of it. The Majority Party senators caucus every time there's a new Congress in the Conference Room of the Senate Office Building to select a temporary presiding officer to sit up there with the gavel and pound it. The idea is to select one of their own as a substitute or alternate for the Vice-President when he's out of town. Nine times out of ten, they cast their caucus vote for the member among them who has seniority. There's no rule about it, but it's a kind of gesture of courtesy, a custom, to select the senator who's had the most years of service. That's why Rydberg had the spot so long. 'Papa Methuselah' they called him. Then his doctors make him quit, so the Senate needs a replacement, what with Porter traveling all the time. They've got to caucus again. So what happens this time? All those riots, the bloodshed, in Detroit, Chicago, Memphis, Dallas, all of it from Negroes, with those protest marches and boycotts worsening—so a couple of smart guys get the big political brainstorm, let's give the honorary presiding post to a Negro, a democratic gesture, and shut up those demonstrators, prove to them we mean well. So Senator Selander, the senior member, who normally would have become President pro tempore, seconds the suggestion. That makes it okay. So Selander steps out of the caucus, phones me, and tells me to pass it on to T.C. to find out if he approves. Well, T.C. was so damn busy that day he didn't give a hoot who held that unimportant President pro tempore of the Senate job, so he said okay, maybe it'll look good for the Party, let them do what they think best. So the Party caucus elects Douglass Dilman, and puts the resolution naming him to the whole Senate. Then, a routine thing, the opposition offers an amendment putting forth their own candidate, Senator Riggins, and a roll call is held and the opposition amendment voted down. Then the original resolution on behalf of Dilman is put to a voice vote, and the ayes have it, and Dilman has that idiotic do-nothing post. Who in the hell would know that the Vice-President would drop dead soon after that? Who in the hell would imagine that the fourth in line of succession could ever become President of the United States? In fact, who in the hell, on that day they routinely caucused and voted, even knew that the President pro tempore of the Senate was the fourth in line? I always thought it was the Secretary of State. I thought it was you, Arthur, not that it mattered a damn at the time. So for political and publicity reasons we put that poor Party hack in there, and we had our showcase colored man up there for all to see, a man with no qualifications for leadership whatsoever—"

"How do you know that?" asked Eaton quietly.

"Douglass Dilman's been in the House four terms, in the Senate two terms, and what has he ever done or instigated?" said Talley heatedly. "He was sent to Washington because of the temper of the times, and given an honorary gavel in the Senate because of the times, and then a once-in-a-thousand accident happens, and blooey, we're stuck with a tenth-rater whose presence means potential trouble, and plenty of it." He lifted his hands to the ceiling. "The fourth in line becoming President —I repeat, Arthur, who could've imagined it?"

"It was always a possibility," said Eaton. "I was reading this morning that what happened now might very well have happened during the last six weeks of 1961. At that time Speaker Rayburn was dead, and not replaced, and had President Kennedy been assassinated then, and Vice-President Johnson with him, we would have had the fourth in line, President pro tempore of the Senate Hayden, as President of the United States."

"But this Dilman, anyone would have been better than Dilman."

"Well, if he doesn't work out," said Eaton, "you and your senator friends have only yourselves to blame. As an expediency, you played politics instead of exercising judgment, and you did it once too often."

"Arthur, don't lecture me from hindsight. We always play politics. That's our business. Politics—why, that's not necessarily a dirty word. It implies bargaining, giving and taking, it means tuning in on the times, doing things people want even when you're not sure it's best for them. More often than not, politics produces good results. And usually, when we play politics, we guess right, and what happens is right not only for us here but for most of the people out there. This time, this once, though—" He shook his head sadly. "Well, like I said, we were dealing with a minor decision, and we dusted it off to placate a pressure group. Who in the hell knew that it would lead to this?"

"Yet it has led to this," said Eaton. "I suggest that we forget the past, and consider what is to be done in the present. This is the time to be realistic, to make the best of a—a difficult situation." He paused and considered Talley. "I believe T.C. would have wanted that."

Talley's cross-eye jumped, and he swallowed, as ever cowed by the mention of T.C.'s name. "Yes, I guess you're right," he said. He came away from the desk, rattling the sheet of paper in his hand. "Well, you can see that I, personally, am trying to make the best of it. I'm trying to get up a reasonable list of the first duties Dilman must discharge. God knows how well he'll be able to manage them."

"Wayne, certainly he will expect expert counsel and guidance," said Eaton softly. "Long ago the office became too big for one man. After all, what are the demands on the President today? He is Chief Executive, overseeing the execution of our laws, exercising important powers of appointment and removal. He is chief of state, national host to an endless stream of native and foreign visitors. He is Commander in Chief of the Army and Navy and Marines and Air Force, with the Pentagon dangling from his civilian lapel. He is arbiter of both Houses on Capitol Hill, able to influence Congressional activity, able to nullify its accomplishments by veto. He is Ambassador to the world, making deals with international leaders, ironing out treaties, selecting foreign diplomat puppets, using my own Department of State as little more than a computer. And that, Wayne, is but the start of it, for any President. Consider his lesser jobs—he runs his political party, he molds public opinion, he sees that his voice is heard in the United Nations, he acts as a super-policeman in areas ranging from strikes to race riots to big-business monopoly."

Arthur Eaton saw that Talley was becoming impatient, and he smiled. "Forgive a résumé of what you are already too well acquainted with, but this is a morning in which to remember the facts of a President's life. What lone man, in our complex age, can perform as so many men at one and the same time? There's enough here to give Hercules a nervous breakdown. Every modern President knows that. Roosevelt, Truman, Eisenhower, Kennedy, Johnson knew that, and delegated power to specialists. The only one who tried to go it alone was The Judge, and that lasted about one year, and his cranky ego put him in such a hole that it took several hundred experts to dig him out. Why, T.C. once told me our method of electing and depending on one President was as outmoded as the horse-and-buggy, that what this country needed today was the election of a board of Presidents, at least five serving at once. Since he could not have that, T.C. did the next-best thing. He took on you, Wayne, after you lost your election, and myself, and a half-dozen others of the Party as assistant Presidents, and it worked nicely, very nicely."

Talley sniffed. "Great, Arthur, I know that. You know that. Maybe every schoolboy knows that. But does our new Mr. President know that?"

"He may. If he does not understand delegation of power, I think he will come to understand it within a week."

"I wish I could be as sure of that as you, Arthur. We're not dealing with an ordinary man. We're dealing with a colored man, the product of a race that's been pushed around for a century or more, and is used to being told what to do, and resents it. You give someone like that power, the power to do the pushing, and he may not want to let go of one inch of it. He can ruin us."

Eaton was briefly preoccupied. At last he looked up. "You may be right. On the other hand, it is quite possible that his color, the history of his racial background, can work to our benefit. Based on what I know of his performance on Capitol Hill, he is a timid and uncertain man, a good listener, orthodox and agreeable in every way. Last night I asked Senator Selander to read me Dilman's voting record for this last session. He went along with T.C. and the Party on every piece of major legislation. I think that augurs well for all of us."

"Arthur, he wasn't President of the United States then."

"No, but now that he is, he may be more frightened and eager for our help than ever before. At least, I choose to think so. I cannot fire up enthusiasm for those extremist challenges and measures being proposed to void Dilman's Presidency or to hamper him if he legally remains our President. I see no reason to antagonize him, where there is no shred of evidence that he will be uncooperative. I believe we must make him see matters as T.C. saw them and would have acted upon them in the future. If we succeed, it'll be a certainty that we will

survive the rest of the term unscathed. And I think the
time to begin our guidance is right now, from this moment onward." He pointed to the sheet of paper in
Talley's hand. "Tell me what is on Dilman's agenda."

Still troubled, Talley sat on the edge of the sofa, and
consulted the scribblings on the sheet of paper he held
before him. "Let me see—umm—he signed the proclamation for T.C.'s funeral and the period of national
mourning last night, didn't he? Yes, I remember. Well,
now, he'll have to go over and meet the funeral plane
tomorrow."

"I wish Grover Illingsworth would take care of that,"
said Eaton. Then he added, "Anyway, let him make arrangements for the procession, the services in the White
House, and the funeral itself. He's the best Chief of
Protocol we've ever had, but he's even better at—at delicate affairs like this. I've already packed him off in
T.C.'s jet to bring Hesper back from Arizona."

Talley brought his head up sharply. "What about
Hesper? Should Dilman see her?"

Eaton did not reply at once. He thought of Hesper,
T.C.'s gracious wife, now a widow, with one fatherless
son, isolated in the summer home in Phoenix. He had
already spoken to her. She was taking it courageously,
as might be expected of a woman of her background.
Like his own Kay, she was Social Register and independently wealthy, but unlike his own Kay, she was
well-balanced and friendly. Passionately devoted to her
child, her numerous charities, she would survive her
loss well. "I don't know, Wayne," Eaton said. "Perhaps
Dilman should pay his respects to the First Lady, but I
think it would be uncomfortable for both of them. We
have a day or two. Let me think about it." He waved
his hand at Talley's notes. "Let's go on."

"He has to swear in the White House staff—"

"This afternoon."

"—and fill some sudden vacancies, mostly female secretaries, Southern."

"I see. Fine, Edna can begin screening applicants."

Talley went back to his notes. "Tim Flannery says the
press reports show considerable concern. The country's

had a bad jolt." He looked up. "Maybe it would allay everyone's fear if they could have a look at him, see that he's harmless. I thought we could prepare a short, rather self-effacing speech for him, and put him on the television networks—"

"No," said Eaton firmly. "Too soon. His appearance might inflame rather than soothe. Let's try to keep him out of sight for a while, let the country know that even under Dilman the government has not been disrupted, that business is going on as usual."

"What about letting him address a Joint Session of Congress? Truman did it after F.D.R.'s death."

"He did it over his colleagues' protests. No, Wayne, I don't like that either. I still say keep him close to his desk for a while, until everyone settles down."

"Well—"

"Arrange to have him lunch tomorrow with selected leaders of the Senate and House."

"Excellent," said Talley, making a note of it. "What about the Cabinet? Shall I summon all hands for a meeting today?"

Eaton shook his head. "Not today. Not tomorrow, either."

"Won't it look funny if he doesn't—"

Eaton licked his lower lip. "I do not want him running a Cabinet meeting until we've had a chance to brief him thoroughly. We've first got to inform Dilman of T.C.'s desires, wishes, plans. Then he will know how to handle himself." He sat up straight. "I'll tell you what to do, Wayne—beginning this afternoon, and during the next few days, have the various Cabinet members drop in on courtesy calls, but make sure none of them discusses business. As to Dilman, for his part he must request each one to remain in office and to serve him as each served T.C."

"What if he objects or has reservations?"

"He won't resist, Wayne. He doesn't know them, and he does need a knowledgeable Cabinet at once. He hasn't had time to consider anyone else. Oh yes, be sure to remind him that after F.D.R. died, Harry Truman did just this, asked each member of Roosevelt's Cabinet to stay on. And Lyndon Johnson did the same. Very well, what next?"

"At least a dozen ambassadors have applied this morning for appointments. Ambassador Rudenko wants to discuss resumption of the Roemer Conference——"

"I'll see him myself."

"Then the Ambassador from Baraza, Nnamdi Wamba, is most anxious——"

"I'll have Jed Stover stall him. I'm flying someone over to Baraza tomorrow to sit down with President Amboko. I want to do what T.C. was intending to do—pave the way for a settlement with the Russians by making the Africans ease up on their Communists in return for our ratifying the African Unity Pact. I want to feel Amboko out. When we are ready, we can tell Dilman how to behave with the Barazans."

"Then the Indian Ambassador and——"

"Limit them to courtesy calls, too. No official business until next week. Is that enough to keep Dilman occupied?"

Talley nodded. "Of course, but there's——"

The knocking on the door behind them made both of them turn. "Yes?" Talley called out.

The door opened and Edna Foster poked her head into the room. "Secretary Eaton, since it's personal, I thought, rather than buzz—there's a call from Miami Beach for you. It's Mrs. Eaton. Can you take it now?"

Eaton hesitated and then quickly said, "Yes, certainly. Thank you, Miss Foster."

"Line two, please," Edna said, and closed the door.

Eaton rose stiffly from the sofa and crossed to the telephone.

"Arthur, if you'd like to be alone——" Talley called after him.

"Stay where you are."

Eaton punched a plastic key on the telephone and brought the receiver to his ear. "Kay dear, how are you?"

He listened to her soprano mockery of his greeting. "'Kay dear, how are you?' Oh, my, somebody should hear you. They'd think you had just come off the tennis court. How do you do it, Arthur? How do you stand calm and collected in a massacre? I thought you'd be in the middle of a wake, at least, beating your breast and loaded to the gills over your poor T.C. Doesn't anything drive you to drink, Arthur?"

"You may succeed where others have failed, darling."

Her laughter rattled through the receiver, and then there was a pause, and she came on more soberly. "I heard it when we all drove back to the hotel before midnight. They broke in on the music, every station. Quite an uproar down here in Florida. And this morning, too. The colored waiter wouldn't even take a tip for breakfast. 'Got enuff for one day, ma'am,' he said. And the whites down in the lobby, glowering and complaining and nigger-hating all over the place. It's enough to scare you. Know anywhere to hide, Arthur? Or don't you run scared any more?"

"Not any more, Kay."

"That the best you can do, Arthur? You sound so restrained. Is there someone in the room with you?"

"Yes, there is."

"Well, that shouldn't inhibit the Eatons, should it, now? We're public property, we belong to all ages. Did you know Reb Blaser's column is syndicated? Indeed it is. I read about us right down here in the sand. I hear the Eatons are heading for the divorce court. Should I believe everything I read?"

"Cut it out, Kay. He was gunning for bigger game in that column."

"I should think there's no bigger game than you personally right now, my dear one. What's the saying— ah—you're a heartbeat away from the Presidency, I read."

"I haven't had time to think about it."

"Well, I have, Arthur. I have nothing but time these days. I could hardly fall asleep last night speculating about it. I kept thinking how close it had been. What if that Negro—whatever his name is—had been with T.C. and MacPherson in Frankfurt? Why, you'd be the President and I'd be the First Lady. Now, you couldn't divorce a First Lady, could you? Could you, Arthur? Has it ever been done?"

At last her chiding anger had penetrated his control. "Kay, stop it. I'm busy right now. We can——"

Her voice was suddenly serious. "Arthur, do you want me to come home now? If you need me——"

He thought how much he had needed her how many times in the past, but now he needed only peace of mind. He had a desire to tell her so, but he was aware that Talley was in the room, and he restrained himself. "Finish your vacation, Kay. That would be best for both of us."

"Drop dead," she said calmly, and hung up.

He was left with the receiver still uplifted, without the chance to say good-bye, always an embarrassment when others were in the room. He made a lame pretense. "Be well, Kay," he said into the dead phone, and he returned the receiver to its place.

He observed that Talley was too busily occupied making notes on that crowded single sheet of paper. He was sure that Talley had guessed what had gone on between Kay and himself, and he was even more resentful of Kay for baiting him when she knew he was not alone.

Remaining near the telephone, Eaton inquired, "What about the rest of Dilman's agenda?"

"Oh," Talley said, sitting erect, as if he had been deeply absorbed in work and unaware that the telephone call had ended. Quickly he began to announce what was left for Dilman to do. "He'll have to reply to a ton of foreign dispatches from heads of state. Maybe something short and sweet, to instill confidence in them. Perhaps a longer cable in response to Premier Kasatkin. I think Tim Flannery and the two of us should get to work immediately helping Dilman draft a dignified, somewhat ambiguous statement to the press telling them that he enters the office with a sense of responsibility to T.C. and to the American people who voted T.C. into office, and that the ship of state is still T.C.'s ship, and he is only temporarily at the helm, but will do his best——"

"Good," said Eaton. "Inform Dilman and Flannery we'll meet at three today."

"Next on the schedule——"

The telephone beside Eaton rang out. He picked it up, praying that it was not Kay again. It proved to be Edna Foster from across the hall. She reported that Congressman Zeke Miller and one of his assistants were in the press lobby. Miller had said that it was imperative that he see both Eaton and Talley. He had promised not to take up more than a few minutes.

"What should I say to him?" Edna Foster asked.

"Tell him we're crowded for time, but—" He weighed the necessity of seeing Congressman Miller, whom he found gauche and distasteful, but then he realized that if he were to act as T.C. acted, he would have to be a politician as well as a diplomat. "Very well, Miss Foster, send him in."

He moved toward the corridor door.

"Who is it?" Talley inquired.

"Zeke Miller wants to see us for a few minutes. I suppose we have to."

"Absolutely," said Talley. "He packs a lot of power, especially right now."

Eaton opened the door, noticing that the "In Use" sign still hung from its peg, and then, as if on cue, Representative Zeke Miller, thin briefcase tucked under his arm, charged into the Fish Room, shaking hands with Eaton, and with Talley, who had come to his feet. Then Miller introduced the gangling young man with thick spectacles and flabby lips and overloaded brown briefcase, who had followed him inside, as one Casper Wine.

Zeke Miller circled the Fish Room, hot with perspiration, and imperiously ordered his assistant to a chair. "Sit down over there, Casper." Then he said to Eaton, "Casper Wine is the goldarn smartest young constitutional lawyer on the Hill. Does a lot of homework for those of us on the House Judiciary Committee."

Miller swung away, yanking a blue handkerchief from his hip pocket. He brought it to his nose, honked into it, and then, balling up the handkerchief, wiped the perspiration from his forehead, face, and neck. Eaton watched Miller's activity, these nervous gyrations, with growing distaste. On those occasions when he had been thrown together with Miller, he had always left feeling

that he would have been more comfortable with a pit
viper. For one thing, Eaton found the Southern Congressman's appearance repulsive. Not that Miller was
technically ugly, Eaton conceded, but his aspect was
that of the bigot incarnate. Miller was not quite short,
was wiry, and was perpetually in motion. There was
something meanly threatening about him, like a coiled
spring ready to tear loose, explode, and shred anyone
within range.

Miller was semibald, with a long, thin, veiny nose,
tiny gray eyes, and an almost lipless mouth that continually worked over discolored teeth. His small frame,
like his small mind, was tough and supple. His suits
were expensive but garish. Neither his father's textile
money nor his inheritance from his mother had given
him polish. His years away from the Deep South had
modified his Dixie accent which, it was said in the cloakrooms, he turned on at will during electioneering years.

When taking to the hustings down home, traveling the
red clay roads and magnolia groves, Zeke Miller re-
verted to being the complete "Southroner," and the voice
that twanged away like the plucked strings of a banjo
on the floor of the House became softer, rounder, as its
rich mellifluosness inveighed against the Communist-
African conspiracy "to undermine America by reducing
us to one mongrelized family, and thereby bringing on
the Biblical Armageddon which will wipe our Christian
government from the earth." America's hope, Miller
often said, was in containing the spread of the Black
Plague through strict segregation, and ultimately shipping off the carriers and spreaders of destruction to their
native Africa. In his infrequent cheerier moments of oratory, Miller was given to attributing his jokes to his
father's decrepit green parrot, or to revising suitable quotations from the Old Testament. He would not forget that
his grandpappy, Braxton Z. Miller, had owned slaves,
and they had been peaceable and grateful, and "the
Nigra's lot" had been the better for this paternal segregation. "As the Prophets have told us," Miller often liked
to say, " 'Thou shalt not plow with an ox and an ass
together.' "

Now Zeke Miller had finished drying himself, and was folding his handkerchief and returning it to his hip pocket. "I tell you," he muttered, "those reporters out there sure downright bugged me. Trying to make me out a Bilbo or worse. Anything for a story. They sure can be mighty rough boys."

"You should know, Zeke," Talley said cheerfully, "you own half of them."

"Aw, no, that's not true, Governor," Miller said. "The few newspapers my Dad and I control, they don't amount to a hill of beans." For the first time Miller became conscious of Eaton's stare. He half faced Eaton. "I've got too many more serious matters on my head than to bother about my newspapers. Just for the record, Mr. Secretary, I had no part in what that goldarn fool, Reb Blaser, put in our papers. It got me sore as could be, and I told Reb off good, and said if he picks on my friends once more with goldarn scandal rumors, I'll see that he winds up on one of those nigger newspapers. Just so there's no misunderstanding, Mr. Secretary, I've got nothing against you and your lady. I'm for you. I'm for all of T.C.'s team and everyone in our constitutional government. Fact is, I'm closer on your side than I've ever been before. No, sir, you've got my word, no more subverting rumors."

"You're protesting too much, Congressman," said Eaton, "and it's not necessary. I take your word it was a mistake. I accept your promise that it won't happen again. I've quite forgotten the whole incident. You're right, there are more important matters to contend with now."

Miller's mouth cracked into a smile, and his nicotine-stained teeth were revealed. "There's more important things on my mind, too. If you sit down, I'll be quick, I'll give you a report on what's been going on up on the Hill to save this poor country."

Eaton and Talley eased themselves down on the sofa, but Zeke Miller stayed on his feet, snapping open his briefcase, extracting a wad of clipped papers. "Know what this is?" he asked, holding up the papers while dropping his briefcase. "This is the American people joined and united in one voice of protest against the greatest humiliation and danger of our century—against having an ignorant nig possum politician dirtying the White House and shoving us around."

Eaton did not suppress his displeasure. He knew that Miller used the words "nigger" and "nig" when trumpeting for white votes in the South but, like most of his colleagues, he confined himself to Negro ("Nigra," his accent made it) in the public arena of the House. Now he had slipped back to "nigger," and this, Eaton decided, came from inner fury. "Congressman Miller," Eaton found himself saying, "President Dilman is not shoving anyone around. He hasn't had the time to do so, even if he had the desire."

"You wait, you just wait and see," Miller shot back. "Before you can turn around, you'll find yourself staring down at a nigger Cabinet, with every administrative aide and every ambassador a black jigaboo, and you can be sure he'll be hiring white men for his servants and white girls for his secretaries. That's what all of them have been waiting for."

Miller belched, strutted in a tight circle, and came to roost before Eaton and Talley once more. "For a minute, forget about the side issues. I'm worried sick about the big issues. See here in my hand, tallies of the telegrams that have come flooding in to Hankins and myself and the rest of us, and not all from the South, either. I'll leave them for you to read. Over two thousand telegrams since last night, demanding we keep that Dilman out of office and protect our country. Now, don't give me any cool racist and segregationist back talk, because this is bigger than that. Almost three years ago the people of this glorious country heard the issues and elected the man they wanted to represent them, and suddenly they find themselves saddled with someone they never wanted who plumb hates their guts. I call that legal crime. I tell you here and now, and I'm willing to shout it from the rooftops, if that Nigra Dilman is allowed to sit in T.C.'s chair, we're in for rebellion. Inside a month we'll be wading through blood from white and nigger bodies. Letting this stranger be foisted upon us disrupts our unity and progress, degrades us in the eyes of the world, and promises corruption and ruin."

He paused, his pinpoint eyes darting from Eaton to Talley, and then he hiccuped and went on. "I know what you're both thinking, or maybe I don't, but I'm no redneck, I tell you. I'm an educated, progressive legislator who wants what is right. Sure I was raised to believe that we have our place, and the niggers have their place, and that's the way Jehovah arranged it. But I'm a Party man, and always will be, so help me. When the Party had to bow to the Supreme Court and force us to give in to niggers, I went along. And that's what I'll still do. I eat with niggers, and ride with them, and let my youngsters enter the same school with them, because that's the law. Good enough. I've done everything with niggers, like it or not, but goldarn it, there's sure one thing I won't do—I won't let an African black man sit in the chair where General Washington sat, and try to rule me. Maybe if one day it was the wish of the electorate out there, black and white, I'd go along. If he was voted in by popular vote, I'd live with it. But the way it is now—no, never!"

Miller had the blue handkerchief out again, and angrily mopped his wet face.

Talley wrung his hands nervously. "Zeke, he was voted into the Senate—"

"By damn Northern Communists," interrupted Miller.

"Nevertheless, he was voted into the Senate, and the Senate voted him President pro tempore, and legally he was in the line of succession. I don't see what you can do about it."

"Aha!" exclaimed Miller. "That's why I brought Casper Wine over here. He knows the Constitution so thoroughly, he could've signed it with Hancock. A group of us who are concerned about what's happening to our country, who believe in justice, we met most of the night and this morning, and we brought Casper in with us, to find out what could be done before Dilman becomes President."

"He is already President," said Eaton calmly. "I saw him sworn in last night."

"Illegal procedure's what you saw," said Miller. "Casper and the rest of us have covered that point. There are plenty of loopholes in the Succession Act. We're fixing to have the whole thing nullified. We're getting up this preliminary challenge for the House Judiciary Committee. I'm here because I'm of the mind that you should be the first to know what we're doing, Mr. Secretary. After all, if we win, you're the one person directly affected. If we can disqualify Dilman, then you're the one to replace him, by special election, if necessary. We're only trying to make you President, Mr. Secretary."

"I should be grateful," said Eaton coldly, "but I am only interested in upholding the law."

Miller had spun away. "Casper, read them our findings."

Casper Wine was already tugging a massive legal brief out of his brown case.

Eaton shook his head. "We don't have time to hear a reading of any brief. President Dilman is on his way here, and there is a good deal of business to transact. . . . Mr. Wine, forget any reading. Tell us in your own words what you have in that appeal."

Casper Wine squinted despairingly through his convex spectacle lenses at Miller.

Miller shrugged, then said, "Okay, give it to them in a capsule, Casper."

The myopic constitutional attorney brought the legal brief up high, close to his eyes, until it all but obscured his face. Slowly he peeled the pages, reading to himself, and at last he lowered the brief to his lap. He began to speak in a hesitant falsetto, his magnified eyes not on Eaton or Talley but roaming his brief, the carpet, the shoes of his sponsor.

"It is difficult—uh—difficult to reduce our appeal to a few generalities without—uh—without reciting our researches into precedent, previous Acts—uh—Acts of Succession and constitutional history," he said. "I shall attempt to condense our case." His eyes closed behind his fat lenses, and then his eyes and his mouth opened. "If you will read the Constitution, you will see under Article II, Section 1, Paragraph 6, that should both the

President—uh—President and Vice-President die, then
Congress shall have the right to declare—I quote—'what
Officer shall then act as President' until 'a President
shall be elected.' Now then, Congress three times passed
bills clarifying—uh—clarifying the succession, and the
last bill in 1947 provided that the Speaker should be
next in line, the President pro tempore of the—uh—the
Senate after him, and the Secretary of State after him.
Under this bill of 1947, within the framework of the
Constitution, it is highly questionable if—uh—Dilman,
this Douglass Dilman, can be sworn in, that is, can become in actuality President of the United States. First,
the wording of the Constitution makes it clear—uh—
clear that the successor must be an 'Officer,' and the
weight of legal opinion is that Dilman as a Senator, and
the Speaker before him, and the—uh—the Secretary of
State after him are not technically officers at all. If Dilman is not an 'Officer,' how can he be eligible to become
President?"

Talley turned to Eaton. "That's a point, Arthur."

Eaton wrinkled his nose and shook his head. "Too
weak. I think it is doubtful if you can overturn an Act
of Succession on a minor semantic issue."

"We shall see," said Casper Wine. "But let us suppose
—uh—suppose you are found to be right, Mr. Secretary.
Next, we come to a stronger challenge. The Constitution
states plainly that the successor shall—uh—shall—and
I emphasize this—shall '*act* as President' until 'a President shall be elected.' In short, Senator Dilman may act
as President, in an honorary custodial sense as he acted
as chairman in the Senate, until a special election is held
across the country to give us a new and legal President
for four more years."

Once more, Eaton was shaking his head. "I don't see
that. In the recent past, eight Vice-Presidents succeeded
eight dead Presidents, and they did not act as Presidents,
they performed as Presidents."

"True, but they performed unconstitutionally," persisted Wine. "The first mistake was made when William
Harrison passed away in 1841. The Cabinet informed
and addressed his successor, John Tyler, as Vice-Presi-

dent of the United States, Acting President, which was correct. Tyler, wishing the power, honors, and title of full President, ignored—uh—ignored the Cabinet, and made himself full President and spoke—uh—spoke of his 'accession to the Presidency,' despite protests of many senators. Other successors merely followed his high-handed illegal custom. Almost all—uh—all of these successors have been challenged in the press. Harry Truman and Lyndon Johnson were so challenged. But nothing more happened."

Zeke Miller jumped into view, and stood over Eaton. "This time, Mr. Secretary, we're seeing to it something happens. We're abiding by our beloved Constitution. If Dilman is not an officer, he is not eligible for the Presidency. If he is an officer, then he is eligible to act as President only until we can have a special election in this country to vote for a legal President—hopefully, Mr. Secretary, yourself."

Eaton stood up. "Forget about me. I am not the issue."

"You are the issue," said Miller excitedly. "Six former Secretaries of State have become Presidents, but no President pro tempore of the Senate ever did. You are our best candidate."

"Congressman Miller," said Eaton wearily, "you can have no candidate for another year and five months, because you have a President. . . . Mr. Wine, I appreciate your legal briefing. I can have no part of it. I will not deter you or the Congressman from presenting your findings before the House Judiciary. I can only remark that I must serve President Dilman until I am told not to do so."

Congressman Zeke Miller began to grin. "Fair enough, fair enough. You let us carry the ball, and you stand by. Believe me, Mr. Secretary, you won't regret it." He sought his briefcase, and signaled Casper Wine to his feet. He paused before Talley. "I'm looking out for all of us, Governor. I am all-fired determined, by legal means which exist, to prevent that there Dilman from selling out our heritage to that parcel of black terrorists in the Turnerite gang and to those whining hymn singers in the Crispus Society and NAACP. You can tell Dilman he can play President for a couple days, but you better also tell him not to go to the expense of moving into the White House." He winked. "I like that old House, I like the color it is right now."

After Miller and Wine had gone, the clatter of their footsteps on the tile corridor quickly receding, the Fish Room was silent. Eaton and Talley did not look at one another. Eaton occupied himself inserting a cigarette into his silver holder and lighting it. When he had taken several puffs, he met Talley's gaze.

"I do not like that man, I do not like him at all," Eaton said.

"He's a nasty customer, no question. You'd think he'd know better. But I understand his kind. I've been through his state with T.C., and there are loads of Millers down there. When you've seen that, you can know how he feels about having Dilman in here."

"Wayne, you must believe me, I have nothing against Dilman because he is black. I simply have no prejudices about color."

"Neither have I," said Talley hastily.

Speaking more to himself than to Talley, Eaton went on. "I could never be on Miller's side or Hankins' side or anyone's for such a reason. In fact, I would feel an obligation to defend President Dilman against such attacks." He considered what he would say next. "I could find myself resisting Dilman, and being unwillingly thrown in with the Miller crowd, for only two reasons. If Dilman were, indeed, to perform as a Negro President instead of the President of the entire nation, if he were to show favoritism to men of his race to the detriment of the country as a whole, I would have to oppose him. And if he were to fall under the wrong influence, jettison T.C.'s program and T.C.'s team, I would have to fight him." Then he added, "I do not anticipate either of these problems arising."

"Well, up on the senior side of the Hill there's a little more concern, Arthur," said Talley. "Senator Hankins feels that the only way to preserve T.C.'s program is to preserve his Cabinet. They've been trying to figure out a way of curbing Dilman's power of removal."

"Yes, I guess I heard something of that last night."

"They're worried about Dilman moving in, feeling his oats after a bit, and then firing you and replacing you with a Negro friend or some white liberal who will toady to him. They're worried this would not only end T.C.'s program but weaken the rightful line of succession."

Eaton pursed his lips. "I believe that they are building straw men to knock down."

"They want to play it safe, Arthur. As long as you're around, they feel there is someone to oversee Dilman, make sure he speaks T.C.'s language and signs bills with T.C.'s pen. Then, too, they're all feeling a little fatalistic —with good reason—and they want to make sure that if anything happens to Dilman, you'll be around to succeed him, you and not someone, Negro or white, who does not represent the Party's platform."

"Yes, I see," said Eaton thoughtfully. "Whatever they do, they had better make sure it is within the limitations imposed by the Constitution."

"I'm curious to know exactly what they're up to," Talley said. "We know what Miller and his House boys are doing, but I keep wondering about Senator Hankins. I think I'll give him a ring." He started for the telephone, but hesitated when he reached it. "No, I don't think I want to talk to Hankins. That'll be Miller all over again." He snapped his fingers. "I know—" He lifted the receiver and dialed one digit. "Edna? This is Governor Talley. Be a good girl and hook me up with Senator Hoyt Watson. He's probably still at home. . . . Yes, I'll wait."

Across the room Arthur Eaton waited, too. When he heard Talley get his connection and begin to question Senator Watson, he ejected his cigarette butt from the holder and replaced it with a fresh cigarette. It was the first time in a decade, to his surprise, that he had found it necessary to chain-smoke.

CONCENTRATING on the postcard-sized screen of the miniature Swiss television set, which stood on the white Formica breakfast table between them, Sally Watson heard her father say, "One second, Governor Talley, hold it a second."

She glanced up from her coffee to find her father jabbing a finger at the television set. "Sally," he called to her over the din, "would you mind lowering it a trifle?"

"Of course not, Dad." She put down her coffee, reached out and turned down the volume.

"That's better, baby." Senator Hoyt Watson's long Percheron face had gone back to the mouthpiece from which he removed his hand. "Okay, Governor, would you repeat your question?"

As she picked up her coffee cup again, Sally Watson's attention returned to the television screen. The horrible newsreel film of the Frankfurt catastrophe had ended, and now the network was beginning to project a hastily prepared documentary biography to acquaint its viewers with President Douglass Dilman.

Fascinated, she watched the unreal scene in the Cabinet Room of the White House the night before, as Senator Dilman took the Presidential oath. Although she had seen Dilman a number of times in the corridors of the Old Senate Office Building and at Washington social affairs, she had never really been aware of him as an individual, she realized. In close-up on the television screen, he became a person, a very dark person, to be sure, but a man with neat wavy hair, kind eyes, and a habit of rubbing his upper lip with his lower one. Now the film took viewers back to Dilman's beginnings. There were scenes of a Midwestern city slum area, where Dilman had been born over fifty years ago, and still photographs of an unattractive infant in absurd lacy dresses, and then dull shots of school buildings, and Sally Watson's interest began to wane and her head began to throb.

She poured herself a third cup of black coffee, hoping her father would not see this, and she wondered at what point during the gruesome party last night she had switched from vodka to Scotch. She could not remember, except that she had made the change because the vodka had done nothing for her and she had wanted something that would make the evening bearable, especially with all that incessant and tiresome Grim Reaper chatter provoked by T.C.'s death. More and more, she knew, she was mixing her drinks at parties, determined to attain euphoria swiftly, and more and more often the hangovers were persisting late into the next day, when she was forced to rid herself of them with fresh drinks and new pills.

Drinking the third cup of black coffee, she tried to devote herself to the television screen. But now her father was replying to Talley, and since the sound volume on the set was low, it was superseded by her father's basso, so that his voice and the image on the screen blended and created utter confusion.

Because her father's voice was more alive than the pictures on the screen, and dominated them, she surrendered viewing for listening. Her father, a large, impressive, authoritative figure, with his trademark shock of white hair and his trademark black string tie in evidence, was drawling into the telephone.

"Certainly I'm not happy about the turn of events, Governor," he was saying, "and neither will my constituents be happy. I don't like to have truck with Hankins and Miller and their Ku Klux Klan adherents, but at the same time I must agree with them that the country is today faced with a crisis. I don't like having a Negro as Chief Executive any more than they do, but I don't like it for different reasons. I don't think the country is ready for a colored man as President, and I foresee endless strife. I don't think Dilman, the little I know of him, is up to the rigors of the office. He is adequately educated, modest, a good Party man, but I don't think he is cut out of Presidential cloth. He may blunder us into considerable grief, unless we hold a firm rein on him. However, this I can assure you, Governor, and you may repeat my words to the Secretary of State—I cannot in good conscience go along with Miller in attempting legal gymnastics to prevent him from holding an office allowed him by the Constitution. I will not subscribe to that. On the other hand, I believe that what Senator Hankins is proposing to do does make a certain amount of sense—"

He halted to listen to Talley, nodding his head slightly at whatever he was hearing.

Since her father was not speaking, and the audio part of the television set was merely an indistinct hum, Sally concentrated on her coffee, as if this concentration would help eliminate her hangover. If she had not drunk so much at the Leroy Poole affair last night, she might have been in better shape now and this might have been an absorbing morning. In twenty-six years she could not remember a morning that gave so much promise of excitement, of an exchange of tidings and rumor.

Sally Watson was a girl who thrived upon turmoil. It stimulated her and gave her empty days meaning. When there bloomed confusion, scandal, the possibility of adventure, she was enriched. She would not have known this about herself, except for three short and almost fruitless efforts at self-understanding and adjustment with three concerned psychoanalysts in the last eight years. She knew also that when life did not provide this stimulation, her days became devoid of meaning, and she sought to fill them with drugs and drink.

She despised this need in herself, this weakness, and envied other women who controlled their restlessness with husbands, children, or careers. She was tangibly marked by her failure. She could see the mark now, as she drank her coffee, the white line across her right wrist, a permanent reminder of the dreadful time when she had slashed her wrist in an effort to solve everything. That had been seven or eight years ago, after she had been dropped from Radcliffe for the marijuana party (Senator Watson had "arranged" to have her quietly withdrawn from the school), and after she had tried to work for the advertising agency in New York City (Senator Watson had "arranged" the job), and after she had eloped to Vermont with the Puerto Rican musician (Senator Watson had "arranged" to keep the marriage out of the papers, and have it annulled, and have the boy deported). That feeble effort at self-destruction had been one institution and three analysts ago, very long ago, but the scar reminded her of what was possible, and for this she blamed her father, although she loved him, really, and her mother, in Rome with that parasite second husband who was a count, whom she hated and admired, and her stepmother, whom she disliked only for being an intruder and a bore.

Yes, she told herself, this morning—with T.C. dead and a Negro in the Presidency—might have been a ball. As one who had nothing but affection for the idea of death, who equated it with peace, she felt no loss at T.C.'s extinction. In truth, she had not cared for T.C. because he had refused, despite her father's weighty intervention, to give her a job in the White House, and when she had mentioned it at the annual Congressional Dinner the President had given, he had teased her, and she had not been amused, only humiliated. So the events of the last day and night offered not loss but gain on the scales of adventure. A Negro President—my God, what must be going on around the city? If she had not had the damn hangover, she might have been on the phone at daybreak.

She had drained the cup of coffee, she realized, and her father was speaking once more. She tried not to listen to him but to herself, but his voice was too forceful to be ignored.

"All right, I'll explain it to you, Governor Talley," Senator Hoyt Watson was saying into the mouthpiece. "As you've remarked, the Senate has always reserved the right to approve of the President's Cabinet appointments. He makes his choice, and we consent. After that, he retains all removal powers. He cannot hire alone, but he can fire alone. You mentioned the Tenure of Office Act of 1867. Hankins has a complete rundown on that. It was vindictive. It was meant to give the Senate complete control of President Andrew Johnson. It was the one and only time the Senate tried to curb the President's removal powers. But it was known to be unconstitutional at the time, and, indeed, it was pronounced unconstitutional around sixty years later by the Supreme Court. Now, Hankins isn't falling into that trap, and neither of us wants any repetition of the past. Therefore, Hankins —what? What was that, Governor?"

He listened a few seconds, and apparently interrupted Talley.

"No, hold your horses, Governor. I repeat that if we do something, it has to be under the law of the land. Now, Hankins hasn't worked the wording out yet—I think we'll have that in a day or two—but it is his intent to submit a revised—or new—succession bill at once. The idea would be that if this kind of tragedy ever took place again, the successor to the Presidency would merely act as a caretaker, a temporary Acting President, until the Electoral College could be reconvened and a full-time President and Vice-President be elected to finish out the unexpired term. As for our present situation, Hankins wants—and I think I subscribe to this—a retroactive clause stating that in order to preserve the present succession to the Presidency, as set up in 1947, so that this can't be tampered with politically, those next in line to the office cannot be removed without a two-thirds consent vote of the Senate. In short, Secretary of State Eaton could not be removed, fired, willy-nilly. Neither could Secretary of the Treasury Moody or Attorney General Kemmler, the next two in line, be removed without our approval. I think—"

Abruptly he halted, his white-maned head cocked sideways, and then he resumed.

"No, I don't know if it is constitutional. But it can serve us until it is tested. I haven't the vaguest idea if Dilman would sign it or veto it—I don't know that man at all, Governor, no one does—but if he has good faith, I think he will see the reasonableness and come along. I think this bill can be moved through to his desk quietly, without too much ballyhoo and fuss. I'm the last one to want it to appear that we are trying to manacle Dilman because of his race. As a matter of fact, Governor, I am approaching this New Succession Bill of Hankins' not as something that may serve us only now, in this emergency, but as something that can serve us in the future, so that other successors cannot recklessly unseat their potential heirs and pack the Cabinet with persons of their own race or creed or party, or with incompetents who happen to be sycophants or relatives. In fact, I'm trot-

ting over to the Hill now to see if I can assist Hankins
with the language. I don't want it to be a vindictive
measure, but one that can be useful in the present and
future. What's that, Governor? Arthur Eaton wants to
say—all right, put him on."

With the second mention by her father of Secretary
of State Arthur Eaton's name, Sally Watson had become entirely alert and attentive. Now that her father
was listening to Eaton, she bent forward, hoping to hear
Eaton's seductive voice on the phone, but it was impossible to hear a thing at this distance across the table.

At last she shut off the television set, rose, and noiselessly began to gather the breakfast dishes from the table.
Normally, on maid's day off, she and her stepmother
did the dishes. But her stepmother had gone early to a
Daughters of the Confederacy breakfast, and Sally
lacked the patience to do this menial work by herself.

She emptied the leftovers into the garbage disposal,
and waited for her father to finish.

Senator Watson was speaking into the telephone. "I
concur, Arthur. I subscribe to everything you say. It will
be judicious. I shall lend my weight to that. I will keep
you closely informed. . . . Let me add, I don't seem to
have had time up to now to tell you how sorry I am
about the tragedy. I wasn't as close to T.C. as you, but
I respected him. It is a horrendous blow to the country.
Nevertheless, the realities of life. We live with them. Let's
do our best. . . . Good luck today, Arthur, good luck
to both of us."

From where she stood quietly at the sink behind him,
Sally watched her father put away the telephone, pull
free his napkin, wipe his mouth, and stand up. He appeared too self-absorbed to notice her. Yet she waited,
eager to speak to one who had just spoken to Arthur
Eaton.

"Dad—"

"Oh, hello, baby. I thought you were dressing. I've
got to rush off. I'm late already."

"Dad, I was listening to everything. It's all very dangerous, isn't it?"

He studied her for a moment. "Well, dangerous isn't

precisely the word. Nothing as ominous as that. Any new President creates certain problems for everyone, but a new one of Dilman's race, in times like this, well, the problems are definitely heightened."

Sally ran her fingers through her thick blond hair. "It gives me the chills to think how close Arthur Eaton came to being the President. Wouldn't that have been wonderful?"

Hoyt Watson disappeared into the next room a moment, and reappeared with his hat and birch cane. "Well," he said, "with Eaton we'd have had an easier time of it, no question. Good man, Eaton."

Sally was not satisfied. "Do you think Arthur Eaton could still become President?"

Thoughtfully Hoyt Watson tapped his cane on the kitchen linoleum. "Unlikely, Sally. If you understand what I was discussing with Talley, you know what is going on."

"I have an idea."

"Representative Miller likes to imagine that he is John C. Calhoun. It was Calhoun, you remember, who used to remark that it was false to believe that all men are born free and equal. The assumption, he used to say, was based upon facts contrary to universal observation. Well, now, time has passed Calhoun by, and the time and the law say all men are free and equal, no matter what the realities. In short, no matter how nostalgic I may be for the past, I've founded my entire career on progress and observing the law. Representative Zeke Miller thinks otherwise, and where once he might have had an overflow auditorium to applaud and support his sentiments, he will today find the auditorium only one-third filled. He wants to prevent Dilman from becoming President. He is acting out a dream of the past. He won't succeed in ousting Dilman simply because Dilman is black, and in getting Eaton elected because he is white. Dilman is our President, improbable as that is to conceive."

"What about the new law you were discussing?"

"Well, even if we get it, that won't change things very much, not in actuality. It will only prevent Dilman from discharging Eaton, Moody, Kemmler, the rest of T.C.'s Cabinet. Our idea is that we want this Cabinet so that Dilman is encouraged to follow T.C.'s ideas and the Party's wishes. Then, as a show of goodwill on our part, we've agreed not to elect either a new Speaker of the House or a President pro tempore of the Senate, so that no one precedes the succession line of T.C.'s Cabinet for the rest of the unexpired term. Instead, our House and Senate members will rotate the job of presiding on an alphabetical, weekly basis. That would be in the bill, too."

"If the law passes, it would make Arthur Eaton the President—I mean, should something happen to Dilman, wouldn't it?"

"Yes, of course," said Hoyt Watson. "But nothing's going to happen to Dilman. We've had all the accidents we're going to have, and Dilman is a young man, Arthur Eaton's age, and strong as a bull, I'm sure." Watson paused, and eyed his daughter keenly. "Why this sudden interest in politics, Sally? This is more than I've heard from you in a year. I'm gratified."

Sally moved toward her father, eased his hat from his hand, and placed it on his head. "I'm not interested in politics especially, Dad. I'm interested in Arthur Eaton. I have enormous admiration for him. I'd like to see him the First Man in the country—after you, of course."

Hoyt Watson chuckled. "You can forget about your father. He has everything he wants out of life. As to Eaton—" He looked down at her, and then he said, "Your interest in our Secretary of State wouldn't be personal, would it? I'm just remembering. I thought I saw you spending an inordinate amount of time with him at Allan Noyes's party."

"I think he's the most attractive man in Washington."

"His wife thinks so, too," Hoyt Watson said with a wink. He pecked Sally's cheek, turned to go, then halted. "Tell your mother I may be late for dinner. I'll try to call her later."

He was gone, leaving Sally with a flare of resentment at his having referred to her stepmother as her mother. But the irritation was quickly dispelled as she tried to recollect everything her father had said about Arthur Eaton and his position in government today.

After stacking the dishes on the side of the sink, she went to her vast cream-colored bedroom. She pulled the drapes open, to find the day halfheartedly sunny. She went to her double bed, a mess from the gyrations of her restless, drunken sleep, and quickly drew the blanket and quilt over it. She moved to her tall mirrored dressing table, pulled her long green housecoat around her, and sat on the bench to make up.

Her gaze fell on the framed color portrait of her taken two years ago, just after T.C.'s inauguration, when she had played the Southern belle in that silly satire at the Press Club. She examined the portrait with detachment. When Arthur Eaton looked at her, was this what he saw? Her blond hair was combed high and curling to one side, her frank, emerald eyes were what countless crude young men had called "bedroom eyes," her nose was small and agreeably tilted, the beauty mark at the left of the mouth accentuated her full crimson lips.

Of course, she reminded herself without swinging to the mirror, the portrait was two years old. It did not reveal the shadows under her eyes, born of twenty-four months of drinks and barbiturates. Nevertheless, she remained hypnotized by her color portrait. Her complexion was marvelous, milky white and flawless, then as now. Yet, it was not a usual pretty-Southern-girl face. There was something hidden behind it that was wild and pitiful, although its outer aspect was childish and moody. But interesting, she decided, interesting, and not too much of its attraction had been traded for the liquor and pills that she used to fight the insomnia and emotional self-hate of unlovely fornication. Then, too, there was more for Eaton that no portrait could reveal.

Impulsively, not bothering about the morning's make-up, she came to her feet, unfastened the housecoat, and threw it across the bench. She made her way to the center of the bedroom, and slowly paraded, as poised as one can be in lace brassière and clinging panties, before the high mirror. The ravages of inner imbalance had not marred any feature of her slender, lithe figure. Her breasts were high and large, her belly flat, her hips boyish, her thighs and legs long and nearly perfect.

Satisfied, she returned to the bench and, casting the housecoat aside, sat down to devote herself to her make-up and Arthur Eaton, lucky man. Merging memory with hope, she relived her short, happy life with Arthur Eaton, and almost miraculously her hangover evaporated.

She had always been conscious of him, at least in the two and more years he had been Secretary of State, conscious of his incredibly handsome face with its contained sensuality, and of his breeding and manners. But then, she had not thought about him too much, certainly no more than she had ever thought about a motion picture hero, because he had often had his wife, that immaculate, haughty icicle, Kay Varney Eaton, on his arm, and there was no real connection to be made with him.

But Sally was a receptacle for gossip, sought gossip, welcomed it, stored it, and among the tidbits of gossip that had come to her was one, from a reliable source, that Eaton and his wife had separated. This rumor had been given some credibility six weeks ago, four large parties ago, when she had found herself sitting next to him at the dinner party given by Secretary of Defense Carl Steinbrenner. Eaton had been alone. No Kay Varney Eaton anywhere. She had discovered him similarly unattached at Tim Flannery's crowded and raucous outdoor barbecue. And when the national Party chairman, Allan Noyes, had given his large cocktail and dinner affair during the hot spell, and many of the guests, including herself, had gone swimming in the pool late at night, she had been more certain than ever that Eaton had rid himself of that monstrous wife.

Finishing her eye makeup, she reexamined her relationship with Arthur Eaton. The first of their three public meetings, the Steinbrenner one, had been largely exploratory. She had perceived that Eaton had become conscious of her not only as an individual but as a glamorous and pretty girl. He had wanted to know about her, rather formally but persistently, and she had told him all that she believed he should know.

At the Flannery party he had come in sports coat and

slacks—gorgeous man—and she had been wearing the
open-necked jonquil silk blouse and yellow shantung
skirt, and been bare-legged and gay, and he had sought
her out, remembering things she had told him about herself, and then for the first time telling her something of
his own life and feelings.

The Noyes party had been the best. After most of the
guests had departed, he had been one of the few top-
level ones to remain. He had sat in a deck chair near
the pool, drinking brandy steadily, and his eyes had followed her from the cabaña to the pool. She had known
that in her tight white two-piece swimming suit she was
a feast for any male's eyes. Later, drying, she had sat
at his feet, joining him in the brandy, and when it was
very late and they were almost the last, she had realized
that her father had gone and that she must call a taxi.
Eaton had insisted upon driving her to Arlington.

She still remembered the drive. They had both been
drunk, or rather she had been drunk and he had been
high, and she had sat curled close to him and held one of
his hands when it was free from the wheel, and he had
covered hers firmly with his own. In the darkened street
before her house he had kept the motor idling, and then,
never taking his eyes from her face, he had turned off
the ignition.

"You are quite a young lady," he had said. "I don't
think I have ever met anyone quite like you before."

"I hope not. There's no one anywhere like me."

"I suppose you have a hundred young men to keep
you occupied."

"I could have. I don't. Not one." She waited, but he
was silent, troubled, and so she had helped him. "I have
no patience, any more, for immature children. I've had
all the young intellectual buzzards, dedicated patriots,
ex-collegians-on-the-rise I can stand. Too tiresome. If I
can't have what I want, I'll pass."

He had taken an eternity to say the next. "What do
you want, Sally?"

Despite her intoxicated state, she had maintained her
control. "Oh, I don't know. Someone like Mrs. Eaton's
husband."

"You're teasing an old man, Sally. Not fair."

"You're not old at all, and I'm not teasing one bit."

"I see . . . I must make a confession, too, Sally. I've found you more refreshing than anyone I've met in ages. I don't have much free time, except occasional evenings. Perhaps you would let me call you for dinner sometime."

Her heart had almost burst. "Anytime!" She had sat up in the front seat, gone across the wheel, taken his surprised face in one hand, and kissed him on the lips. "There," she had said. "Now I'm a fallen woman, and you can't abandon me. I'll be waiting for that dinner."

The morning after had been her best morning in years. But that entire day, and in the several days following, he had not called, and she had begun to believe that she had invested too much in his promise and her hope. Either he had been drunk and indiscreet, and had now sobered and forgotten the flirtation, or he had weighed it and decided that a married Cabinet officer could have nothing to do, no matter how innocent, with the neurotic half-his-age daughter of a senator. Then, in her misery and consequent drinking, Sally had decided that it was his wife who was to blame. Despite flimsy rumor, Kay Varney was his wife, and was coming home or was home already, and that was it, the fact of it, and good-bye rendezvous and good-bye dinner.

And then, the other evening or morning, she had forgotten which, she had read Reb Blaser's column. Arthur and Kay Eaton were—it was in black print, rumor or not, it was in print—separated, with divorce imminent. The effect upon her was like that of a half-dozen vodkas. She soared. She walked on air. She was ten miles high, and almost in orbit. Her prospects rose with her. The fact that Arthur Eaton had not yet telephoned her, as he had said he would, meant only that he was busy with man's work and not that he was confined by husbandhood.

In her exhilaration Sally had wanted to telephone him, chide him for not keeping his word, but her instinct restrained her from this aggressive act. Also, she had told herself, it would have been in poor taste, after that wonderful Reb Blaser story. Eaton would call. Of this she was more certain than ever. If he did not, they would meet soon, and this time she would make sure that he knew of her desire for him. Yesterday she had even begun to think about contriving accidental meetings, when the Frankfurt tragedy had broken over her. As the daughter of a senator, she knew what that meant. Arthur would be busy for a while, busier than ever.

She had completed her makeup and was content with the result. She went to her wardrobe to search out the proper dress for this first day of a new administration, a day that had brought her Arthur (since Reb Blaser's column, she had determinedly begun to regard him as *her* Arthur) to within a step of the Presidency. Holding out and rejecting dresses, she wondered how she could prove her love to Arthur Eaton. She could, of course, give herself wholly to him—not difficult—and let him be young once more and enjoy what he had certainly been deprived of by Kay Eaton. Still, such giving was too easy and rarely guaranteed endurance of a relationship. Mature men required much more. They wanted a woman interested in them, interested in their lives, their careers, a woman as concerned about them as they were concerned with themselves. At night a woman could resurrect a man's ego in bed. But day had more hours. Successful women, the great courtesans of France, for instance, the mistresses of the rulers, women like Madame de Pompadour, survived and remained on top because they were not only love partners but helpmates. How could she be a helpmate to a public figure already so successful, the foremost member of the President's Cabinet? How could she be of any use to a public figure who already possessed everything?

Just as she settled upon the simple blue Galletti suit and removed it from the hanger, something crossed her mind. She recalled her father's conversation with Talley, and her own conversation with her father. Evidently Arthur Eaton did not have everything, yet. Overnight his position in the Cabinet was insecure. At the same time, overnight, he was the next in line to the Presidency. Senator Hankins and her father were working to keep him in the Cabinet, and believed that they would succeed. Representative Miller was working to make him

President at once, but her father did not think this was possible. Clearly Arthur Eaton could use help. She wondered what help she could offer. If she were to come to know this Dilman, know him well, she might succeed, as a woman, where august councils failed. She might convince Dilman that Arthur Eaton was indispensable to him and to the country, that he must not only be retained as Secretary of State but must be given a heavy share of the Presidential powers. But she did not know Dilman, and it was hopeless, and then it occurred to her that she *felt* she knew Dilman, and then she remembered why.

It was because of last night's party, the one that had given her the hangover, the one young Harriet Post, a Senate secretary who was as crazy as herself, had taken her to, a boozing, literary party of the avant-garde Washington crowd, lower-level, black-and-white. A Negro poet, reedy and homosexual and maybe talented, had given it in his unkempt, sparsely furnished, barnlike upstairs flat, above the hall with the sign over it, JESUS NEVER FAILS, on Georgia Avenue.

There had been at least forty persons coming and going, most of them Negro, all drinkers, all too full of T.C.'s death, all discussing the implications of Speaker MacPherson's accession to the Presidency, and Sally had not enjoyed it particularly. Lately she had grasped at every invitation to a black-and-white party, because it was different, because it might mean a charge of excitement. Unlike her family, she had no feelings against Negroes. In fact, because of her sheltered upbringing in the South, she had always considered them attractive since they were forbidden and hence exotic, and because there were stories she had heard about the men. The stories were not true, she knew, from firsthand experimental evidence. After college, when she had met the jazz crowd from Harlem, she had slept with two of the colored boys in a band before running off with her Puerto Rican. Both brief affairs had been tiresome disappointments, no better, no worse than those with most of the white boys with whom she had slept. Perhaps she had expected too much. Perhaps the Negro musicians had not been able to give enough because they were inhibited by her Southern-supremacy origins.

The affair or wake last night had been a drunken bore. She had heard from Harriet about the guest of honor, Leroy Poole, and in fact thought that she had read some of his powerful essays on his years as a Negro in Harlem and on civil rights, and she had expected too much, again. Leroy Poole had looked like anything but an author. He had proved to be short, fat, perspiring, resembling nothing more than a jet-black eight ball. He had been supercilious and self-centered, too knowing and opinionated about everything and everyone in Washington and on the earth. He had repeated several choice anecdotes ridiculing MacPherson, who everyone had thought was the new Chief Executive.

Sally remembered that Poole had read aloud several passages from his second novel (still in the works, stream-of-consciousness), bitter narrative sections that made no sense and gave no fun when you were half drunk. After the applause he had explained the novel, and for a while his idea had held Sally's attention. It was hard to recall it clearly the morning after, but there was something about the near future in the United States, something about a sudden outbreak of bubonic plague in the heavily Negro-populated county of a state similar to South Carolina or Louisiana (where some counties are 80 per cent Negro), but where the minority whites keep control because of their ties to the outside world. Overnight, to prevent the raging epidemic from spreading, this county is quarantined from the rest of the state and nation. No one can enter or leave. After a few months this isolated county has a population 90 per cent black, and 10 per cent white, and must live this way for several years.

"There it is, see?" Leroy Poole had squeaked, waving the manuscript in his pudgy fist. "Shoe on the other foot, see? Now we are the Ins and they are the Outs. How come? 'Cause gradual-like, the Negroes begin dominating the voting, buying and spending, law enforcement, the works. And pretty soon Negroes are running government, schools, business. And the poor whites left, the minority, what happens to them? Well, now, don't you know? Negroes hire white women for their maids and white gents for their handymen. Now the whites go to the back of the bus, to the segregated lousy puking little white schools, and the Negroes got the run of the county. What do you say, friends, how's that for an acidy parable?" She could recollect little more of it, or perhaps Leroy Poole had refused to tell any more. She had thought it rather novel and cruel, and wondered if he would finish it, and if he did, how it would be received.

Now, dressing, she realized that, by coincidence, Leroy Poole's way-out fantasy of last night had—well, a small portion of it had—become a reality with Douglass Dilman's accession to the Presidency. Her mind, remembering Dilman, remembered last night when she had found herself on a torn sofa beside Leroy Poole, listening to him discuss Dilman.

It all came back to her, the connection, Poole and Dilman, not what Poole had been saying. A Negro publisher had given Poole a sizable advance against royalties to write a biography of Senator Douglass Dilman, since Dilman was one of the highest-ranking Negroes in government. Poole had not been enthusiastic, for some reason, but had needed the cash to finish his novel, and had undertaken the chore. He had come to Washington weeks ago, received Dilman's cooperation, and had been practically living with the Senator, gathering information on the Senator's background and political career and ideas, and had already begun writing the made-to-order book. She recalled a thread of Poole's conversation, to someone, to Harriet or herself. "I've gotten to know Senator Dilman better than he knows himself, I've been that close—but don't hold it against me, sister!" He had screamed with laughter, a disconcerting high-pitched laughter, and after that she had left Poole for the bottle of Scotch.

Suddenly the creative process began to work inside Sally. She could almost feel it working, and she ceased buttoning her blouse to let it happen. Poole had said that Dilman was a widower, with a son, no one else. That was last night when Dilman was a senator. This morning

he was the President of the United States, still a widower, with a son, and no one else. Who would run
his life for him, the social part, the feminine part? A
new President always made new appointments, hired
new personnel. Whom would Dilman hire for his First
Lady, his social secretary, his party giver? He might hold
over some of T.C.'s staff, and the First Lady's staff, but
there would still be openings that would have to be filled,
and there would certainly be resignations. Sally's mind
went to at least a half-dozen of her Southern girl
friends who would not, or whose husbands or families
would not let them, work under a Negro, President or no.

That was it, that was surely it, Sally exulted to herself. There would be an opening in the White House for
a white girl of high social breeding and with a political
background, to assist the new President, a girl who had
many Negro friends and so could, in a natural way, give
the President guidance in the world of white socialites
about him. There would be an opening which she could
fill, and in filling it give aid to that wonderful, kindly-
looking Negro who had become Chief Executive, and in
aiding him, gaining his dependence upon her, she could
represent Arthur Eaton inside the White House. She
could become Arthur's helpmate on the highest level.

Only one piece of the puzzle was missing, and once
that was in place the picture was there, made sense, and
her future was assured. The missing piece was the image
of the go-between who could get her offer of service to
the new President himself. And she had that, too. Last
night, last night, Leroy Poole, living with Dilman, writing
about Dilman, last night a senator's biographer, this
morning a President's historian.

Her mind fitted the last piece into the puzzle, and the
picture that she saw and embraced was that of herself
and Arthur, captioned by the lettering of her imagination: Secretary of State Arthur Eaton and Mrs. Sally
Watson Eaton.

She ran to the cream-colored French telephone beside
her bed, and then, as her hand clutched it, she tried desperately to remember the hotel where Leroy Poole was
staying. Not the Shoreham, not the Mayflower, not the

Hilton or Willard, no. What would that poor, struggling, fat little Negro writer be doing in one of those expensive big places? She eliminated the big hotels. She tried to think. It was some cheap hovel, ridiculously named, in the heart of town. She had heard it mentioned several times last night. It was on—yes, on F Street—heavens, but where—heavens—yes! That was it—Paradise—the Paradise Hotel on F Street.

She picked up the telephone and dialed for information . . .

The instant after the alarm clock went off, Leroy Poole opened his eyes, reached out and shut off the bell, flung aside his blanket, then settled back on the pillow and, lying perfectly still, began his daily morning exercise.

For five minutes, he performed this Spartan drill, a system of valuable and mystic calisthenics of his own invention, one known only to himself. As he engaged in it, he knew that his daily ritual would have astounded an outsider, especially a white outsider. Where most men did vigorous bends, push-ups, sit-ups to strengthen their muscles, to give tone to their physiques, Leroy Poole practiced an exercise consisting solely of remaining immobile on his bed, first contemplating his gross body, then conjuring up his gross past.

Once, wondering if this physical inactivity could be rightly regarded as exercise at all, Leroy Poole had looked up the word in Webster's Dictionary. *Exercise* was, among other things, "Exertion for the sake of training or improvement, whether physical, intellectual or moral." Pleased with the definition, he had continued to practice his peculiar form of exercise under its familiar name.

Leroy Poole's morning exercise followed an unvarying routine. After awakening, and removing his blanket, he set his eyes on the mound of flesh before him, gazing at the flabby chest and jelly protrusion of stomach encased in capacious cotton pajamas. Sometimes he studied his hands, the fatness of the sausage fingers. He was not concerned with this obesity of the flesh, the distorted plasticity of it, for he had been told that it was the result of glands, not gluttony. Instead he was concerned that the outer softness so unfairly contradicted the inner hardness, making it more difficult for others, and himself as well, to take his aggressive word sermons and crusading pen seriously.

Since no physical exertion could reduce his body to the same hardness as that of his mind and heart, Leroy Poole compensated for this by toiling daily to invigorate and fortify what lay invisible beneath his skull and skin. Like Richard Wright, a boyhood idol, Leroy Poole had learned long ago that "there existed men against whom I was powerless, men who could violate my life at will," and that their savage and unjust superiority must be combated, even unto death. He had to toughen his will against white men's bribes: no money, no comfort, no intellectual rationalizing, no compromise promises of future Green Pastures, no white token acceptance and approval could be permitted to negate the searing helplessness and humiliation that he and his family had suffered, were suffering, or allowed to modify and weaken the determination in his mind and heart. These were the muscles—the inner muscles of righteous hate—that Leroy Poole sought to energize and sustain every morning. The exercise performed was a simple one: he remembered his past, and was strong again.

It was not always easy. It had not been easy this morning. Last night's party had left him weakened, and a residue of this weakness remained. It had not been the drinks. He did not drink. His abstinence he owed less to the hellfire Baptist upbringing of his childhood than to the fact that drinks made black men as foolish as white men, but while white men could afford such lapses, black men could not. The weakness that carried over from the party was caused by the fact that he had been induced to read aloud a passage from his new novel, and relate some of the story, and he had been applauded and been made prideful and been lulled into believing, briefly, that life might not be so bad after all.

That was one impediment to his exercise this morning.

Another was that he despised the work he must do in
the next hours, days, weeks. He resented having to abandon his polemics, his angry and effective articles and
essays on his experiences as a Negro and on his ideas
about equality, for which he was poorly paid, to undertake a hack political biography that would profit him
nothing but money. He resented, too, delaying his great
novel, a moral earthquake that would shake the mossbacks and crackers of the South and the pretentious tol-
erators of the North from their fixed poles of prejudice.
He resented delaying it in order to feed the vanity of
stupid and ignorant Negro readers who wanted to enjoy
vicariously the rise to Congress of one of their own color.

And there was more that distressed him after the alarm
clock had jarred him from his sleep. He was ashamed
of himself for the small corruption of making heroic, to
his people, an undeserving ward heeler who, through
servility and errand-running and ass-licking, had become
a senator. If only he was presenting to his people the
figure of a brave and true Negro leader like Jeff Hurley,
his beloved friend, his superior in the Turnerites, it would
be a worthwhile and noble endeavor. But then, he knew,
the Hurleys did not become congressmen in the paleface
world. Only the handful of Dilmans could make it, because they were puking counterfeit whites. It distressed
Leroy Poole that he must spend this precious day typing
up notes of his last meeting with Dilman, preparing
questions for the next interview, and then spend several
months more writing the crummy, phony biography.

If he could not do his own work, he told himself upon
awakening, then at the very least he should be at the
barricades, where the action was, where the freedom
fight would finally be won, just the way the whites had
won their fight at Concord and Bunker Hill. He was miserable about the Turnerite fiasco in Hattiesburg, Mississippi, yesterday. He had known for some time, having
learned about it from Hurley, that the first step in the
new program was planned for yesterday afternoon. He
had not known the result until last night. His mind went
back to last night.

Because he had been offered a ride, and had research

to do, he left the party early, over much protestation. The streets were curiously desolate, but then he supposed this was because T.C. had been killed and everyone was at home or in bars glued to television sets. There had been some talk between his driver, a Howard University boy, and himself about the President's demise and what it might mean to their cause, and they agreed it meant nothing at all. Since the time Theodore Roosevelt had invited Booker T. Washington to the White House, no white President had proved any better than another for them. It was not yet ten o'clock when Leroy Poole was deposited before the small, three-story hotel, rising between an alley and a grocery store, its broken red neon sign shining out: PARADISE HOTEL.

He entered the minuscule lobby, with its spotted rug and seven threadbare chairs, and waddled to the reception desk. No one was there. Peering off, he saw the pimply young clerk at a table in the office, head in his arms, snoring softly. Leroy Poole went behind the desk, pulled down his key, and then walked toward the rickety self-service elevator. He paused at the newspaper rack, to buy the late edition, but the rack was empty. Disappointed because he had anticipated seeing the space the Mississippi demonstration received, he considered going out in search of a newspaper. At that moment he sighted one newspaper folded on a chair. It proved to be a discarded early evening edition, and the headlines proclaimed T.C.'s death and Speaker MacPherson's succession to the Presidency.

Leroy Poole took the newspaper up to his second-floor room, and once he had bolted his door, he sought the results of the Turnerite demonstration in Hattiesburg. As page after page made no report of it, he began to believe that the newspaper had been printed too early to carry the news. And then, on page eighteen, he found it.

The wire service story was brief: To counteract the terror of the revived Ku Klux Klan in Mississippi, a Negro activist group, the Turnerites, had sent twelve members, wearing black hoods and robes, to picket a department store owned by the local Klan's Grand Dragon; the white proprietor had rushed out, unmasked one Turnerite picket, and thrown sulphuric acid in his face, permanently blinding him; the Negroes had gone berserk, beating the white Klan leader, smashing his store windows and damaging most of the showcases inside; the armed police and their dogs had come, and two of the Turnerites were in the county hospital, critically injured, and the other ten were in jail.

The news report infuriated Leroy Poole in two ways. First, it related that the Turnerites had retaliated for Klan violence with peaceful if dramatic picketing, and, as always, had been brutally attacked; and second, this horrible story, deserving of a page-one notice which might inspire national revulsion and action, had been buried on a back page because, unluckily, the President of the United States had died.

This defeat, as well as all his other frustrations and disappointments, had again filled his head, the instant the alarm jangled this morning. It would not be easy to undertake his daily exercise, and for seconds he considered skipping the exercise this once, but then he knew that he must not permit himself any inner flabbiness.

After that, he began his calisthenics.

Alabama. State flower: camellia. State tree: Southern pine. Motto: We Dare Defend Our Rights. Whose rights, you bastards? Father, a cotton picker, old, old at forty, dead at forty-one of malnutrition, pneumonia, fright. Mom, maid, cook, laundress, slavey ("Look, old lady, we know that lying nigger talk of yours, so if you're too sick to come to work, you stay sick and stay home for good"). Older sister, prostitute for peckerwoods, not even mossbacks, but red-neck peckerwoods, the gutless bitch. Older brother, high I.Q., a shoeshine entrepreneur. His favorite cousin, grave outside Mobile. Almost a teacher. Walking in the woods with an educated white girl. Seen. Next day, six grabbed him, putting a blowtorch in his face. Leroy, Mom's hope, youngest, running scared, hiding scared, hungry. Jewed by the hunchback, kicked and stoned by the squat red-necks, stealing once, twice, three times, wanting books, wanting everything, having nothing, but shoved, spat upon, threatened, cursed at, slapped, scared, always scared.

Pennsylvania. State flower: mountain laurel. State tree: hemlock. State motto: Virtue, Liberty, and Independence. Job in a trucking firm. Bullied and underpaid. No friends. No service in restaurants. No rooms in rooming houses. No nothing. Only freedom to read and read and read. College. Himself lonely, isolated, freakish. Scared, writing good English papers, amusing one white girl. She curious. Some meetings to talk literature. Discovered. Boy friends "protecting" her. Behind the gym at night. Holding him down, pulling off his pants, shorts, brandishing knives, then laughing ("Not enough to cut off, black boy, but keep it buttoned or you'll lose it"). Humiliated, scared, quitting. North worse than South, because of pretense. North worse, because no place else to go.

New York City. New York Harlem. Flower: none. Tree: none. Motto: Don't Want Your Daughter, Mister, Just Want Half Her Freedom. Black ghetto Harlem. Squalid, stinking, poverty, danger. Knives, booze, heroin, hot goods. Fleabags and tenements, and dinner out of garbage cans. Listening to New York voices, white: They're illiterate, they're shiftless, they're not dependable, they're criminals, they're best in their place. Listening to Harlem voices, black voices: They sure is mean folk, they smells more than us, they is gougin' crooks, they scared of us more than us of them, they no good never. Talk a waste. Learning, improving, escaping, all that counts. Reading books still free. Finding writer's magazine in library, finding writing is paid for. Writing, writing, writing, first writing foolish white writing for money, can't sell, then writing the Leroy way about what's inside, crude, true, and the small magazine saying come over, and the Jew editor, a good Jew, saying you write, we'll buy. Writing, writing, writing, and never stopping until his people make the scene, the American scene, but all of it still too slow. Need to cry out, to protest. Need to talk to someone, Mom too far, too scared. Joining everything. NAACP. Too slow. Crispus Society. Too slow. New thing, Turnerites, doers, not scared. Better. Much better. Mister, what's wrong with me marrying your daughter? What's so special about her? And, mister, who in the hell are you that's in any way better than me?

As this exercising went on, strength growing through hot memory of oppression, Leroy Poole began to feel invigorated and purposeful. He decided that he would do one more minute of it before rising. His mind returned to the South, to personal offenses, to recollections of being shoved off the street, hustled to the rear of a bus, to degradations that he had witnessed, to recollections of his cousin being turned away from the polling place, his best friend being hooted away from the white high school. His mind did these push-ups, sit-ups, bends; his mind shadowboxed and ran a mile, until the blood throbbed in his temples, and his breathing came in gasps, and the rage coursed through his blood to quicken his heart and his determination never to relent.

It was the ringing of the telephone that stopped his exercise.

Satisfied with his preparation for the day, he shoved himself off the bed, hitched up his pajamas, and on bare feet hastened to the chipped telephone next to the armchair. Sitting, taking up the phone, he hoped that it would be Jeff Hurley, with a full report of the Mississippi trouble, and anxious to enlist Leroy Poole's advice as a member of the Turnerite strategy board.

"Yeh, hello?"

"Oh, hello there. I hope I have the right room. Is this Leroy Pool, the writer?" The voice from the other end surprised him, for it came from a female, unmistakably from a refined Southern female.

"That's right. This is Leroy Poole."

"I hope I'm not interrupting your work, Mr. Poole. This is Sally Watson. Remember me?"

The name reminded him of no lady of his acquaintance. This did not surprise him. There were not many. However, occasionally club-women called, to request him to lecture or sit in on a civil rights panel. "I'm not sure, ma'am. The name is familiar."

"Last night," she was saying, somewhat distraughtly. "We met last night at the party for you. I was there with a friend. I'm Senator Hoyt Watson's daughter—"

He placed her now. The well-shaped, edgy blonde.

"Of course," he said, "of course. How could anyone forget you?" He swallowed, restrained himself, not yet prepared to go on in this vein with a white girl, not while the remembrance of his cousin's grave outside Mobile and his own humiliation behind the college gym were alive within him. "I enjoyed the pleasure of meeting you, Miss Watson."

"And I enjoyed hearing you read from your new novel. I think it's wonderful."

Wonderful, he thought, a savage novel in which whites were reduced to a ten-per-cent minority in one imagined American county. "I'm glad you were open-minded enough to like it," he said.

"Don't let my accent or my father's voting record fool you," she said. "I'm quite my own person, and I count at least fifty Negroes among my good friends." She paused, and then she said, "You must be very excited about the news this morning."

"What news?" he asked.

"The new President, I mean."

"Oh, that. I read all about it last night. I don't think there's anything especially exciting about MacPherson becoming President. He—"

"MacPherson?" She almost screamed the name through the telephone. "You mean you don't know?"

He was utterly bewildered. "Know what? I just woke up, and I—"

"MacPherson died, too. One of your own people was sworn in as President last night. Your friend Douglass Dilman."

The news vibrated in his ear. He sat thunderstruck, speechless and uncomprehending.

"Mr. Poole, are you there?"

"I—yes—I—are you sure? I can't believe it."

"It's the truth. It's all over the place. Everyone's talking about it. Well, I'm glad I could bring you the news—"

"Miss Watson, you've knocked me out. I'd better turn on my radio and find out what's been going on. I sure appreciate your—"

"Mr. Poole," she called to him urgently, "I really

phoned about something else. I wanted to discuss a personal matter—"

"Look, jingle me back in ten minutes, will you? I'll be right here. Thanks, Miss Watson."

He slammed the receiver down, almost certain that he was having his leg pulled, jumped up, and found his tiny red transistor radio. As he switched it on, he became positive that she had been teasing him. How in the devil could a rabbit-hearted twerp like Dilman become President of the United States? He was only a second-rate senator, and a Negro besides. That dizzy, sick dame, with her sadistic Southern joke, damn her.

The volume on the transistor radio was turned high, and the pontifical voice of a network editorial philosopher engulfed him. He listened, incredulous, and then began spinning the selector to other stations. There were news broadcasts. There were interpretive analysts. There were discussion panels. There were taped reports from the man on the street. There were faded reports from London, Paris, Moscow, Rome, Tokyo. Miss Watson was right. It was true. His boy Dilman was the Chief Executive of America the Beautiful. Lor' Mighty! I'll be John Browned!

He listened for five minutes, until he had the facts and they had sunk in, and then he turned the radio off. He wheezed about the room in his baggy pajamas, trying to sort it out, convert it into a facsimile of reality. Once he interrupted his walking, thinking, to ring the desk downstairs and ask the clerk to send the handyman next door for a carton of coffee and a doughnut, overcoming resistance with the promise of an extravagant half-dollar tip.

He resumed his heavy pacing, which finally led him into the closet-sized bathroom. By the time he had finished his quick shaving, nicking himself twice, his washing, and had changed into sweat shirt, corduroys, and moccasins, his mind had moved from the enormity of the news and narrowed down to himself. What did this upheaval mean to Leroy Poole?

His weeks of intimate conversation with Dilman made it clearly evident that the Senator, now President, was a loner. Whenever Poole had begged for relatives or friends whom he might consult for more objective information, Dilman had turned him aside. "I have almost no one close to me," he had said. Eventually Poole had extracted several names: Dilman's son, Julian, at Trafford University; Dilman's maiden aunt, Beatrice, in Los Angeles; Dilman's old sponsor and still political boss in his home state, the union leader, Slim Dubowsky; Dilman's tenant, the Reverend Paul Spinger; Dilman's acquaintance, the national chairman of the Party, Allan Noyes; Dilman's good friend in the Second World War, the liberal trial attorney, Nathan Abrahams, in Chicago. "That's about it, Leroy," Dilman had said on that occasion. "Fact is, except maybe for Nat Abrahams, you yourself know me as well as, maybe better than, any of them."

Of this list of friends, Poole now saw, he himself was one of the three who were in Washington, near at hand, ready with friendship and counsel. In short, his association with Dilman could be turned to profit, now that Dilman was the head of the country.

First off, the hack biography, since its subject was on all lips, would not be just another book that sold three thousand copies, but would be an intimate, inside look at a new President that might sell a hundred thousand copies. It could make Leroy Poole wealthy and give substance to his by-line. Second, and more important, far more important, there was his relationship with the President; their scheduled meetings in the coming weeks would give Leroy Poole access to the ear of the most powerful figure in the United States.

Dilman, as Leroy Poole saw him, was a weak and tentative public servant, who had spent so many years mouthing the Party's pronouncements that he had become a mere ventriloquist's dummy for his white superiors. He was unoriginal, without a single dynamic or progressive idea or program of his own. His head was a receptacle of platitudes and ayes. But it was a head, and it could be filled with ideas by one near enough to him. The possibility excited Poole. With real effort he might make Dilman swallow, digest, and regurgitate the Tur-

nerite demands for full equality now. And even more
might be accomplished. Great Negroes—forceful ones,
brilliant ones, like Jeff Hurley—might be appointed to
high and key government offices, possible, possible, provided there was one at Dilman's arm to guide him in the
right direction, even push him ahead.

Leroy Poole left the bathroom to answer the knock at
the door with the conviction that fate had made his own
future role unique. At last, as never before, in a way
more effective than his essays and books, or his work on
the Turnerite board, he could help promote his people
to their rightful place.

He accepted the carton of tepid coffee, learning the
cream and sugar were already in it, and the crushed
doughnut, and reluctantly handed out a quarter and a
half dollar for the breakfast and tip. After closing the
door, he felt less worried about his extravagance. He was
way up there now, potentially rich, potentially the savior
of his people.

Then, gradually, as he squatted on the armchair to
drink his coffee and munch the tasteless doughnut, the
conviction that he might serve himself and every Negro
through Dilman became fainter. Dilman, no matter what
had happened, was still no more than the man Poole had
come to know and despise. Dilman was as scared of
whites as Poole himself had once been. Dilman had never
once tried to break out of the servile, bowing, watermelon world of the Uncle Toms and Aunt Jemimas. He
was a figurehead fink, using his color in a state where
it mattered, to gain office, rejecting his color in the gentleman's Chamber of the Senate, where it mattered more.
How could a person who trembled so constantly even
hold onto a new idea? How could a person always back-
ing away from responsibility be reached?

In fact, Old Chub the Rabbit-Hearted might even re-
nege on the biography now, Poole realized with a shud-
der. In the last minutes, the biography had become as
valuable to Leroy Poole as a First Folio Shakespeare.
As an obscure senator, Dilman had been afraid of the
biography, recoiling from any attention. It had taken the
intervention of the foremost Negro publisher in America,

and pressure from several Negro leaders, including Spinger, to convince Dilman that a short, innocuous, political biography would be more useful to him than harmful.

Immediately after Poole had arrived in Washington, he had found Dilman reserved and tongue-tied about discussing his personal life. Cleverly Poole led the Senator into discussions of his public career. Since the facts had been published, Dilman had proved easier, more amiable, more talkative. Recently Poole had led him back to his private life, and Dilman, at last conditioned to these interviews, more trusting of his interrogator (who had not told him of his connection with the Turnerites), had been more helpful, but still not frank and open. If Dilman had been so timorous before, Poole wondered, how would he be now, when his every word might be examined by a suspicious or hostile citizenry? Would he call Leroy Poole in and tell him that the project was finished? Or would he simply evade Poole, postpone interviews, and allow the project to languish and die?

Leroy Poole put aside his coffee container, wiped the crumbs from his mouth as he brought the telephone to it, and put in a call for Dilman's secretary, Diane Fuller, in the Old Senate Office Building. Told that her line was busy, Poole waited. Presently he heard her harassed voice, her speech ungrammatical as it was whenever she was under tension. Poole had always been flattering to the scrawny, nervous colored girl, because he had long ago learned that personal secretaries were important, sometimes alter egos, and even if Diane did not measure up, it paid to play it safe. As ever, Poole greeted her effusively, and congratulated her on the elevation of her boss.

"Oh, what a day," she groaned. "Everybody's callin', and it ain't—isn't—no fun. I don't know what's goin' on here, Leroy."

"Then I won't keep you, honey chile," Leroy Poole said sympathetically. "I just want to know where I stand. I have an appointment with him day after tomorrow, around two in the afternoon. He was going to give me a full hour. But now that he's moved from the Senate to

the White House, I want to be sure the date's still good
and to know where to come. Has he had time to mention it?"

"Leroy, so much is happening, *I* haven't even seen
him yet. Got to talk to him once on the phone, no more.
I don't know where he is or what he plans. I have your
date on the calendar. First chance I get today or tomorrow, I'll remind him."

"That's my sweetie pie. And look, I want to be reasonable. The poor guy's been hit on the head with a
country. If he's crowded day after tomorrow, you tell
him I can wait. But try to get a firm appointment out
of him for this week, even if it's a shorter time."

"Sure thing, Leroy. I'll call you . . . whoa, there's
three other phones. Good-bye."

Leroy Poole sat back deeper in the chair, still holding
the telephone in his lap. Of course, he had almost enough
material to do the biography without any additional interviews with Dilman. He could see other people, which
he had not done yet, and use clippings. Still, that was not
the point. He wanted to maintain his person-to-person
contact with Dilman. He must fight for nothing less.

The telephone in his lap shrilled at him, and he
juggled it, undoing the receiver, then retrieved it.

"Yeh, hello?"

"Mr. Poole? Sally Watson again. Remember, you told
me I could call back."

"That's right."

"Have you heard the news for yourself by now?"

"Miss Watson, I not only heard the news, I'm trying
to make some of it myself," he said cockily. "It's quite
an experience, having someone you know, someone
you're dealing with, become President."

"That's why I'm calling you, Mr. Poole. I hope I'm
not being presumptuous. If I am, you tell me. To be perfectly honest, even though I hardly know you—well, actually I feel that I do—I've read so much of your work
—I want to ask a favor of you." She paused. "There,
I've said it."

He puzzled over what on earth he could possibly do
for a rich white girl whose father was a senior power-

house in the Senate. "You name it, Miss Watson. If it's something I can do, I'll be glad to oblige."

"I mean, I don't go around asking people favors like this," she said. "I've never done this before. But maybe you won't mind. I know a lot of people on my own. Maybe one day I can be of help to you—not that you need it, with your genius."

Impatience nudged Leroy Poole's curiosity. "Like I said, name it."

She seemed to exhale her request through the earpiece. "I want you to help me get a job with President Dilman."

The request bewildered him. "A job with him? Why, I don't know that I have all that much standing with him, Miss Watson," he said. "Can't your father do that better for you? After all, they were fellow senators, on the same side of the aisle."

"Yes, I know," she said hastily, "but that would be awkward for a hundred reasons. Besides, my father doesn't know President Dilman as well as you do, and even if he did, it would be a little difficult for him to pop right in and ask for Party patronage." Her tone became a plea. "You'll be with the President constantly. It would be easy for you. I'm sure he'd listen."

Leroy Poole straightened, gratified to have become Dilman's adviser. He weighed her request. Her background was important. Intervening on her behalf was no skin off his ass. You did a favor, you had a debtor. It was good to have investments outstanding. When he saw Dilman—*if* he saw him—he could just toss it out, and if Dilman said yes or no, at least he had his debtor. "Miss Watson, I think you'd better tell me, what kind of job have you got in mind?"

"I want to be his social secretary."

"Forgive me for being naïve, Miss Watson, but exactly what does that mean?"

"Every President has a White House social secretary. Sometimes his wife has one, too. But now there's no First Lady, so the President will need someone competent and experienced for both jobs. The social secretary helps the President with his—well, his social life, getting up lists, sending invitations, calling around to arrange cocktail parties, dinners, informal gatherings in the White House. Both T.C. and President Johnson had marvelous social secretaries, but President Dilman needs someone even better. His problems are more complex. Not having a wife or daughter, he'll have to have someone who knows all levels of Washington society. And, well, the fact that he is colored, he may want someone who—well, Mr. Poole, you know—who is understanding, and so forth. I fill the bill."

She had entered Poole's grounds, and he challenged her. "Where you from, Miss Watson?"

She sounded disconcerted. "You mean where I was born and raised? I was born in Louisiana. My mother lives in New Orleans. Well, now she's in Rome, but— and my father, well, you know, he's—"

"How's it going to look, Miss Watson, a daughter of the Confederacy working so close to a Negro?"

"I told you how I feel. I don't have those die-hard sentiments. I was educated in the East. You saw me at the party last night. I like your people."

"I don't mean how's it going to look to you, Miss Watson. I mean how's it going to look to your father? Even if Dilman took you on, do you think your father'd allow it?"

"Mr. Poole, not my father, not anyone, waves me around like a Confederate flag," she said with a tinge of anger. "I'm over twenty-one. I'm an American like you and the President. I belong to me and I do as I please. I want a job where my background can be useful. I think that's the right job for me. Above all, I think I might be of use to the President. I can send you a résumé of my experience and abilities, to show to him. I can send you a list of persons, high up as Cabinet members, who would recommend me. Won't you help me?"

"Miss Watson, I like your sound, and I dig you. Yes, I'll try to make a pitch for you. I'll do my best."

"When? Do you have an idea? I'd like to apply before everyone else begins pestering him."

"I'm supposed to see him this week. If we speak on the phone earlier, I'll mention you right off. Like I said, I'll do my best. Whatever happens, I'll call you."

"Let me give you my number—"

"Wait, I don't have a pencil."

"Well, no matter, I have my own phone. I'm listed as Watson, Sally, in the Arlington book. I don't know how to thank you enough."

"Only thank me if I'm lucky. If I am, just see that I'm invited to one of those White House dinners someday."

"I'll do more. I'll have hundreds of copies of your book there, waiting to be signed. Thanks, Mr. Poole. I'll be living by the phone. Good-bye."

Setting down the telephone, Leroy Poole crossed to the cheap pine desk on which his portable typewriter rested, located a pencil, and jotted a reminder to mention Sally Watson to Dilman, if and when. He then knelt, opened his suitcase under the desk, and pulled out two unwieldy legal-sized manila folders. One contained the typed transcript of his interviews with Douglass Dilman. The other was filled with typed research notes, newspaper clippings, photostats of magazine articles, and mimeographed handouts, all giving data on Dilman and his public record, on the Senate's rules and history, and on Dilman's home state and its politics; and there was also associated material on other Negroes who had served, or were currently serving, in Congress.

Returning to the armchair, he set the research folder on the floor and opened the folder of typed transcripts before him. He put aside the pages covered with penciled notes of his last talk with Dilman, four days ago, which still had to be typed. He began to study what had already been typed, the result of at least two dozen sessions with Dilman, his questions, Dilman's answers.

The ringing of the telephone shattered his concentration. Hastily he closed the folder, shoved it between his leg and the arm of the chair, and brought the receiver before him, hoping that this was the call he wanted.

"Yeh, hello?"

"This is Memphis, Tennessee, long-distance operator. Is this Mr. Leroy Poole?"

"Right."

"Please hold on a moment. Your line was busy. I'll have to ring your party."

"Operator, who's calling?"

"Uh—Mr. Jefferson Hurley. One moment, please."

Leroy Poole could feel the smile creasing in his face. Hurley had not neglected him after all. Busy as he was, having moved from Topeka down to Memphis, obviously to set up a base closer to Hattiesburg, Mississippi, Hurley still had found time to consult with him. Poole gloried and preened at the compliment, not so much of being a member of the Turnerite inner circle as in being Jeff Hurley's friend.

Waiting to hear the deep, thick voice, which never failed to move him, he visualized Jeff Hurley, whom he had seen too infrequently in the three years since they had met at a Crispus Society meeting on New York's East Side. Hurley was a beautiful giant, at thirty-three but a year older than Poole, a self-educated, spellbinding, coffee-colored genius, determined and fearless, cleverer than any white man, unafraid of any human being, white or black. The Turnerite Group had been Hurley's creation, hewed from the Crispus Society's dead heartwood, a great and pulsating splinter committee secretly set upon a course of direct and immediate action to achieve equality now.

Hurley had given the Group its arrogant name because of his admiration for the brave Negro farmer and preacher, Nat Turner, who had dared to rebel against Virginia slavery in 1831. With five followers Turner had ranged through Southampton County, a vengeful black Moses determined to lead his children out of Egypt to freedom, and in the course of his rebellion he had slaughtered sixty whites. Freedom had not been won, and over one hundred colored men were to die from retaliation, but a point had been made. Never again would the South feel safe with its slaves.

Hurley's Turnerites wished to make no point. They desired to lead no chosen people to a Promised Land. Their goal was to make the United States that Promised Land, the one promised in the Constitution, and to do so by force, if necessary. The black-hooded picketing yesterday, in Hattiesburg, Mississippi, had been their first move. If it, or the Turnerite actions to follow, were thwarted, Hurley had promised, like the white Moses of the Jews, like the Moses of the blacks, Nat Turner, to respond with "an eye for an eye." The Southern leaders had ranted against Hurley, the Northern leaders had chastised him for intemperance and impatience, and Spinger's Crispus Society (in which many Turnerites still retained membership) had pleaded with him to observe due process of the law. Now, in Hattiesburg, Hurley and his Group had been assaulted bodily and hurt without just cause. Those who still recalled Hurley's fiery press pronouncements would be wondering: Would his Old Testament warning be acted out?

Waiting at the telephone, Leroy Poole had no doubts. In all communities of people, you separated the men from the boys by determining which were the doers and which the talkers. Hurley was a doer. Leroy Poole adored him. It was not only Hurley's authority that appealed to Poole, but the gorgeous physical aspect of the man, his short-cropped, glossy dark hair, his liquid brooding eyes, his aquiline nose, his gleaming teeth. This was the human being Leroy Poole wanted to be, but since the metamorphosis was an impossibility, it gratified Poole simply to stand beside that human being forever. For Poole, the best safety that he had ever known had been that offered by Hurley's mammoth arm around him, Hurley's hearty laughter, Hurley's electrifying instructions. Leroy Poole had given only a part of himself, in friendship, to many black men and a few black women, but Jeff Hurley (whether Jeff knew it or not) was the only one of either sex for whom he would have given his life.

From far Memphis he felt Hurley enfold him. "Leroy? You there?"

"Jeff—Jeff—how are you?"

"I guess I'm the guy who knows the guy who knows the new President of the United States. How about that, Leroy? Speak of shocks—"

"I still can't believe it."

"I don't know the reaction up your way, but down

here you'd think old Nat Turner himself had overthrown the government of the United States. Almost every Memphis white is apoplectic. Even here on Beale Street our brothers are numbed, full of joy and fireworks inside but afraid to display it."

"The question is—what do you think, Jeff?"

"I don't know what to think yet. I know nothing about Dilman except for a couple of cracks you've made in your letters. I gather you haven't much high regard for him. You once called him a doughface."

"Did I? Well, maybe that was too strong. He doesn't exactly support the Southerners. Up to now I've just sort of felt he was less interested in equality than in self-survival. You know, Jeff, the kind of person who doesn't even want to stop and help out when he sees someone in trouble or being wrongly hurt. He just wants to be left alone. Maybe that was understandable yesterday, but today's a new day, and he'll find no one's going to leave him alone. What it comes to is who's going to get to him first and strongest, and then he's going to have to show if he's nothing but a scarecrow stuffed full of bought ballots or if he's a colored man with guts. I don't have high hopes, Jeff."

The voice from Memphis was momentarily still. Poole waited patiently, and at last he heard Hurley speak. "We'll see soon enough, we'll find out if they've made our man into another hanky-head. Things are moving fast, Leroy, and we're not letting anyone ignore them."

"That was awful, what happened down there in Hattiesburg. Was someone really blinded?"

"Yes, Simon was, poor bastard. Completely sightless, of all the rotten things. And Marvin's sustained a skull fracture, but he'll live. The other ten are okay, as okay as anyone can be in those stinking cell blocks."

"When are they going to be let out?"

"Let out?" Hurley snorted bitterly. "They come up for sentencing in a day or two—"

"*They* come up for sentencing?" Leroy Poole shouted. "Je-sus, what did they do but peaceably picket in some Halloween costumes? What about the Grand Dragon who threw the—"

"Leroy, Leroy, you know better than that. Those folks can't do anything wrong, just like we can't do anything right. The charges against our boys are a mile long. Disturbing the peace, inciting a riot, assault and battery—you name it; whatever's in the book is being thrown at them. Worst of all, a county judge named Everett Gage is going to be on the bench, reading the sentence. We've got the biography on him. Twice in ten years he let off proven lynchers. And they've built a special cemetery, in some swamp, just to hold the Negroes he's sentenced to hard labor."

"What are you going to do, Jeff?"

"I'm heading down to Little Rock in an hour, and if Judge Gage does what's expected, I'll probably set up a base of operations in Shreveport. Then, if necessary, some of us'll do what has to be done."

"You mean—?"

"Yes, that's right."

Leroy Poole was suddenly unnerved. "Jeff, one thing. You talk about the sentencing. Didn't our boys plead Not Guilty?"

"Sure thing."

"Well, what about the trial first?"

"I omitted it to save long-distance charges. Leroy, you've been away from your South too long."

"Yeh."

Hurley's voice came on more forcefully. "There is one thing that does count, and that's an appeal carried on our behalf by an important attorney. Something to stir up pressure, force them into second thoughts, into moderation. That's primarily why I called you."

"What can I do, Jeff?"

"I'll tell you what I've done, and what you can do. You've heard of Nat Abrahams—?"

"The lawyer?"

"The one who got those Mexicans off in California, and did that great job for the NAACP in Ohio. I tried to get through to him in Chicago. He was gone. His associate, fellow named Hart, said he was on his way to Washington. I explained the urgency of our case, and asked where we could contact him in Washington.

Hart said Nat Abrahams was turning down all criminal cases, was involved with something new in your city. Leroy, I'd like to—"

Poole interrupted, remembering what had been nagging at him as he listened. "Wait, Jeff, something just came to mind. This Nat Abrahams, he's the one—when Dilman gave me the names of relatives and friends to interview, he named Nat Abrahams of Chicago as one of his best friends."

Hurley whistled. "Great. Better than I hoped for. I was going to ask you to look up Abrahams when he arrives, make a special plea for him to intervene for us on the appeal. But this is better, much better. When are you seeing Dilman again?"

"Well, now that he's become President—"

"See him." It was a command, and Leroy Poole came to attention. "See him," Hurley repeated, "and when you see him, make sure he knows what's happened to the Turnerites down in Mississippi, what's happened to *his* people. Tell him you'd like him to get his friend Nat Abrahams to give us a little help. Tell him we're desperate, anything you like. We need Abrahams, and no matter how busy he is, I can't see him saying no to the President of the United States."

Poole was worried. "I can't see Abrahams saying no to Dilman either, but I sure can see Dilman saying no to me. You should look at the notes of my talks with Dilman. He's chicken. He's a let's-make-haste-slowly fink."

"Did you ever feel him out on the Turnerites?"

"I sure did. He hemmed and hawed, weaseling all the way. It's in my notes."

Hurley's tone had become fiercer. "Send me a copy of your notes on Dilman. Everything. In return, I'll send you something today, some information that'll maybe help you turn Dilman from a chicken to a bantam cock. Try your best, Leroy, any way you can. Get your man in the White House to deliver Abrahams to us. If you succeed, you've done a great service for us, and we've got a real fighting chance."

"What if I can't make it, Jeff?"

"Then we're going all the way, like we agreed."

"I—I'd hate that, Jeff."

"You think I'd like it? But it's that or nothing now. We've been knocked around long enough. Maybe it's time we punch back hard."

"All right, Jeff."

"First things first. Before you pitch the President, make sure Nat Abrahams is in Washington. Once you're sure, you get in there with Dilman, because right now it's either the lawyer way or the other way, one or the other, but whichever, it's got to be fast. We're going fast from here on in."

Even an electric razor did not make the task of shaving easier on a swaying, speeding train. Ridding oneself of a thick stubble, while in rapid transit, required the steady hand of a surgeon and the concentration of a yogi. He possessed neither attribute this sulky gray morning. He blamed his unsure hand and his wandering mind on the stunning news that he had heard in Akron last night. He had been up half the night with it, following its implications along every dead-end tangent, and back again, and over again, and a few hours' sleep had not alleviated the disturbance.

Grunting surrender, Nat Abrahams gave up.

Unplugging the cord, wrapping it around the electric razor, he considered the results of his shaving in the dim yellow mirror of the cramped, rattling compartment lavatory. A sadly uneven job, but then God had been there first, he decided wryly. No electric gadgetry could smooth the Maker's work. Nor did Nat Abrahams really care much. The twin in the mirror with its shock of unruly brown hair, lined forehead, bushy eyebrows, sunken eyes, hooked nose between high cheekbones, amused mouth, prominent jaw, all gaunt, sallow, keen, had been faithful friend and partner through most of his quixotic idiocies and adventures for most of his years. The six-feet-and-one-inch twin—not only the face, but the lanky, ungainly, sinewy structure appended to it—had frightened off few clients (well, maybe a few fastidious ones),

lost few juries, antagonized few judges. It had won him
Sue. It had collaborated to gain him mighty pleasures and
minor reputation. Who could ask for anything more?

He smiled with self-mockery. Who could ask for anything more? He could. He could ask for one thing more
—money—money, and plenty of it. The unselfish need
of it, after years of treating it as a time-wasting intruder,
was the only thing on earth that could have put him on
this rushing train from Chicago to Washington, D.C., in
his busiest August yet. He had turned over his crowded
calendar to Felix Hart, he had turned over the three
children to their grandmother, he had dragged Sue away
from her thousand wife-mother activities, to obtain what
he had spent a lifetime ignoring: the pot of gold that had
become a necessity at last. Nothing but necessity would
have sent him careening forth on this questionable treasure hunt.

Nat Abrahams reached down, pulled up his suspenders, and snapped them over his shoulders. The suspenders, regarded by his opponents as a corny affectation, had become so much a part of him now that he
was hardly aware of them. When he was aware, he was
happy to remember that they were not and had never
been an affectation. In his first year in law school he had
purchased his first pair and worn them as a talisman,
to help him attain and honor the kind of shingle he had
always wanted: Lincoln, of Lincoln & Herndon, Counselors, or Darrow, of Darrow & Sissman, Attorneys-at-
Law. He had deserved half of neither shingle, he was
certain, but he was equally certain that the talisman had
reminded him always to remember the ideals of Lincoln
and Darrow.

Yet this morning the suspenders felt as tight and uncomfortable as a guilty conscience. Was the journey to
Washington right for him? The cardiac specialist, his old
friend Greenberg, had reiterated that there was no
choice. "Nat, surely the American Bar Association does
not disapprove of its members being well paid. So why
all the Old Country guilts? Enough already. Your whole
life you have lived by the Golden Rule, 'Do unto others
as you would have them do unto you.' So now it's time

to do unto yourself as you have done unto others. Survival, Nat, not at any price, no, but what Avery Emmich offers is not any price, but your price, your terms. Younger men with younger hearts will swing your broadsword to protect every minority, every civil liberty, so let go, let them. You have had your warning, one early coronary insufficiency. Not every man is so lucky. So do what I tell you and what Sue wants. Let go of the crusade. Go to Washington, sign the contract, make the fortune, and then come back and buy the farm. Live so your children can honor their father, not his tombstone. Go to Washington, Nat."

The words rang in his ears, in duet with the train's whistle. Well, if he was nothing else, he was obedient. Here he was, on the Capitol Limited, little more than one hour from Washington's Union Station.

He left the lavatory and groped his way into the compartment bedroom, where only the tiny bed light over his upper berth and the slit of morning beneath the green shade provided visibility. He took down his vest, and then his suit coat, and pulled them on. Fixing the silver watch chain, he squinted to make out the time. Yes, one hour and five minutes more to Washington.

He bent to see if Sue was awake. Her back was to him. Her small, fragile face was buried in the pillow, and her short bob was a tangle. He listened to her inhale and exhale, and loved her now as he had for every moment of their eighteen years. She was so sound asleep, so far from turmoil, and he regretted having kept her awake last night with the news that he had heard in Akron.

He touched her bare shoulder. "Sue, darling—"

Her shoulder lifted, fell, and her head, eyes still shut, came around. "Mmm?"

"Time to wake up. We're almost there."

"Thanks."

"Are you awake, Sue?"

"I'm fine."

"You've got an hour to dress. If you make it fast, you can join me for breakfast. The diner's two cars back. I'll be there."

"Okay."

He straightened, flexed his shoulder muscles, picked up his attaché case, and went to the door.

"Nat—"

He halted, returned, to find her on an elbow, eyes wide-open, staring up at him.

"Nat, is it true, what you told me last night—or was I dreaming?"

"You weren't dreaming, dear."

"No," she said slowly. "I was afraid of that. Poor Doug in the White House. I don't mean just that he's colored. It's that he's so—so sensitive and—and withdrawn. Nat, they'll crucify him."

Abrahams frowned. "He's tougher than a lot of people think, and smarter, too." He paused. "Maybe it's the best thing that could have happened—I mean, to the country."

"Do you really believe that?"

"Honey," he said evasively, "I never know absolutely what I believe until I've had breakfast and a pipeful. You ask me then. Now, hurry up. I'll see you in the diner."

Once he was alone in the train corridor, wending his way between the compartments and windows, he tried to understand what he did believe. Stopping before the last window, he placed a palm against the glass pane, briefly conscious of the blur of green trees flashing past him, but soon inattentive to the scenery. His mind had gone back to the scene he had witnessed at the depot, during the time of their departure yesterday.

When he and Sue had boarded the Capitol Limited in Chicago ten minutes before it left at three-forty yesterday afternoon, they had already known of the President's sudden death in Frankfurt. All through the depot, and outside the train, and in the train itself, Abrahams had seen in the expressions of passengers and porters the same evidences of disbelief and anguish that he had observed that other terrible time when President John F. Kennedy's life had been extinguished by an assassin's bullet in Dallas.

Pushing himself away from the window, Abrahams tried to sort out the different qualities of grief. He felt sure that the public had reacted to T.C.'s death in Frank-

furt in very much the same fashion that they had reacted
to President Kennedy's death in Dallas, which was considerably different from public reaction to Franklin D.
Roosevelt's death in Warm Springs. T.C. had been almost as youthful as Kennedy, and as vigorous. Most people had regarded T.C. more as an older brother than as
a father, because he had been their Chief Executive less
than three years and they had not become totally dependent upon him. His sudden death had shaken them
badly—that was evident everywhere yesterday—but
what seemed to shake them more was the realization that
invincible youth and strength, carrying hope and ambition, shielded by the indestructibility of success and
power, could be brought down and stamped out so swiftly
and easily. Thus, Abrahams guessed, public lamentation
had taken on the form of disbelief. When Roosevelt died
—and this, too, Abrahams remembered very well—the
President had been an intimate part of people's lives and
experiences for so many years that the loss had been
not only the loss of the ever-present head of the family,
but each man's loss of a great segment of his personal
life.

After their train left Chicago, Nat and Sue Abrahams
had talked over the tragedy and its meaning at length,
and pored over the latest newspapers, and then he had
devoted himself to his work. While Abrahams had voted
for T.C., supported him, he had felt no passionate involvement with him, and so he suffered no feeling of
passionate loss. He had thought, as he worked over his
notes for the Washington meeting with Gorden Oliver,
Emmich's lobbyist there, that MacPherson might do the
job as well as T.C. had done. There would be no national trauma.

The rest of the short afternoon on the train had been
lost to working, napping, reading, and desultory chatter
about the children, the new position that was in the offing,
the utopia that was possible after that. They had gone to
the lounge for martinis, and then eaten too much dinner.
Abrahams had seen Sue back to their compartment,
where the berths were already made. She had told him

that she was tired, and would read some more, and go to sleep early.

With his attaché case he had returned to the lounge car to study the proposals from Emmich's attorneys, to mark modifications and changes after them. He had hardly been aware that they were in Akron, and that it was eleven-fifteen and they were running a little late. But then, casually peering through the window, he had noticed, with growing curiosity, a large gathering of the train's porters and conductors, and lips moving excitedly and considerable gesticulating from everyone.

Minutes later, as the Capitol Limited had begun to move again, the wizened Negro bartender had hurried into the lounge with the news. MacPherson had also died in Frankfurt. Senator Douglass Dilman, a colored man, had just been sworn in as President of the United States.

Doug Dilman.

It had taken Nat Abrahams a long time to calm the chaotic emotions he had felt about his old friend and his friend's incredible promotion. At midnight Abrahams had gone back to his compartment. In the darkness Sue's sleepy voice welcomed him and said good night. He had sat down on the edge of her berth, and told her what he had heard. She had snapped on the blue night light above her head, and he could see that she was upset and trembling. He had given her a sleeping pill, and then they had discussed it, until her voice had thickened and fallen silent, and she had drifted off to sleep again. Later he had stretched in his upper berth, but he had not slept. He had been awake, his mind a turmoil, for at least an hour after they left Pittsburgh.

And here it was early morning, and here he was drawing closer and closer to the nation's capital, a city so jolted overnight, so changed, by the rise to highest office of the only colored man he had ever known well and one who had been his friend since their first meeting during the Second World War. Only the previous week Abrahams had had a letter from Dilman, who was overjoyed that Abrahams was coming to Washington. Dilman insisted that they must see one another as often as possible during Abrahams' visit. Dilman had even set a date for their dinner of reunion. Abrahams speculated as to whether that engagement still existed and, if it did, what his friend would be like.

Sighing, Nat Abrahams drove further speculation from his mind and walked quickly, opening heavy resisting doors, into the lounge car, and then continued into the immaculate dining car. Except for a sprinkling of white passengers, absorbed in the Pittsburgh newspapers, the dining car appeared to be the scene of a Pullman porters' convention. At least a half dozen of them, joined by the Negro waiters, were congregated at the far end, engaged in deep conversation.

The short maître d'hôtel, rimless spectacles pressed into his Prussian face, bounced forward, signaling Abrahams to a table. As Abrahams sat before the spotless water glasses and gleaming silverware, dancing to the click of the wheels and rails, the maître d'hôtel placed the menu, order pad, and pencil in front of him.

"I won't need a menu," Abrahams said. Taking up the pad, he wrote his order: cereal, French toast, tea. Then he filled in Sue's order: grapefruit, melba toast, coffee. He handed the pad to his host. "Hold the coffee until my wife comes in."

"Very well, sir."

Abrahams nodded off to the far end of the car. "I'll wager they're talking about President Dilman."

"Nothing else but that. They can't keep their minds on their work since it happened." He bowed closer to Abrahams and whispered, "You'd think it was the Second Coming."

"Let's hope so."

The maître d' was about to say something, but seemed to change his mind, and said something else. "Are you, by any chance, with the government, sir?"

"Heaven forbid," said Abrahams, "unless that covers all suffering taxpayers."

The maître d' lingered. "We're expecting our next trainloads, the coming months, to be more heavily Negro, if you know what I mean."

"I don't see why," said Abrahams sharply. He motioned to the pad. "May I have my tea right away?"

After the maître d' had hurried away, Abrahams remained inspecting the picture that the man had planted in his mind—thousands of Pullman cars, overflowing with black men pouring into Washington to accept their new appointments. However, he could only visualize the picture in broadest caricature. For, knowing Dilman as he did, he was aware that it was wildly ridiculous. One of Dilman's shortcomings, Abrahams had always felt, was that he leaned too far backward, and away, from those worthies of his own race, lest he be charged with favoritism. Dilman believed that all men were created equal, and should inherit equal rights, yet he was too inhibited by fear to practice his beliefs. Instead he had a tendency to practice a sort of inverse segregation, one turned inside out. This was too harsh a judgment of so good and suffering a man, Abrahams knew, but it was largely true.

His memory went back to early 1945, when, as a captain, he had been assigned to the Military Justice Division of the Judge Advocate General's Corps, Department of the Army, in the Pentagon Building. He had found himself situated at a desk in the same glassed-in olive green cubbyhole as Lieutenant Douglass Dilman. Abrahams had known a few Negroes when he attended the Law School of the University of Chicago, but he had never known them intimately. Abrahams had never possessed any strong, special feelings about Negroes, except intellectual resentment at their oppression and slum history and bondage in America. His bookish, impecunious father, a philosophy professor, and his active-in-causes, fearlessly vocal mother (a sort of Margaret Fuller whose Master's thesis had been on the Abolitionist movement) had raised him so naturally that he had come to manhood without any racial prejudices.

As a matter of fact, Abrahams was not even possessed of tolerance for Negroes, as many of his intellectual and progressive friends were. To Abrahams, the word *tolerance* bore, in itself, a flick of prejudice—one was nice to certain people, treated them equally, accepted them, but by being tolerant of them thus, one implied that they were different. To Abrahams, Negroes had been men

who were light black or dark black as white men had
been swarthy white or pasty white. All men were men
together, and some were stupid and others were intelligent, some more boring than others and some more fascinating, some more bad than good and others more good
than bad, whether they were black or white, brown or
yellow. Abrahams had entered the Army with this attitude, and it had not changed.

Being confined in a cubbyhole with a Negro officer
had been unusual only because he found Dilman shy
and deferential beyond the requirements of their difference in rank, and because he had been uncertain about
Dilman. His uncertainty was not related to his own feelings about Dilman's color, but rather to Dilman's own
sensitivity about his color and to Abrahams' whiteness.
But because they had been thrown together a couple of
feet from each other, devoting themselves to the same
cases and working under the same pressures, Dilman's
defensiveness had gradually dropped.

Their closeness had begun in the common language of
military legalities, and had eventually shifted to the common language of intellectually equal men. Not only had
they worked together, but they had dined in the Pentagon
cafeteria together daily and left the river entrance together in one car pool for their respective lodgings. They
had come to know of each other's lives, although Dilman
had always been more guarded here, and of each other's
likes and dislikes, human weaknesses, human aspirations.
They had become fond of each other as men, and when
they had been assigned together to London, and then
Paris, and then Occupied West Germany, their friendship had solidified. The triumph of it, Abrahams had
finally realized, was that Dilman had one day ceased to
consider him white and therefore alien.

After the war they had both practiced in Chicago, he
with offices in the Loop, and Dilman on the South Side.
While he had known that Dilman was married, he had
never met Dilman's wife during the war, because she had
not accompanied him to Washington. In Chicago Abrahams met her three times and, knowing Dilman as he
did, understood why Dilman had not brought her with

him to Washington. Aldora Dilman, although of Negro ancestry, had proved to be of fair complexion. Abrahams had thought her tense, embittered, ashamed of her darker husband, and he had observed that she drank too much. Eleven months after setting himself up in Chicago, Dilman had abruptly moved himself and his wife to another city in another Midwestern state.

Occasionally, in the next years, Abrahams had his reunions with Dilman, often going out of his way to enjoy one. After an initial constraint, Dilman had always accepted him as an old friend. Abrahams had become aware of Dilman's work for Negro organizations and great labor unions. He had not been surprised when he read that Dilman had agreed to run for the House of Representatives, and he had been thrilled when Dilman won. Since Abrahams' cases had often taken him to Washington, D.C., he had been able to see his old friend more frequently.

In these meetings, during which almost every subject was covered, Abrahams had learned to avoid one area, although he perceived much about it. He had silently understood Aldora's refusing to accompany her Congressman husband to Washington. He had been pleased to learn, indirectly, that Aldora had given Dilman a son some years before. And it had come to him as no shock, somehow, when Aldora died at the age of forty. He offered Dilman no words of sympathy. He had always known that this dark area of personal life was one that Dilman did not like to discuss.

The years that had made them older had given each of them, in different ways, national identity. Abrahams' name had become known for his successful intervention in cases involving legal oppressions of minorities. Dilman's name had become even more widely known for his four terms in the House of Representatives, his appointment to a vacancy in the United States Senate, his election to the Senate, and finally his widely heralded election as President pro tempore of the Senate in the Vice-President's absence. And now, overnight, this improbable upheaval in Dilman's life, and the life and history of the United States.

Abrahams had been jounced out of memory by the dining car waiter staring at him, and he realized that he was shaking his head over the turn of events and the waiter was worried that he was shaking his head over the breakfast that lay before him.

"Is everything all right, sir?" the waiter was asking.

"Perfectly fine, looks excellent, thanks."

He ate his cereal hastily, so that the French toast would not be cold. Eating, he realized that he must remove the problem of Doug Dilman from his mind. His immediate concern must be the personal business that was bringing him to Washington, D.C. In forty minutes they would be arriving at the Union Station, and not long after they would be in a taxi entering Massachusetts Avenue and heading for the Mayflower Hotel. Sue would be calling the children and her mother, and unpacking, while he would be making arrangements to meet with Oliver, the veteran lobbyist empowered by Avery Emmich, chairman of Eagles Industries Corporation, to negotiate with him. What would result from these meetings could be crucial to the future years of his life—and conscience.

Putting down knife and fork, Abrahams snapped open his attaché case and extracted the most recent proposals submitted by Emmich's legal advisers. As he sipped his tea, reviewing the already familiar proposals, Abrahams was amused at how the formal legal language had bent to Emmich's imperious personality. One could almost visualize the cowering corporation lawyers listening to Emmich's flat commands on the Dictabelt, and then trying to couch them ever so little more in corporate phraseology. Every paragraph gave evidence of being pure Emmich. Straight declarations, bombastic imperatives, the highly limited and inflexible linguistics of millionaire patrons, the power elite, who had almost forgotten the sounds of reply that used words like *possibly* and *compromise* and *suggest*. In their lofty towers, protected by the magic weapons of money that brought all opposition to its knees, the Emmichs had made the word *no,* spoken to them, virtually obsolete.

He had met Avery Emmich but once, less than a year

ago, and their conversation, or rather Emmich's monologue, had been short and pointed. Emmich had been
in Chicago to conclude the acquisition of several chemical plants. The millionaire had summoned Nat Abrahams
to his suite, and Abrahams, surprised that he was even
known to Emmich, had gone out of wonder and curiosity.

Avery Emmich, the son of a German immigrant, had
proved to be a dyspeptic, glaring, squat man in his late
sixties. In their twenty minutes together he had been as
humorless and efficient as an imported calculating machine.

"I wanted to see what you look like," Emmich had
said at once. "You don't look like a bleeding heart."

"I'm an attorney," Abrahams had said, "a hard-
working one."

"Yes. Recently some of your trial cases were brought
to my attention. I was impressed."

"Impressed?"

"You appear surprised," Emmich had said.

"I guess I am," Abrahams had said. "From what I've
heard about you, and read, I wouldn't have imagined
you'd be impressed by someone who has defended Mexicans, Negroes, small unions."

"Young man, I don't give a hoot in hell whom you defend. I'm impressed because you took on tough cases
and won them. I'm impressed by skill and toughness.
What do you make a year?"

Abrahams had told him. Emmich had grunted with
self-satisfaction, and revealed a slip of paper on which
he had surmised what Abrahams' income would be.
Without further interrogation, Emmich had told Abrahams what he was after. He was, he had stated, after
Nat Abrahams himself. He wanted Nat Abrahams in
Washington, D.C. He made it clear that Eagles Industries and its multiple interests—cotton production, textile
factories, chemical plants, brass and copper mills, insurance companies, shipping lines—had a vast network of
legal representation, even in the nation's capital. He
made it clear that he was never satisfied with what he had,
that he always demanded the best help, and that he was
ready to pay for it. He made it clear that Washington,

D.C., was a sore spot for him. Even under a sensible President like T.C., the government was putting its nose more and more into private enterprise. Emmich wanted the best there, the best minds, voices, legal lookouts.

Abrahams had heard all of this with detached fascination, but without interest. Even as he had listened, he could not conceive of himself abandoning the desperate and wretched people who needed him, for a more lucrative job with a mammoth combine. The Emmichs of the world, he had always known, advocated free enterprise —laudable; but they meant free enterprise for themselves and not a free economic society—less laudable. The Emmichs, he had always known, wanted competitors, consumers, workers, the government itself, controlled by their own definitions of freedom.

Abrahams had begun to shake his head, when Avery Emmich had announced Abrahams' worth to the corporation in dollars and cents. Abrahams had been taken aback by the sum announced. The annual salary offered had been more than he had made in the last four years of exhausting work. After that, dazed, he had not shaken his head again. He had listened attentively, and with interest. It had amazed him the way Emmich had anticipated his unspoken reservations. He was being asked to represent the corporation as an attorney, no more, no less. He was being asked to speak for the corporation on legal matters and legislative matters, and to inform and advise the corporation on activities pertaining to its business. He was not being asked to compromise his ideals or attitudes. He was not being asked to perform contrary to his good conscience. He was not being asked to forfeit any part of his freedom as an individual. Eagles Industries would be his employer. Nat Abrahams would be its employee. He would not be lobotomized. He would be himself. Emmich wanted *him*.

And then it was that Abrahams had understood the sense of the offer. Every big company needed its basic liberal, to showcase, as every big company needed its basic Negro.

That visit in Emmich's suite had been the beginning of it. Despite Sue's squealing excitement over the offer,

and his own headiness at what was suddenly made possible, Abrahams had clung to certain reservations about
it, about the change itself. He had hated the thought of
giving up a practice he loved, of dislocating himself and
the family, for money. Yet it was only money that might
guarantee him added years of life, and provide his wife
and children with security. He had hated the thought of
devoting himself to an impersonal financial combine,
with headquarters in Atlanta, that had no motivation except profits and that regarded people as Social Security
numbers. Yet it was a corporation that promised him un-
restricted individual freedom.

While Eagles Industries bombarded him with telephone calls and memoranda, Nat Abrahams had remained indecisive. He had stalled his reply, and then he
had made negotiations as difficult as possible, hoping that
this would make decision unnecessary. He had refused
to bind himself to Eagles Industries for seven years, and
had insisted that three years were enough. Emmich had
countered with five years. Abrahams had remained adamant. Emmich had agreed to three years. Abrahams had
demanded more money, better side benefits, expense accounts, thorough definitions of his position, and to everything Emmich had acceded. Finally Sue had told him
that he had been trying to create an encroaching monster,
when the monster did not exist. And he had admitted
that she was right.

There had been serious talks between Sue and himself. Both had circled the reality of his coronary warning, and both had finally faced it. They had also faced
the fact that they lived on what he made, that aside from
his life insurance policies, a still-mortgaged house, a
pitifully small reserve of government bonds and blue-
chip stocks, their financial future was bleak. He would
never get far enough ahead to ease up, to enjoy semi-
retirement, to buy the farm they both wanted.

On a warm Sunday morning, with Roger, David, and
Deborah churning about the back seat of the four-year-
old sedan, they had driven down near Wheaton, Illinois,
to look at the farm once more. The beautiful cottage,
the freshly painted red barns, the smell of the machinery

and livestock and brown-green grass and wheat and corn fields had overwhelmed them again. Driving home, the children happily napping in the back, he and Sue had speculated upon what his life could be on such a farm. He could retain an interest in the firm, serve as a once-a-week consultant on vital cases. He could give time at last to writings about what he believed in, writings that might accomplish more than his private cases had. He could manage the farm. He could be outdoors, live more easily with himself, have more time for Sue, for the children. Above all, he could live. In three years he could have this if he wanted it.

The following morning Nat Abrahams had telephoned Avery Emmich to draft a contract. In a month, he had promised, he would be prepared to go to Washington, to sit with Gorden Oliver, and mold the contract into its final form. And then he had taken an option on the farm outside Wheaton.

"Nat—"

His head came up at the sound of Sue's voice, and he found her settling into the chair across from him.

"Where were you?" she was saying. "You were a million miles away."

He smiled. "Not quite that far." He thought: only the distance away you can reach in three years.

As she went at her grapefruit, he reminded the waiter of her coffee and melba toast, and then stuffed Emmich's proposals into his attaché case.

"How are the waiters here taking Dilman?" she asked between mouthfuls.

"I gather they're pleased. That is, if this had to happen, they're pleased the next in line was one of their own."

"They're not all pleased," said Sue. "I was just talking with our porter. He says most of his friends are glad a Negro will have a chance to show he can perform as well as anyone else. But our porter says he's not as happy as his friends, because he says he's a thinking man and they're not. He says he's thinking ahead, and he's frightened. He doesn't think this country is ready for any Negro to head it. He thinks this focuses the wrong kind of attention on the Negro, and is bound to cause worse

resentment and antagonism. Nat, you should have seen
his face when he was speaking. So—uneasy."

For Abrahams it was too early in the day to concur,
and to bare his own uneasiness. As he tried to determine
what to say to Sue, he observed that her attention had
been diverted by three persons taking seats at the table
across the aisle. There was an elderly, obviously well-off
couple, and opposite them a slick-haired, smooth-
shaved, jowly, overweight, middle-aged young man in a
tailor-made Oxford gray business suit.

The overweight middle-aged young man, wiping his
spectacles with his napkin, was speaking, and not
quietly. "Well, after that, the meeting broke up, and we
hung around the television set," he was saying. "I tell
you honestly, we weren't so worried about this Dilman's
competence, because that doesn't matter these days. The
government is run by committee rule, and T.C. had some
good heads there. Our worry is in the area where a
President can't be controlled as well. You know, appointments, policy speeches and such. Those people—I mean,
like Dilman—are leftist, no question. I can show you the
facts. Now that one of them has power, he's apt to coddle
the Communists—don't get me wrong, Harold, I'm not
saying Dilman is a Red; I'm saying he's apt to have a
sympathy for them, rapport, let them slip in and take
control here, and go soft on them abroad. Well, Harold,
we're not going to let that happen—no, sir."

The speaker lowered his voice to address some confidences to his companions, and Abrahams turned his
head away. He found Sue looking at him, gray and
helpless. Before he could placate her, there was the sound
of a fork against a glass. The middle-aged young man
kept up the noise, half turning for the waiter. A tall,
skinny waiter came on the run.

"About time!" the middle-aged young man boomed
with mock joviality. "What's happening to the service?
You all too busy running our government today?"

"I'm sorry, sir," the waiter said. "I was waitin' for
you to fill in your order."

"Aw, give us a break, we poor folk can't write," the

middle-aged young man said, winking. "Come on, Sam, one round of Sanka."

The waiter stood a moment, unspeaking, and then slowly, with calm dignity, he turned away and walked toward the dining car kitchen.

The three across the way were laughing together now, and then huddled, whispering, and Abrahams did not want to overhear a word of it. He fumbled for his tea, head bent to avoid Sue's eyes. He finished the tea, and, in no mood for his pipe, picked up the complimentary newspaper.

"Oh, Nat—"

Abrahams was forced to look up.

Sue was near tears. "I'm like our porter, Nat, I'm plain frightened. Doug needs friends so much."

"He has friends," Abrahams said curtly. "I'm sure no one in Washington is worried about that."

She was staring at the back half of his folded newspaper. "Nat, if you're right—I—I can read your paper upside down—why have they doubled the guard around him?"

"Honey, stop fretting. It's routine. Whenever there's a new President, they assign twice as many Secret Service men to him. Now, let's hurry up and get out of here." He tried to smile. "You concentrate on taking care of your husband, and let the Secret Service take care of Douglass Dilman."

After securely buckling the strap that connected his revolver in its shoulder holster to his waist, Otto Beggs pulled on his dark, conservative, worn suit coat. Going to the bureau that he and Gertrude shared, he took down his open leather wallet, for good luck rubbed his thumb across the silver star of his Secret Service badge pinned inside, closed the wallet, and slipped it into his inner coat pocket.

He felt the constriction of hunger in his stomach, and yet he was not ready to join Gertrude and the boys for breakfast. He felt unnaturally elated this morning, and wanted to savor it minutes more, alone, before risking the loss of this rare well-being to his enemies downstairs.

Humming to himself, Otto Beggs strolled about the mussed and used bedroom, tidying it, then continued to his desk to straighten the three scrapbooks with his name imprinted in gold upon each. Considering his activities of the last twenty-four hours, it was strange that he should feel so fit.

He had worked not eight hours but eleven hours yesterday, after his boss, Lou Agajanian, Chief of the White House Detail, had awakened him to tell him to come in earlier and replace one of the night-shift agents who had become ill from a virus. Then there had been that pressure and strain, after the news that the President and Speaker had been killed, when the correspondents and half the government officials had overrun the West Wing. To make matters worse, not only Agajanian but Hugo Gaynor, the Chief of Secret Service, had been all over the place, on everyone's tail, out of temper. It had been nerve-racking. And then, instead of giving him any rest at home, Gertrude had kept encouraging her relatives to come over, including her hotshot brother, Austin, and his wife and brats. It had been a nut house, and once, around midnight, he had tried to escape by saying that he was out of cigarettes. He had headed straight down the block for a couple of beers at the Walk Inn, but the joint was jammed with wild, drunken Negroes, and he had gone back to the house, embittered, to stay with television until three in the morning.

Before turning off the set he had heard one added interesting piece of news, and it had been confirmed, and it had kept him wide-awake and speculating about it until almost dawn. The interesting piece of news had been that the collapse of that ancient ceiling in the Alte Mainzer Palace had not only killed T.C. and MacPherson, but it had also crushed to death two Secret Service men. Beggs had known them both well. One had been Agajanian's aide, Assistant Chief of the White House Detail Gene Sonenberg, and the other had been mobile White House special agent Les McCune, the only one of fifty on the House Detail who held seniority over Beggs.

Lying in bed, stimulated by what tragedy had made possible for him, Otto Beggs had done some simple subtraction and addition. The subtraction had consisted of removing Sonenberg from his position as Agajanian's aide, and removing McCune as the next in line to fill that position. They were gone. The addition had consisted of putting a plus sign before his name. He was next, the one next eligible to move up and replace Sonenberg as Assistant Chief of the White House Detail. This promotion would make other promotions more likely. Once you got off your feet, taking orders, and on your seat, giving orders, the world was yours. After that, he might one day became Chief of the White House Detail, and then Deputy Chief of Secret Service, and then Assistant Chief of Security, until at last he became Chief of Secret Service under the Secretary of the Treasury. With the first giant step accomplished, the rungs above would be easier to grasp. And he had time. He was only in his early forties. In recent months Gertrude had made that seem too old for him to achieve anything better, and he had begun to believe her, but now, in a flash, he was young again, and once more on the road that had seemed so straight and easy when he had entered onto it at Corvallis, Oregon, and continued up it outside Seoul, Korea.

Last night, twisting and turning on his bed, he had wondered when he had lost the road, and where, and how, or if he had lost it at all. He had tried to relive his short journey, so much with him in recent years that he could only relive it as an experience ever present and not of the past.

At Oregon State University he was invincible. He had come to the campus on an athletic scholarship. Except for his innocent, pugged, smiling baby face and small head, everything about him was formidable. He was powerful, husky, amazingly agile and fast for his 190-pound weight. Swiftly, at fullback, he became the mainstay of the football team, carrying it in his senior year to a victory in the Rose Bowl and himself achieving singular recognition by being voted to Associated Press's All-American second team. He was popular. The girls competed for his favor. Gertrude was one of them, not beau-

tiful but attractive and smart. She earned his gratitude
by helping him with his homework, and she earned his
respect by letting him kiss and pet her but not letting
him go all the way. By the time he graduated, they were
dating steadily.

When he was commissioned a Second Lieutenant in
the First Marines, and before he was shipped off to
Korea, he married Gertrude and spent a three-day
honeymoon with her in Yellowstone National Park. After
arriving in South Korea, the tension of battle evoked his
football days and he was fearless. When a superior officer rebuked him for an unnecessary risk on a patrol,
calling him "too goddam stupid to be afraid," Beggs was
proud. On a cold and icy night before Christmas, during
his eleventh month in Korea, in the wintry scrubs outside Hagaru-ri, he became an authentic hero. Four
wounded Marines lay trapped in enemy-held territory, as
Chinese gunfire kept medical-aid corpsmen from reaching them. Enraged, Beggs snatched up a machine gun,
and, darting forward, falling and rising, he decimated the
Red Chinese, personally rescuing his four wounded buddies. For this he received America's highest military
award, the Congressional Medal of Honor, for valor in
action.

In the Oval Office of the White House, the medal was
pinned on Otto Beggs by President Eisenhower. There
were columns of photographs and feature stories, and
one of Gertrude's gifts was the first scrapbook. There
were dozens of well-paying executive jobs offered him,
and he took the best, and left it, and took another, and
then a third and a fourth, and left these also. After Oregon and Korea the jobs were too tame and caging. He
wanted challenge and danger. He wanted—Gertrude's
word—"clippings."

His nostalgia, in his waking dreams, was for that climactic moment in the White House when President
Eisenhower had given him the Medal of Honor. He was
jobless, but not concerned, because Gertrude had saved
their money, and he was telling friends that he was
"looking around for the right sort of thing." Then one
noon, in a barber's chair, leafing through a magazine,

he found exactly what he was seeking. There was a cover-line article commemorating the death of a White House police officer who had been shot down before Blair House in the assassination attempt on President Truman by two Puerto Ricans. The alert and gallant White House police and Secret Service agents on guard had saved the President's life in a gun battle. The story then went on to explain the role of the White House police, as a branch of the Secret Service, and told about the history and the daring adventures of the Secret Service itself, from the time after the murder of President McKinley when its prime responsibility became that of protecting the life of the President.

Intrigued by this one rare job that put a premium on courage, that promised drama, Otto Beggs wrote to the Chief of Secret Service, Treasury Department, Washington, D.C., relating his background, his keen interest, and applying for a position as a special White House agent.

What followed came quickly. Beggs was summoned to prove himself. With enthusiasm, he took the United States Civil Service test, the four-hour written observation and memory test of the Secret Service, the thorough physical examination. He overcame each obstacle, including the personal interviews, with ease. He received his appointment to the Secret Service at the beginner's salary of $5,000 a year, with the assurance that once he had experience he would be raised gradually to $10,000 a year, and once he became a supervisor of top grade he could earn $16,000 a year.

While the money was not what he had earned in business, as Gertrude kept reminding him, he pointed out to her that it was more than sufficient for their needs. He told her that he would be serving his country again, which was worth any monetary sacrifice, and the prestige that he would acquire through the years might make him a political figure with the attendant wealth necessary to insure their future. He did not tell her that he felt he was being paid for having fun.

And, indeed, for Otto Beggs the beginnings were challenging. His enthusiasm mounted as he attended the Secret Service's special training school in Washington.

He was instructed in the use of the most modern sub-machine guns, revolvers, riot guns. He was instructed in judo, first aid, fire fighting, parachute landing, wrestling, psychiatry. He was indoctrinated into the mysteries of atomic, biological, and chemical warfare. When his basic training was concluded, he was casually asked what position in the Secret Service interested him the most. He was frank. He knew that the procedure was for a new-comer to spend two years in the field, apprehending counterfeiters and forgers, before being considered for an elite job in the Executive Mansion. Nevertheless, he felt that his background warranted his requesting imme-diate assignment to the exclusive White House Detail. He had no interest in chasing petty criminals. He desired only to protect the nation's leading official from assassins. Having spoken his piece, he waited with confidence. He did not wait long. The word came from the Secretary of the Treasury himself. Otto Beggs had been assigned to become a member of the White House Detail. He was not surprised. He knew that the old Medal of Honor had counted for something.

The first year was agreeable, if somewhat disappoint-ing. He had expected his supervisors, on the second floor of the East Wing of the White House, to recognize his unique merit by assigning him, at once, to be at the President's elbow. Instead he found himself with the po-lice at the East, then the South, then the West guard-house entrances to the Executive Mansion. When he was assigned to what was cheerfully labeled "the diaper de-tail," off and on watching over President Kennedy's daughter and son, President Lyndon Johnson's two daughters, his hopes soared again.

Encouraged, optimistic about his future in the early days of the "diaper detail," he had insisted upon buying a house that would be their own. Impulsively he pur-chased a small, comfortable two-story residence off lower Connecticut Avenue. He crowed over his bargain, but Gertrude did not hide her apprehension. While the neighborhood was still genteel middle-class, it was only a few blocks from a bursting lower-class Negro section. Beggs was not concerned. The Negroes, he was positive, would stay in their place. If they invaded his neighborhood, he and Gertrude could sell at a profit. By then he would have his promotion, raise in salary, and they could find their way to one of the more expensive locations in suburban Washington. Gertrude was not convinced. She felt that the Negro invasion was on its way and her husband's promotion was not.

As ever, Gertrude was proved right on both scores. The Negro invasion began slowly, at the perimeter, and then cut in deeper and faster. White homeowners, prospering at their government jobs and businesses, seeing a chance for additional profits, sold off and moved elsewhere. The neighborhood streets that Beggs liked to stroll along in the evening were soon one-third black, and several years later two-thirds black. Beggs's favorite haunt, a congenial corner tavern known as the Walk Inn, with its bar and booths and variety of pinball machines, began to undergo a transformation, too. In the beginning, when he went there for his evening beer, Beggs joined a community of white neighbors, men who were his equals and who respected his important job and contested with him over the pinball machines. Gradually his friends disappeared, one by one, and there remained strangers with dark skins, men with whom Beggs had nothing in common.

From time to time, bowing to Gertrude's increasingly shrill demands that they move, he accompanied his wife to suburbs like Silver Spring and Bethesda to see what the housing developments had for sale. It was for his sons, Ogden and Otis, for their better school conditions, that he did this. But the new pseudo colonials were too expensive. After each of these frustrating explorations, Beggs promised his distressed wife that a promotion was forthcoming and the move would soon be made possible.

Incredibly, the promotion did not come. Within the White House, and about its spacious grounds, Otto Beggs was transferred from one inconsequential job to another. Other agents surrounded the President's Oval Office, walked with the great man, traveled with him. Beggs remained chained to routine and peripheral duty. When T.C. was elected, his hopes lifted once more. A change

in the occupancy of the White House always gave promise of a change in his duties. And, indeed, there was a
change. He found himself assigned to the West Wing
lobby, occupied mostly by the press and visitors who
called up T.C. He did not mind, because he liked the
reporters, who were important and who occasionally
mentioned him or quoted him in their feature stories.
But Gertrude would give him no peace.

One day, before his shift, he called upon Chief of
Secret Service Hugo Gaynor, waited in the oak-paneled,
red-carpeted receiving room, and had his embarrassing
interview. Gaynor was impatient, evasive, and pledged
to Beggs that he would be kept in mind for the next promotion. Upset, Beggs sought his immediate boss, Lou
Agajanian, in the Secret Service office off the West Wing
lobby, and Agajanian said that he, too, would see what
he could do. A short time later, eating in the President's
Navy Mess in the downstairs basement, he overheard
some of his fellow agents gossiping, unaware that he was
within earshot. They were analyzing one another and
their absent colleagues. He thought he heard his name
mentioned. He heard expressions like "workhorse" and
"not too bright" and "living in the past." He was not
certain if they were referring to himself, and chose to believe that they were not. He did not repeat what he had
overheard to Gertrude, who was too antagonistic to be a
confidante any longer, but he thought about it for a number of nights in the Walk Inn, where his beer intake had
gone up from one to three steins per sitting.

What he thought about was that while he liked his
job, he had become increasingly disappointed in it. From
the first, he had assumed it promised responsibility and
danger and high adventure, countless opportunities for a
fearless individual to prove himself under fire. Instead it
had proved a job like almost any other, no more hazardous than had he remained a stockbroker or public relations man. Perhaps the disappointment, the monotony
of each day's shift, had dulled him. Perhaps the routine
had made him less lively, less enthusiastic, less sharp and
aggressive. Perhaps Gaynor and Agajanian saw this, and
felt that he could not be trusted as one of the six to ten

agents assigned to be closest to the President, or as one who deserved to be made a supervisor. He did not know.

Yet, despite Gertrude's recent nagging that he quit the Secret Service and go into the real estate business with her successful rebuke of a brother, Austin, he could not bear to make the change. As a realtor, he might acquire money, but there would surely be the grave of anonymity. As an agent, he could always hope for recognition. He could also, no matter what the routine, feel he was in the center of life, where anything might happen. Once, some unimportant newspaperman, a kid named George Murdock, had interviewed him. Well, despite what the big reporters said, Murdock wasn't that unimportant. His Tri-State Syndicate did have twelve newspapers, even if half of them were only weeklies. Anyway, this kid, George Murdock, had asked him what he liked about being an agent and what he did not like. He did not remember his reply, but what Murdock quoted him as saying was, "To me, the appeal of the Secret Service is the same appeal most law enforcement jobs hold. But I don't consider it a mere job. If I did, I would have left it long ago for higher-paying executive positions that have been offered to me. There is more to it than merely doing a job. As an agent, you feel you are doing a real service to everyone. There is enough going on to keep you on your toes. There's no routine or rut to bore you. Maybe it's not as glamorous as people think, but there is plenty of pressure every minute, and there's no margin for error. Our most important training is to cope with suddenness. Well, when you have to be alert for suddenness, you haven't time to be bored." George Murdock had given him a clipping of the interview as it appeared in the Sandusky, Ohio, *Register*. He supposed no one important, like the President or Gaynor or Agajanian, ever saw it. But he had seen it. It was on page seven of his third scrapbook.

All that had gone through his head last night, before he fell asleep as dawn came. Now, fully dressed, ready for breakfast and his daily shift that began in an hour, he stood immobilized in front of his scrapbooks. He opened the uppermost one and turned to page seven.

There it was. He reread Murdock's quote. He had remembered it correctly, word for word.

"Otto!" It was Gertrude screaming at him from the foot of the stairs. "Otto, you want to see your sons before they go to school, or not?"

"Coming!" he shouted back almost gaily.

He felt *good*. He could not wait to get to work. The West Wing lobby would be a madhouse today. He would be interviewed about Sonenberg and McCune, who had died last night in Frankfurt with the President. He would think of what he should say, on the way to work. He might be too busy to say anything. He knew that Agajanian or Gaynor would be waiting for him.

He went, light-footed, out of the bedroom and down the stairs, as light and quick as he had been at Oregon and in Korea. Although he now weighed 210 pounds instead of 190, and maybe his face was a bit fleshier and blotched from beering, he was proud that he was still strong and fast and without an inch of flabbiness.

Almost breezily he entered the dining room, where Gertrude, in her usual early morning disarray, was trying to force Ogden, his ten-year-old, and Otis, who was eight, to eat their plates clean. Settling down to spear a waffle, he noticed, as he often had recently, that Gertrude, once pleasantly thin of face and trim of figure, had become sharp around the nose and mouth and baggier beneath the spotted housecoat. He noticed, too, that neither she nor his sons had acknowledged him with so much as a good morning. This time he would permit no disrespect to intrude on his good cheer.

"Well, Gertie, what's the bad news today?" he said with a grin.

He had almost forgotten how much this greeting, which he had been using lately to anticipate and blunt her shrill attacks, infuriated her.

Her head swung toward him, threatening as a machine gun. "What unholy hour did you get to sleep?"

"I don't know. Two or three." He buttered his waffles and poured syrup over them. "I couldn't take my eyes off the television screen. What a night."

"Apparently you were able to take your eyes off it long

enough while my brother was here. I suppose you went
to that frightful saloon?"

"Just for cigarettes." He sliced off a piece of waffle
and was pleased to find it limp and cold. "Then I guess
I walked around. I was pretty shook up by that Frankfurt thing."

"I didn't know what to say to Austin. He only wants
to help you. Even if he is my brother, he doesn't have to."

"I appreciate it," Beggs said grimly. He stared at the
tops of his sons' heads. "Ogden—Otis—where's your
manners? I haven't even heard hello."

Both their sandy-haired heads went up and down.
"Hello, Pop . . . hello."

He might have been a stick of wood for all they cared,
he thought. Gertrude had done a thorough job of brainwashing them against him. A few years ago they would
have been swarming over him, tugging, hugging, pestering him for more stories of derring-do on the Oregon
gridiron, on the Korean battlefields, on the perils of his
White House job. They had looked up to him, admired
him. Only Gertrude's increased and open daily hectoring
had reduced his past heroism and authority to his present
symbol of failure.

He determined not to lose them. "Well, boys, it should
be quite a day in school today, with a new President, eh?"

Gertrude's querulous voice drew a discordant curtain
between her sons and their father. "You sound like it's
good news You have a Negro President. You have two
sons in a predominantly Negro school. They're both
afraid they'll be hooted at and kicked around."

"Why make out that it's so bad?" Beggs demanded.
"Why does everything have to be bad?"

"Because it *is,* it just is," Gertrude said, throwing her
crumpled paper napkin on the table. "Do you want some
really bad news now? I don't mind telling you. I just
heard it from the milkman. The Schearers are moving
out of the neighborhood. They've put their house up for
sale. They didn't even have the nerve to tell us. I had
to hear it from the milkman."

Automatically Beggs's eyebrows had arched with surprise. The Schearers were the last of the old crowd, their

old friends in the neighborhood, who had stayed on with them. He and Gertrude saw the Schearers at least twice a week.

Gertrude was going on. "He must've gotten that new position he applied for. Well, at least they've got some sense. They've had enough, even if you haven't. And I'm thinking of the boys now, especially now, and nothing else."

"I think of them, too," he said angrily. He paused, to control himself, and then he said, "There's going to be a change right here. Didn't you hear it on television or read it in the papers?"

"What? Read what?"

"Sonenberg and McCune were in the same room with the President in Frankfurt. They were killed, too. That means the Assistant job to Agajanian in the White House is open, and I'm next up. It means a solid raise."

Gertrude seemed to deflate into weariness. "Oh, that one. I heard that one before. Do you have a contract that says you'll get it?"

"It's my turn, Gertie. Chief Gaynor knows I'm next in line. Besides, I was thinking"——he felt shrewd, his old confident self——"the fact that we stayed on in this neighborhood is going to work for me. Look at it any way you want, but the new President is a Negro, and knowing Gaynor's politicking, he'll be wanting to play up to President Dilman. Gaynor knows where we live. It shows I have no prejudices—in fact, shows I like the Negro people and get along with them. Gaynor'll figure my promotion will look good to Dilman."

"I'm sure Dilman doesn't know you exist," said Gertrude, "and I'm not sure Gaynor knows either, considering these past years." He was furious at her remark, in front of the boys, but before he could reply, she was on her feet, hustling Ogden and Otis to the door, stuffing their arms into their jackets. "Get on your way," she was saying, "and watch the crossings, and if there's any trouble you report it to the principal."

Otis had gone through the door, but the older one, Ogden, hung behind. "Pop, last night Junior Austin said there's a holiday off when a President dies. I hope so."

"When I get to the White House, I'll arrange it," Beggs said expansively.

"Ha," Ogden chortled, "that'll be the day."

Flushed, Beggs shouted, "If I can get you those damn stamps from the President's secretary, I can——" It was too late. His older son had gone.

Put down, he waited, as Gertrude came back into the dining room. She tried to push her hair out of her face, and buttoned her housecoat, and then she lifted her head and stared at her husband. The tight, unyielding lines of attack had left her forehead and mouth. When she spoke, her tone was more imploring than accusing.

"Otto, I know what that promotion means to you, and I——I hope you get it, for your sake," she said. "I know what the Service means to you, and all that business, and the excitements, and the scrapbooks. But there's more to life, Otto. Even if you got the promotion——"

"I'll get it," he said fiercely.

"So you get it. But even then, we'd have to borrow and scrape to make a down payment on a better house in a ——a decent, proper neighborhood for the boys."

"We'll manage, that's all that counts."

She came forward a few steps. "Why do you make it so hard for yourself and for us, Otto? It's been——I guess it's over a year since Austin agreed he'd like to have you in Chevy Chase as a partner. It was no favor to a brother-in-law. He's making money hand over fist. He wants to expand. He respects you, no matter how——how carried away he gets sometimes with his success. He's always saying a person of your background would be a definite asset to his business."

"I don't need his charity——him, of all people."

She was pleading. "Otto, there's no charity. You'd have to work for it. Six months ago you seemed to be more agreeable. That's why I got him to loan you those textbooks, so you could study up for the realty board examinations. I think maybe you opened them once. They've been rotting inside the desk ever since. But you're smart enough to do it. Look how fast you got in the Secret Service, passing those tests when you wanted to. You could become a licensed realtor in no time. You'd triple Austin's business."

"Doing what? Standing in drafty houses and showing couples still wet behind the ears the view, the goddam new plumbing, the bedrooms? That's a life, after what I lived? Listen, Gertie, you stick with me, let me do it my way, and I promise you—"

The telephone in the living room rang out, and he stopped, wondering.

"I'll get it," Gertrude was saying. "Probably Mae Schearer to gloat about—"

She was gone. He started to eat his bowl of yogurt, when he saw her return.

"Otto, it's Chief Gaynor calling from the White House."

He jumped to his feet, suddenly beaming, his temples throbbing. "I knew it, I knew it. Tell him I'll be right on. I'll take it upstairs."

He wanted this triumph alone. He rushed out of the dining room and bounded up the creaking stairs two at a time. Breathless, he snatched up the telephone on the desk.

"Hello . . . I've got it, Gertrude . . . hello."

He heard her click off, and heard a remote secretary tell him to hold on, and then he heard Gaynor's gruff voice, so welcome this morning.

"Beggs? Chief Gaynor here."

"Good morning, Chief. I was just leaving for duty. Glad you caught me. I'm sure sorry about Sonenberg and McCune."

"It happens, it happens," said Gaynor impatiently. "We just wish they could have done something to save the President. Well, that's behind us. We've got a job to do, and today it's harder than ever. Beggs, I'm calling you to tell you we're forced into some changes around here—"

His heart swelled. "Yes, sure."

"—and we've upped the guard detail, and have to do some switching around on the three shifts. I know you're on the morning-to-afternoon shift. But for the time being we're putting you on from afternoon to evening. You don't have to come in now. Rest up. You check in at four o'clock and stay until one in the morning."

His heart thumped faster. "You—you mentioned changes, Chief. Is that all? I mean, just the time?"

"Matter of fact, no, glad you mentioned it. One second, I think there's another call—no, it's okay. Yes, you'll be undertaking a new job. Lou Agajanian tells me you get along well with Negroes."

"That's right, Chief," he said hastily. "Been living right here off Connecticut among them for years. Some of my finest friends—"

"Excellent," Gaynor interrupted. "We're assigning you to being one of the twelve special agents who will personally be guarding President Dilman. How's that?"

Confused, he waited for Chief Gaynor to tell him the rest, but realized there was no more. "I—I don't understand, Chief. You want me to guard the President? Is that my new job?"

"I knew you'd be pleased. Agajanian told me it was a duty you'd always wanted."

Beggs felt sinking and frantic. "Chief, it's what I wanted four or five years ago. But there's a lot of water under the bridge now. I—I've got seniority, now that McCune is gone. I know that Sonenberg left a supervisory vacancy. I figured it was regular procedure—I mean, I thought that the Assistant to Lou, that opening, would—"

"It's already filled, Beggs." Chief Gaynor was brisk and businesslike. "An hour ago I submitted Special Agent Roscoe Prentiss' name to the Secretary of the Treasury and he okayed it."

"Prentiss?" Beggs could barely restrain himself from shouting at his Chief. "He came into the Service four years after I did. He's way down the list. I'm supposed to get—"

"Wait a minute, Beggs, easy there. You're creating a seniority system that doesn't exist. Going by length of time in the Service is not in the regulations. It's a factor, of course—always has been when we consider promotions. But just as often we try to angle the right man for the right job at the right time."

Beggs felt himself shaking with righteous indignation.

"Who's Prentiss? What has he got that I haven't got?"
Then it came to him, and he knew. "Don't tell me. I
get it. He's colored. He's being upped to supervisor because he's a Negro."

There were empty silent seconds on the telephone, and
then Chief Gaynor came on less gruffly. "I'm not in a position to say that was the decisive factor, Beggs. I—" His
tone of voice lowered, offering confidence, man-to-man
equality. "I just want to put it to you as one reasonable
human being to another—what would you do in my
boots? Overnight we've got an unusual situation, we've
got a Negro President. Don't you think it's only fair that
one of the six Secret Service executives should be of his
people? If I didn't do this he might feel we were being discriminatory, and feel unkindly toward the Service."

"Did President Dilman ask for this?"

"No-no, he doesn't even know about it yet. It's just
something we felt would be fair at this time."

"Dammit, Chief, it's not fair, say whatever you want.
It's discrimination against me because I'm white. It's not
giving me what I deserve. I don't like it."

"Beggs, this is a time to be reasonable. I appreciate
your disappointment. The fact is, we're giving you something better, something you always wanted, an assignment right next to the President of the United States. In
fact, and Lou'll go into this with you, there'll be a—a
token raise. As for the future, we'll keep you in mind.
We take care of our own, Beggs. Now, you take it easy,
and check in with Lou at four. Be seeing you."

Listlessly, Otto Beggs returned the telephone to the
desk. Life had spat in his eye again. He knew when he
was licked. His glance went to the door, but he had no
stomach for facing Gertrude.

He lumbered to the bedroom window and glared
down into the busy street. There were people down
there, and most of them were black. Until now his attitude toward them had been boxed between resentment
and toleration. Now he was bitter toward all of them.
Because his Chief wanted to apple-polish a new President, who was Negro, who did not deserve to be President, Otto Beggs had been elbowed aside to make room

for a callow colleague whose only qualification was his black skin. And the worst of it, they were throwing him a few pennies more and telling him to risk his life to protect the life of a colored politician.

The injustice of it gagged him. He, a war hero, who almost gave up his life for his country, almost got killed trying to protect those watermelon eaters in the safe rear lines doing soft KP and shooting craps and knocking up Korean girls. He, who had received the Medal of Honor from Eisenhower, having to be at the beck and call of a black President, whose war record consisted of keeping records in the Pentagon. Chrissakes, what in the hell was the world coming to?

He was ready for Gertrude at last.

He strode out of the room and down the stairs. She was waiting below, unblinking, as her fingers picked at the fringe of her housecoat, watching his descent. He felt that his cheeks were livid, and knew that she knew, and did not give a damn.

He looked fixedly at her. She did not utter a word.

He said, "My shift's been changed. I'm not going to work until four. I've got time on my hands. I want to use it. Where in the hell are those real estate textbooks?"

She swallowed, quickly nodding her head. "I—I'll find them for you, Otto. I'll get them right away."

She raised the long skirt of her housecoat, to make movement and speed easier, and hastily she climbed the stairs. For once, he was satisfied with her. For once, she'd had sufficient respect for him to say nothing more.

Late in the afternoon, still behind her desk in her office next to the President's Oval Office, Edna Foster sat with hands clasped tightly, observing George Murdock as he read the short letter she had moments before pulled out of her gray electric typewriter.

Her gaze did not leave her fiancé. He was running his fingers through his sparse blond hair, and then scratching at his acne-pocked pale cheeks, and then scratching at his beaky nose and receding chin, about which she felt so possessive.

His small, translucent eyes were smaller as they came up from the page to meet her own. "No, Edna, don't show it to him, not yet."

She took her neat, two-paragraph letter of resignation to President Dilman back from George, coughed wretchedly, since her cold had settled in her chest, and said, "It's expected of the whole staff."

"Flannery told us President Dilman was keeping on T.C.'s entire staff. And there'll be an announcement he's keeping on the Cabinet, too. Just like Harry Truman and Lyndon Johnson did, at first."

"George, it's impossible. How can I work for him after working for T.C.?"

Murdock's eyes became even smaller. "Is that the reason, Edna?"

"I don't know," she said quickly. "He has his own secretary over in the Senate Office Building. She's colored. She'd understand him. It—it would be so difficult for me."

George Murdock shook his head. "No, it would be wrong, Edna. You know this job. The other girl doesn't. Give him a break. You admitted you didn't even know him. You haven't even talked to him today."

"He's been locked up in the Cabinet Room for hours, with Eaton and Talley and everyone. Even if I did know him, it would be—"

She halted, and listened. She could hear the tread of many feet leaving the Cabinet Room for the tiled corridor outside.

She said, "They're breaking up now, George. You'd better leave me. He might come in, and it wouldn't look right."

George Murdock came to his feet and so did she, and she was pleased that she was no taller than he, even if it was, as she suspected, because he wore lifts in his heels. He started for the corridor door. "Think twice, Edna, before you quit. You can help him. It might be better for both of us, you being busy right now. See you tonight."

Alone with her letter of resignation, she reread it, then, with a pen, supplied a missing comma. George, she

knew, was wiser than she, and she was attentive always
to his counsel. But this time he was wrong because he
could not see the turmoil inside her, and there had been
no time to talk it out. Yet George had perceived what
was at the bottom of her discomfort. He had doubted
that she wanted to resign because of her loss of T.C.
He had forced her to confess that she thought a colored
secretary could serve a Negro President better.

She wondered now what her admission had meant.
Why did she think Dilman should have a colored secretary? She had never possessed strong feelings for or
against Negroes. In fact, throughout her career she had
had no close contact with them. To her they were not
people, but a controversial issue that had swirled about
T.C.'s Oval Office these last two years and that had gone
in and out of her typewriter as a civil rights problem.
Like T.C., she had been for them. Like Lincoln, she did
not believe in slavery or discrimination or prejudice. She
had always considered herself open-minded and progressive, and wanting the right thing.

She had never been faced with the problem of knowing a Negro really well, or working for one really closely.
Last night the problem had come to her, and all through
the hectic and emotional day she had tried to evaluate
it. Without precisely defining why, she had come to the
conclusion that she must resign. She had drafted several
versions of her letter, when she could find the time, and
at last it was typed. She had called George in from the
West Wing lobby, where the members of the press were
crowded about for every news flash, but the two of them
had had only five minutes together.

She wondered if she would see President Dilman at
all today. He had arrived at the West Wing entrance late
in the morning, had been hurried past the television and
radio microphones outside, stopping just long enough to
speak, brokenly, no more than thirty words of his grief
over the nation's loss, and to promise that the continuity
of orderly government would not be impaired and that a
formal statement would be forthcoming.

After that, he had spent the entire afternoon in the
Cabinet Room, flanked by Secretary of State Eaton and

Governor Talley, seeing Congressional leaders and several ambassadors, approving funeral arrangements, signing a more elaborate proclamation of a period of mourning, preparing a statement to the nation. There had been, as far as Edna had been able to make out, only one change in plans. She had scheduled the members of the Cabinet to see him, one after the other, separately. Apparently Dilman had insisted upon seeing them as a group for five minutes. Talley had emerged to tell her, and Edna had made the arrangements. The first Cabinet meeting had lasted seven minutes, and, according to Tim Flannery, President Dilman had requested one minute of silent prayer for T.C. and MacPherson, and then he had made a little impromptu speech promising that he would try to serve the country, try to carry out T.C.'s programs with their help, and he had concluded by pleading with all of them to stay on in their posts.

She heard muffled voices in the corridor, and then the tramp of footsteps toward the Oval Office, followed by lighter footsteps. Her intuition told her that President Dilman was on his way to his desk for the first time in his first day in office, followed, no doubt, by his Secret Service bodyguards.

She wanted to make certain.

She went quietly to the thick door that separated her room from the Oval Office. In the middle of the heavy door, at eye level, was a minute peephole with a magnifying glass inside it. Very few visitors, even members of the government, were aware that this peephole existed. Occasionally, with glee, T.C. had pointed it out to distinguished foreign guests. He had liked to say, to Edna's embarrassment, "My wife Hesper had the hole drilled, so that Miss Foster can keep an eye on me. We have a lot of pretty secretaries here, you know." Actually, as Edna knew from the first day, the peephole was there so that a President's personal secretary could unobtrusively peer inside, to make sure that the Chief Executive was not occupied with visitors, before she entered or dared to disturb him.

Edna Foster stood on tiptoe and placed her right eye to the peephole.

The magnifying glass enlarged T.C.'s elaborate desk, made up of the oak timbers of the *H.M.S. Resolute,* a ship turned over to Queen Victoria by American Minister to Great Britain James Buchanan in an effort to aid the British search for a lost Arctic expedition. Years later Queen Victoria had returned a portion of the rescue vessel to President Hayes in the shape of this White House desk. And forever after it had been known as the Buchanan desk.

Clearly visible to Edna's eye now, as she studied the venerable desk, were the numerous knickknacks and gadgets surrounding the green blotter, all favors that emissaries from Japan and Ecuador, Italy and Baraza, had brought to the President. Almost visible, too, were the silver-framed portraits of T.C.'s wife and adolescent son.

Dropping her gaze, Edna could make out the center of the room, even to the Presidential seal woven into the green carpet. Shifting her eyes to the right, Edna could see T.C.'s cushioned antique captain's chair, set between the two curved sofas.

Beyond the furnishings, the Oval Office was empty.

Suddenly the open doorway to the corridor was filled by a Secret Service agent, the one named Beggs, who was unfastening the chain. A moment later President Douglass Dilman came into the room. No one followed him.

Knowing that this was his first visit, as Chief Executive of the land, to what was now his office and had been the office of every President since 1909, Edna Foster watched with fascination.

Douglass Dilman had come to the middle of the room hesitantly. He simply stood there as if uncertain where to turn, what to do, like one who was not sure that he had found the right address. Edna examined him. Although the peephole brought him closer, made him larger, he appeared smaller than she remembered him to have been last night. His broad black face reflected confusion. He rubbed one side of his flaring nostrils and slowly pirouetted, staring at the three windows behind the desk, at the two standing flags, the American flag and the Presidential flag. Then he stared down at the desk itself.

He was full in the peephole once more. Edna's heart ached, not from the fact that T.C. was not there, not from the fact that a stranger was there instead, but for Dilman's forlornness. His charcoal suit looked too new, too uncomfortable, and long at the sleeves. He might have been a proprietor of a shoeshine-stand concession in his Sunday best, waiting for an interview on the new lease.

She must go to him, at once, before he came to her.

Withdrawing from the peephole, Edna Foster folded her letter of resignation, located the memorandum of urgent calls and messages that she had prepared for the President. Holding the letter, the memorandum and her shorthand pad in her left hand, she nervously opened the door to his office and went inside.

"Good—good day, Mr. President."

"Miss Foster, how do you do. I—I was about to find out where you were."

"There've been endless phone calls and messages. Some may be important. I didn't want to break in on your meetings, the—the first day—but—" She removed the memorandum from her left fist and handed it to him. "I've typed it out for you, in detail. If you want to dictate—"

She had started for her familiar chair next to T.C.'s desk, but Dilman did not move. She halted, and waited.

His eyes were on the desk. Then they swung toward the sofas across the room. He indicated one sofa. "I think it'll be more comfortable over there."

She nodded, then remembered a procedure. She went quickly to the open French door leading to the Rose Garden, waved to a Secret Service agent, then closed it. She started toward the other open door leading to the corridor.

Dilman, having reached the captain's chair, said, "What are you doing?"

Puzzled, Edna replied, "I'm closing the doors for privacy."

Dilman did not hide his concern. "No. Leave that one open."

"I—I've always been told to do it, to shut them. What

you may be dictating—it might be personal, I mean privileged—"

"Leave that door open," Dilman said.

She was surprised at his severity. "Well, I—" She shrugged. "Very well, Mr. President."

Before she could move to the sofa, he intercepted her. His distress was obvious. "Let me—I think I'd better explain," he said quickly. "I think I can be honest with you. After all, you were T.C.'s confidential secretary."

"Yes," she said, bewildered.

Dilman hesitated. His eyes were cast downward at his shoes. "Once, President Eisenhower appointed a Negro, E. Frederic Morrow, to his staff in the White House, in an executive capacity. Morrow required a secretary from the White House pool. They were all specially trained white girls. Everyone refused the job. According to Morrow, 'None wants the onus of working for a colored boss.' So Morrow sat alone in his White House office, without a secretary, not knowing what to do. Then, late in the day, a white girl timidly appeared. She was from Massachusetts. She was religious. She knew Morrow was having trouble. She felt that she could not be true to her faith unless she volunteered for the job. When the white girl appeared, Morrow said, 'She kept the door open behind her, as if for protection, and refused to come in and sit down.' " Dilman paused. "I could never forget that. In the Senate I always kept one door open when I had a white secretary or female visitor in. I—I guess I've brought the same feeling with me into the White House. Forgive my sensitivity, Miss Foster. Now, at least, you understand it."

Shaken, Edna wanted to burst into tears. When Dilman raised his eyes to look at her, she tried to control her voice, but it quavered. "I think the President's door should be closed."

She went to the corridor door, shut it firmly, and without meeting his eyes she went to the curved sofa and sat down.

Dilman was behind the captain's chair, still standing. He ignored the memorandum that he held. "Governor Talley tells me that I should announce to the White

House staff that I am keeping all members on. Is that right?"

"Yes, Mr. President."

"I'll begin with you, Miss Foster. Will you stay?"

As he spoke, she had separated her shorthand pad from her folded letter of resignation. Now she stuffed the letter of resignation deep into her skirt pocket. "Yes, Mr. President," she found herself saying. "I'd be honored to stay. Thank you."

"I thank you," he said with a wan smile. "Then you're my first appointment as President of the United States. I'll take care of the others later."

Efficiently, she had opened her shorthand pad and held a pencil poised, waiting.

He had not yet consulted the memorandum. His eyes were directed toward the three naval paintings over the mantel of the fireplace. "Miss Foster, do you remember what Harry Truman said after F.D.R. died and after he himself had become President? He said, 'I felt like the moon, the stars, and the planets had fallen on me.' He said to reporters, 'I've got the most awful responsibility a man ever had. If you fellows ever pray, pray for me.' And Lyndon Johnson. Will we ever forget his leaving the plane at Andrews Airfield with President Kennedy's coffin, and his going to the microphones? Do you remember, Miss Foster? He said, 'I will do my best. That is all I can do. I ask for your help—and God's.' Well, Miss Foster, that's how I feel, like Harry Truman did and like Lyndon Johnson did."

Edna tried to find her voice. "I think everyone understands that, Mr. President."

"Do they?" He looked at her absently. "I wonder."

"They'll pray for you and—and they'll help you. I know they will, the way they helped Harry Truman and Lyndon Johnson. It's no different now."

His eyes were fixed upon her. "It is different now. . . . They weren't black." Then, suddenly, he smiled. "Of course, if there's no one's help, there is always God's. After all, we don't know if He is white or black."

And he sat down in the captain's chair, and was ready to begin.

III

RECLINING LOW in the rear seat of the bulletproof White House limousine, Douglass Dilman felt, this early morning, as he had felt every morning of the past week, like a prisoner being transferred from his home to his cellblock.

Up ahead, through the distortion of the bent windshield, he could make out the motorcycle escort, red lights flashing. On either side of him were more roaring motorcycles. Behind him he could hear the higher pitch of the protective sedan, which contained the remainder of his complement of bodyguards.

Within the luxurious limousine there was little freedom. In the front seat, the driver and the man next to him were Secret Service agents of the White House Detail. In the back, an arm's length from Dilman, sitting sideways on one jump seat, was agent Beggs. True, none of them had their eyes upon him. The chauffeur's gaze was directed straight ahead, the other agent in front examined the passing panorama of Sixteenth Street to their right, and Beggs examined the passing pedestrians and buildings to the left.

Douglass Dilman pressed his brown fedora more tightly to his skull as the wind whipped in through the opening of the electric window beside the driver. Wistfully, Dilman took in the landmarks that he had passed so often in the years when he had belonged to himself, and almost no one had cared if he were living or dead. He recognized the Hebrew Academy, the Methodist Church, the blue Woodner Hotel, the all-female Meridian Hill Hotel, the Hotel 2400, the Bulgarian Embassy, the

white-pillared, red-brick, bogus English houses with their
porches and stoops, which so many affluent Negroes had
purchased from whites. In minutes the limousine would
take him away from all this, around Lafayette Square,
and to Executive Avenue and the south entrance of the
stately Executive Mansion.

Dilman had awaited with dread the inevitability of
this important day. It was his moving day. And now it
was here. T.C.'s widow Hesper, Dilman had been told,
had overseen the removal of the late President's and her
own personal effects and furniture from the White House
yesterday, just as Governor Talley and Edna Foster had
removed T.C.'s personal belongings from the Oval Office
of the West Wing three days before.

For long, painful hours last night, Dilman, with the
help of his housekeeper Crystal, his Senate secretary,
Diane Fuller, Rose Spinger, and two nervous Army enlisted men, had assembled and packed into cartons and
crates his pathetically limited and long-used possessions.
Dilman had refused to allow anyone from the White
House to help him, not Edna Foster, not T.C.'s valet
Beecher, and not any of the White House staff that included the housekeeper, the houseboys, the ushers. Although Flannery had talked him into permitting newspapers to publish photographs of his simple living room
in the brownstone row house, he did not want any critical outsiders to see or poke through his home. Nor had
he permitted the Reverend Spinger or Wanda Gibson
to come downstairs to assist him. In his new role, Dilman realized, he could no longer treat Spinger as a
friend, only as one who headed America's foremost
Negro pressure organization. As for Wanda, her presence might have made the Secret Service men wonder
about her relationship to him, and someone might have
divulged it to the press, which in turn might distort it.
While he had spoken to her briefly on the telephone
every night before going to bed, he had not seen her
personally since assuming the Presidency. She had not
chided him for his neglect, for that was not her way.
But he suspected that she commiserated with him, knowing his weaknesses, which was justifiable on her part.

Through the window he could see that they were turning off Sixteenth Street. Suddenly he was terrified. He tried to define his terror. It was not simply that he was giving up the safe anonymity of the ground floor of his modest two-story brownstone to spend a year and five months of life in the unfamiliar, awesome, museum-like, constantly exposed second story of the White House. That was bad enough, being the intruder-lodger in a mansion supported by a population that had never before permitted him to live among them, as part of them, in their easy streets and developments and tracts. The worst of it was that he was being carried farther and farther away from the only woman on earth whom he loved, and who cared for him. In short minutes he would be entombed in a prison that she could not visit, to which he dared not summon her. He wondered how long she would wait for his release, or if she would wait at all. He might lose her. He would lose her. Then he would be alone, utterly alone, in a hostile world. It was this terrifying possibility that had chilled him.

He brought his eyes from the window to the ominous radiophone beside him, and then to the sour face of the Secret Service agent in the jump seat. Fleetingly he wondered what the agent was so unhappy about. Perhaps, Dilman decided, his expression was really that of anxiety over his responsibility.

The agent's full name was Otto Beggs, Dilman remembered. He had been on the afternoon shift, on guard outside the Oval Office, throughout the week. This morning he had appeared at daybreak, introducing himself again, saying that he was on a split shift today, four hours now and four hours late in the afternoon. With the three women, Beggs had helped supervise the Army privates who carried the cartons and crates into their huge military truck. There had also been several pieces of Dilman's furniture, a small bedroom desk and bench, a maroon leather armchair, a tall lamp with a shade that Aldora had painted so long ago, and the Revels chair, that Dilman had permitted to be moved. The Revels chair was the possession of which he was most proud. He had received it as a gift from the state Party organization upon his election to the United States Senate. Although it was a genuine John Henry Belter rosewood chair with an upholstered panel in its scrolled back and with an upholstered felt seat, handmade in New York in 1865, he had been told its real value lay in the fact that in the 1870s it had belonged to Hiram R. Revels, of Mississippi, who had become the first Negro to sit in the United States Senate.

The rest of the furniture Dilman had left behind, so that Rose Spinger could lease his old quarters for him furnished, to bring a better rental. After the Army truck had wheeled away toward the White House, followed in a Presidential staff car by Crystal and Diane Fuller, who would direct the unpacking, Beggs and the other Secret Service agents had waited to escort Dilman himself.

Still filled with the panic induced by his thoughts of losing Wanda forever, Dilman determined to question Beggs. He must be discreet, he reminded himself. But he must also know what was possible.

"Uh, Mr. Beggs——"

The Secret Service agent turned his head. "Yes, sir—yes, Mr. President?"

"I'd like to ask you a question."

"Anything, Mr. President. Pardon me if I keep my eyes on the street while I talk. Duty, sir." He was attentive, but his eyes were pointed to what lay out beyond the limousine window in the gray morning.

"While I haven't had time to acquaint myself with the functions of the Secret Service, I do gather your Detail is assigned to protect me at all times."

"Yes, sir, since 1901. Title 18, United States Code, Section 3056, amended and approved by the 82nd and 83rd Congress," recited Otto Beggs. Then he went on, " 'Subject to the discretion of the Treasury, the United States Secret Service, Treasury Department, is authorized to protect the person of the President of the United States and members of his immediate family.' "

"I gathered that," said Dilman dryly. "I haven't been out of your sight for a second this week, except when I've gone to the bathroom or have been asleep. Does it always have to be that way? Isn't there some time when

I can go out alone, privately, to see certain—certain friends?"

Beggs shook his head. "Sorry, Mr. President. How can we protect you if we're not with you?"

"I can't believe every President has been followed every minute of his term by agents," said Dilman.

"It's true, sir. Mr. Truman tried to get off on walks without us, and General Eisenhower tried to get rid of us to play his golf in peace, and Mr. Kennedy tried to escape for some swims, but they never succeeded one minute, far as I know. Mr. Johnson was more coopera- tive in some respects, but T.C. once tried to sneak off to a stag party in Foxhall Road at one in the morning. We caught up with him."

Dilman was thoughtful. "Let us say I kept it perfectly secret, yet insisted I had to see some friends alone?"

"You can see anyone alone, Mr. President, but you can't travel to them unguarded."

"What if I ordered it?"

Beggs turned his head, his puffy red face showing astonishment. "You couldn't, Mr. President—begging your pardon, sir, but it's the law. Chief Gaynor is em- powered by the law to prevent you from any physical movement that he considers dangerous. This is sort of embarrassing, Mr. President, but like I said, it's the law —sir."

Dilman surrendered. "Thank you, Mr. Beggs." The conversation left him more agitated than ever about Wanda and himself. Circumstances had made any fu- ture relationship impossible for them. He could not see her again on his terms, which demanded complete pri- vacy. He could visit her only on the Secret Service agents' terms and, he supposed, her own desired terms—publicly —and this would for the first time make known to one and all their longtime association. He considered the last, and then one more possibility came to his mind, and he thought about it.

"Crowding up a bit," the chauffeur called out. "Take us another five minutes, Mr. President. Mind if we go on sirens?"

"I'd prefer not," Dilman said. "There's no hurry."

There was no hurry inside him to face what lay ahead. He put the meeting with Wanda out of his mind. He would tackle that dilemma later. He tried to consider his more immediate problems. Edna Foster had telephoned him at breakfast to read him his schedule for today. He would have one hour in the living quarters of the White House, to become further acquainted with the historic rooms that were now his home, and to meet his staff, to brief them on where his furniture and personal effects should be placed. After that, there were his morning engagements: a half-hour meeting with Secretary of State Eaton and Governor Talley; a one-hour full-dress Cabinet meeting, his first, not counting the brief gathering when he had asked the members to stay on; a short meeting with his son, Julian, who was coming down from Trafford to see him; a short meeting with his biographer, Leroy Poole, who had so insistently been telephoning.

Lunch, he remembered, would be with the Joint Chiefs of Staff, who were coming over from the Pentagon. This afternoon would be packed, conferences with the Majority and Minority Leaders of the Senate and House of Representatives, conferences with the Directors of the CIA and the FBI, a conference with Tim Flannery, a conference with the Federal Loan Administrator, a conference with the Ambassador to Russia. Only the hours between five and eight had been left free, so that he might catch up on his official reading. After eight in the evening there would be the best time of the day and the week, a private and informal dinner in the White House, his first as President, with Sue and Nat Abrahams.

Thinking of everything he had to do before dinner made him acknowledge the tension that was overlaid on the weariness and uneasiness that had accumulated in the seven days behind him. It was incredible to him that a week, an entire week, had passed since he had become President of the United States. Even now, in his protective, mechanized capsule that moved toward the White House, he did not feel the way the President should, however it was that a President was supposed to feel. Perhaps, he realized, this was because he had not yet been made answerable to the demands put upon the executive branch. The events of the past week had been out of his hands, had rolled in pomp and tragic splendor to their climax, as if motivated by the force of a Supreme Being. He had been an observer. And he had been grateful for this, and for Governor Talley and Secretary Eaton, who had both possessed the kindness and intelligence to speak for him when his voice was supposed to be heard.

Vividly he recalled T.C.'s funeral. His memory turned like an orderly kaleidoscope, yet showing him only hasty, quickly changing fragments of color, almost abstract vari-colored impressions of sliding glass. There was the impression, streaked by the rain of the late afternoon, of himself and the Cabinet and the Congressional and military leaders at Dulles International Airport, when the jet known as 809 Air Force One landed after its trip from Frankfurt and disgorged the coffins containing the bodies of T.C. and MacPherson. There was the impression of the morning after, when T.C.'s widow Hesper, back from Arizona, stately and contained in her grief, supported by her awkward, adolescent son and by Secretary Eaton, had met him. They had gone together into the East Room of the White House to find T.C.'s flag-draped bier beneath the dimmed chandeliers, surrounded by the flickering candles and the rigid guard of honor. There was the impression of the following noon, the yellow sun shining down upon the massed thousands who lined Pennsylvania Avenue, as he plodded behind the muffled black-draped drums, behind the horse-drawn caisson with its coffin, behind T.C.'s widow and son and relatives. He walked side by side in step with The Judge and two other ex-Presidents, toward the public Rotunda of the Capitol, where the 21-gun salute rang out and the Marine Band played "Hail to the Chief," and the brief Episcopalian services were observed. There was the impression of the funeral itself, once more in the noon sun but screened from the general public's view, with himself and The Judge and other ex-Presidents and T.C.'s Cabinet in the landscaped family burial plot on the grounds behind the family manor near Concord, New Hampshire.

There was the change in the kaleidoscope of his memory from yellow to muted and mixed colors. There was the impression of himself, with Eaton and Talley on either side of him, in the Cabinet Room—he had been unable to bring himself to return to T.C.'s Oval Office—greeting and reassuring the countless heads of nations who had participated in the cortege and attended the burial. He remembered meeting the Prime Minister of Great Britain, the President of France, the Deputy Premier of Russia, the Chancellor of Germany, the King of Belgium, the Premier of Japan, and half a hundred more coming, chatting, going, in those bewildering hours. There was the impression, even less bright, more settling, of himself in the Fish Room the day before yesterday, engaged in the lively but brief discussion with The Judge, so forthright, so encouraging, then the more formal discussions with the other ex-Presidents, the short exchanges with senators and representatives whom he had known, with the Party heads, with the members of T.C.'s advisory team. There was the impression of himself, in Tim Flannery's press office yesterday behind closed doors, being informed of the ugly riots that had broken out like bursting boils, riots between whites and blacks, unorganized but savage, in Tennessee, in Louisiana, in Texas, in California, in Missouri, in Michigan. And the impression of Tim's reading aloud the first public opinion poll on President Douglass Dilman—in favor of him: 24%; against him: 61%; undecided: 15%—and the remembrance of his secret dismay at this harsh factual appraisal of him, so at variance with the optimistic guess and hopes of the moderate New York newspaper editorial that had heartened him the week before. And then the impression of Tim, and others, afterward, helping him hastily draft the statement requesting national unity and support, promising adherence to the principles T.C. advocated, reminding Americans that the eyes of the world and of history were upon them.

"Mr. President—"

It was Beggs addressing him, and quickly he collapsed the kaleidoscope of memory and hid it in his mind, and he looked up.

"—here we are at the White House."

The limousine had, indeed, drawn to a halt before the South Portico. A group of men, three of their number brandishing large cameras, were gathered between the curved driveway and the canopy. Beggs leaned forward to open the rear door, but a uniformed White House policeman had already opened it. Before stepping out, Dilman looked off to his left. The view, that would now belong to him for a year and five months, as it had belonged to Jefferson and Jackson and Lincoln and F.D.R., momentarily lulled his apprehension. There was a sylvan, pastoral quality about the sloping expanse of green lawn, flecked here and there with autumn's rust, and between President Cleveland's Japanese maples a circular fountain threw off its steady clean spray. Behind the birch and elm trees in the distance he could make out the high iron fence that enclosed the President's private park and protected it from the traffic on South Executive Avenue. Beyond the fence he could see the majestic white marble obelisk of the Washington Monument pointed to the cloudy sky. The greatness demanded of the Mansion's occupant pierced his peaceful mood, and apprehension suffused him again.

Beggs and the policeman were outside the car in attendance. Dilman pushed himself from the deep upholstered seat, ignoring their offered assistance, and stepped out onto the driveway. Only one of the clustered dozen waiting, Tim Flannery, was familiar to him.

Flannery darted forward to grasp his hand. "Welcome home, Mr. President," he said.

"This isn't much pleasure to me, Tim," Dilman said, "considering the circumstances."

"No," Flannery agreed. Then he was all business. "Mr. President, I've allowed three from the press pool to grab a few pictures of you." He turned, waving. "Go ahead, boys."

As the limousine rolled away, leaving Dilman stiffly posed against the backdrop of the south lawn and the Washington Monument, the photographers hustled toward him, crouching, clicking. Dilman nodded, unable to smile, and then he moved toward the canopy. The photographers went crabwise alongside him, shooting more pictures, as the onlookers, White House police, Secret Service agents, gardeners and yardmen parted to give him passage.

He was halfway under the canopy when a medium-sized Negro with tight curly white-cotton hair that matched his white bow tie, with jet-black solemn face that matched his immaculate dark suit, stepped forward.

"Mr. President," he said, "I am Beecher, the late President's valet."

Dilman stopped and extended his hand. Hesitantly the valet shook it.

"I'm glad to see you again, Beecher. I remember you from the Congressional receptions I attended here." He paused, and then added, "I don't know what your plans are, but I'd be pleased if you stayed on, that is, if you'd like to work for me."

For the first time a smile wrinkled the valet's bland face. "Thank you, Mr. President. I would like nothing better." He indicated the south entrance. "Many of the White House staff are in the Diplomatic Reception Room, waiting to welcome you. After you've met them, I'll escort you to your apartment on the second floor."

"Very well," said Dilman.

The valet leaped ahead to open the door, and Dilman went through it into the Diplomatic Reception Room. Inside the door, he hesitated. At least one hundred persons lined the vast and stately circular room with its eighteenth-century furnishings. There were women in domestic white or blue uniforms, many wearing aprons, and several dressed in crisp daytime secretarial suits or blouses and skirts. There were men in overalls, in fatigues, in dark suits with black ties. They were everywhere, aligned against the ornately framed oils of many First Ladies—he recognized the likenesses of Dolley Madison and Jacqueline Kennedy—and they waited along the cupboards of gold-edged plates, amid the scattering of yellow-upholstered furniture, against the scenic wallpaper depicting Niagara Falls and New York Bay.

"This is part of the White House day staff," the valet whispered to Dilman.

All eyes were upon Dilman, curious eyes, speculating eyes. Slowly Dilman crossed the oval carpet, until he had progressed to the middle of the Reception Room.

He cleared his throat. "I do not have time to meet you individually right now and shake your hands, but I am touched by this turnout. I would like you to do this for me—I don't think it will take very long—but I'd like each of you, starting from the door, to raise your hand and give me your name and job title. I would appreciate that."

He turned to his left, toward those nearest the entrance and before the glassed cupboard, and as each one lifted a hand, some tentatively, some high and assured, each announced his name and position in the White House. While the roll call went around the room, Dilman murmured an acknowledgment of each one's identity. He was astonished by the diversity of personnel. He had read or heard that there were 132 rooms in this house to be looked after, and that thirty-eight policemen guarded its many passageways, entrances, exits, and that four thousand persons possessed full-time or semipermanent security passes to service the Executive Mansion from within or without.

Yet Dilman had never expected anything as overwhelming as this. The men and women identifying themselves included police, chefs, kitchen help, chambermaids, butlers, carpenters, air-conditioning specialists, launderers, electricians, maintenance engineers, house painters, floor boys, telegraphers. Some were more important than others, Dilman knew, but he gave them no warmer recognition. Among the important ones were the housekeeper, Mrs. Crail, and the members of the Social Bureau from the East Wing, T.C. and Hesper's social secretary, Miss Laurel, with her twelve assistants that included two secretaries.

It had taken longer than Dilman had anticipated, a full fifteen minutes, and when the last to introduce himself, the wispy chief calligrapher—who wrote all White House invitations, place cards, seating charts by hand—had finished, Dilman cleared his throat a second time.

"Thank you, each of you. It is a pleasure to meet

you," he said. "Some of you, I know, have become indispensable to the operation of this nation's first house.
Some of you have served Presidents as far back as Her-
bert Hoover and Franklin Roosevelt, and others of you
have been here under Mr. Truman, General Eisenhower,
Mr. Kennedy, Mr. Lyndon Johnson, and The Judge. But
all of you, I know, old and new, have served T.C. and
the First Lady efficiently and loyally. Some of you, missing them, having other plans, may wish to leave for different employment. You may do so, of course, and I
will understand your motives. Most of you, I hope, I
trust, will stay on, knowing your—your loyalty is to a
high office and not to any individual. If you will stay
on, this is simply to tell you that I want you and depend
upon you. I can't promise life in this house will be as it
has been. No one can replace T.C. But the life of the
house itself, the routine, the service to those who come
here, must remain unchanged."

He paused, blinking at the cream-colored carpet, and
then he said with the faintest smile, "Perhaps, even, your
work will be easier now. You see, except for my son,
who is away at college, I am alone, quite alone, a widower, and I have few friends and little interest in social
affairs except those which are expected of me. Yes, my
personal demands may make it easier, but remember
that this White House is not only my house but your
house, too, and I want you to continue to take pride in
it and in your jobs. I hope you will stay. I hope to know
each of you better in a short time. Thank you—thank
you very much."

The valet, Beecher, was at Dilman's side, and from
the crowd of personnel, the Chief of the Secret Service,
Hugo Gaynor, and T.C.'s military attaché, Brigadier
General Robert Faber, swiftly emerged to join him. There
was a light spatter of applause as General Faber, Chief
Gaynor, and Beecher led him straight ahead, out of the
Reception Room, into the wide ground-floor corridor
with its seemingly endless ribbon of red carpet.

"Excellent, Mr. President," the buoyant military attaché was saying. "I'm certain they will be eager to serve
you." He guided Dilman to the left. As they started up

the corridor, Chief Gaynor said, "Over there is where you will come in from your office every day. Next to it is the service entrance for employees and tradespeople." He pointed ahead. "Miss Crail's office, she's the house-keeper, a demon, and next to her, Admiral Oates's of-fice, he's the White House physician, and across the way the flower shop—they keep the old house decorated—and those doors open to the main kitchen, all electric and stainless steel. It has a dumbwaiter that runs up to a pantry on the first floor, and to your private pantry or kitchenette on the second floor. Ike put the second-floor pantry in—liked late snacks and raiding the refrigerator." General Faber and Chief Gaynor threw half salutes at a plainclothes agent and a police guard seated at a table in the corridor, as both leaped to their feet and returned the greeting.

"Here we are," said Chief Gaynor. He swung off the red carpet, passed under an arch into a small vestibule. "Here is your private elevator, Mr. President. Takes you straight up to your second-floor apartment every day." He pushed the button, and Dilman watched the floor lights on the wall indicator drop from 3 to 2M to 2 to 1M to 1 to G. The valet opened the elevator door and held it.

"Gaynor and I will leave you here," said General Faber. "I'm sure you'll want to oversee what's going on in privacy. If you need anything up there, Beecher and Miss Crail will be at your beck and call."

"I appreciate your help," said Dilman.

He ducked into the miniature elevator, as Beecher closed the double doors and pressed the button for the second floor. While the mobile closet climbed upward, Dilman inspected it. The elevator was carpeted in green. There were three mirrors on its three walls, and two mir-rors on the double door before him. For the first time since shaving, hours ago, he could see himself. His kinky hair, despite the tonic, was as stiff as ever. His wide dark face was as Negroid as ever. The improbability of it all hit him with fresh impact. He was black and he was *here*.

He emerged into another small vestibule, almost

bumping into an umbrella holder. The valet had gone to the left, and Dilman followed him.

"This is the second-floor West Hall," said Beecher.

The hall, too long and too wide to be called a corridor—to Dilman it resembled a gallery—appeared to run almost the width of the White House.

"It goes from east to west," said the valet, "and divides the second-floor apartments. Every important room opens into this hall. Down that way"—he pointed to the east section—"on the other side, the south side that looks down on the back lawn and Washington Monument, are the main rooms—the Executive study, although the Kennedys, Johnsons, and the late President used it for a living room, also. That is where the Truman Balcony is, sir. Next is the Treaty Room, and then the famous Lincoln Bedroom."

"What's down at the end there?" Dilman asked.

"The state bedrooms, Mr. President. The Rose Guest Room, the Lincoln Sitting Room, where there's a fine television set, the Empire Guest Room, that's the most of it, sir."

Dilman stood studying the enormous hall. There were bookcases against one wall, and along the opposite wall were grouped a settee and chairs, beneath early American prints of Indians. At the farthest part of the hall stood a desk, and then a Baldwin piano.

Dilman gestured to his right. "What's over there?"

"A private suite, Mr. President. You can see, it opens into T.C.'s sitting room, and on either side are the bedrooms that were used by the President, First Lady, and their son. Also, the pantry is there. It all looks down on the Rose Garden. I'd be glad to show you around—"

"Not yet, thanks," said Dilman. "First, I'd like you to show me where my own things are being unpacked."

"Oh, in the Queen's Bedroom—the Rose Guest Room, really—way down at the end of the hall. We figured it wouldn't be in use immediately, and it was the best place to uncrate everything until you could sort it out and become acquainted enough to know where you wished your effects to be placed. I'll take you there, Mr. President."

They marched briskly to the end of the hall, then

through an entry, past a carpeted bathroom, a sitting room where the sofa and chairs were done in blue slip-covers, and into the Rose Guest Room. Dilman stepped aside as two Army privates carried out the last of the empty crates.

In the bedroom, he found Crystal on her knees upon the white tufted rug, stacking his embarrassingly limited collection of law books, history books, encyclopedias, synthetic leather-bound sets of Booker T. Washington's writings and Dickens' novels, and all the garishly jacketed mystery stories he enjoyed. Diane Fuller, her back also to him, was sorting out his papers on a table draped in red velvet.

Without disturbing them, he glanced around the room. It probably had been breathtakingly beautiful yesterday, he guessed, but this morning it was a mess. Except for the Revels handmade Belter chair, his cheap pieces of furniture, drab and scuffed, were eyesores that littered the magnificent room, so gaily decorated in red and white. Heaps of his belongings, from humidors to ash-trays, from photograph albums to laminated plaques, stood like dozens of unattractive molehills. Piled across the canopied bed, across the rose-patterned quilting, was a rag mountain of his clothes, on hangers, encased in plastic garment bags.

"It's not fit for any royal Queen visiting us today," he muttered.

"We'll have it orderly in no time," Beecher said quickly. "You know, many Queens have stayed in this room, one of the last being Queen Elizabeth II of Great Britain. She left behind, as a gift, that mirror over the fireplace. The bed was said to have belonged to Andrew Jackson. The shield-back chair—"

But Dilman was no longer listening. Crystal and Diane Fuller had turned around at the sound of voices, and now, grunting and heaving, Crystal was lifting her rotund bulk upright. "Thanks, Beecher," Dilman said. "I think I'll pitch in and help them here. I won't need you right now."

The moment that the valet was gone, Dilman went directly to Crystal, taking hold of her thick arm, smiling down into her shining face. "Well, Crystal, how are you managing? It's a little different from my beat-up five rooms on Van Buren, isn't it?"

"Mr. President, I'll sure take them beat-up five rooms any day. This ain't no livin' home. This is a museum, sure is. Why, I'd be 'fraid to go to the bathroom here!"

Dilman chuckled. "You'll get used to it, soon enough." He was suddenly serious. "That is, if you want to. Crystal, I haven't had a real chance to speak to you, or I would have asked you before. Will you stay on and help me?"

Her shoulders went up and down, and her fat arms shook. "Doin' what, Mr. Dilman—Mr. President? I'm willin', but doin' what with all that fancy help around?"

"Taking care of me, that's what you can do, Crystal, as you always have done. Those servants you see are for other people—visitors, dignitaries, guests. I need someone who knows how to make my breakfast, and keep starch out of my collars, and where to put my bedroom slippers. Let's make believe nothing has changed, Crystal, except our address. We'll continue on the same basis, only I'll try to arrange a raise. What do you say?"

"I say yes, and how, bless the Lord!" Crystal exclaimed. "Maybe I'll wind up writin' a famous book about you, what the President is really like, and I'll get rich and famous, too, and—"

Dilman grinned. "I knew I could count on you."

He became aware of Diane Fuller watching, listening, from the velvet-draped table. He tried not to frown. Oddly enough, while Crystal belonged here, Diane did not. Her scrawny, deferential manner, her lack of poise, her unseemly loud dresses (the one this morning was orange polka dots on yellow), her bowlegs, her stutter and nervous mannerisms, made her less of an asset here than in his Senate office, where he could relegate her to the typewriter and file cabinets. Moreover, he did not want to bring in too many of his own color. That would create unpleasant talk. Still, there was Diane, waiting. Something must be done.

"What about you, Diane?" he asked. "Would you like to stay on?"

She spoke with difficulty. "Of-of course, S-senator. I have—haven't no place else to go, and besides—"

"Besides what?"

"This is—is—is sure enough real exciting."

"All right. Now, it won't be the same as before, I'm sorry to say. I've kept on T.C.'s personal secretary, because she's familiar with the Executive Office routine and can guide me. However, they can always use another secretary in the East Wing downstairs. I'll tell them I want you hired."

"I—I'd sure be grateful, S-s-senator." Then she amended it hastily, "I mean—Mr. President."

Crystal had approached, taking in the entire room with the arch of her hand. "What do we do with all this stuff?"

"You keep sorting it out so it is neat and so that you know where every item is," said Dilman. "As soon as I find out which rooms I'll be living in, we can start moving everything where it belongs. Don't worry about it." He consulted his wristwatch. "Matter of fact, I don't have much time to look around. I'll see if I can learn which is to be my bedroom."

He left the Rose Guest Room, lost his way a moment, then escaped the maze of rooms to find Beecher, the valet, patiently tarrying in the hall.

"Sorry to keep you," Dilman said. "Let's start with a bedroom for tonight. What do you suggest?"

"Well, there's these guest bedrooms—"

"No. Too fancy."

"That leaves two others on this floor that are used," said the valet. "Way down there at the end is the one most used by other Presidents. It's huge and has a good cedar closet and bathroom—why, even the bathtub has the Presidential eagle on it. It was T.C.'s bedroom before he—"

"I'm not sure about that, either," Dilman said. He did not repeat what had passed through his mind: that the electorate might unconsciously resent a minority black politician immediately sleeping in the bed where their popular T.C. had slept for two years and seven months, a Negro enjoying that bed while their choice slept in a coffin in the earth.

"What else is there?" Dilman asked. "You mentioned another—"

"Yes, sir, Mr. President. There's the Lincoln Bedroom right over there."

"I thought it was a show piece. Has it ever been used in modern times?"

"Often, Mr. President. Will you have a look?" Beecher started down the hall, with Dilman a half step behind him. Unexpectedly the valet veered to his left, opened a door, and waited for Dilman to go inside.

Dilman almost entered, had meant to go right into the room, but something about it brought him to a stop, made him hang back. For the first time this morning, he had the feeling that he was neither visitor nor intruder. An accident of history had brought him to this place, and suddenly, in this room, he was a part of this place, engaged in its role, a part of its story. For the first time this morning, he felt that he belonged. It was his fancy, he told himself, yet the warmness of being wanted radiated beneath his flesh.

Hushed, he surveyed the Lincoln Bedroom. It was an old-fashioned and simple room, too calming, too reasoning, too good to permit here the invasion of violence and hate and fear. It had once been Lincoln's Cabinet Room, he knew, and the plaque on the mantelpiece was a reminder that within these plain walls Lincoln had signed the Emancipation Proclamation, prohibiting slavery in the United States and giving four million human beings of Dilman's race their freedom.

Lincoln's own bed, massive and grand, dominated the room.

"What's it made of?" Dilman asked.

The valet came beside him, puzzled. "Pardon, Mr. President?"

"His bed. What's it made of?"

"Oh. It's solid rosewood, sir. Look at the beautiful carved headboard. That's eight feet high above the bed. The bed itself is nine feet long."

"Not long enough," said Dilman. "He was taller than that."

Dilman studied the velvet-covered tables and Victorian lamps on either side of the large bed. He studied the bureau and mirror, and the stained table on which rested one of the five copies of the Gettysburg Address written in the sixteenth President's own hand. All these pieces had been purchased by Mrs. Lincoln, and everything in the room was probably Lincoln's own, the painting of Andrew Jackson, the chairs in yellow and green Morris velvet, the desk, the Empire clock, everything. Even the figured rug gave Dilman comfort, a rug so much like the threadbare ones that had covered the floor of the hovel in which his mother had raised him to adulthood. Straight ahead, framed by the windows, was the spire of the Washington Monument once more.

He walked deeper into the room, and on an ashtray lay a white book of matches with the imprint "The President's House."

Over his shoulder he said to the valet, "You are certain this is a bedroom that's been in ordinary use?"

"Positive, Mr. President. Theodore Roosevelt and Calvin Coolidge slept in that bed. Teddy Roosevelt's children, six of them, often slept in it at once. F.D.R. had Colonel Louis Howe, his aide, sleep in it, and Margaret Truman slept in it, and so did Mamie Eisenhower's mother, Mrs. Doud. President Kennedy and Mrs. Kennedy used this bedroom while their other one was being painted. Mrs. Jacqueline Kennedy, particularly, loved that bed. She liked to say it looked like 'a cathedral.' Later, whenever President Kennedy's parents, former Ambassador Joseph Kennedy and Mrs. Rose Kennedy, visited, they were put up in this room. Lyndon Johnson's relatives were here, and T.C.'s son Freddie always slept in the bed when he came here during school holidays."

"And Lincoln," said Dilman.

"Yes, Lincoln."

Dilman stared at the towering rosewood headboard and green-fringed white spread. No one on earth, he told himself, could object to his occupying the Lincoln Bedroom, and least of all Abe Lincoln of Illinois.

"Very well, this is it," he said curtly, and he went into the hall.

When the valet had caught up with him, Dilman stopped, something on his mind.

"Is there anything else, Mr. President?"

"I was just wondering what room is accessible when I want to work at night."

"Well, sir, there's the Lincoln Sitting Room on one side, and the Treaty Room on the other, but one more room beyond that is where T.C. and most of the Presidents have worked and relaxed at night."

"Which room?"

"It's been known by several names, including the Yellow Oval Room and the Executive study. May I show it to you?"

Dilman strode in step with the valet across the parquet floor. "Is it a study?" Dilman asked.

"It's a catchall room, Mr. President. Right up until he left the country, T.C. used it for a living room, library, informal office. Dolley Madison did it up in yellow damask, and—you'll see—most everything in it, the oval rug, the wallpaper, the covering on the two sofas, and some of the Louis XVI chairs are in bright yellow. T.C. would sit in a green leather padded captain's chair at the green inlaid desk—behind one of the sofas—while the First Lady sat across from him and read. On balmy nights they'd go out on the Truman Balcony, stretch on the patio furniture, and have iced tea, and just talk and talk. When some head of state was visiting, they would receive him in this room, and then go with him down the grand staircase, across the way, to the White House Entrance Hall, where the Marine Band would play their ruffles and flourishes, and then they'd go on into the first-floor State Dining Room. . . . Here we are, Mr. President. The Yellow Oval Room."

The white doors were wide-open, and Dilman went into the great golden chamber, slowed by its breadth and brightness, by its richness, impressed by the chandelier with its chains and crystals, the candelabra guarding the central window to the right, the Cézannes on the wall nearby.

Dilman wheeled slowly, to take it all in, when suddenly his neck stiffened and he stepped back with surprise. He and the valet were not alone. There was another in the Yellow Oval Room.

She was bent over the flat table desk behind the nearest sofa, opening and closing drawers, concentrating on her search. When she straightened, and sighed, Dilman could see that she was not as tall as she appeared to be, but held herself so regally that it gave her added stature. She was attired in an unadorned black afternoon dress, and lifted from her face and lying across her coiffured blond-gray hair was a mourning veil. Even as she turned at his movement, Dilman knew who it was he had stumbled upon.

T.C.'s First Lady arranged her mourning ensemble. Her wide-set eyes betrayed nothing except recognition. Her high-cheeked, well-bred, fiftyish face did not change its expression, but retained its cool, phlegmatic sadness.

Dilman felt his Adam's apple drop and rise. He was too tongue-tied to know how to address her. He had met her fleetingly at T.C.'s annual dinners for the members of the Senate. He had seen her three times during the week of grief and burial. He had never exchanged more than an incoherent phrase with her. He could hardly recall her maiden name, only that her given name was Hesper, the renowned and admired Hesper who had been one of the few First Ladies to bring style and grace to the White House. He could not force himself to address her so quickly by mere proper name, like any ordinary citizen, although he knew that she was no longer First Lady, her title and eminence stolen from her by Fate. Yet, she was what she was, T.C.'s widow.

He turned for the valet, as if for help, but realized that Beecher was retreating, readying to withdraw from the room.

Dilman faced her. "Good morning. I'm sorry to walk in on you this way. I'd been told that you had left—"

"The apology should be mine, not yours, Senator Dilman. I did, indeed, move out yesterday. It was kind of you to be so patient, to give me the entire week. But last night I remembered some of my husband's personal correspondence I had overlooked." She touched the table desk behind her. "It was in this desk, the one he always used late at night."

"I hope you found what you wanted," said Dilman lamely. "Perhaps you wish to look around some more? I—I have other things I have to—"

She lifted a gloved hand. "No, please, Senator." She took up the packet of letters, bound by a rubber band. "I have everything now. I know this is your moving day, and I must not be underfoot. But, in a way, I'm pleased this happened, our meeting like this, away from the crowds, the misery."

"I don't know if I've adequately extended my deep feeling of grief," said Dilman, "or my condolences. I welcome the chance to repeat both. All of us are less, without T.C."

She was quietly observing him. "Thank you. You are very generous, Senator Dilman."

Dilman's sensitivity had come closer to his skin, and now he was acutely conscious of her manner of addressing him. Despite her good breeding, her infallible manners, she was not addressing him as Mr. President. To her he had been a senator, and he was a senator still, and she would not recognize his accession. Or worse, she regarded him as an inferior, a Negro inferior, unworthy of replacing her husband as Chief Executive.

But then Dilman rejected the motive of intended, or unconscious, insult. She was not demeaning him in any way. He was being ungenerous, overly susceptible to his own conviction of his inferiority, and he was better able to understand this suffering woman. She had come through the long, ambitious political years, with their gains and setbacks, clutching the hand of one mate. She had encouraged him, yearned and aspired with him, shared the ultimate victory with him. Overnight, at the height of reign and glory, his crown had been torn from him, his page in history ripped in half. She could not let herself lose both for him yet. For her, beneath her controlled sorrow, there was a refusal to accept unfair reality. For her, still, there could be only one President, one Mr. President, and that one her dearest, her own one. She would not let him be dethroned, not so soon, perhaps not ever. She would not be unfaithful to his love and their dreams. She would acknowledge no usurper.

Dilman knew what was required of him. He must reassure her. "I do want to add this—this one thing," he said. "I consider myself a temporary tenant of this house. If it belongs to anyone, it still belongs to your husband and yourself. You earned your residence here. I have not. I am keenly aware of the fact. I want you to continue to feel it is your house. The doors will forever be open to you and your son."

"Yes," she said absently. "Thank you again."

She paced a few steps, nervously, then moved to the yellow sofa nearest the fireplace and sat down, head bowed.

Dilman's uneasiness increased. He wanted to escape. "I—I think you deserve some privacy. I'll go."

Her head came up, and she spoke as if she had not heard him. "You have a son, too, have you not, Senator? I can't remember."

"Yes. A twenty-year-old boy at Trafford University. In fact, he's coming down to see me today."

"It is wonderful, having a son. My own is at Andover." Her eyes took in the room. "He so enjoyed coming here. He was so proud and thrilled. Like his father, he has a sense of history."

Dilman did not know how he could reply or comment. He wanted to move the conversation away from the White House. Because it was difficult speaking to her across the table desk, he walked around it and sat on the corner of the other sofa. "Have you made any plans yet? Will you stay on in Washington?"

She shook her head. "I don't think so. Of course, Freddie will return to school. I believe I'll settle in our Phoenix house. There's so much, so very much, to be done. I want to go through T.C.'s papers. Princeton is preparing a special Presidential Wing to receive them. Then many fine scholars, historians, want to write biographies about my husband. I think they should. I think it's my duty, difficult as it will be, to cooperate." She paused. "By the way, Miss Laurel—she's been our social secretary—Miss Laurel has consented to come along with me, to help handle the thousands of letters that have poured in, to help with the rest. I believe that you'll have her resignation today. I hope you won't mind?"

"Not at all," said Dilman hastily. "She belongs with you."

She was inspecting him once more. "You're alone, I'm told. Who will run this place for you?"

"I'm sure it will run itself."

"No. It needs someone. There is so much that goes on. It needs a woman. Find one—an experienced social secretary, at least."

"I—I'll try to find someone," he said. "I'm fortunate to have Miss Foster."

"She'll be helpful, but she is limited. I might add, I've requested her to empty my husband's files, and put them in some kind of order, and send them to me—you know, for the biographers. I promise, she won't take too much time away from you."

"Miss Foster and I will do anything to cooperate. I want to do whatever is possible to commemorate T.C.'s achievements and his leadership. No matter what, do not hesitate to call upon me."

She was staring at him. "There is one thing," she said slowly, but said no more.

"Please, anything—"

She pulled herself erect. Her manner was more candid now, more firm and forthright. "Perhaps what I am about to say I should not say. Perhaps it is out of line. Do not misunderstand. I am not being presumptuous. I may be moved by private emotion, but I choose to think that what is giving me strength to speak out is my concern for the millions of Americans who voted for my husband, backed him, depended upon him." She caught her breath, and then rushed on. "Nothing I can do from this day forward, no gathering of his letters and documents, no publication of his speeches and life, can be one-tenth as useful as what you can do, Senator Dilman. You alone can truly perpetuate T.C.'s memory and the ideals for which he gave his life. You, and no other, can serve his voters and the future generations who will be grateful for what he accomplished. You yourself can be his best memorial."

Her urgency troubled and bewildered Dilman, and the burden she was settling upon him made him wince inwardly. He did not speak, but waited, hoping that he was masking his dismay.

She went on. "You will be sitting in the chair T.C. was to have sat in these next critical seventeen months. You will be holding the pen he was to have held when his proposals and legislations come to your desk. You will be implementing decisions on matters here and abroad, decisions he had already made but had had no opportunity to carry out. You will be surrounded by good and wise men, Governor Talley, Secretary Eaton, Attorney General Kemmler, General Fortney, whom T.C. appointed, counted upon, whose advice he would have continued heeding, but whose words he can hear no longer."

She paused. "I—I have no right to ask it, Senator Dilman, because now my husband is gone, and I am no longer a President's wife but a private citizen and a widow. Nevertheless, I will ask it as a private citizen, one of the millions who put him in office to lead us. I will ask that you try—try your best—to—to perform in the next seventeen months as if the Saviour had resurrected T.C. inside your head and your heart." Suddenly her voice broke, and her composure with it. "Oh, I know you can't be T.C., but—" Her hand went to her wet eyes, and she murmured, "Oh, forgive me—"

He had come off the sofa, stirred, to embrace this good woman, but then, as he neared her, arm extended, he could see the blackness of his supplicating hand groping past her white face. He froze, then straightened, trying to find the right words to speak.

There was a light knocking on the door behind him. Startled, he spun around.

"Mr. President?" A platinum-haired, smartly dressed young female was speaking to him from the doorway. "I'm Miss Laurel, the White House social secretary. I have a worried call from Edna Foster. She's trying to locate you. She says you are running behind schedule.

Secretary Eaton and Governor Talley are in your office, and then the Cabinet meeting—"

Dilman nodded, distraughtly, then turned back to look down at the former First Lady. She had found her handkerchief and was dabbing at her eyes.

His voice thick, Dilman spoke to her. "You have my promise, ma'am. On any matter that confronts me, from this day on, I will think before I act—I will think of T.C. first. I can never be the man he was, except in one respect. I love my country as much as he did, and I will do everything I can to preserve its security and well-being, no matter what lies ahead."

Quickly he left her, and as he did, he exposed T.C.'s widow, for the first time, to the full view of Miss Laurel, who was still standing at the doorway. Miss Laurel gasped at the sight of the handkerchief and tears, and ran past Dilman, crying out, "Hesper, dear—what is it? What is it? Don't, my dear—everything will be all right."

Dilman fled from the room into the hall, but Miss Laurel's promise to T.C.'s widow, repeated over and over again, followed him to the elevator. *Everything will be all right.* These moments, if the alchemy were possible, he would have sold his soul to the devil to bring T.C. back. For he knew that he could never be T.C., because he was weak and he was black. Then, he thought, he crazily thought: an original sheet of paper is white, but the carbon is black, and often the carbon copy, no matter how weak, is almost as useful. He would try. He would try with all his strength.

When he punched the elevator button, he felt better.

Slouched in the wooden antique chair alongside the Buchanan desk in the President's Oval Office, Arthur Eaton crossed his legs, dropped the memorandum he had prepared for the Cabinet meeting in his lap, and tightened the navy blue knit tie higher between his button-down shirt collar. He brought out his silver holder, twisted a cigarette into it, lit it, puffed contentedly, and watched with amusement Wayne Talley's impatient dartings about the office.

"Easy, Governor," Eaton called out. "Save yourself for the Cabinet meeting."

"If there's going to be any," Talley growled. "Why does he have to be late on a day like this? We'll have only half the time we need to cram him."

"It won't require as much time as you think," said Eaton.

He continued watching Talley, as the stocky aide went to the French doors, peered across the Rose Garden, made some indistinct sound, tramped to the first window overlooking the south lawn, then came around to the almost barren Presidential desk.

Talley's arm swept across the desk. "Look at it. Everything gone, even the clock, even his pens, and the captain's chair. Not a damn thing of T.C.'s left—"

"Except us," said Eaton, with a smile.

"Yeh, sure. If they get that New Succession Bill through, you're safe. What about me? How do I know who'll get to him a month from now?"

"Nobody'll get to him a month from now, Wayne." Eaton uncrossed his legs, and held the Cabinet memorandum in his free hand. "Look, Wayne, Dilman is President. Learn to live with it. I knew from the start that Zeke Miller's protest would be thrown out of the Judiciary Committee and it was. After all, when the written law is obscure, you follow the unwritten law, which is historical precedent. The precedent was, nine times, that the next eligible in line becomes President, and no ifs, no maybes, about it, and no special elections either. Dilman was the next eligible, and now he is the Chief, and let us not waste any more energy fretting about it. Let us get on with business."

Talley had planted himself in front of the Secretary of State. "Okay, business, Arthur. Do you know that the New Succession Bill sponsored by Senator Hankins is being approved by the full committee in the Senate Caucus Room today? Only one change suggested by the Legislative Council. After a President dies, and the next in line is serving as temporary Acting President, the new President and Vice-President are elected by the existing Electoral College for a full four-year term and not merely the unexpired term."

"Yes, I heard about the change. I didn't know the hearings were done and the bill was being approved today."

"The committee isn't touching a word in the language about you and the rest of T.C.'s Cabinet. It stays right in there. Dilman cannot remove you or any other member of the Cabinet without Senate consent. In fact, the line of succession as it was the day T.C. and MacPherson died stays untouched for the rest of the unexpired term. No new Speaker, no new President pro tempore of the Senate is to be elected to take precedence over you. The chairmanship will be revolving. That's it, Arthur."

"I know."

"As committee chairman, Hankins is bringing the bill to the floor tomorrow or the next day. It'll pass."

"Will it?"

"It certainly will. And now, to expedite things, Zeke Miller is introducing a companion bill, same language, in the House. The House Rules Committee won't stymie it. When it gets to a roll call there, it'll go through in a flash."

"Maybe."

"For sure, Arthur. The question is—will Dilman sign or veto?"

"I haven't the faintest idea," said Eaton with annoyance. It irritated him to be dragged into these grimy, tricky, bartering legislative matters.

Eaton allowed Talley to drift out of his vision. He closed his eyes and smoked his cigarette. As much as he had tried not to, he had thought of that damned New Succession Bill, of course. How could he help but think of it? Everyone in T.C.'s inner circle, in the Party, in the press, his own wife, Kay, in fact, had kept reminding him that he was the next in line to the Presidency. Even if he had been able to remain deaf to the talk of the past week, it would have been impossible not to recognize his new position with the arrival of the three Secret Service agents, assigned by law to protect him as the Number Two man in the government.

Now, like it or not, he had Senator Hankins' New
Succession Bill, with language that retroactively froze
him into the position of succeeding Dilman as President,
no matter whom the House and Senate selected for
chairmen, no matter whom Dilman might prefer in his
Cabinet. It was an embarrassment in many ways, the
kind of act Eaton ordinarily deplored, for it was so
nakedly political and unreasonable. If it passed, it told
Dilman that the Congress did not trust him as a person
(and a Negro), that the Senate was stripping him of his
inherent removal powers, that the Senate was taking over
as his guardian. Furthermore, no matter how ambigu-
ously written, it told the country to shut one eye to the
Constitution, for while the Constitution gave the Senate
the right to approve of a Presidential appointment, it
did not give that body the right to control a Presidential
removal. In short, one paragraph of the language of the
act was clouded over by doubtful legality, yet it was skillfully hidden behind the verbiage of an otherwise valid
New Succession Bill. The political cynicism and ra-
tionalization that wrote the bill, put it in the hopper, had
it introduced on the floor, had it powerhoused through
the subcommittee, the full committee, and to a roll call,
was appalling to Arthur Eaton.

Moreover, Eaton hated himself for being thrown into
the Hankins and Miller camp. They were not his kind of
people. He despised their talk. Publicly, they were pleading that an unusual situation in government had called
for an unusual measure to meet it and to secure the continuity of government. Privately, secretly, these same
men were agreeing that even if the doubtful paragraph
made the bill unconstitutional, it would take so long a
time to reach a test before the Supreme Court, take so
long a time to be thrown out, that by then President Dilman would have served his one year and five months
under Senate restraint, and what happened after that did
not matter. All that mattered was that the nation would
have been protected from its own current President.

Eaton wanted no part of those politicians and their
bill, and he promised himself that he would stay aloof,
as far above and beyond the questionable intrigue as

possible. He had one task, and it was enough for one human being—to see that the United States was steered in the direction that his friend T.C. had set for it.

He opened his eyes to find Wayne Talley before him once more.

"Arthur," Talley said, "Dilman mention anything to you about the Hankins bill?"

"Not to me, no."

"What if it's brought up at the Cabinet meeting?"

"I doubt that it will be brought up," said Eaton. "Since it concerns each of the Cabinet members, protecting them against their President, why should any one of them bring it up? Certainly I would not have the nerve to speak of it myself."

"What if Dilman himself brings it up?"

Eaton thought about this. "No, he won't bring it up either," he said with confidence. "You've seen him in action throughout the week. He's afraid to open his mouth. He listens. He worries. He retreats. He has no strong or definite opinions about anything in government, except that he doesn't want trouble. I think he wants to remain unobtrusive and accepted. If he can get through T.C.'s term without rocking the boat, I believe he will feel that he has accomplished all he wished to accomplish."

"Which is?"

"To prove a Negro can be President and leave the nation no worse off."

Talley did not seem convinced. "I hope so. Let's see how he reacts to that first television speech we hammered out for him. If he goes for it verbatim, every point we made, promising the country he will serve merely as a caretaker for T.C.'s program, then I think you're right."

"When did you give him the draft of the speech?"

"When he was leaving here last night."

Eaton nodded. "Then we should know today. After all, if he is going on the networks with it tomorrow—late tomorrow afternoon, isn't it?—he should—"

Eaton left the sentence unfinished, as he cocked his head to listen to the approaching clack of footsteps on the cement walk outside. He came to his feet, and he and Talley stood respectfully attentive as the Secret Service agent near the garden greeted Dilman and the White House policeman opened the screen and turned the latch of the French door.

Dilman was inside the Oval Office, nodding his head. "Mr. Secretary—Governor—"

"Mr. President," said Arthur Eaton.

"Good morning, Mr. President," said Wayne Talley. Dilman remained uncertainly before them, revealing a troubled smile. "I know I'm late. I apologize. I was trying to supervise the moving, and trying to find where everything was, when I ran into the—the First Lady— you know—"

"Oh, Hesper, you mean," said Eaton. "I thought she'd moved out yesterday."

"Well, there were a few bits of unfinished business, I guess," said Dilman. "Anyway, we got to talking—a lovely lady—and that's why I'm late. Do we still have a little time before the Cabinet meeting?"

"Only fifteen minutes now," said Talley. "We can cover the ground, if we go right at it."

"I'm ready," said Dilman. He started for the desk, and with obvious reluctance sat down behind it in the straight-backed, light green leather swivel chair that had been substituted for T.C.'s widely photographed ebony chair with the electrically controlled lifting and reclining device built into its massive frame.

Eaton settled back into the seat he had been using beside the President's desk, and Talley pulled up a cane-bottomed chair.

As Talley took the memorandum from the Secretary of State, Dilman held up one hand. "Before you start," he said, "I—I've got to remind you I've never attended a real Cabinet meeting, let alone chaired one. I assume our gathering last week was merely a brief prayer get-together. As to a full-dress meeting—" He shrugged helplessly.

Talley glanced at Eaton, and then addressed Dilman. "While there are no set rules as to procedure, Mr. President, there are a few certain practices that are traditional. As you know, you are the presiding officer, and, as you know, the ten Cabinet members are seated in their order

of succession. Generally, you meet with the Cabinet twice
a week, usually Tuesday and Friday, but that is highly
flexible. Truman and Eisenhower believed in these regular Cabinet meetings. Lincoln, Wilson, Kennedy did not,
preferring to work out problems in individual conferences
with Cabinet members or advisers. Other members of
the government that you feel can be helpful can also be
invited to attend. F.D.R. usually had Harry Hopkins in
the room—"

"I'd expect you to be present, too, Governor Talley,"
Dilman said.

"Thank you, Mr. President. Now, the meeting is nothing more than a sort of clearing house—you know, clearing house for ideas, opinions, exchanges of specialized
information, and so on. It gives you a chance to get a
diversity of advice, reactions to your own notions, and
to pick up some expert knowledge. The whole thing is
informal, and because no official records of the conversation are kept, it can be pretty freewheeling. Truman had
a private secretary take rough notes. Eisenhower appointed a special Secretary of the Cabinet to prepare the
agenda and keep minutes of what went on, but that hasn't
been done much since. You are expected to open the
meeting by presenting any problems you have on your
mind. Or you can simply ask the members, from Secretary Eaton here down to the Secretary of Health, Education and Welfare, what they have to report or discuss."

Listening, Eaton pushed forward. "Excuse me, Governor. . . . Mr. President, I want to interject one observation I have made while attending so many of T.C.'s
Cabinet meetings. Don't be disappointed if not too much
is accomplished. Your Cabinet members are specialists
in different fields. T.C. found that the Secretary of the
Interior had neither interest in nor knowledge of our
problems in—well, say my Department of State. And the
Postmaster General is apt to be more concerned about
the design of a new stamp issue or political patronage in
the Post Office Department than the Attorney General,
who is full of facts and figures and concern about Negro
voting. I think it was to avoid this bureaucratic self-
interest, as much as for any other reason, that President

Kennedy chose to depend on small task forces to dig up facts for him, so that he could thrash them out beforehand with a handful of intelligent advisers. Certainly he had no fixed schedule of Cabinet or National Security Council meetings. Neither did T.C. He liked to get his facts from any one of the ten government Departments, from experts among the more than two million civil servants in the executive branch, and then sit down with Governor Talley and myself, maybe one or two others, and debate the specific problem and arrive at a conclusion." Eaton paused. "I think, Mr. President, you will be able to determine, shortly, if you prefer to lean on the Cabinet as a whole or on advisers you find intelligent and sympathetic."

Dilman's fingers twisted the cigar visible in his upper suit-coat pocket. "I don't imagine I'll go wrong following T.C.'s procedure. Only—"

Eaton waited, curious to see if Dilman had any unexpected qualification.

"—I keep wondering if the country might not feel easier about me if they knew I was meeting regularly, formally, with T.C.'s Cabinet. They can then see plainly what I am doing. Whereas, well, they might be worried about what I'm up to behind closed doors, you know, with a kitchen Cabinet."

It was sensible, a fine point, Eaton told himself, yet he could not be sure that Dilman was not offering resistance to their guidance or attempting to assert his individuality.

Eaton decided to proceed cautiously. "You may have something there, Mr. President. I believe you will be able to decide which course to take in a few weeks. Certainly give the regular Cabinet meetings a tryout."

"Yes," said Dilman. He swiveled toward Talley. "What are we going to talk about in there today, Governor?"

Reminding the President that they had only seven or eight minutes before the meeting, Talley went rapidly through the problems on the agenda. There was the African Unity Pact. Renewal of the United States as a member nation, pledged to defend the independence of the new African democracies, was being scheduled for consideration in the Senate. T.C. had wanted ratification, had planned to speak out for it and then sign the Pact. This would satisfy Africa. At the same time, T.C. had intended to pressure President Amboko of Baraza into dropping anti-Communist legislation on a local level, and into resuming cultural exchanges with Moscow. This would satisfy Russia. Then, to conclude the peace parley left unfinished in Frankfurt, President Dilman and Premier Kasatkin would have to arrange another international conference. Talley thought it wrong to resume the talks in Frankfurt. The President of France had already offered the hospitality of his country. A site near Paris might be considered.

"As to domestic affairs," said Talley, "the major effort, the one T.C. gave most of his energy to, is the Minorities Rehabilitation Program. I'm sure you are well acquainted with it, Mr. President."

"Not as well as I should be at this point," said Dilman. "Naturally, as a senator, I've followed its development. Lots of people have had lots to say to me about it, inside Congress, and on the outside, too. But it's been in the Legislative Council so long that I've been waiting for the final form of the measure."

"It's in its final form right now," said Talley. "It's in the hopper. It's being introduced. It'll go to the Subcommittee of Employment and Manpower. Anyway, as you'll soon hear, the majority of the Cabinet are involved in support of it. Attorney General Kemmler, Secretary of Interior Ruttenberg, Secretary of Labor Barnes are prepared to go to the Hill to fight for it. T.C. felt that not only would it give our economy a shot in the arm, but it was the only reasonable solution to the—the civil rights issue. We've found the majority of responsible white and colored leaders are behind it, Mr. President."

"Yes, I know," said Dilman. "I know the Crispus Society, the NAACP, and the Urban League have approved, with reservations."

Eaton had been not only listening to Talley, but watching the President's broad, black face. Except for an expression of unceasing anxiety, nothing else, either affirmative or negative, was betrayed. On familiar Caucasian faces, Eaton was always able to detect inner response, a closing, a widening, a dilation, an expansion, a wrinkling of some feature, that was often as eloquent and revealing as words. On this unfamiliar black face Eaton could read no subtle definition of reaction. The blackness hid Dilman's thoughts as successfully as the darkest moonless night.

Eaton's instinct, which he and T.C. had regarded as unerring, led him to a quick decision. To continue overwhelming Dilman with a landslide of information would be useless now. He had been made aware of the key issues, the immediate ones, and of how T.C. had felt about each. It was enough for the time. If more indoctrination were required, the Cabinet meeting might supply it.

Eaton straightened, and squinted down at his wristwatch. "I'm afraid we're expected in the Cabinet Room."

Talley protested. "There's still some more to—"

"You've briefed the President on the main points, Wayne. That's enough." He rose, and smiled at Dilman. "I'm sure you're ready to say uncle to this stuff, Mr. President. I know that I am."

Dilman smiled back. "I appreciate your understanding, Mr. Secretary. I feel like a computer that's been overloaded with data. I'm afraid something might clog or short-circuit."

Eaton waited for the President to rise and precede him. Then, with Talley, he followed Dilman across the Oval Office, through Edna Foster's cubicle, and into the cool chamber that was the Cabinet Room.

T.C.'s team was present and seated, and immediately upon Dilman's entrance they rose to their feet. Dilman took his place in the handsome chair at the center of the twenty-foot mahogany table, the only spot on the table covered by a desk blotter, near which a telephone rested. About the table were ceramic ashtrays, some partially filled, silver carafes of water and trays of glasses, and sheaves of notes and documents belonging to individual members of the Cabinet.

Once the President was seated, and Eaton had taken

his chair next to Dilman, the others in the room sat down. Talley found his place at the far end of the tapering table, near the fireplace and the portrait of George Washington above it. Across from Talley sat the only other non-Cabinet member in the room, Ambassador to the United Nations Slater.

Eaton's gaze swept the table, taking in the attendance: Secretary of the Treasury Moody, Secretary of Defense Steinbrenner, Attorney General Kemmler, Postmaster General Guthrie, Secretary of Interior Ruttenberg, Secretary of Agriculture Allen, Secretary of Commerce Purcell, Secretary of Labor Barnes, Secretary of Health, Education and Welfare Mrs. Cummins. They were each well-known to Eaton. Despite their differences in years, their varied backgrounds—some had been university professors, some businessmen, some career politicians— they had always been a lively and unceremonious clan. But that had been at another time, under the informal leadership of the one who had appointed them, and knew and respected them.

This morning they were different, Eaton could see. They were quiet, almost hushed, inquisitive about their new Chief Executive. They were strangers to him, and he to them. In the afterwave of shock, Dilman had asked them to stay on, to assist him. They had agreed. Now they were confronted by one with whom they had had little previous contact, a man whose mind they did not know, whose desires were a mystery to them, a man separated by a color barrier that made understanding of him almost impossible. It was reflected in their cautious eyes, and probably loomed large in the brains behind those eyes, Eaton guessed. He could be wrong, he told himself. He doubted it.

He wondered why the meeting had not begun, and then he realized that Douglass Dilman had pulled an envelope out of his inner suit-coat pocket and was reviewing some notes penciled on the back of the envelope.

Dilman placed the envelope on the blotter, and scanned the Cabinet personnel surrounding him.

"I'll call our first meeting to order," Dilman said. "I know that we met once last week, but I cannot think of it as a conference on government business. Now we must not fall out of step with one another. We must go ahead together. I do not know you. I have inherited you. And you do not know me. You have inherited me. However, we do have one mighty factor in common, and that is our belief in the ideals T.C. represented."

Dilman reached forward and picked up the envelope upon which he had scribbled.

"Leaving the second floor of the White House for this meeting, I had occasion to run into the late President's widow. We talked, and coming down in the elevator I jotted a few reminders of our talk. I was moved that, in this period of her deep personal grief, her one concern was that I, as her husband's successor, continue to uphold his program for the welfare of all the people of the nation. This good woman was thinking not of herself but of others. She hoped I would be the transmitting agency of a solution to her concern over the fate of her husband's vast and dependent following."

Dilman laid down the envelope and looked around the table.

"I am here to pledge to you that I shall, to the best of my ability, within my limitations, serve the United States in such a way as to relieve the First Lady's concern about our program ahead, and in such a way as to assure the millions who voted for and backed T.C. that their support was not given in vain."

The ringing out of applause was spontaneous, and it surprised Arthur Eaton. He could not remember ever having witnessed such a demonstration during T.C.'s tenure. He cast a glance at the black man to his left, sitting hunched forward, head lowered, one hand folded over the other on the blotter. The blackness still made Dilman impenetrable, but now, for the first time, Eaton wondered if behind the stolid, dull mask there lay astuteness and the intuition needed for winning favor. Now it occurred to Eaton that perhaps Dilman had not been elected to Congress by political accident and shenanigans, but that he had been elected because he was clever enough to judge people and use them. Yet this evaluation of Dilman was so drastically the opposite of Eaton's judgment of the man the past week that he was not ready to accept it. More likely, Dilman had just scored because of the emotional climate created by T.C.'s death, which had affected not only his listeners but Dilman himself.

Eaton looked down the table at Talley, who winked. Then Eaton understood why Talley had winked, and what had just happened. Dilman had made his pledge. He would not walk outside of T.C.'s shadow.

Dilman was addressing them once more.

"At this first meeting, I have no specific problems or legislation about which to ask your advice. It is too soon. Except for my knowledge of what is going on as a senator, and from briefings by the former President's advisers, I am not yet fully conversant with what T.C. had to face and what I must now face in his stead. I require all the information I can get, as fast as possible, and I need any suggestions you have to offer. So let me say, for this get-together at least, I would like each of you, specialists in your own fields, to speak of your problems, so I may understand my problems. You do the talking today. I'll be only too ready to listen. At the next meeting, perhaps, I'll be able to be more constructive. There are ten of you, and the Ambassador, eleven of you, and if you each take five minutes, I'll be sufficiently befuddled and informed to feel we've got off to a good start, and I'll still be out of here in time to keep a heavy day of other appointments. . . . Mr. Secretary Eaton, do you wish to start off my education?"

Eaton tried to smile. "Mr. President, you are doing so well that I feel you can educate us. As a matter of fact, there are a number of foreign-policy problems of the most pressing nature to remark upon."

Eaton found himself vividly reporting to the Cabinet the last conversation with T.C., and T.C.'s desires up to that moment when he had been killed. Carefully, he elaborated upon what Talley had tried to tell Dilman in the Oval Office. Premier Kasatkin and the Russian Presidium were suspicious of United States intervention in emerging Africa.

"The Russians," said Eaton, "feel that our renewal

of membership in the African Unity Pact, promising
these African countries economic aid and military support if their independence should be threatened from
the outside, is a provocative slap at Moscow. In short,
another NATO. However, T.C. said, the Russians
would overlook our Pact if we would cease to encourage
anti-Communist legislation in Baraza. Almost the last
words T.C. spoke were that we must compromise with
honor, maintain a moderate course, to insure world
peace. While he wanted the Pact ratified, he also wanted
to give the Russians their bone—our promise that
Baraza would lift its anti-Communist measures. This
week, as Secretary of State, I did two things—I brought
Ambassador Slater from the United Nations meetings to
hold talks with the Barazan Ambassador to this country,
and I sent Assistant Secretary for African Affairs Stover
to Baraza City to feel out President Amboko. Perhaps
Ambassador Slater would like to tell you about his conferences?"

The United Nations Ambassador, a diminutive, onetime history professor celebrated for his eloquence,
launched into a detailed account of his talks with Ambassador Wamba of Baraza. The talks had made it clear
that while Baraza was fearful of American abandonment
by its not joining the African Unity Pact, the little
country was equally fearful of giving its minority of
Communist-trained natives a free hand. Ambassador
Wamba would make no promises. The decision would
have to come from President Amboko.

Here Eaton took over again. Stover's one long conversation with President Amboko had reflected the same
fears and indecision.

Eaton turned in his chair to Dilman. "Amboko wants
to see you in person, Mr. President, before he makes up
his mind. If I may be frank, I think he suspects that because you are an American Negro, while he is an African Negro, you will be more sympathetic toward his
views, perhaps let him have his cake and eat it, and
promise to defy Russia." Eaton could see Dilman squirm
slightly at his undiluted candor, but he felt that it was
time to let Dilman know that there were those abroad

who might make use of his color. "Mr. President, no matter what our African friend may have to say to you, our own course has been distinctly charted by T.C. We cannot risk a nuclear war to serve the self-interests of one tiny African country. This can be discussed in detail before Amboko's arrival. I suppose you will have to receive him."

"Yes," said Dilman quietly, "I think I'd like to."

Now Eaton brought up the resumption of the Roemer Conference, and promised to see Russian Ambassador Rudenko about a mutually satisfactory date and the possibility of holding the conference in or about Paris. Then, feeling that he had dominated the table long enough, Eaton hastily told Dilman that foreign policy had become so complex it overlapped from his Department of State into numerous other Departments, notably those of the Defense and the Treasury.

As if on cue, Secretary of Defense Steinbrenner, a mirthless, ponderous, shrewd aircraft millionaire, made a statement about the country's current standing in the weapons race, emphasizing the number of stockpiles of nuclear warheads, and the country's situation as to overseas bases. Except for the recent development of the Demi John guided missile, mainstay of the nation's highly mobile airborne rocketry force known popularly as the Dragon Flies, Steinbrenner deplored the fact that in readiness for limited warfare the United States was woefully behind the Russians. He wanted greater expenditures devoted to select units like the Dragon Flies. Furthermore, he wanted reorganization of the Pentagon, especially in the areas of enlarging the military manpower draft and in enforcing speed upon government-subsidized contractors' production schedules.

Immediately Secretary of the Treasury Moody leaped into the fray, protesting the cost of a Pentagon reorganization and opposing part of Eaton's foreign-aid program. Listening to the contentious banker's rasping voice, Eaton took out a cigarette and his silver holder, fitted them together, and smoked. He had heard all this before, and he could see that Dilman had heard it, too, in the Senate, and Eaton tried to hide his boredom. As Moody went on about deficit spending, lower interest rates, tax cuts, economy, Eaton shut him out. Then, suddenly, the Secretary of the Treasury mentioned the budget of the proposed Minorities Rehabilitation Program, and immediately there were six voices, one from every part of the table, superimposed upon each other.

Eaton tried to distinguish one voice from another, but it was difficult, and then, he knew, unnecessary, for the voices were saying almost the same thing but in different languages of self-interest. Unanimously they favored the Minorities Rehabilitation Program and they wanted no paring of the budget. Secretary of Labor Barnes was saying that the Program would create jobs and guarantee prosperity. Secretary of Agriculture Allen was saying that farmers were satisfied that the Program would absorb their own surplus foods for use in depressed areas at home and abroad. Secretary of Interior Ruttenberg was saying the Program would help him develop and conserve natural resources, as Ickes had done with the WPA. Secretary of Commerce Purcell was speaking of his public highways, and Secretary of Health, Education and Welfare Mrs. Cummins was speaking of her expanded school-building program, and Postmaster General Guthrie was speaking of the promise of more post office branches and more carriers.

Ideas were flying, and despite the initial unanimity, there were suddenly acrimonious exchanges. Hearing the cross fire, the participation of almost the entire Cabinet, Eaton was pleased. T.C.'s genius, he told himself, had made such intellectual vitality and excitement possible. Here they were not suffocated by the tedious monologues that had often taken place in earlier Cabinets, ones divided by departmentalism. Eaton recollected a conversation, long ago, with a member of one of Franklin D. Roosevelt's Cabinets, about a typical meeting during which Secretary of Labor Frances Perkins had lectured the others on her problems, and Harry Hopkins, James Farley, Cordell Hull had been inattentive, and Robert Jackson and Henry Morgenthau had exchanged jokes about other matters. Only President Roosevelt, the catalyst interested in everything and everyone, listened to Madam Perkins.

Eaton cast a sidelong glance at President Dilman. His black face was as set and unchanged as ever. His hands were immobile, but his cautious eyes moved from speaker to speaker.

Then came the slapping of a palm on the mahogany table, and a voice louder than the rest. Immediately the others fell silent, fully concentrating on Attorney General Clay Kemmler, whose flinty eyes were colder than ever and whose prominent jaw was extended farther than ever.

"Why don't we stop this economic and prosperity nonsense about the Minorities Rehabilitation Program, and all the sidetracking and disagreements about the money aspects, and speak right out about the only damn thing that is important about that bill?" Kemmler demanded. "We've had a Negro problem since Reconstruction days, and it didn't get attention until the Eisenhower, Kennedy, and Johnson administrations, because the Negroes kept quiet and were poorly organized, and then all hell broke loose. Under T.C., all hell was still breaking loose. His administration had to dig up something fast or be witness to daily massacres of whites and blacks. So he thought of how F.D.R. pulled the WPA out of his hat, to keep the unemployed busy, keep them from open rebellion. Then he thought of the Urban League's old notion of a domestic Marshall Plan to help Negroes, who have been deprived so long, to bring them up quickly, through increased income and education, to ready them for complete equality. That's how MRP was born and that's the sole reason for it."

Attorney General Kemmler seemed to gulp for breath, and then he whirled toward President Dilman, and leaned against the table, wagging a finger at him.

"Mr. President, there's no aspect of that bill for you to consider except one—that it's designed to help your people, and therefore your country."

Eaton could see that while Dilman's broad face held to its impassivity, one hand folded over the other more tightly, until the dark knuckles lightened.

"Mr. President," the Attorney General went on, "I

hope you will find time to visit our Department of Justice someday soon, and walk through our Civil Rights Division. Under Kennedy and then Johnson we had a hundred men and women, lawyers, investigators, secretaries, working there. Under T.C. we had two hundred in this Division. In the past week, since you, a Negro, sir, have become President, we have had to bring our personnel up to two hundred and fifty and in a month it should be three hundred and fifty. Why? Because your sudden accession has doubly reminded the average Negro of what he is missing. He is tired of standing in line with his hungry belly, waiting for his citizenship and his book learning. He is tired of the Crispus Society and the NAACP fighting his battles with law books. He wants action. There's this Turnerite Group, to name only one of a hundred others springing up, all putting on the heat, not merely demanding our action but acting themselves, and threatening all kinds of unnamed horrors. And there's the Klan, and its offshoots, militantly revived, and doubly revived because they fear your administration may be anti-white and vindictive, and they're getting ready for every kind of violence. Only one thing can stop the civil warfare that's right ahead, and that is immediate passage and effective implementation of the Minorities Rehabilitation Program. Maybe it won't solve everything permanently, but it'll get this country back to normal right now, and give my Department a fighting chance to handle what is going on. I recommend strongly, because of the race issue and nothing else, that you, like T.C., throw the full weight and prestige of your office behind the bill."

The Attorney General halted, chest heaving, and Eaton could observe that after this outburst there was little left to discuss. Eaton looked at President Dilman, whose expression still had not changed.

Eaton said, "Mr. President, I think we've used up our allotted time. If you are to keep to your appointment schedule—"

Dilman nodded, stuffing the envelope still before him back into his pocket, and then, blinking at Kemmler, and then at the others, he tried to speak. His voice, caught low in his throat, was almost inaudible.

"I will begin a thorough reading of the Minorities Rehabilitation Program Bill tonight," he said. "Before our next meeting is convened, I may call upon some of you, individually, for more information about it, as well as on Baraza and other matters. . . . Secretary Eaton, I appreciate the speech that you and the others among T.C.'s advisers prepared for my television debut tomorrow. It is excellent, and represents my sentiments entirely. I shall deliver it as written, with but one insignificant modification that I must make. I will not be explicit about the minorities bill in this talk to the nation, until I've studied it and understand it better. In all respects, I believe the speech will assure the country that I am not going to give it a—a black government—or a different government—but a government such as it enjoyed under the late President. . . . Thank you, one and all. The meeting stands adjourned."

He rose, and went hastily across the thick green carpet, and disappeared into Edna Foster's office.

At once the Cabinet meeting broke up, and few lingered behind to hold postmortems, since each of them had a heavy engagement calendar. Going to the door, most of them expressed satisfaction that Dilman would "toe the mark" and "cause no trouble" and "listen to advice." Eaton was the last member in the room, and before he could leave, he found Talley holding his elbow, guiding him to the privacy of the nook between the far wall and the farthest French door.

"What do you think, Arthur?" Talley asked.

"I thought it went very well," said Eaton. "He seems prepared to go all the way with us. He's delivering our speech to the country tomorrow. We can't expect more."

Talley had a reservation. "Yeh, but what about that last little thing, about his saying he wants to modify the outright endorsement of the minorities bill we put in his speech, wants to study the bill so he can understand it? What does that mean, Arthur?"

"It means, Wayne, he needs to display some dignity as an individual, to prove he is not simply a parrot. He is a person, a person who happens to be Negro, and he wants at least to read the most important bill presented to Congress in twenty years involving the people of his race. It makes sense. In his shoes, I would do the same."

"But you think we have him?"

Eaton frowned. "Forgive me, Governor, but I would not put it precisely that way. I'd say that T.C. has him, and he has T.C., and that is good enough for me."

"Amen," said Talley. "And I say you deserve the entire credit."

"Not all," said Eaton. "Hesper deserves some of it."

"I still say—you," said Talley. "You convinced her to be upstairs when he was there, and to speak to him the way she did. Nobody can resist a widow. That would be like pushing Mom out the window or stepping on the flag. You're a genius, Arthur. I feel now—why, it's almost like having T.C. back in the President's office."

"T.C. *is* in the President's office," said Arthur Eaton. "And we're going to keep him there."

Douglass Dilman sat back in the green swivel chair and contemplated his son across the Buchanan desk.

Since his arrival ten minutes ago, the boy had remained in a state of high enthusiasm. He had congratulated his father profusely. He had happily recounted the details of his train trip down from New York, accompanied by the Secret Service man who had shown up at Trafford University six days ago. He had reported proudly that every passenger aboard was absorbed in a newspaper or weekly magazine filled with pictures of President Dilman. He had recounted the excitement of his ride in the White House limousine, of the photographers who had surrounded him outside the West Wing lobby, of his rescue by Tim Flannery.

Momentarily muted by his first visit to the Oval Office, Julian had then wanted to know everything about it. Dilman had quickly led his son on a tour of the room, pointing out the historical curiosities about which he had recently learned. He had shown Julian the Chief Executive's seal impressed upon the white ceiling, the .51 Spencer carbine first shot by Lincoln now hanging on a wall, the cork floor between the carpet and French doors still pitted from the spikes of Eisenhower's golf shoes, the faint heel markings on the wood of the Buchanan desk left by Kennedy's young son when he crawled under it, the mounted leopard head presented by the President of Baraza to T.C., which the First Lady had permitted to remain behind. When they had returned to the bare desk, Julian wondered if his father would be allowed to put his own effects upon it. Dilman had replied, "Of course, when everything's unpacked. Next time you come you'll see the Forensic League trophy on the desk, and those framed pictures of your mother and yourself." Both had been conscious, fleetingly, of the name and picture unmentioned.

Now Dilman observed his son, rather than listened to him, as Julian rattled on. Julian was relating how the events of the past week had thrilled the student body of Trafford University. Studying the boy, Dilman was surprised again that Julian was almost twenty years old. Julian's dudish attire—narrow-shouldered, tapering suit coat, tight trousers, high-collared, starched white shirt with the Italian-made tie, pointed, glossy English shoes —accentuated his chicken-breasted, slim and slight five feet seven inches. Julian's short-cropped hair was pomaded, his white-brown eyeballs bulged out of the coal-black face across the center of which his nostrils were distended. His constantly animated hands, scrubbed clean, the fingernails manicured, were almost overdelicate, in contrast to his African visage. One day he would be wizened.

Julian had, Dilman feared, a certain lack of maturity, balance, judgment. Where his sister resembled her mother physically, Julian had inherited some of his mother's character traits, too quick to become manic and too quick to become depressive, too often reckless and too often venomous. It was these traits that had made Dilman determine that the boy would be safer in a Negro school, among his own, than in a Southern nonsegregated school, which might be a potential ammunition dump.

Considering his son, Dilman wondered if he had acted wisely. Julian had pleaded to enter the famous university in South Carolina which had been desegregated by force—five Negroes had then been attending it, and they did so under guard—arguing that he wanted to get used to the equality he deserved and arguing that he had every right to benefit from the university's renowned School of Law. Dilman had refused to let his boy enter that explosive institution. At the time he had said, and tried to believe, that he was doing this for Julian's own good, to shelter him from the hatred, ostracism, and possible physical violence that were bound to result. Often, afterward, following troubled discussions of his decision with Wanda, Dilman had wondered if he had acted less on his son's behalf than on his own. The entry of a senator's son into a South Carolina college would have put Dilman into the news, underlining his Negroness and differentness to his constituents, and this would have been a political detriment rather than an asset to him, and harmed the Negro cause in general.

Yet, Dilman could see, enrollment in a once entirely white college might have had a salutary effect upon Julian. Not only would it have answered his youthful demands for equality, but it would have enforced upon him a sense of social and scholastic responsibility, modified his flare-ups of resentment, given him a greater maturity. Certainly, Dilman could see, Trafford University had not served Julian well. If anything, it only served Dilman himself, kept the public surface of his own life smooth. The peace that Dilman had won by placing his son in the isolation and safe shelter of a Negro school had been costly to the boy. Julian's frustration was fuel for his anger. Segregation among his own—"that crummy academic Harlem," Julian had once called Trafford— had made him less fit to become a citizen of the country at large. The parentally enforced segregation, with its withdrawal of rights and challenges, had made Julian disinterested in the life around him and in his education.

Continuing to inspect his son, Dilman tried to tell himself that he had performed sensibly, with a consideration of reality that Julian did not possess. As a father, Dilman had been and was still protecting his child. This morning there was none of the usual bitterness, resentment, imbalance of temperament in Julian. He appeared stim-

ulated, even happy. But then, listening more carefully,
Dilman could not deceive himself. The boy was not happier with Trafford, but with the fact that overnight he
was a President's son at Trafford. His pleasure was not
that he had won more attention and respect from his colored classmates. He had already had an undue amount
of that, unearned, as a senator's offspring. His pleasure
was that members of the white faculty, and members of
the white press, and white social arbiters in nearby New
York towns, had been fawning upon him.

"Geez, Dad, I wish you could have been to that tea
in the Law School library yesterday," Julian was saying.
"Except for some of the honor students, I was the only
undergrad there. You'd think I was a celebrity or something the way those white professors kept coming around
me to ask about you and your law background, and how
you did in Commercial Law, and where you practiced,
and if you kept up your interest in law after you got
into Congress. I tell you, you should have seen. Even
the Dean of Admissions kind of tried to get my ear, to
find out my plans, and to find out if I had talked to
you, and if I was going down to the White House to see
you. Imagine, old frostpuss, the Dean himself—"

Dilman knew what was foremost in his mind. It was
time to end his son's false ticker-tape parade. Dilman
interrupted. "Julian—"

Julian stopped, saw his father's face, and waited suspiciously.

"I'm glad you're so popular," Dilman went on, "but
tell me one thing. Was Chancellor McKaye among those
eager to seek you out?"

Julian's expression showed that he suspected a trap,
and his protruding hyperthyroid eyes rolled, as they always did when he was wary. "No," he said. "Why?"

"Well, he sought me out," said Dilman. "I had a letter
from him the day before our late President's death."

Julian attempted an evasive tactic, but it was half-
hearted. "You mean about having you come up to the
school to speak on Founders' Day? I heard some talk
they were planning to invite you. I hope you—"

"You know that was not the invitation Chancellor

McKaye sent me," said Dilman with annoyance. "It was an invitation, yes, but to discuss what's happening to you. He informed me you're heading for an F in at least one course, and you may not maintain a passing grade in two others. If your grade point average goes below a C, he will find it necessary to put you on probation. You know what that means. You not only need to get passing grades, but you need a B average in order to be accepted in law school. I must say, I was surprised, Julian. You were averaging between a B and C. You've been complaining that the curriculum was too easy. Now, suddenly, this nose dive. The Chancellor indicated that you are rebellious, inattentive, and more interested in outside activities than in your classes. Before going to him, I wanted to hear you out. We've always been honest with one another, Julian. More than ever, this is a time for honesty. What's happening with you at that school, Julian?"

Julian had been wriggling in the antique chair. Now he was sullen. "Nothing," he said. "I've been busy, that's all."

"Busy with what?"

"Well, you know, I'm on the students' administrative board of Carver Hall, and there's the Debate Club, and lately they've been overloading us with homework."

"You've managed up until now."

"And then the Crispus Society. Now that I've become the campus rep to National Headquarters, and I'm on the Students' National Advisory Council of Crispus, I have to go into New York more often. Ask your friend Spinger the amount of work that entails. Anyway, don't worry, I'll—"

"I am worried, Julian. I've not stood in the way of outside activity. As far as I'm concerned, have it, but only if it doesn't interfere with your real job, and your real job is getting through the university, and later getting a Bachelor of Laws."

Dilman could see the venom shooting across his son's face, and Julian's lips puckering to contain their trembling. "I don't care what, but I disagree with you," said Julian, his voice cracking. "My real job isn't in that in-

tellectual Catfish Row, getting a black sheepskin so's I
can practice on Chicago's South Side like you did, protecting my people from petty civil suits. My job is protecting my people's rights under the Constitution, seeing
they're not subjugated. I can do that better devoting more
time to the Crispus Society, fighting for my whole people, than by trying to do graduate work in a Negro college, so's I can become a Negro lawyer to represent
Negroes over matters that don't count. My first duty is
to help the country straighten itself out, so that when I
get my law degree, I'll have one as a lawyer, not as a
Negro lawyer, and I can live among people, not just
Negro people, and can represent clients of every color—
that's my duty and my job. I don't care what you say to
it, Dad, but you went and put me in that school to keep
me in my place, to keep me a Negro, like the whites
do—"

Dilman had heard much of this before, but never
spoken with such indignation. He held his own temper
in check, determined to reason with the boy. "I didn't
try to keep you a Negro or anything else, Julian," he
said. "What you are, what you become, is in your own
hands. Certainly there are gross inequities being practiced against us, but we've made gains and we'll make
more, and one day, under due process of law, this country will be everyone's country."

"The payment's overdue more than a hundred years,"
said Julian angrily. "We're not waiting any more. We're
collecting."

Dilman stared at his hands on the desk. "We're being
gradually paid up," he said quietly. "Slavery and bondage are gone. Segregation is going. You'll have it easier
than I had it, and even the way times were, look what a
Negro like your father could accomplish in this country.
Both whites and blacks put me in Congress—"

"On the white man's terms," said Julian. Hastily he
added, "I'm not being disrespectful, but I mean—"

"Julian, look where I'm sitting, look around the room
you're in—"

Julian had grasped the desk. "They didn't mean for
you to be here, Dad, they don't want you here. We want

you, but they don't." His voice was cracking again. "I haven't told you everything I've been hearing."

Dilman wanted to end this painful scene with one who was of his own blood, one who would not understand. "I know what's going on, Julian," he said. "Nevertheless, I'm here, and that speaks well of our situation in our country. It is proof of what is possible. I'll do my job here, and all I want of you is that you stop trying to turn over the country with one push and concentrate on learning some reason in school—"

"Dad, I'm going to tell you, I'm going to tell you," Julian interrupted. "All of us think it's like a miracle, your being put here. You've got the chance of a lifetime to do in a little while what our people, and the ones who died and suffered, all the societies, couldn't do in a century. You can force the whites—"

"I'm not forcing anybody to do anything." Dilman's tone had become harsh. "I'm the President of the United States, not the President of the Negro population, and whatever's best—"

"I'm still going to tell you—listen, Dad, please listen —you've got to know what our people are saying outside—they're saying if you were the President of the United States, all of it, that would be fine, too, but you're not—won't be—you'll be like the ones before—the President of the whites—"

Dilman's hands balled hard. "That's enough from you, Julian, that's quite enough. You remember who you are and who I am, and that I'm the one who's still in charge of seeing you think right and behave right—me, not your callow friends."

Sulkily Julian released his grip on the desk, and pushed back into his chair. "Okay, if—if you don't want to talk—"

"Don't bait me. And stop being childish."

"I'm not baiting you the least bit. I'm only thinking how you always wanted us to be your kind of Negro, and none of us wanted it, not Mom, and not Mindy, and not me either. I always envied Mindy because she was born lucky, and got away, and I was born this way and got stuck. When I wanted to do something about it, become a person like everybody else, like Mindy, you wouldn't let me, and you still won't."

At the first mention of his daughter's name, Dilman had automatically begun to scan the office, to make certain that every door was closed to hostile ears. He could see that the doors were shut tight.

He brought his gaze back to his son. "I don't want to discuss Mindy here."

"And you don't want to discuss me, either," said Julian bitterly. "I'd trade places with her tomorrow, if I could."

"Don't be so sure of that," said Dilman. "All Negroes who pass aren't so happy. The deceit—"

"She's doing all right," said Julian.

Dilman looked at his son sharply. "How do you know?" he demanded. "How do you know she's doing all right?"

Julian's immediate discomfort was evident. "I—I'm guessing. If she weren't, wouldn't you have heard from her, now that you're President? If she weren't better off playing white, wouldn't she come forward to live in the White House?"

"You seem to know a good deal about her," said Dilman. "You've been in touch with her, haven't you?"

"Suppose I have?"

"I'm surprised, that's all," said Dilman, and his heart ached at her rejection of him, and then he was ashamed at the fear that had entered his head. When Mindy had gone across the line separating white from black, she had gone entirely, disappeared from every phase of the old life she had ever known. Only she knew her secret and her identity. Now she was not alone. She had shared her secret. The threat of it oppressed him. "Isn't she afraid? Why should she take the chance of letting you know—"

"I don't know who she is or where she is," said Julian. "One day, a year and a half ago, I had a brief note from her at school, right out of the sky. She needed money desperately, for some emergency. She figured I was on an allowance from you. She asked for a loan to be mailed in cash. She told me to mail it under a different name to General Delivery at the main post office in New York City. I did. After that, I tried to find that name she gave me in the New York directories. There was none like that. Maybe she uses many names. Anyway, I wrote her, using that name, and a couple of months ago she paid me back in cash. There was another note from her. She's got a better position, whatever it is. She's going with a great crowd, and she made it clear they were white. Oh, she's doing fine, she's doing just great. She's got equal rights, because she was born color-lucky like the white folks. And all I'm asking is that you let me work harder on the outside for the same acceptance and decency."

"Mindy's wrong," said Dilman. "Deceit is wrong. Julian, you'll have your acceptance and decency in the open, on your own terms. T.C. was fighting for it, and you tell your friends I will, too." He suddenly felt tired. "I moved today, I moved into that"—he pointed through the French doors—"plantation house." He smiled weakly. "That's our home for the next year or so, Julian. There'll be a room for you, for weekends and holidays. When are you going back to Trafford?"

"Late this afternoon."

"Very well. Why don't you go up there—someone will show you the elevator to the second floor—and have a look around? It's something to see. Crystal's there right now. She'll whip you up some lunch, and after that you get the valet to show you a room for yourself. I'll catch up with you before you leave."

Julian rose, softened, chastened by the realization of the White House. "I'm sorry to—to disagree with you, Dad, with all you've got on your mind. I'm staying on with my work in the Crispus Society, but I'll try to do better in school, too. You can write the Chancellor that."

Relieved, Dilman smiled fully. "Thanks, son. Just open that door, and go around the ell and through the ground-floor door. You won't get lost."

The moment that Julian had gone, Dilman consulted the typed card slipped into the silver holder on the desk. The card read: *The President's Engagements.* Beneath his son's name was the name of Leroy Poole.

Dilman picked up the console telephone receiver and pressed the buzzer. Instantly he heard Shelby Lucas, the agreeable, somewhat courtly, prematurely gray engagements secretary, inherited from T.C., reply on the other end. "Yes, Mr. President?"

"How am I running, Mr. Lucas?"

"About—about ten minutes ahead, Mr. President."

"Is Mr. Poole here?"

"In the Fish Room, sir."

"Please send him in."

Putting down the console telephone, Dilman attempted to disengage his thoughts from his son, from the accusations of his son and Mindy, and concentrate on what he must say to Poole. He remembered how impressed Julian had been that an author of Poole's stature had undertaken to write his father's biography. From the first, Dilman had been less impressed. He had found Poole repulsive in appearance, deficient in objectivity, and more unreasonable than Julian about equal rights for Negroes. He was a race chauvinist, the Negro counterpart of the Zeke Millers. His perspiring journalistic professionalism seemed barely to perform on a jellied foundation of emotionalism. There was something oily and insincere about him. His questions, well researched, well prepared, often seemed to have no relationship to his own curiosity or interest.

Behind Poole's deference to his subject, Dilman suspected, lay mockery and contempt. Dilman could not be sure, but his sensitivity always entertained these suspicions when his biographer left the Senate office or the brownstone living room. Time and again Dilman had been tempted to call the project off. He had not wanted a researcher rummaging through the storeroom of his past life. He had not wanted this book written about himself, even though it was to be published by a Negro press, presumably for Negro readers. Dilman had feared that it would be read by white constituents, too, who might decide that he was not representative of them, and next time vote against him. Yet because the Reverend Spinger and other Negro leaders wanted the book as an inspiration for the Negro young, to turn them away from violence, to show them what one of their own had accomplished in a democracy, Dilman had continued cooperating.

Several times since he had been sworn into the Presidency, Dilman had thought fleetingly about the book, wondering if he should permit its publication now that his role had changed. Of course, previous Presidents had made themselves available to biographers during their terms of office. But his own problems were ones that they had not possessed. He had been unable to come to a decision. There had been so many calls from Poole during the week, which he had avoided, that at last he had been embarrassed into taking one. On the telephone, he had been aware at once that Poole's approach had become even more self-effacing and deferential. Dilman had accepted his biographer's congratulations and good wishes, and heard out his set speech about the increased importance of the book now that its subject had graduated from senator to President. Without committing himself to the book's continuance, Dilman had agreed to see Poole as soon as possible, and requested him to work out a date with the engagements secretary. Since then Dilman had been too busy to give Poole or the book another thought, but now this was one more minor matter that he must settle.

The corridor door had swung open, and engagements secretary Lucas was saying to someone not yet visible, "Right in here, Mr. Poole."

Leroy Poole came through the door like a beach ball. The door closed behind him, and he stopped, dipped his obese face, murmuring, "Mr. President of the United States," and then he advanced toward the desk, pudgy hand outstretched. "Once more, my sincere best wishes, Mr. President. I think all of us are very lucky we have someone with your experience to carry on."

Dilman half lifted himself from the swivel chair, and lost his hand inside Poole's chubby clasp, thinking how much it was like shaking hands with a boxing glove. Dilman waved toward the chair. "Sit down, Leroy."

Poole eased into the seat, his arms aloft, as if to bring all of the office down into their laps. "The office looks so different from any of the photographs I've seen. Somehow you come to expect a throne room, considering that this is the most important office in the world."

"One of the most important," Dilman corrected him.

"Yes, I guess the others consider theirs just as important," said Poole.

"They do, and they're demanding equal time. I don't want to be abrupt, Leroy, but I'm afraid they won't let me be as casual about appointments here as I was in the Senate Office Building. So let's get right on——"

Dilman paused. The French door behind Poole had opened, and Julian was standing there, worried and harassed, and at his elbow was the Secret Service agent called Sperry.

"I—I'm sorry to break in like this," Julian was saying, "but I went into the ground floor like you said, and this gentleman grabbed me and asked for my pass, and I had none. I told him who I was, but he frisked me, and then said I couldn't get upstairs until I was cleared."

Dilman calmed his son with a gesture. "All right, Julian. . . . Mr. Sperry——"

The Secret Service agent came alongside Julian. "Sorry, Mr. President, I was sure he was your son, but I couldn't take any chances unless he was identified or I was instructed."

Dilman nodded. "You were correct. Consider him identified as my son, and ask Chief Gaynor to make out a permanent White House pass." Dilman realized that Poole was on his feet, studying Julian. Hastily, Dilman performed the introduction. "Julian, meet Leroy Poole, the writer you so much admire."

Julian's eyes protruded more noticeably as he eagerly stepped forward to shake Poole's hand. "Gosh, Mr. Poole, this is an honor——"

"A pleasure for me, too, Mr. Dilman. I'd been looking forward to meeting you at least once before completing your father's biography."

"I've read every one of your articles," Julian said. "I even heard you lecture once at our school."

"Your school? I remember your father telling me. You're at Trafford. I don't recall——"

"It was the students' branch of the Crispus Society."

"I remember," said Leroy Poole.

Dilman's cough interrupted the exchange. "Sorry, Leroy, but I am crowded for time. . . . Mr. Sperry, will you take my son up to the second floor?"

"Thanks, Dad," said Julian. His eyes lingered admiringly on Poole. "Pleased to meet you, Mr. Poole."

When the French door closed, Poole resumed his seat. "That's a mighty fine boy you have, Mr. President. I don't remember your telling me that he was a member of the Crispus Society."

"It's in your notes, I'm sure," said Dilman. "In fact, he's now on one of the national committees at their headquarters. Shall we get on with our business?"

"I'm ready, Mr. President. I've been giving some thought to the book——"

"So have I, Leroy. I've come to a decision. I don't like the idea of its publication right now, but I want to be fair. You've worked hard and long on it. You're expecting certain income from it. I have no right to deprive you. So——"

"You have no right to deprive the country," said Poole, fingers wiping his brow. "The book was conceived as an inspirational story for our people. Due to circumstances, to your elevation, Mr. President, I now feel positive it will be inspirational for all people of this country, no matter what their color. It will lead to an understanding of you, better feeling between the races, and it will present the best image of you, the most accurate one, the only firsthand one extant."

Listening to Poole's salesmanship, Dilman remembered hearing from Edna Foster what she had heard a few nights ago from her fiancé, George Murdock, that many members of the press corps had been approached by New York publishers to write their reminiscences of T.C., and several had been asked to write hurried biographies of the new President. It occurred to Dilman that not one of the press corps, who might undertake a paste-up story of him, knew him as well as Poole or was in possession of so many actual facts. If biographies were inevitable, it behooved him to encourage one that might be a good one.

"All right, Leroy," he found himself saying, "you don't have to sell me on the biography. I agreed to this, and no matter what has happened, I'll go through with it. I'll make only one qualification. When I was a senator, it did not seem unreasonable to permit a Negro publisher to bring the book out. Now that I am, by fate, President of the country, I think that would look wrong. I think the book should be published simultaneously by the Negro press you've contracted with and by a reputable white publishing house in New York. I must insist upon that."

"Suits me fine," said Poole. "In fact, that's a great idea. I'll call my literary agent in New York today. Tell him it has to be two publishers or none. That'll be no problem. The big thing is the ending of the book. I've got to change that. Now there's a new climax and finish, and we'll have to talk it over, and—"

"Leroy, I don't have time any more. I wish I could, but—no more interviews."

Poole looked stricken. "Senator—Mr. President— Good Lord, I can't write about you and not tell of your becoming the first Negro President."

"Don't get upset," said Dilman. "I'll tell you what— you conclude the book on the note of my moving into the White House, which I did today. You end the book where I've been President for a week."

"That'll still require some interviews."

Dilman hesitated. "I can't promise you, Leroy. Here's what I suggest. Draw up one last set of questions and send them to me through Miss Foster. I'll dictate the answers some night soon when I have a spare hour. You have my word—I'll do it soon. If there's anything you've missed, you can poke your head in here once or twice in the coming month. That's the best I can promise, Leroy."

"It'll have to do," said Poole unhappily. "Yes, I'll manage somehow. It'll be a good book, I guarantee you."

"I'm sure it will." Dilman pushed his swivel chair away from the desk. "That's it, then. Everything's settled." He waited for Leroy Poole to rise and leave, but Poole had not moved. Puzzled, Dilman waited.

"Uh, Mr. President," said Poole, "there is just one other thing, if you can give me another minute or two."

"Well—" Dilman began doubtfully.

"Only a minute or two," Poole implored.

As he watched the beads of perspiration on the writer's brow increase, Dilman felt sorry for him. He relaxed slightly. "Very well, Leroy, what's on your mind?"

"All the oppressions going on around the country against our people," said Poole with urgency. "Especially one case I happen to be following. It seems to symbolize the worst of everything. Have you been reading about the trial down in Hattiesburg, Mississippi?"

"You mean those Turnerite boys?" said Dilman. "I've seen it in the morning papers this week. I haven't followed it closely."

"It's a shocking matter," said Poole with growing agitation. "The Turnerites were peacefully picketing a Klansman. They were violently attacked, one blinded, one crippled for life. They were jailed, instead of their white attackers. Now they're waiting sentence by County Judge Everett Gage, one of the most flagrant segregationists and vicious warthogs in the white racist underground. The trial was a farce, and it seems to me it is the perfect battleground to stop discriminatory practices in those local Southern courtrooms and introduce some vestige of legal democracy. I keep telling myself the Attorney General should intervene—this is one place he should intervene. Has he sent you a full account?"

Dilman's forehead had contracted, trying to read Poole's anxiety and interest in one out of more than a hundred similar cases. "No," said Dilman. "This is not a Federal matter. It is a state matter, a community matter."

"But our whole judicial system is being made a clowning—"

"Leroy, I don't understand you. Why this concern over one obscure and isolated trial?" He paused. "Is it because you're a Turnerite? I never asked you before. Are you?"

"My God, no," said Poole. "I'm dragging along with the Crispus Society. I'm too sedentary and timid for anything as vigorous as the new Turnerite Group. It is just that I admire them, as every thinking minority should. This is, after so many words, their first public move, and they're being legally lynched. That's all there is to my interest, Mr. President. I have deep sympathy for them."

Although he was inexplicably troubled, Dilman tried to hold a stern expression on his face. "I'm sorry, Leroy, but I have less sympathy for those Turnerites than you have. I don't like most of that irresponsible and inflammatory talk their leader has been giving out."

"Jeff Hurley? Why, Senator Dilman——Mr. President ——he's a great man. I——I had occasion to meet him several times, hear him speak. He's no rabble-rouser or savage red-neck like those white segregationists. He's intelligent, kindhearted, and he's only reflecting the mood of ——of the Negro population."

Dilman felt weak, but would not weaken. "Leroy, we've gone over this ground indirectly in our interviews for the book. You know my stand. I'm a Negro, I'm conscious of it, I'm proud of it. I'm more aware of my birthright today than ever before. I want justice done for us, as Negroes, the way I want it for every Mexican and Puerto Rican and Jew and Catholic. But, Leroy, this is still a civilized country we have, educated to abide by the laws enacted by the majority. You don't get what you want by breaking other people's heads."

"In war you do. There is war in this country."

"No, Leroy, as Americans we gave up that kind of solution at Appomattox. We've come a long way by using better means. We'll go farther the same way."

"But, right now, you can do so much more for us, for justice, now that you are President," Poole pleaded.

"Leroy, no matter what I feel inside as a Negro man, I can do no more as an American President than T.C. or The Judge or Johnson or Kennedy did before me."

Poole came forward, his moonface crunched with anguish. "Then I appeal to you not as a President but as a Negro man. There is one personal act you can perform that would help those Turnerite martyrs and bring the issue more strongly before the whole country. I heard there's a great attorney come here from Chicago, Nathan Abrahams, the kind of man who is conscious of these injustices. He could save the Turnerites, even with the trial over, then by appealing the verdict and sentence. I know you once mentioned him as an old friend of yours. His prestige would——"

Dilman shook his head vigorously. "No, Leroy. I can't go to Nat Abrahams. He is an old friend, true. He is in the city. We spoke on the phone only two days ago. In fact, he's coming to dine with me tonight. But I would not dream of influencing his activity. If you want him so badly, why don't you call him? Or have that man Hurley do so?"

"Hurley tried. I heard that. He was told Abrahams is tied up on other business right now. But if you, as his friend, with your position——"

"Absolutely no," said Dilman. "If he can't do it for Hurley, I don't feel I should put him in the position of having to do it for me." Then he added, "Especially since, in spite of what the details of that trial in Mississippi may be, I still don't like how Hurley is going about things. Sorry, Leroy."

"Well, I'm sorry, too," said Poole softly. "Forgive me. I think you are making a mistake."

"I've made many mistakes as an individual," said Dilman. "I hope to make fewer as this country's Chief Executive. I'm as conscious as you of my color and of injustices to men of my color. Perhaps what's happened— my being put in this seat, this office—and acting with dignity and responsibility toward all races in the full view of the whole nation and the world—will, could, do more to break down barriers of prejudice than anything else. It is a dream I hold. I don't want to destroy it by diverting myself to lesser skirmishes or using my influence on friends. Be patient, Leroy. Much will be done." He paused. "Our conversation, of course, is privileged. I don't want to see any of it in your book."

Leroy Poole rose. "Of course not, Mr. President. One thing has nothing to do with the other. . . . Thank you for your time. I'll write up some questions for you to answer. I hope to see you again soon."

He had turned to leave, when he seemed to remember something and hurriedly came back to the desk.

"Mr. President, I almost forgot, but I promised someone to mention this to you. There's a young lady I met, very well known in Washington—very capable, I'm told—who wants to apply for the position of your social secretary. She's—"

"I was thinking of promoting one of the girls already on the White House staff. I don't think anyone from outside—"

"She's Senator Watson's daughter."

Dilman could not conceal his surprise. "Senator Watson? Are you sure? He's the Southern—"

"That's right. But his daughter, Sally Watson, is different. I don't know her well, but we've talked. She's absolutely color-blind, progressive, liberal, and knows everyone in the city, naturally. She's dying to apply for the job, if it's open."

"Oh, it's open." Dilman tried to think. At least three top secretaries on T.C.'s staff had resigned. Mary Lou Rand, the First Lady's press secretary, had been one of them. Miss Laurel, the First Lady's social secretary, had been another. He hated to examine their real motives in quitting. He remembered the advice given him by T.C.'s widow this morning. Hesper had said that he needed a woman in the White House to manage the many executive social functions. The right woman was imperative. Through the morning, Dilman had thought of hiring a clever and personable Negro girl. Then he had rejected the idea. There was no Negro girl among those he knew who had the social background to conduct formal dinners, play hostess to heads of state and Supreme Court justices and congressmen and ambassadors. There was not one he knew, even if he waived experience, who had the education and poise. Moreover, a Negro girl brought into the White House by him on this level would invite more angry speculation from the press that he was peopling the White House with those of his own race.

Yet, he had thought, a white social secretary invited

as many difficulties, if different ones. While he expected that, by making inquiries, he could find the right young lady, one who had mingled in the government and Georgetown set, the idea of having a white girl so close to him in the White House was dangerous. That, too, might create suspicion and resentment. Nevertheless, it had to be *someone,* and if he was to do what Hesper advised, find an efficient person, it would have to be a white girl.

He considered the name of the one whom Poole had suggested. He had a vague recollection of reading about Sally Watson in the Washington *Post,* the *Star,* Zeke Miller's *Citizen-American.* As a senator's daughter, she would know everyone, know what was proper and correct. And Poole had said that she was liberal and open-minded, and "dying" for the position. Gradually Dilman warmed to the suggestion. The act of appointing a Southern senator's socialite daughter to a social job in the White House might be more valuable than harmful, from a public-relations point of view.

Dilman found Leroy Poole standing before him. Dilman nodded. "Yes, the position is open," he repeated. "I was just thinking pro and con, but I suppose that is pointless without meeting the young lady and knowing more about her."

"I think you should at least see her, Mr. President. I think you'll be impressed."

"All right, I'll see her. Can you call her for me?"

"Immediately."

Dilman's eyes went to his engagement card and then to his wristwatch. He was still running ahead of schedule. There would be a free span of fifteen minutes or so between his last morning appointment and his luncheon with the Joint Chiefs of Staff.

"All right, Leroy. Tell Miss Watson to be here at twelve-fifteen. Don't give her any false hopes. Simply say I'll see her briefly."

"I'll take care of it, gladly, Mr. President." Poole began to turn away, when the view of the South Portico of the White House beyond the Rose Garden arrested him. "My, that's a beautiful sight out there." Suddenly he snapped his fingers. "One last thing, Mr. President. Since I'm ending your biography on your moving into the White House, I think it would be the smart thing to have a quick look at what's going on up there."

"It's a mess today—"

"Exactly," said Poole with heightening enthusiasm. "I want to see the moving in, the unpacking, the various rooms. I've never been up there before."

"The press and public are not usually invited into the President's private apartment."

"I wouldn't repeat the intimate details to a soul. I simply need a general visual picture for the book. That'll be the tag of the book."

Dilman shrugged, indifferent, his mind already going to the next names on his engagement card. "Go ahead, Leroy, if you require it. But don't get in the way and don't be long. I'll inform the Secret Service where you're going."

He buzzed Edna Foster to alert Secret Service that Mr. Poole could be admitted to the second floor for a short visit. Then he buzzed Mr. Lucas to tell him to pencil in Miss Watson at twelve-fifteen, and to send in the next visitor.

He sat back in his green chair, exhausted by the hammerings of guilt from his son, by the special pleadings of his biographer, and resentful of this jabbing at his repressed consciousness of being a Negro, of being the first colored man in America who could (if he wanted to, they said) lead his people out of servitude to a Promised Land.

Through the French doors he could see the waddling, ridiculous figure of Leroy Poole making his way toward the ground-floor entrance. How could anyone as ineffectual and verbose and foolish-looking as that make him, a man in his position, feel so reproached and uneasy and afraid? Damn the Pooles and the Hurleys, he suddenly thought. They had no larger responsibility and so they could think, say, do anything. They had only a little ax to grind. But he, as President, had inherited a big stick. He must remember, he must never forget, to use it with wisdom, if at all. Unaccountably then, his mind revolved to Wanda Gibson, whom he could not see, and to the solution that had been taking form in his thoughts, and he began to feel more assured about what lay ahead. . . .

After Leroy Poole had embraced Crystal across the expanse created by their equal corpulence, after kidding her gently and dubbing her Mammy Dolley Madison (for he adored her because she exuded the warmth he had enjoyed from his Mom in childhood), he made a mock ferocious charge across the litter in the Rose Guest Room toward Diane Fuller. While the skinny secretary feigned resistance and squealed, Poole pecked at her hollow cheek and pinched her behind.

Then, elaborately, he again extracted his small spiral notebook, and began to scribble notes describing this historic room on Dilman's unpacking day. Without meetlng the eyes of the fink Uncle Tom of a valet, he was conscious of the haughty servant's disapproval of his uncouth extroversion.

Writing, Leroy Poole thought how much the valet Beecher had in common with Douglass Dilman: Man, you are sure enough a counterfeit white, like Massah, and, man, maybe it gets you along fine today, but it won't stand you no good on Judgment Day, because you ain't white, no matter what, and you ain't black, no matter what, and you won't rise no higher than purgatory and limbo.

Before coming upon Crystal and Diane in the Rose Guest Room, Poole had been taken on a careful tour of the second floor of the White House by the valet. At another time in his young life, he imagined, the visit might have been memorable. To know that a poor shanty black boy like himself could be led down hallways and up elevators by the President's bodyguards, could be shown the intimate splendors of the White House by the President's valet, would have been a high spot of his life. This morning it was next to nothing, and he was as inattentive as if he were going through the modern office building on 44th Street in Manhattan to visit his publisher.

For ten minutes he had been guided in and out of the great hall, in and out of the Yellow Oval Room, the Treaty Room, the Lincoln Bedroom (here he had his only start, seeing that fink Dilman's clothes piled on the long bed), all the while listening to that Uncle Tom valet's supercilious history patter. While Poole had made a pretense of taking notes, had indeed taken several, knowing all the while that he could get what he needed from the excellent guidebook the White House Historical Association had published, his entire attention was focused on a confrontation with one person somewhere in one of these stodgy, phony rooms.

Christ, he had thought, what had this junk cost to keep one bum politician in luxury for four years while millions of his people couldn't buy their way out of the countless filthy, overcrowded, rotting and stinking slums? The hell with all this, the crappy Victorian chairs in the Treaty Room, the crappy crystal chandeliers bought by that nitwit President Grant, the crappy Monroe vases in the Yellow Oval Room, the crappy Greuze painting of Ben Franklin, another white fink—all this cared for by more overpaid people than there were working in the Civil Rights Division of the Justice Department or than were publicly able to work for the Turnerite Group.

His lousy meeting with that servile black Judas, Dilman, more yellow on his spine than black, had infuriated him, blinded him to everything but his failure. There were his gutty, beaten brothers handcuffed in that stinkpot town in that Devil's Island of a state in the deep torture chamber of the South, suffering kangaroo trial before a foul vermin of a county judge. There was his friend Jeff Hurley, and that smart good Dago, Valetti, and the rest of his brother blacks risking their lives in Little Rock or Shreveport, where every segregated hotel was about as safe as the Alamo. And here was he, one of the secret unlisted members they counted upon most, commanded by their leader to convince a fink President to get a maybe fink Jew lawyer to lend a hand to justice.

They were on the firing line, waiting on word from him, their hopes and last appeal for decency depending on him, and he had failed. Would Hurley understand how desperately he had tried? Would Hurley believe that he had been unable to turn a black man who was yellow into a black man who would be Negro? Yet three days ago the mails had brought him a hasty letter from Hurley and one last hope. If this hope was fulfilled, they could be optimistic again. If this, too, failed, then hell would break loose, and when Poole remembered the Turnerite plan of last resort, he had shuddered. And so he had tagged after the valet, looking not at the *objets d'art* which were America's pride and heritage—not his, for America rejected him—looking not at this alien decadence but for the one animate object he must meet.

Finishing his note-taking in the Rose Guest Room, he once more slipped on his fat-man jester mask of good cheer, teased Crystal and Diane, and bade them good-bye for today.

"Have we seen every room?" he asked the hovering valet.

"Not quite. Please follow me."

They entered a corridor, then entered the red-and-white Empire Guest Room, then looked into the small bathroom with a carpet—a carpet in the can, Je-sus!—and then moved toward the southeast corner room.

"This is the last one you haven't seen," the fink valet was announcing. "It is the Lincoln Sitting Room, adjoining the Bedroom, which you visited. You'll find the furniture somber, late Empire and Victorian. The side chairs are backed by laminated rosewood, quite unique. The room offers solitude, retreat, and an excellent view of Washington and Georgetown. Perhaps the only modern, discordant note in the Sitting Room is—"

The valet had gone into the Lincoln Sitting Room, and at once halted and drew himself upright.

"Excuse me, sir," he was saying to someone in the corner. "We won't disturb you, Mr. Dilman. I was taking one of the President's guests on a—"

At the mention of the name, Leroy Poole squeezed past the valet into the Sitting Room, where Julian Dilman sat slumped in a red-patterned, upholstered chair drawn up before a going television set.

Poole rotated his palm in greeting. "Hi, Julian," he said breezily.

Julian leaped to his feet, as filled with consternation and pleasure as if Lincoln himself had come into the room.

"Why, hello, Mr. Poole. It's sure good to see you again. It was a great honor and pleasure meeting you downstairs. You don't know what a fan I am of yours. I'd sure like to talk to you sometime about your essays."

"Why not right now?" said Poole, all affability. He pivoted toward the impassive valet. "Do you mind, Jeeves?"

"Not at all, sir," said Beecher. "We've completed the tour, sir. Ring for me when you are ready to leave."

The valet backed off to the doorway, then through it, then hastened away.

Poole had followed the retreat of the valet to the door. Now, closing the door, he said to Julian, "That butler—I bet Harriet Beecher Stowe's writing a book about him this minute."

Julian clapped his hands, and beamed at being the solitary recipient of a Great Author's *bon mot.* Going to the side chair nearest the President's son, Poole silently exulted that he had found the *objet d'art,* animate, he had been hunting, and that it would not be difficult at all.

"Sit down, Julian," Leroy Poole said. "I have only a couple of minutes, but I'd enjoy a little chat."

Poole settled easily into a chair, while Julian, displaying embarrassment at the unreeling of an old Western motion picture filling the television set screen, said, "I—I was just eating up some time before catching my train back to Trafford. Let me shut it off."

"You'll never know how it came out," Poole said.

"I don't care," said Julian. He went awkwardly to the television set and turned it off. Then, shyly, he took a place beside Poole. "My taste is better than that, believe it or not," he said. "I read a lot, that's what I do."

"What sort of thing?" asked Poole.

"Well, the classics, of course," said Julian nervously.

"I thought you said you read my stuff."

"I do! That's the truth, Mr. Poole, that's what I really read the most now, the protest literature, that's what I find important."

Poole dropped his teasing demeanor and nodded solemnly. "Good boy," he said. "I wish your father felt the same."

"What do you mean, Mr. Poole?"

"I've come to know your father quite well, Julian, so I mean no negating or adverse criticism of his remarkable mind and achievements, but—no, I don't think it's fair to discuss this with—"

Julian almost fell from the chair in his eagerness. "Please, please, Mr. Poole, go ahead! I know my father pretty well, and I know his shortcomings as well as his good points."

"Ummm," murmured Poole. "Okay, then. It's just that I don't think he's as close to his people, their problems, as he should be. I think he's been in this antiseptic center of compromise too long, and he's been separated from the realities of Negro misery and injustice too long."

"You're right, absolutely," Julian said fervently. "He's always been that way, at least long as I can remember, long as he's been a politician depending on support from whites. To tell the truth, I was having a fight with him—well, a disagreement, let's say—about just that before you came in his office."

Poole wore his mask of innocent wonder. "No kidding?"

"He forced me into a Negro college," Julian rushed on. "Now he objects because I'm giving so much time to the Crispus Society. I accused him of not facing what he is, what we're up against, and he gave me a good dressing down."

"No kidding?" Poole repeated. "Well, we gave him quite a morning, the two of us. You know that trouble down in Mississippi over the Turnerites—?"

"Oh, yes!"

"I begged your father to get the Attorney General into the matter, to straighten out that crooked trial. If he couldn't do that as President—I know the pressure he is under—I asked him to do Jeff Hurley a personal favor. I asked him to have his friend Nat Abrahams—"

"I know Nat. He's a great guy."

"Okay, I asked your father to persuade Nat to step in and appeal the conviction, when it comes. Apparently, Nat's tied up with something else, but he couldn't say no to your father, to the President, if he were asked. No soap. Your father wouldn't ask."

"He wouldn't?" said Julian. Then he nodded knowingly. "That's right, he wouldn't. Especially now. He has strong feelings against equality by force. I'm like you, like what you write, Mr. Poole. I think that's the only course there is left for us. Yet nothing can change Dad. He's wrong, but that's the way he is."

"*You* can change him," said Leroy Poole. He had timed it. A pause, and then this opener before the real bombshell. He could see the beginning. Julian's repellent eyes had inflated.

"Me?" Julian grimaced. "You mean you want me to ask him to help them down in Mississippi?"

Leroy Poole allowed his last mask of affability to slip away. His fat face was grim. He was Jeff Hurley's envoy and final negotiator before the cataclysm.

"Julian, I didn't come upon you in this room by accident. I pretended to be on a tour. That was crap. I was looking for you. You know why? Because those Turnerites down in Hattiesburg have got to be saved. No Negro can give in to such flagrant injustice and humiliation. I know Hurley has drawn the line in Hattiesburg. If those bastards step over it, there'll be real trouble—not talk, Julian, but trouble—for your father, for the whole country, for you and me. I'm trying to prevent it being done the hard way. I want to be law-abiding like your father. Okay, either he's got to intervene, or get someone in the government or in private practice, someone with weight, to throw it around and show those bastards that the Middle Ages are done and over with forever. That's it, Julian. I just tried. I failed. You're the last hope. I want you to go in there and convince your father to act."

Julian pushed a little dry laugh, false and fearful, out of his unsmiling mouth. "Mr. Poole, I—I'd do anything —I'm trying all the time—but this is one thing I can't do. My father just practically threw me out of his office over a lesser matter. If I even opened my mouth about this, he'd pin my ears back—he'd cut my allowance, make me quit Crispus, God knows what else. We've had it out about active protest. No use. I can't go back to him again."

Leroy Poole held his breath. This was it, the cold, chilling moment to strike, the clear air and exact time for the bombshell.

"Julian, I'm not asking you to go to your father, I'm ordering you to go—as one member of the Turnerite Group to another."

He was pleased at the result of the impact. Julian's eyes almost popped from their sockets, his mouth gaped, his jaw went slack. Some instinct of self-preservation appeared to draw his thin body into itself, as if trying to shrivel itself into invisibility. Julian's terrified eyes went from Poole to the door and back again.

Julian sought helplessly to articulate some coherent reaction, and then he managed to stutter, "I—I—you shouldn't—I—Jeff made the blood pledge with my pledge—that it would be secret—no one would know in a million years—it was the condition—to be in the secret corps. This is—this is—"

"There's no betrayal, if that's what you're going to say, Julian," said Leroy Poole briskly. "We have a small public organization, but the mass of the iceberg hidden below is the most of it and the most effective section. I'm an unlisted, undercover member, and so are you. I wouldn't have known you belonged, except that Hurley wrote me the information the other day. No one knows, will ever know, except Hurley, Valetti, and now me, and I was okayed because I'm on the Advisory Board. When you and I went in, we vowed to do whatever we were ordered to do. I was ordered to write the pamphlets and propaganda. I did. Then I was ordered to get your father on our side. I followed orders, I tried. You—you were ordered to stay in the Crispus

Society, get on their Student Council in New York, and
you did, and then you were assigned to get inside information for us, about the trouble spots, the hard and soft
spots—"

"I've done it, that's what I been doing, that's enough,"
Julian whispered.

"Not now, Julian," Poole went on relentlessly.
"Now you've got more to do, because your situation has
changed. Your father is President of this country. You're
his son, and that counts for something. You're one of us,
and we are your brothers, and that counts for more. You
go to him—"

"What if I fail like you did? I know I'll fail, I know.
What'll happen then?"

"We'll worry about that later. All I want to know is
that you don't chicken out on Hurley and the Group.
Will you see him today? Will you speak to him?"

Julian's voice was a croak. "Yes."

"Good boy." Poole placed his hands on his knees and
stood up. "What time are you going to be at the Union
Station?"

"Five o'clock."

"I'll see you there," said Leroy Poole.

He started for the door, but Julian's quavering voice
caught him before he could touch the knob.

"Mr. Poole—it—it's supposed to be secret—that's the
whole thing."

"Julian, what do you take us for? It's as secret as it
ever was, about me, about you. No one's ratting on either
of us. Trust Jeff Hurley. He's the greatest Negro this
country ever gave birth to. He's our savior, our future.
Let's just do as he says, every one of us, and then maybe
soon we'll all be free, and won't be scared any more, not
scared of anyone, not scared of being secret and being
found out. This is it, Julian. You get in there. You
make your father's first real Presidential act a gutsy one,
and he'll go down in history and deserve Lincoln's bed
—and so will you."

Waiting for the President to finish his telephone call,

Sally Watson glanced at her wristwatch. The time was twenty-three minutes after twelve. She had been with the President nearly eight minutes, had done most of the talking, and still was not certain if she had impressed him. There were seven minutes left—ten at the most—to prove that she could be an asset to him in the White House.

She was still breathless with the suddenness of Leroy's call, the careening drive to Pennsylvania Avenue, the bantering passage through the crowd of newspapermen in the West Wing lobby, the immediate face-to-face interview with the new President.

She tried to review the first half of this important meeting. His blackness had not disconcerted her. Indeed, she had found his heavy features rather exotic and his general aspect not at all unattractive. What had disconcerted her was his remoteness. The few questions he had posed, about her upbringing, education, and previous jobs, had seemed directed not at her but at the blotter on his desk. Her replies, carefully detailed, confident yet reserved, well edited, had seemed to slide off the top of his kinky-haired head. He had hardly met her eyes at all. He had not reacted to anything she had told him. She could not be sure he was even listening. Sally Watson was not used to inattentiveness from men, black or white. Even T.C. used to *look* at her.

The President was still on the telephone, and she was worried now. Had his inattentiveness been due to a natural reticence, or preoccupation with his busy schedule? Or had he been bored by her? She could not believe that she had bored him. She had been composed and controlled, bright but not silly, and when she had left the house she had never looked better. Perhaps, between the house and here, with all the frightful rush and tension, she had unraveled.

Quickly, quietly, while there was time, Sally Watson brought her expensive lizard purse to her lap, located her enamel-inlaid sterling compact, and snapped it open. Her bouffant blond hair was still set perfectly, not a strand out of place. Her eye shadow and mascara were still fresh and right. Her lips—possibly they were overdone.

Furtively, she found a Kleenex, brought it to her mouth, and pressed her lips against it. The compact mirror congratulated her on the improvement. The last touch of Aphrodite was gone. What was left, she prayed, was modest Pudicitia.

She dropped the compact into the purse and sat erect, waiting. President Dilman's call was proving interminable for her. Every minute that he was so occupied was a minute subtracted from her chances. Could he even imagine how desperately she wanted the position? She would be "inside." She would be "high up," in the rarefied power hierarchy. She would be Somebody. Her circle of friends would envy her. Arthur Eaton would respect her infinitely more.

She *must* win the job. Yet there was not a single indication that President Dilman was seriously considering her for it. Of course, he had sent for her, but maybe that had been to satisfy Leroy Poole or toady to her father. A pin of discouragement perforated her grand hopes. Well, anyway, she told herself, if nothing came of it, well, anyway, she'd been the first of the crowd to see him up close, the strange one, the one on everyone's lips. She would have a conversation piece and attention grabber for a month. But—oh, dammit—she didn't want a conversation piece. She wanted a real occupation and identity, to make her eligible for continued living and for Arthur Eaton's love.

She heard the telephone bang into its cradle, and she started, and then, to her surprise, she found President Dilman appraising her.

"Forgive me for the length of that telephone call, Miss Watson," he said. "If Alexander Graham Bell had not lived, I guess we'd have anarchy instead of a centralized democratic government today."

She knew her responding laugh was strained. She said, "It's kind enough of you to see me at all."

He had a pencil, and absently drew circles with it on a scratch pad. "Everything you've told me up to now, Miss Watson, indicates you possess the right background for this type of work. But I must add, to be perfectly honest, I do have one or two reservations about you."

She felt stricken, as if sentenced to doom without being told the reason behind it. Desperation made her bolder. "What reservations, Mr. President? Please tell me whatever is on your mind. I feel I'm so perfectly qualified for the position, so right for it, that I can't imagine—" She threw up her hands helplessly, then remembered the scar and turned her right wrist inward. "I can't imagine anyone on earth not seeing how useful I could be."

Dilman made some kind of muttering sound—approving, disapproving of her outburst, she could not judge— and then he said, "Very well, Miss Watson, we don't have much time, and I must fill this job, and I mustn't make a mistake. To be specific, my reservations are three. Let me put them before you."

Sally said, "Yes, please do," and she held her breath.

"First," said Dilman, "you've skipped around a good deal in your job training and positions—"

"Because I've never found what I wanted or what I'm best suited for," she said quickly. "This is where I belong."

"Very well. Let us say this is where you belong. The second question is—have you ever served in a position similar to that of White House social secretary?"

"Not exactly, except in my personal life. It's such a special position, the only one like it in the United States, that I suppose few girls have had experience like that. But I have known most of the White House social secretaries from Miss Laurel back to Miss Tuckerman and Miss Baldridge, and I believe I can bring to the job as much know-how as any of them brought to it, to start with. I can bring you a dossier filled with every kind of endorsement, from Eastern boarding schools to Radcliffe, from Park Avenue editors to the Junior League. I believe I am attractive, well groomed, well dressed, with the best of breeding and manners. I have imagination, taste, adaptability. I know how to handle and direct correspondence, plan and conduct an informal luncheon or a formal dinner, oversee the housekeeper while she manages the help. I've done this, Mr. President, I've done it for my father, ever since my mother divorced him. My

stepmother has never been good at this, and I am, so
I've done it. You know how long my father has been in
the Senate. He is acquainted with everyone and everyone
knows him, and we've been visited by princes, mahara-
jahs, ambassadors, millionaires, and astronauts, and I've
entertained for most of them. You are acquainted with
my father. Call him and ask him. He'll verify every word
I've spoken."

Dilman smiled. "I don't believe I need to call your
father as a reference, Miss Watson, but perhaps I should
call him about something else—that third reservation I
hold."

"What is it?"

"Miss Watson, as a Negro I have never had much in
common with my Southern colleagues in the Upper
House. The only one I've had any liking for is Senator
Watson, and I've not known him too well, either. He is
a decent man, a gentleman, but he is still a product of,
a representative of, an area, a people, who regard persons of my color as inferiors. What will your father think
of his daughter serving as social secretary to a Negro?
Does he even know you are here?"

"He does not know I am here, but if he did know, he
would not have stopped me from coming, or even have
tried to. He treats me as an individual, and he lets me
have my freedom. We disagree about many things. We
love each other none the less for it. As to what he would
think of my being your social secretary—I don't think
he would like it. But I don't think he would make his
objections known to me or to anyone. He would not interfere. And I know he would understand that my affection for him would always be a thing separate from my
loyalty to my employer."

She paused, seeing how intent Dilman was upon her
every word, and then she went on. "Mr. President, my
father is not applying for this job. I am. While he is an
enlightened Southerner, he still carries ancient prejudices. I do not. Please, Mr. President, in all fairness,
do not visit the sins of the parents on their children."

She sensed that she had convinced Dilman on this
point, and his receptive expression confirmed it. "I be-

lieve you, Miss Watson," he said at last. "If there were a First Lady in the White House to help me, I'd feel safe in hiring you on the spot. Being without a First Lady, I must burden the woman I hire with the social duties of two women. If there were only someone in Washington, beside your parent, who could assure me that you were absolutely capable of—"

That instant, it came to her. "I know someone," she said.

"To recommend you?"

"Yes. Well, I hope he would. I mean Secretary of State Eaton."

She had thoroughly impressed him, at last. It was evident in his reaction. And she knew why: not because Eaton was second in the government, but because he had Style. No Negro, she thought, would dare turn down an applicant who had the social sanction of the suave Secretary of State.

"Let's hear what Secretary Eaton has to say about you," said Dilman. He reached for the white console telephone. "Do you mind going into Miss Foster's office for a moment? Right there, the door behind you."

Sally could hear the President speaking on his direct line to the Department of State as she left the Oval Office and went quickly into Miss Foster's office. She interrupted Miss Foster's staccato typing to introduce herself and remind Miss Foster that they had met briefly at the White House Congressional Dinner two years before. After that, Sally allowed Miss Foster to resume her work, and she nervously moved around the small room, pretending an interest in the framed photographs on the wall and the reference books on the shelves.

She had done all that could be done, and now her entire future rested on Arthur Eaton's word. If he said yes, her life would become new and meaningful. If he said so little as maybe, her life would be shattered. She would kill herself, for she would not only have lost the job, but she would know that she had lost Arthur.

Miss Foster's telephone shook the room, or so it seemed to Sally. Her heart thumped. Miss Foster had hung up and gestured toward the President's office. "You can go back in, Miss Watson."

President Dilman was standing before his desk when she entered.

Suddenly his broad face offered her a wide smile, and he extended his hand. "Welcome to the White House, Miss Watson. Secretary Eaton's praise and enthusiasm for you were so unbounded that for a moment I was almost too timid to think of hiring you. Apparently you are everything I hoped for, a remarkable young lady who's going to safeguard my social life. Well, I am delighted."

She clutched his hand in both of hers, squeezing it in her excitement, shutting her eyes and whispering, "Oh, thank you, thank you, you won't regret it a day." She wanted to faint, but whether from pride over the prestigious job or from knowledge of Arthur's reciprocal love, she didn't know.

She realized that Dilman was guiding her to the corridor exit. She tried to fasten on what he was saying. Something about calling Miss Foster tomorrow. Security papers, payroll papers, résumé blanks, all to be filled out. Something about seeing her office in the East Wing the day after tomorrow. Something about officially starting the job Monday. Thank you, Miss Social Secretary. Thank you, Mr. President.

Dazed, she found herself gliding past the secretarial cubicles outside Flannery's office, found herself wandering into the press-filled lobby, found Reb Blaser and George Murdock and others watching her. Before they could question her, she left swiftly, half running up the White House driveway, past the guardhouse, and into busy Pennsylvania Avenue.

She walked on air, lofted and propelled by her unrestrained fantasies of bliss, and when she came down to earth she was on Fifteenth Street, in sight of Keith's RKO Theatre. There was only one thing she wanted to do to fulfill her perfect day. She reached a drugstore, and then a telephone booth inside, and closed herself in a glass cocoon of privacy.

She dialed DU 3-5600.

The Department of State. The seventh floor. The chief receptionist. *The Secretary's* secretary. Who? Miss Sally Watson? One moment please, I'll see if he has gone to lunch.

"Hello, Sally?"

"Arthur, I hope I'm not bothering you in the middle of a conference or——"

"What happened, Sally?"

"Arthur, I got it! I can't believe it. The President says I start Monday. I can't believe it. And my thanks to you. I don't know how to thank you enough."

"You have the position because you deserve it. I told him honestly that I thought he would find no one your equal in Washington. I told him not to let you go. I told him that had I known you wanted a job, I would have released half my girls to make way for you. I'm delighted, Sally. Congratulations."

"Arthur, that buildup you gave me. How can I live up to it? You can't believe——"

"I believe more than that about you, Sally. You know I do."

"Arthur, I want to do anything I can for you."

"You do your job."

"I want to repay you."

"Mmm——well, my dear, there might be one way, as I suggested the last time we were together. It becomes fairly lonesome at home in the evening, especially at the dinner hour."

"Invite me, Arthur, go ahead, invite me."

"You are invited. I'll get to you tomorrow with the date."

"You won't forget, this time?"

"I hadn't forgotten, Sally. I've been busy. I am still busy. Except now that you are a government girl, I can justify it as mixing business with pleasure. I must run, Sally." He paused. "There is only one thing I want you to do for me. When we meet, I want you to be wearing the white sequined gown. You know, the décolleté one. Good-bye, Sally."

When she floated out of the booth, she was surer than

she had ever been. She would be a First Lady of sorts yet—not Dilman's, but Arthur Eaton's.

It was a quarter to seven in the evening. The after-work, going-home traffic had abated. The Presidential limousine sped through the red lights and darkened thoroughfares toward the brownstone row house on Van Buren Street.

This morning, when he left his private residence, the journey had taken twice as long, and Douglass Dilman had not imagined that he would return so soon. All through the busy, depleting, and eventually upsetting day, the conviction had grown upon him that he must return as soon as possible.

Because of his second argument with his son, his appointment schedule had dragged on longer than planned. His last visitor had left him a half hour ago. Then he had requested Edna to inform Nat Abrahams at the Mayflower Hotel that their dinner must be postponed from eight o'clock to eight-thirty. Before she departed for the night, Edna had confirmed the change, adding that Mrs. Abrahams was confined to bed with a cold and that Mr. Abrahams would be coming alone.

After that, Dilman had telephoned Reverend Paul Spinger directly.

"Paul, is Wanda back from work yet?"

"She's in the kitchen. I can get her for you, Mr. President."

"No. I'd rather not speak to her on the phone. Simply ask her to stay there. I want to see her alone. Just for a few minutes."

"I'll tell her, Mr. President. How was your first day in the White House?"

"I don't know, really, Paul. I've been too busy. . . . Look, Paul, I want my visit kept hush-hush. You understand? It's not easy to arrange on this end, but I intend to manage it. See you all shortly."

After notifying engagements secretary Lucas and press secretary Flannery that he was through for the day, and would spend the entire evening in his new dwelling,

Dilman had stepped outside. He had come upon the Secret Service agent, Otto Beggs, the one who had accompanied him from the brownstone this morning. Beggs had been waiting beside the colonnade to accompany him again in the short walk to the ground-floor elevator. Dilman had remembered the husky agent was on a split shift, which might explain his disgruntled expression. Dilman also remembered that it was Beggs who had warned him he could travel nowhere alone.

As they strode through the chilled darkness, he had taken his measure of Beggs. It would not be easy, he had told himself, but he was determined to have this one important private visit. When they had entered the ground floor, Beggs had turned left, but Dilman had turned right. Almost comically, Beggs had scrambled back to his side.

Dilman had informed the agent that he wanted to make a short visit to his brownstone residence before dinner. There was a civil rights matter that he had to discuss informally with Reverend Spinger, his upstairs tenant. Dilman had insisted that he did not want the press alerted to this unscheduled meeting. Therefore, he wished minimum security maintained in order to allow his going and coming to be unnoticed. There had been a brief disagreement, nervous on both sides, and, at last, Beggs had consented to reduce their protective escort to three agents in the limousine, and one motorcycle policeman ahead and one behind, without sirens being put into use until they left the immediate White House area.

He had been pleased at how quickly and quietly the limousine had been made to appear, and how swiftly and stealthily their departure had been accomplished.

During the ride to Van Buren Street, he had known that he could not repeat this kind of rendezvous many times. Despite the ease of this slipping away from the President's House and its prying eyes, there were always too many others, elsewhere, watching and whispering. Sooner or later he would be caught in the act. He could not constantly use Spinger as his camouflage. And, at the same time, he could not risk the possibility that his friendship with Wanda Gibson might be made public. It would be misunderstood and misinterpreted. Being a

colored Chief Executive was bad enough. Being a Negro
President with a mulatto lady friend was impossible. To
survive, he must reinforce his public image as the loner,
the bachelor. It would make him less threatening, less
publicized, and make the resentful electorate feel more
secure. Nevertheless, this one personal meeting with
Wanda was imperative. If it developed as he expected
that it would, the result would solve everything.

Dilman felt the automobile braking to a halt beneath
him, and through the rear window he could make out his
beloved Victorian-style residence. The street was empty,
except for parked cars and a Negro boy carrying a cumbersome filled grocery bag, whistling off key, as he me-
andered toward his home.

Beggs stooped and got out, and Dilman followed him.
He noticed that the two other agents, who had left the
front seat, were consulting in undertones. As he started
for the entrance, Dilman saw one agent planting himself
before the house, and the other hustling up the sidewalk
to the rear.

When Dilman reached the front door, he realized that
Beggs was a half step behind him.

Dilman opened the door and said, "Mr. Beggs, from
here on in, I'd prefer to be alone."

Stolidly Beggs replied, "Sorry, Mr. President, I'm not
allowed to do that."

"Well, I can't let you sit in on the meeting. It is private government business."

"I won't invade your privacy, Mr. President," Beggs
promised. "I simply got to be near where you are. It's
risky enough as it is, sir."

He would not be dissuaded, Dilman could see, and so,
with a shrug, Dilman went inside, followed by Beggs.

They strode down the hallway and mounted the stairs
to the upstairs landing. As they arrived, the door opened.
Reverend Spinger, his wife behind him, both conscious
of the Secret Service agent, greeted Dilman formally as
Mr. President. Dilman introduced Beggs, and then entered the warm, old-fashioned living room. When he
turned to address the Spingers, he was surprised and

alarmed to find Beggs still behind him and inside the room.

"Mr. Beggs," said Dilman, "you promised me some privacy."

Beggs's ruddy face was helplessly apologetic. "You're on your own from this point, Mr. President. I'll just remain standing here inside the door."

Dilman frowned, and looked at Spinger. "Reverend, is there anywhere I can see you alone for five minutes?"

"We can go to my study in the rear," said Spinger.

Permitting Spinger to lead him out of the living room, Dilman could hear Rose offering to heat Beggs a pot of coffee, and Beggs accepting with thanks on the condition that he could drink it standing at his post.

Dilman trudged after his friend, until they came to Wanda's bedroom.

"She's waiting," Spinger whispered.

Dilman nodded. "Paul, you'd better not go back. I told him we're having a conference. Can you keep yourself out of sight for a little while? It won't be long."

"I'll go to our own bedroom."

Dilman lingered until Spinger had gone, then he started to knock, but suddenly restrained himself. He did not want Wanda to call out. Instead he turned the knob several times, rattling it, and went inside.

She was at the window pulling down a shade, her back to him, when she heard his entrance. She came around slowly, smiling, and Dilman's heart quickened at the sight of her. Although he had telephoned her every evening from downstairs in the past week, he had not seen her for what seemed an eternity.

He stood motionless on the far side of the tastefully decorated bedroom, enjoying the sight of her. He was positive that no woman on earth at thirty-six was at once so youthful and so serenely mature. Her brunette hair was swept back from her refined cameo face, each diminutive feature crinkled upward in genuine pleasure. Her softly draped chartreuse blouse clung to her small bosom, and her slim, forest-green skirt accented her shapely legs. She appeared taller than her five feet three inches, and she looked definitely mulatto rather than

white. Dilman would not allow himself to believe that
he was shading her in his mind's eye to make her duskier,
because he wanted her that way, and wanted what he
planned to be possible.

Wanda Gibson spoke first. "Doug, I can't tell you how
wonderful it is to—to see you."

He crossed to her, embracing her more spontaneously and closely than he had in months. He enjoyed
her soft hands behind his neck, and he kissed her cheek,
and then her lips. "Wanda, I can't tell you how much—
how difficult it has been without you."

She disengaged herself. "We're together right now.
That's all that matters." She took his hand and led him
to the love seat before the portable television set. "How
were you able to get away, Doug?"

They both sat down, and he said, "I wasn't able to,
but I did. The Secret Service, the advisers, the press,
they keep you on a leash like an unruly pet. I sneaked
away. I don't know if I'll be able to do it twice."

Her brown eyes had been studying every movement of
his face, he knew. "Doug, you're not sleeping," she said.
"I can tell."

"I'm not eating, or living, or thinking, either. From
early morning till night you're on a roller coaster, it
feels, going, going, and when you try to sleep, you're
still going, like there's no place to get off. Why did this
have to happen to me? I'm the wrong man for it, Wanda.
I'm not geared to it. I try not to let anyone know, but
I'm scared and confused."

"Doug, you are as well prepared for the position as
any man on earth. We've been through all that."

"In the House, in the Senate, it was different," he said.
"What you did was part of shared responsibility. Your
ayes and nays were in chorus, not solo. But as Harry
Truman once said of the Presidential desk—the buck
stops here. No one to pass it to, Wanda. End of the line.
Certainly, I understand what is going on. None of the
legislation has any mysteries. It's the final responsibility
that's getting me down. You turn around, to hand some
document to someone else for the final decision, and

you know what? There is no one there. Yours is the final decision. That's what is so damn oppressing."

"I don't think that is your worry at all, Doug."

He was taken aback. "No? What do you think is my worry?"

Wanda bent toward him, took a cigar from his coat pocket, and began to unpeel the cellophane. "Your color," she said simply. She handed him the cigar. "Here. You need it. Besides, I like the fragrance. It's more you, and like old times."

He bit off the cigar end, and she lighted it. He viewed her through the first cloud of smoke. "My color," he repeated dully.

"That's always the worry with you," said Wanda. "If you were white, you might be shocked and a bit over-whelmed by the job, but you'd fall into it, manage it. Now what you've always been trying to—oh, not to have it noticed by anyone—hide—has been exposed to every person in the country, in the whole world, and that's what is scaring you. That's it, Doug, and don't deny it. You are afraid you can't make ordinary mistakes like other ordinary human beings. You are afraid of making Negro mistakes in front of your white peers."

Her bluntness startled him. He was immediately defensive. "Well, there's some truth in what you say, but I think you're exaggerating it, Wanda."

"I'm understating it, Doug. I know your strengths, and you know them, too, and we don't have to go into that. You can't hide your blackness any longer, not by putting your head in the sand, not by losing yourself in the crowd, not by being a yes-man so no one will re-member you have a voice. I won't discuss this part of you in relation to your family, or to me, or to your work in Congress. It's not the time for that, and I have no right to bring it up when you are so engulfed by other demands. But, Doug, there you are, there you are in the White House, and nothing can change it. The whole wide world knows the color of your skin, and like it or not, they've got to accept it, and, more important, so have you. Once you accept that in your mind, you can begin to act as a human being. Then I think you won't be so troubled."

Momentarily he was annoyed with her, because she was speaking the truth, and he did not want the truth, least of all from her. "Act like a human being?" he said. "Do you think anyone'll let me? Don't you read the papers, any more, or listen to the radio?"

"Doug, I know what's going on, exactly. Our people are singing Moses, they've got Moses, and that's an unfair pressure for you. And the bitterest whites are hating more than ever, and persecuting us more than ever to get their hate out of their systems, because they can't get at you. And the in-betweens—I listen, I overhear them —they don't know what to think. They feel threatened and uneasy because your presence makes them feel like members of a minority for the first time. They don't believe you'll rule as a white, like T.C., but as a black man, and they're worried you'll make their precious purewhite Christian land into a Dark Continent. They should know how little they have to fear from you."

Dilman winced at the last. He fought to keep his dignity and manhood in her eyes. "Wanda, believe it or not, I only want to do my job now, do it, get it over with, and go back to where I came from. Yet it seems no one will let me. The Negroes want this and that because I'm Negro. The whites want this and that because I'm not white. T.C.'s gang wants me to be T.C., when I'm not him at all. You want me to be—to be something else. God, even my own son—"

He broke off, lost in misery, and she waited, and then she said, "You saw Julian?"

"He came to the office today. I had to talk to him about his grades and about doing better in school, something more important than ever now. So I had to listen to that Negro-versus-white-school business all over again. I know, Wanda, I know what you've said, but there it is, and he has to do well. I told him he was spending too much time with the Crispus Society, and he owed more time to himself and his future. Well, I thought we had it settled, and then suddenly he had to see me again, in the middle of the afternoon, so important it couldn't

wait. So I saw him. You've never heard anyone so unreasonable and agitated. Now it wasn't the Crispus Society
he was defending, but those damn Turnerite hoodlums.
Sure they got the raw end of the stick down in Mississippi, and there'll be more of that. But it's not a Federal
matter."

"What did he want from you?"

"To use my influence to get Nat Abrahams to intervene. Heaven knows, Nat does his share helping us. Now
he's busy with something for himself. His office has already told the Turnerites he is unavailable. I have no
right, either as his friend or as the President, to influence
him. Julian wouldn't listen. He was practically frothing."

Dilman kept working his fist into his palm. "I didn't
know what got into him, and then I finally figured it out
before coming here. He must have run into that writer
who's been doing my biography, Leroy Poole, up in the
White House. They were both up there at the same time.
And Poole—he talks Crispus, but he acts Turnerite. I
suspect Hurley is a close friend of his. Poole's a very eloquent and inciting young man, and to someone like Julian, who is so much younger, and so impressionable,
who in fact admires Poole's writings, that Turnerite
talk can be unsettling. I'm sure that's what was behind
Julian's tirade. Anyway, I had to be very firm with Julian. I told him no and that was that. He didn't like it. I
don't even know if we're on speaking terms at this
point."

Wanda's hand reached out to touch Dilman's fist.
"I'm sorry, Doug."

Anxiously he asked, "You agree with me on this,
don't you?"

Wanda nodded. "Yes. They're being mistreated in
Hattiesburg, but that's not unusual, wrong though it is. I
don't like Hurley's talk and what he stands for. Neither
does Paul Spinger."

Dilman put another match to his cigar. "Good. You
make me feel better already." He glanced at her, and
then he said, "That's why I need you, Wanda. That's
one of the reasons. You're the only frank and honest
person I can discuss my problems with, personal or

otherwise. That's why I came here to see you right now, hard as it was."

"Why did you come here, Doug?"

"To ask you a favor." He waited for her blanket promise, but she was silent. He went on. "Wanda, now that I'm—I'm President, seeing you on the old basis is going to be impossible. You know that."

"I know that, Doug."

The trace of sadness in her voice accentuated his growing fear of losing her. He said, "I don't want to lose you." He added, "I need you to—to push me forward. Wanda, I figured it out early this afternoon. I was hiring a white Southern girl for my social secretary—"

"Well, that took courage."

"Senator Watson's daughter. She's exactly right for the position. There'll be some dirty digs, but there would be whatever I did."

"What about Diane Fuller?"

"I'm getting her another job, secretary in the press section of Miss Watson's department. But there remain a couple of key openings, secretarial openings, administrative ones, on the White House staff. We've had resignations, as you can imagine."

"Yes."

"Now there are these openings." He paused. "Wanda, I want you to accept one of those jobs."

She did not appear surprised. "That's thoughtful of you, Doug. Unfortunately, I already have a good job."

"Vaduz Exporters? Wanda, this is the White House. You've told me yourself, a dozen times, you don't like your boss—who is that director?—Gar, Franz Gar. Well, here's a chance to leave him. I know you have a well-paying setup at Vaduz, but you told me it is mechanical and dull, and you have no contact with people. It would be different in the White House. The work might not pay as much, but I'd look after that soon enough. It would be fascinating for you. Most important, it would be helpful to me. I could see you every day. We could talk."

"And no one would know we were friends? How nice," she said bitterly. "How shrewd of you, Doug. And courageous, too. What if someone found out I was also your girl friend?"

Her caustic challenge disturbed him. "Don't become angry, Wanda. It would only be temporary, a temporary arrangement, like my own job. Later, we——"

"No, thanks," she said flatly. "Until now our relationship, platonic as it is, has at least been honest. Even if it means not seeing you, I refuse to change that. I won't let what there is between us become surreptitious and back-door."

"Wanda——"

"Absolutely no, Doug. You're having a rough time, and I hate to make it rougher. But I'm not moving into Harding's closet. When you have the nerve to see me again, you'll know where to find me, if it's here or someplace else. Doug, I——"

The soft knocking on the door stopped her, and brought Dilman to his feet. "Yes?" he called out.

The door opened partially, and Reverend Spinger slipped in, and closed it behind him. He looked from one to the other. "Haven't you been hearing it?"

"What?" Dilman asked.

"The noise out front ——" He started for the covered side window.

Dilman listened. What he had been too engrossed to hear above his conversation with Wanda, he heard now. There came through the walls the rumble of many voices. "What's going on?" he asked apprehensively.

"I couldn't get a good look from our room," said Reverend Spinger. "There seems to be a lot of people gathering in the street. I can get a better peek from here."

He flattened against the wall, and parted the shade from the window by several inches. At last he let go and shook his head. "Just from what I can see, there must be a couple hundred out there. There's the press, for sure, 'cause I could see the television trucks, and I'd guess some more Secret Service, and, of course, the neighborhood is all spilling out."

Dilman's immediate reaction was one of annoyance. "How in the devil did my coming here get out?"

Reverend Spinger scratched his cottony pate. "Doug,

you abdicated privacy when you were sworn in to this job. No matter what you attempt, you won't know privacy again for a year and five months. To restate in another form what Voltaire told us, the public is a heartless monster, and since you can't do as he suggested—chain the monster or flee from it—you must be on guard against it every minute of every day."

The clergyman's words reminded Dilman of his precarious situation. He saw Wanda standing, staring at him, and his annoyance melted into shameful trepidation. He detested himself for his cravenness, and for Wanda's knowledge of it. Yet he could not be other than what he had always been.

"Wanda, I've got to go. Will you—?"

Tactfully Spinger drifted out into the corridor.

Dilman moved closer to her, and at once, by a trick of lighting, or from the anxiety in his mind, her mulatto coloring was again more white than dusky. "You see what it's like, my dear. There's only one solution for the present. Please reconsider taking a job in—"

"No, Doug. I'll wait for you to phone."

He wanted to beseech her, but she had turned away from him. "All right," he said at last. "Only, don't give me up."

He joined Reverend Spinger in the corridor. As they started for the living room, Spinger said, as if to give support to the fiction, "You were conferring with me."

Dilman nodded absently. "Yes . . . encouraging the Crispus Society to cooperate with the government in playing a—a more aggressive role in furthering civil rights by legislation and legal means, and joining us in condemning vigilante action and violence on both sides."

They emerged into the living room, and Reverend Spinger said, "Yes, that would sum it up, Mr. President."

Dilman went to the door that Otto Beggs had opened. He halted before his bodyguard. "What's all the racket downstairs?"

"The press missed you, and I guess found out where you were, Mr. President. The minute they started charging after your scent, Chief Gaynor knew it might attract crowds. So he rushed over quite a few of the White House Detail. I'm sorry, but I had nothing—"

"Forget it," said Dilman.

Dilman looked around to say good-bye to Rose Spinger, when suddenly Wanda Gibson burst into the living room.

"Doug—!" Then she stopped, teetered in her tracks, and froze, horribly aware that they were not alone with the Spingers, that a stranger was also in the room.

Dilman's Adam's apple jumped. He could see Beggs staring at Wanda. Dilman felt an onrush of panic. He tried to keep his voice even. "Is there anything that wasn't clear, Miss Gibson?"

"N-no, Mr. President," said Wanda, her voice flat and emotionless.

"I'd like a copy of your shorthand notes," said Dilman. He waved a good-bye, and then went across the landing and rapidly down the stairs, followed by Beggs.

As he emerged into the night, it was not the impact of the reporters' shouts and bellows that momentarily unnerved him, but the battery of lights from the television kliegs and the explosion of flashbulbs. Beyond the rim of lights, the cordon of Secret Service agents, he could see hundreds of black neighborhood faces and fluttering hands, and could hear shouts of encouragement.

Fingers gripped his arm, and he was relieved to find that they belonged to Tim Flannery. The press secretary's mouth was close to his ear. "Mr. President, don't ever leave me flat-footed again. Somebody in Chief Gaynor's office leaked it. Don't let them interview you. Let me go to the microphones and tell them it's too late tonight to answer questions, but that you'll make a short statement."

"Very short, Tim."

He allowed Flannery to precede him down the stone steps to the three standing microphones. He could hear the shouted questions: "What were you doing here, Mr. President? . . . Did you see Spinger alone or with other Negro leaders? . . . What were you talking about? . . . Was it about the Turnerites, Mr. President?"

Flannery held up his hand, then bent over the microphones. "Gentlemen, no questions. Save them for the press conference. The President will make a brief statement, and that's it for tonight."

Flannery stepped aside, and Dilman made his way to the microphones. He felt wooden and insincere. He said, "Friends, because Reverend Spinger, head of the Crispus Society, was confined to his quarters with a cold, I decided to call upon him. Our meeting was partially social, partially devoted to discussion of immediate domestic problems in the civil rights area. We did not touch upon any specific Negro groups besides the Crispus Society and its role in working with the government in the civil rights legislative program."

"Did you talk about the Minorities Rehabilitation Program?" a reporter yelled.

Dilman looked blankly at the semicircle of men and cameras in front of him. He said into the microphones, "We discussed the MRP Bill, among many other legislative acts. We are in accord in our belief that progress toward equality can be attained only by due process of the law, never through the actions of vigilante groups of any race who would take the law in their own hands."

There was a spattering of applause, and, from afar, a shrill catcall and a solitary boo of disapproval.

"Reverend Spinger and I spoke privately about these matters, and informally. In the near future I expect to hold more formal meetings with all national leaders, Negro and white, who are eager to cooperate with the government in maintaining peace, and finding an orderly solution to our mutual problems. That is it for tonight, my friends. . . . No, no questions, or I'll collapse of starvation."

With Beggs and a wedge of other agents leading the way, Dilman hastened to the limousine and ducked inside. As he sank into the cushioned back seat, and Beggs squatted on the jump seat, the car began to pull away. Covertly, Dilman lowered his head but lifted his eyes to catch sight of the illuminated upstairs living room windows. He could make out both Spingers in one. The other window frame was empty. For the heartless monster public there was no Wanda Gibson.

Then, sitting back, Dilman caught Beggs looking at him oddly. And then, with a sinking sensation, he knew that you could guard and guard against the monster, and in the end there was no defense. Somehow, someway, there was always one, as Beggs might be one, to let the monster come through. He wondered what Beggs thought. He wondered if the monster would be loosed, and if it might strangle him.

He shut his hot eyes and behind them cursed his foolhardiness—and his cowardice.

At precisely nine o'clock, Nat Abrahams noted, they entered the Family Dining Room on the first floor of the White House.

As a liveried butler opened the door from the Main Corridor, and Dilman went inside, Abrahams thought again what a strange experience this was for both of them. They had eaten together in so many mean and contrasting places, in crowded cafeterias of the Pentagon and officers' messes of Army bases during the Second World War, in cheap *bistros* of France and hostile *Bierstuben* in Germany, in self-service restaurants and automats of Chicago and Detroit. Often, during their reunions in the Midwest, when Abrahams had been the host, he had made numerous preliminary calls to find a decent eatery where his Negro friend would be accepted and in no way embarrassed. Incredibly, and in short years, here they were once more, together, dining in the White House, Dilman's first dinner in the nation's first house as President of the United States, and Nat Abrahams his first guest.

Following his host across the floral carpet, Abrahams had an opportunity to examine the Family Dining Room briefly. The walls were yellow, the ceiling white. To the right a gilt convex mirror, with a gold eagle perched upon it, hung over the marble fireplace. To the left stood a Philadelphia breakfront filled with blue-and-gold chinaware. Ahead were two windows looking out toward Pennsylvania Avenue. Abrahams was able to identify two oil paintings: one plainly President John Tyler, re-

sembling somewhat Truman's first Secretary of State
James F. Byrnes; the other, reproduced in the guidebook
that Sue had purchased, was of a brigadier general
mounted on a black horse, John Hartwell Cocke of Virginia, he thought.

They had reached the mahogany pedestal table, and
Abrahams counted eight chairs of richly grained wood
set off by white upholstery surrounding the table. The
White House maître d'hôtel, a smiling South American
in cutaway coat and striped trousers, held the President's
chair for him at the head of the table, and a white-coated
colored waiter attended Abraham's chair next to the
President's. Dilman sat first, and then Abrahams took his
seat.

Abrahams could see that Dilman was ill at ease,
brushing nervously at his rumpled business suit, blinking
up at the chandelier, at the flower centerpiece, then at
the ostentatious table setting, classic tulip-shaped glassware, elegant Limoges plates, sterling knives, forks, and
spoons. While the tomato soup was ladled out from a
silver-gilt tureen, Dilman glanced sheepishly at Abrahams in the manner of one who wonders which spoon to
use first. Abrahams smiled, winked, unfolded his gold-
crested napkin and dropped it over his lap. Dilman did
the same.

When the soup had been served, and the maître
d'hôtel and waiter had backed away, Dilman said,
"You'd never guess I told Mrs. Crail—she's the official
housekeeper—I wanted an informal dinner, no fuss,
absolutely no fuss. Look at this. Anyway, Nat, I won
the battle of the menu. She had in mind—let me think
—oh, yes—boiled rolled flounder, roast turkey with
something called jelly celestial, scalloped sweet potatoes, and God knows what not. She kept saying that
was the kind of small menu T.C. liked for informal dining. But I put my foot down, so I'd get off on the right
one. I said, 'Mr. Abrahams is my oldest friend, and we're
going to eat what we always enjoyed most, the kind of
food you can talk over.' I don't know how it'll come out,
but I think it'll be a reasonable facsimile of old times."

Abrahams had been spooning his soup. "Brisket of beef?" he asked.

Dilman grinned. "Exactly. The beef, and a green salad with oil and vinegar, a noodle-and-ham casserole, hot sliced carrots, and—hold your hat—potato pancakes with apple sauce."

"Latkes," said Abrahams, giving them their Jewish name.

"I don't think they'll come out quite the way Sue's mother used to make them. Oh, yes, and I remembered red wine—they have the best years, Bordeaux, the kind that makes me sleepy. Just like those nights sitting in between the zinc bar and pinball machine in that joint off the Champs-Élysées."

A waiter appeared and poured water, followed by the maître d'hôtel, who placed the wine bottle on a side table. Dilman lapsed into silence, and sipped the tomato soup.

Abrahams enjoyed the thick soup. Except for the constricting black bow tie that Sue had made him wear, as being appropriate for high places, he felt relaxed. When the Lincoln limousine had picked him up at the Mayflower Hotel, and was bringing him to the South Portico of the White House, he had suffered a mild attack of apprehension, wondering if some protocol would be imposed, worrying whether Dilman would be as he always had been. The apprehension had been dispelled at the moment of their impulsive bearish embrace of greeting.

The months that separated them from their last meeting had visibly changed Dilman. Although he appeared more friendly, less withdrawn, than he had as a senator, his eyes were red-flecked, tireder, Abrahams had seen, and there were rigid lines of tension around his mouth. Also, he walked more ploddingly, like an elderly person recovering from major surgery. Yet the week as President had not inwardly transfigured him, had not weighted him with any more reserve or aloofness than he had normally possessed. Abrahams guessed that his friend was too new to the post to comprehend it fully. If anything, he seemed uncertain about his role, as if misplaced in some Dantesque purgatory between the Senate and the White House.

After Abrahams' congratulations and Dilman's inquiries about Sue and the children, they had gone from the elevator into the Main Hall of the first floor. There had been an empty stretch of seconds when Dilman did not know where to take Abrahams, or what to do next, but this impasse had been resolved by the dignified Negro valet, Beecher, who had seemed to materialize from nowhere.

"I almost forgot, Nat, but I asked Beecher to take us on a quick tour of the first floor," Dilman had said. "I could use a refresher myself. Besides, the walk will give us both appetites."

They had been led to the vast East Room, with its gold drapes and gilt benches and Steinway piano (Beecher: "Each of the three chandeliers weighs 850 pounds and has 50,000 pieces of crystal, and each requires two houseboys a week to clean it"). They had been led to the Green Room, with its Daniel Webster sofa and Martha Washington armchair and James Monroe clock (Beecher: "Please take note of the portrait of President Eisenhower over that door and President Kennedy over this door, and, of course, the portrait of The Judge"). They had been led to the Blue Room, with its velvet upholstery and gold Minerva timepiece and white bust of George Washington (Beecher: "The three windows looking down on the south lawn may be converted into doors by sliding them upward and opening the wall panels beneath"). They had been led into the Red Room, with its cerise silk-covered walls and Jacqueline Kennedy breakfast table and crimson Empire sofa (Beecher: "This portrait of President Wilson was painted in Paris in 1919 by an English artist, but as you can observe, it was left unfinished").

By the time they were in the immense and drafty State Dining Room, Nat Abrahams had become less attentive. Because Dilman appeared absorbed, as if soaking in and memorizing every fragment of data, Abrahams had not wished to spoil it by reminding his friend that he had been through these rooms not once but on two occasions before. The first time, Abrahams and a dozen other attorneys involved in civil rights causes had been brought to Washington by President Kennedy for a two-day conference, and they had toured the ground and first floors of this mansion. The second time, Abrahams and officers of the American Bar Association, then meeting in Washington, had attended a reception given by President Lyndon Johnson, and again Abrahams had been part of this tour.

During T.C.'s abbreviated term of office, Abrahams had not been invited to the White House. He had supported the minority opposing the Party's nomination of T.C. and Porter, and even though, once T.C. had been nominated, Abrahams had backed him, he had not been forgiven. Abrahams suspected that it was T.C.'s aide, Governor Talley, notable for a mastodon memory (if little else), that separated the good ones from the bad ones, and who had listed Abrahams as lukewarm. Abrahams had, in fact, cast his ballot for T.C. only as the lesser of two evils, and because T.C. had been committed to the Party platform, which had extended lofty if generalized promises to the restless minorities.

Abruptly, his recollection of the last half hour's tour was brought to an end by the waiters removing the empty soup bowls.

He looked at Dilman, and he said, "You know, Mr. President—"

Dilman's scowl was immediate. "Cut it out, Nat. You want me to call you Barrister Abrahams?"

"I was merely testing you," said Abrahams with a chuckle. "Okay, Doug, it's an *informal* dinner." He felt better, very good, indeed, about his friend, about tonight, and he scratched his hooked nose and jutting jaw, and said, "I was simply going to say how sorry I am that Sue is missing this, not only seeing you as President—she's so thrilled about that—but being able to eat amid this splendor. She could keep her mother silenced and put the kids to bed with it for months."

"Well, I want Sue here as soon as possible," Dilman said. "You said it's only a mild cold."

"The hotel physician promises she'll be up in a day or two."

"Then I want you both over for a rerun of this meal in a few days." He took up the glass of Bordeaux and held it toward Abrahams. "To you and your new future, Nat."

Abrahams toasted him back. "Happy Presidency, Doug. You'll make out."

They sipped the wine, and then Dilman said, "I want to see as much of you and Sue as you can spare of yourselves. I'm busy as a beaver all day, and have plenty of homework at night, but I'll be eating alone a good deal. With Julian up at school, and—well—I don't have anyone around I can really kick off my shoes with. I need you both, Nat."

He was about to say something more when the servants came in with heaping platters, and he fell into silence. Abrahams guessed that Dilman would not speak during the evening while any of the White House staff was within earshot. He is wary and defensive, Abrahams thought; he's afraid of letting anything slip, anything that might be misconstrued, whispered behind the stairs, and create gossip and paragraphs for enemy columnists. Sensible enough, Abrahams thought, and decided to go along with his friend and hold his own tongue until they were alone.

While they were being served their slices of beef, potato pancakes, and more wine was being poured, Dilman spoke only once. He pointed to the vegetables. "Those peas, Nat, savor them, because you'll be digesting history. Mrs. Crail says they were grown and picked from Teddy Roosevelt's mint garden."

After the waiters had retreated, the two of them ate quietly for a full minute. Abrahams, his mouth full, said, "Mmm, the pancakes aren't bad, Doug. You're running a fine kosher kitchen."

"I'm sure that confuses them. That and the fact that I don't like watermelon." He spoke the last without bitterness, but with dry humor. He went on, "I meant what I was saying before, Nat. I want you and Sue here as often as you can come. This is the loneliest time I've ever faced. It's bad enough being a widower President, in the White House by accident. But being a colored one, to boot, makes it—"

"Enough of that nonsense," Abrahams interrupted. "You're not getting any sympathy from me, unless I get my share. Don't forget, I'm only a white darky whose grandfather was beaten to death in a Polish pogrom." He had spoken lightly, but suddenly he became serious. "Plenty of white Presidents have been unpopular and lonely, Doug. I remember reading a letter in some collection—R. H. Dana wrote it to one or another of the Adamses, wrote it from this town in the 1860s—to the effect that Lincoln—it was about President Lincoln—that 'he has no admirers, no enthusiastic supporters, none to bet on his head.' I'm sure for a time Lincoln felt like an outcast locked in this house . . . but yes, we want to see you whenever you're free, which I'm sure won't be as often as you think. And we want to see you not because we're sorry for you but because we need good companionship, too."

"How long are you going to be here, Nat?"

"A week or two, maybe even a month. If it works out, I'll take Sue back, spend a few days straightening out my things at the office, and leave her to pack or sell off the furniture and maybe stay on with the kids until the end of their semester. I'd return here, and she could follow me later." He paused. "Under the new plan, I'd be living in Washington for three years."

"That would be great, Nat." Dilman grinned. "You'll be living here longer than I will." He ate slowly, thoughtfully. Then he said, "I think I was a little surprised when you wrote me about Avery Emmich's offer, and that you were considering it. Didn't I write you, asking you more about it? Maybe I didn't. But even what you told me on the phone the other night doesn't make it—well, entirely clear to me."

"What do you mean, Doug?"

"You can't live up on the Hill as long as I have without picking up a good deal of information about big business, big private enterprise. Not many come bigger than Eagles Industries. Nothing wrong with them, or any other corporation, except that Eagles isn't notorious for being liberal or progressive. And Emmich, I gather, is a sort of throwback to Cornelius Vanderbilt, Astor, Gould. One of the public-be-damned gents, I always thought. Maybe I'm wrong. Anyway, I've found it hard to fit you into that framework. The mental pictures I have of you and Eagles don't harmonize. I know I'm wrong."

Abrahams put down his fork. "You're right, Doug. I've been through all that, until my conscience collapsed of weariness. Doug, it comes down to this—I've looked into Eagles, and if I had found out they were crooks, real crooks, or special bastards, or anything like that, I'd have blown the deal immediately. They're no better or worse than the rest of American big business. The anatomy is the same, always—hard head, no heart, all hands in a thousand tills, mechanized, automated, conservative, with a single goal—profits. Okay. The democracy we fight to save. Eagles Industries needs me, men like me, with the liberal lapel button. For them, that's good business, too. And I—I need a fat patron, Doug, because I'm threadbare, and have responsibilities, and can't get any more life insurance. If the patron is willing to let me get fat, too, without putting me on a leash, it's a good deal."

"No more life insurance, you said?"

Abrahams could see the flick of concern in his friend's dark countenance. He shrugged. "I'm exaggerating, self-dramatizing. It wasn't a real coronary, only a yellow light that warned me to slow down. I want to slow down before it turns red and stops me dead. Nothing serious, no sword hanging overhead, but I love Sue and I love those kids and I want that farm. So I'm playing it safe. I'm trading three years of doing what doesn't particularly interest me for a lifetime of living, of puttering around with what does interest me, after those three years. That's the whole of it, Doug."

"I agree with your choice," said Dilman solemnly. "I'd do exactly the same in your place. Have you seen Gorden Oliver yet?"

"Twice, briefly. He came to the hotel. We're still trying to reach agreement on several of my recent demands."

"What do you make of him?" Dilman asked.

"Oliver? I don't know. I must say, he threw me off balance on first meeting. I always fall prey to preconceived notions of what people will be like—I should know better, and I do. Anyway, word association, you say lobbyist and I say rotund, foxy, devious, greenbacks, call girls, et cetera. I was surprised to find him rather outdoorsy, literate, direct, a qualified attorney, a family man."

Dilman had been listening to every word. "Yes, he's all you found, Nat. He's also a little, just a little, of what you expected him to be. He's been in and out of my offices on the Hill, with talk, free information, free tickets and invitations, free services, free jokes, for years. I have no reason not to trust him or like him. He's been useful to me at times. And registered lobbyists do as much good as harm. But somehow, even though he's New England—I think he's from Vermont—I keep remembering he is a company man and his company is headquartered in the South. Anyway, that's nothing that need bother you, Nat. You are sharper than I am about people. You'll stay on top of him."

The waiters had returned, and were busily removing the empty plates and platters, and used silverware. Both men waited for the table to be cleared, and for the ice-cream cake and coffee to be served, so that they had their privacy once more.

Something had entered Abrahams' mind, and would not go away. While he knew that his friend was sensitive and secretive about his personal relationships, Abrahams was curious and he determined to investigate one area. He had finished the dessert, and as he filled his crusted, straight-stemmed pipe and lighted it, he said, as casually as possible, "Doug, I was thinking of what you were saying before about being lonely, and then I couldn't help thinking of someone you've mentioned several times in your letters. The lady you once introduced to Sue and me when we had dinner at your place. I mean Miss Gibson, Wanda Gibson."

Dilman did not raise his head from his coffee. "What made you think of her?"

"As I said, your loneliness. I had a suspicion—Sue did, too, the night we met her—that you were fond of the young lady."

"I am," said Dilman.

"You still see her? I didn't know. You haven't mentioned her name in—why, I guess in over a year."

"Aside from you, she's been the person closest to me. Until now, we've kept company all the time. She's very unusual."

"Pretty, too," Abrahams said, "and I thought sound and intelligent."

"Yes, all that. Now I don't know what'll happen to us. This President thing came right down between us like— I was thinking recently—like a steel grill. You know, this is privileged talk, Nat, strictly, like everything else—but I tried to call on her alone tonight, first time since all that happened to me—it was awful—"

In a subdued, almost compulsive spate of recollection, Dilman recounted the details of his effort earlier in the evening to see Wanda alone at the Spingers'. He told of his offer to her of a job in the White House, and of her absolute refusal to accept one.

"That's what happened," Dilman concluded, "and here we are, wanting one another, and farther apart than ever before. I wish she weren't so prideful. I'd give anything to have her in the White House."

"Anything, Doug?"

Dilman looked up sharply, eyes narrowing. He started to retort, but did not. He waited.

The sensitive area, Abrahams thought. And then he thought, we're either friends all the way or not at all. "You could have her here in an instant, Doug. It would take only four words: 'Will you marry me?' That's the only anti-loneliness, Doug. Have you asked her?"

"No."

"Okay, I can't pry further."

Dilman said, "It's all right. If anyone has a right to ask, it's you, Nat. I know you want to help me. But I can't go into it. I haven't gone into it deeply enough with myself. Maybe someday I'll be able to discuss it with you. All I can say—the only explanation I can make is

—well—I can't see myself with Wanda in a big ceremonial state wedding in the White House. Having one lone colored man in the White House is churning up enough trouble. Maybe it'll calm down, because they'll see I'm sort of alone and inoffensive, not threatening to anyone. But a Negro man and his wife in this Southern mansion? That would be too much for them out there to take—too much, and I'm not ready for it. I know it's a shameful infirmity in me, Nat, but it is an infirmity I can't overcome, like a limb missing, and one simply can't will that limb back on. I haven't the strength of character."

Embarrassed, Dilman fumbled for a cigar. Abrahams watched him, leaned across the table corner to light the cigar, and then sat back.

"Doug," Abrahams said at last, "how can I lecture the President of the United States? I can't. But I can lecture one of my oldest and best friends. I'm going to."

Dilman grunted. "I've been lectured at all day, by the boy who's writing my biography, by my son, by Wanda, by myself. I don't mind one more, only I'm afraid the ground's been pretty well covered."

"I'm sure it has," said Abrahams. "But since I'm giving up making jury speeches, I'd like to hear the sound of my voice on a similar issue one last time, in valediction." He knocked his pipe against the heel of his hand, then packed and lighted it once more. "Doug, there's never been a Negro as high up as you, politically, in our country's entire history. I know all there is to know about that. Most Negroes are happy about this, but many are scared of your sudden exposure and the subsequent white resentment. You are one of these. The nigger-hating whites are doubly inflamed, that's for sure. You did worse than marry their sisters, you became the head of their plantations, their Massah, their Colonel. The rest of the whites are—what? Uneasy, edgy—let's leave it that way. If the country had a say now, you'd be out in the street in ten seconds flat. The country has no say, so it has to sit still for you, until this Presidential term is over. But no matter how much hate there is out there, everyone knows you are here by law, the white man's law. Nothing can alter the historical fact of your succession. You are rightfully their President, our President.

"Okay, so how are you to behave? Just be yourself? Who in the hell are you, anyway? I'm sure you don't know. Maybe I don't know, either, but maybe I have a better idea than you do. You are our President. That's a fact. You are an American citizen. That's a fact. You are a Negro American. That's a fact. Because of the last, the pigmentation of your skin, you are different from any other President in our history. That's a fact. What does this mean to you? Does it mean you act like a minority party who's now king of the hill and going to put his heel in everyone else's face? Does it mean you act like somebody who wandered into the wrong house, and you better beat it quick before you're arrested? Does it mean you act like you know you don't belong because you are different, and you back away and hide? Or does it mean you act like a human being who has inherited, through no wish of his own, the toughest job on earth, and you know it, and they out there know it, and you are going to fill that job like any human being fills any job he has to do?"

Dilman stared past Abrahams' shoulder, twisting his cigar, twisting it until the tobacco leaf flaked. "Thank you, Nat. Very good in a Northern courtroom, where there's a sanctified air of reason. Not very good here, where I'm servant to a mass of two hundred and thirty million who don't always observe rules or reason." His troubled eyes met Abraham's eyes. "Your premise is not built on solid ground, Nat. You need one more fact, and it's missing. Out there, even to the best of them, I'm not a human being. That's it. I'm not a human being."

"Doug, for God's sake—"

"Facts, Nat, two lawyers addressing themselves to facts. You don't want me to be a mean Negro or a servile Negro or a Negro in white face. You want me to be a human being who has a job called President, and to serve the job as a human being. How can I? Who'll let me? What happens if I slip out of here one day, unrecognized, with Wanda for my wife, with nobody knowing who we are, and travel across the country? What am I then? Human being? I'm a nigger like any other nigger—you can't tell one from another, you know——in the South and Southwest, and a Negro in the East and North and West. That's what I am, Nat, when I'm not pretending to be senator or President. I'm a black man, nothing more. None of the government and organization language, like education, employment, equal suffrage, good housing, public accommodations, none of that is out there. It's a simpler language out there. It says if you stand in line an hour in a market or store, and it's come to be your turn, and a white man walks in, he gets served first. It says if you've got a hunger pang in your belly, and want to park at the first hamburger slop-joint you see, you can't, because they won't let you in. It says if your wife's got to go to the bathroom, and there's no public rest room she can get into, she'd better have a good bladder. It says if your throat is parched, and you want a Coke, just a lousy Coke, you can't find a place to buy one, nowhere, no, sir. It says if you're exhausted and grimy on the road and want to stop overnight, there's not a hotel or motel with a vacancy when you ask. It says what Roy Wilkins always used to say, that every time you step out of your front door in the morning, until you come home and shut the door in the evening, you run the risk or certainty of all this kind of mistreatment and denial and humiliation. That's the real language out there, Nat, and it reminds you, in case you ever tend to forget, that you're not a human being, not here, not now, but a black man, meaning a half man.

"Sure I am President, Nat, but I'm not forgetting, and no one will let me forget, I am a black man, not yet qualified for human being, let alone for President. No matter how I feel, I can only act one way, Nat, only one way, and that's as if I'm a servant of T.C., keeping the house in order while he's away. . . . It's the old story I used to hear a Negro deacon tell when I was a little boy. He told it from the pulpit. 'Ef yo' say to de white man, "Ain't yo' forget yo' hat?" he say, "Nigger, go get it!" ' That's got to be my job, Nat, getting T.C.'s hat."

Nat Abrahams was too deeply moved, too filled with white man's guilts, to plead further with Dilman. He knew that he should accept Dilman's view of reality but

try to broaden it, to help him see more clearly his role
and future. It was no use now, impossible, after this confessional. For years he and Dilman had openly discussed
the Negro problem, and yet he could not recall any other
time when he had heard his friend sound so passionately
embittered.

"Okay, Doug," Abrahams said quietly, "you'll get
T.C.'s hat. But there are a few other things you have a
right to do, to instigate, to press, on your own. You have
a right—"

Dilman held up a tired hand. "Nat, I have no more
rights here than I have out there. Maybe fewer here.
Someday, it might be different. But this is here and now.
Don't you think I'm aware of what's going on? Don't you
think I know everything there is to know about the New
Succession Bill they're rushing through? Why all this
speed from my colleagues on the Hill? Because they
can't forget I'm Negro and they don't trust me, don't want
me to put in an Ethiopian Cabinet, with a black Secretary of State who might one day succeed me. And you
know what, Nat—I'm not going to veto it. No, sir."

"You should."

"No, sir. I'm not going to sign it 'Approved,' either,
but I'm not going to veto it. I'm going to let it sit on
my desk ten days and a Sunday, and let it pass into
law without either my approval or disapproval. It'll get
knocked out eventually by the Supreme Court, anyway.
But I'll play their little game, so they feel safer, so they
know I'm not peopling the succession line with recruits
from the Crispus Society or NAACP. I'm letting them
know that I know my place, and I'll do what I'm supposed to do, like it or not. If I didn't, Nat, I'd be inviting real trouble for every Negro, let alone for myself,
and for the unity of the country at large."

"Maybe it's time for that," said Abrahams.

"It'll never be time for that until my wife can go into
any restroom in the land, and until a Negro can walk
through the front door of the White House by popular
demand." He pushed himself away from the table. "It
could be worse, Nat. I inherited some pretty good people
from T.C. I know Governor Talley isn't too smart, but

he gets things done. Secretary Eaton is crafty and help-ful, and a gentleman. As far as I can tell, the Cabinet is a good one. As for the bills pending, the minorities bill, the crisis in Africa, I think I can't go far wrong lis-tening to T.C.'s advisers. After all, they want what's best for the country, too."

Abrahams slipped his pipe back into his coat pocket. "Everyone wants what's best for the country. Everyone isn't always right." He tried to smile. "Read the fine print, Doug. There's always fine print."

"Don't worry, Nat. Maybe I'm serving T.C., but I can't rubberstamp his name. It's got to be my name affixed to everything. And I always read what I sign."

"Good enough," said Abrahams. He saw Dilman stretch and yawn, and he stood up. "First session ad-journed, Doug. I'd better get back to poor Sue, and you'd better get what sleep you can."

"I think that's best, Nat. I'm bushed. Let me walk you to the elevator."

Only later, when he was by himself in the elevator, was Nat Abrahams relieved that Sue had not come to dinner. He knew that she would have wept.

Douglass Dilman was alone in the dimly lighted in-timacy of the Lincoln Bedroom, in his baggy pajamas, slumped in the Victorian velvet-covered chair, downing the last of his sherry and trying to read the completed Minorities Rehabilitation Program Bill.

It was no use. The long day, the dinner, the Bordeaux, the sherry, had made him heavy-lidded and drowsy. He cast the printed bill on the marble-topped table, placed the sherry glass next to it, and tried to think of what Nat Abrahams had said and what he had said. He was too fatigued to recall exactly. His memory slid off to Wanda, to Julian, to Leroy Poole, to Arthur Eaton, to Sally Wat-son, to Clay Kemmler and the Cabinet, and then slid past them, searching for respite.

He heaved himself out of the chair, tightened the cord of his pajama trousers, and peered at the Empire clock. It was after midnight. He turned off the lamp, padded in his flopping slippers to turn off two more, pausing once to examine the handwritten copy of Lincoln's Gettysburg Address and then giving up because the words ran together and blurred.

Yawning, he shuffled to the giant rosewood bed, sat on it, kicked off his slippers, stuffed his weary, middle-aged body between the white sheets, and reached over to turn off the last global lamp.

In the welcome darkness he fell back against the pillow.

He knew that sleep was coming swiftly, and his tired mind groped for one noble good-night thought, one lofty sentiment, to commemorate this unique historic occasion, a black President ready to slumber his first night in the white man's White House.

He tried to evoke something of Abe Lincoln's wisdom, since he rested in Abe Lincoln's bed. He sought words . . . noble . . . lofty . . . historic . . . malice toward none . . . charity for all . . . firmness in the right . . . in the right . . . in the right . . . in rights, rights, rights.

It had gone, as sleep suffused him, and what remained was an old Negro jingle chanted among the shanties . . . noble . . . lofty . . . historic . . .

> *Nigger an' white man*
> *Playin' seven-up;*
> *Nigger win de money—*
> *Skeered to pick 'em up.*

Sorry . . . Mistah . . . Lincoln . . . ah's skeered . . . skeered . . . skeered.

He turned on his side, curling beneath the thick white blanket, seeking and nearing the warm encompassing safety of night oblivion. There was one moment's lucidity before sleep drew nothingness over it.

One moment's thought: How hard this bed is, how hard and big and white, too hard for a soft man, too big for a small man, yet maybe, maybe, not too white for a black man. Maybe.

Douglass Dilman, President of the United States, slept at last.

IV

THE Stars and Stripes, whipping from the pole above the White House, was no longer at half-mast.

It had given Douglass Dilman a small shock when Crystal, fifteen minutes ago, had delivered this fact to him with his breakfast tray, in the second-floor Yellow Oval Room. She had proudly described the event as an eyewitness: yesterday, coming to work, she had seen the flag hanging limply midway down the pole; today, coming to work, she had seen it billowing in the wind at the very top of the flagstaff. She had reported the change as if it were a momentous event.

Remembering Crystal's glowing face now, as he gulped down his coffee, Dilman supposed that she was right. The returning of the nation's banner to its normal position meant that the thirty-day period of national mourning had ended. On this day, four weeks and two days since he had taken office, the beginning of his second month as President, his fellow countrymen would do an about-face. They would cease looking backward. They would look ahead again, and find him before their eyes. They would begin looking at him, at him and no one else. Not that they hadn't already done so, he thought wryly.

A vicious editorial, in one of Zeke Miller's more Southern newspapers, came to mind: "Citizens, keep your Old Glories at half-mast for the rest of Dilman's term, not in mourning for T.C., but in mourning for the death of our dignity and stature as a nation." But now Crystal had told him, in effect, that Miller's advice had not been followed, that this day the flag once more celebrated at full-mast a living President.

Yes, he thought, today it's official. They would all be looking at him, and he did not like it. He was not ready for their total scrutiny and judgment.

He drank his coffee in haste, knowing that today would be another busy and trying day, even more trying than the ones that had preceded it. When the telephone at his elbow rang genteelly, as befitted its station in the gracious damask room, and then musically rang again, Dilman was not surprised. Lately Edna Foster had been starting off his mornings with these calls from her office because there were more and more messages awaiting his reluctant arrival, acting like so many powerful magnets trying to draw him into a day that he shrank from attending.

With a sigh he gave the saucer back its cup, and answered the telephone before it could begin its third summons.

The caller was Edna Foster.

After assuring her that she had not disturbed him, not at all, that he was dressed and fed and almost prepared to come downstairs, he listened for the inevitable.

"There are several messages, Mr. President—"

"Yes, Miss Foster."

"Grover Illingsworth called in a terrible panic—I mean for him."

Dilman enjoyed good humor for the first time this morning. Visualizing Illingsworth in a panic was as difficult as picturing a waxen Prince Albert in Madame Tussaud's trying to slap a fly off his nose. Ever since Kwame Amboko, the President of Baraza, had arrived two days ago, the tanned, tall patrician Chief of Protocol had been a dominant part of Dilman's life. Everything about Illingsworth was formidable—he was Back Bay Boston, his English so precise as to sound faintly foreign, his chalk-striped gray suits as impressive as a military uniform, his knowledge of *Burke's Peerage* and *Almanach de Gotha* as thorough as his fluency in French, German, Italian, Spanish was expert—yet he did not make Dilman cower. And this instant, Dilman realized why: because, as Chief of Protocol, Illingsworth regarded all heads of state as equals without regard to

their race, religion, or background. When you rode in
jet planes or jeeps or on horseback with leaders of millions of people in Ireland, in Spain, in Nigeria, in Iran,
in India, in Japan, you charted men by their position in
life and not by their color. To Illingsworth, Dilman was
one more head of state, like so many black or yellow
ones he had known and dealt with, and he was easy and
casual with Dilman, and Dilman felt relaxed and natural
with him. But this man phoning in a panic? Had Miss
Foster taken leave of her senses?

"What is he upset about?" Dilman asked. "Is anything
really wrong?"

"Tonight's State Dinner you are giving for President
Amboko. Mr. Illingsworth knows the menu is set, but he
just found out Amboko is a vegetarian!"

Dilman laughed. "Is that all? Well, you have the
housekeeper prepare a special meal for Amboko. What
does a vegetarian eat besides grass?"

"I already asked Mr. Illingsworth. He said he hadn't
had a chance to inquire, but he supposed that a vegetarian could eat anything that, in its original state, would
not have bitten back. Anyway, he's very anxious about
this State Dinner, since it's your first, and Baraza is such
a hot spot, and—"

"Miss Foster, you call Illingsworth right back, and
have him get in touch with Amboko's aide-de-camp at
the Barazan Embassy, and have him find out exactly
what our guest will or won't eat. Then have him pass it
on to Miss Watson, and she'll take care of Mrs. Crail and
the chef. Put in a call for Illingsworth at the New State
Department Building right now—I'll hold—"

Waiting, Dilman tried to review the two meetings that
he had already held with Kwame Amboko. In some
childlike way, he had expected that the meetings would
be informal, lively, easier than those with his own Cabinet members, because both he and Amboko were black,
and that would be enough to bind them in quick understanding and agreement. It had astonished him how
wrong he had been.

He had found Amboko a young man, no more than
thirty-five, a scholarly and withdrawn young man with

woolly black hair, suspicious eyes behind rimless glasses, and a flat nose that seemed to cover his countenance from cheek to cheek. His puncture of a mouth was ringed by flabby lips that revealed a quarter of an inch space between his upper center teeth. While Amboko's accent was Harvard, and he possessed many agreeable memories of his time in the United States, and had tried to model his newly independent democracy along the lines laid out by the United States Constitution, he had appeared unconvinced that the United States was an entirely trustworthy mentor and friend.

Dilman could see that Kwame Amboko was not impressed by a fellow colored man's ascension to the Presidency in a mammoth white nation where colored men were a minority. Amboko seemed to be suggesting, without saying so outright, that Dilman was merely a front for an undependable white cabal. The African had implied that Dilman was a puppet repeating white men's words, and therefore could bring no more understanding to the problems of an all-black nation than could his white masters.

Dilman had been able to discover only one common bond between President Amboko and himself. He and his visitor appeared to be equally sensitive to disregard and disrespect from whites. But even this one bond, which might have drawn them closer, was slack, because their sensitivities were activated by different hurts. Whereas Dilman was sensitive to slights reflecting on his human and democratic rights as a man, Amboko was sensitive about the weakness of his small country and the threats of foreign domination. To Dilman, President Amboko was like a longtime prisoner, paroled at last, uncertain that his freedom is real, constantly glancing over his shoulder at the gray walls that had incarcerated him to make sure that someone more powerful than he is not reaching out to pull him back inside. When Dilman had mentioned this to Sue and Nat Abrahams two nights before, Nat had said, "Yes, I think all newly independent nations are at once paranoid and egocentric——they think everyone is against them, and they have no interest in anyone but themselves. Not so long ago the United

States suffered those same adolescent growing pangs."

Dilman's policy talks with Amboko had been inconclusive. Dilman had been frank about the necessity for a compromise. He would sign America into the African Unity Pact, which the Senate had ratified, he would guarantee continued economic assistance to help industrialize Baraza, if Amboko would be less repressive toward native Communists and the Soviet Union. Dilman felt that this was the least Amboko could do, in order to help the United States pacify Russia.

Doggedly President Amboko had resisted this compromise. True, the Barazan Communist Party was small. True, there was no evidence of subversive activity by the Soviet Embassy in Baraza. True, there was no conclusive evidence that young Barazan natives on cultural exchanges to Moscow were being indoctrinated with Marxist ideas. Yet, despite this, President Amboko felt that his country, in this transitional period, was a fertile field for the rise of Communism. Because Amboko had abolished rule by chieftains, broken up the ancient social structure (which had scattered warring tribes over the grasslands of the plains and through the dense forests of the mountain ranges), supplanted it with not yet effective elected inter-village councils, there was discontent. Furthermore, the per capita income in Baraza was still only sixty dollars a year, and industrialization had hardly begun. The impoverished and unemployed might easily be turned against democracy.

Above all else, President Amboko did not trust the Soviet Union. He feared that Russia coveted his little nation's resources—the gold, iron ore, diamonds—and, in a power grab, might try to put his people back into a colonial stockade. He had reminded Dilman of the experience of one of his neighbors, Guinea, with Russia. After the French had left Guinea in 1958, the newly independent nation, tempted by the Soviet Union's anti-colonial talk and its offer of economic credit, had invited the Russians to help them. Within three years Guinea had been forced to expel the Russians because the Soviet Embassy, it was learned, had been working with native union leaders against the democratically elected government. President Amboko feared that the same Soviet activity might occur, if it was not already taking place, in Baraza, and he wanted to anticipate and thwart it.

Impressed as he was by Amboko's concern, Dilman had felt that he must not be sidetracked by a small nation's problems to the detriment of world peace. He had tried to behave as T.C. might have behaved. He had insisted upon the compromise, promising that Montgomery Scott, Director of the Central Intelligence Agency, would assign a sufficient number of his agents to Baraza to keep a watchful undercover eye on any subversive activity there. Amboko had agreed to think the matter over further, and to give his final reply to Dilman before returning home. He would be leaving for Baraza, Dilman remembered, after tonight's State Dinner.

"Mr. President." It was Edna Foster on the telephone again. "I spoke to Mr. Illingsworth. He'll take care of everything."

"Fine."

"There are two messages from Leroy Poole. He wants to discuss the last chapter of the biography with you. Shall I have Mr. Lucas give him an appointment?"

Dilman tried to interpret Poole's calls. If there had been only one, the writer might indeed have wished to discuss the book. But two messages indicated something more urgent. Dilman suspected that it was the Turnerite business, still. For one who had insisted that he was not a member of that avowed direct-action group, Poole's interest in the organization was unaccountable. Three weeks ago he had agitated Julian into fighting with his father. A week ago he had cornered poor Nat Abrahams in the Mayflower lobby, without success. Now, no doubt, because of the Hattiesburg sentence rendered by Judge Gage, he was trying to get to Dilman once more.

While Judge Gage's verdict of "guilty" in the Mississippi trial had probably been technically exact, his sentence had been unduly harsh and vindictive. Two days before, in his Southern courtroom, he had sentenced all the Turnerite pickets, including the blinded one, to the maximum ten years' imprisonment in the Mississippi

State Penitentiary at Parchman, under State Criminal Code Section 2011. While the Crispus Society had agreed to review the legalities of the case with an eye to an appeal, the Turnerites were too outraged to be patient. The Jeff Hurley statement to the press yesterday had been an uncomfortable threat, understandable, yet imprudent. "We are told this is justice, and to abide by the law of the land," Hurley had announced. "We are also told to abide by the words of the Old Testament, that 'Vengeance is mine; I will repay, saith the Lord.' But this cautious and creeping Lord is not our Lord. We find a better Lord with better guidance in the words of Nahum, 'The Lord revengeth and is furious; the Lord will take vengeance on his adversaries.' "

Dilman had deplored Hurley's injudicious statement. Such pledges of lawlessness gave further ammunition to the enemies of the Negro race, and made Dilman's own situation that much more difficult. No, he would not discuss the Turnerite activity with young Poole again. There were other ways to proceed, better means, within the law, and he would hasten them when he felt that it was possible.

"Miss Foster, you call Poole and tell him I'm too busy right now," he said. "I'll discuss the book with him—well—tell him next week."

"I think he wanted to see you this morning."

"Impossible."

"Very well, Mr. President. Then there is Chancellor McKaye's letter, the invitation to Trafford. I have a notation on my calendar that it must be answered by today."

Dilman had forgotten. Chancellor McKaye and the Regents of Trafford University had written to him, inviting him to appear on Founders' Day to accept an honorary Doctor of Philosophy degree and to be the principal speaker at the gathering of the student body, alumni, and faculty.

Even his son had put aside his pique to congratulate him and to beg him to make the appearance. Dilman had avoided any decision, but now he knew that he must reach one. His instinct, he admitted, was against the appearance. If he could not turn down the honorary degree, he must turn down the invitation to speak. Julian would be disappointed, perhaps upset, but there were more important considerations. To date, he had avoided public speeches, accepting the advice of T.C.'s advisers that they might be inflammatory no matter what he said. While he must give his first television press conference this afternoon, and hold others later, this contact with the public would be buffered by reporters. When the time came to speak in public, he would have to do so, but certainly it would be unwise to make his first such appearance at a Negro school.

"Miss Foster," Dilman said, "you write Chancellor McKaye to this effect—that I'm moved and pleased to be offered the honorary degree and that I will accept it later if I may, but that I regret I cannot accept the Founders' Day speaking engagement. Tell him my overloaded schedule will not allow my leaving Washington. Make it—make it as tactful as possible. Leave the door open for the future. Say maybe on another occasion, when things ease up, I can pay Trafford a more informal visit. Tell him I'm not unmindful of the good job they are doing there, and I speak not only as Chief Executive but as the father of one of their undergraduates. You know how to write it. I'll read and sign it later in the day. Anything else?"

"Mr. Flannery and Governor Talley have just walked in. They're ready to brief you on the press conference."

"Tell them to wait in my office. I'll be right there."

After hanging up, Dilman considered a second cup of coffee, rejected it for lack of time, rose, tugged his jacket straight, and found his briefcase. He left the Yellow Oval Room and went into the West Hall.

As he started for the elevator, he heard his name. He spun around, to observe Sally Watson, waving a sheaf of papers, hurrying toward him. Once again he was aware of her dress. The variety of her attire—he could not recall seeing the same garment on her twice in three weeks—fascinated him, as usual. She was wearing a claret-colored sheer blouse and magenta skirt, costly, unornamented, the subtle colors contrasting pleasantly with her sleek blond hair. She had more the appearance of a hostess than that of a secretary, Dilman decided, and he did not mind. At first he had worried about her conspicuous beauty, but by now it blended into the stately beauty of the White House itself. Besides, to his relief, with one exception, the press had played down and been uncritical of her being chosen to fill the position of social secretary. The expected exception had been Reb Blaser, acidly writing that the wily new President was trying to disarm the Southern bloc in Congress by embarrassing bribes, beginning with the hiring of the daughter of Senator Hoyt Watson. Dilman's annoyance at this gratuitous observation had been teased away by Sally herself. "Now really, do I look like a Southern Trojan horse, Mr. President?" she had joked.

However, whimsicality from Sally Watson was rare. For another surprise about her had been her seriousness. Somehow Dilman had expected a certain degree of frivolity in a wealthy, spoiled child. Instead, he had a social assistant who had proved punctual, earnest, dedicated, agreeable to working all hours, and who had the initiative to go beyond the scope of her East Wing office, to take over the handling of his engagements outside the White House. Once or twice he had almost forgotten to be cautious with her about his private affairs.

As she approached, smooth brow furrowed, it was difficult for him to reconcile with the young lady's angelic face one bit of gossip that he had heard. A few evenings ago Sue Abrahams had repeated a tidbit that Mrs. Gorden Oliver had passed on to her: that Kay Varney Eaton had been out of the city an uncommonly long period of time, and that the Secretary of State had been seeking solace in the company of Miss Sally Watson. Sue Abrahams had not repeated the gossip to titillate, but to keep Dilman informed of all that she heard behind his back. She doubted if the Arthur Eaton-Sally Watson thing was true, and had been pleased when Dilman discounted it entirely. Dilman had said that he could not conceive of an amorous relationship between a dignified, circumspect, older career diplomat like Arthur Eaton and a relatively superficial, inexperienced,

too-well-known young single girl like Senator Watson's
daughter. What had Nat thought? Nat had shrugged,
hummed a few bars of "September Song," and they
had laughed and dismissed it.

Now, waiting for her, Dilman superimposed Nat's
shrug on Sally's gilt-headed Aphrodite loveliness. Anything was possible, of course, but in this central city of
professionally prying eyes it was unlikely that a sophisticated statesman of international renown would dare risk
his reputation over any bachelor girl. Improbable, he
told himself again, and accepted Sally Watson in her
previous virginal and unsullied state.

"Good morning, Mr. President," she said, trying
to catch her breath. "I need you for a few minutes—tonight's dinner—"

"I'm sorry, Miss Watson, but can't it wait? I'm running behind—"

"Just one minute, then. I suppose it's not all that important, but—"

"All right, Miss Watson. Do you mind telling me on
the way to the office?"

They walked to the elevator as Sally checked the
markings on different sheets of her papers.

"The platform is up in the East Room, and it's completely decorated," she said. "Very pretty. I just called
the Hay-Adams and the Statler Hilton, and the whole
Hollywood contingent is in, safe and sound. I can't wait
to hear Herbie Teele, and I adore Libby Owens, don't
you?"

Entering the elevator, Dilman was less enthusiastic
than his social secretary about the entertainment that
was to follow the State Dinner. Allan Noyes, the Party
chairman, had been the first to suggest it. The six famous
Hollywood and New York performers had been staunch
and vocal supporters of T.C. and the Party, and had
raised a small fortune to help finance his election campaign. Now they had been the first to volunteer their
support of the new President. Their quotations in the
syndicated movie columns had been embarrassingly extravagant in praise of Dilman, whom none had ever met.

This type of show-business liberal, no matter how sin-

cere and well intentioned, had always made Dilman uneasy. They made too much of a point of loving anyone
black or yellow or brown, no matter what the character
and worth of the object of their extrovert affection. When
the entertainment group had heard of Dilman's first State
Dinner, they had offered their services through Noyes.
Dilman had been indecisive about them, preferring no
entertainment at all, or, at least, something more conservative. And then Illingsworth had learned that President
Amboko was an inveterate moviegoer, and that he would
be delighted to enjoy some of his American cinema idols
in the flesh, and that had pushed Dilman into agreement.

Dilman had not minded Trig Cunningham, the rough
and fearless star of a half-hundred swashbuckling and
soldiering epics, or Betsy Buckner, the sinuous national
Love Object, or Tilly Reyes, the rubber-featured lady
clown, or Rick Wade, the disheveled guitar-strumming
adolescent. They were white. His objections were to two
other members of the troupe, Herbie Teele, the lanky,
fork-tongued comedian known for his acid integration
monologues and his coterie of young white female wor-
shipers, and Libby Owens, the magnificent singer of sad
blues songs. They were Negro. Dilman did not want
them, not so soon, not the first day after the national
mourning ended. But President Amboko wanted them.
So did Sally Watson, apparently. And so they were here
and in the wings.

"Yes, it'll be interesting," he found himself saying. "I
hope they exercise some caution. President Amboko may
be a little touchy about certain jokes." He meant himself and not Amboko, but he could not bring himself to
be so naked in front of this girl. He hated Negro jokes
told by Negroes, and Negro songs sung in public by
Negroes.

"Oh, don't worry, Mr. President. Mr. Illingsworth's
assistants are attending a rehearsal at the Hilton this afternoon." Sally was busy with her bundle of papers. "The
routine for the dinner has finally been worked out."

"Go ahead."

"All but the honored guests will arrive by the south
grounds—go through the South Portico entrance to the

first-floor corridor, where the Marine Band will be playing. I'll be there with my staff, and we'll show everyone
the seating plan and give them their escort cards. Then
we'll get them into the East Room. They'll have about
twenty minutes there before your arrival."

The elevator had stopped. Quickly Sally opened the
door, and waited for Dilman to step out before following
him. Dilman, whose mind was on the press conference
briefing, walked hurriedly, so that Sally had to skip every
few steps to keep beside him. As they traversed the
ground-floor red carpet, she continued to speak.

"President Amboko and his entourage, with Mr. Illingsworth, will come in by the Pennsylvania Avenue side
—the North Portico entrance—around five minutes after
eight. You will welcome them in the Yellow Oval Room,
and have perhaps ten or fifteen minutes to chat with
President Amboko. After that, all of you will go down
the stairway. Photographers will be permitted to take pictures—"

"Is that necessary?"

"I'm told it is the custom followed by T.C. and most
others before him." She glanced at Dilman, who nodded
assent, and then she went on. "The Marine Band will be
playing 'Hail to the Chief' as you take Amboko into the
East Room. Then, since we've been forced to combine
the reception with the dinner, you, Mr. President, and
Amboko, and his entourage, will form the receiving
line, and as guests file past, they will go on to their tables
—one main table, and smaller ones—in the State Dining Room and wait for you to take your seat. You will
offer the first toast, after the dessert."

A White House policeman had sprung forward to open
the door, and Dilman emerged outdoors with Sally onto
the colonnaded walk that went past the indoor swimming pool, and turned toward the West Wing executive
offices. He sniffed the air, cold and invigorating, peered
at the blue-gray cloudless metallic sky, and resumed his
march to the briefing.

"According to Mr. Illingsworth," Sally was saying,
"after dinner you can lead President Amboko upstairs for
a private conversation in the Yellow Oval Room, while

the other guests go into the Red, Green and Blue Rooms for champagne. Then, Mr. President, you will show him to the East Room for the performance." She slowed, searching her papers, and Dilman slowed his stride with her. "The final total—we sent 104 invitations and admittance cards—"

"Is everyone coming?" Dilman asked.

"Ninety-six have accepted," she said. "The others are either out of town or ill or—oh, yes, there is one guest —no, two—I haven't heard from. Senator Bruce Hankins—"

"I predicted that. I told Talley we shouldn't bother, but he wanted to play politics."

"—and Miss Wanda Gibson. She and the Reverend and Mrs. Spinger were invited together. I heard from the Spingers, but I have not heard from Miss Gibson." She looked up. "I'll telephone Miss Gibson—"

"No," said Dilman, and at once, from Sally's inquisitive eyes, their widening, he knew that he had uttered his order too hastily and too strongly. He sought to rectify it. "You needn't bother. She lives with the Spingers, and I am sure she assumed their acceptance was her own."

"Very well." But he could see that Sally was reluctant to drop it. He wondered if she would go further. She said, "I think I am acquainted with all of the guests, or at least know about them, except Miss—Miss Wanda Gibson. Since I want to be as useful to you as possible, Mr. President—you know, introductions, making outsiders feel at home—is there anything I should know about the lady?"

Dilman cursed himself for having added Wanda's name to the invitation list. He had known the hazard of doing so. He had done it only to prove to Wanda that he was not afraid to see her in public. He had expected questions from Illingsworth and received none, and Sally Watson's curiosity caught him momentarily off guard.

He halted before the French doors leading into his Oval Office, returned the greeting of a Secret Service agent, and then confronted Sally as casually as possible. "You needn't fret about Miss Gibson," he said. "As a senator, preparing for committee hearings, I sometimes

found her a valuable information source. She is employed by a Liechtenstein corporation, the Vaduz Exporters, in Maryland. I believe her firm carries on a good
deal of trading with African nations, Baraza among
them, and I thought that President Amboko and his Ambassador—what in the devil is his name?—Wamba, yes,
Wamba—that she'd be one more person for them to
talk to. That's all. You needn't bother about her tonight.
She'll be well taken care of. The Spingers will have her
in tow. And Mr. Abrahams—you met him—I think he
knows her slightly, professionally, and he'll pitch in."

He realized that he had explained too much, and that
Sally Watson had been listening too closely.

He said, "Is that all? I've got to—"

She said, "Well, there are a couple of minor—"

"You take care of the rest of it, you and Illingsworth.
I haven't time to be nervous about tonight. I've got to
save my anxiety for the press conference. Forgive me,
Miss Watson. You're doing wonderfully on your own."

"Thank you. And I'm sorry, Mr. President. I didn't
mean to distract you. Good luck, if I'm allowed to say so."

He turned to the closest French door, and could see
Tim Flannery holding it open. He thanked his press secretary and went into the office, which was agreeably
warm. Talley, making corrections on the typed pages in
a loose-leaf folder, began to rise, but Dilman signaled
him to remain seated.

After taking his place behind the desk and apologizing
for his tardiness, Dilman said, "Well, gentlemen, I've
been doing my homework the last couple of nights.
What's next?"

"This," said Talley, closing the vellum folder and holding it up. "I've tried to anticipate every question that
might be put to you in the press conference. Then Tim
here kind of had drinks with some of the boys, and
picked up a few clues as to what you might expect. We
listed the questions, circulated them to every department,
and each one sent over lengthy replies on policy, supplemented with facts and figures. Tim and I condensed
this to five typewritten pages. I don't think we've missed
a trick." He came out of his chair and handed the folder

to Dilman. "You have enough time to go over them by yourself now. Most of it will be familiar, but if anything puzzles or confuses you, we can talk it out right here."

Dilman picked worriedly at a corner of the blue vellum folder. "What if I don't remember some figure or—"

"You're not expected to be a memory expert, Mr. President," Talley said. "Tim will be seated beside you with that folder, and you can always turn to him for some elusive fact or number."

"Won't that look amateurish on television?" he asked.

Flannery shook his head. "Not a bit. It'll make you appear fallible and mortal, serve to put viewers at ease."

Dilman did not feel reassured. There had been several hours of debate on how his first press conference should be presented to the public. Dilman had turned down a huge televised press conference from the New State Department Building auditorium as being too impersonal, and as demanding histrionic talents that he knew he did not possess. He had considered an informal gathering in the Indian Treaty Room across the street. Flannery had been against this, arguing that Dilman had yet made no contact with the American public or with the majority of the press, except through brief, impromptu remarks or dictated statements, and that full exposure was now a necessity. A compromise had been reached only two days before. Forty to fifty members of the press would be admitted to the Cabinet Room. The television networks would cover the event. The atmosphere would be comfortable and unstaged. Dilman would make a series of news announcements, and then answer questions for perhaps twenty minutes.

Dilman opened the folder. On the first page there was typed in capital letters:

FOR THE PRESIDENT—MORNING BRIEFING ON PRESS CONFERENCE

As he turned the page, he heard Tim Flannery saying, "One thing, Mr. President." He looked up, and Flannery went on, "You'll notice a star in the margin, and the name of a newspaper or wire service beneath it, alongside several questions. There are not many, but those are the ones we planted to be sure they were asked. They're the ones we feel you have good replies to and can come off well with."

"I knew it was done," said Dilman, "but how do you manage it? Don't the reporters resent it?"

"Not at all," said Flannery. "It gives them added news, even if canned or controlled, as they may think. These are men we can depend upon. They do us a favor, and at the right time we repay them with an exclusive lead. It's not too obvious. Yesterday I called in one of the bureau chiefs representing a New York paper, handed him a written question, and I said, 'Look, if you ask the President this question, in your own words, you might get an interesting answer. I'm just tipping you off.' He looked at the question and said, 'You mean, he'd like to get an official policy statement on this off his chest?' I said, 'I think so. It won't be pap. It'll be solid and definite.' He said, 'Okay, Tim, good enough.' " Flannery smiled at Dilman. "It's the way we've worked in the past, with excellent results."

"Fine," said Dilman. "You two do whatever you wish until I've gone over this. If I have any questions, I won't be reticent. I'll need every bit of direction I can get today."

Dilman studied the second page in the folder. Under the heading, YOUR OPENING REMARKS, there was a concise list of the subjects that he would cover in his reading of the mimeographed text. Next, under the heading, QUESTIONS ON OPENING REMARKS AND OTHER MATTERS (IF ASKED), there were fourteen short queries. Turning the page, Dilman found the heading, YOU MAY RESPOND AS FOLLOWS, and here each possible inquiry was repeated, followed by a suggested reply, severely condensed to one paragraph. This ran almost two pages. The last heading read, BACKGROUND, with numbers keyed to the questions and answers, and tight paragraphs filled with authoritative quotations and statistics from government departments elaborating upon the suggested responses.

Flipping back to the second page, Dilman quickly went over the outline of the prepared statement already in his briefcase, which he was to read to the reporters and television cameras. The general tone was humble and conciliatory. He was to begin by saying that he welcomed the opportunity to meet with the men and women of the fourth estate upon whom the electorate depended for all information concerning their government. He was to say that he felt they would perform with the same sense of responsibility with which he would try to perform. Never in our history, he would say, was a President or the public more dependent upon news media for accuracy and reliability. There would be the quotation from Thomas Jefferson: "The press is the best instrument for enlightening the mind of man, and improving him as a rational, moral, and social being." Tim Flannery had calculated that these remarks, this initial flattery, would soften the cynical reporters, make them preen with self-importance, make them know that here was a Chief Executive who would cooperate with them. Remembering the writings of Reb Blaser and his kind, Dilman felt less confidence in the uses of flattery, but he liked Flannery too much to disagree.

After that, there was the repetition of all of Dilman's press statements of the past month. He had not sought the Presidency, he had not wanted it, but since it was his duty by law to undertake the office, he would do so to the best of his ability. He had, he was to say, only a short time—short time was underlined—to be the caretaker of T.C.'s ideals. As a senator, he was to say, he had always admired and supported T.C., and he was to cite his voting record as a congressman. The country, he was to say, need expect no drastic detours from the peaceful and prosperous road along which the former President had been leading it. Had he not already given evidence of good faith in retaining every member of T.C.'s Cabinet and personal staff of advisers?

Troubled, Dilman looked up. Talley and Flannery were across the Oval Office, leaning against the fireplace, smoking, whispering. He considered telling them that he did not like these opening remarks. They seemed too humble, as if he were apologizing to the press and the 230 million Americans for having a Negro in the wrong place, as if reassuring everyone that the fact that he was a member of a minority race would not destroy them. Yet he had no courage to bring it up this late, for he realized that these were not Flannery's words but the language of politically expert white men like Talley, Eaton, and the Cabinet members, and perhaps they knew what was best for him.

He concentrated on the rest of his opening remarks, mostly official news announcements: he had met with the National Space Council and agreed that within three months the advanced Apollo rocket would catapult a team of three astronauts into orbit; he had given assurances to Brazil and India that A-11 flights would not be continued over their embattled borders; he was being kept closely informed of Secretary of State Eaton's meetings with Russian Ambassador Rudenko, and could reveal now only that progress had been made, and it was likely that the interrupted Roemer Conference with the Premier of the Soviet Union would be resumed at another site, probably on the European Continent; he had sat in on one meeting with labor leaders, heads of the steel industry, and Secretary Barnes, and he was confident the impending strike would be averted; he had been informed of the exclusive story in the Chicago *Tribune* that Frank Valetti, second-in-command of the Turnerite Group, was a member of the Communist Party, and he had already urged the Justice Department to investigate; he had written a letter to Annapolis, appointing T.C.'s young son, Fred, to the Naval Academy when he became eligible.

Dilman unwrapped a cigar, bit off one end, and lighted it. Although his opening remarks were filled with news, he knew that they would not be enough, and that Flannery and Talley knew it, too. Puffing the cigar, Dilman went down the possible questions that he might be asked, and then he examined the answers offered to him.

Question: Will you sign the African Unity Pact Bill? *Suggested Response:* Yes, we affirm our determination to support free peoples and democratic ideals throughout the world, et cetera.

Question: Can you discuss the subjects that you and Kwame Amboko of Baraza have covered, and relate them to the AUP and the recent Roemer Conference? *Suggested Response:* The meetings with President Amboko have been fruitful, and progress has been made in many areas. We will conclude our talks after tonight's State Dinner. There will be a joint statement from President Amboko and myself upon his departure tomorrow.

Question: Do you feel that, as a Negro, you can be more effective in making activist organizations like the Turnerites behave more moderately? *Suggested Response:* I do not believe my color is an issue one way or another. As a senator, and now as President, I am certain my views about immoderate activity and violence are well known. Like my predecessor, I believe in progress under the law and through the courts of the land, such progress as is being made on behalf of Negro Americans by the Crispus Society and NAACP.

Question: Do you believe passage of the Minorities Rehabilitation Program will alleviate the current tension, and do you intend to support and sign the massive work and education bill? *Suggested Response:* I believe that MRP has much to offer minorities in this country, but at the same time I do not believe it should make us relax our other efforts to secure civil rights for all men and women, et cetera. I am still studying the bill, and will make my views known shortly.

Dilman put down his cigar and rubbed his eyes. The last question was the only one, so far, to which he had written the response. He realized now that his statement was ambiguous, and might not satisfy the press.

"Tim," he called out, "do you think they'll try to pin me down on the MRP Bill?"

Flannery nodded. "I think you can expect it."

Talley took a few steps from the fireplace. "Mr. President, I'm positive you'll avoid a lot of nettlesome questions by simply coming out in flat support of—"

"Governor," Dilman interrupted, "I'm not saying I'm against it, God knows. It's just so damn big and important, I want to feel sure it is right—will ease off the tension—"

Flannery said, "Then whatever you're asked, keep saying you are consulting with your advisers, seeking the best and most efficient legislation possible. You know the sort of thing."

"I understand," said Dilman.

He reviewed the remaining possible questions and suggested responses quickly. How often would he hold press conferences? There was a star after this one. It had been planted. He was to say that he hoped to air ideas with the press every two weeks, depending upon circumstances. Had he approved of the Postmaster General's new commemorative stamp bearing T.C.'s likeness? This also had been planted. He was to say that he had instigated the idea of the memorial stamp. Would he permit his name to be offered as a candidate for the Presidency at the Party convention in Baltimore next year? No star after this one. He was to say that such political considerations were premature, that he preferred to make no comment at this time, except to say that he had never had, and had not now, any political ambitions beyond Congress.

There were several more questions, and then the last one, and reading it, he sat up. For the first time, the New Succession Bill, which would freeze his Cabinet by giving the Senate authority over him, lay coldly and boldly before his eyes, not in speculative newsprint but as a fact presented by his advisers.

Possible Question: Since the New Succession Bill seems assured of passage through Congress, will you sign it into law or veto it?

Without lifting his head to look, he sensed that the watching Talley knew that he had arrived at the yet unspoken question and that, in a way, it was being asked of him by his staff rather than by the press.

Suggested Response: For a long time we have needed reforms and better precautionary measures in our Presidential succession system. The possibilities of multiple deaths in the line of succession, in this nuclear age, are too real to be ignored. I approve of Senator Hankins' proposed bill as one more security measure to safeguard the nation at large.

The omission glared out at Dilman. There was not a word about the embarrassing addendum to the bill, the one amputating his removal powers. Did Talley and the others think the members of the press were blind to it, that they would not ask it?

He took pen in hand, and looked at Talley. "Governor, about the last question here. I don't think I'll get away with your suggested response. It covers only three-fourths of the New Succession Bill. Someone is surely going to inquire about the final paragraphs, and I'd better be ready."

Talley came toward the desk, with Flannery behind him, and Dilman was pleased to see that his aide was flushed with consternation.

"I—we didn't know what you'd want to say about that, Mr. President," Talley was saying. "We've never discussed the clause—"

"Because no one brought it up," said Dilman. He faced Flannery. "Tim, I'd better be ready to say something about that. If I'm asked about it, and I will be, I'll try to make up my mind what to say extemporaneously. I just want to jot a note here for you, after my suggested response, to the effect that—let me think—well—that I have examined the clause shifting the removal powers of the President over his Cabinet to the Senate, in the special case where the succession has gone below Vice-President, and—and while I understand the motivation behind it—the desire of Congress to preserve the nature of the elected and appointed government—I must remark that I believe the clause to be of debatable legality and designed to weaken the executive branch of government. Will I let that one questionable feature turn me against an otherwise excellent piece of legislation or will I approve it? I don't know, Tim—Governor—I'm afraid if I suggest veto, it will create an uproar, make the Southern bloc in Congress, the racists around the country, positive that I'm going to dump T.C.'s Cabinet for an all-black Cabinet. I can't afford that, no matter how I feel—"

"Exactly, that's the point, Mr. President," said Talley anxiously. "The whole piece of legislation was merely made to alleviate fear—"

"But I think the legislation is wrong because it is unconstitutional," Dilman said. "I'll make a note here that I cannot say how I will act until I observe the conditions under which the final New Succession Bill reaches my desk. Then, if I find it necessary to approve it in order to preserve national unity, I will do so after making my legal opinion, and the opinions of the best constitutional lawyers, known to the country."

Hastily, he scrawled several sentences after the last suggested response.

He looked up. "There, that should keep everyone satisfied—for the time."

"Very wise, Mr. President," said Talley, exhaling a gust of relief.

Dilman turned the page. "Let me bone up on the backgrounds to my responses—"

Talley quickly retreated, as if his proximity might provoke the President into second thoughts.

Studiously Dilman devoted himself to the information. He had gone through five of the capsule briefings when the buzzer sounded from Miss Foster's office.

Since he had told her to hold all calls except the most urgent ones, he picked up the telephone immediately.

"Mr. President," said Edna Foster, her voice quavering, "the Attorney General is here. He must see you at once. He says that it is imperative."

"Shoot him right in."

He hung up. "Clay Kemmler's here. Apparently, something critical—"

"We can step out until—" Flannery began.

Dilman waved Flannery and Talley back to the sofa. "No, stay put. Let's—"

Edna Foster's door swung open, and then shut, and Attorney General Kemmler stormed in, flinging his hat at the sofa, ignoring Talley and Flannery as he shed his coat and moved toward the President. Dilman could see that Kemmler was the personification of spleen. His close-set, flinty eyes narrowed, and looked as if they were giving off sparks. Head back, his square jaw thrust forward beyond the point of his nose, he resembled a beset dragon carrying *banderillas* in its backside.

"Mr. President, there's trouble for us," he announced angrily, almost bumping into the Buchanan desk. "I thought you'd better hear it in person, not on the phone, because we'll have to make some fast decisions."

He paused, leaned over the desk, and said, "Those goddam Turnerites went and started their retaliation program. I just got the flash from Mississippi. Some of Hurley's hoodlums crossed into Hattiesburg, grabbed Judge Everett Gage at gunpoint, and kidnaped him. They left a ransom note for local, state, and Federal officials. They'll free Judge Gage when Mississippi frees those Turnerites who were sentenced to ten years. Now what in the holy hell am I supposed to do?"

Involuntarily, Dilman had shivered when Kemmler spat out "kidnaped him." The full realization that his people, a segment of them, had ceased talking terror, were practicing it, performing it, involving him in their insane deed, frightened him.

"It's crazy," he said. "Are you sure Hurley is responsible? I can't believe it."

"He's already sent a denial to the Birmingham and Jackson papers—but who else can be responsible for this act except Hurley and his Turnerites?" Kemmler demanded impatiently. "Naturally, he gave out a statement denying his Group had anything to do with it, but he added something to the effect that he couldn't disapprove of any of his fellow Negroes standing up for their rights. We're trying to locate him for questioning, but no luck, so far. But whether he denies it or not, whether he makes it look like an individual action or not, it's got to be something he sanctioned. Hasn't he been threatening us with retaliation and violence in all his speeches? And who else on earth would risk their necks in a foolhardy act like this—trying to spring a bunch of jailed Turnerites—except other Turnerites?"

Within Dilman there beat a faint hope. "So far, as much as you know, the kidnaping was done by individuals?"

"So far, yes," said Kemmler. "But, Mr. President, there's no doubt over at Justice that the crime is a direct result of announced Turnerite policies."

Dilman's gaze went from the Attorney General to Talley and Flannery, who had come forward, both deeply disturbed. Dilman shook his head. "Well, whether it was the act of individuals or an organization—whichever—how in the devil do they expect to accomplish anything by it?"

"I'll tell you how," said Kemmler. He pushed past Flannery, and came around the desk to stand over the President. "It's all been thought out, every detail. The unsigned ransom note demands that the ten Turnerites in the penitentiary at Parchman be released from jail at once and be delivered safely to Tampico, the Mexican seaport—very smart, since you know and I know how goddam uncooperative the Mexican government has been lately about extraditing our fugitive citizens of Mexican, Japanese, or Negro descent. When the Turnerites are released and landed in Tampico, the kidnapers promise Judge Gage will be returned unharmed. That's the deal."

Dilman sought to rally his authority. "What's this got to do with us? From what you've told me, it's strictly a state affair."

"No, Mr. President, it's *our* affair," said Kemmler emphatically, slapping his thigh. "I spoke to Lombardi at once, and ordered him to sic the FBI after them, because there were indications that the victim was being taken across the state line. Now there's concrete evidence from the FBI that Gage has been carried from Mississippi into Louisiana, and the hoodlums are probably trying to get him to Texas and into Mexico. That makes it our business. That brings it under the Lindbergh kidnaping law. It's a clear-cut Federal offense."

"Well, all right, you're on top of it," said Dilman. "You're doing what you can—"

"My God, Mr. President," exclaimed Kemmler, slapping his thigh repeatedly in his agitation, "this is only the beginning. Can't you see what this means? It means Hurley, Valetti, the whole Turnerite gang—no matter what their phony denials—are starting their eye-for-an-eye policy. If we let them get away with this, they're going to go on with it, take the law into their own hands. Every time they can trump up an injustice practiced upon a Negro, they're going to retaliate with a kidnaping, blaming their act on unknown individuals and mocking us with their innocence as a group. Can't you see what this will lead to? Anarchy, crime compounding crime, with counter-vigilante outfits galloping around the country. Goddammit, we're going to have the Civil War all over again —but twice as bad, because it'll be black against white this time—unless we do something fast."

Shaken, eyes now downcast, Dilman began crumbling the cigar butt between his fingers. "I suppose I could make some kind of personal appeal to Hurley to join us in apprehending—"

"No, absolutely not," said Kemmler.

Talley snapped his fingers for attention. "Mr. President, I'm inclined to agree with the Attorney General. You, personally, can't treat with a possible abductor as an equal, bring him up to your level, or demean yourself by going down to his. The consequences—"

"I'm flatly against any bargaining," Kemmler interrupted. "The situation is too explosive. We can't let one man who is outside the law, heading up one organization, decide what is just and unjust, and mete out his own punishments. We can't have two governments, Mr. President. If there are biases and delinquency on our side, and there are plenty of these, we'll find ways to right them under due process, but no gang of activists is going to supplant us." He straightened, breathing heavily, and then continued. "The FBI'll nail the kidnapers soon enough, you can be sure. Then we'll be able to prove their link to the Turnerites and prosecute them. But we can't wait for that, believe me. What we need from you, Mr. President, is foresight and firm intervention right now that'll put an immediate stop to any more Turnerite violence. In this way you'll discourage lawlessness from other activist groups, black or white. You've got a press conference today, right? You can bet those reporter hounds will be howling after you and after me.

Okay, I think you should be ready for them, beat them to the punch. I think you should announce that the Federal government is moving immediately to outlaw and disband the Turnerites, and that any person found to be a member—"

"Wait a minute," Dilman interrupted, rolling his swivel chair back, and swinging his bulk directly toward Kemmler. "I haven't the power to ban or restrict any private society or organization in the United States, be it the Turnerites or the Ku Klux Klan, unless—"

"Unless it is proved subversive," Kemmler finished for him. "That's right. Well, we've got the goods on the Turnerites. It was because he anticipated a situation exactly like this that T.C. forced Congress into beefing up the Subversive Activities Control Act. He and Congress knew that the $10,000 fine and five-year imprisonment for failure of a Communist to register wasn't going to scare anyone, especially since it was always being questioned in the courts. That's why T.C. pounded through this stronger act—any Communist Front organization engaging in subversive activity, to the detriment of the nation, against the safety of the government, can have its leaders punished and its membership disbanded, and those not complying—"

"You don't have to read the law to me, Kemmler," Dilman broke in. "I voted for it in the Senate. I just don't see how the Subversive Activities Control Act can be applied to the Turnerites. They don't—"

"We can pin a Communist Front tag on the Turnerites and make it stick!" Kemmler exclaimed triumphantly.

"The Turnerites—Communist?" said Dilman with disbelief. "Come, now. I know you're investigating that newspaper scoop about one of the Turnerite directors— whatever his name—Valetti, yes—being a Red, but—"

Kemmler shoved his face almost into Dilman's own. "We *have* investigated Frank Valetti. He's been a Communist Party member for years, and he still is. He is also Hurley's second-in-command. That's point one. And here's point two, the clincher. Over in Justice we wondered where the Turnerites were getting their money.

Who was financing them? Either they were being kept in business by the Crispus Society, which I doubted, or by the Communist Party. Well, we're now satisfied that Valetti has been carrying money from the Commies to the Turnerites."

Dilman shook his head vigorously. "I'm not satisfied. It sounds flaky. Accepting the fact that a member of the Turnerite leadership is a Communist is one thing, but proving the Turnerites, as a group, are part of a conspiracy to overthrow the government—I don't think anyone will buy that."

"You don't?" Clay Kemmler was obviously indignant. "Mr. President, forgive me, but your people have been wide-open to Communist manipulation for years. Remember what J. Edgar Hoover said years ago? He said the Communists were trying to divide and weaken America from within. He said the Communists were trying to exploit misunderstandings and take advantage of areas of dissension and unrest in this country. He said, 'This is especially true in the intense civil rights movement, for America's twenty million Negroes and all others engaged in this struggle are a major target for Communist propaganda and subversion.' Well, okay, that's what is going on right now. Valetti and the Commies are trying to use the Turnerites for their own ends, and Hurley and the Turnerites are fanatic enough to accept anyone's help to achieve their goals."

Dilman stared at Kemmler. "You still haven't proved that the Turnerites are being financed with Communist funds."

"We have a dossier a mile high on Valetti, Mr. President. Here's an unskilled man, whose education ended with grammar school, banking a fantastic yearly income. From whom? From registered Communists, that's who. And no sooner does Valetti deposit this money than out it goes in big cash lumps. Where does it go? Do I have to spell it out? Our file is wide-open to you."

Dilman gripped the arms of his big green chair and heaved himself to his feet. He studied Kemmler a moment, and then left his desk, circling the office. He knew that the three of them were watching him, waiting for him to speak. He tried to think. Desperately he tried to sublimate his feelings as a Negro and coolly judge what he had heard and what was wanted from him, by applying his critical faculty as a onetime practicing attorney-at-law.

At last he faced them. "Gentlemen, this much I know now—I don't intend to do anything rash, anything I'll regret later. Ever since the stronger Subversive Activities Control Act has been in effect, there have been five hundred specific organizations posted for public notice on the Justice Department's questionable list. To my knowledge, not one has ever been prosecuted and disbanded under the act. Is that correct?"

"Well, yes, but that doesn't mean—" Kemmler began.

"It doesn't mean such banning can't be done or shouldn't be done," said Dilman. "When the safety of the country is at stake, and the enemy within is proved guilty, it will be done. I remind you, Mr. Attorney General, I've got a law degree, as you have, and I tell you I am not satisfied that we possess sufficient evidence to invoke the Subversive Control Act now against the Turnerites. Until I know beyond a shadow of doubt that Hurley and the Turnerites, as a group, are responsible for that kidnaping of Gage, and until I am certain that they are Communist-financed, I cannot restrict, ban, or dissolve them."

Kemmler was unable to conceal his dismay. "But, Mr. President—you've got to do something."

Dilman had started for his desk. "I intend to. I want to satisfy myself on one question. And then I will do something."

He dialed Edna Foster, and requested her to put through a call to the Reverend Paul Spinger at the Crispus Society Building. Standing, telephone in hand, he suggested that the others make themselves comfortable. Talley and Flannery retreated to the sofas, but Clay Kemmler refused to sit. He went to the French doors and glumly looked out at the south lawn.

In less than a minute, the Reverend Spinger's concerned voice greeted Dilman.

"Reverend," Dilman said into the mouthpiece, "have you heard what's happened down in Hattiesburg?"

"Yes, Mr. President, it's dreadful. Those irresponsible and ornery gangsters couldn't have done a greater disservice to our cause."

"I agree with you, Reverend. Now I'll tell you why I'm calling. I have here in the office with me the Attorney General, as well as Governor Talley, and Mr. Flannery. We've been discussing the abduction, and the possible repercussions it will have. We must be prepared to act. Reverend, do you consider the kidnaping as something done by an isolated bunch of hotheads or as something instigated by Hurley and his Turnerites?"

"Mr. President, I can't say. Certainly we have no information here, one way or the other."

"All right, you don't know." Dilman looked over his shoulder at Kemmler, whose back was still to him. "Reverend Spinger, we've touched upon this matter many times, but I have never put the question directly to you. Now I am going to do so, and do so officially." He could see Kemmler turning to catch every word. Dilman concentrated on the telephone. "Since many Crispus Society members left you to form the Turnerites, it is imperative that we know what ties you have, if any, with the Turnerites. I must—"

"None, Doug, you know that." Dilman could detect the fervent emotion in Spinger's voice, as the clergyman went on. "We disapprove of Hurley, his threats, his inciting activities, just as he and his group disapprove of us, of our adherence to legal procedure, our qualified support of the Minorities Rehabilitation Program, our—"

"Then, Reverend, you disavow any ties with the Turnerites. Two final questions. Has your organization now, or at any time, by any means, ever financed the Turnerites?"

"The answer, Doug, is an unequivocal no. Not now, not before, never."

"Never. Very well. Then the second question. Do you have any information as to who *is* financing Hurley's group?"

"I have no factual information, Mr. President," replied Spinger, more controlled. "There's been some hearsay—you know, Valetti, the—"

"I'm not interested in hearsay, Reverend." He paused, then asked, "Have you ever met Jefferson Hurley? Do you know him?"

"I've appeared on several speaking platforms with him, at one or two rallies, on a television show once, that's the extent of it."

"Does he have a fairly high regard for you, Reverend?"

Spinger grunted. "He thinks I'm a doddering and reactionary has-been who ought to have been interred long ago."

"I see," Dilman said. "Would Hurley speak to you if you requested a meeting?"

"I don't know why not . . . yes, I think he would."

"Very well, Reverend Spinger, I'll tell you what we're up to, here. When the news of the kidnaping gets out today, we expect an uproar, and considerable unrest and agitation. Based on some evidence in the hands of the Justice Department, I have been asked to outlaw the Turnerites—"

"Doug, don't do it, don't do it unless you are positive," Spinger pleaded with passion. "You have no idea how this might affect the Negro community. It might give the impression that you're in the hands of vindictive whites, that you've been whitewashed, so to speak. It would create a terrible reaction against you, your administration, and, worse, create automatic sympathy for Hurley and his Turnerites. Our people might look upon them as the persecuted underdogs, identify with them in a way they have not done up to now. Our people might begin to equate the Crispus Society with any repressive government action, and pull out on us, and—"

"Wait, Reverend, I haven't said I'm ready to disband the Turnerites. I've only said it is under consideration, until I have the facts, all the facts. You have as great a stake in ferreting out the truth as I have. I want you to do something for me, if you can."

"Anything, Mr. President. Whatever you say."

Dilman measured his words carefully. "Reverend Spinger, I am appointing you my official representative, the President's intermediary, to meet with Jefferson Hurley for a discussion of this whole affair." As he spoke, Dilman's eyes shifted from Kemmler's reaction of disgust, to Talley's expression of bewilderment, to Flannery's show of approval. He drew the mouthpiece closer to his lips. "Reverend, I want you to locate Hurley, and converse with him by phone, if you can't in person. I want you to find out, as best you can, whether the Turnerites are behind this crime or not. If he denies any part of the crime, as he has done already, I want you to tell him exactly what the Justice Department is considering doing. And I want you to tell him that if he wants to prove himself clean, and keep his organization intact, he must publicly condemn the Hattiesburg crime, and come forward to open his financial records for your eyes. If he will do this, I can promise him I will not enforce the Subversive Activities Control Act. If he refuses, I will promise nothing. Are you prepared to undertake the assignment, Reverend Spinger?"

"I am, Mr. President. When should I begin?"

"You begin this minute, and report your findings to me directly. Good luck, Reverend."

After he had hung up, he remained still, knowing the others were gathering before his desk.

Dilman lifted his head. "That's it for now, gentlemen."

Kemmler was doing a poor job of containing his displeasure. "You're making a mistake, Mr. President."

"You might be right," said Dilman. "I think it would be a greater mistake to act in haste."

Talley had sidled up alongside Kemmler. "Mr. President, I'm still inclined to agree with the Attorney General. Reconsider, please. The appointment of Spinger only delays the inevitable. It may make the administration appear weak and vacillating and——and even encourage more lawbreaking and violence——I mean, giving the Hurleys encouragement to go on and commit more crimes because we're reluctant to do anything but talk."

"I'll have to take the gamble, Governor." He looked

at Kemmler, who was still seething. "Give Spinger twenty-four hours," Dilman said in a conciliatory voice.

"Then give me twenty-four hundred more FBI agents," Kemmler snapped. "Okay, you do it your way, Mr. President. I'll be in my office, sitting on my hands. The responsibility for whatever this leads to is in yours."

Dilman suffered a sudden ache of abandonment and a sinking heart, as he watched the Attorney General stalk out of the Oval Office.

As he lowered himself into his swivel chair, he met Tim Flannery's questioning eyes. Dilman's fingers touched the loose-leaf folder. "I guess some revisions are in order for the press conference, Tim. What are they going to ask me *now*—and what am I supposed to say?"

After drawing up to the curb in his rented Ford, a block from the Capitol, Nat Abrahams kissed his wife, reminded her where to pick him up and when, and then relinquished the wheel of the car to her. He waited until she had safely driven off, then he walked to the stairs of the Capitol and slowly mounted them.

While he knew it troubled Sue that they had already been in Washington a month, and he missed the children as much as she did, he found that he was neither annoyed nor impatient over their protracted visit. More than ever, Washington was stimulating. The fact that he and Sue had enjoyed the opportunity to dine in the White House three times since his private reunion with Doug Dilman had made his stay doubly interesting. Of course, if his negotiations with Gorden Oliver continued at this snail's pace, he had promised Sue that she could go back to Chicago and the children this week. He was positive he would not be much behind her.

The half-dozen meetings with Gorden Oliver had been profitable. What had caused the delay was the fact that Oliver did not possess final authority to approve of Abrahams' demands and revisions. Whenever a contractual clause came under discussion, and Abrahams requested improvement of it, or clarification, Oliver would promise an immediate answer and then disappear for several days. It was clear to Abrahams that Oliver was consulting not only with the Eagles Industries Corporation crowd in Washington, but with Avery Emmich in Atlanta. Abrahams suspected that Oliver had even flown off to Eagles' main headquarters to meet with Emmich once or twice. Then Abrahams had read that Emmich had been out of the country last week, and that had explained the most recent delay. Despite this, Abrahams felt that his last meeting with Oliver might have concluded the preliminary give and take. He expected that the next time he saw Oliver, there would be copies of the contract ready for his approval. Then he would be able to take Sue home and help her wind up their affairs, before moving the family to Washington. In fact, he had encouraged Sue to occupy herself by looking for a roomy brownstone to lease in the city.

It was not Oliver's telephone call last night that had surprised him, but rather the fact that Oliver wanted to see him about a matter other than the contract.

"The contract is routine now, Nat," Gorden Oliver had said. "It's at the home office for final review and retyping. It should be here any day. You can assume you are now a representative of Eagles Industries. No, what I want to see you about, Nat, is not the contract——I'm as sick of it as you are, old boy——but something pertaining to your first duties here in Washington. I'll go into it when I see you tomorrow. Why don't you meet me in the private Speaker's Lobby of the House at noon? I'll leave your name with the Capitol police." Abrahams had accepted the invitation.

Now he found himself, as he had so many times in the years past but for the first time on this trip, standing before the elevator beneath the Capitol. When it arrived, he followed a woman and two men into it. In seconds, he was upstairs. He went past the sign MEMBERS ONLY to the swinging doors leading into the Speaker's Lobby, gave his name to the uniformed policeman, and was admitted. He reflected briefly on the power of a lobbyist like Oliver, who was able to get his friends and associates past that excluding sign so easily.

The long lobby, with its rich red carpet, contained
only a few visitors studying the Department of Commerce
weather map and the framed portraits on the walls of
former Speakers of the House, the one of MacPherson
still draped in black. None of the visitors was Gorden
Oliver.

Puzzled, Abrahams turned left and entered the Members' Reading Rooms that ran parallel with the lobby.
He saw a group huddled beneath the globular light fixtures, once picturesque gas jets, near the teletype machine. Gorden Oliver was not among them. Abrahams
inspected several members standing before the library
stands of newspapers, reading the front pages. For a moment Abrahams was diverted. These newspaper stands
fascinated him. There was an individual rack for each
state of the fifty in the Union, and every day upon these
racks were hung the newspapers from the leading cities
in that state. Abrahams paused before the stand with
the sign MISS. above it. Tilting his head, he cast his eyes
down the file of dangling newspapers from Greenville,
Columbus, Vicksburg, Meridian, Natchez, Hattiesburg,
Biloxi. The majority of the headlines were several days
old, and were devoted to Judge Gage's sentencing of the
Turnerite demonstrators, or to the debate of the Minorities Rehabilitation Program Bill in the House, or to the
announcement of Dilman's first State Dinner to entertain
a fellow black man from Africa. Before many days the
rack would carry the dated headlines screaming of
Judge Gage's abduction by Negro terrorists, and segregationists' vows of retaliation, which Washington newspapers had carried only an hour before.

Nat Abrahams continued through the Members' Read-
ing Rooms, but nowhere was Gorden Oliver to be seen.
He realized that a burly, blue-coated Capitol policeman
was observing him. He went over to the policeman. "I'm
Mr. Abrahams," he said. "I was to meet Mr. Gorden
Oliver here. Have you seen him around?"

"Oliver? Is he the columnist—?"

"No, he's—"

"I'm new on the force," the policeman apologized.
"Let me check with someone else."

As the officer left for the lobby, Abrahams thought that he heard a familiar voice. Even as he pivoted, he recognized it was Doug Dilman's voice, low and strained, competing with the hum of a television set. The small set was on a reading table, and several representatives had pulled up chairs and were watching and listening. Nat Abrahams came up behind them, to see how his friend was faring in his first press conference.

The picture projected on the screen, momentarily wavy, showed President Dilman seated at the mahogany Cabinet table, flanked by Flannery and Governor Talley. He had reached the last page of his prepared speech, and was reading the final news announcement: that he deplored the kidnaping of Judge Gage, that the FBI was on the trail of the terrorists, that there was no information yet as to whether the abduction was the work of individuals or an organization, that he had already appointed the Reverend Paul Spinger, head of the Crispus Society, as the President's personal representative, and that Spinger was to investigate the possible participation of any extremist organization in the crime, and to sort fact from rumor.

As the camera pulled back for a full shot, the battery of microphones before President Dilman was revealed, and then the forty to fifty journalists with their pencils and note pads pressed around the far side of the table, and the still photographers taking their pictures.

Dilman put down his prepared statement and looked up tightly. The distortion of the television screen made his Negroid features seem broader and blacker than they were.

Dilman said, in almost a whisper, "That completes the news announcements, gentlemen. Do you have any questions? Hold up your hands, and Mr. Flannery will recognize you in order."

Like marionettes' limbs jerked by strings, at least a dozen arms shot up and a dozen hands beckoned for recognition. Flannery acknowledged each with a nod, and scrawled the name of each on a sheet before him. Finishing his jotting, Flannery called out, "Mr. Blaser, of the Washington *Citizen-American* and Miller Newspaper Association."

Nat Abrahams searched the mass of reporters on the television screen, and then could make out a short, stocky middle-aged man with a high pompadour and an unattractive carbuncle of a face—"I don't mind most of those reporters," Dilman had told Abrahams at their last dinner, "but that Reb Blaser is like a toad in a flower bed." Blaser was elbowing through the crowd of reporters to get closer to the table.

"Mr. President," Blaser began, his wheedling, oiled tongue seeking to cover his renowned cantankerous, liverish manner, "about your announcement of that dastardly Turnerite kidnaping in Mississippi—"

To Abrahams' surprise, Dilman leaned forward and interrupted. "Mr. Blaser, I did not announce that the kidnaping was done by any organization. I believe I made that point clear. We can make no accusations until our investigation is completed."

Blaser was smiling regretfully. "I beg your pardon, Mr. President. I assume—you see, our papers have information that the act was performed by a parcel of Turnerites—"

"Then you should turn your information over to the Department of Justice," said Dilman grimly. "If it's not fiction, they'll welcome it."

There was some laughter, but, viewing the exchange on the television screen, Nat Abrahams squirmed. Dilman was allowing himself to be baited. He was not standing aloof. Abrahams told himself that he must speak to Doug about this.

Framed in a close-up on the television screen, Blaser's face had lost its unctuous smile. "I'm fixing to have my editors follow your advice, Mr. President. Meanwhile, I would like to inquire what you instructed Reverend Spinger to find out about, in relation to this dastardly kidnaping. Also, how do you expect to get objective facts from the head of a Negro lobby pressure group, who goes into this with well-known prejudices?"

The camera cut back to Dilman's face, and Abrahams

was relieved that it was outwardly passive and that he was considering his reply carefully.

"I appointed the Reverend Spinger," Dilman said, "because I felt that the kidnapers, if they are Negro, be they individuals or members of an organization, would trust him more than anyone else. I believe the Reverend Spinger is the best-qualified person I know to reason with anyone so involved, and to gain their confidence. As to his exact assignment, I think it would be unwise to disclose what I have ordered him to do, especially at a critical time like this. When the Attorney General and I have the facts, we shall act upon them without hesitation. . . . Next?"

Flannery called out, "Mr. Paletta of *U.S. News and World Report.*"

"Mr. President, concerning the New Succession Bill now on your desk. Do you expect to approve it or veto it?"

Nat Abrahams felt someone touch his arm, and spun around. It was the burly young policeman again. "Sir, I'm sorry about keeping you, but I found out that Mr. Oliver did leave a message. He's across the Chamber in the House Majority cloakroom. He said for you to meet him there. Will you follow me?"

Reluctantly Abrahams turned his back on Doug Dilman's excruciating ordeal by press, and followed the policeman out of the Reading Rooms and lobby, past the elevator, through the library, and into the rear of the mammoth House of Representatives Chamber.

Treading as silently as possible behind the last row of leather-covered benches, Abrahams could see that the House of Representatives was about two-thirds filled with members, some slouched and listening to Congressman Hightower's speech, others gathered in knotted groups whispering together, and still others reading the daily *Congressional Record* they had found in the compartments under their seats.

Abrahams knew that the Minorities Rehabilitation Program Bill was in its climactic stages of debate. Congressman Hightower, representing the opposition party from a California district, was vigorously endorsing the

seven-billion-dollar public-works bill, and especially the
apprentice and job-training provisions designed for un-
educated and unskilled Negroes, Puerto Ricans, and
Americans of Mexican descent.

"When we have passage of this bill," the Congressman
was promising, "we won't have repetitions of the sort of
violence we saw in Hattiesburg, Mississippi, today. Our
minority citizens will enjoy a law of restitution to make
up for their educational and financial losses under slavery, under segregation, under bondage. They will be
trained. They will be gainfully employed. They will be
indemnified for their long history of inequality. Thus
satisfied, they will know peace of mind, and we will all
know the peace of harmony that comes with justice and
economic improvement."

They are slugging the big bill through, Abrahams
thought, and in two weeks, less perhaps, it will be on
Doug Dilman's desk. Poor Doug, he thought, how much
these elected politicians are throwing at him, and how
little time he has had to prepare for the deluge of vital
legislation. Still, Abrahams thought, if Doug's only going
to get T.C.'s hat, he has no decisions to make. If he
were going to fit a hat for himself, one of his own, that
would be another matter. A pity, Abrahams thought, for
if Doug Dilman remains as subservient to a ghost as he
insists that he must be, his own keen intelligence and
fine judgment will be wasted and the nation will never
know its loss.

Abrahams looked up at the press gallery above the
Speaker's rostrum, and then at the curved mezzanine of
public galleries, almost filled, and he knew that the minorities bill had captured the national interest. It was
the most crucial domestic legislation in years.

The policeman had halted, waiting for Abrahams, and
then said, "Right through this door, sir." Abrahams
thanked him, took hold of the doorknob, realizing that
while he had been inside the House Chamber many
times, he had never visited the legendary cloakrooms,
where national decisions were supposed to be made by
horse trading in secrecy.

He entered the Party's cloakroom, not knowing what

to expect and yet finding less than he had supposed he would find. The cloakroom was narrow and dimly lighted. There were a half-dozen soft sofas along the walls, about the same number of deep used leather armchairs, then the room stretched off behind the House and turned a corner. At the far end three men were assembled before a semicircular bar. Only when Abrahams approached them closer did he see that it was an innocuous ice cream and soft drink counter, with many telephone booths nearby.

He recognized Gorden Oliver, even though the Eagles lobbyist had his back to him. Identification was possible from Oliver's distinctive high starched collar, navy-blue wool sport coat, gray flannel slacks, and brown metal brandy-flask cane (his trademark).

"Gorden—"

Oliver wheeled around at once, and when he did so, Abrahams could see that the Eagles lobbyist and the two others beside him were watching Dilman's press conference on a television set.

"Hello, hello, Nat. I was beginning to worry whether you'd find the way." Oliver pumped his hand, and then took him in tow. "Nat, I want you to meet two of our most influential House members—Representative Stockton, of Colorado, Representative Kramer, of West Virginia. . . . Gentlemen, this is Nathan Abrahams, Eagles' answer to Rufus Choate."

After the handshaking, Representative Kramer said, "Gorden here tells us you are a personal friend of the President, Mr. Abrahams."

Embarrassed, Abrahams said, "Yes, the President and I have known each other since the Second World War. We were in the Judge Advocate's Department together."

Representative Kramer assumed a dour visage. "Well, if Dilman got out of the service uninjured, then he's certainly earning a Purple Heart today. They've been grenading him for twenty minutes."

Abrahams' eyes went to the television screen, to Dilman's worn expression as he listened to one more question. "Most people haven't had a chance to find out yet, but President Dilman is very sharp," Abrahams said loyally. "I saw some of the press conference on my way in. I think he can handle them. When you've made it all the way up to Congress as a Negro, you've been through worse inquisitions. He'll survive."

"We didn't mean he won't," Oliver said hastily. "It's simply that this is his first time out, and they've mined every inch of it with dynamite. You should have—"

"Quiet, Gorden," Representative Stockton interrupted. He pointed to the television set. "The *Time-Life* man just asked him about the minorities bill."

The four men directed their attention to the close shot of Dilman, gnawing his lower lip, fingering the blotter in front of him. "You want to know why I have not spoken out in favor of the Minorities Rehabilitation Program?" he was saying. "In reply, I remind you I have spoken neither for it nor against it. I have been examining the bill. It has much to offer minorities in this country, and can make a great contribution to bolstering our economy. At the same time, I think it would be a mistake to regard this bill as the cure-all for the civil rights problem. The bill may alleviate certain pressures brought down on minority segments of our population. Still, whether it passes into law or not, it must be supplemented by continued and unceasing efforts to secure for each and every citizen those equal rights guaranteed by our Constitution. I am closely watching the debate over the bill in Congress, and await seeing in what form it reaches me for signature."

Gorden Oliver dug an elbow into Abrahams' rib. "Cagey, Nat. Your friend is playing it cool and cagey."

For an instant Abrahams was irritated, but he contained himself and kept his eyes on the screen, where Flannery had nodded to someone off scene. On cue, the correspondent from United Press International called out, "Thank you, Mr. President," and the first press conference was over. As the picture on the screen dissolved to one of the Presidential seal, Representative Stockton turned the set off.

The Colorado Congressman addressed Abrahams. "Mr. Abrahams, since you know our new President personally, you might do well to inform him for us—since nobody else seems to be able to get to him—that we hope he doesn't drag his feet on this bill or on putting that Baraza President in his place. Tell him that's what the boys in the back room are saying."

"You tell him yourself," said Abrahams stiffly. "I'm afraid I have no influence over the President."

Gorden Oliver emitted a false, cackling laugh. "Aw, Nat, don't take it so seriously. None of us are worried about Dilman. He's pledged himself to the Party platform and T.C.'s policies. We know he'll deliver. . . . Say now, Nat, you've never been in this sacred sanctum before, have you? Well, have a gander down there, past those fourteen phone booths, and what do you see? A stretcher, yes, sir, and a first-aid kit. Know what? After those Puerto Ricans began holding target practice from the House gallery in 1954, wounded five of our members, the boys here became scared it might encourage more open-season hunting. Now they're prepared. . . . What say we have our lunch? I'm starved. I've a table reserved at the Hotel Congressional down the way. . . . See you later, boys. I'll tell Emmich you're reading his breakdown."

Gorden Oliver led Abrahams out of the cloakroom, through the rear of the House Chamber, still resounding to oratory on the Minorities Rehabilitation Bill, past Room H-209, which he pointed out to be the Speaker's quarters, past the House Reception Room, and then downstairs.

They came out into the east front of the Capitol and started in the cold sunshine of midday toward the Hotel Congressional.

"It's only a couple of blocks," said Oliver.

But the few blocks, Abrahams soon realized, would take as long to traverse as a mile. Gorden Oliver knew everyone, and everyone knew him. It was not enough for him to greet each acquaintance with a wag of his metal brandy-filled cane. Each person met—a photographer for the Republican Party, a public relations man for the Democratic Committee, three Capitol policemen, two senators, four young giggling female secretaries going to lunch—was stopped, introduced to Abrahams, regaled

with a warmed-over joke or bit of innocuous gossip, before being passed.

There was neither business nor political conversation
between Oliver and Abrahams as they walked. The
lobbyist's eyes were scanning the pedestrians for more
acquaintances, while he filled Abrahams with petty chatter about Washington and calumny about congressmen,
past and present. According to Oliver, there was one congressman and his wife who, to save money, had set up
and maintained living quarters in a corner of the House
basement, until they were discovered and evicted. There
was another who, to make ends meet, sold ready-made
suits at a discount out of his office. There was a third
who had enjoyed a reputation for hard work by staying
on in his suite in the Rayburn House Office Building long
after his colleagues had gone home, until it was discovered that he was using his suite to entertain call girls.

"Yet the work of government gets done," said Oliver,
as they crossed the street and entered the modest lobby
of the Hotel Congressional. He halted, after waving his
cane at the desk clerk and at two congressmen who had
entered behind them, and he added, "I only wanted to
show you, Nat, that you won't be dealing with sacred
cows but with plain, ordinary human beings, possessing
their share of mortals' frailties." He poked his cane toward a sign to the right of the lobby, indicating the direction to the Caucus Room and the Filibuster Bar.
"Caucus over food, Nat, or filibuster over drinks first?"

Abrahams held up his vest-pocket watch. "Sue's
picking me up here in an hour," he said. "She wants to
show me some houses she's been—"

"Food it'll be," said Oliver.

Abrahams allowed the lobbyist to take his arm and
guide him through a corridor, decorated on one side with
framed photographs of the current members of Congress.
They entered the spacious dining room, already nearly
filled, and were shown to a reserved table next to the
curved window overlooking the hotel's lawn and garden.

As they were seated and given their menus, Oliver
winked at Abrahams and said, "Best table in the room,
Nat. Eagles Industries rates here, and so will you. Con-

gressmen come and go, but Eagles stays on forever. . . . What'll you have?" He began recommending dishes, but Abrahams ordered only a small green salad and a mushroom omelet. Automatically Oliver ordered a steak. "We're on an expense account, you know, Nat," he reminded Abrahams.

"I'm on a diet," Abrahams replied. "I'm at my best when I'm lean and hungry."

"Good, good—" the lobbyist said absently, his attention again diverted by his recognition of familiar faces. He began to salute diners at other tables, calling out, "Hi, Mike. . . . How you doing, Jim fellow? . . . Hello, Ruthie girl." Then he excused himself, and for five minutes, cane in hand, he went table-hopping, ending each visit with an uproarious peal of laughter.

When he returned to Abrahams, who was eating his salad, he offered only an oblique excuse for his absence. "My trade consists of contacts," he explained, "making them and maintaining them."

"I'm not good at that, Gorden."

"You?" said Oliver, with pretended horror. "We can't waste a genius like yours on this sort of Rotary-Kiwanis activity. My rounds are the National Press Club, Burning Tree Golf Club, Metropolitan Club, and right here. That's for me, not you. Avery Emmich wouldn't be paying you what he is paying you—hell, my salary is picayune tip money beside what you're going to get— for public relations. He's hiring your brain, Nat, not your glad hand."

"As long as that's understood, that's all," said Abrahams.

The lunch proceeded into the entrée, and Oliver spoke less and became preoccupied with his own thoughts. Abrahams searched the Caucus Room, trying to match faces to headlines he remembered, and then, finishing the omelet, he stared up at the rough yellow-and-white textured plaster ceiling and speculated on the reason for this lunch.

While the lobbyist was drinking his Sanka, Abrahams sipped his hot tea and decided to make certain that the meeting had nothing to do with the contract.

"Gorden, last night you said you wanted to see me about my first duties here in Washington, not about the contract. Are you sure?"

Oliver's ruddy, weather-beaten Vermont countenance immediately offered an open expression of distress that his motive should even be questioned. "Nat, I told you, the contract is routine. It'll be in final draft shortly. The delay has been caused by Emmich's visit to Dallas for a speech before the National Association of Manufacturers."

"Well, I'd like to be able to send Sue home and let her close up shop."

"Send her, by all means, send her. But you'd better hang around here for the final reading of the contract and the signing. After that's done, you can get back to Chicago for a week and turn over your keys."

Glancing off, Abrahams caught the time on the wall clock. "Okay, Gorden. Then what did you want to discuss with me? I've only got fifteen minutes."

Oliver blew across the rim of his cup, drank the Sanka, and then set the cup down. "Nat," he said, "you heard the little speech Congressman Stockton made to you in the cloakroom."

"About what? You mean the President dragging his feet on the minorities bill and Baraza? I sure did."

"Well, I think he was really concerned about the minorities bill. That's a big thing. Nobody gives much of a damn about that little African football field."

"Soviet Russia does," said Abrahams.

Oliver took his cane, which had been leaning against the table, and began unscrewing the top. "Oh, you know what I mean. The minorities bill is the thing that counts right now for the boys on the Hill. A wrong move can lose a lot of votes back home. That's what matters to them." He paused. "I know that Stockton got your dander up a bit, but he means well. He was only trying to tell you how the majority of both parties in the House feel."

"Why tell me?" said Abrahams.

"Because he heard you knew the President and—" Then, as if to prevent Abrahams from interrupting him,

Oliver went on more urgently, in a rush, "Look, Nat, listen, the boys on the Hill—forget the Southern bloc —the others, they're not too worried about Douglass Dilman. He's behaved well. He's made it clear he's standing on the Party platform and listening to T.C.'s best minds. Only one curious fact gives them pause. The single major legislation the President has made no private or public commitment on is this minorities bill, the very bill he should be behind hot and heavy. It's the only pacifier we have to stop the racial unrest in this country. Once it is law, all rioting and demonstrations will cease. No more repetitions of what happened down in Mississippi today. The Negroes will be too occupied and prosperous to complain. We'll have solidarity." He considered Abrahams a moment, and then he asked, "Have you read the MRP Bill yet?"

"No," Abrahams answered flatly. He felt vaguely irritated again and put upon. He had guessed, at once, what Gorden Oliver was leading up to, and he wanted to make it difficult for him. "No," he repeated, "I haven't. Should I?"

Oliver screwed the top of his brandy cane tightly, and leaned it against the table once more. "Only because it is a vital piece of public works legislation, and a great part of your job for Eagles Industries will be to advise Emmich on any new bills affecting his interests."

Abrahams was more determined than ever to be difficult. He forced his eyebrows upward, ingenuously. "Is the minorities bill of that much concern to Emmich?"

Now it was Oliver who was irritated and trying to control his feelings. "Really, Nat, you must know what passage of this bill can mean to Eagles. There's a seven-billion-dollar—*billion,* mind you—Federal pie to be cut up among private industry. Eagles wants its share, and is ready to underbid all competition. And Eagles can do the job. We're strong in the South, strongest there, where much of the money will be spent. We have the know-how and equipment to build those new vocational trade schools, those highways, those housing tracts, those factories. Sure we're concerned, damn concerned. Nothing is more important to Emmich right now. I thought you knew that."

Abrahams was suddenly impatient with games. "I suppose I did know it. I guess I was leading you on a little, Gorden. I wanted to find out how involved you were in this legislation."

"Then you have read the bill?"

"No, really, I have not. I know what it is about, generally, but I haven't read it. I didn't think I was on the payroll yet."

"Well, you are, in a way you are."

"Then I'll get a copy."

"You won't have to." Oliver patted his chest complacently. "I brought a copy for you."

"So reading pending legislation is one of my first duties here," said Abrahams. "Assignment one is the MRP, is that right? Okay. What am I to do after I've read it? Tell Emmich I think it's great? He knows that. Tell him I think it won't help him very much? He doesn't want to hear that. Tell him what, Gorden?"

"You have to tell him nothing," said Oliver uneasily. "He wants passage of the bill—of course. I think he'd like to know that you want it, too."

Abrahams could feel the involuntary tension in the cords of his neck. "What's the difference whether I want it or not?"

"Nat, you're being tough on me." Oliver was frowning down at the cane. He took it, laid it across his lap, and turned it several times before looking up. "Christ, we're on the same team. We're getting money from the same mint. We have our jobs to do."

"I only want to know my job, I suppose."

Oliver appraised Abrahams with a quick glance. "Harv Wickland, the Majority Leader, feels the Party can push the bill through the House. It'll be landing on President Dilman's desk any day. Dilman is the one worrying Emmich, all of us. He's the only unknown factor."

"You heard him say that he wants to read the bill in its final form."

"Come now, Nat, there won't be many late changes. It's in the open for everyone to read. Dilman has had plenty of time to read it and make up his mind. Really, Emmich is deeply concerned. He feels what Dilman does here is the test of him as the new President."

"You mean the test of him in the eyes of Eagles Industries."

"Well, whether he is for us or against us."

Abrahams found himself appalled at this constricted, selfish vision of a piece of legislation which carried with it so many broader ramifications. "Perhaps Dilman feels there is more at stake than whether this is good or bad for big business."

"I don't know," Oliver said. Then he added quickly, "Maybe you happen to know. Has President Dilman— after all, everyone is aware you've been in the White House with him pretty often—has he ever mentioned how he honestly feels about MRP? That could tell us a good deal. Emmich would be very grateful if he could get some inkling of—"

"Gorden, I don't know whether the President is for or against that bill, but even if I knew, even if he had discussed it with me, I wouldn't tell you about it. I've been visiting with him as an old friend, not a lawyer-lobbyist for Eagles Industries."

"Touché," said Oliver, with a twisted smile. "I'm nicked and I deserve it. But I've got *my* job, too, you know."

Abrahams crumpled his napkin and threw it on the table. He pushed back his chair. "Gorden, I know what you've been trying to get at. The MRP is an Eagles Industries type of bill. You want to be sure that, once it has passed both Houses, the President approves it. You'd like me to go to him right now and find out if he's intending to sign it. If he does, you'd like to know first, so you'd have the jump on your competitors when it comes to submitting bids. If he's on the fence or negative, you'd like me to use my influence on your—okay, our —on our behalf. That's the sum of it, of this lunch, isn't it?"

Gorden Oliver almost beamed with relief. But then, aware of Abrahams' taut face, he converted his smile to an appearance of moderate seriousness. His caution was obvious. "If you think Avery Emmich and I are asking you, as your first job for us, to go in and use your friendship with the President to make Eagles a few millions, you are mistaken. We're not such fools, and we don't favor using such tactics. No, that's not it. All we want you to do is to study the MRP Bill, and then study a little homework we at Eagles have done on the bill, a sort of breakdown on its value to our economy and—and to domestic peace—" He reached inside his suit coat, and drew out one bulky document and one folded memorandum. He handed the bulky document across the table. "There's the text of the MRP."

Abrahams opened it, and read the heading: *"Be it enacted by the Senate and House of Representatives of the United States of America in Congress assembled—* Section 1. This Act may be cited as the 'Minorities Rehabilitation Program.'"* He carefully folded it. "Okay," he said quietly.

"And this is a concise breakdown and memorandum of the high points of the bill," said Oliver, handing over the other folded pages. "Anyone who reads this will know in five minutes how this five-year works program will help the Negroes, all minorities, economically, socially, educationally, improve and integrate them, to the best interests of the majority white community as well. It may be brief, but it is thorough, Nat. You'll see how this bill can be helpful to every one of the fifty states, naming names, facts, figures. It's irresistible."

Accepting this document, too, Abrahams shoved both in his pocket. "I'll read them. Then what?"

"If you approve—I think you will, most everyone has, except for a handful of left-wingers and right extremists —I wish you'd tell us so. Then, if it comes up, only if it comes up, you understand, I wish you'd let President Dilman know how you feel. That would be natural. But, Nat, even if you find it awkward, then—well, at least ask him to have a look at our patriotic little breakdown of the facts and figures. He might find it an eye-opener, if he needs one. I suspect he's on our side, anyway. . . . Don't promise me anything, Nat. I just want to be able to tell Avery Emmich you are studying this, and will do what you believe is right and best for the country."

"For the country," Abrahams murmured, rising quickly. "I'll be in touch with you, Gorden. Thanks for the feed."

Departing from the Caucus Room, Abrahams could see Oliver's worried face pretending to study the restaurant bill as, out of the corner of one eye, he watched his guest and tried to gauge his feelings.

Going up the corridor, Nat Abrahams' feelings were red with anger, not at the idiot lobbyist's effort to use him to coerce the Chief Executive of the land, who happened to be a friend, but at himself for having allowed himself, for the first time in his entire life, to be put in a position that might compromise his honesty as a responsible human being.

By the time he had left the Hotel Congressional and crossed over to the corner before the Old House Office Building where Sue was to pick him up, his anger had subsided. The bright cool air was not only refreshing but prickly, stinging to life his numbed sense of reality.

His abiding human fault, Abrahams had come to realize, was that he constantly clung to the saber of romanticism. This satisfied his ego and conscience, but it had provided him with a poor weapon in a progressive, mechanized age, a weapon shown to be inadequate for the protection of his wife, his children, his weakened heart. He had known from the start of the Eagles negotiations that he could not slay dragons with obsolete sabers and broadswords to rescue his family and save himself. This was a new world out here, and to get by the dragons you did not blindly slash at them—they were too big, too many, and you were too small, too ill-armed —instead, you reasoned with them, you compromised, you gave something so that they would give, too. What was it that wise old Edmund Burke had said? That all government, almost every human benefit and enjoyment, almost every virtue and prudent act, was founded on compromise and barter. As his own grandfather used to say, holding him on one bony knee, his grandfather licking his saliva and croaking, "Boychick, you bend some-

times so maybe you won't break." Or, Abrahams now
thought, so you won't break others with you when you
fall.

He searched for his mottled briar pipe, filled it with
tobacco from the rubbed pouch, and lit it. He had taken
no more than one puff when the rented Ford blocked
his vision and Sue was framed in the car window, her
left hand hitting the horn.

He climbed inside, kissed her cheek, and the Ford
jolted forward. He asked her what she had been doing
and where they were going, and she began to tell him,
but he hardly listened. If you must bend, he thought, how
far do you bend?

As the car turned a corner, and he was forced against
her, he realized that she had become silent and was trying to study him as she drove.

"What's the matter, Nat?" she asked.

"Matter? What makes you think—?"

"You haven't heard a word I've said. You've been a
million miles away."

He tried to smile. "Only a few blocks away, in the
Hotel Congressional with Gorden Oliver, errand boy between Mephistopheles in Atlanta and Nat Faust right
here."

"So that's the way it is," said Sue. "Tell me. Don't
leave out a thing."

She drove, and he talked. He told her what Oliver
had wanted, and how he himself had reacted, as much
as he could remember of it in a ten-minute monologue.
When he was done, he turned his head. Her pretty face,
still unlined except at the brow, was pointed straight
ahead at the windshield, wifely grave.

"That's it, Sue," he said. "Beneath all the verbiage it
comes to this, a command from on high—go in there
and influence Doug Dilman, no matter what he believes,
to approve the minorities bill. Persuade him, get him to
sign it, and you've earned your salary from Emmich
and big business."

"Gorden Oliver didn't tell you to do that in so many
words."

"He told me without the words."

She continued watching the street before them. "Nat, maybe you've got your hackles up for no reason at all. You are simply assuming that whatever is good for Eagles Industries is bad for the country, for Dilman, for yourself, and you are against it. Can't it be that what they want might also be what everyone else wants and needs?"

"We-ll—could be."

"The odds are Doug Dilman likes most of the bill and will sign it. He hasn't told you he won't, has he?"

"No, he hasn't."

"I read the papers too, and from what I have read, almost the entire press and the political organizations and Congress seem to be behind this legislation."

"That doesn't make it right."

Sue glanced at him. "That doesn't make it wrong either, darling. I think you're misplacing your hostility. You feel guilty about leaving your practice, abandoning your underdogs, making so much money in a short time. You feel ashamed, and so you're taking it out on Eagles and Emmich and Oliver and anything they propose. Nat, you're smarter than that. Study all that stuff in your pocket objectively, like you study a legal brief. Then decide how you feel. If MRP is a sensible compromise program, speak up for it. And there's nothing wrong in telling Doug you're for it, whether he's President or not. He may welcome discussing it with you. If you don't like it, shut up."

She took her right hand from the steering wheel and covered her husband's hand. "Nat, maybe it *is* good for the country. Don't be like some angry kid who has to be against everything his elders are for, to show he's a man. You are a man, the best and most wonderful one on earth. You are a man who can still serve himself and the public while protecting his own life and his children. Don Quixote wasn't for real, darling, but you are. No more dragons, either. Freud scared them away. And all that is left are human problems to be solved by human beings like yourself in a mature way. I know you'll handle this and the next three years that way."

Her literary allusion, so exactly and uncannily reflec-

tive of his own on the street corner earlier, swept aside
the last vestige of his anger. Wives, he thought, wonderful wives who grow your minds as you grow theirs, until
you and they are one and the same till death do you
part. He was amused by her and loved her, for herself
and for the better part of him that she possessed, and
he wanted to hug her and hold her close to him and
enjoy her.

Instead, he leaned over and kissed the corner of her
mouth. She seemed startled, and wary, and then pleased.

"Mmm," she whispered, "nice, even if I did almost
hit that truck." Then she said, "What brought on that
affection?"

He continued to smile at her. She would never know
what had moved him. Nor did it matter. He could only
say, "Because you make good speeches, and you are sensible, and you think I am a man, and I love you. I'll
always love you."

He settled back, at ease at last, lighted his pipe again,
and felt strong enough to bend a little, a little, if it would
be necessary.

When Otto Beggs caught sight of the broken, un-
lighted neon sign jutting out from the Walk Inn a long
block away, he automatically slowed down. For the second time in a week he had lied to Gertrude about his
hours, to get away from home early, and for the second
time in a week he was deliberately timing his arrival at
the tavern because he knew that Ruby Thomas would
be there, and suddenly he felt furtive and uneasy about
what had previously come about so naturally—well, almost.

Except for those times in Korea, which did not count
because he was in the Army and in danger and the tiny,
submissive girls were foreigners, and except for four or
five times on special assignment trips around the country,
which did not count because he had been drinking in his
off hours and the women were prostitutes, not women,
Otto Beggs had never been unfaithful to his wife. He was
prim and correct about living up to the responsibilities

of a husband and a father, and about remembering the obligations of his position in the Secret Service, and especially the extra obligations thrust upon him as a Congressional Medal of Honor holder, and he would do nothing to sully his reputation. He looked down, with an attitude of superiority (and a tinge of envy), upon those of his colleagues who cheated on their wives, proud that there was as little likelihood that a scandal would find its way into his scrapbooks as there was that Tom Swift would accept a bribe or that an astronaut would beat his wife.

Yet what had made Otto Beggs feel furtive this time, for the first time, was not the lie to Gertrude (he had already lied to her two days ago), not the fact that he had told Ruby Thomas he would be there (he had been there with her three times before), but that he had lain awake several hours last night enacting a fantasy relationship with her. Even worse, late this morning, and again after lunch, with Austin's lousy real estate primers open on the desk, he had been unable to study a line because Ruby had sat on the pages before him, Ruby dressed (which was like any other woman undressed), Ruby naked (which was like no sight on earth, he imagined), Ruby opening her arms to him (which had excited him as much as if he were a schoolboy).

It was this sudden obsession with her, and the realization that she might not be averse to fulfilling his dreams, that gave today's meeting a special significance, and gave him pause in his advance toward the Walk Inn, where she waited. For now this was no more, at least to him, a casual meeting between chance acquaintances. It was something strange to him: an assignation. It was the kind of surreptitious activity of which he disapproved as being indecent, almost un-American, and yet it moved him like a force powerful enough to overwhelm his puritan will and fear of danger. Much as his mind resisted it, his body had become a partner to this rendezvous with Ruby. For in a life of disillusionment, where he was being ignored on a job he loved, being degraded into studying for a new and anonymous and sedentary career he detested, being disapproved of by those closest to him,

being made less and less a virile male of action, there
was one radiant light of hope. Ruby. It was Ruby who
admired his looks, his position, his dreams. Ruby, who
was young, magnificent, passionate (he was sure). It
did not surprise him that he could not resist her. What
did astound him was that the one radiant light of hope in
his life, in this gray time, should shine from one so
black. For Ruby Thomas, twenty-four, was a Negro.

He had progressed halfway up the block, and the neon
in front of the Walk Inn loomed larger and more distinctly against the silver-gray midafternoon sky. His reluctant stride shortened, for he wanted added time to
think, to decide if he was plumb crazy or plain lucky, to
determine whether the lie he had told Gertrude a second
time in three days was worth the risk.

Almost two weeks ago—an afternoon such as this one,
he remembered—he had pulled the battered Nash
Rambler up before the Walk Inn before continuing to
work, because he was out of cigarettes. Once inside the
dim interior of the saloon, reviving his resentment against
the shiftless colored boys who had appropriated his
place at the pinball machines, he had gone to the horseshoe bar for his cigarettes. Then, realizing that he was
thirsty, he had lifted himself up on a stool and asked
Simon, the former pugilist now a bartender, for a root
beer in a frosted stein.

As the soft drink had been placed before him, Ruby
Thomas had set herself on the stool beside him. She had
made him-conscious of her presence by pointing at his
root beer and telling Simon, "That sho' looks yum—I'll
have some of the same, but git me a J an' B on the
rocks on the side." Immediately, two facts had made
themselves clear to Otto Beggs: one, that this was the
prettiest Negro girl he had ever seen; two, that despite
her reserve she must be interested in him, for most of the
stools at the bar were unoccupied, and yet she had deliberately and boldly chosen to sit beside him.

At first he had tried to ignore her, for fear that she
was a streetwalker. This concern was quickly dispelled
by her appearance and manner. She was attired in a
crisp white uniform—he would learn she was a dental

assistant, only recently moved into the neighborhood—
and there was a fresh, unused look about her and a self-
contained air of minding her own business.

Against his will, without being too obvious, he had inspected her several times from head to toe. She sat
erectly on the stool, one leg crossed over the other, exposing a knee and shapely calf. She was, his thumping
heart told him, breathtaking. Not since he had enjoyed
and suffered through a long-distance crush on the singer
Lena Horne, way back when he was a sophomore at
Oregon State University, had he known a colored girl to
attract him so instantly and engage him so totally. This
one had tousled gamin hair, silken, brunette, sort of
French, and widely spaced, large almond eyes, a short
cute nose, and pouting lower lip. He guessed that she
was no more than five feet two, and he thought it therefore remarkable how firm and large her breasts were beneath the white uniform, and how broad her thighs were
against the tightened skirt. And she was black, although
it kept amazing him how her color enhanced rather than
detracted from her prettiness.

She had not spoken, and he had not spoken, that
first time, until he had emptied his stein and was sorting
his change. Suddenly she had turned to him and said, "I'm
guessin' who you are—Lordy, I kin tell—y'all the famous
Mr. Beggs, the Secret Service hero." He had flushed with
pleasure and pride, and mumbled that he was no hero
at all but that yes, he was Otto Beggs and he was a
Secret Service agent. He had wondered how she knew.
She had told him that everyone in the neighborhood
knew—Lordy, he was the big celebrity in the neighborhood—and that he had been pointed out to her last week.
She had been apologetic about intruding upon his privacy—"I knows you must git mighty tired of bein' a celebrity"—but she wanted to brag to the girls in the office
that she had met him. He had asked her name, and she
had told him, and had told him where she worked, and
he had said that he hoped to see her around, and he
had fled (alive and young as that young one) into the
brightening street.

That had been the first time, and that had been last

week. The second time had been a few days later, again
on his way to work, and this time she had been sitting at
the bar, and he had summoned up the nerve to sit beside her, making some kind of joke to which she had responded with delightful laughter. They had talked inces-
santly, for twenty minutes maybe, this second time, until
she had to leave to return to her dentist and his drills.

For five successive days after that, he had come into
the Walk Inn in search of Ruby Thomas, and she had
not been there. At last, casually, he had inquired of
Simon what had become of her, and Simon had explained
that she had to take her coffee break earlier now, that
she was usually in at three o'clock instead of three forty-
five. And so two days ago, motivated by this intelligence,
Otto Beggs had contrived his first small lie for Gertrude.
His shift at the White House began at four o'clock, and
he had been leaving for work as late as twenty-five or
even twenty minutes to four. At lunch he had told Gertrude that his new shift began at three o'clock, an hour
earlier, and he would be leaving around twenty minutes
to three. Gertrude had thought nothing of it, except to
worry that he would have an hour less to bone up for
his real estate examinations. He had promised her that
he would make up the lost reading time at night.

Thus two days ago, he had driven to the Walk Inn
and found Ruby at the bar, as he had known that he
would, and had sat beside her and enjoyed an entire
half hour with her. By the end of this meeting, the best
there had been yet, he had learned a good deal about
Ruby Thomas. She had lived in Louisiana and Indiana,
and was an only child. She had managed to have one
year of high school before being forced to quit and help
support her family. She had wanted to be educated,
though, and had saved up for mail-order courses, and
tried to take one a year. She had been a photographer's
model—"but when them white boys kept wantin' me to
pose in the way it ain't fittin' to be seen, in my altogether, I sorta got it in my cottonpickin' haid they was
wantin' more than pitchers an' I told them where to go"
—and so she had quit. She had been quick to assure
Beggs that she was no prude—"I got as much lovin'

naycher in my bones as any no'mal gals"—but she did
not believe in mixing business with pleasure.

She had seen an advertisement in *Ebony* magazine,
and enrolled in a mail-order course that would graduate
her as a dental assistant. Her diploma, she had learned
later, had not been enough to make her a qualified dental assistant, but only a sort of assistant to an assistant,
as well as a receptionist, file clerk, telephone operator,
and jane-of-all-trades. She had held three such jobs already, including the new one, and she liked working for
dentists because they were on their feet so much during
the day, they were too tired to chase her at night. She
ate lunch in the office, in order to get this daily midafternoon break, which she found picked her up when
she most needed it and left her refreshed for the evening.
She had located a pleasant, inexpensive double apartment a block from the Walk Inn, a furnished apartment
with a private entrance, which was important to her because she liked her own business to be her own. Her
only extravagance was a recently acquired hi-fi phono-
graph—she would pay it off in eighteen months—and
her avocation was collecting classical jazz records. Did
Otto Beggs like Jelly Roll Morton? Beggs had never
heard of Jelly Roll Morton, but he had told Ruby he had
never heard anyone better.

Best of all, she had enjoyed listening to Beggs, enjoyed
questioning him and listening to his lengthy answers, her
wide almond eyes concentrating on his lips. She was
curious about his life, his achievements, his work in the
Secret Service. He had been able to talk to her more
easily than he had talked to anyone in years. The latter
years with Gertrude had dammed up his pride in himself,
and now he was able to release what had been too long
held back. He had told Ruby of his boyhood, of his athletic triumphs at Oregon State, of his war days in Korea,
of his Medal of Honor, of his numerous jobs, of his years
in the Secret Service. He had avoided telling her about
his family. All he had recounted to Ruby Thomas, every
minute detail, every anecdote, even to the contents of
his beloved scrapbooks, impressed and awed her. "Dog
my cats!" she would exclaim. "You really done that?"

Above all, she held his work in high esteem. Where Gertrude considered a Secret Service agent as nothing more than an underpaid game warden, Ruby considered the role of guarding the President an honor next to the Presidency itself.

Only one truth marred their relationship, and it trailed doggedly after him, following their third meeting. She was black.

Otto Beggs had long taken pride in his tolerance. Sure, Negroes were different from white folk, they were lazier, less dependable, trickier, less smart, but hell, they weren't to blame, because look what they came from; they came from Africa and from plantation slavery. He had not known any Negroes, except Solly, who ran interference for him on the football team in Oregon, and a few others in the Army, and he had liked them well enough. Of course, he didn't like Prentiss too much, because Prentiss had got the job as assistant to the head of the White House Detail that had rightfully belonged to himself. Still, he could not hold that against Prentiss personally. It was not Prentiss' doing. If anyone was to blame, it was Chief Gaynor. Beggs couldn't prove it yet, but he was willing to bet money Gaynor intended to promote as many colored agents as he could, which was natural when you played politics. As to President Dilman, Beggs wasn't definite about him. He didn't like him in general, that was for certain. On the other hand, he could not say he disliked him entirely, either. What he did dislike was having to track around on the heels of a Negro. Beggs knew that he was smarter than Dilman, more courageous (as he had once proved), and had more personality, and yet, look what that lumpy politician was paid per annum and look what he was paid. And worst of all, for the lousy money he was getting, Beggs was pledged to lay his life on the line to protect that colored man. For one of Beggs's stature, gifts, potential, it was demeaning. Imagine Dilman doing anything to deserve a Medal of Honor? Ha!

Without being able to define it, Beggs felt uncomfortable around Negro men, especially the ones in this cruddy neighborhood, which even his so-called friends, the Schearers, had now abandoned. About Negro women, however, his feelings were more lenient, although still confused. After all, he had loved Lena Horne in his youth, well, when he was younger. He had always liked to watch Negro women in the street from his bedroom window. The young ones carried themselves great. And their builds, they were built for heroic men. Sometimes, but not often, in his pre-Ruby days, he had entertained wild thoughts about Negro women and their secrets. But then he would always get mixed up in his thoughts, for sometimes he would think they were below him, not in the street below but socially beneath him, and not good enough for him, with their secrets, those builds from Africa, and only Negro men could manage them.

Several times he had recalled the night that he had escorted President Dilman to that brownstone where the Reverend Spinger lived, and the crazy thing that had happened before they left, that colored girl, an older one but a swell looker, who had come dashing out after Dilman. The President had called her Miss Gibson and acted like she was a secretary, which she probably was, taking notes on the conference with Spinger, which she probably had done, yet Beggs could not forget that when she had come out, she had been kind of informal, calling after the President, "Doug." Beggs had never heard of a secretary calling her boss by his first name, especially a boss who was President of the United States. He had tried to picture Miss Gibson exactly in his mind, but could only remember that she had been kind of light-colored and slender, and not bad for her age. He had wondered if she was Spinger's secretary and had just called Dilman by his first name because she had known him a long time, or if maybe she was Dilman's lady friend and nothing else. The latter thought had been so disrespectful, so Communistic, especially for one in his job, that Beggs had driven it from his mind as best he could and had not dared repeat the juicy speculation even to Gertrude.

But it had come back to him, the thought, in a different context last night when he could not sleep, when he

had enjoyed his daring dreams of Ruby. If Dilman, he
had told himself, could manage to take care of a pretty
fair-looking light-colored girl—lady—then he, Otto
Beggs, could do ten times better with any one of them.
This feeling of superiority had brought some order to
his confusion, and reinforced his ardor for Ruby
Thomas. He had not waited for lunch to tell his lie to
Gertrude. He had done so the moment that he had sat
down to breakfast.

Suddenly he realized that he was standing before the
Walk Inn. No more last night's dreams. No more last
week's accidental meetings. He was here, now and
today, because he had planned it. He had even left the
Nash for Gertrude, being gracious and considerate
about it, announcing that he would take the bus (because he did not want the car parked so dangerously
long in front of the nearby tavern). He had planned
everything. His first assignation.

He went inside, past the clanging pinball machines, and
headed straight for the horseshoe bar.

He stopped in his tracks. There were three men at the
bar, two colored, one a white laborer, but there was no
Ruby. His disappointment was as sharp as if he had received a physical blow. He had started toward the bartender, Simon, who was busily drying his glassware,
when the flutter of a distant brown hand crossed his vision. He stood on tiptoe, elevating his bulk to its utmost
height, and peered over the bartender's bent head. The
hand fluttered still, and then he could see it belonged to
Ruby.

Quickly Beggs made his way between the bar and the
wooden tables and chairs, to the farthest of the three
leatherette booths hidden deep in the rear of the tavern.
She was waiting for him in a corner of the dark booth,
fingering the rim of her drained glass. What perplexed
him was not that for the first time she was waiting in the
intimacy of a booth, but that for the first time she was
not in a white uniform.

As he clumsily slid into the booth, he could not help
but gape at her across the table. Since he had never seen
her out of the dental uniform, he had not imagined that

any different garment could improve her good looks. This instant he could see that he had been wrong, that a new dimension had been added to her. She wore a ruffled pink chiffon blouse, one that almost indecently revealed the well-filled pink lace brassière beneath, and could not adequately contain her breasts. Her waist was tied tightly with a red flowered sash above her red skirt. She was ravishing.

She smiled timorously, showing him even white teeth and a deep dimple. "I was hopin' y'all be comin', Otter," she said. The first time that his Otto had become her Otter, it had made him squirm, reminding him that he was white and she was not, but the intimacy of it had quickly appealed to him, as it did now. " 'Cause," she went on, "I didn't wanna be made to feel foolish, 'cause I done come here 'specially today expectin' you to come, like it was an occasion."

"Ruby," he said, "where's your usual outfit, the uniform?"

"Doc done come down with the flu bug last night, and we been cancelin' the customers. So today's off for us-all, an' I been fixin' an' messin' 'round the apartment, and done some shoppin' for records, but still thought to git me here case you come, too."

His head swam, and last night's fantasies began to grow real in the daylight. "That's awfully nice of you, Ruby. I guess you knew I'd, well, I'd be hoping to run into you for a drink."

"You were ackin' like you was meanin' it day 'fore yesterday."

He opened his hands. "Here I am," he said. "You been here long?"

"One drink's worth."

He felt expansive and rich. "Well, have another."

"You gonna?"

"I've got to go on duty, but—what the hell—one beer never made anyone cockeyed." He twisted, raised his arm and snapped his fingers. "Simon! One J and B on the rocks, and one tap beer. Bring some pretzels, too."

She reached for her folded coat to find a cigarette, but

he took one from his pack, handed it to her, and then put a match to it.

"I was thinkin' 'bout you last night, Otter."

"If it was something bad, don't tell me."

"I was thinkin' how I hopes you don't go sellin' real estate land. Maybe I should hush my big mouff, but—"

"No, go ahead, Ruby, please."

She set her elbows on the table, and stared at him. "I been thinkin' you is too much man—Lordy, too much man—to be givin' up bein' a hero and protectin' our Pres jes 'cause of extra money. Bein' a richcrat ain't no more impo'tant than what you is."

"Well, I don't know that I'm so important, Ruby—thank you, anyway—but I do think the job is certainly important. I'm beginning to feel the way you do about giving it up. But my pay's sure not up to what I could make in real estate, and everybody can use extra money."

"Bet if you eggs 'em 'bout leavin', Pres Dilman would git you a raise but fast. Bet he wouldn't wanna lose you."

He wanted to tell her that Dilman probably did not know he was alive, but he did not want to run himself down in her eyes. "Maybe," he agreed. "You think a lot of Dilman?"

She brushed the air with her long thin hand. "Aw, Otter, I don't mess 'round much studyin' politics or race stuff an' nonsense like such. Like my mothah always used to be sayin'—'Sweetheart, live an' let 'em live, and don't fuss 'round none with such p'ofessional matters.' Sep, 'course, I wanna git an education an' be smart so's I kin live good an' be right for the right man, but I don't fuss my mind with Dilman this and Dilman that—I jes mostly wanna have me a good time, swing it 'round a little, 'joy my days."

Beggs had tried to assess what she was saying, and wondered if it was meant to be provocative. Since he was not certain, he said pedantically, "You have a healthy attitude, Ruby."

The drinks had come, and she drank hers and he drank his, and then she said, " 'Course my not messin' with politics don't mean I'm not fascinated 'bout your impo'tant job. Otter, what you do day 'fore yesterday when you left here, an' what you do yesterday?"

He was on, and liking it, and he went on and on, without interruption, except for a reverent "Sure enough?" or "Ain't that somethin'!" from her occasionally. He narrated his activities of the day before yesterday, and of yesterday. He told her of his colleagues and their duties. He presented her with the highlights of the history of the Secret Service. He described the West Wing offices and the people and life in them, and he described what sections of the White House he himself had visited, with himself always in the foreground of these descriptions.

She listened raptly, and drank, and exclaimed or clucked her admiration.

His monologue took him a half hour, and when he was done, he was hoarse and happy. "Christ, Ruby, I've been bending your ear to death. You shouldn't let me go on that way."

"You-all a good teacher, Otter. I was lovin' it."

He finished what was left of his beer. "What about you, Ruby? What have you been up to today?"

"Like I told you, nothin', 'cept sleepin' too long this mornin' to git me my naycher back full stren'th— nothin', Otter—"

But then she went on about her hi-fi set, and the fun she'd had shopping for rare jazz records to add to her collection of classics. With enthusiasm she evoked names little known or unknown to him, mystical names like Bix Beiderbecke, Joe Oliver, Fats Waller, Muggsy Spanier, Bunk Johnson. She spoke of Storyville jazz and gut-gone bands and Bessie Smith's "St. Louis Blues" and King Oliver's Creole combine belting out "Froggie Moore."

After ten minutes she stopped. "You diggin' it, Otter? No, you ain't, you not with it, you a orfan from the blues. You need educatin', Otter."

He swallowed. "I'm always open to improvement, Ruby."

"Man, you gonna go limp when you hear what I bought me this mornin'—know what?—piano solo of Jelly Roll doin' 'The Pearls.' You gotta hear that, an' then you gotta come up to my place an' hear Duke Ellington an' his Wash'tonians doin' 'Rainy Nights'— listenin', you ain't ever gonna be exactly the same, Otter, you gonna be no more orfan, you gonna join up an' belong like Ruby Thomas here."

He had been holding his breath. Now he let it go with a wheeze. "Are you extending an invitation to me for a musical concert in your apartment, Ruby?"

Her almond eyes held on him a moment. Then she said softly, "You always been welcome, Otter. Fact is, my machine needs some adjustin' an' I ain't got the money for it yet, but you always sayin' you got mechanical ways—"

"I'm a wizard with a monkey wrench, Ruby. I've never tinkered with a hi-fi, but I bet I'll have yours perfecto in two seconds and a jiffy. That's a deal, if you say so. I'll bring a bottle of J and B, and some tools, and you can give me my first jazz lesson."

She pushed her glass aside. "You done got a deal. When you wanna come up?"

Before he could reply, a hollow, echoing voice intruded upon their conversation, coming from the left. He looked off. A well-dressed Negro customer had walked through the door, holding a transistor radio, and was making his way to the bar. The radio's volume was on high, and an announcer's voice boomed, "—gave his first press conference in the Cabinet Room of the White House today. President Dilman told fifty reporters very little that they did not already know. He sidestepped any direct commitment to the Minorities Rehabilitation Program, was evasive about reporting the results of his conversations with the visiting President of Baraza, and would make no comment on the New Succession Bill. However, the President did speak of reopening a summit conference with the Russians. He came under greatest fire, during the questioning period, over his appointment of the Reverend Paul Spinger, director of the Crispus Society, to investigate the electrifying kidnaping, down in Mississippi, of—"

As abruptly as the radio news program had assailed him, it now ended. Beggs could see that Simon had leaned across the bar to speak to the customer, who had then lowered the volume.

Turning back to Ruby, Beggs suddenly realized that he had lost all track of time. The radio program reporting on Dilman's press conference reminded him that he was to report for duty, to guard Dilman, at four o'clock. He looked at his watch and was horrified that it was seven minutes to four.

"Ruby, what time do you have?"

"Five to four."

"Christ, I'd better find a cab." He pushed free of the booth and jumped to his feet. Fumbling for his wallet, he found it and laid down three dollars. "Sorry to run out on you like this, Ruby."

She smiled. "Like I was sayin', you is doin' man's work. But, Otter, you ain't answered my lil question—when you fixin' to come up an' see me?"

The haste went out of him. Impulsively he reached down and touched her hand. "Soon as I can, Ruby. My first free day off. Tell you what, see you here same time, day after tomorrow, and we'll set a—a rendezvous."

"I'll be waitin', Otter dear." She turned her palm upward, caught and caressed his fingers, then released them. "I wanna be with you."

He winked at her, started away, turned once to wave back, and then hastened outside to hail a taxi. For the first time in the Secret Service, he would be late on the job. Yet he did not give a damn what Agajanian said or Gaynor said, or in fact what President Dilman might say. All that mattered was what Ruby Thomas had said: Otter dear, I wanna be with you.

Sighting the parked taxi down the block, he hummed to himself as he hurried toward it. The girl had said that she wanted to educate him. Great. Nothing suited him more. He had reached the time in his life where he wanted action, action and a little more learning. Whatever Dilman did with that colored broad of his, if he did, he could do better, if he dared.

"The White House, Pennsylvania entrance," he ordered the cab driver. "Half a buck extra if you make all the lights."

He was moving again, he was rolling, Jelly Rolling along, and everything was good, real good, once more.

Edna Foster and George Murdock ate an early and hasty dinner at the Chez François on Connecticut Avenue near H Street, and by five-thirty they had left the modest French restaurant and headed in the direction of Lafayette Square.

Edna had not enjoyed the rushed meal. She liked the comfort gained from leisure with George, their time for small talk and confidences, and she resented any deadlines imposed upon their dinners. Lately she had been more and more burdened by work, so that she often stayed on at night to clear her desk for the following day. Not that President Dilman was being more demanding than T.C. had been, for, in truth, he was almost diffident about summoning her for dictation or special assignments. No, it was not Dilman per se, but rather the atmosphere of conflict and tension that his presence in the Oval Office had created. Her desk, it sometimes seemed, had become a fort (her typewriter a machine gun), a surrounded outpost in an alien land, vainly trying to survive the cannonading and strafing of an overwhelming enemy.

More difficult than the upsetting atmosphere was the concrete problem that she was no longer a *personal* secretary to the President alone. Under T.C., she had worked for him and no one else. Under Dilman, a subtle change had occurred. She worked not for the Commander in Chief exclusively, but for his aides, his staff and allies as well. It was as if a half dozen of them did not trust Dilman to perform solo, and intruded themselves as a chorus (so there might be less likelihood of detecting a sour note). Edna found herself doing what Dilman wanted, little enough, and also what Talley, General Faber, Eaton, to think of only three, wanted done for Dilman.

Tonight would be one more night for her to reduce the overload of work. Besides, Dilman was having his last conferences with Kwame Amboko before and after his first State Dinner, and Flannery and the wire-service men and syndicated columnists (like George) would be standing by in the press lobby. She might be required to help Flannery and his girls if there were any press releases, which she did not mind as much, since indirectly she would be helping George.

But more than the haste of their dinner, what disturbed her right now, as they strolled hand and hand toward the square and the White House across from it, was George's mood. Whatever his shortcomings—no one is perfect, her father always used to say, although it does not hurt to try—George Murdock was almost consistently cheerful and lighthearted. Rarely was he pensive. When he complained, and usually he did it in a joking way, it was not about the $150 a week he earned from Tri-State Syndicate, but about the fact that the twelve newspapers in his string were small, obscure, and so no one in Washington ever saw his stuff. As a consequence, he had no permanent slot in the Press Room off the West Wing entrance, and no standing among his colleagues or with the administration. This indignity, added to the chore of having to be his own photographer, sometimes became a matter of annoyance to him. Yet most of the time he enjoyed his work, what standing it did give him, and he lived economically in his bachelor's quarters, his only extravagances being his numismatic collection, Indian-head coins his specialty, and his gifts to Edna.

From the time they had begun going together, she had wanted to help him succeed, because instinctively she knew that she might be helping to liberate herself from spinsterhood and improve her own condition of life. While she could have been of enormous value to him numerous times, by slipping out to him scoops or beats or whatever the reporters called exclusive stories, she had refrained from doing so. By her rigid standards it would have been unethical and unthinkable. George had always been a darling about this, and had never pressed her. Sometimes she had ached to let him in on a secret a few hours or days before it would become public, so that he could benefit by it and become famous. She had never done so. The main consideration was not that such an act might cost her the job she had once cherished, but that the respect in George's eyes would have been lost to her. They had always discussed T.C., of course, but usually in relation to his public politics or known gossip or nonsense about her own work. However, since Dilman had come to office, there had been even fewer of these discussions, because her intuition had warned her that Dilman was more vulnerable to loose talk and more opposed by the press.

Yet, in her own way, Edna had tried to give assistance to George. She had made it known to T.C. that she was going steady, that her boy friend was a habitué of the West Wing lobby, so that T.C. would be more aware of George Murdock. And T.C. had been, for on several occasions George had been invited to intimate off-the-record briefings (reserved for the select handful of White House veterans) and paid-for administration trips that he would not have otherwise rated. Recently, whenever the opportunity presented itself, she had begun to mention George's name to President Dilman, too. ("If you need me, Mr. President, I'll be dining with my boy friend, George Murdock, of Tri-State Syndicate, at the Iron Gate Inn.") She was never sure that Dilman heard her.

Even though George did not complain about his meager income, she was certain that it was his economic straits that inhibited him from discussing marriage. Except for the small amount he had been able to put into a few speculative stocks, she knew that he did not earn enough to save. Until he did, there was little chance of his proposing marriage. There was one hope on the far horizon, hinted at by George. He had an Uncle Victor in Hawaii, wealthy, retired, and now seventy-nine years old. George was a favorite of this uncle, and was undoubtedly written into the old man's last will as the heir to a considerable sum. But the Waikiki sun appeared to have rejuvenated Uncle Victor. He had not been ill once since Edna had been going with George. Still, that was a hope, a possibility, *something*.

Sometimes Edna became desperate at the waiting. Once, on her own, she had planned to go to Tim Flan-

nery, who was so nice, and ask him if he would take on
George as a Press Department assistant. She had rehearsed her request, a beautiful and touching one. When
the occasion had arisen, she could not make her speech.
She had perceived that Flannery would have had to consult T.C., and whatever he might decide, it would put
her in a bad light. *Using* her confidential position.

And so her directionless life with George had gone on
with no merging of their separate paths into a single path
in sight. Her father brought the situation up at least once
every other month in his short, stilted letters from the
farm outside Milwaukee, but she never tried to explain,
beyond saying that George was still her good friend
and implying that she was still behaving in a way that
would not disgrace anyone back home.

In fact, most often, it was she, not George, who was
disturbed by their seemingly pointless relationship. She
had tried to tell him, without telling him, that she was
the kind of girl who did not need much, who was not demanding. She had tried to tell him that the only riches in
life to which she aspired were someone she cared for
and a decent home where she could bear and raise wonderful children. Did he understand? He had never let on.
How she wanted to tell him, if only he would bring it up,
that she was ready to move into his confined apartment,
ready to continue working while he worked, ready to
skimp and save for their family and their future. This
was her workable vision of tomorrow. She knew that it
was not his. A man who wore lifts in his heels, she supposed, who was sensitive about his acne marks, she supposed, who wrote marvelously but was not read, she
supposed, would be too proud for another second best.

Tonight—it was becoming dark, no longer day, not
yet night—she could see from his mood, so unusually
low-spirited, so ingrown and silent (he had not uttered
a word in all their walk to this point), that until now it
was his own good nature and ebullience that supported
both of them. But not these minutes, not tonight. His
depression was only too apparent. She wondered what
had caused it. She was afraid to find out.

They had reached the square.

He released her hand. "One second, Edna. Late edition of the *Citizen-American* is out. I want to see how Zeke Miller let his paper handle your boss's first press conference."

She waited in the gloom while he went to the heavily sweatered newsboy. She enjoyed observing George when he was apart from her. His thinning blond hair was so neat, his pointed nose and receding chin made him appear so intellectual (which he was), and the tweed topcoat, even if it was not exactly the latest fashion, gave him the appearance of Fleet Street's best.

He returned to her, the newspaper opened, his gray eyes darting across it from side to side, then up and down. He was, she remembered, a remarkable speed reader. He clucked his tongue.

"What is it, George?" she asked.

"Congressman Miller's unloading his big guns," he said. "Look at the headlines over Reb Blaser's by-line lead story."

He pushed the front page before her, sharing it with her, an intimacy she appreciated tonight. She had meant to glance at the front page only briefly, for this kind of news was the last thing on her mind. But the headline pulled her eyes toward it.

The banner headline read:

IS THE WHITE HOUSE REALLY BLACK?

The second headline read:

DILMAN BEGINS TO COLOR LOOK OF NEW ADMINISTRATION

The three columns of bold type over Reb Blaser's by-line read:

PRESIDENT DEFIES ATTORNEY GENERAL
REFUSES TO ACT AGAINST TERROR KIDNAPERS OF
JUDGE GAGE
APPOINTS NEGRO FRIEND SPINGER TO "INVESTIGATE"

Edna's eyes took in the three paragraphs of Blaser's lead. Blaser had it from a source "close to the President" that Attorney General Clay Kemmler had demanded Dilman "outlaw" the Negro Turnerite Group for being behind the Mississippi kidnaping and for being supported by Communist Party funds. Apparently the President had rejected advice based on "well-known facts," and had taken the first step in reducing T.C.'s brilliant Cabinet into "Uncle Tom's Cabinet." Dilman had appointed the Reverend Paul Spinger, a Negro apologist, to sustain his stand with "fiction" about the colored abductors. Dilman's Black Hand had shown itself today, and it was redecorating the nation's first and proudest house in its own dark hue. Not only had the President demeaned his high office and violated the nation's trust, by attempting to treat with a known subversive and criminal like Jefferson Hurley, but he was dealing "softly" with a fellow African, Kwame Amboko, and risking our peaceful coexistence with Russia; he was refusing to come out in full support of T.C.'s minorities bill that would enable Negroes to "earn their citizenship" instead of commit crimes for it, and he was "reluctant" to sign the New Succession Bill on his desk that would assure every American that its Executive Mansion would remain as President Washington had wanted it to be and as President John Adams had known it.

Edna's eyes skipped down to the end of the story. She read: "Tonight President Dilman is presiding over his first formal State Dinner in the very room where President Adams' prayer is carved beneath the mantel: 'I pray Heaven to bestow the best of Blessings on this House and all that shall hereafter inhabit it. May none but honest and wise men ever rule under this roof.' Poor Adams! Tonight President Dilman will sit with his back to our country's prayer, having for his first honor guest to our House an African who is tampering with our lives, enjoying for his first official entertainment the anti-American wit of several entertainers of his own race. As one well-known congressman remarked, 'We on the Hill are worried that we have a black Andrew Johnson in the White House, one with no regard for other branches of government or for the wishes of the majority of all decent Americans. We have grave apprehensions about the future. If the remaining days of Dilman's one-year-and-five-month term are like today, then, alas, America has been pushed into a time of trial and infamy that will come to be known as its own Dark Ages.' "

Edna Foster was surprised at her shivering indignation as she looked up from the newspaper. "How dare they! Did you read that? As 'one well-known congressman remarked'—meaning who? Zeke Miller, that's who!"

George Murdock withdrew the newspaper and carefully folded it. "I suppose it is Miller—after all, the paper is his plaything—but there are dozens more who are apt to say the same thing."

Edna could not control the quaver in her protesting voice. "It's terrible, terrible, George. I've read some bad things—the President insists on seeing everything—but this, his painting the White House black, creating an Uncle Tom's Cabinet, it's—it's scurrilous libel. He ought to sue. George, I wish you wouldn't buy that newspaper any more."

He had taken Edna's arm, and when the street was free of traffic, he guided her across it and into Lafayette Park. As they passed the Kosciusko statue, he said, "I disapprove of this as much as you do, Edna, you know that. But what the devil, I can't say as I blame Reb Blaser. He does what he's told. He's got a job to do like the rest of us. I will say one thing, he's a darn good writer."

"Then why doesn't he write for someone decent? I think there is simply no excuse—"

"Edna, be reasonable," pleaded George Murdock. "We newspapermen try to be truthful and honest in our own way. Blaser has to give in a little, just the way I do. Do you think I like slanting my stories the way I have to, full of corn-shucked pap, because my employer and audiences are conservative hayseeds? Still, I have to. I'm sure you don't like working overtime, like tonight. Yet you have to. Do you think Dilman likes reading newspapers like this one any more than I do? No, but he has to and I have to, so we both know what's going on. The country's full of many kinds of people, Edna, and we have to live with them."

"Well, I don't want to if I can help it," Edna said. Her wrath had diminished as they reached the center of the park. George's objectivity and good sense always calmed her, and Lafayette Park, too, always had the effect of soothing her. Even as she listened to George, she had been peering across the artificially lighted grass toward the tree trunks, looking for the brown squirrels, and sparrows and pigeons, that gave her so much pleasure. They reminded her of the farm in Wisconsin and her childhood when there had been so little conflict and so many rosy dreams. She saw two squirrels at last, one scampering up the rough bark-covered trunk of a tree, the other following, and she felt even better. "The poor President," she said. "I can see him opening up the paper tomorrow morning or before lunch. I always try to avoid him then. I can't stand the——the way his face looks——"

"How does it look?"

"How does it look? Sort of like the face of one of those Negroes they knock down in the South, after they pull back the dogs and close in around him and start kicking him——I remember the series of pictures of one on the ground being kicked, his first look of automatic shock, sort of, then pain but not letting them see it, then finally a look of resignation, keeping the hurt inside so as not to give them satisfaction. That's the way the President looks when he reads the papers. He doesn't show much. But I'd hate to see his X rays."

George Murdock scratched one scarred cheek and then the other. "I guess I can only say I hope your boss is tough underneath, Edna. This vilification is just the start. Every President is a target. He asks for the job and he's got to be prepared——"

"President Dilman did not ask for the job."

"He did when he ran for the Senate, and he did when he accepted the gavel as President pro tempore of the Senate. Dilman is a bigger target than the others, because he's black on white and can't be missed. There he is. Everything he does will be judged not only for its wisdom but for what it means coming from a Negro. The facts of life, Edna. Every day is going to be worse for him."

Her gaze went to George, and for once she was not calmed by his matter-of-factness. "You think it'll be worse?"

"Unquestionably."

She resolutely prepared herself to speak what had grown in her mind. "If it is, George, then, well—maybe he can take it, but I can't. I'm going to quit."

He was so startled that he stopped abruptly to study her, to gauge how serious she was. She knew that her upset expression convinced him. He took her arm. "Come here a minute," he said. He led her to the last bench before Pennsylvania Avenue. After they sat down, he said, "Edna, I thought we settled your quitting that first day, when you took my advice and decided not to resign."

"It's never been completely settled in my mind, George. The first day I made up my mind to stay because you convinced me he needed help and because—you know—I felt so sorry for him. But I'm too close to what's going on, and I can't stand it. How can I explain it to you?"

She clasped her hands and looked down at the pavement. "I've had enough of the mental strain, George. The position is hard enough without that. I'll be honest with you, I really will. I finally figured it out. It's not that I suffer every day with him, get hurt because he's hurt, the way I felt with T.C. No. I—I'm as liberal as anybody, but I can't somehow identify with him in the same way. He's so different from me. I know this is awful, but it is his color, I guess, his whole background, so different from anything I know. Yet I can *understand* him. So I'm outside him, but I have to be there. You know what—it is like a bullfight—having to go to a bullfight and watch. He's the bull, practically helpless, no chance, and the men with the *banderillas* and the picadors with their lances are sticking him till he bleeds, goading and hurting him, until he's weaker and weaker, and the matador comes out and finally drives the sword in behind his neck. If I have to be close up, watching, maybe I can't feel like the bull, I can't suffer that way, but I can hate what I see of all the torturing before he is finished and dragged away. I can be revolted and sickened by it. Well, George, that's the way I feel, being in those offices with Dilman. I can't stand it. I hate having to go in and see him tomorrow."

George Murdock squeezed her hand. "Edna, he has only one year and four months left in office. Surely—"

"How many days is that? Four hundred, four hundred and eighty or more? That's four hundred and eighty bullfights. No, George. He can find other help now. He's settled into his office. And me, I can find a better job, without agony, typing for someone who doesn't have to worry about anything more than sales volume or competitors undercutting him."

"You couldn't stand it after these years. You'd go stir-crazy. You'd wither."

Edna Foster shuddered. The word *wither* made her think of spinsterhood. Maybe this was the time to test him on that, too. "Then I could do something more interesting. I didn't tell you, but Hesper kind of subtly asked me if I'd like to move to Phoenix and help her and Miss Laurel with T.C.'s papers and documents, and her correspondence. She's—"

"Edna, no, I can't have you leaving me now."

She met his eyes, which were genuinely anxious, and she felt a wave of relief. "George, that's nice of you, but—"

"I mean it," he said, almost desperately. "I've got no right to ask you to do anything for me. I realize that. But you know, I haven't been able to—to sort of talk to you more seriously—about the future—because I've been trying to get myself set, better established."

There could be a moment of truth, she knew, far from any bullfight. "George," she said firmly, "as far as I'm concerned, you are well enough established. I mean, from my point of view." She had never been more eloquent about her longings for their future, and she awaited his reply with trepidation.

He sighed. "Maybe," he said. "I suppose I always set my sights too high. You know how I feel about you. Nothing is too good for you. Maybe I've wanted too

much. Tonight, if things were the way they were yesterday, I—I might say more than I have up to now. But
tonight I can't, Edna. I got a one-two punch today, both
on the button, and I'm shook up, I'm badly shook up."

She turned fully toward him. She had *known* something was wrong. Why had she not penetrated his moodi-
ness from the outset? "I suspected you were worried,"
she said. "Tell me, George. Maybe I can help."

"First off, I had a cable from Honolulu this morning.
Uncle Victor, the senile bastard, he went and got himself married. Can you beat that? After twenty years a
widower? Some island social dame nailed him. And him
seventy-nine. I didn't think the old bastard was that
feebleminded. Well, that blew it—good-bye, nephew
George. I bet they're collaborating right now on the new
will."

"George, my God, you were depending on that pie in
the sky? I never gave it a second thought."

"Well, I don't know if I counted on it or not. But
somehow it was always there to think about. So that's
out." He hesitated. "That's not the important thing,
though. Something worse happened in the mail."

"What?"

He ran his fingertips across his pocked cheek. "Edna,
I lost three newspapers today. They—they dropped me.
Far as I can figure out, I'm not 'in' enough. They switched
to the big wire services instead of keeping their own correspondent. They figure the big ones, exclusive or not,
are closer to the inside."

She felt weak, helpless, and faintly guilty because he
was not inside. "You still have nine papers."

"For the time," he said, "and for now, less income."

"I don't understand, George. I know you'll make less,
but—"

George Murdock's nails dug at the bench between his
knees. "The whole tone of Weidner's letter," he said.
"There's a point of no return with Tri-State. If I lose another paper, I'm through. They'll buy some other columnist. In fact, if they can't sell my column to more outlets,
I may be through anyway. I didn't even have to read between the lines. He wrote, 'If you don't pep up that daily

column, don't come up with something hot, in place of those warmed-over handouts, we'll have to reappraise the whole situation. I can't understand why you're not doing better.' Then he said something dirty." George Murdock glanced at Edna worriedly. "I don't know if I should tell you."

"Tell me, go ahead, tell me everything."

"He wrote, 'I can't understand why you're not doing better. After all, you are going steady with the personal secretary to two Presidents. Who has a better pipeline into the White House, especially today?' Goddammit. Can you imagine?"

She felt sick. "Oh, George, how could he!"

"He did . . . I tell you, I've got a good mind to quit. Here you were talking about quitting, when that's all I have on my mind. The effrontery of the bastard, thinking for one minute I'd risk the respect of the only decent woman I've ever known, for personal advancement."

She wanted to hug him for his perception and gallantry. What held her back was a heavy anchor of failure, tied to a rope of guilt. "Maybe I have let you down, George—"

"Stop it, Edna. You're not involved."

"I mean, you've always been so wonderful, knowing my responsibilities, what my position entails, never even being curious. So maybe I am a little to blame, George. Maybe I've been leaning over backward to your detriment."

"Forget it. I don't want to even discuss it."

"You're so kind, George. There *are* story leaks, let's face it. Every day it happens. That Blaser story we were just reading. Kemmler and the President did have a disagreement today about the kidnaping. But it was secret. How did Blaser find out? Someone must have leaked it to him."

"You bet your life. Somebody over at Justice. Maybe even Kemmler himself. They want to look good, get on the record. All the big press correspondents have inside contacts whom they use, and who use them."

"Except you, because of me!" cried Edna. The resolve came to her, and she gave voice to it. "I won't have you penalized any more, simply because you happen to be seeing me. I'm going to keep my eyes and ears open, and if there is something that—that doesn't endanger security—that I know someone else will let out beforehand anyway—I'll tell you first. I promise, George."

"I told you—forget it," he said gruffly. "Tri-State isn't the only syndicate. I'll look around. We'll make it yet." He stood up. "Come on, we'd better check in."

She came to her feet slowly. "George," she said, "I think I want to keep my seat at the bullfight."

"Not for me," he said. "Don't do it for me."

"For us," she said. "I want to do it for us."

His thin lips curled upward, and he pulled her arm through the crook of his elbow and propelled her toward Pennsylvania Avenue. "That's different," he said. "That makes me very happy. We'll make out somehow, together."

They crossed Pennsylvania Avenue in silence, and entered through the open driveway gate leading to the White House, both automatically flashing their passes and greeting the police guards, now doubled in number for this evening's State Dinner.

As they walked in step to the West Wing lobby, they heard someone hurrying behind them. Edna glanced over her shoulder and grimaced. Reb Blaser, skipping on stubby legs, was alongside them, a grin on his frog face.

"Hiya, Edna—Georgie, old boy," he drawled. "How are the love doves?" He did not wait for an answer, but gestured toward the front entrance of the White House, ablaze with light. "Looks like a big night, eh?"

"To paint the White House black," said Edna indignantly.

"Aw, come now, Edna girl," Blaser said, still grinning. "I got me a job to do, that's all. Matter of fact, might be some truth to what I wrote, even though I admit to applying a trifle too much tar and feather. But that's Zeke for you. Don't blame you none for being loyal to your employer, though."

Before Edna could speak again, George Murdock said hastily, "It was a little too rough, Reb, like you said, but that was quite a thing about Kemmler and Dilman disagreeing. Where'd you get it?"

One of Blaser's warted eyelids winked. "Connections, George. Comes of being slavey for a big-time Congressman." They had reached the door to the West Wing, and all three halted. "Incidentally, George, my Congressman brought up your name to me day before yesterday. Meant to tell you, but been too plumb beat out to remember."

"Zeke Miller mentioned me?" asked George Murdock cautiously.

"Nobody else but you. Seems one of our stringers sent him a clip of the piece you did on Miller's speech on farm subsidies. He liked it, liked it powerfully. 'That's a smart young man, that Murdock,' he said to me. 'Sharp nose for news. Let's keep an eye on him.' "

"That's nice of Miller," said George Murdock.

"Oh, he's not half as bad as everyone makes him out," said Reb Blaser. "Hell, he's a successful business tycoon from the South, and he knows what side his bread is buttered on. Yes, he's right impressed with you, George."

Edna turned her glare from Blaser's nauseating face to George, and she disliked the way George was swallowing this syrupy flattery whole and enjoying it.

She said briskly, ignoring Blaser, "Good night, George. Don't work too hard. See you tomorrow."

"Yes—good night, Edna. I'll call you."

She started into the lobby, but at the door, turning sideways to let a correspondent slip past her, she had one more glimpse of George and Reb Blaser. The frog was still croaking, and George was still listening, eager, deferential, pleased. For an instant she wished that George wouldn't stand there, that he would be more than that, but then she knew that she was being unfair. It had been a bad, bad day for George, and now for her also.

She would have to do something for him. But what?

Unhappily, she went inside to resume her seat at the bullfight.

The one emotion that Douglass Dilman suffered, as
he stared at the dessert being placed before him, was
deep mortification.

He had suspected what was happening earlier in the
evening, when he and Kwame Amboko had stood
against the wall of the East Room, he uncomfortable in
his new white tie and long-used unstylish dinner suit,
Amboko at ease in his blue-and-white-striped silk peaked
hat and matching cape draped over his dress suit, the
two of them receiving the splendidly garmented guests.
Dilman had suspected something was wrong, because it
had gone so quickly. He had meant to draw Sally Watson
aside and put it bluntly to her, but she had been busy,
her fashionably coiffured blond hair and bare shoulders
and shimmering white satin evening gown everywhere,
and he had been unable to catch her eye.

Only when Dilman had arrived in the enormous white-
and-gilt State Dining Room, and had taken his place in
the gold-covered Queen Anne chair at the head of the
immense horseshoe table, with Kwame Amboko to one
side of him and Amboko's older sister at the other side,
and the guests had seated themselves at the main table,
and at the four smaller tables near the Red Room, had
his earlier suspicion been fully confirmed.

Once the guests had been seated, in the interval before the waiters swarmed through the room from the pantry hidden behind the Chinese screen, Dilman was able
to see the truth. Of the 104 invitations sent out, Sally
Watson had advised him this morning that ninety-six had
been accepted. The seating plan, which Illingsworth had
shown him before he had dressed, had provided for
fifty-six guests at the three sections of the main horseshoe
table, and forty more guests at the four smaller tables.
Ninety-six guests in all. And when these were seated,
Dilman was reminded—he had almost forgotten in the
excitement—that he was not Washington's social Commander in Chief, but T.C.'s humble orderly.

Humiliation had filled every pore of his being: naked
shame before his honored guest and the latter's entourage from Africa, before his official family, before the
White House waiters. He had been witness to a similar

scene twice in his life, as an onlooker, when he had viewed the old motion picture, *Stella Dallas,* on television, and when he had attended a screening of the silent film, *The Gold Rush,* with pathetic Charlie Chaplin. Both times he had been moved, for, as a Negro, he had understood. Now he was witness to it a third time, not witness but participant and the solitary object of this shattering ostracism.

Every second gold-covered chair at the horseshoe table, it seemed, was empty. The four smaller tables mocked him with their gaping vacancies. Ninety-six important guests had accepted the invitations to his first State Dinner. No more than fifty had appeared. To all intents and purposes, President of the United States or not, he was still segregated, and the house he lived in was segregated too.

From that moment on, the formal evening had been for him an embarrassment to be tolerated and a disaster to be survived. He could not now remember one dish he had eaten, or the sense of anything that Amboko had spoken about or what he had replied to Amboko.

Dipping his spoon into his dessert, an ice-cream mold of a miniature White House, he raised his head, one of the few times he had done so during the dinner, and quickly his eyes roved over the room. He had to be positive that he had not been oversensitive and mistaken, to be sure that the seats had not been filled in the interim. But there they were. Nothing had changed. More than forty were empty still.

His gaze crossed Nat Abrahams, then darted back and fastened upon his friend. Nat, adjusting his bow tie, lifted his fingers slightly toward him in a private communication of understanding and assurance. Dilman's furtive gaze moved to Rose and Paul Spinger, and the empty seat next to them. *That* was disappointing too, but in a different way. Wanda had made her terms clear. She would come to the White House, not as his employee, not in the guise of someone else's guest, but only as his own guest.

The Spingers, he remembered, had been the very last to arrive, Rose plainly distressed, her husband harried.

The receiving line had already broken, and Dilman had begun to engage Amboko in diplomatic conversation once more, when he had seen the Spingers and excused himself to intercept them.

He had addressed Rose, searching past her. "Welcome, Rose. Where's Wanda?"

"She refused, Doug. I scolded her, but—" Rose Spinger had shrugged. "She said you'd understand."

The Reverend Spinger had joined them. Dilman had inspected the clergyman's face, appraising it to see if he bore encouraging tidings, and at once he saw there was nothing to give him optimism.

"I received your message earlier, Paul," Dilman had said. "You were still waiting for Hurley to return your call. I thought you'd be on your way to him by now. What happened?"

"I'd be on my way if there was some place to go," Spinger had said unhappily. "I just hung up on Frank Valetti in Little Rock. It took a lot of—of wheedling and prying to find out he was there—and a half-dozen calls to get him to phone back." Spinger had glanced around, to be certain that no one else was within hearing, and then he had gone on in an undertone. "I made it clear to Valetti that I was personally representing you, but he already knew that from radio and television reports. I told him I had to see Jefferson Hurley. I told him I would fly out and see Hurley anywhere, under any conditions. No use. Valetti insisted that Hurley was away on a trip, out of touch, and he did not expect to hear from him for at least two or three days."

"What about Valetti himself?" Dilman had demanded. "Did you say you'd see him?"

"Yes—yes—I certainly did, Mr. President. I told him that since he was second-in-command of the Turnerite Group, perhaps he would do as well as Hurley. I told him I could be in Little Rock tonight to confer with him." Spinger had paused, and shaken his head. "He was evasive and—and I'd say distrustful. He kept saying that no meeting with him would prove helpful. He kept saying only Hurley could speak for them, and Hurley was not available. I persisted that there were some questions that he could answer. He said flatly no, that he was in seclusion, that he didn't want to be hounded and harassed by the press and Federal investigators, who'd only persecute him without good cause, and that my coming was sure to put everyone on his trail. Besides, he said, he was on the move, leaving the city. Well, I could see it was hopeless—"

Dilman, conscious of the time he was spending away from his honor guest, had quickly interjected, "Paul, did you get anything out of him?"

"There was nothing left to do but pose your inquiries to Valetti on the telephone. I told him you were deeply disturbed by the Hattiesburg kidnaping. I said that both you and the Attorney General wanted to be assured that the Turnerites had no part in that heinous crime, and that if they had not, it would do much for their cause if Hurley came forth and condemned such acts of violence. I reminded him that the Justice Department was investigating the Turnerites as well as other similar associations for possible Communist affiliations, and that they could forestall and thwart any repressive government action by voluntarily coming forward, opening their membership records and financial ledgers for the Justice Department. I implored him to cooperate. I begged him to get Jefferson Hurley to cooperate. I asked him if he would—" Spinger halted, swallowed, blinked down at his shoes.

"What did he say to that, Paul?"

"One word, Mr. President. A crude four-letter word. I am unable to repeat it. Then—then he hung up."

Dilman had scowled. "That's it?"

"That's all of it, Mr. President. I'm afraid I failed you, but that's the most I could do. They're a mean, secretive bunch. One thing. Somewhere in our talk, toward the end, I did leave the door open. I told Valetti that he or Hurley could call me at any time, any hour, and reverse the charges, if they had a message for you."

"They won't call," Dilman had said. "What do you make of it now? Do you think the Turnerites played any part in the abduction?"

"We don't know a thing more than we knew this

morning. Maybe yes, maybe no. As long as there is reasonable doubt, I don't see how you can ban them."

"I don't either. . . . Well, Tim Flannery is down in his office, waiting to put out some kind of statement. When you get a chance, slip out and call him on the Entrance Hall phone. Tell him what you reported to me, in substance, and tell him that I suggest a noncommittal statement over my name. Something like—you have made contact with a high Turnerite official, conversations are proceeding—the Group admits no complicity in the Hattiesburg affair—meanwhile, the Federal Bureau of Investigation is being reinforced with additional manpower for its pursuit of the criminals. Have you got that, Paul?"

"Yes, Mr. President."

"Now I'd better return to Amboko. He's being about as cooperative as Valetti. What an evening."

He had remembered all of this earlier failure as he studied the Spingers across the State Dining Room. Absently, he finished his dessert. From his close friends his gaze went to the dazzling gilded chandelier with its flame-shaped electric bulbs, then down to the gay flower-filled centerpieces on the table, and at last to the empty Wedgwood plate on the white damask linen cloth in front of him.

He hoped that his face did not reflect his shame at the massive rebuke of the empty seats. He was still that kinky-haired, thick-featured relative of the orangutan, one of Zeke Miller's Nigras, barely a second-class citizen. He could not help but be conscious of the oil portrait above the white marble mantelpiece directly behind him. Healy's Abraham Lincoln. Would anyone but himself, Kwame Amboko for instance, appreciate the irony of it?

He glanced at his guest and realized that Amboko had been squinting at him thoughtfully through his rimless spectacles.

"A marvelous meal," Amboko said with his always startling Harvard accent. "I regret it is finished."

"You must come back soon for another," Dilman said. Then he added wryly, "I'll invite you, if I'm still here." Down the table he saw a napkin fluttering. It was Chief of Protocol Illingsworth, pretending to wipe his mouth but actually signaling to him that the dinner was ended and that there was one more formality before the champagne and entertainment.

One more formality—and then he remembered it. Quickly Dilman pushed back his chair and came to his feet. Immediately the clatter of ice-cream spoons and the hum of conversations ceased. All eyes in the half-filled room were upon him.

Dilman reached for his hollow-stemmed champagne glass, and his unsteady hand held it before him. "Ladies and gentlemen, I offer a toast," he announced, "a toast from the people of the United States to the health and prosperity of the President of Baraza, Kwame Amboko, and the people of his free republic."

Throughout the room, glasses tinkled and sparkled as the assemblage rose and joined in the official toast.

Awkwardly Dilman sat again, spilling some of his champagne on the tablecloth. He could see that Amboko was already standing, proffering his champagne, and piping out in his cultivated voice, "To the President of the United States of America, to the republic for which he stands, I reciprocate with our wishes for your health and prosperity and"—he half turned, lifting his glass toward the portrait of Lincoln—"to paraphrase the blessing and hope of your Emancipator, may *our* nations, under God, enjoy a new birth of freedom, so that government of the people, by the people, for the people, shall never perish from the earth."

Dilman drank, with everyone, and the champagne was curiously stale. He tried to fathom his honor guest's toast. Had Amboko shrewdly tried to remind the whites in the room that not only must his own primitive land continue to know freedom, with America's help, but vast America needed to begin re-evaluating its own attitudes toward freedom? Or had he been merely paying lip service to the greatest President and his most familiar quotation in the usual Fourth of July manner?

The toasts were continuing, from Secretary of State Eaton, from Secretary of Defense Steinbrenner, and were being answered in turn by Baraza's Foreign Minister and

Baraza's Ambassador Wamba, and automatically Dilman responded to each and sipped the flat champagne.

Suddenly the ordeal was ended. He rose with Amboko, and both watched the dinner guests rising, the women in their formal gowns being led by their escorts or military attachés to the Red Room and Blue Room and Green Room for more champagne.

Again Dilman found Amboko squinting at him. He felt tired of formality and protocol. "Well, President Amboko," he said, "I guess the rules say we're supposed to have a few minutes alone upstairs to settle our problems. We're supposed to make some kind of joint statement tonight or tomorrow. Ready to climb the stairs again?"

"Not necessary," said Amboko. "I have made up my mind. I can say what I have to say right here."

Dilman hesitated. "Very well." There was something about Amboko's expression, a warmth, a comprehension, that he had not seen before. For the first time, as they stood there—the two of them, isolated from the departing guests—they were not African and American, but two black men struggling in the power world of whites.

"I tried to hint it in my toast," Amboko said. "I will be less cryptic now." He paused to form correctly the words he wished to speak, and then he spoke. "I will take the risk. I will compromise. I shall return to Baraza and rescind all pending plans to repress our Communist Party. I shall not oust the Soviet Embassy or forbid the cultural exchanges with Moscow. In short, we shall attempt to maintain an open but watchful society such as you have here. You have shown good will in ratifying the African Unity Pact, and we shall display good faith by giving you what you need for bargaining with Soviet Russia when you meet with them."

Dilman was overwhelmed by a sudden surge of affection for this scholarly young man. "I can't tell you what good news this is, President Amboko. I can't tell you how gratified I am."

"If I may suggest one tactic, Mr. President. Let us make no mention of my concession in our formal announcement, only say that our talks were valuable to both of us and the agreements we reached will be jointly given out in the near future. This will afford me the opportunity to put my house in order back home. It will also equip you with something unexpected when you sit across from Premier Kasatkin to barter. Agreed?"

"Agreed," said Dilman. He was still bewildered by the African leader's change of heart. He wondered what had moved Amboko to make the concession that he had so recently opposed.

Amboko's eyes had narrowed behind his spectacles. He said, "Perhaps, Mr. President, you are curious at my reversal of position. I can see you are perplexed that—"

"I *am* curious," said Dilman quickly. "Of course, I am pleased. Your cooperation means so much. But I was wondering—"

"I will tell you," said Amboko. "I will address you frankly, as I hope we will always address one another in the days to come. Until tonight I was reluctant to trust you wholly. Until tonight I thought you were the puppet of your Master Race in this country. Forgive me, but this I thought. Then tonight I saw the truth. I observed you look around this room, and I looked around it too, and the truth was clear."

Dilman's shame rose in his throat. "The chairs, you mean, the empty chairs?"

"Yes, my friend. I realized that you were not one of them, because they would not let you be. I saw you were on your own, because of your color. I saw you for the first time as a black like myself. I knew then that our problems were one. The freedom problem. You must win your freedom here as we must maintain our own in Africa. You must convince yourself that democracy in America is real as I must convince myself it is possible in Baraza. The guests who did not come tonight, the hurt they visited upon you, the illumination of your battle that they gave me, those absent guests were the ones who swayed me. I knew that you would always understand me and my people and our aspirations because, in a larger sense, they are your own. I can now trust you. I can now return to my homeland and take the risk of letting my people be freer, because I know you will never let us down. I am prepared to help you, because I believe you will always stand ready to help me. Not because we are both black, finally, but because we have both known bondage and we have the common human desire not to suffer it again." He smiled beneath his broad expanse of nostrils and said in a kindly tone, "I thank the empty chairs, no matter how they may grieve you, for bringing us to friendship at last."

Amboko extended his ebony hand, brightened by its large sapphire ring, and Dilman warmly gripped it in his own. He wanted to express his gratefulness further, but he was too choked with emotion to do so. At last he said, "Come, President Amboko, we can tell our visitors we are ready for some well-earned relaxation."

Comforted by their agreement, the two men crossed the State Dining Room and entered the crowded Red Room. Dilman could see Grover Illingsworth's towering, impeccable, waxen person rising above the crowded champagne drinkers. He beckoned to his Chief of Protocol.

"Mr. Illingsworth," said Dilman, "why don't you get President Amboko and his party settled for our little gala? In fact, you might start shooing everyone into the East Room." Dilman turned to Amboko. "I won't be a minute. I must find my Secretary of State, inform him of what we've agreed upon, so that he can have a joint press statement drafted at once. A copy will be at Blair House for your approval later tonight."

Satisfied, Amboko gathered his entourage and followed Illingsworth out of the Red Room. As others began to move toward the door, and the crowd thinned, Dilman looked around the room for Arthur Eaton. He saw him finally, in a corner, deep in conversation with Sally Watson. For a moment he recollected Sue Abrahams' gossip about the pair, and how he had dismissed it because Eaton was too circumspect and too old for Senator Watson's child. But now, seeing them so close, he had second thoughts. They seemed right together: Eaton, despite the striking gray at his temples and through his hair, so much like a youthful aristocrat, bronzed, perfect in his faultless white tie and dinner jacket, and Sally Watson, despite her smooth, innocent countenance, so much like a mature lady with her beautiful carriage, and her bare shoulders set off by her costly white evening gown. They appeared scientifically matched. Dilman wondered where Eaton's wife was this night, and if still in Florida, why she had not returned for this occasion.

He hesitated to separate them, yet knew that he must. Before he could move to do so, Eaton's head turned toward Dilman, and Dilman was able to summon him. Eaton whispered something to his partner and came to Dilman at once, an inquiry on his features.

Dilman led his Secretary of State to the red silk Empire sofa against the wall, where they could have relative privacy. "I've finished with Amboko," Dilman said. "He's agreed to everything—everything."

Eaton's long diplomat's face, used to shrouding reaction, this time could not conceal his surprise. "Really? Splendid, Mr. President. How did you accomplish it?"

Dilman would never let one like Eaton know the truth. He said, "Oh, we'd talked so much, and then suddenly, a few minutes ago, he threw in the towel. He said that he would put his entire trust in us, to protect him against his native Communists and Soviet meddling."

"And we shall," said Eaton. "I'll speak to Monty Scott tomorrow. I'll see that he has his best Central Intelligence agents over there. Were there any reservations?"

"Not one," said Dilman. Then he snapped his fingers as he had an afterthought. "Except this. He wants our news release to be optimistic but ambiguous. He doesn't want his concession made public until he's had time to return home and secure his position there. Also, he thinks we should be silent about his concession so we can spring it on the Russians as a bargaining point."

"Of course, of course," agreed Eaton with a trace of impatience. "I suggested from the start that if we won this agreement from Baraza, we withhold it until we sit down with Premier Kasatkin. When Kasatkin begins to rave and rant about our ratification of the African Unity Pact, we hand him this concession to prove our good will. Will you sign the AUP?"

"Tonight."

"Excellent, Mr. President. I'll reopen negotiations for resumption of the Roemer Conference at once. The Russians seem to be agreeable to holding the talks in France, in Chantilly. Are you?"

"Perfectly."

"Consider it done."

"One thing, Mr. Secretary." Dilman was conscious of his continuing formality with Arthur Eaton. Try as he would, he simply could not call this formidable person Arthur. "Edna Foster and Tim Flannery are standing by downstairs. Could you slip away for a few minutes and notify them? I promised Amboko a rough draft of our joint press statement at Blair House tonight. If he has any amendments, we can incorporate them in the morning. You can tell Flannery to let the press gang know they can go home and get some sleep. We'll have nothing for them until nine in the morning."

"I'll do that at once, Mr. President. I'll go upstairs and call Edna and Tim immediately." He did not leave. He said, "I think we can agree, then, your first State Dinner has been a success."

"In some respects," said Dilman. He decided to say no more. "I'd better get to the East Room. They may be waiting for me."

"I shall not be long," said Eaton.

He left the room without a glance at Sally Watson.

Sally Watson had remained stationary in the corner of the Red Room, watching Arthur Eaton go into the Main Hall. He was moving purposefully, with concentration, and so she guessed that he was not yet on his way to the entertainment in the East Room. Restlessly she stayed on, waiting for the room to be emptied of all but herself. The moment that she saw President Dilman take his leave she gathered her long skirt a few inches from the floor for greater mobility. Just as Dilman disappeared into the Green Room, she hastened into the Main Hall.

She had the briefest glimpse of Arthur Eaton, beyond the central pillars, as he turned off to the wide staircase that led to the private apartments on the second floor. Except for the chief usher, the Secret Service agent Beggs, and a White House policeman, there was no one to observe her as she hurried along the red carpet of the arcade to the stairs. There she found two more Secret Service agents, who greeted her admiringly. For their eyes she made her ascent with more reserve and dignity.

The State Dinner had been a thrill for her, because of its success and despite its failure, although the failure part made her feel insecure about her position as social secretary. From the instant, however, that Arthur Eaton had sought her out in the Red Room, all thoughts of the dinner had vanished from her mind. Arthur—now really her Arthur, her darling, since she had visited him twice alone in his Georgetown house, and had had the one midnight drive with him to that tiny bar near the Normandy Farms, off the River Road in Potomac—had dominated all her waking hours. Arthur had been beautiful tonight, and in their minutes together, considering the important guests around, he had been almost daring. She suspected, from his lack of inhibition, that he had been drinking more than he ordinarily drank. She had not minded, indeed, loved it, because it had made him more open and romantic.

She remembered: he had teased her about their evening last week in his house that nestled behind the trees on Dumbarton Avenue. After dinner, after the maid and cook had retired, he had poured the brandies, while she had studied the antique-filled gracious Tudor living room with its two fireplaces. She had felt drunk with excitement that night, reckless, and following the brandy she had blurted out, "Arthur, I don't want to embarrass you, but where is your wife?"

"In Florida," he had replied calmly.

"No—no—" Her hand had drawn an arc around the room. "I don't see a single framed photograph of your wife. Isn't that peculiar?"

He had remained unruffled, smiling. "Not at all, my dear. You see, I put them away in drawers before you came the first time. They're still in the drawers."

"Oh." She had speculated upon that act. "What if she came home suddenly?"

Still unperturbed, he had said, "I doubt that she will be here for many months."

Sally had then wondered if they were quietly being divorced, and prayed for it, but had not bothered him with it, for she wanted no definite answers so early, not until she was indispensable to him. "I see. Well, it is cozier this way. I wouldn't want her glaring at me. You were thoughtful, Arthur. You think of everything."

He had come to sit on the sofa beside her. "I don't want you distracted when you are with me. These evenings mean too much."

She had held out her arms, and he had gone into them, embracing her passionately, kissing her eyelids and forehead and ears and lips. And then the special telephone from the Pentagon had come between them. That had been that.

The next time together, he had kissed her again, caressed her, in his car in the parking lot outside the café in Potomac, and had briefly resumed after driving her to her home, but he had done no more.

She had desired him, and was ready to satisfy his desire when he made the demand. He had not yet demanded her, at least not until tonight in the Red Room, when he had been somewhat drunk and was dazzled by her low-cut white gown. After she had teased him about that time in his living room, the hiding of Kay's photographs, he had become serious and so had she. He missed her every day, he had whispered. He wanted to see her more, be with her alone, know her better. She had waited expectantly for the final overture, the ultimate invitation, and then President Dilman had stolen him away.

She could not let go of their precious exchange, its promise and potential, and she was determined to play their scene out to its conclusion. Perhaps, because of whatever Dilman had told him, his mood had been altered and he would not go further with her. Or perhaps nothing had changed. She must find out. And so instead of going to the East Room to help direct the seating, her duty as President Dilman's social secretary, she had followed Arthur Eaton upstairs.

She stood now, uncertainly, in the vast West Hall of the President's private second floor. No one, not even the valet, was in sight. She wondered which of the fifteen rooms Arthur had gone into, and then she wondered if he would be conferring with someone or be by himself. The champagne bubbled behind her eyes, reinforcing her adventure, making her intrepid.

Stealthily she went to the Monroe Room, tried the door, peered inside. It was empty. Shutting the door softly, she started toward the Yellow Oval Room, and then, nearing it, she heard his voice. She stopped beside the partially open doors, listening, trying to determine whether Arthur was speaking to someone in the room or on the telephone.

He was addressing Tim—that would be Tim Flannery —but still no evidence whether it was the press secretary in person or on the telephone. She listened harder. Only Arthur's voice could be heard, then silences, then Arthur again. No question now. Telephone. To hell with discretion.

She released the folds of skirt gathered in her hand. She peered down at the cleft between her breasts, which were pressed high by the built-in brassière cups of the evening gown. She took hold of her bodice at the waist with both hands, pulling it down an inch (the way it was meant to be) so that the milky rise at the top of her bosom was defined as her most attractive accessory. Lightly touching her hair to be sure every strand was in place, she straightened. Boldly she opened the first entrance door and walked into the Yellow Oval Room.

He was standing with the receiver at his mouth and ear, leaning against a sofa. When he saw her, he lifted his hand in welcome, smiling, but continued to listen to the voice on the other end. Suddenly he cupped the mouthpiece tightly and called out softly, "Be right with you, darling."

Sally closed the doors, then wandered about the lustrous room, hardly listening to him, knowing only that he had apparently dictated something about Baraza, and was hearing Flannery read it back, and was suggesting revisions. On a fragile Louis XVI end table she noticed three books in a neat pile, the President's reading, and when she bent to read the titles, she found them strangely incongruous with the furnishings of the living room. One was the latest *Congressional Staff Directory,* another *Our CIA Defense* by Montgomery Scott, and the third, at the bottom of the pile, a faded, mottled, second-hand volume, *My Bondage and Freedom* by Douglass. She drew the bottom book out from under the others and opened it to the title page, which read "My Bondage and My Freedom, Part I—Life as a Slave. Part II—Life as a Freeman. By Frederick Douglass." It had been published in New York and Auburn by Miller, Orton, and Mulligan, in 1855. Sally turned to the lengthy dedication and then to the following page, and there, above the "Editor's Preface," was an inscription in pale blue ink, a slanting, definitely feminine inscription that read, "For my favorite Senator—the first Douglass would have been so proud of the present one. With enduring affection, Always, W." The date was last year, the day and month President Dilman's birthday, she remembered.

Sally examined the inscribed "Always, W.," closed the book, lifted the others, and returned it to its former place. Going to the wall to the right of the fireplace, intending to study the two Cézanne paintings once more, her mind lingered on the inscription to Dilman. Her feline curiosity reached for, pawed and clawed for, a female W. connected with the President. Mrs. Wickland, wife of the House Majority Leader? No, unthinkable, not a *personal* inscription like this one. W.? At once, it came to Sally. W. for Wanda, Miss Wanda Gibson, the friend of the Spingers, whom Dilman had invited to the State Dinner tonight, who had neither responded to the invitation (gauche), nor appeared, although Dilman had insisted that she would (interesting). So Wanda Gibson, probably Wanda if she was the W., was a personal friend, even last year on his birthday. Intriguing.

Before she could speculate further, she felt cool, strong hands on her naked shoulders, and turned around to find herself looking up at Arthur Eaton.

"Business concluded," he said. "I'm glad you came up here, Sally."

"I thought you might need a secretary."

He held her arms, squeezed them. "I might need someone who needs me."

"I hoped you'd say that. I—I was unhappy the President interrupted us. It was going so well."

"I was sorry, too, but it was important. He brought Baraza into line tonight. Not that it was so difficult. But I'm afraid he needed something affirmative to shore up his pride. In all my existence I've never been witness to anything like the social rejection that took place downstairs."

"It was terrible. I hope he doesn't blame it on me."

"On you? Nonsense. You did what you could."

"I swear, ninety-six of them accepted—*accepted*. Do you know how many showed up tonight? I counted the cards. Fifty-seven. I checked with my office right before dinner. And then with Edna. There was such a flurry of notes, telegrams, telephone calls, terribly apologetic, everyone fallen ill at once. I've never known an epidemic like that to sweep Washington. And the worst part of it was the cruel timing, the heavy last-minute declining, so that by the time I realized what was actually going on, it was too late to remove the table settings and chairs. I mean, it couldn't be done, there was no time left. So there they were, those embarrassing chairs. I'm sorry for him. It's so humiliating. It'll be in all the columns tomorrow, you can be sure. No matter how many faults he has, he didn't deserve this."

"I don't like it either," Eaton said. "Whatever one's views, there is such a practice as observing the social amenities. We have a generation of gauche boors."

His usage of *gauche* brought to her mind what had been there a minute ago. "At least his friends showed up, the Spingers, the Abrahams, all—except one."

Eaton's eyebrows raised. "One?"

Sally savored her tidbit. "Have you ever heard of Miss Wanda Gibson? She works for Vaduz Exporters . . . no, of course you haven't. Well, she lives with the Spingers, and as far as I can guess is an old friend of the Presi-

dent's. He specifically invited her for tonight, and when
she didn't answer and I asked him what to do this morning, he went into a long thing about how she would show
up anyway with the Spingers. He disowned any personal
interest. He said that her export company traded with
Baraza, and she would be someone Amboko and Wamba
could feel at home with. Well, the President was mistaken. Miss Gibson did not appear. And also, I don't
mind telling you, and this I don't understand at all, he
was mistaken about Miss Gibson's Vaduz company
being involved with Baraza. I wanted to make conversation with Ambassador Wamba before dinner, so I mentioned Vaduz, and he looked blank, perfectly blank.
He'd never heard of it. Do you think Wamba was bluffing? Or that the President didn't know? Or—I know this
is awful of me—that the President invented an excuse for
inviting Miss Gibson?"

Eaton's hands still held her arms, and he smiled and
said, "I haven't the faintest idea, Sally, but I do know
you are the best representative the State Department has
ever had in the White House."

"Arthur, don't make fun of me. I only want to be of
help. I'd do anything for you."

"Well," he said lightly, "there are some of us who'd
give a good deal to find out what the devil the President
has in mind about that minorities bill, and a few other
matters."

"I can find out," she said eagerly.

He shook her playfully. "I was kidding, Sally. We don't
need a secret operative in the White House. We're both
working with the President. If we do our jobs well,
that is enough." His smile went away. "I prefer you as
you are, not as Mata Hari."

She lifted her fingers to his neck and caressed it.
"Arthur—before—you were saying before how much
you missed me—how you wanted to see me more often
—alone. . . . I'd like that."

"Right now I want to kiss you," he said.

Her eyes went to the entrance door, worriedly, and
then to the balcony doors to her left. "Let's go outside
a minute."

"You'll freeze."

"You'll keep me warm."

He released her, and she went to the first sash wood door. Opening it, she stepped out into the darkness of the Truman Balcony and stood beside the moist green pad that covered the white metal settee. He came to her in the shadows, and she went quickly into his hard arms, feeling her breasts flattened against his chest as his parted lips rubbed against hers and finally held to them. They clung to one another, and when his lips freed her, she gasped, "I love you, Arthur. I want you—you say it."

"Tonight," he said.

"Tonight."

"When you're through here, come straight to the house. You don't have to go home tonight."

"Will the servants—?"

"They are off. Just us, alone."

"Yes, Arthur." She heard her exultant heart beating wildly, and brought her hands up to hold his face, and kissed him quickly. "There'll be a million years of time tonight." She pushed herself from him and sought his hand. "Let's get downstairs, before we're missed. . . . No, wait, I'll go first, then you . . . I can't stand these next hours. You do love me, don't you, darling? You won't be sorry, you won't be sorry at all."

In the middle of the front row of seats in the white-and-gold hall that was the East Room, President Dilman sat impassively, his arms resting motionless on the arms of his chair like the paws of a sphinx, as he watched with distaste the show being performed by the Hollywood and Manhattan entertainers.

His mood had been good an hour ago when he sat down with President Amboko and waited while the guests noisily took their places. His good mood had continued as the entertainment began with the five-piece orchestra on the raised platform before him doing its lively medley of George M. Cohan songs, ending on the rousing "Yankee Doodle Dandy."

Then after the provocative blues singer, Libby Owens, backed by her own accompanist at the ornate mahogany grand piano with its gilt eagle legs, had rendered "St. Louis Blues" sweet and low, Dilman's mood of well-being had begun to deteriorate. Just as he and so many of his fellow Negroes resented aggressive liberal whites who buttonholed them in ostentatious and determined displays of equality, speaking to them with proper indignation of nothing but Negro problems, he resented the slant and content of this show. The white entertainers, out of misplaced eagerness to parade their tolerance (look-we-are-on-your-side-fellow), had loaded their program heavily with both serious and humorous Negro sketches and songs. Dilman detested this kind of patronizing, well-intentioned though it may have been. If a Jew were President, he asked himself, would this same crowd have presented Yiddish jokes and songs?

He stared at the stage with displeasure. There was Herbie Teele, the brash nimble-limbed colored comedian, propped high on a stool, derby lopsided on his head, homely black face feigning solemnity, then wide-grinning after each burst of applause, twirling his cane and spouting his half-bitter inside integration stories and jokes. Why Herbie Teele tonight? Why this special routine? Would this same crowd have offered the same program to T.C., to The Judge, to Lyndon Johnson, to John F. Kennedy? Dilman doubted it.

He cast a sidelong glance at Amboko and then down the row at other members of the Barazan entourage, and they seemed appreciative enough. They were chuckling, beaming, and the constant eruptions of laughter from the rows behind indicated that Allan Noyes, the Party's national chairman, had cast the evening right. At last Dilman once more had to blame himself for his own thin-skinned sensitivity, but he felt the way he felt, and there was no use trying to feel any other way.

He tried to be more attentive to the stage.

Herbie Teele, elastic mouth, brace of white chipmunk teeth, was concluding his routine.

"Well, all that I am, all that I hope to be, I owe to one of the pioneers of topical humor, my fellow Afro-

American, Dick Gregory," said Teele. "He went to jail so's I could come to the White House. Like Dick used to say, these days I'm gettin' a couple thousand a week for saying the same things I used to say under my breath. No matter what the goings-on in Mississippi, they're really not readying to pass a law banning mixed drinks. So, like ol' Dick, I'm not worried. The President is doin' his best. He's got the Reverend Spinger in there, and the Reverend is the only famous man I know who's given out more fingerprints than autographs. The kids down South used to collect his signature on police blotters. Well, folks, let me bow out with one more to my mentor, Dick Gregory—like he used to think, I was just thinkin' " —Teele jumped off his stool and came to the edge of the platform and rubbed his cheeks vigorously—"now, wouldn't it be a helluva joke if all this on me was burnt cork and all you folks were being tolerant for nuthin'?"

He slapped his hands, reared back and roared, and the audience behind Dilman gave out a great whoop of laughter and joy in unison, and applauded for a half minute as the audacious Teele pranced off the platform.

Dilman clapped halfheartedly, and when he had ceased, the two chandeliers above had dimmed, and Libby Owens, in her tight sequined skirt slit thigh-high, stood center stage, while her colored accompanist slid onto the bench behind the piano.

She drew the microphone to her and announced throatily, "For the finale, I shall render three haunting Negro spirituals by unknown bards."

She began, and the room was hushed in the soft light. She sang:

> "I know moon-rise, I know star-rise,
>   Lay dis body down.
> I walk in de moonlight, I walk in de starlight,
> To lay dis body down.
> I'll walk in de graveyard, I'll walk through the
>   graveyard
> To lay dis body down.
> I'll lie in de grave and stretch out my arms;
> Lay dis body down."

The melancholy lyric moved Dilman, sent memory clutching backward for an almost forgotten part of his childhood, and he was too lost in the distant past to realize that someone, bent low, had hurried past the front row and crouched before him. He stirred, then was startled to find Beecher, the valet, on a knee waiting to address him.

"Mr. President," the valet whispered, "Attorney General Kemmler is in the Blue Room. He must see you at once. He says it is urgent."

Dilman's heartbeat tripped. *It is urgent.* He had been so far away, rocking in the helpless cradle of the past, that he was unprepared to cope with crisis in the world of tall men.

Dilman shivered. "Tell him I'll be right there."

Silently the valet slipped away, and Dilman waited for the last of Libby Owens' lyrics. As she finished the spiritual, and the room rang with applause, Dilman excused himself to Amboko, speaking under his breath, then hurriedly rose and went past the guests sitting in the front row and to the exit. He could see that first Eaton, then Nat Abrahams, were observing his sudden departure, and he shrugged to both. He went into the Main Hall, just as the piano resumed and Libby Owens sang, "Oh, Mary, don't you weep, don't you moan."

Coming into the Main Hall of the first floor, Dilman found himself immediately flanked by two Secret Service agents.

"Why don't you keep your eye on President Amboko," Dilman suggested. "I'll be all right."

Nevertheless, they accompanied him up the corridor, past the Green Room, until they came to the entrance to the Blue Room, where Otto Beggs was on guard, and Beecher had pushed the door open. Dilman hung back a moment, steeling himself for this crisis that was as yet unknown to him, and then went into the large formal chamber, hearing the door click closed behind him.

There were two of them waiting for him, he observed. Robert Lombardi, the Director of the Federal Bureau of Investigation, bald as a cannonball and as inflexible and physically round, was pacing in short, quick steps near the velvet-draped circular table in the middle of the room. His usual forced public smile was missing. His forehead was damp. Beyond him, fingers laced together behind his back, loomed the presence of Attorney General Clay Kemmler, still wearing his coat.

"Gentlemen," said Dilman, announcing himself.

Lombardi's pacing stopped. He moved to one side of the room in token deference to his superiors as Kemmler spun around from the lofty center window, and as he did so, the spire of the Washington Monument in the distance appeared to emerge from his head, making him resemble a unicorn rearing on its hind legs. Immediately, Kemmler came forward to where the FBI Director had been, and Dilman, advancing to meet him, could see across the circular table that the Attorney General's cold eyes glittered, but that his tight lips, a slash in his craggy face, were severe and implacable.

"Mr. President," he said, "what I've been expecting has happened. The second that Bob Lombardi received the flash from his field operatives and brought it to me, I came right over. I hated to break in on you, but I think you'll agree the news is of critical import."

Dilman placed his fingers on the draped table to steady himself, and then remained immobile.

"We don't have every detail yet, but the essential news is this," Attorney General Kemmler said. "The Hattiesburg kidnaping was committed by a gang of Turnerites led by Jefferson Hurley himself. They have since killed Judge Everett Gage in cold blood, and the FBI has apprehended Hurley. The others in his gang got away. But we have Hurley, we've got him good, and now you can have no more reservations."

Dilman allowed the sensational report to sink in, rocking on his heels, cursing himself for not having believed Kemmler this morning and in consequence having been made to look like an indecisive fool—or worse, like a prejudiced black. "You have Hurley?" he repeated woodenly. "And they actually murdered Gage? What more do you know?"

Kemmler jerked his head toward the FBI chief. "Bob—" he said.

Robert Lombardi came back to the table. The dampness on his forehead had spread to the top of his pate. His high-pitched confirmation came out as if strained through his nostrils. "Mr. President, as of a half hour ago, this is what happened, and this much is accurate. My men trailed the kidnapers from Mississippi, across Louisiana, into southeast Texas. They were moving fast, those kidnapers, but they weren't too hard to follow, being amateurs and, begging your pardon, being of dark skin. They holed up on some ranch before reaching Beaumont, and laid low, and my field agents spread a pretty wide net to catch them in. Then there were a couple of pistol shots on this ranch, and as luck would have it, some of our men were nearby. We sent out an alert, surrounded the farm, and nabbed Jeff Hurley and found Judge Everett Gage's corpse. The rest of the gang —don't know how many there were yet—got away. Hurley's not telling, but evidence indicates there may have been two more of them."

"You know that it was Hurley who killed Judge Gage?" Dilman asked.

"He confessed it, Mr. President. Well, not at first, of course. What we figured out was he'd stayed behind a minute too long, to clean up things—burn some papers and hide his gun. We found the revolver. Two chambers empty, and two bullets were in old Judge Gage, one in his chest and one in his abdomen. Ballistics says the markings on the bullets were made by the barrel of Hurley's revolver. Then we—we put a bit of pressure on Hurley— he's a sullen bull—and he finally admitted to doing it. We've got his signed confession to the murder. Well, what he said, actually, at first, was that they intended Gage no physical harm, they weren't killers like Gage and his Southern Klansmen—lots of propaganda like that —but in trying to hide out from us, trying to find a real concealment until they could continue to Mexico, they let down their guard on their victim. Gage worked his wrists free, got his hands on one of their rifles, and instead of trying to escape, prepared to gun them down. Hurley came into the room, and Gage fired at him. Hurley said that it was a matter of self-defense, his own survival, and instinctively he pulled out his pistol and began firing back, got Gage with his first two shots."

Lombardi shook his head. "Mr. President, you can discount that kind of whining. We always get that song at the Bureau. It was murder, pure and simple, compounded by the Federal offense of kidnaping, crossing two state lines. As Clay here says, Hurley is the secondary issue. He's caught, he's confessed, and he's as much as buried. The bigger issue, and that's what the Bureau is proud of, is that we've proved it was a Turnerite Group plot and crime. Since we know they're a pack of Red scum anyway, this gives us what we've been hoping for."

Something inside Dilman prickled, and he said, "What have you been hoping for?"

Kemmler's arm went out, forcibly pushing Lombardi from his spot near the table. "Let me take it from here, Bob. My department. . . . Mr. President, I laid it on the line with you this morning. I said we have evidence that Valetti, the Turnerites' Number Two man, is a member of the Communist Party and is a go-between, financing violent racial groups like the Turnerites so they can commit acts of subversion, create an atmosphere of hate and rebellion in this country, and weaken us at home and abroad. I said that the first major crime of this sort had been perpetrated by the Turnerites, and I demanded that we act at once to outlaw them, to discourage further organized violence. You felt I was being hasty about such a big move. I said Turnerites definitely, and you said Turnerites maybe. You wanted more evidence before acting. Now you have the evidence. You can't have any more doubts. I want to invoke the Subversive Activities Control Act at once. This is our first clean-cut opportunity to show these damn agitators the law has teeth. I've got to use it, and put an end to insurrection."

During this demand, Dilman's mind had gone to the consequences of invoking the control act. It would place a terrible onus on his race. Worse, and here his cooler legal brain was at work, it would strike a blow against civil liberties, setting a precedent that could soon be misused. Still, there was the law, and there was the crime

against this law—Kemmler was right about that—and
justice must be observed, and national security (his prime
concern) must be preserved. But there must be no mistake, no margin of error, no matter how small or narrow. Lombardi had a reputation for being ruthlessly if
not sadistically anti-Communist on the United States domestic front, not wrong in itself, but often he had been
too eager to interpret every coloration of opinion and
action as Red, and consequently had had his arrests re-
versed by more unbiased minds. Was he too eager now?
Was he being honestly patriotic, or subconsciously using
this as a grand opportunity to make headlines and raise
himself even higher on his pedestal as the public's foremost law enforcement officer and superpatriot?

As for Clay Kemmler, he, too, was eager and ambitious, yet Dilman could find no reason to fault him for
bad judgment or overriding vanity. Kemmler had been a
district attorney, a Federal judge, T.C.'s Cabinet member, a person of spotless reputation. Still, he had shown
himself to be impatient, which Dilman regarded as injudicious, and to be motivated less by considerations of
political advancement, probably, than by some kind of
absolute view of what was just and unjust. He was a man
to be listened to, but not one to be overwhelmed by, not
without deliberating upon every word he spoke first.

Dilman deliberated, teetering on his dilemma, not
wanting to jump or be pushed, yet not wishing to fall.

"I believe you have a sound case," Dilman said at
last. "I'm not concerned about Hurley as an individual.
He committed the crime of kidnaping, clearly. Did he
commit premeditated homicide or homicide in self-
defense? That will be for the Federal courts to determine.
So you see, I, too, am concerned only with the larger
issue. Was this so-called crime of subversion an organization crime or an individual one? There is still no air-
tight—"

"Please, Mr. President, don't start that again," interrupted Kemmler. For the first time, his rigid face was
clotted with anger. He tried to control himself, with little
success. "Mr.—Mr. President—how can you have second thoughts about cracking down on an overt and out-

rageous crime like this? Over in Justice, we have a file on every one of Hurley's public utterances as head of the Turnerites. Even if his motives were the best, to give your people equality overnight, to be their black Moses, it's not enough to offset what he's done. Time and again, in public, he promised violence if the Negroes could not have their way. Then a crime of violence was performed, kidnaping and confessed murder, and who did it? Hurley and his gang. He practiced what he preached for the Turnerites. Are you going to go before the American people and say you doubt that?"

Dilman weakened under his Attorney General's righteous wrath. Desperately, Dilman tried to fortify himself with Blackstone and the Constitution. "I'm not doubting anything, when there is factual evidence to support it. Yes, I'm inclined to believe this is a Turnerite crime, an organized and planned crime, and I'm inclined to punish the group responsible. But, Mr. Attorney General, when I do something unprecedented, that is necessary to protect us now, in spite of attendant harmful aftereffects, I must be positive I am right, 100 per cent positive, not 99 per cent positive. Did the Turnerite Group meet and plan this crime and vote for it, and then did Hurley and several others, representing the Group, carry it out? If that is the case, it is subversion, and to be punished instantly. Or—and here is my one per cent legal doubt—did the Turnerite Group vote against this as being impractical and inflammatory, and did their leader, hardly a reasonable man at any time, go off on his own, with one or two accomplices, and did they perform the heinous deed as individuals? I must know that the last did not happen. I must learn which it was from Hurley himself, or from his accomplices, when and if you catch them, or from any other reliable Turnerite members you question, or from Turnerite records that you find." He held up his hands. "That's my view of it, gentlemen."

Kemmler glared at him. He said coldly, "What if we can't find any more evidence?"

"I'll see then. I'll study Mr. Lombardi's findings, the interrogation of Hurley, and make up my mind. I sup-

pose I'll let you invoke the control act. But until I do,
I suggest you not make any rash moves or statements."
He made an effort to gain their friendship, to mollify
their anger. "Look, gentlemen, you have Hurley. Go
ahead with that. Announce it. As to banning his organization, give me a day or two, overnight at least——"

"Good night, Mr. President," said Kemmler curtly.
"Come on, Bob."

"I'll be in touch," said Lombardi to Dilman. "Good
night, sir."

Regretfully Douglass Dilman watched them leave him.
He had not merely disappointed them, he had infuriated
them with his indecisiveness. Would they believe that
he was motivated by a true concern for justice, or solely
by a sympathy and partiality toward hounded men of
his own color? He knew their answer. He was less sure
of his own.

They had gone, but the door was still open, and now
he noticed the bulky Otto Beggs waiting to speak to him.

"Mr. President," Beggs said, "we've been holding a
phone call for you. Miss Foster downstairs says she must
talk to you. Do you want to take it in here?"

"Yes, please."

Beggs closed the door, and Dilman walked tiredly to
the indigo-colored French telephone that sat on the pier
table.

He took up the receiver. Edna Foster was on the line,
sounding as harried as he felt.

"Mr. President," she was saying, "I have Leroy Poole
on the other phone. It's the sixth time he's called tonight.
He insists upon speaking to you personally. He sounded
so frantic that——"

"No," said Dilman irritably. "I have no time for him
tonight."

"I'm sorry to bother you," Edna Foster apologized.
"I wouldn't have, except he said it was so important,
something about Jefferson Hurley being arrested in
Texas——I didn't know what he was talking about——"

Ready to hang up, Dilman suddenly gripped the receiver hard. "Wait a minute, Miss Foster. You say Leroy
wants to talk to me about Hurley's arrest?"

"That's right, Mr. President."

Dilman's brain aligned this information beside another piece of information. The two facts did not belong side by side. What had brought them there together? Apperception told him the answer to this might be the answer to what had made him so indecisive before Kemmler and Lombardi.

"I've changed my mind, Miss Foster. Put him on."

For a few brief seconds the telephone was dumb, and then it had Leroy Poole's squeaky, hysterical voice. "Mr. President, is that you—you—Mr. President?"

"Yes, Leroy, what is it?"

The words tumbled forth in a torrent. "Mr. President —have you heard?—geez, the FBI caught Jeff Hurley in Texas, and they're indicting him for the murder of Judge Gage. Mr. President, you can't let them frame him —it was justifiable homicide—it can be proved—even the kidnaping wasn't exactly that—they were taking the judge to reason with him, show him new information— but then Gage became violent, got hold of a weapon, tried to kill Hurley, and Hurley did what any man on earth would do—what you and I would do. He defended himself, he acted in self-defense to save his life. That's the truth of it, I swear, and it's in your hands. If you haven't heard, they got poor Hurley—"

"Leroy!" Dilman broke in, and his stern command checked Poole's hysteria. "Leroy—I *have* heard—I know *all* that—but how do *you* know?"

"Me? How do I know?" Leroy Poole sounded confused. "I don't understand. What do you mean?"

"I'll spell out what I mean. Minutes ago I heard of Judge Gage's death and Hurley's arrest in Texas from the FBI chief and the Attorney General. Except for the three of us here in the White House, and a handful of FBI agents in Texas, and a couple of Hurley's friends who got away, nobody knows about this incident. It couldn't have happened more than an hour ago. And the news just got to us. So how do *you* know?"

It was as if the phone at the other end had gone dead.

"Leroy, are you there?" Dilman said. "Listen to me.

You're calling, asking for help for Hurley. If you want my help, you'd better give me yours."

Still the other end of the line was silent, but now Dilman could hear Poole's labored breathing.

"Leroy, if you don't want to get involved with the FBI yourself, and I mean that, you'd better level with me. You'll find me easier to talk to than those agents." He hesitated, then resumed harshly. "I think you've given me the picture already. Many times as you've denied it, you are in the Turnerite movement, aren't you? Apparently a secret member, isn't that right? Now a lot of things you've said recently make sense. Jeff Hurley's your friend, at least your boss, isn't he? And now someone has gotten to you—not Hurley, he's incommunicado this minute—but the others, one of his accomplices in the killing, he or they, they've got in touch with you from wherever they are and told you what happened, and they're desperate, and they know that you know me, and they asked you to appeal to me. Is that right, Leroy?"

He heard Poole's disjointed whine at last. "Mr.—Mr. Pres-President, I swear on my mom and everything that's holy, one of the members called long distance, which one, who, I don't know, no names on the telephone, and simply told me what happened to Jeff Hurley, the truth of it, and asked me to help him, see the truth gets known. That's all I know, I swear to God in Heaven."

"All right, I take your word for it, Leroy. But you still haven't told me what I want to know. This abduction of Judge Gage, it was done by your gang, by the Turnerite Group, wasn't it?"

"What if it was? Sure it was. You don't think a man of Jeff Hurley's moral character and standards would go out for some personal revenge, do you? He and whoever was with him, they agreed to lead the way, to be the first like John Brown, to set an example, not order others to do what they wouldn't be willing to do themselves. So they did it for the Turnerites—not kidnaping, either—but merely taking that sonofabitching, persecuting magistrate to another climate where they could reason with him about his abortion of justice, make him rescind it or admit he was wrong, make him agree to be the instrument to let our poor guys free. This was no hoodlum act, Mr. President. It was a protest act by the only decent, uncorrupted protest society in America today, doing something, not just talk and compromise, but doing something to dramatize the plight of every beat-up and degraded colored man and woman and kid in the country. You—you of all people—should be the first to see that, Mr. President. And you can become the greatest President in history, a hero of our people, if you will shake off those white bastards around you and intercede for Jeff Hurley—"

Dilman felt ill with the knowledge of the truth, with the realization of what had happened and what he must do. His loathing of this truth, its consequences, filled every bone of his body with a creeping dullness.

"Leroy," he said wearily, "Hurley is no longer the issue. The Turnerite Group is the issue, the whole society, you and every one of them, your membership, your financing, your program—that's the issue. You may as well know. The Justice Department is going to take legal action against you, to disband and outlaw you, and arrest and fine those who resist."

There was shock in Poole's trembling voice. "You—you can't let them do that."

"I have no choice. I must."

"No, listen, Senator—Mr. President—don't, don't let them. If you kill Hurley, disband what he's fought for, you kill me and yourself. With one act, you hurl us back where we were before the Civil War. Freedom now becomes freedom never. Ban us, and the fiery crosses and police dogs win. Every activist group will have to close shop and get off the street when the white man passes. We're niggers again, with no hope but those ass-dragging old Uncle Toms in the Crispus and NAACP. We're niggers again, and when we want white men's food, they'll throw us our watermelon rind like the Minorities Rehabilitation Bill, so's our mouths will be full and we'll have to stay shut up. Mr. President, don't do it, don't go bowing and scraping after the ones who're lording it over you, don't sell us out, because if you do, you'll not only kill us, like I said, but you'll make every one of your people your enemy and the enemy of your Party for life."

Annoyance at the offensive little writer's presumption and disrespect momentarily overrode Dilman's guilts and fears. "I've heard enough, Leroy. I have no more time to talk to you. I've got my job to attend to. I'm going to do what has to be done. Good-bye and—"

"Hold on, Mr. President," Poole called out across the wire. "You're sure, you're absolutely positive, *nothing* can change your mind?"

Dilman hesitated, not because of what Poole said but because of how he had said it. Poole was no longer hysterical or wheedling, no longer begging. There had been a new undercurrent in his voice, of slyness, even cruelty. Perhaps, Dilman told himself, he was imagining too much.

He still held the receiver, and now he brought the mouthpiece closer. "No, Leroy, nothing can change my mind. I will instruct the Department of Justice to observe the law immediately. I have no more to say."

"I have," said Leroy Poole. "One last thing. Listen. You indict the Turnerites for criminal subversion, and you indict your own son, too. You hear me? You indict your own son. Maybe it is news to you, but Julian is one of us. Julian is one of our secret members assigned to the Crispus Society, to get at their private files of statistics on cases of white persecution, like the information that Hattiesburg was a hot place to begin our crusade, If you condemn us, you—"

Dilman's hand clenched the telephone until his fingers were nearly bloodless. The nausea that welled high in his throat was not of fear but of disgust. He said, "You're no better than Hurley—you'll do anything—you're a rotten, sick liar, dragging my boy into it."

"Am I?" said Poole. "Okay, Big Man, ask him—and then let's see what you'll do!"

He banged the telephone in Dilman's ear.

Douglass Dilman stood motionless, the receiver still poised at his mouth and ear. Kemmler and Lombardi were right, and Poole had confirmed it. And they were right about another thing, too. There was no room in America for Turnerites, black or white. They were savage. They were vicious. No tactic, no matter how slimy and foul, was too low for them to accept, with their psychotic minds, and to brandish as a club. Kidnaping. Murder. Now—family blackmail. The Lord damn them and curse them every one.

He jiggled the telephone for the White House operator, and demanded she get him Edna Foster.

When his secretary came on, he said, "Miss Foster, I'm coming down to the office. Ring up Attorney General Kemmler. If he's not home yet, leave a message with anyone there. Tell Kemmler to come back to the White House immediately. Say the President has made up his mind and must see him at once."

"Yes, Mr. President. Will that be all?"

"All?" He wondered: Could there be more? Something nagged. "Uh, one last thing. Before you go home, Miss Foster—that letter you wrote to Trafford University, turning them down—tear it up. I've changed my mind. Write Chancellor McKaye I consider it a privilege to accept that honorary degree, and I'm glad to accept the invitation to make the principal address. Inform him I will speak not only to his student body and faculty, but to the nation, on a policy decision of national importance. Have you got that, Miss Foster?"

"Yes, Mr. President."

"And then write a short note to my son—to Julian— tell him I'll be at the school on Founders' Day, and that I want him there, because—because after the ceremony —I want to have a private talk with him about a matter that concerns us both. Is that clear, Miss Foster? Leave both letters on my desk for signature, and then go home. Now, you'd better get that call in to Kemmler first."

He hung up, and then he strode to the door, opened it, and went into the corridor. The ever-present Otto Beggs was still on duty.

"Is the show over with?" Dilman asked.

"Fifteen minutes ago, Mr. President. They kept it going with encores, hoping you'd get back. The guests are gone. Except there's one gentleman—"

It was then that Dilman sighted Nat Abrahams

slumped on a red chair in the Main Hall, puffing his pipe. Abrahams came to his feet, waved, and started toward Dilman.

"I thought I'd hang around a little bit," said Abrahams as he approached, "in case you needed a friendly ear. I was worried the way you left the East Room. Anything I can do, Doug?"

"Damn kind of you, Nat. Thanks. There's nothing anyone can do for me tonight—except me." Dilman tried to smile. "Believe me, Nat, I'd rather be talking to you than to the Attorney General. But he's the one I've got to go downstairs to see."

Nat Abrahams nodded agreeably. "Another time, then." His eyes did not leave Dilman. "I'm not prying, Doug, but is everything all right?"

"Nat, everything is lousy, and I'm afraid it'll get worse. Maybe I'll be able to tell you about it someday soon. Anyway, what was that girl singing in there before? Yes. 'I'll lie in de grave and stretch out my arms' and 'Lay dis body down.' That's what I'd like to do tonight, Nat."

"Not yet, Doug."

"No, not yet. . . . Good night, Nat. And, Nat. Don't let your kids grow up to be President. They deserve better. Remember that."

THE WHITE HOUSE

**ADDRESS OF THE PRESIDENT AT THE FOUNDERS' DAY
CEREMONY, TRAFFORD UNIVERSITY, NEW YORK, AFTER
RECEIVING AN HONORARY DEGREE IN PHILOSOPHY.
COPIES OF THIS SPEECH ARE BEING DISTRIBUTED TO
THE PRESS AT TRAFFORD UNIVERSITY AND
FROM THIS OFFICE.**

Chancellor McKaye, my fellow citizens:

It is a great pleasure for me to participate in this ninety-second celebration of the founding of your illustrious school. I am deeply gratified by the academic distinction being conferred upon me. This is not simply because the award has been given by a Negro university to one who is Negro, but because the award has been given by an institution—whose program and teachings have risen above the narrow confines of racial thinking—to one who is working as an American member of our national community and not as an Afro-American member of our country.

Indeed, it is about our relationship to our nation as a whole, as Americans, and nothing else, that I wish to address you today. You are aware of the racial unrest in our country.

You are aware, also, that the Department of Justice and I
have been studying evidence of the activities of these super-
government, super-American societies and organizations,
composed of extremists of the right and left, of white and
black, responsible for fomenting such dangerous unrest in
these critical . . .

———————

IT WAS a cool, shining autumn morning, and President
Dilman, feeling slightly ridiculous in his tasseled mortar-
board and warmed by his dark gown, sat comfortably
on the outdoor, flag-decorated stage, basking in the sun,
only partially attentive to Chancellor McKaye's laudatory
introduction.

Except for the Washington press corps, predominantly
white, seated in rows down to his left, busily engaged in
reading and marking the mimeographed advance release of his address which Tim Flannery had passed out
minutes before, the sea of faces stretching before and
around him was black. The faculty and alumni, the ones
he could see clearly because they were directly below in
folding chairs, appeared interested and hospitable. The
mass of the student body beyond, crowded and standing
(and Julian probably among them, having rejected a
place on the platform), represented a jagged inky blur
offering no visible clue to its friendliness or hostility toward him. The fact was, they were there, orderly and
silent, and to Dilman this seemed a good sign.

While he was no judge of crowds, Dilman guessed
that there must be more than three thousand persons
present, an amplitude of humanity that blanketed every
foot of the rectangular grassy quadrangle, and the walks
and shaded malls leading into it as well. What gave the
scene its added dignity, even majesty, were the old stone
buildings, vine-covered, rising behind the audience, the
Social Science Building, Medgar Evers Memorial Library, the School of Law Building, and Garrison Hall,
the student union.

Trafford University was, he told himself again, a

gracious and resplendent school and campus. He would never understand why Julian had not made peace with it.

He shifted in his chair to enjoy the sun more, and was surprised again at the lack of tension and fatigue in his body. Certainly he had every reason to feel tired. His administrative duties in recent days had been hectic. He had affixed his signature to the African Unity Pact, previously ratified by the Senate. He had, after some brief soul-searching, allowed the insulting New Succession Bill to become law, not with the approval of his signature but by letting it remain in his desk drawer for ten days and a Sunday, whereby it had automatically become a statute. He had released, through Flannery, his only comment on the New Succession Bill: that he had not been able, in good faith, to sign it or yet to veto it. Since he doubted its constitutionality, he preferred it to be the House's law and the Senate's law until it could be judged properly by the Supreme Court in the first test case that should arise.

Certainly, too, he had had every reason for feeling worried in recent days. The White House press room, and his own Oval Office, had been filled with nerve-racking reports about the Hurley trial, the pros and cons on the possible banning of the Turnerite Group, the latest outbreaks of racial violence in Raleigh, Fort Lauderdale, Wichita, Oklahoma City, Cincinnati, Houston, San Diego, Oakland. He had not looked forward to this visit to Trafford, to the potentially explosive announcement he would make on this occasion, and, equally disagreeable, to the private confrontation with his son.

Yet here he was, and it was not bad at all. He felt relaxed. He felt welcome among his own. The speech would likely be well received. And as for Julian, whom he had seen momentarily with the reception committee, that small, reticent boy seemed utterly miscast for the violent role that Leroy Poole had said he was playing. Yet, reconsidering the last, Dilman retained one misgiving: would Poole have dared hurl such a charge as a lie, knowing how easy it would be for him to check it out?

Suddenly, he heard the words "—give you, ladies and gentlemen, the President of the United States!"

He realized that the learned, dusky face of Chancellor McKaye was turned toward him, that there was scattered applause from up front, and that his turn had come at last.

Dilman rose, accepted his degree, accepted the Chancellor's handshake. Then, putting the beribboned degree aside, he mounted the rostrum, extracting his triple-spaced typed speech from beneath his gown, placed it on the lectern under the curve of microphones, and smiled at the unsmiling black sea stretching before him. "Chancellor McKaye, my fellow citizens—" he began, hearing not his voice but its curious echo in this building-encircled outdoor arena.

The first of the speech went well, he felt. Although Talley, Flannery, Kemmler had all had a hand in the writing of it, had in fact written it, the third sentence had been inserted by himself, after a discussion with Nat Abrahams. This was the sentence about his pride in not being honored as a Negro by a Negro university, but in being honored as a fellow American by a distinguished school of learning that had broadened and risen above racial chauvinism.

Now, a little more uneasily, but keeping his voice deliberate and clear, he entered upon the controversial portion of his address. What he might say had been speculated upon in the press, on the airwaves, the entire week. Today what he said would be official. T.C.'s advisers had agreed that the announcement be made in his speech at Trafford University, because the atmosphere would be one of intellect and reason, and because the audience would be largely Negro, receptive to him, proud of him.

Now, as his eyes skipped to the words ahead, his voice faltered. He was not used to announcing agonized-over decisions in public. But there it was, in unmodified pica lettering on the page beneath the microphones, already released to the press, and he must read what had been written. Controlling his voice, enunciating with care, he plunged ahead.

"You are aware, also, that the Department of Justice and I have been studying evidence of the activities of these super-government, super-American societies and organizations," he read, "composed of extremists of the right and left, of white and black, responsible for fomenting such dangerous unrest in these critical times when we must preserve unity and peace at home to maintain strength abroad."

He held his breath, and then, leaving his deliberate manner behind, rushed in where former Presidents had feared to tread.

"Extraordinary challenges to our way of life, we have decided, must be met promptly and firmly by extraordinary countermeasures within the law. Drastic crimes against our government must be met and punished by drastic executive action. Recently, whatever its motivation, a deplorable crime occurred in Hattiesburg, Mississippi. A county judge was kidnaped and taken across two state lines, to be held for human ransom. The leader of the abduction was caught by the Federal Bureau of Investigation, and is now standing trial, and his individual case will be decided, without prejudice, on its own merits. The concern of your government, however, has been with the factors behind the crime itself."

He no longer looked up from the printed words. His gaze was directed to the carefully prepared text. He read from it with measured emphasis.

"Irrefutable evidence, examined by objective minds, has made it clear that the Federal crime was not perpetrated by irresponsible individuals, but was an act of organization policy. The abduction, we now know, was committed by the activist Turnerite Group, which has been financially backed by the Communist Party, as the first act in a premeditated strategy to subvert our laws, our country, and take the administration of justice into its own hands. Such activity cannot be permitted in a democratic government by the people, of the people, for the people. And so, to halt its cancerous spread, and with full knowledge of my accountability of our tradition of civil liberties, I take this occasion to announce to my fellow Americans that I am invoking the Subversive Ac-

tivities Control Act against the leadership and membership of the Turnerite Group. As of eleven o'clock this
morning, the Turnerite Group is outlawed and banned,
and any further activity of any nature by its members
will be regarded as criminal and dealt with under the
statutes that provide—"

There was a thin crackling sound that interrupted
Dilman, a sound similar to that of an eggshell breaking,
and it distracted Dilman and made him lift his face to
the microphones. He saw at once that it had been an egg,
a raw egg that had hit the microphones, broken and splat-
tered, now spilling its liquid yolk down upon the page of
his manuscript.

Bewildered, he looked out over his audience and saw
that a curious thing was happening before his eyes. The
black mass, so inert, so silent, had come alive like dark
amoebae breaking apart, moving, under a giant micro-
scope lens. The rear two-thirds of the throng was surging
forward, pushing and upending the faculty and dignitaries
from their folding chairs on the fore part of the campus
lawn.

Suddenly there were red, white and blue signs and
banners rising above the dark, animated pack of three
thousand. Squinting, Dilman could make out the crude,
savage lettering on one sign, then another, and another,
and still another: GO HOME, UNCLE TOM! . . . HE'D
RATHER BE WHITE THAN BE PRESIDENT! . . . BLACK
JUDAS! GIVE BACK YOUR THIRTY PIECES! . . . DILMAN,
WIPE OFF THE BURNT CORK! SHOW YOUR TRUE FACE!
. . . TWO RAT FINKS—DILMAN AND ZEKE MILLER!!

And, assaulting him like so many angry black fists,
from beneath the signs, behind them, around them, he
could hear a single choral chant screamed out by the infuriated horde: "Down with traitor Dilman! Down with
traitor Dilman! Down with traitor Dilman!"

Petrified, eyes wide, mouth agape, Douglass Dilman
saw the air suddenly filled with flying, churning objects.
Dozens of eggs exploded on the platform around him,
against the front of the rostrum, and then followed the
rotten apples, gnawed chicken bones, chunks of red
watermelon and green rinds.

The single chant, hoarse and hating, began to fragment into a hundred shouts of individual protest, shrieks dinning against his ears: "Beat it, you bastard! . . . You're puttin' us back in slavery! . . . Doughface, doughface! . . . Give Simon Legree the white man's degree! . . . Sellout! . . . Down, down, down, with the Jim Crow President!"

Instinctively he recoiled at the fury of protest, lifting his arm to shield his face. He could hear police whistles, see the swaying comber of officers in blue, clubs out, bowling over the photographers, as they formed a chained line to protect him from his people. The wood platform on which he wavered now rocked with footsteps, the Chancellor, regents, deans, and Secret Service agents crowding about him to save him.

Someone was tugging at his shoulder, wrenching at it, and he gave way a little to stop the hurt, twisting his head, and he saw it was the Secret Service agent Otto Beggs. As he tried to speak, he was struck sharply on the jaw. His free hand went to his jaw and came away with a handful of gooey, dripping white and yellow egg and pieces of shell. There had been no physical pain in being struck, only psychic pain, followed by shock and fear.

"Come on, come on, outa here, Mr. President, outa here. Got to get you to where it's safe!" Beggs was shouting.

They had surrounded him entirely now, his white Praetorians, almost lifting him from his feet as they hustled him across the platform, down the rear steps, and through the heavy lines of gathering police officers and faculty members, into the Main Administration Building behind.

Once, breathless, before being shoved inside, he had turned, wanting to call out something to the misled multitude, to explain why he had announced what he had announced, to explain that it would save them in the end. But it was no use. While the raised platform hid the eye center of the vortex, he could make out the rest of the wild mob on either side, the black students swinging their homemade signs and banners and yelling their foul epithets, and the police, reinforced by state troopers, retaliating with their clubs and curses and whistles.

Presently—he would never know how he had arrived there—he found himself on the tan leather couch in Chancellor McKaye's high-ceilinged, oak-paneled office. The swift transition from the animal bedlam of the disorder outside to the hushed quiet of the soundproofed office left him limp and dizzy. Familiar persons came and went: Beggs wiping the egg from Dilman's chin, Chancellor McKaye with his endless apologies, and Admiral Oates with his stethoscope and tranquilizers. After the dour White House physician had barred all visitors but those who were absolutely necessary and then himself had left, Dilman had received Tim Flannery.

"I'm sorry, I'm damn sorry, Mr. President," the press secretary said, scratching his head through his rumpled red hair. "That was unexpected. Even the reporters were thrown."

"What are they saying?" Dilman wanted to know.

"Most of them think it was planned by the Turnerites themselves," said Flannery.

Dilman thought about this. "No, I don't think so," he said at last. "I don't think one organization would be big enough. I think—I believe all of us misjudged Negro sentiment here and around the country. I can see it now, after the fact. Because the Crispus Society, the NAACP, the Urban League were still for going slowly, for the minorities bill, outspoken against the activist outfits like the Turnerites, we thought that was the heavy majority of Negro opinion. We're wrong, Tim. I think those young Negro boys have had it. They may not be Turnerites, but they're sympathetic, they want action. Gradualism is out. They're rebelling against their fathers, who accommodated themselves to the segregation system. The young are disenchanted by the recent past. Their fathers failed. Hurley and his leaders represented a new look in paternal authority. And now, without thinking it out, they expected the first Negro in the Presidency to see things their way. And I refused. I went along with their fathers and the white men who fenced them in. I used a legal instrument to cut off their momentum and make their goal harder to reach. They weren't positive I'd do it, but they suspected I would, and they came here prepared for it, with their signs and slogans, waiting. That's the sum of it, I'd guess, the gospel truth."

"Do you want to say anything like that to the press?" Flannery asked. "They're clamoring for a statement."

"Now? Lord, no. Now's no time for reason and psychological explanations. Let this break up, and die down. Maybe we can issue something later."

"Well, I'll keep the correspondents away from you," Flannery said. "I'll tell them you're safe and sound, and will have some statement to make tomorrow or the day after. They'll be busy enough trying to interview some of the student demonstrators, find out what drove them to this."

"Good luck to Reb Blaser," Dilman said with a grimace.

Flannery stood up. "Mr. President, I'm still not so sure that demonstration was representative of all Negro feeling. I think you'll see most of them are behind you when the minorities bill becomes operative."

"I think you'll find you're wrong," said Dilman. "They'll look on the minorities bill as a white man's bill. They'll look on that as a forgiveness bribe, after today's announcement, curtailing their right to direct action."

"Maybe," said Flannery.

"I hope maybe, Tim," said Dilman. "When are we supposed to leave here?"

"After the Chancellor's luncheon and——"

"Cancel it," said Dilman. "McKaye'll understand."

"Done," said Flannery. "Then you wanted a brief meeting with your son."

"Yes. Is he safe? Will you find out about him? Give me a little while alone here to get my bearings, and then send him along."

"Okay."

"Tim, I could stand a drink, nothing too potent. Maybe a small brandy or some wine——"

Dilman had been alone ten minutes when Beggs opened the door to admit his press secretary once more.

Flannery came in with a well-filled crystal decanter and a wine glass. He set both on the coffee table.

"The Dean of the Law School provided this," he said. "Sherry. Will that do?"

"It'll do fine."

"The mob is gradually dispersing," Flannery said.

"Any serious injuries?"

"A few bloody noses, one fractured wrist, that's all. By the way, someone located Julian. He's in his dorm room with his friends. He's shaken up a bit, naturally, but he's okay."

"I'll be ready for him in—in fifteen minutes."

Alone once more, Dilman unwrapped a cigar, readied it, but was too distracted to light it. He put it down in the tray, reached for the decanter with his trembling hand, then realized that Flannery had already poured his drink. He took up the sherry in his right hand, steadying it with his left, and sipped it.

He reconsidered what he had done today. He had urged his people, already so grievously hurt, to uphold white men's laws. He had alienated his Negro support. But conversely, had he gained white support, restored the majority of the people's confidence in him? He was doubtful of this. The white electorate probably felt that he was carrying out, with reluctance, what T.C.'s advisers insisted he carry out. He had lost much, won little.

Yet these mathematics were not what concerned and bothered him. If he had felt positively in the right, nothing on earth would have disturbed him. What bothered him, as it had from the beginning, was that the Turnerites had qualified for condemnation only if they were Communist-financed. Yet he was still uncertain of the truth of this accusation. He had bought Attorney General Kemmler's flimsy case after that bad telephone exchange with that damn Leroy Poole, after learning from Poole that the Mississippi abduction had been inspired by Turnerite policy, which frightened him, and after hearing the lie that his own son was a part of this terror, which had emphasized for him how far the members of that gang would go in maligning the innocent to gain their ends. But the reasonable part of his brain doubted that the Turnerites were literally subversive, dedicated to overthrowing the government. His black skin knew what all of Kemmler's Justice Department attorneys would never understand, and what that rioting throng that had stopped his speech did understand, that the Turnerites were out to overthrow inequality, not government but inequality. Now it was too late for these second thoughts. If injustice this was, he must find other means to correct it.

He had finished his sherry, and then realized with a start that not fifteen minutes but twice that time had gone by. He jumped up, went to the door, and opened it. Beggs, who was planted outside, quickly turned.

"Has my son——?" Then he saw Julian, miserably huddled in a chair of the reception room. "Oh, hello, Julian. Come on in." As Julian brushed past him with only a muttered greeting, Dilman asked Beggs, "How is it going?"

"We got it under control. Only a few handfuls of them hanging around."

"Good. Tell Tim Flannery to have the car here in fifteen minutes. He can notify the helicopter crew."

He closed the door carefully, to make certain it was fastened securely, and then he turned to his son. Julian was standing beside the coffee table, patting his checkered sport coat against his dark-gray slacks. His short hair was plastered down and glossy as ever, and his thyroid eyes were fixed on the sherry decanter.

Dilman indicated the decanter. "Want some?"

"No."

"All right, sit down. We don't have much time. Let's talk."

Defiantly, Julian remained on his feet, but once Dilman had settled on the couch, the boy yanked a chair nearer the coffee table and lowered himself into it.

"I don't know what we're supposed to talk about," Julian said sullenly.

"We'll see. . . . Were you out there in that mob?"

"For a while. When the guys with the signs started infiltrating in, I decided to get out. I went with two of my friends back to my room."

"Did you know this was going to happen?"

"If you did what they hoped you wouldn't, yes, I knew it would happen. Everyone's been steamed up since Hurley was arrested."

"Have the other students been giving you a rough time?"

Julian examined his polished nails. "Not especially. I told them I didn't know what you'd do. I told them if you did the banning, I was against it, and on their side."

"I see."

"I don't have to listen to white men," Julian said angrily. "I make my own decisions."

Dilman picked up his unsmoked cigar. "Maybe I'm not listening to white men or colored men either. Maybe, in my position, I have a higher responsibility. Maybe I'm listening to the Constitution."

"Oh, sure."

Dilman knew that he could not continue to be high-minded and pretentious. He was dealing with his son, who was once more disillusioned with him and, in effect, disowning their relationship. "You know my feelings about the law, Julian. Possibly it would help if you'd transmit them to your friends."

"Help who?" said Julian. "I'll be lucky if I can find anybody to speak to me."

Dilman's heart ached. He put the cigar down again. "Do you want to transfer out of here, Julian?"

"A month ago, yes. Now, no. Not now. I'll show them I belong to me."

Dilman sighed audibly. The time had come. It was the wrong time, but then, perhaps, there would never be a right time to speak what was foremost in his mind. "Are you sure you belong only to yourself, Julian? Are you sure of that?"

Julian's bulging eyes left the examination of his fingernails. He glanced suspiciously at his father. "What does that mean?"

"Do you have any allegiance elsewhere? I know you're

an officer in the student end of the Crispus Society—"

"That crud. Are you serious? I joined them before I grew up."

"And after you grew up, Julian, what else did you join?"

Julian's brow wrinkled, once more wary, and his pointed English shoe dug at the carpet. "What else did I join? I don't get you, Dad."

Dilman edged forward toward his son, until his knee hit the coffee table. "All right, cards on the table, Julian. I forget how many days ago—the night after the FBI caught Hurley—I received a call from the young man you so much admire—from Leroy Poole—pleading Jefferson Hurley's case for self-defense and begging me not to ban the Turnerites. I said I'd have to ban them. Do you know what he said?" He watched his suspicious son carefully now. "He said to me, 'You indict the Turnerites for criminal subversion, and you indict your own son.' He said 'Julian is one of us, stealing information from the Crispus people, getting statistics about persecutions in places like Hattiesburg.' To that effect. That's what he said."

Julian's face was filled with wrath. "Leroy Poole? *He* said that to you?"

"That and more. Yes, Julian. And I told him he was a rotten liar. He said, 'Okay, ask Julian.'" He paused. "I'm here, Julian. I am asking you."

"Asking me what? You mean you even listened one minute to that sonofabitchin' smelly satchel-mouth? Him? He said all that?"

Dilman had never heard his son use such language before. Yet he was relieved by the boy's indignation. "I'm quoting him almost exactly. I told you I did not believe him. I came here to make sure."

Julian was on his feet, agitatedly wringing his hands. "That bastard, that dirty troublemaker."

"Julian, I wouldn't press this further, but obviously there's a lot at stake for both of us. Were you ever, even for a day, for a minute, a secret member of that Turnerite Group? Just give me a simple yes or no, and that's it."

"No, I never was. I swear to it. Now are you happy?"

Dilman stood up. "I'm not happy. But I feel better. I'm glad you had the good sense for which I always gave you credit."

"I never belonged," said Julian shrilly, "but that doesn't mean I don't think they're righter than you are."

"I'm not interested, Julian. Thanks. Be well. I'll see you soon in Washington."

He tried to go to the door, but Julian blocked his way. "Dad, you can be President or whatever, but there's a lot who put more faith in Jeff Hurley's ideas than yours."

"I told you I'm not interested." He went around his son to the door.

"You'd better be, you'd just better be!" his son shouted.

He refused to be baited or engaged further. He had come here to ask his son for a plain answer. He had heard his son's answer and it was satisfactory. That shone bright as a jewel on a dismal day. He would not allow this tiny gem of happiness to be tarnished so soon.

FOR RELEASE AT 8:00 P.M. EDT
Office of the White House Press Secretary

THE WHITE HOUSE

PRESIDENT DILMAN RETURNED FROM NEW YORK CITY AT 6:30 P.M. HE SPENT A HALF HOUR CONFERRING IN HIS OFFICE WITH ATTORNEY GENERAL KEMMLER AND SECRETARY OF HEALTH, EDUCATION AND WELFARE MRS. CUMMINS.

AT 7:15 P.M. THE PRESIDENT MET WITH THE REVEREND PAUL SPINGER AND DIRECTORS OF THE CRISPUS SOCIETY. FOLLOWING THE MEETING, THE PRESIDENT MADE AN IMPROMPTU STATEMENT TO THE PRESS.

PRESIDENT DILMAN: The unfortunate incident that took place on the campus of Trafford University this morning,

after my announcement of the banning of the Turnerite
Group, underlines the necessity . . .

———————————

" '—for every American citizen to be alerted to the subversive dangers of extremism, from wherever it originates,'
President Dilman told the White House press corps gathered about him in the West Wing lobby earlier this evening.
Showing no ill effects from the egg-throwing episode at
Trafford, which is creating controversial headlines abroad,
the President went on calmly to tell his listeners that he was
taking further steps to align Negro moderates alongside—"

A voice from the far corner of Leroy Poole's motel
room bellowed, "Shut that goddam fink announcer off!"
Immediately Poole got out of his chair and hopped to
the transistor radio propped against the bag of fruit, and
with a roll of his thumb muted the news report.
Pocketing the tiny radio, Poole wheeled to face the
others, who were sitting or lolling about the large motel
room he had rented the morning after the night he had
put the zinging old filial arrow into that bastard Dilman.
Once having revealed to Dilman that the kidnaping had
been an official Turnerite action, and having zinged him
with the news of Julian's secret membership, he had
begun worrying that Dilman might sic the FBI bloodhounds after him for more information. Losing no time,
Poole had borrowed a car and removed himself and his
effects from his hotel in the center of Washington to this
obscure second-class motel on Canal Road, near Fletch-
er's Boat House, three miles from Georgetown.
Since then, Poole had decided that he probably was
not being sought for more information after all. Most
likely, for fear of compromising his kid Julian, the President had told no one of the call from his biographer.
Finally Poole had felt safe enough to let the word of his
whereabouts be known to those who mattered. One by
one they had converged outside Washington, the last of
the Turnerite leaders, to determine what could be done
for Hurley and for the survival of their organization.

There were seven of them here——Poole excluded himself——and they had been gathered for at least four hours,
drinking beer and eating cheese and ham sandwiches.
They had reported, they had debated, they had speculated, taking breaks to listen to the news broadcasts,
and the time had come for a settlement.

Frank Valetti, Hurley's second-in-command, product
of a Negro-Italian interracial marriage, who resembled
a bronzed Indian brave (and was the most persuasive
and sophisticated among them, excepting Leroy Poole
himself), had informally presided. He had already
burned the membership records and minutes of meetings. He had accounted for the cash on hand and suggested how it be spent. The vote had been seven to one
in favor of Valetti's proposal that the funds be turned
over to a white leftist lawyer, a good headline maker in
Manhattan, to be used to reinforce Jeff Hurley's defense.
The lone dissenter had been Burleigh Thomas, one of
the two men who had assisted Hurley in the kidnaping
of Gage, and who had gotten away unrecognized, to be
the last arrival at the motel. Burleigh Thomas, a constantly fuming, short-tempered, squat and muscular
truck driver with matted hair, a low broad-bridged nose,
a cleft chin and an abrasive voice, had wanted most of
the remaining Turnerite funds held out to support further underground violence.

"Jeff Hurley's a stuck pig, scalded, skinned, and ready
to be cooked," Burleigh Thomas had said. "Why throw
the dough down the drain? Let those of us who wants
to, go on and use it for getting in a few more licks against
the whiteboys."

Valetti had replied reasonably that Dilman's banning
had left them disorganized, in danger, and further activist resistance was pointless at this time. Later, perhaps, but not now. Leroy Poole had added that Jeff
Hurley was not dead yet, that there were means to save
him, that it was their duty to try, and to make a good
propaganda campaign for their ideals along the way.
This would take what was left of the money. And so the
vote had gone seven to one.

Settlement time had arrived. Disposition of the *corpus sine pectore*.

"Well, gang," said Valetti, uncrossing his legs and bringing his hands together, "I guess that does it. I think we're all of a mind to disband. Our head man is gone. Our records are gone. Our funds are disposed of. We're through—at least for now."

"What are you going to do, Frank?" Poole asked.

"I'm going abroad for a while."

"Abroad, listen to him," Burleigh Thomas mocked. "Abroad, eh? Chickening out, you mean."

Valetti shook his head gently. "Don't try to bug me, Burleigh, we're on the same side. Yup, I'm going abroad, because I don't want the Federals badgering me or using me against Jeff Hurley. Besides I want to raise some dough for our cause, lots of it, and then come back and reorganize something new."

"Who's giving you dough abroad?" Burleigh Thomas snorted. "Who gives a damn about us anywheres else? Them that does, they ain't got the green stuff, and them that has, they don't give a damn."

"Settle down, Burleigh." Valetti's lips curled in a knowing smile. "I've got my means. I suggest you join up with our old friends in the more respectable societies, and do what you can to rouse them up a bit. Just do your best, and when the climate here is ripe, and I have a nest egg for us, I'll be back and calling on you, all of you. As for Jeff, I guess we can trust the lawyers to do what can be done, and if they get nowhere, we can depend on Leroy here to try to intervene with the President for clemency."

"I don't know if Dilman'll even see me again," said Poole.

"You've got enough to make him see you again." Valetti winked. "Maybe one or two of our records weren't burned."

Burleigh Thomas was on his feet, hiking up his overalls. "I wouldn't spit on that goddam yellowbelly Dilman, let alone go asking him any favors. I'd see him for only one thing, to bust his goddam face wide open. He's the cause of all our trouble, I tell you. I could see it from the

day he came in that job, told Jeff Hurley as much from
the start, that Dilman would be our worst enemy, bad
or worse than some goddam whiteshirt Kleagle. Like I
said to Jeff from the beginning, we better be prepared to
fight that there white nigger of ours hard as we fight the
whiteboy skunks. Well, you guys can see I was right,
wasn't I? Lookit him, lookit Dilman. When you got a
Rastus nigger up there, you got someone doing the backward bends, so's he not even treating us like some
stumblebum white politician would, let alone like a nigger should. I tell you, I'd sure enough give my left gut to
see T.C. still President, or even that Yankee man, Eaton,
because they'd at least remember our voting power, and
they wouldn't be hacking us down with that subversive
controls business. But Dilman——" Thomas glared at
Poole. "I'd rather let my pal Jeff Hurley die in the chair
than ask that yellowbelly nigger Dilman one favor."

"I don't have to ask Dilman any favors," piped up
Leroy Poole. "Like Frank says, we've got other means
to deal with turncoats."

"You bet we have, but not by asking favors," Thomas
growled. He stared at the others. "Okay, you fraidcat
punks, do whatever you want to do. Some of us ain't
giving up so easy, no sir. We're not letting any crappy
control laws put in by that possum slummock make us
run for cover."

"You haven't got a chance on your own," said Frank
Valetti. He threw his raincoat over his arm and went to
the motel door. "I'm hitting the road. Good luck to each
of you. We'll win what Jeff and all of us are after—one
day, someday soon. Good night."

After Valetti had gone, the others shook hands with
Poole and one another and departed, singly and in pairs.
Presently the room was empty of all but Burleigh
Thomas and Leroy Poole.

Thomas pulled on his heavy sweater as Poole waited.
Poole could see that Thomas was deliberately fussing
too much with his garment, as if he wanted to speak
about something on his mind.

Poole felt uncomfortable. It often amazed him that
one organization, with one purpose and goal, could have

room for men so dissimilar as Thomas and himself. For Poole, the ones like Thomas were aboriginals, too brutish and demoniac to appreciate the refinements of rebellion and freedom, as did ones like himself. The Thomases were the easiest targets for whites like Zeke Miller and Bruce Hankins and Everett Gage, the late Everett Gage, who did not believe such beings were prepared for civilized equality. When you agreed to set them free, you opened the cage. But what then? Could untrained, barbarous, vindictive primates be let loose to live with skilled, educated, law-abiding higher creatures?

Instantly Poole hated himself for entertaining redneck thoughts. His mind went to his morning mental exercises, and he knew that Burleigh Thomas was as deserving of freedom, no matter how ill-prepared he was for it, as he himself, and he felt kindlier toward the truck driver.

He found Burleigh Thomas scrutinizing him. Poole suffered a lump of guilt inside. "Well, Burleigh, I wish you—"

"Leroy, what you going to do next?"

Poole was surprised that his primitive companion could have such concerns. "Do next? Why, first off, I'm kind of low on eating money. I guess I'll knock off my book, the one I'm writing on Dilman, and get what is owed to me. And then I'll start pounding my typewriter pulpit for real, trying to heat our people up some more. Guess I'm still a poor preacher boy at heart."

"Naw, I mean about our movement."

"What's there to do? I'm keeping an eye on Jeff Hurley's trial. I already heard from his old lady, Gladys, in Louisville, and his other relatives. They're depending on me. I don't think the Feds will give Jeff more than a stiff sentence, manslaughter or some such. They don't want more trouble. If it goes past that, well, I guess I'll have to go to Dilman. I can make him see me. And from what I've read, he's got it in his power to save Jeff." He could see that Thomas was not satisfied, and then he remembered. "Our movement, you asked? Like Frank Valetti said, the Attorney General and Dilman shot us down. I guess I'll play dead until the shooting stops."

Burleigh Thomas covered his matted hair with a wool cap. "Not me," he said. "There are maybe a half dozen of us who ain't letting those big shots think they won the crap game because they got the loaded bones. Nope. We're going to keep moving in on them holy Joes, the way Jeff would want."

"I wish you luck, Burleigh, but the dice are still loaded. Valetti's a pretty smart guy. Why don't you do what he suggests—take it easy until—"

"To hell with Valetti. He's got his Commie friends to go back to. That ain't got a friggin' thing to do with us. We got no nothing waiting for us but to keep fighting." He paused, and considered Poole through slit eyes. "You're a mighty smart kid, Leroy. I been listening to you. They ain't housebroke you yet, for sure."

"Nobody has, and nobody ever will."

"I don't think we're so far apart, except like in education. Knowing Dilman the way you do, I sorta have a hunch you agree with me he's the worst yellowbelly son-ofabitch ever got born black."

"Basically, I can't disagree with you," Poole conceded. "However, his fault isn't that he's mean, but that he's scared—"

"Shivering scared, yup. Old cullud-boy-in-the-cemetery-scared, yup. But to me there's nothing badder, because that makes him suck around those whiteboys, barking and standing on his hind legs when they give him their finger-snapping. It's like he's afraid to recognize us, to prove he don't know us, so he's twice as tough against us. I think even that scrotum-face, rumdum Zeke Miller would be better—"

"We-ll, I wouldn't go that far, Burleigh."

"You're going to see I'm right," insisted Thomas. "Before Dilman's finished in office, we'll all be back on the plantations picking cotton. I'm just saying to you, do what you want, but there are some of us not letting him get away with it. What Jeff started, we're finishing. We're going to bug that Dilman until he's gotta tell difference between black from white." Thomas hesitated. "You sure you don't want to stay with us?"

Leroy Poole patted his belly. "I'm not built for the

muscle part of it, Burleigh. I'm strictly a word man. Words can be fists, too."

Thomas made two hamlike fists. "Not like these, no words like these. Okay, Leroy, you do your doings your way, I do them mine." He went to the door, wrenched the knob, but turned back before opening it. "Maybe you'll have a change of heart. If you do, I'll be here a few days. If you want to talk, you can always get hold of me through my kid sister. She's a good kid. Leave a note for her at the Walk Inn—that's a booze joint on Seventeenth—and say you want me to call. Just leave a note for my sis."

As he opened the door, Poole called out, "What's her name, Burleigh?"

"Ruby—same last name like mine—Ruby Thomas. She knows where I am every minute."

FOR IMMEDIATE RELEASE
Office of the White House Press Secretary

THE WHITE HOUSE

FOLLOWING THE ORDERS OF THE WHITE HOUSE PHYSICIAN, ADMIRAL OATES, THE PRESIDENT IS SPENDING THE DAY ABOARD THE PRESIDENTIAL YACHT "FREDDIE BOY." THE YACHT DEPARTED FROM THE WASHINGTON NAVY YARD DOCK AT 9 A.M., EDT. EXCEPT FOR CONFERRING WITH SECRETARY OF STATE EATON ON THE FORTHCOMING CONFERENCE WITH PREMIER KASATKIN, AND REVIEWING THE FINAL MINORITIES REHABILITATION PROGRAM BILL DELIVERED TO HIM BY CONGRESS, THE PRESIDENT WILL DEVOTE HIS TIME TO DEEP-SEA FISHING AND RESTING.

BY ONE o'clock in the afternoon, Douglass Dilman knew that the cruise was a mistake, and that he was in for another fiasco.

When Admiral Oates had suggested the brief nautical outing, his need for a relaxed day away from his office, especially because of the agitation induced by the Trafford University incident and the slight flare-up of his blood pressure, Dilman had not been able to reject the idea. Somehow, he had felt, it would make him lose face in front of Governor Talley, Secretary Eaton, and several other advisers in his office at the time. With feigned enthusiasm, he had agreed to the cruise. He had not told any one of them that except for one trip on a Great Lakes steamer and several ferryboat crossings to Staten Island, he had never been on a boat, and he had never in his life been on one that went out to sea.

His apprehension had been somewhat alleviated in the early morning, after he had been piped aboard and been made welcome by Commander Chappell, and been saluted by the six enlisted men on deck. As the ninety-two-foot yacht—once christened Eisenhower's *Barbara Ann* and Kennedy's *Honey Fitz,* and last and still T.C.'s *Freddie Boy* (so lettered in bright gold on the stern)— proceeded down the Anacostia River, and into Chesapeake Bay, Dilman had been taken on a tour of the vessel by Admiral Rivard, the veteran Navy Chief of Staff.

Hardly conscious of the rocking of the yacht, the steady creaking of the timbers, Dilman had admired the white, mahogany-trimmed ship from stem to stern, from port to starboard—or was it starboard? Wasn't it aft? Or fore? Or bow? He had been as baffled by the Admiral's language as he would have been by Latin or Hebrew, in fact, more so. Nodding constantly, to display his pleasure and comprehension, Dilman had covered not only every inch of the deck, but the Commander's cabin where the helm could be seen, and then he had gone down the companionway—or was it hatch?—no, companionway, absolutely—between the nauseating, freshly painted walls to the cabins below. He had visited the dining room, which seated forty, and the large Presidential stateroom or bedroom with its two bunks, and the attractive lounge with its green carpet, chairs, television set, radiotelephone, and Currier and Ives nautical prints. On the afterdeck—he was sure Admiral Rivard had called it the afterdeck—Dilman had gratefully settled into a bamboo chair on the hemp rug. He had tried to be attentive to Secretary Eaton, as the Secretary reported on his recent conversation with Soviet Ambassador Rudenko. Dilman had assimilated the gist of it—three-day summit conference to be held at the château in Chantilly, twenty-six miles north of Paris, with the final meeting capped by the French President's farewell banquet, to be held in Versailles Palace—and all the while he had been hypnotized by the yacht's rising and falling rail over Eaton's shoulder. Dilman had measured, secretly, the distance the rail heaved above the horizon line and dipped beneath it. The upward motion had taken in two inches of perfectly blue and cloudless sky. The downward motion had taken in three inches of pea-green, sea-green water. The more his stomach gurgled, the more his gorge heaved toward his throat, the more attentive he had tried to be to Eaton's voice.

He had not known how long his Secretary of State intended to go on, but he had been thankful when Edna Foster interrupted him with a shore-to-ship message. After that, Commander Chappell announced cheerfully that they were in the Atlantic, in the open sea, and the fishing tackle was ready for him on the port side. To Dilman, the obstacle of locating the port side (without daring to ask) through this floating maze, and the sickening knowledge that they were bouncing about in the middle of the ocean had given him the courage to state that he was not prepared to fish yet.

"I've got too much work," he had said.

The Commander had persisted. "Mr. President, you ought to take advantage of a warm windless day like this. Not many this time of the year, I'll tell you. But look there, the sun, not a breeze, sea smooth as glass, and some channel bass and marlin waiting to be caught."

"Thank you, Commander, soon as I can."

He slunk off, making a pretense of finding Miss Foster, but when he reached the companionway, Sally Watson had intercepted him. The sea change had made her more exuberant and prettier than ever. Her blond hair, swept back, was partially covered by the hood of her brightly striped Italian sweater. Her slim hips, as she walked, moved provocatively under her snug white raw-silk slacks.

"Magnificent, isn't it?" she had asked joyously, lifting her sunglasses.

"Fine, fine," he had said.

"I'm utterly famished. The salt air really gives one an appetite. But we're not allowed to eat lunch, Mr. President, until you lead the way. The steward is all set."

"Lunch already?" he had said, and inside, his stomach again climbed toward his gullet. "Too early for me. You tell the steward I'll eat later. Go right ahead, and let everyone know they can get started."

While the others went below to be served by the white-jacketed messboys, Dilman had remained on the deck alone. For a while he had sat in a deck chair, warm in his gray wool suit coat and constricting starched collar, shutting his eyes to the slight roll of the yacht, trying not to think of the work that awaited him in the lounge, wondering if Nat Abrahams had received his message last night and would be able to come out and visit him.

Too quickly an hour had passed, for he could hear the chatter of the diners as they came out on the deck, and he had pushed himself to his feet. He had not wanted to be found slumped in a deck chair, wilted and ailing. It would have been embarrassing and un-Presidential. The least that he could do, he had decided, was to assume some casual, more presentable pose. He had walked unsteadily to the bow section of the ship, and propped himself with elbows upon the rail, striking an attitude of deep meditation.

And here he was at one o'clock, suffocated with nausea, increasingly dizzy and bleary, and sorry for himself.

From the corner of his eye he could see Arthur Eaton, so natty in his white yachting cap, foulard, brass-buttoned Navy coat and immaculate white trousers, joining Sally Watson at the prow, joking, laughing, enjoying this perfect day on the water. For the first time, the very first time, Dilman envied Arthur Eaton, not because Eaton was white and he was black, but because Eaton had had the advantage of being raised to this kind of life, being a natural part of it, belonging to it. Eaton was to the Presidential yacht born. Himself, he was strictly a ferry commuter, a Chicago elevated or New York subway type.

Bitterly he turned away from that pair and looked out to the hostile sea again. How he envied his predecessors, those natural outdoor maritime Presidents like Franklin Roosevelt and John Kennedy and T.C., gifted with sea legs, their class and breeding inborn—but all *born,* all with the advantages from their day one. Weakly, elbows stiffening on the rising and falling rail, he indulged his self-pity. This goddam yacht was only a symbol of the whole impossible thing. It was rotten to grow up and live one's entire life as an outcast, a fringe man, and that went not only for Negroes but for many whites, too, whites without background and money and training. It was rotten to live and die dampened by inferiority and awkwardness, never really knowing which fork, which spoon, never knowing etiquette, or the games of leisure, surfing and polo, and that latest South American dance, never knowing sumptuous family gatherings at Thanksgiving or Christmas (with Mother, the matriarch, not Ma, with knobby washboard hands), never knowing foundations and charities and old school ties and stock portfolios and—and assurance, confidence, acceptance—never knowing yachts.

This was not just himself, a usurper here, a crasher, a servant made up like his master; this was most people everywhere, crippled for leisure by the exhausting striving to make good, make ends meet, make it until coronary time. That was Nat, too, in a way; Nat, like himself, knowing there was better while you pressed your nose to the pane, and knowing you had not the price of admission. There were greater inequities in life than this, but this was one that stayed with you forever. Like your skin, if it was black. His throat was filled with his gut, and he wanted to vomit it all overboard, but he fought it down, clenched his teeth and fought it, so as not to be what he was in front of Eaton and the Admiral and the women, and the Zeke Millers of the earth.

"Mr. President——"

He turned from the rail to find his physician, Admiral Oates, contemplating him.

"Are you all right?" the physician inquired.

"Why, yes, of course." His Adam's apple hardly had room to deny it.

"I've had an eye on you. Mmm. You seem a trifle distressed."

"I'm tired. It's hard to get off the treadmill. I'm tired."

"Why don't you go down into the bedroom and grab forty winks? Let me catch some fish for you."

He wanted to buss the doctor for the face-saving order. "That's a good idea. Maybe I will try to nap."

He had started for the companionway when Oates caught his hand. He felt the physician press something hard and square into his palm. He looked at Oates questiongly.

"You wear this with your lifebelt," said Admiral Oates, and he left.

Not until Dilman had reached the bottom of the stairs did he open his palm to see what Oates had given him. It was a tiny pillbox. He turned it over. On the label was printed "For motion sickness, 1 every 4 hours." Ill as he was, he felt comforted, not only for the physician's understanding but for his discretion.

Entering the bedroom cabin, Dilman yanked a silver pitcher out of its holder beside the lower bunk, filled a thick-rimmed glass with water, then swallowed a Dramamine pill and water. Squeamishly, he held on to the upper bunk and waited for the result of the silent civil war inside his throat. Either the pill would make it through the enemy line and save him, or the enemy would throw up the pill and overwhelm him. It took twenty minutes to a half hour for a pill to dissolve and work, he had read in some digest magazine, and he waited, hot with anguish, moist with perspiration. He wanted to lie down on the bunk and die. The defeat would be too enormous, and he resisted bowing to it.

After fifteen minutes, hearing a roar outside, he staggered to the porthole to see what was happening. What he saw was the PT boat *Guardian,* filled with Beggs and several other armed Secret Service men, slicing through the water thirty yards away. Far off there was the speck of what appeared to be a cabin cruiser, growing gradually larger. He left the porthole, once more tempted by the bunk, and then, blindly determined to survive, he walked out of the bedroom.

Within a minute, he was inside the yacht's Presidential lounge, where the pitch and roll of the vessel were less apparent. He surveyed the off-white walls of the lounge, the green-and-white curtains with their nautical pattern, the soft aquamarine-colored chairs, the painting of the *Independence* hung over the television set. The lounge was as gracious as any room in the White House, and he knew that he was best off here, because he would not dare to be ill in a room like this.

Observing his locked briefcase propped against a deep chair, he made his way to it, sat down heavily, and devoted himself to the combination that sprung open his lock. There was only one thick sheaf of printed sheets, fastened into a manila binder, inside the briefcase. This was the Minorities Rehabilitation Bill that the Senate and House had passed, and that was now in his hands awaiting his signature. He had read it thoroughly last night, made some notes and put question marks in the margins about certain provisions, and now he must reread the seven-billion-dollar bill once more and do what needed to be done, what the majority of his staff, of Congress, of white America and black America were apparently waiting for him to do.

He opened the manila binder to examine the bill a final time, but his vision was double, and his stomach heaved higher and higher toward his throat. He dropped the folder on the end table and gagged, clutching the arms of his chair, willing for himself the sea legs and stomach and mind and inner ears of F.D.R. or Kennedy or T.C. And then his convulsions stopped, and he lay back limp, arms flopped on his thighs, legs outstretched, a minor skirmish won, praying for the Dramamine to put down the enemy and save the beleaguered battlements of well-being and dignity.

Half reclining in this state of stupor, Dilman tried to remove his mind from water to land. His memory sought out Wanda, Julian, Mindy, Aldora . . . piteous Aldora of their long ago . . . it had gone wrong the second-to-last day of the last week of their honeymoon, driving home through Joplin, Missouri . . . going into that nice-looking bar for a late afternoon drink, because Aldora from the start had always liked a late afternoon drink, and when inside having their cocktail, these two drunken young business fellows had come up, hey-buddying him, hey-buddy-what-you-doin-with-one-of-our-white-girls, hey buddy? . . . and knowing they were loaded to the gills, trying to explain, not fight, explain that Aldora was colored like himself and his bride . . . and trying to leave until they grabbed him and held him, saying hey-buddy, you-not-leavin, no, not leavin with any white girl . . . and him trying to pull free, until they wrestled him down and pummeled him bloody and Aldora began screaming . . . and the men going at last, hooting and whooping . . . and he and Aldora . . . the real beginning of the trouble had been then, but not the real beginning, for it had begun when she was born more white than black, fair skin, unfair heart . . . displacing her bitterness at fate, life, for making her *almost* white but not enough, displacing it by resenting her lot with him, his dark skin . . . and his striving to show her he was no poor black trash, but more a man, worthy of her, big lawyer, big politician . . . but no good, because there was Mindy, *almost* white like herself, so white she also had the prospects Aldora had abandoned too early, and Aldora's growing contempt for him and her hoarding and segregating of Mindy, as if he would contaminate his daughter . . . and then Aldora wanting another Mindy, to prove something, maybe flee from him, but again no good . . . worse . . . getting Julian, black as coal, reminder that her husband was black and she was black and Mindy was black too . . . and his own trying to lift them up in politics, lift them high as white men, to make up for being Aldora's black albatross, and Mindy's, too . . . but too late to lift them up with him, because they had escaped, both escaped . . . Mindy, with Aldora's conspiratorial help, into a white private school in Colorado, the name of which he'd never known, and then into the East, the white white East . . . and Aldora escaping too, into a bottle, a bottle a day, as insulated by glass as a model ship in a great big bottle . . . and his trying everything to reach her and help her escape, even trying to crawl into the bottle with her, no good . . . even taking a room in the sanitarium with her, no good . . . until she'd escaped at last, in a coffin, in the ground, where no one is *almost* white, where all are equal, still and equal, possessed of one mind, dead, one flesh, dead, one face, dead, white-wanting, free-wanting Aldora, in the subterranean planet of nothingness where there were no demons of *almost*.

He envied her, too, and wanted to escape the drowsy too-oft-relived nightmare, and now he had the Dramamine, and he escaped.

He dozed.

An eternity? An hour? How long had it been? He did not know, after the rattle of the door and then the persistent knocking upon it and then the calling out of his name had aroused him.

Blinking, he sat up, rubbing his eyes. He swallowed. The Adam's apple had running room. There was still a clogging thickness in his throat, but the nausea and dizziness were gone, and so were Aldora and those dreadful years.

"Who is it?" he called out. He shook himself fully awake. "Who's there?"

"Mr. President—"

He recognized Miss Foster's muffled voice, and he said, "Come in, come in."

She poked her head into the lounge. "Mr. President, Mr. Abrahams is aboard. Would you—?"

"Of course, send him in. I've been waiting for him."

She left the door open, and the squishing of her sensible rubber-soled shoes receded up the corridor, to be replaced in seconds by the solid smack of Abrahams' leather heels.

Like himself, Dilman was pleased to be reminded, Nat Abrahams was not to the sea or manor born. Abrahams' husk of brown hair had been tangled by his boat ride, and the bulky tweed coat he carried slung over one white shirt sleeve, and his tie pinned down by a gold-plated tie clasp, and his uncreased heavyweight wool trousers, and his scuffed brogues gave him the appearance of a landlubber adrift on a raft.

It occurred to Dilman, as it had occurred to him once before, years ago, how much resemblance his friend bore to Frederic Dorr Steele's profile drawings of Sherlock Holmes, especially this moment when Abrahams, having greeted Dilman, stood in profile, too, his bony, falcon countenance adorned with pipe and jutting jaw, and all the admirable cold wisdom of the great detective. Could one imagine a hearty and windblown nautical Sherlock Holmes? Inconceivable. As impossible, Dilman decided, as Nat Abrahams and himself on this luxury yacht. With an ally of the anchored earth present, Dilman felt well for the first time. He felt as restored as if he had disembarked on terra firma.

Abrahams strode across the lounge, billowing a trail of smoke, clutched Dilman's hand heartily, and pulled up a side chair.

"Quite a layout," he said, his hand taking in the yacht's lounge. "Been enjoying it?"

"It's a hell ship, Nat," he said. "This is what must have inspired Edward Everett Hale to write *The Man Without a Country*. I know how Philip Nolan felt. Any day, give me my own, my native land."

Abrahams studied him. "Mal de mer, Doug?"

"Times ten," said Dilman. "I became seasick going up the gangplank. You have no idea what it's been like, Nat. All my advisers and officers and aides up there, inhaling, exhaling, full of salt air and the bounding main. Everyone telling me what a perfect day it is, great riding vessel, ocean like a carpet, and me alone, the only one, staggering around, trying to hide from them, not to let them see that all I want is to upchuck. I couldn't fish, couldn't eat, couldn't even make sense talking to Eaton. I've devoted every minute to concentrating on not throwing up. I guess I wanted to uphold my position of authority. Tell me, how can you be Commander in Chief of the Navy and have your head in the toilet bowl the whole lousy voyage? They're born to it, up there, their stomachs trained for it. How can I let them know their Commander thinks a knot is something you tie——and that the closest he ever came to a yacht was when he turned the pages of *Holiday*——and that all the President accomplished today was that he didn't vomit? But I haven't fooled them one bit, Nat, not Eaton or any one of them. They know I'm as out of place here as in the White House. . . . What's the idea winding me up like this, Nat? But anyway——you brought it up. How do I feel? Sick and demeaned, and thanks for coming to hear me complain."

Nat Abrahams, pipe between his teeth, was shaking his head, so that some burning flakes drifted to the floor. He stamped them out, and then he said, "Doug, what are you trying to prove? You feel sick and demeaned? Demeaned about not being an old yachtsman with social background? Holy Daniel, look over your shoulder—— what did Andrew Jackson and Zach Taylor and Abe Lincoln and Harry Truman know about yachting and Exeter or Yale? And they did right well, you bet they did. And sick, you feel sick? Well, you're the boss, and if bouncing around on this roller coaster makes you queasy, get off, just get off. Tell them you don't like it and want to go home. I've said this before, so forgive me, but why try to wear T.C.'s shoes, or even Arthur Eaton's, if they pinch? You can afford your own."

At last Dilman was able to smile. "Thanks, Dad. I feel better already. In fact, I could stand a tall cool drink. What about you?"

"Nothing would please me more. . . . Sit still, I'll make them."

Abrahams went to the bar and made a bourbon-and-soda for Dilman, and sloshed some Scotch over ice for himself. After he returned to his chair, and they drank awhile in silence, Dilman said, "Better, much better." He set his half-finished bourbon down beside the MRP Bill, and loosened his tie. "I know I'm cheating you, Nat. I invited you to fish——"

"Nonsense."

"—but I guess I really wanted a chance to talk to you. There hasn't been much time lately. I haven't seen you since those Trafford boys used me for target practice, have I?"

"No. I was tied up, too. I got Sue off to Chicago, to pack. And while waiting for that final contract, I've been meeting your legislators. Oliver has practically made me an honorary congressman." He hesitated. "Trafford? I gather it was rough on you and Julian."

"It was. But I had no choice. From the demonstrations going on, I guess I've alienated what Negro sympathy I had. I think that's what surprised me most."

"You'll win it back, and fast," said Abrahams. "Once you sign the minorities bill, you'll have 70 or 80 per cent of the Negro population on your side. Nothing you do will satisfy the rest, the extremists." Abrahams' glance went to the end table and back to Dilman, who sat bemus '. "Have you signed the Minorities Rehabilitation Bill yet, Doug?"

"Not yet. I don't know. I suppose that's why I wanted to see you today. Fishing, yes, I guess I wanted to throw out a line and fish for your opinion." Dilman thought that his friend had fidgeted uneasily, and he was puzzled. "Unless, of course, you haven't kept up on the bill and don't particularly care to talk about it. If—"

"Oh, I've read it, Doug. Don't forget, I'm the new Nat Abrahams, and I'm supposed to be conversant with all pending and active legislation. And the minorities bill— let's face it, it *is* the biggest domestic spending program to go through Congress in years."

Dilman watched Abrahams tap the ashes out of his pipe and then refill it and light it. Dilman said, "The cost doesn't bother me, if I could be as positive as T.C.'s crowd and Congress that it would do some good. I keep having the sneaking feeling that—that it's a sort of—oh, give-them-bread-and-circuses sort of thing."

"It's more than that," Abrahams said, too hastily. Drawing on his pipe harder, he dug for something in his hip pocket. "As a matter of fact, I happen to have a little item here——" He pulled out several sheets of paper that had been folded and stapled. He unfolded them. "I——I have here the——the salient points of the bill——facts and figures, and some authoritative notes, projecting its effect on the country as a whole. I even penciled in several of its questionable aspects. But overall, there's no doubt, it can give our economy a big boost, a big one——" His voice had trailed off. He held the papers forth tentatively. "Maybe you'd like to see this."

"I certainly would." Dilman took it, and since it was concise, he read every word of it, acutely aware that Nat Abrahams was watching him nervously, exactly the way Leroy Poole used to watch him nervously when he read the author's manuscript pages.

Reading on, flipping the pages, Dilman felt a growing sense of bewilderment. The logic was there, the statistics and authorities were there, but there was something real and important missing. What was missing was the Nat Abrahams that he knew, or, my God, thought he knew. There was none of Nat's keen intellect, his humanity, his understanding, his language. There was a complete omission of the central issue, the kind Nat liked to tackle head on. Dilman hoped to find it toward the end. When he reached the end, it was not there. He felt cheated and deeply confused.

He looked up, unable to disguise his disappointment. "Interesting. It does make a solid case for priming the economy. I just sort of——missed——any case for how it'll close the racial gap between the have-nots and the haves."

To Dilman, there was no question about it this time: his friend *was* squirming. Abrahams set down his drink. "Well, we take that for granted."

"Take what for granted, Nat?" Dilman sat up. "We're friends——don't take this in the wrong spirit——I'm not being critical of you——but this *is* a *minorities* bill. That, to me, is the primary point. What will the seven billion dollars of taxpayers' money do for minorities, not for the economy? Will the spending buy equality for all, or merely greater prosperity for industry and labor? Dam-

mit, Nat, as a matter of self-interest, there's every reason
why I should sign the bill. Everyone wants me to, and
God knows I need every possible bit of support now, and
I probably will sign it. Only, foggy as I am, indecisive
as I've been, one factor seems to be wanting in the entire bill, as it appears to be missing in your précis. I
miss the sum allocated to give the Negroes, Puerto
Ricans, Mexicans, Indians, Japanese—let's stick to the
Negroes—I miss the sum that will guarantee them all
they really want, first-class citizenship."

Abrahams had reddened. "Doug—" he began.

"No, let me finish. Here we have it, seven billion dollars for public highway construction, desegregated but
quota-limited schools, dams, factories, forest conserva-
tion, and sure, preferential treatment so Negroes do the
work involved and receive the benefits. But, Nat, despite
all those watered-down civil rights bills passed in recent
years, when we talk about the American Negro today,
we still talk about five rights being kept away from him—
five, not one. The right to work, and not be the first
to be fired, the last to be hired, and not be exiled to
menial jobs. All right, this bill takes care of that. What
about his other four rights? Will this bill really give the
Negro the right to use public facilities? To have first-rate
education? To occupy integrated housing? To enjoy freedom to vote like any other American? No. There are
a few crumbs, sure. Sweep them together and what do
they represent? No segregation in buildings constructed
under this MRP Bill. Higher salaries for teachers who
go into slum areas or work in desegregated schools, and
some free tutoring programs and scholarships. Better
and cheaper housing in the tracts the bill subsidizes for
those who will move into these mixed neighborhoods.
And on voting, nothing specific, the usual patriotic promises and hopes. So there it is, and our Negro leaders are
ready to accept the crumbs because they're tired of fighting for the loaf, when they've been hungry more than a
century. I can understand that. But I'm troubled. This
bill may rehabilitate the minorities financially, but it
won't raise them up to full equality. And in the end, it

may be only a delaying action, and solve nothing for the white population either. Yet I could be wrong, dead wrong. Maybe fights are won one skirmish at a time, and this would gain my people one right they desperately want. And who am I to worry it so, be indecisive again, when smarter minds support this bill? Still—" He stared directly at Abrahams and then held up the stapled sheets of paper. "I guess it was unfair of me to expect you to include all that other in your summary, because I felt lame and sort of wanted a crutch. It's just that this didn't sound like you'd written it."

Dilman sat back, and fumbled for his drink.

Quickly Nat Abrahams leaned forward and took the papers from Dilman's lap. "I didn't write it, Doug. Eagles Industries wrote it. Avery Emmich wrote it. Gorden Oliver wrote it. They wanted me to transmit it to you —first assignment—and I did. I'm ashamed of myself now. I knew, the second I handed it to you, I could never go through with it, pretending it was mine."

Embarrassed, Dilman tried to stop him. "Forget it, Nat. You did what you had to do, and some of the points in there are well made."

Abrahams stood up, ripped the paper in half, worked it into a ball, and stuffed it into his trouser pocket.

"It stinks," he said flatly. "I'll never do this to you again, no more harmonizing with others on what they believe. I'll rely on solo. Doug, you've said it, there's good in the minorities bill and there's bad. It's a big decision you have to make, and there are a lot of considerations to keep in mind, but you'll do what you must do for yourself and others. No one's going to influence you. You wanted my opinion, and I'll give it to you if you still want it."

"I do, I sure do, Nat. Who else can I listen to?"

"Yourself. But let me have my own honest say, and then I'll shut up. . . . Doug, I hate this minorities bill. I hate its pretense. Every reservation you hold is true, as far as I'm concerned. T.C. and most of Congress invented this legislation as an emergency measure. The country is splintered apart—always has been—but these years it's been worse than ever. Negro revolution, you bet, and about time. So how does one put down a revolution, especially a just one? By force? Impossible in our democracy. Unthinkable. By giving in to those discriminated against, giving them justice and making democracy a true one? Difficult. Too much ignorance, blind hatred, senseless fear, and politics, for which read compromise. By bribery? The old Roman trick? The only way. So they came up with this MRP. Put down the insurrection and buy peace with money. Money is cheaper than decency. So here is a vast hog-barrel, boondoggling bribe to buy off the Negroes. And the Negroes can't resist. They are weak, tired of the long slow fight, and—you said it— they're hungry. If you've got to choose between having three square meals a day and money in the bank and all the wonders and advantages of materialism, as against waiting for the less tangible advantages of full liberty, which will you choose? So the Negroes, most of them, have given in. And the whites, big business, big labor unions—they love it. They've paid off the revolutionists and their guilty consciences, and they've purchased safety. And a good deal more besides, because they'll make profits, giving with one charitable hand, taking it back with the other.

"Everyone is happy, almost everyone, except those few of your people who are willing to go hungry a little longer to get five-fifths of what belongs to them, not one-fifth, and except the impractical liberals like myself who know better and want better for your people—but, of course, can afford to despise this bill because our stomachs are full. Now you've heard all I have to say, Doug, and don't listen to it. I don't have to make the decision. I don't have to worry if I've done a disservice to minorities or expediently helped them endure the near future. I don't have to worry if my opinion is weightier than those of several hundred experts. I don't have to worry how I feel if I do sign or what will happen to me and the country if I do not sign. Don't you listen to me, the man from Eagles Industries with a full stomach, Doug. I teed off this way because I wanted you to know I am still the man you've always known me to be. As for you, I know—"

There was a sharp knocking, and Dilman's attention was diverted to the lounge door.

"Mr. President," a voice called out, "it's Secretary Eaton."

"Come in."

The door swung open, and Eaton entered. He appeared disconcerted to find Abrahams with Dilman, then recovered his poise. His manner toward Dilman was concerned and sympathetic. "I missed you on deck, and I only wanted to know that you were all right, Mr. President. Is everything satisfactory?"

Dilman stood up and offered his Secretary of State a half-humorous grimace. "Mr. Secretary, to be perfectly frank with you, everything couldn't be worse. I've been seasick—"

"I'm sorry, Mr. President."

"—and while there has been an improvement, I'm still uncomfortable. If I am Commander in Chief of all the troops on land and all the ships at sea, I'd like to issue my first naval order. Have someone turn this damn yacht right around and deposit me safe and sound on God's good earth."

Eaton's conditioned countenance betrayed neither approval nor disapproval. "As you wish it, Mr. President. I'll transmit your order to Commander Chappell at once."

"And my apologies to our guests for cutting short their little outing."

Eaton nodded, and hurriedly left. The second that the cabin door closed, Dilman pivoted toward Nat Abrahams and gave him a wide grin and an elaborate salute.

"How was that, teacher?"

Abrahams smiled. "You're learning. You get an A."

Dilman had become solemn once more. "Now what I need is an A where it counts more, in political science." He took up the manila folder holding the minorities bill and balanced it thoughtfully. "Of course, it all depends on who does the grading, doesn't it?"

He stuffed the folder into his briefcase, pressed it shut, then went to Abrahams and took him by the arm. "For some reason, I feel better now. I think everything is settling into place, anatomically speaking. I'm ready to fish

awhile, if you are. Who knows, Nat? We might even catch
something we'll be proud of. . . ."

FOR IMMEDIATE RELEASE
Office of the White House Press Secretary

THE WHITE HOUSE

THE PRESIDENT HAS REQUESTED SPECIAL TIME OF ALL
MAJOR TELEVISION AND RADIO NETWORKS TONIGHT TO
ADDRESS THE NATION AT 7:00 P.M., EDT, ON THE SUB-
JECT OF THE MINORITIES REHABILITATION PROGRAM
AND THE BILL CONCERNING THIS PROGRAM AWAITING
HIS SIGNATURE. THE FULL TEXT OF HIS ADDRESS WILL BE
DISTRIBUTED TO THE PRESS FROM THIS OFFICE TEN
MINUTES AFTER HE IS ON THE AIR.

ALTHOUGH it was too soon for Governor Talley to have
arrived upstairs for their private meeting, before the
others came, before the President's television address
began, Secretary of State Arthur Eaton found it impossible to sit out the intervening time in the loneliness of his
huge seventh-floor office.

Ever since receiving Governor Talley's cryptic, but
definitely frantic, telephone call from the White House
ten minutes ago, Arthur Eaton had been worried and on
edge. He had not liked the tone, and the inconceivable
implications, of Talley's abbreviated call. Apparently,
even in the privacy of his own White House office, Talley
had been suspicious of being overheard or monitored. Yet
what he had said, guarded as he had been, had been made
meaningful and eloquent enough by his nettled speech
and its unnatural brevity.

Pacing, Arthur Eaton reconstructed what little he had
heard:

"Arthur? This is Wayne Talley. I've just come from

Edna Foster's office. The President wouldn't see me. He had Miss Foster give back the speech we wrote. He's written his own."

"His own? What are you talking about, Wayne? What kind of nonsense is that? Are you pulling my leg?"

"Arthur, I swear—"

"What in the devil has he written? What is in it?"

"Arthur, I can't speak. I'd better see you as soon as possible, before the others. Shall I come to your office?"

"Yes—no, wait—I think we want some seclusion. You use the E Street entrance. Take my private elevator right up to the top, to the eighth floor. I'll leave word for them to let you come up, and the others, also. I'll be waiting in the Madison Dining Room. . . . How does it look to you, Governor? He's going to sign the bill, of course?"

"I think so, I think so, there's nothing else he can do. It's what he's going to *say* about it that bothers me. I'll get over to State right away, Arthur. Good-bye."

That was all the evidence Eaton had to go by, ten minutes ago and now.

The degree to which the news had flustered him was a surprise. He had been schooled to be poised for the unexpected. Even international masters of the unexpected, like Premier Kasatkin, could be anticipated. One studied their arcs of reasoning, from the top curve of predictability to the bottom curve of unpredictability, and if one knew their backgrounds, ambitions, pressures, one could be ready to bisect and contain them at any point of the arc. But Dilman, apparently, had proved himself to be unlike other men.

This, then, was a part of what had unsettled Arthur Eaton, jolted his superior complacency. He had, of course, made his study of the new President, a shallow study, to be truthful, but then, the man had appeared to have no subtle resources that would require an examination of more depth. Dilman had given the impression, from the first, of a person obvious and simple to divine, or so it had seemed to one of Eaton's wide experience with more clever and devious men.

Of three dozen important demands made upon him, Dilman had been agreeable to all, well, all save two,

and even in these two matters he had finally performed
what was requested of him. He had not signed the New
Succession Bill into law, that was true, but he had weakly
permitted it to become law, with only the mildest legalistic protest. No one had minded that too much, considering Dilman's color and sensitivity and his need not to condone publicly a legislative insult. The fact was: he had
come along.

Then, in the invoking of the Subversive Activities Control Act, he had displayed faint resistance, evidenced by
hesitancy and delay. Yet his hesitancy, if one was reasonable, could not be regarded as unexpected. He had been
asked to outlaw a segment of his own race, and suffer
their ire, and had recoiled from it as long as possible.
Too, his behavior toward the Turnerites, if one studied
these matters as Eaton did, was the natural result of his
personality. Time and again he had shown himself to be
fearful and uncertain, and therefore indecisive and slow.
This was simply his style. In the end, predictably, he had
banned the Turnerite Group.

But this new development of ten or fifteen minutes ago,
this was unusual. To date, his slowness in signing the
Minorities Rehabilitation Program Bill was not unexpected, but part of his pattern. His sudden announcement
yesterday, before the Cabinet meeting adjourned, that he
had decided to address the nation on the bill, had been a
minor surprise to Eaton and all of them only because they
did not expect an act of impulse on Dilman's part. Yet,
once more, it was an understandable desire. Many Presidents, before approving of a crucial or gigantic piece of
spending legislation, liked to explain their belief in what
they were doing, mention minor reservations (as political
self-protection if anything went wrong or there was dis-
sent), and to dramatize their own roles in a useful action.
No, it was not unexpected that Dilman, conscious that the
minorities bill was T.C.'s bill, would wish to reap some of
T.C.'s popularity and curry some favor (when he needed
it most) by projecting himself before the public on millions of television screens as one of the authors of the
bountiful bill.

It had been routine for T.C.'s writers and special counselors to spend the remainder of yesterday afternoon, following the Cabinet meeting, and most of the evening, sketching out and molding into final form a public speech, in this case the fifteen-minute address on the minorities bill that explained its virtues and Dilman's own approval. Dilman had known that they were preparing his address, and had offered no objections. Late last night Dilman had received the polished final draft from Talley, with no indication of protest, indeed with thanks. And to Talley's suggestion that should Dilman desire any changes today, everyone would be standing by to help him, Dilman had again been appreciative.

And now, for the first time, the unpredictable: Dilman had rejected their speech in favor of one he had written, was writing, himself. He had displayed his first evidence of decisive action, of individuality, of independence, of ignoring advice from his betters—no, not his betters—his more experienced advisers.

Eaton had tried to penetrate the President's motivation for this silly and small rebellion. It did not mean that Dilman was opposing their wishes, the wishes, in fact, of Congress, the country, his own race, in regard to the important bill. No, one unaccountable action did not imply or indicate a more drastic one to follow. All Dilman was doing was demanding to write their speech *his* way. A sensitive colored man was asserting his rights. That was it. Eaton could see it more clearly now. By overlooking consideration of that one dimension of President Dilman's color, Eaton had almost erred in anticipating his behavior. Dilman's color had been largely responsible for his quick servility, his readiness to come along, his indecisiveness. This same color, Eaton saw, must occasionally drive him into some action of immature self-assertion, as if to remind the whites around him that he was their equal, a man with a mind of his own. That was it, of course, the complete explanation. Dilman was doing their bidding, whatever his secret qualms, on the Minorities Rehabilitation Bill, but was reminding them that although he must do what he was being told to do, he still would not allow himself to be held in utter contempt. In

short, Eaton saw, the President must at least be permitted
to say in his own words what his advisers wanted said.

Eaton told himself that his analysis made sense. He
congratulated himself on clearing up the enigma. Yet, he
realized, he was still unnerved. Why? Well, dammit, what
President of the United States had ever shielded the contents of a vital domestic policy speech—in this case the
most vital one in a decade—from everyone around him?

Tired of trying to solve mysteries with insufficient
clues, impatient to learn the details of Talley's encounter
with Dilman, or with the protective Miss Foster, Arthur
Eaton left his office. He proceeded through his stenographer's office—reminded, those moments, that he was
to have met Sally Watson in his home shortly after the
speech, resenting the fact that he might now be delayed,
and had better phone her to come later—and then he entered the small reception room and went on into the main
reception room. The desk there, too, was empty. He
noted the time. It was eleven minutes after six o'clock.
Everyone had gone home.

Yet not quite everyone, Eaton realized. Two clerks
passed busily through the corridor. Assistant Secretary
Stover, in his shirt-sleeves, carrying a dispatch, waved at
him. The sight of such activity pleased Eaton. At least
here, in his dominion, there were no mysteries, and nothing was unknown to him. Under his exacting rule, guided
by his cool intelligence and supported by a five-hundred-
million-dollar annual budget, his army of seven thousand
foreign affairs specialists toiled, and one thousand of
these worked through the night. It gave him pride that his
palace, the Department of State Building, was never dark
—as, so suddenly, the White House had become dark.

Restlessly, to kill time, Arthur Eaton wandered into
the corridor. He turned right, made his way across the
rich blue carpeting, absently glanced at the framed pictures of the nation's previous Secretaries of State on the
wall, then came to a halt before Room 7228, the corridor
entrance to his own office. He studied the two words lettered on the walnut panel of his door. They read simply:
THE SECRETARY. He thought of the many persons who
saw these two words daily, and how few understood the

encompassing, far-reaching nature of his responsibility, reaching back to T.C., reaching ahead to every American citizen everywhere, reaching now into that suddenly secretive Oval Office at 1600 Pennsylvania Avenue.

It was time for Talley to arrive, he decided.

Quickly he went to his private elevator, found and inserted his special key, observed the arrow light up red. Once inside, he was whisked to the eighth floor, a treasure house of history visited by no one except himself, his luncheon guests, and those he invited to attend diplomatic functions and State Department dinners during the evenings.

Leaving the elevator, Eaton hastened through the lounge, past the bar, and pulled open the two doors that led into the small, dimly lighted Madison Dining Room, the private hideaway where he ate lunch almost daily. None of the dozen chairs around the center table, nor the chairs drawn up before the television set, were occupied.

Annoyed, Eaton crossed the room, entered the adjacent dining room, also empty, and then he continued through this room and made his way to the outside terrace. The night air had turned cold, and he shivered. He went to the cement rail, kept his balance by holding onto a metal pillar, and peered down into E Street, studying the area between the parked automobiles and the green canopy that covered the walk to his private elevator. There was no one to be seen.

He looked up, and in the distance he could make out the Lincoln Memorial and the mass of the Pentagon Building behind it. Tonight he wished that he could see the White House half so clearly. He became aware that as he exhaled, his breath was condensing into visible clouds of vapor. Why the devil was Talley being so slow? Well, he told himself, it was not worth risking pneumonia to catch sight of his arrival.

He left the terrace for the heated interior of the eighth floor, and then returned to the Madison Dining Room. As he entered, he saw Wayne Talley bustling in from the lounge, tugging off his camel's hair overcoat, and dropping it and his hat across a chair.

"My God, Wayne, it's about time." Eaton tried to keep

the peevishness out of his voice. "Where have you been?"

"The traffic," said Talley breathlessly. "Even Moses couldn't have made that sea of cars part, let alone a White House limousine."

They met at the dining table. "What happened?" Eaton demanded. "Try to remember everything."

"I wish there was much more to tell you besides what I told you on the phone, but there isn't," Talley said. "When I gave him the draft of the speech last night, I assured him I'd be waiting to consult with him on any changes. He said he was grateful, and I thought he was. I waited around in my office all morning, and not a word from him. After lunch I dropped in on Edna Foster and asked if the President had been looking for me. She said no, he was tied up. I asked if he had the speech on his desk. She said she thought she had seen it there. I told her to be sure to tell him I was standing by for any last-minute changes or modifications. She said she'd tell him. Well, the whole afternoon passed and not a word——"

"Didn't you see Dilman at all today? I mean, on anything else?"

"Not even a glimpse of him," Talley complained. "I think this is the first day that's ever happened. Well, about an hour ago I couldn't stand it any more, so I went back to Miss Foster's office and again I asked if he'd been looking for me. She said no, not as far as she knew. That was too much, so I said, 'Edna, I'd like to see the President.' And she said—you know what she said?—she said, 'I'm sorry, Governor Talley, but he canceled every one of his appointments and left strict orders not to be disturbed.' How do you like that, Arthur? Well, I didn't, not at all, so I said, 'What in the heck is he so busy with?' She said, 'I really don't know, except he's been writing the entire morning and afternoon.' Writing? That exasperated me——"

Eaton looked up from his watch crossly. "Governor, do you mind skipping your feelings and traumas, and sticking to what happened? In a few more minutes, we won't be alone."

Hurt, Talley said, "Geez, Arthur, I was only trying—okay, okay—so I said to her firmly, 'Edna, I'm his aide, and if he knows I'm out here he will probably want to see me. So you go in there, you tell him I sent you in, and tell him I'd like to know what he thinks of the speech, and if he'd like to talk it over.' She was kind of hesitant, but I insisted. So she went inside, and I cooled my heels for maybe a minute. Then she came out, and you know what she had in her hand? This." Wayne Talley reached inside his suit coat and jerked forth the folded typescript of the speech they had jointly prepared for Dilman the night before. Talley opened it and pointed to the pen-written scrawl across the top.

Eaton cocked his head, squinted his eyes, trying to decipher the scrawl. Haltingly, he read the President's notation aloud. " 'Thanks for all your trouble. D.D.' " Eaton frowned, and pursed his lips. "I wonder if he even read it."

"I don't know," said Talley. "All I know is Miss Foster stuck it in my hands and said, 'President Dilman asked me to tell you he appreciates this, the work that went into it, but he won't need it because he's writing his own speech.' I was so appalled, I blurted out to her, I said, 'Edna, for Chrissakes, no President in living memory has ever written his own speech. It takes writers, real writers, and in this instance, specialists in domestic matters. No man can do it alone. He'd botch it.' And she said, 'I don't think you have to worry, Governor. He didn't do it entirely alone. When I told him you were standing by to help, he said to tell you he'd had plenty of help all day long from friends of his.' I got sore, and I said, 'I thought you told me no one saw him today.' She said, 'That's right, at least not through this office or Mr. Lucas' office. But he may have seen someone in his own apartment at lunch. Besides, I didn't say that no one *talked* to him today. There were plenty of telephone calls.' I couldn't ask her who he called or who called him, so I thanked her, double-checked with Lucas to see if there'd been any visitors through his office—there weren't—and then I hopped right back to my desk and telephoned you. That's the whole of it, Arthur. What do you think?"

"I think I don't like it, and I think our President is a

fool," Eaton said. "He is liable to make a bloody mess of it. I can only pray he is literate and lucid enough to make the meaning and intent of the bill clear to the people."

"Well, I've had time to cool off, and I'm becoming philosophical about the whole thing," Talley said. "What difference what he says about it, as long as he signs it? I only resent his being so high-handed, and ignoring us. Besides"——Talley smoothed the typescript almost lovingly where it lay on the table——"it was such a damn beautiful bit of rhetoric, would have kicked the whole minorities program off in high. Christ, what T.C. could have done with this. Lookee here——"

He began to read snatches of the rejected speech. " 'This magnificent Federal program follows in the great American tradition of the WPA at home and the Marshall Plan abroad, both milestones in our democratic effort to lend a strong, undemanding hand to those of our citizens who need a hand, and to give aid and comfort to those millions who desire their country's help even as they help themselves. It is with pride in my fellow citizens, and with the greatest confidence in our future well-being and security, that I endorse the Minorities Rehabilitation Program approved by our Congress, and that I put my name to it before all of you.' " Talley looked up. "Not bad, Arthur?" He dipped his head again. "I like this part best. 'This bill, my fellow Americans, will stand a monument more enduring than granite to the name and memory of my predecessor, the late President, who——' "

"That's enough, Governor," Eaton interrupted. "It's a waste of time. It has as much meaning now as a letter that was never mailed." He paused, and listened. "Is that the elevator?"

Quickly Talley folded the speech and shoved it into his pocket. He sidled up to Eaton. "What do we tell them?"

"Nothing, except that Dilman told you he was revising our draft at length, and we have no idea how he has altered the language." He looked off. "Hello, Allan. . . . Evening, Senator——"

The Majority Leader of the Senate, John Selander, came into the room, followed by Allan Noyes, chairman of the Party. Minutes later, Gorden Oliver, full of cheer and carrying a bottle of Cutty Sark as his entry pass, arrived with Harvey Wickland, Majority Leader of the House of Representatives. Shortly after, Secretary of the Interior Lionel Ruttenberg was the last to arrive.

Arthur Eaton found that he had no patience for the usual small talk and gossip, and he drifted apart from his guests to smoke and think. When he consulted his wristwatch, it was only three minutes to speech time.

He returned to the group, but hung back while Gorden Oliver finished the latest addition to his endless store of jokes.

"—stood waiting on the Montgomery street corner for his transportation," Oliver was saying, "and when it came, this dark-skinned gentleman climbed on, paid his fare, and started to sit down in the front seat. Then the driver yelled at him, 'Get in the back of the bus!' Then the man said, 'But I'm Jewish.' Then the driver yelled, 'Get off the bus!' "

They all roared with glee, and Oliver, encouraged, was about to embark on another story when Eaton said loudly, "The President is speaking in one minute. Let's settle down."

As Talley hastened to turn on the television set, find the clearest channel, adjust the volume, the others took their places in the semicircle of chairs set before the screen. Eaton did not join them, but propped himself against the table edge, arms folded across his chest.

The television screen was filled by a commercial, and then the station break with the network's emblem.

Senator Selander, tipping his chair backward, twisting, whispered to Eaton, "What's this that Wayne was telling me about the President doing considerable rewriting on the address we prepared? I thought it was a gem. Are you sure you have no idea what parts he changed?"

"No idea whatsoever, Senator. Apparently it was a last-minute thing. In all probability, he beefed up the sections on civil rights. I think he's trying to woo back his Negro following. But quite honestly, I don't—" Eaton uncrossed his arms and pointed past Selander. "There it goes. We'll know soon enough."

They concentrated on the screen, which now showed the Presidential seal.

Eaton's memory of the many times he had been in that Oval Office when T.C. had waited to address the nation enlarged the screen in his mind. A minute or two before, the still photographers had been shooed out, and what remained were four or five television cameras and their operators focusing on T.C.'s hearty figure, solid and ready in the big leather chair behind the Buchanan desk. Eaton remembered too, with an ache of nostalgia, the little things that prepared T.C. for this moment: the thick cables leading from the cameras across the rug and through the French doors to the colonnaded walk where the Secret Service men stood; the black drape hung and pinned across the windows behind the President; the brown felt cloth thrown over the desk from which the gadgets and framed photographs of Hesper and Freddie had been temporarily removed; the tilted stand atop the desk, holding the cards on which the President's address had been typed; the two members of the press pool, sitting out of view at the President's left; the television monitor set off screen at his right, but facing him so he could see the image that he was projecting; the two secretaries in the rear, holding transcripts of the speech, to check his spoken words against the printed words, and pencil in any changes he improvised or ad-libbed.

"Ladies and gentlemen, the President of the United States."

The camera cut from the close-up of the Presidential seal to a full shot of the President behind his desk. And to Eaton's surprise, he had succumbed completely to memory's sorcery. For it was not T.C. who sat there at all, but a black stranger. The camera moved in until the screen was entirely occupied by Douglass Dilman's broad African visage and features. These features, blended and made indistinguishable by his blackness, contrasted with the lightness of his suit and shirt, but matched the blackness of his hands resting on the sides of the stand. For the first time in many weeks, Eaton sensed his loss, the nation's loss, and felt deeply embittered by the sheer insanity of human existence.

"Good evening, my fellow citizens."

If not T.C., Eaton thought, then at least a reasonable facsimile. Thank the Lord, he thought, that all of them here were alive to see that T.C. would not be wholly dead.

By an effort of will, he ceased his thinking of what could not be. He listened. President Douglass Dilman was addressing the nation.

"One week ago there reached my desk the original enrolled bill, printed on parchment paper, certified and signed by the Acting Speaker of the House of Representatives and the Acting President of the Senate, that has come to be popularly known as the Minorities Rehabilitation Program. It requires only the scratch of my pen to enact it into public law—or, on the other hand, it takes only my returning it unsigned to the House in which it originated, with my objections stated, to institute a Presidential veto.

"To this date, I have neither approved the bill nor rejected it, because I have needed as much time as possible to consider every aspect of it, to weigh its cost against its value to all of us. Before rendering my decision, I felt it necessary to discuss briefly with you, the people, certain aspects of the bill, of this Minorities Rehabilitation Program.

"The preponderance of opinion is behind this program. Four out of five of your representatives in Congress are behind it. They are behind it, they say, because they feel that it will repay a minority of the population, largely Negro, for years of deprivation, it will restore economic dignity to those who have suffered loss of it because of their color, and it will bring a dramatic end to racial strife. Business leaders, as well as labor leaders, are behind it because they believe that the program will boost the national economy, bring prosperity to all, and bring civil peace to the land. Even the majority of Negro organization directors favor the bill as an expedient measure of restitution that would, to a degree, make up for losses suffered through a century of actual slavery and continued segregation thereafter.

"Without bothering to explore in detail every provision of the bill, and speaking to you in the plainest of language, what are the general arguments for and against the Minorities Rehabilitation Program?

"Those who want me to sign this bill—and they are, I repeat, the overwhelming majority—sincerely believe that by dispersing in various ways seven billion dollars of your tax payments, over a period of five years, to the underprivileged racial minorities of this nation, they will be bringing internal peace to the United States. They feel that the Federal government can now accomplish, by this massive outpouring of money, what the prejudices of private industry and restrictions of labor unions have heretofore prevented doing: close the economic gap between black and white. They feel that this financial restitution to the colored man will make up for a century of oppression. And they feel that, by giving twenty-three million of the nation's blacks economic equality, by giving them higher wages, jobs or better jobs, subsidized training, by so occupying their minds and hands, by so filling their stomachs, they will have brought tranquility and order through the democratic process to the United States.

"However, there is a smaller, less vocal number of Americans, as concerned about the deprivation of minorities, as desirous of bringing about tranquility and order, who strongly believe this nation cannot afford the minorities bill, not because of its financial cost but because of the means by which it will bankrupt our ideals, our democracy, our Constitution.

"What are their arguments against the bill? You have seen little discussion of their reservations in the press, and heard few of their protests on the floors of Congress or on the airwaves. In all fairness, their objections should be heard tonight, and considered by you, as they have been considered by me.

"The dissenters believe that this bill is a governmental conspiracy to bribe the oppressed into silence. It may bring racial peace, but at what price to our democratic integrity? The Constitution will be converted into a checkbook. We will have given our minorities not civil rights, not equality, but a giant payoff to end their clamor. Under this bill, the Negro will not have gained his vote, his equal place in public accommodations, his dignity as a

free American. Instead, he will have gained employment.
He will have been detoured from the hard, uphill road to
that place where free men live, to remain at the roadside
beneath and below them, diverted from his goal by the
dollars he has suddenly found. And when the money is
spent, where will he be? Still too far from freedom, and
perhaps unable to find the public road again.

"Yes, my fellow citizens, there are thoughtful men,
Americans as decent as you and I, who believe in their
deepest conscience that one cannot substitute dollars for
the dignity of liberty. By so doing, we undermine the
humanity of the giver as well as the taker, we weaken the
majority as well as the minority. And worse, by so doing,
we reinforce the anti-American caricature of Uncle Sam
throughout the world by showing him not as a man but as
a figurehead in the shape of a dollar sign, an Uncle Sam
who offers his flock cash instead of love, respect, and
freedom.

"The proponents of the Minorities Rehabilitation
Program believe that through a seven-billion-dollar out-
lay they will have bought time. The opponents of the program wonder, time for what? And how much time? There
are those who believe that the time to solve our minority
problem is today, no matter how high the cost in civil
strife and discontent, and that the means to solve it is
not through huge Federal bribes, but through total Federal support of any human being who is treated as less
than an American and less than a man because of his
race, religion, color, or national origin.

"My fellow citizens, there is something to be said for
both sides, but as your President I can choose only one
side, and for me the moment of decision has arrived. Addressing you then, not as one who is prejudiced by white
or black demands, not as one heeding majority or minority wishes, but rather addressing you as one who has come
to believe that any travail or sacrifice is worthwhile if it
will strengthen the foundation of a stronger, totally democratic United States of America that can stand before the
world unashamed, indeed, proud, for having practiced
those noble ideas upon which it was founded, I hereby
notify my former colleagues in Congress, and my fellow

citizens everywhere, that I cannot and shall not sign the Minorities Rehabilitation Program into law.

"Tonight I am vetoing this bill, and returning it to the House where it originated, with the prayer that never again will I or any President be forced to consider an example of legislation so cynical as to pretend that freedom has a price tag.

"Yet we do need powerful legislation to replace this bill. We need legislation concerned with equality, not tranquility, and in due time I intend—"

Before the gasps, groans, and angry exclamations from those in the Madison Dining Room could drown out the remainder of the President's speech, Arthur Eaton leaped forward, cursing under his breath, and savagely turned off the television set.

White-faced, trembling, he stood with his back to the others, unable to face them until he had regained his composure.

He heard Talley say, "I'll be goddamned, that sonofabitch torpedoed us!"

He heard Oliver demand, "That bastard, who does he think he is?"

He heard Noyes explode, "The Party can't let him get away with it!"

He heard Senator Selander predict, "He's split the country, even if we can override his veto."

As the voices became increasingly furious and uncontrolled behind him, Eaton tried to block out the din, to assemble his thoughts. His first thoughts were of T.C. The minorities bill was to have been T.C.'s enduring monument. Tonight, no matter what followed, it was a monument no more. Until tonight T.C. had been alive, his government kept alive, through the works he had instigated and the men he had left behind to see them through. Yet tonight a semiliterate black man, defying the wishes of his superiors and the majority of the nation, had trampled on moderation to cater to extremists of his color. Tonight a black interloper, employing the rankest demagoguery in a crude and inciting play for power, had sold out national unity to dress his personal pride.

Then, filtering through Arthur Eaton's initial shock and

disgust, the real implication of Dilman's rebellion could be seen: It was not T.C. who had been ousted from the White House Oval Office, for T.C. was a ghost, but it was himself, Arthur Eaton himself, T.C.'s heir, who had been banished from decision making and rule.

"What's left without Party rule?" he could hear Congressman Wickland cry out behind him. "Anarchy, that's what is left!"

Eaton heard the telephone across the room. Glad of an excuse to escape from the others, he hastily went to answer it.

Immediately he recognized the excitable voice, with its mean Southern slur, on the other end.

"Oh, hello, Zeke."

"Arthur?" shouted Congressman Zeke Miller. "What do you think, Arthur? Don't answer. You're too goldarn gentlemanly for your own good. Let me tell you what I think, Arthur. I'm not afraid of speaking out the truth. You know what I think, Arthur? I think that there black Nigra just did us and the country the greatest goldarn service in history. He showed us he's ready to dump all branches of government, executive, legislative, judicial, all, to make himself the Nigra dictator like they once had down in Haiti. He stripped and showed his true colors— ha, you betcha—showed us he's making a black republic exclusive for his brother Nigras—banning the Turnerites, then showing himself to be worse than—"

Eaton had little patience for this line. "Zeke, he's already alienated the Negro extremists. This won't win them back. What he's done, for whatever reason, is simply to alienate most everyone else. I think he's left himself high and dry—"

"All the better!" Zeke Miller shouted. "Now we can bring him down. Now he's in the open for what he is, and no more bleeding hearts to guard him, no more poor oppressed black Tom mask to gain sympathy, but just a big black bull Nigra as mean as Mr. Hyde himself. He downright showed his hand, his malignant hand, with that veto, Arthur, and made a mess for us on the Hill and all over the country. Now he's in the open, and we're coming out in the open, too. You've got to get off the dime now,

Arthur. You're not going to let some all-fired ignoramus lout of a nigger do that to T.C.'s memory, besmirch our great friend, and drag the country to hell and deeper because he's fixing to make us into another Africa. Arthur, you're not letting him get away with that, are you? For the sake of the country and our prestige, you got to play ball with us. We're suffering this together. We're going to put old Sambo on the hot seat good, and we're going to roast his ass plenty, until he yells enough, and begs us to get him off it. I'm going to force him to resign, to resign because of disability or whatever, but to resign, and if he refuses, I'm going to resign him by force."

"How do you intend to do all of that, Zeke?"

"You'll see. Watch and see. Meanwhile, the boys want to know, I want to know, are you with us, Arthur?"

Eaton said, "Let's not do anything rash, Zeke. Let Dilman dig his own grave for a while——"

"Takes too long!" snapped Miller. "I want to hustle him into it before we wind up in that hole, too."

"Well, let me think awhile, let all of us think, and play it by ear until——"

"You play it by ear. You just remember what that ear heard from our Nigra President tonight. There's only two sides left, Arthur, his and ours. You've got to be on ours. I'm counting you in. I'll have more for you later, Arthur, a lot more."

Although holding less distaste tonight than he usually did for the Southern Congressman, Arthur Eaton was relieved to hang up on him.

He turned to find Wayne Talley behind him. "That was Zeke Miller," Eaton explained.

"I guessed it would be," said Talley. "What's he after? Throwing Dilman out?"

"Something like that. All kinds of wild, impractical talk. You don't throw someone out because you disagree with him."

"Sometimes you do," said Talley. "But if you don't or can't, at least you try to control him."

"How can we control him? Look what happened tonight."

"Arthur, when someone's dangerous, you isolate him

from causing any more trouble." Talley paused meaningfully. "Certainly, you don't give him a gun. You know what I mean?"

"I think so—I think I do."

Talley looked around, to make sure they were out of hearing of the others, and then he said, "Arthur, I wouldn't send him that CIA report, not that one."

"Aren't you worrying too much? It may be inconsequential. It doesn't have a very high reliability evaluation."

"No matter," Talley persisted. "Dilman's irresponsible. He could make a mountain out of a molehill—before we get to the summit meeting in Chantilly. I think we've got to start right now, this instant, keeping the seat of government where it belongs."

"You may be right."

"If Zeke Miller's too wild for you, then somebody else has got to do something. I think it's up to us to save the country."

"What there is left of it after tonight," said Eaton bitterly. He considered this, then added, "You are right, Wayne. We have no choice. Dilman has just had his fair trial in public. He can be judged honestly. He is irresponsible, and therefore potentially dangerous. If we cannot punish him, we should seek means to contain him. That should be our private policy. As you so succinctly put it —no gun; we are not going to give him another opportunity to shoot this country down."

FOR IMMEDIATE RELEASE
Office of the White House Press Secretary

THE WHITE HOUSE

THE PRESIDENT IS LUNCHING TODAY WITH MAJORITY LEADERS AND MINORITY LEADERS OF BOTH HOUSES OF CONGRESS TO DISCUSS HIS VETO OF THE MINORITIES REHABILITATION PROGRAM AND DISCUSS AN AMENDED BILL.

FOLLOWING IS THE FULL TEXT OF A CABLE FROM
NIKOLAI KASATKIN, PREMIER OF THE U.S.S.R., STATING
HIS OPTIMISM CONCERNING THE CHANTILLY CONFER-
ENCE TO BEGIN IN FOUR DAYS. FOLLOWING ALSO IS THE
TEXT OF PRESIDENT DILMAN'S REPLY.

AT 3 P.M., THE PRESIDENT WILL MEET WITH SECRET
SERVICE CHIEF HUGO GAYNOR TO APPROVE SPECIAL SE-
CURITY MEASURES BEING PREPARED FOR THE PRESI-
DENT'S TRIP ABROAD.

———————

AT four-fifteen of an overcast, chilly afternoon, a time
when he was normally posted between the President's
Oval Office and the Rose Garden, Otto Beggs sat sprawled
deeply and comfortably in the foam cushions of Ruby
Thomas' sofa and listened to the high-fidelity phono-
graph he had repaired an hour ago.

He was tieless and shoeless, and filled with a single-
minded lust he had not felt in years, a passion gradually
heightened by his second gin-and-tonic and the perfume
and fleshy scent of Ruby's dusky sensuous person so near
to him. The insinuating rhythms were part of it, too, he
supposed, all that Bunk Johnson, Muggsy Spanier, King
Oliver, Louis Armstrong, Jelly Roll Morton that he pretended to understand but only felt.

But mostly it was the drinks. Ordinarily Otto Beggs
was a beer man, a Coca-Cola man, because sobriety was
a cornerstone of his exacting job, and an integral part of
his devotion to physical fitness. Only at rare times had he
ever indulged himself in gin-and-tonic (on his vacation,
and at Christmas, and on Big Occasions like his wedding
anniversary or when he received a raise in salary or chose
diversions after hours on assignments away from Washington, but never on an ordinary weekday—and during
an afternoon yet!). But this afternoon, at first guiltily,
then as the gin took its potent effect, its taste becoming
less medicinal, more pleasurable, he drank, because this
was, indeed, a Big Occasion.

"What you thinkin', Otter?" Ruby Thomas asked.

He looked at her, feasting his gaze upon her tousled dark hair, almond eyes, perfect dark complexion, open-collar orange-yellow blouse, bare feet tucked under her skirt. He said, "I'm too relaxed to think much, Ruby. This is great."

"Now you talkin', 'cause I'm 'joyin' this, too," she said. She brought her second J and B on ice to her lips, and drained the glass. "Yum. Sure gits this pickaninny's naycher up. Yum, good." She studied him over the glass. "Hope you not gonna leave me too quick like, Otter, jes when I'm gittin' to 'joy myself. Can you stay awhile?"

"Remember, I told you before, Ruby, I took the day off. I can stay all day and evening, if you're up to it."

"Up to it? Mothah! I never been happier, man, you bet." She set the glass down. "How you manage it, Otter? I mean, takin' all day from you p'ofessional duty? Ever done this before?"

"Never done it before, Ruby. There's always a first time, though, if there's good enough reason. I figured you're a good enough reason. So I made up to go to work, then parked behind the Walk Inn, then phoned my boss and told him I had a bellyache and was going to the doctor. Nothing to it."

He thought about that call to Lou Agajanian, which had been taken, ironically, by the Negro, Roscoe Prentiss, who had been promoted to the position that was rightfully Otto's own. If he had been hesitant before making the call, the fact that Prentiss answered had hardened his resolve to have some things his own way. Beggs had said that he was unwell, and was on his way to his doctor, and would then take it easy, but he'd probably be okay tomorrow.

Prentiss had been definitely upset. Ten of the White House Detail had been dispatched to Paris to look things over at Chantilly and Versailles nearby. Two others were in bed with influenza. There would be no one to substitute for Beggs but that new kid, Ross, transferred to the Detail from Baltimore only a week ago and still unfamiliar with the White House routine and the President's habits. Maybe the doctor would give Beggs a clean bill of health, and he could report for duty anyway, even if a little late.

Momentarily, Beggs had wavered—duty—but then he had revived his resentment toward Prentiss and Dilman, Negroes who had put him down, were still trying to put him down, trying to keep him from one of their girls. It had been difficult for him, but he had insisted, in a pained voice, that he was just too sick, and he'd check back with Agajanian tonight.

Working his way through back streets toward Ruby's apartment, to be sure that no neighbor would observe him, he had worried briefly that Agajanian might be concerned and call the house, and Gertrude would learn of his deception. But that was unlikely, he had decided, for he had told Prentiss he would be at the doctor's long enough for a complete physical examination. Furthermore, Agajanian was too busy to give him a second thought at any time. The new kid, Ross, could do the job.

A half hour after his arrival in Ruby's small walk-up apartment through the private entrance to which she had carefully directed him, his last lingering guilt about dereliction from duty had been washed away by the two generous servings of gin and Ruby's provocative warmth.

She had asked how he had managed to arrange seeing her, and he had told her that there had been nothing to it. It had not been really easy, yet it had been easier than he had expected.

He saw her pleased face, and was in turn pleased himself by his aggressive independence. This was worth any risk. She was the most beautiful dark animal on earth, and he was alone with her.

She was saying, "You mean, Otter, I'm more impo'tant for you to see than the Pres? You mean you don't mind givin' up p'ofessional work jes 'cause you wanna be with me?"

The gin, and the scent of her, now mixed together behind his temples and made him light-headed and reckless. "Honey, I'd rather be here than anywhere on earth. This is all I've been dreaming about, day and night, being with you like this."

"Whee!" she exclaimed, and suddenly she was up on her knees, reaching out for him. "Man, I sure like you sweet-talkin' me, makin' me tingle all ovah—you is de-servin' a reward——"

She was over him, to his surprise, playfully mouthing little kisses upon his cheek. The fluttering opening and closing of her soft lips aroused him. Unable to control himself further, he threw his arms around her, and han-dling her as easily as a flexible plaything, pulled her down to his chest, pressed his lips hard against her half-open mouth. She responded with her lips, and wriggled her body in his grasp, until the sensuous movements of her back and the sides of her breasts against his palms al-most suffocated him.

When she came away from him, eyes now open and staring up at him, gasping to breathe as he gasped too, she said, "Man, you sure is potent—you gittin' poor Ruby's naycher stirrin' up a mile high an' wantin' to go——"

"Honey——"

She pushed herself off his lap and came around to stare at him solemnly. "Man, you know what you is doin' to me?"

"Ruby——"

"You sure enuff full of powers, man, got me hot and full up with naycher—better lemme change—wanna let lil Ruby change?"

Bewildered, frightened, Beggs said, "Whatever you want, Ruby. Yes, you'd better."

"Yum," she said. She jumped off the sofa, and then abruptly sat on his lap again, her back to him, one finger pointing behind her. "Unbutton me, darlin', so's I can change."

His thick fingers fumbled at the buttons, and he had difficulty opening them, but at last the back of her blouse fell apart revealing the smooth black shoulders and ridge of spine and the white band and clasp of her brassière. Her head came around, and her lower lip pouted. "Otter, you been 'round too much for this lil pickaninny. Ummm——" She kissed his nose and stood up, chastely holding up the front of her unfastened blouse with her palm. "Won't be more than a minute changin'. Wanna freshen the drinks?"

"Sure thing."

"You be waitin' for lil Ruby—oh, mothah me! Dog my cats! I loves you, man—"

She went quickly, hips and skirt swinging, out of the small living room into the bedroom, half closing the door behind her.

Otto Beggs sat unmoving. She was gone, but the fragrance of her flesh still enveloped him, entered his pores, kindled his desire for her even more intensely. She had said that she wanted to "change." What did that mean? Change to what? He had an idea to what. Still, would she? Was it possible? Of course, it was possible. She had said that she was hot and full up with "naycher"—meaning, he woozily deducted, that her natural instincts, her primitive instincts, had been aroused by him. Criminy, what did a colored girl do, how did she behave, when she felt like that? It was a mystery to him, yet his wonder at the unknown was secondary to his great expectations. Shortly, if he had not misread her, he would be initiated into the club—the club of coarse jokes—to be one with all those who had changed their luck.

He left the sofa for the kitchenette, dropped ice into the glasses, poured a double amount of J and B over her ice, and a long shot of gin over his, and forgot about the tonic. He walked back into the living room, holding her drink, taking a swallow of his, and suddenly he stood still. There she was, and he had never seen anything like it except in the movies and men's magazines.

She posed, one hand on a hip, standing between the mosaic coffee table and the sofa.

"How you like it, Otter?" she asked, and as she pirouetted gracefully, the dark definite lines of her body were clearly revealed from behind the flimsy, long lemon-colored negligee. "I had to git myself some expensive underwear, price of three LPs, jes for this occasion with my Otter."

"It fits you great," he said, embarrassed by the thick huskiness of his voice. "This is sure a treat."

"Don't sweet-talk cottonpickin' me—you a big hero with all them fancy whitegirls fussin' 'round you—"

He took another drink, and protested, "None of them

hold a candle to you, Ruby. You look like a movie star, no kidding."

She lowered herself to the sofa, crossing one leg over the other in a new pose, this one of languor, and watched him. He placed her drink before her and looked down at her, at the ebony flesh running from the hollow of her throat to the exposed cleft between her breasts. She raised her hands behind her head, and he was hypnotized by the shifting and spreading of the mounds of her bosom, no longer covered by the brassière, hardly concealed by the transparent negligee.

She patted the soft sofa beside her. "Come on, Otter, ain't you gonna show this woman no friendshipness?"

Stiffly, almost asthmatically wheezing, he moved between the sofa and table, drinking again. Then, daringly, he sank down beside her, one arm high on the sofa behind her, his free hand holding the drink. Without trying to look, he could see the reddish bikini panties she was wearing, and the flesh of one broad dark thigh as it lay over the other. He tried to lift his eyes to her face, but he could not help holding his gaze on her protruding breasts.

"Thirty-eight," she said.

His head came up quickly. "What?"

She cupped her hands beneath her breasts. "Size thirty-eight," she said. "Figger you'd wanna know exactly."

He brought the trembling glass to his flushed face. "You should be an actress, Ruby, something like that." He drank to reinforce his giddy hopes.

"Naw, like I told you before, I been there bein' leered at by the whiteboys. I don't like paradin' myself before any ol' body. You—you is somethin' special, Otter—"

She reached out, gently but firmly removed the glass from his clutch, set it on the table, and squirmed closer to him, head against his shoulder, fingers playfully opening his shirt, and then her hand slipping underneath his shirt and caressing his hairy chest.

He dropped his arm from the sofa down around her shoulders, loosely, listening to the throaty sounds of her, like a cat's motor-purrings. He was not positive what he should do next, take the plunge at once, grab her, start it, or tell her first what he wanted, or be more subtle and find out if what he thought was being led up to was really understood by both of them. If he came right out and made the move, or the demand, and she was just teasing around, it would be embarrassing and ruin everything. He had to be positive. Also, there were some women, even among the paid ones, who liked to go slow, and maybe she was one of these. If she was, he didn't want to spoil his chances. There was time, plenty of time.

"Why do you think I'm so special, Ruby?" he asked, feeling foolish. "I like hearing it, believe me, but you must've known plenty of young men."

"Not so many, Otter, an' no somebody like you—you is handsome and strong—Jee-sus—you feels all muscle—an' a hero with them medals, botherin' 'bout lil pickaninny me—nobody me, sep I admit to bein' thirty-eight where it counts—" She enjoyed this, and giggled. "You knows what, Otter, I was thinkin' last night. You is too impo'tant to be wastin' time even guardin' the Pres of the U.S.A.—you knows that? You too impo'tant in you own right to be wastin' time on a finky cullud-man Pres who ain't half the man you is. Thass what I think of you, Otter. You is better than him. Mothah an' Lordy, you sure is."

"Thank you for the compliments, Ruby, but he is President of the United States, and nobody's more important."

"Ummm. You smell jes good . . . you is more impo'-tant. That black man in the White House ain't fit to shine you shoes."

A little more, he thought, a little more of this aimless chatter, and he'd be sure, and take the plunge. "Last time we talked, you had no feelings one way or the other about President Dilman. What's happened since, Ruby? You don't have to answer—who gives a damn about him—except I'd think you'd be happy about a Negro in—"

Suddenly she removed her hand from his chest and turned on her side, her silky, cooing voice turning resolute and strident. "I ain't happy 'bout him no more. Lots been happenin' to him and us. Dilman ain't good enuff to be colored man or whiteboy, either. He ain't good enuff to be any ol' thing. He a turd, nothin' better. Lookit him bannin' the Turners, not liftin' a finger for poor ol' Jeff

Hurley. Lookit him even takin' away the crummy mimority law money from my kinfolk. Otter, that man you guardin' with you life no good for nobody—he spellin' only evil—"

Silently Beggs cursed himself for inciting her with a conversation that he had meant to use only as a bridge to the ultimate seduction. Now, judging from the indignation in her eyes, he saw that her mood was anything but sensual. Desperately, he tried to sidetrack her. "Ruby, just as you said before, he isn't important enough to get riled up about. I don't like him much either, I can admit it to you since we're so close, and not because he's a Negro or for what he's doing to Negroes—I don't know much about that, except the whites are plenty sore at him too for vetoing that bill, throwing his weight around—I don't like him because he's a weakling. That's the main thing. That banning, somebody else did that for him, that's how weak he is. And the veto, hell, that showed no guts, only he got scared of the banning and tried to make up for it—"

Ruby shook her head. "You too charitable, Otter—my friends and relatives, they don't think that Dilman weak—they think him evil all day long, 'cause he resents his color, thass what."

There was imagining and there was performing, and Otto Beggs had had enough of the imagining and was ready for the performing. He lowered his arm further, and encircled her tighter, feeling the spongy give of her breast beneath the lingerie.

"Aw, forget him, Ruby. He's not worth you and your friends getting so sore about. Believe me, and you know how well I know him, take my word for it from the inside, he's scared of his shadow, and that's why he acts the way he does."

She seemed hardly aware of Beggs's arm or hand or increasing ardor. She sat up a little. "What is you meanin'—thass why he acts way he does? Don't tell me he ain't 'shamed of his own people an' actin' against us." Her tone had become concerned. "You knows somethin' different, bein' with him? I won't believe anythin', sep if you—"

"Ruby, listen." He was determined to end this conversation fast, and get going with her. "Like I said, I hold no brief for the guy, and I don't like being put in the position of defending him. At the same time, I think enough of you not to want to see you all worked up and angry, for no reason. So let me tell you the truth of it, between us, strictly you and me——"

"For sure, I promise, Otter."

"——and let's get you relaxed and at ease again, and have ourselves a ball. Few people have had as close a look at the President as I have. You agree to that?"

"Sure enuff, Otter, but don't you think he——?"

"He's no more against Negroes than you are or your friends are or I am. He's just on the spot being President, being a colored President, and he knows it and feels it. He knows whatever whichway he turns, a whole bunch of people will think he's wrong, simply because he's a minority person. Whenever I get sore at him and at myself for having to spend my good time guarding him, guarding a man who is contributing nothing to improve us, I remember a couple things I've seen and heard, and then, instead of being sore, well, I pity him. That's true, Ruby, I'm not puffing myself up, but me, *I* pity *him*." He paused. "You know why? Because even though he's sitting where F.D.R. and Harry and Ike and J.F.K. and Lyndon and The Judge and T.C. sat, he still feels he's sitting in the back of the bus, because that's where a lot of people around him make him think he belongs. I don't know politics, but I've got eyes and ears. Certain people are trying to run him, and to make it easier they're pressuring him, letting him know he doesn't belong, and he feels it and suffers like a dog, and that's the only thing he's got from me, my sympathy."

Ruby seemed curiously chastened and troubled. "What you mean with that there talkin', Otter? What you mean?"

Beggs was becoming increasingly furious at the time this was taking. "Okay, I'll give it to you quickly, and then you promise, no more politics or Dilman?"

" 'Course, Otter, I promise. But what you mean by——?"

"Remember that big speech he delivered the other night, vetoing the minorities bill everyone wanted? I was outside his open door, the door to his office, during it and afterwards. I could see and hear everything. You should have seen him after that speech, almost sick with nervousness and worry. Then there were a lot of phone calls, apparently from big shots in government and all over, and most of them must have been awful, calling him names, giving him hell. Anyway, later, I heard him on the phone with somebody who's a friend of his, a lawyer from Chicago, and I heard Dilman saying—these aren't the exact words, but something like this—'Don't kid me, Nat, they want to crucify me. There's a whole race of people around here like them, not white or black, but selfish, thinking of themselves and no one else and not the country. I could've been popular, a little popular, by playing along the way I have all my life, but I figured just once I'd like to be myself and do what I think is right. I thought everyone would see I have nothing to gain by doing wrong. I don't have to play politics, because I don't have to worry about getting re-elected. I have only a short time to go, so I can afford to be honest. I figured everyone would see that, and kind of think twice about the veto, and sit down and talk out a real bill and not a bribe. I didn't think they'd come down on me like this. I can't repeat what I've been called tonight. How do you reach people like that? How do you reach anyone at all?' And he went on, Ruby, not in those exact words, but like that. Well, Christ, I never felt sorrier for him than I did then, until the next—"

Beggs found that Ruby was holding his arm, clutching it. "Otter, that really did happen? I can't—it's sorta—"

"It happened, you bet it happened," Beggs said. "It's just more of the same. You read about the time he gave his first official dinner for the African President, and half the big guests never showed up? Can you beat that? It's true. I was there."

"Oh, no—" said Ruby. She released Beggs's arm, reached for her drink, and took a long swallow of it.

Fascinated now by the way his words were upsetting her, feeling there was some strength and ascendancy to win over her in this way, Otto Beggs went on. "One more little thing I started to tell you. The next day, after the television speech, I happened to be alone with Dilman's secretary, and she was kind of disturbed and unraveled from the way he was being beaten up on the phone and in the papers, and we got to talking about it. She's a white girl, you know, from Wisconsin, and usually cool and steady, but she was kind of emotional, and when I said it was too bad the way the President was getting knocked around for his color, she said that I didn't know the half of how he really felt."

Ruby was staring at her drink, not at Beggs. "What— what she mean by that there talk, Otter?"

"Miss Foster, her name is. She said she'd never forget his first day as President. She was alone with him the first time, planning to hand in her resignation, and when she'd come in his office, there was one door open. She started to shut it, so they could be in privacy, and he wouldn't let her close the door, he didn't want it shut. She couldn't understand, and then he said that Eisenhower once had a Negro adviser who found that white girls always left a door open when they came in to see him, sort of as protection, as if he was a lower animal or habitual rapist. And so Dilman took to the habit of being sure one door was left open whenever a white girl came in and—" To Beggs's astonishment, Ruby had jumped up from the sofa and gone to the center of the room, her back turned to him. "Anyway," he concluded lamely, "Miss Foster said she wanted to cry for him, and she shut that door and did not resign. So whatever your friends think about Dilman being evil—"

He halted, and listened.

It was incredible. Ruby's shoulders were shaking, and her face was in her hands, and she was sobbing.

Utterly confounded, Otto Beggs left the sofa and hurried to her side. "Ruby, what the hell—" He grabbed her arms, and pulled her around, and then drew her hands from her eyes. She was crying, mascara running, and tears streaking her face. "Otter—Otter—Otter," she kept repeating.

He shook her a little. "Ruby, what's got into you?"

She swallowed, trying to control herself. "Otter, the

devil's in me an' I'll burn in front of Jesus if I don't tell you—Otter, from what you told me, you swear it—"

"What I told you? I only told you the truth about—"

"Jesus in Heaven, I done did an awful an' wicked act, I think I did, I think, I don't know, but I'm worryin', Jesus, I'm worryin'—'cause I don't wan' Pres Dilman hurt if he's like you say."

Beggs felt the blood coursing to his head. "What—what do you mean—?" A chill of apprehension, intensified by guilt and fear, crept across his chest and forearms, leaving goose pimples. "How—how could anything you do hurt him—the President?"

"Otter—listen—I didn't know a thing, sep some certain cullud folk were wantin' me to meet you long time ago from right after Dilman become Pres, 'cause they not likin' his weaslin' 'bout the Turners, so they bein' my folk, I agrees. But meetin' you, I fo'gits 'bout them, 'cause I gotta admits y'all been excitin' to me—then when those there certain cullud folk, they see Pres Dilman killin' off the Turners an' Hurley, they gits to fussin' an' fumin'—an' they remembers me—an' come askin' if I is still friendly-like with Otter Beggs, an' I says I is, sorta, an' they says for me to git you up here in my 'partment today, git you off the job today, 'cause they didn't want you 'round when they see the Pres—I—Otter—I don't pay no mind to who tell me this, don't remember who told me—Otter—don't look like that, Otter—only there's some who hate the Pres like you don't know, like I was tellin'—hate him from the start, hate him with real hate now—an' wanna have a showdown with him—an' figgerin' it was hard to git to him exactly private-like, with you always there, a hero man like you readyin' to shoot everybody—so they say for me to keep you busy till they can see the Pres when he finishes with his office workin' today an' goes up to—"

Beggs was violent with rage. "Goddammit, you little whore!" he shouted, wrenching her arms. "If you're lying to me or not telling everything—!"

"Otter, Otter, don't! You hurtin' me—Otter, it's true, every word I'm tellin'. Why should I tell, sep I sinned—I know I sinned—"

He could not release her arms. "Damn you, who are your friends—what are they planning—?"

"I don't know—don't know—swear to Jesus—"

He flung her arms down fiercely. "I ought to kill you—boy, I ought to kill you for making me such a sucker—"

"But I was likin' you, Otter—truth, I swears it—"

He was no longer listening.

He looked at his watch. It showed sixteen minutes after five o'clock. Almost every afternoon President Dilman quit his office at five-thirty. Ruby's friends wanted to see the President when Beggs was not around, when someone less experienced and able than Beggs was there, when someone new was there. It could mean but one thing, one horrifying, life-shattering thing. There were only fourteen minutes for him to intercept Dilman or alert Agajanian.

He looked up and saw that Ruby Thomas had retreated to her bedroom door, frightened, watching him wide-eyed.

"I ought to beat you to a pulp and drag you to the FBI!" he hollered. "My duty's more important than you, you little whore—"

He spun around, snatching up his coat and holster, and strode to the door.

She cried out, "Otter, I did tell you aforehand—you ain' sayin' I didn't tell you—don't let them hurt him, please, Otter—!"

He slammed the door on her, hastily buckling on the holster, then yanking on his coat as he went down the stairs two at a time. As he rushed outside, his first instinct was to locate a telephone booth, call Gaynor or Agajanian or Prentiss, any of the Detail, and warn them to keep the President in his office, and throw up a double—a triple—guard, and search for Ruby's hophead friends. Then, suddenly, he realized it was impossible for him to make such a call. They'd ask him who and what—and how had he got his tip? What could he say? He had a hunch? He'd overheard something? He'd got a crank note with a lead? He possessed no instant evidence—except the truth—Ruby—and if he dared mention her, and she was hauled in, and they found out that he had not been sick, had been trying to have an affair with her, a *colored* girl, he'd be cooked, through, his present a scandal, his future no more. He'd lose the Secret Service, and Gertrude and the kids. No, the call was out. He'd have to do it himself.

He had been moving fast, now half running, all the while he had been thinking. He arrived at the alley behind the Walk Inn, with its parking slots, leaped into the Nash Rambler, started it, backed up, shifted, and wheeled out of the alley into the street. He gunned the car, running a yellow light, and twisted the vehicle toward the White House.

He drove fast, fast as he could over the route that he had traveled so many days of his life, jumping lights, beating the changing signals, weaving in and out of traffic, knowing he must be there before the President left his Oval Office. If a policeman flagged him down, he'd have to flash his Secret Service badge and bellow emergency. He drove on the brink of recklessness, ignoring the angry horns and curses that chased him briefly and then died away.

There were intervals of lucidity. He had sobered, he knew, but his breath still reeked of gin. If he came into the West Wing lobby like a madman, like some fugitive from a cops-and-robbers television show, and there was nothing there, and Ruby Thomas' story was a cock-and-bull story, he would not only be the laughingstock of the Service but in real trouble for being drunk in public. Anticipating this, determined to prevent it, he dug into his pocket for the peppermints that he always carried and sucked on after having a beer or two, and was grateful that there was still a half roll. His nail loosened and freed three of them, and he popped them into his mouth.

With difficulty, as he neared his goal, he tried to organize his thoughts. Had that black bitch lied to him, fed him that whopper of a tale? It was possible, if she was some kind of psychopathic nut, a schizo, a fruitcake. Another possibility: maybe—and he hated this, hated the comment on his manliness—maybe she had led him on, for the kicks of it, and then, when the chips were down, had backed off, not wanting to go the distance with him, wanting to go so far for kicks and no farther, wanting to be rid of the whiteboy. There were women like that—teasers. And so she had pulled this wild story out of left field to get rid of him. Maybe. But, unhappily, that made little sense. After all, Beggs remembered, he had got her onto the subject of Dilman, challenged her opinion, changed her, touched the emotional part of her femininity and Negro feeling, and then she had done the about-face, the confessional. More than that, it was unlikely that she would invent so dramatic and serious a lie, knowing as she did that he could cause her so much trouble with the authorities.

Unless she was a psycho—she did not look like one, behave like one, except that Jelly Roll idiocy, and playing around with a white man like himself, who was respectable and married and could offer her nothing—well, there was no other explanation for what had happened except the worst one. And the worst one was: she was telling the truth. Someone she knew personally was plotting to hurt the President, and had used her to divert the best shot in the Secret Service.

The possibility that she had spoken the truth sickened him, and automatically made him thrust his foot harder against the gas pedal as his car rattled and shook out of another turn. My God, he thought, in five minutes it could happen, be happening, whatever it was, and he, Otto Beggs, Medal of Honor winner, Secret Service bodyguard, would not only be absent, derelict in his duty, unable to protect the President's life, but would have innocently collaborated, in a way, with those who would be harming the President.

For a second he was tempted to skid to a halt, run to a telephone, and, since he could not admit he was calling, place an anonymous call. Then he knew that time had run out for that. There were always so many crank calls, and they were sifted and checked, and before his could be treated seriously, the five-minute leeway, less now, would be gone. Besides, even if there was time, supposing the President had been delayed in his office, Beggs knew that he would be no good at disguising his voice. He was no actor (the word *actor* was associated in his mind im-

mediately with John Wilkes Booth, to whom he was uncomfortably close in infamy this moment), and it was no
use. He kept the Rambler speedometer at fifty-five miles
per hour.

The possibility of a real assault on the President, even
an assassination attempt, grew on him, refused to go
away, and became a firm conviction. These were bad,
unsettled times. In Beggs's experience, he had never
known so many people to speak out viciously—not chidingly or satirically or with irritation, but viciously—
against a Chief Executive of the land. Perhaps in no
rooms of the 132 rooms in the White House was this savagery felt, or known, as thoroughly as in the rooms occupied by the Secret Service. Never in its history had the
Protective Research Section of the Secret Service been so
overworked. Since President Dilman had outlawed the
Turnerites, since he had vetoed the minorities bill, there
was evidence that eight out of every ten Americans were
against him, and half of the threatening and obscene letters that had poured in recently, and had been referred to
the Protective Section, were still unread, a mounting pile
of anonymous letters to be analyzed and broken down by
geography, writing habits, vocabulary tricks, so that the
potential killers could be identified and observed or apprehended.

Whenever Chief Gaynor thought that his agents were
becoming complacent and sloppy about routine, he made
them read a sampling of the letters. Most, he would admit,
were harmless, penned by ordinarily rational citizens
letting off steam. But some, he would remind them, came
from paranoid personalities, with little hold on reality,
with obsessive beliefs that with one tug of a trigger they
could right the wrong and save the nation. These were the
ones, they existed. Oh, they existed, yes. Remember
them, Gaynor would warn, remember Richard Lawrence,
John Wilkes Booth, Charles J. Guiteau, Leon F. Czol-
gosz, John Schrank, Giuseppe Zangara, Oscar Collazo,
Griselio Torresola, even the puzzling Lee Harvey Oswald
—remember them and do not be deceived by the preponderance of foreign names. Enough of them were Americans, Gaynor would say, Americans who read the papers,

went to amusement parks, shopped for groceries, celebrated holidays, saved their money, ate their meals, voted
at election time, slept and woke, and walked crowded city
streets, and carried instruments of destruction to bring
great men down to their size and to their feet, to settle
grievances. They existed. They acted. Expect the unexpected, Gaynor would say, never go slack, be ready and
prepared for *suddenness*.

Otto Beggs saw the White House across the street. He
screeched around a car, slowing for the red light on
Pennsylvania Avenue, roared across the thoroughfare,
and braked as he entered the Northwest Gate.

He began to show his pass, but a grinning White House
policeman waved him through. "Hi, Otto. How come the
VIP entrance? You being decorated again?"

"Yeh, decorated!" he shouted back. Yeh, with thirty
pieces of silver, he thought.

He rode up the driveway, jerkily parked, came out of
the car fast. He realized that he was still tieless, and that
would draw attention, but there was no time to put on the
necktie stuffed in his pocket. He must make haste without
causing a commotion, without letting himself be waylaid
by press or colleagues. He must get where he was going
quickly, yet without creating panic, lest he be exposed for
a fool over a false alarm.

Striding to the West Wing lobby, he glanced at his
watch. If the timepiece was correct, it was five thirty-two.

As ever, at this hour, the press foyer with its three
telephone booths was teeming with reporters. He shoved
past them, ignoring their curiosity at his disheveled appearance. He swallowed the last of his peppermints, hurried into the Reading Room, keeping his back to the Secret Service offices to the right, curtly acknowledging the
greeting of the blue-uniformed policeman at the desk to
the left. He swung off, past the reporters lolling about on
their leather sofas and chairs, past Tim Flannery's office,
and into the corridor with its black-and-white checkered
floor.

Alone at last, now unobserved, he ran heavily past the
Cabinet Room door and Miss Foster's door, until he
reached the open corridor entrance, with a chain across it,

leading into the President's Oval Office, where Agent Winkler stood guard.

"Hey, Otto," the agent called out, "where you been?"

"I got a special message for the President. Where is he?" He poked his head into the office. It was empty.

"Left five seconds ago for upstairs."

Beggs unfastened the chain with one hand as he unbuttoned his coat with the other. "Got to see him, important message," he said, flipping the end of the chain to his colleague.

Moving swiftly, for his size, Beggs bounded across the President's office toward the one French door that was still open to the Rose Garden.

Outside, heart hammering, he halted, and in the gloomy dusk of late afternoon scanned the L-shaped colonnaded terrace walk that led from the West Wing offices, past the indoor swimming pool, to the ground-floor entrance into the White House proper. He did not see them at first, and then, at once, he did, as they emerged from behind a white pillar. They were close together as they moved ahead, first President Dilman, then the new young fellow, Agent Ross, a short man, shorter than the President, a half stride behind.

The scene was peaceful and serene, the activity as familiar and routine as every five-thirty stroll he himself had enacted with Dilman in the last two months. Nothing unusual, nothing unexpected, nothing sudden.

False alarm, thank God, Beggs reassured himself, sagging with relief. His pleasure was mitigated only by the anger he had hoarded against that bitch of a colored girl, who had put him through a quarter of an hour of hell simply to be rid of him.

About to turn back into the office, he saw that the President had stopped to point out something concerning the barren hedges that separated the cement walk from the historic garden.

Automatically Otto Beggs's trained eyes examined the leafless hedges, then lifted to inspect the White House Rotunda and Truman Balcony across the way, then lowered to study the bushy Andrew Jackson magnolia tree, then casually took in the depleted flower beds, the group of empty metal patio chairs around the outdoor table, the busy gardener in olive-drab overalls on his knees digging a hole with his trowel for a new plant, the rectangle of the Rose Garden itself off to the right, the—and then it came to him—the unusual and unexpected.

Beggs's neck stiffened. His gaze shifted back to the gardener, the gardener in olive-drab overalls, their color almost blending him and losing him against the magnolia tree. The gardener straightened, stood up, rubbing his back, then reached down to pick up his plant, and slowly began working his way from the magnolia tree, unobtrusively, diagonally, across the carpet of lawn toward the spot where the President and Ross still stood, absorbed in their horticultural conversation.

As if propelled by instinct, Beggs stealthily moved to his left across the cement walk, toward the corner turn, toward the ramp leading down to where the President and Ross were talking. Beggs's narrowed eyes never left the gardener. From eighty feet, he could not make out the laborer clearly, except to see that he was a squat, husky Negro carrying a plant, to all outward appearances absorbed in his work, going toward the chrysanthemum bed and naked hedges and white colonnades.

An innocent and customary pastoral scene, a prosaic scene to be observed daily from his post outside the President's office, the gardeners, their plants, their tools, something that went on in the daylight and sun of repeated mornings and afternoons. But—Beggs's mind wondered, as he moved: oddity one, an unfamiliar Negro gardener, he could not remember a Negro gardener, no, he was mistaken, there was one, a lanky, skinny, elderly Negro, the opposite in build of this husky person, yet Dilman, being Negro, could certainly have hired another recently; oddity two, a gardener at work in the dusk, scant minutes before night, a gardener alone when all the regulars had gone home, a gardener planting at an hour when planting was never done, impossible.

Beggs had arrived, unseen, at the corner colonnade that now separated the two on the walk from himself. Straight ahead of Beggs, Dilman and Ross were still talking, Dilman listening to the new Secret Service agent, and the new agent, his back to the garden, unaware that there was anyone else nearby. And even if Ross should turn, and the walk to the ground floor be resumed, the agent was too unfamiliar with the personnel and routine to realize that this was an unknown gardener who was engaged in planting at an unlikely hour. There they conversed, the unsuspecting pair, there straight ahead, to the left of the corner colonnade. And to the right of the colonnade, at the center of the garden, fifty feet away, the Negro gardener had strangely halted, put down his plant, was reaching inside his overalls.

Overcautious or not, Beggs had a pattern he must follow, one spurred by a foolish warning from a colored chippy and reinforced by a suspicion born of the unusual.

He started down the ramp, then called out, "Hey, Ross! Ross!"

President Dilman looked up, startled, as the new agent started to whirl around.

Beggs cupped his hand to his mouth. "That gardener behind you—check him. Who is he?"

Neither Ross nor the President had been listening when he began to give his order, and now as if by reflex action, to Beggs's petrified amazement, the new agent quickly left Dilman and started toward Beggs, head cocked, one finger tipping his ear forward.

For a split second, Beggs was too horrified to speak. It was understandable, that reflex to catch more distinctly what had been called out, to draw nearer, but it was a lapse that broke the cardinal rule of Presidential protection. By his action, Ross had left Dilman momentarily alone and unguarded.

"What?" Ross called back, as he came toward Beggs. "What is it?"

Infuriated by a freshman's stupidity, Beggs sprinted down the sharp decline, shaking his fist. "Dammit, you're not supposed to leave the President! I told you to check on—" And then, as he was almost upon Ross, the corner of his eye caught the flash of motion, the *suddenness* of motion.

The Negro gardener had yanked some object from inside his overalls, and at once, from an easygoing planter he had become transformed into a purposeful aggressor, springing forward, dashing across the remaining lawn and flower bed, rapidly closing the distance that separated him from the President.

Beggs's response was instantaneous, as swift, as positive, as mindless as it had been that memorable frozen night in Korea. Beggs clutched Ross by the shoulder, forcibly flung him aside, sent him pancaking against the wall.

As his free hand plunged to his holster, whipping out his revolver, Beggs stumbled, recovered his balance, and then he raced down the walk toward the President. Ahead, Dilman, hand massaging his forehead in bewilderment, remained inert, as if hypnotized by Beggs's incredible action. To the right, converging on the President as he himself was, Beggs could make out the Negro gardener running, slipping on the wet grass but retaining his footing and bounding toward the President. The object in his fist, shockingly vivid now, was a Luger that seemed to grow monstrously large.

"Down! Drop down!" Beggs screamed at Dilman.

The President's head spun from the charging Beggs to the sound of the running on his left. As he saw the looming black figure with its weapon, unmistakably an assailant waving a gun, hurtling from the lawn across the flower bed in order to take dead aim in the near-darkness, Dilman's strangled throat cried out, "No!" and his arms went up to cover his face.

"Down!" Beggs roared again.

Rooted by fear, Dilman turned only his head and torso from the attack, helpless and a perfect target. Beggs was fifteen feet away when the burly assassin landed in the flower bed, pointing his Luger, sinking in the soft turned soil just as he pulled the trigger.

The explosion, so near, was like a clap of thunder against Beggs's eardrums. He could see the erratic, tilted shot go high, ripping the cement and plaster above the President's head.

In a frozen moment, imprinted on Beggs's mind, there was the tableau of their coming together—murderer, victim, protector. Frozen, and insanely joyous, the white eyes and gold and white teeth of the matted dark Halloween head, over the hedge. Frozen, as unready and incredulous as a defenseless yearling about to go down, the wide, red-flecked eyes of the President, the lifted and ineffectual arms of the President with the sleeves too short and ridiculous. Frozen, Beggs himself, the length of a man's length away, the length of mortality, his one leg high, high off the walk, his other driven against the cement, his catapult, the Corvallis Beggs, the Korea Beggs, the has-been who would-never-be, the faded physique glued and pressed into the scrapbook page.

The frozen moment heaved and blew sky-high, as the eruption and detonation came simultaneously.

Beggs erupted, vaulted into the air, knees and legs smashing the President's chest. The assassin's pistol, at the end of his unwavering arm, the barrel an accusing and avenging metallic finger, came over the hedge and discharged its point-blank, vehement, deafening blast.

For an infinity, Beggs felt himself being lifted higher and higher by the blast, and then he was plummeting downward, legless, as if the folding body beneath him were his lower limbs. He heard Dilman groan as they crashed to the cement walk, Dilman beneath and doubled over, and himself atop Dilman.

Trying to rise, Beggs teetered on the rim of a deep invisible canyon, swaying, knowing he must fall. It was all feeling now, feeling and nerve ends, feeling the moist blood on Dilman's cheekbone, the soaked blood that had pasted his own trousers to his own leg, feeling the security of the metal in the grip of his right palm.

The reverberations from the assassin's blast still pounded inside his head. He came around on his side, lightning-fast, trying not to expose the President. He came around as the assassin above shook his gun, raised it unsteadily, as if unsure that he had killed the President and determined to try again, determined to find an opening. All this in the shaving of a second. As the other's gun came up, steadying itself, Beggs's wrist snapped the revolver in his palm upward. His proud Medal of Honor reflex. His forefinger tugged the trigger as immediately and gently as once it had pulled the thumb from his infant son's mouth. The response, the report from his revolver, was as quiet and as firm as his finger's reproof. There was a muffled metallic cough, a swooshing, humming sound.

He was not surprised to see the assassin's black face let go its venom, open and broaden in wonder. He was not surprised to see the assassin's fingers fan outward, like those of a mechanical doll, until the Luger was released and clattered to the cement walk. He was not surprised to see the person above touch both hands to his chest, as if to open the overalls at the reddening stain, and then drop his chin, and then gradually surrender life, and then fold downward and downward into a lumpy heap behind the stark branches of the hedge.

Beggs turned his head at the footsteps, so many hurrying footsteps. Sluggishly, with disinterest, he watched them coming from everywhere, from everywhere, it seemed, from the guardhouse, the Oval Office, the entrance above the ramp, and probably from the ground floor behind him. His vision was poor. There were police, Ross and Prentiss and a half-dozen others of Gaynor's boys, Miss Foster, Flannery, Talley, countless more.

He heard the babel of voices, the shouts, the yelling, the commands.

"Get the physician—get Oates—right through there, around the corner!"

"Move Beggs—move him—lift him off!"

"The President—is he dead?"

It was pleasant for Beggs, all the hands, all the attention. He found himself on a blanket, on his back, staring up at blurred faces and the overhang above them.

From a distance he heard Ross's voice. "—the gardener fired, missed, then Beggs jumped on the President and bowled him over as the colored guy fired again. Then Beggs rolled over and just shot him dead. . . . The body's over there, Chief—"

He thought that he heard Admiral Oates's voice nearby. "Mr. President—Mr. President—" Then silence. "He's alive—I don't think he's been touched—the blood's not his—here, nurse, give me the spirits of ammonia—Mr. President, there now, that's better—"

Then he heard President Dilman, weak but irritable.

"I'm all right. Leave me alone. Beggs, he took the shot instead of me. Get over there and help him."

Beggs opened his eyes. What was wrong with them? Nothing was distinct. Admiral Oates's face floated into his vision, a face less grouchy because it was not clear. He was saying, "Easy, Mr. Beggs, let me have a look—oh yes, yes—see here, it's his right leg—really chewed up—Miss Foster! Get an ambulance to take him to Walter Reed Hospital at once! Beggs, do you feel any pain? No, I suppose not. Shock. I'll give you a shot—"

He felt the sting of the needle and its extraction, but no pain; then he was diverted by Chief Gaynor's voice behind him somewhere. "Mr. President—you all right, sir? Just wanted to tell you the assassin's cold dead. Beggs got him with one shot straight through the chest. His wallet here—Burleigh L. Thomas, twenty-eight—truck driver's license—the clippings—Turnerite stuff—that's it, I'm sure. . . . This, this is the regular map of the guided tour through the White House. You can see the line he drew in red ink. See? Followed the ground-floor tour upstairs, then into the State Dining Room, and when the others went on to the Red Room, he must have hung behind, slipped into the Family Dining Room—something we've always been afraid of—hid out then, apparently had the overalls inside his suit coat or jacket, changed, picked up two plants—Hawkins says he saw a colored man carrying plants downstairs around three-thirty—he must have kept himself busy but out of sight until the regular gardeners left—then kind of blended himself with the magnolia, puttered around, waiting for you. . . . What? No, Mr. Flannery, not yet, give us a chance to cover the grounds. We'll have something definite for the press in the morning. Just tell them the attempt was made, the President is fine, just fine, and the assailant was shot dead."

Beggs heard Dilman's voice, shaky but loud. "Tim, you see that Otto Beggs gets all the credit—you hear? All the credit. Admiral, I want him to receive every bit of care available to—"

Someone was shouting, "That's spelled B-u-r-l-e-i-g-h, yeh, Burleigh, Burleigh Thomas."

Miss Foster's voice, he thought, distinct but so far off. "The ambulance is on its way, Admiral! How is poor Mr. Beggs? Will he—?"

He heard Oates's distant voice. "He's a brave man. Thank God for men like that."

He felt soothed, no pain, too tired and sleepy to listen.

He thought: You hear that, Gertrude? You hear that, Otis, Ogden? Brave man.

He thought: You're right, Ruby, your Otter here is impo'tant. Brave man.

He thought: Ruby Thomas, Burleigh Thomas. Fair enough, Ruby, all square.

He thought: Am I dying? To save a nigger? Dirty, lousy trick, goddam.

He thought: History books'll say a President, he saved a President. Not bad, not bad, eh, Gertie girl?

He thought: Dear God, be merciful to me a sinner . . . dear Lord Jesus, see this, greater love hath no man than this . . . dear Saviour, cast me not into darkness . . . lemme live, please lemme live to fill the scrapbook, please, thank you, amen.

FOR IMMEDIATE RELEASE
Office of the White House Press Secretary

THE WHITE HOUSE

ADMIRAL OATES, PERSONAL PHYSICIAN TO THE PRESIDENT, ANNOUNCED TODAY THAT, EXCEPT FOR SEVERAL HEAD BRUISES AND A GENERAL CONDITION OF FATIGUE, THE PRESIDENT IS IN EXCELLENT HEALTH, FOLLOWING YESTERDAY'S ASSASSINATION ATTEMPT. ALL OF THE PRESIDENT'S APPOINTMENTS HAVE BEEN CANCELED, AND HE HAS BEEN CONFINED TO HIS ROOMS FOR "A MUCH-NEEDED REST." HE WILL ATTEND THE CHANTILLY CONFERENCE IN FRANCE AS SCHEDULED.

ADMIRAL OATES ALSO ANNOUNCED THAT OTTO BEGGS, WHITE HOUSE SECRET SERVICE AGENT WHOSE ACTION

SAVED THE PRESIDENT'S LIFE, REMAINS ON THE "CRITI-CAL" LIST AT WALTER REED GENERAL HOSPITAL. DECI-SION WILL BE MADE IN NEXT FORTY-EIGHT HOURS WHETHER BEGGS'S INJURED LEG CAN BE SAVED OR WHETHER AMPUTATION WILL BE NECESSARY.

COMPLETE TEXT OF ADMIRAL OATES'S MEDICAL BULLE-TINS ONE AND TWO ARE ATTACHED.

EDNA FOSTER sat alone in a shadowy recess of the faintly lighted Promenade Lounge of the Mayflower Hotel. She was the small and elegant room's single occupant in this pre-cocktail hour, lost in thought as she prepared to finish her third vodka Gibson.

She was to have met George Murdock here, their favorite secluded and somewhat-beyond-their-means meeting place when either of them needed a lift, at a quarter to six. Normally she would have finished her day's work, and taken a taxi up Connecticut Avenue, and arrived here nearly on time, to find George waiting.

However, today had been anything but normal. Because the President had been indisposed, suffering acute hypertension (if the truth were known) induced by the horror of last night, and was confined to his quarters, Edna's work load had diminished and her workday had been curtailed. Dilman's usual engagements had been shunted off to the occupants of other offices, and her own duties had been distributed to other White House secretaries. By four-thirty in the afternoon her desk had been clean. She had telephoned the second floor, and the President had insisted that she close shop and go home early. She had found it too late to go to the apartment first, before meeting George, and too early to time her arrival at the lounge with his own. She had decided to go by foot, by some roundabout route, to the Mayflower, to use up the extra time. Once outside, she had found the air too nippy, the sky too bleak, for her thin skin and frayed nerves, and she had immediately altered her plan. She had known, then, what she wanted. Alone or not, she wanted to be drunk.

Now, forty-five minutes later, her little finger excessively crooked as she downed the last of her third Gibson, she was warm and resolute and nicely drunk.

A waiter in a red jacket, a servant gray and smooth as an old British family retainer, glided in from the adjacent Presidential Room, hovered a moment, then came forward and removed her long-stemmed cocktail glass.

"Another, ma'am?"

She was tempted, but then she might forget what she had so carefully rehearsed for George. "I think I'll wait, if you don't mind. I'm expecting a friend."

After the waiter had gone, she took out her compact to prepare for her friend. She peered into the mirror with distaste. That's what came of buying cheap compacts with cheap mirrors, she told herself. The cheap reflecting glass was always grainy, always gave you lines you did not deserve. But then, she was too inebriated for deceit. It was a good compact, the best she had ever owned, the gift of her generous aunt in Madison. The looking glass was flawless. The lines belonged to her, fact, no argument, and for those new creases engraved on her forehead, under her eyes, around her mouth, she blamed not time but her employer.

A person did not age that much in a couple of months, any scientist would tell you that, except if there was a reason, like the way you read of some person's hair turning white overnight because of what they'd been through. She had her reason, and his initials were Douglass Dilman. If you were not inhuman, if you had half a heart, if you empathized with even a dumb animal, you had to suffer while being around that colored President eight to ten hours a day. It was like, as if, Dilman was William Tell's son and she had to hold the wormy apple on his head, and all the Gesslers, or whatever their names, were shooting arrows to knock the apple off—we-ll, nobody was really aiming for the apple, everybody was aiming for him, President Tell, and lots of them missed and naturally hit her, because she was there holding the apple. Like perfect example last night. That Thomas brute-murderer with his surplus-sales gun. Bang. Bang. Bang. Missed Dilman. Hit Beggs. Hit her. Poor Dilman, vomiting afterwards. How must it feel always going around with an apple on your head? Poor Beggs, too. For that salary. She must remember to send over those foreign stamps to his boys. Most of all, poor Edna, she herself, personal secretary to a target, getting hit so often that the compact mirror finally showed it.

She wondered why three drinks had not made her drunk. She knew. They made profits serving domestic vodka, which was as potent as bottled water. At those prices, yet. What a gyp!

There was the cheap grainy mirror, still. She powdered her forehead, nose, chin, then combed her messy brown hair, then tried to give herself lips, then gave up, closed the compact and put it away.

She lifted her head and there was George, talking to the waiter. He was neat as always, but had grown shorter —was it possible? Yes, because maybe he had worn out his shoe lifts. He stooped and kissed her caked forehead, and squeezed her hand, and sat across from her, pushing the table lamp aside.

"Have you been here long, honey?" he wanted to know.

"George," she said, "I'm quitting." She hiccuped. "I'm quitting next week after I come back from Paris."

Poor George looked not stricken exactly, but sort of moody. "Edna, we've been through this two times already—"

"And three times is out. The President can call me out."

George Murdock, possessing the impatient air of one who had wanted to speak about himself but had first politely inquired how-are-you, and then had had to listen to his companion at length, said, "What is it now, Edna?"

"Don't you read the papers, George? Huh? Last night. Most secretaries put the cover on their typewriters, lock the files, wash out the coffee cup and go home like anybody. Me, I have to be scared out of my wits, right outside my office, the President lying there, Otto Beggs half dead, that—that Thomas completely dead, a corpse. They never taught me that was part of it in secretarial school. I couldn't sleep most of the night, George. I took three sodium butisols and had ten nightmares. That's why I look so haggard."

He reached out and touched her hand. "No matter how you feel, honey, you look great."

"Thank you, George, but I mean it."

His fingers left her hand, and began pinching his pitted cheeks. She wished that he wouldn't. He said, "Edna, these things happen. They've been happening ever since that Lawrence fellow, the house painter, took a pot shot at President Jackson in 1835, and practically in the same place. That's part of being President, knowing certain people will be sore at you and some of them are nuts. I'm sure Dilman was not surprised. That Burleigh Thomas was an out-and-out extremist, and he decided Dilman was hindering the Negro cause. So he took matters in his own hands. No one approved of it. Even the anti-Dilman press was dismayed."

"Hypocrites, the papers, George. Forgive me. Next week they'll resume their hate campaign and inflame some other assassin. No, George, this time I mean it. Don't try to stop me. The first time, I wanted to resign because I missed T.C. and didn't see how I could work for a stranger. Last time, I was just getting too sorry for Dilman, sickened by the hate he was suffering from. This time it's different. He's in danger, and so is everyone around him, and I'm scared."

"Well—" said Murdock. He shrugged, then sat back, resigned and waiting, as the waiter served the Gibson and the Scotch-and-soda.

They both took their drinks and sipped them, and then, worrying about his displeasure, she said, "Don't be mad at me, George."

"I'm not mad at you," he said curtly. "I'm mad at myself."

She was too befogged to understand him. She said, "Why do you want me staying on that miserable old job? It's not as if I've been able to be of any help to you, like a real girl friend should. Each time I want to give you a tip, without hurting security, I choke up, because I know so much, too much. I'm a detriment to you, that's what.

You see, you'll be better off when I'm somewhere else. Pa called from Milwaukee this morning. Can you imagine? First time in all this time. Even *he* wanted me to quit."

"I'm not saying you should stay on, Edna." He drank, coughed, put down the Scotch. "I was just trying to buy a little time for us. If I thought you were in danger, I'd bodily remove you from that office, you believe me."

She felt comforted, but determined. "Thank you, George. I—I just don't think you can see the position I'm in like any ordinary person would. You're a newspaperman, and it's natural for you to—to look on what happened like a story—like part of a play that isn't real—but if you'd been in the garden last night, not as a reporter—"

"Edna," he said.

The quavering urgency in his tone made her stop. "What?"

"Edna, I'm not a newspaperman or reporter any longer. I'm unemployed. I haven't had a chance to tell you."

Her concern with herself, tied to her dream of their future, popped like a pricked balloon and disappeared into thin air. She stared at him. "Oh, George." Her hands went to his sleeve. "No," she said. "Did they fire you?"

He clutched to self-esteem as firmly as he now held his highball glass. "Not exactly, although it might look that way." Involuntarily, his thin nostrils quivered. "Tri-State lost another of my papers. That brought me down to eight, and the low-paying ones at that. Weidner called and said carrying the column was a losing proposition— like hell it is, but that's what he said—and unless I wanted to continue on a so-much-per-published-inch rate, making me virtually a stringer, he was taking on one of the more established names. So I told him, in effect, not on your life, you skinflint. I was even a little abusive about his ingratitude."

"Good for you, George."

"Then he backed down a bit and said—" Murdock hesistated. "Aw, what's the use. Let's have another round. I can use it." He held up his glass, called the order, and finished his drink.

"What do you mean, he backed down?" Edna asked.

In her heart she knew what was coming and wanted to run away from it, but this was too important, her whole life in the balance.

"You won't like it, so never—"

"Please, George."

"He said, 'Of course, there's still that so-called friend of yours right on the inside. If she'd become a source for you, one like all the name columnists have, and you'd promise to deliver a couple of whoppers in the next few weeks, we'd reconsider.' I said, 'Not on your life, Weidner, I don't mix business with my personal life,' and so I quit, two days ago I quit."

Edna had been holding her breath. She let it go in a gasp. "George, why didn't you tell him yes? Really, if I had known this before—how serious—George, I can help without hurting the President or my job. After all, what can hurt him or me any more? Look, George, maybe I can tell you some real exclusive things nobody has about the assassination attempt, or when we go to Chantilly and Versailles, maybe I can see if—"

"You're sweet, darling. No use, now. I wouldn't know what to do with the copy. I told you I quit. I'm out of work. I don't have a column." He considered her. "Don't look so—so tragic, Edna. You can take the newspaper away from a boy, but you can't take a boy away from the newspaper. I've got my lines out. There are some big people who think more of me than that crumb-bum hayseed in the Midwest does. You yourself heard Reb Blaser tell me how much his publisher thinks of my writing."

"You wouldn't work for *them?*"

"I'd work any place where I could be independent and write as I please. That includes the Miller chain or any other. What the hell, Edna. I'd rather be reporting for a reactionary paper where I can get a chance to give them a breath of fresh air, proselytize, than a paper whose readers believe what I believe and know what I know."

As ever, George's infallible logic subdued Edna. "You're right, I guess," she said.

The fresh drinks came. They drank in silence. It was wonderful, she thought, despite all this, how positive and clearheaded she felt.

"Let's enjoy ourselves," George Murdock was saying. "Rome hasn't burned yet. Leave it to your Georgie. I'll find another spot."

"And I'll help you!" she cried out. "This time I will, I promise. It's only right. This time, every evening, I'll tell you what I can about what goes on in the President's office."

"Edna, I repeat, no need for that. Besides, you're quitting, too, next week. Did you forget?"

"Oh," she said, and slumped. "That's right."

He kept looking at her, until she was uneasy, and then he kept looking at the Scotch, and then he said quietly, "Edna, when big things happen to you, your life sort of changes—know what I mean? You're forced to take stock —and that's what I've been doing myself these last two days, taking stock. I have a better picture of myself. I've been too conservative, not taking any chances, and to get anything out of life you've got to—well—stick your chin out and say to yourself and everybody, I'm me, I'm somebody, I deserve more out of life, out of my career and out of life, and I'm going out and get my share of life, no matter what. Know what I mean?"

Her mind had gone blank, but she said dutifully, "Yes, George."

"I'm making a fresh start from tonight on. That's what I decided. Like the next job. No more looking for anything second-rate. I'm shooting straight for the top. And like us, the two of us, no more waiting for the big doubloons at the end of the rainbow. Live for today, that's all there is to be sure of, and if you have to make good, somehow you make it, and meanwhile you're getting something out of life. Do you understand, honey?"

"Yes, George."

"No, you don't," he said, "or you wouldn't be sitting there like you're miserable." He put aside his drink and leaned across the table. "Edna, I've denied myself long enough. I want to start over again from scratch. Maybe it's the wrong time, both of us going to be out of work, but maybe it's the best time to start living. Edna, the minute you come back from France, let's get married."

She had not quite heard him, with her mind wallowing

in self-pity, with the Gibson in front of her face, and she had been about to say "Yes, George" when comprehension forced its way into her stultified brain. "What? What did you say? I'm sorry, I—I've been drinking."

He was smiling. "I said, darling, let's get married. Forgive me for keeping you waiting this long, but if I'm going to be big, think big, I've got to show I can live big like—"

"Married?" She was about to weep. Could it be? Could it possibly be? "George—I—I think I'm going to die—you said—darling, you want to marry me?"

He continued to smile. "Nobody else, if you'll have me. The minute you return—"

"Oh, George, I'm coming apart—come here, don't let me cry—I'm so excited, I've never been happier—to think—George, kiss me—"

Nervously he glanced around the cocktail room, confirmed that they were still alone, and quickly he picked the chair up under him and moved it around the table beside her. She was sniffling as she accepted his kiss.

"I haven't heard you say yes," he murmured.

"Yes-yes-yes—a million times yes." She had his shoulders, held him off, searched his face. "George, you mean it? I'm tight now—I don't want to wake up in the morning and find out I was dreaming—we're going to be married?"

"I'll pin a note on you to remind you and to tell everyone else, 'No Trespassing.'" He saw the waiter appear in the inner door. "Hey," he called out, "two more of the same!"

"Oh, George, I've had enough to drink. I don't need—"

"You haven't had a drink as Mrs. Murdock-to-be."

She enclosed both his narrow hands in her own, and snuggled against the wondrous safety of him. "When, darling, when will we do it?"

"Just as I said, right after you return from France. Of course, you'll want to give Dilman a week or two's notice —I mean, you owe him that much. It's not easy for a President of the United States to replace his personal secretary. Then we can marry. We'll work out exactly where and how, and I have a few bucks to tide us over while we're both looking for jobs—actually, maybe you won't have to work any more, if I can find something fast, something good—"

He had become solemn again, and she squeezed his hands and said, "Darling, don't look so worried. I don't want to start off with me being a burden. I want to quit that job, but it doesn't have to be right away. Of course, I'll stay on until you're set. It's the least I can do." She kissed his cheek. "In fact, I'll insist upon it."

She parted from him, sat back in a ladylike way, as the celebrating round of drinks was served. Her eyes made out two Gibsons—two and a half—two waiters, two Georges; and the room reeled. She had never been so excited, so happy, so floaty, so lucid in her head, and, after the waiter discreetly left the lounge, so much at one with another person. He was no longer a separate being, a desirable object, a goal, an idea. He was her own, and she was his own, and the merging was miraculous.

After they toasted, she had no notion if she made sense, but she bubbled over and talked and talked about her life and hopes, and their life and future, and what she would do for him and what it would be like, the most perfect marriage in history.

How long she went on she did not know, except her first drink as Mrs. Murdock-to-be was drained, and she was being very serious now, practical, to show him he had not been mistaken because she was practical and would make his life an eternal Christmas.

She knew that her tongue was thick, but she knew also that on this memorable evening he must be reassured that he had not made a mistake.

"I'll make it better than any marriage there's been on earth, George, no bickering like my folks, or bossing around like my girl friend, Dorothy, did, no unfaithfulness from either of us like the people we know about here—the Arthur Eatons—that kind. You won't want to chase, George, because you'll have no need to. I'll keep a beautiful house, and raise the best-mannered, smartest children, and give you interesting meals, and help you with your work, and charm your friends so you'll be proud of me. You'd be surprised what I'm really like,

George, how much better I am—better-groomed, and brighter, more fun—like when you first met me—remember? It's just been worse recently, and you appreciate that, you know why. But once you have the right job, the one that's perfectly right for you—and there's no rush, George, I won't quit until you tell me to—but once you're settled and happy, then I can give up the White House office. You'll see how different I'll be, how relaxed, devoted, better-looking, once I get away from that horrible job and that poor miserable man I'm working for."

"I'm sure of it, Edna," he said.

"You can be surer than being sure of being sure of it," she said grandiloquently. "Once I'm free to devote myself to you, and be with our kind of people, who are happier, as we will be, and not tied down to a friendless, tormented, heartbroken black man, with his black thoughts, who is worrying about being killed, who doesn't even have a wife to console him because she drank herself to death, whose son is failing in school, whose daughter is passing for white—who is so afflicted with personal problems, nobody would believe it, let alone what he goes through in public where—"

She realized that her beloved George's cool hand was upon her hand, caressing her hand lovingly, lacing his fingers through hers like they were married and in bed together. "Edna, what are you saying?"

"What am I saying?" she repeated, not remembering.

"About the President having a daughter. You must be mixed up. No more drinks. What if someone overheard you?"

"George, stop teasing. I haven't been drinking any more than you. I'm very sober. I know everything I'm saying, and I never make up anything, like other wives do. You'll see. You'll find out. It's one of my virtues from my father. You'll always know your wife says everything true."

"Everyone knows Dilman has that son in college, but—"

"George, I told you I never, never lie," she said indignantly. "He has a daughter, too, older than Julian, and it's a secret because she's passing for white in New York, so he doesn't recognize her maybe, or she him, I don't know which, so that's why nobody knows, but it's true." Through bleary eyes, she decided that he was still unconvinced of her integrity, and this was no way to begin a marriage. "George, he calls her Mindy, so does Julian call her Mindy, except her made-up passing name is Linda. Linda Dawson."

"I can see where that would make him worried," said George Murdock sympathetically. "It's just odd, somebody as black as the President having a daughter hidden somewhere, white enough to pass."

"Hormones," she said knowingly. "Or is it genes?" She studied George's many faces and tried to bring him into focus. "I don't lie or exaggerate, George——"

"I didn't say that you did."

"But maybe you are thinking it—Edna, you are thinking, she is the kind of wife who'll get drunk and make up stories and embarrass you socially. You said he's black so how could he have a daughter who could pass? I can prove it, George. I wrote it down word for word in my diary. Did you know I have a diary? I started one the day T.C. moved into the White House. I thought some day—I'm not pretending to be a writer like you—but my job, I thought some day maybe my diary could be history. It isn't much, but I am a President's confidential secretary, two Presidents', and maybe some day when we're all dead, our children can make a million dollars getting a writer to fix it up. You hear of those things."

"Very intelligent, Edna. I see I'm going to have an intelligent wife. Just don't put me in your diary."

She started to giggle and could hardly stop. "Of course you're in it, George, but nothing you won't like. You and T.C. and President Dilman——"

"And Mindy Dilman alias Linda Dawson. Pretty exotic company." He brought her hand to his lips and kissed it, and released it. "Did Dilman tell you all of that stuff about his family?"

"Heavens, no—George, do you think we can have just one more drink to celebrate, a short one?—Dilman? No, he's secret as a clam or something, and I don't blame him, do you? But about the daughter, it came from him, sort of, well—I'm not sneaky, don't think that—I'm very integrity, full of—you know—I never leak things to you —isn't that so, George?"

"I've never known anyone with as much integrity as you, Edna."

"Thank you. So you understand. Part of my job is, you know, to monitor his calls, the business ones, like I did for T.C., listening on the extension and taking down the gist of it shorthand so he has a record to refer back to. Standard procedure. So whenever Dilman makes a call, I've got to listen, except when it's something real personal, like when he calls old friends like Nat Abrahams or the Spingers or some woman who lives with them named Gibson or his son, he tells me to get off, and let it be personal and I do. Well, this day he was letting me monitor calls, and maybe he was busy or upset, I don't know, but he called his son and didn't tell me—to get off, I mean— maybe he didn't know or forgot I was on the line—and there it was, the President and his son Julian talking, and when I heard what they were saying to one another, I knew I shouldn't be hearing it but I was too embarrassed to get off and let him hear the click and then always have him suspicious of me, so I suffered through it, and when they hung up, I hung up simul—same time—and that's how I heard the argument about his daughter and her passing, and about her, the daughter, being like her mother, Dilman's wife, who wanted her to be white like she wanted to be white herself, and because Aldora, Dilman's wife, couldn't, she took to drinking—I don't believe in drinking except socially, do you, George?—until she even became an alcoholic in that sanitarium in Illinois —in Springfield—and died after, except that was a long time ago. Isn't it all horrible, George, how people let their lives become? Ours won't, will it? For my part it won't, I promise you."

"I promise you, too."

"I'll be the best wife ever, George, once I'm away from that horrible atmosphere."

"You're the best wife in the world right now, darling. Let's have one more for the road on that. Okay?"

They drank, and a half hour later they had a hamburger and gallons of hot black coffee—she was determined to give evidence of her wifely frugality—at the counter of the Mayflower Coffee Deck.

After that, they strolled for a long time in the cold, and George bought her a gardenia corsage in some place that was open late and warm inside, and then they walked through Lafayette Square until she felt the cold and began to sober. Then, so thoughtfully, so generously, he hailed a taxicab and took her home, and because it was late and she was wonderfully weary and he was inspired to get up early in the morning and look for the right job, he did not come in, except inside the hall of her apartment. She stayed in his arms, and as they kissed this time, she permitted him to pet her bust as long as he wanted to, because her bust and all of her belonged to him, and it felt good, so good.

When he was ready to go, and she could make out one of him, not two or three, she said, "You meant everything you said tonight, George, didn't you?"

"Everything, sweetheart."

"I think I bored you, talking so much, but I was so excited. It's not every day a girl is proposed to and accepts. I hope I didn't say anything foolish or—or indiscreet. Did I?"

"Of course not."

"Well, if I did, it doesn't matter, because we belong to each other now, no secrets, never, promise? You can trust me with everything and I can trust you. Isn't that right, George?"

"Sweetheart, from now on you're not Edna Foster and I'm not George Murdock. We are Mr. and Mrs. Murdock, almost, for all intents, and whatever we say to one another, and that goes for both of us, is sacred as pillow talk. Agreed? Agreed."

"I love you, George. You'll be famous, I know."

"That's not important. I love you too, that's all that matters. You have a great trip to Paris, and stay away from those seductive Frenchmen—"

"George, silly—"

"—and when you return, I'll be right here, with the

wedding band and a job, a real big job this time. That I can promise you for sure."

FOR RELEASE AT 9:30 P.M. PARIS TIME
Office of the White House Press Secretary Abroad

THE UNITED STATES EMBASSY, PARIS

COMPLETE TEXT OF PRESIDENT DILMAN'S SPEECH AT APPROXIMATELY 11:00 P.M. TONIGHT CLOSING THE FIVE-DAY CHANTILLY CONFERENCE FOLLOWS. THE PRESIDENT IS DELIVERING THE ADDRESS AT THE CONCLUSION OF THE STATE BANQUET BEING HELD FOR HIM AND FOR PREMIER NIKOLAI KASATKIN OF THE U.S.S.R. BY THE PRESIDENT OF FRANCE IN THE HALL OF MIRRORS OF VERSAILLES PALACE. SIMULTANEOUSLY THE TEXT OF PREMIER KASATKIN'S REPLY WILL BE RELEASED AT THE SOVIET EMBASSY.

IMMEDIATELY AFTER THE BANQUET, PRESIDENT DILMAN WILL RETURN TO PARIS FROM VERSAILLES. HE WILL SPEND THE NIGHT IN HIS SUITE AT THE QUAI D'ORSAY BEFORE FLYING TO WASHINGTON IN THE MORNING.

WHILE THE five-day conference had been successful, the long hours had been strenuous, and Douglass Dilman had intended to return to Paris the moment that he and Premier Kasatkin and the French President had finished their public speeches. But when the formalities in the Hall of Mirrors had ended, and the bewigged, liveried servant had assisted Dilman from his chair, the Russian Premier energetically charged to his side.

"Mr. President," Kasatkin had said in his guttural yet clearly understandable English, "you do not leave so soon to go to bed, no? In my country, to lie down after much rich food and wine is like lying down in the grave. Always, after feasts, I walk for thirty minutes in the court inside the Kremlin walls. We must enjoy a breath of air together in the magnificent gardens of Versailles, not to observe how tyrants built and lived, but to see that we live in health, now that we are friends and in accord."

For a moment Dilman's mind went to the five days of arguments, concessions, bartering in the drafty Grand Château at Chantilly. Although the Soviet Premier had been generally reasonable, his occasional flare-ups of temper had been irritating, as in the instance of his demands for freedom for native Communists in Baraza and other AUP countries. Too, his sporadic sarcasm had been annoying, as when he had chided Dilman and Eaton for finding a Communist bogeyman under every American bed. "You outlaw the Turnerites on the pretext they are using our good Moscow gold to overthrow you," he had said. "Do you think we are crazy to waste money on your oppressed minorities, to incite them, when they have more anger against their capitalist overlords than we ever had or will have? Bah. When you are in trouble, you try to wriggle out and divert your masses from your own shortcomings by making them see Red, at home or in Africa." Yet the gibes, the tantrums, had been fewer than Dilman had expected, and after Kasatkin had spoken his pieces for his Presidium and *Pravda* back home, he had always proved ready to trade. He was not a fanatical crusader, Dilman had guessed early. He was a pragmatist. When he spoke as Communism's voice, with Lenin's intelligence, he was perverse. When he spoke for himself, with his own intelligence, he was reasonable.

Now the Russian had extended a friendly and spontaneous invitation to Dilman, and Dilman found the other's brusque, forthright, roughneck warmth difficult to resist or offend. Yet Dilman was tired. "Well," Dilman said hesitantly, "I had promised Mr. Illingsworth and Secretary Eaton we'd try to get back at——"

"You promise nothing to the ones who work for you, you owe them nothing," Kasatkin said with mock severity. "You owe only your proletariat, the working people, your allegiance and health to do good."

Dilman cast a sickly smile at the Russian leader. "I'm less certain than you that my proletariat—or yours, for that matter—are all so unanimous in worrying about our good health."

"You speak for yours, I shall speak for mine," said Premier Kasatkin cheerfully. "Come now, Mr. President, some air, the two of us together, no advisers, no specialists, no petty bureaucrats. Five days we have been surrounded. One night, the last, let us be alone together, a social promenade to cement our continuing good relations. What are thirty minutes in a lifetime, after all? And who knows?" He winked broadly. "Our thirty minutes may mean more to the world than our other accomplishments of a lifetime."

The Russian seemed so determined to end their meeting on a friendly note that Dilman could deny him no further. "Very well," he said. "A short walk, then, in the gardens."

Arthur Eaton had come upon them during the last exchange, and he appeared pained, trying to indicate that he disapproved, but Dilman avoided his eye. Dilman had permitted the Russian to take him by the arm, when Eaton finally protested. "Mr. President, we're expected to depart—"

Premier Kasatkin brushed his hand toward Eaton as he might brush off a bothersome fly. "You go have some champagne with the other courtiers, Eaton. You keep busy with my pretty secretary with the yellow hair over there—Natasha. She admires you. Give your President and me, two simple men of the streets with bad table manners, a chance to discuss earthier matters alone—like our children, and our hernias. A half hour, Mr. Secretary."

And now Dilman and Kasatkin were crossing the ancient cobblestone courtyard of the seventeenth-century Palace past the saluting Garde Républicaine, marching through the gate of the iron grillwork fence, preceded and followed at short distances by United States Secret Service men and Soviet KGB agents.

As the two leaders entered the 250-acre gardens, Dilman could see that the autumn season had already stripped the ancient trees of their green foliage. Yet the night was mild, refreshing, and the varicolored gush and spray of the spotlighted fountains lent their walk a festive air.

Dilman indicated a path that led in the direction of the

Trianons, and the Russian Premier nodded and turned off with him, while the bodyguards ahead scampered back into line. Out of the corner of his eye Dilman glanced once again, as he had so many times in the past five days, at his Soviet counterpart and marveled at the familiarity of his face. What there was about Kasatkin, he had realized from the moment of their first handshake in the Grand Château at Chantilly, what there was that had partially disarmed and captivated Dilman, was the Russian leader's uncanny resemblance to old Grandpa Schneider.

In the pantheon of Dilman's memory, the brightest eternal flame honored Grandpa Schneider. When Dilman was seven and eight and maybe nine years old, surrounded by squalor, poverty, anger, deprived of all love except that which his mother could find strength and time to spare, the only male affection and guidance that Dilman had known had come from Grandpa Schneider. The old man—although lately Dilman had realized the old man could not have been *that* old then—had not been a grandpa and his name had not been Schneider. He had been an immigrant Jewish bachelor and a tailor (which, in Yiddish, was *schneider*), and because, when he was not hunched over the sewing machine or over the steam presser, he sat in a rocker, wearing a shawl and spectacles low on the bridge of his nose as he stitched, he had become Grandpa Schneider to the colored neighborhood and had been as pleased as if he had been crowned.

For Dilman, as a child, that rickety hot tailorshop had been the manor hall of a bountiful prince. Sitting crosslegged at Grandpa Schneider's feet, while the old man repaired his shirts or patched his knickers or black stockings for free, Dilman would listen big-eyed to anecdotes of a faraway duchy named Bialystok in a kingdom named Poland. From Grandpa Schneider he would receive at no cost, and in equal quantities, Jewish aphorisms, licorice sticks, revised stories from Sholem Aleichem and Tolstoi, cinnamon rolls, and capsule biographies of such intellectuals as Emma Goldman, Lincoln Steffens, Elbert Hubbard, and Arthur Brisbane.

Long years later Dilman had often thought that more

than the material deprivation of his youth, the oppression of his race, the goading of his mother, it was the magical goodness and encouragement of that kindly, improbable old tailor that had sent him to books, to schools, to law, to whatever he had become in life. During the hard years much had gone out of Dilman's memory, or faded into the hinterland of memory, but not Grandpa Schneider. Dilman's love for the old man was ever there, burning bright.

And that was why, although he had come to the Chantilly Conference tense, prepared to be aggressive, he had been immediately softened by Nikolai Kasatkin, despite the latter's subsequent bombast. For the faces of the Soviet Premier and the immigrant tailor of cherished memory were almost the same face. Thereafter, Dilman had been unable to be anything but friendly, amiable, and receptive toward Kasatkin, who, himself disarmed, most often responded in kind. If the Chantilly Conference between two of the mammoth powers on earth were a success, and its success one day recorded by learned professors in weighty historical tomes, would there be any mention in any index of "Schneider, Grandpa"? Well, so much for definitive histories, Dilman had thought.

Tonight, observing Premier Kasatkin strutting beside him along the Versailles garden path, Dilman still saw the old tailor's knobby peasant profile matching the Russian leader's profile, but he observed more. For all his sixty years, Kasatkin was taller, heavier, more muscular than the one residing in Dilman's memory. Too, Kasatkin's silver hair was fuller, his nose more pugged, his bridgework (startling, when he laughed) made of stainless steel and not gold.

Kasatkin had moved his head, caught Dilman's glance, and smiled. "Yes, you are familiar with this dynastic relic, I see. It is my first visit. Has it changed much since you were here after the Second War?"

Dilman blinked. "How did you know I'd been here before?"

"I have no time for strangers," Kasatkin said. "I must know of a man before I consent to meet with him."

"Yes, I came to Versailles, this place, twice, with an

attorney friend from Chicago. It was during the liberation period. We were flown over. We were officers, Judge Advocate's Division of the Army." He searched off. "As far as I can make out, it hasn't changed much, though I'm not sure I recognize everything. I knew the way to the Petit Trianon—you know, Louis XV built that little palace for Madame Du Barry, then his son gave it to Marie Antoinette—because my friend, a very learned man, told me a modern-day ghost story about it, which I never forgot. It was one of those things that sticks in your mind."

Dilman turned toward Kasatkin, as they continued walking. "Have you ever heard about the two lady tourists, English schoolteachers, who came here to do some sightseeing one afternoon in 1901, and about the people they ran into and the objects they saw that did not exist then or now, but did exist over a century before? I mean, those two schoolteachers, walking through the Versailles gardens in 1901, just as we are walking tonight, they somehow walked backward in time and stumbled on Versailles as it had been in 1789."

Kasatkin was staring at Dilman. "Surely, my friend, you give no belief to that story?"

At once, Dilman felt foolish. Here he was speaking to the hard-headed, materialistic graduate of the Moscow Industrial Academy, the boss of the Presidium of the Central Committee of the Russian Communist Party, the dictator of 280,000,000 people, with whom he had spent nearly a week discussing trade agreements, ballistic missiles, outer space, Baraza, Berlin, India, Brazil, peace and coexistence, and here he was telling him a psychical experience as if it were as real as the issues over which they had debated. Kasatkin must think him mad or drunk or, worse, a moron. Dilman's instinct was to puncture the tale good-naturedly and change the subject, but his loyalty to Nat Abrahams and to Nat's intelligence, imagination, curiosity, would not allow such defection. There was nothing to do but go on, commit more of his forces to what had originally been a casual and innocent conversational foray.

"I don't presume to say whether it's true or not," Dilman said. "I know only that we are insignificant mortals, not certain of where we came from or where we are going or why we are here. Nor am I certain that all there is of ourselves or the world around us can be comprehended with our five known senses. How can we be sure we know everything?"

Kasatkin's shrewd eyes twinkled. "We'd better be sure, my friend." Then he added, chidingly, "Go on, go on with your tall tale. It will give me something to tell my grandchildren when they refuse to sleep. Evidence, my friend—what is the evidence that those school spinsters of yours broke the time barrier and were witnesses to events of the past?"

Rapidly, to get it over with, Dilman went on. "Both those schoolteachers—one was named Anne Moberly, the other Jourdain—taught in the city of Oxford. They were intelligent, sober, conservative ladies. When they went on a vacation to France together in 1901, and decided to visit Versailles, they knew next to nothing about Versailles except for the information they had got from the Baedeker they carried with them. During their walk in the gardens, one such as we are making, they came across Frenchmen strangely attired in what appeared to be masquerade costumes. There were officials in green coats and tricornered hats. The Moberly woman thought the scenery unnatural and lifeless, one-dimensional, no breeze, no light and shade, no sense of aliveness. Then, and this is important, they crossed a small, rather rustic bridge over a ravine. And on the lawn, before the Petit Trianon over there, they saw an aristocratic lady in a large straw hat and full skirt, sketching at an easel. Not immediately, but afterward in Paris, they discussed the eerie, haunted quality of their day here, and they decided they had undergone a unique adventure, and secretly they began to research it."

"A playlet," said Kasatkin. "Maybe they saw actors in a playlet being put on for them?"

"No, there had been nothing like that. Anyway, they researched for nine years. You know what they found out? There was no ravine and no bridge over it in 1901, even though they had crossed it together. La Motte's map of the gardens, done in 1783, did not show the ravine or bridge either. But listen to this—two years after they'd had their adventure—the original map done by Mique, the Queen's architect, from which La Motte had made an inaccurate copy, was discovered in the chimney of some French house. This original map showed the ravine and bridge that no longer existed. Furthermore, from a portrait done by Wertmuller, and from the journal of the Queen's dressmaker telling what the Queen wore in the summer of 1789, our two schoolteachers ascertained that the aristocratic lady sketching on the lawn in 1901 was none other than Marie Antoinette herself. . . . There you have it—well, a small part of it—what psychic experts have called the best-authenticated account of Serialism, stumbling backward through time, on record."

Premier Kasatkin was silent as they tramped over a worn footbridge, and then he said, "Amusing . . . amusing, Mr. President, especially if one dreams of escaping present-day realities of possible nuclear horror by being transported into the past of 1789." He made a short gesture toward the mist-clad grounds and trees and Petit Trianon. "The atmosphere invites escape. But it is false, a Potemkin lie to beguile and lull. All that is truth is our nuclear age, our power to destroy one another and life itself. For us, the two of us, we cannot be two old ladies running away into the past, Mr. President. The past is dead. It does not exist today. We have only ourselves and tonight and the future. Our unique adventure is to save, to guarantee, the reality of the future."

"That is another story," Dilman said with a smile, "still unwritten."

"We are writing it," Kasatkin said flatly. He sniffed the air. "The weather is changing. France can be unhealthy for common men if we are to read its dead past. Come, let us leave the Trianons and return to the present and the future."

Kasatkin veered left, to a new path that would bring them to their motorcades waiting outside the Palace. The bodyguards, both American and Russian, were hastily doing their turnabouts, falling into position as the two leaders resumed their walk.

It was Premier Kasatkin who was speaking once more. "Mr. President, to be blunt, I like you more than the one who was President before you. The other one, he was a stranger. He came from a life that never knew oppression or want, he was like a sterile machine, and his ministers, such as your Secretary Eaton, were no better." Kasatkin held up his hand. "Do not protest, do not defend. It is only my way of being complimentary to you. We understand each other because we have both been underdogs, like most of the people on the earth. When I use the word *underprivileged,* I know your experience makes you define it as I do, and not with the numerals of statistics and reports."

"That much of what you say is true——" Dilman began.

"I have not spoken everything that is on my mind," the Russian said. "More than any American President that has come before you, I think you understand my people and myself. You are surrounded by a reactionary clique, an elite class of capitalists, interested in promoting only their white-skinned version of freedom and prosperity. They regard us, as Communists, their enemy, as threats to the privilege and special interests they wallow in like hogs, just as they consider you, as Negroes, their enemy, and will allow you no freedom and no prosperity. Since you suffer, and therefore understand, such selfishness, I feel you and I are better able to——"

Listening, Dilman perceived Kasatkin's unsubtle strategy. Deftly the Russian was trying to sever Dilman from his American citizenship, leave him as a second-class Negro citizen who would have more in common with the U.S.S.R. than with his own country.

"Premier Kasatkin, let me interrupt you here," Dilman said. "I am an American who happens to be Negro. I am one person, not two who can be separated. I am more aware than you of inequality and injustice in my country. Nevertheless, progress has been made, is being made. Once our Negroes were slaves. Now they are free men. Once they were kept entirely segregated in certain areas. Now they are not. Once it would have been unthinkable for a colored man to be the Chief Executive of the United States. Now——well, here you see me."

"Yes, you may think of yourself as an equal of the whites in your own country, but the ruling clique does not think so. I have read the reaction to your speeches and acts. Your life is in peril every second—"

"It was a Negro who tried to kill me," said Dilman.

"Because he believed you were bending to white masters," said Kasatkin shrewdly. "American you may be, very well," he added. "But Negro you are, no matter what you tell me. I have observed it the entire week. What other reason could there be for your passionate interest in that little, unimportant tribal nation in Africa?"

For the first time this evening Dilman was pricked by annoyance. "Are you implying my interest in Baraza stems from my being a Negro rather than an American? If that is what you mean, you are wrong, dead wrong. Baraza chose, by plebiscite, to live under our democratic system rather than yours, and I am committed to see that their wishes are safeguarded and that nothing they have rejected is imposed upon them."

"Come now, do not tell me they know what is best for them. What is this Baraza, really, truthfully—eighty tribes, fifty languages, primitives, leprosy-ridden and starved. You guarantee them alleged freedom, when they want food. You give them newspapers and radio stations and books and electricity, when they want wheat and livestock. No matter, no matter—as you remark, they will find their own way, decide for themselves, as we in Russia did one October week. All I have been saying is that your former President, as a white American capitalist, saw them for what they were, and saw how they could be used, as a potentially rich pawn for trading and bargaining. You see Baraza as an African American, and your interest is out of proportion to that little country's worth. But, no matter. I understood this from the start at Chantilly, even admired it, and that was why I did not make a greater argument in our own bargaining. I appreciated the Negro feelings in you as you must appreciate the peasant feelings in me. I said to myself, Nikolai, let him have the good feeling of defending his fellow Negroes in Baraza, as long as he allows me to have the good feeling of defending the open freedom of the impover-

ished natives there who wish the right to support ideals
of socialism. Now we understand each other fully, no?"

Moving through the light and darkness of the gardens
of Versailles, Dilman had heard the Russian out with a
rising sense of hopelessness. The gulf that separated them,
that had almost been closed, now seemed wider than ever.
He said, "I am sorry, Premier Kasatkin, but I still am
unable to agree with your analysis of me, of my interest in
Baraza. It absolutely does not spring from my color—"

"You cannot be unconscious of your color, Mr. President," Kasatkin cut in. "When you go back to your America, what awaits you? Brutal racial riots on every street
corner, fury, dissension. Why? Because you do not and
cannot practice the democracy your white salesmen try
to sell."

Dilman had tired of being defensive. "You," he said,
"do you practice what you sell? True communism? The
system of social organization in which goods are held in
common? The system of Plato and Karl Marx?"

"The system of Karl Marx, yes," said Premier Kasatkin coolly. "And not only goods held in common, but
brotherhood, respect—"

"You read our newspapers, but I read yours, too, Premier Kasatkin." Dilman tried to keep his tone level, reasonable, to save what had been gained these last five days,
yet let this mule-headed adversary know that he knew the
U.S.S.R. was anything but a utopia. "You speak of your
brotherhood, your equality, in Russia. You have twenty-
three members of your ruling Presidium, yet not one is
a Georgian, a Uzbek, a Ukrainian. Not one is a Jew. Why
the discrimination? Why the starvation purges? Why the
constant treason trials? Why only one political party instead of two or three or many? Why the deposing or killing of those who are anti-Party? Why the persecutions of
Molotov, Kaganovich, Malenkov, Beria? Why no kosher
shops and the dwindling handful of synagogues for one-
fifth of the world's Jews? Why the growing anti-Semitism?
Why the beatings and ridicule of African students from
Senegal and Nigeria at Moscow State University? Why
those endless rural revolts against fixed prices and goug-
ing taxation? Why the KGB *and* the MVD secret police?

Why half a dozen Hungarys under your fist? Why do thousands flee from East Berlin, from all of your satellite provinces, when they can, if there is so much brotherhood? Why do your masses protest threadbare clothing and several families live cramped in one apartment while members of your entourage wear handsome suits and live in palatial *dachas* outside Moscow? Is this the comradeship you sell, Premier Kasatkin?"

He halted, winded, and was relieved to hear Kasatkin chuckling. "Good, good," the Russian was saying, "spoken like a true son of the robber barons. I miscalculated. You feel you have more equality than I thought. Well, my friend, we would have to be here five more days for me to reply to you, and correct you, and I would get nowhere with you, and you would accomplish less with me. Let us forget ideologies, their strengths and weaknesses. Let us concentrate on coexistence in peace. We have glued together much these last days. Let us make it stick."

"That is all I wish," said Dilman.

They had arrived at the Palace. Ahead, their counselors and aides, and their French hosts, waited in curious groups beside the fleet of gleaming Citroëns.

Premier Kasatkin halted. "Our last moment alone, Mr. President." He extended his hand. "We will keep the peace. As for Baraza, you have my pledge, we will not interfere with *your* people there."

Dilman took his hand. "I shall reassure Kwame Amboko you will not interfere with *his* people there."

Their grips relaxed, their hands parted. As they moved ahead, separating as they walked, Dilman remembered two lady schoolteachers who had once come to Versailles. He envied them their magical escape to the past, where all had already happened and where there could be no terror of the unknown, unlike Kasatkin's realistic future, where there lurked tomorrow and the day after tomorrow.

Dilman mourned leaving what was behind, as he mourned Grandpa Schneider, who had not been at his side after all, and he said cheerlessly, "All right, Secretary Eaton, let's head for home. There's work to do."

VI

HIS life was so filled with telephone calls from so many varied persons, at all hours, on all subjects, with so many degrees of urgency, that it was surprising how one more call, no matter how unusual, could have possessed the devastating power of an earthquake.

All of this he would remember later.

It was five days since his return from Europe, and Douglass Dilman sat at the head of the mahogany dining table in the intimate Family Dining Room on the first floor of the White House, enjoying the informal luncheon with United Nations Ambassador Slater and key members of the American delegation. In spite of the necessary presence of Arthur Eaton, who had been disapproving and excessively formal with him since his veto of the Minorities Rehabilitation Bill, the friendliness of his United Nations colleagues made the meal pleasurable.

Dilman had reported upon every detail of his foreign policy talks with Premier Kasatkin. His listeners agreed that the air had been cleared, and peace was probable and wonderful, and that the President had achieved a real success. Basking in the unanimity of this favorable opinion, Dilman had the appetite for a second helping of the baked salmon loaf.

Then it was, with the luncheon almost over, that Sally Watson appeared, and came quickly to him. While Ambassador Slater politely shifted his discourse from the President to Eaton, Dilman leaned toward his social secretary as she bent close to his ear.

"A telephone call, Mr. President," she whispered.

"Miss Foster says that the party calling insists it is important."

"Who is it?"

"Miss Foster didn't say, except—"

"I'm sure it can wait, then."

"—except it is personal, from someone with the Vaduz Exporters."

Dilman's immediate reaction of concern broke across his features. He was sure that Miss Watson was not unaware of his reaction. "Yes," he said, "I suppose I'd better take it."

"Shall I transfer it in here, or—"

"No, no." He pushed his chair back, made hasty apologies, and followed Sally Watson into the State Dining Room, and then into the Main Hall.

She was leading him to the Red Room. "Right in here," she said. By the time he entered the nineteenth-century Empire parlor, he could see Miss Watson taking up the receiver from the marble-topped circular table. "Miss Foster," she was saying, "I have the President. One moment—"

Dilman accepted the telephone. "Thank you. That'll be all, Miss Watson. Please close the door when you leave."

He waited. The moment that Sally Watson had gone, he turned away, receiver pressed to his mouth and ear, and said, "Miss Foster? You can put the call through."

Again he waited.

The call had unsettled him. Not once before, in all his weeks in the White House, had Wanda Gibson telephoned him here. This was the first time. Of late, he had kept their tenuous relationship alive by trying to telephone her at least once a week, during evenings only, when the Spingers were home to answer the phone, and so avoid arousing any suspicion in the minds of operators or anyone else who might overhear him.

Now here was Wanda coming to him openly. He wondered. Of course, the message had not said that Miss Gibson was calling, but rather, someone from Vaduz Exporters. Perhaps Wanda had fallen ill, met with an accident, and someone in her office, or her employer, Franz Gar, was trying to notify him. But no, Wanda would have told no one in her firm that she was a friend of the President. He was baffled.

Suddenly, unmistakably, he heard Wanda's voice in the earpiece. "Mr. President—is this President Dilman?"

He understood her hesitancy immediately. "One second, hold on," he said. "Uh, Miss Foster—"

"Yes, Mr. President."

"Personal call. You need not monitor this one. Thank you."

He listened for the audible click of his secretary's telephone, heard it, and was assured that Wanda and he were now alone. "All right, Wanda—"

"Are we private?"

"Absolutely." The restrained tightness of her voice troubled him. "Wanda, what is it? Are you all right? Is there anything wrong?"

"I don't know, Doug. I wanted to phone you all morning, but it was dangerous, so—"

"Dangerous?" What could be dangerous on a crisp, beautiful American morning? "Wanda, I don't—"

"Wait, Doug, listen. I had to hold back until lunch, so I could get away without being obvious. I'm in a grocery store booth now. There's so much that's been—" She paused as if to organize her thoughts, and then her low modulated voice came through the telephone swiftly but clearly. "Our office was chaos this morning. Mr. Gar had summoned all the Vaduz associates from New York, Savannah, Galveston, San Francisco. There was so much pressure and haste, I think half the time they forgot I was there. Anyway, I was able to piece things together, and I could see how it might affect you, and thought you should know about it." She caught her breath, then continued. "Doug, the agricultural equipment Vaduz Exporters has been sending out these last months to their home warehouses in Liechtenstein, it wasn't entirely farm equipment, but weapons, small arms, machine guns, ammunition. My company was using Liechtenstein only as a cover-up. The weapons were actually being shipped on behind the Iron Curtain to Bulgaria and Albania, and from there to—to certain parts of Africa."

"You mean Baraza? The Communists are shipping weapons to Baraza?"

"I heard Baraza mentioned once. I'm almost certain of it."

Shaken, Dilman said, "And your company, Vaduz Exporters, they're actually a Communist Front over here?"

"A trading corporation for the Soviet Union. I'm positive."

"Wanda, did you ever have an inkling of this before?"

"Never, not once. Everything exploded early this morning. There were these people pouring in, rushing around like insane, and I was one of several ordered to burn duplicates of procurement orders that had gone out, duplicates of orders I had never seen, typed by someone else, kept by Gar in his office vault. I could read bits and pieces before the stuff went into the incinerator, and I could see Vaduz was shipping weapons and they were winding up eventually in Communist hands in African ports. But the main thing—"

"Wanda, what alerted them to destroy everything this morning?"

"I was just going to tell you, Doug. That's the main thing. I heard CIA mentioned twice. I was all ears for everything by then, but I don't think anyone realized I was listening. But Gar said their informant knew of a special CIA report that had gone to you about a Communist weapons buildup in or around Baraza, and by now Vaduz was probably under surveillance, and orders were—whose orders, I have no idea—orders were to take precautionary measures. This may all be unreliable, Doug, but something *is* going on. You probably know the entire story, and this is silly. You do see all the CIA reports, so—"

"I'm supposed to, Wanda, but I haven't seen any CIA report like that one. I know nothing about a weapons buildup around Baraza. In fact, I was just having lunch with the United Nations delegates, telling them how the Russians promised me hands off."

"Doug, maybe—" Wanda's tone had become uncertain. "I'm sure I haven't got any of this wrong, but maybe I'm reading wrong things into what I've heard and seen. It's just that I'm so worried about you. Maybe you should —I mean, don't depend too much on what I've said—but on your own, I think—"

"You did the right thing, Wanda, calling me. If there is nothing to it, fine, nothing lost. On the other hand, if what you've reported can be verified—" He was full of it now, his mind straining in every direction, until he realized that Wanda was still on the other end, in a telephone booth, worried, perhaps frightened. "Wanda—?"

"Yes—?"

"Thank you for this. I'll look into it immediately. There's one thing I want you to do for me. I want you to quit Vaduz, get out of there as fast as you can."

"Yes, I had decided to do that myself, even if it's a false alarm. I'm afraid of them, what might happen. Even if I've blown this up out of all proportion, the money isn't worth the worry in staying on. I'll give Mr. Gar notice to-night. Doug, I'd better run. No matter what, do be careful."

"You be careful, Wanda. I'd give anything to see you. Well—I'll call you, let you know at home—tonight, to-morrow night latest. Good-bye."

After hanging up, Dilman remained very still. He suffered a curious sensation of loss, and then of inertia induced by helplessness. He tried to liken his reaction to that which he had known the evening he had vetoed the Minorities Rehabilitation Bill. On that occasion, after his act of rebellion and the bitter response to it, he had felt that he had cut himself adrift from his crew. He had been pervaded by, almost overwhelmed by, the awesome experience of loneliness. He had turned the ship of state into an open boat on a running sea, and he was not sure that he could navigate it, without help, to port. But the sense of aloneness then had not engulfed him. He had gone on. He had tried.

This was different. If the danger to which Wanda had alerted him had any reality—and she was not one to panic, to convert rumor into fact, to exaggerate—then he had not cut himself adrift from his crew by his own choice, but had been forced into the helpless isolation of an open boat by hostile mutineers. His own crew had conspired against him, to take over the ship of state and to let him sink.

For the first time, the full realization of what might be happening struck him: he was President in name only, while those around him, without his knowledge, were at the helm, performing the functions of high command.

If this was the case—and now his strength was revived by growing anger—he would not go down, and let the country go down, because other hands had tried to heave him overboard and themselves take control. He was still President of the United States, possessed of the total authority of the executive branch, and he still had enough of a crew at his beck and call to use this authority.

He lifted the telephone from the hook, identified himself to the White House operator, and asked for Edna Foster.

"Miss Foster? Two things. Confidential. Contact Bob Lombardi at the FBI. Notify him I want to see the complete files on every foreign subversive organization, and especially those under suspicion of being Communist Fronts, located in this immediate area. Do you have that?"

"Yes, Mr. President."

"I want the information on my desk by two-thirty today. Second thing—" He thought about it. He had met the Director of the Central Intelligence Agency only three times, and never once in private. He wondered if he could trust him, or if the Director was in the conspiracy against him, if such there was, and then he decided that he had no choice of action. If he could not trust the CIA, he was lost anyway. "Get hold of Montgomery Scott at Central Intelligence. Tell him I want to see the original, unedited daily reports, for every day of the past month, on every one of the African Unity Pact countries, especially those on Baraza."

"Mr. President, if I may say so, we do have a complete file of these CIA reports in our—"

"I know we have copies, Miss Foster. And I know the Secretary of State has copies. I need the originals. Tell

Scott I want to see him personally, along with the original reports, in my office at three o'clock sharp."

"I'll have to rearrange your appointments. And I want to leave you time to rest up before tonight's dinner—"

"Do whatever you have to. But Scott is top priority. Understand?"

He hung up, then recalled that he had left the United Nations delegation in Eaton's hands. He was in no mood for the delegates now, especially when he was less certain about the durability of the worldwide peace he had achieved at Chantilly, but he must return to the table. At least they must be prompted to remember that he was President.

Quickly he crossed the Red Room, and as he reached out to open the door, he realized that it had not been entirely closed during his telephone conversation. He must remind Miss Watson to be less hasty and slipshod in the future. He would hate to have had the valet or the other servants overhear any of his conversation with Wanda, and then use it as fodder for their backstairs gossip.

He looked down the vast hall, and in the distance he could see a girl in a white blouse and blue skirt rushing to her work. Not until she had gone around the corner and out of sight did he remember that Sally Watson had worn a white blouse and blue skirt today. It was too late to call out to her and reprimand her. It was also unimportant, considering what was on his mind and what the afternoon ahead held for him.

Bemused, he started back to the Family Dining Room to take his place at the head of the table.

Edna Foster brushed the limp brown strands of hair from her eyes, left the President once more buried in the heap of files delivered to his desk by the FBI twenty minutes earlier, and unhappily returned to her own office to get the disagreeable task over with.

The instant that she returned, before she could prepare herself for him, Leroy Poole was out of his chair, forehead perspiring, swollen eyes moist, black porcine face beseeching her. She tried to escape behind the moat of her desk, but doggedly he trudged after her and hung over her electric typewriter.

"What did he say, Miss Foster?" Poole begged to know. "Did you tell the President that the Federal judge of that lousy U.S. District Court sentenced Jeff Hurley to death, to be executed in the lethal gas chamber?"

Edna Foster squirmed. "Yes, the President had heard the news from Mr. Lombardi." She hated this scene, and tried to avert her gaze from Poole. It was evident that the grotesque little Negro had been crying all morning, and over the death sentence of a man, not even one of his family, a man crying over another man. It embarrassed her and made her slightly ill.

"Will he see me, or is he still sore at me?" Poole asked.

Edna summoned a vestige of dignity. "I really can't say if the President is—is sore at you, as you put it—but he definitely cannot see you, even for a minute. This is honestly one of his busiest days. I can vouch for that."

Leroy Poole seemed to sag into some emotional morass, nodding, nodding, and then whining, "What about my request that he commute the sentence? He has that power. I have new evidence, and we've filled out the application for executive clemency in the Justice Department. If I have to wait for all those investigations and recommendations from the pardon attorney and the Attorney General, Jeff Hurley will be dead and buried before my appeal gets to Dilman's desk. Did you tell him that?"

"Everything, Mr. Poole." She flipped a page of her shorthand pad. "I passed on to him everything you asked me to, and the President answered—I have it here word for word—'Inform Mr. Poole to go through proper channels at the Department of Justice on his appeal for executive clemency in the case of Jefferson Hurley. For my part, I will personally contact Attorney General Kemmler and request that he cut the red tape and expedite the appeal. When I have the new evidence, and the Attorney General's recommendation, I shall review the appeal and summon Mr. Poole to hear my final decision. I promise him this will be done before Mr. Hurley can go to the gas chamber.'" Edna looked up. "That's all."

A gust of air escaped Poole's mouth, as from the neck of a balloon, yet his puffed features did not deflate. "Okay, fair enough," Poole said. "I'll go ahead. I'll see the appeal is in order. You just see that I'm here to talk it over with the President and hear his pardon before Jeff Hurley is gone."

"You have the President's word, Mr. Poole."

"Okay. Goddam them down there, legalizing murder of the best, most decent human being in the country. I won't let them, and Dilman won't either, once he reviews the facts and hears what I have to say. . . . Okay, I know you're busy, Miss Foster. Just remember to call me."

Temporarily appeased, Leroy Poole shuffled across the office, out the door and out of her sight, and Edna Foster dropped into her hard swivel chair with a sigh of relief. She laid her notebook aside, and waited to see if the pinch behind her eyes was going to develop into another migraine headache. It was getting worse and worse, all this pressure, and all these people, like just now, a black man in here, a black man in there, and all their anger and self-pity.

Why had she fastened on Dilman's color again? She tried to think. Was it the tension of the job, created by Dilman's color, or simply, simply the discomfort of being secretary to a Negro? How far had she come since that first day when she had agreed to work for Dilman, just as she had so long ago for T.C.?

Intellectually, she supported all the *right* things for Negroes, their right to vote, to sit like anyone else in any school classroom, to be equal under God and the Constitution. All the right things she believed in, without equivocation, yes—yet in some mysterious way her emotions continued to dominate her intellect, and at such times she felt that those black people were a threatening and inferior people. Threatening because black was threatening, because black was evil, like blackmail, black arts, blacklist, black magic. Threatening because, no matter what common sense you had, when you walked in the street, in the dark, alone, and you saw a Negro man walking toward you, you felt unsafe, because black was African and black was night, meaning uncivilized, meaning oblivion. And, illogically, you considered them inferiors. When she was on a bus, and looked out the window to find a Negro at the wheel of a large new car that had drawn up to the light, she was always surprised if he was not a chauffeur, surprised and vaguely resentful. How could a lesser person have more than she, who was white, meaning good and decent, and educated and chaste? After such internal bouts, and with difficulty, brought on by shame, she would recall her popular readings on race: these were not inferior people, only different-appearing people. Desperately she would evoke the names of Booker T. Washington and Carver and Bunche, but it was no use.

Yet when those stupid Southern-born secretaries made their jokes, Edna was resentful of them, too, and felt superior because she was not so prejudiced as they. She would never stoop so low, she thought then, as to believe that Negroes, because of their color, made so by God's choosing, were more criminal, more shiftless, more smelly than whites. Whenever she was thus intellectually rein-forced, she had easier days with Dilman, treated him with more deference and regarded him with more re-spect, as if to make up for her fluctuating emotional preju-dices and those of her friends. Yet she never wanted to defer too much to Dilman, because tolerance was a form of feeling superior, too. Then she tried to treat Dilman as she would George or Tim Flannery or any other white man. But then she couldn't, not truly, because since he was black, his presence in the Oval Office meant threat-ening danger to him, to the country, to herself, and his inferiority made things a mess, and no matter what, she was sure he smelled different. Damnation. And then she blamed George. He was at fault for her miseries, her pre-dicament.

Because of George, she was still on this horrible job. His proposal of marriage, true, had been the high spot of her whole life. Because of it she had not enjoyed her trip to France at all. When she had not been working, she was mooning and wanting to get back to George and mar-riage. She had not even taken the time to visit the

Louvre. And after all that, when she had flown back so full of high hopes and expectations, George had not been waiting for her, which was really too much. There had been a note under her apartment door, nothing more. He was in New York City investigating a possible job. He'd be back in a day or two with good news. The day or two had frustratingly become almost a week, and his brief, enigmatic telephone calls gave her nothing more definite to expect from his trip.

Less than an hour ago she had received his daily call, the call for today. He was still in New York City, he said. He could not promise to be back tonight or tomorrow, but maybe tomorrow. For the first time she had not hidden her irritation. Was this the way to start a marriage, he in New York, she in Washington, not even seeing each other in ten or eleven days? To pacify her, he had stayed on the phone longer than usual, full of hints about a terrific job, a quick marriage, so on and so on. This had soothed her somewhat, but after he had hung up, the long-distance operator had called her. There was an overcharge. The party had telephoned from a public booth and left without depositing the extra coins. Would she pay the overcharge? She would. Where should she send the one dollar and ten cents? To the telephone company in Trafford, New York, she was told. Not to New York City? No, to Trafford. Very well, Trafford.

What in the devil was going on with George Murdock, she wondered now. Why tell her that he was calling from New York City, and then have it turn out he was calling from Trafford? What could there be for him in Trafford? It was a one-street college town, Negro college town at that, and neither of them knew a soul there—except the President's son, if that counted for anything.

So here was she, stewing, and there he was, *somewhere,* mysterious and behaving like anything but a bridegroom, and she was—all right, to use Leroy Poole's word—she was *sore* as heck.

The buzzer at her elbow startled her.

She snatched at the telephone. "Yes, Mr. President?"

"Miss Foster, put a hold on all calls, and then come in. Bring your shorthand pad."

She diverted incoming calls to Mr. Lucas, the engagements secretary, took up her notebook and pencils, and went to the door. Momentarily she hesitated, and then placed her right eye against the peephole.

There were two persons at the Buchanan desk, looking oddly magnified by the glass she peeked through. One was President Dilman, seated, features bunched in concentration as he licked a broad thumb and turned page after page of the pile of bound papers on the desk before him. The other was Montgomery Scott, standing over Dilman, watching and speaking, and when not speaking, dryly working his lips.

Edna had known Montgomery Scott since the day T.C. had appointed him Director of the Central Intelligence Agency. She had never been able to reconcile his appearance with his record. Scott's silky brown hair was parted low and combed up and over his head to disguise a bald spot. Yet his Vandyke beard was full and pointed. In between, his pink, bland, ageless face, with little pulls and punctures for features, was innocent and noncommittal. His long frame, slouched, carried his familiar sports jacket and dark-gray slacks. His carved meerschaum, the gift of some Middle Eastern potentate, added to his sedentary, scholarly aspect. Yet, Edna remembered, Scott had once been an active cloak-and-dagger man for the OSS. Later, while with the CIA, he had been involved in the overthrow of the Arbenz government in Guatemala, the instigation of the U-2 espionage aircraft, the onetime invasion of Suez, the assassination of Trujillo. Except for the incisiveness of his speech, his incongruous braying laugh, the spade of a beard, there was nothing to indicate that Scott was unique, yet he was the Director of derring-do, with a half-billion dollars of funds (never publicly accounted for) and 15,000 employees (rarely publicly recognized) at his disposal in Langley, Virginia, and around the world. The reporters who admired him referred to him as "Great Scott," and those who disliked him referred to him as "Great Scott!"

Edna Foster opened the door and entered the President's Oval Office.

Not until she reached the desk did both men look up.

"Hello, Edna," Montgomery Scott said to her. "Long time."

"Yes, good to see you, Mr. Scott."

Dilman pointed to the chair next to his desk. "Sit here, Miss Foster. I'm going to interrogate Mr. Scott. It's important, so take down everything. Transcribe it and have it ready for me today. I may want to study it after dinner tonight."

Edna sat, pulled down the hem of her skirt, pad and pencil waiting. "Any special security rating for this, Mr. President?"

"One copy, for me and no one else, stamped 'Eyes Only' and 'Top Secret.' " Dilman indicated the chair on the other side of the desk. "Please sit down, Mr. Scott."

"If you don't mind, I will." The CIA Director slumped into the chair and, propping himself in it like a fishhook, tugged at his short beard, then massaged the orange-stained meerschaum in his other hand.

"All right, Miss Foster," Dilman said over his shoulder as his eyes remained upon Scott, and he finally swerved his leather chair to face him completely. "Mr. Scott, I'll tell you why I wanted to see the original file of your daily reports, and why I wanted to see you. Shortly after one o'clock today, from a private source, I learned that the Vaduz Exporters, a Liechtenstein corporation with offices in Bethesda, is a Soviet Union Communist Front organization, operating illegally, shipping arms and ammunition through Liechtenstein to Iron Curtain countries, and from those countries to Africa. I have now found this confirmed in the FBI file on foreign subversive organizations in this area."

"Oh, yes, Mr. President, we gave the FBI the lead on that two weeks ago, two weeks ago yesterday," said Scott, with obvious satisfaction. "Unlike Amtorg, the Vaduz people are unregistered enemy agents. Lombardi told me they were already under surveillance, but what came in from our Barazan operative was the first concrete evidence of what was actually going on here. I think the FBI intends to crack down any day now."

"Tomorrow," said President Dilman. "The FBI is rounding them up and closing them tomorrow."

Edna Foster's mind, which had still been trapped by the mystery of George's peculiar telephone call, now released itself to the new mystery she was recording in shorthand on the pad resting upon her knee. As her interest focused upon the two men in conversation before her, her pencil darted across the ruled lines, hooking, looping, scrawling.

"Excellent," Montgomery Scott had said. Then he added, "Of course, that's no longer strictly a CIA matter."

President Dilman leaned forward. "I'll tell you what is a CIA matter and a matter that seriously concerns me. How did you know that Vaduz weapons were pouring into Africa, the Baraza area, for native Communists?"

Scott sat straighter. "It's in the special daily report I sent you—as I said, I remember the day—two weeks ago yesterday."

"Mr. Scott, I received no such report from you," said President Dilman grimly. "It's not in my file here. Miss Foster brought my file in before you came, and I was able to see what I had overlooked before. One day's report is missing from my file. As you said, the one dated two weeks ago yesterday. How is that possible?"

Montgomery Scott had shoved the meerschaum into one capacious pocket, and was entirely erect in his chair now. "I can't imagine, Mr. President," he said. Then he poked his forefinger at the second mound of sheets before Dilman. "In any case—"

"It should be in your original CIA file that you just brought in," said President Dilman, finishing the Director's sentence. "Well, sir, it isn't. You saw me go through your original reports a few minutes ago. That one daily report is missing from there, too." He leafed the sheets backward, and then said, "I find only a blue memorandum slip inserted, with the date and the note, 'Talley/ Eaton to return.' " He looked up. "What does that mean?"

Scott, who had become increasingly disturbed, suddenly rapped the desk. "Of course. I remember. Following our usual procedure, that morning I sent out two copies from Langley, one to Governor Talley for you, and the other to Secretary of State Eaton. Later in the day

Talley telephoned me that both you, Mr. President, and Secretary Eaton were concerned about the report, and wished our entire file, including the original from which the two copies had been made."

"Wasn't that unusual, Mr. Scott?" asked President Dilman.

Scott pulled at his Vandyke. "Why—yes—reconsidering it, I suppose it was. But I saw no reason not to comply. After all, President Truman established our Central Intelligence Agency primarily as a source to supply him, and future Chief Executives, with vital foreign data and information, unedited, unslanted, uninterpreted." He bent forward, eyes narrowing. "Are you telling me, Mr. President, that although Governor Talley and Secretary Eaton sent for every scrap of that daily report on Baraza in your name, you saw neither our direct copy nor the original?"

"I saw nothing," said President Dilman, "and until two hours ago I knew nothing. That is why I brought you here."

"Well, I don't understand," said Scott, scratching his jaw through a portion of his beard. "Of course, I can't become involved in politics, but speaking on a purely factual level, there can be a simple and quite understandable explanation of why your aide and the Secretary of State acted as they did."

He appeared to be considering what he would say next. At last he spoke. "On occasion, a Secretary of State or some other Department head will withhold information from the President until it is fully confirmed or simply because, at that point, the Department head believes it to be unimportant.

"I can't vouch for this, but I am told that during the Eisenhower administration the American Ambassador to Mexico learned that Fidel Castro had long been a Communist and had been trained to take over Cuba and convert it into a satellite of the Soviet Union. The top-secret report went to Washington. For some reason it was put aside, never shown to President Eisenhower. As a result, the President and his aides knew too little of Castro's Red leanings. They blessed him as a democratic rebel, as did most Americans in those early days—only to learn later that he was, in truth, a puppet of the Soviet Union. The original warning report to Eisenhower? Who knows? Maybe somebody thought it was too idiotic and untrustworthy to be treated seriously."

President Dilman held up his hand. "Mr. Scott, this missing report on Baraza, the one that has been kept from me—do you feel it was such as could be justifiably regarded as idiotic and untrustworthy, or not fully confirmed?"

The Director of the CIA was, in Edna Foster's eyes, definitely uncomfortable. "Mr. President, I really feel I should not get involved. We are a fact-finding organization. We dredge up the facts, evaluate the source, and present them to you for consideration, and you decide what happens after that."

"Very well," said President Dilman, "then you dredge up the facts in that missing report on Baraza. You evaluate the source for me, and I shall do the judging. Since I prefer not to go to Talley or Eaton for the actual report just yet, I must depend upon someone else for the information it contained. Do you have that information in your head?"

"Yes, I have, Mr. President."

"All right, shoot."

"The information we received was precisely this: In the hills, on the entire northern frontier of Baraza, there is now taking place a buildup of a native Communist rebel army. Crates from the Vaduz Exporters have been coming in, along with Russian officers who are training these African Communists. The Soviet Embassy in Baraza City is paying for, and directing, the secret buildup. We do not know the size of this Communist force yet, or the extent to which it is being armed. So much for the information. Now, you want the source?"

"The source," said Dilman.

"The first information came to our Embassy in Baraza City from a Communist defector, a native. To look into it further, our head CIA undercover agent there recruited an educated native, good clearance, who was, as we say, 'in place,' on the scene of the buildup. Our report, two weeks ago, was based on this source."

"And your evaluation of the reliability of the source?" demanded President Dilman.

"As you know, Mr. President, we rate all incoming information on a scale that starts at 1—meaning positively reliable—and this scale grades downward to 6—meaning probably unreliable. Most of the reports that we give further attention to are those rated 2, 3 and 4. The Baraza report? I remember the rating exactly. It was rated between 3 and 4, meaning fairly reliable but requiring more investigation."

"What have you done about it since?" asked President Dilman.

"We've ordered our field men to continue probing for information."

"Not enough," said President Dilman firmly. He stood up, stared at the windows behind him, then slowly turned back to Scott. "Whatever Talley or Eaton determined—whether they kept this information from me because they decided it was unimportant or because they refused to trust me—I am not yet ready to let them usurp my powers, the powers of this office, and make decisions for me. This can be serious, serious beyond belief. Mr. Scott, I persuaded President Amboko to relax his guard against Communism, give the Russians a freer hand in Baraza. Five days ago I received Premier Kasatkin's assurance that this democratic freedom we had insisted upon in Baraza would not be misused by the Soviet Union. No matter how others in our country may feel about Baraza, I will not break faith with Amboko or with other African leaders who trust us and depend upon us. Nor will I let Russia deceive us, play us for fools, make us keep hands off while they are getting ready to take over the independent, underdeveloped nations of Africa through intimidation and terror. Mr. Scott—"

Montgomery Scott had come to his feet. "Yes, Mr. President?"

"We're way behind, and Baraza may be in danger and we may be in danger. I want to make up for lost time. I want the number of undercover CIA agents in Baraza doubled, and redoubled, if necessary, and at once. I want the secret funds committed to this investigation doubled, tripled. Hereafter I want every CIA report on Baraza brought to me, by you in person. Let Talley and Eaton keep their heads in the sand. I cannot, and shall not. I want a final report on Baraza rated up to 1 or down to 6. Whatever it becomes, I want the truth, and I want it fast!"

By five minutes after ten o'clock that evening, Sally Watson, fortified by the three Bloody Marys before dinner, the two glasses of wine and one full-grain energizing pill during dinner, the second refill of champagne in her hand now after dinner, felt at last possessed of the daring to go through with her scheme.

Her bare shoulders backed against the striped satin wallpaper of the Blue Room, Sally Watson stood removed from the clutter of military guests some feet away. The informal reception and dinner for the Pentagon crowd, in the State Dining Room, had gone off smoothly. There had been no last-minute dropouts, no ostracizing of Dilman, since the military needed the President's support in their next budget battle. Now the thirty-two guests, the beribboned, bemedaled men in their brown, blue, gray, green uniforms, and their wives in semiformal dress, were enjoying their after-dinner drinks, a choice of champagne or brandy.

Sally drank, and through the tipped curve of her champagne glass, somewhat distorted, she could make out President Dilman, surrounded by Secretary of Defense Steinbrenner (a clod), Chairman of the Joint Chiefs of Staff General Fortney (a lecher), Admiral Rivard (a bore), Air Force General Ormsby (a social climber). Undoubtedly, she guessed, they were discussing with the President the trip he would be leaving upon late tomorrow, a one-week swing around the nation to visit military installations and deliver three speeches: on his Chantilly accord with the Soviets, on defense spending, on the forthcoming culmination of

Project Apollo with the three-man orbital flight and moon reconnaissance under the direction of that attractive young General Leo Jaskawich.

It was interesting, to Sally, to watch how the President made a pretense of attentiveness, when she could see how disinterested he really was—in fact, how self-absorbed and moody he was, as he had been throughout the evening. He's bugged, absolutely neurotic, about that telephone call he received during lunch, she decided. She knew that she was right. It takes one to know one. For she was bugged too, absolutely psycho, about what she had overheard and had reported to Arthur Eaton, and about how Arthur had reacted and what she had promised him.

With quiet desperation, before she lost her courage, before she became undone again, she wished that the damn after-dinner drinking would cease, and that they would all go down to the projection room for that Air Force film and leave her alone. Instead they stood there, lapping up the free booze. She considered her own empty glass: not that she was one to protest.

She peered down at her sea-green chiffon cocktail gown and wished that she had worn something less provocative. The next thing, General Pitt Fortney would be leering over at her again, and trying to make her come down to the projection room as his partner so that he could put his hand on her knee in the dark. She had her speech all made up for Dilman. She did not want any Texas lunkhead spoiling it.

From the top brass in the drawing room, her thoughts careened to the golden Galahad splendor of her lover. Tonight she was putting it all on the line for Arthur Eaton. Not that she had not already put plenty on the line for him, but tonight would cinch it. After tonight he would know for sure that she was not only good in bed, but good for a wife, a perfect wife for an entire life. After all, where had that snotty Kay Varney, his wife in name only, been during this crisis in Arthur's life? What had Kay ever given him but a bank account and a cold in bed? As for herself, Sally was giving him more —everything, in fact. She was giving him an excitement in loving that he had never known before—he had admitted it the last time—and now she was preparing to undergo any risk to protect and elevate him.

The issues at stake were cloudy to her. She had no mind, she was the first to admit, for politics. She knew only that what was going on was of life-and-death importance to her Arthur, and that if she saved him, he would save her. He would have to, whether he wanted to or not, and he would want to anyway. They were together in this. Besides, they were in love, not kid love, lifetime love.

In front of her, some jazzed-up darky was starting to splash more champagne into her glass, and she pulled it away and let the rest of the champagne pour on the rug. She did not want to be intoxicated. Too much at stake. What at stake? She relived the highlights of the hectic afternoon.

During lunch, after leading Dilman to his Miss Gibson on the telephone, after leaving him, Sally had deliberately left the door slightly ajar. Why? She did not know. Why not? She had heard what she had heard, not comprehending fully, knowing only that it was something terribly surprising to the President, terribly involved with foreign affairs, and that she must convey to Arthur what she had learned. Whew, it had been close, getting away just in the nick of time. She was certain that Dilman suspected nothing. He was a dimwit, nice but a dimwit, through and through.

The second that she was back in the privacy of her office, she had telephoned Arthur at the Department of State. She did not get far. Brusquely, he had cut her short, asking her not to tell him any more on the telephone, but to come over at once. Pleased to have struck a spark, she had made some excuse to Diane about an errand, and hastened downstairs to her sports car.

When she had arrived at the Department of State and entered Arthur's marvelous office, she was dismayed. She and Arthur were not alone, as she had expected they would be. A third party, Wayne Talley, was also present. At once, Arthur, perceiving her embarrassment, considerately had placed an arm around her, assuring her that she could speak as freely before Talley as with him.

She had recounted everything that she could recall having "accidentally" overheard of the President's conversation with Miss Wanda Gibson. When she had mentioned that the President had said he had not "seen any special CIA report like that one," Arthur's face darkened and there was a rapid exchange between Talley and himself.

Arthur had said, "Dilman knows. He'll try to see that CIA report now."

Talley had said, "There's none to see."

"You are certain of that?"

"Arthur, I am positive."

"Good . . . I know we have acted in the right. T.C. would have commended us."

"No question, Arthur. How could we let someone like Dilman have that information—and possibly misuse it? He'd not think of what was best for us, only what would be best for his African friends."

Then Sally had resumed her story, and when she finished with the news that Dilman was meeting with Scott this afternoon, Arthur had turned to Talley once more.

"Wayne, I'm worried. This could be dynamite."

"We've got the percussion cap."

"I'm not so sure. Depends on what Scott tells him. I'd give anything to know."

After promising to meet with Arthur again in the evening, Talley had departed. For Sally, being alone with Arthur was reward enough, but when he also embraced her and kissed her, it was almost too much to bear.

Before leaving, Sally had clung to Arthur briefly. "Honey," she had whispered, "did you mean it, what you told Governor Talley, about giving anything to know what Dilman and Scott are going to discuss this afternoon?"

"It would be of inestimable importance to me, yes."

"What if I could find out for you?"

"You find out? How?"

"Never mind—what if I could? That's something your wife wouldn't do for you, would she?"

"Kay?" He had smiled wanly. "If she saw a tree about to fall on me, she probably wouldn't raise her voice."

"There, then," Sally had said triumphantly. "You can see I'm not Kay. To me, you're the most precious person on earth—"

"Darling, I—"

"I mean it, Arthur. Anyway, let me go after this for you."

"Sally, I wouldn't want you attempting anything foolish or risky."

"I wouldn't be. I'm only saying, I can try to help you, I want to, because I love you."

"I love you, too, darling."

"If—if I find out anything, I'll see you tonight."

He did not stop her, she remembered. He had told her not to attempt anything risky. He had not told her that he preferred she do nothing at all. Therefore it was important to him, whatever she could learn—and therefore it was equally important to her to learn something for him, for both of them.

She looked up from her glass, and was glad to note, while she was still keyed up, that the after-dinner drinking was coming to an end. There was a spontaneous breaking up of groups, a realigning into couples, a general movement in her direction, toward the exit beside her. They were streaming out of the room now, going down to the East Wing projection room, with its front row of soft armchairs and seven rows of stiffer chairs behind, which they would not more than half fill.

The stocky figure of President Dilman, momentarily separated from General Fortney, drew nearer. He glanced at her, and she stared blearily at him.

"Coming, Miss Watson?" he inquired.

" 'Fraid not," she murmured beneath her breath, a trick of underplaying that usually brought her prey, unable to hear her, closer to her to find out what she had said. It worked.

Dilman was beside her. "I didn't catch what—?"

"Mr. President, do you mind if I skip the movie? I— I'm embarrassed, but 'fraid I drank too much, an' I feel a bit woozy. Maybe I'd better lie down somewhere, an' come in for the end of it."

"Not necessary, Miss Watson. If you don't feel well, you go home, go to bed."

"Thank you. Matter of fact, I'm not up to that either yet. Really, if you don't mind, I'd just like to find a place to rest a few minutes, and then—"

His military aides were cluttering the doorway, and Dilman said absently, "Whatever you think best, Miss Watson. Come down and join us later, if you like. You did a fine job with the dinner. Thank you."

He was gone. The others were gone. In seconds, the Blue Room was emptied of all but herself and two white-coated waiters retrieving the empty glasses. She waited a short interval, until there was no more sound in the Main Hall outside. Then, setting down her champagne glass, taking up her beaded evening purse, she started to leave the room. At the doorway one of her knees buckled, she staggered, but she quickly recovered, surprised to realize that she was really a trifle woozy after all.

She intended to climb the state staircase, go up the quiet red carpet to the second floor, but then remembered that the glass doors at the top were automatically locked on the inside to anyone approaching from below. Immediately she took the President's private elevator and, seconds later, emerged into the upstairs foyer.

Cautiously she made her way into the West Hall. She expected to come upon the valet, Beecher, or the housekeeper, Mrs. Crail, and she had her professional excuses prepared. She was almost disappointed when neither one was in sight. She turned left, going past the Yellow Oval Room, going more briskly, ready for any Secret Service man who might accost her and then recognize her. In her brief passage up the corridor she neither saw, nor was seen by, any other person.

At the door of the Lincoln Bedroom, which Dilman had recently converted into his permanent night study as well as sleeping quarters, she paused. Lightly, she knocked, to learn if the valet was inside, readying the room for the night. There was no response. Satisfied,

THE MAN 529

she looked up the corridor, then down it, to confirm once more that there were no witnesses to her adventure. There were none.

Swiftly, heartbeat quickening, she opened the door and stepped inside, shutting the door silently behind her.

The somber stillness of the chamber quelled her rising nervousness. The valet had been here and gone. The white trapunto coverlet had been removed from Lincoln's rosewood bedstead, and the pillows were in place, with a corner of the blanket cover folded back diagonally. The President's pajamas were laid out neatly across the foot of the bed, and below, on the rug, were his misshapen brown bedroom slippers. The room was shadowy, lit dimly by only the round glass-shaded lamps on either side of the bed, and by the one on the marble-topped circular table.

Holding her beaded purse tightly, she went slowly around the bedroom, examining the tops of the bureau and the Victorian table against the wall, the couch, the end tables, the slipper chairs for the object of her search. They offered her no help. Distressed, yet positive that it must be in this room (if it existed at all), for she knew the President read and studied and made notes late into the night, Sally continued around the bedroom. Then, on the figured carpet, propped against the leg of the end table on the opposite side of the bed, she saw it.

With a tiny, audible gasp of elation, she ran to the stuffed leather briefcase. Kneeling, praying, she tugged at the heavy flap. It pulled up, the bag opening wide without resistance, and she wanted to cry with gratitude. The President had released the combination lock before leaving, probably intending to do some work while dressing for dinner.

Settling on the floor beside the enormous bed, lifting her skirts and tucking her legs sideways beneath her, she dipped one hand into the first partition of the briefcase. What she came up with were several green-covered pamphlets and booklets from the Department of Defense, on military weapons and equipment currently in use. With care she returned them to their slot, and then pulled a thick wad of papers out of the second partition. She skimmed the headings in haste, and saw that these consisted of the President's speaking schedule around the country, with several rough drafts, marked with blunt pencil, of the addresses he would be delivering. Disappointed, she returned these to the briefcase too.

There was one partition remaining, and in it were more clipped sheets. She extracted them. The first two listed his tentative engagements for tomorrow. The next, bound in a light-blue folder, bore two block-lettered, ominous, rubber-stamped red-ink warnings upon it: EYES ONLY and TOP SECRET.

She opened the folder. The first page had the type-written heading: "Following is a Transcript of the Conversation Between the President and Director Montgomery Scott, of CIA, from 3:15 P.M. to 4:22 P.M. Today. (Q means Question by the President; A means Answer by Mr. Scott.) Transcribed by E.F."

A thrill of intrigue and accomplishment shot down Sally Watson's bare and shaking arms, into her fingers holding the valuable document. How proud Arthur would be of her, she thought, how proud and pleased, as pleased as he had been after their first night of fulfilled love not many weeks ago.

She turned the pages one by one, counting them. There were seven in all, single-spaced, but with generous skips. Even though her shorthand was rudimentary—she had never had the patience to acquire such a menial skill—she had concocted a homemade short-hand of her own, employing mostly abbreviations and silly symbols that she understood. Unfortunately, her system, efficient as it was, would take considerable time, perhaps too much time to enable her to copy the entire document.

She squinted at the diminutive dial of her wristwatch, finally making out the minute and hour hands. Almost fifteen minutes had passed since the President had led his guests to the ground-floor projection room. They were watching a movie. If it wasn't a spectacle, merely an ordinary movie, it would take an hour and a half.

Then, when it was over, there would be some discussion of it, and there would be more time consumed bidding good night to the officers and their wives. At the least, based on past experience, this should take Dilman another half hour. So she had two hours, minus fifteen minutes, leaving one hour and forty-five minutes. But, assuming there was no lingering after the film had been shown, assuming the President was anxious to return to his homework, she had better shave off a half hour as a margin of safety for herself. That left one hour and fifteen minutes of assured privacy.

She weighed the folder and its precious pages. No, the time left to her might not be enough to copy everything, considering the amount to be done, the pressure, and, she had to admit, her somewhat groggy condition. She decided upon a course of action: even if she did not completely understand the contents of these pages, she would copy out fully whatever looked important or factual, or concerned foreign affairs, especially whatever Scott had told Dilman. Then, if there was still time left, she would go back and fill in the rest, or what she could of it.

She came to her feet, folder in one hand, purse in the other, wobbled on her high-heeled pumps, then went hastily to the marble-topped circular table in the center of the room. Pulling up one of the velvet-covered chairs, she laid the folder on its face, snapped open her purse, and brought out her two dozen blank index cards and her gold pencil. Putting her purse aside, she turned over the bound transcript, flipped a page, and read:

Q. Mr. Scott, I'll tell you why I wanted to see the original file of your daily reports and why I wanted to see you. Shortly after one o'clock today, from a private source, I learned that Vaduz Exporters, a Liechtenstein corporation with offices in Bethesda, is a Soviet Union Communist Front organization, operating illegally, shipping arms and ammunition through Liechtenstein to Iron Curtain countries, and from those countries to Africa. I have just now found this confirmed in the FBI file on foreign subversive organizations in this area.

A. Oh yes, Mr. President, we gave the FBI the lead on that two weeks ago, two weeks ago yesterday. Unlike Amtorg, the Vaduz people are unregistered enemy agents. Lombardi told me they were already under surveillance, but what came in from our Barazan operative was the first concrete evidence of what was actually going on here. I think the FBI intends to crack down any day now.

Q. Tomorrow. The FBI is rounding them up and closing them tomorrow.

A. Excellent. Of course, that's no longer strictly a CIA matter.

Q. I'll tell you what is a CIA matter, and a matter that seriously concerns me. How did you know that Vaduz weapons were pouring into Africa, the Baraza area, for native Communists?

A. It's in the special daily report I sent you two weeks ago yesterday.

Q. Mr. Scott, I received no such report from you. It is not in my file here. Miss Foster brought my file in before you came—

Sally caught herself. She had become so absorbed in reading, she was forgetting to copy. Of course, most of this she had already relayed to Arthur, it being similar to what she had overheard in Dilman's conversation with Miss Gibson, but nevertheless, Arthur would want the essence of it.

She slid the first of her small rectangular index cards next to the transcript, took up her gold pencil, and began to write clearly: "Q—Mr. Scott, I'll tell you why I wanted to see the original file of your daily reports . . ."

She wrote on. The first part was tiresome, for she had read it and there were no surprises, but then, after she reached the new dialogue, it was more interesting and more sport, and her cramped writing hand hurt less and the time went more swiftly.

Once, as her filled index cards began to form an exhilarating pile—like a square slice of wedding cake—she glanced at the time. More than forty-five minutes of her allotted one hour and fifteen minutes had passed.

She had, she realized, covered less than half the transcript, and there were fewer than thirty minutes remaining. What she had put down, she hoped, would be useful to Arthur, but she was being too meticulous, writing everything out in full, and much of what she had written out suddenly did not seem vital. With a pang, she wished that she possessed Miss Foster's stenographic skill, and her knowledge of what was usable and what was chaff. But then, Arthur would not have been interested in a girl whose talents were so circumscribed.

She determined to resort to her own brand of shorthand, and hoped she would be able to decipher it later tonight. She also determined to skip ahead, setting down only what seemed to touch upon Arthur's life and interests.

She resumed reading, copying nothing for a few minutes, then realized that Scott was orally filling in for the President what had been in some kind of missing report, and this she duplicated on her cards in detail. Then she skipped more, and then Arthur's name leaped out at her in the transcription of the President's words, and the words were threatening to Arthur, and she knew that she must capture them for his eyes. She reread the passage:

Q. What have you done about it since?
A. We've ordered our field men to continue probing for information.
Q. Not enough. Whatever Talley or Eaton determined—whether they kept this information from me because they decided it was unimportant, or because they refused to trust me, I am not yet ready to let them usurp my powers, the powers of this office, and make decisions for me. This can be serious, serious beyond belief.

The words blurred to her eyes, and the champagne's bitter aftertaste was in her throat, and her writing hand was painful from spasms of cramp, but she knew that she must write this down too, and fully. She suspected it would be more important to Arthur than anything else. When one had knowledge of what other people thought of them, were planning against them, one was forewarned and as strong as one's self and one's opponent combined. How much she herself would want such a transcript of Arthur's private conversations by long distance with his impossible wife. Armed with that, she would know how to behave to perfection. But then, she supposed, such information was superfluous. Every time Arthur lay in her embrace peacefully asleep, his beautiful repose told her what he thought of Kay, what he thought of Sally, and what she herself could depend upon in the future.

She shook off the lassitude of drink, pulled a fresh index card before her, and began copying again.

Her wavering pencil had neared the bottom of the card, when abruptly it stopped, and hung there as if impaled.

There had been a sound outside the door.

Her head went up, her back arched, her heart thumped.

She listened.

Then there was a voice, and another voice, both muffled, barely audible, but as strident as fanfares against her ears, amplified and amplified again by her mortal terror.

Beyond the closed door, the voices seemed to converge upon her until they were recognizable, one that of Douglass Dilman, the other that of Beecher, his valet.

A cold sweat bathed her, and her clammy fingers tightened about the pencil as panic gripped her heart and head.

Impossible, was all that she could tell herself. But, simultaneously, the shock of fear cleared her head. She remembered for the first time since she had stood drinking her champagne after dinner: it was not an ordinary feature-length film they had seen, but two Signal Corps short subjects (running time, twenty-eight minutes) and one Air Force documentary (running time, seventeen minutes). No wonder it was over. No wonder the President was outside the door.

She was trapped, she and Arthur trapped, because of

her stupid miscalculation, caught red-handed without prepared explanation or lie.

The voices, indistinct outside the door, rose and fell. Desperately her numb fingers sought help from her numbed brain. She threw the pencil into her purse, shoved the index cards together and jammed them haphazardly into the purse; then, holding the purse, she grabbed up the folder and stumbled out of the chair. Blindly, choking, she darted to the side of the bed. Casting the purse on the bed, she knelt, tore open the briefcase, and stuffed the folder into it.

She leaped to her feet, wildly searching the bedroom. Across the bed, past the towering headboard and Lincoln portrait on the wall, was another white door, the one leading into the adjoining Lincoln Sitting Room. It was her escape hatch, her only hope. If she could only get out before he came in. She went swiftly around the endless bed, half running, reached the door to safety, was about to open it, when she realized that she was empty-handed.

She spun back into the room, and then wanted to scream with anguish. There it was, the sonofabitching purse, the indicting purse fat with her notes for Arthur. There it was, glittering and mocking her, lying on the far side of the bed.

She bounded to the bed, reached over it for the purse, lost her balance, and fell across the blanket cover. She had snatched the purse and rolled over to regain her feet when she heard the creak, like the report of a firing squad, outside the corridor door. On an elbow, hypnotized, she watched the doorknob turn. She was lost.

In that living instant of horror, a flash of recollection was illuminated out of her past: she had got into José's dingy flat in Greenwich Village, while he was playing with the band uptown, to rummage through his effects and find out if he had left a wife down in Puerto Rico. She was still on marijuana, and insanely jealous, and would not have an affair or marriage with a bigamist, and she would not take his word. She had heard his footsteps on the wooden boards outside, the key rattling in the unlocked door, and she had been trapped. She had thrown herself on his mattress, sprawled and in disarray, and pretended sleep. Thus he had found her, the first time in his room, and had accepted the fact that she had got drunk in the saloon downstairs waiting for him, and come up to sleep it off. It had deceived him completely, poor bewildered primitive, and she had blotted out his suspicions by giving herself to him. They had eloped the next day, the silly annulled episode, but the point was, he had not found out why she had been there, because of her cleverness. Had he found out, he would have cut her throat. He had been a nut, like herself in those sick days, and he would consent to any degradation except question of his word, his only wealth of pride.

The memory passed through her mind with the speed of enlightenment.

Her gaze remained riveted to the doorknob. It had turned once, yet the door had not opened. She heard Dilman's voice call out something to his valet. Still the door did not open, as she heard the distant reply from Beecher.

Could she lift herself off the bed, retrieve her now fallen evening shoe, reach the second door, get through it and close it, before the President came inside? Maybe. She started to sit up, then saw the door beginning to open, and more clearly heard Dilman wearily relate the last of some instruction for the morning to his valet.

Too late.

Breath locked in her lungs, she kicked off her other pump, lifted her legs high, and rolled to the middle of the bed. Her hair was mussed, which was all right, and one of the thin straps that held up her green bodice had slipped loosely down her arm, and the skirt of her cocktail dress, a part of it, she knew, had caught to the blanket in her falling back and rolling, so that her garters and a portion of one thigh were exposed. She did not know which to cover first, her thigh or her lace brassière, but then she covered neither, for the door was opening and she must pretend sleep, pretend to have passed out, and this way she would look it. Besides, in this privacy, he wasn't a President or politician or any big shot at all, but just a poor, lonesome colored man who'd had no attractive woman around for weeks, and she was the best-looking female in the White House. Let him know, let him know. José had been diverted. The colored man would be diverted, too, diverted and flustered, and would not bother to reason and concern himself with why she was there. She'd make it, she was sure, confident now, if only the champagne didn't make her nauseated. She released her taut muscles, threw one arm out limply, so that her bodice dropped even farther and one spidery cup of the white brassière was almost fully revealed.

The door opened.

Her eyes closed tightly, and she tried to contain her breathing to the natural shallow breathing of sleep.

She waited for the exclamation from him, astonishment or harsh annoyance. Neither came. There was only the soft sounds of shoes rubbing on the carpet, of human movement, of a stifled yawn.

She eased one lid open to form a slit of vision. He filled the thin, long frame: his broad back was to her, his dinner jacket already removed, his white suspenders and dress shirt sharply contrasting with his thick growth of kinky inky hair. His stubby black hands were unfastening the white bow tie. He undid it, dropped it on the table, opened his collar. He began to turn, and knowing middle-aged men, she guessed what was next. He would make his way to the bed to sit, remove his shoes and socks, and stick his feet into comfortable bedroom slippers before settling down to read.

He had come around quickly, before she had closed her eye. For a second, she had the record of his petrified expression at discovering her: at once startled, at once confounded, at once agitated.

Her eyelid covered the slit. She feigned deep sleep, inhaling and exhaling through her mouth. She sensed, not heard, his advance toward her.

"Miss Watson—Miss Watson—"

She must seem to be too drunkenly unconscious to hear him. She breathed on, squirming slightly to her side in his direction.

"Miss Watson?"

Her bare arm felt the light touch of his blunt fingers,

and involuntarily the nerves beneath the skin jumped, but she remained inert. His fingers pressed into her arm, and then pulled at her arm, shaking her. The pretense was over. She must do what must be done well and speedily.

She opened her eyes slowly, dazed eyes, closed them, then suddenly opened them wide in a double take, and instinctively hunched her shoulders in a position of self-protection. Her hand went to her mouth. "What—what are you doing here? What—where am I?" She tried to make her voice disoriented, distraught.

He remained standing over her. "I'm afraid, Miss Watson, you fell fast asleep on my bed. You said before that you felt you'd had too much to drink, and you wanted to lie down. I don't know how you found your way up here, but—"

"Oh, heavens, did I? What an awful thing. I—I guess I wanted to find some out-of-the-way corner—I meant to lie down on the bed in the Rose Guest Room, but I—oh, I remember—I couldn't make it, that's it. I was going past here, and I felt suddenly ill, and your bathroom was the nearest, and after that I simply collapsed on the first thing I saw. I'm afraid I've made a spectacle of myself. I'm sorry."

"Not a bit. It happens sometime or other to everyone. It's just that—" His Adams apple bobbed up and down, and he smiled weakly. "If I had come in with someone, it could have been embarrassing for both of us. Of course, it's ridiculous—"

She had not moved, lying there, her eyes on his Adam's apple and his nervous fingers. She could see his gaze go helplessly from her naked thigh between the bunched hemline and the upper sheath of her silk stocking, to fix once more on the protrusion of her brassière cup. "I don't know what to say," she found herself saying. "What you must think of me. I'm ashamed. I hope you won't hold this against me, I mean, against my keeping the job."

He swallowed, and tried to chuckle. "Hardly," he said. "What I should do is offer you a drink, or something, to get you on your feet. But I think you've had quite enough. What I will do is send you right home in a White House car, Miss Watson."

"Thank you, Mr. President, thank you so much. You're very kind." She came up on an elbow, and then groaned, even as she forced a smile, groaned and touched her brow, to give validity to her having passed out. "Ouch. I have a cage of buzzards in my head."

He was instantly solicitous. "If you don't think you can make it, I'll have Mrs. Crail find you a room on the third floor."

"Oh no, not that, Mr. President. Mrs. Crail? She'd have me branded Hester Prynne——S for scarlet sinner ——in ten seconds flat. I can make it under my own steam. I'm grateful to you."

She began to sit up, and as she did, Dilman started to turn away. "I'll step out while you fix yourself."

"Oh," she gasped, pretending to see for the first time her dropped bodice and revealed thigh. "Heavens, what a sight. Don't leave——I'll be out in a second."

In a rapid motion, knowing she had survived the ordeal, eager to escape, she swung off the bed. As she did so, her hip struck the bulging evening purse on the edge of the bed, and the purse hurtled to the floor, hit hard, burst open, and spilled its contents widely over the figured rug.

She was momentarily horrified by what lay strewn about the rug, not her lipstick and compact, not her handkerchief and keys, but the bent index cards filled mainly with her clear writing, everywhere. She wanted to throw herself across them, hide them, gather them, but it was too late.

Out of automatic gallantry, Dilman had crouched, gone down to one knee, retrieving her beaded purse, returning to it the lipstick and compact, the handkerchief and keys, and now he began to pick up the scattered index cards.

"I—I'll—please let me—don't bother——" she cried out, yet she was unable to move from her sitting position on the bed.

He had gathered some of the cards, but the frantic pitch in her voice made him glance at her with surprise, and then, almost as a reflex, down at the uppermost card in his hand.

"It's nothing—" she gasped out.

He stared down at the index card, ignoring her, while his free hand groped for the rest of the cards on the floor. He placed these on the others, and stared at the new top card, which was also crammed with writing. He rose silently, leaving the purse on the floor, blinking at the cards in his hand.

She could not see his full face; it was averted from her, lowered over the cards. She crossed her arms, dug her nails into her flesh to make the trembling cease. There was nowhere to hide, nowhere to go, no way to brazen it out. She wanted to die, but could only wait for the first blow.

His voice, issuing from the lips and face not fully visible to her, was surprisingly controlled, level, though chillingly soft and restrained. "You *have* embarrassed both of us, Miss Watson—you have."

"Don't believe—it doesn't mean what you—"

"It's my own fault, of course." His Negro modulation, the slurred vowels, had become more pronounced. "I should have known there is no one to be trusted. I should not have breached security by leaving my briefcase unlocked. Yet, I suppose I felt that my bedroom was—my own."

The blood and drinks had coursed to her head, and the room rocked, and she felt palsied by insane desperation and recklessness. "Believe what you want—but try to believe me—I swear it on the Bible—I was drunk—I came in here to—to use the bathroom, and then lie down —I bumped into your briefcase—and something was sticking out—I figured it couldn't be important if it was sticking out—so I took it to read, to help me nap—I read only a few pages—then I started copying a few things because—because—you want the truth? I want to write a book about you one day, about being your social secretary, and I wanted these notes as inside stuff to put in my diary, to remember years from now when there'd be no security involved—I swear—it was just something that—that happened on the spur of the moment—believe me—"

He turned toward her at last. She expected his features to be hardened into anger. She resented that they were only pitying, like those of a father listening to his daughter recount an improbable fib. "I see, Miss Watson. Do you mean to say that you're in the habit of always packing note cards in your evening purse?"

"No—no, of course not. I was taking those home from my office. I'd picked them up just before dinner, to use before coming to work in the morning."

He had moved closer to her, and was staring down at her now. "Or did Arthur Eaton put them in your purse, Miss Watson? Was that why you came here? For him?"

She tried to summon up indignation. "Eaton? What ever has he got to do with it? Why would I come here for him?"

"It's all over Washington, Miss Watson. I don't listen to gossip, but everyone seems to know about you and Eaton."

"Filthy troublemakers!" She was truly angry at last. "Filthy, dirty tongues. How dare they!" She was panting, but tried to be as controlled as he. "What would I have to do with that old man? I have my own crowd. Besides—how can you? He's married, he has a wife. I know him only socially, because he's an old-time friend of Daddy's, and—"

Dilman's expression remained placid. "And he would like my job. In fact, as you now know, he has been trying to do my job, just as you have been trying to do Mrs. Eaton's job. Very well. Now you can go to him and tell him I know." He stepped forward to hand her the index cards, and his knee touched hers, and the contact, the proximity of him, his lack of anger, gave her a last made surge of hope.

"No," she said, refusing the cards, "I wouldn't do that to you. I think too much of you."

He lowered the cards to drop them into her lap, eyes avoiding her eyes and the exposed brassière. With a sob, Sally clutched both his arms, not allowing him to turn away and leave her.

Dilman made no resistance. "Let go of me, Miss Watson."

"No," she sobbed. "Listen—all right—I'll tell you the truth—all right, you're forcing me to—it's terrible—but I'll tell you. I—I didn't come here to lie down, or for anyone else, but just for you, to be with you awhile alone and talk to you. I deliberately came here to wait, and became lonesome, and poked around—looking at your work—it has moved me, the way you work so hard, and nobody understands you except a few of us, like myself—and the cards, the notes, I did take them to keep busy, for my diary, honestly—that's what it was. I'm not ashamed, I wanted to be alone with you, to tell you I understand what you go through, that you have a friend in me who—"

Forcibly, he removed his arms from her grasp. "Miss Watson, I suggest you leave here at once."

"No, listen—" She believed it now. Who had known Secretary of the Treasury Hamilton as well as Mrs. Maria Reynolds? President Cleveland as well as Mrs. Maria Halpin? President Harding as well as Miss Nan Britton? She believed those stories as much as she believed in herself, now and here, and in what was possible. If she were to lose Arthur because of her failure, she might still have more than any woman on earth. Casting the index cards aside, she leaped to her feet, and the room went topsy-turvy, and she almost collapsed, grabbing Dilman's arms, holding herself erect. She knew she was drunk, but she knew what she wanted. "—listen—I do care for you. I want to help you. Don't you—don't you want to know me better?"

She had pulled close to him confidently, knowing the offer of her flesh had never failed her before. She waited for his concession to the inevitable, his embrace, and their friendship.

"Miss Watson, get out of here."

Her hands released him, and she recoiled, looking at him with disbelief. For the first time, his face was set in pure black anger.

There was one thing left. She'd had her elementary school in Negroes. She knew them too well. "You're afraid of me, that's all," she heard herself say. "You're afraid of getting in trouble because I'm white, Southern white, and somebody, and you're colored. Don't—don't be that way. I've known plenty of Negro men. I consider them to be like—like anybody else—and when they get to know me, they appreciate me. Now you know, so—"

She halted, frightened by the way his red-rimmed eyes protruded and blazed at her.

"You're a drunken, silly, sick young lady," he said. "You get out of here, and you stay out of here, and never show your face in this house again."

As her self-assurance faded, her face became contorted by humiliation and rage. "You—*you* throwing *me* out—?"

He turned his back to her, picked up her purse, took the index cards from the bed, fitted them into the purse, and placed the bag in her hand. "I'm throwing you out, Miss Watson. I'm sure Mr. Eaton will take you in."

She glared at him, reeled past him to the door, held the knob, and over her shoulder considered him contemptuously. "You hypocritical pig," she cried shrilly. "You —with that nigger girl you've got stashed away—I *know* —I'm not forgetting—no low nigger is going to insult me. You're damn right I'm going to Arthur Eaton. He won't be forgetting either. . . . Enjoy this house while you can, because, mister, your lease is running out, and from now on we want only gentlemen on the premises, nothing lower—you hear? No more of your indecent kind, only two-legged beings, you hypocrite!"

Reluctantly Arthur Eaton reopened the concealed wall bar of his Tudor living room and took down the bottles and glasses. He prepared a Jack Daniel's, with water, for Senator Bruce Hankins, and poured a generous amount of sweet liqueur from the Grand Marnier decanter for Representative Zeke Miller. Behind him, he knew that the elderly Hankins had settled on the sofa across from Wayne Talley, while Miller remained on his feet, spread-legged, in the pose of a public speaker impatient to begin a harangue. Talley, Eaton had observed, still had two-thirds of his Seagram's whisky, and required no refill.

About to take the two drinks to his recently arrived guests, Eaton, who had not been drinking, reconsidered his own need. The sight of the newcomers definitely left him with a bad taste in his mouth. To remove this taste, a counter-potion was required. Eaton studied the two rows of bottles on the shelves of his bar, brought down the Remy Martin cognac and an amber-tinted snifter that Kay had long ago purchased in Vienna, and he covered the bottom of the glass with the cognac.

His eye caught the Roman numerals of the early English lantern clock on the mantelpiece of the fireplace. It was twenty-three minutes after eleven, too late for this, and too late for Sally Watson. When Talley had come over, after dinner, they had quietly reviewed the entire Baraza situation, from start to the present, as well as the withholding of the single CIA warning from Dilman. They had justified their act, one to the other, and Talley had been reassuring about the safety of their position. Sally's precious news that Dilman had found out, or at least suspected what they had done, had been useful in alerting them to possible trouble. However, more important would be the degree to which Dilman could confirm, through the Director of CIA, exactly what they had withheld. If Scott was uncooperative or vague, Dilman would have no evidence with which to endanger the peace of the country. (If new evidence came—better, worse— the problem could then be handled by them openly.) On the other hand, if Scott had been informative and explicit this afternoon, Dilman might be foolhardy enough to act both against Talley and himself, and against the Russians, and the rift in foreign policy would have to be taken to the public—T.C.'s public still, he trusted.

Eaton had hinted to Talley that Miss Watson had indicated she had means of learning what had transpired between the President and Montgomery Scott. Also, she had indicated that she might have the information for them this evening. Fortunately, Talley, who was anything but well-bred, had accepted this with delicacy. He had not questioned why Miss Watson should trouble to help Eaton, or, indeed, what her relationship was with Eaton. Of course, Eaton guessed, Talley knew about Sally Watson and himself. Eaton was never one to indulge in self-deception. There were few personal secrets anywhere between Foggy Bottom and the Hill. Yet, to Talley's credit, he had behaved like a gentleman, an unnatural behavior no doubt induced by Talley's realization that his own future was insecure and entirely linked with Eaton's future.

Without discussing it further, they had waited, both of them, for Sally Watson's telephone call. At eleven o'clock, when they were discouraged and had talked themselves out, the telephone had finally rung. Hopefully, Eaton had answered it, only to find that the caller was not Sally but Representative Zeke Miller. If Eaton had not known of Miller's temperance, he would have thought him intoxicated, so excited and unrestrained had been his outpouring.

"Remember, Arthur, how I was telling you, after that there Nigra vetoed the minorities bill, that we were setting out to put him in a kennel where he belongs? Well, Arthur, we were dibble-dabbling here and there, digging up a case or two, when tonight we cracked it wide open. Yayss sir, my friend, cracked it open with a Jim Crowbar." Miller had cackled with glee over the telephone. "We were having a caucus, five or six of us on the Hill, me and Bruce Hankins presiding, when this certain information about our Nigra President fell plumb in our laps, came right to us, dropped down in our laps like manna from the sky. Yayss sir. This is it, Arthur, and me and Bruce are scooting right over to Georgetown to share our intelligence with you in person."

Eaton had meant to protest that he was expecting someone else, but then he decided that Sally would not be heard from tonight. Still, he was in no humor for Miller's white-supremacy pipe dreams. "Zeke, I appreciate this, but it is terribly late. If this is some idea or plan of yours, can't it wait until tomorrow?" Yet, considering the precariousness of his own position with Dilman, he had been unable not to leave the door slightly open to a possible ally. "Of course, Zeke, if you are not being carried away by wishful thinking, if you have some information that is vital—"

"Vital and factual!" Miller had shouted. "Important enough to make our Nigra tender his resignation, and to make you, as next in line, the President of the United States."

Eaton had winced at the bluntness of the last. Nevertheless, it had been useless to resist further. "Very well. You and the Senator come right over. I have Governor Talley with me."

"All the better. See you in a jiffy."

And now they were here in his living room, awaiting his full attention. Wondering what was so "vital and factual," Arthur Eaton carried the lacquer tray of drinks to the sofa. He held the tray out to Senator Hankins, and followed the elderly lawmaker's horny hand as it took the Jack Daniel's and brought it up to his pickerel face. Eaton did not know Hankins intimately, but only as a thirty-year public legend on the Hill who had been at once a thorn in T.C.'s side in matters of domestic legislation and an asset to T.C. and Eaton himself in matters of foreign policy.

Hankins wore a wavy gray toupee, so cheap that the hairpiece appeared pasted on with schoolboy's glue. His ancient sad eyes, moist nostrils, flaccid puckered lips were surrounded by curlicues of deep wrinkles. The broad black silk ribbon to which his pince-nez was attached dangled from under his high starched collar. Unlike the younger Zeke Miller, he was not vocal. He was a senior citizen given to long silences and grave nods, which had conferred upon him the mistaken reputation of having wisdom. Since he had a son and grandson serving the government abroad, and because he enjoyed Congressional junkets to London, Madrid, Tokyo, he had come to consider himself a specialist on international affairs. He led foreign-aid programs and treaty agreements and was pleased to read often that he was a progressive Southerner. Where he was not progressive, however, was in his attitude toward the Negroes in his state and in the Black Belt beneath the Mason-Dixon line.

For Senator Hankins, the elevation of Douglass Dilman to the nation's highest seat had been a trauma that would have been comparable only to seeing General William Tecumseh Sherman ascending to the Presidency of the Confederacy. To Hankins, the nigger President was beneath human contempt, an abomination and eyesore on once-beautiful America.

Yet, until now, he had not led his colleagues in the fight against Dilman. It was as if he would not dignify Dilman's position by voicing his disgust. He permitted the yeasty young Miller to lead the Christian forces, letting it be known that he was in his palace, ready, available to come down into the field to administer the final coup.

"Well, Mr. Secretary," he said now to Eaton, after gingerly tasting, then relishing, his Jack Daniel's, "looks like you been to Tennessee to oversee the proper distilling of this celebrating libation."

"You feel we have something to celebrate, Senator?" Eaton asked, as he took the tray to Zeke Miller.

Senator Hankins nodded. "As I was relating to Governor Talley, I'm a mighty cautious old coot, Mr. Secretary. These eyes of mine and ears of mine have seen and heard too much fable to be unwary of those bearing good tidings. But what I witnessed and heard a few hours back gives me hope we will be able soon to see the last of our nigger tenant on Pennsylvania Avenue, and restore prideful Christian government to this land of the Founding Fathers. Zeke there, he'll tell you what is in our possession, and like ourselves, you will sleep easier tonight. . . . Tell the Secretary, Zeke. Tell him and the Governor."

"Well, goldarnit, Senator Bruce," Miller said, "I've only been waiting for Secretary Eaton's undivided attention, like not wanting to open a Christmas present till everyone's all assembled round the tree."

Miller had taken the liqueur glass, and without tasting it had immediately put it down on the coffee table. His lipless mouth curled apologetically at Eaton as he slicked his bald spot. His wiry frame appeared to dance with eagerness and restlessness, although he remained stationary on his spread legs.

Dismayed by this unattractive pair, yet increasingly curious as to what they had learned, Eaton set the tray down, retaining his cognac, and then sank into the sofa beside Talley, opposite Hankins.

"I am quite ready for you now, Zeke," said Eaton.

Talley bent forward and pleaded, "Make it good, Zeke. For the country's sake, we need something to control our—our President."

Zeke Miller's thin nostrils jumped, and he grinned, baring his yellow teeth. "This is no lasso we found, to tie our Nigra down. This here is a regular blowtorch we got, to singe his black behind and send him hightailing back where he come from."

"Tell them, tell them," Senator Hankins grunted, "before my kidneys give out. This isn't the House Chamber, Zeke. Make it short and sweet and *factual*."

Zeke Miller moved a few feet nearer to Eaton. "While I deplored, much as you, that assassination attempt, it gave us a clear mandate to proceed against Dilman. It showed us he not only has no white support—South, North, East, West, except for a handful of liberal-Commie punks and bleeding hearts—but he's got none of his brethren Nigras behind him neither. So Senator Bruce here and I, and the party leaders both sides of the aisles, been yakking around, casting about, then meeting to see what we'd come up with. Till tonight, not much. We had some information he might be locked into the Crispus Society, giving his pal Spinger and those law-spouting darkies certain advantages over the rest of us. I've had my legal beagle, Casper Wine, looking back into some of Dilman's old court cases for possibilities of unethical practices, and checking back into his campaigns and elections to find out if there's anything that smells fishy-like. Sooner or later, I figured we'd come up with something concrete to hold over his head, and make him resign like he should. Then, the way Senator Bruce says, tonight the facts fell right plunk in our lap."

"God sake, boy, quit being garrulous," said Senator Hankins testily. "Tell them, boy, tell them."

Irritated at the prodding, Miller snapped, "I'll tell

them in my way." He yanked out his maroon handkerchief, honked into it, returned the handkerchief to his hip pocket, and looked squarely at Eaton and Talley. "Ever hear of a lad named George Murdock, gentlemen?"

Talley said, "The reporter? Yeh, he's Miss Foster's boy friend."

"Right and o," said Miller. "And who is Miss Foster but Dilman's private and confidential white secretary, yes? Okay. So one night not so far back, the two of them are dating, real cozy, and Murdock proposes marriage, and Miss Foster, who's an old maid, like comes apart, gets plastered with booze in her joy, and begins to spill the goods on our Black Mose in the White House. Hold your hats, Arthur, Governor, but here's the goods." He paused dramatically, grinning. "Fact one. Dilman's got a daughter in New York passing for white—hear that? —the President's daughter deceiving, subterfuging, passing for pure Aryan white, and she with blood black as ink in her veins. Fact two. Dilman's got that scrawny son up at the Nigra school in Trafford—and you know what?—the President's son was and is a bona fide, one hundred and one per cent, all-out, scummy underground member of the Commie Turnerite Group. Fact three. Dilman's wife died of booze, and he was an alcoholic with her, and spent time drying out once in a drunk tank of a sanitarium with her, and there's evidence he's a boozer now, which can best explain some of his behavior since—"

Eaton's original astonishment on hearing these charges was now replaced by doubt. The accusations that Zeke Miller was announcing sounded as intemperate as the conduct of the one who conveyed them. Eaton came out of his slouched posture, sitting erect as he interrupted the Congressman. "One second, Zeke. That is almost too much to believe. No one, I am sure, has a spotless background or life, not you, not I, and quite possibly Dilman has his shortcomings and made some errors in the past. But until now, if he had nothing else, Dilman, at least when he was a senator, had a reputation for sobriety and commonplace decency. Now you would have us believe—"

"Let me finish," Miller interrupted.

"Wait, you allow me to finish," Eaton said. "Suddenly, overnight, you are painting him as a secret drunkard, as a bad family man and a discredit to his race, as a Negro in public life who would permit his daughter—if there is a daughter—to pretend that she is white, condone her deception and disavowal of him and of her heritage, as a father who would let his son, utterly dependent economically on his favor, be a secret terrorist. Zeke, I—"

"You're doggone right his son's a terrorist," said Miller indignantly. "Why else do you think Dilman thwarted the Attorney General, stalled on banning the Turnerites, until one of them murdered a good and decent helpless judge? Dilman's more responsible for Judge Gage's murder than that ape Hurley—and the public will say so, too, once the facts are out."

"My God, these facts could change—" Talley had begun.

Eaton's hand silenced Talley. Eaton fixed his gaze on Miller. "Facts," he said. "Facts depend on sources. What are your sources, besides some unknown reporter who is used to contriving stories for his keep, and a foolish secretary full of liquor? You'll have to do better than that, Zeke."

"I can do better than that!" Miller said angrily. "Give me a chance and you won't be questioning me no more. The source for all these facts is Douglass Dilman himself, in person, no other. Miss Foster monitors most of his calls, as she did with T.C. Once, or a couple of times, Dilman forgot to tell her not to monitor, and she listened in to him talking to his son. That's how she found out about that daughter, Mindy, passing for white, and about his wife and him being in that Springfield sanitarium for drunks. Miss Foster's no maker-upper. She's even got it all set down in black and white in a diary, believe it or not. Drunk or sober, it's there in writing for us to demand, if we need it."

Eaton continued to frown. "And what about that Turnerite nonsense?"

Miller's wiry frame danced again. His veiny nostrils quivered. "Okay, now the rest of it. . . . Look, Arthur, I'm not ready to give credence to just any old defamation or garbage that comes my way. I want proof, good proof, too. When Reb Blaser brought this Murdock kid to me tonight, and said, 'Congressman, this is the reporter fellow you wanted me to keep an eye on, and now he's come up with a zinger of a story he wants to sell you,' I heard Murdock out, and was about as downright skeptical as you and maybe the Governor are now. But when he finished the whole thing, and then backed it up for me, I was ready to buy. I said to Murdock, 'Okay, kid, what's your price?' He said, 'A permanent editorial job on your Washington paper, starting $200 a week, and going up, with a contract for five years.' Know what, Arthur? I said, 'Murdock, you're too smart not to be in our camp. You're hired. We sign and seal the deal on Monday.' That's what I think of his evidence."

Senator Hankins had a fit of coughing, hacking and wheezing, and Miller quickly moved to help him with his drink. When Hankins recovered, he sputtered, "Thanks, boy, but damnations, tell them the whole of it."

Eaton waited, sipping his cognac, trying to assess the possible accuracy of what he had already heard, and the value of these revelations to all of them if the evidence could be proved. He heard Miller blowing his nose, and he looked up. "Is there more?" he demanded.

"When this George Murdock got this information from Miss Foster, who got it from Dilman himself, he kept his head. That's what impressed me about the lad. He didn't come to me or anyone else half-cocked. If he had, we'd probably have thrown him out. No. Smart kid. He went out on his own, to verify what his girl friend told him. He went to New York last week and just came back today. Know what he did in New York? Listen. He'd remembered the two names Dilman's daughter had— her real nigger name, and her phony white name. Her nigger name is Mindy Dilman, and her white name is Linda Dawson—how do you like that? Linda Dawson, ever hear anything whiter? So Murdock looked her up, and went calling on her, and right off rocked her back on her heels, greeting her with 'Hi there, Mindy.' That nigger-white girl sure let him in fast. I won't go into details now, except Murdock said she was practically white, sure enough, and a looker, a good-looker, but sarcastic and mean, and twisting and squirming away from what he knew. But, tough as she was, she finally caved in and confessed it. Then she started fussing and weeping. If Murdock let it out, she kept saying, her life was ruined. Said she'd been white since being grown up. Said she had a white boy friend who was with a brokerage house in Wall Street, and they were almost engaged, and all her friends were white, and this was the end of everything. Said why did anyone pick on her, when she only wanted to be lost and did no harm to anyone, least not like her brother Julian, with his rotten Nigra friends and his Turnerite hoodlums. Well, now, Arthur, you bet our Mr. Murdock pricked up his ear high as a radar beacon."

Eaton contemplated the cognac, warming in his palm, and the terrible scene provoked by that unsavory Murdock in a New York apartment, a scene he found unbearable and which Zeke Miller apparently relished. Eaton said, "You mean that girl informed on her brother?"

"You're goldarn right she did," said Miller, "because she hates him like she hates her father, our biggety Nigra President. Anyway, Murdock wanted to know if she could prove her brother was a Turnerite. She said sure she could, and she would, but only if she had to. She told Murdock if he wanted to know more, go and talk to Julian personally. So Murdock rode out to Trafford, cornered our President's son, and accused him of the Turnerite membership. Julian got sullen, then downright nasty, and said it was a lie to hurt his father, and he was never a Turnerite in his life, and Murdock couldn't prove it, and his sister couldn't prove it, and besides she was a psychopathic liar, and so forth. So our kid reporter, Murdock, he hotfooted it back to New York and got to Mindy again, and said she was a liar, because Julian said so and had denied everything. Mindy was pretty keyed up that day, I mean on some kind of pills or something, and she got pretty hysterical against her brother. She went and dug out some letters, and held them while Murdock read them. They were from Julian, and the first one, with the oldest date, was full of resentment about being stuck in the Nigra school, and his father being too yellow to act for the Nigra race, and Mindy turning her back on her people, but he was going to be different, the one in the family who wasn't yellow, because he was planning to join up secretly with a new outfit called the Turnerites who were going to give all Nigras equality. Well, there it was. In the other letters, written later, when he was involved with Hurley and learned his membership was supposed to be secret, I guess, he wrote his sister he'd been kidding, and denied ever joining, but he wasn't kidding. There it was in writing. Is that proof, Arthur, or is it not?"

Eaton put down his empty cognac glass. "Can you get that first letter?" he asked.

Miller grinned. "I got it, my friend."

"You have? How?"

"Mindy agreed to turn it over to Murdock for his written and signed pledge that he would never disclose her identity, that he would leave her alone, leave her keep passing, so's she can give some poor white Christian young fellow her nigger blood in a coon baby. Murdock gave me the letter, and all his statements are to be made into affidavits tomorrow, on the condition that Mindy's passing not be exposed and his fiancée, Miss Foster, and her diary with the facts, not be dragged into this in any way." Miller paused, and added solemnly, "I gave the lad my word, and I gave him the job. And now we got the goods on our biggety Nigra President."

Senator Hankins coughed and wheezed. "Mighty powerful case, gentlemen."

Talley echoed, "Mighty powerful case."

"For what?" asked Arthur Eaton. He stood up, and went to find a cigarette. Not bothering about his holder, he lifted a silver table lighter before him as he said to Miller, "What do you intend to do with all that—that research?"

Zeke Miller opened his hands and raised his shoulders. "Simple. I intend to go—or have you and the Gov-

ernor go—straight to our beloved President Dilman and
say, Mister, you're here ruining the country, and we're
here with our minds made up to save the country. The
way for you to help us save the country, Mr. President,
is for you to become incapacitated and be forced to resign because of ill health—maybe you been pretty sick
since that assassin almost got you—maybe you got a
heart condition and it's been kept hushed, but now your
family physicians say you can't go on—so you resign because of disability, for the sake of the country, and the
Party, and your health, and let the next in line, namely,
our able Secretary of State and close friend of T.C., Mr.
Arthur Eaton, become President for the rest of this term.
If you won't resign, Mr. President, we got to tell the
country the truth about your son being a Commie Turnerite, and you condoning it and giving those subver-
sives aid and comfort, and we got to tell about your
wife's death, and your past, your unreliability because
you're a drinking tosspot of a Nigra, and we got to tell
your own people how you're so ashamed of being a nigger you encouraged your daughter to pass deceitfully
for a white girl. Now, what'll that do for you and your
family, Mr. President, all that coming out? So for reasons of your health, you better resign."

"Impressive," said Eaton with irony.

"You betcha," said Miller, pleased.

Suddenly Eaton ground out his cigarette and said,
"And what if Dilman refuses to quit?"

"Aw, Arthur, cripes, you know he'll shrink up and
have to."

"American Presidents don't resign," said Eaton flatly.
"Not a single one ever has, not even Woodrow Wilson
when he was bedridden by a stroke. They die. They are
killed. They become ill, even incapacitated, but they do
not resign. And Vice-Presidents, they're the same. Only
one ever resigned, Jackson's Vice-President, John C.
Calhoun, and that was with only two months to go and
he had already been elected to the Senate, and that was
as far back as 1832." Eaton shook his head. "No, I'm
afraid President Dilman might not fold up and quit. He
might prefer to have you expose him, suffer his family

to go down the drain, rather than give in to your pressure. Have you allowed for that?"

Before Miller could reply, Senator Hankins snorted and trembled on the sofa, as he raised his hand. "I allowed for it, Mr. Secretary. Actually, so did Zeke. We talked about it with our friends before coming here. We decided this. If that nigger won't leave the White House on his two feet, then we'll carry him out."

Eaton contracted his brow. "Carry him out?"

"Remove him, sir, remove him by force," said Senator Hankins. "Your Constitution, young man—never forget your Constitution. Article II, Section 4. 'The President . . . of the United States shall be removed from office on impeachment for and conviction of treason, bribery, or other high crimes and misdemeanors.' The law of the Founding Fathers, young man."

Arthur Eaton tried to maintain his poise, but he was deeply shaken. He stood still, eyes averted, staring at the carpet. He had never before, not until this moment, heard the monstrous word *impeachment* used in this way by men elected to high offices of responsibility. He had heard it employed in gossip, he had read it in the columns of the lurid tabloid press, but he had not heard it used by members of the United States Congress. It was as impossible an American word to him as *secession* or *revolution* or *assassination*. All of his background and breeding—his intelligence, his faith in orderly settlement of any crisis, his belief in the give and take of gentlemanly compromise—was offended by this word.

"That's right," he heard Miller saying, "if Dilman won't get out, we'll evict him out under due process of law."

"Gentlemen," Eaton said, "I find even consideration of such a solution repugnant. I think such a solution could do the country as much injury, in these times, as Dilman's own bumbling. Even if I stand to gain by the outcome, I'm afraid I could not support you in such a drastic act."

"But the Constitution—" Miller said.

"The Founding Fathers, riding to their meetings in horse-drawn carriages, creating the Constitution with their quill pens, could not have anticipated what every article of it would mean in a nuclear age, with Communists in front of us, with racial strife behind us," said Eaton. "No, impeachment would be dangerous. Jefferson said it was merely a 'scarecrow' in the Constitution, presumably not to be used except as a scarecrow. But Jefferson aside, and given real cause to use impeachment powers, and even if it could be managed quickly and safely, I do not believe that Dilman would merit removal, at least not on the evidence you have at hand. What you possess is criticism of the character of a man in high office, what you have is scandal, but that is not evidence of treason, bribery, or high crimes against his country."

Miller pounced forward, confronting Eaton. "It can all be made to add up to treason and unfitness for office," he insisted.

"I have strong doubts," said Eaton.

"Anyway, we don't have to prove that much," said Miller. He turned to Hankins. "Senator Bruce, you got that—"

"Got it right here handy," said Hankins, holding up the photocopy of a book page. He adjusted his pince-nez, studied the photocopy briefly, then looked up at Eaton. "There's no precise exact definition of impeachment crimes, Mr. Secretary. Fact is, it's a pretty wide umbrella, and our evidence fits under a fair amount of it. Example, this little definition of impeachment I have here. George T. Curtis, the historian-attorney, made it back in 1889. He said"—Hankins read from the photocopy—" 'A cause for removal from office may exist where no offense against positive law has been committed, as where the individual has, from immorality, or imbecility, or maladministration, become unfit to exercise the office.' "

"See!" Zeke Miller exclaimed triumphantly to Eaton. "Like it's tailor-made for Dilman."

"Nevertheless, I have my doubts," said Eaton.

"Well," Talley called out, "I think we're barking up the wrong tree, and wasting our breath. It'll never come to anything so serious. Arthur, I'm inclined to side with

Zeke and the Senator on what'll really happen. If they pull together what authentic findings they already have, and hit Dilman smack between the eyes with them, I think he's got to back off. I think he'll run up the white flag and call it quits."

Eaton bit his lip. "I wish I could be as confident as the three of you. I can't be. I believe you have enough evidence right now to hold over the President's head, and make him reconsider any further rash and self-serving behavior. I believe you can slow him down, and force him to listen to our advice. I think you can manage that, and more power to you. But, I reiterate, I do not believe you have enough evidence to impeach, and, I repeat, I doubt that you even have enough to frighten him out of office." Eaton shrugged. "This is my opinion. You do what you will. I feel it only fair to say that if you take more drastic steps, based on what you have, I cannot let myself go along with you." He saw their unsmiling faces, and he said, as lightly as possible, "But I will go along with you for one more drink, before we—"

The doorbell chimes melodiously interrupted him. Puzzled, he looked at the clock over the fireplace. It showed ten minutes before midnight. The chimes played again, followed by the metallic hammering of the brass door knocker.

"Who can it be?" Talley wondered.

"I'll see," said Eaton. "Excuse me, gentlemen. The Governor will pour you one for the road."

He left the living room, went into the high-ceilinged entry hall, and pulled open the door.

Sally Watson stood there, one hand clutching the doorframe. Eaton had never before seen her this way, in this condition, and for a moment he was taken aback.

"That's right," she said thickly, "it's me, or whatever's left of me, believe it or not."

"My God, Sally, come in."

He reached out and drew her into the hall, examining her with disbelief. Her blond hair was in disarray, and strands of it hung down over her eyes. Her mascara had run, and there were tear streaks along her cheeks. The bodice of her green cocktail gown was half on, half off, one strap torn loose, the front of the dress ripped, so that part of her brassière was in view.

She covered her bosom with the coat on her arm, and looked up at him. "Quit staring, Arthur. It's not my fault. Blame him. He did it to me, the sonofabitch, blame him."

"Who?"

"Who do you think?" she said angrily. She had worked the index cards out of her purse. "Here's what you wanted. I promised you I'd get it, and I got it. I did that anyway. Lemme get cleaned up and I'll tell you plenty, that filthy bastard."

She started toward the living room, lurched off balance, and Eaton quickly grabbed her elbow. Then, taking the coat from her, he led her swiftly into the living room. With her appearance, Zeke Miller, who had just sat down, immediately leaped back on his feet, and Bruce Hankins rose with a grunt. They greeted her with courteous surprise, but Sally did not reply, only stared at them as she wobbled past.

"Miss Watson's been in some trouble," Eaton explained. "I want her to lie down. Be right with you."

Talley had wheeled around at the bar, and his eyes followed Sally with incredulity. "What the devil happened?" he wanted to know.

"Your goddam drunk President," she said viciously. "He did it—he thought I was like all the rest of his chippies!"

Eaton's expression was pained. "Please, Sally." He shoved the index cards at Talley. "Here. The notes on Dilman's CIA meeting with Scott. Better read them." He hustled Sally out of the living room, but not before he heard Zeke Miller shout, "Hey! Wait a sec—what was that she was saying?"

With difficulty, trying to steady her, Eaton hurried Sally through the corridor. He knew that she could not make the stairway to the upper bedrooms. Instead, he guided her into the book-lined library, one hand supporting her, the other slamming the door behind him.

"There's the bathroom," he said.

"I changed my mind," she said.

He studied her face and could see she was not only

intoxicated but on the verge of hysteria. He forced her to the sofa. "Then lie down for a moment."

She sat on the sofa, and dropped her face into her hands. "I don't want to lie down. I want to kill that bastard."

"I think you need something to settle your nerves," said Eaton anxiously. He rushed into the bathroom, turned on the light, and hunted for Kay's tranquilizers. He found the container, spilled out two, prepared a glass of water, and returned to Sally. "Take both of them."

She obeyed him.

"Good," he said, "now the water."

She took one swallow, made a show of distaste, and pushed the tumbler back at him. "I've had enough to drink."

Eaton set the glass aside, knelt before her, and considered her. "Do you think you need a doctor?"

"What can a doctor do for me? It's all inside, what he did, humiliating me like one of his whores. If anybody knew——" She beat her fist helplessly on the sofa cushion.

Eaton rose and sat on the corner of the coffee table. "When you——you feel ready to speak of this, Sally, I'd like to hear what——"

"I'm ready now."

"Whenever you say."

"I was trying to figure out how to help you," she said excitedly, "and then I got the chance, because he invited me to his bedroom again——"

"Who? Dilman?"

"Not Calvin Coolidge, you bet. Of course, Dilman."

"What do you mean——he invited you *again*?"

"Jesus, Arthur, I can't always bring myself to tell you everything. He's had a lech for me, and at least three times before he's invited me to his bedroom in the evening, to go over social affairs, so he says——ha, social affairs. I always got out of it. But tonight, when he whispered it again, to meet him about some plans after the guests had gone, I saw a chance to help you, and I agreed. I went to his bedroom a little early, and the transcript of the meeting he had with Scott today was lying open, so I just read it, you know. Made those exact notes on the cards. You're lucky to have it—"

He found her hands. "Sally, darling, I am grateful, but I'm worried—"

She withdrew her hands, and brushed the hair from her eyes. "Well, about ten he came in—everyone had gone—and I could see he was plastered, drunk as a lord. I wanted to leave, but he insisted on business talk, and hell, you can't insult the President, I mean—how? He kept insisting I drink with him. What could I do? He must've poured me a triple, and himself, too, because I got real tipsy, and him, you should have seen him."

She kept shaking her head angrily, and Eaton said, "What does that mean, Sally?"

"I can't give you the details, it's too embarrassing, considering his position. But I guess those politicians are only human, like Harding and Nan Britton in the White House closet, but who'd expect this from a weaseling, hymn-singing black nigger who's lucky he's alive, let alone President? Sure, he came after me, and I fought him, weak as I was, and he even got me on the bed, desecrated that bed, tried to rip off my dress—look at it— but I got away—oh, we had a scene, what a scene—"

"Sally—Sally—wait a minute. Are you saying Dilman got you drunk and then—"

"You're damn right that's what I'm saying."

"But—Sally—there was a dinner party there tonight. Surely you had something to drink on your own first?"

She was silent for a moment, staring at him warily. "Suppose I did? Who doesn't have one or two before dinner?"

"Did you have any more after dinner?"

"What do you mean, Arthur?" she said. "I told you —with him—he forced me—"

"Yes, of course. I meant, after you got away from him. If you saw him at ten—and let's say you left him an hour later—that still leaves almost an hour unaccounted for and I was wondering—"

She had become rigid. "I went to my office for my coat. If there'd been a gun there, I'd have shot him. I went downstairs. I was too agitated to drive my car. I walked up Pennsylvania Avenue. Then I decided to call you to pick me up. I went into the first place I came to, a bar. I was too upset even to call. So I decided to have a drink or two to steady my nerves, until I could get hold of myself. Then I took a cab——" Abruptly, she stopped, mouth compressed. "I don't like your expression. You think I'm lying. What are you, a prosecutor or something——?"

"Please, Sally. I'm simply questioning you because this is serious, and——"

"You're telling me I'm lying. I don't have to take that from you—you, of all people—the hell with that." She jumped to her feet, almost pitched forward, caught the coffee table, and straightened. "If you're not going to stand beside me, I know some people in the next room who will!"

Head held high, the rest of her tottering, she groped her way to the library door.

"Sally, come back here, don't be foolish——"

Without turning, only tossing her shoulders, she pulled the door open and left him.

Eaton was on his feet now, but he did not follow her. Her tawdry adventure was so bizarre—and improbable —that he needed a few minutes of solitude to turn it over in his mind.

He lit a cigarette, then paced the room thoughtfully. What weighed against the story was Sally herself, for he knew her character thoroughly. She drank. She drugged herself. She was unstable, given to exaggeration and flights of fancy. She had drawn a picture of Dilman that bore no resemblance to the stodgy, frightened Negro politician that he and everyone else knew. Yet, to balance the scale in his quest for the truth, what possible motivation could Sally have for making up in its entirety such a farfetched story? He could think of none, not one advantage to her in this, unless there was some semblance of truth in it and she wanted Dilman punished. Moreover, she was sexually attractive to men, as he well knew, and Dilman was alone, and just a few minutes earlier Miller had spoken of some evidence about Dilman's secret drinking.

Still, dammit, Eaton found the whole thing inconceivable. Whatever idiotic rumors of infidelity and adultery and lechery, fanned by political partisanship and the instinctive desire of all common people to bring the highups down low to their own level, whatever rumors surrounded the Presidency—and hardly any President in decades had escaped such malice—there was not one clear-cut shred of evidence that a single Chief Executive, while in office, had ever behaved as Sally had just accused President Dilman of behaving. No matter what the former habits of its chief tenant, the White House was simply not a seraglio, never had been, never would be, because it had glass walls. Or, perhaps, because its grandeur seemed to convert its chief resident from mere mortal into abstract symbol. This was true not only of the President, but of his Cabinet members and—and then, suddenly, with astonishment, Eaton realized that the wall of invincible virtue he was building around the Chief Executive and his Cabinet members was made of cards, and had collapsed.

What about himself? He was the Secretary of State of the United States, mentor of America's international destiny, next in line to the Presidency—and still, in the camouflage of night, he was mere mortal. How many times had he lain naked beside this beautiful young girl, who had been naked, too, and was not his wife?

Anything *was* possible.

There were no symbols for men, no matter how august and exposed their offices. There were only the men themselves.

He peered down at his wristwatch. Nearly ten minutes had gone by since Sally's angry departure from the library. He had best join her, and the others—Good Lord, the others!—and hear out the rest of her adventure, and do what he could to sift proven fact from alcoholic and neurotic invention.

He left the library, and when he entered his living room, a not unexpected tableau presented itself to him.

Sally, her back to him, sat lurched forward on the nearest couch, with Senator Hankins beside her on the same couch, and Wayne Talley perched on a chair he had drawn up alongside, intently listening, and Zeke Miller, squatting upon a footstool directly in front of her, his countenance redly twisted with outrage.

Moving into the room, Eaton could hear Sally saying, "And then, and then I pushed and punched at him, and started to scream, until he backed up, and then I got away—no, first—I remember—before going I told him what I thought of him—"

"Pardon me, Miss Watson, if I may interrupt," said Zeke Miller, "but I want to get this clear—I want to get this crystal-clear—because I have never been so roused and angered—never heard such degradation—but do I understand you to be saying—this Nigra buck, this Dilman, he made—forgive my language, you being a lady well brought up, the daughter of an esteemed colleague —but are you saying that this Dilman made improper advances to you tonight, improper advances against your express will and desire?"

"Improper advances?" she cried out. "That animal tried to rape me—practically—I can prove it. You want me to prove it?" She became aware of Eaton, standing behind Talley, and she shouted, "You can see for yourself, Arthur. Now you'll know I'm not prevaricating one word."

Suddenly she reached down, grasped the hem of her skirt, and yanked the dress up over her knees, and then higher, until both her full thighs, and part of her garter belt, and the lace fringe of her panties were revealed. She half fell on her side, to show her right thigh and buttocks more fully, and drew her finger along her flesh. "Look at this. I'm not ashamed. Look for yourselves, see what he did."

Eaton wanted to shut his eyes, but he did not. He could see the deep nail scratches, ugly crimson, several blood-encrusted, across Sally's perfect white flesh. He could see Miller's gray eyes widen, fastened to the sight, and Hankins' old eyes narrowing.

"You've seen enough?" Sally said, straightening, and throwing her skirt down over her knees. "I'll show you more. Look."

She held up the torn shoulder strap of her gown,

dropped it, pushed down one side of her bodice until the protruding webbed brassière cup was entirely unveiled. Eaton wanted to halt her, to tell her no more exhibits were necessary, but before he should speak out, she had loosened one brassière strap. Quickly, she pulled the freed cup down the smooth mound of her round breast, baring it to an inch from the point. She did not have to draw attention to what could be seen by all of them. The nail marks were even more stark here, and the bluish welts, too.

Eaton could contain himself no longer. "That's enough, Sally."

She glared up at him, covered her breast, and then pulled her bodice over the brassière, and said to Miller, "That's from my resisting, and don't think anybody could have done it but that nigger. I was alone with him tonight, in his room, and Governor Talley is holding the proof of it in those cards, some things I copied from Dilman's papers in his room."

A rumbling came from deep in Senator Hankins' throat. "Young lady, in all my years in public service, I never heard of a more dastardly indignity perpetrated on helpless young womanhood. I pledge you——" He slapped his hip. "I pledge my last resources to drive the culprit responsible for this from our capital city."

Sally seemed momentarily mesmerized by Hankins' gallantry. "Thank you, Senator. I——I only want justice done."

Zeke Miller was in a fury. "Justice is too good for that drunken lechering Nigra, Miss Sally," he shouted. "Lynching is what he deserves. Your word is enough for us to——"

"It's not me alone," said Sally. "It's not as if this were an isolated example of his immorality."

"Meaning what?" Miller demanded. "Be free to tell us everything you know."

Sally looked at the men around her. "You mean you don't know about his mistress?"

Miller's exhalation of amazement and pleasure became a whistle. "You know this for sure?" he bayed.

"Of course!" Sally exclaimed heatedly. "When I was

leaving him tonight, I told him to his face I wasn't going to become another Wanda Gibson—being kept by him in some back street—well, you should have seen him. It stopped him in his tracks. He didn't know anyone but the Spingers knew about it, but I know, and I'm positive Edna Foster knows."

Senator Hankins stirred erect, some confusion on his wrinkled face. "What was the lady's name again?"

"Wanda Gibson," said Sally. "She's a young nigger woman. Dilman had her living upstairs in his brownstone when he was—before he became President. She's still there, and he went over there the night after he moved into the White House. In fact, he tried to bring her into the White House, invited her to the State Dinner for Amboko—I know, because I sent the invitation—but I guess she was afraid to show up. Anyway, this Wanda Gibson, she's the one who called him today—she works for the Vaduz Exporters in a highly confidential job— she called him today to say they'd been found out— meaning the FBI found out her boss and company were a Communist Russian Front, and to warn him—"

Eaton stepped forward. "No need going into that now, Sally."

"Hey, now, Arthur, one minute, now. Goldarn, this sounds like something big," said Miller. He touched Sally's knee. "Are you saying that the President of the United States, Nigra or not, the President of America has been living clandestinely with a Nigra female who's working for the Soviet Russians?"

"That's right."

Miller had become transformed into a quivering hunting dog. "Hey, now, if those are the facts—"

"They are the facts," said Sally fervently. She pointed to Talley. "He's holding some more of the evidence on those cards, copied directly from a meeting Dilman had this afternoon with Mr. Scott. It's all there."

Miller turned to Talley, eyes gleaming. "True, Governor?"

Talley fanned the cards nervously. "Well—uh—in so far as Vaduz Exporters being a Red Front—yes—it's been uncovered that they've been shipping arms to—to

Soviet countries, who dispose of them mainly in Africa. And the President evidently has a woman friend who has been working in that firm, Miss Gibson—yes—but, of course, I'd have no knowledge about their relationship."

Miller held his palms apart and then smacked them together vigorously. "Open-and-shut!" he announced. "You want treason, bribery, and high crimes, Arthur? Okay, what's this? The President of this country consorting regularly with a lady friend who works for the Communists, talking bedroom talk, letting out secrets on purpose or inadvertently, on purpose to help his fellow niggers in Africa or inadvertently because he's trading secrets for sex. If that's not treason, what is? The President delaying prosecution of nigger extremists like the Turnerites in return for them not squealing about his son being a member, and then a pure white judge getting killed as a result. If that's not bribery by blackmail, what is? High crimes and misdemeanors? Meaning loose morals, maladministration, intemperate habits? If the President's fornicating with a mistress, trying to seduce his helpless white social secretary, added on to his record for drunkenness, if that doesn't qualify him, what does? Arthur, it's open-and-shut. The Nigra goes out, and you come in."

For Eaton, it was rolling too fast now. He wanted time to think. "We'll see," he said quietly, "we'll have to see."

Talley stood up. "I'm afraid Dilman won't give us much time, Arthur." He indicated the index cards in his hand. "Miss Watson recorded most of the private meeting with Scott. Dilman knows everything. He knows for certain we withheld the report from CIA on Baraza. He knows what was in that report, because Scott was able to tell him. Dilman was apparently angry as hell, and ordered more agents and funds to be allotted to investigate the situation in Baraza. He told Scott to bypass us from now on and come straight to him. He said from now on he's running the government, not letting us do it for him." Talley massaged his jowls worriedly. "I tell you, Arthur, we're in for trouble from that man."

"What kind of trouble can he give us?" said Eaton testily. "Be realistic. What has he got on us now—considering what we've got on him? After tonight, that incident with Sally, he knows what he's in for. He won't lift his voice to us. He won't dare say a word."

"Maybe you're right," said Talley.

"I know I'm right," said Eaton.

He could see that Miller and Sally had been holding a whispered conversation, and that now Sally was trying to rise and Miller was assisting her. Eaton hastened to them, and took Sally's other arm.

"Are you feeling better?" he asked solicitously.

"Arthur, Arthur," she said, "I'm suddenly so sleepy. Did you give me something? I forget. Did you give me pills?"

"Yes, I wanted you to rest. I'll take you into the library—"

Zeke Miller blocked them from leaving. "Only one thing, Arthur, and I've asked Miss Sally and she's agreed, fully agreed. I'm notifying Casper Wine and his boys to come on the double right over here. I want to dictate everything Sally told us as it came straight from her lips. He'll type it up as a legal affidavit, and then Miss Sally said we could waken her and she'd sign. She's cooperating to the limit."

"Whatever she wishes is agreeable to me," said Eaton.

Sally was leaning heavily on his shoulder now, and Eaton's arm encircled her as he began to lead her from the room.

He heard the telephone ringing—strange, at this improbable hour—and he waved at Talley to take it. Then he waited, propping Sally up, watching Talley on the telephone, unable to hear him. The call lasted no more than twenty seconds, and then Talley slowly hung up.

Eaton's gaze stayed on Talley as he came from the telephone and approached them. Talley's face was drawn and grave, a portrait of apprehension.

"Arthur," he said in a hoarse whisper, "that was Edna Foster, from the White House. She's just left the President. He ordered her to call you, to wake you if necessary. Dilman wants you in his office at nine o'clock sharp tomorrow morning. He wants to talk to you about an important and personal matter. She hit the *personal matter* pretty hard."

"I see."

"I think this is it, Arthur. The fat's in the fire. I think this is the showdown. He's got the gun now."

"So have we—now," said Eaton grimly. "Only what we possess is not a gun but a howitzer." He freed himself from Sally Watson, who was half asleep, and offered her limp arm to Talley. "Here, Wayne, you take her to the library, and see that she is comfortable. Treat her with care. She may be worth her weight in ammunition."

He remained immobilized, deep in thought, until Talley had led Sally Watson out of the living room. Then Eaton turned and walked slowly to the couch, where both Zeke Miller and Bruce Hankins were busily scratching notes, one in an address book, the other on the back of an envelope.

Eaton stood over them until first Miller, then Senator Hankins, looked up inquiringly.

"Gentlemen," Eaton said, "I have changed my mind. I don't believe that I can stand by idly, as a neutral, any longer, and allow you and the Party to fight this man alone. I'm with you tonight, and all the way."

Miller beamed, and his hand tugged at Hankins, who was also smiling happily. "By God!" Miller exclaimed. "I knew you'd see it right!"

"However, there is one thing I want both of you to understand," Eaton went on. "If I fight Dilman, join with you in forcing his resignation, it is not because he is a Negro but because he is a fool."

At one minute past nine o'clock the following morning, President Douglass Dilman stared through the rear windows of his Oval Office at the barren trees scattered across the south lawn, and at the cloudy, overcast November sky. He tried to equate his inner spleen with the threatening turbulence of the new day.

At last he swung his swivel chair back to the telephones, lifted one, and buzzed.

"All right, Miss Foster," he said, "send him in."

He girded himself, and waited.

The door opened, closed, and Secretary of State Arthur Eaton entered, solemnly greeted him, and carefully arranged his topcoat and homburg across the back of the sofa. Dilman, who had not spoken yet, was satisfied that Eaton's features were as severe as his own. But there, he suspected, their similarity of mood, as reflected in their countenances and carriage, ended. If Eaton was concerned, then the emotion was camouflaged by the pale, bloodless pallor of his aristocratic negotiator's mask and his easy, elegant Saville Row attire. Dilman felt that his own emotion, that of persistent displeasure, showed in the rigid lines along his tired eyes and bitter mouth. After Sally Watson's disgusting behavior last night, after his rereading of the Scott interview and his realization of what must be done, he had slept fitfully.

"You can sit there," he said, pointing to the Revels chair across from the corner of his desk. "I won't keep you long."

Eaton took his seat, crossing his legs, extracting his silver cigarette case and silver holder. He offered the open case to Dilman, who ignored it, and then Eaton fixed his cigarette and lighted it. After exhaling the first puff, he said easily, "Since your message stated that you wished to see me on a personal matter, I did not bother to bring any of my papers."

Dilman pulled himself closer to his desk and to the one so imperturbable before him.

"Eaton," he said, "I want your resignation from my Cabinet and from the Department of State."

To Eaton's credit, Dilman observed, there was no surprise, no reaction whatsoever, in his expression. Not one muscle moved beneath his patrician visage. He considered the President coolly, then he considered the smoke curling from his cigarette, and then, at last, a thin smile appeared. "A rather inhospitable beginning for so early a morning," he said. "Are you serious?"

"I want your resignation today," Dilman repeated.

Eaton remained outwardly unruffled. "Don't you think you owe me at least an explanation for this extraordinary request?"

The Princetonian's aloof insolence goaded Dilman's anger. "I didn't think an explanation would be necessary," he said. "I was sure your spy, and whatever else she is to you, I was sure Miss Watson gave you ample reason last night to know I was on to you and Talley. I will not suffer the continuing presence of a Secretary of State who is trying to usurp my office and its constitutional functions. Nor will I suffer the company of any man who sends, or permits, or uses a member of my White House staff to pry among my confidential papers. I hold ambitious disloyalty next to treason. I suggest that I will be better off, and the nation will be better off, if I remove you and your antagonism. That is my explanation, which I thought unnecessary."

Eaton had made no effort to interrupt and refute what the President was saying. His poise had not wavered. He betrayed no hidden concern, beyond the evidence of his inhaling and exhaling of smoke, which came faster now.

"There can be two versions of the truth to every matter," Eaton said at last. "I find that, for whatever real reasons you may have, you have chosen to believe a warped version of the truth, and have not been judicious enough to wait for my version. Shall I go on? I think I should. No one spied upon you, at least on my behalf, last night, or ever. If Miss Watson took it upon herself to prove to me, as an old friend concerned about your— your questionable behavior, that you were my enemy, it is not my offense or concern—any more than is my knowledge of your private behavior with female members of your staff and your unseemly activity and habits after hours."

Dilman stiffened. "What in the devil does that mean?"

"It means, Mr. President, in matters not affecting the welfare of the state, I have no right to interfere with your personal life. However, I, too, carry a public trust, and in matters concerning the life or death of my country, where I feel you have performed or may perform to the national detriment, I believe that I have the right to pass judgment on you, and interfere patriotically to correct you. I will not deny that Governor Talley and I temporarily withheld a Central Intelligence document concerning Baraza. We did so, for the time being, because of our knowledge of your temperament and—if I may say so—prejudiced judgment. We evaluated the rumor of a Communist buildup around Baraza as being ill-founded, and of minor consequence. Yet we foresaw that, because of your affection for Amboko, your understandable affinity for the struggling tribal people of your own color in the new African nations, you might have overreacted and committed the United States to a course of action from which there could have been no retreat. You displayed your favoritism, with dire results, in ignoring our advice to disband the Turnerite Group immediately. You displayed your arrogance and rashness in ignoring the majority will, the interests of the country at large and the pledges of your Party, by vetoing the Minorities Rehabilitation Program. I could not stop these disasters that you perpetrated in domestic affairs. But when I saw that you might perform as improperly in foreign affairs, which are my primary responsibility, I felt it my duty to guide you, whether you wished it or not. My motive was not to usurp your powers, but to preserve the peace."

Throughout the last, delivered as if by a prep-school headmaster to a gauche poor boy in on a scholarship, Douglass Dilman's wrath had been leavened by wonder. How unbelievable, he had thought finally, that this man could really justify his actions to himself by his self-hypnosis, this distorted rationale that he alone knew what was best for America and what was not. Could Eaton not see that he was doing no more than asserting his feeling of superiority, ergo: no second-class black citizen was able to possess the same wisdom and objectivity toward other peoples that an expensively educated, well-bred, white Protestant possessed by birthright.

Dilman had not meant to debate with Eaton, only to be rid of him. Yet, the Secretary of State's last remarks could not go unchallenged before their interview ended.

"Mr. Eaton, did it ever occur to you that by your act of withholding information from me, in effect taking it upon yourself to bury a grave warning to the government, you might be endangering the country you want to protect? What if I had not found out what was going on, and no one else in the executive branch had? What if the Soviet buildup of native Communists about Baraza proved to be true, and continued while we slept, what do you think would happen then? There would be an overnight takeover of the Barazan government by the Soviets. Then we would be forced to honor the African Unity Pact under the worst of circumstances, to try to save an ally, many allies, even a continent, where circumstances would put us at a military disadvantage. Can't you see that preventive treatment is less costly than desperation surgery?"

Eaton shook his head, smiling disagreeably. "Mr. President, forgive me, but you are more naïve about foreign affairs than I even suspected. Do you honestly believe that T.C. or Congress or the Department of State or the Joint Chiefs of Staff ever intended, from the start, to honor the African Unity Pact to the letter? Yes, we ratified it to bolster the strength of our democratic friends in Africa—but only on paper, for diplomatic propaganda. No one, not ourselves, not the African states, not Soviet Russia, ever believed we would commit our armed forces to uphold that pact." He shook his head more vigorously. "No, my good man. Only an unsophisticated and overemotional Afro-American—and I put this in the kindest way—could so misunderstand the intent and purpose of our foreign policy. Do you believe any of us, who have experience in these affairs, would ever risk a nuclear war with the Soviet Union over Baraza? It grieves me that you have to learn the facts of life and politics this late in the game. But better now than never. In any event, all this conversation is pointless, as you will shortly learn. In fact, your wish to see me on a personal matter this morning coincided with our Party's wish that I see you on a personal matter, also. I'm afraid I am on a painful mission. If you are prepared to listen to—"

Dilman's disgust, his loathing for this diplomat's crawling sophistries, was now complete. "Mr. Eaton, I have nothing more to discuss with you. Consider this interview our final meeting, and consider it now terminated."

He placed his palms against the edge of his desk and rolled back his chair, and then, hands on knees, he said, "I shall expect your resignation within an hour. Good day, sir."

To his utter surprise, Arthur Eaton did not move, but remained complacently settled in the Revels chair, casually ejecting his cigarette butt into the standing tray. Without bothering to look at the President, Eaton said, "Your bravado is admirable, Dilman. But do you honestly feel you are in a position, this minute, to ask anyone in your government to resign?"

Dilman, about to rise, held to the arms of his chair. "Do I feel I'm in a position to—?" He paused, then said slowly, "I feel I'm in a position to do whatever I believe to be right."

As he absently examined his silver cigarette holder, the Secretary of State spoke. "I have been assigned to tell you—I find it painful, but no less my duty—that you are the one who is no longer wanted in our government. For many hours now, all through last night, the leaders of the House of Representatives and the Senate and your Party have been meeting to weigh the evidence they have uncovered about you. They have agreed, unanimously, that you are dangerously incompetent, and consequently unsuited for the high office accidentally thrust upon you, and that your continuing services are a detriment to the future of the United States."

Eaton stared at Dilman.

"They desire to impeach you for high crimes and misdemeanors in office. Because I feel that such a method of publicly disgracing you and removing you from the Presidency is abhorrent, I have prevailed upon them—it was not easy, but I prevailed upon them—to accept a more moderate means of disposing of you. They would prefer, and I would prefer, that you do what is necessary to be done as a gentleman would, do what you so childishly requested of me earlier, and that is, tender *your* resignation immediately, for reasons of disability brought on by ill health. However, I was able to foresee that such a natural solution might antagonize you, and understandably—that is, embarrass you and make you lose face before your own people. As a consequence, I was able to convince Miller, Hankins, Selander, Wickland, Noyes, all of them, that there was yet a third course. They do not like its moderation, any more than I like the extremism of their course of impeachment. Yet they will go along with me, if you are tractable."

He paused, then continued. "The plan is that in the next few weeks, you fall ill, become more and more confined to your White House bedroom, and as the months pass, your disability becomes permanent. As you recover from this disability, perhaps a severe coronary, to which we can arrange that a committee of physicians attests, those of us who have been your assistants will continue to conduct the business of the executive branch in your name. You will remain President in name only, of course, as were Woodrow Wilson and Eisenhower when they were invalided. You may sign the documents that require your signature, but you will leave the actual performance of your duties to your committee of successors in the Cabinet. I find this solution simple, orderly, completely sensible—and in the best interests of the country. In return, of course, you have our pledge that the Articles of Impeachment in our possession will never be made public against you. Well, now, Dilman, there you have it."

Douglass Dilman had listened to this plan unfold as if helplessly caught up in a mad nightmare. And emerging from it now, finding himself face to face with an actual human being who had spoken these fantastic words as if they were ordinary words, he was for seconds too stunned by the reality to speak.

But then the full impact of what had occurred hit him, and he felt the blood rushing through him and felt the pounding beneath his chest and temples. The effrontery of the proposition, the degrading insult of it, at last transformed his shock into rage.

He stared at his black hands knotted together on the Buchanan desk, watched with fascination their trembling. Never in his entire life had he suffered such a monstrous attempt to humiliate him. As a Negro, he was a scarred veteran of white men's jeers and ridicule, blasphemy and vilification. Yet now he could conjure up no agonized instance out of his past, from childhood to manhood, not even that revolting occasion on his honeymoon with Aldora, when he had been treated so inhumanly.

As his fury rose, and his head pulsated, he wanted to grab the heavy inkwell from his desk and fling it at Eaton's face. Or strangle him, strangle him until he admitted indecency and confessed shame.

But then, seeking an ally to justify his right to violence, he remembered Nat Abrahams, and knew that Nat would restrain him, remind him that knocking someone down solved nothing except the question of which was the more muscular, and justice would not be served. What had this monster Eaton and his so-called cabal, what had they threatened him with—yes, impeachment for high crimes and misdemeanors, unless he crept into an invalid's bed with a feigned disability for the rest of the term and allowed them as palace conspirators to run the country their way. How had that Sally put it last night? Two-legged beings, yes, that's what they wanted on the premises. And anything lower than that they wanted kept in its place leashed and muzzled, like a bothersome house pet, tucked into the doghouse where its bark could not be heard, while two-legged men kept the house clean and in order. They wanted Eaton, and Eaton wanted Eaton, to run a comfortable white country, and comfortable white world, for privileged, superior white people, cynically bribing with Federal charities the susceptible minorities at home, cynically betraying through lies and peace-bartering the helpless small nations abroad.

That they felt they could accomplish this, that they believed he would readily and gratefully acquiesce to their offer, was what astounded and infuriated him. Desperately he tried to think with Nat's mind. Obviously, they were confident because they believed they had a club over him. If he would not accede without resistance, they would employ legal force. Nat's mind inquired: What legal force do they possess, Doug? What case can they build against you? Either they have something or they have nothing, and if you know they have nothing, then they are bluffing you, trying to intimidate you, scare you out. Nat's mind instructed: Call their bluff, Doug, call it, and then decide.

It required his last powers of restraint to exercise this control. All right, Nat, I'll try.

He saw Eaton placidly waiting for his reply.

Dilman said, "Eaton, I don't know where, not even in stories about Central American politics, I ever heard a more bizarre or outlandish proposition. You have it all figured out, have you? I'm put away, and you play President. I'm to cooperate with you in this—this palace revolution, and if I refuse, you indict me for high crimes and misdemeanors, and then you try me and then you convict and remove me. But first, you kindly offer me the choice of abdication and self-exile."

"If you prefer to put it that way, that's right," said Eaton agreeably.

"Well, I'll tell you what, Eaton—I think you're bluffing. I don't think you or your ambitious crowd have a single shred of evidence against me, not one thing, that would stand up and convince a majority of the 448 sworn members of the House of Representatives to send Articles of Impeachment to the Senate. Unless you can—"

"One moment, Dilman." Eaton uncrossed his legs and sat straight. "If it requires this to make you realize that we are dead serious, that your situation is hopeless, then you should see it."

He extracted three folded sheets of yellow foolscap from his inside coat pocket, elaborately unfolded them, patted them straight, half rose, and dropped them on the desk in front of Dilman. He fell back into the Revels chair. From beneath hooded eyelids, he kept his gaze on the President.

Douglass Dilman looked down at the topmost yellow sheet, filled with typewritten paragraphs, resting on the desk blotter between his elbows. At last he unclasped his hands, picked up the three pages, spun his chair away from the Secretary of State, and read the heading, and then the first paragraph of each numbered section. He read:

INTRODUCING PROCEEDINGS
IN THE HOUSE OF REPRESENTATIVES FOR
THE IMPEACHMENT OF DOUGLASS DILMAN,
PRESIDENT OF THE UNITED STATES,
FOR HIGH CRIMES AND MISDEMEANORS

Upon the evidence collected by the Committee on Judiciary, which is herewith presented, and in virtue of the powers with which they have been invested by the House of Representatives, they are of the opinion that Douglass Dilman, President of the United States, should be impeached of high crimes and misdemeanors. They therefore recommend to the House the adoption of the accompanying resolution.

Zeke Miller, Chairman.
Harvey Wickland
John T. Hightower

Resolved, That Douglass Dilman, President of the United States, be impeached of high crimes and misdemeanors in office.

Articles of evidence for the House of Representatives of the United States against Douglass Dilman, President of the United States, in maintenance and support of the resolution of impeachment against him for high crimes and misdemeanors in office.

ARTICLE I.

That said Douglass Dilman, President of the United States, at Washington, in the District of Columbia, unmindful of the high duties of his office, of his oath of office, and of the requirement of the Constitution that he should preserve, protect, and defend the Constitution, did unlawfully and in violation of his oath of office, commit treason against the United States by conveying, with knowledge beforehand or through gross indiscretion, national secrets concerning internal security into the hands of the U.S.S.R. and its allies through his hitherto covert friendship with one Wanda Gibson, an executive secretary of the Vaduz Exporters,

Limited, of Bethesda, Maryland, said corporation having been indicted by the Department of Justice as a Communist Front organization conspiring with the U.S.S.R. to overthrow democratic institutions wherever . . .

ARTICLE II.

That said Douglass Dilman, President of the United States, unmindful of the high duties of his office and of his oath of office, in violation of the Constitution and laws of the United States, at Washington, in the District of Columbia, did unlawfully hinder the Department of Justice in its prosecution of the Turnerite Group, a subversive organization, and thus cause the loss of one life and internal unrest, because of unlawful and covert conspiracy with the Turnerite Group in an effort to protect from public knowledge the membership in this subversive organization of a relative and offspring, Julian Dilman . . .

ARTICLE III.

That said Douglass Dilman, President of the United States, unmindful of the high duties of his office, and the dignities and proprieties thereof, did disgrace and bring into contempt the Executive Branch of the United States government, and show himself unfit to perform the duties of his office, through certain intemperate and scandalous behavior involving loose morals, intoxication, partisanship, and maladministration.

Specification first.—At Washington, in the District of Columbia, in a private chamber of the Executive Mansion, said Douglass Dilman, President of the United States, while under the influence of intoxicants, made improper advances upon the person of a member of the Executive staff, namely Sally Watson, White House social secretary, and did attempt to seduce said Sally Watson, and did commit bodily harm to said Sally Watson when she resisted.

Specification second.—At Washington, in the District of Columbia, for five years including the time of his ascension to the Presidency, said Douglass Dilman,

President of the United States, widower, conducted covertly an extramarital liaison with the aforesaid Wanda Gibson, unmarried, in a house owned by said Douglass Dilman, on whose premises Wanda Gibson dwelt. In the same house there dwelt also the Reverend Paul Spinger, National Director of the Crispus Society, an organization of Negro Americans, and his spouse, Rose Springer, who were treated to certain special favors by said Douglass Dilman, in return for aiding and abetting his liaison with Wanda Gibson and keeping it secret.

Specification third.—At Washington, in the District of Columbia, said Douglass Dilman, President of the United States, did attempt to bring into contempt and reproach the Congress of the United States, and impair the powers of Congress, by obstructing its legislative activity through veto of the Minorities Rehabilitation Program Bill, because of intemperate habits, partisanship, and inefficiency, to the detriment of the national welfare. Without study of the aforesaid legislative bill, while under the influence of intoxicants and Negro extremists, said Douglass Dilman . . .

Specification fourth.—In his various residences at Washington, in the District of Columbia, in Chicago, in the State of Illinois, in Springfield, in the State of Illinois, where he was a registered patient in a sanitarium for alcoholics, and in his residences in the States of Michigan, Ohio, Indiana, said Douglass Dilman, President of the United States, was habitually addicted to . . .

Dilman came around in his swivel chair, and with great deliberation he held out the three yellow sheets until Eaton took them. Dilman was pleased to see that his own hands no longer shook, because there was no fear in him. One felt fear when there was something real that threatened, a person, a charge, that might subject one to physical injury or mental harm. This preposterous document, its grotesque half-truths and whole lies couched in the false dignity of Congressional legal verbiage, was too ridiculous to be treated seriously.

He considered Eaton with new confidence. "Is this all of your blackmail, Eaton?"

Carefully Eaton folded the three yellow sheets of paper. At last he looked up.

"These are, without the supporting affidavits and testimony of witnesses, the Articles of Impeachment against you that will ultimately be sent to the Senate, after the House of Representatives has voted to indict you. This evidence will first be presented to the House not as formal articles, but as a series of charges, written in similar language, supporting a resolution for impeachment. This is the case against you which I have managed so far to prevent from being introduced on the floor of the House."

"I see. . . . Well, I'm sorry for you, Eaton. If you want to become President of the United States, as you do, you are going to have to work and sweat for it, gain it the hard way, and not by trying to frighten me out of this chair with three pages of poppycock. Yes, I'm going to make you work for it in a way that will revolt your fastidious self, by making you live and sleep and hold hands and cast your lot with that gang of inhuman bullies and ignorant red-necks on the Hill. You are welcome to them, and to this trumped-up pack of lies, a nigger indictment wrapped in a package of Constitutional parchment. It'll get you nowhere."

Eaton appeared incredulous. "Are you telling me, in the face of those irrefutable facts, you will not step aside?"

"I'm telling you more," said Dilman, standing up. "I am telling you I will no longer give you the right to the dignity of resigning, because you do not deserve it. As of here and now, Mr. Eaton, you are fired!"

Eaton leaped to his feet and moved to the front of the President's desk. "Dilman, I think you are too distraught to realize what you are doing."

"I know exactly what I am doing. I am removing you from office and from my Cabinet."

"I won't let you commit suicide, Dilman. You've taken leave of your senses. There is a law—the New Succession Act—that prevents you from removing any Cabinet officer without the consent of the Senate. Have you forgotten? You can no more fire me than President Andrew Johnson could defy the Tenure of Office Act of 1867 by trying to fire Secretary of War Stanton without consent of the Senate."

"Andrew Johnson did it, and I am doing it."

"Dilman, for heaven's sake, he was impeached for exactly this."

Dilman nodded. "Yes, and he was acquitted."

Eaton planted his knuckles on the desk, and bent forward. "Listen to me, Dilman. You won't be that lucky. If you fire me, you won't have me standing between you and your bitterest enemies. Nothing will hold them back. And now they'll have their strongest ammunition against you, a new article of indictment, and the most powerful one: a charge that you flagrantly violated the law of the United States, that you ignored the rights of the Senate. They'll be all over you like a pack of angry wolves, and they'll have teeth for their final attack. Dilman, for once, for one last time while you still can, show good judgment, at least the good judgment of self-preservation. Step aside, as I have suggested. Don't force us to parade all your friends, your misconduct, before the nation and the world. Don't force us to drive you from this room in disgrace."

Dilman had waited patiently for the finish. When he saw that Eaton was done, winded, his chalky cheeks flushed with color, he knew the time had come.

"Eaton, I have no more to say to you, except what I said to your lady friend last night—get out of this room, or I shall have you thrown out. And clear out your office in the Department of State, or I'll have the United States Marshal dump your effects in the street."

For silent seconds, as if the firing had come with bullets, Eaton hung suspended before Dilman, riddled with disbelief. Finally he shook his head, turned on his heel, and crossed the room to his hat and coat. When he had picked them up, he shook his head once more.

"Dilman," he said, regretful as an executioner, "I'm sorry for you, I really am, but you have given us no choice." He paused, and then concluded, "As of twelve o'clock noon today, the resolution recommending your impeachment goes before the House of Representatives. I would wish you luck, but you don't deserve it, and besides—it wouldn't help you anyway."

With that, Arthur Eaton, former Secretary of State, quickly left the Oval Office.

Holding the telephone receiver in one hand as he waited for Miss Foster to put through his call to the Mayflower Hotel, Douglass Dilman noted the time. Two hours had passed since he had fired Eaton and since he had learned that an effort would be made to impeach him.

It was now a quarter to twelve. He could visualize the scene on the Hill. Right now, bells were ringing throughout the Capitol corridors, buzzers were sounding in the offices of the representatives and in their committee rooms, announcing that the formal session of the House was about to begin.

Soon the corridors and elevators would be filled, and soon the House Chamber, too. At exactly noon, the mace would be placed on its marble column, and the acting Speaker would be announcing, "The House will be in order. Please rise while prayer is offered by the chaplain."

Immediately after, the Speaker would receive the copy of the urgent resolution that Representative Zeke Miller had deposited in the hopper at the desk of the clerk. He would permit Miller, as author of the top-priority measure, to read out to his assembled colleagues and the gallery, "Resolved, that Douglass Dilman, President of the United States, be impeached of high crimes and misdemeanors in office." Then there would be instantaneous pandemonium in the press gallery, among the visitors —in fact, among much of the House itself—and then, at last, all the world would know what was taking place.

By two o'clock the Speaker would have referred the impeachment resolution to Miller's committee, a formality, since the committee had already secretly completed its investigation and voted its recommendation.

By tomorrow, the resolution's position on the House calendar would be waived, Miller's committee would have given its recommendation, and the membership of the House would have resolved itself into the Committee of the Whole House on the State of the Union, a maneuver that allowed it to act on important legislation with a quorum of one hundred members, instead of more than twice that number which it normally required. Then the limited debate on the charges in the resolution for impeachment would begin, the debate preceding the vote on whether the President should or should not stand trial before the Senate for high crimes and misdemeanors. But that would be tomorrow, and the day after. For today, it was business enough to let the nation and the world know, for the first time, the scandalous and delinquent conduct of the President of the United States.

But right now, that was fifteen minutes to one hour and fifteen minutes away. The creation of the indictment, the speeding of it into the hopper, and out of it into committee, and out of committee onto the floor—this procedure accomplishing in hours what often required days and weeks—was still anticipated by only a relative handful of persons. On the Hill, the leaders and most influential legislators of both parties, and a few of their favorite newspapermen, already knew of it. In the White House, only Governor Talley and himself, and in the past hour Edna Foster and Tim Flannery, knew of it. On everyone else in Washington, in the United States, in the world, it would fall as a thunderclap.

Dilman was glad that he would not be present in the city for the sordid debate, for the vile lies and disgraceful calumny, for the charges and countercharges. Outside, on the south White House lawn, he was aware that the huge, blunt-nosed Marine helicopter was standing on its steel pad in readiness to lift him into the sky and spin him to Andrews Air Force Base, where the scarlet-and-silver jet airplane, with its Presidential emblem still on the door, would take him on his five-day inspection and speaking tour of the nation.

Eager as he was to escape the maelstrom of impending scandal, he had been made to reconsider his flight one hour ago. A distressed Tim Flannery had felt that leaving the scene of the impeachment fight at this time might be a tactical error. Since the debate would not be a trial, but the airing and consideration of an indictment, Flannery felt that the President would have no place to respond to the charges against him except in the press. From the Oval Office he might best, and most effectively, ridicule and refute the resolution for impeachment. From a distance his voice might be heard less distinctly.

Giving short shrift to his press secretary's plea, Dilman had determined to adhere to his schedule. Once the impeachment effort was official, he would issue a single statement, perhaps from St. Louis or Cleveland, and after that, dignify the effort no further. He was confident, he had reassured his press secretary, no more would be required from him. The charges were so oversensational and so lacking in solid proof as to collapse readily from lack of factual foundation.

Yet there was one act that he must perform before his departure, and that was to speak to Nat Abrahams. He wondered why he had not told Nat Abrahams what was in the wind, and why he was not going to reveal it to him now. Then he knew. The two things he had in mind to discuss with Nat must not be discussed in the emotional atmosphere of his personal needs. It would not be fair to Nat, who had his own life to live.

And then, through the telephone at his ear, he heard his friend's voice at last.

"Hello, Nat."

"Doug, I'll be damned. I thought you were already airborne."

"Oh, I will be in ten minutes. I wanted my Dramamine to have a head start. How are Sue and the children?"

"Sue's right here with me. She arrived this morning. She's got everything under control back home. The kids are with the family. We didn't want to pull them out of school until the beginning of February when the semester ends. I think we'll go back for the Christmas holidays, though."

"What about your Eagles Industries contract, Nat? Signed yet?"

"In four or five days. About the time you finish your tour. We'll have to have a drink on it, although I'm not sure if it should be champagne or cyanide. . . . What about you, Doug? Anything special?"

"Nat, every day is special, it's one endless crisis here."

"Hey, that reminds me, Doug. What's that in the morning paper about the FBI clamping down on the Vaduz Exporters? Isn't that the outfit your—the firm that Wanda Gibson's been working for?"

"Yes. That's really why I'm calling you, Nat."

"Is she in trouble?"

"No, no, nothing like that. She's no more Communist than you and I are. She was, after all, just another employee there. She didn't have the faintest idea that her boss was a Red agent or the company a Communist Front until yesterday morning. When she told me, I told her to get out. Anyway, what worries me is that she may be served a subpoena or something while I'm gone—"

"Doug, they have nothing on her, so why should anyone bother her?"

"We-ll, they might. You know our overzealous bloodhounds on Capitol Hill. And—and the case may have other ramifications—and there may be a lot of questions. I wouldn't want Wanda feeling abandoned and scared, and without legal counsel. Now, I know you are up to your ears—"

"Doug, I'm doing nothing except waiting to affix my autograph to a contract. Of course, I'll pitch in."

"I'd be grateful. It would be a load off my mind. Maybe you can kind of look in on her—say, in a day or two."

"Absolutely, Doug. In fact, I'll nose around Justice a bit, and the Hill, to learn what's going on. Then I'll drive over and see Wanda."

"Thank you, Nat. You're the one person I can depend upon. Too bad I'm losing you to Avery Emmich. Maybe it's not too late. Have you ever thought of coming into government? The pay is lousy, but the cocktail parties are free, and you get a lot of press clippings."

"Me in government? Of course you're kidding, Doug. Can't you see me trying to conform to the Party? And compromise with the Attorney General? I'd last a fast eight hours in any Federal job. Of course, I can't say it would be worse than what I am about to do. But in Eagles, at least they pay top wages for sin. I'll come out only slightly sullied, and at least with cash and the farm to keep me warm. . . . You were just kidding me, weren't you, Doug? I mean—"

"Yes, I was only kidding. You belong in government about as much as I do, except you'd be good at it. . . . Well, I can hear the helicopter's choppers beating out there. I'd better be off. Good luck with your contract. Kiss Sue. And—and thanks again for keeping an eye on Wanda."

Gently Dilman returned the telephone receiver to its cradle.

Well, he told himself, as expected: yes on Wanda, no dice on the other. He would have to go it alone, not that it had been different with Talley and Eaton as part of his administration

He stared down at the last-minute papers waiting to be signed. He reached for his pen. He signed the note to Admiral Oates requesting that the foremost civilian orthopedic surgeons be brought in to try to save Otto Beggs's leg. He signed the memorandum to Attorney General Kemmler, reminding him that Leroy Poole's appeal for executive clemency must be expedited, now that the date of Hurley's execution was drawing nearer. He signed the order for the Federal Marshal to barricade Arthur Eaton's office in the Department of State, if necessary, to keep him out. He signed his own curt acceptance of Governor Wayne Talley's resignation from his staff, as well as that of Talley's friend and his own military aide, General Robert Faber. And finally, he reread the electric news announcement, prepared by Flannery, stating that he had removed Arthur Eaton from the position of Secretary of State because of their irreconcilable differences over foreign policy, and then he signed that too.

He called Miss Foster, to let her know what he had done, and to remind her to take care of the letters, and especially the news announcement, at once.

He pushed himself to his feet, gathered together the

copies of the speeches he was to deliver, the briefing notes on the military installations he was to visit, the memorandum he had written to himself on what he could remember of the House's impeachment charges, and he stuffed them into his already overcrowded briefcase. Once he had secured the lock of the briefcase, he found his hat and took down his heavy overcoat.

Thus laden, he went outside where the Secret Service men and Tim Flannery were waiting on the dry grass of the Rose Garden lawn. He fell in step with them, and headed for the noisy, vibrating bulk of the helicopter.

The weather was good, he noted, the sky over the Potomac clear. He wondered how long it would stay that way, and if, when he returned, he would be under a cloud at last.

Nat Abrahams' shoe pressed down on the brake, and he brought the rented Ford to a standstill at the red traffic light on Sixteenth Street. Once more he gave his attention to the half-open newspaper, purchased when he had left the Mayflower Hotel, with the double-banner headline reading:

PRESIDENT DILMAN IMPEACHMENT! SCANDAL DEBATE OPENS IN HOUSE!

It amazed him that only yesterday, little more than twenty-four hours ago, Doug Dilman had telephoned him before leaving the city, and talked without giving a single hint or reference to this monstrous attack on his integrity. Dilman, he reasoned, must have known at that very time about the impeachment charges being mounted against him; yet, except for his concern over Wanda Gibson's future, he had omitted discussing anything connected with them. He had pretended that his concern over Wanda was merely to see that she was protected from harassment by Congressional Red-baiters. Now, it was evident, he wanted her protected from the charge of having collaborated with the President in committing a treasonable act.

How typical of Doug Dilman, Abrahams thought, to seek no advance advise or help about the impeachment as a whole. Dilman had always been secretive about his personal family relationships. But this impeachment attempt was another matter. Yesterday Dilman had been at the brink of facing public infamy, and yet he had kept his silence. How difficult it must have been for him, privately knowing that he had discharged three of his inner circle, had left himself alone to fight against his slanderers, to refuse to seek the aid of his closest friend. His damnable pride, Abrahams thought, pride, which Defoe had once defined as "the first peer and president of Hell." Yet, knowing Doug Dilman as he did, Abrahams could see that his reluctance to spill out his troubles might have been otherwise motivated. It might have been his Negro sensitivity that had so muted him, the feeling that he did not wish to overdraw his friendship balance with a white man, that he had no right to do so. On the other hand, perhaps he had sought Abrahams' assistance after all. Hadn't he said something to the effect that he was sorry to lose Abrahams to Avery Emmich's corporation, that maybe it wasn't too late to bring him into government? Had that been Dilman's tentative feeling out of his friend, privately aware as he was of what lay ahead? Had Dilman wanted to sound out Abrahams on the possibility of his replacing Talley? Probably not, Abrahams decided, for if Dilman had desired him for so responsible a job, he would not have been afraid to mention it openly.

A car honked behind him. Nat Abrahams realized that the red light had turned green. He shifted his shoe from the brake to the gas pedal, and continued up Sixteenth Street. He remembered his upset yesterday, in midafternoon, when he had been half dozing over an out-of-print history of the early days of Congress, and Sue had awakened him with the flash bulletin she had just heard on the radio. After that, neither the radio nor television in their Mayflower suite had been still. With his intimate knowledge of Dilman, the personal charges made by Zeke Miller yesterday had been preposterous. Yet there had been enough validity in each, just enough, to force

Sue and himself to discuss them compulsively all afternoon, through dinner, and into the night.

As he drove now, gradually guiding his car into the right-hand lane, watching for his turnoff, Abrahams' mind centered particularly on the sections that related Doug Dilman to Wanda Gibson. It was difficult for Abrahams to conjure up a sharply defined image of Wanda Gibson. He and Sue had met her once, about a year and a half or two years ago, and Doug had mentioned her a number of times in letters he had written. Nat could recollect only that she had been a rather mature and striking woman, well educated and well mannered, and with a lovely tan complexion that appeared lighter when contrasted with Dilman's own color. She was, Nat remembered, a mulatto.

He recalled, too, the frank discussion he had had with Dilman, the first night Dilman had moved into the White House. His friend had not concealed the fact that he was close to Wanda, in love with her, hoping to marry her one day if he possessed the courage. But there had been no indication of anything more. Trying to match what he knew of his friend and of Wanda to Zeke Miller's lurid picture of them was impossible. Doug Dilman, that sedentary, bemused, middle-aged, frightened Negro, suddenly a Casanova with a mistress? Miller's accusation would be hilarious if it were not so serious. Doug Dilman, a reeling drunk in a love nest spilling Presidential secrets to a mulatto Mata Hari who was employed by Soviet Russia? Dilman seduced into performing treason? An insane fantasy.

Yet Nat Abrahams' legal mind permitted the House charges in its resolution for impeachment to revolve in his brain, as he examined their many sides. In three decades he had not seen Doug drink more than Bordeaux wine, perhaps an occasional highball or sherry nightcap—still, still, there might have been more. Since he had not known much of Dilman's family life, he had been dumbfounded by Miller's revelation that both Dilman and Aldora had once spent time in a Springfield sanitarium for alcoholics. If that was true, if Miller and his cohorts could prove it, there might also be proof, or some circumstantial evidence, that Dilman had been conducting a love affair with Wanda and had unwittingly betrayed a government secret. But Abrahams had his strong doubts, derived not merely from loyalty to his friend, but from knowledge of his accusers. Their charge of treason, based on intemperate habits, partly disguised their true reason for impeachment: they would no longer countenance a colored man sitting as their leader. They refused to forgive him not only his blackness, but the effrontery of his veto of the Minorities Rehabilitation Program. No Nigra—wasn't that what Miller called Doug?—was going to be permitted to chastise the majority white legislative branch. It was time for an object lesson to all Nigras who were getting out of hand. This would put them in their places, send them back to carrying hats for their genetic superiors.

Driving more slowly, Nat Abrahams caught the street sign that read "Van Buren N.W." He flipped his turn indicator up, and wheeled into the residential thoroughfare.

Nearing his destination, he remembered that he had awakened early this morning filled with righteous indignation and legal curiosity. He had telephoned one of Attorney General Kemmler's assistants about Wanda, and then he had telephoned and personally visited with Robert Lombardi at the Federal Bureau of Investigation in the forbidding Justice Department building. After that, he had returned to the hotel and telephoned Wanda Gibson herself. She had responded with recognition to his name, and had been formal, but his persistence in addressing her as Wanda and not Miss Gibson had finally forced down her defenses to accepting him as Nat—and as friend. At first she had not wanted to see him, vaguely speaking of other appointments. She had sounded more shy than troubled. When Nat had invoked Doug Dilman, Doug's desire that Nat as attorney if not friend look into her predicament, the vague appointments had evaporated, and she had capitulated entirely. Abrahams had told her that he would visit her after lunch, around one-thirty or so.

Cruising slowly along Van Buren Street, keenly conscious of the upper-class Negro women on the sidewalks with their shopping bags, Nat Abrahams sought the residence. Midway up the block, his gaze rested on the two-story brownstone row house, and he knew it immediately. He slid the Ford up to the curb, parked, and pocketed the keys.

Before his reunion with Wanda Gibson, he decided to review the evidence supporting the resolution for impeachment one more time. He unfolded the newspaper, propping it against the steering wheel, and absently packed tobacco into the crusted bowl of his straight-stemmed pipe and lighted it. The lead story reported Zeke Miller's dramatic introduction of the impeachment resolution, then went on to say that although it had been referred to the House Judiciary Committee, almost all necessary evidence against Dilman had been gathered from witnesses and documents, and therefore Miller promised that the committee, after meeting through the night, would present its recommendation to the House of Representatives at noon today. Majority Leader Harvey Wickland was quoted as stating that he expected the committee to recommend impeachment unanimously, and that he expected the full contents of the charges embodied in the resolution for impeachment to be read and put to limited debate by early afternoon.

Nat Abrahams' attention was drawn from this story to the impressive black-bordered box in the upper center of the front page reproducing four Articles of Impeachment in boldface type superimposed over a faint photograph of Doug Dilman's portrait, a not too flattering portrait at that.

Beneath the photograph there ran a lengthy caption. Abrahams studied it:

"The Articles of Impeachment reproduced above—this newspaper has been informed by a reliable Congressional source—may be the form the House of Representatives charges will take when presented to the Senate, presuming the House does indict the President of high crimes and misdemeanors. These charges, in less stately language, are a part of the resolution of impeachment that will be debated today in the House of

Representatives. If a majority of House members vote to
impeach the President, the charges will be turned over
to a special appointed committee, drawn from the House
Judiciary Committee, which will formalize them as Articles of Impeachment, and return them to the House for
routine approval, before sending them on to the Senate
for final judgment. But the raging question today is—will
the House of Representatives vote yes or no on the grave
matter of converting its resolution for impeachment
into actual Articles of Impeachment upon which the
Chief Executive would have to stand trial?"

Scowling, Abrahams began to read the evidence that
had been prepared against Doug Dilman. He skimmed
the contents of the first three articles, more notable for
their questionable sensationalism than their proof of
high crimes and misdemeanors (although the first charge
of treason, if substantiated, might be grave), until he
reached the last article. The fact of this one, of course,
could not be disputed. Nat reread it carefully:

ARTICLE IV.

That said Douglass Dilman, President of the United
States, at Washington, in the District of Columbia,
unmindful of the high duties of his office, of the oath
of office, and in violation of the Constitution of the
United States, and contrary to the provisions of an
act entitled "The New Succession Act Regulating the
Line of Succession to the Presidency and the Tenure
of Certain Civil Offices," without the advice and consent of the Senate of the United States, said Senate
then and there being in session, and without authority
of law, did, with intent to violate the Constitution of
the United States, and the act aforesaid, remove from
office as Secretary of State the Honorable Arthur
Eaton. Then and there being no vacancy in said office
of Secretary of State, whereby said Douglass Dilman,
President of the United States, did then and there commit and was guilty of a high misdemeanor in office,
not only for his disregard of the law and his contempt
of said Senate, but for his malicious desire to sustain
himself in office by illegal removal of the next in line

to his succession, whose popularity with the electorate he resented and feared.

This charge, Nat Abrahams could see, would be the most difficult to refute, the one Doug Dilman would find the most menacing and formidable to contest. Whereas his opposition might be challenged on their proof of his commission of treason, through Wanda, with the Vaduz Exporters and Soviet Russia, there was no denying the fact that Doug had broken a law (no matter how unconstitutional it might be) by firing a Cabinet member without the consent of his onetime colleagues in the Senate. Of course, a sound case might be made on Doug's behalf in the House debate today, but Nat was not sure there was anyone prepared to make that case.

Abrahams' eyes left the box of articles, and moved to the farthest left-hand column. There was another dismaying headline, and beneath it a dateline from Cleveland. Doug had spoken before a convention of war veterans, of which he was one, and his speech had been met with continuous boos, hisses, and catcalls—the epithets were shocking ("Traitor! . . . Commie! . . . Whoremonger!"), and although the police had evicted two dozen hecklers from the auditorium, the disturbance had not ceased. The speech had been an utter disaster. Abrahams' heart went out to his friend. He was tempted to telephone him, and beg him to return to Washington, but that made no sense either.

As he was about to fold the newspaper, one more story caught Abrahams' attention. The Secret Service agent who had saved Dilman's life, Otto Beggs, had successfully come through his latest surgery, had not lost his shattered leg, but his use of it would be considerably impaired. Even this was related to the impeachment. Miller's investigators, eager to question the President's personal bodyguard for evidence of what he might have seen or overheard, had been rudely turned away by Admiral Oates.

It pleased Abrahams that someone had shown a shred of decency, but it distressed him to know to what lengths the House investigators were going, to build their case

against the President. Apparently they felt that even if
they already were in possession of enough evidence to
indict the President, there was always use for more, and
again more, if he should go on trial.

Abrahams' vest-pocket watch told him it was twenty
minutes to two, and that he had been sitting outside the
brownstone for over five minutes. He pulled down the
rearview mirror, to see if he was entirely presentable
for Wanda Gibson. A tuft of his chestnut hair stood up
in back, and no amount of water had been able to slick
it down. The extraordinary amount of sleep and relaxation he had enjoyed in Washington, while awaiting the
last draft of his contract and while casually acquainting
himself with his future duties for Eagles Industries, had
not eliminated the lines in his gaunt features or made his
deep-set eyes appear more rested. Nevertheless, he felt
energetic and revived, all senses alert and questing, as if
resurrected from fat lethargy by his antagonism toward Doug's prosecutors.

He swung his long legs out of the car, slammed the
door, and strode to the brownstone. Emptying his pipe
against the heel of his hand, he told himself that if he
could not help his friend in the House of Representatives,
at least he could be of some use to Wanda. It was little
enough, but in a time like this it might mean much to
Doug. And anyway, it was good to be active.

Inside, he took the stairs two at a time. When he
reached the upper landing, he was pleased that he was
not winded, and knew that his physician would be
pleased too. Approaching the door, he could hear the
sounds of television behind it. He knocked firmly. Almost immediately the door opened, and he was inside
the parlor, face to face with Wanda Gibson.

He was delighted to find that she was as attractive as
he had remembered her. Her glossy dark hair was caught
back in a ribbon, and her tawny smooth face was devoid
of any makeup except at the lips. Her dark eyes tried to
smile, and failed. She wore an apricot-colored cotton
blouse, and wide navy-blue leather belt, and a simple
tailored blue skirt. Her countenance and her figure were

classic, and Nat Abrahams silently congratulated Doug Dilman for his good taste.

Taking his overcoat, she told him that she remembered both him and his wife very well, and she inquired about Sue and the children. As they walked to the couch, she waved a disdainful hand at the television set. The screen showed a panoramic shot of the overflowing galleries in the House, and then moved down to a cluster of representatives gathered before the Speaker's rostrum.

"Look at it," Wanda said. "It's like watching a motion-picture revival of some old spectacle about the Roman Colosseum, with the caged lions rumbling, waiting to be released to rend apart and chew up one poor Ethiopian martyr. Have you been watching, at all?"

"No, I haven't had the opportunity—or the inclination."

"A television first," said Wanda bitterly, finding a cigarette on the coffee table and allowing Nat to light it for her. "A special public service, the network said. Produced by the Marquis de Sade, directed and written by the Spanish Inquisition, they didn't bother to say. I tell you, I don't know what we're coming to. All the sham and pretense. That little monster, Miller, jumping up and announcing the House committee recommends impeachment. Then all kinds of parliamentary business. Then, just now, Wickland—I thought at least, as a Far Westerner, the Majority Leader, he'd be something more—but no, there he was droning out those awful blasphemous four charges as evidence to back their resolution for impeachment. Now there's a point of order, then Miller is going to elaborate on the charges in detail, before the debate begins later." She stopped, looking sorrowfully at Abrahams. "It's terrible. Poor Doug, getting it here—and as a result, look what's happening to him on the road. Who is there to contest these libelous lies?"

"There'll be someone when the debate begins, Wanda. At least a dozen congressmen, white and colored, have come out against this."

"Where are they?"

"They'll be heard, believe me."

She nodded uncertainly. "I have some coffee ready—"

"It's not necessary."

"I have it ready," she said. "I'm sorry the apartment is a mess. The Spingers are in New York on this business. They're meeting with Crispus lawyers on the charges against the Reverend as well as those against Doug. . . . Excuse me a minute."

After she had gone, Nat Abrahams filled his pipe, settled into the chair between the couch and television set, and smoked as he watched the screen. There was a close shot of Representative Zeke Miller rising from his bench, notes in his hand, grinning, waving a greeting to someone, then addressing the chairman and the House.

"My honorable colleagues," Miller was saying, "we on the Judiciary Committee who have recommended this distressing action are not unconscious of our responsibility to our constituents, and to our traditions of justice. We are fully aware that this is only the second occasion in two centuries that it has been found necessary to bring such all-fired powerful proceedings against a Chief Executive of the United States. It is for us a distasteful undertaking. Yet we must have the courage to face our duties and back up our convictions. We must accept the shocking facts as they have come to us, and we must elevate our patriotic concern for our beloved America's future above any sentimental concern over a single weak and dangerous—yes, downright dangerous, for the tyranny of the weak is the worst tyranny of all—individual. Aware as we are that we may face the opprobrium of the squeamish, as well as the protests of Communist appeasers, misguided and devious liberals, sanctimonious and professional minority lovers, we must suffer their slings and arrows to perform the greater good. We beg you not to let your intelligence be hamstrung by the propagandists, but to permit cool reason to accept and weigh the incontrovertible facts in this case."

The camera revealed a close-up of Zeke Miller, mopping his forehead with a handkerchief, gulping water from a glass, and then it held tightly on him as he continued.

"In speaking of the one who was the object of another Presidential impeachment in another time, namely, Andrew Johnson, two of our predecessors in this very chamber, both from the great state of Illinois, remarked that the object of the impeachment was 'as mendacious as he is malignant,' that 'this nation has been too long disgraced by this man, this accidental President. Let him be removed.' I say, let that wise American injunction guide us in our deliberations today."

On the television screen, Miller consulted his notes, and then looked up. "Allow me to elaborate on the four major points in our resolution for impeachment, one by one in their order, and offer to you the evidence of how President Douglass Dilman has degraded himself and debauched our democratic government, through reptilian cunning and unsavory habits. Let us begin with our first charge, the astounding and appalling conduct of this accidental President of the United States in his relationship with the mulatto female, an employee of the Soviet Union, known as Miss Wanda Gibson, and the serious consequences of this allegedly illicit relationship. First of all——"

With a start, Nat Abrahams became aware of Wanda's presence behind him. She was standing stock-still, holding the tray of coffee, cream, sugar, her hurt eyes trained on the television screen.

Every instinct of decency impelled Nat Abrahams to rise swiftly, putting himself between Wanda and Miller. He reached to the set, found the right knob, and turned it off. Miller's harangue was interrupted in mid-sentence, his image blotted from view.

Wanda closed her eyes briefly, then said, "Thank you, Nat." As he pulled his chair to the coffee table, she inquired, "Cream and sugar?"

"Sugar. I need it."

He laid his pipe in the ashtray and began to drink the coffee.

Wanda Gibson circled the coffee table. "Doug telephoned me from Cleveland last night, after the speech," she said. "He didn't want to talk about that though, only to find out if I'd read Reb Blaser's column in the Miller paper. He'd read it. Apparently it appears in Cleveland too. Have you seen it?"

"I don't read Blaser's column," Abrahams said.

"You should, because lots of others do, and they're people too, and they have as much to say as we do." She plucked the folded newspaper off an end table. "You want to hear the column? Well, the first paragraph, anyway. The heading says, 'The Red and The Black.' Then it goes on, 'Now then, good citizens, if our illustrious President has done nothing else during his short term in office, he has revived an interest in the classics, especially in Stendhal's *The Red and the Black*. The difference is that Douglass Dilman has rewritten the sordid and immoral French yarn, and given it a peculiarly modern twist. The Red, in the new version, is the infamous Soviet undercover agent, Franz Gar, and the Black is his executive office assistant, Wanda Gibson, the comely Negro paramour of the President of the United States.' " She lifted her eyes. "Enough?"

"Too much, considering the source," said Abrahams. He hesitated, frowning, and then he said, because he felt she was one that he could tell the truth to, "Wanda, you've got to steel yourself for more of the same. This could be only the beginning."

"Oh, I know." She sat down, one hand massaging the other. "I've turned away two dozen photographers and reporters today."

Abrahams put down his coffee cup, and took up his pipe. "Mind?"

"Please—"

He passed a lighted match over the tobacco. "I'm here to help you, if you require help, not only because Doug wants it, but because I want it."

"That's kind of you, but—"

"Wanda," he went on, "I'm not interested in newspaper dirt, any more than you or Doug should be. I'm interested in seeing that you are treated fairly under the law. I've already been to the Department of Justice. I've been assured that there is absolutely no evidence in their files that would enable them to charge you with being a Communist. As of today, Justice has no plan to prosecute you in any way. Yet, inevitably, you will be questioned, and I wanted to see you before that begins."

"Too late," she said calmly. "It's already begun."

"Who?"

"The legal counsel for the House Judiciary Committee, a Mr. Wine. He was here at the crack of dawn today, with aides, to hand me a subpoena. Either I had to appear before the subcommittee, or testify before him and sign my statement. That's what I did, the last."

"What did he want to know?" Abrahams demanded hastily.

"Everything. Where I was born, educated, how I lived, jobs, family, everything. Most of it was about Doug and myself, when and where we met, how often we saw one another when he was a senator, after he became President, how frequently we talked on the telephone, how—"

"How many times did you see Doug after he became President?"

"Only once, I'm sorry to say, once and no more. He came here to offer me a job in the White House. I turned it down. Of course, we had a number of telephone conversations."

"What else were you asked?"

"Exactly what our conversations were about. That Mr. Wine was so obvious and embarrassing, all those suggestive questions. Did Doug tell me about what went on in the Oval Office, at Cabinet meetings, the National Security Council meetings, and so forth? Did I discuss Doug with my employer?"

"What did you tell him, Wanda?"

"The truth. What else was there to tell? I have heard no secrets, so I had none to pass on. I doubt if Franz Gar even knew Doug was a friend of mine. Then—then all kinds of nasty stuff about my having lived here when Doug did—both of us under the same roof—the illicit love routine."

"I hope you told him to—"

"To drop dead? No. I'm a straightforward person, a defect of mine, but it makes sleep easier. I said the President and I never had an affair. We have known each other nearly five years, and he has never done anything more aggressive than kiss me, embrace me, hold me, hold my hand, and that yes, we have always been fully clothed in one another's company. Good Lord, you know Doug as well as I do. To him, all women are Vestal Virgins, unless sanctioned by the church and state to procreate. That's why I almost laughed at their other charge of immorality—Doug, the libertine, trying to rape that daughter of Senator Watson. Can you imagine them swallowing that?" She halted and looked hard at Abrahams. "No one will believe that, or the things about me, will they?"

Abrahams shifted uneasily. He could never lie to this woman. "People believe what they want to believe, Wanda."

She was immediately disturbed. "Then you think he might be impeached? He doesn't think it is possible."

"Anything is possible, but he is most likely correct in his estimate of it. This may amount to no more than a means of public censure. I did some superficial browsing on the subject this morning. Impeachments by the House of Representatives are few and far between. Since 1797, the House of Representatives has considered innumerable impeachment charges, yet voted to send Articles of Impeachment to the Senate only twelve times in history."

"*Only* twelve times," repeated Wanda, aghast. "I thought only once—Andrew Johnson."

"No. He was the one President ever impeached. But the House has the right to consider impeachment of other civil officers, too. Besides President Johnson, impeachments were voted against an associate justice of the Supreme Court, a secretary of war, a senator, and eight Federal judges."

"What happened to the twelve who were impeached? Was that the end of them?"

"God, no, Wanda. Impeachment by the House is not a trial but a hearing. If the majority of the House votes against the evidence, the whole matter is dropped for the time, although the House brought impeachment proceedings against Andrew Johnson three times before it got a favorable vote. If the majority votes in favor of impeachment, that is but the first step. It means the person facing impeachment has been indicted for high crimes, and then, and only then, does his case go before the whole Senate, which is converted into a High Court, with the Chief Justice of the Supreme Court presiding if the President is being tried. Then the person being impeached can have a defense, can retain a staff of attorneys—managers, they are called—to combat the charges of the House managers. Of the twelve men who have gone on trial before the Senate since 1797, eight were acquitted, and four were found guilty, all the guilty were judges, and none was punished beyond removal from office."

"And eternal disgrace."

"Yes, I suppose you might say that. The legislator who was impeached, Senator Blount, was not actually tried but was expelled from the Senate, because it was determined that a congressman was not strictly a civil officer."

"To go back to one point you made, Nat. You said that many impeachment cases have been put before the House, like Doug's today. Only twelve were sent to the Senate, you said. What happened to the rest?"

"The indictments did not gain a majority vote. They were not passed. Most of the time, however, civil officers whose names are introduced by the House for impeachment don't let it come to a vote. For example, fifty-five Federal judges have been investigated for impeachment. Eight were impeached, eight were merely censured, twenty-two were acquitted, and seventeen simply resigned their offices and put an end to the proceedings."

"Nat," Wanda said quietly, "Doug told me that he was given a chance to resign yesterday—yesterday morning."

Abrahams felt his hand tighten on the warm bowl of his pipe. "He was? I didn't know that."

"Arthur Eaton came to him on behalf of the others. Eaton told him to step aside or quit, on some health pretext, or—or be prepared for what's going on today." Wanda fiddled with the buttons of her blouse, eyes downcast. "Nat, you can do something for me, and for Doug. Make him resign. Please do it for both of us."

Abrahams studied her unhappy profile. "Why, Wanda?" he asked.

She lifted her head, and her eyes had filled. "Because I—I love him—love him too much to see him stripped and tarred and feathered and lynched in front of the whole world. It'll destroy him, and any happiness he—both of us—might have had. Please make him quit."

Abrahams felt helpless. "If Eaton couldn't make him resign, what makes you think I can, even if I believed it was for the best?"

"I know Doug, his sensitivity. Coming from Eaton, it was an insult, got his hackles up. Coming from you, his closest friend, he would listen, knowing you want the best for him."

Abrahams sucked at his empty pipe, and thought about it. Finally he met her anguished gaze. He shook his head slowly. "Wanda, I truthfully don't know what is best for him. If he sees this through, he has two chances to survive, to win, to prove he deserves to be President. If he quits now, he loses, he has no more career in public service, he admits incompetence and worse."

"He'll be *alive!*" she exclaimed fiercely. "Everyone on earth will know the professional haters forced him out because he is colored; everyone will know. He might conceivably be popular again, have supporters, come back. And if he didn't, he could go into private law practice, and we could make a life for—"

"Wanda, you can't decide this for Doug, and neither can I. Please believe me. Even if he has been goaded beyond common sense, no one can make such a pivotal decision for him. He must make it for himself. That's all I can say to you."

"Yes," she said wearily.

Nat Abrahams wanted to comfort her, but further words would be useless. He rose, and went to the coat tree. As he pulled on his overcoat, he said, "I'll be on my way. I'm at the Mayflower. I want you to promise me, if any more of the House investigators come snooping, you'll pick up that telephone and summon me. No more answers to questions without legal counsel at your side. Will you promise?"

She said nothing.

"Wanda, it's for Doug's sake as well as your own," he said sternly.

"I promise," she said.

"Fine. Now, no more television, either. Keep yourself occupied. Not all of our congressmen are witch hunters. Let's trust there is a majority who still cling to sensibility and decency. If there is, this will be as forgotten as a bad dream. I'll see you soon, Wanda."

"Thanks for everything."

Not until he had fully emerged into the cold afternoon, and gone down the walk to his car, did he realize how relieved he was to escape Wanda's problems and Doug Dilman's problems and the whole impossible situation. Closing himself into his sedan, he felt momentarily insulated from all constricting, suffocating evil, and grateful that he was the lucky person he was, free of torture and punishment, free to return to his untroubled and loving mate, to a new career that promised him wealth and security, to a life unfettered by savage scandal and constant cruelty. Never had he been more grateful than now for being who he was, with so snug and tidy a niche in so seething and blazing a world.

Then, as he turned the ignition key and heard the engine whine and catch, heard its power idling, his conscience was awakened by the smooth mechanical purr.

Before the bar of his conscience, the blood went to his cheeks, and he felt the heat of shame. For he knew that he had allowed himself the vain corruptions of superiority and safety, and in his heart he knew that he possessed neither. He and Douglass Dilman were both men on this earth, with minds and hearts and limbs like one another and every man. His own position in life was high, but no higher than Doug's position, and he was no more secure on high than his friend. If Doug was vulnerable today, and could be brought down, then so could he. He possessed nothing that Douglass Dilman did not possess. And his shame now came from the vanity of his one safe possession that Douglass Dilman did not have and could never own—the thin sheath of his conforming white epidermis.

Nat Abrahams shifted gears, and the car leaped forward. He was satisfied to know, at last, what he fervently prayed that the honorable members of the House of Representatives would know in due time—that any impeachment of Douglass Dilman, because of his difference, would also become an indictment of themselves, and of half-civilized men everywhere, for all of history.

On the fourth day after his departure from Washington, President Douglass Dilman stood hatless and coatless in the wind and the sun of Cape Kennedy, near Cocoa Beach on the east coast of Florida. He stood flanked by the Chairman of the Joint Chiefs of Staff, by the nation's most famous astronaut, by several members of the National Aeronautics and Space Administration, posing for pictures being taken by the dense swarm of press photographers around him.

Following the wintry weather (and receptions) endured elsewhere on the trip, the Florida sun now baking down on his bare head and the Atlantic breeze now gently nipping at his brown suit represented an agreeable change. Yet Douglass Dilman was uncomfortable.

Staring back at the clicking shutters being manipulated by the crouching, kneeling, shouting photographers, Dilman experienced the sinking sensation of one who suddenly realizes that he is having his picture taken for some nefarious purpose. Under different circumstances, the excessive photography might have been innocent and natural: news shots heralding the Commander in Chief on his first inspection of his country's foremost missile test center. Under today's circumstances, the excessive photography was suspicious: news shots recording for posterity and editorial morgues the nation's leader on his last outing as President of the United States.

The darker side of Dilman's mind wondered what the caption would be on each still shot, as it was transmitted to New York and from there around the world. Then he knew that there would not be one caption to every photograph, but two, and with cynical amusement he wrote the alternate captions in his head: (A) "The grim and embittered President, shown minutes before learning he was impeached for high crimes and misdemeanors by a majority of the House"; (B) "The determined and courageous Chief Executive at Cape Kennedy minutes before hearing of his vindication by a majority of the House, who voted down the charges against him."

In an effort to supply appropriate art for the happier caption, Dilman tried to reset his face, tried to look determined and courageous, but he knew that he was not succeeding. He still looked grim, because his innards were poisoned with disappointment and bitterness.

The swing around the country had been an unremitting disaster. Everywhere, he had been preceded by the one-sided, unrefuted charges introduced into the House of Representatives, the charges of his treasonable conduct, his immorality, his intemperance, his contempt of the people's own elected Congress, all trumpeted into every municipality and hamlet, into every ear, via newspapers, radio, and television. Everywhere, the seeds of hatred had been sown, and everywhere, he had reaped the harvest of malice and malevolence.

There seemed no color line that divided the nation in its united aversion to his presence. The white folks screamed at him as if he were a dangerous orangutan on the loose. The colored folks condemned him as if he were a black Quisling who had sold his people back into slavery. If the demonstration against him in Cleveland had been a horror, his violent reception in the Shrine Auditorium of Los Angeles (where his life had been briefly imperiled by young hotheads who rushed the stage) had been worse, equaled only by his reception in Seattle, where not one word of his fifteen-minute talk had been heard.

The hurried visits to widespread military installations, under the reluctant guidance of General Pitt Fortney, had been no less distressing. At Fort Bragg, North Carolina, at general headquarters of the Strategic Air Command outside Omaha, Nebraska, at the ICBM site near Cheyenne, Wyoming, at Fort Bliss, Texas, Dilman had been maddened by an entirely different kind of contempt.

At the military installations, the Commander in Chief could not be met by placards and fists and curses. Instead, disdain and low opinion were implied subtly, through mock formality, extravagant courtesy, lack of social warmth. On every inspection and tour, he had found his hosts, his guides, his companions, his servants, to be low-ranking Negro officers or Negro enlisted men. Wherever he had appeared, television sets and radios had been flicked off, newspapers had been hidden, and nowhere had mention been made, reasonably or unreasonably, encouragingly or discouragingly, of his impeachment being debated in the House of Representatives—and throughout the nation. From the seething rage and turmoil of the big cities, he had been dropped by jet airplane into the chilly, soundless atmosphere of ostracism by silence. He had been kept at arm's length (and a salute), as if he were a leper forced in among them, a leper who would soon, by the vote of his betters, be removed to some political Molokai.

When his jet aircraft had put him down at Patrick Air Force Base, south of Cape Kennedy, this morning, he had known what to expect. With dread he had entered the motorcade, expecting vocal censure from the citizenry and silent rejection from the military once more, and in both instances he had been surprised. While there had often been a hundred thousand persons lining the route to cheer every successful astronaut from John H. Glenn to Leo Jaskawich, and, by Flannery's estimate, there had been no more than ten thousand along the route to receive him, Dilman had been anything but dismayed. If there had been no cheers, there had also been, for the first time, no catcalls, no shouts of disapprobation, no visible hatred. The onlookers watching him ride past had proved orderly, and their sunburned faces had reflected only interest and curiosity.

Even after his entry through the main gate of Cape Kennedy, acknowledging the saluting security guards and uniformed staff and workers, he had found the atmosphere more courteous than hostile. His short speech to the assembled personnel and the press, promising full support of the administration to the Apollo program, to its forthcoming three-man reconnaissance of the moon, had been received without snickers or protest, with full attention and respect.

Yet, after visiting the sprawling Central Control Building, with its four intricate IBM electronic computers, after arriving at the Gemini launching pad to pose for the photographers, Dilman's sense of anxiety had been revived. The session of picture taking, much of it by cameramen who had trailed him constantly from the White House to this site, had reminded him of the whole disastrous trip and of what was taking place on the floor of the House of Representatives this moment.

Leaving the Control Building, Tim Flannery had whispered to him that the members of the House had reconvened, and that the summations had been concluded, and that there had been heartening support of Dilman from several Western representatives, notably Collins of Montana, who had warned his colleagues that their evidence for impeachment was "built on quicksand" and "if they indicted a President for his personal habits and his friends and his opinions," they were opening the way for future Congresses to control the executive branch completely, and "punish Presidents for the cut of their clothes or the behavior of their wives or the score of their intelligence quotients."

Nevertheless, the knowledge that the debate had come to an end, and that the final vote on impeachment was about to begin, had filled Dilman with oppressive concern. If the House, which more closely reflected the feelings of the voters than did the Senate, felt the same hatred for him that he had recently witnessed around the nation, he was doomed.

Still he could not believe it would happen. His firm belief was that the House members, having enjoyed the catharsis of vituperation, would now realize the historic gravity of the decision they faced. They would realize that an impeachment in modern times was unthinkable, that the legal instrument of reproof and discipline in the Constitution had become obsolete. In fact, just the other night, unable to sleep, Dilman had come across the words of an eminent political scientist who had once charac-

terized impeachment as a "rusted blunderbuss, that will
probably never be taken in hand again." Surely, the more
judicious of the House members would see that, would
think twice before signifying aye or nay. In the end, these
members would not give their vote to Zeke Miller, whose
own political motives were more questionable than those
he had attributed to Dilman. There could be no question about it. When the vote came shortly, cooler heads
would prevail.

Dilman heard General Fortney's Texas-accented voice
drawl forth, "All righty, you fellows, you've had enough
of your picture taking for now!" Fortney turned to General Leo Jaskawich. "What next? Want to put us into
orbit?"

Jaskawich offered the Chairman of the Joint Chiefs
of Staff a restrained official smile, then he said to Dilman, "Mr. President, I hope you'll allow me to ride you
up to the top of the pad. There is a wonderful view from
there."

"I'd certainly like to see it," said Dilman.

Dilman stepped into the elevator, followed by Fortney, Jaskawich, and the Operations Director. Slowly
they ascended alongside the upper portion of the Titan
rocket until they rattled to a halt 100 feet above the
concrete pad.

Emerging onto the platform between the rocket's nose
and the steel tower overhead, Dilman found it windier
and cooler. He followed Jaskawich's arm and hand,
straight as a signpost, as the astronaut pointed out the
blockhouses, the Test Annex, the workstands, the service towers, the other launch rings, the moonport on
Merritt Island. For the most, Dilman was inattentive, absently gazing out at the indigo-blue ocean to the east,
the ocean that led to Washington.

Suddenly he became conscious of the fact that Jaskawich was looking at him, and that they were alone.
Fortney and the Operations Director had moved to another section of the platform.

Jaskawich offered an understanding smile. "I can't
blame you for not listening, Mr. President," he said. "I'm
sure your thoughts today are more concerned with what's

happening on the ground than with what's happened in outer space."

The young man's directness and quick perception nudged Dilman's interest in him. He attempted to smile back. "As a matter of fact, you are quite right, General."

"I—while I can speak to you like this—there is something I wanted to say to you, sir. I've been reading about your trip around the United States. I've been following the debate in the House of Representatives on television. I've never been more ashamed of my fellow Americans, or their representatives, and I wanted you to know. I want you to know also, there are many of us who feel this has been rigged, blown up out of all proportion, and that you are being judged solely because of prejudice against your color. Maybe I'm out of line, but I had to tell you."

Not in days had Dilman been so genuinely moved by the friendliness of another human being. His eyes moistened, and he averted his head. "I thank you," he said, almost inaudibly. "I sincerely appreciate your understanding. I—in fact, I was impressed from the moment I arrived here—by the courtesy, an air of decency, such as I have not seen in four days."

Jaskawich's frank, open face had become intensely serious. "We are another breed here at Cape Kennedy—not everyone, but certainly the men who have finally gone up, and the handful most closely involved with them. We're trained to be cast closer to heaven and its planets. And when you leave the earth for orbit in space, as I have three times, you can see how small our little mudball of a world is in true godly perspective. When a one-and-a-half-million-pound thrust puts you up there, alone in the Mercury capsule, or with one other in the Gemini capsule, and you swing around the earth for several days, you come to have some spiritual knowledge of what the Maker meant when he packed our pattycake together, and populated it with living beings, and gave this mudball a semblance of order and its men a modicum of intelligence. Believe me, Mr. President, you lose all petty poisons that corrupt men and spoil life. You lose all that in outer space. You come to understand how lucky man is even to exist, how fortunate he is to survive, and you come to speculate on why he lacks appreciation of his lot, and why he destroys so much of his own pleasure and the enjoyment of those around him with incredible pettiness of mind and action. One period, when I was up there, I thought—I know this will sound odd—but I thought, if only men like Caligula, Attila, Torquemada, Hitler, the jurors of Socrates, the witch burners of Salem, the bombers of Birmingham, the ravagers of reason and decency had been made to don our twenty-pound pressurized space suits and been hurtled into orbit, to look above and look below, and then had fired their retrorockets to descend to earth once more, they would come down like resurrected saints. That's what can happen, Mr. President. No matter how many or few your failings, when you return from there to here, you are never the same again. You've left prejudice, hatred, destructiveness, lying, cheating in the reaches of outer space. You look upon your fellow men with the eyes of eternity, as your equals on the earth, and you want to live and let live. That's why so many of us here—"

He stopped in mid-sentence. General Fortney and the Operations Director had walked back to join them again.

Fortney said to Dilman, "Had enough of this?"

Dilman smiled. "I find I like it up here. But I guess it's time to get down to earth."

In the elevator he studied General Leo Jaskawich with new interest. During an era already becoming jaded from continuous space exploits and achievements, Jaskawich was a special hero. He was the only astronaut to have been in orbit three times, once alone and then twice in the two-man Gemini capsule for six days. His physical aspect was deceptively average, in no proportion matching his legend. Dilman judged the astronaut to be perhaps five feet ten inches in height, and weighing around 160 pounds. His hair was short-cropped and sun-blanched, his eyes quick and kind, his nose the most prominent feature on his swarthy Lithuanian face. He wore his uniform not as a martinet would, but with the confidence of one who had earned it through calculated and accepted risk. Not since Dilman had first met Nat Abrahams, and later The Judge and Tim Flannery, had he so quickly allowed himself to like and trust another being.

After that, for the remainder of their ground tour about the heart of Cape Kennedy, Dilman was entirely attentive to Leo Jaskawich. Especially in Hangar R, where rested the enormous Apollo spacecraft, with its two outer bays for equipment, that would hold three astronauts and bring them within 40,000 feet of the surface of the moon, did Dilman appreciate Jaskawich's eloquence and become infected by the astronaut's enthusiasm over the approaching lunar exploration.

The last stop before riding out to the beach was the horseshoe-shaped, one-story dormitory where the new astronauts, twelve in number, now training for the next Apollo flight, were supposed to reside while on the base.

As they examined the neat, furnished rooms, Jaskawich stated, "Ten of them live here, while their families live in Cocoa Beach."

Some inconsistency joggled inside Dilman's head. "Ten live here? I thought you said there were twelve in training."

Before Jaskawich could reply, General Fortney brusquely intervened. "A couple of them preferred to stay in the old barracks. It's the same as this. They're doing special work that keeps them up later. Let's move on."

As he started away with the directors and public relations officers, Dilman held Jaskawich back. "Those other two, who are they? Why are they living separately?"

For the first time, Jaskawich appeared uneasy. "They are Negroes, sir," he said.

"But I thought this place was—"

"I know, Mr. President," Jaskawich said sadly. "When I spoke of a new breed of men that had grown out of this program, I meant the ones who had experienced orbital flight or been thoroughly indoctrinated for it. The new trainees are just groundlings, and while they are superior in some respects, they still carry the infection of groundling education and prejudices. Officially, like all military installations since 1951, this is a desegregated base, entirely so. But if two newcomers are made to feel—well—different, and know they'll have more peace of mind for concentrating on their training if they can remove themselves from social abrasion, they do so, they volunteer. I don't think our two colored astronauts give a damn. They're too devoted to the work. That's all that counts. Eventually, I promise you, the others will be inviting them back to this building." He hesitated, and then added, "Even when done on a so-called voluntary basis, I didn't back this segregation. I'm not running the show, but I stepped out of channels long enough to buck a note up to Fortney at the Pentagon. I never had a reply. Maybe Fortney never saw it."

"Maybe he did," said Dilman. "He knows what is going on here."

"Dammit, I'm sorry, Mr. President."

"You've done your best. Now I'll do mine. You see that I have a memorandum waiting for me at the White House, reminding me to order that all the astronaut trainees on the Cape henceforth, whatever their wish or anyone else's, live in the same quarters, receive the same food and teaching, without discrimination or favoritism. You can bet I'll act on it."

Jaskawich's eyes were bright. "You'll have that memo. Thank you, Mr. President."

"To everyone else I may be a groundling, but you and I know, General, I've been up there and returned." Dilman started to go, then had an afterthought and stopped. "Tell me, General Jaskawich, are you permanently assigned to Cape Kennedy?"

"Yes, sir."

"What do you do here?"

"I'm supposed to teach," he said, and then he grinned. "I don't really. There are a hundred men who can handle that better than I can. I'm not a teacher, I'm a doer type. I was supposed to direct the Apollo operation, but that was just publicity. I'm really based here to guide eminent visitors around, like congressmen, especially the ones on appropriation committees, or columnists, who can give us the right public image. I'm reduced to the profession of being an animated monument or showpiece. I make commencement addresses, too. Very good ones, I might add."

"Are you going to be sent up again?"

"I'm afraid not, Mr. President. I'm past my thirty-fourth birthday, and the limit for men going into space is now thirty-five."

Dilman took out a cigar and busied himself with it, and then remembered to offer Jaskawich an Upmann. "Allowed to smoke?"

"Absolutely," said Jaskawich. "But no, thanks, that cigar is too much for me. Mind if I have one of my own?"

"Go ahead."

Jaskawich took out a slender cheroot and his crested lighter, hastily lit the President's cigar first and then his own cheroot. He inhaled. "Good," he said.

"Tell me," Dilman said, "do you like Washington?"

"I like any place where there's action and challenge, and I guess that describes Washington."

"It certainly does," said Dilman. He resumed walking, with Jaskawich keeping in stride beside him. "I was thinking," Dilman went on, "how much we could use—in the Pentagon, maybe even in the White House—the judgment of a person who has been a little closer to heaven than any of us are ever likely to be." He cast the astronaut a speculative glance. "Think you'd be interested?"

"Mr. President," said Jaskawich fervently, "you signal retrofire—and Washington's where I'll land."

"All right," said Dilman, "you stand by, and when I—"

Dilman came to a jarring halt, teetering for a moment, waiting, as he stared straight ahead. He could see Tim Flannery, rushing up the dormitory corridor toward him. At once, discerning the upset expression twisted across the press secretary's usually pleasant countenance, Dilman's heart began to hammer. Gone were his cheer and high hopes of the past minutes.

"Mr. President, I wanted to catch you before you

went outside," Flannery said breathlessly. "The reporters and photographers are piling up out there, waiting for you. I had Fortney order guards to hold them in line a few minutes. It's just happened, Mr. President—goddamit—" The redhead's freckled face became contorted, and Flannery looked as if he might weep. "The vote in the House, it's over—" he said brokenly.

Curiously, Dilman suffered no pang of fear, and no hurt. He said quietly, not as a question, as a flat statement of fact, "I've been impeached."

"Yes—goddamit, it's terrible—I don't know what—"

Dilman's hand touched Flannery's shoulder. "Easy, Tim. Details are unimportant, but—was it close?"

"The vote was 287 for impeachment, 161 against it."

Dilman nodded. "I see. The voice of the people."

"The voice of bigotry!" Jaskawich exclaimed fiercely.

Dilman licked his lips, and was embarrassed by his uncontrollable Adam's apple. "Well," he said, with a slight shrug. His eyes moved from Jaskawich to Flannery. "What next, Tim?"

"According to the radio, an announcement just came from the Senate Office Building—no wonder they call it SOB—it came from Senator Hankins. He said the Senate will be convened as a High Court, and be ready to try you a week from now. Mr. President, about those newshounds yelping outside the door—"

Dilman's knuckles crept to his forehead. He felt dizzy and displaced. "I—I can't see them yet, Tim. Get me out of it."

"What can I do?" Flannery said wretchedly. "They're fifty feet deep outside the front door and even in back. There's no—"

Jaskawich clutched Dilman's arm. "I can help you. There's a fire exit at the side of this building—no one'll know—we can slip out of there—give you a two- or three-minute jump on them before—"

Immediately Jaskawich started off, with the President and press secretary following him.

Five minutes later, dusty and panting, Dilman reached the Cadillac limousine behind Jaskawich and Flannery, as the surprised Secret Service agents and Cape security guards closed in from either side.

Quickly Dilman shook hands with Jaskawich. "Thanks for everything, General. Too bad, but I don't expect I'll have the authority, very soon, to send for you. You'd have liked Washington."

"I don't like it now," said Jaskawich angrily. "That's why maybe I'll show up whether you send for me or not. You've still got a big chance——"

"I don't know," said Dilman. "I just don't know."

As Dilman settled heavily into the back seat, then made room for Flannery, he could observe, through the curving surface of the car's bubble top, the herd of reporters and photographers on the run in the distance, hurrying to assault him again.

"Patrick Air Force Base," Dilman ordered the chauffeur, as two Secret Service agents slammed into the limousine. Up ahead, the motorcycles were forming a protective wedge. The Cadillac moved, wheeled right, and pointed toward the exit gate.

"Mr. President, I was just thinking," Flannery began earnestly, "when you make your last speech in St. Louis tomorrow, you'll have a chance to answer the impeachment. The minute we get to St. Louis tonight, we can sit down and revise——"

Dilman had been immersed in thought. While the car sped through the gate, leaving the Cape Kennedy missile site, he suddenly said, "Tim, there's going to be no St. Louis. No St. Louis. Do me a favor, do you mind?" His limp hand indicated the radiotelephone beside Flannery. "Ring the airport for me, and notify the crew we're changing our flight plans. Have them get clearance to take me straight to Sioux City, Iowa. Then locate Noyes in Washington and have him cancel the St. Louis speech, the whole visit. Tell him to make any excuse. Tell him I'm sick. I *am* sick." He alleviated the press secretary's instant concern with the faintest smile. "Not the way you think, Tim."

Dilman pointed to the mobile telephone unit again. "Book me into a Sioux City hotel for overnight. No engagements, not that anyone except the reporters would want to see me. I've got no patronage to hand out now. I'm nothing more than a politician under criminal indictment, and that's like being a typhoid carrier. I think we'll have our privacy in Sioux City."

Flannery had heard this out with unconcealed anguish. "Mr. President, please reconsider the St. Louis speech. You've still—"

"No. I need time to think, and I know what must be done first. After you've finished the other calls, get The Judge for me. He lives outside Sioux City somewhere—"

"Fairview Farm."

"Yes, that's right. Tell him I'd like to drive out and have breakfast with him tomorrow morning, ham and eggs and a little talk, the two of us, an ex-President and one about to join his club, and nobody else. Tell him I won't need much of his time, maybe an hour, before I head back to Washington."

For quiet seconds Douglass Dilman listlessly watched the business section, the stores and offices and nightclubs of Cocoa Beach, flash by. Then, still staring outside the window, he said, "Funny how, the moment everything collapsed around me ten minutes ago, my mind went back to my father. Funny, because I never really knew my old man, except from some pictures and what my mother used to tell me. He died when I was just a child. My mind went to him, I guess, because I felt like a helpless kid they're after, and I wanted someone old enough and strong enough to stand in front of me, between them and me. But then, I knew I had no father. So I had to adopt one, someone who was tough and sure and unafraid, someone who was—was old enough for me to respect and talk to. So automatically, in my head, I kind of adopted The Judge. Crazy, because he hardly knows me and I hardly know him either. But he's as irascible and durable as an Assyrian goat. You know, Tim, my first morning as President he called me from his farm, and after he finished lecturing me, he said, 'Young fellow, you listen and remember, if you ever need my advice or a helping hand, both of which are untaxable and both of which we got plenty of, you come out here and visit the Missus and me, and we'll have a good farm breakfast and set you straight.' That's what he said, Tim."

Dilman turned away from the window and met Flannery's eyes. "I'd have no way of knowing, but I guess that's the way a father would talk. . . . Now, what in the devil's keeping you, Tim? We haven't got all day. Get on the phone there and start making those long-distance calls, charged to the White House, while I can still spend the government's money."

It was a luminous, pure, autumn-crisp Iowa morning. Overhead, the disc of sun was too fresh to the new day to have yet warmed the air or the soil, so that the air still livened the flesh and entered the lungs with the bracing coolness of a natural spring, and the patches of grass and springy earth underfoot were damp with the night dew. There was a strange, tangy, life-giving smell all around, a mingling of rural odors of livestock and poultry, of corn and wheat, of red barn paint and crackling skillet.

They made their way back from their hike, in step, without haste, strolling leisurely, the President of the United States and the ex-President of the United States, both holding to their own ruminations as they crossed the barnyard toward the sprawling gray-and-red farm house.

The Judge held his gnarled Irish shillelagh aloft, to greet the arriving farmhand clad in patched blue overalls, and then he brandished the walking stick at an indignant rooster. "Guess you've got yourself an appetite at last, eh, young man?" he said to Dilman.

"Yes, Judge, I'm about ready."

Dilman had been too impatient for a hike when it had begun, and had gone along only out of courtesy to his aged host. Now he was grateful for the tonic of the walk, and his respect for the ex-President's instinctive folk wisdom was reinforced.

Upon his arrival at Fairview Farm, ten miles outside Sioux City, Dilman had been abashed by The Judge's unceremonious welcome as they shook hands on the wooden porch.

The Judge had snorted, expectorated, and rasped out, "So, they crucified you up on the Hill yesterday, eh, my friend? Hell and tarnations, I've known them for muddleheads and blockheads half my life, and firsthand, but I sure didn't expect them to take leave of their senses, insulting our office of President, making our Party into a white demagogue's party, slapping the Negro vote in the face. Couldn't have done better if they wore white hoods when they indicted you, the blasted fools."

"I'm glad we're of one mind," Dilman had said, his hand still gripped in The Judge's hand, as they remained in sight of Flannery, the Secret Service agents, the state police.

The Judge had let go of the handshake. "Young man, I hold a strictly zoological view of our legislative branch. Taken as a whole, Congress reminds me of nothing more than a dinosaur—the Stegosaurus, to be specific—a giant body with a peewee head and a collective brain the size of a walnut. Taken individually, the members are either dodoes or dingoes—understand?—the dodo bird pretending to be a bird, yet unable to fly, and heading for extinction because of self-importance, pretension, unadapability—the dingo dog of Australia, half domestic pet, faithful and serving, other half wild beast, roving in packs and killing sheep. Congress!" He had glared off. "Who in the hell is invading our serenity?"

Three sedans, crammed to overflowing, had come bumping up the rutted main road into Fairview Farm.

"The press," Dilman had said.

"Let them stew," The Judge had growled. He had considered Dilman, eyes narrowing. "Young man, you're not fit to enjoy our food, not yet. Come on, let's you and me take a brisk half hour's hike over the farm—show you how the middle of America lives—you'll find it good for your juices—cleanse out all the spite from your gut before breakfast."

They had fled from the press into the inner hall and parlor, and emerged through the back door, and gone on their hike. The Judge, entwining a knitted scarf around shoulders and neck, taking up his walking stick, had led Dilman to the towering silo, where green corn and feed were already stored and ripening for the winter, and past the windmill, and through the sheds where the gleaming four-row cultivators, plows, harvesters were parked. They had paused at the hogpen, where the pigs lined the troughs, jostling, squealing, eating their swill.

They had gone inside the vast red barn to watch the milking machines attached to the udders of cows, and to observe the buckets of milk being taken to cream separators. The Judge had pointed out the haymow on the upper floor of the barn, proudly announcing that he labored up there three times a week, pitching hay down to the mangers.

They had rested briefly before a second farmhouse, smaller and newer than The Judge's own, where his niece and her young son and daughter lived. "Kids are in school now, or I'd show the tykes off to you," The Judge had said with pleasure. "Smartest ones you ever seen. Good having them all here with me, makes me young again, but too bad it had to be. She was married to my younger brother's boy, and he got himself sniped at and killed some years ago in Vietnam. So I took them in. She does my typing, letter answering, editing of my books for her board and keep." Then he growled, " 'Course, if she knew the truth, I'd pay her just to have those young ones around."

After that, they had cut across a soft field, freshly plowed and planted with winter wheat, and then entered a wooded area, stopping only when they had arrived at the gurgling, swift-running creek. "Better than the Potomac," The Judge had said. "I spend every hour of the summer I can spare just lazing on the bank over there, fishing with live bait, chewing my cud, and catching stray memories. I don't know a better way of living. Too bad it's going out of our giddyup life." He had dug his stick into the soil in several places near the creek. "Sometimes you can kick up an old Indian arrowhead. Can you imagine that? Let's head back to the chow line before the Missus has my scalp for starving a guest."

As they returned to the main house, The Judge spoke

several times, in his nasal fashion, of his book reading.
He had pride, like most largely self-educated persons,
in his thorough knowledge of several subjects. His collection of volumes on American history, one of the most
extensive private collections in the nation, now reposed
in the Presidential Library that bore his name. He could
quote at length from almost any book in that library.
He had read deeply, if not selectively, in the works of
philosophers, and he would remember an anecdote about
Diogenes as readily as a passage from Thoreau. Once,
encompassing all of his feudal domain with a swing of
his stick, he said, "I love this because it inspires meditation. 'Life is a ticklish business. I have resolved to spend
it in reflecting upon it.' Know who said that? Dutchman
named Arthur Schopenhauer. Don't subscribe to some
of his ideas, but like that one. Trouble with a job like
the Presidency is it's a job where you should do more
thinking than anyone in the world, and yet you have
less time to think than a shoe clerk."

Twice, approaching the large farm house, Dilman had
opportunities to inspect carefully his famous, cantankerous host. The Judge was short, overweight, certainly
eighty years old, but he was confident in his opinion,
lean-minded, jaunty. His chapped globe-face with its
pimple triangle of a nose resembled, except for the myopic eyes, nothing so much as a squashed pumpkin left
outdoors long after Halloween. Above all, he was earthy,
common, colorful, and knew it, and promoted the image.
In their walk, he had characterized Representative Zeke
Miller as "a kind of adolescent who likes to step on flowers," and he had dusted off Senator Bruce Hankins as
"ineffectual because rigor mortis set in on him two decades ago." As to Arthur Eaton, he had hooted at the
name, remarking that "he wants to be President more
than any man in this country, yet he thinks it's bad table
manners to admit it, but take my word, you could fit all
his supporters in a telephone booth." Best of all, The
Judge had said wryly, he preferred to discuss more dependable and trustworthy animals, such as the livestock
on his farm.

When they entered the homey parlor, Dilman realized

to what extent the hike and the fresh air had fatigued him. And for the first time there was the hollow need for food in his belly. He was about to flop into the widest armchair when the Missus came in, scolding her husband for his tardiness and warmly taking Dilman's hand.

Seeing her this way, in her inexpensive cotton print housedress and white apron, Dilman was reminded of how impossible it was to believe that she had once been the First Lady of the land and the hostess in the State Dining Room. Her thinning blue-gray hair was set neatly above a smooth, plump face, broken only by the bifocal spectacles perched low on the bridge of her potato nose. She was dumpy and grandmotherly, like senior models shown in advertisements for pancake mixes or hot cereals, and although she would brook no nonsense from The Judge, she was adoring of him, and sweet and concerned about everyone else in the world.

She had been, early in the century, a county librarian, Dilman remembered, and her choice of language was less erratic and more refined than that of her husband.

"Right now I want to apologize for The Judge's behavior," she said to Dilman, "treating you like some delegate from the 4-H clubs rather than President. He and his farm! And walking you nearly to death. Why did I have to marry the world's number-one pedestrian? Now, you come right in and eat, Mr. President. You look famished. And as for you, Judge, take off that abominable scarf, and wash your hands, and don't keep us waiting."

After they had gone into the dining room and settled themselves around the circular colonial table, The Judge tucked the corner of his napkin into his shirt, bowed his head, muttered grace, then smacked his lips and poked his spoon into the steaming porridge. As Dilman finished his own porridge, and consumed the rest of the generous breakfast—the waffles, the browned ham and scrambled eggs, the oven-hot biscuits, the still-warm, creamy glass of milk—his mood perversely altered from mindless well-being to vague depression.

He had made this visit outside Sioux City to seek advice—or confirmation—of a political and personal decision that had possessed all his thoughts from the second that he had learned of his impeachment. For more than a half hour he had been diverted from unhappy reality by the outdoor interlude with the ex-President. Briefly his healthy exhaustion and hunger had distracted his mind. But now, with breakfast almost ended, with his stomach filled and his calves strong, he was no longer diverted. The truth of his painful situation permeated his thinking. No rural sight-seeing, no return to nature, no amount of fresh air or delicious food, could anesthetize him longer.

He was about to speak what was uppermost in his mind when the Missus rose from the table. "I'll leave the dishes and let you gentlemen talk," she said. "I can't stand having those poor men and women out front starving, while we stuff ourselves in here. I'm going to see they at least get coffee and biscuits in the shed. . . . As for you, Judge, don't go smelling up this room and getting soot on my curtains with that foul corncob."

The Judge, who was already lighting his brown-yellow corncob pipe, grunted, "You go attend your chickens, Missus." As Dilman peeled the wrapper from his cigar, The Judge said, "Now we can talk peaceably." He puffed with contentment. "I know you got lots on your mind, Douglass, or you wouldn't be out in this godforsaken place. I wasn't unconscious of your problems when I ran you ragged out there and peppered you with all my fool talk about harvesting and horses. I did it on purpose, to try to settle you down."

"I appreciate that," said Dilman. "Matter of fact, while we were walking, I kept envying you—not only you but a friend of mine, Nathan Abrahams, the lawyer—"

"The Chicago fellow? Good man, good man. Followed his handling of tough civil rights cases for years."

"I envied you both because, when your work was done, you had someplace to go. You did your service, Judge, and then you came back to the farm. Nat Abrahams has served in his way, and when he's earned a few more dollars, he, too, has a farm outside Wheaton waiting for him. It must be gratifying to know you've undertaken the tasks on this earth you were born for, have finished them as best you could, and now deserve and can enjoy a reward beyond that of a career alone."

"No reason you can't do the same one day."

"Not a chance," said Dilman, "not any more. I haven't earned my peace. Not that it will be my fault, but that's the way it is working out. I've been impeached—that's an awful thing—the second President ever to be impeached for crimes, existent or nonexistent. Already I'm burdened by a half disgrace. Now I've got to go on trial, like the worst kind of felon, in the biggest, most public courtroom in the world, and hear lies told about my supposed immorality and incompetence and lawbreaking, see these lies become a permanent part of my record and biography, and of American history. They'll convict me, Judge, no matter what their lack of evidence or my rebuttal, because they have one piece of criminal evidence against me I can't refute—and that's that I'm black. I'll be thrown out, the first President in history, and my half disgrace will become full disgrace. My work will be undone. I'll spend the rest of my life, I suppose, like some persecuted fanatic, buttonholing people to convince them I was innocent, to justify my few months in office. I can't seek a farm, a reward, a pension, for a job well done, because I will have been fired. That is why I feel such despair, and why I so much envy you and my friend Nat."

"Sounds to me, young man, like you're beginning the self-pity and buttonholing a mite prematurely," said The Judge owlishly. He sniffed at the bowl of his corncob. "You're impeached. You're not tried yet. You had your years as an attorney. Did you ever give up a client before he went into court?"

"Maybe I practically did, once or twice, when my client was black and his jury was white, and outside the courtroom the papers and the public clamored against him."

The Judge sat straight. "Hell and tarnation, fellow, then you were dead wrong. This is still these United States of America, and not just white America, and you're still innocent until proved guilty. Do you think you're guilty of any one of those loaded Articles of Impeachment they're sending over to the Senate?"

"I'm not guilty of a single one, not even the fourth one, because I contend I had the executive right to remove a Cabinet member, since there's Presidential precedence, and the kangaroo law restraining me was vindictive, prejudicial, and unconstitutional."

"Then you're innocent. Go in there and show them."

"Show whom?" said Dilman bitterly. "Those House advocates—managers—who prosecute me? The full Senate that sits as a jury on me? They're not experienced and uncommitted magistrates. They're elected representatives of the people, mostly voted in for their popularity rather than for having common sense, and so they're the mass public's alter ego. They hear the voice of the people, and they echo that voice. If they don't, they're out on their behinds come next election. I tell you, it boils down to the emotional, unthinking public in the final analysis. Remember, I've been out on the hustings, tramping through the grass roots, these last four days—five days, counting this morning when my hotel in Sioux City was picketed for giving shelter to a Communist traitor—"

The Judge gave a nasal trumpet of disgust and waved his hand in dismissal. "Forget those provincial farmers. Any stranger who comes around these parts, who's been to Paris twice and Moscow once, he's an international scoundrel and Soviet spy. I know my Middle Western brethren. Except for some of our fringe progressive movements, these boneheads are traditional, conservative, close-minded, all hoarding, saving, clinging to one-hoss-shay ideas in their silo heads. But they're not all bad either, only slow. Give them time, a warm stove to sit around, a chance to reason in a language they understand, and they come around, they come around. A section of the country that nurtured Battling Bob La Follette, John Peter Altgeld, Eugene Debs, even produced nuts like Ignatius Donnelly, can't be written off. There's hope for it, and hope for you."

"Too little hope too late, Judge," persisted Dilman. "Let me finish. My fate is in the hands of the voting public right now, and for four days I've seen that public up close, cheek by jowl, and I don't know if any President ever endured such unanimous vilification and hatred. The voice of the people wants me out, and that voice will call the Guilty's in the Senate."

The Judge touched a match to his corncob and said, "I declare, Douglass—and this I didn't altogether expect from you—you're becoming what the Missus' fancy books call a paranoid, meaning you're down on yourself because you've built up a case for believing the whole world's against you, and you won't allow nothing to bring you up."

"I'm facing the harsh facts, Judge—what I've seen firsthand."

"Bah," said The Judge. "You're so beat-up inside, you can't handle a fact when one comes along. Here's a few real facts, the way I see them. I read about your speeches in Cleveland, Los Angeles—where else?—Seattle. You got rough-handled, for sure, but there were lots of people, lots, who weren't booing and stomping their boots against you. There were some clapping for you, I read, not many, but some, and there were lots who were silent, listening, giving you a chance, withholding judgment. There's that part of the public you can't ignore. Then there's that impeachment vote in the House yesterday. Sure, the majority voted against you. But there were plenty who spoke up on your behalf, and out of 448 members there were 161—no small number—who voted for you. They're the people's voice, too. Now, we got the Senate next week. What were most of the senators before they were elected? Most were attorneys-at-law; the Senate's top-heavy with lawyers. That means you'll have more educated men than in the House hearing your trial. Then, also, to be considered is the fact that the House is pretty much overturned every two years and a lot of new members are elected, so the old members have to parrot their constituents word for word if they want to avoid being replaced come next election time, true? Those senators, though, they're in for six years, and they don't have to parrot, knowing in six years their constituents won't remember much or will maybe have mellowed. So you got a body that has its share of donkeys from the

North, and linen suits and Panama hats from the Confederate South, but you got a body of judges apt to be more independent of public hysteria. Young fellow, you remember this: old Andrew Johnson got impeached by the House, but there was no two-thirds against him in the Senate, and contradicting the asinine House, the Senate set Andrew Johnson free."

Dilman shook his head. "No comparison, Judge. Andrew Johnson had everything but the kitchen sink thrown at him, and he barely squeaked by. Me, I've got everything *and* the kitchen sink thrown at me—because, Judge, cards on the table, President Johnson wasn't black, and I am. The electorate and the Congress simply won't have a Negro running their affairs in Washington. They never have and they won't allow it today."

"The hell they never have, Douglass." The corncob in The Judge's hand now went up and down like a schoolteacher's ruler. "Don't tangle with me on matters of history, young fellow. There were fourteen colored congressmen in the House of Representatives between 1869 and 1876, and there are eleven in the House this year. There were two Negroes in the Senate between 1870 and 1881, and there are three in the Senate today. Maybe the public crawls along the way, but each decade it gets a bit closer to the State House in Philadelphia where the Constitution was drafted, signed, and sealed. Americans let some Negroes run their affairs far back as the 1870s and—"

"And what happened right after?" Dilman said. "You're telling half the story. I'll tell you the rest. For sure, no one lived happily ever after. The unreconstructed Southern Democrats powered Hayes into the Presidency, and he paid them back by pulling Federal troops out of the South, troops who'd been protecting Negro voters, and then came the Klan and segregation and the Negroes were niggers again."

"Today it's different," insisted The Judge, "because today Negroes are gaining their rights by using the ballot, not by relying on the force of Federal troops. I don't say you've gotten enough fast enough. What's the old mammy spiritual of yours?—yes—you 'keep inchin' along.' The public's more prepared to allow a Negro to govern than ever before. Maybe not this morning, because they've been whipped into a frenzy against you. But maybe two weeks from this morning, when your side of the case is aired for the first time, maybe then their temper will change and their intelligence be restored. Maybe it's a long shot. I say it's at least a shot. You've still got a good chance."

Dilman had listened thoughtfully, and now he pushed his chair back, hardly aware of the act, and stood up and went to the window. "All right, Judge," he said. "It's no use beating around the bush any longer. I'll tell you what compelled me to come here. But before that, I'd better fill you in on how this impeachment came about."

Quietly, half facing the pondering ex-President, Dilman recounted the entire story, beginning with the CIA report on Baraza that had been withheld from him by Secretary of State Eaton and Governor Talley, and including Miss Watson's effort to help Eaton by her bizarre espionage in the Lincoln Bedroom. Then he told of how he had summoned Eaton to his office to ask him to quit his Cabinet post, and described what had followed— Eaton's refusal to quit, Eaton's demand that, instead, Dilman either resign from the Presidency outright or back off because of a pretended disability and turn the reins of government over to T.C.'s crowd, or prepare himself to face impeachment and trial.

Dilman took a few steps toward The Judge. "At first I braved it through, Judge, because I couldn't believe the House would even consider their phony case. Now I see how wrong I was. I misunderstood their consuming need to believe the charges against me, I miscalculated the degree of their hatred of me, and the public's hatred. I was stubbornly optimistic, and the vote yesterday proved me a fool. Since yesterday I've been faced with one last decision—"

The Judge tugged his chair around, directly toward Dilman. His eyes were hard. "What decision?" he demanded.

"Whether or not to undergo this excruciating trial before the Senate and the world, to go through the personal agony of it, permit my poor dead wife's miserable history of alcoholism to be paraded before all eyes, permit my one son, with all his emotional problems, to be tortured for his alleged and fictional affiliation with anti-white terrorists, to let the one woman I love in the world, a decent, innocent woman, be marked for life as no better than a prostitute—to decide if it is right and humane to undergo all of this myself, to let all of this happen to the ones I hold dear, out of selfish anger and vanity, knowing all the while that inevitably I'll be grabbed by the scruff of the neck and thrown out of the White House and into the street. I've got to decide whether to do that or accept the one alternative that Eaton and Miller and their gang offered me, and that is to give in, meekly quit my post, resign, save myself the indignity of defeat, spare those dear to me the scandal, protect my country from a trial that can only, ultimately, intensify racial hatred. Shall I turn the Presidency back to the white majority who want it for their exclusive club? That's the decision I must make today."

The Judge filled his corncob with a practiced hand. His eyes stayed on Dilman. "Okay. How say you?"

"Judge," said Dilman, "I intend to resign from the Presidency."

The Judge's pipe was halfway to his mouth, but now it hung in midair. "Resign?" he said. "You're going to quit?"

"I have no choice."

"The hell you haven't!" the old man roared. His corncob clattered to the table, and so quickly and vehemently did he jump to his feet that Dilman backed against the wall. The Judge was upon him like an angry, pecking rooster, waving his finger under Dilman's nose. "You resign, you slink out of that greatest office in the world, you give up the best opportunity a President and a minority citizen ever had to improve this country, and I swear—Dilman—I swear on the Missus, and on my niece and her kids, you'll never set foot in my presence again. I'll receive and respect any race of man on earth —black, white, yellow, purple—but I won't receive and respect a puling, wailing coward."

"Wait a minute—"

"You shut up!" shouted The Judge, vibrating from head to toe. He glared at Dilman, hands on his hips. "You came here for advice, and goddamit to hell, you're going to get it, like it or not. I'm through coddling your self-pity. I'm through exchanging intellectual statistics with you. What you need is a good boot in the behind, and I got seniority in that Oval Office, so I got the right to give it. Young fellow, you hear me out. I don't care if they were putting you before a firing squad tomorrow unless you resigned, you still couldn't resign. No President of the United States who's marched into that Oval Office either by popular acclaim or by accident ever quit under pressure. You're not going to degrade the office, be derelict in your duty, thumb your nose at the Constitution, by being the first. No sir, young fellow, no sir! Resigning from the Presidency is the real high crime, not being tried for a pack of partisan lies. Resigning from your opportunity to show a Negro can lead would be the real crime, not being found guilty of adultery and incompetence. If you quit because you're a Negro President who's scared stiff, if you go down that way, it's not only your race that loses, it's the Missus and me and every decent white person in this democracy that loses, because it shows us and the world we got a country where a Negro is afraid to perform as a man, act as a man, live as a man, because he's scared we won't let him do it. Well, goddamit, Dilman, if you know it or not, in the eyes of the Lord and our Saviour and the Constitution, you are a man, not a Negro, not a Baptist, not a Rotarian, not a war veteran, but a human mammal who is a man under God in heaven before he is anything else. You can be a bald man, or a long-nosed man, or a crippled man, or a colored man, or a dago man, or a kike man, but first, last, and always, you are a one-headed, two-legged man, whose complexion happens to be black and whose Social Security file says he is President of the United States."

The Judge was livid, gasping for breath, punching the air with his right hand. Frightened, Dilman held to the wall, watching him advance, nostrils dilated, nose quivering with indignation.

"For a half minute there, while you were working in the White House," the ex-President went on in his nasal rasp, "I thought, 'Maybe that fellow's going to find out what he is.' That was when you had the guts to veto that foul-smelling Minorities Rehabilitation Program Bill. I thought you were standing up for your principles as a man equal to any other man, and more, as a leader who wanted good for his people. Now I see I was bamboozled. You vetoed it as a single act of spite, and out of vanity, to show the ones kicking you around that they better let up once in a while, just once in a while. But that was all it meant, 'cause now I see you're so afraid of being kicked around some more, and kicked out, that you're ready to get down on all fours and crawl away voluntarily. Hell and tarnations, fellow, stop crawling. Stand up on your two hind legs like a man, and when somebody kicks you, boot them right back in the ass. You believe in the Republic. You've got ideas for this country. You've got the most important desk in the nation, full up with unfinished business. Don't let any man force you to walk out because you think he is a man and you know he thinks you're not. You've got too much to do. Like President Lyndon Johnson said back a time, 'Until justice is blind to color, until education is unaware of race, until opportunity is unconcerned with the color of men's skin, Emancipation will be a Proclamation but not a fact.' That's one piece of your unfinished business, Dilman—to make it a fact, and to make it a fact not as a Negro who is President but as an American man who is President. And that's only the beginning of what you've got to do. Don't tell me they won't let you, won't give you a chance. If they obstruct you, you knock them aside. If they charge you with crime and misdemeanor, you answer them and you charge them with ignorance and medievalism, and you battle them as their equal, knowing you're a human being, and as their superior, knowing you're still the legal holder of the highest-ranking office in the land. The way President Kennedy wrote in that fine book of his on courage—it's the most admirable of human virtues, courage is—he knew, 'cause he owned enough of it for ten men—and the way he said—compromise is okay in its place, but only compromising on issues, not your principles—but nowhere did I read in that book of his any praise or defense of quitting, turning tail and running, under any circumstances. You came for my advice and—"

The Judge suddenly stopped, bent his head sideways, listening. The front doorbell was ringing insistently.

The Judge cursed under his breath, glared once more at Dilman, and said curtly, "A grown man's got to decide for himself."

He strode from the dining room into the parlor, and Dilman slowly followed him. The Judge had opened the door, and the Missus appeared. "You locked me out," she said crossly, then peered over his shoulder at Dilman. "Mr. President, there's somebody important to see you, and Mr. Flannery says you have to see him."

Dilman had come forward. "Who is it?"

"I don't know—somebody just flown in from Washington." She had turned around to beckon to the person. "Right in here, sir, the President will see you."

He came through the open doorway, a diffident, embarrassed, well-built gentleman in his late forties, his fingers playing nervously across the brim of the hat he held in his hand. "Mr.—Mr. President," he said, "I don't know if you remember me—Harold L. Greene from—"

That moment, Dilman recognized him. "Of course, Mr. Greene, I couldn't make you out for a minute—so far from the Hill. You're the Sergeant at Arms of the Senate."

"Yes, sir." He wriggled in his ill-fitting overcoat. "I was sent here by plane from Washington on official Senate business. I'm supposed to serve you with this"—he reached inside his bulky coat and pulled out a document that resembled a folded legal brief—"summons. It's an order for you to stand trial, sir, a week from today, before the Senate constituted as a court of impeachment. It's all in here, sir. I'm sorry to have to do this, but—" He shrugged unhappily and held out the summons.

Dilman stepped forward, reached out and accepted the summons. "Thank you, Mr. Greene, for going to this trouble. I suppose I shouldn't send you back to Washington empty-handed."

The Sergeant at Arms appeared puzzled as The Judge, who stood beside him.

"You can take this message back with you," said Dilman. While he faced the Sergeant at Arms, his gaze had shifted to The Judge. "Tell the Senate of the United States that the President of the United States looks forward—looks forward to seeing them in court!"

The second that the Sergeant at Arms had gone, The Judge let out a whoop. Beaming from ear to ear, he descended upon Dilman and gave him a wrestling hug. "Mr. President, spoken like a man!" he exclaimed hoarsely. "I knew you wouldn't quit, knew you'd fight, felt it in my bones."

Smiling, Dilman pocketed the summons. "I guess I came here, Judge, knowing that too. Only I needed somebody wiser and tougher than I am to give me a kick in the pants, so I'd get mad enough to remember I was right, and do some kicking myself."

The Judge pounded Dilman's back affectionately, then held him off. "Mr. President, no matter what comes of this, when you come to be my age, you'll look back and won't regret it, never for a minute."

Dilman nodded gravely. "I hope so," he said softly, "because I'm going to take an awful licking."

"No matter what," said The Judge. "Ever hear of an ancient Roman philosopher by name of Seneca? Ever read what he wrote about a company of Romans trapped and decimated in an ambush? He wrote, 'The three hundred Fabiae were not defeated, they were only killed.' Remember that when it gets real bad. It's enough to make it worth while. Now go, and God bless you."

Dilman returned The Judge's powerful handshake, and then he was surprised to find the Missus, holding his coat and hat on her pudgy arm, waiting at the door. Dilman allowed her to assist him with his overcoat. When he took his hat, and began to thank her, he could see that her eyes were brimming. Impulsively she went up on her toes and kissed his cheek. "Be brave, Douglass," she said. "There's lots of us who need you."

Too choked by emotion to reply, Dilman fumbled for

the doorknob. As he opened the door, he heard the immediate chorus of shouts from the photographers beyond the porch, but louder than the rest was The Judge's admonition behind him.

"Braveness is good," The Judge had called out, "but a smart lawyer is better. Get one, and get one fast, the best there is, Mr. President!"

From over his shoulder, Dilman forced himself to smile at The Judge. "I'll try," he said. "I know the best attorney there is—but he wants to be a farmer like yourself, so it's hard to say if he'll be able to take time off from his harvesting. I'll try, you bet. That's all a man can do."

Behind the closed doors of their bedroom on the sixth floor of the Mayflower Hotel, Nat Abrahams finally hung up the telephone receiver and remained standing over the instrument, lost in thought.

At last, mechanical as an automaton, he wandered past the double bed to the window. He stared down into darkened Connecticut Avenue, his mind still on the call he had taken, hardly aware of the early evening foot and vehicular dinner traffic in the street below.

The glow from a neon light across the way caught the glaze of the window, and its angled illumination intensified the reflection of himself in the glass. He realized then that he was attired in his best suit, dressed for a festive night out, and with a start he remembered that Gorden Oliver and Sue were still waiting for him in the living room of the suite. His activity in the ten or fifteen minutes before the telephone had interrupted him was instantly revived.

Gorden Oliver, professionally hale and hearty, his ruddy New England features aglow, his brandy cane in one hand, an impressive manila envelope in the other, had arrived precisely on time. With the air of one Caesar conferring a laurel wreath upon another Caesar, he had handed the long-delayed final draft of the Eagles Industries employment contract to Abrahams. While Sue, bubbling and pretty in her rose sheath dress, had mixed the highballs, Abrahams had sunk into a corner of the sofa to review one last time the legal language of a contract he had almost committed to memory during these past months.

As he read on, Nat Abrahams had tried to shut his ears to the cheery conversation between Sue and Oliver, to the lobbyist's political gossip and anecdotes and Sue's merry, appreciative responses. Only once, when he had covered the paragraphs announcing his astronomical salary, bonuses, deferments, stock options, had he been forced to look up. Oliver had been patting his narrow-shouldered, tight-fitting, tailor-made suit coat importantly, and telling Sue that nothing was too good for the spouse of Eagles Industries' soon-to-be-number-one barrister, and therefore it was only befitting to cap the occasion with a regal dinner at Billy Martin's Carriage House in Georgetown, the swank restaurant on Wisconsin Avenue so renowned for its cuisine. Sue Abrahams had squealed with delight, and Nat had enjoyed seeing her so happy, and then returned to the contract.

That had been his only distraction until he had finished his reading of the contract and raised his head to Gorden Oliver. "Okay," he had said to the lobbyist, "this is it. Now you want my John Hancock?"

"Sure do!" exclaimed Oliver, uncapping his gold fountain pen. He had handed the pen to Abrahams. "Historic occasion. Sign all copies where they're x'd and initial in margins where stamped."

As Abrahams spread the numerous copies on the coffee table before him, and, with pen in hand, bent over the original, the second distraction of the evening had occurred.

The telephone had started to ring.

Sue had leaped to her feet. "I'll take it," she had said to her husband. "You go on and get that over with."

Yet Abrahams had held the pen poised over the contract, not touching the point to the sheet, waiting to hear whom the call was from.

Sue had cupped her hand over the mouthpiece. "Nat," she had said, "it's the White House for you."

Abrahams had placed the pen on the table and quickly stood up. "I'll take it in the bedroom," he had said.

And then, going into the bedroom, before shutting the door behind him he had heard Gorden Oliver cheerily call out, "Well, that's the only other corporation I'll give equal time to—even though Eagles is more solvent."

The call had lasted no more than three or four minutes, and Abrahams had mostly listened in the quiet room, his festival mood gradually receding and being replaced by one of serious concern.

Now, as he stood at the hotel window, the call had become the dominant prodder of his judgment and conscience, and it was difficult to ignore it and resume the business awaiting him on the coffee table in the living room. Yet his wife was there, his new career partner was there, his future was there. With reluctance he left the solitude of the bedroom.

He could see Sue's wondering eyes, their gravity contradicting the curved smile of her lips, following him to the sofa.

He sat on the sofa, fingers interlocked between his long legs, chewing the corner of a lip, looking past the pen and contracts.

"Well, Nat," said Gorden Oliver with hearty cheerfulness, "let's get the formalities over with—and let me have the honor of taking one of the richest attorneys in America out on the town!"

Abrahams hardly heard him. His gaze had gone to Sue and fixed upon her. He said, "That was the President on the phone."

"Doug Dilman?" she said with surprise. "I thought he was still off in—?"

"He just flew back," Abrahams said. "He's decided to fight them. He's decided to go on trial in the Senate and defend himself."

"Oh, no," said Sue with a groan. "After that terrible impeachment? He hasn't a chance, Nat. I hope you didn't encourage him. I can't understand it. Why, the rumor around town was that he'd resign rather than——"

Abrahams' eyes stayed fixed on his wife. "He's not quitting, he's fighting." He hesitated, inhaled, and then he said, "Sue, he has asked me to take over his legal defense before the United States Senate."

"You?" Her hand had gone to her mouth. The fun and frivolity had disappeared from her eyes. "But, Nat, how —? What did you tell him?"

"He wouldn't let me give him a yes or no right off. You know Doug. You know how sensitive he is, how reluctant he is to make demands on anyone, or ask a favor, or impose on anyone. It took him all the way from Sioux City to here, and then a couple of hours more, to get up the nerve to—to lift the phone to tell me he would stand trial, and explain his problem. Even then he didn't ask me right out. He said he desperately needed the best attorney in the country—preferably me, but if it couldn't be me, then anyone I might suggest. I suspect he must have been awfully scared and—and lonely—after making his decision—to call me at all. . . . No, he wouldn't let me give him an answer. He asked me to give it some thought, and call him soon as I could, and if my answer was no, he'd understand, because he knows how tied up I'm going to be. So I said I'd get back to him later this evening. That's the gist of it, Sue. That's it."

Abrahams became conscious of the third person in the living room. The New England lobbyist's expression had lost its bluff cheerfulness and had become intent.

Abrahams decided to bring Oliver into it. "Of course, Gorden, if I did this for the President, I'd need a short leave of absence to—"

"*If* you did this?" interrupted Oliver, his face a portrait of incredulity. "You're kidding me, Nat, aren't you?"

"I'm not kidding you or anyone," said Abrahams. "I'm thinking out loud. I said if I represented the President in this impeachment trial, I'd—"

"Nat, whoa, wait a minute, wait a minute." Gorden Oliver held the arms of his side chair and crouched forward. "You can't be serious about giving Dilman's request two seconds' serious consideration?" He searched Abrahams' face, then said, "Because—if you are—you'll have to realize there's only one answer you can give him, no matter who he is, no matter what your relationship with him has been: There's only one answer, and that is no—no, you can't do it, you wish you could for a friend, but first things first, and so sorry, old chap, no."

Abrahams felt his back arch, but he controlled himself. "I think you're a little out of line there, Gorden. I hadn't said either that I would defend the President or that I would not. In fact, I haven't made up my mind yet. But frankly, Gorden, I don't feel anyone has the right to make up my mind for me."

"Under the circumstances, maybe I can claim the right," said Oliver. "Considering your situation—your obligations—I don't think it's proper for you even to entertain the idea of going before the Senate and the whole country on behalf of a politician whose behavior leaves much wanting and who is under criminal indictment. Chrissakes, Nat, of all things—I don't want to quarrel with you—with anyone in Eagles—we've gotten along so perfectly up to now. Look, I can understand how this can be upsetting to you—the fact that he's been your friend, throwing himself on your mercy, the fact that he's an underdog, a Negro besides—but that's all by the way. Life goes on. You've got to think of yourself first, and your first responsibility is to—to us—to Eagles."

Abrahams knotted his fists more tightly in his lap. He measured his every word. "Maybe I don't know all the facets of the position I'm to have with your corporation. Maybe there is more I should know, and right now. My responsibility to you in this matter—what is it, Gorden? You'd better—"

"Please, Nat," Sue called out frantically, "don't get so—"

"Come on, Gorden," Abrahams persisted, "let's have it. Lay it out on the table right beside those contracts. Tell me about the clauses that haven't been written in."

It fascinated Abrahams then to see Oliver's face take on a look he had never seen there before. The winning charm, the howdy-hi geniality, had disappeared, and what remained was the granite rock bed beneath.

"We're not keeping any secrets from you, Nat. By now, you should know all there is to know of what Avery

Emmich expects of you. If you don't, I'll be only too glad to make it clearer."

"Do just that," said Abrahams. "Make it clearer why you won't let me defend Doug Dilman, if I choose to do so."

"All right, then, if you're putting me on the spot, if you refuse to understand, if you want it the hard way, all right, there's no time like the present." Oliver glanced at Sue, with no smile, then pointed the unyielding face back to Abrahams. "Nat," he said, "when I say I or we, I mean Emmich and Eagles, right? Okay. We contributed heavily to T.C.'s campaign and election, because we knew he was our friend. We paid for four years of his friendship, and we've received only two-thirds of our investment back. To put it crudely, we paid for a blue-chip stock, and then at the end it turned black, and, for our purposes, worthless. Dismayed as we were with the succession of Dilman to President, we were assured by Governor Talley that he was sensible and tractable and would stay in line. Then he double-crossed us. Talley said it would never happen, but it did. We wanted that Minorities Rehabilitation Bill passed into law. It was Emmich's pet, important to all of us with Eagles. Instead, your Mr. Dilman wrecked it. We knew what we had on our hands then, someone we couldn't trust or depend upon. Still, we figured that Congress would pass the bill a second time, over his veto, and we'd salvage something. We didn't figure those labor unions would swing enough weight to force the bill back into committee for a rewrite, but they did, and there it's bogged down, all because of Mr. Dilman. Well, look, Nat, I'll tell you straight out, there's nobody in the United States big enough, powerful enough, to cross Avery Emmich or work against the best interests of this country he loves. Emmich swore that if it was the last act he could perform as a patriotic citizen, he would get rid of Dilman and get the country back on the road to peace and prosperity. Well, I guess other equally patriotic citizens had the same feeling, because Emmich didn't have to lift a finger. Our friends in Congress took matters into their own hands. The House impeached your bumbling friend, and the Senate will convict him. And we'll be rid of him."

Abrahams had listened, hand massaging his chest as if to keep the heavy beat inside from his wife's ears.

"You seem pretty sure Emmich will have his way," Abrahams said.

Gorden Oliver's smile was frosty. "I am *positive* Emmich will have his way."

The whole thing was clear to Abrahams now. It would have been clear to a child. The powerful head of one of America's largest corporations had pitted himself against a weak head of state. The president of Eagles had more allies in the Senate than the President of the United States possessed. The president of Eagles could dispense more patronage than the President of the United States. The president of Eagles had secret weapons and the President of the United States had none. For Nat Abrahams there was one mystery: how was it done? What masks did bribery wear? Was the disguise a future campaign contribution? A gift of bonds and stocks to a grandson? The annuity of an apartment building investment? A year of prepaid call girls? A silent partnership in an oil lease? A lifetime membership in an exclusive golf club? A high-paying, permanent job for a brother-in-law? Or simply the gentlemanly request for a favor in return for an IOU to be cashed in on some distant, needier day?

Still, Abrahams told himself, if he did not know how it was done, here was one more clear implication that it was being done. The largess of the lobbyists was there, no question now. Were there takers in the Senate? Of this Abrahams was less positive. When you counted one hundred men, you could expect that most of them were decent men, else the penitentiaries of the land would have standing room only. Abrahams was satisfied with his textbook view of history. No Senate could be bought. Only some senators. And Oliver was wrong. Emmich was big and Eagles was big, but neither was bigger than the Presidency and the United States itself. Still, the armies of Eagles were on the move, and Dilman was the object of their assault, and now Oliver's dismay was un-

derstandable. Abrahams had pledged his allegiance to
the armies of Eagles, and yet had dared request a leave
of absence to help build the defenses of their enemy. But
then, in fairness to himself, he had not realized until this
moment the extent to which Eagles was dedicated to
liquidating Dilman. Now he knew.

"I didn't know," he heard himself say to Oliver, "how
set you were on opposing Dilman."

"Now you know," said Oliver flatly. "Now you can
understand how flabbergasted I was that you even considered siding with that man." Oliver softened slightly.
"Look, Nat, I don't want to be impossible, to go against
the grain. We're not asking you to join in our active opposition to Dilman during the trial. What the devil,
you're a friend of his. All we're asking is that you don't
oppose us, take our money with one hand and expect us
to let you punch us in the nose with the other. We just
want you neutral in this matter."

"There is no neutral, Gorden. Either I help the President or I don't. If I do, yes, I'll be in opposition to you
with every ounce of my strength. If I don't, I'll be de-
priving the President of the counsel he needs to help
save him, and in that way aiding you, actively aiding
you."

"Nat, my God, he can obtain a hundred other counselors, black or white. They'll welcome the chance for the
headlines. Look, I'm not saying you're not better than
the others available. If you weren't, we wouldn't be hiring you. I'm saying in a special trial like that, he can get
all the help he wants."

"True enough, except for one thing," said Abrahams.
"He wants me." He considered that a moment, and then
added, "I don't think it's because he believes I'm more
skilled than the others. I think it's because I'm one of
the few human beings on earth he trusts completely."

Oliver's brow had contracted ominously, and he said,
"You mean, after what I've said, you're still seriously
considering going over to that man?"

"I'm considering it."

Oliver rose, started to speak, then agitatedly circled
the room. He came to a halt beside Sue.

"All right, Nat, consider it," he said. "But then I think I've got to tell you—I hate telling you this, but I'm speaking for the company now and not myself, I've got to level with you—if you go to the mat for Dilman, you can consider yourself out of Emmich's camp, for now and forever. If you agree to defend the President, I will be able to see no other course than to withdraw our offer to you." He waited. "Does that help you make up your mind?"

"I'll make up my mind when I'm ready to do so, Gorden, and not a minute before."

"Okay," said Oliver, "you give me no choice but to pick up my marbles and go home, and wait to see if you're ready to play the game by the rules."

He went to the coffee table, retrieved the copies of the contract and the pen, then slipped the contracts back into the manila envelope. He looked at Sue. "Under the circumstances, I don't imagine any of us has too much of an appetite. Maybe we'll have cause to—to hold our celebration tomorrow."

He found his coat and hat, as Sue ran to the door to see him out. At the open door he offered Sue a courtly bow. "Thank you, Sue. Do your lobbying best." He considered Abrahams. "We'll wait for you to call us, Nat. I hope you think straight. At this stage in your life, you owe nothing to anyone on earth except yourself and your family." He held up the manila envelope. "This would be an awful lot of boodle to throw away—like throwing away ten years of life. Good night."

Abrahams did not move from the sofa. He watched his wife shut the door, then saw her sag and lean against it, her cheek pressed to the panel.

When she came away toward him, her face was drawn and pale, and he knew that she was fighting tears.

He averted his eyes as she came nearer and stood over him, but he could avoid her no longer. "All right, Sue, you've heard Oliver and you've heard me. What do you say?"

"What do I say? Do you care for one second what I say?" she said, voice rising. "Gorden Oliver said everything for me."

"Even after hearing that rotten stuff about Emmich and Eagles?"

"You wouldn't have to be mixed up in that. He promised you. I heard him."

"You want me to sit by, up there in the Senate gallery, as an employee of Eagles, watching my fellow hatchet men go to work on the body, and tell myself I'm not their accomplice, I'm only an innocent bystander? That's not like you, Sue."

"What is like me? Do you know? Do you bother to try to understand? You've spent your life, and your health, in musty back halls and dirty courtrooms giving everything you have for people who've had nothing to give you—or us. You've spent years putting every underdog who whined for help ahead of Roger and David and Deborah and me—yes, me. I didn't complain. I didn't obstruct you. In fact, I encouraged you, because I was proud of your love for others and because I loved you for that and for yourself. But I was glad when this Eagles offer came up. I never forced it on you, but I was glad, because I felt at last you were getting what you deserved, and you'd have your health, and we'd have a better life together for years ahead, and live it normally like other people. And now, suddenly, when we've got it, you turn your back—you want to think—now, suddenly, Eagles is dirty—what isn't dirty as well as clean, what business, what profession?—and now, suddenly, Doug Dilman is lost without you, and you'll throw over everything, your future, your wife, your sons and daughter, to help him—to help a lost cause—when you know and I know that he hasn't the chance of a snowball in hell, and if he has, as Gorden said, there are dozens of attorneys who can defend him as well as you. You want to know how I feel? That's how I feel!"

He waited for her hysteria to subside, and then he said, "Sue, while I often take a dim view of myself, I know my virtues and my capabilities. I feel I can do more for Doug than any other attorney on earth. Maybe you're right, and no one can save him, but if anyone can, I have a feeling I might. He *is* my friend—"

"And I'm your wife, and I'm the mother of your children! What about us? Do we have to put on blackface to get your help?"

"Sue!"

"Oh, dammit to hell for everything coming apart." She covered her eyes with her hand.

"Nothing's come apart," he said sternly. "I truly haven't made up my mind yet. I'm just nagged by the lousy feeling that the meaning of our whole lives is being put up on the block for inspection at last—that everything that came before, our paper liberalism, our talk liberalism, our real fiber as two decent people—is being challenged for real, for the very first time. Now it's not contributions to Crispus or CORE. Now it's not having a Negro friend to dinner, knowing he'll go home afterward. Now it's as—as if a Negro family has moved into the neighborhood, really moved in, and every penny we have in the house, in the world, is being threatened—and—how do we act? Turn our backs, move on?"

"It's not the same at all!" Sue exclaimed indignantly. "Don't twist things up with your lawyer sophistries. Nat, how can you? What are you trying to make me out, a heel? You know me, you know I love Doug as much as you do, but I don't love him or anyone as much as you and the children." She was pleading now. "Can't you see that? Won't you think of us first? Doug will survive or sink without you. But we can't survive, not without you."

Abrahams shook his head. "Darling, it's not all this or that, one thing or another. If I gave up Emmich for Dilman, the world wouldn't come to an end. Remember that—"

"Is that all you've got to say?"

"I'm only trying to—"

"To hell with you, then. Do whatever you damn well want to do. I've said all I've got to say to you!"

He was startled to see her spin away and dash into the bedroom, slamming the door. He considered following her, but then, instead, he went to the tray of drinks near the suite entrance. He poured himself a whisky-and-water, and was stirring it with a martini mixer, thinking, thinking, when he heard her noisily emerge from the bedroom.

He turned as she brushed past him. She had changed from the dinner sheath and pumps to a woolen blouse and skirt and flat-heeled shoes, and now was taking her heavy corduroy coat out of the closet.

"Sue—where in the devil do you think you're going?"

"I don't know, I don't care. Maybe I'll look for a truck to walk in front of. What difference does it make to you? I just want to be by myself, not that I haven't been since Oliver left!"

She was gone, the door resounding behind her, and he was alone with his drink.

After that, he walked the carpet, pacing back and forth, weighing his neatly planned future on some unseen scale against his need to become involved with Doug Dilman and what Doug Dilman represented.

Crazily his mind careened backward to that time, late in the last century, when Father Damien, the Belgian who had worked among lepers on a lonely Pacific island, had been viciously attacked by a Reverend Hyde for having been "coarse, dirty, headstrong." It had been Robert Louis Stevenson, risking all of his earthly possessions against a libel suit, who had defended Father Damien, counterattacking his traducer as one who was suffering conscience pangs for his own inertia. "But, sir," Stevenson had written to the Reverend Hyde and the world, "when we have failed, and another has succeeded; when we have stood by, and another has stepped in; when we sit and grow bulky in our charming mansions, and a plain, uncouth peasant steps into battle, under the eyes of God, and . . . dies upon the field of honour—the battle cannot be retrieved. . . . We are not all expected to be Damiens; a man may conceive his duty more narrowly, he may love his comforts better; and none will cast a stone at him for that. But—"

But.

Abrahams reflected, meditated, and finally saw that it must be settled tonight. Well, then, he would settle it. He would think a lot and drink a little, or better yet, drink a lot and think a little, and when it was clearer, when he was certain, he would telephone the White House.

And so he began to think a lot and drink a lot . . .

There was a pressure on his right shoulder, gentle, but it was there and real, and he opened his eyes.

To his growing surprise, as he oriented himself to his surroundings, he found that he was seated at the bedroom dressing table, his head nestled in his folded arms. The travel clock behind the telephone told him he had drowsed off and slept over two hours.

There was the pressure on his right shoulder again, and then he could see it was Sue's hand, and Sue herself above him, and except for her eyes, red from weeping, and the tear stains on her cheeks, her expression was softer than he had ever remembered it.

"Nat, are you all right?"

He sat up, wagged his head like a shaggy dog, rubbed his eyes and ran his fingers through his rumpled hair. "I guess I'm a one-drink man," he said. "Tonight I had three." Then, badly, it all came back to him, and he was fully awake. "Where have you been all this time, Sue?"

"Walking," she said, "walking endlessly, prowling through Washington. It was nice and cold, and it—it did things for me. Know where I wound up? I went all around and back, and there I was on Pennsylvania Avenue, standing there like a goon, like I'd never been there before, in front of the black iron fence, looking at the White House in the nighttime. It looked so different tonight, Nat, like an abandoned fort on a lonely island, and I kept picturing him alone in there, alone in those empty rooms, lost, trapped, no one to turn to. And then a young couple came along, young marrieds, out-of-towners, the Midwest, I suppose, feeling good after dinner and walking it off, and she said she heard there was a White House tour every day and she wanted to take it, and he said sure thing but not this time, but next time, on the way back from wherever, because by then they'd have gotten rid of the tenant and fumigated the place and redecorated it right proper. And you know what, Nat, she laughed, she thought he was clever, so clever and right, and she was pleased with him, and they both laughed, and I was left there by myself staring through the iron fence and thinking about Doug in there, and you, and the children, and all of us. I couldn't get back to you fast enough."

He had taken her hands. "Sue—"

"Nat, forgive me for everything I said before. I don't know what got into me. I wouldn't want you with Eagles. I mean it. I couldn't live off that kind of money, and raise the children on it. And if I were to know that you could have—have helped Doug—and didn't—I couldn't look at myself again, or you. I'm not worried about us, I'm really not. You have your practice. We can save. I'll show you what I can do. And we'll be together, that's all that matters. And if we save, maybe one day we can get ourselves a farm, not that one, but another, even if it's smaller." He had tried to draw her to him, but she resisted. "Nat, call the White House and tell him."

He came to his feet, smiling. "I've already done it, Sue. I called him an hour ago and told him he had his attorney. I told him we were in this together, sink or swim, from tonight on. I thought he'd—he'd cry." He encircled her with an arm. "Well, it's done. I don't know if I can help him, but one thing I do know. I didn't do it for him alone, Sue, I did it for us."

She kissed him, and she whispered, "I love you so." And when he released her, he could see that her face had never been more alive with excitement. "Nat, let's call the children, and then let's celebrate with dinner up here, and then—then let's love each other, tonight and forever, and never stop."

He reached for her again, but she laughed and slipped away and went to change into her robe. Only at the bathroom door did she hesitate and half turn to him, her sweet face grave and troubled. "Nat, can you save him? You must. I want this to be the kind of country we'd like to leave for our children to grow up in, one where they can live unafraid, one they'll be proud of. That would be the best thing we could leave them—not a farm, not a hundred farms or a million dollars—but a country like that."

VII

As the time for combat drew closer, Douglass Dilman had taken to rising earlier each morning. He was living, he found, two wholly separate lives: in one, he continued to perform the endless exacting duties of the Presidency; in the other, he strenuously prepared for the criminal trial that would determine if he was fit or unfit to perform those duties.

He sought and found extra hours he had not previously known existed. Sometimes it astonished him how many there were of these, stolen from sleep, from daydreaming, from inconsequential engagements. Amazingly, these hours he subtracted from himself, for himself, seemed to cost him little loss of energy or hope. It was as if he had discovered, and tapped, a new reservoir of stamina. His single-minded determination to fight back gave him a vigor he had never before enjoyed. His ceaseless activity left him no time to brood about the prosecution that awaited him or to anticipate its likely results.

This morning—because it was the morning of one of the most crucial days in his life—had begun earlier than any other.

Beecher had entered the Lincoln Bedroom at six-thirty, awakened him, opened the drapes to the dark, ominous sky, and then had drawn his bath. After that, attired in the blue terry-cloth robe that Wanda had given him one Christmas, Dilman had padded through the West Hall to the sitting room of the private apartments so many other Presidents had used, and where he had only this week begun to eat his breakfast.

Eight newspapers, among them the New York *Times,*
the New York *Herald Tribune,* the Washington *Post,* the
Washington *Star,* were piled high beside his place mat.
He took pride in the fact that one of the eight was Zeke
Miller's scurrilous Washington *Citizen-American,* and
that his ego was sufficiently reinforced by the knowledge
of injustice being done to him to read it, and he
was prouder still that one week ago he had again subscribed to the Washington *Afro-American.* Beneath the
pile, he knew, like an intelligence report on the enemy
camp less than two miles away, lay the *Congressional
Record.*

This morning, he had been too preoccupied with ideas
for the forthcoming and final meeting with his legal defense staff, and then too devoted to the folder with the
label "Application for Executive Clemency re Jefferson Hurley, Petitioned by Mrs. Gladys Hurley (Mother)
and Mr. Leroy Poole (Friend)" to open a newspaper.

After breakfast, having gathered the newspapers
under one arm, still reading the petition for commuting
Hurley's sentence from death to life imprisonment, he
had gone up the corridor, meaning to change into his
clothes. But then he had wandered into the Monroe
Room, next to his bedroom, and dumping his newspapers
on the pedestal table, he had sat in a Victorian chair
and read on through the folder submitted by the Department of Justice.

It was there that Nat Abrahams and Nat's associates
had found Douglass Dilman at seven forty-five, his petition laid aside, his newspapers strewn about him on the
carpet, still in his terry-cloth bathrobe, absorbed in the
fantasies of the *Congressional Record.*

Dilman had read that the House of Representatives
had named five of its most forensically able members to
the task of trying him, with Representative Zeke Miller
the chief prosecutor. He had read that the Senate, after
the formality of converting itself from a legislative
body into a high tribunal of justice, had voted upon sixteen rules of parliamentary procedure to govern its behavior as a court of impeachment. He had started to read
about other arrangements being made for the Roman

holiday scheduled to commence at one o'clock sharp this afternoon, when Nat Abrahams, pipe streaming smoke, had arrived, followed by Felix Hart, Walter T. Tuttle, and Joel Booker Priest.

Dilman gestured toward the chairs around the table, and apologized for his bathrobe. Then, as they unstrapped and unlatched their briefcases, Dilman became conscious of the chamber in which they were about to confer.

"Isn't it strange I wound up in this room?" he said. "I wonder what compelled me to come into the—into this room—the Treaty or Monroe Room, it's called. I've never used it for a meeting before."

"What's so strange about it?" Felix Hart, Abrahams' young Chicago partner, inquired.

"Look at the inscription over the fireplace," Dilman said.

Felix Hart scurried over to the white fireplace and, bending slightly, read the mantel inscription aloud. " 'This Room Was First Used for Meetings of the Cabinet During the Administration of President Johnson.' " He looked up, awed. "I assume that means Andrew Johnson, not Lyndon."

"It does," Dilman said. "Maybe this is a good omen. I hope I get off as lucky as he did in his trial."

Without glancing up from the sorting of his notes, Nat Abrahams said, "That was a one-vote acquittal, Mr. President." Dilman was once again disconcerted by his friend's formality. Ever since his legal associates had been brought in, Abrahams had taken to addressing him as Mr. President, instead of Doug. Then Abrahams added, "We've simply got to do better than that. . . . Ready, gentlemen? We don't have much time. Let's review the whole business again, before heading up to the Hill."

Promptly, they plunged into the last-minute summary of Dilman's defense. For Dilman, the discussion was comforting. These were attorneys, and he was an attorney, and their language had the mathematical precision of Law School and his legal practice of long ago, so dear to his memory. The talk was rooted in tradition and precedent, and great names of the American bar, some heroes, some rascals, all geniuses in their fashion, were evoked. Dilman listened to the names of Webster, Choate, Stanbery, Darrow, Steuer, and many more.

Dilman gave his complete attention to his four managers—even the title "managers," as applied to attorneys in a Senate impeachment trial, had a comforting ring, as if these were men who not only defended, but controlled, guided, administered, directed their respondent, who might otherwise be helpless. Dilman heeded every exchange, as they examined the Articles of Impeachment point by point, sentence by sentence, and even word by word. They were trying to anticipate the course that Zeke Miller's prosecution might take, and foresee what damaging evidence the House's witnesses, signed affidavits, submitted exhibits, might present.

Then they reviewed one more time how the House's case could best be refuted.

In replying to Article I, they appeared to be confident they could show that Wanda Gibson had never been privy to any government top secrets that she could have passed on to her Communist employers. They had other former Vaduz employees standing by to swear that Miss Gibson's connection with Franz Gar was no more than that of secretary to employer, and that she had never been heard speaking to him about matters that were not concerned with her immediate job.

Dilman's managers displayed little concern about Article II. Their interrogation of Julian Dilman had convinced them that he had never been a member of the Turnerite Group, and that even if he had been, there could be no proof that the President had conspired with his son and the subversive Negro organization to obstruct the Department of Justice.

However, Dilman was surprised at the massive dossier his managers had assembled in an effort to knock the underpinnings out from under Article III, an omnibus of scandalous accusations. They had put such extra effort into their rebuttal of this charge not because they believed the charge had legal substance, but because they saw that it might have effective propaganda value for the prosecution. First, they had investigated Sally Watson's entire erratic history, but apparently Senator Hoyt Watson's long influential arm had thwarted them at every turn.

As to answering Miller's allegation of the President's extramarital affair with Miss Gibson, the success or failure of the defense would depend entirely on how Miss Gibson conducted herself testifying and under cross-examination on the witness stand. In replying to the House charges of Congressional contempt, Negro favoritism, alcoholism by Dilman, once more the defense managers were ready to rest their case entirely on the impression made by their own eye-witnesses and expert deponents.

It was Article IV, Dilman observed, that continued to disturb his managers the most. This would resolve itself into a battle over the constitutionality of the New Succession Bill, and the degree to which Congress might ever be permitted to limit the powers of the executive branch.

To reinforce his rebuttal of Article IV, Nat Abrahams had, the morning after accepting Dilman's defense, insisted that the President make a new appointment to the office of Secretary of State, thus replacing Eaton. After hours of indecision, Dilman had finally settled upon Jed Stover, the Assistant Secretary for African Affairs, as the career diplomat best qualified to succeed Eaton. Happily, Stover had been enthusiastic about permitting his name to be used in this token gesture. Not unexpectedly, the Senate, without seriously considering Stover's appointment while in committee, had rejected the replacement with a heavy vote. Then, to put their rebuke of the President indelibly on the record, the Senate had again declared Dilman's removal of Arthur Eaton illegal, and had sustained Eaton as Secretary of State (and next in line to the Presidency) until the disagreement could be resolved during the trial of impeachment. As a gesture, Abrahams had submitted the issue of the unconstitutionality of the New Succession Bill to the Supreme Court, aware that it could not be considered before the impeachment trial ended.

For forty minutes, Dilman heard out the give-and-take on these points among his managers, offering only an occasional comment himself. Now, glancing at the marble-encased clock, with its time-piece, calendar, barometer, a clock that went back to the time of Ulysses S. Grant, Dilman could see that it was almost a quarter after eight.

As the morning's vital strategy session approached its conclusion, Dilman studied the men whose clever minds, vast legal experience, honest interest in justice would represent him before the bar.

Dominating the four, of course, was Nat Abrahams himself, chestnut hair rumpled, seamed profile drawn, long frame slouched into the heart-backed Victorian chair, as he chewed the hard rubber stem of his briar pipe and listened. His trusted junior partner, a brilliant graduate of the University of Chicago School of Law, was animatedly speaking. Felix Hart was deceptively callow-looking, cherubic, ebullient, imitative of Nat's careless manner of dress—deceptively, because his easy outer aspect hid a pertinacious, clawlike, investigative brain. It was he who had supervised and directed the dredging up of all of Dilman's earlier life in the Midwest, trying to pinpoint what might be harmful to their case and at the same time watch for what might be useful.

Listening, also, was the elder statesman of the quartet, the renowned Walter T. Tuttle, a onetime Attorney General during The Judge's administration, whom The Judge had rousted out of recent retirement to join the defense team. A courtly old-school gentleman in his late seventies, Tuttle had a countenance as American as any that had been sculptured on Mount Rushmore. The opaque eyes screened a slow but direct mentality. The tone of his utterances was dry, yet often tart. Tuttle's affectation was not that he was a country squire, which he was, but that he was a farmer in citified clothes, which he was not. He had been widely quoted for a remark made during his service in The Judge's Cabinet, that he "always avoided any dinner where there were three forks beside the plate." His specialty was constitutional law, and as a youngster he had sat behind his father, an eminent attorney turned congressman, when his father had been one of the House managers trying Judge Halsted L. Ritter before the Senate during the Seventy-fourth Congress, in 1936. Judge Ritter had been impeached, like Dilman, on four articles. Acquitted on all but one charge, which was that of "misbehavior" in office, he had been found guilty by the Senate and removed from office.

Speaking now was the fourth of Dilman's managers, a slight, pensive attorney still in his thirties named Joel Booker Priest. Conservative and immaculate, Priest had attended every meeting with his slick, shiny hair smoothly in place, his person exuding a pine-scented cologne, and his body always garmented in one of his costly single-breasted suits. Joel Booker Priest was a Negro, of dark tan complexion, who now and then had handled special cases for Spinger and the Crispus Society. His law firm was in Washington, and quietly, but with the eager persistence of a bird dog, he had retraced Dilman's life in the capital city and had attempted to ferret out what Miller, Wickland, and the other opposition managers were planning to present to the Senate.

Observing Joel Priest this minute, as he tried to surmise the House's case in support of Article IV, and as the others hung on his every word, Douglass Dilman was incredulous at how much he himself had changed in short days. Not long ago, the very thought of a Negro defending him in any action would have been frightening. It was Spinger who had suggested Priest's services to Abrahams, and Abrahams who had then studied the Negro lawyer's career and met him. And when Abrahams had recommended him, surprisingly, Dilman had asked only one question, "Why do you want him, Nat, because you think it might look good to have someone of my own color on the team?" Nat had snorted, "I want him because he's *good*." And Dilman had replied, without reservation or hesitancy, "He's hired."

Suddenly Dilman was aware that the others were pushing back their chairs and standing.

"Well, that's it, gentlemen," Nat Abrahams said. "We're as ready as we'll ever be. Remember, we've been assigned the Vice-President's formal office next to the Senate Reception Room for our private headquarters. They're turning over two of the late Vice-President Porter's other offices for our stenographers and researchers, but the formal office will be the brain center. You can unpack there. I'll catch up with you about eleven, and we can have a quiet lunch together, and then be ready for the fireworks at one o'clock. Oh, there's another thing, Mr. Tuttle—" Abrahams turned to Dilman. "Mr. President, I'd better walk with them to the elevator. Then I'd like to come back and have a few more words with you alone. Can you spare ten minutes?"

Dilman nodded. "Certainly, Nat. I think I'd better get dressed first. I'll only be a short time. I'll meet you in here."

He preceded his managers into the second-floor hall, then thanking them warmly and wishing them luck, he parted company with the four. As Abrahams went left down the hall, deeply engrossed in conversation with his associates on the way to the private elevator, Dilman turned right and entered the Lincoln Bedroom.

After throwing aside the terry-cloth bathrobe, he dressed slowly. As he was getting into his shirt, pulling on his trousers, his thoughts dwelt on the impeachment, and then, as if by a force of will, wishing a respite from the suspense of it, he temporarily shoved it to the back of his mind. He reviewed the week of days that had brought him from the Iowa farmhouse, and his resolve to fight for his life rather than quit, to this forbidding morning in the Andrew Johnson Cabinet room of the White House, and the last meeting before his actual trial would begin.

Most of that week gone by had been given over to building his actual defense against impeachment, to the seemingly endless meetings with Nat Abrahams and the other managers, and yet there had been other persons who had populated his world in the last seven days.

In many respects, since the impending Senate trial cast a shadow over his every activity, it had been a mean and arduous week. The language of law used this last hour permeated his thinking, and when he recalled the week he had lived through, he considered it in concise legal terms.

Specification one: the said Douglass Dilman and Wanda Gibson. He had telephoned her at the Spingers' the midnight after his return from the Midwest. He had told her of his decision to fight, and she had broken into tears, and contained them, and been only slightly heartened after he had added the news that Nat Abrahams had thought enough of his chances to undertake the defense. She had dreaded his impending Calvary, the vilification to which he would be subjected, the disgrace that would probably be his, but in the end she had accepted his decision fatalistically. He had telephoned her twice more, once learning that the House had served her with a subpoena to appear as a witness (this had made him miserable and apologetic, and he had blamed himself for her suffering so much over a relationship from which she had derived so little fulfillment), the second time learning that she had decided, after working it all out in her mind, that she was proud that he was going to stand up to his traducers. Wanda's devotion to him had been unreserved, yet now he could not be positive that it was the product of love rather than pity.

Specification two: the said Douglass Dilman and Julian Dilman, relative. The second evening, he had brought his son down to Washington for a last talk before the trial. Julian had sworn to Joel Priest that he had no connection with the Turnerite Group, and since Priest had a complete account of this denial, there was no more need for Dilman to go into it further. Rather, Dilman and Julian had dined together as father and son. Dilman had learned that because of the impeachment, there had been some sentiment among the Negro undergraduates of Trafford University which had turned in his favor, even though the greater proportion of the student body still resented him for the discredit his alleged conduct had visited upon the Negro population. It was clear to Dilman that his son was undergoing an unspoken trial of his own on the campus, and that he was torn between emotional sympathy for his father and intellectual sympathy for his fellow students, who felt that his father's weakness had led to the scandalous court action. With gravity, so that there would be no question in his son's mind, Dilman had explained to Julian the answers that his managers were preparing against the widely publicized indictments. Once only had Mindy's name been mentioned, and then by Dilman. He had wondered what she, unfettered and free in her white world, must think of all of this. Julian had offered no comment. They had said good night awkwardly, and not until the next morning had Dilman learned that Julian had received his subpoena from the House while boarding the train that would take him back to New York City, and then on to Trafford.

Specification three: the said Douglass Dilman and Sally Watson. He had not seen his former social secretary since the night that he had dismissed her. Yet he had not been able to avoid her sick vengefulness. At least three interviews that she had volunteered to the press had made national headlines, the latest and most sensational having appeared in the middle of the week under the joint by-lines of Reb Blaser and George Murdock. In print she had been quoted as remarking, "President Dilman likes to pretend he's a celibate deacon, but I can tell you, and his impeachers have photographs of my cuts and bruises to prove it, he's no better than some illiterate oversexed buck Negro who's gotten tired of his 'cullud gals' and wants to make time with the whites." In the same libelous story, too, Senator Hoyt Watson had stated, "I don't intend to demean myself by contesting with the President, more rightfully His Royal Accidency, in the public press. I shall wait to hear the legal evidence. But if the House charges are supported, then his personal conduct, the degradation he has visited upon our most exalted office, will be uppermost in my mind, in the minds of my fellow senators, when we sit as his judges." The story had concluded with the sidelight that Miss Watson had placed her subpoena to appear as a witness for the prosecution in a gold frame on her mantelpiece.

Specification four: the said Douglass Dilman and Edna

Foster. Upon his return from the Midwest, it had surprised him to find his Negro Senate secretary, Diane Fuller, making a shambles of his affairs in Miss Foster's office. It appeared that Miss Foster had fallen ill of a kidney ailment, and would be both indisposed and incommunicado for several weeks, at a time when he needed her most. Then, two days ago, from Tim Flannery, he had received some inkling of the true nature of Miss Foster's illness. She had been served with a subpoena to be a prosecution witness against the President. Dilman had been disturbed and confused by the information that his confidential secretary would appear as a witness for the prosecution. Until now, he had considered her a loyal and tight-lipped assistant. Unless she was collaborating with the enemy against her will, her defection was inexplicable. Besides, Dilman had wondered, of what value could Edna Foster be to his opposition?

Specification five: the said Douglass Dilman and Montgomery Scott, CIA. He had spoken with Scott three times in the past four days. Scott had reported that by now the CIA had a network of native agents, working hand in hand with Kwame Amboko's own security force, throughout the back hills and frontiers of Baraza. Scott had expected definitive intelligence information on the Russian buildup any day. Then, last night, he had requested a meeting with the President for this afternoon, and had hinted that it might be wise for the President to arrange a conference with his military advisers immediately afterward. Dilman had taken the hint. After seeing Scott this afternoon, he would meet with Secretary of Defense Steinbrenner and General Fortney. Normally, he would not have looked forward to the conference with these formidable Pentagon chiefs. He suspected that most of the military had contempt for him, hoped for his conviction in the Senate, regarding him as no better than another "big-shot boogie getting too large for his breeches," a phrase attributed to General Fortney. One new mitigating factor, however, made this confrontation with his Pentagon advisers seem less disagreeable. It would be the first meeting that Brigadier General Leo Jaskawich would attend as the President's newly ap-

pointed military aide. For, once Dilman had returned to
Washington, he realized that he would require not only a
replacement for his former military aide, but for Governor Talley as well. Immediately, his mind had gone back
to Jaskawich, and their talk atop the launching pad at
Cape Kennedy and their conversation afterward. Then
Dilman had known that what he desperately needed as
much as an adviser was another human being on his team
he could trust. He had telephoned Jaskawich in Florida,
offered him the position, and quickly reminded him that
it could be both short-lived and detrimental to his career. If Dilman were convicted, as he likely would be,
Dilman had said, Jaskawich's Washington job would be
ended in a matter of weeks. Worse, Dilman had warned
him, was the danger of guilt by association. Jaskawich
was an authentic American hero. If he wore his spotless
armor in the wrong cause, the cause of one soon to be
purged for high crimes and misdemeanors, the astronaut's own image would be irreparably tarnished. It
would be absolutely understandable to him, and he would
think no less of Jaskawich, Dilman had said, if the astronaut turned down the position being offered. Jaskawich
had replied simply, "Have armor, will travel. See you in
twenty-four hours."

From somewhere, musical chimes interrupted Dilman's specifications of activity past and future. What
remained was the immediate present. The hands pointing to the Roman numerals on the Empire clock told him
it was eight-thirty. The south windows, on either side of
the clock, were spattered with rain. For several seconds
Dilman listened to the downpour outside. Often, in the
past, he had found that a rainy day had a comforting
effect upon him. It confined one's activities. It heightened
one's appreciation of shelter. It made one feel, if one
was indoors, apart from the uncontrolled nature of the
universe, safe and apart from it, and in complete repose.
Perhaps the pleasure was primitive, harking back to the
dry Paleolithic man, snug near the fire in his cave, as the
tempest raged outside. Yet, this morning, the rain disappointed Dilman. It seemed the enemy's rain, imprison-

ing him, daring him, adding portentous urgency to the need for survival. His was an unquiet cave.

Quickly, Dilman knotted his tie, buttoned his suit coat, slipped a handful of cigars into one pocket and hastily made his way back to the Monroe Room for his last exchange, this first judgment day, with the one who had sacrificed so much in an attempt to save him.

Nat Abrahams was there, scanning and discarding the newspapers that Dilman had left behind.

"Quite a splash you're making, Doug," he said. He held up the front page of the newspaper in his hands. The banner headline announced:

MOST DRAMATIC TRIAL IN HISTORY BEGINS TODAY.

Beneath the headline, side by side, were two photographs. One was a picture of Dilman being hustled off the platform at Trafford University while eggs erupted around him. The other was a shot of members of the Senate at their desks in the Chamber. The bold caption read:

IN THIS CORNER THE PRESIDENT— IN THIS CORNER THE SENATE— ONE MAN AGAINST ONE HUNDRED—ARE THOSE THE RINGSIDE ODDS AGAINST DILMAN?

"Yes," said Dilman. "Did you see the lead? Read it."

Abrahams brought the newspaper into his line of vision. He read aloud:

" 'At precisely one o'clock this afternoon, in the hallowed Chamber of the United States Senate, there will unfold what promises to be one of the most memorable trials in the history of the Western Hemisphere—rivaling in drama and importance the great trials of our civilization—those of Socrates, Jeanne d'Arc, Galileo, King Charles I, Mary Queen of Scots, Lord Warren Hastings, President Andrew Johnson——and matching in raw sensationalism and fevered public interest the lesser trials of our time—those of Aaron Burr, the Tichborne claim-

ant, the cadet Archer-Shee, John Brown, Sacco and
Vanzetti, John T. Scopes, Bruno Hauptmann. For the
second time in the history of the United States, a Chief
Executive of the land will go before the tribunal of the
people's Senate to be judged guilty or not guilty of high
crimes and misdemeanors—' " Abrahams suddenly
crumpled the newspaper and cast it aside. "Bunk," he
said. "Thank God the people will be able to see it for
themselves on television. I think that's an advantage,
don't you, Doug?"

"I don't know," said Dilman.

"I think so. If we didn't have television, we'd have, in
effect, a closed chamber hearing, sort of a secret kangaroo court, with the senators less responsive to their
constituents' wishes. The news of the pros and cons
would be funneled out by maybe twenty-five regulars of
the White House press and maybe one thousand other
correspondents, and everything could be angled for
reader interest rather than truth. As it stands now, the
people will be able to see for themselves what goes on
and make up their own minds, not get the story second
or third hand through other minds. For the first time in
history, an impeachment will be judged not only by the
senators and press, but by the voters concerned. You'll
have 230 million judges, Doug, not merely 100."

"Is that necessarily good?"

"Not necessarily, but probably. The masses become
impatient with absurdity much faster than a narrow
group of locked-in legislators. Witness what happened to
Senator Joe McCarthy. I've always thought that if we'd
had television back in 1868, President Andrew Johnson's
impeachment trial would not have lasted three months,
but three weeks, if that long. The people would have
seen through the politics and prejudices of the so-called
impartial judges, their congressmen, and they'd have
risen up and demanded Johnson's acquittal at once. In
fact, they would have probably demanded that two-
thirds of the Senate be impeached. No, Doug, I'll take
my chances on the electronic eye. If it helps us in no
other way, it at least guarantees us that Zeke Miller and

Bruce Hankins won't dare to bamboozle their Hill clan
with any bigoted anti-minority sleight-of-hand."

Dilman had unwrapped his first cigar of the morning.
He lighted it, enjoyed the aroma briefly, and then took a
chair across from Abrahams. "Well, Nat," he said, "now
we're alone, the two of us, a few hours before the showdown. Truly, what do you think are my chances?"

"Honest to God, I can't say, Doug. Usually, going into
any trial, I have a suspicion of what may happen, I can
make an educated guess as to the outcome. But this impeachment business is so unique—the procedure so
damn irregular—that no matter how much homework
you've done, you can't predict what is going on in those
100 senatorial heads today or what will be in those heads
two weeks from today. After all, we have only a single
precedent to go by. Just as the newspaper said, there's
only been one Presidential impeachment trial before
this. Of course, that gives us several guideposts—" He
stopped, and considered Dilman. "How familiar are you
with the Andrew Johnson trial?"

"Shamefully ignorant of the details, I'm afraid," Dilman confessed. "I remember some of it from school, and
side reading, of course. And lately the papers have been
full of it, highly colored, and the radio and television
have been dinning it in our ears, but somehow, I've been
unconsciously avoiding it. I don't know. I have the impression that President Johnson was given a bad time
of it. My survival instinct tells me not to relive his hell
when I'm about to undergo one of my own. It's like—I'll
tell you what—like you're about to face an unusual life-
or-death major surgical operation. You know there's
been one similar case. Well, you're not inclined to study
the gory details beforehand. You sort of prefer to shut
your eyes and let them roll you in, the mystery of it still
a mystery, holding your layman's blind high hopes before you go under."

Abrahams had listened solemnly, full understanding
in his face. "Yes," he said. "Nevertheless, if you can
bring yourself to it, I believe you should try to understand something of that other impeachment trial."

"If you think so, Nat. But why?"

"Because, far from being dead history, the facts of it will become a living part of your own trial. I repeat, it is the single precedent both sides have to go by. The House managers and the four of us will quote from it, refer to it, whenever it is to advantage, you can be sure. Furthermore, not surprisingly, President Johnson's impeachment crosses and touches yours in several important areas. I do recommend you acquaint yourself with the salient facts, Doug."

"All right, then, I will."

"I'm not saying you must go out and get some weighty tome from the Library of Congress. I know you haven't the time. But——" He leaned sideways, riffling the file folder tabs in his briefcase on the floor. "I have something here, if I can find it . . . ah, here it is." He came up with what appeared to be a stapled typescript. "We all read what we could on the Andrew Johnson trial. Then Tuttle condensed the proceedings of that trial into eighty pages, for easier reference." He handed it across the table to Dilman. "Take a look at it when you can. Of course, the great amount of offstage byplay, the cloakroom hanky-panky, isn't in there——"

"Like what?" asked Dilman, fingering the manuscript.

"Like——well——to be quick about it——when Booth's derringer pistol killed Lincoln, it was Vice-President Andrew Johnson who became President in 1865, when he was fifty-seven. It makes me laugh, Doug, when I read those columnists who say you weren't prepared for the Presidency. You were ten times better prepared for it than half our past heads of state, and a hundred times better prepared than Andrew Johnson. He'd been a tailor in North and South Carolina, and owned a tailorshop in eastern Tennessee. He'd never had a single day's formal education. So he went into politics, and made the United States Senate. Lincoln took to him because, even though Johnson owned slaves and was a Southern Democrat, he fought against secession. Well, anyway, by the time Johnson became President, he had few friends left. The Southern Democrats considered him a traitor. The Northern Republicans considered him an untrustworthy rebel-lover. He was lonely as hell in the White House.

He had a wife, but she was invalided by tuberculosis, and I believe she made just one public appearance beside him in four years."

Dilman nodded. His heart went out to that vilified President who had been treated like some sort of white nigger. "I never knew any of that," he said.

"Oh, there's more," Abrahams said, "but to get to the crux of it, his impeachment. Why was he impeached? Basically because the Northern Republicans, who controlled Congress, wanted to treat the defeated states as a conquered and occupied country, wanted to keep the South disenfranchised and in bondage. President Johnson, on the other hand, following Lincoln's policy, wanted to heal the wounds of war, conciliate the Southern states, bring them back into the Union. So that was a bad breach. Almost every time Congress passed some bill of reprisal keeping the South under the military heel, giving freed slaves control there, Johnson would veto it, and then Congress would override him. Finally, it resolved itself into a fight for power between the executive and legislative branches of government. Congress felt that it should run the Reconstruction of the South, and the President felt that this task belonged to him. There were endless secondary factors against Johnson, also. He was hated as a man who was neither fish nor fowl, neither true Southerner nor Northerner. He was resented for going soft on the ex-rebels, when they were being blamed for Lincoln's assassination. He was feared by the Republicans, who didn't want him to bring the Southern Democrats back into power on the Hill by admitting the Southern states back into the Union. So the House decided to get rid of him. They started impeachment proceedings against him, not once but three times, and the third time they succeeded in getting their impeachment. And on March 5, 1868, his case went on trial before the Senate."

"There were eleven Articles charged against him, weren't there?" Dilman asked.

"That's right," said Abrahams. "Most of them, like most of the charges against you, were pure stuff and nonsense. Andrew Johnson was charged with using foul language, with drinking intoxicants, with ridiculing Congress in his public speeches. But the whole thing came down to the three Articles accusing Johnson of breaking the law by defying the Tenure of Office Act. That was the grandfather of the New Succession Act that you defied by firing Eaton. The tenure act handcuffed Johnson to his Senate, told him he could remove no one in the Cabinet he had inherited from Lincoln without the approval of the Senate. Well, the President saw that his Secretary of War, Edwin M. Stanton, was performing not as his adviser but as his enemy and as a spy for his opposition in Congress, and so he asked Stanton to resign. Stanton refused. So the President, in effect, threw him out without consent of the Senate, arguing that Stanton didn't come under the tenure act since Johnson hadn't appointed him, and insisting the tenure act was unconstitutional anyway and the Senate had no right to tell him who to keep and who to fire. Shades of you and Eaton, Doug."

"I'm afraid so."

"It was a nasty eleven-and-a-half-week trial, the House's seven managers pitted against the President's five attorneys. But there was considerably more that went on than oratory and cross-examination of witnesses. The majority of the Senate was determined to get Johnson, whether the charges against him were proved or not. They arranged to have witnesses favorable to him kept out of court. There were attempts at bribery. And as for sitting as an impartial body of jurors —listen to this, Doug—the President pro tempore of that Senate was Benjamin Wade, who hated Johnson, and who was next in line to become President if Johnson was found guilty, and yet he was allowed to sit and vote on Johnson's impeachment. In fact, Wade was so sure he and his friends would convict Johnson, and that he himself would be the new President, that he picked his Cabinet before the trial was over and before he had cast his vote!"

"Incredible," said Dilman.

"Yes, it was incredible. Of course, while you don't have a President pro tempore eligible to succeed you, sitting in judgment of you, you do have some senators—notably Hoyt Watson because of his personal involvement, Bruce Hankins because of his regional prejudices, John Selander because of his affection for T.C.—already committed against you. But, to get back to precedent. In order to convict President Johnson, two-thirds of the Senate had to find him guilty, that is, at least thirty-six senators against eighteen. Well, you know the result. One senator, Edmund Ross of Nebraska, though he personally disliked Johnson, disliked even more what he had observed and heard from his fellow congressmen during the trial. He determined that the office of President should not be disgraced and degraded by an impeachment based on partisanship. And so at the last minute, after sleepless nights, he went over to Johnson. His vote, which cost him his political future, was the President's life belt. The final tally showed thirty-five for guilty, nineteen for not guilty. The two-thirds required for conviction had fallen short by one. Andrew Johnson remained President of the United States."

The cigar in Dilman's hand had long gone cold. Deliberately, he flicked the gray ash into a tray and lighted the end again. He waited for the first cloud of smoke to lift, and he said, "Nat, I think I have far less chance to remain President than Andrew Johnson did."

"Less chance? No, there's no reason to believe—"

"Nat, in our careers as attorneys, we've both tried all kinds of cases before hundreds of jurors. You know as well as I do that jurors are not legal-minded, often subject to being moved to vote guilty or not guilty because of their emotions and prejudices. They will ignore or discard the logic of a case, and simply vote for or against a defendant because they like or do not like his manner, personality, nervous habits, clothes. It's happened to us in court, and it still could happen here, despite the early judicial background of so many senators, because they're politicians now, not level-headed jurists, and you can't deny it."

"Yes," admitted Abrahams, "that occasionally has happened, and conceivably it could happen here."

"Very well. I feel certain Andrew Johnson lost as

many votes because his jurors didn't like his crudities, bad temper, immoderate speech as because of the legal case against him. I've said this before, and I'll say it a last time. I suspect it will be worse for me. In my trial, the defendant is a black man, whatever else is against him, and the emotions and prejudices this may evoke among the jurors, and not Southern ones alone, is not too difficult to imagine." Dilman shook his head sadly. "Why—dammit, why does it have to be? Why does so much judgment of me—not only me but all men like me —have to be influenced by some instinctive rejection or acceptance of so superficial a thing as my color? Why are we still darkies, shines, coons, spooks, jigs, or, at best, hanky-heads, and not people? Why are we isolated, forced into our squalid ghettos, our Niggertowns, from Atlanta's Buttermilk Bottom to Chicago's South Side to Los Angeles' Central Avenue, with tin plates feeding us morsels of tokenism, concession, slight adjustment, un-fulfilled promises? Why this callous and subhuman mis-treatment? It—it's bewildering, Nat. I won't go further, no, I won't say that the white men, not the lunatic fringe but the otherwise decent Caucasians, can't really under-stand how we Negroes feel, can't fathom what it is really like to be a Negro, because that would concede to them their argument that Negroes are inherently different, which we are not."

Then an embarrassed smile crossed Dilman's lips. "Silly of me, Nat, at a late date like this, bringing it up again. That's like trying to obtain an Instant Answer to a tired and complicated old question—how can civil rights still be an issue in a free country? And yet, I keep asking myself—how is this possible? Why? Ridiculous. Let's for-get it, and—"

Abrahams had been thoughtful, but now he said, "No, Doug, you've posed a legitimate question, familiar as it is to both of us. We all know the endless reasons why American whites are prejudiced against Negroes. We've heard it from anthropologists and psychiatrists, from intellectuals and segregationists. We know there is a basic prejudice in all human beings that grows out of xenophobia—the dislike of foreigners, the fear of persons who look and seem to act differently. In the case of Negroes, this phobia is severely heightened. We know there is a widespread psychological, as well as an esthetic, antipathy toward black-skinned people. We know there is a belief, hidden or overt, that Negroes are of inferior mentality. Don't segregationists always quote Arnold Toynbee to the effect that of history's twenty-one great civilizations, Negroid Africa produced not one? We know that there is a fear, a deep unreasoning fear, among whites that Negroes are closer to savagery than to civilization, and therefore are unpredictable and threatening. I was thinking about this point just the other night. We've kept the Negro down so cruelly and for so damn long, denying him equal housing, employment, education, transportation, public accommodations, justice at the ballot box and in the courts, that despite the Supreme Court demand that we assimilate him 'with all deliberate speed,' we find we are reluctant to do so, to open up the Niggertown stockades and let him out. You see, by now, Doug, we're simply afraid to let him free. Do you understand?"

"I'm not sure," Dilman said uncertainly.

"Well, let me put it another way," Abrahams went on. "By now, we suspect that the most meek and submissive Negro servant in our kitchen harbors a strong resentment toward us. And outside the kitchen, in the city streets, we know there are colored men who have been so long deprived, whose lives are so hopeless, that they no longer have anything to lose by employing force and violence against us. We know we have shoved too many of them beyond the safe boundaries of adherence to custom and law. We fear that, given half a chance, they may invade our secure boundaries to confiscate what is rightfully theirs, and more, and beat us up in the process, take our women by force, maim and kill, because they do not recognize the rules that we have for so many years forbidden them to live by. That's part of the picture we both know, Doug, but in your case there is one more thing, I believe."

Dilman waited, and then he asked, "What more can there be?"

"This. The men who are prosecuting you, and the public out there that has denounced you, they have done this for many of the reasons I've enunciated. But the quality of their antagonism toward you is different from what it is toward the Negro-on-the-street. This antagonism doesn't spring from fear of you—since they know you are educated, oriented to the white world, surrounded by whites of strength and importance—and they know you are in the full glare of the spotlight, unable to initiate any violence, always subject to their laws and accountable to their decision. If they hate you, and want to be rid of you, and are trying you, I suspect it is for a different psychological motive than fear."

He hesitated, and Dilman said, "For what, then, Nat? Why do they want to get rid of me?"

"Not because they fear you, but because—because they are *ashamed* of you. There are a hundred truths, but this is the main one, I would suggest. Men live by pride, and the predominantly white population of this country is mortified by the fact that their beautiful land and their beautiful lives are being run by a person who is —they have been brought up to believe—so shockingly their inferior, by a person whom one and all think they are superior to, and whom consequently they cannot respect, and whom they cannot have pride in before each other and the world at large. There is a kind of unvoiced national desire to regain national pride by liquidating, through due process, through civilized process, the one blot on the pure white landscape—and also, in doing so, sleep and play with less guilt for not having to look up constantly at you, Negro, so long wronged, who towers as a blatant rebuke to the national conscience. So, by legal hook or crook, out, damned spot. And that, I suppose, is why you go on trial in four hours."

Dilman sat back in his chair, and his eyes did not leave those of his friend. "Nat, I intend to help you, not for myself but for what it means to everyone, the tormentors and the tormented. How can I help you?"

"By staying right in the Oval Office. By doing your job as President as well as you can. By letting us fight to keep you there."

"Nat, that's not enough. I want to confront the Senate and the country. I want them to see me and hear me on trial. I want them to see the man they're ashamed of. I want to be the last witness for the defense."

"No."

"Why not?"

"Andrew Johnson never appeared in the Senate during his impeachment trial. His managers would not permit it. They felt that he might be goaded into losing his head and into saying things that could never be taken back. They felt his appearance could only endanger his cause. Johnson complained and protested, but he gave in."

"Nat—why not?"

"Listen, you nigger lover, don't you give me any more trouble. I've got headaches enough," he said lightly, and he stood up. Then, looking at Dilman, he became serious. "Why not, Doug? Because I won't throw a sheep, even a black sheep, to a slobbering pack of jackals. I may be your counselor, but I am also your friend. . . . Now, you wish both of us luck, and if you believe in St. Christopher, it wouldn't hurt to give him a jingle on the hot line, and ask him to hold a good thought."

At five minutes to one o'clock in the afternoon, Nat Abrahams was witness to a sight that had been seen only once before in American history.

Jittery and impatient, he had left his three associates awaiting the official summons in the Senate Office of the Vice-President, slipped past the emptying Senate lobby, and come to the filled doorway on the Minority's side of the Senate Chamber. The two doors had been fastened open, and the entry was crowded with curious, blue-uniformed Capitol police and gawking, scrubbed Senate page boys.

A policeman recognized Abrahams, and started to make a place for him just inside the Chamber, but Abrahams declined the offer. He did not yet want to be seen by the assembling congressmen and the eagle-eyed occupants of the press gallery. Instead he hung back, partially hidden from public view, but, because of his height, he was able to survey the scene inside fully.

The scene of this second Presidential trial for impeachment was, Abrahams felt sure, twice as hectic and highly charged as the first one over a century before. When the Andrew Johnson tribunal had convened, in those horse-and-carriage days, there had been 54 senators in attendance, and 190 representatives of the House present as onlookers, representing a United States populated by 30 million constituents. This early afternoon, there were packed in the Chamber before him 100 senators, to sit as jurors, and behind them 448 representatives of the House who had voted to become a Committee of the Whole to present themselves as guests in court, and these represented 230 million constituents. In 1868, the Andrew Johnson trial, beyond settling the balance of power in the government, as well as a political vendetta, possessed no central issue that would affect the lives of the citizens of the country. Today's trial, Abrahams knew, possessed an issue of incalculable importance, that of the hidden reason for which President Dilman was being tried, the color of his skin, an issue that touched the life of every American. The outcome of the judgment on this issue would seriously affect America's future at home and abroad.

Peering upward over the heads of the page boys, Abrahams' eyes roved across the three sides of the galleries visible to him. As in Andrew Johnson's time, the House had ruled that public admission to the trial would be by ticket only, a different-colored ticket to be printed for each succeeding day. The top-priority tickets had been passed out according to rank. Of the 1,250 tickets printed daily, 50 were given to President Dilman, 60 distributed among the foreign diplomatic corps, two went to each senator, one went to each representative, and only a few hundred were made available, on a first come, first served basis, to the quarter of a million persons, the public, who had been applying for them by telephone, telegram, and letter.

Except for the space requisitioned by the television cameras and technicians, the five steep tiers of the public galleries on high, with a sixth row for standees, were jammed tightly with humanity, and had been so for over an hour. Even the aisle steps above were occupied, and in the doorways could be seen the conservatively attired, ever-watchful agents of the Secret Service. By squinting, Abrahams could make out several familiar faces, among them Hugo Gaynor's and Lou Agajanian's. Then, as last-minute arrivals appeared with their dripping umbrellas, removing their wet raincoats, he could distinguish other persons known to him—Dilman's chubby housekeeper, Crystal, the lobbyist, Gorden Oliver, the Party chairman, Allan Noyes, and then, dressed smartly in flagrant red, as if for an afternoon's party, Sally Watson. In vain, Abrahams tried to locate his wife, and then gave up.

Turning slightly, to take in the desks of the press gallery directly over the Acting President pro tempore's rostrum, Abrahams could see the reporters, feature writers, and columnists squeezed elbow to elbow, strips of their long white writing pads hanging down over their desks as they bent to their notes. Side by side, chatting, laughing, were Reb Blaser, of the Miller chain, and a young man whom Abrahams guessed to be George Murdock.

Now his gaze dropped to the floor of the Senate Chamber, shortly to be the arena of ceremony and then fierce conflict.

Never in its venerable life, Abrahams supposed, had the Senate Chamber undergone such a chaotic physical transformation as this. The comfortable, spacious, club-room seating was no more. Within the beige walls and veined marble pillars of the Chamber, the spacious semi-circle of proud senatorial desks had been rudely shoved together and pushed forward to the very lip of the rostrum. Every senator, ailing or not, appeared to be in his brown leather straight-backed armchair. On each mahogany desk, as if a last determined genuflection to tradition, sat those hangovers from the quill pen period, the paperweights that were once crystal shakers of blotting sand. Arranged on almost all the desks, also, were note-pads as well as copies of the Articles of Impeachment. At each senator's feet rested an unused polished cuspidor.

Here and there, Abrahams could identify a juror he must soon confront: the smiling visage of the Majority Leader, Senator John Selander, the testy countenance, decorated with its pince-nez, of Senator Bruce Hankins, the vaguely Negroid features of Senator Roy Sampson, the perpetually snarling face of Senator Kirk Bollinger, the unexpected feminine profile of Senator Maxine Schultz, the leonine head of Senator Hoyt Watson.

Arrayed behind the jurors, standing, sitting, kneeling in conversation, but compressed like so many sardines, were the less dignified members of the House of Representatives.

Suddenly Abrahams heard a Capitol policeman to his left announce, "Well, fellers, here she goes."

Abrahams' gaze swung directly ahead. Everyone on the Chamber floor who had been standing or crouching was now finding a seat. The Acting President pro tempore of the Senate, John Selander, and his colleagues, Hankins and Watson, were marching single file toward the rostrum. Immediately in front of the elevated bench, with the marble counter beneath which the clerks sat, they closed ranks. They passed the empty long oak table and tooled leather chairs at the right of the podium— similar long wooden table and chairs were on the opposite side, and Abrahams remembered these were reserved for the managers—continued past the vacant seat perched between the rostrum and the counter, where the witnesses would sit in turn, and they disappeared through the two doors opened for them. The doors remained open.

The august Chamber was hushed, as if a mammoth blanket had been thrown over it and smothered it. Senators and representatives alike leaned forward attentively. The occupants of the gallery were stilled, craning their necks to see what would come next. The reporters in the front row of their gallery were half on their feet, hanging over the cream-white rail of the balcony.

Through the gaping doors that led from the Senators' Private Lobby into the Senate Chamber there materialized the lone, erect figure of a patriarch, as imposing and aloof as an austerely draped statue of Eternal

Lawfulness and Righteousness. Abrahams recognized him at once. This was Noah F. Johnstone, Chief Justice of the Supreme Court, resplendent in his billowing black robe of office. For a fraction of a second, his keen, sunken eyes took in the scene before him, and then, as his committee of escorts, Selander, Hankins, Watson, clustered around him, Chief Justice Johnstone entered the Chamber proper.

Immediately, in a human wave that broke from the front to the back of the auditorium, senators and representatives came respectfully to their feet. In the balcony above, the spectators and journalists also rose.

Gathering the skirt of his judicial robe in one hand, Chief Justice Johnstone climbed to the summit of the rostrum, then wedged himself between his high-backed chair and desk, and waited. His escorts had hurried back to the door, where a second robed figure, the senior Associate Justice of the Supreme Court, Irwin Gray, a younger, smaller judge, waited. Speedily, Senator Selander showed him up to the top of the rostrum.

Now the two justices of the Supreme Court were alone, with every pair of eyes upon them. Justice Gray held forth a Bible, and Chief Justice Johnstone placed his right hand upon it and raised his left hand high.

In his rumbling bass, the Chief Justice intoned, "I do solemnly swear that in all things appertaining to the trial of the impeachment of Douglass Dilman, President of the United States, I will do impartial justice according to the Constitution and the laws: so help me God."

And now Chief Justice Johnstone, dismissing his associate with a nod, settled into the high-backed chair of the presiding officer, and held his silence while the congressmen and visitors and press followed his lead and sat down.

The Chief Justice lifted a heavy gavel, struck it once, and its wooden sound echoed throughout the Chamber.

"The Senate will come to order," the Chief Justice announced. "Since the senators present did yesterday take the oath required by the Constitution, the Senate is now organized for the purpose of proceeding to the trial of the impeachment of Douglass Dilman, President of the United States. The Sergeant at Arms will make proclamation."

Chief Justice Johnstone sat back, and directly beneath him the Sergeant at Arms of the Senate, Harold L. Greene, clearing his throat, bellowed out, "Hear ye! Hear ye! Hear ye! All persons are commanded to keep silence on pain of imprisonment while the Senate of the United States is sitting for the trial of the Articles of Impeachment against Douglass Dilman, President of the United States."

Immediately after the Sergeant at Arms had lowered himself to his chair, Senator Selander came to his feet from behind his front-row desk. "I move that the Secretary of the Senate notify the managers on the part of the House of Representatives that the Senate is now organized for the purpose of proceeding to the trial of the impeachment of Douglass Dilman."

The Chief Justice assented with a nod. "Since the rules of proceeding were adopted unanimously by the Senate yesterday, to the effect that the Senate is now organized as a separate and distinct court of judgment rather than as the Senate sitting in its legislative capacity, the Secretary of the Senate may now notify the managers of the House of Representatives that the Senate is ready to receive them."

As the Secretary of the Senate, officious as a dapper Pekinese, hastened into the Private Lobby, and the Chief Justice pulled at his nose and then inspected his gavel, many members of the Senate fell to putting their heads together and consulting in whispers.

Nat Abrahams touched a wide-eyed, neatly dressed adolescent page boy on the shoulder. "Young man, I'm one of the attorneys for the President. Will you go to the Formal Office of the Vice-President where three of my colleagues are waiting—tell them, 'Nat Abrahams says it's time'—and you bring them right here. Do you know your way?"

"Yes, sir!" The page boy was off at a run.

When Abrahams gave his attention to the Chamber again, he saw that the five managers of the House had aligned themselves in a straight row before the bar. The

Sergeant at Arms was once more standing, announcing the presence and readiness of the prosecuting managers of the House, and introducing them by name, one by one.

Narrowly, Nat Abrahams studied his opponents in this death struggle. The easiest to identify was their leader, Representative Zeke Miller, because of his semi-bald head, his cocky spread-legged stance and continually fidgeting fingers, and his customary showy attire, this afternoon an inappropriate (almost defiant) unseemly Glen plaid suit in shades of blue and green. To his right, more conservatively garmented, standing ramrod-straight, was the veteran Majority Leader of the House, Representative Harvey Wickland. Beside him, scratching a thigh, was the gawky, uneasy Minority Leader of the House, Representative John T. Hightower. Next to him stood the stunted, potbellied Representative Seymour Stockton, renowned for his drawling, long-winded oratory. Finally there was the boyish, intellectual, new-breed Southerner ("new-breed meaning they quote University of Virginia geneticists instead of Calhoun to prove Negroes are inferior," one liberal newspaper had remarked), Representative Reverdy Adams, with his pyramid tuft of hair, thick sideburns, horn-rimmed glasses.

Nat Abrahams counted noses: two Southerners, one Easterner, one Northerner, one Westerner; three Protestants, one Catholic, one Mormon; five graduates of Law Schools who had become politicians and members of the House of Representatives. A formidable and colorful crew, Nat Abrahams decided, thinking of the President's own managers who were, like himself, relatively staid.

There would be a problem here, Abrahams foresaw: since the Senate was not a usual courtroom, it would be more receptive to emotional argument and pleadings. The House managers had been schooled by countless campaigns to speak the Senate's language, which was also the people's language. Dilman's managers possessed no elective political experience, and their legalistic pleadings might be considerably less effective. Nat Abrahams promised himself to remind Hart, Tuttle, and

Priest that they had better incorporate into the wisdom of Blackstone some of the wisdom of such eminent American philosophers as Dale Carnegie, Harriet Beecher Stowe, Bruce Barton, Dr. Benjamin Spock, Robert Ripley, and Artemus Ward.

He realized that Chief Justice Johnstone was speaking. "The managers of the impeachment on the part of the House of Representatives will please take the seats assigned to them."

Led by Zeke Miller, the five opposition managers made their way to the chairs behind the oak table to the right of the rostrum at the far end. Of the group, only Representative Miller did not sit. Instead, he raised a hand to catch the Chief Justice's eye.

"Mr. President of the Senate," Miller called out, his voice high-pitched, "we are instructed by the House of Representatives, as its managers, to state that since the Senate has already taken process against Douglass Dilman, President of the United States, that he now be made to appear at the bar of the Senate in his answer to the Articles of Impeachment heretofore preferred by the House of Representatives through its managers before the Senate."

The Chief Justice plainly scowled. "Are you suggesting, Mr. Manager Miller, that the President of the United States be present to answer the Articles against him?"

"Mr. President of the Senate, I am suggesting that he appear in person, or have competent persons appear on his behalf, so that his trial may proceed with punctuality."

"I am quite well acquainted with the proper procedure, Mr. Manager Miller," said the Chief Justice, sniffing. He waited, while Miller shrugged and sat down. Johnstone then squinted at the rows of senators. "I have been informed that the President of the United States has retained competent counsel, and that counsel was duly sworn in at noon. I understand that the President's counsel have been awaiting notification to appear. They are in the Vice-President's suite attached to this wing of the Capitol. Will the Secretary of the Senate bring them before the bar?"

Seeing the Secretary of the Senate clamber down from his marble counter and start toward the doorway behind which he stood, Nat Abrahams nervously turned to seek his associates. He almost bumped into Felix Hart, directly behind him, as Priest and Tuttle quickly joined them.

"Okay, gentlemen," said Abrahams, "what's the look of the defense counselors to be—cheerful confidence? Remorseless concentration? Benign aloofness?"

"Unalleviated terror," said Hart with a grin.

"Well, if you're going to quake, Felix, restrict it to your boots, not your jowls. Set, Walter? You ready, Joel? Swell—"

Abrahams turned around just as the police and page boys parted for the hurrying Secretary of the Senate. He stopped short breathlessly at the sight of Abrahams.

"We couldn't hold back," Abrahams said with a smile. "We're raring to go."

The Secretary did not smile. He beckoned them with his hand. "This way, gentlemen."

Nat Abrahams walked into the Senate, followed closely by Tuttle, then Priest, with Hart bringing up the rear. Abrahams directed his gaze to the back of his escort's neck, trying to avoid any and all of the almost two thousand pairs of eyes following his progress past the senators at their desks. He came to a halt, arms stiffly at his sides, while his three colleagues formed a group around him.

The Secretary of the Senate announced the appearance of the defense managers, and identified each of them aloud by name. When he had finished and returned to his first-level chair, the Chief Justice squinted down at Abrahams.

"You are the authorized counsel retained by the President?"

"We are, Mr. Chief Justice," replied Abrahams. He extracted a document from his left coat pocket, and unfolded it. "I have here, Mr. Chief Justice, President Dilman's authority to enter his appearance which, with your permission, I shall read."

"Proceed."

Abrahams read aloud, " 'Mr. Chief Justice. I, Douglass Dilman, President of the United States, having been served with a summons to appear before this honorable court, sitting as a court of impeachment, to answer certain Articles of Impeachment found and presented against me by the House of Representatives of the United States, do hereby enter my appearance by my counsel, Nathan Abrahams, Walter T. Tuttle, Joel B. Priest, and Felix Hart, who have my warrant and authority therefor, and who are instructed by me to ask of this honorable court that they fully represent me in this court of impeachment. Signed, Douglass Dilman.' "

Abrahams folded the document, handed it up to the Secretary of the Senate, who lifted himself from his seat to receive it and turn it over to Chief Justice Johnstone.

"The court stands so instructed," said the Chief Justice. He gestured toward the vacant chairs and oak table to his left. "Will the managers of the President of the United States please take the seats assigned to them."

As Abrahams and the other three promptly found their places, the fifth chair was quickly occupied by Leach, the perspiring White House stenotypist, who hoisted a weighty briefcase to the table, unstrapped it, and then shoved it toward Felix Hart. While Abrahams' partner began to distribute legal papers, pads, pencils, Leach located a note in his breast pocket and passed it down the row. Tuttle handed it to Abrahams, who opened it.

The lettering at the top of the half sheet read *The White House*. Beneath it, hastily penned, was the following:

Dear Nat, Before going to work, I got down on my knees beside the Lincoln bed and I prayed for the Lord Almighty to join in judging our cause and our worth. I don't know if He heard, but I was kind of loud, so maybe He did, or maybe St. Christopher did. Anyway, make yourself heard beyond the Senate Chamber, just on the chance He is Up There listening. Win or lose, you try for Heaven. But give them Hell. Your eternally grateful friend, Doug Dilman.

Tenderly, Nat Abrahams refolded the note and deposited it in his pocket. He would be heard loud and clear, he silently pledged, but first the traducers and haters would have to be heard.

Chief Justice Johnstone's bass was booming across the Chamber. "The Senate is now sitting for the trial of the Articles of Impeachment. The House of Representatives and the President of the United States appear by counsel. The court is now prepared to hear the opening arguments." He bent to his right and looked below. "Gentlemen managers of the House of Representatives, you will now proceed in support of the Articles of Impeachment. . . . Senators will please give their undivided attention. Proceed—proceed—Mr. Manager Miller."

Had Zeke Miller dared to wear galluses and snap them before this dignified assembly, as he had often been pictured doing during campaigns in the Deep South, they could have been no more real than the illusion of them at this moment. He exuded humble folksiness, as he hooked his thumbs into his lapel buttonholes and came in short, uneven strides to center stage. His stained teeth were bared, and his thin lips curled in an attempt at a winning, self-deprecating smile, as he examined the faces of the expectant senators.

"Mr. Chief Justice and gentlemen of the Senate," he began, "it was on a similar day to this one, back in 1868, that your honorable predecessors sat forward in their chairs in this Chamber to hear and judge evidence against another Chief Executive of the United States, who had attempted to render ineffective the constitutional prerogatives of the legislative branch of government and who had otherwise proved himself unfit for the highest office in the land and a detriment to the domestic well-being of our beloved nation. The fact that, by the luck of a single vote, he escaped removal from the Presidency in no way lessens the integrity and patriotism of the House of Representatives that had the courage to impeach him and the Senate that had the onerous duty to try him. Had the charges against him been more objectively drawn, fewer in number and better prepared, he would have been driven from office, crude and malevolent turncoat that he was, and although my native South would have suffered more intensely, time and good judgment would have tempered vengeance, and American justice would have prevailed the sooner. Nevertheless, the legislative branch of the government of our fathers proved then, and it proves today, that it will forever serve as the watchdog of democracy over incipient tyrants who are elevated to the executive office by accidents of fate.

"We gather here, today, on behalf of 230 million American people, as watchdogs once more, guardians of life, liberty, and the pursuit of happiness. Our responsibility, however, is far, far graver than that assumed by our predecessors in 1868. In that other time, the one impeached, for all his reckless malversation in office, presided over a Union he could harm but could not liquidate. The world was slow and small then, and the island of the Union, no longer riven, only hurt and bloodied, was a fortress unto its own, and withdrawn enough so that no single fumbler, no single incompetent, no lone traitor, could bring it to disaster.

"We, today, live in another and terrible age, the nuclear age, a clouded and fearful time where the jet, the rocket, the hydrogen bomb can liquidate life on this wondrous planet of the Maker in minutes, fulfilling the terrible prophecy of the Apocalypse. Contracting, momentarily, our view of our era, we live in the one great free republic of this planet, where intelligent and God-conscious men have laboriously, through two centuries, constructed a utopia of peace-loving, free and independent citizens, who dwell in prosperity and equality. We are the fortunate heirs of a society that is sinless and decent, lawful and just, a Christian society so brilliantly arranged that in our government, in our government of the people, by the people, for the people, there are three branches of government, with their magnificent checks and balances, one upon the other, assuring the preservation of our democracy.

"A world such as I have described, sensitive to every national indiscretion, capable of self-extinction in the blink of an eye, a democracy such as I have described, delicately responding to any mutinous hand that would rock and sink the ship of state—a world such as this, in this new epoch of ours, cannot afford executive leadership which, out of ignorance or wickedness or selfishness, can destroy us all through the madness of a perverted bias. Because we are the elected caretakers of the life of our proud country and of our good neighbors, to preserve ourselves under the judgment of the Supreme Being who made us all, we are met here today to cast down from his high seat a pretender and usurper who has placed himself above the law, above every standard of common decency, above and outside the pale of respect, wittingly or unwittingly leading the United States and the world toward inevitable total extinction.

"Who is this evildoer among us? You know, and I know, but I shall enunciate it clearly for the world beyond this Chamber to know, and to realize that we are men of good will. The one I refer to is not a man among ordinary men like ourselves. He is not possessed of our good intention and good purpose. I hesitate to identify him for what he truly is, as we know him and this trial shall prove him to be. He is—no, let not the words be mine, but those of one of greater stature than myself, an immortal American liberal who loved black Americans with the same fervor as he loved white Americans, yet who loved America more and would not see it wrecked by the one other President in our history whose disgraceful conduct earned him impeachment. The words I shall repeat were spoken in the House of Representatives by Thaddeus Stevens, upon hearing that President Andrew Johnson had committed his most notorious act of treachery and infamy. 'Didn't I tell you so?' Stevens thundered to his colleagues. 'If you don't kill the beast, it will kill you!'

"The beast. Yes, the beast, he had branded that earlier dangerous and delinquent President—and the appellation, I say to you honorable gentlemen, is far more aptly suited to the one who sits in the White House today. On behalf of the entire country, I paraphrase the warning of a great dead statesman—I entreat you, I implore you —if you don't remove the beast, it will kill you and me

and all of us—and the beast that you must expel from
the government, from the company of civilized men, is
the one under trial today, the one already entered in the
roll call of history's blackguards and villains. He is the
beast who dares bear the name of a man—I refer to
Douglass Dilman—known to the press as His Accidency
—known to our shame as the President of the United
States!"

The viciousness of Zeke Miller's opening attack
elicited from the audience not what Abrahams had
hoped for, which was shock and revulsion at such lese
majesty, but surprisingly, a reaction of understanding
and approval. In Abrahams' eyes, it was as if Miller had
thrown a spear near a large, coiled, dozing snake, not to
harm it but to awaken it and warn it of danger from a
beast in the jungle. And now the snake writhed awake,
twisting and rising and hissing.

The senators, the House members, the gallery spectators stretched before Abrahams had been momentarily
transformed into that malignant serpent. They were
alerted to the beast at their back.

Abrahams watched Miller strut a few steps this way
and that, satisfied, regaining his composure, as he waited
for the audience to settle down. Abrahams did not bother
to look at his own associates. He knew that they must
feel as he felt, and he concentrated his contempt upon
the House prosecutor. Hatred was an emotion almost
unknown to Abrahams. For even the most unregenerated
criminals, the most dangerous bigots, he had always
been able to leaven disapproval with charity, trying to
understand their motives, born of heredity and nurtured
by environment. Yet, for the first time in as long as he
could remember, he felt the awakening inside himself of
blind hatred for Miller and Miller's colleagues and all
the ignorance and malice on earth that they represented.

As he assessed the content and tone of the opposition's
initial attack on Dilman, another thought came to Abrahams. The boundaries of the forensic battle were now
more clearly drawn. Definitely, the conflict between the
managers would not be warfare within the limits of legalistic weapons. The boundaries had widened to include

emotional demagoguery at its basest level. How well Ben Butler had understood the value of this when he had opened his first barrage upon President Johnson in 1868. Snatches of Abrahams' reading of that earlier impeachment trial came back to him now. Butler had made it clear at the very outset that the arena for an impeachment battle was not to be a gentlemanly courtroom but a political cockpit. What had he told his senator-jurors in that other time? This proceeding "has no analogy to that of a court." Each step must be different "from those of ordinary criminal procedure." Then, "A constitutional tribunal solely, you are bound by no law, either statute or common, which may limit your constitutional prerogative. You consult no precedents save those of the law and custom of parliamentary bodies. You are a law unto yourselves . . ."

Abrahams had begun to jot a note to his colleagues, reminding them of this precedent established by Ben Butler, reminding them this was not gloved fighting, but bare-knuckle, when, to his amazement, he realized that Zeke Miller had resumed, and that Zeke Miller had done homework at the same source.

"—and so, I repeat, able gentlemen, I repeat the words of my illustrious forebear who had opened for the House in that first impeachment of a President—I repeat—you are not tied down to the steps of ordinary criminal procedure, because you are an elected parliament. You don't have to follow any precedents except those established by Congress. 'You are a law unto yourselves, bound only by the natural principles of equity and justice, and that *salus populi suprema est lex*.'

"More and more as this trial progresses you will find me, and my fellow managers, harking back to the noble wisdom of our watchdog legislators of more than a century ago, the legislators who desperately tried to preserve the Union and government against the dictatorial encroachment of mad, drunk Andy Johnson. Again, with your leave, I echo the injunction of Ben Butler in 1868. In other times, in other lands, he pointed out, despotism was removed by assassination and rebellion. 'Our fathers,' he said, 'more wisely, founding our government, have provided for such and all similar exigencies a conservative, effectual, and practical remedy by the constitutional provision that the "President, Vice-President, and all civil officers of the United States shall be removed from office on impeachment for and conviction of treason, bribery, or other high crimes and misdemeanors." The Constitution leaves nothing to implication, either as to the persons upon whom, or the body by whom, or the tribunal before which, or the offenses for which, or the manner in which this high power should be exercised; each and all are provided for by express words of imperative command.' "

Miller paused, surveyed his listeners, and then he said:

"We assemble here as warriors enlisted in the holy cause of the United States Constitution. Despotism has cast its black shadow across our fair land. As warriors of righteousness, we have heard the imperative command, and now, at any cost, we shall obey it.

"Honorable gentlemen and impartial judges, fellow warriors in this crusade, what are the charges we bring against the despot reigning in the White House? Are these four Articles of Impeachment, approved so overwhelmingly by your colleagues in the House, merely vindictive paper charges, indictments created out of envy, pique, spitefulness, and based on hearsay and conjecture? No! One thousand times no, and no again! The case of the People versus Douglass Dilman, President, motivated by patriotism and Americanism and nothing less, nay, motivated by a loftier purpose, motivated by duty to flag and country—this case is firmly based on the bedrock of truth and fact. Hear me—truth and fact!

"Let us proceed to examine the Articles of indictment one by one, and permit me to elaborate upon their fuller meaning, upon their intent, and upon the support of evidence we are prepared to give to each."

Miller's hand had gone into his pocket, extracted a rolled wad of notes bound by a rubber band. With deliberation, he removed the rubber band and spread out the notes.

"Article I," he read, and then looked up. "Indictment number one arising from the heinous and treasonable behavior of the respondent . . . ."

Nat Abrahams settled back, tightly crossing his arms over his chest, prepared to hear the outline of the prosecution's case. There was no need for him to make notes. The pencils of Tuttle, Priest, and Hart would be busy. The stenotype beneath Leach's fingers would capture it all for later reference. For Abrahams, it was enough to hear and weigh the slant and direction of the speech, so that he could make a final judgment about his own opening remarks.

Attentively, he listened.

Slurring the words, Miller hastily read Article I. Then, at a more deliberate pace, with greater care, he defined the indictment. The charge was treason. President Dilman was in possession of the nation's topmost defense secrets. He was also possessor of a lady's affection, and this lady, this Miss Wanda Gibson, who had once been tutored by, mesmerized by, employed by a professor of leftist leanings, had naturally gravitated to other employers who were of leftist persuasion. For five years she had worked as a confidential executive secretary for a Soviet Russian spy, who had since fled the country, and she had accepted a high salary, Judas money, from him and from his Vaduz Exporters, a secret Communist Front organization. Subsequently, from the President of the United States, who had perhaps been seduced by her beauty and proffered love, who had either innocently trusted her or deliberately sought to help her hold and improve her position, whose tongue had been loosened by a brain befogged by drink, Miss Gibson had acquired precious military secrets. Then, either because of her desire to impress her Soviet Communist employer or because of her long indoctrination in socialistic beliefs, she had passed on the American President's confidences to Franz Gar, who had in turn speedily relayed them to Premier Kasatkin in Russia. Thus, knowing the secrets of our then current policy and strength, the U.S.S.R. had been in a position to anticipate and best us in divided Berlin, in India, in Brazil, and elsewhere.

In the immediate days ahead, Miller went on to explain, the House managers would fill in the details of this traitorous design. They would provide witnesses, from Vaduz employees to White House employees, to prove—to prove beyond a shadow of a doubt—that the President of the United States had this close relationship with Miss Gibson. They would bring to the stand the President's own personal secretary, and enter a diary she had kept as Exhibit A, and they would bring to the stand the President's own social secretary, to prove his extramarital liaison with Miss Gibson. They would bring forth subpoenaed witnesses, ranging from the leftist-minded professor who had taught Miss Gibson at the University of West Virginia, to the Director of the FBI, to prove that the President's indiscretions had opened every file in the Pentagon, in SAC, in Cape Kennedy, to the Premier of Russia.

Now Miller read Article II, and in his explanation of it, gave it little elaboration. Because the President had placed a blood relationship above his oath of office, because of "a natural and unfortunately understandable passion for a member of a minority race and a desire to help militant members of that race," the President had been in secret collusion with the infamous Turnerite Group and its condemned and soon-to-be-executed leader, Jefferson Hurley. There would be ample evidence to convince the eminent Senate members of the President's criminality. There would be entered into the record Exhibit B, a letter in the hand of Julian Dilman, confessing his intent to become a secret member of the Turnerites. There would be subpoenaed witnesses who had seen the President and his son holding their surreptitious and questionable meetings in the White House and at Trafford University. There would be read an affidavit signed by the Attorney General of the United States himself, to reveal by what means the President had obstructed the Department of Justice in his effort to protect the Turnerites, and thereby protect his son. And because of this prejudiced interference, it would be shown how the President was as responsible as the murderer Hurley for the death of a noble and selfless Southern magistrate, namely, Judge Everett Gage, now in his Mississippi grave, a martyr to executive selfishness and conspiracy.

With the lip-smacking, leering delight of a young boy slowly turning the pages of a nudist periodical, Representative Zeke Miller fluently rolled out the charges specified in omnibus Article III.

"We are grown men, men of the world, and we know that Babylon has existed, and that weak men are weak in the flesh," said Miller, his words winking out across the Chamber. "Seduction of the innocent, the fair, the frail, lechery imposed upon other men's daughters and wives and widows, exists. *However*"——and his high-pitched voice rose several decibels, like a Confederate bugle, until its shrillness knifed across every portion of the auditorium——"when the leader of our democratic and spiritual renaissance, through wicked and sinful behavior, profanes the sacred sanctum where once slept the illustrious Abe Lincoln, profanes the hallowed halls of the President's House where the tread of Jefferson, Jackson, Wilson, and both Roosevelts was once heard, it is a time not for revulsion but for retribution."

The President, said Miller, grown coarse and intemperate in his long years of solitary bachelorhood, often inflamed by drink, had become disrespectful of the opposite sex. One extramarital love affair, with one of his own race, had not been enough to satiate him. He had sought out and hired the sweet and innocent daughter of one of the nation's most respected and beloved legislators. He had brought close to him this young lady, little qualified though she was for the position he had offered her, baiting her with it for no other purpose than ultimately to satisfy his carnal needs. Yes, he had degraded his office, and his manhood, and his race, by attempting to force himself upon Miss Sally Watson while intoxicated, seduce her, and only through the grace of the Lord had she escaped. In due time, the victim herself, agonizing as reliving the experience would be for her, would recount the details of the horrifying episode. Photographs of her injuries, taken immediately after the terrible ex-

perience, would be entered into the record as Exhibit C
by the managers of the House.

Miller went quickly over the other specifications in
Article III, and from his table Abrahams grudgingly had
to concede the effectiveness of his tactic. Miller sensed
that he had made an impression with the details of the
Sally Watson charge. It had been strong stuff, as the
faces of the senators indicated, and Miller was too clever
to water it down.

He glossed over the Wanda Gibson affair. Mainly, he
emphasized that the President had dwelt under the same
roof with this single woman for five years, encouraged
by the Reverend Spinger (who would be a witness to the
fact), because the Reverend had offered her up as a
bribe to get preferential treatment for his Crispus Society. Suffice it that, even after leaving his licentious
house on Van Buren Street and moving into the White
House, the President had been compelled to return in
the night, against all security advice, in order to be by
the side of his mistress.

Dilman's veto of the Minorities Rehabilitation Program required little explanation, according to Miller.
There would be a host of specialists of every race to
show how severely the veto had hindered America's economic advance and had damaged domestic peace.
Soon enough, the House managers would spell out in
detail the reasons behind the President's incredible veto:
his inability to study the bill with a brain sodden with
alcohol, his persistent desire to placate Afro-American
extremists who had no desire for the domestic tranquil-
lity that passage of the bill would insure, above all, his
determination to insult Congress and take all the reins
of government into his own hands.

As to the President's history of alcohol addiction, that
would be put forth in irrefutable affidavits collected
throughout the Midwest, and in Washington, D.C., and
its environs.

Now, his voice having become ragged, Zeke Miller
paused and swallowed a few times. He laid aside his
notes, and then standing wide-legged, hands on his hips,
he surveyed the crowded Senate Chamber.

"At last," he said, "we have come to Article IV, the gravest crime we can charge against the President, the one beside which all others seem petty misdemeanors in their meaning and portent. For, in commission of this single misdeed, the Chief Executive has, like an insane Samson, attempted to crumple the pillars of our institutions and bring our proud temple of democracy down into rubble and ruin. It was mainly for this high crime that Andrew Johnson was haled before the bar of justice, and it is for this same act of arrogant lawlessness, if for no other, that we are met here this afternoon.

"Once more, permit me to quote Ben Butler's remarks, on a similar issue, in the first impeachment trial. 'Has the President, under the Constitution, the more than kingly prerogative at will to remove from office, and suspend from office indefinitely, all executive officers of the United States, either civil, military or naval, at any time and all times, and fill the vacancies with creatures of his own appointment, for his own purposes, without any restraint whatever, or possibility of restraint by the Senate, or by Congress through laws duly enacted? The House of Representatives, on behalf of the people, join this issue by affirming that the exercise of such powers is a high misdemeanor in office.' "

Miller halted, pulled himself to his full bantam height, and scanned the rows of senators directly before him.

"Honorable gentlemen, need more be said today? Has there been, in this century, in these United States, a Presidential act more overtly and nakedly tyrannical? No, never, never, in any century. The offense may be read on your desks. The crime admits of no discussion. What remains is only punishment for the crime.

"Honorable gentlemen, we of the House do here and now charge the President of the United States with contemptuously breaking a major law of the land, a law almost unanimously passed by Congress, a law not vetoed by his pen. We, of the House, do here and now charge the President of the United States with summarily removing from office the Secretary of State of the United States, without the legal consent of the Senate, and of so doing not because his first Cabinet member had been disabled or was incompetent, but because his first Cabinet member advocated policies that were and are desired by the majority of the American people. For this adherence to democracy, our Secretary of State was beloved by the American people as he was beloved by our late President. And because our Secretary of State earned this popularity, because he was the next in line to succession of the Presidency, because his popularity posed a threat to the uneasy holder of that primary office, he was fired illegally by a horn-mad, jealous, spiteful President. For this vicious act, honorable gentlemen, we of the House do here and now charge the President of the United States with violation of the Constitution of the United States."

Zeke Miller paused, sucked in his breath, drew back his shoulders, lifted his arms high above his head in an evangelistic posture of beseeching both the Lord above and the Senate below.

"Fellow Americans!" he shouted. "I close our argument with the prayer that the historic warning be emblazoned from this memorable day of justice undertaken, to the day of reckoning and final judgment in this Chamber. Fellow Americans, kill the beast before the beast kills you!"

The galleries broke out into an unrestrained burst of applause, and here and there senators, and the majority of the House members behind them, came to their feet, clapping their hands. Zeke Miller gave a short nodding bow, turned on his heel, and went swiftly to his table, where his colleagues waited, all standing, faces wreathed in smiles of congratulations and triumph.

From above, Chief Justice Johnstone's gavel fell steadily, its pounding drowned out by the tumult and clamor.

Nat Abrahams, arms still crossed over his chest, sat grimly, observing the spectacle, the animated congressmen and spectators, the swiveling television cameras. He knew that Miller had scored, hit low, scored high.

Engaged in a trial, Abrahams always divested himself of self-delusion, not hope but self-delusion. The opposition, he calculated, was far ahead at this point. They would have to be caught. It would not be an easy matter overtaking them. Miller's hour and twenty minutes of oratory had worn down the senators, undoubtedly exhausted the attentiveness of millions of television viewers. How could reason hold them now? When you were sated with a rich feast and heady wine, what taste would there be for health foods and the milk of kindness?

Behind Abrahams, the Chief Justice's gavel monotonously pounded, and gradually the din of mob celebration began to subside.

Aware of activity to his left, Nat Abrahams looked down the table. Felix Hart had passed an open note to Priest, who read it, nodded, gave it to Tuttle, who glanced at it noncommittally, and then handed it to Abrahams.

Abrahams stared at the note. "Nat," it read, "that was rough. We've lost them, unless you can bring them back sharply. Need an immediate attention grabber, what writers call a narrative hook. Suggest you discard agreed-upon opening, and alternate as well, and go all out with third possibility we discussed. What do you say?" The note was signed "Felix."

Abrahams' mind had already been made up. Taking up a pencil, he scrawled across Hart's note, "I say YES!"

He passed it back, observing each of his associates read his reply. He waited for their decision. Felix Hart was the first to answer, vigorously nodding his approval. Then Joel Priest ducked his head twice in affirmation. Abrahams waited upon Tuttle, who sat with his jaw on his fist, thinking. Tuttle's head turned. "Hate to fight their roughneck style," he said gruffly, "but when you're set upon in a dark alley by ruffians, guess you got to knee as well as punch. No choice, Nat. Yup, better bring that audience back, right quick, or nobody'll know we have a case or a President."

Abrahams was relieved, and now edgy but eager for the counter-attack. He glanced behind him and upward.

The sputtering Chief Justice had hit his gavel down one last time. The Chamber had finally lapsed into silence. Abrahams' gaze returned to the senators at their

desks. While respectful and half attentive, most of them
were slouching and slumping in attitudes of relaxation,
as if they had heard it all, as if there was no more to
be said, as if the show was over and only the necessary
and boring closing formalities of the first day remained.

The Chief Justice had rolled his chair forward and
leaned across the side of the rostrum.

"Mr. Managers for the President," he called down,
"are you prepared to proceed with your opening statement?"

Adjusting the knot of his tie, Nat Abrahams came
swiftly to his feet, hearing the crack of his knee joints
and feeling the strained pull on his back and calf muscles.

Facing the Chief Justice, he replied, "Yes, Mr. Chief
Justice. I am instructed by my associates to say that we
are ready to proceed with our evidence against the Articles of Impeachment exhibited by the House of Representatives against the President of the United States. I
am Nathan Abrahams, Your Honor, and I have been
assigned to present the opening testimony for the defense."

"Very well, Mr. Manager Abrahams, proceed with the
evidence."

Abrahams lifted a document from the table. "Mr.
Chief Justice, before undertaking the defense, I should
like to offer first, on behalf of the managers, a certified
copy of the oath of the President of the United States,
which I will now read." He read aloud from the document: " 'I do solemnly swear that I will faithfully execute
the office of the President of the United States, and will,
to the best of my ability, preserve, protect, and defend
the Constitution of the United States.' Signed, 'Douglass
Dilman.' "

Handing it up to the Chief Justice, Abrahams announced in a voice penetrating enough to be heard not
only by the presiding officer but by the legislative jurors,
"That is our prime exhibit, and the cornerstone of our
case—evidence, first, that Douglass Dilman is the legal
President of the United States, and evidence, second,
that he was and is fully cognizant of his oath of office,
which we contend he has entirely lived up to and is con-

tinuing to live up to, and which contention we shall support through select witnesses and further certified evidence. Now, Your Honor, I shall enter upon my opening argument."

Walking slowly to the spot on the carpet between the rostrum and the jammed Senate benches, his face rigidly set and unsmiling, Nat Abrahams was prepared to begin. He had left his multitudinous notes on the table. He had committed to memory ever fact and shred of evidence. All the stored knowledge he possessed of the case, provoked by his opponent, had been electrified, and now pulsated with life inside his brain, waiting for his summons. He required no written reference. He was alert, anger controlled, ready as he would ever be to even the score. If it was possible, he would do it. He would try.

"Mr. Chief Justice, gentlemen of the United States Senate, fellow citizens," he heard himself say, surprised at how firm and even was the pitch of his address. "As the document I have turned over to the Chief Justice of the United States confirms, we have for President of the United States a man, a man who has sworn, before the presiding officer now seated on the bench above, that he will preserve, protect, and defend our Constitution and our nation under God. We have, I repeat, a man for our President of the United States.

"Perhaps, from the outset, since the managers of the House have raised the point, some clarification is necessary. What is a *man?* Is he, indeed, Emerson's 'golden impossibility'? Or is he, in the definition of Noah Webster, simply 'a male human being'? Is he, to give the anthropological view of him, 'an individual (genus *Homo*) of the highest type of animal existing or known to have existed, differing from other high types of animals, especially in his extraordinary mental development'? Is he Pindar's 'a shadow and a dream'? Or is he more? Is he, in the words of Genesis, that one whom God created in his own image, that special and holy being whom God formed from the dust of the ground, and into whose nostrils God breathed 'the breath of life' so that he became 'a living soul'? Or is he, as the poetic Psalms would have it, a creature 'fearfully and wonderfully made' and made only 'a little lower than the angels'?

"You see, then, man is defined as many things, but of one fact I am positive, and all higher authority is positive, one thing he is not. Man is not a beast.

"A beast, again quoting Noah Webster, is plainly, precisely, 'any four-footed animal,' and an animal, as apart from a plant, is most often 'a brute or beast, as distinguished from man.' There are many beasts on the earth, quadrupeds all. A lion is a beast, a panther is a beast, a rhinoceros, a dog, a jackal, a wolf, a hyena, each is an authentic beast. But only among the unknowing and the ignorant, or the malicious and unbalanced, is a man ever confused with a beast. Sometimes, in the North of our nation, I have heard pathetic and psychopathic perverts called beasts, even though they were men. Sometimes, in the South of the United States, not the South of Africa, in the South of the United States and occasionally in the North, I have heard our citizens of black skin called beasts. But I have always attributed that confusion of identity to ignorance or malice, and believed the only corrective measure to be education.

"Forgive me the biological discourse, honorable senators, but since my able opponent mistook the nature of the subject on trial today, I thought it but proper, indeed necessary, to correct him. Let there be no confusion among you from this moment on. In 1868, the President of the United States was a man, a man made in the image of God, Thaddeus Stevens notwithstanding. Today, the President of the United States is another man, a man created in the image of God, Zeke Miller notwithstanding. The President is not a four-legged brute, but a man, as you are men, no more, no less, as even the managers of the House are men.

"I am determined to keep the definitions in this trial precise. You are here to sit in judgment on the future of a human being who is the President of the United States. The managers of the House are here to prosecute a human being and try to remove him from his rightfully held office. My colleagues and I are here to defend a human being and retain him in the highest position in the land. If that is understood and agreed upon, I am prepared to enter into our argument against the Articles of Impeachment voted upon by the House of Representatives."

It was time for a breather. Nat Abrahams halted. With unfaltering gaze, he surveyed the faces and the profiles of the senators arrayed before him. He had gained and held their attention, he guessed, shamed some, annoyed others, but he had opened the path for what must now, of necessity, follow. Along this path there was danger, but there was no other way.

Bending his head to organize his thoughts, he took several paces to his right. When he raised his head, his eyes met those of Zeke Miller, and it pleased him to see that Miller's balding warm pate was beaded and his eyes burning and his thin-lipped mouth compressed with contained bile.

Abruptly, Nat Abrahams swung back to confront his audience.

"Gentlemen of the Senate, I shall now enter into my argument against the five Articles of Impeachment—wait, it was not a slip of the tongue, I repeat, the *five* Articles of Impeachment pronounced against the President this afternoon."

There was puzzlement on many faces, he could see, and there were rustles and whisperings of wonder from behind some of the desks. Rapidly, Nat Abrahams resumed. He almost had them; now he must grab them and hold them and bang their skulls against the truth.

"It is not the fourth Article, as my distinguished opponent has stated, that stands as the gravest charge and the one most crucial to the welfare of our government and our democracy. No, gentlemen, it is the fifth Article of indictment against our President, the covert, hushed fifth Article, unannounced, unwritten, unmentioned yet in this judicial court, that pervades the atmosphere of this Chamber, that dominates this trial, and that exists as truly as if it had been made public from the first—it is this Article, I submit, that is and shall be the head and heart of the House's case against our President, and the disposition of which shall affect the future existence of our democracy most seriously.

"This vaporous, invisible, elusive Article V, if the opposition had possessed the courage to set it down in writing against President Dilman, would have read as follows: 'That said Douglass Dilman, President of the United States, at Washington, in the District of Columbia, unmindful of the high duties of his office, of his oath of office, and in violation of the Constitution, did irresponsibly, and without regard for the will of the majority of the public and its elected legislators, accept the high office of the Presidency, despite his origin and color. And said Douglass Dilman, President of the United States, did then and there commit high crime and misdemeanor by daring to undertake his duty as Chief Executive and perform as President, while knowing that in the eyes of zealots and bigots he was unqualified and unfit for leadership because he was of the Negro race, and therefore not a full citizen but a second-class citizen, and therefore semiliterate, shiftless, mentally arrested, socially inferior, addicted to whiskey and violent behavior, possessed of unnatural inherited desires, if not to marry, then at least to molest daughters of Caucasians, and contemptuous and sullen in his determination not to know his rightful place and in his refusal to serve his racial betters.' "

Nat Abrahams could hear the vocal storm rising before him, around him, the legislators barking their indignation, or pounding their desks, the lung-filling intake of shock followed by scattered outbreaks of applause from the galleries, the enraged protests from the House managers' table.

He tried to go on. "Gentlemen!" he cried out over the tumult. "This unannounced Article, I submit, is what lies behind the announced four Articles, colors them, shades them in the hue of darkness, and unless this fifth indictment of President Dilman is brought into the open and aired, and considered by honest and courageous men, there can be no justice done in the impeachment trial of Douglass Dilman!"

He wanted to say more, but he could hardly hear his

own voice now over the hubbub, and so he stopped and waited for what would happen next.

Chief Justice Johnstone's gavel smashed down three times, and the sounds of it were as deafening as a cannonade, and at once the tumult receded, settled into order, except for a pocket of continuing protest at the rear of the Chamber.

Then Abrahams realized that Senator Hoyt Watson, gray hair disheveled, string tie out of line, was standing, arm aloft, attempting to hail the chair.

"Mr. Chief Justice! Mr. Chief Justice!" Senator Watson roared. "Objection! I submit a question on a point of order!"

At last, the room fell silent.

"The chair recognizes the honorable Senator on a point of order," Chief Justice Johnstone announced. "Your inquiry, Senator?"

"Mr. Justice, we have just been subjected to the most insolent performance I have ever been witness to in my many years on this floor. That Mr. Manager Abrahams, on behalf of the President, should dare to insult our intelligence, impugn our integrity, by implying that we fly under false colors, that the four Articles under consideration are lies created to mask some horrendous racial plot, that he should dare assail the honesty and human decency of the Senate of the United States, and the House as well, by charging that we want that miscreant Dilman out of the White House because he is black, and not because he is incompetent, offends me, offends every one of us, beyond conceivable expression. . . . Mr. Chief Justice, I demand that the manager's offensive grandstanding tirade be stricken from the records forever. I suggest that he be reprimanded by the chair for attempting to convert this august Chamber into a Turnerite meeting hall. I demand that he not be permitted to discuss again his ludicrous and inciting fifth Article, this rabble-rousing figment of his imagination, at the pain of being ordered to withdraw from the case and from this Chamber for the remainder of the trial. I trust, Mr. Chief Justice, that you will instruct Manager

Abrahams to confine himself strictly to a discussion of the evidence against his client that is known, that exists, that is the subject of this impeachment trial, and if he should arrogantly persist in disobeying, that he be held in contempt of court!"

As the flushed Senator sat down, his colleagues and the House members crowned him with a smashing round of applause.

Nat Abrahams had turned to the bench. "Mr. Chief Justice—"

Chief Justice Johnstone nodded. "What say you to the objection, Mr. Manager Abrahams?"

"It was not my purpose or intent to incite or inflame through demagoguery, or to imitate the manner and method of the opposition," said Abrahams calmly. "I submit, Your Honor, that it is President Dilman's difference of color that has antagonized his opposition, and inspired them to build their cleverly diverting Articles of Impeachment. I submit that the President's color will in turn color and affect the mind of every prosecution witness, and a majority of the jurors, and largely to the detriment of my client. I submit this is the real hard-core issue, and no mere figment of my imagination. I stand prepared to offer concrete evidence in the form of affidavits—signed editorials from newspapers, speeches in the *Congressional Record,* off-the-record statements made by biased Senators—to prove that the President's color is the central issue of this trial. I am prepared to contend with the four Articles as voted, to fight them with all my heart and soul, but I suggest that they are windmills, Your Honor, and that the real dragon to be slain is racial prejudice. I beg your leave to be permitted to speak further, with as much restraint as possible, and when it is appropriate, on this invisible Article of indictment."

Chief Justice Johnstone huffed, gathered his judicial robe around him, and looked past Abrahams toward Senator Hoyt Watson.

"The Senator's objection is sustained," he announced. He peered down at Abrahams. "The counsel will not allude to a fifth Article again in this trial, but devote himself solely and entirely to the four Articles before this court. Proceed as directed, Mr. Manager!"

Abrahams tried to accept the rebuke graciously. Turning his head from the bench, he could see his three associates watching him, and while their faces remained phlegmatic, there was applause in their eyes.

Slowly, Abrahams continued around until he was once more face to face with the Senate. Legally, his accusation was stricken, but in fact the entire nation had heard his charge, and now it was a living issue that would hang over the conscience of every man in the days to come. If he could no longer allude to the fifth Article, it was nonetheless now made visible for all to see and reckon with. Officially, the color prejudice against President Dilman had been segregated from this hostile and limited Chamber, but now it ran rampant across the breadth of the broad country.

By his reckless offensive into the exposed high ground of truth, Abrahams decided, he had lost hard votes for Doug Dilman as a President on trial for impeachment, but perhaps he had won something more important for Doug Dilman as a man. He hoped that his choice of tactic had been the right one, and that Doug would, somehow, understand.

Inaudibly, Abrahams sighed. Well, he told himself for the last time, the truth was in the open. He had done what had to be done, in a manner most repugnant to him, but there had been no other choice for one who believed his cause was just.

And now, he could see, he had accomplished something else, also. He had won the eyes and ears of the Senate, the House, the galleries, the entire nation. He had them even as Zeke Miller had not.

Satisfied with this one victory, Nat Abrahams, relieved to be able to resume the role of attorney once more, quietly began to address his audience again.

AT approximately a quarter to three in the afternoon, Edna Foster had suddenly turned off her television set, blotted the loathsome spectacle from her screen if not

from her mind, impulsively changed into a severe suit,
set a hat on her bunned brown hair, pulled on her transparent olive-colored raincoat, telephoned for a taxicab,
snatched up her umbrella, and gone downstairs to wait
for it.

Now, at a quarter after three, she walked purposefully through the puddles of rainwater gathering across
the circular driveway leading from the Pennsylvania
Avenue entrance to the West Wing lobby of the White
House. What she had relived, during the short taxi ride,
she continued to relive intensely, unmindful of the steady
drizzle spattering upon her umbrella overhead.

It had been a horrible week of lies, lies and indecisiveness, and she was glad she had finally brought it
to an end.

She had seen George Murdock only once after her
return from Paris and his belated return from the extended visit to New York City.

Their meeting had taken place during the early evening
of the day that the President's impeachment had been
introduced into the House of Representatives. It had
not been her best evening, from the moment George had
picked her up to the moment he had left her at her apartment door after dinner, because her mood had been at
such odds with his. She had been stunned and unhappy
over the fantastic attack on Dilman. George had been
alive and gay because of his new high-paying job with
the Zeke Miller chain of newspapers, which he had announced to her that night. She had hated his taking the
job, somehow equating it with her misery over the
threatened impeachment, and not even George's naming
an actual marriage date had improved her mood. She
had desperately tried to evince some pretense of pleasure, but she had failed. She had hoped that a long evening
together—she was relatively at liberty, with the President off on his tour of the Midwest, Far West, and Atlantic Coast—would work its miracle, restore her joy in the
knowledge that she would soon be Mrs. Murdock, but
then George had had time for only a short evening. He
was, he had apologized, toiling nights as well as days
now, to impress his new employers, anxious to get off

on the right foot. Then, after he had hastened away to the Washington Citizen-American Building, and she had wearily returned to her living room, the orderly, well-regulated, promising personal world around her (which excluded the Dilman part of her world) had disintegrated completely (because Dilman could not be excluded from it, after all), and since that time, by choice, she had not seen George again.

The events of that unforgettable night still haunted and possessed her like a recurring hallucination. She had been too occupied with the last of her work during the hours before seeing George to inquire into every detail of the impeachment charges, to watch and hear the indictments read on television and radio, or read them in the newspapers. During her incessant typing, and hectic taking of telephone calls, she had become aware of several of the general charges. Something incomprehensible about the President having broken the law in his firing of Eaton, she had heard. Something ridiculous about his having frequent bouts of intoxication. Something utterly absurd about his having made improper advances toward that stupid, spoiled Sally Watson. But not until George had left her so early, and she had been able to kick off her shoes and be alone with the day's newspapers, had she fully read all four of the Articles of Impeachment.

Then, before they had made their full impact upon her, her privacy had been invaded, and her apartment had teemed with officious and threatening men. She had found herself cornered, with warrants and subpoenas thrust under her nose. She had found herself being questioned by the stuttering Casper Wine and two other attorneys or investigators sent by the House Judiciary Committee, and she had protested against the Federal Marshal turning her premises inside out.

In desperation, she had tried to locate someone, anyone, to advise her during the barrage of questions, but there had been no one. Curiously, her first thought of succor had been the President, but he was traveling and out of reach. Then she had sought to reach George by telephone, but he was nowhere to be found. A last gasp had been a telephone call to her accountant, the one who made out her annual income tax, but neither his office nor residence number had brought an answer.

And when the inquisitors had departed at midnight, they had left her with the extra copy of the shocking confession or affidavit or whatever it was called that she had been forced to sign (for everything in it was true, and could not be denied under oath). They had left her with a subpoena to appear (if needed) for the prosecution against the President. They had left her without her precious diary (located, impounded, carried away by them over her tearful protests). Worst of all, they had left her with the wreckage of herself, her shattered self, and the first full realization of her unintended perfidy and disloyalty to the persecuted man who was her boss before he was her President.

It had been a horror night, with a more dreadful week to follow it, because then the self-questioning had come, and for a long time she had refused to face the one unacceptable answer. How had they known that she had once inadvertently monitored a private telephone call from the President to his son? How had they known that she alone, among outsiders, had knowledge that the President possessed a daughter who was passing for white? How had they known that the President's wife had once been a patient in a sanitarium for alcoholics? How had they known—no one, no one on earth knew—that she kept a private diary and had recorded every event and bit of knowledge on its lined pages?

All of this information had been hers alone, unshared, as private as the date of her last menstrual period and the petite electric razor she used to remove the unattractive hair from her legs, and yet it had been known by someone, and now it would be known to the world. And then searching, searching, rummaging through the attic of memory, she had discovered the traitor, and first was disbelieving, and then unwilling to believe, unwilling to fasten the blame fully upon him.

Her dreadful sin had burned her with shame, until she was nearly mad. For, and there was no avoiding it any longer, she had committed the only real wickedness a confidential secretary could commit. She had committed Indiscretion.

And so she had exiled herself to her lonely apartment. For, difficult as it had been to face herself, it would have been completely impossible to face anyone else, either the one she had betrayed or the one who had betrayed her. She had lived her week of lies, and sent a message to the White House that she was unwell and would have to rest in bed for some time, and left a message for George not to call because her mother had fallen ill in Wisconsin and she was flying home to be at the bedside, and she would write.

Only one human being, and then it was by accident, had even had a peek into her private inferno. Late during the fifth afternoon of her absence from work, there had been a knock on the door. She had expected the grocer's boy with some cold cuts, bread, and milk. Instead, to her dismay, she had found herself confronted by the solicitous Tim Flannery. He had apologized for dropping by unannounced, but he had been concerned, he said, as the President had been concerned, about her health. It amazed her that anyone decent, let alone the harassed President, gave a damn about her, now that her disloyalty to her boss was known.

She had meant to turn Tim Flannery away, and continue to nourish her self-pity and self-hate, when suddenly she had realized that she wanted someone near, anyone kind and good, and Tim Flannery was both. She had invited him inside, barely listening as he spoke of the difficult trip around the country, the untriumphant return, the President's decision to fight back. The moment that he had lapsed into silence, she had bared her soul to him, determined to expiate her guilt. First haltingly, then with a torrent of words, she had revealed herself to him as she might to a father confessor. She had divulged everything, her weeks-ago drunken babblings to George Murdock, her next-day regrets lulled by her utter and reassuring trust in George, and she had gone on this way, unable to prove it was George who had given over so many of the President's secrets to the enemy, but adding that she was almost certain of it, else why had the enemy so quickly knighted him with a reward?

"I meant no harm to the President, I swear on my mother and father I didn't," she had told Flannery. "But I'm still one of the ones who has hurt him most, I know that, I'm not denying it. What'll I do, Tim? I can't go back to my office now, I can't face him, and even if I could, he'd probably throw me out, and have every right to."

"Well, Edna, this is one of those times I can't speak for him," Flannery had said, "and I really—well—I don't think it's my place to advise you what to do next. It depends on how you feel about the President and—well—how you feel about Murdock. After all, George is the man you've been planning to marry. I wish I could help you. I can't. But I believe you didn't mean to do any harm. I believe that."

After he had gone, she had felt better but was no less confused. Flannery had reminded her, as the modest sparkling crest of tiny diamonds on her finger reminded her, that she was engaged to be married. To whom, then, did a girl owe her loyalty—to a boss she had sold out (not that these truths about him would not have been uncovered elsewhere, anyway), or to a fiancé who had sold her out (*if* he had done so, which he probably had, but then, perhaps, he had felt he was doing it for both of them, and it was not wrong because he loved her so)?

She had slept on it, and wakened with it, this insoluble dilemma, and she had spent hours playing out little fantasy games, with herself the heroine.

In one version, she had married George (for his explanation had been satisfactory), and she belonged, and she had dozens of other married lady friends, and they had teas and played bridge, and she marketed and cooked for George, and dutifully attended the PTA meetings, and they had marvelous summer vacations each year, in Palm Beach or Atlantic City or Province-town, the young and happy marrieds, she a doting mother and the wife of the eminent columnist.

In a frighteningly different version of her fantasy, she had refused to marry George (for his explanation had *not* been satisfactory) and, discharged by the President, or losing her position after the President's impeachment conviction, she had been forced to take one of those gray mouse-on-the-wheel jobs in the Commerce Department or the Pentagon, and she was a spinster and would always be one, gulping her lunches in dank basement cafeterias where the thick crockery was never quite dried, going to Hecht Company sales every Saturday with the other "girls" who had taken to dyeing their graying hair, collecting her cheap reproductions from the National Gallery of Art, spending summer vacations with her parents outside Milwaukee, growing fat and resentful and old alone, alone, and bitterly remembering that she'd had her chances (one chance anyway) and turned her back on them (well, on it), and garrulously recollecting (even for those who had heard it before) that she had once been the personal secretary to two Presidents of the United States, one killed, the other crucified.

She had awakened late this morning fortified to act out her last deception in the week of lies. George Murdock, she had almost convinced herself, could not be at fault, and if he had been, it might have been a slip of the tongue like her own, and even if it had not been that, but had been intentional, there was nothing that George could have given to the enemy forces that would have damaged the President more than he had already been damaged by himself. So, that was settled.

But then, at one o'clock sharp, she had turned on the television set, as everyone in America was doing, meaning to watch only a little of it out of curiosity, expecting to see no more than a tedious enactment of the kind of quasi-technical or irrelevant or senile verbiage you came across in the *Congressional Record* every morning. Instead, she had found herself absorbed in the trappings and opening grandeur of a drama that gripped her as much as any historical drama by Shakespeare that she had ever seen. And then there was that horrible Zeke Miller spouting his foul calumnies, and her numbed absorption had become inflamed to the point of sickening wrath. And then there was Nat Abrahams, making public the invisible fifth Article of Impeachment, and her wrath had melted into sickening shame.

It was all of that week behind her, and the morning and early afternoon of this day, that she had relived and dwelt upon as she splashed across the White House north driveway to the entrance of the West Wing lobby.

Closing her soggy umbrella, shaking it twice, she went into the small hall, and, avoiding the Reading Room straight ahead, filled with so many journalists with whom she was acquainted, she turned to the open doorway that led into the cramped pressroom.

To her surprise, the narrow work enclosure was abandoned except for a single reporter in the rear, tilted back in his green chair, swallowing from a soft-drink bottle while he studied a yellow sheet of teletype. She took in the room that she had so infrequently entered. A cardboard sign, tacked to a square pillar, read: WHITE HOUSE CORRESPONDENTS. There were aisles to her left and right, and in the center of the room were the two rows of reporters' cubbyholes, back to back, each slot separated from the adjoining ones by perforated, soundproof plywood dividers. She hesitated, wondering which one was the right one.

Then, with determination, she went up the left aisle, between the green wall—unevenly decorated with framed photographs, many faded or yellowing, of former press regulars and Presidents—and the line of nine cubicles on her right side. Reaching the sixth cubicle, peering into it as she had into the others, her eye caught a typewritten notice Scotch-taped upon the blue center partition. It read: "Poachers Stay Out! Private Property Of Miller Newspaper Association. R. Blaser. G. Murdock."

Shoving the chair aside, she searched around the battered standard typewriter, telephone, spindle with its sheaf of impaled handouts, and reference books. At last, she located a memorandum pad upon which was imprinted, *Quickie-Note*. Tearing off a sheet, she found a pencil stub and wrote, "George: Sorry, it doesn't fit. Edna." Then, easing the engagement ring off her finger, she placed it atop the note that she had written, and then she hurried out of the press quarters.

Approaching the Reading Room, returning the White

House policeman's hearty greeting, she intended to turn left and duck into the corridor that led past Flannery's office to her own office. But the entrance to the press secretary's corridor was blocked by a crowding, heaving, elbowing mass of correspondents, and in their midst, his rust-red hair tangled, his tie yanked down from his open collar, in shirt-sleeves and suffering harassment, was Tim Flannery.

The reporters milling around him were noisy, vociferous, and profane. Although Flannery kept raising a hand to silence them, his tormentors continued to wave their pads and shout questions: "Tim, is the President watching the impeachment on television? . . . Hey, what did he think of Zeke Miller's opener? . . . Did Dilman himself get his counsel to inject the Negro issue? . . . Say, Tim, how is he taking it? . . . What about a statement? What time is he making a statement?"

"Pipe down, will you?" Flannery bellowed. "Now listen, fellows, I only stuck my head out here because you've been driving my poor secretaries nuts with notes and questions that you know they can't answer and I can't either . . . wait a minute—quiet—listen—I told all of you every day last week, I told you yesterday, I told you this morning, and I'll repeat it once more for those of you who need ear trumpets: the President, and correctly so, believes it would be improper to make any public statement about his impeachment trial while it is in progress. He may have something to say afterward, but right now—"

"Afterward will be too late, and nobody'll want to listen!" someone croaked out, and Edna could see the speaker was the repulsive Reb Blaser. "Tim, you tell him, for his own sake," Blaser went on, "he better take advantage of any free space while he can get it. Two weeks from now he won't be able to get mention in a single paper unless he takes out want ads!"

Another voice shouted angrily, "Can it, Reb, will you? You'll always have Jeff Davis to write about anyway! . . . Hey, Tim, what about—?"

There was a chorus of laughter, and then Flannery stilled it. "Boys—repeat and stet—no comment from

the President until the trial is over. However, he will continue to make statements and give out releases on other
matters of government. Right now, I have two or three
routine—"

The press crowd had quieted, bringing pencils to their
pads, as Flannery read the White House news of the day.

Edna Foster realized that she would have to take the
long route to her office, or whoever's office it was by
now. She started across the lobby, and had just passed
the heavy center table adorned by the White House police pistol-shooting trophy, when she heard her name
called aloud.

Slowing, she turned her head in time to observe George
Murdock, decked out in an expensive smoke-gray suit
she had not seen before, his pitted face beaming, as he
hastened around the table to intercept her.

"Honey," he said, grasping her forearms, "what a
sight for sore eyes. Why didn't you call me? When did
you get back?"

The obligatory scene, she told herself. There was no
use trying to escape it. A phrase from the trial crossed
her mind, and she altered it for George and herself: kill
the beast before it—even if it—means the end of your
own life.

"Edna, when did you get back?" he repeated.

"I've never been away, George."

"Never been away?" he echoed, puzzled, slowly releasing her arms.

"That's right. I was here all the time. I didn't want
you to know, because I didn't want to see you."

"Edna, what in the devil do you mean—you didn't
want to see me?"

"I mean I want nothing to do with a person I can't trust.
You took what I told you in confidence, you sold it to
Zeke Miller in return for a filthy job, and you are as
responsible as anyone for the President being on trial,
and that makes me ill—and you make me ill."

At first, from the crimson hurt on his face, she thought
that he would deny everything. To her surprise, he did
not. He said, "Look, sure, but there was no question of
breaking trust—I've never double-crossed anyone in my

life—and you, I wouldn't—" Suddenly he was aware that the conference around Tim Flannery was breaking up, and his colleagues were spreading about the room. "Edna," he said urgently, "we can't talk here. Let's go out for something and I'll explain—"

"I'm not going anywhere with you, now or ever."

Pained, he dropped his voice low. "Look, honey, you promised to help me hold my old job or get a new one by tipping me off in advance to any news—and I thought, maybe I was mistaken, but I thought what you told me that night was meant to be in the nature of offering me something I could use—to help both of us. Well, I was just going to use a little, and that's all I did use, but Reb and the Miller staff, they added two and two and came up with more. My own part in it was next to nothing."

She would give no ground. "If your part was next to nothing, how come Zeke Miller paid you off so handsomely? For next to nothing?"

"Honey," he whispered, "the ammunition that maybe they got from me, that I hinted at, was practically a dud compared to what they had found out and stored up already. Miller, he was just being grateful that I—I was on the side of people who want to see this country run right, that's all. You don't know him, Edna. Miller is actually a generous man beneath that political bombast. Anyway, I really believe it, that stuff about the President, and I really believe I've done something good for my country. Is that wrong? It's all out now. And you know it as well as I do. Dilman isn't fit to be our head of state. So be sensible—"

"Be sensible? For what? So we can be married, and you can have a cheap source of hot news for—"

"Stop it, Edna. Dilman'll be out on his butt in two weeks, and you'll be out of a job, so what kind of news source will you be? I want to marry you because I want to, that's all. I can afford it now, and I want to be a family man—"

"Well, I can't afford it now, because you've cost me too much."

She saw him glancing off nervously, and then she became aware that Reb Blaser was hovering nearby, pretending disinterest. She was perversely pleased with George's discomfort. She placed the soggy umbrella under her arm and started to go around him.

"Wait a minute," he said, attempting to block her, "we're not through."

"Oh yes, we are."

"You mean you're choosing Black Sambo over me?" he said tightly.

"I'm choosing to go back to work for a man who's trying his best, if he'll have me, rather than live with a—a—with whatever low, slimy thing you've become. Goodbye, George. You and Blaser go on writing good lynch stories. I'll be watching for them in print. Only don't bother to call me ever again, especially not when you can't sleep nights."

"Edna, for God's sake—"

She heard no more. She rushed out of the lobby. In the corridor, she was pleased with only one thing: that she was tearless.

Entering her office, she could see that nothing had changed except that her swivel chair was now occupied by the scrawny colored girl, Diane Fuller, who was busy on the telephone. As Edna put down her purse, propped her umbrella in a corner, and took off her raincoat, she realized that Diane was regarding her with popeyed disbelief, as if she were an apparition from another world.

Diane Fuller said, "Yes, Mr. President," into the telephone. Then hanging up, rising, fumbling for her shorthand pad and pencils, she nervously said, "Hello, Miss Foster. I somehow didn't expect you."

Edna reached the desk. "Where are you going?"

"Inside. There's a meeting about to start. The President wants me to take it down."

"Well, you never mind." She held out her hands for the pad and pencils. "I'm ready to go back to work."

Diane Fuller clutched the pad and pencils. "I—I don't know if—"

"I don't know either, Diane," she agreed, "but I intend to find out." Firmly, she removed pad and pencils from the colored girl's fingers. "You stand by for a while, take the phone messages. If I remain inside over five minutes you can go back to your office in the East Wing. If I come flying right out, you've got yourself a permanent position right here."

Without bothering to check her appearance in the mirror, Edna Foster opened the heavy door to the Oval Office and walked into the room. At first, as she advanced toward the Buchanan desk, she saw him in profile, and she realized that President Dilman was unaware of her entrance. He stood behind the desk, his attention entirely fixed on the television screen. The volume was turned low, and not until Edna reached the desk could she make out the words spoken by the voice coming from the television set, that of Nat Abrahams, as it gently chided the House for having included Article II as one of the impeachment charges.

Reaching the desk, Edna Foster coughed discreetly. At the sound, President Dilman's head jerked toward her. His brow contracted slightly, but there was no astonishment in his reaction. He turned off the television set.

"Good afternoon, Miss Foster," he said. "Are you fully recovered?"

"I've been ill, Mr. President. But now, yes, I am fully recovered. Whether or not I am well enough to work, that's entirely up to you. I do feel—I feel I owe you an honest explanation—"

Dilman fussed with the papers on his desk. "No further explanation needed. I heard the whole thing from Tim Flannery at lunch today. He finally confessed to seeing you, and took it upon himself to repeat what you had told him."

She was thankful that Tim had made at least a part of her task easier. Still, she felt that she must speak for herself. "Then all I can add—whether it means anything to you or not—but I must say it for my own sake—it's this—I've had to make an important personal decision, and I've made it. Sooner or later, I guess, everyone is called on to choose sides. There's no avoiding it. Well— not that it matters to you any more—but I am on your side, whatever happens, and I won't tolerate or have anything to do with anyone who is not on your side. I'd like to work for you, not because it's the most rewarding secretarial job in the world, but because, like Mr. Abrahams, I want to do my part. I know I'm not being fair to you. You have every reason to tell me to leave. If you do, I won't blame you a bit. I know in your shoes I'd—"

"Miss Foster," the President said, with a trace of impatience, "this is a busy day. Please sit down and let's go to work."

Her heart, its beat momentarily suspended, or so it seemed to her, suddenly resumed its thumping. She wanted to embrace him. She murmured, "Thank you, Mr. President," and quickly occupied her accustomed place. The President pushed a button on the intercom, and spoke something to his engagements secretary.

Almost immediately, Shelby Lucas' door opened, and the Director of the CIA, Montgomery Scott, entered, unzipping his portfolio. He was followed by General Jaskawich. Both men greeted the President, and then Scott saluted Edna, and Jaskawich warmly introduced himself to her. Edna, whose years around the Senate and the White House under T.C. had made her incapable of hero worship, found herself awkward and thrilled in the presence of Jaskawich. She had read that he had been sworn in as the President's new military aide, and somehow, she had expected that he would be as aloof and remote as the Joint Chiefs of Staff. Instead, as if refusing to take his rank, uniform, and orbital flights seriously, he was as friendly and natural as, well, as Tim Flannery. To Edna, it was as if one of those stone statues in Lafayette Square had leaped down from the saddle to enlist itself on their side.

"Where shall we sit, Mr. President?" Scott asked.

"You sit here, right next to Miss Foster," Dilman said. "General Jaskawich, you pull up a chair next to me, so we'll be facing them."

"I've been watching television," Jaskawich said, lifting a chair and moving it to the indicated spot. "If ever I laid eyes on an animated cuspidor, I did today, watching that Zeke Miller. But you know, I think your Mr. Abrahams is spitting him right back in the eye."

"Do you think so?" Dilman asked. "It's difficult for me to judge."

"You may lose the first round by a shade in the Senate," said Jaskawich, "but you may have won it by a mile around the country."

Dilman nodded thoughtfully, then suddenly pulled up his swivel chair and again buzzed his engagements secretary. He studied Jaskawich and Scott, and then he said, "They'll be coming in now. . . . When I think of what we're up against this second, that show on television seems about as important as a cartoon short for children. Mr. Scott, you've got to lay it on the line."

A door opened and closed, and at once, with the arrival of the Secretary of Defense and the Chairman of the Joint Chiefs of Staff, the atmosphere of the Oval Office seemed to become highly charged. Secretary Carl Steinbrenner, embodying in his every movement the irreproachable solidity of the self-made successful aircraft manufacturer, exchanged guarded courtesies with the others, while General Pitt Fortney, after flinging his braid-trimmed cap and military trench coat on a sofa, strode forward with a more aggressive helloing.

"Well, now, Mr. President," drawled General Fortney, settling himself beside the Secretary of Defense, "what's so pressing that Carl and I have to come hopping over here in the middle of the day? Far as I could learn, everything that's been coming in this afternoon on our restricted communications wires and the command lines might as well have been delivered by doves. All's pretty much at peace around the world—no rumbles, except for that little brush-fire conflict down on our own Senate floor maybe." He chuckled. "Guess that's pretty much outside our province."

Dilman appeared to endure this calmly, and then, gripping the edge of his desk, ignoring General Fortney, he addressed himself wholly to Steinbrenner. "Gentlemen, I summoned you because there is a very real and grave crisis developing abroad. As of and until yesterday, Mr. Scott and I have kept you fully apprised as to the situation in and around Baraza, and—"

"Oh, *that,*" General Fortney interrupted with a snort.

Dilman stared at the Chairman of the Joint Chiefs. "Yes, that," he said. "So long as there is a place on earth where the Soviet Union, secretly or overtly, is prepared to challenge the independence of a democratic government, no matter how large or small, to which we have pledged support, that is a place with which we must concern ourselves. Baraza is such a place. We persuaded Baraza to relax its guard against Communism, as a barter for Russia's good will and promise of peace. Now there is ample evidence that Russia is about to break its promise by helping overthrow President Amboko. Our responsibility is to see that Amboko is not overthrown."

"Mr. President," said Secretary Steinbrenner, "based on the information that I have seen up to and through yesterday, it would seem extremely doubtful that Premier Kasatkin has any real intention of fomenting rebellion in Africa."

"That was yesterday," said Dilman. "Today's another day, and the additional information we've been waiting for came in late this morning. . . . Mr. Scott, repeat right here and now what you told me an hour ago, the latest intelligence that just came in to CIA."

Montgomery Scott had emptied his portfolio, and shuffling the papers in his hands, he looked gloomily at Steinbrenner and General Fortney. "Unhappily, gentlemen, the prospects for maintaining peace in Baraza are deteriorating with each updated report. Our last intelligence from our agents in Baraza, you recollect, we rated as being from a 4 to 3 in dependability, meaning fairly reliable. Enough for us to become concerned, and to suggest that we investigate the situation further. We have investigated further. It has cost us the life of an outstanding CIA agent to obtain today's report, and this one we have evaluated at 2, only a shade under positively reliable, and that makes the situation sufficiently serious to warrant consideration of military countermeasures."

"Monty," said the Secretary of Defense, "what's in that last report?"

"You'll find a complete copy on your desk when you get back to the Pentagon," said Scott. "What's in it? Briefly, the information that Soviet Russian officers are just outside the Barazan frontier, mainly in the high country, whipping together and preparing a Russian-sized division—that would make it somewhat smaller than our divisions—or native Barazan Communists. Maybe as many as 13,000 men. The infantrymen are equipped largely with American small arms, M14 rifles, AR-10 Armalite rifles, 3.5-inch rocket-launching bazookas. However, most of this Communist division is both mechanized and armored, having been supplied with Soviet-manufactured tanks, mortars, Gaz jeeps, medium artillery. They have even hurriedly constructed several hidden airfields, and delivered a limited number of MIG-17 jet fighters and some two-engined light jet bombers. We know that the buildup and equipping of this native Communist force is nearing completion, and all that remains is to find out precisely when—at what date—the rebels intend to strike. We expect to discover this date sometime between tomorrow and the end of the week. Several of Kwame Amboko's own security agents have infiltrated the enemy camp, and if one of them gets out alive, Amboko hopes to relay his vital information to us by then."

Steinbrenner's attention went to Dilman. "Do you trust Kwame Amboko, Mr. President?"

"Completely," said Dilman.

"I don't," snapped General Fortney. "He's sure to come up with something alarming, merely to drag us into that swampland of his and use us to liquidate his political opposition. Mr. President—"

"General," Dilman interrupted, "I trust him. . . . Go on, Mr. Scott."

The CIA Director patted his Vandyke beard. "Of course, the CIA will also evaluate Amboko's sources, as we evaluate the findings of our own agents. If Amboko's findings match ours in rating, are found to be nearly positively reliable, I am afraid you will have to act swiftly."

Chafing, General Fortney exploded, "Wait a minute there, hold your horses, Scott! You trying to egg us on into a shooting war, based solely on some inciting literature you double-domes over at CIA are producing? Not on your life!" He leaned on the desk, across from Dilman. "Mr. President, there's too much at stake to put our country's future completely in the hands of CIA. There're plenty of us who've been keeping an eye on Mr.

Scott's Spy Palace over in Langley. What do we see? A bunch of collegiate amateurs. Why didn't CIA tell us Red China was coming into the Korean War? Where was the CIA when we fell on our faces in the Bay of Pigs in Cuba? How come they let us fly U-2 planes over Russia when we had a big summit conference pending? Is that the outfit you want us to listen to—to listen to and then send us charging into Baraza?"

"Pardon me, Mr. President, if I may reply," said Montgomery Scott, maintaining his composure with difficulty. "General Fortney, I daresay the CIA has done as much as, if not more than, the Pentagon to safeguard this nation and its interests. We gave you advance intelligence on the Arbenz gang in Guatemala, we told you about Sputnik before it went up, we predicted and alerted you to the rise of both Khrushchev and then Kasatkin, we supplied the information that has so far enabled us to thwart the Communists in India and Brazil. I suggest you pay heed to our CIA intelligence on Baraza, although I am not suggesting you act until our report is confirmed by Amboko's own statement as to the date of the expected Communist attack."

General Fortney scowled, muttering to himself, as he fingered the four stars on his right shoulder.

"We have two courses of action," said Dilman. "Either we sit back and wait for the Communists to make their actual attack, or we anticipate it and prepare for them, holding a mobile force in full battle readiness, and letting Soviet Russia know we mean business and will brook no evidence of bad faith. I don't like the first course, sitting back and waiting, because then if we have to move, we may be too late, and it may cost us too many American lives to recover lost African territory. I prefer the second course. I want a full division alerted and ready to move on fifteen minutes' notice, if required. Have you such a force, Secretary Steinbrenner?"

"I have," said Steinbrenner, moving restively in his chair. "There is only one modernized force I can recommend that could swiftly and economically, yet successfully, pull off an operation of this kind. It has artillery battalions together with a guided missile, our new Demi

John, and it has units incorporating the latest airborne cannon, and mobile rocket platforms with their movable launching ramps, along with standard, air-transported infantry units, and fighter-bombers, to give us diversified airborne firepower. This group is trained for speed and flexibility. It cuts in fast, sets up faster, opens full blast, and then zooms away before the enemy can zero in on it. This is our elite and most advanced division, Mr. President—you know—the Dragon Flies."

"The Dragon Flies," repeated Dilman thoughtfully. "Excellent. I want them put on battle alert."

"Mr. President—!" It was General Fortney again, his scarred face glowering. He stood up and demanded heatedly, "Isn't someone in this office going to listen to some reason? Do you mean to say that it's worth the risk of a nuclear war with the Soviet Union, worth sending American soldiers into some black hole that isn't on half the maps, so's we can uphold a piece of parchment that says they're a democracy when everyone knows they're only primitive tribesmen who haven't even learned how to read yet? Baraza isn't worth the loss of a single American life, not one, let alone thousands, and if such a war spreads, maybe millions. Only yesterday, when I was talking to the Scretary of State—"

"General Fortney," said Dilman, "you must be mistaken. There is no Secretary of State."

Momentarily, Fortney lost his poise, stood bewildered, then recovered his equilibrium. "Okay," he said shortly, "let the Senate settle that. I'm not interested in politics. I simply had to see Eaton about some old diplomatic problems—whom else was I to see? Anyway, I can't condone any rash decision that will commit my most highly trained force, the best-equipped military outfit in the United States, the most technically proficient, to some unimportant jungle hell spot. If you want me to make ready a couple of ordinary infantry divisions, as a token gesture to the AUP—"

"General Fortney," said Dilman firmly, "I want to make ready the Dragon Flies."

"Mr. President, you can't do that," General Fortney insisted emphatically. "Do I have to spell it out for you because"—he looked disdainfully at the others in the room—"because no one else here has the guts to spell it out for you?" He stared at Dilman once more. "Okay, I've got the guts. I'll spell it out, I sure will."

General Fortney's cold eyes seemed to fasten harder on Dilman. His thin lips by now seemed bloodless. He said, "No matter what you've heard, do you know what the Dragon Flies are, what they really are? They are a fighting force that is 100 per cent—not 99 per cent, not 89 per cent, but 100 per cent—Caucasian white. This is a division composed from top to bottom, from Lieutenant General C. Jarrett Rice at the top to the lowest one-striper on the bottom, of militarily educated, all-white, fighting veterans. And in case this gets anyone's dander up here, it is not all-white for discriminatory reasons —if Rice and I could've included colored boys, we'd have welcomed them—this group is what it is because when it was created, developed, and ever since then, it required fighting men with advanced technical know-how, good education, plenty of savvy, to handle this new-fangled complicated airborne rocketry hardware, and we've found such men only among the white troops and white population. That's the way it worked out, and that's the way it is."

Dilman's expression neither evinced surprise nor conceded compromise. Not a muscle in his dark face moved. He waited.

"Now you know the military facts of the situation," General Fortney continued relentlessly, "and knowing them, maybe you'll have some second thoughts. Because I tell you, Mr. President, it's my duty to tell you—you send that 100 per cent white elite corps of ours into that 100 per cent black hellhole, send our white lads in to fight and die for a pack of ignorant tribesmen and savages, and, Mr. President, you'll have yourself a nation-wide rebellion on your hands right here at home. You think the Congress of this country, or the people out there, will sit still and allow such an action for one solitary second? You bet your life they won't. . . . Look, don't think I'm not considering you, too. You've got yourself enough problems with that impeachment trial under way.

Why ask for more? Why try to commit suicide? Even one hint in public that you're putting the Dragon Flies on combat alert for Africa, and you're politically dead and buried. It'll look just one way—like you are absolutely determined to sacrifice only American whites for African blacks, all the while keeping your Negro brethren who are in uniform safe at home—"

"General Fortney, if I may interrupt, sir." It was General Jaskawich speaking for the first time. "If we are being absolutely frank, sir, why not go a bit deeper? I think it is well known in military circles that the Dragon Flies are today an exclusively white force because that's the way you and your Pentagon command willed it to be ten years ago. If you had permitted young Negro recruits to have the same advanced education, technical training, military opportunity as those of us who are white, I venture to say that 30 per cent of that force would be colored today. I think the blame, sir, falls not only on your shoulders but on the whole country. Now we must all face the consequences."

General Fortney shook an angry finger at Jaskawich. "Young man, don't you try to tell me what's going on right here on terra firma, because I'm the only one with enough military experience to know. You stay way out there in outer space where you belong, and leave the real problems down here to men who have to tend to them." He turned upon Dilman. "Mr. President, you listen to me, for your own sake if not the country's. You let me alert a couple of substantially Negro outfits, or evenly mixed ones. They'll do well enough, and then we can stall along until we see what the future brings—"

For Edna Foster, absorbed in the verbal give and take, as well as her own pothooks on the shorthand pad, the sum total of Fortney's resistance gradually became clearer. He was trying to stall for time until the impeachment trial ended. Then Dilman would be out, and Eaton would be in. Eaton would never commit any racially mixed American divisions, let alone an all-white battalion, to action in distant Baraza. She wondered: Does the President perceive this? She had her answer almost instantaneously.

President Dilman was on his feet. "General, if it is your hope that the near future will bring a more reasonable white President into this office, you may be right, but I cannot permit you to wait for him or for his orders. Nor will I endanger our integrity by allowing the country to wait. Right now, it will be my orders that count. I want the Dragon Flies readied."

Steinbrenner was standing. "Of course, Mr. President——"

"If you insist," General Fortney said bitterly to Dilman. "But——"

"I don't merely insist," said Dilman, "I command it, I command it now."

After Fortney, Steinbrenner, and Scott had gone, there were three of them left alone.

"Brassy bastard," said Jaskawich.

"Never mind him," said Dilman. "What's next, Miss Foster?"

She came out of her chair to take up the engagement holder. Her eyes traveled down the card. "At five you are seeing Mr. Poole and Mrs. Hurley, and at—oh, before that, in fact, almost any minute, you're scheduled to go to Walter Reed Hospital——"

Dilman slapped his desk. "That's right. I want to get over there. . . . General Jaskawich, I'd like you to draft a short note to Soviet Ambassador Rudenko. Let him know that we have a good idea of what's going on around Baraza, and the part his country is playing in that skulduggery, and that we are taking necessary steps to prevent any Communist takeover. Just rough it out, and let me see it later. . . . Very well, Miss Foster, better have the car brought around to the South Portico. I want to get right over to Walter Reed Hospital. This is something I want to do——while I'm still President of the United States."

It was the first full day during which Otto Beggs's body was not racked by excessive postoperative spasms and his mind was not fogged by pain-killing drugs. It was a day during which he could think clearly. This lucidity he had at first welcomed as a blessing, but now he could see it was leading him steadily toward morbidity and dejection.

An hour ago, a nurse had been in to roll up the head of his hospital bed so that he could more easily look over his splinted and bandaged right leg, suspended in traction, and divert himself with the doings on the television screen.

Every network channel at this time carried the same picture: Nat Abrahams, on the Senate floor, methodically attempting to refute the lurid charges brought against President Dilman by Zeke Miller, spokesman for the House of Representatives. For a viewer who found his own condition and situation more pitiable than that of the President, the on-the-screen coverage of the momentous trial provided little diversion or escape from his increasing depression.

By now, Otto Beggs's attention had drifted entirely away from the screen to turn inward on himself and his own trial. Automatically his thumb pressed down on the volume key of the remote control unit beside him on the bed. He clicked the key several times, until the sound of Nat Abrahams' voice had become inaudible and only the image of him on the screen ahead remained.

Wearily, Otto Beggs turned his head on the pillow and stared out through the rain-streaked window at the limited square that was his view of the 113 acres of the Walter Reed General Hospital and Army Medical Center, the compound which had become his world and prison. Although the steady downpour had abated by late afternoon, the rain still fell in thin slanting lines, creating a gray shrouded and vaporous effect that obscured any view he might enjoy of the outdoors. Directly below him, marking the hospital entrance, was the high-spouting fountain, centered in the now muddy flower bed, and Beggs could make out the top of the fountain's geyser as it reached up to meet the weakening rainfall.

Of his treatment in Walter Reed General Hospital he could not complain. He was not even sure that he belonged here. He knew that its doors were open to career soldiers, ranging from generals, like Pershing (who had made it his home in the seven years before his death) and MacArthur, to ordinary privates. He knew that Presidents like Eisenhower and T.C., and even Dilman, had come here, and that Cabinet members like George Marshall and John Foster Dulles and Arthur Eaton had been treated here. He did not know what had made him eligible for the free treatment and care. Unless it was that he had once been in the service. Unless it was his Medal of Honor. Unless it was that he had saved a President's life. This much he did know—he had heard it from the talkative anesthetist—that the consulting orthopedic surgeons, brought down from Johns Hopkins, had been ordered by President Dilman himself. Beggs had accepted knowledge of this special treatment with mixed feelings. Instinctively, he had been grateful for the President's unpublicized assistance. At the same time, he had not liked the idea of being indebted to anyone, let alone Dilman, especially in this period of helplessness. Yet, when his head was clearer, as it was today, he realized that Dilman was the one who was really trying to pay off a debt.

Leaving the window, his eyes took in the close hospital room that had come to resemble a hothouse. Among the elaborate banks of flowers, from everyone, from his onetime neighborhood friends, the Schearers, from his brother-in-law Austin and family, from the proprietor of the Walk Inn, from the White House correspondents, from Miss Foster, and dozens more from dozens of others, the least ostentatious was the modest pot of violets placed on the medicine table next to his chrome water pitcher. Gertrude, the other day, examining and impressed by the cards of the various senders, had found no card among the violets. "Who's this little thing from, Otto?" she had asked. He had replied, "I don't know, Gertie. Crazy, but it came without a card attached."

Of course there had been a card attached, addressed simply to Mr. Otto Beggs and not, correctly, to Mr. Otter Beggs. The card had read: "You are the bravest man in the world. Will you and the Lord Jesus ever forgive me? Ruby."

He had tried to trace Ruby Thomas through the card. He could learn only that the order had come to a

Washington florist in an envelope postmarked Los Angeles, along with the card pinned to a ten-dollar bill and the typewritten request that whatever the money would pay for in a flowering plant be sent to Mr. Otto Beggs.

In his early drugged fantasies he had hunted Ruby down and punished her, or meant to punish her, for the fantasies had always ended with his embracing her nude, flawless, coffee-colored body. In moments of clarity he had wondered if he would ever see her again and, if their paths crossed, how he would behave.

Then, slowly, in his recuperation, Ruby had receded to some hazy dream of make-believe, and Gertrude, less sharp-featured, less baggy, better groomed, and more kindly than at any time since their early married years, and ten-year-old Ogden, and eight-year-old Otis, as awed by their father as when they were younger, had taken over and dominated his real world. They had visited him early every evening, and every few days the boys proudly presented him with a cardboard box of newspaper clippings which they had cut out themselves or received from friends, clippings proclaiming the heroism of Otto Beggs. The seven boxes of clippings stood piled against the wall. Except for the first box, which he had undone to find out what was inside, he had not bothered to open them. He was pleased to have these from his sons, but the contents no longer interested him as once they might have.

For Otto Beggs, each clipping was not a new merit badge proclaiming his courage, but an obituary. He could not bear to read the last of himself that he would ever see in print. For Beggs, the assassin's bullet had, to all intents and purposes, ended his useful life. While Admiral Oates had considered the surgery a great success—because his smashed right leg had been repaired and not amputated—Otto Beggs had considered the medical victory a hollow one. His leg had been saved, true; but for a man of action, for a Secret Service agent, it was no longer an effective limb but a paralyzed appendage that could do no more than give him the appearance of being a man, when he was, in fact, a cripple. Admiral Oates had assured him that he would be able to walk under his own power, with the aid of a crutch or cane, and he would be able to drive a specially modified car. But never in his remaining years would he be able to run, jump, crouch, to be the Otto Beggs of West Coast gridirons and Korean battlefields again. Or even the Otto Beggs who had sprinted toward the President, brought him down with a flying tackle, taking the assassin's bullet and answering with the fatal shot of his own. Gone forever the whole Beggs. Left merely the half Beggs.

"Hey there," he heard the colored registered nurse say to him. "What you got your face so crunched up for in that nasty look? You in pain?"

She was offering him the tiny paper cup with its pink pills, and a glass of water.

"I'm okay," he said.

"Well, take these anyway. Good for digestion. Hey, is this a new fad, looking at television without the sound? You should turn it up. Whole ward's seeing and listening. That smart lawyer fellow for the President, he's giving back as good as he got. He's closing his speech."

Beggs washed the pills down, and after the nurse had gone, his thumb manipulated the remote control, and the volume came on full blast.

On the screen, the President's attorney, Abrahams, had paused. The camera closed in on his worn countenance. In measured sentences, he began to speak once more.

Dutifully, because all the others on the hospital floor were listening, Otto Beggs watched and listened, too.

"Honorable gentlemen of the Senate, allow me to conclude my opening address to you by quoting from the words spoken over a century ago by that legendary member of Congress upon whom the opposing manager lavished so much affection earlier in the day," said Abrahams. "I refer to Thaddeus Stevens, and to his last anguished tirade before the Senate, after that Senate had rejected his demand for conviction and had acquitted President Andrew Johnson.

"Gentlemen, I quote Thaddeus Stevens' bitter words following that other trial. 'After mature reflection and thorough examination of ancient and modern history, I have come to the fixed conclusion that neither in Europe nor America will the Chief Executive of a nation be again removed by peaceful means. If he retains the money and the patronage of the government it will be found, as it has been found, stronger than the law and impenetrable to the spear of justice. If tyranny becomes intolerable the only resource will be found in the dagger of Brutus. God grant that it may never be used.' "

Abrahams seemed to weigh this, then he appeared to address the camera lens and its unseen audience. "Gentlemen, these are words worth pondering tonight. For little could Thaddeus Stevens, that champion of the colored people, yet enemy of the executive branch of government, have known how a future generation would distort his warning to its own ends. For today, at the bar of justice, stands a Chief Executive of the United States, unarmed with money or the power of dispensing government patronage, weakened by unconstitutional laws that have been devised to do him harm—today he stands alone to oppose the intolerable tyranny of his accusers, who, literally, have attempted to wrest control of his office from him, and have defied his necessary resistance by wielding, figuratively, the dagger of Brutus.

"Yes, honorable gentlemen of the Senate, this trial of impeachment, instigated by members of the House as a vengeful means of slaying a lawful leader so that he may be replaced by one of their own choosing, this trial of impeachment is the true dagger of Brutus. The blade has been drawn from its sheath today, by the opposition, for all the world to see. With its challenge to reason, to law and order, to democracy itself, the naked dagger of Brutus is being flourished, ready to be plunged again. I entreat you, I implore you, to heed the plea of Thaddeus Stevens: 'God grant that it may never be used.' . . . Thank you for the courtesy of your attention."

Otto Beggs's thumb pressed the remote control key, and the television screen went dark.

Disturbed—for he suffered the curious sensation that a second assassin, weapon bared, was approaching the President and he was helpless this time to intervene—Beggs reached for his package of cigarettes on the medi-

cine table. As he fumbled for it, he was surprised to see
Gertrude, one arm around Ogden, the other around Otis,
standing in the doorway. She was in her best dress, the
boys spick-and-span in their going-out suits, and their
unexpected appearance at this time of the day, before
visiting hours, made no sense.

"What are you doing here?" he demanded, trying to
sit upright, but pinned down by his suspended leg.
"What's going on? Is something wrong?"

"Otto," Gertrude called out, "are you wide-awake—?"

"What do you mean—am I wide-awake? Of course I
am."

She was mysteriously beckoning to someone in the hospital corridor, and then she came into the room, pushing
the boys before her. "Otto, this is a special occasion."

Puzzled, he watched the sudden parade of Very Important Persons through the doorway into his hospital
room. First came Secretary of the Treasury Moody, and
then Chief Hugo Gaynor and Lou Agajanian, and then
came Admiral Oates and Tim Flannery and Edna Foster,
and finally, disregarding protocol, preceded and followed by more of the Secret Service men, came President Douglass Dilman.

The room was filled with smiling faces, and Otto
Beggs's head swam.

"What's going on here? What's going on?" he demanded worriedly.

President Dilman had circled the bed to the right side,
and even he was smiling, which was incredible to Beggs,
considering the impeachment trial he had just been
watching.

"How are you doing, Mr. Beggs?" the President
asked.

"I'm okay—I guess—" Beggs gestured in bewilderment at the roomful of people. "I don't understand
what's going on."

President Dilman nodded, digging both hands into his
coat pockets, and extracting a black box with one hand
and a small sheet of paper with the other.

"Mr. Beggs, I hope you can endure this brief and belated ceremony, well overdue and well deserved by you."

The President unfolded the sheet of paper. "Permit me to read the citation. 'To Mr. Otto Beggs, veteran agent of the White House Secret Service Detail: At the recommendation of the President of the United States, and the Secretary of the Treasury, I hereby bestow upon you the highest award the government can give to a civilian, the Exceptional Civilian Service Honor, which is reserved for those who demonstrate outstanding courage and voluntarily risk personal safety, in the face of danger, while performing assigned duties, and whose performance results in direct benefit to other employees of the Department and to the government. Otto Beggs, for outstanding bravery in shielding the person of the President while under fire from an assassin's gun, I do here and now cite you for your action and present you with this gold medal, gold lapel button, and certificate testifying that your country has bestowed this honor upon you.' "

Tears welled in Beggs's eyes, and he was too choked to reply. He had the gold medal, and then the President's hand, and he tried to smile at the applause, and at the photographers who swarmed into the room to shoot pictures of the bedside ceremony.

After posing with the President, and then with Gertrude and the boys, and then with the Secretary of the Treasury and the Chief, Beggs fell back against his pillows exhausted. The President held up his hand.

"Mr. Beggs," he said, "you are now a unique American hero, the sole citizen in our land who is the possessor of both the nation's highest military award and its highest civilian award. One might imagine there is no place higher for you to go. However, it is our belief that there is much more you deserve, and can attain, in your chosen career. The Secret Service is waiting for your return to active duty, Mr. Beggs, although not at the same old stand. I am pleased to announce your promotion, effective as of today, to the position of Chief of the White House Detail. Our good friend, Lou Agajanian, is moving on to New York, and you, Mr. Beggs, will have his responsibility, his desk. We need you. Get back to us as soon as you can!"

Beggs, tears trickling down his cheeks, whispered, "I'll be there, you bet. Thank you, Mr. President."

The room was emptying now, and Gertrude herded the boys against the wall and held back, as the President went to join Flannery, who was waiting for him.

It was then, as Dilman and Flannery were about to leave, that Beggs remembered something he had meant to tell the President.

"Mr. President," he called out. "May I speak to you for a moment, sir?"

"Why, yes, of course——"

Dilman nodded for Flannery to go outside, and then he came back to the bed and stood beside Beggs.

"Mr. President, I just have to tell you one incident I wasn't going to tell anyone," Beggs said in an undertone. "Zeke Miller himself, and some fellow named Wine, they were here last night. They sort of sneaked in. They tried to get me embittered about being crippled, tried to work me up against you——but what they were really after was a signed affidavit from me for the trial——a statement confessing that I saw you with Miss Wanda Gibson, behaving like they pretended you behaved——and claiming that I saw you drinking from time to time——and that I saw you, overheard you, at Trafford University talking to your son about the Turnerites. Know what I told them?"

President Dilman waited, silently.

Beggs said, "I told them to get the hell out of here before I knocked their crooked heads together and dropped them both out the window." Solemnly, he stared at the leg suspended in traction. "You see, Mr. President, men like that don't understand the first thing about the Secret Service. If they did, they'd have known my responsibility is to protect the President of the United States from every harm including assassination, even if it's character assassination. I guess they didn't know I was still on duty——and always will be. That's all I wanted to assure you of, Mr. President."

It was the President's turn, Beggs could see, to be emotionally moved, much as Dilman was trying to hide it.

"Thank you, Mr. Beggs."

"Nothing to thank me for. Like I said—I was doing my job."

The moment the President was gone, Beggs wanted to be alone, but there were Gertrude and Otis and Ogden rushing toward him. Gertrude was over him, smothering him with her thin kisses, sniffling and wheezing, while the boys fought to clasp his free hand in panting joy. All Beggs could find to say to Gertrude, keep mumbling to her, was that now, with his promotion, there would be a sizable raise in salary, and now she could start hunting seriously for a different house, something in the suburbs where the Schearers lived, a house in a neighborhood that would make her happier. And she kept saying that it wasn't a snob neighborhood that she would look for, only a larger place, a ranch-style house with sun, something roomier, that offered better surroundings for the boys. And he kept saying, wearily, that the task was in her department, and he was sure she would find something, and maybe it wouldn't hurt if she left some time for herself to shop for a new dress or two, maybe that wouldn't hurt.

When the nurse pried them apart, and led Gertrude and the children out of the hospital room, Otto Beggs was thankful to be by himself at last. There was a good deal to think about, the gold medal in his hand, its luster dimmed and its size diminished only by his bandaged hulking leg in traction. There was that, and the new executive job with its higher salary, and the new house in a classier neighborhood, and the family with their new respect and new clothes, and yet his mind touched each of these wonders briefly, then impatiently left it behind.

He turned his eyes toward the modest violet plant standing on the medicine table beside him.

Upon this, his thoughts lingered at length.

Otter.

He wondered what it would have been like, when he was still a man of action . . .

"I WONDER," said Leroy Poole, "what's keeping the

President. It's twenty minutes already. I'm sick of looking at that stupid fish."

Poole grimaced at the fish mounted on the board above the fireplace of the White House reception room, then glanced at Mrs. Gladys Hurley.

Gladys Hurley, seated straight, her shoulders back, mouth pinched, continued to look at the carpet and said nothing.

Fretfully, Poole wandered to the desk, picked at the museum-piece typewriter that was supposed to have been used by President Woodrow Wilson (another overrated fink, half his Cabinet members Southerners, ordering Negro Federal employees in Washington to be segregated, so busy trying to make the world safe for democracy he'd let sixty-nine lynchings take place in one year of his administration). Then irritably, Poole returned to the center table, yanked up a chair, and squatted in it, drumming his pudgy fingers on the tabletop.

He tried to keep his mind from imagining how Jeff Hurley felt this late afternoon, in his debasing prison garb, in his chilly death-row cell in the State Penitentiary. It made Poole tremble to think what Jeff Hurley himself might be thinking this minute: in six days from this day, this hour, he would be strapped into the big lethal chair, held helpless while the cyanide capsules dropped, and he would be gassed until dead because of kidnaping for ransom and murder. He would be dying for a crime that was not his own but America's crime, an innocent saint rubbed off the earth because the guilty who remained did not want to hear his accusations. This minute this good giant, this Gulliver pionioned by pygmies, was helpless, voiceless, impotent. Noble Jeff, great Jeff, poor Jeff, lost to life and the future, unless the two of them in this reception room, his protesters by proxy, could save him.

This was it. They were it.

Leroy Poole wished that he had obeyed his instinct and traveled down to see Jeff Hurley for himself. When he had proposed the visit, through Hurley's lawyer, he had learned that Hurley would not have it. Hurley's sole request of Poole had been to give his mother in Louisville a few bucks to make the trip to Washington, and there to help in building up the appeal for clemency—clemency desired not out of fear of death but out of fear of leaving his scattered but militant armies leaderless.

There had been little enough of the Turnerite funds left to work with, that for sure. Just recently, Poole had learned to his dismay that Frank Valetti had produced no more than half of the war chest for Hurley's New York defense lawyer, and had skipped off to his Commie friends behind the Iron Curtain with the rest.

Poole's own available funds had been meager. Except for a hundred bucks sent him by Valetti before taking off, except for what Burleigh Thomas (the ignorant numbskull with his stupid assassination attempt) had left behind for Hurley, delivered to Poole by that sister, Ruby (who had disappeared from town fast enough), there had been only his own dwindling bank account, the blood money, the last of the advance against the future royalties from the Dilman biography, which he had not yet had either the time or the interest to complete.

Poole had spent the Turnerite money and his own savings with care, as if every paper bill contributed another year to his beloved Jeff Hurley's life. Poole had allotted some of the money for the New York lawyer, and used some for his own side trips and payoffs in order to gather the fresh evidence needed for the appeal. He had doled out some cash in treating influential Negro correspondents in the capital to dinner, bending their ears with the injustice mounted against Hurley, and a good deal of the press space his pleadings obtained had been gratifying, had whipped up further sympathy for Hurley among the Negro population, had even provoked one petition for clemency signed by eight hundred Northern Negroes. Then, when time had all but run out, and the money, too, Leroy Poole had purchased the round-trip bus ticket for Mrs. Gladys Hurley, mailed it to her in Louisville, brought her here to Washington yesterday, put her up in his hotel, all to have her on hand for this last, last climactic act.

Abruptly, Leroy Poole ceased drumming his fingers on the table. Once more he considered the mother of his

idol, and was again vaguely disturbed and disappointed.
Most often, Poole had observed, and made note of it
for some future writing, the mothers of celebrities proved
disconcerting. You might consider a novelist or scientist
or philosopher or military hero so great, so invincible,
so perfect as to believe that he had burst upon this mun-
dane earth full grown, without the process of human
birth and with no previous habitat except Olympus. And
then, sometimes, you learned he had a mother, a living
rag, bone, and hank of hair, and it amazed you that a
womb belonging to one so unattractive, mean, stupid,
or merely garrulous and mediocre, could have produced
Greatness. Especially was this often true in the case of
celebrities renowned for their beauty, actresses or actors
—flawless idols, all, until their mothers came out of the
closets, shrill and repulsive crones.

From the moment that he had sent for her, to the time
he had awaited her arrival, Leroy Poole had expected
Gladys Hurley to be such a mother, a parent the complete antithesis of her sublime son. And what confounded Poole the most last night, when he had set eyes
upon his idol's mother for the first time, was that Gladys
Hurley appeared to be the Olympian mother incarnate.
Nothing about her, neither her appearance nor her manner, had contradicted her son's heroic proportions.

Secretly, emotionally, Poole had been pleased that
Gladys Hurley was worthy of her great son; secretly,
intellectually, Poole had been distressed. He had wanted,
when he went before President Dilman in these critical
moments, someone to supplement himself and his own
appeal in the confrontation. The brief that he and the
lawyer had prepared, Poole hoped, would provide the
argument that would be acceptable to Dilman's intelligence, what little there was of that. The mother, he had
hoped, would be the woeful and pathetic universal
mother, perhaps the mother of Dilman's own childhood,
who would shake and soften Dilman and reach his deepest feelings.

For once, in the shrewdness of his preparations, Leroy
Poole had prayed for a nauseating pudding of a mother,
a weeper, a mammy talker, a servile, menial mother, a

shawl and Good Book mother, a breast-beating, psalm-sniffling, kneeling, begging mother capable of making the hardest heart crack. Instead, he had been handicapped by Gladys Hurley, and the final touch to his grand design had been botched.

He inspected her now. She was tall and thin, neat and respectable in her dark Sunday-meeting dress. The gray in her hair had been blue-rinsed. Her square, taut, dignified visage was as impressive and tough as that of a plains squaw. She carried silence like a sword. Except for her lack of formal education, which showed itself during her brief forays into speech, except for her work-roughened hands, except for the stoicism in her bearing, there was nothing that betrayed the oppressed and embittered Negro mother. She was worthy of Jefferson Hurley, yes, but she was wrong, all wrong, for a sentimental yahoo like Dilman.

Nevertheless, between them, they would have to make do, Leroy Poole decided. The cautious confidence he had brought along with Mrs. Hurley to the White House now became surer as he recalled his lengthy petition for executive clemency, his detailed review of the unjust trial and sentence, his documentation of new evidence (the prejudicial remarks to the press by the Federal judge presiding, the refusal of the court to grant immunity to the one surviving Turnerite—since Burleigh Thomas was dead—who had participated in the kidnaping with Hurley but escaped, and had been prepared to vouch for the fact that Judge Gage had threatened Hurley's life before and after the kidnaping, as well as other new and important facts), and his closing moving plea that the President commute Hurley's death sentence to life imprisonment.

Leroy Poole wondered how carefully Dilman, with his self-absorption, the distractions occasioned by his impeachment, had studied the appeal. The last time he had spoken to Dilman—it seemed another age by now—he had been threatening, even insulting, to the President. Would the residue of his resentment weight the scales as part of the President's judgment? Poole feared it might and then he did not. For when he had last been here in

Miss Foster's office, she had come straight from Dilman to inform him that the President had promised he would see that the cumbersome process of appeal for Presidential clemency would be expedited. If Dilman had still borne him a grudge, he would not have made the concession.

Indeed, Poole had definitely received cooperation from the Department of Justice. His appeal of the sentence, in the case of the *United States v. Hurley,* had been rushed through all five stages. His application had been swiftly processed. His affidavits, in the hands of the appointed pardon attorney and United States Attorney, had been rapidly investigated, considered, acted upon, and the Attorney General's personal recommendation, along with the original appeal, had moved speedily on to the President. Now the petition for clemency was on the threshold of the fifth and final stage—notification of the President's decision.

Surely, Poole thought, the Dilman who had read this appeal could no longer be the faint, vacillating, half-ostrich, counterfeit-white Dilman he had known months ago as a senator and as the repugnant subject of his hack biography. Surely, Poole thought, the Dilman who read this appeal had been altered by the events around him, which would explain why Dilman himself was unjustly on trial (yes, even Poole would concede this, because, as Dilman's smart attorney had said on television today, he was being indicted under an invisible Article of Impeachment directed at his black skin).

Suddenly Poole was distracted by a movement from Gladys Hurley. She had opened her imitation-patent-leather purse and found her compact, and was phlegmatically examining herself in the mirror.

As she returned the compact to the purse, Leroy Poole said, "I was just reviewing the case, Mrs. Hurley. I think we have everything on our side."

She said, "I hope so, Mr. Poole."

He said, "Of course, we've got to allow for anything to happen. If—if it goes the wrong way—you remember our discussion last night, don't you? I mean, we're of one mind about that?"

She said, "Yes, sir, if that's what'll save my boy."

Satisfied, Leroy Poole began to consult his wristwatch for the twentieth time, when the corridor door opened.

A White House policeman said, "The President is back. He'll see you now. Right this way to Mr. Lucas' office. He's the engagements secretary."

Hastily, Mrs. Hurley and Leroy Poole followed the policeman across the checkered tile of the hallway, until they were shown into a modest antechamber with two brown desks. Shelby Lucas, the bespectacled engagements secretary with the Hapsburg lip and undershot jaw, was standing.

"Mrs. Gladys Hurley? Mr. Poole? Sorry to have delayed you," he said. "The President had to attend a ceremony, and he's only now returned. I'm afraid he's running behind schedule, but you may have ten minutes."

Poole liked the sound of that ten minutes. Bad tidings took more time. One did not snuff out another's life without lengthy explanations. Good news needed no hour hand.

Lucas had opened the door beside his broad desk, signaled his visitors, and they obediently followed him through a little corridor. Lucas rapped, opened the next door, and announced to the occupant inside, "Mr. President, Mrs. Gladys Hurley and Mr. Leroy Poole."

They went inside, and Douglass Dilman, on his feet beside his desk, shook Mrs. Hurley's hand, murmuring some amenity, and then he took Poole's fat hand. "Hello, Leroy. It's been some time. Do sit down over there by the fireplace. It'll be more comfortable."

Poole trailed his miscast mother to the sofa, waited for her to sit stiffly, then sank into a cushion beside her. Dilman, the appeal folder in one hand, sat in the ornate Revels chair. He opened the folder in his lap, licked his thick lips, and peered down at the first page.

Poole strained to discover a clue to the decision in the President's face. His visual exploration detected the fatigue of one overtaxed, detected stress, detected despondency. But no facial feature provided a hint of judgment made.

"Mrs. Hurley—Leroy—" Dilman said, turning a

page, still reviewing the bound folder, "I have given considerable time to reading, and rereading, your request for clemency. It is well conceived and well put together. I have also, since, received the report and recommendation on your appeal from Attorney General Kemmler and his staff. I want you to know that I am fully cognizant of every aspect of the case, from the public protest activity of the Turnerites that inspired Judge Gage to treat the demonstrators harshly, imprisoning them for ten years, to the details of the retaliatory action by Mr. Hurley and his accomplices. I have studied the FBI reports on the kidnaping, and on the shooting in Texas, as well as the transcripts of Mr. Hurley's interrogation by local police officers and Federal agents, the statement of Mr. Hurley's refusal to defend himself once his witness would not be admitted under the conditions his attorney requested."

Quickly, Poole blurted out, "Jeff Hurley pleaded guilty only after he and his attorney were promised a deal. They promised him an unpremeditated manslaughter sentence and imprisonment with eventual chance for parole, if he would plead guilty. So he pleaded guilty, and then the Federal judge double-crossed him and slapped the death penalty on him."

"Yes, I saw that in your brief, Leroy. But the only affidavits you could supply, to support the existence of such a—such a deal, were those signed by Mr. Hurley and his attorney, who are concerned parties. You have no impartial confirming evidence to this deal. According to the United States Attorney's investigation last week, the other participating parties—the United States Commissioner and Federal judge—vehemently, and under oath, denied that such a deal was ever made, and so did the stenographer present at all meetings."

"Well, they're liars," said Poole. "What do you expect them to say now?"

Dilman nodded. "Be that as it may. I simply wanted both of you to understand that, busy as I am, I have given this case much study and reflection. Now, besides your eloquent appeal, I also have here on my lap the Attorney General's remarks and recommendation, as I said." Dilman lifted his head and gazed at Mrs. Hurley. "The Attorney General recommends, without reservation, that clemency be refused and the death sentence stand as ordered."

Mrs. Hurley did not move or speak, but Leroy Poole, his round forehead perspiring, jumped up indignantly. "That Kemmler—that lousy rotten racist—"

Dilman ignored the writer and resumed addressing Mrs. Hurley. "Of course, as President I have the right to disapprove the Attorney General's recommendation, override it, return the papers with instructions that they be revised according to my wishes. This rejection of a Justice Department recommendation is the exception to the rule. It has been exercised by Presidents in the past, but in very, very rare instances."

"Well, thank God, thank God you got that right to do justice," Poole cried out, and sat down, anxious thyroid eyes fixed on the President's mouth.

Dilman appeared to gather his strength.

"Mrs. Hurley, I was once an attorney myself, and as an attorney, and now the last judge in this case, responsible for the ultimate decision that must be made on the life of your son, I must tell you honestly—I cannot—I cannot, with any pretense at honesty, countermand the recommendation of the Attorney General. There is nothing here, none of Leroy's so-called new findings, that convinces me that the decision of the Federal court was wrong, the Department of Justice was wrong, and that your son should not be punished, as he is to be punished, according to the law of the nation and not according to my personal beliefs, for kidnaping and for murder. Mrs. Hurley, it grieves me, but I must reject this appeal to commute the death sentence. I am sorry. I hope that —eventually, if not now—you will understand."

Leroy Poole fell back into the sofa, covering his face with his hands. His anguish was too overwhelming for an immediate protest or contention. It was as if he had been axed, split from head to toe, by a black brother whom in his desperation he had decided to trust.

To his surprise, he heard Gladys Hurley speak, and her voice was low and composed.

"Mr. President," she said, "when they stuff my boy into that gas chamber, they're doin' to him like the Nazis once did to the Jews—they're punishin' him and killin' him off for what he is, an' not what he did."

"Mrs. Hurley, believe me," Dilman said with intensity, "if I could prove that—*prove* it—I would commute his sentence immediately. I cannot prove it. Jefferson Hurley is a confessed kidnaper and murderer. The essential truth is that he was a self-appointed Messiah of our people, taking the law into his hands, and the government cannot condone such action. I have no grounds on which to give Jefferson Hurley his life, to overlook his crime, except the fact that he is black like I am, like the three of us in this room are, and if I commuted his sentence, he would be getting preferential treatment, special consideration which a white kidnaper or murderer would not get in this office. Can't you see that, Mrs. Hurley?"

"No," she said flatly. "I see one thing. He's goin' to die because of his skin. The Federals and Southerners are puttin' him to death because he's a black man who won't crawl, like the Senate is puttin' yourself to death because you're a black man who suddenly stopped crawlin'."

Poole had recovered his wits. "It's the invisible prejudice law against him!" he shouted. "Same as there's the invisible Article V of impeachment against you!"

Dilman said sternly, "Mrs. Hurley—Leroy—however we feel about the prejudice that we know exists—and we feel as one in this—there is still the law of the land we live under, our law, the law that keeps us a civilized community and not a pack of roving barbarians. In this case I am the final symbol of that law. Despite the passionate forensics of my good friend and advocate on the Senate floor today, you heard his invisible Article thrown out of the court. It does not enter into my trial, and will not, unless he can legally prove I am being prosecuted as a Negro and not as a criminal. There is little chance he can prove that. And there is no way for you to prove Jefferson Hurley is going to the gas chamber simply because he is a Negro. Jefferson Hurley is going to the gas chamber because, as a man, he committed a crime against men, and against their law. If I am convicted by the Senate body, and punished and disgraced by removal from office, it will not be because I was tried as a Negro but as a government official who committed high crimes. I may have other feelings or views about this, but in court there is the law, and I will abide by it shortly, as you must abide by it now."

Mrs. Hurley's inflexible composure broke slightly. "There is—is more than law, Mr. President. There is human bein's' compassion, one for the other, there's that, and sometimes it's above the law."

To Poole it appeared that Dilman, perturbed, shaken, would reach out to touch her hand. He did not. He said softly, "Mrs. Hurley, I am not inhuman. I have a son, too, and I know, and I can feel for you."

Dilman's mention of his son aroused the last crouched hope inside Leroy Poole, and suddenly he found himself standing again.

"Mr. President, Mr. President!" Poole cried out, his voice a shriek. "Listen to me, listen! This is just for the three of us in the privacy of this room, this one more thing. You keep saying you're a human being, not just a Negro like us. Okay. Then like a human being you're fighting for your rights and your life in the Senate, you sure are. I listened some today, and it's not going good for you, no, but you've got a chance, maybe a chance, if it doesn't get any worse. Okay. That Article II of Zeke Miller's, one-fourth of all the case against you, that's leveled at your conspiring to protect the Turnerites because you knew your son was a member, right? Okay. What have your enemies got to support that serious accusation? Nothing much except circumstantial evidence, and some exhibit of a letter from Julian to someone who's name was not even mentioned, in which he said he was planning to join the Turnerites. That's all their evidence is, and it's nothing, because Julian answered, through your attorney, that he was only angry when he wrote that letter, and talking big, and that he never actually joined and there's no proof he ever joined. Isn't that the way it is, Mr. President?"

"What of it?" said Dilman suspiciously.

"What of it? Listen to me, man to man. What if that

crummy, flimsy evidence in Article II against you overnight became real factually proved evidence, huh, what
then? Well, I told you before, and you blew me down,
I told you before that your Julian was a member of the
Turnerites. I once had it in a letter from Jeff Hurley.
But no, father and son, your son, you wouldn't believe
me then. Okay. Mitts off. We, the two of us, Mrs. Hurley
and yours truly, we got the living, breathing proof that
your Julian was an extremist agitator, an extremist Turnerite—a member of a subversive outfit, as you put it.
We have the proof. After you banned the organization,
and before he took it on the lam, Jeff, who was personal
custodian of every secret membership application and
pledge, filled in and signed by every Turnerite, he gave
this file over to the one person he trusted in the world, to
his mom, to Gladys Hurley here. She has that file, and
there is one application and blood pledge in it, swearing
to work underground for the cause and die for the cause,
and it is signed by none other than your son, namely,
Julian Dilman, in his own handwriting, which you'll recognize and an expert can prove."

Poole had the satisfaction of seeing that the blow had
struck its mark. Dilman's self-assurance appeared to
falter, give way. Dilman's troubled eyes darted from
Poole to Gladys Hurley. She gave a slow nod of confirmation.

For Poole the exalting moment had arrived. On the
success of his surrender deal depended Jeff Hurley's life
or extinction from the world of the living. With all the
power he could muster, Leroy Poole pressed home his
last effort.

"Okay, there's the membership evidence Zeke Miller
wished he had, but doesn't have, doesn't know exists,
somewhere in Louisville, somewhere in the keeping of
Jeff Hurley's mother. Okay, inside the four walls of this
room, let's come to a businesslike understanding. You've
been a politician most of your life, and you know there'd
be no politics, no economics, no survival, no nothing
without bartering and trading, without wheeling and
dealing. Mrs. Hurley and I already discussed this, and I
hoped it wouldn't be necessary to speak of it, but she

agreed that I could if it was necessary. I'll offer you a deal here and now, Mr. President. You do what should've been done anyway, you commute Jeff Hurley's death sentence to life imprisonment, and Mrs. Hurley will turn over her file to you instead of to Representative Zeke Miller."

He waited, out of breath, now that the final terms were in the open. He waited for reasonable capitulation.

Curiously, Dilman had seemed to regain his poise. He contemplated the Negro author with equanimity. When he spoke, his tone was almost gentle. "Leroy, that is no deal, that is blackmail."

"An eye for an eye, like Jeff used to say," said Poole. "You spare Jefferson Hurley, we spare Julian Dilman —and yourself. It's take it or leave it, because——"

The buzzer on the President's desk pierced through Poole's threat, and then urgently persisted.

Dilman left the Revels chair, hastened to his desk, and snatched up the telephone. "Yes? . . . What? No, bring them right in, right in now, Miss Foster!"

Confused, Poole's gaze went from the President to the secretary's door, and then back to him. Dilman had gone behind his desk, suddenly so agitated, so nervously distracted, that he now seemed entirely oblivious of the presence of Poole and Mrs. Hurley in his Oval Office.

The door flew open, and into the office, striding fast, came a tall, long-legged African, turban on his head but otherwise garmented in a conservative blue suit. Behind him came a slender, uniformed Air Force officer, whom Poole recognized a moment later as the hero of outer space, General Leo Jaskawich. Bringing up the rear, pad and pencil fluttering, came a disheveled Edna Foster.

All of them crowded around the desk. There were no greetings, there was no formality, there was only an electric air of emergency.

"Ambassador Wamba," Dilman was saying to the African, "Miss Foster says you have definitely heard. What is it?"

Before the Barazan Ambassador could reply, General Jaskawich, after a nervous glance behind him at Mrs. Hurley and Poole, quickly said to Dilman, "Mr. President, your other guests—this may be confidential——"

Impatiently, Dilman dismissed Jaskawich's concern with a gesture. "Forget them," he said. His attention was again entirely concentrated upon the Barazan. "Ambassador Wamba, do you have news?"

Wamba's speech, with a lilting English accent, precise and Sussex public-school, was forceful. "I have heard from President Amboko directly on our Embassy telephone. The word is in, sir, and the evidence is being flown to you by the CIA. Our own best agents have discovered that our Communist insurgents in the hills will launch their attack at daybreak, in ten days from tomorrow morning."

Anxiety bunched Dilman's features. "There can be no mistake? This is positive?"

"Positive," said Wamba, without equivocation.

Jaskawich stepped forward. "This is it, Mr. President, no question. Scott said for sure they'll raise the reliability rating from 2 to top 1 on this."

"Then it is clear-cut," said Dilman. "We've got to prevent their first offensive, and we can only do it by letting the Soviets know we are onto it and that we are prepared to stop it. Very well, Ambassador Wamba, speak to President Amboko at once. Tell him to convene the Foreign Ministers of the African Unity Pact nations in Baraza City, and brief them, and request that they mobilize their forces, and inform them that the United States stands ready to honor its mutual defense treaty with them. Unless Premier Kasatkin gives me absolute assurance there will be no further action, I shall order dispatched by air and sea, within ten days, our fully equipped forces, our very finest troops and rocketry teams, to fight side by side with the armies of the African democracies. . . . General Jaskawich, notify Secretary Steinbrenner of this development. Tell him I want the Dragon Flies battalions on red alert, and I want them quietly, speedily positioned at points of takeoff. When you're through with him, let's get out our note of protest and warning to Ambassador Rudenko, for immediate transmission to Premier Kasatkin. Is that clear?"

"Yes, sir," said Jaskawich.

Jaskawich had Ambassador Wamba by the arm, and

hastily the two of them, in whispered consultation, left the office.

President Dilman was about to sit down to his eighteen-button telephone console, when he became aware of Edna Foster still standing at his desk.

He considered her curiously. "What's the matter, Miss Foster?"

"Don't—don't do this!" she blurted.

He appeared confused. "Don't do what?"

"It's not my business, except I don't want you convicted for impeachment. Mr. President, I hate General Fortney, I abhor him, but what he said to you before, about sending an all-white military force into Africa to die for those underdeveloped people, it'll ruin you in the Senate, it'll create a storm against you. Can't you see? It'll be used to prove what Zeke Miller's been insinuating all along, that the New Succession Bill had to be made law so you wouldn't show favoritism to Negroes, even if they're African Negroes, and that here you are, ready to sacrifice the best of our white troops to do that very thing. I'm not saying don't defend Baraza. You must —I agree, you must—but can't you send mixed white-and-Negro battalions to fight there? Can't you—?"

"No, Miss Foster, I cannot. There is only one counter-guerrilla force that can act effectively, that is equipped to do so with a minimal loss of life, and that, as Steinbrenner said, is the Dragon Flies."

Edna Foster persisted. "Don't, Mr. President. Please don't. This will ruin you—this'll be the end of you—"

Dilman did not disagree. "It may be," he said. "But whatever happens to me right now does not matter. It's what happens to a good neighbor, black or white, one that's put its entire faith in our decency, its trust in our way of life, that does matter. I can't make deals with Fortney, or anyone else, to compromise my country, and I won't. I appreciate your feelings for me, Miss Foster, I really do, but I must handle it this way. Now, please, tell Tim Flannery to notify the networks that I wish air time to deliver a short, major address—fifteen minutes, say—on a matter of national emergency—

make it tomorrow at six o'clock our time. Thank you, Miss Foster."

She shook her head sorrowfully, then ran from the office.

From the sofa, Leroy Poole had witnessed these scenes with fascination. He continued to watch as the President, by now completely unaware that there were others still in the room, swiveled toward his telephone console once more. Then, to Poole's bewilderment, Gladys Hurley was on her feet and advancing toward the desk. Poole leaped up and chased after her.

Dilman's hand was on the white telephone when he saw Mrs. Hurley. He blinked, perplexed, then seemed to remember, and pushed the chair back and rose. "Mrs. Hurley," he murmured, "forgive me, but—"

She stood tall, head high, shoulders thrown back, worn fingers working over her smooth shiny purse.

"You forgive me, Mr. President," she said. "I am sorry you cannot see fit to save my boy, but from what my eyes have seen, I have seen your goodness. If you cannot help my son, I *can* help yours and yourself, because you are deservin' of help from every American. I am goin' home and I am burnin' those files of Jeff's, Mr. President, because even if your boy was in it too, like Jeff was, he did no wrong against the people's law like Jeff did, and if I will appeal anywhere, it will be to the Lord Jesus Christ, to punish Jeff's misdeeds and give him mercy so he can become the companion of the holy angels in heaven above."

Then her voice trembled, as she went on. "Mr. President, no matter what, my Jeff was always a good boy, attendin' church and learnin' the scriptures, keepin' to cleanliness, never fibbin' or runnin' wild in the streets, behavin' and readin' his books. And when he growed up, he always respected his father, when his father was alive, and was obedient to his father, and he took care of me, always took care of me and his younger brothers and sisters and needy kin with money and letters. He was a good boy, Mr. President, and he only meant well, but there was no one to understand. . . . Come on, Mr.

Poole, let's leave the President be. He's got his work to do for all of us."

At nine-thirty that evening, the West Wing of the White House was still ablaze with light.

In the Reading Room of the press section, a handful of hardy correspondents, aware that the President was still at work, lolled about, hopefully waiting for some fresh morsel of news. In the antechambers beyond the Oval Office, numerous secretaries, on overtime, pecked away at their typewriters. In the corridors, the special police and the Secret Service men of the White House Detail ceaselessly maintained their vigils.

And, in the Cabinet Room, before an audience of three, Douglass Dilman was concluding his rehearsal of the latest draft of the crucial speech that he would deliver to the nation the next evening.

Nat Abrahams, recovered from his ordeal on the Senate floor, puffed his mellow pipe, picked at the rumpled napkin on his depleted dinner tray and listened. General Leo Jaskawich, chewing a half-smoked cheroot, absently doodled on a scratch pad and listened. Assistant Secretary for African Affairs Jed Stover, one hand forming a hood over his shaggy eyebrows, followed the circling needle of the stopwatch cupped in his other hand and listened.

Across the glossy Cabinet table, seated in the high-backed leather chair bearing the diminutive brass plate engraved THE PRESIDENT, Douglass Dilman, without exerting himself, without emphasizing the key phrases, approached the end of the television address that the four of them had hammered out before their informal dinner.

Dilman flipped the page, and then, in a voice becoming horase, read aloud:

"It is my fervent prayer that these powerful battalions of this democracy, now battle-ready and on full alert, will not have to leave our nation's boundaries. It is my fervent prayer that even if we should commit ourselves to a limited conflict, it will not spread into a worldwide holocaust, and that our ICBMs will rest forever in their silos, and our jet bombers will continue confined to their runways or routine missions, and that our Polaris submarines will cruise under the seas with their nuclear rockets safely unarmed."

He paused, and then he resumed.

"This is my fervent prayer and I know that you share it with me, one and all. But let not the enemies of freedom misconstrue this wish for peace as an evidence of weakness. There are many abroad who may think the United States speaks in many voices, and who may choose to hear, and believe, the voice that pleases them the most. They may prefer the American voice that reflects our normal, two-party political wrangling and discord, so that they may suspect we are disunited. They may prefer the American voice that reflects our onetime isolationist ideology, that promises we will not trade a single American life to preserve the independence of an African democracy whose entire population can fit into one of our largest cities, so that they may suspect we are disunited. They may prefer the American voice that reflects our own domestic racial strife, the one vowing we will not protect our colored brothers in other lands any more than we will integrate them in our own land because they are inferior, so that they may suspect we are disunited.

"To the hopeful cynics abroad, I can only say—do not be misled by the discordant sounds of opinion and disagreement so much a part of our democratic system—for, in times of danger, America has always and will always speak out in one single united voice, and that will be the voice of the majority of its free citizens.

"Tonight, fellow Americans, the words to be spoken by our united voice, the voice we want our friends and enemies around the earth to hear and heed, may best be taken from the words spoken by our beloved former President, John F. Kennedy, who said, 'The free world's security can be endangered not only by a nuclear attack, but also by being nibbled away at the periphery . . . by forces of subversion, infiltration, intimidation, indirect or nonovert aggression, internal revolution, diplo-

matic blackmail, guerrilla warfare or a series of limited
wars. . . . Let every nation know, whether it wishes us
well or ill, that we shall pay any price, bear any burden,
meet any hardship, support any friend, oppose any foe
to assure the survival and the success of liberty.'

"Thank you, and good night."

Dilman exhaled, tossed the typescript on the table,
and looked up.

"Well, how did it sound to you?" he asked. "There
are a few rough spots, but I think we can smooth them
out in the morning. Otherwise, I believe it says what
should be said."

Jed Stover was all enthusiasm. "I think it's great, and
about time!" He held up the stopwatch. "Almost on the
nose, Mr. President. Only fifteen seconds over." Then
he added, "This is going to make Amboko and the African Unity Pact nations very happy."

"I'm not so sure it'll scare Premier Kasatkin," said
Jaskawich, "but it's sure as hell going to scare the living
daylights out of the Senate!"

Revolving his empty teacup in its saucer, Nat Abrahams said nothing. He saw Dilman's attention focus on
him.

"What about that, Nat?" Dilman asked. "I've given
you a tough enough job, asking you to handle that trial,
without making it tougher. Anything you want me to
reword or tone down?"

Nat Abrahams removed the pipe from between his
teeth. "Hell, no," he said. "The devil with the Senate.
Sure they won't like this, but it's only a big stick you're
waving at Russia, not a bazooka. It probably won't influence a single senator's vote, one way or the other, not
yet."

"Then you think it should read as it stands?" asked
Dilman.

"Not quite," said Abrahams. "If anything, at least in
one passage there, I'd be a little more explicit. I mean
earlier, when you go into our military resources, and
when you detail the power potential of the Dragon Flies.
I think you should come right out and explain why you

and Steinbrenner have selected this all-white force for the African assignment."

Dilman's features revealed his worry. "I don't know, Nat——"

"Why not, Mr. President?" asked Abrahams. "It's in the open anyway——"

"It sure is," said Jaskawich. "Mr. President, I'm inclined to agree with Mr. Abrahams. You heard the late afternoon broadcasts, saw the early evening papers. 'A reliable top-level Pentagon source admitted today that the military chiefs are doing their best to dissuade President Dilman from throwing only white troops into the African inferno.' " Jaskawich snorted. " 'A reliable Pentagon source'——ha! Spelled Pitt Fortney. You'll never be able to prove he leaked it, but one gets you ten he did. You're his superior officer, Mr. President, so he can't blow you down face to face. What he's doing is the next-best thing, whipping up a tornado against you among the general public. If anybody's going to fight and die for us in Africa, he's going to make damn sure it'll include our Negro soldiers with our whites, even though the mixed battalions aren't prepared for that kind of warfare. Or maybe he just wants to solve our race problem by shipping as many colored men to Africa as possible. No, seriously, Mr. President, Fortney's tidbit has been out for hours, burning across the country like a prairie fire, prejudicing more and more misinformed people against you. Mr. Abrahams is right. Douse that fire while you can."

"Maybe I should," Dilman mused.

Abrahams bent forward, leaning on his elbows. "It wouldn't take much, another line or two in the speech. You know, 'Fellow Americans, concerning the Dragon Flies, you may have heard irresponsible talk that this entirely Caucasian battle force will be committed to the defense of Baraza, if required, because of your Commander in Chief's desire to protect those of his own race. This canard could not be further from the truth. The Secretary of Defense recommended the Dragon Flies because their units are the only ones equipped and trained for the type of defense indicated. Unfortunately, there are no colored soldiers in the Dragon Flies, because none have been given the long training necessary for handling weapons of such complex—' " Abrahams shrugged. "That sort of thing, and that would be enough. It may blunt a good deal of criticism from around the country, and it'll certainly show Fortney you're not going to take any of his treachery lying down."

Dilman hit his fist on the table. "Sold. We'll write it in." He stared at Abrahams. "Do you think all of this will become an issue in the trial, Nat?"

Abrahams emptied his pipe. "Mr. President, everything you say or do is an issue in the trial. But you wouldn't be making this speech at all if you didn't believe there are some things more important than the trial."

"That's right, Nat."

"So—"

There was a sharp rapping on the corridor door, and Nat Abrahams stopped and looked over his shoulder as the door came open and a distraught Tim Flannery rushed into the room. His face was as fiery as his hair, but then, as he started toward Dilman, he seemed to realize there were others present.

"Sorry to bust in on you like this," he apologized, "but—" He hesitated, as if wishing to speak to the President, yet unsure if he should do so in front of Abrahams, Jaskawich, and Stover.

"What's wrong, Tim?" Dilman asked. "Is anything the matter?"

"I hate to tell you, Mr. President," said Flannery, "but your boy's out in the press lobby—"

"My boy? You mean Julian—he's here?"

"He just popped in from nowhere, and before I heard about it and could stop him, he had gathered the wire service men around him and begun making a statement. When I got out there, it was too late, dammit. Now he's answering their questions—wouldn't listen to me—so I thought I'd better find you—"

Dilman came to his feet. "What kind of statement? What's Julian saying?"

Flannery hesitated, then blurted, "He just now confessed that he had for a long time been a secret member of the Turnerite Group. He——he said that young Negroes like himself got sick of seeing how their parents had been bought off by white men's lying promises—sick of seeing the way the old folks were still in the anteroom, twiddling their thumbs, waiting for their citizenship papers—and he was one of the ones who had decided to do something about it. So he joined the Turnerites and pledged himself to secrecy."

"He confessed to all of that?" said Dilman quietly.

Flannery nodded. "Right off. Then he told the reporters that if they believed that much, they had to believe more—that he never did a single violent thing or subversive act for the Turnerites—only did clerical work for them—and shortly after the Turnerites were banned, he telephoned Frank Valetti and resigned. Then he said——" Flannery faltered, and glanced uncertainly about the Cabinet Room.

"Go on," Dilman said, "what else did he say?"

"He—he was sorry about only one thing—that he had to lie to you from the start. He told the reporters you never really knew he was a member, and that Zeke Miller's Article of Impeachment concerning him was idiotic—because not only you didn't know, but if you had, you wouldn't have obstructed the Justice Department or made a deal with Hurley, because you disliked the Turnerites and their policies and their methods." Flannery paused, and shrugged helplessly. "That's as much as I heard. I was afraid to stop him, haul him in here. I didn't want to start any commotion. But if you'd like me to go out there now and——"

Flannery halted, suddenly aware that no one in the room, not Dilman or any of the others, was listening to him any longer. Their attention had been diverted to someone behind him. Puzzled, Flannery turned around, and then he, too, saw Julian Dilman standing in the open doorway.

For once, Julian's hair was not sleekly pomaded, and his form-fitting suit was wrinkled. Fidgeting, his tremulous eyeballs rolled, and his gaze went from Abrahams to Dilman to Flannery, and then back to his father.

With an effort, he seemed to gather up his courage and finally entered the room.

"You heard what I did?" Julian said to his father. Julian nodded toward Flannery. "He told you?"

"Yes," Dilman said.

"I—I know it's going to count against you in the—the trial—but I had to do it."

"Why?" Dilman asked.

"Why?" Julian repeated. "Because when they impeached you, I figured you'd quit, and you didn't. You set out to fight in the open the ones I tried to fight in secret. And then, from what I heard on the radio today, I knew you meant it—not being scared to punish Hurley because you believed he should be punished, and then—what I figured out from that 'reliable source' Pentagon story against you—that you were not afraid of the big-brass Charlies in uniform because you believed our best troops, no matter what color, should go to Africa. It—it just made me sick of my lying, when all I had wanted to do was to fight back in the open like you—so I took the plane here and figured the best way to begin was to stand up and tell the truth." He paused. "I—I hope you'll forgive me for what I did in the past, and what I did out there just now."

Dilman considered his son evenly. "I already knew what you did in the past, Julian. I found out this afternoon," he said. "As for what you did out there in the press lobby, that's all right. I guess it had to be done. . . . Now get yourself upstairs and find some nourishment in the pantry. I'll be up in a little while."

Quickly, awkwardly, Julian left the room, and when he was gone, Dilman turned slowly back to Abrahams.

Dilman stared thoughtfully at Abrahams for several seconds, and then he said, "Yes, I know, Nat, this can help lose me the Senate trial. Well, I suppose this was a sort of trial, too, in a way—only this was one I couldn't afford to lose." He tried to smile, but no smile came, and then he said, "That's something. At least, it is to me."

VIII

FOR THE FIRST TIME in the nine days since the impeachment trial in the United States Senate had been under way, the front page headline of the morning edition of the Washington *Citizen-American* made no direct mention of the legal proceedings against the President.

This early morning, the top and banner headline, bolder and inkier than any that had appeared before, read:

SCANDAL! EXCLUSIVE! DILMAN HAS DAUGHTER PASSING AS WHITE!

The second headline, scarcely smaller, as brazen and black, read:

PRESIDENT'S HIDDEN OFFSPRING ASHAMED OF HER RACE—AND PRESIDENT KNEW IT ALL ALONG!

Slowly, Douglass Dilman folded the newspaper until the headlines were no longer visible, and then he folded it again and dropped it into the wastebasket beside the Buchanan desk.

He slumped in his chair for a moment, feeling old and feeble, sickened to the marrow of his bones, but then he forced himself to lift his bowed head and meet Tim Flannery's angry look and Nat Abrahams' worried one.

"Why?" Dilman asked despairingly. "Doesn't that Zeke Miller have enough without this?"

"No," said Tim Flannery. "He wants to be sure you're

752

a dead horse, a real dead horse, before he stops beating you."

"But can't he see, it's not I who am the victim?" Dilman said. "It's poor Mindy, that poor, poor girl. Why go after her? Why ruin her life? It won't get him any more Senate votes. . . . Nat, explain it to me—I mean it—this is not only revolting, it's mad, it's senseless."

Nat Abrahams sighed. "I know, Doug." Restlessly, he came out of his chair, crossed the Oval Office to the French doors, and stared into the bleak gray of the morning. Then he said, "When you're locked in a death fight with a fanatical enemy, Doug, don't expect rational motives for his actions. If there's any rhyme or reason to this—this so-called exposé in the paper—well, trying to fathom a mind like Zeke Miller's—I suppose the sense of it would be this." He came around and spoke directly to Dilman. "Miller doesn't care a hoot about your daughter. She doesn't exist, as far as he's concerned. You are the target, and all he cares about is hitting you, high or low, anywhere. He's prosecuting you before two sets of jurors, so he needs as much heavy buckshot as possible, and if there's no legitimate buckshot, then nails or anything else will do."

"What do you mean, Nat, two sets of jurors?"

"Your first jurors, the real ones, are the great outside public, and the members of the Senate are actually only a vulnerable second jury. If Miller can keep the voters antagonized toward you, he knows their feelings will press down on the Senate, and encourage their continuing antagonism. This Reb Blaser story about Mindy passing, for instance. Try to see its value through Miller's distorted vision. Despite your turning down the Hurley appeal, and his execution the other day, you've captured more and more Negro and liberal white sympathy because of your willingness to fight your tormentors. The big television speech on Baraza and our pledged defense, over a week ago, is a good case in point. The majority of the audience didn't like it, true, because they think you're fomenting a needless war to help some worthless African blacks. But American Negroes and white liberals liked it, for the wrong reasons, and many mod-

erates and independents liked it, for the right reasons.
Miller understood their growing sympathy for you. He
doesn't want those people going over to your side. How
to turn them against you once more?

"Well, however he did it, he found out you had another child, a daughter named Mindy, who is ashamed
of being a Negro and is passing, and he found out that
you knew that she was doing this, yet you had not
stopped her. Okay. So today he shouts it to the world—
he yells out—hey, American Negroes, lookee here, your
Negro President has a daughter who's ashamed of being
the same color as you, and her old man approves. Do
you see, Doug? He's desperately trying to turn the ones
who are for you against you, trying to tell your Negro
following that you hate their skin and your own, trying to
tell everyone—Dilman, he's ashamed of his skin. Then
he's trying to tell the liberals, and the members of the
Senate, Look, look at the kind of man you are judging,
a man capable of perfidy and lies, constantly saying he
had one child when he had two, hiding a grown daughter,
condoning her masquerade. Is this kind of man fit to remain President? He's not only untrustworthy, he's positively un-American.

"That's it, I think, Doug. That's the level of Miller's
mentality, and the thinking of his fellow managers. They
are appealing to the public, trying to get the public so
whipped up against you that if the Senate dared to
acquit you, there'd be marchers from four directions
bearing down on Washington to burn the Capitol. You
saw the caliber of witnesses they threw up against you
all week long. Experts? Authorities? Judicious men to
explain and defend their Articles of Impeachment?
Hell, no. Not one. Instead, plain people, just-folks people, brought here for the holiday, swearing to hearsay
and depending upon faulty memory to insist you were a
drunkard, a lecher, an extremist—anything, as long as
it is foul and inciting—and all declaiming your shortcomings in language the public can understand. No,
Doug, it is not Mindy, it is you—they're after you, by
means foul or fair. It's bad luck your girl has been

caught in the middle. This news story is lousy. The whole thing is rotten lousy."

Dilman pushed himself up from the desk and walked heavily toward Abrahams, joining him at the French doors. For a long and silent interval he looked out upon the barren Rose Garden. Then, as if addressing himself rather than Abrahams and Flannery, he said, "I'm so sorry for Mindy, so sorry. She was like her mother. She wanted so badly to be white, and average, and part of life. This thing, I don't know what this'll do to her, publishing both her names. I'd give anything to be with her now, just to comfort her and try to talk to her, try to explain and soothe her. But I don't even know where she is. Edna says the phone number listed under Linda Dawson no longer is connected. It was changed to an unlisted number a couple of weeks ago. Now Mindy has seen the papers, she knows the truth is out, the fact of her being Negro, and now all her white friends know, and her employer knows, and her life—what'll it be? And I can't even get to speak to her."

He looked at Abrahams. "Nat, it's my fault for not resigning when I could, for being a selfish and prideful mule and bucking the men with the whips, and all I'll have succeeded in doing is to harm everyone—Wanda, Julian, the Spingers, and now the worst of it, my little girl Mindy. I knew I was up against mudslingers, but I thought I'd be taking most of the mud. I didn't know it would spatter so wide, so wide and far and destructively. Well, I guess there is no turning back now."

Absently clasping and unclasping his hands, he wandered back to the middle of the office floor. Aware of Tim Flannery again, he said, "What can I do for my girl? I don't know."

Flannery said, "Fight the mudslingers in the press, the way you're fighting them in the Senate, Mr. President. Is there any statement we can release to offset this—I don't mean just for your sake—for hers, too, to ease it for her?"

"No. What could I say that would do anything but make it worse? Thanks, Tim. You'd better get back to your work." Then, as Flannery shrugged and prepared

to leave the office, Dilman said to no one in particular,
"If people only understood what makes a colored person
pass for white." Suddenly, he exclaimed with wonder.
"Wait now—why not tell them? Why not tell them what
it is like?"

He saw Flannery had hesitated at the door. "Tim, if
Mindy can't speak for herself, maybe her father should
speak for her. I think I *will* make a statement."

As Flannery returned, Dilman looked at Abrahams.
"Any comment before I do, Nat?"

Abrahams said, "Don't worry about my problems.
This is something altogether your own. This is personal.
Act the way I know you want to act—like a father, and
not like the President."

"Yes," said Dilman.

"Do you want to dictate this statement now?" asked
Flannery.

"Dictate it? No. I just want to go out in the press
lobby—yes, that's what I'll do—and speak my mind.
You go ahead, Tim. Alert the correspondents that I
want to make a few brief remarks, and that's all."

Flannery hastened out. Dilman remained lost in
thought for long seconds, then he went to the wastebasket, retrieved the *Citizen-American,* unfolded it,
studied the headlines, and scanned the story.

"Poor child," he said, and then he left, with Abrahams
following him.

After Dilman went through Edna Foster's empty office
into the corridor, where two Secret Service men fell into
step behind him, and turned toward the Reading Room,
he was conscious of his press secretary's staff watching
him curiously from their desks as he passed them.

Nearing the open door leading to the press lobby, now
blocked by Tim Flannery, with Edna Foster and her
shorthand pad and pencil behind him, Dilman could see
Flannery holding up his arms to quiet the clamoring
reporters. Dilman hung back, listening, until Flannery
finished his speech.

"—I repeat, gentlemen, those are the rules. He's decided to make an impromptu statement about the unfortunate story that appeared exclusively in Zeke Miller's

Washington *Citizen-American* this morning. When he has finished his remarks, no questions about the matter will be entertained. None, boys."

"Hey, Tim," someone shouted, "after he does that, would he mind a couple of questions about the impeachment trial? I'd like to ask him about the House witnesses yesterday from the Vaduz Exporters, who insisted—"

"Absolutely no," Flannery replied. "Nothing's changed about that. No comment on the impeachment trial, or the Dragon Flies and Baraza, or anything else this morning. And no questions about his daughter. If you refuse to abide by our stipulations, I'm afraid—"

Several voices yelled out, "Okay, Tim! . . . Bring him out! . . . Let's go! Where's the President?"

Tim Flannery turned and nodded to Dilman, who came forward, easing his way between his press secretary and personal secretary, until he stood within the thickly massed assemblage of eager and impatient correspondents. For a moment Dilman scanned their familiar faces, then dropped his gaze to the pencils and notebooks or pieces of paper their hands held ready. They were waiting, and behind him, behind the Secret Service agents, Flannery, Miss Foster, Nat Abrahams, and many of the White House staff were waiting.

Dilman's lips were dry. His Adam's apple had grown huge in his throat. His lungs felt hot. For a hanging second he wondered if this was wrong, feeding fuel to the scurrilous Blaser story, and then his eyes picked out Blaser's toad face, puffed and important, toward the rear. At once, he knew that he must speak what was in his heart, because somewhere in New York his poor girl child might be waiting also, and listening.

Dilman opened the newspaper in his hand, studied it, then held it aloft.

"You all read this—this news, I'm sure," he said. He cast the newspaper aside, heard it flutter to the floor. "It is quite true, every word of it. Despite its tone or interpretation, these are the facts. The facts are correct. I have a twenty-year-old son named Julian, who has returned to his studies at Trafford University. I also have a daughter, yes, she is older than my son, she is twenty-four, and her legal name is Mindy Dilman. I have not seen her, not set eyes upon her, since shortly before my wife's death, when my daughter was eighteen or thereabouts. With my wife's encouragement, Mindy left the Midwest for the East, to seek a career. Like my wife, more than my wife, Mindy was fair-skinned, and had delicate features. On my wife's side, for perhaps three or four generations back, and to a lesser extent on my own side, there were Caucasians and Indians, white and brown forebears."

Dilman hesitated. "I might add, this is not unusual. I am well acquainted, as are most literate Negroes, with the history of our common ancestry. The information about ourselves comes to us largely from white sociologists and anthropologists. According to these authorities, there has always been miscegenation—racial mixing with consequent propagation—in the United States. This began in colonial times, although the most intensive interracial contact among Caucasians, Negroes, and Indians, as Dr. Gunnar Myrdal has pointed out, occurred during our period of slavery and immediately thereafter. It was a time when Negro women were sexually exploited by white men. As a result, according to Dr. Myrdal and numerous other sociologists, as a result of this mixing between whites and colored peoples, with or without the benefit of marriage, there are today estimated to be 70 per cent to 80 per cent of American Negroes who have some degree of so-called white blood or, more accurately, white genes. Because of this, my wife and I, like eight out of every ten Negro Americans, have some white heredity, no matter how minute. I might add that conversely, because of this mixing, at least 20 per cent and perhaps as high as 40 per cent of the whites in the United States have some degree of so-called Negro blood in their veins, whether they know it or not. In any case, because of these heredity facts, many Negro families will, every generation or so, produce offspring who more closely resemble their one or two Caucasian ancestors."

Dilman studied the tops of the reporters' heads encircling him, and then he went on.

"In our family of four, there were two of us who were black-skinned like myself and two who, because of the old admixture, were fair-skinned. My wife Aldora was fair-skinned, what is called, in a certain section of the country, 'pumpkin yellow.' I, her husband, as you can see, am unmistakably black. My son is also unmistakably black. But my daughter Mindy, from birth to maturity, was as fair as her mother. Her complexion was, and no doubt is today, more light-colored than many Mediterranean whites.

"Now, it is a regrettable fact, or so I believe, that among American Negroes themselves, most of them, the lighter-skinned ones, often feel superior, and are envied or looked up to by their brethren. Why is this? I think the reasons are obvious. Just as whites consider white skin more esthetically satisfying than dark skin—despite the widely prevalent effort, constantly, to become sunburned or tanned by the sun, since this is a status symbol equated with leisure time and therefore wealth—despite this, whites find whiteness more attractive than blackness, just as in India and Brazil, the natives consider the lighter ones of their communities more attractive—so this same color scale has invaded and infected the American Negro community. But ahead of pure esthetics, there is a more compelling reason why American Negroes are frequently pleased to have, and are envied for having, tan or pink or almost white or totally white skins. It is that these lighter Negroes get closer to the majority of the white population, are more acceptable to the dominant white community, more apt, by mistake or their own intent, to escape discrimination and persecution. And often these almost white Negroes, seeing how much easier and better life is for them when they are taken for white instead of Negro, become tempted to cross the color line, to live permanently in the white world as whites, to enjoy being a part of the aristocratic majority with all its advantages and privileges.

"Yes, every Negro like myself, especially one who has had a nearly white wife and an almost white daughter, knows a good deal about this subject. I can tell

you, with considerable authority to support the statement, that at least three thousand American Negroes
with light-colored skin, at least three thousand a year,
maybe as many as six thousand a year, take advantage
of their appearance, slip away from their Negro homes,
communities, family, friends, and cross over and join
the white race. I can tell you, also on excellent authority, that of the one million mixed or interracial mar-
riages in the United States at the present time, and there
are that many, at least nine hundred thousand are mar-
riages in which the white partner does not know his or
her mate is Negro, or of some other color, because that
mate is passing as white and has got away with it.

"For the most part, Negro parents do not like it when
their fairer-colored children quit their race and surrep-
titiously join the white classification, the white world,
the white census, pretending to be white when they are
not. Negro parents will condone the action of one of
their children if he passes as white in order to acquire
a better education or get a better job that might not
otherwise be available to him. This is condoned on the
condition that the one passing remembers he or she is
Negro, and returns from the school or business world
to resume family and social life among his or her Negro
brethren. What Negroes resent is permanent passing by
one of their number who resigns entirely from his race,
attempts to blot out his blackness, pretends to be white
in school, in work, and in his social life. Yet, as much
as Negroes resent permanent passing, only rarely do
they expose or give away to whites the true origin of
their defectors. They will guard a passer's secret because, as black Americans, suffering as a minority group,
they can understand how driven one of their kind must
be to risk this form of escape into equality."

Dilman halted. The circle of heads came up. He inspected the faces, nodded, then resumed speaking, and
the heads went down to the note-taking.

"Now you have the background explaining my daughter's defection. She was reared as a Negro, and around
her she could see the terrible injustices and inequities
that were to be her lot. When she realized that she alone,

of the four of us, need not endure the suffering, like a curse on her for the rest of her years, she fled it, she escaped it, she ran over the line and far away, and lost herself in the white world of New York City, where there was no reason for anyone to suspect that she was not white. I will not stand here and say I approved of Mindy Dilman's action. I will simply say I did not try to stop or dissuade her then, and I would not now, because I understand her and the three to six thousand other Negro girls and boys who annually cross over.

"I understand Mindy and all like her who pass as white, because I can understand, as many of you around me cannot, what it is to rid yourself of second-class citizenship, of poverty, of receiving contempt, of inferior social status, and to take on in their place, even if the pleasure is acquired through a deception, the advantages and joys of equality under the law, a respectable job, the feeling of belonging, new friendships based on one's personality rather than color. It grieves me that this has to be so, that this is the condition in our country, but I understand it.

"And I understand more. I understand the deep rage within Negroes, the deep and helpless rage that defies all reason and sense, against not only their present lives but against lives in their past, rage at the accidents of heredity and of environment that made them as they are, and put them in the wrong place at the wrong time. Do you have the slightest idea of what truly makes one human being black and another white? When you consider how violently a person's life is affected from birth to death if he is born black rather than white, it is almost impossible to believe that such a slight change within the human body creates this vast and traumatic difference.

"According to the foremost geneticists, blacks and whites possess within them the same pigments, the same skin-coloring elements, exactly the same red blood. Then what creates the difference in their skin shading which so affects their lives? The decisive factor is a particle that cannot even be seen by the naked eye, and it is called a gene. Yes, a gene. What is a gene? Bear with me briefly, gentlemen.

"To create a human life, a Mindy, requires two factors —a male sperm so minute that a hundred million sperms can be counted in a single drop of seminal fluid, and a female egg so tiny that it is smaller than a typewritten period on a printed page. Both this liquid drop and this period-sized egg contain something even smaller called chromosomes, and they in turn contain something yet smaller called genes, and these invisible genes are what give each newborn child his hereditary characteristics and control his skin color. If a newborn child has a dominant gene that will cause the production of excessive melanin, a dark pigment, he will be black on the outside. If he possesses a different kind of microscopic gene, he will be brown or yellow on the outside. And if he has an unseeable gene that produces hardly any melanin, he will be some shade of white. And so, what a Negro is comes down to no more than a slight shake and blend of genes, like tiny dice rolling out of the past, and when the shake is done, one goes before the world as a black-skinned individual or a white-skinned one, or somewhere in between, and that's it for life. And because of this luck of genes, a man or woman comes forth a Negro, sometimes a fair-skinned Negro, but a Negro nevertheless, and because of this luck of genes, a human being is labeled for the rest of his days, in certain places, as an inferior. No wonder the Negro rages, both against this accident in his past, and against the conditions in the present that insensibly penalize him for his ancestry. No wonder one like Mindy, light-skinned through a haphazard blend of white and black genes, makes use of this avenue of escape.

"My daughter Mindy committed no crime, no matter how vicious the tone of the condemnation in Representative Zeke Miller's newspaper. She committed a deception, yes—but that is a minor human frailty, not an exclusively Negroid characteristic. Who among us, at one time or another, has not engaged in deception? Husbands lie to their wives, and wives to their husbands, and children to their parents, in order to make life easier. I do not condone this, either. I say simply, it is there, it is life. Businessmen exaggerate and boast untruths, to improve their business. Clerks and white-collar workers lie about their accomplishments and skills, and products, to sell themselves or their goods, in order to succeed, to get ahead, to improve their lot. Some Jews pretend not to be Jews, in an effort to obtain a desired position, a country club membership, a house they long for in an anti-Semitic neighborhood, in order to escape the onus of being different. Some Catholics pretend not to be Catholics, because of feelings against the Holy See, to get along, just to get along. I deplore the deceptions in our culture, but more, I deplore the conditions that seem to make them necessary.

"Mindy's deception? Whom would it have harmed but herself? Would her secret blackness, hidden by white skin, if never revealed, have given a fatal disease to her men friends and women friends? Would it have infected them with bad or despicable notions or ideas? Would it have made her work less adequate or contaminated her living quarters? No, it would have done no harm to anyone—until now—except to Mindy herself. Can you picture my girl's life these years since she ran off at eighteen? I often have. For all its advantages, her life, I imagine, has not been easy or uncomplicated. See her, as I have, escaping from a segregated black neighborhood of the Midwest into a white private school and then into a wide-open white world in New York. To do this, Mindy has deprived herself of mother, father, brother, and every other relative. She has disowned every childhood and school friend she had, except a handful of friends made while passing in a white school. She has sprung up, literally, from the earth afresh, with no past, no background. How impossible this seems in our world of curiosity and rapid communications today. Mindy, I suspect, had to find new friends, white friends, in her apartment building, in her white church, in her white social clubs, in her chance encounters, and in her job. What does one say to new friends, male or female, or on the employer's application form and to his questions? Mindy must invent a white family, somewhere remote, that is actually nonexistent. She must create a cardboard white community, somewhere remote, where she grew up, and early schools that for some convincing reason cannot be contacted. And as she draws a circle of friends about her, she must fabricate a living past—find photographs of a white mother and father to put in frames, buy gifts for herself and send them to herself from her nonexistent white parents so that she is not alone giftless on Christmas, or unremembered on birthdays. She must compose and send herself occasional letters from distant places and pretend they are from white relatives or friends.

"But not enough. Once this fiction is completed, accepted, she cannot let down her guard. Will she, someday, while intoxicated or under anesthetic or even through some casual verbal slip, disclose that she is really colored? Will some astute newcomer to her circle begin to wonder about an expression she has used, an old habit of speech like 'G'wan, man' or 'Look heah' and begin to scrutinize the texture of her hair, breadth of her nose, thickness of her lips, moons of her fingernails? Will she, someday, while with her white friends, run into that one-in-a-million visitor from the Midwest, from her old place of life, who is Negro, and recognizes her, and comes up to her, a pretended white girl, and inadvertently exposes her? Will she, falling desperately in love as an equal with a young white man, unable to confess the truth and lose him, keep her secret, marry him, and awaken from the hospital table to find with horror that she has delivered an infant with features and hair more Negroid than white?

"I have not seen Mindy Dilman in all these years, not because I have not deeply wished it, for I love her, but because she chose it to be this way, so this is the way it had to be.

"Of course Mindy has been passing for white! Of course I have known it! I would not interfere, because I would not strip from her the advantages she deserves and would otherwise be denied. But I repeat, what is Mindy's crime? Is it her fault that she was born to Negroes, and in a country where such birth is a sin? If there is crime in this, the crime is not Mindy's, but yours and mine, that of the American government and the American people, who would not let her grow and develop in dignity and grace.

"Now, this morning, for the sake of boosting a newspaper's circulation, for the cause of a politician's prejudice and quarrel, Mindy's secret is out. Now, for motives of sensation and hate, the camouflage of this harmless young girl has been stripped off, so that she is naked and alone and black, though no whit blacker or less worthy than yesterday or the day before. And for this my heart is heavy. I sorrow for my daughter, and over what she will endure, and what must become of her—but more, far more, gentlemen, I grieve for the nature of those in this country, and for the situation in this country, that drove Mindy to pass—and I grieve that such minds exist, in government, in the press, who feel that her pitiful masquerade was so monstrous a vice and transgression that they publicly had to brand her not with a searing scarlet letter but a burning black one, to destroy her, to hope to damage me as her father and as the nation's President, in order to preserve the racial purity of the republic in which we live.

"Thank you for your attention, gentlemen. Thank you, and good morning."

The Senate, sitting as a tribunal for the impeachment trial of President Dilman, had been convened promptly at one o'clock in the afternoon.

This was the tenth day of the trial, the first day having been given over to the opening speeches of the opposing attorneys, and the eight days since having been given over to the testimony of the witnesses for the House and the cross-examinations conducted for the defense by Abrahams, Tuttle, and Priest, with Hart confining himself to the paper work. Actually, excluding the Sunday during which the Senate had been adjourned, there had been only seven days of witnesses.

This afternoon's session had begun with the House managers summoning Julian Dilman to the witness chair, set at eye level with Chief Justice Johnstone's raised dais, to testify. Representative Zeke Miller's interrogation of the President's son had started mildly enough, with questions about the young man's early years, elic-

iting information that traced his growth to the time of
his entrance into Trafford University. Even though the
interrogation had not been fearsome, Julian had appeared frightened, constantly twitching and twisting, his
replies sometimes barely audible, sometimes too loud.

When, after twenty minutes of this, a senator had risen
on a point of law and Chief Justice Johnstone had called
a fifteen-minute recess to consult his associates and to
review published precedent, the stately rectangular
Chamber on the second floor of the Capitol had become
an informal clubhouse once more.

Leaving his associates at their table on the Senate
floor, their heads huddled together over some legal strategy, Nat Abrahams had quit the Chamber to smoke his
pipe and to evaluate the position of the defense. He had
gone through the Senators' Private Lobby, meaning to
turn off to his own assigned office, but then he had wandered into the Marble Room, so called for its circular
Italian columns, had wended his way past a group of
legislators chatting at the round reading table beneath
the ornate crystal chandelier, and had then come to a
stop next to one of the towering white columns. Still lost
in thought, desiring to remain inconspicuous and undis-
turbed in this lair of the enemy (although every room,
apparently, belonged to the enemy), Abrahams had
gone behind the pillar, leaned back against it, and lighted
his pipe.

Now, isolated and smoking, he could perceive the
House managers' strategy, all of it dominated by a public relations concept and intended to overwhelm the general public (and through them, the Senate jurors) in one
emotional spate of accusation. After Miller's frenetic
opening address, the opposition had built the case for
their Articles of Impeachment slowly and not too powerfully. Except for their presentation of several witnesses
from Vaduz Exporters, to bolster their Article I charges
against the President's treasonable relationship with
Wanda Gibson, except for their questioning of the Reverend Spinger and then his wife to further solidify Article I and give some credence to the extramarital liaison
and preferential treatment to Crispus specifications in

Article III, except for their parade of Washington experts to prove the New Succession Act was constitutional and the law of the land, and the questioning of Governor Talley to prove it had been violated by the President, which had invited Article IV, the House managers had presented only a series of shabby and inconsequential witnesses.

Analyzing it now, weighing the effect of the defense's own cross-examinations, Abrahams was able to see better what progress the opposition had made. Miller had done a fairly good job, not legally but emotionally, in shoring up Article I, charging the transfer of secrets through Wanda Gibson. Until three-quarters of an hour ago, he had offered no witnesses on Article II, the Julian-Turnerite charge, except one affidavit, from the Attorney General, relating the President's delaying tactics on the banning of the extremist society. As yet, Miller had made little progress on the specifications of Article III. He had made no mention of Sally Watson, and the witnesses he offered to prove the liaison with Miss Gibson, favoritism toward Spinger, political partisanship, and intoxication had been so vague and irrelevant, and had been so rattled under the relentless cross-examinations of Abrahams and his colleagues, that Article III had become more an embarrassment than an asset.

Miller's case for Article IV, that the President had broken a law by firing Eaton in defiance of Congress, had been more impressive for the quantity of his witnesses than for their quality. Under Abrahams' ceaseless bombardment, many of the witnesses had lost their assurance and authority. However, the question of whether the President had removed Eaton because he believed his Secretary of State was usurping his Presidential powers, or because he feared his popularity, was still not settled. And the question of whether the President had removed Eaton without consulting the Senate because he believed the New Succession Act to be unconstitutional and therefore believed that there was no need to consult anyone, or whether he had merely determined to defy and humiliate the legislative branch, and be headstrong and break a law, was still not decided. To this moment, the battle over Article IV was probably a draw.

Today, Abrahams guessed, Zeke Miller would be unloading his big artillery in one concerted and smashing effort to scatter the defense and send it into hopeless retreat. Today, no doubt, Miller would bring forth those who were still missing: Wanda Gibson to build up Article I, Sally Watson to save Article III, Secretary of State Arthur Eaton to clinch Article IV, just as he now had on the stand Julian Dilman to prove Article II. Miller would try to bring his case, through the evidence of these witnesses, to a peak in one shattering afternoon, rocking the public and the Senate with the President's criminality, so that nothing Abrahams or the defense managers could offer in rebuttal, after that, would be able to halt, or even slow down, the assault.

Why, Abrahams asked himself, had the House managers determined to crowd the best of their case into a single afternoon? Because, he decided, they felt the timing was right, the climate never better.

The steady if gradual shift of sympathy and support to President Dilman, among the public, had faltered in the last nine days. Miller's weather eye was keen. Eight days ago the President had admitted to the nation that he might, if necessary, sacrifice the lives of an all-white American fighting force in the defense of a little-known African nation. The Negroes and liberals approved, but the larger part of the nation boiled with resentment. Then Julian had confessed to his Turnerite affiliation, and while the majority of twenty-three million American Negroes may have been sympathetic once more, and some whites impressed, the greater part of 230 million Americans were increasingly suspicious of the President's past activities. Now, this morning, Zeke Miller's revelation about the President's daughter passing for white, with the President's knowledge and lack of disapproval, would once more turn the Negro population against him and infuriate most of the white population. And, Abrahams saw, even Doug Dilman's profoundly moving explanation of his daughter's passing, and of his own role in it, would fail to counteract the damaging publicity. For the rest of the press, who had missed Miller's sensational scoop, were trying to make up lost ground by excerpting portions of the President's remarks, lifting them out of context, angling and distorting them to make headlines anew and sell copies of their newspapers.

Abrahams rubbed his shoulders against the pillar, put a flame to his pipe again, and considered the situation. Yes, for Zeke Miller, the national climate was right to bring out, from the principal witnesses, the last of the evidence against Dilman. There was momentum in the sentiment against the President, and whatever headlines Miller could create and throw forth today would ride with the momentum, until the charges would be too many and too powerful for it to be stopped.

Abrahams did not like the defense's position. If the prosecution concluded its testimony today, it would be the defense's turn, either late today or tomorrow, to summon up its own rebuttal witnesses. These were good witnesses, but not colorful, not space grabbers, not names, and they would receive scant attention. Abrahams needed what Miller possessed—a cast of stars—and he had none, not one.

Only a single faint hope remained, Abrahams decided, and that was to make Miller's stars his own stars. He must build up Julian and Wanda, even though subpoenaed by Miller, as defense witnesses. He must tear down Eaton and Sally Watson, so that resultant headlines would favor the President over his prosecutors. It would not be an easy game to play, if it could be played at all, but, he thought mournfully, it was the only game in town.

He heard an agitated voice call out, "Congressman— Congressman Miller—"

Looking off, he was surprised to see George Murdock, fugitive from the press gallery and Blaser's collaborator, hastening in his general direction. Then Murdock hurried past him, and abruptly halted. Abrahams poked his head around the pillar, and he recognized Zeke Miller, profile to him, considering the reporter with annoyance.

"What are you doing here?" Miller demanded. "You're supposed to be up there doing what you're paid to do."

"Congressman, I've got to speak to you," Murdock insisted, clawing his acned, pasty face. "That story you and Reb broke this morning—about Mindy passing—"

"Don't bother me now. I have no time. I've got a trial to conduct."

"Listen—wait—I signed a paper for that girl, promising if she gave me the letter Julian wrote her, I'd never in my life whisper a word of who she is or what she is. I told it to you in confidence—remember? It was part of our deal—you could use everything else I got you, as long as you never used that. You promised, like I promised. You pledged your word."

Miller's lipless mouth was drawn back so that his yellowed teeth were exposed. "Boy, I don't remember making no foolish promise like that there one, you understand? When Zeke Miller makes a promise, he keeps it. You're not questioning my integrity, you're not doing that, are you? That wouldn't be sensible—would it?— for a reporter in an editorial room to doubt the word of the proprietor, would it now? I've seen my daddy, in his day, have his cotton pickers thrown off his land for less than that."

Murdock shriveled. "I—I'm only trying to say—"

"Boy, what burr you got up your behind? You mean an important proud writing person like you is worrying about some cheating cullud girl, some Nigra tar baby who's painted herself white because she wants to insinuate her class into our class? What's happening to you, boy? Keep that up and I got a good mind to make you a foreign correspondent and send you off to cover Harlem permanently. Know what I mean? You wouldn't like that, would you, feller? Come now, would you?"

"No—no—I wouldn't."

"Then get yourself back up to that gallery and write like you're told, and don't bother Zeke Miller again with any of that Northern weeping-willow crap." Miller waved off to someone. "Hiya, Senator Watson. Time to get back to the combat field, I guess."

Abrahams watched Miller leave, in step with Senator Hoyt Watson. Quickly, he glanced at Murdock. The reporter's face was sallow gray, like a scrap of ancient papyrus. Some kind of involuntary utterance came from him, more moan than sigh, and he turned, head down, and went slowly back to the press gallery, as Abrahams, aching for his humiliation, averted his eyes.

Then, seeing that the Marble Room was quickly emptying, Abrahams tapped out the ashes from his bowl, pocketed the warm pipe, and fell in line behind those returning to the Senate Chamber.

When he took his place at the President's managers' table, he could see the Chief Justice already on the bench above, Julian Dilman in the witness chair timidly prepared for anything, and the last of the absent senators squeezing back in behind their desks.

Chief Justice Johnstone's gavel came down. After calling the court to order, announcing his decision on the point of law which conceded the correctness of the senatorial challenge and therefore required no vote by the body of legislators present, the magistrate ordered, "Senators will please give their undivided attention. The counsel for the House of Representatives will proceed with the examination of the witness."

Zeke Miller bounced up from his table, came to the front of the podium, and planted himself before Julian Dilman.

"Well, now, Mr. Julian Dilman, we have arrived at the core of the charges in Article II of this impeachment. You have confessed, in a public statement, that you were an early and secret underground member of the subversive Turnerite Group. There is no arguing about that now, is there? We can accept your public confession of membership in full, can't we? Or do you wish to retract it?"

"I was a member, yes," said Julian, "exactly the way I announced it last week."

"I am pleased Mr. Witness confesses to the confession." Miller waited for the laughter from the gallery to subside, and then he asked, "Before the day of your public confession, did the President, your father, know you were a member of the subversive Turnerite Group?"

"No, sir."

"You say, 'No, sir'? Let me explore this further. Did the President, your father, ever make mention of the Turnerites to you, in speech or writing?"

"Well, yes, but——"

"Oh, he *did* discuss the subversive Turnerite Group with you? Did he inquire if you were a member?"

"Yes, he did, but——"

"Why would he inquire if you were a member? Was it just paternal curiosity or did he have suspicions of you?"

"He'd heard I was a member. Someone told him."

"Ah, 'someone' told him," said Miller. "In other words, he was in contact with someone who definitely knew? He was in touch with other secret Turnerites?"

"No, not exactly——"

"Never mind. The point is that the President had been informed that you, his son, were a Turnerite, and he went to you, and desired for you to confirm the news of your membership?"

"He didn't know I was one of them, but he had heard a rumor, yes. He was upset. He tried to pin me down. I denied everything. I lied to him, because—because I was afraid."

"Afraid of whom, Mr. Witness? Afraid of your real boss, the late murderer, Jefferson Hurley—or afraid of your father's wrath?"

"Both."

"So you lied to your father. Are you in the habit of lying often, Mr. Dilman?"

"No. But my situation made it necessary that one time."

"If you could lie to your parent, if you could lie to the President of the United States, might you not be capable of lying to this high tribunal?"

Abrahams leaped to his feet. "Objection, Mr. Chief Justice! Mr. Manager Miller is baiting and leading the witness."

Miller looked up at Chief Justice Johnstone, all bland

innocence. "Mr. Justice, I am merely attempting to establish the devious character of—"

The Chief Justice's gavel rapped. "Objection sustained. The witness is under solemn oath, Mr. Manager Miller. Avoid further speculation on his veracity."

Miller shrugged good-naturedly and considered his witness once more. "Let's see, Mr. Julian Dilman, what have we established up to now? That you were covertly a blood member of a subversive organization. That your father heard about it. That your father confronted you with the fact, and you denied it, you lied to him. Now, from his subsequent actions, we must wonder if your father, the President of the United States, believed your denial—or if he knew more about your affiliation than he had told you. Let us see, let us see. The Turnerites, in their efforts to overthrow the established government of the United States, perpetrated a planned kidnaping of a municipal official. Despite this, as the Attorney General has testified in writing, the President refused to outlaw the society which had been responsible for this outrage. Instead, he appointed a friend and tenant of his, a Nigra lobbyist, to talk and deal privately with the Turnerites. Then, when your organization committed foul murder, the President still refused to condemn your friends until he was forced to bend to the pressure of the Justice Department and outlaw your organization. Would that not clearly indicate that Hurley had threatened to expose you, unless your father, the President, went soft on the Turnerites? Would that not clearly indicate your father, the President, *knew* his son was a member of a lawless society, and, to protect his son, treated with the Turnerites, went easy on them, until a life was lost? Would that not indicate that your father, the President, putting his own interests, the interests of his family, before the interests of his high office, was guilty of high crime and—"

"That's not true!" Julian protested. "He didn't believe I was involved, and he made no deals with them."

"How do you know, Mr. Julian Dilman? You weren't there when the President's emissary was treating with the Turnerites."

"Neither were you!"

Miller's face darkened. "You are being insolent, young man. Who taught you your manners? The Commie terrorists and Nigra extremists in your crowd? Or the President himself?"

"Objection!" Abrahams called out.

Miller held a hand up to the bench. "Never mind, Mr. Chief Justice. I retract. I fear the younger generation can often be provoking. . . . Very well, Mr. Julian Dilman, your father had heard you were a bona fide member of this violent, now outlawed, society. Let's find out what nefarious activities you performed while serving—"

Half listening to Miller's continuing examination, Nat Abrahams jotted notes on the pad before him. Miller, he realized, was making his best of a bad thing. Miller had failed to prove that the President knew of his son's membership and had therefore promised the Turnerites he would go easy on them if they kept Julian's membership quiet. Yet, proof or no proof, Miller was succeeding, by using the tactic of repetition, in lending some credulity to the charges in Article II. Had not the President "heard" his son was a member and accused him of it? Therefore, he might possibly have "known" for certain. Had not the President appointed a "friend," instead of a government official, to arrange a compromise with Hurley through Valetti? Therefore, he may possibly have been party to an underhand "deal."

After five minutes more, Miller concluded his examination, and Nat Abrahams stood before the shaken young Negro boy.

In as kind a tone as possible, Abrahams said to Julian, "Since the House managers have no witnesses, no firsthand evidence whatsoever, that the President believed you were a Turnerite, that the President made a deal with the Turnerites to protect you, the charge embodied in Article II stands or falls completely on your word. Julian Dilman, you have taken solemn oath before the Senate body, at the risk of being charged with perjury, that you will here tell the truth, the whole truth, and nothing but the truth, so help you God. You are entirely cognizant of that?"

"Yes, sir."

"Did the President, in a private room at Trafford University, ask you if you were a member of the Turnerite Group?"

"He did."

"And you told him you were not a member?"

"I told him I was not a member."

"Did he believe you?"

"Yes, sir."

"Did he ever bring up the subject again?"

"He did not, sir. He believed me."

"In short, Julian Dilman, as far as you know, the President was satisfied from that day on that you were not a member of the Turnerites?"

"Yes, sir."

"Therefore, he would have no reason to compromise himself with the Turnerites in order to protect you?"

"He would have no reason whatsoever, sir."

"You have told the learned manager of the House that the President did, on several occasions, discuss the Turnerite movement with you, other than discussing your own possible involvement. Is this so?"

"Oh, yes. We talked about them. I mean, he didn't discuss the Turnerites with me. I discussed them with him. I always brought them up."

"Why did you bring them up?"

"I felt worried about secretly belonging, without his knowledge, and wanted to convince him that the ideals of the Group were good ones. Then, at the time, I believed in the society, and he did not, and we used to argue about it."

"What were the President's feelings about the Turnerites?"

"He thought they were all wrong. He detested them. He hated every extremist and pro-violence organization, black or white, left or right. So we would argue. But now I can see my father was correct."

"Julian Dilman, one thing puzzles me. Allow me to pose the puzzle in the form of several questions. You were a member, yet you never told your father about it. Why did you not tell him? Why did you lie about this one thing? You informed Mr. Manager Miller you were afraid of revealing the truth to the President. What were you afraid of?"

"Well——"

"Were you afraid of breaking your pledge of secrecy to Hurley?"

"Only a little. That was the least part of it."

"What was the major part of it, then? Were you afraid of your father's disapproval?"

"I——I knew how much he was against those extremists. I knew how much he hoped for me and expected of me. I knew that if I told him, he——he would be horrified, and disappointed by the way I'd turned out, and think less of me. I knew he loved me and——I didn't want to lose his love."

"I see."

It was a fine moment to dismiss the witness, but Abrahams knew that one more question needed to be asked. "Is that why you finally confessed your secret? It was your secret, and you might have kept it forever. Yet, last week, you made it known to the press and the world. What compelled you to do so? Why did you—— when it was no longer necessary——jeopardize your character, make your veracity questionable, and give ammunition to the smallest and weakest part of the House managers' indictment?"

"Why?" Julian paused. "Because——I guess because I was so proud of my father's integrity——and——and ashamed of my own lack of it——and my own ambition was to grow up to be a man like he was, and is——and I decided the way to start was to be honest like him."

"Thank you, Mr. Witness."

After Julian had left the witness box, Abrahams returned to his table. He could not calculate, from the reaction of his associates or that of the senators, how effective his cross-examination had been. He decided that if it had accomplished nothing else, it had shown the legislators that the President's son was sincere and trustworthy, and that although Julian had lied once, it was not likely that he was lying under oath today. If this image had been created, Abrahams decided, it was something, little enough, but something, a small victory. And perhaps the scale of justice (or injustice) so heavily weighted against his client had been lightened, and was better balanced, if only a trifle.

Suddenly Abrahams realized that Miss Wanda Gibson had been summoned, and was already standing before the Secretary of the Senate, right hand raised.

The Secretary of the Senate droned forth, "You, Wanda Gibson, do affirm that the evidence you shall give in the case now depending between the United States and Douglass Dilman, President of the United States, shall be the truth, the whole truth, and nothing but the truth: so help you God."

"I do, so help me God."

"The witness will kindly be seated."

It pleased Abrahams to see her there, so composed, so attractive in her blue jersey dress and matching jacket. Wanda's luminous eyes, shining out of her solemn tan face, fleetingly caught Abrahams' gaze, and they flickered as if to reassure him, and he was grateful for her piquant maturity. He hoped that Doug Dilman was watching on television. Perhaps he would be less worried about the ordeal to which he had subjected her.

But then, as Zeke Miller materialized, Abrahams' confidence in her buckled slightly. She would have to be as resilient on the inside as she appeared to be poised on the outside, if she were to survive without serious hurt.

"Miss Wanda Gibson, I have it," said Miller, slurring the syllables of her name. "According to Articles I and III of the impeachment, according to the testimony already received, you are the great and good friend of the President of the United States. How long have you known him?"

"Five years."

"How long have you lived under his roof?"

"I have rented a room from the Reverend Paul Spinger and Mrs. Spinger, the upstairs tenants, for six years. The President purchased the building, occupied the lower half of the duplex, and became the Spingers' landlord, and, in turn, mine, five years ago."

"Do you pay rent for your room?"

"Of course I pay rent for my room."

"Have you always paid rent? Did you pay rent when the President lived in the same building with you?"

"If you are trying to say, Mr. Congressman, that I accepted special favors from my landlord in return for special favors—the answer is no, I did not." There was a wide tittering across the gallery, and Wanda looked up with surprise, and then down at Miller. She said, "I have never missed payment of a single month's rent."

Miller sniffed. "Miss Gibson, were you ever, in those five years, alone with the President, either in his down-stairs flat or your own?"

"Never in his flat. Occasionally in the Spingers' living room. Most often, we were alone on the outside, when we went to dinner or the theater, that is, when the President was a senator."

"Miss Gibson, in this dwelling on Van Buren Street where you live, which the President owns, is there any means of private access one could use to go from the downstairs to the upstairs, or vice versa?"

"Do you mean, is there some kind of private stairway or hidden passage by which the President and I could have seen one another without being seen by others?"

"I will request you to refrain from rewording or de-fining my questions, Miss Gibson. I mean precisely what I asked. Did the President have any private means of getting to your quarters or you to his?"

"No. Unless he used a ladder—or the vine that grows on the back wall—but I doubt if the President is, or ever was, that athletic or romantically foolhardy."

The spectators in the gallery roared with laughter, and some stamped and whistled.

Chief Justice Johnstone's gavel slammed down hard. When peace was restored, the robed magistrate warned, "The Chief Justice will admonish strangers and citizens in the galleries of the necessity of observing perfect order and profound silence—at the penalty of being evicted."

Zeke Miller was staring at the witness. "Miss Gibson, previous witnesses who were acquainted with both you and the President, when he was a senator, have agreed that you had a close relationship with him. How close was it?"

"For the most part, about as close as you and I are right here."

"Previous testimony indicates otherwise."

"What does previously testimony indicate, Congressman?"

"That you, Miss Gibson, and the man who is now President had a relationship which might be regarded, by some classes, as an illicit liaison."

"Can you prove that scandalous allegation? What do you possess, beyond a desire to defame the President, to support it?"

"Miss Gibson, circumstantial evidence, strong circumstantial evidence, is enough. The records of your visits and dating together, your telephone conversations, they are enough. The affair is indicated plainly. That is enough."

"Enough only for backstairs gossips and vindictive persecutors—"

"Watch your tongue, Miss Gibson. You are sworn—"

"Watch yours, Mr. Manager. You have no proof. You have hopes. You have hopes, and hearsay, and indications. And on that you are trying to build a straw Romeo and a straw Juliet. What you are building is a nonexistent affair, a fabrication, and I am the only one in this Chamber who knows the truth, and that is what I am telling you."

"Miss Gibson, do not insult the intelligence of this court. Do you mean to tell me that you, a grown single woman, enjoyed a friendship with a mature widowed male for five years, and there was no intimacy between you, not once in five years?"

"Intimacy?"

"Come now, Miss Gibson, you know very well what I mean."

"I suspect I do, and I am appalled. Congressman Miller, the friendship I had with the President was based on mutual respect, common intellectual interests, and the simple pleasure of being together. We had an abiding affection for one another. We held hands. We embraced. We kissed. But, sorry as I am to disappoint you, there was nothing more furtive or lurid that ever occurred."

"I am not disputing your sincerity, Miss Gibson, but do you mean to tell me that a person like the President —his intemperate habits have already been introduced into—"

"What intemperate habits?"

"Drinking, excessive drinking, for one thing."

"Drinking? The President? Surely you're joking. All he ever drank in my presence was carbonated water, celery tonic, and occasionally wine at dinner. Two glasses of wine and he fell asleep. The sight of a bourbon advertisement made him take me home early. You're joking."

"And you, Madam Witness, are flippant, excessively so, to the detriment of the person you, understandably, are trying to protect."

"If I am flippant, it is because your questions inspire only my contempt, and yet I do not think they deserve the honest emotion of contempt, not from a lady and not in a court."

"I will leave it to the honorable members of the Senate to judge your performance. However, before entering into the serious matter of how your close relationship with the President, your kiss-and-tell Vaduz relationship—"

Abrahams was on his feet. "Objection, Your Honor!"

Miller gave a disdainful gesture toward Abrahams. "Forget it. I'll rephrase. . . . Miss Gibson, before entering into the series of questions designed to extract from you the full story of how you were able to acquire from the President privileged state information, and pass it on to your Communist employers, in support of Article I of the House indictment, I wonder if you would be kind enough to reply to one more question about your friendship with the President. Did the President find your companionship so rewarding, so fulfilling, for five years, that he did not think it necessary to ask your hand in marriage?"

"Congressman, I suspect the implication behind your question is an insult."

"No offense intended—"

"You are implying, despite my sworn denial, that the President and I did have an affair, and that this satisfied him sufficiently to keep him from proposing marriage."

"Miss Gibson, you said that, I didn't."

"Congressman, when a snake rattles, you know it's just a rattle, not a bite, but you know the meaning of the sound, and what comes next."

"Miss Gibson, I will not be diverted by a lecture in zoology. I want the facts of your relationship with the President set before this tribunal. Miss Gibson, after five years, why did the President and yourself not legalize your relationship?"

"Not legalize our relationship?"

"Not marry, Miss Gibson. Why did you not marry?"

"Because he never asked me. I think he meant to, but I think he was afraid."

"The President—afraid?"

"Of people like you, Mr. Manager, who might think him too black for me, and me too white for him, and who might cry out that our union would be mongrelizing the Congress, where he was once a member, or the White House, where he is now the President. If you are through with the Madame du Barry part of my life, Mr. Manager, can we go on to the Mata Hari part? I'm eager to know how it all comes out."

Ten minutes later, when Zeke Miller, mopping his wet bald pate, had finished the Mata Hari part and grimly gone back to his table, it was Nat Abrahams' turn.

Abrahams rose. "Mr. Chief Justice, the President's managers waive cross-examination. The witness may be dismissed without recall."

He smiled at Wanda Gibson as she left the stand. Maybe the Senate had another view of it, but for Abrahams, the President's lady needed no further defense this day or ever. Perhaps, Abrahams reasoned, her

flippancy—how difficult the attitude must have been for
her, considering her essential seriousness and concern,
yet how unwaveringly she had maintained that pose,
determined to ridicule the outrageous charges—may
have offended some senators, coming, as it did, from a
mulatto. Nevertheless, Abrahams believed she had more
than adequately defended herself and the man she loved.
She required no counsel's assist. If most of the Senate
appreciated her sparring with Miller, her ridiculing of
Miller's charges, then her triumph was not a small one.

Scanning the inscrutable public faces of the senators
as they watched Wanda Gibson leave, Abrahams could
detect nothing decisive, neither favorable nor unfavor-
able reactions.

Looking past the podium, Abrahams saw Zeke
Miller's manner change. He appeared to light up. Then
Abrahams beheld the witness who was approaching, the
witness whose deceptively innocent face was set firmly
in cold determination.

Sally Watson, blond hair combed bell-like for the occasion, taupe wool sheath accentuating her feminine
contours, mink stole on her arm, had gone up before
the witness chair and the Secretary of the Senate.

Tuttle, beside Abrahams, leaned closer. "She looks as
if she's going to be hard on us," he whispered.

"She will be," Abrahams whispered in return.

Zeke Miller, rubbing his hands with apparent relish,
dipping his head to the seated witness in a gallant welcome, addressed her with the deference he might have
accorded Varina Howell Davis—Jefferson Davis' Varina
—flower of the Confederacy.

"Miss Watson, considering the nature of your familial
ties, the fact that your brilliant and beloved parent is
a member of this august body, considering the ordeal
you have recently undergone, it is an act of uncommon
bravery and patriotism for you to have volunteered to
appear here in public this afternoon. All of us in the
legislative branch are appreciative that you are ready to
become a collaborator in our search for the truth, in
our desire to purify and strengthen the executive branch

of our noble government. For my part, I shall attempt to make your appearance as brief as possible."

"Thank you, Representative Miller."

"I understand that you have insisted upon coming here against your physician's wishes?"

"Yes, sir."

"Because you felt that no affidavit could adequately reveal what injury and humiliation you have suffered?"

"I believed the Senate should know what I know, sir."

"We will proceed. Why did you, one week after Douglass Dilman assumed the Presidency, apply for the position as his social secretary?"

"Certainly not for reasons of personal advancement, Representative Miller. My father, as you know, has always been able to educate and care for his family. I had heard—because of my wide acquaintance in Washington —I had heard that many of the White House staff were resigning, since their loyalty had been only to T.C. Also, I had heard that Miss Laurel, the First Lady's social secretary, was leaving the White House with her. I read and heard that the new President had no woman to bring into the White House to assist him with the ordinary refinements and duties that only a lady versed in the social amenities could help him with. Of course, at that time I did not know he had a grown daughter passing herself off as a white person in secret."

"No, none of us knew that, Miss Watson."

"I knew also that it would be difficult for President Dilman to find someone to fill a specialized position such as social secretary. Because of his—his background— his lack of knowledge of formal entertaining—it would make the position doubly burdensome. Few qualified ladies were prepared to undertake such responsibility for such meager recompense."

"So you applied as a duty, in the same way a socialite might lend herself to hospital work?"

"If you want to put it that way, yes. I wanted to be of use, to do my part in maintaining the continuity of the social life in the White House."

"You felt you were qualified?"

"I believed so. I had attended Radcliffe. I had handled

the entertaining of account executives for an advertising agency in New York. I had often served as my father's hostess. I believed that I was qualified, and apparently I was, for the President hired me during my first interview with him, and often congratulated me on my ability in managing his limited social affairs."

"Did you find the position agreeable, Miss Watson?"

"In every respect except one."

"Except one? Do I dare inquire in what area you found the position disagreeable?"

"I don't mind. It is time the——the truth came out. Some of my friends begged me not to take the position. They said it was known that the President had been, well, carrying on with an unmarried white woman——of course, I later learned she was an unmarried mulatto woman—— and that his morals were questionable. I ignored that as the inevitable rumor that precedes every new President into office."

"You were generous, Miss Watson."

"I don't like to listen to petty gossip. And at first, the first few weeks, I believed that I was right. President Dilman behaved circumspectly. But then——"

"Go on, please, Miss Watson. Then what happened?"

"I don't know. He——the President——seemed to begin to feel more confident about his office, his belonging up in the White House, and once the mourning for T.C. ceased, and he knew he was really the head man, his behavior altered. It was at first subtle, but it altered."

"Can you give us any instances?"

"Oh, yes. His language became more imperious, coarser, and he was more demanding. Since we had many matters to confer about daily, he would insist, more and more frequently, that I come to see him in his bedroom or study, during the morning, while he was still in his pajamas. Sometimes he would demand that I stay on later at night, to meet with him the same way, and sometimes he drank in my presence and became heady."

"Heady, Miss Watson?"

"Intoxicated. Perhaps Miss Gibson was right. He cannot hold drinks. Nevertheless, he drank. When he was under the influence of drink and we were alone——he

would never permit me to bring another member of my
staff along, not even his former secretary, Miss Fuller—
he would become excessively informal. By that I mean he
would make flattering allusions to my appearance, my
features or my clothes. It made me uncomfortable. I
hated to see him this way, and each time I couldn't wait
to leave him. I'm not a child, but there was something
about him, the way he stared at me, that made me
afraid."

"I see. Until the night we shall discuss in a moment,
the awful night he gave his true intent away, had President Dilman made an improper advance or gesture toward you?"

"No. He hinted at—at our dining alone sometime—
spending a social evening together—but he never came
out with it. I think he was inhibited by the possibility of
gossip or what my father might say if I repeated it."

"And, no doubt, he was put off by your own demeanor?"

"Oh, definitely. I was chilly and businesslike with him.
It was so difficult, especially knowing, as I did, of his
affair—or whatever you wish to call it—with another
woman on the side."

"But the President never touched you, physically, until
the night in question?"

"No. If he had, I'd have quit on the spot, and told my
father."

"Miss Watson, we have arrived at the awful scene,
the one that inspired the House of Representatives to
condemn the morality of the nation's President in Article
III. I refer to the evening that the President, as specified
in our charges, 'while under the influence of intoxicants,
made improper advances' upon you 'and did commit
bodily harm' to you."

"It was an ugly experience."

"The Senate and public will judge fairly the degree of
the President's degradation of his office, Miss Watson. I
know their decision will never free your mind of the nightmare visited upon you, but you will know justice has been
served. Let us, then, quickly and briefly recapitulate the
events of that night. It was the evening of the dinner you

had arranged on his behalf for the Joint Chiefs of Staff. There was a movie shown after dinner which you did not attend. Why did you not attend?"

"As we were leaving for the movie, the President drew me aside and whispered to me. He had a private conversation with me."

"Yes, General Fortney has attested to that. What was the nature of the conversation?"

"The President said he wanted me to get out files on several of T.C.'s dinners given for the legislators, and review them with me, because he thought it was time to start buttering them up. He said he wanted to go over our future social program that very evening. He asked me to get the material and meet him in an hour in the Lincoln Bedroom. I had misgivings, because I could smell alcohol on his breath, but I had no choice. So I was there when he came."

"What transpired next, Miss Watson? I know this is painful to you, and the evidence has already been introduced, but I desire that the Senate hear it from your own lips."

"He came in—"

"President Dilman?"

"Yes, the President. He came in, and mumbled something about the movie, and brought out drinks, and kept insisting I have a drink of whiskey with him. I didn't want to, but he forced one on me. He must have had three in the next fifteen or twenty minutes. I was sitting in a chair next to the bed, and he was sitting on the bed. He was babbling on about his life, what it was like to be Negro, how he was going to prove a Negro and other Negroes he'd bring into the Cabinet could run the government better than white politicians—then suddenly he asked to know if I had anything against him because of his color. I said no. There was more of this, his wanting to know how I felt toward him, then he began saying how he felt toward me, that I reminded him of his wife who was practically as white as I am. Then, suddenly, he asked me to bring him the papers I had in my hand, bring them to where he was sitting on the bed. So I did."

"And then, Miss Watson?"

"He took the papers, threw them aside, and grabbed hold of me. He tried to kiss me. I refused, and that enraged him. He wouldn't let go of me, and I tried to get free. He tore my dress, and then he became brutal, and I slapped him, and he pushed me down on the bed. Then he was after me again, and his hands, he bruised and scratched me—you have the photographs the doctor took that night—and finally I said I'd scream if he wouldn't let go, and pulled away and stumbled to the door, unlocked it, and escaped. I never went back to the White House again."

"What happened immediately afterward, Miss Watson?"

"I—I told some people high up in government—I was afraid to tell my father—I didn't want him to do something terrible—and my friends then acted, decided to take action, against the President, and they told my father, and he agreed, and that was all."

"You've been under the strict care of your family physician ever since?"

"I was in a state of shock. I have been confined to our house. The doctor comes by daily."

"Miss Watson, you have performed a service to your country. Thank you for your soul-rending testimony."

Zeke Miller bowed his head, and then turned away. Keeping his head low, shaking it sorrowfully, he returned to his table.

There was a buzzing through the Senate Chamber, much twisting, turning, consultation, as Sally Watson rose from her chair to leave.

Chief Justice Johnstone's stentorian voice halted her. "The witness will remain in her place for the cross-examination by the President's managers."

Surprised, Sally Watson sat down.

The Chief Justice called out, "The senators will please be attentive. Gentlemen of counsel for the President, if you desire to cross-examine, you will proceed."

Nat Abrahams had taken up a manila folder of documents and come out of his seat. "Mr. Chief Justice, by your leave, the defense does have a number of inquiries to make of the witness."

Abrahams confronted Sally Watson. He had in his mind Dilman's story of the night in question. He had, in his folder, the thorough research accomplished by Priest and Hart. Abrahams knew that he would not be able to shake her from her story, for as one psychiatrist had pointed out to him, by now she believed it to be true, as was often the case with latent paranoid schizophrenics. If he attacked her ego, her id would make the response. His task was formidable. If he overplayed, and she became hysterical, she might gain sympathy for herself while building more resentment toward President Dilman. Abrahams knew that he would have to feel his way, push where there was give, withdraw where there was resistance, and stop hastily if she got out of hand.

"Miss Watson," he said, his tone chatty rather than severe, "like the honorable manager who preceded me, I appreciate what an ordeal this appearance must be for a young lady such as yourself. I will do my part in making it as endurable, and brief, as possible."

Sally Watson eyed Abrahams suspiciously. "Thank you."

"Be tolerant of me if I cover some of the same ground covered by the learned House manager. Now let me see, according to my notes, you stated that you volunteered, applied, to the President for the position of his social secretary, because—what was it now? Oh, yes—because you wished to serve your country. Is that correct?"

"Yes, sir."

"Very laudable. When you applied in person—I believe you saw President Dilman in the Oval Office of the White House—did he hire you immediately? Or do I understand correctly that he had some doubts about your qualifications until you said that there was a personage of importance in the government who would give you the strongest of recommendations? Is that true?"

"Yes—yes, it is."

"Who was the person in government who recommended you?"

"The Secretary of State."

"Secretary of State Arthur Eaton? I see. He recommended you for the position? He knew you personally and said you would be perfect for it?"

"Yes, that's right."

"As a result of Secretary Eaton's favorable recommendation, you were hired as White House social secretary?"

"Well, there were also my other qualifications."

"Of course, Miss Watson, your other qualifications. Let me see." Abrahams opened his folder and examined the photocopies of documents already entered as exhibits in the trial. "Miss Watson, you spoke of attending Radcliffe. The record shows you attended the college for ten months, and then you were dropped, no cause for the school's action being given. Can you enlighten us?"

"I tested very well, or I wouldn't have been there, but my grades slipped. I was impatient with school. The girls were too immature. My mind was on a career. I wanted to go out and have a career. So I moved to New York."

"Yes, I see. You had one job there. With the advertising agency, which is headed by Senator Hoyt Watson's former law partner. You received a sizable salary for a young lady who had no advertising experience. Yes, an excellent job, I must say. I am surprised it lasted only six months. Why was that, Miss Watson?"

"There was too much drinking and fooling around. I couldn't stand it. Besides, I wanted to take voice lessons. I was told I could sing unusually well, and that I might have a future in that field."

"Yes, there is some evidence you possessed a devotion to popular music. I see here that you were married to a young man connected with a Greenwich Village orchestra. Further documentation makes it clear that the marriage was annulled two weeks later. The young man with whom you eloped, evidently he was deported to his native Puerto Rico."

"When I learned about his bad habits—he was a dope addict—I sought the annulment and disclosed his vice to —to certain people. I guess that was why he was deported. I think it is a good thing, too."

"I have no doubt. Such vigilance is admirable. . . . Now, Miss Watson, we have in our possession evidence that, in the next several years, you were attended by three different psychoanalysts, and for one short period you were confined to a mental institution. In itself, nothing wrong. Such treatment is not uncommon. In fact, it shows good sense to take corrective measures when you are emotionally ill. Naturally, and properly, your psychoanalysts and the mental institution would not open their confidential files on your illness to us. We have only the information that you were placed in an institution because you made an attempt upon your own life, made an attempt to commit suicide by self-inflicted wounds that—"

Zeke Miller's voice shrieked, "Objection, Mr. Chief Justice! The testimony the manager is trying to elicit is irrelevant and immaterial to the case on trial, and an obvious effort to damage the character of the witness."

Abrahams appealed to the Chief Justice. "Your Honor, I believe this line of questioning is highly relevant. I am not interested in damaging the character of the witness, beyond bringing to light the factual evidence of her consistent instability, and therefore her lack of capacity for the position for which the President had hired her."

"The President did hire her!" Miller shouted.

"Because he was misled as to her qualifications by Secretary of State Eaton, and for reasons that have a direct bearing on this case," said Abrahams.

"Objection sustained," announced the Chief Justice. "Mr. Manager Abrahams, henceforth confine yourself strictly to questions that will bring out testimony concerned with the charges in Article III."

Abashed, Abrahams closed his folder, walked over and handed it to Tuttle, then returned to Sally Watson.

"Miss Watson, since Arthur Eaton was partly instrumental in helping you become the President's social secretary, I am curious to know how long and how well you have known him."

"How long? Always, I guess. He is a sort of friend of my father. I would see him at social functions."

"And that acquaintance was enough for him to know your qualifications for the White House position?"

"Well, we often talked. I think he thought I was intelligent, and had social experience."

"After the catastrophe in Frankfurt, you knew that Secretary Eaton was the next in line in succession to the Presidency, did you not?"

"I may have read it. I never gave it a thought."

"You mean you never discussed this with Secretary Eaton, not even when you two were alone together?"

"We were never alone togeth—I mean, not actually—"

"Miss Watson, since you are under oath, and before you complete your recollection, I hasten to refresh your memory. We have evidence, entered into the record, to prove that you were seen dining with the Secretary of State outside Washington, and that, later, you were frequently a visitor to his Georgetown house after dark. Do you deny that?"

"I told you he was an old family friend. I saw him sometimes because he was nice to me, gave me advice at times when my father was busy. When I had a personal problem, I always ran to Mr. Eaton. That's not unusual."

"Did you know the Secretary of State was married?"

"Of course."

"Was his wife ever present at these—these fatherly private meetings you had with him?"

"No. She was traveling."

"Then, perhaps I am old-fashioned in suggesting your conduct *was* unusual."

"You're twisting it, that's all. We were hardly ever alone. When we went out a few times, there were other people around. When I went to his house, there were sometimes other guests, well, the servants were there."

"Did you know that the Secretary of State, who was your friend, and the President, who was your employer, were having important political differences?"

"No, I did not."

"Since you spent so much time in the company of the President, in his private quarters, and in the evening, where confidential documents of state might be seen and phone calls overheard, did you ever hear anything—let us say, concerning our nation's foreign affairs—that you repeated to Secretary Eaton?"

"No, I did not."

"Miss Watson, about the night under discussion, the night the President allegedly made improper advances to you, you have stated that he was intoxicated. Were you?"

"No, I was not."

"Yet you were seen, at the dinner for the Joint Chiefs of Staff, consuming champagne before and after the meal, and wine during it."

"Wine does not make me drunk. It is a part of the meal."

"And then, according to your testimony, you drank in the President's bedroom?"

"He forced me to."

"Forced you? How is that possible? He offered you a drink, if he did, and you accepted it. Is that what you mean?"

"I had to take it."

"Miss Watson, you stated you were waiting in his bedroom before he arrived. How long?"

"I don't know. Ten or fifteen minutes."

"What did you do in his room?"

"Do? I—I smoked, and reread the papers he sent for, and kept thinking how I wished I wasn't there."

"The President had left his briefcase open in the room. It contained top-secret documents of such a nature as to have been useful to your friend Arthur Eaton. Did you even casually look at any of those documents?"

"Of course not! What do you think I am?"

"Then the President came in and pressed his attentions upon you, and because you resisted you were injured—is that still your story?"

"It is not my story, it is what happened."

"Miss Watson, I have shown the photographs of the scratches and bruises on your chest and legs to three highly competent physicians. It is their opinion that while the wounds may indeed have been caused by another person, they may also, like the scar on your wrist, have been self-inflicted. Now—"

"That's a filthy dirty lie!"

"I am merely repeating expert—"

"A lie!"

"I am sorry to have so upset you, Miss Watson. You must remember there were two persons in that bedroom, not one—"

"You bet your life there were."

"—and you have given the court one view of what took place, but there is quite another view held by the other person who was present. In any event, let's leave behind us the scene of our disagreement. Let's get you out of that savage bedroom. You escaped, as you have told us. Where did you go? What happened next?"

"I ran to my office in the East Wing, to the washroom, to stop the bleeding, and clean up. Then I went home."

"You went home. A little while ago, when learned counsel for the House asked you what you did immediately afterward, you said you promptly told some friends high up in government what had happened to you. How did you tell them, by telephone or in person?"

"In—in person. I couldn't go right home in my condition. Now I remember. I had to speak to someone. So I went to my friends."

"Could one of your friends, perchance, have been the Honorable Secretary of State Arthur Eaton?"

"Yes. I thought of him first."

"You went to his house in Georgetown to tell him?"

"Yes."

"But he was merely one friend. You say you spoke to several friends. Perhaps, when you went to Secretary Eaton, he had gathered about him others to receive you. Who was there when you arrived?"

"Mr. Eaton, and—and Governor Talley and Senator Hankins were there, and also Representative Miller. They were horrified by the way I looked."

"Did you tell them all what had happened to you?"

"Not right away. I told Mr. Eaton. I was afraid to tell Senator Hankins and Representative Miller, knowing how outraged they would be at how a nig—a—a Negro —had acted."

"You mean you were afraid they would be more outraged that a Negro had, as you say, made improper advances than if he had been a Caucasian?"

"I don't mean that exactly."

"What do you mean, Miss Watson?"

"I mean, they were already mistrustful of Dilman—President Dilman—and I was scared this behavior of his—they are very touchy about nig—about such behavior toward young ladies where we come from—I was afraid this would overexcite them."

"Did it, when you told them?"

"Yes."

"After that, was impeachment of the President mentioned in your presence?"

"Yes."

"Because of what you told them?"

"Because of other things. This was just one more offense to them."

"And Secretary of State Eaton—how did he take it?"

"He was revolted by the President's behavior, and angry, naturally. He was restrained, because that's part of his background and training."

"But Secretary Eaton was pleased?"

"What?"

"He was pleased when you produced a set of file cards with notes taken by you in the President's private bedroom, notes made from a transcript of a top-secret meeting between the Director of the CIA and the President, notes that gave warning to Secretary Eaton that the President was aware of Secretary Eaton's efforts to usurp the Presidential prerogatives of office?"

"You're insane!"

"Our relative sanity is not the issue here, Miss Watson. I told you that only two persons know what occurred in the Lincoln Bedroom. One is yourself, and you have given us your view of it. The other is the President, and in due time I shall introduce an affidavit signed by him proving that your story is fabricated out of whole cloth, and that your real motive in stealing into that bedroom—"

"He's a liar like you! He's a dirty lying black—"

She halted abruptly, staring at Abrahams, then at everyone around her, gasping.

"Are you all right?" Abrahams asked.

"I won't be insulted!"

"I don't think you are in any condition to go on, and I do believe I've heard all I want to hear. Thank you, Miss Watson. As far as the defense is concerned, you may be dismissed."

He turned his back on her and returned to the table. When he resumed his seat, he could see that she had a handkerchief to her eyes, and, assisted by the Sergeant at Arms, was stumbling, then half running from the Chamber.

In the third row of Senate desks, Abrahams could also see Senator Hoyt Watson, livid, white mane wagging, as his colleagues crowded about him.

Abrahams sighed. He had challenged an ego, and when he thought that he had demolished it, he had found the id in its place, the immortal id that could not be demolished.

He looked up to realize that Zeke Miller was standing before the bench, glaring at him. Then Miller directed himself to the magistrate on high. "Mr. Chief Justice, the House managers offer their final witness in the trial of impeachment against the President. I shall examine the Honorable Secretary of State of the United States, Arthur Eaton."

Abrahams' eyes followed the tall, slender, faultlessly attired Secretary of State as he made his way to the raised dais. While Eaton ascended the podium and took the oath, Abrahams touched the arm of Walter T. Tuttle beside him.

"Walter," Abrahams said in an undertone, "I can handle ordinary people, for better or worse, but I'm not sure I'd be any good at cross-examining someone who believes he wrote the Constitution. Think you can take him when the cross-examination comes?"

Tuttle glanced up at the witness stand, then said dryly, "Not sure anybody's going to take him, Nat."

"I suspect Miller will handle his last star witness on a loftier note," said Abrahams. "He'll evoke T.C. and

Congressional dignity and the law of the land, and argue that Eaton was a symbol for all three, and in firing Eaton, our client sullied T.C.'s grave, spat on the Senate, and broke the Federal law. If that's the gambit, I suggest we leave personal considerations out of the cross-examination. Equate the unconstitutionality of the New Succession Act with the proved unconstitutionality of the similar Tenure of Office Act back in 1868, and say it was slyly slipped through to keep Doug from performing as President and to keep Eaton serving as T.C.'s proxy in the White House, as evidenced by Eaton withholding CIA information from the President. I think that should be the note. That's your cup of tea."

"I think my cup of tea is weak, and so is theirs," said Tuttle in a whisper. "I think it's the stronger stuff everyone swallowed, or refused to, upon which the trial vote will depend. Legally, the Article supporting Eaton is the important one. Popularly, in fact, it will be the other Articles that will determine acquittal or conviction."

Abrahams said, "I still say this technical stuff is your cup of tea. Want to handle it?"

"Gladly, even though the potion turns out to be hemlock."

Exchanging smiles of agreement, Nat Abrahams and Walter Tuttle settled back to listen to Representative Zeke Miller begin his respectful examination of the closing witness, the man he was trying to make the new President of the United States.

For almost a half hour, Douglass Dilman had been gloomily sitting at his desk in the Oval Office, watching the spectacle on the portable television screen, watching and listening to Arthur Eaton grandly offer himself to the United States and the Senate as T.C.'s mind and conscience. Eaton had given the impression of being one who had done his utmost to save the country from a pretender, on T.C.'s behalf, in everyone's best interests, but could do no more unless the nation took legal steps to oust the pretender and fill the vacancy with the one who alone was qualified to give the voters what they had wanted in the first place. His behavior was that of a person who fully realized he was giving a preview of what the next President would be like, and who displayed each patriotic and learned digression on domestic and foreign affairs like a model showing off a new garment the public might, and should, buy.

As Eaton's underplayed performance, responding to Miller's direction, came to a close, Douglass Dilman silently acknowledged its magnificence. For a while he stared out through the windows at the White House south lawn, with its stark elm and oak trees, and the long shadows of the late afternoon creeping across the expanse of brown-patched grass.

He was faintly depressed. Eaton's poise and sophistication, his modulated eloquence, the ease with which he faced questions about far-flung nations and their problems and America's historic role in their future, his impeccable attire, above all his superior whiteness—these, and not his actual replies to the interrogation, were what depressed Dilman. The Secretary of State appeared to be the perfect archetype of a national leader, while he himself did not, and never would. If the Senate vote came down to a popularity vote, a vote for an image, then Eaton would be in this chair next week, and he himself would not see this view of the White House lawn again in his lifetime, except in tortured memory.

A familiar voice brought him back to the television screen. Abrahams' colleague, and The Judge's friend, the redoubtable Walter T. Tuttle, had begun his cross-examination of Eaton.

Tuttle's stature in political history would match Eaton's own. Tuttle's tart sarcasm, his piercing inquiries, thrown from catapults built out of his wide knowledge of precedent and the country's past, appeared to jolt the witness. Now and then Eaton's invincible and arrogant confidence would give way to human uncertainty, and there were glimpses of a man no more a man than was Dilman or any other man. Did others see this, or was it only Dilman himself? Imperceptibly, his depression lifted.

He was entirely absorbed in the cross-examination when the telephone buzzer sounded. Absently, eyes still focused on the screen, his hand brought the receiver to his ear.

The voice was Edna Foster's.

"Mr. President, it's your son Julian, telephoning from New York City. He says that unless you are terribly tied up, he must speak to you, and even then he'd like a minute—he sounds—"

"Put him through, Miss Foster."

He reached out, shut off the television set, then cupped the earphone and mouthpiece closer, and tensely waited.

"Hello, Dad?"

"Yes, Julian, what is it? You said—"

"Don't be alarmed, everything'll be fine," Julian was saying in great agitation, "but I felt it best to call—it's about Mindy—I'm in her apartment right now. Dad, she tried to kill herself, she tried—but she's going to get well—everything's working out—"

"Kill herself?" Dilman was aghast, chilled and shivering. "Are you sure she's all right? Is there a doctor there? How is she, Julian? What happened?"

"After she saw the newspapers—the ones telling about her passing—and then heard the radio—she finally made up her mind and took an overdose of sleeping pills —my God, the amount of pills! Then, when she thought she was beyond help and ready to go, she telephoned me at Trafford. She wanted to clear her conscience before dying, I guess. Anyway, I could hardly understand her. She kept mumbling about some reporter who found her out, and to save her own neck she got him after me and my Turnerite membership, and now she was sorry and wanted to apologize. I tried to keep her talking, because I couldn't understand her and I knew something was wrong. Finally she blanked out, but luckily, when I got the long-distance operator to say we were cut off, she gave me Mindy's unlisted number—then I made the operator get the police and police doctors. Whew, it was close, Dad. They found her sprawled on the floor, but the stomach pump did it. A few more minutes and she'd have been a goner. She's all right, though. By the time

I got her address from the police, and whizzed into New York from Trafford, she was half sitting up in bed, and her own doctor was—he's still here. She's okay now."

Dilman slumped back, unable to overcome his anguish. "Julian, give me that address. I'm flying right in. I want to see her."

"No, Dad, please—that's the first thing she said when she knew I was calling you—she doesn't want to see you or anyone else, no one for a while. The doctor agrees. She's pretty weak. It would only upset her, I mean badly, that's what the doctor says. She needs rest, some time to think, think by herself. Of course, I knew you'd want me to hire nurses to be with her—"

"She really tried to kill herself?" Dilman repeated, still aghast at what had taken place.

"Well—it was awful for her, Dad—being revealed naked in public like that, and—wait, one second, she's trying to say something . . . what, Mindy? . . . Sure, sure, okay. . . . Dad, I—I showed her the newspapers with the statement you made in reply to the exposé. She was just repeating something from what you said, about the crime of passing not being hers but everyone's, for not letting her grow up with dignity. It's hard to understand her, the way she's talking—so indistinctly."

Dilman understood her, if his son did not. "Julian, let me have a word with the doctor."

The physician, impressed by the opportunity to speak to a President, was verbose and clinical, but his prognosis came down to no serious aftereffects. Mindy had taken a lethal dose of Nembutals, and been discovered, and her stomach emptied in the nick of time. With proper care and rest, she would be on her feet in forty-eight hours. As for her mental outlook in the days to come, that, of course, was beyond the province of a general practitioner. Right now it would not be advisable for the President, for her father, to visit her, considering her emotional state. Perhaps it would be permitted in the near future, if she wished it. At this time, unwise.

When Julian came back on the telephone, Dilman said, "I want you to remain there in her apartment, nurse

or no nurse, at least overnight. Mindy may want someone close to talk to when she wakes up."

"I'll stay right here, Dad."

"And you keep in touch with me. Understand?"

"Absolutely. I'll call you later tonight."

Dilman shook his head, although there was no one to
witness his despair. "Poor baby. I only wish she'd see
me. I have so much to say to her."

"She's alive, Dad. That's all that matters. Maybe one
day—"

Maybe one day.

Slowly, Dilman hung up.

He could envision, with sorrow, Mindy's probable destiny. Condemned and ostracized in New York City, truly
alone, of no people, no race, she would—like the Wandering Jew, the cobbler who had pushed off the Lord—
become an eternal wanderer, too, in search of identity
and belonging. As long as she could endure it, there
would be for Mindy, endlessly, another city, another lie,
another fearful life lived within the fragile lie, and another exposure. Perhaps the only peace she would ever
know would be the peace of the oblivion she had
sought, and been denied, today. How soon would she be
driven to seek it again?

Aching with grief, Douglass Dilman left his desk, circled the room, and then finally he opened the door to
Miss Foster's office and went inside. He had no specific
business with his secretary. He wanted only the solace of
companionship.

Edna Foster, partly attentive to the letter she was
typing, partly attentive to the television screen, halted in
her work and greeted him with a guilty nod.

"I guess I'm being compulsive about it, Mr. President," she said. "I can't keep my eyes off the set."

On the small screen, Tuttle and Eaton were no longer
in view. The camera was offering a panoramic picture
of the crowded Senate floor, galleries, and press section.
The volume had been turned down too low for Dilman
to hear the announcer.

"What's happening?" he asked Miss Foster.

"There was a motion for recess," said Miss Foster.

"After Mr. Tuttle finished with Eaton, the prosecution rested its case. I don't think they've made such a good case—I mean, there are no facts, if you think about it."

Dilman said, "Unfortunately, Miss Foster, too few people watching, including the senators, may think about it. Did they say what comes next?"

"Yes. Mr. Abrahams said that, except for introducing and reading the defense affidavits, he has only to examine the five witnesses for the defense that he has subpoenaed. Then somebody from the floor made a motion which was passed by a voice vote. It was agreed that Mr. Abrahams could begin his examination of defense witnesses at five-thirty this afternoon. Then the court will adjourn at seven for dinner and convene again tonight, for a night session, at eight-thirty, continuing until all the defense witnesses have been heard and cross-examined. Tomorrow the Senate will convene at ten o'clock in the morning for the closing speeches. The House managers will be given one hour, then Mr. Abrahams will be given one hour. Then there will be a lunch break, and Johnstone said if there were no undue delays, no further points of law to be discussed, the voting should begin at two o'clock tomorrow."

It came as a small shock to Dilman that the trial, which had become a way of life for him, was almost over. There was left only the rest of this fading day, some drugged sleep, and then tomorrow the final decision to acquit or convict. He was not prepared for judgment day, not so soon, but then, he supposed, no one ever was, really.

"Thanks, Miss Foster, sorry to interrupt your work."

He went back into the lonely Oval Office and closed the door. Hands locked behind him, he walked around the room. He tried to figure out why the trial's end appeared to him so sudden and disturbing. Then he knew the answer. There was a sense of incompleteness about it for him, because he had not been an active participant. It was as if a great vessel was sinking—maybe yet to be saved, more likely to be lost forever—and the captain was not there; the captain was somewhere far away, on land, going over the steamship company's accounts. That would be wrong, as this was wrong.

He called to mind Nat Abrahams' firm injunction of
ten days ago—ten thousand years ago, it seemed by
emotion's calendar—that the President, although legally
permitted to do so, must not stand as a living witness
in his own defense. Like himself, President Andrew Johnson had wanted to be heard and had been kept silent by
his managers. In the end, perhaps, Johnson's managers
had been proved right. But somehow, this second Presidential impeachment trial in American history was different, basically different, from the nation's first. The first
had been important, aside from the opposing two philoso-
phies on reconstructing the defeated South, because it
pitted the legislative branch of government against the executive branch. President Johnson had been tried for being an obstructive politician. This second impeachment
trial, however, was vastly more crucial to the United
States. The basic issue was not the differences between
two powerful branches of government. The basic issue
was the hushed and invisible Article V of the impeachment. Dilman knew that Abrahams was right. As President, he was not being tried for being an obstructive politician. He was being tried for being a Negro.

Yet, the real reason for the historic trial would never
be heard again on the floor of the Senate. The trial had
gone its way, with oratory and testimony, and suddenly,
tomorrow, it would be done, and at no time would the
Senate have been forced, or the public outside have been
forced, to examine themselves openly so they would understand why they were voting as they did. What had
there been, these cruel days, to represent President Dilman? The interrogation of witnesses on peripheral
charges, the speeches on evasive indictments. And now,
tonight, more witnesses, more affidavits, offered to the
Senate and the nation on what they preferred to hear
and see, not on what they should hear and see.

Soon the sounds of battle would be stilled. Dilman
would be ousted, condemned like Mindy to wander the
country and the earth in disgrace. And more than Mindy
—he was aware of this in a flash of clarity now—it
would be his own fault for not helping to emphasize the
nature of the real accusation against him for all the world

to know. It would be his failure for not insisting that the public be forced to see for itself, firsthand, what it was really voting upon, and for not letting the people decide then whether they could, after voting, live with only satisfied minds, eyes, eardrums, or whether they needed to be able to live with their consciences, too.

He started moving toward his desk. It was John F. Kennedy, he remembered, who had so truly written of the Andrew Johnson impeachment trial: "Two great elements of drama were missing: the actual causes for which the President was being tried were not fundamental to the welfare of the nation; and the defendant himself was at all times absent."

This time, he told himself, the great elements of drama would be fulfilled. This time America must not be lulled with a sugared half play, but must suffer, with him, the harsh play in its entirety. This time it had to be shown that the cause for trial was fundamental to the welfare of the nation, and it could be shown in only one way.

He lifted the telephone from the white console, and he instructed Edna Foster to locate Nat Abrahams for him, wherever he was in the Senate building.

Waiting, he thought Nat Abrahams would not be pleased by his casting aside of this one remaining garment of cowardice. No, Nat Abrahams would not be pleased. And might not understand. There was only one who might totally understand his act. Mindy would understand, at last.

He heard Felix Hart's voice on the telephone, and Dilman said that he urgently wished to speak to Nat Abrahams. In a half minute, Nat Abrahams was on the other end.

"Nat, is it true you are putting on your defense witnesses between five-thirty and seven, and the rest later in the evening?"

"Yes."

"Nat, I've thought about it. I want our invisible Article V opened up again—I want it there for everyone to see and hear—"

"But, Doug, you remember the ruling. We can't—"

"There is one way we can." He held his breath, and

then he said it. "Nat, I'm coming right over to the Senate. I have made up my mind to testify. I am going to be your first and key witness."

"Doug, you are the President of the United States."

"I am the black man President of the United States. I don't care what I'm asked or what I say. I only want to stand up there and be seen and heard by my judges. I know my appearance can lose it. But I also know this—something more may be finally won."

By twenty minutes to six o'clock, as darkness covered Washington, D.C., the illuminated rectangular Chamber of the Senate of the United States was ready. Until this crucial moment, it had been filled for every speech and every witness, but now the word was out, and for the first time the vast room was crammed to overflowing with incredulous humanity. Not only was every seat occupied, but every square foot of standing space.

From his high seat, the Chief Justice of the Supreme Court, swathed in his black judgment robe, peered out of his wrinkled, sunken face, peered down at the kinky-haired, grim, thickset black man who stood directly below him, facing the Secretary of the Senate, right arm raised.

"You, Douglass Dilman, do affirm that the evidence you shall give in the case now depending between the United States and the President of the United States shall be the truth, the whole truth, and nothing but the truth: so help you God."

"I do."

"Please be seated, Mr. President."

The Chief Justice's gavel struck. "As presiding officer, I once more admonish strangers and citizens in the galleries to maintain perfect order and profound silence. . . . Senators will please give their attention. . . . Gentlemen of counsel for the President, you may now begin your examination for the defense. Proceed with the first witness."

Douglass Dilman gripped the knob ends of the arms of the witness chair, and stared out at the rows of blurred men, his jurymen, his impeachers, men who would decide, perhaps had already determined, his fate. Strangely, their faces were individually unclear. Angled up toward him there was nothing more than a blended disc of whiteness, curiously punctuated by gleaming varicolored dots of eyes, the eyes around the aquarium in the old bad dreams. He could not see them. It did not matter. He was here. They could see him. They could see their black conscience.

Then there was only one before him, the one he could trust. He had conceded Nat Abrahams but a single promise. He would keep his answers concise and to the point. He would, if possible, not permit himself to plead, rise to any bait, or digress. He was ready.

Nat Abrahams was speaking. "You are Douglass Dilman, President of the United States, solemnly sworn on the Holy Book to preserve, protect, and defend the Constitution of your country to the best of your ability?"

"Yes, sir, I am Douglass Dilman. I have sworn to that oath."

"You are appearing here, before the tribunal of the Senate, at your own request?"

"I am."

"You are fully conversant with the charges in the four Articles of Impeachment brought against you?"

"I am."

"Mr. President, let us swiftly take up the indictments, one by one, and hear your replies, from your own lips, as to their truth or falsity. . . . Mr. President, did you know, at any time before the day of his confession to the fact, that your son, Julian Dilman, was a member of the activist Turnerite Group?"

"No, sir, I did not."

"Did you request that the Reverend Paul Spinger perform as an intermediary between the government and the Turnerite leaders because you wanted to make some kind of special personal deal with them, or because you wanted to have them come forward and confess or deny the Hattiesburg crime, and open their books to the government?"

"No, I wanted no special personal deal. I gave the

Reverend Spinger his only instructions in the presence of the Attorney General."

"Then you deny the allegation in Article II that you unlawfully hindered the Department of Justice in its prosecution of the Turnerites because you were in conspiracy with the Turnerites?"

"I unequivocally deny that allegation, sir."

"Why did you delay the outlawing of the Turnerites, as charged?"

"Because, sir, more facts were required in order to make certain, beyond any reasonable doubt, that this extremist society could be prosecuted legally, under the Subversive Activities Control Act. In our society, every citizen, no matter what his religious or political persuasion, is innocent until proved to be guilty. Once the facts were verified, and it was proved that the Group was guilty of subversion, I ordered the banning carried out."

"Let us examine the specifications in Articles I and III. I have brought them together, because the charges in them are repetitious and overlap. . . . Mr. President, according to previous testimony, you have been a friend of Miss Wanda Gibson, single woman, for five years?"

"That is correct."

"Did you, as accused, engage in an illicit love relationship with Miss Gibson at any time?"

"I did not. The charge is false."

"Was your conduct with Miss Gibson, from the day you met her, anything but proper, in the accepted sense?"

"It was nothing else, sir. We were and are now devoted friends. I esteem Miss Gibson above all the women I have known in the last five years. My affection for her is deep and abiding. Our relationship has been one of respect and utmost propriety."

"You were frequently in the company of Miss Gibson while you were a senator?"

"I was."

"How many times have you personally visited with her from the night you became President until the impeachment proceedings began?"

"Once, sir. I called upon her the evening after I

moved into the White House. The meeting was of brief duration. It took place in the Spingers' flat, while they were present in that flat."

"Since becoming President, did you communicate with Miss Gibson by any other means? Did you write to her?"

"No, I did not."

"Did you exchange telephone calls?"

"Yes, nightly the first days I was in office, but never more than twice a week after that."

"Did you ever, on any occasion, by any means, since becoming President, relate to her information concerning matters of state?"

"No, sir."

"You are sure of that, Mr. President?"

"Positively sure of it."

"Did you discuss any other aspects of your new office with her?"

"Yes. I spoke to her of my worries about having been elevated to such an office. I feared that T.C.'s advisers, the legislators, the military, the Party, in fact, the majority of the public, were not prepared to accept a Negro as President, and that they would resent me and cause me difficulty. I wondered, as all men do when they accidentally have a great responsibility thrust upon them, if I could adequately fill the office and please the electors. But most of all, I told Miss Gibson about my misgivings—my feelings that racial prejudice against me would hamper my freedom to serve my country as a President of all men."

"That was the extent of it? You never discussed with Miss Gibson, let slip to her, any government information of a confidential nature?"

"Not once, sir, not once. I was always mindful of the responsibility of my office."

"Mr. President, did you know, at any time during the last two years while Miss Gibson was in the service of Vaduz Exporters, that she was being employed by a Communist Front organization?"

"I did not know that. Miss Gibson has testified she did not know that either. The FBI did not know that.

I first heard about it on the very day Miss Gibson suspected what was going on, and the FBI informed me of it, the day the director of the Vaduz organization fled. The company was closed down the next morning."

"Then you do deny the entire substance of Article I, that with knowledge beforehand or through unintentional indiscretion, you passed on national secrets to a Soviet organization through Miss Gibson?"

"I emphatically deny it, sir. If it were possible to use stronger language, I would deny it in that language. I have never been a party to treason, and neither has Miss Gibson. The House charge is base fiction."

"So much for Article I, and a portion of III. Let us dispose of the remainder of the charges in Article III. Were you at any time in your past life, or in recent years, addicted to drinking alcohol?"

"No, sir."

"Were you ever in your life treated for alcoholism by a member of the medical profession?"

"No, sir."

"Were you ever committed, or did you ever commit yourself, to an institution for alcoholics because of such a habit or disability?"

"No, sir."

"Let us proceed with the only serious specification in Article III. You have read the indictment presented by the House, and elaborated upon by Miss Sally Watson this afternoon, that you attempted to seduce Miss Watson and did commit bodily harm upon her when she resisted?"

"I have read the indictment. I have seen and heard Miss Watson's testimony on television."

"On the night in question, did you order Miss Watson to meet you in your bedroom to confer with you on pending social engagements?"

"No, I did not."

"But she did visit your bedroom?"

"She did. After the dinner for the Joint Chiefs, I joined them for a documentary film showing. Miss Watson took me aside to say she was intoxicated, and desired to forgo the showing. I advised her to return home.

She said she was too drunk and would prefer to lie down first. I told her to do what she thought best. When I came back from the showing, I discovered Miss Watson lying upon my bed in a disheveled and drunken condition. I awakened her and told her I would arrange to have her escorted home. When she tried to get off the bed, her purse fell on the floor and the contents spilled out. I picked up these contents, and saw that among them were numerous index cards. The cards carried notes taken from a CIA document that was in my personal briefcase near the bed."

"Was the CIA document confidential, Mr. President?"

"It was stamped 'Top Secret' and 'Eyes Only.' Miss Watson could not have been unaware of that."

"What transpired afterward? Did you discuss her motivation in trying to acquire this information?"

"We did."

"Could you repeat your conversation at that time?"

"I would prefer not to."

"Was anything else, besides her motivation, discussed?"

"Yes. It has no pertinence to this trial."

"And then?"

"I told Miss Watson to leave. I told her she was fired. After some vituperation—"

"Can you be more explicit?"

"The usual thing, references to my race, and a few threats. Then she departed. It was a sad scene. I can only say here I bear her no animosity. She was, at the time, neither sober nor balanced. Emotional circumstances had driven her to this incredible act. I am sorry for her, but I cannot despise her."

"You did not, then, in any conceivable way, make improper overtures to Miss Watson, or attempt to detain her forcibly, or do her bodily harm?"

"I did not."

"Have you anything more to say about this charge, Mr. President?"

"It is untrue, every word of it. It is sheer fantasy, conceived by a fantastic mind and nurtured by other vindictive minds who have chosen to be deceived."

"Finally, Article IV of the impeachment. You did dismiss Arthur Eaton from your Cabinet and from his position as your Secretary of State?"

"I did, sir."

"You attempted to replace him with another highly qualified appointee, did you not?"

"I did, sir."

"You dismissed the Secretary of State without seeking the two-thirds approval of the Senate?"

"I did, sir."

"Were you aware that there existed a special law, the New Succession Act, passed by both Houses of Congress since you became President, forbidding you to fire a Cabinet member without Senate approval?"

"I was aware of the law. I had believed from the outset, and was supported by some of the best legal authorities in the field, that the law was unconstitutional, and would be so proved when it met its first challenge before the Supreme Court. I remembered that Chief Justice Charles Evans Hughes once remarked, 'We live under a Constitution, but the Constitution is what the judges say it is.' From my knowledge of precedent, I was certain the Supreme Court judges would say that the New Succession Act was and is a political measure entirely at odds with the Constitution. It was a measure rushed through merely to protect the old Administration from anticipated removals and appointments by a new Negro President. This law encroached upon the Constitution, which gives the Senate the right to advise and consent on a Presidential appointment, but gives the President himself the sole power to remove his appointees from office. I fired Eaton summarily, because I felt it necessary to do so, because I believed I had the legal right to do so, because I believed Congress had no right to dictate to the executive branch or freeze into its Cabinet posts the choices of a deceased President, and because I wanted a disgraceful and illegitimate piece of legislation put to constitutional test."

"And so you found it necessary to dismiss Arthur Eaton? Why, Mr. President? Why, specifically, did you remove this veteran public servant from office?"

"Because I was determined to preserve our government's system of checks and balances, which requires that our three branches—the executive, the legislative, and the judicial—remain separate and strong. I learned, and had proof of the fact, that the Secretary of State, with the approval of the legislative branch of our government, was attempting to usurp the powers of the Presidency and conduct the business of the White House from the offices of the Department of State. To save the Presidency, I had no choice but to get rid of him. I fired him. In retaliation, I presume, he and his associates impeached me."

"Mr. President, since the memorable moment you took the oath of office, do you believe you have performed your tasks diligently, soberly, honestly, without prejudice, with consideration for the rights of all men and a sincere concern for the welfare of the United States, and have you attempted to preserve, protect, and defend the Constitution and this democracy?"

"This I believe—I have tried. To the best of my ability I have tried, Mr. Manager."

"Thank you, Mr. President."

Douglass Dilman's grip on the chair relaxed. He thought that he detected the slightest smile on Nat Abrahams' face as Abrahams nodded at the bench, then turned and went back to the defense table.

Dilman had so concentrated on his friend's questions that he had been unable to observe or evaluate the reaction to his replies in the silent, alert Senate Chamber.

But now the Chamber seemed to come alive, and then the Chief Justice's gavel fell.

"The senators will be attentive. The counsel for the House of Representatives will proceed with his cross-examination."

For the first time since assuming the Presidency, since his travail and then trial had begun, Douglass Dilman found himself face to face with the custodian of all the hatred that had been directed toward him.

Zeke Miller's mocking gray eyes boldly met his own unblinking gaze. Miller's veiny nostrils were dilated, and his mouth fixed in a crooked line. He hooked his thumbs into his lapel buttonholes, assumed his favorite spread-legged stance, and appeared to be inspecting his quarry with a huntsman's pleasure.

Dilman's shoulder and chest muscles involuntarily contracted, as if preparing for a blow. Warily, he waited.

"We-ll, Mr. President of the United States of America, I did not expect to see you come down among us. This is a surprise and a privilege for us, an historic occasion, and we welcome you, heartily welcome you."

"Thank you, Mr. Manager."

"However, at the risk of seeming downright inhospitable after your taking this trouble to ride to the Hill, I am afraid I must pose some questions that may give you discomfort, questions that your friend and counsel overlooked asking, in his blindfolded search for the truth about your behavior and competence. I hope you will be as tolerant of Zeke Miller's questions, the questions the House has requested me to propound, as you were of your friend Nathan Abrahams' questions."

"I will do my best to be tolerant of your questions, Mr. Manager."

"Well, now, I guess it would be fitting to take up the matters under review in the order your own friend and counsel arranged them. Would that be suitable to you, Mr. President of the United States?"

"As you wish, Mr. Manager."

"Like perhaps starting with the youngest in your official family, and then reading from *left* to right. This boy of yours, Julian, who pledged himself with his blood to a terrorist program of violence against the elected government and who pledged himself to extract from all of us white people an eye for an eye—has he ever engaged in similar violence before?"

"No, not before, and not now either."

"Well, I am not saying he did any grave violence, like his boss Hurley, I am only saying he pledged himself to do it, but didn't get time to carry out his pledge because the able Attorney General of this country stamped out—despite your interference—these extremists, before your boy could march with them. You knew all along that your son Julian was a member of that subversive gang, didn't you, Mr. Witness?"

"I have already denied, under oath, that I knew he was a member."

"Forgive me, a slip. I didn't mean to say that you 'knew,' only that you had 'heard' he was a member—I meant you knew because you'd heard. Who'd you hear that from? A Turnerite?"

"Yes. From someone I later learned was a Turnerite."

"Want to tell us who your informant was, Mr. Witness?"

"I see no point in that now. The Turnerites are disbanded. Their leader has been executed."

"Am I to understand you won't reveal to us the name of your Turnerite friend informant who tipped you off about Julian?"

"It would serve no useful purpose."

"Okay. You keep your little secrets. Not important. Well, so you heard Julian was a Turnerite and you confronted him with the fact?"

"Yes."

"Then, the first time Attorney General Kemmler demanded that you outlaw that vicious Group, you refused. You refused, didn't you?"

"Yes."

"Then, against the advice of the Attorney General, you got your Nigra lobbyist and tenant rent payer, Reverend Spinger, to talk privately with those kidnaper-murderers, didn't you?"

"Yes, I did."

"You had no tricky self-serving, family-protecting deals in mind, did you? Just acting on your own for the good of the country, eh?"

"Yes."

"So, Mr. President, what we have is this—you heard your son was a Turnerite, true? You heard the Turnerites were a Communist, anti-Christian violence society, true? You tried to delay their being banned, true? You sent a Nigra personal friend to call them up and negotiate something in privacy, true? Is all of that true?"

"That much of it, yes, that much is true."

"Then I say to you, Mᵣ. President of the United States, I say Article II of the House impeachment—charging you with the high crime of violating the laws of the land by hindering justice against a subversive society—I say Article II is true."

"I say it is not, Mr. Manager."

"Then let the august Senate in its wisdom here on earth, and the Lord of all of us in Heaven, judge which of us speaks truth and which of us speaks falsehood. Let us proceed, as your friend and counsel has done, with Articles I and III. What have we here? Ah, Miss Wanda Gibson. Yes, we have heard Miss Gibson's little tale on this stand today. You have a great and good friend in her, Mr. President. You won't find many woman so loyally ready to go to any ends or take any risk, ready to say anything, to protect someone who is not legally their own mate. Well, now, you've known our Miss Gibson intimately for five years?"

"I have known Miss Gibson for five years."

"You have held her hand?"

"Yes."

"You have embraced her?"

"Yes."

"You have kissed her?"

"Yes."

"You have done all of this for five years, sixty months, more than 240 weeks, but you have never illicitly touched her? Is that right, Mr. President?"

"Yes."

"Yet, could I describe your relationship with her as a close one, a warm one?"

"You might. I think so."

"Sure enough, we know you couldn't keep away from her person very long. The first day you were moved out from under the same roof with her, to be President, you came hurrying back that night, thinking you'd given everyone the slip. You did run back to see Wanda Gibson the first night after you moved into the White House?"

"Yes, I did."

"You tried to get her into the White House, too, didn't you? You invited your lady friend to come to the State Dinner for President Amboko of Baraza, didn't you?"

"Yes, I did."

"Sounds like a close enough relationship to me. And the two of you, when you were together, you had your long chatty talks, didn't you?"

"Yes, of course."

"Seeing her after you became President, talking to her on the telephone, you told her what it was like to be President, didn't you?"

"Yes, I did."

"And she, working for the Communist Front Vaduz Exporters, she talked about her boss and her work sometimes, too, didn't she?"

"Yes."

"So you two, holding hands, hugging and kissing, you two talked about your jobs. You talked about what it was like being President with all the problems of that office, and she, she talked about what it was like being at work for a spying company fronting for the Soviet Union, but despite all the talk and talk, and emotional involvement, you kept your lips sealed when it came to what was top-secret that you knew about as President. True?"

"Yes, that is true."

"And I say, and the House says, untrue—*un-true!* No human on earth can be so long intimate with a single lady, being single himself, and being close to her flesh, and whispering and baring every emotion, and still control and shut off certain things while saying others, as any psychologist on earth will tell you. I'm not saying you set out with your mind determined on committing treason. I'm saying you are a frail human, and a frail human person, be he Nigra or white, suffers from his flesh being weak, and I'm saying from the evidence on hand that you committed inadvertent treason, but serious, real treason nevertheless, against the flag and the country. But you alone will not admit to your flesh being weak. You will not admit your sin."

"There is nothing to admit to, Mr. Manager. The charge is rigged up from hearsay, deductions, suppositions, wishes, an effort to make two and two add up to five, but it is unsubstantiated by factual evidence. Because no such evidence exists."

"There is evidence enough, Mr. Witness, and none of this protesting too much will pull the wool over the eyes of the able, learned, honorable members of the Senate. There is evidence for Article I as there is evidence for Article III. Let's take the charge of your proved record of habitual intoxication. You deny it. Your lady friend denies it. Two *impartial* sources like you two deny it. But the documents, Mr. President, the exhibit documents attest and affirm to the truth of it. Were you or were you not, in Springfield, Illinois, once a registered occupant in a sanitarium for alcoholics?"

"I was, yes."

"Along with your poor deceased wife?"

"Yes."

"You were a patient there?"

"No, I was not. My wife was a patient. I was a guest. I checked in there to live with her, be beside her, help her. I was not a patient. I was a resident guest."

"The photostatic evidence introduced as exhibits show clearly, irrefutably, you were a registered 'patient,' meaning, by definition, one who was under treatment or care by a physician, in this case for alcoholism."

"I don't care how I was registered. I know why I was there."

"Mr. President, I assure you the public cares and the Senate cares how you were registered. There is no disgrace in having been registered for alcoholic cure, once the cure has been successful and a person's health, good sense, and dignity restored. But when a person has attempted to be cured, and not succeeded, has continued to be the servant of this debilitating master, and raged through the President's House of this glorious nation in a condition such as Senator Watson's daughter has described, I say the public must care and the Senate must care, and the addict must be curbed and quarantined, if not for his own sake, then for the survival of the nation entrusted to his leadership. Enough! It is time we discuss a charge no less evil, and far more shocking. . . . Mr. President, the House of Representatives has charged you with improper assault upon the person of your helpless young social secretary, Miss Watson. The lady has confirmed, under oath, your misbehavior. Miss Watson, the only daughter of a great and senior Senator whose adherence to truth is a byword in the land, Miss Watson was raised up to gracious ladyhood under the guidance of this noble Senator. Miss Watson, I repeat, confirms the charge of your scandalous behavior. You deny it. Whom are we to believe? What are we to believe? . . . Mr. President—answer this, sir —can we believe that you and Miss Watson were alone together in the Lincoln Bedroom of the White House on the night in question? Is that so?"

"Yes."

"Can we believe that you had her alone in there, were alone with her, the entire period of time?"

"Yes."

"You did not send for the valet or housekeeper? You remained alone with Miss Watson?"

"Yes. Because of Miss Watson's unsettled state, I rang for no one. I still hoped to protect her good name, for her father's sake as well as her own."

"You claim she invaded your room, yet you summoned no one. I consider that highly unnatural and abnormal. On the other hand, had you brought her to your room, kept her there, your reluctance to call for outside assistance would be more understandable. In any event, no third party was summoned, no third party intruded, and there were the two of you behind closed doors and four walls. That is correct, is it not?"

"I have already agreed that it is correct—the fact of it, not the implication."

"Then, Mr. President, what followed, the truth of it, plainly comes down to our acceptance of Miss Watson's word on what took place or your own. Whose word shall we believe? Shall we believe the word of a naïve, unworldly young lady, educated, of unblemished reputation, the only child reared to the blossom of youthful ma-

turity by the most revered legislator in the land, who has
nothing to gain from the unpleasant ordeal of giving
testimony here today? Or shall we believe the word of a
witness who, according to the serious indictment voted
by the House of Representatives, had secret dealings
with a gang of Nigras bent on mongrelizing and weakening the nation, who kept intimate company with an
unmarried female friend for half a decade, who was
frequently under the unholy influence of alcoholic spirits? Mr. Witness, whose word shall it be? This you cannot answer, nor can I. We will let our peers, dedicated
and objective men, steeped in human insight, decide this
question. And for ourselves, we will undertake to discuss
the final Article of Impeachment. . . . Mr. Witness, the
morning after our beloved T.C.'s tragic death, upon your
assumption of the Presidency, you did meet with the
members of the Cabinet?"

"I did."

"Mr. Secretary of State Arthur Eaton was, by rank,
the first member of that Cabinet, was he not?"

"He was."

"Was the purpose of this meeting a desire, on your
part, to inform the Cabinet members to stay on their
jobs? In fact, did you request them to stay on and serve
you as they served T.C.?"

"I did."

"And the Secretary of State, and the other members,
they agreed to remain at their posts?"

"They did."

"Why did you desire Secretary of State Eaton to continue as the head of the Department of State and as the
leading member of your Cabinet?"

"At the time, I thought him competent in his office and
useful to the government. There was no reason to replace
Eaton or anyone else under the circumstances."

"But after several months, you found reason to fire
your Secretary of State, contrary to the law of the land,
and to replace him with an underling?"

"Yes, I did."

"You knew, of course, that Secretary Eaton was a

close friend of the late President, dedicated to promoting T.C.'s ideals of government, did you not?"

"That was the talk. I had heard it."

"Of course, you were aware, you knew, that should you suffer disability or death, it was Secretary Eaton who would become President of the United States in your place?"

"Yes."

"As time passed, could you see that Arthur Eaton, through the integrity of his behavior, because of his adherence to the policies of T.C., was growing in popularity as a national figure?"

"I would have no way of evaluating that."

"In fact, that as Arthur Eaton's popularity dramatically increased, so, conversely, your own popularity, Mr. President, drastically decreased?"

"That may be. I repeat, I would have no way of knowing the truth."

"No way of knowing you were rapidly becoming the most unpopular President in history? Unpopular among those of your own race as well as among whites? Come now, do not make mockery of the intelligence of the learned senators by pretending you had no way of knowing that the electorate disapproved of you and fully approved of Secretary Eaton. Weren't you hooted into silence by those of your own race at Trafford University? Did not one of your own color, a fellow Nigra, make an attempt to assassinate you? Answer me that."

"Yes."

"In your recent trip around the nation, weren't your public appearances greeted with booing and catcalling? Weren't you castigated and threatened? Answer me that."

"Yes."

"And did not all this unpopularity, along with Secretary Eaton's obvious popularity, convince you that you might be forced and pressured by the American people to resign from your office, so that at last they could have for President a man whom you've just called competent and useful? Weren't you afraid that as long as Arthur

Eaton was in public office, you might be thrown out and be replaced by him, and therefore—?"

"That is an utter falsehood, Mr. Manager, a false assumption, and a vicious accusation."

"You fired Arthur Eaton because his presence was a threat to you. You also fired him because you could not manipulate him, bend him to accept your prejudices, and you tried to replace him with Mr. Stover, who would gratefully comply with any policy and order you wished to impose on the people. I say—"

"Mr. Manager, you are not interrogating me, you are lecturing me. And you are attempting to brainwash the Senate. Your assumptions are a tissue of lies, produced by your imagination, which you are trying to stuff into the senators' heads."

"Is that so? I am sure the able senators may see for facts what you prefer to see as a tissue of lies. Contrary to your reckless claim, the great Secretary of State was trying to preserve you in office, not usurp your office. If you yourself were not conscious of your inept bumbling of domestic and foreign affairs, and the national hostility this had engendered, Arthur Eaton was aware, as a dedicated patriot he was extremely aware, and devoted himself to protecting you from yourself, if only to preserve peace and the continuity of our government. If he withheld certain CIA documents from you, it was because he knew how dangerous they might be in your hands, how you might misuse the information because of your own unbalanced feelings about your race. Secretary Eaton's reward for this act of patriotism was to be fired, illegally and lawlessly fired, by you. It is evident to one and all today, this very day, that Secretary Eaton was acting in the right in temporarily withholding from you certain hearsay information about Baraza. Because as we now see, once you had illegally removed your Secretary of State and learned what he tried to keep from you, you performed and are still performing as injudiciously and as dangerously as he had feared you would. You are ready to send American troops into Africa, are you not?"

"Yes, I am. I have already informed the American public of that possibility."

"You are aware that Baraza has a population that is 100 per cent black?"

"Yes, I am perfectly aware of that."

"Do you admit that, even if you alone think it should be done, you are ready to pour into the defense of this primitive African Nigra tract the peerless product of American manhood, to sacrifice rocketry battalions that are, by coincidence, 100 per cent white-skinned?"

"Yes, that is true."

"Have you read the published accounts, only two hours ago released, that Premier Kasatkin spoke last night, in an address made in Leningrad, and said any American troops sent by you into Baraza would be regarded by the Soviet Union as an act of aggression? And that the Soviet Union would not stand for it?"

"Yes, I have been informed of his speech. I have not read the newspaper accounts."

"Mr. President, are you prepared to risk the consequences of a worldwide nuclear war to protect something called Baraza?"

"Every head of this nation, henceforth, will have to risk the possibility of nuclear war to protect both America's freedom and democracy elsewhere."

"Or, in this case, to protect a patch of foreign jungle because its inhabitants are black, and you are black?"

"I trust that is not a formal question. I would not demean myself by replying to it."

"We-ll, Mr. Witness, I am certain our honorable Secretary of State would be honest enough to reply to any question concerned with our life and our liberty. Nor would Secretary Eaton have countenanced the reckless and suicidal policy you are promoting. That is why I charge that you, knowing his feeling, and in defiance of law and the Senate, decided to thrust him aside. Tell me, Mr. Witness, do you consider yourself wiser than Arthur Eaton? Better versed in foreign affairs? More loving of your homeland than one whose ancestors came to these shores on the *Mayflower* and founded this republic to which your antecedents were later invited? No, there is no need to answer those questions. You need answer only this one: Do you feel that in recent weeks, and today, you have acted and are acting in the best interests of the United States, without being swayed by any outside pressures, without being influenced by any prejudices of any kind?"

"Mr. Manager, no man on earth can say to you in naked honesty that he comes to a decision, arrives at a judgment, entirely devoid of prejudices. All men are possessed of certain prejudices, certain feelings, certain emotions toward every problem they face. These prejudices need not necessarily be harmful or bad. More often, they are good, and collaborate with intelligence and common sense. I have prejudices, strong prejudices, against tyranny, slavery, against arrogance, deceit, against vengefulness, demagoguery, against poverty, ignorance. I can only say to you that my understanding of the Presidency, its responsibilities, has grown inside me these last weeks, and perhaps I have grown with the office, grown in the knowledge of myself and other men, grown in my vision of what our country and the world should be and can be. Today I am trying to act in the interests of every man, white or colored, who believes in a human being's right to possess dignity, independence, equality among his fellow men. Today I am doing my best, doing what I believe to be best. I hope my decisions, and the results of these decisions, will be proved right. But no man, not even such a one as our recent Secretary of State, can always be right. We are both human beings. Human beings are fallible, they make mistakes—"

"Mr. President, forgive me for interrupting your most diverting political address. But your last remark is one I dare not overlook. Human beings, you humbly and disarmingly say, are apt to make mistakes. I suggest to you, sir, that today, in this perilous day and time, this nation cannot afford to retain in office that kind of human being, a leader, a Chief Executive, President who is apt to make a mistake—for a mistake, one mistake born of prejudice or rashness, can today mean the total annihilation of all humanity. And I fear that it is such a mistake, perpetrated by our President, that we must face, and pray to rectify in these somber hours. Mr. President, you have led us to the brink of destruction. But we have come to our senses. You shall lead us no more. . . . That is all, sir. . . . Mr. Chief Justice, as far as the House managers are concerned, the witness may be dismissed."

Douglass Dilman stood up.

He had not done well, he knew. Yet he was curiously relieved. For he had done what he had known from the first must be done: he had made the invisible Article V a part of the conscience of the court, and tomorrow he would be judged on it and nothing less.

Stepping down from the witness stand, then crossing past the podium and the table of opposition managers, he could see a crowd of press photographers, along with witnesses and page boys, jammed before and around the doorway to the Senators' Private Lobby through which he would reach the President's Room of the Senate. Then, as he moved toward the milling mob, he recognized Wanda's distressed face among those waiting for him.

That moment, he knew that there was one act left undone that he now wished done. In seconds, they would surround him, begging him to pose, and he would agree, yes, he would agree, but not before insisting that Wanda pose side by side with him. To some, it might be a small thing, but to him, it was of dominant importance. Yes, he would call her to him, because she was so beautiful, because she was so courageous, but, above all, because he must let her know that today, perhaps, he had finally earned the right to stand in public by her side.

Now, at eight forty-five in the evening, and for the first time since Dilman had become President, certainly for the first time in many weeks, Arthur Eaton felt in high spirits.

Arms folded across his vest, the ankles of his outstretched legs crossed, he sat back in the soft armchair and continued to watch the drama ooze out of the trial on the brilliantly colored television screen near the built-in bar of his living room. Chewing on the stem of his empty silver cigarette holder, Eaton followed Nat Abrahams as he plodded through his examination of the last of the defense witnesses.

For Eaton, the trial was all but ended. Except for a few bad moments in the afternoon, when his own name had been bandied about in the low exchange between Abrahams and Sally Watson, it had been a glorious and heady day. Even when President Dilman had unexpectedly taken the witness stand, no doubt denigrating himself further in the public esteem by his undignified self-pleading, and collaborated with his counsel on that defensive pap about Eaton attempting to usurp his powers, Eaton had not been dismayed. He had known that Zeke Miller would, when his turn came, demolish the President, and Miller had succeeded in so doing. Much as Eaton had formerly disliked the Southern legislator, he had been forced, more and more, to admire him for his clever (if barbaric) forensics. In fact, Eaton had told himself while watching the House manager make mincemeat of the President, if Miller were not handicapped by his inherited racial intolerance, he might make, very well might make, an excellent Attorney General in the Cabinet of a new Administration.

Eaton surmised that not only for himself, but possibly for the millions viewing the live spectacular on television. the dramatic climax of the trial had been the foolhardy exhibition of President Dilman on the witness stand. Why had he risked it? Had he expected, under his counsel's soft guidance, to sway the Senate and public to his side by his posture of persecuted martyr? If so, he had failed miserably. Zeke Miller had shown him for what he was, for the entire nation to see, not martyr but satyr, not public official but pitiful fool. That had been the high point: Dilman's fall.

All else that had followed before and after the dinner recess, and what Eaton could see now on the screen, was tiresome and technical and would change no votes. Tomorrow morning's closing addresses by Miller and Abrahams, while they might provide some pyrotechnics, could do no more than underline and emphasize, and then summarize in capsule, the strongest contentions of both sides, all of which were already known. There was nothing left to feed into the Senate's computing mind. The data had been fed. What was left, of interest, historic interest, was the answer that would be spewed out. When would the jurors vote? He remembered. They would vote tomorrow at two o'clock in the afternoon.

Arthur Eaton wondered which suit he should wear tomorrow afternoon.

The doorbell sounded, followed immediately by the heavy clanging of the antique brass front-door knocker.

Eaton came out of the armchair, perplexed. He had expected no visitors tonight. And Kay, it could not be Kay. He had sent the car to the airport after her only twenty minutes ago, and besides, her flight from Miami was probably not in yet.

Eaton opened the door, and then, to his amazement, he found himself staring at Sally Watson.

"Well, President-elect-by-the-Senate, aren't you going to let me in?" she asked.

"I'm sorry, Sally. Of course, please do come in. I guess I was surprised. I thought you'd be busy, and——I was expecting someone else. I'm going to be tied up in a little while."

"Goody for you, my hero," she said. "Well, I'm not tied up, only fit to be tied."

She went into the living room. Eaton closed the door and hastily followed her. She opened her leopard coat but did not remove it.

Pirouetting on a spiked heel to confront him, she jerked her thumb toward the television set. "Licking your chops, Arthur?"

"What does that mean?"

"Don't be senile, Arthur." She considered him. "I haven't been made very welcome. I guess it has been as long as I thought."

Unhappily, he stepped toward her and kissed her lightly on the lips. Her breath was acrid with the fumes of whiskey, and he stepped back quickly, fighting to hide his reaction.

"Don't tell me, Arthur. Let me guess. Multiple choice. Is she drunk, or sorta drunk, or very drunk?" She tried to snap her fingers, but they missed. *"Very drunk. Kee-rect!"*

"Sally, what's going on with——?"

She lifted her hand for silence. "Multiple choice number two. Is she drunk because she hasn't seen or heard from him for eight days, or because he has broken three standing dates, or because he hasn't answered six calls she made in forty-eight hours? Answer——not one but all, *all*, kee-rect! Fooled you, didn't I?"

"Sally, be reasonable. With this trial going on, every move I make is watched. Besides, I've been busy——"

"I know, darling, busy and ill——what is the illness called?——oh yes, Presidential fever. That's all that is ailing you, my hero."

"Well, what the devil is ailing you?"

"Happy to tell you." She walked farther into the room. "Am I allowed to take off my coat?"

"Sally, I wish you could, but I am expecting company in a very short time."

"Okay. A drink, then."

He was reluctant to go to the bar. "Sally, don't you think you've had enough?"

"You bet I've had enough——enough of everything—— so one more of anything won't hurt." As he reluctantly started for the bar, she added, "And shut off that damn television."

Eaton quickly complied. Then, as quickly, he poured a Scotch on ice for Sally, and a soft drink for himself.

"Here you are, dear," he said, handing her the Scotch.

Accepting the drink in one hand, she tapped his glass with the other. "You used to do better than that, when you asked me to take off my coat and more."

"There is a conference tonight. I'll have to have a clear head."

She drank at length, then she said, "All right." She brooded over the glass, then she said suddenly, "Let's have it out, Arthur. Are you trying to give me the brush, or what?"

"Give you the brush?"

"Are you trying to drop me? You know, you know, Galileo's law or whoever it was. You hold something.

You get tired holding it. You let go. It falls down and goes plop. You're free of it."

"What a mind you have. Of course not, Sally. Don't be silly. You know how I feel about you."

She brought her long fingers to her crimson lips in a feigned pose of profound reflection. "I want to see if I can remember—how you feel about me, I mean. Ah yes, that last time in bed—when was it? Twelve nights ago? That was quite a session, wasn't it?"

Eaton wanted to squirm. There was something about her, her too blond hair, her too darkly shadowed eyes, her too powdered cheeks, her too red lips, something about her flippant and coarsened speech, and something left over from the way she had behaved on the witness stand; there was all that which seemed to cheapen her and make her less attractive than she had ever been.

And now, her vulgar reference to their last time together. He wanted only to be done with her, to file her in his history as finished business, and be left alone to go on with life. But here she was, unfiled, and the vulgar question hung between them.

"Yes," he said, "I—I won't ever forget that evening."

"How could you? I knew you wouldn't. And I knew you hadn't forgotten what you promised. You haven't, have you?"

He had forgotten. The Lord save him from women. They remembered everything, everything. How could they expect a man to remember what he said—men said anything, they were all Alexanders promising empires—under those circumstances? What in the devil *had* he said? He could guess, but he would not, aloud. He waited. She would tell him.

"I've been waiting for you to call me, Arthur. I've been living for that call. What happened when you asked her? Will she give you the divorce, or will you have to go out to Reno and get it?"

Divorce, he thought. That was it. He must have been out of his mind. If treaties were made in bed, he thought, women would own the world. What in the devil could he say to her now, to be rid of her? The diplomatic truth, that was best; that was his style, and none exceeded him at it.

"Yes, of course, Sally, it has been on my mind, too, but you know, divorce is not that simple a matter," he said pedantically. Almost instinctively, he was moving them away from the heated, irrational atmosphere of the bedroom into the cooler, logical surroundings of the civil courtroom. "You know my feelings about Kay, and you've known my feelings toward you, Sally. I have desired a divorce, and kept it no secret from you. However, I've suddenly come up against one hard mathematical fact of life. It takes two to accomplish a divorce, not one. I broached it to Kay on the telephone a few days ago, and she would not have it. She is adamant. Separation she will abide, but not a divorce. So all I can do, until I have definite grounds against her, is to work on her, wear her down, and trust that her own sense of decency—"

Sally's pale face was cold. "She won't give you a divorce? Or is that State Department Eatonese for—you've decided not to ask her?"

"Sally, I did ask her. She doesn't give a damn about me, but she likes the idea of being married—"

"So do I, Arthur."

"—and now she likes it more than ever, since everything seems to be changing in my life. She's been watching that impeachment trial like everyone else. She has a good idea they'll drum Dilman out of office. If they do, she sees herself in the White House as First Lady. There's no use trying to reason with her about a divorce at present, not while the result of the trial is still pending. In fact, well, I'll be honest with you, because you must believe in me, Sally—the fact is, Kay has decided to come back to Washington. She's on her way back right now —she's, well, she is the person I'm expecting in a half hour. She wants to be here for the kill tomorrow."

Sally began to laugh, and then threw back her head and laughed hysterically, and it made Eaton uneasy to watch her. Then her laughter broke into a sob, and she choked to control it.

"This is too much," she cried out, "too, too much, the

irony, to think it's my fault, I'm responsible for creating my own Frankenstein monster—me—doing what I did —snooping, spying, going through hell, suffering that goddam insulting exposure in the Senate today—those questions, I wanted to die—die—and what was it all for? For you, so you could become President, and now never leave that old bag who wants to be First Lady."

"Sally, listen—"

She was breathing like a wounded animal now, and her eyes were glazed and staring. "But you know what's worse, Arthur? That you're lying to me, you are lying. You used me, like you use everyone, and I couldn't see it because I wanted to be used, because I thought there'd be something in it for me, too. I should have known. There's nothing for me. It's all you, everything's for you."

"That is not true, Sally. If you'll calm down a minute—"

She was too furious to listen. "I know what is true! You never asked your bag of a wife for a divorce. She's not coming here to stand in the wings, hoping she'll be First Lady. It's you. You want to be President so badly, it smells, it stinks, the reek can be smelled a mile away. So no more bedroom gymnastics, no more, no more taking changes by you. You want to be there, lily-white and aristocratic and Ivy League, with the one and only wife of foreverness and togetherness on your arm, waiting in home beautiful, living the life beautiful, waiting for your country's call the minute they boot that poor unbefitting nigger interloper out of your White House! Now everything's got to be perfect, everything pure and American! Now you've got to quickly, quickly, sweep all dirt under the carpet, all dirt and maybe scandal, and there I go, under the carpet, too—"

"Stop it, Sally! You're behaving like an insane—"

"Don't you call me insane, you lousy, dirty no-good bastard!" she screamed, and then, before he could move, she drew her right hand back, flung it forward, and emptied the entire contents of her whiskey glass into his face.

As he sputtered, wiping his eyes and shirt with his

handkerchief, she yelled, "I hope the whole world finds you out the way I did, you bastard!"

She ran out of the room, and out of the house; and Arthur Eaton, watching her, continuing to clean the dripping whiskey from his face and clothes, was no longer upset. In fact, he was pleased. It had been less costly than he had expected. For the price of a wet handkerchief, a change of apparel, and a minor indignity, he was rid of her forever.

Then, when she saw the door close, she started running.

Before that, Sally Watson did not know how long she had been waiting.

After leaving Arthur, and reeling down the cement steps into the lonely and darkened Georgetown street, she had not known where to turn, where to go. The two Secret Service men, in the car parked across the way, had pretended not to see her. She had pretended not to see them. She had started off, to nowhere, because there was no place left where she could any longer find peace from rage and shame, and then she had changed her mind.

She had come back toward the house, staying inside the shadows thrown by the stately mansions, hidden from the yellow pools of illumination under the street-lamps, and then, two houses from his, clinging to a chilled metal rail, in a recess out of sight, she had waited, senselessly waited, shivering, hating, waiting.

How long had it been, finally? Fifteen minutes? Twenty? However long it takes to die.

Once an automobile had drawn up, and it was not Kay Varney Eaton who had emerged, but five other persons, three of them male photographers, two of them (one whom she knew) women social columnists, and, chattering and cheerful, they had gathered on the sidewalk before Eaton's residence.

Finally the limousine had arrived, and the chauffeur had leaped out and hastened to open the rear door. And there she was, that *old* woman, Kay Varney Eaton, tall and imperial, in her mink coat and mink hat, giving her diamond-laden hand and condescending stone smile to the serfs of the press. There were shrill questions, and requests to pose this way and that, and flashlight bulbs twinkling on and off, and then she had gone, First Lady-elect-almost, up the stairs. And at the top, horrid traitor's face wreathed in a smile, Arthur was welcoming her, a self-conscious embrace before the cameras, an antiseptic cheek kiss, and then, a husbandly arm around her, he had taken her inside their house.

Then, when she saw the door close, she started running.

Sally went blindly, crazily, drunkenly up the street, and at the intersection fell against the post of a stop-light, gasping for air. A cruising taxi slowed, and she hailed it.

Inside, disheveled, mascara on her cheekbones, she was still too choked to speak, unable to direct the Negro cabdriver, who was attending her with curiosity, where to take her. Again, there was nowhere to go. But the last unimpaired although dying impulse of her self-esteem began to form her utterance. Only in one place, in months, years, a lifetime, had she had a *raison d'être*. So, not she, for she was no more, but the surviving impulse within her gave voice to her suicidal mood.

"Take me to—to the White House," she said thickly.

She tried to look at the domes and spires of this city of monuments which she had dirtied, but she could not see. She tried to smoke a cigarette, but dropped it. She tried to cry, but no tears came, for total wretchedness suffused her heart and dry lungs.

She could not breathe, that was the worst of it. The inside of the careening taxi was dank, foul, suffocating. She made out a patch of wooded area, the tree-bowered walks ahead, and she cried out, "Boy—lemme off there —right there—Jackson and H—lemme out!"

The taxi swung into H Street, and she shoved a bill into the driver's hand, released the door and herself, and went weaving into Lafayette Park, past the frost-bitten Steuben statue, past the wet vacant benches, into the park, deeper and deeper, going nowhere.

Her sickened, self-lamenting brain would not stay behind, let her be free, but remained in the cage of her
skull, mercilessly haunting and chastising her. Down
through the liquor haze, her relentlessly chasing brain
showed her herself as she was: the ghastly scene in the
Lincoln Bedroom, the overpainted woman on the Senate
podium spouting her distorted adventures into Abrahams' pitying face, the degraded sound of her name on
that sorrowful black man President's tongue today.

All at once, through the last trees of the park, she
saw the incredible sight, and seeing what she saw, her
heart and legs quickened at the strange madness of it, a
nightmare, another nightmare, and again she was running, drawn to the brightness ahead like a moth batting
against a light.

She came through Lafayette Park, bursting out on the
sidewalk of Pennsylvania Avenue, and then stood
paralyzed with disbelief at what was happening in the
night.

To be seen through the iron grillwork fence, engrav-
ing itself in licking flames on the slope of the White
House lawn, beyond the fence and before the North
Portico, blazing in the night, burned a fiery cross.

There was more than the mammoth red glowing cross
on the White House lawn, she could see. There were
men around the cross, and in the White House driveway, and men clogging the open gate and straining past
the guardhouse entrance. There were whooping young
white men, rampaging hoodlums with incandescent
torches, fleeing the lawn, then grappling and slugging it
out and rolling on the grass and cement when caught
by the white and colored White House policemen and
Secret Service agents.

The pitched battle between the white marauders and
hooligans who had incinerated a section of the lawn,
now trying to escape, and the White House police trying
to contain and arrest them, centered about the entrance
gate. The convulsive sounds of men become animals,
the sounds of clubs thudding on bone and flesh, of
human wailing and cursing, of shotgun blasts in the sky
and shrilling metallic whistles, made Sally recoil.

And suddenly, so suddenly, there was another sound —that of skidding rubber tires, angry brakes—and there was another sight—dozens of cars surging into Pennsylvania Avenue, erupting with shrieking men, black and white, most of them black, young and old, most of them young, all of them frenzied and armed.

More speeding and jolting cars were emptying out their vengeful cargoes of fierce Negroes or bellowing ofays and pinks. At once, the snarling white bullyboys who had branded the President's House, and those rushing to reinforce them, and the embittered products of the capital's squalid black slums that ringed the White House, who had had enough, enough, who would protect this one of their own, now as persecuted as they were, locked themselves into brutish pitched battle.

From the dark rim of the park, still standing detached, Sally Watson watched as if in a hypnotic trance.

The fighters milled through the street before her, striking and being struck, hurting and being hurt, vilifying and being vilified. And as she watched the race riot —the knives and scissors rising and falling, the broken bottles jabbing, the chains swinging, the hurled rocks flying, the brawling blacks and whites cursing, sobbing, shrieking with pain, the beaten men with slashed bloodied faces and smashed jaws loosened in their sockets, men whining, whimpering, going down—as she saw all of this demoniac barbarity, Sally slowly began to relate it to herself.

The seething caldron of humanity was not the result of her witchcraft, the product of her madness alone, Sally knew. The causes were wider, deeper, older than the provocation of her own evil. Yet it was, this wildness in the night, more her doing than that of any other person present.

She wanted to tell them this, tell one and all, tell them to stop doing this to one another and to do their cruelty to her.

This must cease.

They must punish her.

Unsteadily, tripping once, twice, she left the sidewalk and made her way into the swirling center of the riot.

Dimly, she was aware of the inflamed, gap-toothed, bleeding Negro faces raging around her. Dimly, she was aware of the howling, spattered-nosed white faces fulminating around her. Dimly, she was aware of policemen in uniforms and soldiers in fatigues, hammering right and left with their billy clubs and rifle butts.

The jagged edges of a bottle ripped through her coat. A rock struck her shoulder and sent her plunging to her knees. A heavy combat boot skidded against her mouth.

She crawled between legs, then staggered upright, begging them to stop, but no one heard, and she was buffeted and slapped, and then she felt the spittle and blood mingling down her face. Then, unaccountably, she begged them not to kill her, not to kill her, until she did what she must do. Pushing, tearing, fighting, beating her fists, she tried to free herself from the rioters.

And then suddenly there was room to run once more.

She looked about, trying to make out what was happening, what was breaching and parting the mob, and then she could see. Police cruisers and army trucks were surrounding the thoroughfare. Lawmen with their pistols and leashed dogs, khaki-clad soldiers with their carbines rattling gunfire overhead, helmeted firemen with their swelling and flooding hoses, swarmed through the battleground, dispersing whites and blacks.

She had wanted to reach the White House sentry box, but she could only reach the iron fence. She gripped the metal pickets to keep from falling, and then her legs gave, and she slid to the pavement.

There was the sound of feet, and then she heard her name and opened her eyes.

She blinked up into the worried features of a mulatto woman, blinked up with no recognition.

"Miss Watson—Sally—are you badly hurt?"

"I dunno—no—not—what's your—"

Then, for Sally, recognition came. She had seen the mulatto face before, yes, every day, newspapers, television, Senate, yes, Wanda Gibson, Wanda Gibson, President's lady.

"I'd better find you help—" Wanda Gibson was saying.

Sally closed her eyes, listening to the sirens, and then through stinging, puffed lips, she groaned, "No, Wanda —no—just get me home—please, please, take me to my father—you take me—I—I've got to tell him something, it's important—help me—it's important to both of us."

It was almost midnight, and they were still there in the Oval Office. From the sofa, Nat Abrahams, smoking his pipe, calmly watched, listened, and marveled anew at Douglass Dilman's energy.

The President looked up from his desk at Tim Flannery and General Leo Jaskawich nearby, and he handed the sheet of paper back to his press secretary.

"That release will do fine, Tim," he said. "I think we have given the facts, and it's a fair enough statement about the riot so that it will please both sides or neither. . . . There's been no later news from the city police?"

"No," said Flannery. "Luckily, no deaths, and no one on the critical list, but there were 187 injured, a few concussions, mostly cuts and lacerations, broken ribs, a couple of fractured arms. It was bad, but it could've been worse. Remember that race riot in Detroit in 1943? Went on for a week. Thirty-four killed and almost one thousand hurt. I think fast action saved us here. The whole thing was contained in ten to fifteen minutes."

"Thank the Lord," said Dilman. "All right, Tim, you can roll out that release, give it to the correspondents, and let them go home. Better get some sleep yourself."

After Flannery had left, Dilman's gaze held on Abrahams briefly. "Still puzzles me, Nat, what Wanda is doing over at Senator Watson's, of all places, and what the Senator wants with me at this hour. Well, as long as Wanda is safe and sound."

Before the lighting of the fiery cross on the lawn,

and the resulting riot, Dilman had been expecting Wanda Gibson to come to a late White House dinner, Abrahams knew. The riot itself had diverted Dilman's mind from her for an hour, but once the troublemakers had been dispersed and the area was under patrol and was peaceful again, and Wanda had still not appeared, Dilman had become fretful. His concern was that she might have been caught in the fighting, and injured.

Even when no woman's name was reported on the injury list, Dilman had continued to fret. Then the telephone call had come through. It had been Wanda on the other end, at last, to apologize for not appearing. Something had come up, she had explained, and she was now at Senator Hoyt Watson's house, and no, there was nothing wrong, she would explain later, but meanwhile, Senator Watson had asked to see the President tonight. "Tonight?" Dilman had protested, and then, as far as Abrahams could guess, Wanda had said that she thought the President should see him, that it was something important, for Dilman had replied, "Very well, Wanda, if you think so. Have him come over." All of that had transpired a half hour ago.

Like Dilman, Abrahams wondered what Wanda was doing in the dugout of the enemy, and what Senator Watson wanted with the President at this late hour. It was all highly irregular.

Dilman had swung his chair toward Jaskawich.

"Well, General, any last-minute intelligence from the international-situation room downstairs?"

"Status quo. The pins in the map are unchanged. The teletypes are still. Absolutely no word from Kasatkin, or the Soviet Embassy here. And nothing new from Baraza City. Just what we had earlier. Continuing signs of growing activity on the frontier. And you've already heard from Steinbrenner. The battalions of the Dragon Flies will be airborne and heading for Africa in—let me see—about two hours."

"It looks like a fight, doesn't it?"

"I'm afraid so, Mr. President."

"You know, General, something occurred to me before. I think we all have the same feeling about this action. Not you, or Nat, or I want to see a drop of American blood shed, and yet we agree this is right; as things are, it has to be done. But what occurred to me was—by a fluke of fate—and to our eternal shame—it may never be done. You don't understand me, do you? I'll tell you. Suppose the Communists launch their attack, as planned, tomorrow, and suppose we are there to meet them. At two o'clock tomorrow, the Senate jury starts its vote on me. If I'm convicted, thrown out—why, by late tomorrow afternoon there can be a new President of the United States sworn in—and with Eaton in this chair, I can just see him with Fortney, making our troops retreat, recalling them, agreeing to a phony armistice. In a week from now, Amboko would be in a dungeon, and his democracy, our democracy, there with him. And the Soviets would have a satellite country in Africa. All we're trying to do, all we've done, may be wasted if two-thirds of the Senate tomorrow says I'm a Negro out to trade white boys to save Africans."

"I hope we don't live to see that happen, Mr. President," said Jaskawich fervently.

"We likely will," said Dilman. "You may have worked your last full day as a Presidential military attaché. Hope they still have a place for an unemployed astronaut. Well, you'd better get some sleep, too."

"Good night, Mr. President. . . . Good night, Mr. Abrahams."

Once Jaskawich had departed, the two friends were alone for the first time that day. Abrahams moved from the sofa to the chair across from Dilman. He began to analyze the closing speeches that would be made before the Senate tomorrow morning, first what he anticipated must be expected from Zeke Miller, and then the defense points that he himself wished to stress.

They had been discussing this for no more than five minutes, when they were interrupted by a knocking on the door between the Oval Room and the personal secretary's office.

"Yes?" Dilman called out.

The door swung open, and a haggard Edna Foster stood in it.

"Are you still here?" Dilman said. "I appreciate it, Miss Foster, but I want you to get right home."

"Yes, Mr. President. I was only waiting for Senator Hoyt Watson's arrival. He is here now."

"Oh. All right, show him in."

Dilman stood up, alive with curiosity, and so did Abrahams, as Miss Foster held the door wider and Senator Hoyt Watson came through it. When the door closed, he advanced slowly toward the President.

Abrahams had never seen the formidable Senator Watson this close before, and in this light. It surprised Abrahams how old the Senator appeared as he dragged his feet across the Oval Office. Midway in his passage he had with one hand removed his dark felt hat, and with the other adjusted his string tie, but he made no effort to divest himself of the birch cane hooked on his arm or the velvet-lapeled overcoat. Hatless, his hump of white hair mussed, his horsy, lumpy face seemed longer than ever and more doleful.

"Good evening, sir," he said to Dilman. "It is kind of you to see me at this time. I gather that Miss Gibson telephoned to notify you of my intended visit?"

"Yes, Senator," said Dilman cautiously, confused by Watson's courtesy. "Please sit down." He indicated Abrahams. "Is this anything you'd prefer to discuss in privacy?"

"No," said Senator Watson, sitting with a grunt on the edge of the chair, "no, I would prefer to speak in front of your counsel. I shall be brief. I come here with a heavy heart, and with little to say, yet what I do say must necessarily be said by me tonight since it is important for you, both of you, to hear it tonight. My daughter Sally was caught up in the unfortunate riot outside this evening. She suffered some bruises, a minor laceration, but was otherwise uninjured. What did happen to her, whatever happened, apparently shook her back to her senses. She was found by Miss Gibson on the sidewalk, in a somewhat delirious condition, and Miss Gibson brought her directly to our house and to me."

Senator Watson fell silent, nodding at the desk calendar, and Dilman, for want of anything better to say, said, "I'm glad she's well, Senator."

The legislator raised his head and shook it sorrowfully. "She is not well, sir. She never was, but I refused to face that truth, or accept it. I closed my eyes to her behavior and instability, but no more, no more. Tonight I saw Sally for what she always has been. She is ill, mentally ill, and there is no more hiding from it. You, Counselor Abrahams, surmised as much in your crossexamination. I despised you for doing so, because I suspected the truth but could not accept it. But you were right, and I must learn to live with it."

Senator Watson unhooked the birch cane from his arm and leaned it against the desk front, and met Dilman's eyes.

"Sir," Senator Watson said, "my daughter has confessed what really happened that evening with you. She has confessed it before me, Miss Gibson, and an attorney friend I brought in to record it and witness her signature on it. Sally admitted having—having become involved with Secretary Eaton—then going to your bedroom to take notes from a CIA report, then being discovered by you, insulting you, and fashioning the entire episode into a lie to satisfy Eaton, Miller, Hankins. She did you grievous harm, Mr. President, and perjured herself before the body of the Senate, and I cannot let things rest this way another moment, or neither she nor I shall have peace again."

His hand had gone inside his overcoat, and he withdrew a blue-covered folded document.

"I have Sally's full statement recorded here, signed in her hand, witnessed and notarized. I suggest your counselor make use of it in his closing address to the Senate tomorrow, to let the truth be told, and destroy that specification in the House's indictment. I wish I could offer you further redress. You deserve it. All I can offer you is this document, Sally's wish for forgiveness, and my own deep apology."

Abrahams watched, his mind in turmoil, as Senator Watson bent forward and held the document out for Douglass Dilman to accept.

Dilman stared at the paper. His hands remained motionless on the desk. His eyes went from the signed confession to the legislator.

Slowly Dilman shook his head. "No, Senator. I don't want it. Tear it up and throw it away."

The document trembled in Watson's fingers, but still he continued to offer it. "Please, sir, you will need it, you will need as much truth on your side as possible tomorrow."

"No," Dilman repeated. "She is ill, as you have said, and ill people can be cured and saved. The public entering of this retraction and admission into the trial would destroy Sally forever. She would be beyond help, and as one who also has a daughter, a daughter who is ill and not yet destroyed, I will be no party to this. I appreciate it, Senator, but no. My acquittal or conviction will not be decided by this, by the Article charging this lie, nor by any of the other Articles."

With reluctance, Senator Watson withdrew the deposition, turned it over in his gnarled hand several times, considering it, and then he looked up.

"You are generous, sir, and a gentleman," he said to Dilman. "You must understand, however, that this humane decision on your part can have no influence on my vote tomorrow afternoon. I would not have judged against you if I believed you had behaved against my daughter as first charged by herself and the House, solely on that indictment, and I cannot judge in your favor now, simply in knowing my daughter perjured herself and that the House was misled. You understand that, sir?"

"I do."

Senator Watson tore the document in half, and then tore it into halves again, and he stuffed the shredded paper into his overcoat pocket.

Once more he looked at Dilman. "I must judge you tomorrow on your merits as a President of the United States. I must decide in the matter of Baraza, taking that as being representative of all other matters and the most crucial, whether you acted wisely or unwisely as a President, and whether you acted as an American President or as a Negro President. The majority of my Southern colleagues are against you, and have judged you on other issues. The minority of members are for you, and have judged you on other issues. But the final weight of tomorrow's independent vote falls on a great number of our one hundred who sleep tonight and who have not prejudged you, but must awaken with a final decision based on consideration of your merits as a man who is President."

"I ask for nothing more, whatever the outcome," said Dilman quietly.

Senator Hoyt Watson came wearily to his feet. "Thank you, Mr. President," he said, and then, head nodding, he left the room.

From somewhere distant, a clock struck midnight, and time went on past midnight, and the life of the new day had begun.

IX

Born of some half-remembered superstition from Douglass Dilman's childhood was his hope that the sun would shine on this momentous and decisive day of his life, and its appearance would be a lucky omen, melting the hard hearts of his enemies and reviving the spirits of his allies.

Nature was deaf and blind to human superstition.

There was no sun this late November day. Bellicose, brooding clouds, like threatening hosts of strife, gathered low in the bleak sky. The air was wintry, the temperature twenty degrees above zero, and the steady wind from the Potomac swept rawly over the high-strung capital city.

The headlines slashed across the newspapers on the table behind his Oval Office desk were as chilly and ominous as the weather: CRUCIAL IMPEACHMENT VOTE IN SENATE TODAY; PREVIEW POLL INDICATES "CONVICTION CERTAIN" . . . TENSION MOUNTS IN AFRICA; SECRECY ENVELOPS AMERICAN TROOP MOVEMENTS; U.S.S.R. MAINTAINS SILENCE . . . SAVAGE RACE RIOT BEFORE WHITE HOUSE CONTROLLED AS FLAMING CROSS BURNS ON PRESIDENT'S LAWN; WHITES AND NEGROES CLASH IN DOZEN CITIES.

Douglass Dilman tried to ignore the headlines as he came around his desk.

"All right, Tim," he said. "Let's get it over with."

It was one minute to ten o'clock in the morning as Dilman left his office, preceded Flannery into his personal secretary's cubicle, nodded absently to Miss Foster, and entered the Cabinet Room to make his brief news announcement to the twenty-five White House press regulars who had been invited.

For an instant he was unable to see in the glare of the television klieg lights, but he was nevertheless conscious of the camera lens and of critical eyes following him in his unsteady walk to the table in the center of the room and the open place from which his chair had been removed.

When his full vision was restored, and he was able to make out the familiar faces in the ring of correspondents, who were armed with their yellow pencils and blank notebooks, Dilman tried to discern the amount of hostility or friendliness that awaited him. There were friendly, interested expressions on an isolated few, but mainly the features of the correspondents revealed doubt, distrust, even antipathy. They were orderly and attentive, true, but their attentiveness was that offered by cynical reporters to a nine-day wonder they had come to interview—on the ninth day.

Dilman rattled the paper in his hand. "Good morning, gentlemen. At least, I hope it will be a good morning."

There were no chuckles, no appreciation of his weak jest or concurrence with his sad wish. Three or four correspondents murmured their greetings, but otherwise the more than two dozen apathetic journalists remained silent and uncommitted to confraternity.

"I have a brief but important news announcement to make," said Dilman. He read from the triple-spaced typed lines on the sheet of paper in his hand. " 'Precisely one hour ago Eastern Standard Time, so I am informed by the Secretary of Defense and the Joint Chiefs of Staff, the battle-ready battalions of a full division of the United States Army, motorized and equipped with the latest in rocketry weapons, landed safely, and without mishap, at strategic airfields in Baraza, and at similar sites in surrounding allied African countries which are members of the African Unity Pact. I can reveal only that fifteen thousand of our soldiers are there. For security reasons, I cannot be explicit about their exact locations. These brave and well-trained men represent an elite segment of our defense forces, popularly known as the Dragon Flies. They are under the field command of Major General

C. Jarrett Rice. The military leaders of our combined African allies, in this defensive operation, will also be under the command of General Rice.' "

Dilman read ahead, to himself, and then looked up.

" 'I want to stress the nonaggressive nature of our intervention. The United States is a party to the AUP, pledged to come to the aid of any democratic African nation threatened by attack from an outside enemy. Baraza intelligence agents, as well as our own intelligence men, have supplied us with irrefutable evidence that native African Communists, trained, armed, and now led by Soviet Russian officers, are preparing to overthrow the democratically elected and constituted government of Baraza. The United States has informed the Premier of the U.S.S.R. of our obtaining this intelligence and, in unequivocal language, warned the Soviet Union that we shall honor our treaty with Baraza and the AUP, and intervene to protect our democratic neighbors wherever they are threatened. No formal reply has been received from Moscow. Since this is the case, since the Soviet buildup on the Barazan frontier continues unabated, and there have been unmistakable signs, noted through our Air Force reconnaissance flights, of heightening military activity in the last twenty-four hours, I have commanded our forces, under full cloak of security, to be transported from our shores to Africa. We are there now, and we are ready.

" 'I want to make it clear that no overt aggressive action will be undertaken by the troops of the United States or the AUP countries. They stand alert, to defend Baraza if it is struck. They will counter-attack only if the Barazan borders are invaded. If compelled to fight, the United States force will fight a conventional war with limited weapons, that is, without the use of nuclear warheads.

" 'Otherwise, all of our military establishment, here at home or dispersed around the world, is ready, as it has always been, for any eventuality. Our combat divisions, the air arm of SAC, the ICBM squadrons, our surface and undersea navy, have all been placed on strategic warning—not immediate tactical warning but the more conservative strategic warning.

" 'I repeat, the United States is ready for any eventuality. In my judgment, this is a historic necessity. As the first President of the United States, General George Washington, stated, "To be prepared for war is one of the most effectual means of preserving peace." And as he wrote, "If we are wise, let us prepare for the worst." ' "

He folded the sheet of paper, handed it to Flannery, and said, "End of statement. That is it for now, gentlemen."

About to leave, he saw a hand shoot up. He hesitated. It was the respected and moderate correspondent of the United Press International. "Mr. President—please— your quarantine on all questions, the last week or two, has made our task difficult, if not impossible. In a crisis, the American public deserves at least—"

Flannery had edged forward. "Wait now, boys, we agreed—"

Dilman took his press secretary's arm. "Never mind, Tim." He nodded to the United Press International correspondent. "All right, your question, and four more, and that is it. If I have further news, you shall be informed of it promptly. The question?"

"According to Reuters, this morning, an informant in the British Embassy in Moscow has stated that Soviet Marshal Vladimir Borov was flown to Baraza last night to take charge. Can you confirm or deny this, sir?"

Dilman said, "It is possible, but speculative. I have received no official word to that effect."

The New York *Times* correspondent asked, "Are the United States battalions being kept in their landing areas in Africa, or are they being transported inland to more strategic positions?"

"They are on the move to the frontier. If the Communists strike, we want to be in control of as much ground as possible."

"Mr. President." It was the Chicago *Tribune* correspondent speaking. "Is there any definite information on exactly when you expect the Communist rebels to invade?"

"There is no way of knowing for certain. Intelligence believes the Soviet timetable is set for late today or early tomorrow morning."

The Associated Press correspondent asked, "If an actual clash takes place, and the Russian Premier then suggests a compromise over Baraza, have you considered any alternative or revised policy in regard to our position in Baraza and toward the Pact countries?"

"As long as I am President, there will be no compromise when it concerns defending democracy anywhere."

"Mr. President," a rasping voice called out. It was Reb Blaser, of the Miller newspapers. All eyes were upon him as he pushed forward, and Dilman waited, regarding him with distaste. "Mr. President," said Blaser, "of course, the Senate will have something to say about what you have just announced. Are you aware that a sampling poll made of the Senate members last night, by the House managers, indicates that the sentiment stands eighty senators for your conviction, twenty for your acquittal, and therefore the Senate has thirteen more votes than the necessary two-thirds required to impeach you? Wouldn't that—"

"Mr. Blaser," said Dilman, "the main forces in my command are committed to defending democracy in Baraza, not in the United States Senate. I am here to discuss foreign affairs. Perhaps you might better ask your question of former Secretary of State Eaton, who seems to have become an expert on domestic affairs." For the first time, there was laughter, and then Dilman added, "If you've ever gone to a prizefight, you will know that the judges' ballots are not counted before the first bell, but after the last bell—"

"Except when there's a knockout!" Blaser shouted.

Dilman ignored him. "That is all, gentlemen."

The United Press International correspondent intoned, "Thank you, Mr. President."

Briskly, Dilman left the Cabinet Room, parted with Flannery at Miss Foster's desk, and returned to his own desk in the privacy of the Oval Office.

He switched on the television set and dropped into his swivel chair, exhausted.

When the picture came on the screen, it showed Nat Abrahams, in the latter part of his summation of the defense case, earnestly addressing the senators.

"—absurd even to consider that the President violated the Constitution, disregarded the law, displayed contempt for your noble body, by his necessary removal of Secretary of State Eaton," Abrahams was saying. "Learned senators and judges, as we have attempted to show the other three Articles to be a maliciously woven fabric of falsehoods, let me now remind you that the more serious charges embodied in Article IV represent the autocratic, intemperate vengefulness of a small group of legislators. Let me hark back to 1868, when another President's entire impeachment revolved around his right to override the Tenure of Office Act, ancestor of the New Succession Bill, which President Dilman challenged. Chief Justice Chase, who sat on the bench then, where Chief Justice Johnstone sits now, made the following sage remark, as applicable and important in these troubled times as it was in that day: 'Acts of Congress,' he warned, 'not warranted by the Constitution, are not laws. In case a law believed by the President to be unwarranted by the Constitution is passed, notwithstanding his veto, it seems to me that it is his duty to execute it precisely as if he had held it to be constitutional, *except* in the case where it directly attacks and impairs the executive power confided to him by the instrument. In that case, it appears to me to be the clear duty of the President to disregard the law, so far at least as it may be necessary to bring the question of its constitutionality before the judiciary tribunals.'

"So spoke a Chief Justice, in the only other impeachment of an American President in our history. So speak I, on behalf of our President today. The issue is simple. President Dilman assumed office swearing to preserve, protect, defend the Constitution. How could he do so, how could he carry out his duties, if another branch of government, by means of a doubtful law, and from motivations not necessary to repeat, stripped him of his power to thus preserve, protect, defend? If the President has no longer the power to remove an adviser who is acting as President behind his back, an adviser ready to sell out Democracy in Africa to the Soviet Union while the lawful President himself, determined to save that democracy, is rendered helpless, where, then, is left the executive branch, and where, then, is left the Constitution itself? Learned senators—"

The telephone behind him buzzed, and Dilman sat up, lowered the volume of the television set, and spun around to the console.

"Yes?"

The voice was Miss Foster's. "Mr. President, I'm sorry, but there's a new policeman at the north gate who insists on speaking to you directly. He says there is someone at the gate who claims to be a relative of yours and wants to see you. He wouldn't tell me more."

"A relative?"

"I told him you couldn't be—"

"One moment, Miss Foster." On impulse, he said, "Connect me with the gate."

He waited, wondering.

A troubled male voice came on. "Mr. President—"

"Yes—yes—"

"I know I'm not supposed to disturb you, but the person insisted I contact you directly. I know there are crackpots and impostors every day, at least a half dozen daily coming around like this, but this one, she showed me an old beat-up snapshot of you, a photograph from her purse, signed by you, and she—"

"She?" said Dilman slowly.

"A young lady, Mr. President. She claims to be your daughter. I wouldn't give her the time of day, you understand, because—how should I put it?—she looks white to me—but the newspapers did say you—you have a daughter like that—still, the identification cards in her wallet say her name is Dawson, Linda Dawson, which doesn't make sense, except she says you might recognize that name even though it's not her real name, but I thought I ought to—"

"What does she give for her real name?"

"She says her name is Mindy—yes, that's right— Mindy Dilman, like it's supposed to be, and she says for me to tell the President she's better now, and she's been away too long—"

For the first time in weeks, Dilman felt a real smile ease the muscles of his face.

"Mister," Dilman interrupted, "I have an idea that young lady is neither a crackpot nor an impostor. You show her right in. You tell Mindy—her father is waiting for her. Now, hurry up! Don't leave her standing around!"

In the paneled and book-lined library of their early English house in Georgetown, at ten minutes to eleven in the morning, Arthur Eaton and Kay Varney Eaton sat side by side on the couch, concentrating their attention upon Zeke Miller, who was gesticulating on the television screen as he approached the end of his closing address on behalf of the House managers before the United States Senate.

"And so, honorable senators," Miller was saying, "since the able manager of the defense has chosen to bolster his concluding remarks with words borrowed from the impeachment proceedings of 1868, I feel that I can do no less upon behalf of the House indictment. Let me close my remarks in support of Article IV by referring to the wisdom of Representative Butler, as shown in the remarks made by him on that other historic occasion, and conclude by addressing to you the further remarks made by Representative Bingham before the Senate at that same trial.

"The words of Representative Butler, applicable to Article IV, are these: 'This, then, is the plain and inevitable issue before the Senate and the American public —Has the President, under the Constitution, the more than kingly prerogative at will to remove from office and suspend from office indefinitely, all executive officers of the United States, either civil, military, or naval, at any and all times, and fill the vacancies with creatures of his own appointment, for his own purposes, without any restraint whatever, or possibility of restraint by the Senate or by Congress through laws duly enacted? The House of Representatives, in behalf of the people, joins this issue by affirming that the exercise of such powers is a high misdemeanor in office. . . . Whoever, therefore, votes "not guilty" on these Articles votes to enchain our free institutions, and to prostrate them at the feet of any man who, being President, may choose to control them.' Senators, remember this, remember and do not forget a word of history's warning, when you consider your vote on Article IV charged against President Dilman.

"And remember, too, the considered wisdom of Representative Bingham in that other time, and remember and do not forget his patriotic beseeching when you stand up to be counted for all time in your judgment of one and all of the Articles of Impeachment. He said then, and I say now, 'I ask you to consider that we stand this day pleading for the violated majesty of the law, by the graves of half a million of martyred hero-patriots who made death beautiful by the sacrifice of themselves for their country, the Constitution and the laws, and who, by their sublime example, have taught us that all must obey the law; that none are above the law, that no man lives for himself alone, but each for all; that some must die that the state may live; that the citizen is at best but for today, while the Commonwealth is for all time; and that position, however high, patronage, however powerful, cannot be permitted to shelter crime to the peril of the republic.'

"Glorious words, these, which once ennobled this hallowed Chamber. They are timeless, yet were I to make them entirely pertinent to our cause today, I would paraphrase what that House manager had to say—let not the graves of thousands of martyred hero-patriots, sons of the mothers of America, be dug tomorrow and in days to come in the remote and distant jungles of primitive Africa to satisfy the whims of one ill-motivated, incompetent, intemperate, impermanent President-by-accident. Better that one man figuratively die so that the thousands who share our blood, and the state itself, to which we pledge our blood, shall survive and live. Gentlemen of the Senate—"

The library door had opened, and Governor Talley stuck his head in. "Arthur, the press is ready and assembled."

"Wayne," Kay Eaton said, "do you mind switching off the set?" As Talley hastily obeyed her, she turned to her husband. "That wretched Miller of yours is clever, no question. If I had any doubts, they're gone. What do I wear when you're sworn in, Arthur?"

Eaton had been cheerful, but a frown crossed his brow. "Don't talk like that, Kay. Don't let anyone hear you talk like that. . . . Ready, Wayne? Come on, Kay. Let's make it sweet and simple, and get them to the sandwiches and drinks."

Eaton left the library and strode quickly into the packed living room, followed by his wife and his colleague. There were more than one hundred correspondents waiting, and many applauded as he waved jovially and took a position before the built-in bar, maneuvering his wife to one side of him, and drawing Talley to the other side.

"Hold it for some pictures!" a photographer yelled.

As the shutters clicked and bulbs exploded, Talley called out, "Remember the caption—'T.C.'s Team Together Again!' "

More applause greeted this, and then, as reporters roughed the photographers to the sides of the room, Arthur Eaton held up his hand.

"First," he said, "an apology for these cramped quarters. I'm afraid this is a do-it-yourself press conference, but since I've been locked out of the Department of State, it's the best I can offer you!"

Eaton beamed at the laughter and cheers, and then he quieted the roomful of reporters, and his demeanor became serious.

"I have tried to avoid any communication with my friends of the press until the momentous matter before the bar of the Senate is settled today," he said. "However, I have been so widely and persistently solicited by many of you to make some comment that I have, with reluctance, consented. Perhaps, after all, a few brief remarks are in order."

"Hear! Hear!" someone shouted.

Again Eaton held up his hands for silence. Then, in his well-modulated voice, he resumed.

"I have been made increasingly aware of the fact, not that I have consciously ignored it or should do so, that under the law of the land, I am, as Secretary of State, next in line of succession to the Presidency. Although the

person now in the office of the Presidency has not wished
me in this position, has attempted to place himself above
the law and exercise dictatorial powers to remove me, he
has failed. The people of the United States would not
have it, and the effect of their outrage was felt in Congress, which immediately condemned and rejected the
President's illegal behavior and reinstated me as the Secretary of State, as a member of the Cabinet, and as first
in line of succession to the Presidency."

Since he was speaking without notes, although he had
considered with care what he would say, Arthur Eaton
paused at length to determine what he should say next.
Having organized his thoughts, he went on.

"Contrary to the propaganda mill of the White House,
I have not desired, wished for, or in any way actively
sought, or do now seek, the Presidency. It was enough
for me, these last years, exceeding my fondest dreams,
to be our beloved T.C.'s Secretary of State and Cabinet
adviser. I wish that were my position today. The eccen-
tricities of life, so unpredictable, would not have it, the
Lord's will was done, and my mentor and our former
President went to his premature death. When his successor, Senator Dilman, sought to retain my assistance,
wishing, he then said, only guidance to carry out T.C.'s
policies at home and abroad, I agreed to stay on. Like all
of us, I was weighted down with grief, but I realized
quickly that the welfare of our people, their government,
came first, and grief must be subordinated to duty, and
so I served.

"I will not discuss the events that have transpired
since T.C.'s death. They have been fully and widely aired
these last ten days from the floor of the United States
Senate. Let me say, however, in complete earnestness,
that although deeply concerned about the new President's
deviation from T.C.'s policies, and about certain deficien-
cies in his character and competence, I was reluctant to
approve of his impeachment. When there was no longer
a choice, when the impeachment became the desire of
the American people, when I realized that it was my duty
to stand with the people against one who would endanger
the very life of this republic, only then did I submit to

the inevitable and throw my full support behind the House of Representatives.

"I have no knowledge of what the outcome of the Senate's voice will be this afternoon, and I have no opinion about it. If the members of the Senate choose to acquit and retain the President, I shall, of course, resign from my office, and devote all of my energies, as a private citizen and a personal friend who loved T.C., to opposing those White House actions that I feel are detrimental to the country at large. If the members of the Senate choose to convict and oust the President from his office, I can only say that I shall do my duty under the Constitution and God to serve as your President, and as T.C.'s President, with all my strength, with all of my heart and mind, and with every fiber of my being.

"I repeat, my friends, if serve I must, then serve I shall—yes, serve I shall, as everyone's President, as President of no faction or factions but as President of the entire United States of America.

"Beyond that, there is little more I can say. I appreciate your attentiveness."

Eaton was gratified by the spontaneous outbreak of handclapping, and he ventured a smile.

"Mr. Secretary," the Atlanta *Constitution* correspondent called out, "do you mind a few questions?"

"Gentlemen, you know my position," Eaton said. "It would be difficult to comment on a matter not yet settled by the Senate. Besides, every question keeps you longer away from Mrs. Eaton's groaning board and that portable bar she's stocked."

There was pleased laughter, and Talley added, "Well, fellows, maybe a couple of quick questions if you don't put him on the spot, you know. Okay, what was it, Jim?"

The Atlantan said, "Dilman seems to have rallied a good deal of last-minute Negro support. Everyone thinks that if he's removed, racial rioting will reach a higher pitch. If that happens, do you have a plan for restoring peace to this country?"

"I have T.C.'s plan, I have the people's plan, the one the impeached President has derailed," said Eaton. "I would advocate revival of the Minorities Rehabilitation

Program as the one guaranteed way of restoring peace and prosperity to our people."

"What about Baraza?" the Portland *Oregonian* man asked. "Would you pull out our troops and seek a summit meeting with Premier Kasatkin?"

"No comment," said Eaton. Then he added, "My feelings about the reckless adventure in Africa, this playing hide-and-seek until we catch or are caught by a nuclear catastrophe, are too well known to bear repetition. President Dilman is Commander in Chief, as of now, and what he is doing represents how much he is willing to risk for what he believes, for whatever reasons, to be right. If I were Commander in Chief of our armed forces, I would indeed have a policy statement to make on Baraza and the Soviet Union. Right now, it would be premature and out of order."

"Mr. Secretary, you are practically Commander in Chief right now," Reb Blaser bellowed. "Last night's straw vote has eighty senators going to vote against Dilman—thirteen more than required. Doesn't that impress you?"

"Mr. Blaser, I can't comment on that, you understand," said Eaton.

"Let me just say this, fellows," said Talley, taking a step forward. "Secretary Eaton is quite correct in keeping away from speculation. But the Party has taken its own informal poll of the senators who will vote. I can tell you, frankly, there will be no problem in getting two-thirds of the Senate to announce that the President is guilty of high crimes and misdemeanors. Boys, tomorrow you'll have a new look, a government of the people, for the people, and by the people, a government of all the people, again!"

There was smashing applause, and Eaton acknowledged it with a dip of his head. Linking his arm inside his wife's arm, he called out, "Gentlemen, the press conference stands adjourned—and the stampede for the food and drinks begins. Again, thanks for your attentiveness, and now, follow us!"

And then Reb Blaser shouted, "Thank you, *Mr. President!*"

Immediately, the room was filled with an uproar of

laughter, handclapping, cheers, whistling, and Arthur Eaton, feeling as he guessed T.C. must have felt in those great climactic days before the election, led the stampede to the celebration.

At twenty minutes after twelve o'clock in the afternoon, the tray containing two small mixed green salads, two ham-and-cheese sandwiches on rye bread, one coffee and one hot tea had been delivered to the Oval Office of the White House from the Navy Mess below, and it now rested on the coffee table between the sofas.

Waiting for his friend, Douglass Dilman had just sat down to pick at the salad when Nat Abrahams came in, casting aside his hat, shedding his overcoat, massaging his chilled red cheeks.

"Brrr, what a day," he said.

"You're right, what a day," said Dilman, watching Abrahams sit down across from him. "Nat, I didn't see all of your closing address, but what I saw was great."

"I'm afraid Miller's was as good," Abrahams said.

"Nevertheless, thanks."

Abrahams appeared neither to have heard him nor to have any interest in the lunch before him.

Dilman inspected him. "What is it, Nat? You have something on your mind. I can tell."

Abrahams gnawed his lower lip thoughtfully. "As a matter of fact, I have."

"Shoot."

He looked at Dilman squarely. "We've had an offer, Doug. Political horse trade, but an offer."

"For what?"

"Senate votes in an hour and a half from now."

"From whom?"

"Boss of the Party. Allan Noyes buttonholed me when I was leaving. Took me aside. Said there are nine on-the-fence Party senators who are more concerned about what your conviction will do to the Party tomorrow than about what you are up to today. They feel that if you are kept in office, in the long run there'd be less harm done to the Party. They're considering that there's only a year or so of the unexpired term to go, and they'd lose fewer votes in the next election this way than if you are publicly disgraced and kicked out."

"Lose fewer votes? What votes?"

"Well, the Party has been taking samplings around the country. You've regained the sympathy of most of the Negro population, and of other minorities. The bloc of white liberals behind you has grown. Some independents here and there are shifting toward you. Noyes said it isn't a big switch to your side right now, but an impeachment conviction might gain you more sympathy than ever, and lose Eaton a lot of votes when he came up for election."

"Eaton's election. Is that what the Party is worrying about?"

"Frankly, yes. And that's the proposition. These nine senators put their heads together with Noyes, and here's what they came up with. Instead of splitting over you this afternoon, or going against you, they've promised to vote for you under certain conditions."

"All right, let's have it, Nat. What's the price?"

"If they swing an acquittal for you, then they want a public announcement from you tomorrow that you will neither seek reelection as the Party's candidate nor allow yourself to be drafted as a candidate by a third party, and that you will come out in full support of Arthur Eaton or any other Party choice for the Presidential nomination next summer. That's it. Agree to this, and you've got nine powerful votes for acquittal you might not otherwise have."

Dilman squinted at Abrahams and put down his sandwich. "And I need those nine votes?"

"Wouldn't hurt, you can use them," said Abrahams casually.

"And they want my answer before two o'clock?"

"Before a quarter to two."

"Nat, my answer is no. You tell them no."

Abrahams did not seem at all surprised. He began to eat. "I don't have to tell them no," he said, between mouthfuls. "I've already told them."

"You already told them no?" Dilman fell back, laughing and shaking his head. "You were that sure? What are you, my conscience?"

"Why, I'm your counselor, Mr. President."

"My assistant gravedigger, you mean." Suddenly Dilman sobered. "How badly did we need that deal, Nat, no soft-soaping? At the press conference today, Reb Blaser said the House managers took a straw poll, and while they need only sixty-seven votes to convict me, the poll says they have eighty. Any truth to that?"

"Exaggerated. Allan Noyes took his own poll. He's hardheaded Party. No sleight-of-hand."

"Well?"

"He comes up with seventy-four to convict. Seven more than they need."

"What do you come up with, Nat?"

"How do I know? I look and listen. I hope."

"Come on, Nat."

"Okay. If it is sixty-seven for conviction, they win. If it is sixty-six for conviction, short of two-thirds by one, you win. Right now, wetting my finger and putting it into the wind, I'd say they have—there's no way of knowing—but Tuttle and Hart believe they may have seventy votes."

"In other words, they have what they need plus four?"

"Don't think about it, Doug. It's all guesswork. Let them vote and let's see."

"Oh, I'll let them vote."

"There are other things to think about. . . . Hey, Edna Foster tells me Mindy is here. Is that true?"

Dilman found a way to smile. "Absolutely true. She's hurt, she's not well, I'm going to see that she gets help. But she's back, yes. And beautiful beyond belief. She's upstairs napping this minute." He shook his head. "I only wish I had come to my senses sooner and forced Mindy to come here, permitted Wanda to, while I was still a tenant of the White House."

"You're still a tenant."

"Yes. Only it's beginning to feel like Leavenworth."

The desk telephone rang. Dilman wiped his mouth with the paper napkin, then rose and hurried to the desk.

"Direct Pentagon hookup—I wonder what now—"

He could picture Secretary of Defense Steinbrenner ensconced behind the door with the placard reading "3-E-880," busy at his nine-foot glass-topped desk. Ex-

cept for the deceptively placid view from Steinbrenner's
four spacious windows, lulling one with the sight of the
Pentagon lagoon below and the Jefferson Monument
beyond, it was an office of intense action. Steinbrenner
was on the direct White House line now, but he also had
the gray telephone to all command posts open, and his
military assistants busy at the easel on which they
sketched and simplified tactical problems for him, as
well as the strange wall clock depicting time zones in
defense areas ("For Cincpac—Subtract 6") constantly
in view. So much might come through that office today.

Dilman picked up the telephone. "Yes, this is the
President."

"Mr. President, Steinbrenner here. I have just heard
from General Rice in Baraza City. His aerial reconnaissance has delivered—no more than an hour old—film
showing highly intensified Communist movement on the
Barazan frontier, in fact, throughout the enemy perimeter. All equipment is being mobilized. There is no question but that they have decided to move. General Rice
believes it a strategic necessity that our advance rocketry
units, now positioned, hit first. He thinks an enormous
advantage can be gained. I don't feel empowered to
make such a decision. He is standing by in Baraza City
for the go-ahead. I'm ready to give it, but not on my own
responsibility. I'm passing the buck, Mr. President. Do
you want to give us the green light?"

Dilman's palm was warm on the hand telephone. He
thought of Harry Truman: the buck stops here, here in
this Oval Office, not in the more ornate office of the
Secretary of Defense.

It was a difficult decision to make. If he gave the word,
the Dragon Flies would strike, perhaps topple the enemy
in a lightning stroke, perhaps gain an advantage, perhaps save countless lives. Yet he would have committed
the United States to an action of offense, not defense.
He would have betrayed America's entire historic philosophy of peace for a possible military advantage.

He hesitated, momentarily troubled by the man in the
Pentagon with the command line and easel and zone
clock and maps, and then he heeded his instinct.

"I don't want to be the aggressor, no matter what is

going on," Dilman said. "You order the General to continue to keep a close watch on their movements, but only shoot when shot at."

He heard Steinbrenner's snort. "If that's it, then I'll pass it on. But if it is defense we're thinking of, we've got to anticipate the worst, we've got to anticipate the conflict's broadening, and the possibility of an attack by Russia. I feel it is important to consider putting our defense forces on second-strike standby alert." There was a pause, and then Steinbrenner said, "Mr. President, what about going on DEFCON ONE?"

Again Dilman hesitated. The official order to set in operation DEFCON ONE would poise the entire United States, its military and civilian forces, on an all-out war alert. Dilman tried to visualize this alert: The screens of the DEW and BMEWS radar network would be under double surveillance, and fingers would creep closer to buttons that could order the North American Defense Command to activate 720 different Warning Points. The triple blockhouses stationed throughout the world would begin electronically elevating the fixed Minuteman ICBMs from their concrete casings. The secret trains carrying their mobile Minuteman missiles and squadrons would speed to preassigned positions. The Polaris submarines, each with twenty nuclear weapons, would rise from the ocean bottoms. Beneath the yellow clay of Nebraska, from the concrete command center of SAC, special word would send the B-70 jets and their hydrogen-bomb loads hurtling aloft in greater number. And just as his own Marine helicopter would be readied nearby to spirit him away to the subterranean second White House burrowed deep in a Virginia hillside, Dilman knew that fallout shelters across the nation would be manned for the ultimate signal of war imminent. There would be consternation, fear, even panic. Yet there would be preparedness.

A precautionary measure, this DEFCON ONE, Dilman thought, a drastic measure; perhaps a necessary one, as Steinbrenner was suggesting. Still, it was a hazardous choice. For, Dilman realized, DEFCON ONE could not go unnoticed by the world and the enemies of America in the world, Not many city blocks away, the

Soviet Embassy would be informing Moscow of the highly charged activity—the canceling of all military leaves, the bustling in the Pentagon—and the Soviet radar units in the Arctic and on picket ships in the Alantic would be reporting to Moscow the unusual movements of the United States surface and underseas fleets and its aircraft in the skies. How would the suspicious Kasatkin and his nervous Presidium react to this? Would they look upon this defensive preparation as a maneuver for aggression far beyond the provocation of the Dragon Flies in Africa? Would the concrete walls of Russian mountains then open wide to disgorge Soviet nuclear missiles—perhaps even the Gigaton Bomb that Kasatkin had so often boasted about—all building toward a forty-day assault that could snuff out the lives of 180 million of the United States' 230 million people? Or were the Soviets doing all of this anyway, without the provocation of DEFCON ONE?

There was a pounding behind Dilman's temples. His head ached. Then, suddenly, there was the relief of decision. The defensive value of DEFCON ONE was obliterated by the horrifying danger it invited—that of hastening the triggering of the first shot against the United States itself.

"No," said Dilman, "too soon."

The Secretary of Defense was worried. "They *are* on the move in Africa, Mr. President. Are you sure you want to hold back?"

He was sure. "For an hour, anyway, Secretary Steinbrenner. Stay in close touch with me."

After he hung up, Dilman remained standing behind his desk. Shuffling the papers lying on his blotter to be signed, he told Nat Abrahams what was happening.

Before Abrahams could reply, there was a sharp knocking on the door leading to engagement secretary Lucas' office, and then, without waiting for an invitation to enter, General Leo Jaskawich broke into the room.

Gone was the astronaut's normally reassuring expression. Anxiety was written across his swarthy features.

"Sorry to bust in on you, Mr. President, but I think the fat's in the fire," Jaskawich blurted out. "Just heard from the Soviet Russian Embassy. They asked for an immediate appointment for Ambassador Leonid Rudenko, and before I could hang up and get to you, the southeast gate called in to say Rudenko's car had just passed through. He's coming straight in without an appointment. I guess there must be—"

"Looks like this is the showdown," said Dilman.

"I can stall him," said Jaskawich.

"To hell with protocol," said Dilman. "Let's get it over with. Get out to the South Portico, General, and bring him right in here."

Jaskawich tugged down the brim of his officer's cap and rushed past the President's desk, and then through the French door.

Dilman was still on his feet behind his desk. He felt oddly calm, almost fatalistically calm. He saw Abrahams rise.

"Maybe I should get out of here," Abrahams said.

"You stay where you are," said Dilman. Abrahams nodded, and moved to the shabby Revels chair and sat. Dilman wet his lips with his tongue. "Well, they're not only moving in Baraza," he said, almost to himself, "they're moving in Moscow, too. I guess it is one and the same."

He looked off. He could see Jaskawich snappily leading the Russian Ambassador along the colonnaded walk, followed by two Secret Service men.

Jaskawich held open the screen door, and Ambassador Leonid Rudenko entered the Oval Office while the astronaut closed the French door and hung back in front of it.

Ambassador Rudenko was a small, muscular, middle-aged Russian with a perpetually glowering, unsmiling, pimpled face. He was the antithesis of the international diplomat. His English was exact and uncolloquial, his choice of words often sharp and uncivil, and he was famous for his use of a vituperative tongue in public.

He was unsmiling and gloomy this minute. He had removed his dark fedora as he advanced to the President's desk, but he had not touched his maroon woolen scarf or mountainous overcoat. Under his arm he carried a wafer-thin attaché case.

"Mr. President Dilman," he said, but did not offer

his hand. "I requested my Embassy to telephone, but on the assumption that a matter of such urgency—"

"Never mind," said Dilman. "Sit down."

Dilman lowered himself into the high-backed leather swivel chair, but either Ambassador Rudenko had not heard him or was too preoccupied to accept hospitality, for he remained standing before the desk, pulling off his kidskin gloves, then unzipping his attaché case. He extracted three blue sheets of paper, laid his case on the desk, knocking over several pieces of miniature statuary, and then fixed his eyes on Dilman.

"Mr. President, I have received, as of twenty minutes ago, an urgent communiqué directly from Premier Nikolai Kasatkin in Moscow. I have been ordered to read it to you in person."

"Go ahead," said Dilman. His face was expressionless as he tensely waited.

Ambassador Rudenko cleared his throat and began to read the diplomatic note aloud.

" 'To the President of the United States, Douglass Dilman.

" 'Dear Mr. President. I have been in receipt of your note, communicated by your Ambassador, concerning the necessity of your intervention in Baraza. I did not reply at once, nor did I immediately discuss the matter with the Presidium, or anyone, except for one informal reference to it in a public speech, the contents of which represented my immediate reaction. I have continued to delay reply until I could investigate the Baraza problem, the African situation generally, through my advisers in the Kremlin and abroad, and until I could apply to it the full weight of my thought and judgment.

" 'Mr. President, now that the facts have been clarified for me, there is no doubt in my mind that you have been seriously misled by your militarist clique, pawns of a system that desires only to seize control of illiterate blacks in Africa and exploit them for capitalism. The so-called facts you have presented to me about the African Communist buildup on the Baraza frontiers, about the equipment and leadership supplied by the U.S.S.R., which you have received from your intelligence sources, are both faulty and vastly exaggerated. They were cleverly designed by your military and capitalist cabal to provoke you into a warlike act of aggression, and to frighten us into not responding to this aggression. It grieves me that you have fallen prey to advisers who would see colonialism continued, even at the risk of a worldwide catastrophe.' "

Ambassador Rudenko paused, peered more closely at the tightly spaced transcript, and then resumed reading.

" 'Mr. President, you have met me, and know me for one who will not be easily frightened. You know, too, the might of the Union of Soviet Socialist Republics, of our defensive strength, our unity of purpose, and our will for peace. What we seek for ourselves and every nation is peace, prosperity, and equality among all human beings. You know, too, that I believe the strongest secret weapon we possess is not our hydrogen bomb, but our Idea to free the world of the shackles of slavery and bondage, as we have freed our own people in little more than a half century. For our Idea to triumph, there must be a civilized and populated world to save. If there are only the embers and corpses of a civilization left, there is only a junk heap and a graveyard to save.

" 'All of this I had to consider and weigh, against our own national security, when you rashly moved a division of your armies into Africa in these last hours. Over a local and passive incident in Africa, you—a man of good will, I had believed, but a man at the mercy of advisers now persecuting you—have challenged the U.S.S.R. and brought the world to that minute that precedes eternal and total sleep, the sleep of death by suicide. Through dangerous aggression over a relatively unimportant and overvalued problem, you have challenged the U.S.S.R. to respond with like aggression, in the cause of self-defense, to respond thus, or to withhold its invincible arms and become the nation which, by its belief in an Idea, shall lead the way through nonviolence and good example to preserve humanity.

" 'While reaching my final decision, there came to my mind a curious recollection. I remembered the two little old ladies who walked in Versailles. They, so you told me, were possessed of the gift to see into the past. But for us, to see into the past is useless, for we no longer have much to learn from it, because in the past mankind never had the power to destroy itself. Then I held another recollection. I remembered two leaders of the world's two foremost nations who also walked in Versailles. It occurred to me that perhaps they were gifted to look into the future. Would they see a barren earth come to an end through pride and madness? Or would they see, as one of them saw, as I saw in that clear vision hours ago, a world surviving and immortal, populated by independent nations coexisting as good neighbors in peace and harmony and mutual prosperity?

" 'This, Mr. President, is the world I saw ahead, and by my making the first step toward reaching it, I hope you shall see it, too.

" 'Therefore, I have dispatched Marshal Borov and his military staff to Africa, under instructions to carry out and facilitate, immediately, the complete disbandment and dispersal of native African Communist militia who respect our advice and who have been gathering at the Barazan frontier. I have ordered that any weaponry in their hands be surrendered or returned to the sources from which the arms were purchased. I have ordered that our Soviet technicians and educators, working with these native groups, be recalled at once to the Soviet Union. All of this activity, in the interests of peace, is taking place at this time, even as this note is being read to you.

" 'In return for our forward-looking act of peace, I request only that you display America's similar desire for peace by responding in kind. I ask the immediate dispersal of African Unity Pact forces gathered in and around Baraza, and the immediate withdrawal of all United States military forces and equipment from Baraza.

" 'Mr. President, let us remain the two men we were at Versailles. Let us look into the future, the future of this day, all days to follow, and let us see only peace.

" 'With every good wish, I am, Yours, Nikolai Kasatkin, Premier, U.S.S.R.' "

Ambassador Rudenko had finished, and his words hung in the room. Then he placed the note on the President's desk, and, busily, he closed his attaché case.

Dilman sat stunned, hands clenching the arms of his chair, trying to absorb what he had heard.

The telephone beside him was ringing. It was, he saw, the direct Pentagon line. He answered the telephone, listened to Steinbrenner's excited exclamations, and then he spoke a few words and hung up.

Dilman came to his feet. "That was my Secretary of Defense. Premier Kasatkin's notification of total withdrawal of Communist forces from the Barazan frontier has just been confirmed by President Amboko and by our Ambassador to the United Nations. The United Nations, I understand, is this afternoon flying a team to Baraza to supervise the Communist withdrawal. We have instructed our Ambassador Slater to inform the Security Council that we will pull out our own forces within twenty-four hours after your forces are gone. Your delegation has agreed to this."

"Yes."

"Very well, Ambassador Rudenko. This is a happy day for the world. Please inform Premier Kasatkin that I have heard his note, and that on behalf of my countrymen and all who believe in peace, I am relieved and delighted, and tell him—tell him it is my hope, too, and my belief, that enduring peace is possible, that we shall walk arm and arm into the future—into a world that shall remain immortal."

"I shall convey your message, Mr. President. Thank you."

"Thank you, Mr. Ambassador."

Dilman saw Rudenko through the French door, watched him depart up the colonnaded walk with the now cheerful General Jaskawich, and then he swung around and bounded back into the Oval Office.

Nat Abrahams was waiting, beaming as Dilman was beaming. The two men embraced, pounding each other on the back in their excitement.

"We won! We won the big one!" Dilman chortled. "We've got to get Tim Flannery—got to tell the whole world!"

He had broken away to summon Flannery when he stopped, and slowly came around to face Abrahams again.

"The big one," he murmured, with wonder. Then he said, "What about the small one, Nat? Will this make the difference in—in the Senate?"

"I can't promise it'll make the difference," said Abrahams, suddenly solemn. "I can only promise you this —it'll make it a contest, a real contest, for the first time."

IT WAS a quarter after two o'clock in the afternoon, and although Chief Justice Johnstone's reluctant gavel had sounded several times, the Senate had not yet been convened as a court of impeachment.

In all the days of the trial, Nat Abrahams had never once observed a scene in the Senate such as the one that spread before his eyes. Weakly, he smiled and shrugged at Tuttle, Priest, Hart, and received their nervous smiles in reply, and then, again, he tried to take in what was going on before him.

If the galleries had been filled every day, and filled to overflowing during the occasion the President had been on the witness stand, the galleries seemed bent and sagging with vociferous humanity on this afternoon of final judgment.

On the floor of the Chamber itself, few senators were at their mahogany desks. Most of them had spilled into the narrow aisles, clustering in groups, reading the bold headlines of the special editions of the Washington newspapers or listening to the steady chattering of commentators on their transistor radios, reading, listening, and then discussing the sensational news of President Dilman's victory, of Soviet Russia's backdown and retreat, of peace on earth once more.

Abrahams' keen eyes tried to follow the activity of both sides, that of the senators who were known to be in the camp against the President, determined to convict and remove him, led by aging Senator Bruce Hankins, who was everywhere, and that of the senators who were known to be in the camp supporting the President, determined to acquit him, led by the spry former labor union executive, Chris Van Horn, senior senator from Dilman's own state.

Had a single vote changed from guilty to not guilty,

even one? Abrahams could not tell. The partisans were easy to read. The independents were independent still, and unreadable. Only one emotion in common was evident in all faces, all stances, all movement: intense excitement.

At last, in his carved chair on the rostrum high above, Chief Justice Johnstone slid forward and rapped his gavel down hard once, twice, three times on the oak board, and the sound reverberated throughout the Chamber and stilled it, and gradually the Senate members began to empty the aisles and return to their individual desks, with their personal decisions already made or soon to be made.

"All caucusing will come to an end, and the senators will resume their seats and be attentive," the Chief Justice commanded. He waited for his order to be obeyed, and it was obeyed. Satisfied, in a louder voice he announced, "The Senate is now organized for the purpose of proceeding to the trial of the impeachment of Douglass Dilman, President of the United States. The Sergeant at Arms will make the proclamation."

The Sergeant at Arms jumped to his feet. "Hear ye! Hear ye! All persons are commanded to keep silence on pain of imprisonment while the Senate of the United States is sitting for the trial of the Articles of Impeachment against Douglass Dilman, President of the United States."

Abrahams saw a rangy figure rise behind his desk near the aisle. It was Van Horn, the vigorous outspoken senator from Dilman's state. His arm was uplifted.

"Mr. Chief Justice, I move that the Senate proceed by voice vote to the consideration of the order that I submitted to the bench a short time ago, as to the reading of the Articles of Impeachment."

The Chief Justice looked directly below him. "The Secretary of the Senate will read the order which Senator Van Horn proposes to take up."

The Secretary of the Senate rose, and from a sheet of paper read aloud, "Ordered, that the Chief Justice, in directing the Secretary to read the four Articles of Impeachment, shall direct him to read the fourth Article first, and the question shall then be taken on that Article, and thereafter the other three successively as they stand."

Senator Bruce Hankins, coughing and hacking, stood up. "Mr. Chief Justice, is this legal? Can the Articles be voted upon out of their original sequence?"

Senator Van Horn spoke quickly. "Mr. Chief Justice, I suggest the bench remind the able Senator that there is historical precedent for such procedure, as evidenced in the minutes of the Andrew Johnson impeachment, and other lesser impeachments in modern times. While I am aware that each and every one of the Articles is subject to a separate roll-call vote, it is also legal, and there is precedent for this, to select of the several Articles of Impeachment the one that is most important, and center a vote on that. If the respondent is found guilty on that one Article, he will be guilty and removed no matter what the vote on the others. If the respondent is found not guilty on that one Article, it is unlikely he will be found otherwise on the remaining and lesser Articles, which have considerably less support for conviction. On both sides of the aisle, and in both camps, I find sentiment agreeing that Article IV is the key indictment against the President. That is why I have moved that it be taken up at once, and have suggested a voice vote for or against."

The Chief Justice rapped his gavel. "A voice vote will be taken on the motion. On the question of reversing the order, in the first instance, for voting on the Articles under consideration, how many of you say yea?"

A powerful, lusty chorus of voices rang out, "Yea!"

"How many of you say nay?"

Another chorus of voices, thin and scattered, shouted, "Nay!"

"The yeas have it," announced Chief Justice Johnstone. "The motion as to altering the sequence of the Articles to be voted upon is carried."

Senator Selander, the Majority Leader, was calling for recognition. When he had it, he said, "Mr. Chief Justice, I move that the Senate now proceed to vote upon the Articles according to the order of the Senate just adopted. I have submitted this motion in writing to the chair."

"Very well," said the Chief Justice, "the motion will be read."

The Chief Clerk came to his feet, and he read the motion. Promptly, a voice vote was called for. The motion was unanimously agreed upon.

Twice now the robed magistrate's gavel was heard, and when the Chamber was hushed, he announced, "By direction of the Senate, I hereby, as Chief Justice presiding over this court, admonish citizens and strangers in the galleries that absolute silence and perfect order must be maintained from this moment onward. Persons responsible for disturbance will be immediately arrested. . . . Senators, in conformity with the order of the Senate, the chair will now proceed to take the final vote on Article IV, as directed by the rule. The Chief Clerk of the Senate will now read aloud Article IV."

The Chief Clerk was already standing with the document containing the Articles of Impeachment in his quivering hand. He scanned the assembly, and then, with deliberation, enunciating every word of the language of indictment clearly, he began to read.

"Article IV. That said Douglass Dilman, President of the United States, at Washington, in the District of Columbia, unmindful of the high duties of his office, of his oath of office, and in violation of the Constitution of the United States, and contrary to the provisions of an act entitled 'The New Succession Act Regulating the Line of Succession to the Presidency and the Tenure of Certain Civil Offices,' without the advice and consent of the Senate of the United States, said Senate then and there being in session, and without authority of law, did, with intent to violate the Constitution of the United States, and the act aforesaid, remove from office as Secretary of State . . ."

From his corner of the President's managers' table, Nat Abrahams had been listening to the words of indictment long engraved on his mind. But now his attention wandered from the Chief Clerk to the faces of the five at the table across the way, the House managers, each expression intent and solemn, except that on the countenance of Zeke Miller, sitting back carelessly, lips curled in a self-satisfied smirk, as if relishing every dagger word of the indictment.

From Miller's face, Abrahams' attention moved out and across the faces hung over the Senate desks, some directed toward the reading, some turned downward as if contemplating what judgment they must pronounce in not many minutes.

At once, the suddenness of silence brought Abrahams up short. He realized the reading of the indictment, the crucial one, had concluded, and that everyone, everyone around the room, up high, down low, was staring at the dais. Abrahams looked up, too.

Chief Justice Johnstone had risen from his chair, his black robes flowing. Majestically, he surveyed those beneath him. In a husky voice, he uttered three words.

"Call the roll!"

The moment had come, the moment of hope and dread, and Abrahams was certain that his heart had temporarily ceased its beat.

He thought of the millions everywhere, in America, in Europe, in Asia, hypnotized before their television sets. He thought of Doug Dilman watching, and of all the ones that mattered in Doug's life and his own life. The moment had come, and there was no hiding from it, no turning from it, no stopping it.

The Senate Chamber was deathly still.

No longer, it seemed, were all eyes focused upon the Chief Justice, who remained upright. All eyes were on the Chief Clerk, directly beneath him, who had risen with a scroll containing the names of the 100 senators present who would vote in alphabetical order.

"Mr. Alexander," the Chief Clerk called out.

A pinch-faced, elderly man rose in his place at the rear bench.

"Mr. Senator Alexander, how say you?" the Chief Justice asked sternly. "Is the respondent, Douglass Dilman, President of the United States, guilty or not guilty of a high misdemeanor, as charged in this Article?"

Senator Alexander's reply was a shout. "Guilty!"

He sat down, satisfied with himself.

"Mr. Austin," the Chief Clerk called out.

A dapper young politician in the second row stood up.

"Mr. Senator Austin, how say you?" the Chief Justice demanded to know. "Is the respondent, Douglass Dilman, President of the United States, guilty or not guilty of a high misdemeanor, as charged in this Article?"

Senator Austin hesitated, then answered, "Guilty."

"Mr. Bennatt," the Chief Clerk called out.

A twitching, stunted man leaped up from his desk near the center row.

"Mr. Senator Bennatt, how say you?" the Chief Justice inquired. "Is the respondent—"

"Not guilty, sir!" Senator Bennatt interrupted.

From the gallery came a nervous giggle, then laughter, and the Chief Justice suppressed his own smile, held his gavel poised, but did not use it.

"Mr. Bollinger," the Chief Clerk called out.

"Mr. Senator Bollinger, how say you? Is the respondent, Douglass Dilman, President of the United States, guilty or not guilty of a high misdemeanor, as charged in this Article?"

"Guilty."

Abrahams' heart was hammering again, as if to make up for its loss in suspension, and he stared down at his hands worriedly. Four of the one hundred had voted, and three of the four had judged the President as guilty. It was not promising. Abrahams could hear Senator Campbell being questioned, and now he heard the reply.

"Guilty."

About to return his full attention to the rising, announcing, and sitting of senator jurors, Nat Abrahams found himself mildly distracted by the sounds of whispering beside or behind him. He glanced at Tuttle, then down the table at Priest and Hart, to learn if they were the ones conferring, but they were silent, mesmerized by the drama of the vote.

Perplexed, as the whispering continued, Abrahams quietly turned in his chair, and then saw the source of the sound that had distracted him. A network television camera, which he had not noticed before, had been set up on the ground floor level, near the rostrum, to capture the historic countdown in its glass eye. Nearby two men crouched, one tallying the voting on a pad, as the other, an announcer, whispered the totaled figures, and their significance, into a perforated microphone in his hand.

Abrahams tilted backward, cocking an ear toward the whispering announcer, trying to close out the individual senators rising with their votes in order to catch, if he could, the latest tabulation. He listened hard, heard parts of several sentences, and then became attuned to the television announcer's low-keyed commentary and was able to hear him distinctly.

"The vote is going swiftly, as you can see on your screens," the announcer was purring into the microphone. "We have—let me see—yes—thirty-five out of the one hundred senators have already declared themselves. Of this first thirty-five, the vote summary this moment is twenty-six against President Dilman, nine favoring President Dilman, meaning that the vote to convict is running well ahead of the two-thirds required to remove the President from his office. It is too early to tell if this is a trend, and we are unable to learn if there have been any surprise switches against or for, but the President is trailing, he is behind, and if this count continues, he will be removed. For the first time in American history, a President of the United States will be removed from office for high crimes and misdemeanors. We want to remind all of you it will require two-thirds of the one hundred present to vote guilty, if conviction is to be obtained. Two-thirds means sixty-seven Senate members must declare aloud that they believe President Dilman guilty—wait, one moment—what's that, Kent? —yes, fine. Ladies and gentlemen, while I've been speaking to you, the voting has been going on, inexorably continuing, relentlessly driving to its climactic moment, and now my colleague with the tally sheet informs me—informs me that half of the votes are in—here, I have the halfway total in hand—the vote now stands, this minute it stands, thirty-four votes guilty, sixteen votes not guilty, out of fifty senators who have declared. It would appear—it appears that while the President is still running behind, his supporters have somewhat closed the gap, the voting has tightened considerably. If this ratio maintains, the prosecution will get its two-thirds by two votes to spare, at least, but since the earlier tabulation,

it has narrowed down to a real life-and-death struggle
—let's see now, who's that rising to vote?"

Abrahams sat up, tried to shut the smooth, glib, whispering voice from his hearing. It had begun to irritate
him. Out on the floor before them, not only a human
being's future hung precariously in the balance, but the
continuance of the checks and balances of America's
system of government as well as the integrity of the
American public who prattled about equality and freedom. Yet an announcer, epitome of the best and worst,
now the worst, in the brassy, competitive, public-relations American culture, was trying to report this critical historic event in the same manner he might a game, a
sport, a horse race.

As if his mind refused to accept and suffer, hope living, hope dying, each excruciating vote being announced,
Abrahams' thoughts dwelt on the end result of what was
occurring before his very eyes.

What would happen to this country if Douglass Dilman were convicted and ousted in these next minutes?
What would be on the national conscience as the great
country stirred awake tomorrow morning, sated by its
Roman holiday, but knowing it had crucified a President
not because he was an incompetent leader—the Dilman
triumph in Baraza would be known to all by then—but
because he was black and they were white? How would
neighbor look upon neighbor, and how would they live as
one people in their shame? And Doug, what would happen to Doug? Where would he go? What would he do?
How could he live? Yet, on the other hand, if he were
acquitted in the minutes to come, what would be the
state of the Union then? And Doug's future?

He heard the senators' voices replying to the Chief
Justice . . . "Guilty" . . . "Guilty" . . . "Not guilty." He
heard the watch on his vest chain ticking, ticking, ticking.
He sought it, peered down at its hands. Twenty-three
minutes had passed since the roll call began. Then he felt
fingers tugging at his sleeve.

He glanced up. It was Tuttle, and Tuttle was sliding
a slip of notepaper in front of him. It was a scrawled message from Hart:

"They have 60, we have 26—14 votes left. They need 7, we need 8. I'm dying. What do you think, Nat?"

He took up a pencil and wrote across the note, "I think I'm dying, too, but we're not dead. Stop using your fingers for writing and keep them crossed!"

He sent the note back down the table, turned in his chair, and now gave his full attention to the final fourteen voters. But to his surprise, in the time it had taken for Hart to write the note, pass it on, for him to read it, and reply, ten more votes had been announced, and the eleventh was just being announced, and this he knew because he could hear the damnable announcer whispering into the microphone behind him.

"—Stonehill just voted not guilty, as expected," the tightening voice behind him announced to the nation. "It now stands ninety-seven senators out of one hundred have cast their votes. The tabulation shows sixty-five guilty, and thirty-two not guilty. The prosecution requires two of the remaining three votes to impeach and convict the President of high crimes. The defense requires two of the remaining three votes to acquit and save the President of the United States. . . . There seems to be a lull. . . . The Chief Justice is checking with the Clerk to see what is left to be done. . . . We can tell him what is left. Three votes to be announced, and the impeachers need two, and it looks like they may get them. Only Senators Thomas, Van Horn, and Watson remain on the roll uncounted. Thomas, from a border state, has been outspoken in his criticism of the President. Van Horn was a supporter of President Dilman's intervention in Baraza from the outset, and with the flash of our victory there, it is unlikely he will do anything but continue to support the President. The third and last voter, the redoubtable Senator Hoyt Watson, whose own daughter was involved in the charges against Dilman, is a Southerner—a progressive Southerner, but a dyed-in-the-wool Southerner nevertheless—and so it appears that two of the three remaining votes will be guilty, giving the enemies of the President their sixty-seven required votes, their two-thirds, and unfolding before our eyes one of the most memorable occasions in history, the driving from office of the highest public official—"

The Chief Justice's gavel fell.

Nat Abrahams shut his ears to the announcer, gritted his teeth, clenched his fists, and stared straight ahead. He knew that perspiration had gathered on his forehead and down his back. He knew his worn, worried heart was faltering again. He waited.

"Mr. Thomas."

"Mr. Senator Thomas, how say you? Is the respondent, Douglass Dilman, President of the United States, guilty or not guilty of a high misdemeanor, as charged in this Article?"

"Guilty!"

"Mr. Van Horn, how say you? Is the respondent, Douglass Dilman, President of the United States, guilty or not guilty of——"

"Not guilty."

Abrahams' mind tabulated the count now: sixty-six guilty, thirty-three not guilty. One vote would convict Dilman; one vote would acquit Dilman. And there was but one vote and one voter left.

The one-hundredth Senate member in the room sat erect behind his mahogany desk, arms folded across the desk.

"Mr. Watson," the Chief Clerk called out.

Abrahams watched him, throat and lungs near bursting, eyes strained wide, watched the old gentleman unfold from his seat, grip his birch cane, watched his white thatched head, wrinkled phlegmatic face, rise with his aged body.

Chief Justice Johnstone hesitated, perhaps himself slowed by the weight his question would place on the senior senator's bent shoulders.

"Mr. Senator Watson, how say you? Is the respondent, Douglass Dilman, President of the United States, guilty or not guilty of a high misdemeanor, as charged in this Article?"

Senator Hoyt Watson did not reply. It seemed an eternity as he stood there, cane in his knobby hand, gazing up silently at the bench.

Watson's somber voice last night, in the privacy of the Oval Office, his words to Dilman last night, rang in

Abrahams' ears: "I cannot judge in your favor now, simply in knowing my daughter perjured herself and the House was misled . . . I must judge you tomorrow on your merits . . . if you acted as an American President or as a Negro President." All of this Abrahams heard now. Then, he wondered, what did Senator Watson hear now? Did he hear the thousands jamming the streets of Baraza and every democratic city of Africa, cheering the American flag? Did he hear the ancient cacklings of beloved ancestors, good colonels with good slaves, and did he hear the chant of the million in his state, who had carried him on their cheers into the Senate for twenty-four years, made him the bright white shield of their purity and safety against the ignorant niggers trying to threaten their accommodations, education, prosperity?

What did Senator Hoyt Watson hear these fleeting, suspenseful seconds while the Senate, the House, the White House, the South, the United States, the wide world waited?

The Chief Justice, standing before his carved chair on high, bent forward, and as if to shake another old man from his reverie and have today's history written and done with, he spoke.

"Mr. Senator Watson, how say you?" he repeated. "Is the President guilty or not guilty as charged in this Article?"

"Mr. Chief Justice, I vote the President *not guilty* of any high crimes or misdemeanors!"

Nat Abrahams fell back in his chair, limp with disbelief.

The galleries, the occupants of the floor, sat dumb, as if stunned into muteness by the fall of one giant mallet on their collective skulls.

A half dozen, then a dozen senators, foremost among them Hankins, were leaving their desks, surrounding Hoyt Watson, their irate heads bobbing, their angry arms waving, as Watson stood stonily in their midst, clutching his cane and listening.

From above, almost indistinctly now, Nat Abrahams could hear the Chief Justice intoning, "Upon this fourth Article, sixty-six senators vote 'Guilty,' and thirty-four senators vote 'Not Guilty.' Two-thirds not having pronounced guilty, the President is, therefore, acquitted upon this Article! . . . Silence! Silence! . . . Mr. Senator Bruce Hankins, are you requesting the floor?"

"I am!" shouted Senator Hankins above the rising hubbub of excitement. He hobbled forward to the rostrum. "Mr. Chief Justice, I have conferred with the learned Senator Watson, and with the leadership among my honorable colleagues. It appears that all are adamant in their opinions, that no 'Not Guilty' votes will be changed during this day, and that continued voting on the remaining three lesser Articles will result in an even larger tally and judgment for acquittal. Therefore, setting aside my personal feelings, and out of respect for the judgment passed, concerned only with preserving what we can of the unity and well-being of our beloved country, I hereby move that the Senate, sitting as a court of impeachment, does now adjourn *sine die*—that is to say, permanently—permanently. I ask for yeas and nays on this motion."

The Chief Justice gazed out over the churning Senate floor. "Who says yea?"

"Yea!" The concerted shout was thunderous and unanimous, and it went on and on, "Yea! . . . Yea! . . . Yea!"

The Chief Justice roared, "Unanimous! The Senate, sitting as a court of impeachment for the trial of Douglass Dilman, upon Articles of Impeachment presented by the House of Representatives, stands adjourned *sine die!* The President stands acquitted on all four Articles!"

Hardly anyone except Abrahams heard the Chief Justice, and not even Abrahams distinctly heard the last. For Tuttle, Hart, Priest, were climbing all over him, hugging him, choking him, pummeling him, and senators and press correspondents were all around, wringing his hand.

Beyond the circle of humanity pressing in on Abrahams, there was bedlam. The Senate had become a carnival of whooping, cheering, laughing revelers, whose celebrations drowned out the scattered boos and catcalls. Pandemonium engulfed the galleries and the floor, and spilled into the outer rooms.

Desperately, Abrahams tried to reach Senator Watson, to thank him, but it was impossible. Watson was caught in a crush of reporters and announcers. Abrahams heard someone yell, "Senator Watson, how could you repudiate your lifetime record to support Dilman? Why did you decide to vote not guilty?" And Watson, bewildered by the attention, replied firmly, "Two reasons—two. First, like Edmund Ross who cast the decisive vote for Andy Johnson, I decided that the executive branch of the government was on trial, and if its occupant were drummed out in disgrace on such flimsy political evidence, our nation would no longer be a democracy but what Ross called 'a partisan Congressional autocracy.' And second, I decided even before President Dilman had proved his patriotism and intelligence by saving Baraza and Africa for us, that if I could cease judging him as a Negro person and judge him solely as a fellow human being, I could then judge his true merits as a President. I judged Douglass Dilman as a man, and found him worthy of the Presidency. Coming here, rising to announce my vote, I fully realized that he was guilty of nothing except the accident of his colored skin. So I voted not guilty, and I am proud to have done that, and I hope and pray each and every one of you is proud of yourself today. For President Dilman has shown us he is a man—and now, perhaps, the nation has shown him and the entire world that it, too, has reached maturity at last."

Nat Abrahams felt soft arms encircling him, feminine hands touching his neck and cheeks, and there was Sue, aglow and laughing through her tears, pressed to him, kissing him, kissing him again and again.

Then, holding her close, he was leading her past the celebrating crowds toward the exit.

"Come on, Sue, I want to go to the White House and tell him—"

"Oh, darling, he knows, he knows, he knows."

Abrahams smiled. "He knows he was acquitted of four Articles. I want to tell him he was acquitted of five."

THE SNOW had begun to fall on New Year's Eve, and it

fell all the night, and now, on this bright, fresh morning of New Year's Day, the capital city was blanketed in white.

The snow lay like a silvery imperial mantle on the dome of the United States Capitol, clung to the Corinthian marble columns of the United States Supreme Court, covered the flat roof of the Department of Justice. The frosted, pearly flakes sparkled from the cupola of the Jefferson Memorial, the branches of the dogwood trees surrounding the Lincoln Memorial, the five outside walls of the Pentagon Building, the iced surface of the Potomac River, the square mosque of the Tomb of the Unknown Soldier, and the Stars and Stripes of the flag at full mast above the President's House at 1600 Pennsylvania Avenue.

From the broad center window of the Yellow Oval Room, on the residential second floor of the White House, President Douglass Dilman could make out, more clearly than ever before, the white marble shaft of the Washington Monument. It might have been a trick of the dazzling morning, but to Dilman the soaring monument seemed less distant than it had been four months ago, less distant and less intimidating.

The rising pitch of a television announcer's voice, his exclamations and superlatives of appreciation as he described the colorful floats and elaborately dressed equestrian groups in the Tournament of Roses parade from distant Pasadena, California, this voice, mingled with the remarks and comments of the guests watching the spectacle on the television screen, brought Dilman's attention away from the monument, from the snowy south lawn and frosted Truman Balcony, and concentrated it once more on the activity in the festive room.

The handful of friends whom Dilman had informally invited to drop by this morning to enjoy the Pasadena parade, and then the various football Bowl games, filled the sofas and the chairs drawn up before the immense television set that had been placed in front of the marble fireplace.

Affectionately, Dilman observed Julian and Mindy in their activity across the room from the others. His son was holding out the cups into which Beecher was ladling either eggnog or fruit punch from the deep cut-glass vessels on the sideboard. Mindy was busily assisting Crystal in arranging the tiny sandwiches being transferred from a tray to a large serving platter.

It pleased Dilman that his son, less antagonistic toward Trafford University and the world at large recently, was doing better in school, taking more pride in his learning, as if he had decided that education in itself might be the most effective weapon against racial discrimination.

It pleased Dilman, too, to gaze upon his daughter's delicate profile and lissome gracefulness and follow her fawnlike movements. This late holiday morning, she was gay, but Dilman did not deceive himself about her condition. By now, he knew that she was not always this way, nor would she be so in the future, for Mindy's moods were mercurial, and she was given quickly to apathy, self-confusion, and melancholia. Still, Dilman had been told that she might be better one day, after she had been worse. The eminent psychoanalyst she had begun to visit two weeks before had promised Dilman this. And lately she seemed to enjoy immensely lending a hand with some of her father's personal correspondence. But neither her presence here today nor the psychoanalyst's tempered optimism had fully convinced Dilman. After his consultation with the psychoanalyst, Dilman had wondered—as he wondered this moment—once you've been white, how can you ever be black again? Mindy was not his child alone. She was Aldora's child, too. The psychoanalyst, with all his wisdom and insight, was not black, so he might not ask himself what Dilman asked: How long would it be before Mindy tried to escape once more, escape Aldora's way or her own?

These considerations were too unsettling for the first day of the New Year, and Dilman turned his thoughts to the others in the Yellow Oval Room. Somehow, he liked to believe they had become a part of his family. There they sat at ease, most of them, in various postures of relaxation. There was Otto Beggs, able to cross his good leg over his bad leg but unable to hide entirely the pain he was enduring, pointing out to his wife and two sons a particularly gaudy floral float moving ponderously across the sunny screen. Beggs would begin his executive duties, as special agent in charge of the White House Secret Service Detail, the first of next week when the holidays were officially over. Near him there was Jed Stover, with his wife and grown daughter, his mind obviously on matters far removed from the Pasadena parade. Ten days earlier, the Senate had reluctantly approved Stover's appointment as Secretary of State, and since then three new international crises had sprung up. Then, seated comfortably in a side chair, there was General Leo Jaskawich, sworn in as the President's special assistant to replace Talley, puffing his cheroot and amusing himself by blowing smoke rings. Finally, there was Wanda, so delightful in repose, so intent on the screen as she absently drank her fruit punch.

Dilman had not had Wanda's present ready for her at Christmas, and so he had given her a card, shaped and printed as a rain check, and on it he had written apologetically that her gift would be arriving any day now. It had been delivered yesterday, but he had not given it to her yet. He was saving it for the intimate holiday dinner tonight. She would not be surprised, he guessed. Although Sue Abrahams—who had helped him make the final selection, and had suggested the modifications—had insisted upon disguising the engagemeng ring by wrapping it in a gigantic box, Wanda would not be surprised. But she would be pleased, he hoped, as pleased about it (and about what it meant to them in more ways than one) as he was himself.

He looked forward to the small dinner tonight. By then, the festivities, the games, the resolutions, would be behind them all. Then there would be easy, relaxed companionship, Wanda and himself as hostess and host to The Judge and his Missus, to Admiral Oates and his sister, to the Stovers, to the Tuttles, and—he had almost forgotten—to Edna Foster and to Tim Flannery, if they had finished their work in time.

Then Dilman's eyes came to rest on Sue and Nat Abrahams, side by side on the sofa, and their three youngsters at their feet, and his only regret was that they could not remain for the dinner tonight. But Dilman knew, with a pang of guilt, that he had detained Nat long enough. In the weeks since the trial, and then through Christmas, Nat had stayed on, had volunteered to do so, to help Dilman draft the radically revised version of the Minorities Rehabilitation Program, one which put as much emphasis on giving Negroes and other minority groups equality in education, accommodations, voting, as the old bill had given them in economic parity. The revised version was prepared, ready to be introduced by his supporters in Congress when the members of both Houses reconvened shortly. And now, at last, Nat Abrahams was free to go home to Chicago, to share the holiday weekend with Sue's relatives and to return to the law offices that his partner, Felix Hart, had been manning alone.

As he noticed the bulky morning newspaper on the sofa, Dilman's mind went to the persons who were not here but had been so much a part of his life, for better, for worse, in recent months, and who were now less a part of his life, except as he read about them or heard about them. Hastily, Dilman's mind revived news items, important, minor, of recent days.

Arthur Eaton was being boomed as the Party's candidate in this year's Presidential election, and his vociferous backers had entered his name in the first three state primary elections. But to the surprise of many, Governor Talley's name had also been entered as a candidate in those primaries, and to the surprise of fewer people, Senator Hoyt Watson's name had been resoundingly entered, too. For, although Watson had been dropped by his own state political machine, the curve of his national popularity (led by Southern liberals and independents) had risen, and the Party was now interested in testing his appeal outside the boundaries of the Mason-Dixon Line. In the Deep South, Representative Zeke Miller, basking in the afterwave of his impeachment trial publicity, was trying to organize and gain support of his idea for a powerful third political party, and there was money behind him, but it was too early to tell if there were also votes.

As for Dilman himself, the chairman of the Party, Allan Noyes, had telephoned the Oval Office repeatedly for an appointment "to talk things over"—meaning, no

doubt, to find out in what manner Dilman could be useful to the Party without harming or obstructing it, and
to learn his plans, and to determine what must be done
with him in the future. But as Dilman had now shut out
the past, he refused to peer into the future. He was
entirely devoted to the present, to trying to be the kind
of President he thought he was capable of being and
the kind the nation needed. And so whenever Noyes had
telephoned, Dilman had been too occupied to speak to
him or arrange to see him.

There were other names Dilman knew, and they were
often in other sections of the morning newspaper. On
the society page it had been announced that Miss Sally
Watson was off to Switzerland for a vacation. But Dilman had heard more, that it would be an extended stay
in a renowned mental clinic in Zurich. On the book page
it had been announced that Leroy Poole's authoritative
biography of the President was completed and would be
published in the spring. But Dilman had heard more, that
Poole had quickly brought the book to an end (making
no secret of the fact that he was still Dilman's foe) in
order to obtain the necessary funds to work with Mrs.
Gladys Hurley on an angry protest biography of the late
Jefferson Hurley. On the feature page it had been announced in several columns—as rumor, not fact—that
General Pitt Fortney, since his resignation as Chairman
of the Joint Chiefs of Staff, would become a member of
the board of directors of an Oregon aircraft company, a
newly acquired subsidiary of Eagles Industries Corporation. And occasionally, in the back sections of Miller's
newspaper, there was a minor story bearing the dateline
"New Orleans" and the by-line "George Murdock."

Suddenly Dilman, whose eyes had strayed to the
clock on the fireplace mantel, realized how late it was
in the morning. Holiday or no, half of his staff were
at their desks in the West Wing offices downstairs, Edna
Foster among them, and Dilman knew that there were at
least four or five hours of paper work for him to do, too.

He walked over to the sofa where Nat Abrahams sat,
and touched his shoulder. Immediately Abrahams, still
flushed with the delight he took in his family, jumped
to his feet and came around to join Dilman.

"Well, Nat," Dilman said, "I've got to get down to the galleys and start rowing. I'm afraid this is good-bye until sometime next year—"

"Mind if I walk you to the office, Doug?"

They found their overcoats, pulled them on, then went together into the West Hall and started for the elevator.

"Nat," Dilman said, "we're old friends, and you know how inarticulate I am about my deeper feelings. I've tried to tell you, in my way, how much I appreciate what you've done for me, how grateful I am to you. I don't know what would have happened without you."

"Nothing different would have happened."

"I choose to believe it would not have been the same. No other attorney on earth would have understood me well enough to perceive the real indictment, and been able to invent and throw that Article V at them. Anyway, Nat, what you must know, before taking off, is how conscious I am of the sacrifice you made—"

"Enough of that, Doug. I don't wear a halo well. I'm the bareheaded type. What sacrifice? Three unhappy years, filled with self-reproach, with that inhuman corporation? Thank God, you brought me to my senses. You saved me those wasted years, Doug. You handed them back to me. I'm the one who should be grateful to you for what you gave me."

They reached the elevator and waited. "You know what I mean, Nat," Dilman said. "Maybe you kept the three years, but you lost the farm, additional security, a financial cushion, because of me."

Entering the elevator, they started down to the ground floor. "Listen to me," Abrahams said. "I lost nothing, nothing at all. Farms? There are a hundred more, always will be, and maybe better ones. Instead of having mine in three years, I'll have it, and all the rest, in five or six years. Doug, you have no idea how many calls I've had, fat offers I've received, since that trial. Not only corporations, but labor unions, Manhattan law firms. Some of them sound even better and more corrupting than Eagles ever was. Eventually I may accept one, if I can find one that is clean behind the ears as well as solvent. No hurry this time. I'll sit back and let them woo me. So, you see, Doug, what you think I did for you has done as much for me. And it did something else, besides." He grinned shyly before leaving the elevator. "It put me right smack in the history books, a footnote to you. My children's children, they'll read about me. Now, tell me, what other neighborhood Jewish lawyer ever had a break like that? Don't thank me, Doug. Let me thank you."

Once they were in the ground-floor corridor, with the two Secret Service agents falling in a discreet distance behind them, Nat Abrahams spoke again.

"What about your future, Doug?"

"I don't permit myself to think about it," Dilman said. "I wake up, I work, I go to sleep. I'm trying to handle life a day at a time. That's a big job, a big, strange, new job for a person who only recently found out he has the right to perform as a man and not just a colored man. It's like starting afresh, second chance, with a new mind, new limbs, new nerve apparatus, new outlook. You have to get used to it before you can use all that health and strength."

"Yes. I know," said Abrahams. At the ground exit Abrahams stopped. "Whatever happens, Doug, I think it's going to be better for you from now on." He dug into his pocket and came out with a clipping. "Did you see this in the morning paper?"

"What is it?"

"The latest nationwide Public Opinion Poll taken on you. Listen." He consulted the clipping. "When you came into office, 24 per cent of the people favored you, 61 per cent were against you, 15 per cent were undecided about you. Today, four months later—well, here it is—33 per cent of the people are in favor of you, 28 per cent against you, 39 per cent undecided." He returned the clipping to his pocket. "The significant thing, Doug, is that right now, instead of the great percentage of people being against you, they've moved into the undecided column; they've left behind attitudes of strong resentment to move closer to you and say, in effect, 'Okay —maybe—let's wait and see—show us.' Can you realize what that means, Doug?"

Dilman did not reply. The garden door had been opened for them, and Dilman went outside, with Abrahams following him, then going alongside him. The air was crisp, wholesome, bracing, and as they proceeded up the colonnaded walk, there was no sound other than the crackle of their footsteps on the snow-crusted cement.

Briefly, Dilman strode in silence, lost in thought, and at last he looked at his friend. "Strange, Nat, how whenever you're not sure of the future, you go scampering back into the past. My mind just went back to when I was a kid, maybe seven or eight years old. There was a ditty all of us used to chant. Want to hear it?"

Abrahams nodded.

Dilman hesitated, then he recited:

> *Ef I wuz de President*
> *Of dese United States,*
> *I'd live on 'lasses candy*
> *An' swing on all de gates!*

He shook his head. "Our most fanciful dream of heaven. Little did we realize there was no 'lasses candy, no swinging gates."

"Or realize that it was not a fanciful dream at all."

Dilman glanced up sharply at his friend. "Not a dream? . . . Yes, I see. That's true, isn't it?"

"'Ef I wuz de President.' You became the President, Doug. You still are the President. That's something, I think."

"I suppose—yes, I suppose it is, 'lasses candy or not."

"Because you've grown, Doug, and so has everyone around you—the entire country, it's come of age, too," said Abrahams. "The American people have finally learned what a great Kansas editor tried to teach them years ago, that—that liberty is the only thing you cannot have—unless you are willing to give it to others."

Rounding the corner, Dilman stared out at the lustrous snow-covered garden and the glittering expanse of the White House south lawn. "You think it has been learned, Nat?"

"I believe so," said Abrahams.

They had arrived at the French doors outside the Oval Office. They halted, facing one another.

"Let me put it this way," Abrahams said. "The

country may be uneasy today, but it is no longer ashamed or afraid, ashamed or afraid of you—or itself. The country's learned to live with you, Doug, so now, at last, it can live with itself. It has a better conscience today. It feels right. That's an awful good feeling, Doug. . . . And that's a huge step, the greatest this country's made since the Emancipation Proclamation. Mr. Lincoln had long legs. But now, for the first time, we've found countless men with legs as long, and they've made the next step, the giant one. As a result, the country is closer to becoming one nation than it ever has been before—and by the time it becomes one nation, it may be ready, and qualified, to help make our world one world. . . . Big words, Doug, but these are big times. None of us will ever be the same again—not you—not me—not anyone, anywhere. Thank God."

A French door creaked behind them, and Edna Foster appeared. When she saw them, her worried features reflected immediate relief.

"Oh, there you are, Mr. President. I was calling everywhere," she said. "There have been some messages—emergencies—low-grade, but nevertheless—"

"I'll be right in, Miss Foster," Dilman said, and then he turned back to his friend.

Nat Abrahams was smiling. "I think you belong inside." He extended his hand. "Good luck, and a Happy New Year, Mr. President."

Douglass Dilman clasped Abrahams' hand firmly in his own. "Good luck, and a Happy New Year to you, Nat."

After that, Dilman lingered outside briefly, watching Abrahams leave, and then, feeling assured and purposeful, feeling good, he entered his Oval Office to begin the day's work.

ABOUT IRVING WALLACE

Born in Chicago, raised in Kenosha, Wisc., IRVING WALLACE sold his first magazine piece at the age of 15. After that, more than 500 of his short stories and articles appeared in major periodicals like *Saturday Evening Post, Reader's Digest, Esquire.*

During World War II, he spent three-and-a-half years as a writer in the First Motion Picture Unit of the Army Air Forces, and then worked on the "Why We Fight" documentary series for the Signal Corps Photographic Center. After that, Wallace spent 10 years writing screenplays for major film studios.

In 1955 his first book, *The Fabulous Originals*, a collective biography, was published by Alfred A. Knopf. In 1960 his fifth book, *The Chapman Report*, a novel published by Simon & Schuster, became an international best-seller. In the years since, each of his novels has been a best-seller including such well-known titles as *The Prize, The Three Sirens, The Man, The Plot, The Seven Minutes, The Word, The Fan Club, The R Document.* His latest novel, and 22nd published book, is *The Pigeon Project.* All of Wallace's novels have been acquired by motion picture studios. They have starred such actors as Paul Newman, Edward G. Robinson, Jane Fonda, James Earl Jones.

Among his better-known nonfiction books have been *The Twenty-Seventh Wife, The Sunday Gentleman, The Nympho and Other Maniacs.* Recently Wallace collaborated with his children on a series of best-sellers—he joined his son, David Wallechinsky, to create *The People's Almanac #1, #2 and #3*, his daughter, Amy, to produce *The Two*, and worked with David and Amy to write *The Book of Lists, The Intimate Sex Lives of Famous People* and *The Book of Predictions.*

It is estimated that Wallace's books have sold 116 million copies worldwide.

A resident of Los Angeles, Calif, he is married to Sylvia Wallace, author of the widely read novels, *The Fountains* and *Empress.*